HALLIWELL'S
TOP 1000

By John Walker

TED SMART

Also edited by John Walker

HALLIWELL'S WHO'S WHO IN THE MOVIES
HALLIWELL'S FILM, VIDEO & DVD GUIDE

**All pictures supplied by the Ronald Grant
Archive except 'Bicycle Thieves' supplied by
the British Film Institute.**

This edition produced for The Book People Ltd,
Hall Wood Avenue, Haydock, St Helens WA11 9UL

Harper*Entertainment*
An Imprint of HarperCollins*Publishers*
77–85 Fulham Palace Road,
Hammersmith, London W6 8JB

www.harpercollins.co.uk

Published by HarperCollins*Publishers* 2005
9 8 7 6 5 4 3 2 1

HALLIWELL'S ™ is a trademark of HarperCollins*Publishers*
Limited

A catalogue record for this book is
available from the British Library

ISBN 0 00 774511 7

Designed by Geoff Green Book Design, Cambridge
Set in Helvetica

Printed and bound in Hong kong by
Compass Press

Introduction

Welcome to a book that has been a labour of love, in not only making a list of the 1,000 greatest films, but also in putting them in numerical order. Even before publication, it's involved me in a great many discussions and disputes, but that, after all, is a function of being a critic and one of the pleasures, after the event, of film-going.

The films chosen range from studio masterpieces and popular blockbusters to art house obscurities. While the list is mainly of feature-length films, I have allowed the occasional short to creep in, to do justice to the careers of Charlie Chaplin and Laurel and Hardy. Also included are a few documentaries, though I have left out some brilliant ones from the time of the World War II on the grounds that they have virtually vanished from view. It includes not only Hollywood and British movies, but significant work from most countries of the world, from China, Iran and Japan to Belgium, France, Germany and Holland. Some are demanding, and not easy viewing; but all are rewarding and worth watching more than once.

The main criterion used for choosing the films was, of course, quality, whether of writing, direction, acting, cinematography, music, editing and design. Some films succeed in every aspect, others may be deficient in one or another virtue but are impossible to overlook for the brilliance they show elsewhere. There are many instances of great performances – from Lon Chaney in *Phantom of the Opera*, Laurel and Hardy at their slapstick best, Charles Laughton in *The Hunchback of Notre Dame*, Laurence Olivier as a patriotic Henry V, Robert DeNiro in *Taxi Driver*, to Peter O'Toole as Lawrence of Arabia – that on their own would justify the inclusion of the films they grace. Some movies that have gained an impressive following are missing from these pages. You will not find *The Shawshank Redemption* listed, for instance, although currently it enjoys a mass appeal. I have now watched it three times and it still seems no more than an extremely sentimental, over-extended anecdote that is kept alive, for about half its running time, by the quality of its acting.

One thousand films may be a lot to evaluate, but it's a small number compared to the 140,000 or so features that have seen the dark of the cinema since the Lumière brothers first demonstrated the possibilities of moving pictures in 1895. The selection draws on the expertise of the annual *Halliwell's Film, Video and DVD Guide*, written by its originator, the late Leslie Halliwell, who was an enthusiastic filmgoer from the age of five, and me. Between us, we clock up more than a hundred years of film watching and have spent more than half that period writing about them.

Here are the films, silent and talking, old and new, comic and serious, black-and-white or colour, long and short and widescreen that can enrich your life in one way or another. Enjoy!

Thanks are due to Tom Lindley for researching other critics, directors and producers' Top Ten films and providing information on DVD releases. I am also grateful to Monica Chakraverty for her editorial input, to my agents Rivers Scott and Gloria Ferris for their support, and to my wife Barbara, who occupies the top spot in my life.

John Walker

Individual Entries

All entries follow the same format and the notes are set out below in the order in which they will be encountered.

Publicity tags These were used in the promotion of the film.

Country of origin This is the first item on the second line.

Year of release This indicates when the film was first shown, which is not necessarily the year that it was made.

Running time This is given in minutes, signified by 'm'. So far as possible, this is the original release time.

Colour This is indicated by 'bw' for black and white films and 'colour' for the others. The colour process used, such as Technicolor, is given when known.

Other notable points These are given at the end of the second line, indicating the use of a special process, such as Panavision. 'Scope' indicates a wide-screen process.

Production credit This is the central credit on the third line. To the left comes the name of the distributor, which is followed by the production company if different. To the right comes the name or names of the actual producer or producers.

Family viewing 👪 indicates that the film is suitable for family viewing, i.e. by parents together with young film-goers aged from four to fourteen.

Video 📼 indicates that the film has been released on VHS video-cassette for the British PAL system. 📼 indicates that the film has been released on VHS video-cassette for the British PAL system in wide-screen format. ⯐ indicates that the film has been released on VHS video-cassette in a computer-colourized version. 🇺🇸 indicates that the film has been released in the American NTSC format (which is not compatible with the British PAL system). 💿 indicates that the film is available on laser disc in either American NTSC format or British PAL format. ◎ indicates that the film is available on Video CD. 🎧 indicates that the film's soundtrack music has been released on compact disc. ◉ indicates DVD (Digital Video Disc) releases in Region 1 and dicate indicates DVD releases in Region 2. DVD, video and record releases come and go with great rapidity; all that is possible to indicate is whether a title has been available in this format at some time.

Alternative title This is given on a separate line, usually with a note of the country in which it was used. If no such distinction exists, the formula aka (also known as) is used.

Writer credit (w) This appears first since the script precedes direction. The author of the screenplay is given; if this derives from a novel, play, musical, or story, this is given next, together with the original author.

Director credit (d) This follows next. If the director is also the writer, then there will be a combined wd credit.

Photography credit (ph) This indicates the cinematographer or lighting cameraman, otherwise known as the director of photography.

Music credit (m) This means the composer of the background music score. Sometimes there is only a music director (md) who orchestrates library or classical music. When noteworthy songs are performed, or are specially written for a film, those responsible are indicated by a credit for music and lyrics (m/ly) or simply songs.

Other credits These may include art director (ad), choreographer (ch), costume designer (costume), film editor (ed), production designer (pd) and special effects (sp).

Cast ☆ A list of the principal actors is given, roughly in order of importance.

Italics These denote a contribution of a particularly high standard.

Critical comments Brief quotes from well-known professional critics are appended to many entries, sometimes because they wittily confirm the assessments and sometimes because they provide alternative opinions.

Additional notes Any points of interest about the film are given after the symbol †. The symbol m indicates notable songs which appear in the film.

Academy Awards Awards 🏆 and nominations are listed for all principal categories, including best picture, acting, direction, photography, music score and songs, and some minor awards, such as sound and make-up, when they seem of interest. British Academy of Film and Television Arts awards follow the symbol 🎭.

'Who will survive and what will be left of them?'

The Texas Chainsaw Massacre
US   1974   81m   CFI color
Vortex (Tobe Hooper)
🎞 ▣ 🔊 ⊚ ◎
w Kim Henkel, Tobe Hooper *d* Tobe Hooper *ph* Daniel Pearl *m* Tobe Hooper, Wayne Bell *ad* Robert Burns *ed* Larry Carroll, Sallye Richardson
☆ Marilyn Burns (Sally), Allen Danziger (Jerry), Paul A. Partain (Franklin), William Vail (Kirk) Gunner Hansen (Leatherface)

'An absolute must for all maniacs and blood drinkers in need of a few tips.' – *Benny Green, Punch*

'It's without any apparent purpose, unless the creation of disgust and fright is a purpose.' – *Roger Ebert*

'Remains as disturbing, suspenseful and shattering as the day it first saw the light of a drive-in screen.' – *Kim Newman, Empire, 1999*

1000
The Texas Chainsaw Massacre

Visitors to a cemetery in rural Texas find their house occupied by a homicidal maniac.

The cinematic equivalent of the blood and thunder penny dreadfuls beloved by the Victorians, this flesh-creeping horror has a ruthless intensity that is impossible to resist. Leatherface, its hideously masked murderer stalking his innocent victims, embodied every urban individual's fears of inbred rural decadence. Its cannibalistic narrative can be seen as an updating of *Sweeney Todd, the Demon Barber of Fleet Street* that wowed audiences from the 1840s (which in turn had its origins in stories of a Parisian throat cutter five hundred years earlier). Its subversion of family life and its use of the chainsaw as its weapon of choice lift it to a new level of terror. It was based on the crimes of the mother-obsessed murderer Ed Gein, who was also the inspiration for Norman Bates in *Psycho*, and Jame 'Buffalo Bill' Gumb in *The Silence of the Lambs*, among other films. Its cult success led to many similar slasher movies, though none has reached its level of sustained horror.

'See And Hear It, Our Mother Tongue As It Should Be Spoken.'

Blackmail
GB   1929   78m   bw
BIP (John Maxwell)
🎞 ▣ 🔊 ◎
w Alfred Hitchcock, Benn W. Levy, Charles Bennett *play* Charles Bennett *d* Alfred Hitchcock *ph* Jack Cox *m* Campbell and Connelly, arranged Hubert Bath, Henry Stafford *md* John Reynders *ad* Wilfred and Norman Arnold *ed* Emile de Ruelle
☆ Anny Ondra (Alice White), Sara Allgood (Mrs. White), John Longden (Frank Webber), Charles Paton (Mr. White), Donald Calthrop (Tracy), Cyril Ritchard (The Artist)

'Hitchcock's ending was to have been ironic, the detective seeing the cell door shut on the arrested girl, going home and then being asked if he was going out with his girlfriend that evening. His answer: "Not tonight." This was unacceptable commercially and a happy ending was substituted.' – *George Perry*

999
Blackmail

A Scotland Yard inspector finds that his girl is involved in a murder; he conceals the fact and is blackmailed.

This was Hitchcock's first sound film, though it began as a silent one to which dialogue was later added, with Joan Barry dubbing the voice of Czech actress Anny Ondra. Hitchcock used sound creatively, noticeably in a famous scene where the girl, who has stabbed a man, overhears gossiping women in which the only word that can be made out is 'knife'. It is now a very hesitant entertainment but fully bears the director's stamp and will reward patient audiences in several excitingly staged sequences. The hectic chase of a rapist and murder suspect around the rooftops of the British Museum gave the director an early opportunity to display both his liking for climaxes set in high places and his skill at creating suspense. And, for once, a guilty couple goes unpunished.

998
Tin Pan Alley

Tin Pan Alley
US 1940 95m bw
TCF (Kenneth MacGowan)
w Robert Ellis, Helen Logan *story* Pamela Harris
d Walter Lang *ph* Leon Shamroy *md* Alfred Newman
ch Seymour Felix *ad* Richard Day, Joseph C. Wright
ed Walter Thompson *songs* Mack Gordon, Harry Warren
☆ *Alice Faye* (Katie Blane), *Betty Grable* (Lily Blane), John
Payne (Skeets Harrigan), Jack Oakie (Harry Calhoun), Allen
Jenkins (Sgt. Casey), Esther Ralston (Nora Bayes), The
Nicholas Brothers, John Loder (Reggie Carstair), Elisha
Cook Jnr (Joe Cadd)
♫ 'Moonlight Bay'; 'Honeysuckle Rose'; 'The Sheik of
Araby'; 'K-K-K-Katie'.
♟ Alfred Newman

Two schoolgirls become rivals for the love of the same man.

In this musical, full of Broadway clichés and razzmatazz, Betty Grable and Alice Faye star as two dancing girls who love the same composer. It relies on tried and true standard songs rather than originals. Whenever the pace slackens, there are the tap-dancing Nicholas Brothers to add even more zip, especially in the musical's big number, 'The Sheik of Araby', with the portly Billy Gilbert being serenaded by the two stars. (The number was shortened by the censor, who thought too much female flesh was on show.) Darryl Zanuck encouraged rivalry between his two leading ladies, which added a little edge to their performances. After Faye had become temperamental and unwell, he had given Grable the leading role in the musical *Down Argentina Way*. Her success brought Faye swiftly back to the studio to reassert her position as its leading musical star. The wily Zanuck then cast them both in this film.

997
Fire Over England

Fire Over England
GB 1937 92m bw
London Films/Pendennis (Erich Pommer)
▤ ◔ ◎
w Clemence Dane, Sergei Nolbandov *novel* A. E. W.
Mason *d* William K. Howard *ph* James Wong Howe
m Richard Addinsell *ad* Lazare Meerson, Frank Wells
ed Jack Dennis
☆ Flora Robson (Queen Elizabeth), Laurence Olivier
(Michael Ingolby), Leslie Banks (Earl of Leicester), Vivien
Leigh (Cynthia), Raymond Massey (Philip of Spain), Tamara
Desni (Elena), Morton Selten (Burleigh), Lyn Harding (Sir
Richard), James Mason (Hillary Vane)

> 'Should bring much artistic acclaim but, outside of the urban class spots, business will be stubborn … if it had marquee strength it would stand an excellent chance.' – *Variety*

> 'Pommer and Howard have done one remarkable thing: they have caught the very spirit of an English public schoolmistress's vision of history.' – *Graham Greene*

> 'Swashbuckling nonsense, but with a fine spirit.' – *Pauline Kael, 70s*

Elizabeth I and her navy face the might of the Spanish Armada.

Flora Robson makes the most of the opportunity to play Elizabeth I, sending her navy to overcome the Spanish Armada, in a historical pageant kept afloat and interesting by its splendid cast. She gives a regal delivery to lines used by Elizabeth herself. There is a definite chemistry in the love scenes between Olivier, as a dashing secret agent, and Leigh, as the queen's lady-in-waiting, for they had just begun their affair. (Graham Greene grumbled that such kissing and cuddling would never have been allowed at a Tudor court.) The climactic sea-battle is, unfortunately, a bath-tub business. The patriotic movie carried a less obvious message that Britain was again in danger from a continental enemy.

Starship Troopers
US   1997   129m   Technicolor
Buena Vista/TriStar/Touchstone (Jon Davison, Alan Marshall)
☒ ▤ ◎~ ◉ ◎ ⌒
w Ed Neumeier *novel* Robert A. Heinlein *d* Paul Verhoeven *ph* Jost Vacano *m* Basil Poledouris *pd* Allan Cameron *ed* Mark Goldblatt, Caroline Ross *sp* Phil Tippett, Scott E. Anderson, Alec Gillis, John Richardson
☆ Caspar Van Dien, Dina Meyer, Denise Richards, Jake Busey, Neil Patrick Harris, Clancy Brown, Seth Gilliam, Patrick Muldoon, Michael Ironside, Rue McClanahan

'A spectacularly gung-ho sci-fi epic that delivers two hours of good, nasty fun.' – *Todd McCarthy, Variety*

'Would Paul Verhoeven kindly stop making movies?' – *Tom Shone, Sunday Times*

'The crowning achievement of Paul Verhoeven's film-making career to date.' – *Andrew O'Hehir, Sight and Sound*

● Robert Heinlein had to change publishers in order to get *Starship Troopers* published in 1959; the book was intended for a juvenile audience.
● The film took around $55m at the US box-office.
⚐ visual effects

996
Starship Troopers

In the future, when the miltary rule an Earth facing an invasion from giant bug-like aliens, a group of friends become soldiers to fight the creatures on their own planet.

Robert Heinlein's militaristic novel, railing against the decadence of twentieth-century society, described a future where a military elite instilled honour and discipline that could withstand an interplanetary war against giant bugs. In his film version, Verhoeven wittily subverts the book by showing a dystopian future of mindlessly patriotic young on a killing spree, where all that distinguishes the two competing armies is that one has more than two legs. Yet the movie also remains true to the novel's enjoyment of violent battles and military superiority. The cast of bland young actors suggest that individuality is a luxury the future cannot afford.

The Blair Witch Project
US   1998   81m   bw/colour
Pathé/Haxan (Gregg Hale, Robin Cowie)
☒ ▤ ◎~ ◉ ◎
wd Daniel Myrick, Eduardo Sanchez *ph* Neal Fredericks *ad* Ricardo R. Moreno *ed* Daniel Myrick, Eduardo Sanchez
☆ Heather Donahue, Michael Williams, Joshua Leonard, Bob Griffith (Short Fisherman), Jim King (Interviewee), Sandra Sanchez (Waitress (as Sandra Sanchez)), Ed Swanson (Fisherman With Glasses), Patricia Decou (Mary Brown)

'An intensely imaginative piece of conceptual filmmaking that also delivers the goods as a dread-drenched horror movie.' – *Todd McCarthy, Variety*

'The sort of film that gets its best effects by creeping up on you unawares and whispering scary things in the dark.' – *Kim Newman, Empire*

● The original film was made at a cost of $25,000, though more was spent later on improving its quality. It took more than $140.5m at the US box-office, making it probably the most profitable film so far released.
● It was followed by a sequel: *Book of Shadows: Blair Witch 2*.

995
The Blair Witch Project

Three students set out to film a documentary about a local legend of a witch; they are never heard of again, but the footage they shot is found a year later.

An extraordinary success that looks and sounds like the amateur movie it's meant to be. The movie itself was made in an unusual way. Its cast was shown how to use video cameras and let loose in a wood for eight days. Every day, each was secretly given instructions on his or her role by the directors. The rest was improvised. The result has a palpable sense of unease and hysteria, brilliantly faking a feeling of reality. Its horrors are never quite seen; it relies with great skill on the fearful power of suggestion. It is a movie that is far more skilful than it first appears, and is cleverly edited to emphasize the increasing panic of its partici-pants. Those involved have all gone on to successful careers in movies and TV, though that of the cinematographer Neal Fredericks was unfor-tunately cut short when he was killed in a plane crash in 2004.

994

Kipps

Kipps

GB 1941 112m bw
TCF (Edward Black)

US title: *The Remarkable Mr Kipps*

w Sidney Gilliat *novel* H. G. Wells *d* Carol Reed
ph Arthur Crabtree *m* Charles Williams *ed* R. E. Dearing
☆ Michael Redgrave (Arthur Kipps), Phyllis Calvert (Ann
Pornick as a woman), Diana Wynyard (Helen Walshingham),
Arthur Riscoe (Chitterlow), Max Adrian (Chester Coote),
Helen Haye (Mrs. Walshingham), Michael Wilding (Ronnie
Walshingham), Lloyd Pearson (Shalford), Edward Rigby
(Buggins), Hermione Baddeley (Miss Mergle), Frank
Pettingell (Old Kipps), Beatrice Varley (Mrs. Kipps),
Kathleen Harrison, Felix Aylmer

'It has the old fashioned charm of wax roses under
a glass bell.' – *New York Times*

In 1906, a young draper's assistant comes into money and tries to crash society.

H. G. Wells's novel of a upwardly mobile draper in Edwardian England who inherits money and attempts to enter society became a comedy of snobbish bad behaviour in the hands of director Carol Reed, who wanted the film to be a wartime morale booster. With its excellent cast, Arthur Riscoe given space for his well-observed comic turn as a hopeful playwright, and Cecil Beaton's and Vetchinsky's re-creation of bygone Folkestone, it is a splendidly old-fashioned delight. There is a nicely understated performance as the modest and diffident hero from Michael Redgrave, who wrote in his autobiography that Reed was able to 'bestow on his actors the feeling that everything was up to them and that all he was doing was to make sure that they were seen to their best advantage.'

993

The Great Waltz

'Miliza Korjus – rhymes with gorgeous!'

The Great Waltz

US 1938 103m bw
MGM (Bernard Hyman)

w Walter Reisch, Samuel Hoffenstein *story* Gottfried
Reinhardt *d* Julien Duvivier *ph* Joseph Ruttenberg
m Dimitri Tiomkin *ad* Cedric Gibbons *ed* Tom Held
☆ Fernand Gravet (Johann Strauss), Luise Rainer (Poldi
Vogelhuber), Miliza Korjus (Carla Donner), Lionel Atwill
(Count Hohenfried), Hugh Herbert (Hofbauer), Herman Bing
(Dommayer), Curt Bois (Kienzl)

'Should click nicely, but in these swingaroo days
the waltz part may slow down anticipated b.o.
enthusiasm.' – *Variety*

'A film to set the feet itching, and to make you want
to grab a partner and join in.' – *Film Weekly*

🏆 Joseph Ruttenberg
🏆 Miliza Korjus; Tom Held

Young Johann Strauss becomes Vienna's waltz king.

This schmaltz-filled biopic is an exhilarating, old-fashioned, studio-set musical. Located in Hollywood's endearing vision of Old Vienna, the streamlined production has an excellent cast and an excess of hokum: Strauss, torn between his wife and the opera singer he loves, is shown writing 'The Tales of the Vienna Woods' while taking a coach ride, inspired by the sound of the horse's clip-clopping hooves and by birdsong; he composes 'The Blue Danube' by the dock-side as a ship bears his lover away. Duvivier's soaring camera and Tiomkin's dazzling arrangements give it all an irresistible verve. It is the music that drives the film, aided by Duvivier's virtuoso direction and cinematography that almost swoons as it tracks Miliza Korjus, the flamboyant Polish coloratura soprano who plays Strauss' lover. It is a movie that remains a monument to a less cynical time.

The Group
US 1966 152m DeLuxe
UA/Famous Artists (Sidney Buchman)
🇺🇸

w Sidney Buchman *novel* Mary McCarthy *d* Sidney
Lumet *ph* Boris Kaufman *m* Charles Gross *pd* Gene
Callahan *ed* Ralph Rosenbloom
☆ *Joanna Pettet* (Kay Strong), Candice Bergen (Lakey
Eastlake), *Jessica Walter* (Libby MacAusland), Joan Hackett
(Dottie Renfrew), Elizabeth Hartman (Priss Hartshorn), Mary
Robin-Redd (Pokey Prothero), *Kathleen Widdoes* (Helena
Davison), Shirley Knight (Polly Andrews), Larry Hagman
(Harald Peterson), *Hal Holbrook* (Gus Leroy), *Robert
Emhardt* (Mr. Andrews), Richard Mulligan (Dick Brown),
James Congdon (Sloan Crockett), James Broderick (Dr.
Ridgeley)

'Although it is a strange, inclusive, no-holds-barred
movie that runs the gamut from scenes that are
almost soap-operaish, to amusing scenes that are
almost satire, to outrageously frank scenes that are
almost voyeuristic, it is still greatly exhilarating
while it provokes thought and pushes the viewer
into examining his own conscience.' – *Philip T.
Hartung, Commonweal*

992
The Group

*The subsequent love lives of a group of girls who graduate from
Vassar in 1933.*

Based on Mary McCarthy's best-selling novel, Sidney Lumet's film is
set mainly in New York, and its tight-knit circle includes a lesbian, a
wife who enjoys her pregnancies, a rich girl who prefers to earn her
living and a witty literary groupie who resembles McCarthy herself.
Lumet treats them with a seriousness they may not deserve, but it is a
generally fascinating series of interwoven sketches and character studies, with mainly tragic overtones; good attention to period detail, and a
dazzling array of what was once new talent. It was only the second
time that Lumet had made a film in colour and he was unhappy with
the result. In retrospect, he felt that colour did not look as real as black
and white, and the reason must be that he was not using it correctly.
Yet its gloss and very artificiality now seem a bonus, as indicative of a
style that is redolent of the movie's period.

Jason and the Argonauts
GB 1963 104m Technicolor
Columbia/Charles H. Schneer

w Jan Read, Beverley Cross *d* Don Chaffey *ph* Wilkie
Cooper *m* Bernard Herrmann *ad* Jack Maxsted, Toni
Sarzi-Braga, Herbert Smith *ed* Maurice Rootes *sp* Ray
Harryhausen
☆ Todd Armstrong (Jason), Honor Blackman (Hera), Niall
MacGinnis (Zeus), Andrew Faulds (Phalerus), Nancy Kovack
(Medea)

991
Jason and the Argonauts

*With help and hindrance from the gods, Jason voyages in search of the
Golden Fleece and meets all kinds of monsters.*

One of the most enjoyable film fantasies, in which the actors are constantly upstaged by Ray Harryhausen's stop-motion monsters and
sword-fighting skeletons. The story of Jason bears some resemblance
to the Greek myth, while keeping its tongue firmly in its cheek, and
giving the Olympian gods plenty of opportunity to help and hinder
Jason's quest. The cast are no more than adequate and its leads are
extremely bland, but Harryhausen's bronze giant, winged harpies,
seven-headed hydra and her children, the skeletons, provide enough
excitement.

Tokyo Olympiad

Japan 1965 154m Eastmancolor
Toho (Suketaru Taguchi)
◫ ▤ ⬧
original title: *Tokyo Olrmpikku*
w Kon Ichikawa, Yoshio Shirasaka, Shuntaro Tanikawa,
Natto Wada *novel d* Kon Ichikawa *ph* Shigeo Hayashida,
Kazuo Miyagawa, Shigeichi Nagano, Kenichi Nakamura,
Tadashi Tanaka *m* Toshiro Mayuzumi
☆ Jack Douglas (narrator)

'An epic study of athletes struggling, against their own bodies and each other, to excel. But it reaches even further, as a stirring portrait of fleeting human hopes — some exalted, most of them thwarted — which are preserved and transformed forever by Ichikawa's vision.' – *Desson Howe, Washington Post*

990
Tokyo Olympiad

Documentary account of the 1964 Olympics held in Japan.

Ichikawa (a second choice after Kurosawa proved to be too expensive) organized 164 cameramen to capture his humanistic account of the 1964 Olympics. He was less interested than the participants in winners, concentrating on the muscular effort, the sweat and tears of supreme athletic endeavour. Inevitably, the Olympic Organizing Committee hated his film and it was re-edited before being released; the version originally seen in the US was even more hacked about. A revelation at the time, his methods, including slow-motion photography, have become routine in TV sports coverage, but his immaculate composition, and the sense of community he observes between spectators and athletes, still enthrals.

'Inside the skyscraper jungle! Ruthless men and ambitious women clawing for control of a billion-dollar empire!'

Patterns
US   1956   88m   bw
UA/Jed Harris, Michael Myerberg
▭
GB title: *Patterns of Power*
w *Rod Serling* play Rod Serling d *Fielder Cook* ph Boris Kaufman ad Richard Sylbert ed Carl Lerner, David Kummins
☆ Van Heflin (Fred Staples), Everett Sloane (Walter Ramsey), Ed Begley (William Briggs), Beatrice Straight (Nancy Staples), Elizabeth Wilson (Marge Fleming)

989
Patterns

The tough boss of a New York corporation forces a showdown between a young executive and the older ineffectual man who he hopes will resign.

This tense boardroom melodrama with domestic asides dates from the moment in the mid 1950s when live television drama was attracting young and talented writers, directors and actors. Rod Serling, later the creator of TV's *Twilight Zone,* was among the most aggressive, and *Patterns* reflects his pugnaciousness. Its producer, the much-disliked Jed Harris, tried to take the script away from him, rewriting and re-titling it *The Bitch Goddess, Success*, but director Cook insisted on going back to the original. He had planned to open up the film version to include more background material. Even in its present form, the drama is a pleasure to watch.

'It's a wonderful world, if you'll only take the time to go around it!'

Around the World in Eighty Days
🏃🏃 US   1956   178m   Technicolor   Todd-AO
UA (*Michael Todd*)
▭ ▭ ◉ ◎ ◎ ⌒
w James Poe, John Farrow, S. J. Perelman novel Jules Verne d Michael Anderson, Kevin McClory ph Lionel Lindon m Victor Young ad James W. Sullivan, Ken Adams ed Gene Ruggiero, Paul Weatherwax titles Saul Bass
☆ *David Niven* (Phileas Fogg), *Cantinflas* (Passepartout), *Robert Newton* (Inspector Fix), Shirley MacLaine (Princess Aouda), Charles Boyer (Monsieur Casse), Joe E. Brown (Station Master), Martine Carol (Tourist), John Carradine (Col. Proctor Stamp), Charles Coburn (Clerk), *Ronald Colman* (Railway Official), Melville Cooper (Steward), *Noël Coward* (Hesketh-Baggott), Finlay Currie (Whist Partner), Reginald Denny (Police Chief), Andy Devine (First Mate) and also Marlene Dietrich, Luis Dominguin, Fernandel, *John Gielgud*, Hermione Gingold, Jose Greco, Cedric Hardwicke, Trevor Howard, Glynis Johns, *Buster Keaton,* Evelyn Keyes, Beatrice Lillie, Peter Lorre, Edmund Lowe, A. E. Matthews, Mike Mazurki, Tim McCoy, Victor McLaglen, John Mills, Alan Mowbray, Robert Morley, Jack Oakie, George Raft, Gilbert Roland, Cesar Romero, Frank Sinatra, *Red Skelton*, Ronald Squire, Basil Sidney, *Harcourt Williams*, Ed Murrow
👤 picture; James Poe, John Farrow, S. J. Perelman; Lionel Lindon; Victor Young
👤 Michael Anderson; art direction; editing

988
Around the World in Eighty Days

A Victorian gentleman and his valet win a bet that they can go round the world in eighty days.

Jules Verne's story became an amiable large-scale pageant in Michael Todd's lavish production. It resolved itself into a number of sketches, which could have been much sharper, separated by wide-screen spectacle. What was breathtaking at the time seems generally slow and blunted in retrospect, but the fascination of recognizing 44 cameo stars remains. The film is less an exercise in traditional skills than a tribute to its producer's energy. The film did provide a rare opportunity for non-Mexican audiences to enjoy the performance of Cantinflas, a great comic actor who was here given only a few opportunities to display his talents, which was also true of many of the other stars who popped in and out of the movie, just long enough to be seen. The overweening ambition of the project gives it a continuing fascination.

The Man Who Could Work Miracles

GB　1936　82m　bw

London (Alexander Korda)

w Lajos Biro *story* H. G. Wells *d* Lothar Mendes *ph* Harold Rosson *m* Mischa Spoliansky *ed* Philip Charlot, William Hornbeck

☆ *Roland Young* (George McWhirter Fotheringay), Ralph Richardson (Col. Winstanley), Ernest Thesiger (Mr. Maydig), Edward Chapman (Maj. Grigsby), Joan Gardner (Ada Price), Sophie Stewart (Maggie Hooper), Robert Cochran (Bill Stoker), George Zucco (Moody), Lawrence Hanray (Mr. Bamfylde), George Sanders (Indifference, a God)

> 'Supposedly a comedy. A weakling: little draw power on this side.' – *Variety*

> 'Sometimes fake poetry, sometimes unsuccessful comedy, sometimes farce, sometimes sociological discussion, without a spark of creative talent or a trace of film ability.' – *Graham Greene*

987
The Man Who Could Work Miracles

A city clerk discovers he has the power to work miracles (given him by sportive gods) and nearly causes the end of the Earth.

This film is a pleasing variation on a simple theme that was explored more recently, and less successfully, in Jim Carrey's *Bruce Almighty*. Fotheringay begins with parlour tricks but then decides to bring peace and prosperity to the world, and discovers that it is harder than it seems. He asks others for advice, but is given selfish and unimaginative suggestions; after he summons all the world's leaders to a meeting, chaos results. 'Once an ape, always an ape,' is a god's verdict on the human race. Korda, who had been unhappy with the film when he first screened it, directed some retakes before putting it on the shelf for a year. It was, he knew, an uncommercial film and it failed to earn back its cost at the box-office. But it is a fable that has retained its power to entertain and disturb.

Atanarjuat The Fast Runner

Canada　2001　168m　colour

ICA/Igoolik Isuma/NFBC (Paul Apak Angilirq, Norman Cohn, Zacharias Kunuk)

w Paul Apak Angilirq *d* Zacharias Kunuk *ph* Norman Cohn *ad* James Ungalaaq *ed* Zacharias Kunuk, Norman Cohn, Marie-Christine Sarda

☆ Natar Ungalaaq (Atanarjuat), Sylvia Ivalu (Atuat), Peter Henry Arnatsiaq (Oki), Lucy Tulugarjuk (Puja), Pakkak Innushuk (Amaqjuaq), Madeline Ivalu (Panikpak), Paul Qulitalik (Qulitalik)

> 'Mysterious, bawdy, emotionally intense, and replete with virtuoso throat singing, this three-hour movie is engrossing from first image to last, so devoid of stereotype and cosmic in its vision it could suggest the rebirth of cinema.'
> – J. Hoberman, *Village Voice*

986
Atanarjuat The Fast Runner

In the Arctic, the legend persists of a leader who could outrun his enemies.

A film like no other. The first to be made in Inuktitut, the language of the Inuit, by an Inuit cast, it depicts a way of life, full of strange rituals and magic, that seems other-worldly. The story of a struggle for leadership between two Inuit families, leading to death and betrayal, is based on an Inuit legend passed down from one storyteller to another over a period of more than a thousand years. The desire for power, the deadly nature of family rivalries, and the survival of the wiliest, though, connect with modern life. It is both an action movie and a tale of a spiritual quest for healing and understanding. There is one astonishing scene in which Atanarjuat flees from his would-be murderers, running naked across an endless landscape of frozen snow and splashing through icy water until exhaustion sets in. There are moments, too, of tender intimacy, all suffused with the quality of magic.

'Images of wax that throbbed with human passion. Almost woman! What did they lack?'

Mystery of the Wax Museum
US   1933   77m   Technicolor
Warner (Henry Blanke)
●● ▬ ℚ. ⊚
w Don Mullally, Carl Erickson play Charles S. Belden
d Michael Curtiz ph Ray Rennahan ad Anton Grot
ed George Amy
☆ Lionel Atwill (Ivan Igor), Fay Wray (Charlotte Duncan), Glenda Farrell (Florence Dempsey), Frank McHugh (Jim), Gavin Gordon (Harold Winton), Allen Vincent (Ralph Burton), Edwin Maxwell (Joe Worth)

'Its most telling details are its horrific ones. The fire at the beginning, with lifelike figures melting into grisly ooze; night-time in the city morgue, with a dead body suddenly popping up as a side effect of embalming fluid; chases through shadows as the ghoulish sculptor collects bodies for his exhibit; and the shock when Atwill's homemade wax face crumbles to the floor and exposes the hidden demon.' – Tom Shales, The American Film Heritage, 1972

● A Region 1 DVD release includes this and the 1953 version of the film.

'The mission of the Strangelove generation!'

Dark Star
US   1974   83m   Metrocolor
Jack H. Harris (John Carpenter)
●● ▬ ▬ ℚ. ⊚ ⊚ ⌒
w John Carpenter, Dan O'Bannon d John Carpenter
ph Douglas Knapp m John Carpenter pd/ed Dan O'Bannon
☆ Brian Narelle (Doolittle), Dre Pahich (Talby), Cal Kuniholm (Boiler), Dan O'Bannon (Pinback)

985
Mystery of the Wax Museum

A sculptor disfigured in a fire builds a wax museum by covering live victims in wax.

One of the archetypal horror movies: its writers flesh out the story with a sub-plot about drug-running and an authoritative example of the wisecracking reporter school of the early thirties. The film is also notable for its highly satisfactory use of two-colour Technicolor and for its splendid art direction, especially in the creation of the museum's creepy basement. It creates frissons of fear, as when Charlotte (Fay Wray), threatened by Igor, Lionel Atwill's mad sculptor, pummels his face and watches it crumble. (The movie was remade in 1953 as *House of Wax*, a 3D effort that caused a sensation at the time.)

984
Dark Star

In the 22nd century, the bored crew of a starship on an intergalactic mission become prey to their own phobias and to the alien mascot they are taking back to Earth.

This paranoid low-budget science-fiction comedy was made by John Carpenter and Dan O'Bannon long before they went on to have successful Hollywood careers. It has some great moments of surreal comedy, notably as the crew try to persuade a smart bomb, which is stuck in the ship's bomb bay, not to explode. The movie deserves cherishing as one of the rare examples of the cinema of the absurd. Its alien must be the cheapest-ever special effect: a large, red beach-ball with two webbed feet, who bounces about the spacecraft causing havoc. Carpenter's film was originally made as a student project at the University of Southern California and ran for less than 70 minutes. He added three sequences to bring it up to feature film length, managing to maintain its off-the-wall (and -planet) charm.

The Bowery

US 1933 92m bw
Twentieth Century (Darryl F. Zanuck) (Raymond Griffith, William Goetz)

w Howard Estabrook, James Gleason *novel* Michael L. Simmons, Bessie Roth Solomon *d* Raoul Walsh *ph* Barney McGill *m* Alfred Newman *ad* Richard Day *ed* Allen McNeil

☆ Wallace Beery (Chuck Connors), George Raft (Steve Brodie), Pert Kelton (Trixie Odbray), Jackie Cooper (Swipes McGurk), Fay Wray (Lucy Calhoun), Herman Bing (Mr. Rummel)

'It delivers as entertainment. It should draw by itself, while the cast will be a considerable help.' – Variety

'A model of skilful reconstruction and ingenious research.' – Times

'Fairly reeking with authentic, rowdy, hurdy-gurdy atmosphere … a grand evening of fun for everybody.' – Photoplay

• The Bowery was the first production of Twentieth Century
• Gable was sought for the Raft role, but proved unavailable.

983
The Bowery

In 1890s New York, two boisterous rivals settle their differences after one has jumped off the Brooklyn Bridge for a bet.

Based on an actual feud in 1890s New York between two Bowery gang leaders, this roistering saga of cross and double cross starred two of the screen's tougher guys, Wallace Beery and George Raft, who came to blows during filming. Raoul Walsh achieved a certain authenticity in the fights by telling the extras on each gang that the other side thought they were soft, so that tempers were lost. It is splendidly vigorous in acting and treatment. Walsh was also able to recreate the appearance of the Bowery's notorious McGurk's tavern from his own memories of the place. Raft played Steve Brodie, a Brooklyn bookmaker who won fame in 1886 by jumping off the Brooklyn Bridge into the East River three hundred feet below and surviving (though it is claimed that actually an accomplice threw a dummy off the bridge while Brodie hid below by a pier).

One Hundred Men and a Girl

👣 US 1937 84m bw
Universal (Joe Pasternak)

w Bruce Manning, Charles Kenyon, Hans Kraly *d* Henry Koster *ph* Joseph Valentine *m* Charles Previn *m/ly* Frederick Hollander, Sam Coslow *ad* John W. Harkrider *ed* Bernard W. Burton

☆ Deanna Durbin (Patricia Cardwell), Adolphe Menjou (John Cardwell), Leopold Stokowski (Himself), Alice Brady (Mrs. Frost), Mischa Auer (Michael Borodoff), Eugene Pallette (John R. Frost), Billy Gilbert (Garage Owner), Alma Kruger (Mrs. Tyler), Jed Prouty (Tommy Bitters), Frank Jenks (Taxi Driver), Christian Rub (Gustave Brandstetter)

'Smash hit for all the family … something new in entertainment.' – Variety

'Apart from its value as entertainment, which is considerable, it reveals the cinema at its sunny-sided best.' – New York Times.

'An original story put over with considerable skill.' – MFB

♫ 'It's Raining Sunbeams'; 'Music in My Dreams'
🎼 Charles Previn
♟ best picture; original story (Hans Kraly); editing

982
One Hundred Men and a Girl

A young girl persuades a great conductor to form an orchestra of unemployed musicians.

The 16-year-old Deanna Durbin's success in this delightful and funny musical fable resulted in her salary being doubled overnight. Audiences responded to its tale of a young girl persuading a great conductor to work with an orchestra made up of a hundred unemployed musicians, including her widowed father. She finally achieves it by marching the orchestra into the home of Leopold Stokowski, who then conducts them in Liszt's *Hungarian Rhapsody* while standing at the top of his staircase. It is a lasting example of the Pasternak formula of sweetness and light at its richest and best.

The Ghost Breakers

US   1940   85m   bw
Paramount (Arthur Hornblow Jnr)

🏳️ ⊕~ ⊘

w Walter de Leon *play* Paul Dickey, Charles W. Goddard
d George Marshall *ph* Charles Lang *m* Ernst Toch
ad Hans Dreier, Robert Asher *ed* Ellsworth Hoagland
☆ *Bob Hope* (Larry Lawrence), *Paulette Goddard* (Mary
Carter), Paul Lukas (Parada), *Willie Best* (Alex), Richard
Carlson (Geoff Montgomery), *Lloyd Corrigan* (Martin),
Anthony Quinn (Ramon/Francisco Maderos), Noble
Johnson (The Zombie), Pedro de Cordoba (Havez)

'Bob Hope can joke, apparently, even with a risen
corpse.' – *MFB*

'Paramount has found the fabled formula for
making audiences shriek with laughter and fright at
one and the same time.' – *New York Times*

● Previously filmed in 1914 with H. B. Warner; in 1922
with Wallace Reid; and remade in 1953 as *Scared Stiff*.

981
The Ghost Breakers

A girl inherits a castle and finds herself up to her neck in ghosts, zombies and buried treasure.

Bob Hope is at his best in this well done, archetypal comedy horror as a crime reporter helping a girl who inherits a West Indian castle. By this time, he had perfected his cowardly routine and his timing of wisecracks is impeccable. He and Goddard made an excellent romantic and comedy team. All that has dated is the jokes at the expense of Hope's black valet (Willie Best), which will cause audiences now to wince. The film followed on the success of Hope and Goddard's earlier haunted house mystery, *The Cat and the Canary*, though the tone here is darker and, ultimately, all the funnier for it. For those familiar with the genre only from more modern manifestations, such as the Scooby-Doo series, this provides a revelation in the art of successfully combining wisecracks and scares.

☆ **Geoff Andrew,** Senior Film Editor, *Time Out* ☆

1. L'Atalante (Jean Vigo)
    The greatest (because most honest) love film ever made, and a miraculous mix of drama, suspense, comedy, social observation, eroticism, and pure filmic poetry.
2. Our Hospitality (Buster Keaton)
    Arguably the most exquisitely crafted comedy ever (alongside Keaton's likewise elegant 'The General'), and a delightfully authentic historical movie into the bargain. Keaton's 'stone-face' was never more expressive.
3. Tokyo Story (Yasujiro Ozu)
    A landmark of world cinema; the becalmed simplicity of its methods are matched by the emotional and philosophical depth of its account of human disappointment and the pitfalls of modern life.
4. The Magnificent Ambersons (Orson Welles)
5. His Girl Friday (Howard Hawks)
6. My Night with Maud/Ma Nuit chez Maud (Eric Rohmer)
7. Ordet/The Word (Carl Dreyer)
8. Les Demoiselles de Rochefort/The Young Ladies of Rochefort (Jacques Demy)
9. The Wind Will Carry Us (Abbas Kiarostami)
10. Persona (Ingmar Bergman)

'Growing up isn't easy at any age'

On Golden Pond
US 1981 109m colour Panavision
ITC/IPC (Bruce Gilbert)

🎞 ▦ ⌕ ◎ ◎

w Ernest Thompson *play* Ernest Thompson *d* Mark Rydell *ph* Billy Williams *m* Dave Grusin *ed* Robert L. Wolfe

☆ *Henry Fonda* (Norman Thayer, Jr.), *Katharine Hepburn* (Ethel Thayer), Jane Fonda (Chelsea Thayer Wayne), Doug McKeon (Billy Ray), Dabney Coleman (Bill Ray)

'Moments of truth survive some cloying contrivance; Rydell directs on bended knees.' – *Sight and Sound*

'Two of Hollywood's best-loved veterans deserve a far better swansong than this sticky confection.' – *Time Out*

'The kind of uplifting twaddle that traffics heavily in rather basic symbols: the gold light on the pond stands for the sunset of life, and so on.' – *Pauline Kael, New Yorker*

• A Region 1 special edition DVD includes commentary by Ernest Thompson.

👤 Ernest Thompson; Henry Fonda; Katharine Hepburn
👥 picture; Mark Rydell; Jane Fonda; Robert L. Wolfe; Dave Grusin; Billy Williams; sound (Richard Portman, David M. Ronne)
🏆 Katharine Hepburn

On Golden Pond

An 80-year-old, his wife and his daughter spend a holiday at their New England lakeside cottage.

A well-acted, decent screen presentation of a rather waffling and sentimental play. The film is remarkable not so much for what it is as for the fact that in the sophisticated eighties enough people paid to see it to make it a box-office record-breaker. This was mainly due to affection for Fonda, whose last film it was, and Hepburn, but also to an American desire for a reversion to the old values of warmth and humanity after the sex and violence which the screen had lately been offering. Katharine Hepburn, who gave Henry Fonda Spencer Tracy's favourite hat to wear in the film, found him 'wonderful to play with'. As Jane Fonda, its co-producer, intended, the film belongs to her father. Hepburn's role as the wife was to provide unconditional support; she thought of it as a film about a couple who really liked one another. It also mirrored real life. Like the character he played, Fonda had a heart condition and was near death, which adds an extra depth to his performance.

Witchcraft Through the Ages

Sweden 1922 113m approx (24 fps) bw silent
Svensk Filmindustri
⊟ ▤ ⦾
original title: *Häxan*
wd Benjamin Christensen *ph* Johan Ankarstjerne
☆ Oscar Stribolt, Clara Pontoppidan, Karen Winther

979
Witchcraft Through the Ages

A 'documentary' investigation of the history of witchcraft, with acted examples.

Danish director Christensen's film is a strange mix of documentary, still images and dramatic reconstructions of witchcraft from the earliest times to the twentieth century. Images of demons from medieval texts, strange animal shapes, malevolent hags and human sacrifices fill the screen. Also paraded are the instruments of torture used to extract confessions of demonic possession. The film was banned for many years and also exists in mutilated versions, usually running at around 90m. A restored version, running for 113m, was produced in the late 60s. It still maintains the power to frighten. For its time, it was an extraordinary, pioneering work by a director with a flair for striking imagery as well as a gift for sensational exploitation. He vividly recreates moments of medieval superstitions, ranging from the trials and torture of witches to old hags flying high on their broomsticks and a woman giving birth to a demon.

Lover Come Back

US 1961 107m Eastmancolor
U-I/Seven Pictures/Nob Hill/Arwin (Stanley Shapiro, Marty Melcher)
⊟ ⦾
w Stanley Shapiro, Paul Henning *d* Delbert Mann
ph Arthur E. Arling *m* Frank de Vol *ad* Robert Clatworthy, Alexander Golitzen *ed* Marjorie Fowler
☆ Doris Day (Carol Templeton), Rock Hudson (Jerry Webster/Doctor Linus Tyler), Tony Randall (Peter 'Pete' Ramsey), Jack Oakie (J. Paxton Miller), Edie Adams (Rebel Davis)

'One of the brightest, most delightful satiric comedies … the funniest picture of the year.'
– Bosley Crowther, New York Times

⚐ Stanley Shapiro, Paul Henning

978
Lover Come Back

Rival executives find themselves advertising a non-existent product.

A sharp satire of the advertising business disguised as a romantic comedy, this pits Rock Hudson against Doris Day as two rivals who eventually fall in love so that the maiden can reform the cad. Fast-paced, cleverly-plotted, and with sharp dialogue, it has a joyous performance from Tony Randall as Hudson's neurotic boss. Its sexual attitudes may seem a little dated, and booze flows and cigarettes are smoked with a period abandon, making it almost the last gasp of screwball comedy. It was the stars' second film together, following the success of *Pillow Talk*, which had been Hudson's first comic role after many dramatic parts. By the time he made this, his comic timing had sharpened, so that he was at ease with witty dialogue. More importantly, as Doris Day remarked, 'we looked good together.' There is fun to be had, too, at the expense of the social conventions of the time, as Day protects her virginity with a resolve only matched by Hudson's desire to rid her of it.

Les Triplettes de Belleville

France/Canada/Belgium/GB 2002 81m colour
Metro Tartan/Les Armatuers/Champion/ViviFrance 3/ RGP (Didier Brunner)

US title: *The Triplets of Belleville*
GB title: *Belleville Rendez-vous*
wd Sylvain Chomet *m* Benôit Charest *ad* Evgeni Tomov
☆ voices of: Jean-Claude Donda, Michel Robin, Monica Viegas

'By turns sweet and sinister, insouciant and grotesque, invitingly funny and forbiddingly dark.' – *A. O. Scott, New York Times*

'A wondrous blend of quaint nostalgia and barmy, sometimes spooky strangeness.' – *Nicholas Barber, Independent*

animated film; song 'The Triplets of Belleville' (m/l Benôit Charest, Sylvain Chomet)

977
Les Triplettes de Belleville

A club-footed grandmother, an overweight dog and an aged trio of singers help rescue a cyclist who is kidnapped during the Tour de France to take part in Mafia-run races.

Divertingly original animated film in which there is almost no dialogue but plenty of sound; its narrative style is closer to that of Jacques Tati than conventional cartoons, with gentle, observational humour, jokes that lack punch-lines and surreal moments. It has great fun with national stereotypes: the French singers eat nothing but frogs and the United States is almost exclusively inhabited by fat people and wide-shouldered gangsters. Sylvain Chomet's scratchy drawing style adds a slightly sinister quality to the animation, though it is his exuberantly inventive imagination that gives the film its originality. He manages to leap from one absurd notion – a dog's dream of being an engine driver – to another – an Atlantic crossing by pedalo – without losing his way. It is a remarkable achievement.

Sherlock Junior

US 1924 45m (24 fps) bw silent
Metro/Buster Keaton (Joseph M. Schenck)

w Clyde Bruckman, Jean Havez, Joseph Mitchell *ph* Elgin Lessley, Byron Houck *d/ed* Buster Keaton
☆ *Buster Keaton*, Kathryn McGuire, Ward Crane, Joseph Keaton

976
Sherlock Junior

A film projectionist, unjustly accused of stealing a watch, has dreams of being a great detective.

A fast-moving comedy that ranks among Keaton's best, providing him with two roles to play. The first is of a hapless cinema projectionist, who can afford only the smallest diamond ring for his girlfriend; he also provides her with a magnifying glass so she can get a closer look at it. After he is outmanoeuvred by an unscrupulous rival and unjustly accused of stealing a watch, he dreams of being a great detective, and steps into a mystery movie. Quick-fire gags keep the laughs flowing (though one stunt, in which he grabs the spout of a water tank from the top of a moving freight train, left him with a broken neck). The film has a happy ending, but in reality most critics at the time damned it; it was only later that its hilarious ingenuity was fully appreciated.

The Last Waltz

The Last Waltz
US 1978 115m DeLuxe
UA/Martin Scorsese, Jonathan Taplin (Robbie Robertson)
■ ◎~ ◎ ◎ ∩
d Martin Scorsese *ph* Michael Chapman, Laszlo Kovacs, Vilmos Zsigmond, David Myers, Bobby Byrne, Michael Watkins, Hiro Narita *pd* Boris Leven *ed* Yeu-Bun Yee, Jan Roblee
☆ Robbie Robertson, Rick Danko, Richard Manuel, Levon Helm, Garth Hudson, Eric Clapton, Neil Diamond, Bob Dylan, Joni Mitchell, Neil Young, Emmylou Harris, Ringo Starr, Paul Butterfield, Dr John, Van Morrison and also Ronnie Hawkins, The Staples, Muddy Waters, Ron Wood

975
The Last Waltz

Documentary featuring the last concert of the rock group The Band at the Winterland, San Francisco, on Thanksgiving Day, 1976, after 16 years on the road.

Martin Scorsese's documentary is perhaps the best movie so far of a rock concert, one that also features many of the most influential performers of the era, from Muddy Waters to Bob Dylan, together with some brief but revealing interviews with The Band members. Scorsese, aided by a stellar team of cameramen, ignores the audience for the most part, concentrating on capturing the musicians close-up, professionals at work and play. The timing of Scorsese's film was perfect in its way. It may have been the final performance of The Band, but it also showed what were then the grizzled veterans of rock, a familiar collection of individuals who were comfortable in each other's company, playing at, or near, their best before changing times also changed the music.

The Lodger
GB 1926 84m approx (24 fps) bw silent
Gainsborough (Michael Balcon)
◾ ■ ◎
Subtitle: *A Story of the London Fog*
US title: *The Case of Jonathan Drew*
w Eliot Stannard, Alfred Hitchcock *novel* Mrs Belloc Lowndes *d* Alfred Hitchcock *ph* Baron Ventimiglia *ad* Bertram Evans, C. Wilfred Arnold *ed* Ivor Montagu
☆ Ivor Novello (Jonathan Drew, The Lodger), June (Daisy Bunting), Marie Ault (Mrs. Bunting), Arthur Chesney (Mr. Bunting), Malcolm Keen (Joe Betts)

'It was the first time I exercised my style ... you might almost say it was my first picture.' – *Alfred Hitchcock, 1966*

974
The Lodger

A modern version of the novel about a stranger who is (in this case) wrongly thought to be Jack the Ripper.

The first version of a novel which was to attract three other directors over the years. It is the first true Hitchcock film, full of his familiar dramatic visual touches. Oddly enough it was followed by three years during which he seemed to forget them. Here is one of his favourite devices: having an innocent man accused of a crime he did not commit and forced to flee. It includes a startling shot using a glass floor, so that the lodger's landlady can be seen looking anxiously at her ceiling as he paces overhead. As Hitchcock's French admirers, Eric Rohmer and Claude Chabrol, have pointed out, Ivor Novello is a perfect Hitchcockian actor: 'handsome, disturbing, projecting a strange and melancholy gentleness with romantic overtones'.

Donnie Darko

US 2001 113m DeLuxe Panavision
Metrodome/Pandora/Flower (Sean McKittrick, Nancy
Juvonen, Adam Fields)

☒☒ ▤ ⊙ ⊙ ⌂

wd Richard Kelly *ph* Steven Poster *m* Michael Andrews
pd Alexander Hammond *ed* Sam Bauer, Eric Strand
☆ Jake Gyllenhaal (Donnie Darko), Jena Malone
(Gretchen Ross), Drew Barrymore (Karen Pomeroy), James
Duval (Frank), Maggie Gyllenhaal (Elizabeth Darko), Mary
McDonnell (Rose Darko), Holmes Osborne (Eddie Darko),
Katharine Ross (Dr Lillian Thurman), Patrick Swayze (Jim
Cunningham), Noah Wyle (Dr Monnitoff)

'What a refreshingly different, distinctive piece of
work it is.' – *Peter Bradshaw, Guardian*

'Kelly is unable to give the movie the kind of pacing
that would make us laugh and shock us
simultaneously, because he's too infatuated with an
aura of hand-me-down gloom.' – *Elvis Mitchell,
New York Times*

● A director's cut, running an extra 20m, was released in
2004.

973
Donnie Darko

*In the late 1980s, a troubled teenage boy, who is prone to sleepwalk-
ing, is visited by a large rabbit, who tells him that the world is soon
going to end.*

The time is 1988, and the place is a paranoid universe on the brink of
destruction. This is the world of Donnie Darko, who is not your average
American teenager: a possible schizophrenic and compulsive sleepwalker, he is seeing a psychiatrist and forgetting to take his medication.
Director Richard Kelly, aided by Jake Gyllenhaal's befuddled, charming
Donnie, has made a bracingly original, deliberately puzzling movie with
a circular narrative that is concerned with teenage angst while taking a
few sideswipes at suburban living. He achieves the difficult feat of
being both comic and serious at the same time.

'Meet the ultimate dysfunctional family.'

Tokyo Godfathers
Japan   2003   91m   colour
Mad House/Tokyo Godfathers Committee (Masao Maruyama)
◉
w Satoshi Kon, Keiko Nobumotu *d* Satoshi Kon
ph Katsutoshi Sugai *m* Keiichi Zuzuki *ad* Nobutaka Ike
ed Takeshi Seyama *co-director* Shogo Furuya *character designer* Kenichi Konishi
☆ voices of: Toru Emari (Gin), Yoshiaki Umegaki (Hana), Aya Okamoto (Miyuki), Shozo Iizuka (Oota), Seizo Kato (Mother), Hiroya Ishimaru (Yasuo)

'This is a first-class film that will appeal to anyone who wants to see a plausible, witty, absorbing human story told well – indeed, told gorgeously.' – *Shawn Levy, Portland Oregonian*

'Takes anime to a whole new level.' – *Variety*

972
Tokyo Godfathers

At Christmas in Tokyo, three vagrants – an alcoholic, a former drag queen and a teenage runaway – discover an abandoned baby and wander the city looking for her mother.

Satoshi Kon has emerged in the last few years as one of the best directors of animated films which are aimed at a mature, rather than childish, audience. His *Perfect Blue* examined the world of manufactured pop idols, while *Millennium Actress* traced a hundred years of Japanese cinema and a thousand years of its history through the life of one actress. *Tokyo Godfathers*, his best film so far, is an engrossing stylishly animated drama of the meaning of family that is an urban variation on John Ford's 1948 Western, the much filmed *Three Godfathers*. The story is purged of its usual sentimentality and revels in the complexities of the underside of city life.

Trash
US   1970   103m   colour
Vaughn/Andy Warhol
⬛ ▦ ◉
aka: *Andy's Warhol's Trash*
wd Paul Morrissey *ph* Paul Morrissey *ed* Jed Johnson, Paul Morrissey
☆ Joe Dallesandro (Joe), Geri Miller (Go-go dancer), Holly Woodlawn (Holly), Bruce Pecheur (Jane's husband), Jane Forth (Jane), Michael Sklar (Welfare investigator), Andrea Feldman (Rich girl), Johnny Putnam (Boy from Yonkers)

971
Trash

A drug addict finds that the women he knows are anxious to cure him of his impotence.

A seminal film that, like some of the other movies that emerged from Andy Warhol's Factory, helped broaden mainstream cinema and bring street life to the screen. Paul Morrissey seems at once fascinated and horrified by his characters. Here is the downside of the drug culture, dispensing with its hippie glamour, yet finding a compassion for its human trash, notably in the intimate relationship between the passive Joe and the hectic Holly. The setting is sordid – the opening shot is of Dallesandro's naked, pimpled backside – but the actors are given room to be whatever they want to be. As George Cukor, a Hollywood director of an earlier generation, remarked, 'it's chilling and it's beautifully done'.

Young Frankenstein
US   1974   108m   bw
TCF/Gruskoff/Venture/Jouer/Crossbow (Michael Gruskoff)
🎞 ▤ ⊛ ⊘ ⊚
w Gene Wilder, Mel Brooks *d* Mel Brooks *ph* Gerald Hirschfeld *m* John Morris *ad* Dale Hennesy *ed* John Howard
☆ Gene Wilder (Dr. Frederick Frankenstein), Marty Feldman (Igor), Madeline Kahn (Elizabeth), *Peter Boyle* (Monster), Cloris Leachman (Frau Blucher), Kenneth Mars (Inspector Kemp), Gene Hackman (Blind Hermit), Richard Haydn (Herr Falkstein), Teri Garr (Inga)

'Like a sketch from the old Sid Caesar show, for which Brooks wrote, spun out ten times as long. Ten times too long. Brooks is a sprinter, and there aren't enough good sprints here.' – *Stanley Kauffmann*

'A great deal of low fun.' – *Vincent Canby*

⚱ script

970
Young Frankenstein

Young Frederick Frankenstein, a brain surgeon, goes back to Transylvania and pores over his grandfather's notebooks.

An engaging parody of the cliches of horror movies which, unlike many earlier comic attempts in a similar vein, has the advantage of not having Abbott and Costello meeting anyone. Wilder's nervy young brain surgeon returns to Transylvania and before long is making a monster. It's lowbrow fun, with some splendid moments, notably the encounter between Gene Hackman's kindly blind hermit and Peter Boyle's monster; Hackman spills soup in his lap, smashes their glasses in an enthusiastic toast, offers a cigar and then lights the monster's thumb. Gerald Hirschfeld's gleaming black and white photography deftly captures the style of the vintage Frankensteins, as does Dale Hennesy's production design, down to a laboratory that Colin Clive would have felt at home in.

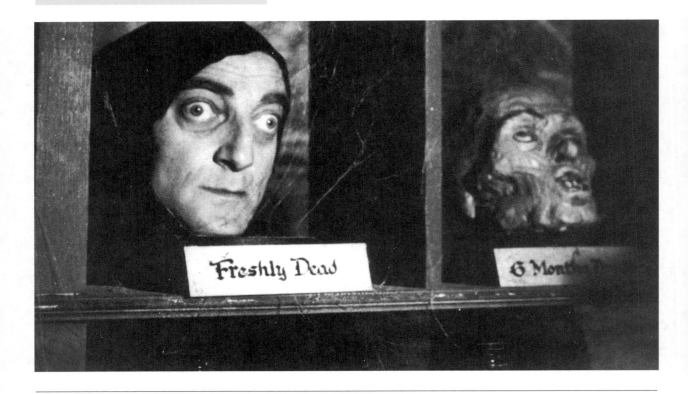

The Black Pirate

US 1926 76m approx (24 fps) Technicolor
silent
Douglas Fairbanks
■ ◎~ ◎
w Douglas Fairbanks, Jack Cunningham *d* Albert Parker
ph Henry Sharp *ad* Oscar Borg, Dwight Franklin
ed William Nolan
☆ *Douglas Fairbanks* (Michel, the Black Pirate), Billie
Dove (The Princess), Donald Crisp (McTavish), Sam de
Grasse (Lieutenant)
● The Region 1 DVD includes a commentary by film
historian Rudy Behlmer.

969
The Black Pirate

A shipwrecked mariner swears revenge on the pirates who blew up his father's ship.

In this first great swashbuckling pirate movie, Douglas Fairbanks created a moment that has been repeated many times since: he plunges his knife into the top of a high sail and slits it as he gracefully slides down to the deck. The athletic panache of his performance, swinging from one mast to another in shipboard battles, brightens the tale. Filmed in early Technicolor, this still communicates an infectious sense of high adventure. Fairbanks availed himself of every boyhood fantasy in his action-packed melodrama. There was buried treasure, sword and dagger fights, a princess in distress who needs rescuing from an evil pirate, and a finale in which he is forced to walk the plank before returning to rescue the girl he loves and revealing himself as a Duke in disguise. What larks!

The Rains Came

US 1939 103m bw
TCF (Harry Joe Brown)
■
w Philip Dunne, Julien Josephson *novel* Louis Bromfield
d Clarence Brown *ph* Arthur Miller *m* Alfred Newman
ad George Dudley, William Darling *ed* Barbara McLean
sp Fred Sersen
☆ Myrna Loy (Lady Edwina Esketh), *George Brent* (Tom
Ransome), Tyrone Power (Maj. Rama Safti), Brenda Joyce
(Fern Simon), *Maria Ouspenskaya* (Maharani), *Joseph
Schildkraut* (Mr. Bannerjee), H. B. Warner (Maharajah),
Nigel Bruce (Albert Lord Esketh), Mary Nash (Miss
MacDaid), Jane Darwell (Aunt Phoebe Smiley), Marjorie
Rambeau (Mrs. Simon), Henry Travers (Rev. Homer Smiley)

'A big box-office picture with the advantage of a new locale.' – *Variety*

'It would be difficult to improve on the direction, the outbreak of the monsoon, a curtain billowing in the breeze, a lamp casting the shadow of lattice work against white silk, servants scattering for cover …' – *Charles Higham, 1972*

'Slick Hollywood film-making at its professional best.' – *Channel 4, 1982*

● Myrna Loy was third choice after Dietrich and Lamarr; Brent second choice after Ronald Colman.
Ω Alfred Newman; editing

968
The Rains Came

High-class parasites in India during the Raj redeem themselves when a flood disaster strikes.

In the monsoon season, a flood disaster strikes, followed by a malaria epidemic, in this lavish, tear-jerking, romantic epic. It is a wholly absorbing disaster spectacular in which the characterization and personal plot development are at least as interesting as the spectacle, and all are encased in a glowingly professional production. Under Clarence Brown's expert direction, Power, in dark make-up as an aristocratic Indian doctor, confirmed his position as a top box-office star (second only to Mickey Rooney, then riding high in the *Andy Hardy* movies). He represents a more modern India, as he works devotedly to save the common people. The film has an ambivalent attitude towards Empire. The British are shown as decadent; but as the womanizing Tom Ransome is saved from the flood by hanging on to a statue of Queen Victoria, he remarks, "It's just me and you, old girl. You're the living reminder of the brave world before it went to seed."

Chicken Run
👥 US/GB 2000 85m Technicolor
Pathé/DreamWorks, Aardman (Peter Lord, David
Sproxton, Nick Park)
▨ ▤ ◉ ◈

w Karey Kirkpatrick *story* Peter Lord, Nick Park *d* Peter
Lord, Nick Park *ph* Dave Alex Riddett, Tristan Oliver, Frank
Passingham *m* John Powell, Harry Gregson-Williams
pd Phil Lewis *ad* Tim Farrington *ed* Mark Solomon
☆ voices of: Mel Gibson (Rocky), Julia Sawalha (Ginger),
Miranda Richardson (Mrs Tweedy), Jane Horrocks (Babs),
Lynn Ferguson (Mac), Imelda Staunton (Bunty), Benjamin
Whitrow (Fowler), Tony Haygarth (Mr Tweedy), Timothy
Spall (Nick), Phil Daniels (Fetcher)

'Always engaging, full of bright humor, marvelous
stop-motion work with Plasticine figures, dramatic
conflict and wonderfully nuanced
characterizations.' – *Todd McCarthy, Variety*

'A smart mix of nostalgia, sweetness and flip
modernity in design and dialogue.' – *Angie Errigo,
Empire*

'Pretty modest fare, with nothing like the style and
invention of the *Toy Story* films.' – *Peter Bradshaw,
Guardian*

967
Chicken Run

*A circus rooster helps organize chickens to escape the jail-like farm
where they face certain death in an automated pie-making machine.*

This charming animated movie has some of the very English qualities
of the old Ealing comedies. In part, it is a parody of prisoner-of-war
films such as *The Great Escape*, which may mean little to its intended
audience. Gradually, though, it develops a comic momentum and
absurdity all of its own, with a quaint, handmade charm that proves
irresistible. Despite the chicken's chirpy optimism and stiff upper-beak
attitudes, the film is at times properly scary. Mrs Tweedy, the fearsome
farmer's wife, grabs one recalcitrant hen and marches off with it. The
next sound that is heard is the thud of an axe. A chicken pie machine,
from which two heroic birds only just escape, is a fatally gruesome
piece of machinery, like a diabolic Heath Robinson contraption. The
overall tone, though, is of a sweet-natured optimism and a delight in
the simple pleasures of life.

The Blue Bird
👥 US 1940 98m Technicolor (bw
prologue)
TCF (Gene Markey)
▤

w Ernest Pascal *d* Walter Lang *ph* Arthur Miller, Ray
Rennahan *m* Alfred Newman *ad* Richard Day, Wiard B.
Ihnen *ed* Robert Bischoff
☆ Shirley Temple (Mytyl), Johnny Russell (Tyltyl), *Gale
Sondergaard* (Tylette (The Cat)), *Eddie Collins* (Tylo (The
Dog)), Nigel Bruce (Mr. Luxury), Jessie Ralph (Fairy
Berylune), Spring Byington (Mummy Tyl), Sybil Jason
(Angela Berlingot), Helen Ericson (Light), Russell Hicks
(Daddy Tyl), Al Shean (Grandpa Tyl), Cecilia Loftus (Granny
Tyl)

'One of the most deliciously lovely productions to
be brought to the screen.' – *MFB*

⚖ Arthur Miller, Ray Rennahan

966
The Blue Bird

*In a Grimm's Fairy Tale setting, the two children of a poor woodcutter
seek the bluebird of happiness in the past, the future and the Land of
Luxury, but eventually discover it in their own back yard.*

An imaginative and often chilling script clarifies Maurice Maeterlinck's
fairy play. The art direction is outstanding, but the children are necessarily unsympathetic and the expensive production paled beside the
success of the more upbeat *Wizard of Oz*, which was released almost
simultaneously. Slashed for re-release, the only existing prints now
open with confusing abruptness and no scene-setting before the
adventures begin. Shirley Temple's mother had complained vocifer-
ously to Darryl Zanuck, the head of the studio, about the script and
characterization. As a result, 'my role became more shameful and despicable,' Shirley Temple later recalled. 'The character appealed to me, a
peevish, greedy spiteful brat, the sort anyone would like to put over a
knee and wallop.' But it upset audiences at the time and it was to take
thirty years before the film found an appreciative audience.

Satyricon

Satyricon
Italy/France 1969 129m DeLuxe
Panavision
UA/PAA/PEA (Alberto Grimaldi)
⬚ ▤ ☍ ⦾ ⦿
aka: *Fellini Satyricon*
w Federico Fellini, Bernardino Zapponi *d* Federico Fellini
ph Giuseppe Rotunno *m* Nino Rota, Ilhan Mimaroglu, Tod
Dockstader, Andrew Rudin *pd* Danilo Donati *ad* Giorgio
Giovannini, Luigi Scaccianoce *ed* Ruggero Mastroianni
☆ Martin Potter (Encolpius), Hiram Keller (Ascyltus),
Salvo Randone (Eumolpus), Max Born (Giton)

'A picaresque satire in fragments ... a series of
tableaux which carry the poetry visually at the price
of coherence.' – *Mike Wallington, MFB*

'Part of the gradual decomposition of what once
was one of the greatest talents in film history ... a
gimcrack, shopworn nightmare.' – *John Simon*

♟ Federico Fellini (as director)

965
Satyricon

Sexual adventures of a Roman student.

Fellini at his most self-indulgent, as he is here, is still more interesting than most of his rivals. In a free adaptation of Petronius's incomplete novel, he vividly creates the decadence and brutality of Rome during the reign of Nero, when the sexual abandon of those times seemed peculiarly modern. The film is a picaresque adventure, centring on two Roman students, whom Fellini regards as proto-hippies. They are both attracted to a pretty slave boy and wander through the ancient world, surviving a series of unexpected encounters. But these actors, picked for their looks, are unable to match his vision of magnificent vulgarity.

'West of Chicago there was no law! West
of Dodge City there was no God!'
Dodge City
US 1939 104m Technicolor
Warner (Robert Lord)
⬚ ▤ ☍
w Robert Buckner *d* Michael Curtiz *ph* Sol Polito, Ray
Rennahan *m* Max Steiner *ad* Ted Smith *ed* George Amy
☆ Errol Flynn (Wade Hatton), Olivia de Havilland (Abbie
Irving), Ann Sheridan (Ruby Gilman), Bruce Cabot (Jeff
Surrett), Alan Hale (Algernon "Rusty" Hart), Frank McHugh
(Joe Clemens), John Litel (Matt Cole), Victor Jory (Yancy,
Surrett's Henchman), William Lundigan (Lee Irving), Henry
Travers (Dr. Irving), Henry O'Neill (Col. Dodge), Guinn
Williams (Tex Baird), Gloria Holden (Mrs. Cole)

'A lusty Western, packed with action, including
some of the dandiest mêlée stuff screened.' –
Variety

'It looks programmed and underpopulated, though
in an elegantly stylized way.' – *New Yorker, 1980*

964
Dodge City

An ex-soldier and trail boss helps clean up the West's great railroad terminus.

Errol Flynn's first Western is plainly inspired by the exploits of Wyatt Earp. He plays a roaming Irishman who has been a revolutionary in Cuba, a cowboy and a soldier for the South in the Civil War. He becomes sheriff and cleans up the town. It is a satisfying big-scale Western with all the usual ingredients intact and very enjoyable, as is the soft, rich, early colour. Its great distinction is its vast and hectic saloon brawl, one of the screen's great fight scenes that begins when the band plays a Northern song and Flynn and his friends retaliate with a chorus of 'Dixie'. The footage turned up in many subsequent movies.

The Sea Hawk

US 1940 122m bw
Warner (Hal B. Wallis, Henry Blanke)

w Seton I. Miller, Howard Koch d Michael Curtiz ph Sol Polito m Erich Wolfgang Korngold ad Anton Grot ed George Amy

☆ *Errol Flynn* (Capt. Geoffrey Thorpe), Flora Robson (Queen Elizabeth), Brenda Marshall (Donna Maria Alvarez de Cordoba), *Henry Daniell* (Lord Wolfingham), Claude Rains (Don Jose Alvarez de Cordoba), Donald Crisp (Sir John Burleson), Alan Hale (Carl Pitt), Una O'Connor (Martha), James Stephenson (Abbott), Gilbert Roland (Capt. Lopez), William Lundigan (Danny Logan)

'Endless episodes of court intrigue tend to diminish the effect of the epic sweep of the high seas dramatics.' – *Variety*

♯ Erich Wolfgang Korngold; Anton Grot

963
The Sea Hawk

Elizabeth I encourages one of her most able captains to acts of piracy against the Spanish.

Errol Flynn swashbuckles with great style in this period piece, which is a stirring example of old-time Hollywood, complete with a soaring symphonic score from Korngold. Warners originally planned to remake the 1924 silent movie of *The Sea Hawk*, taken from a novel by Rafael Sabatini, who had also written the book of Flynn's first great success, *Captain Blood*. In the end, they kept the title but changed the plot to a story based on the exploits of Sir Francis Drake. It is a stirring and exciting seafaring actioner, with splendid battle and duel scenes, captured by a restless camera in gleaming black and white photography.

Stage Door

US 1937 93m bw
RKO (Pandro S. Berman)

w Morrie Ryskind, Anthony Veiller play Edna Ferber, George S. Kaufman d Gregory La Cava ph Robert de Grasse m Roy Webb ad Van Nest Polglase ed William Hamilton

☆ *Katharine Hepburn* (Terry Randall), *Ginger Rogers* (Jean Maitland), Adolphe Menjou (Anthony Powell), Gail Patrick (Linda Shaw), Constance Collier (Catherine Luther), Andrea Leeds (Kaye Hamilton), Lucille Ball (Judy Canfield), Samuel S. Hinds (Henry Sims), Jack Carson (Milbank), Franklin Pangborn (Harcourt), Eve Arden (Eve)

'It is a long time since we have seen so much feminine talent so deftly handled.' – *Otis Ferguson*

'Zest and pace and photographic eloquence.' – *Frank S. Nugent, New York Times*

'A rare example of a film substantially improving on a stage original and a remarkably satisfying film on all levels.' – *NFT, 1973*

'One of the flashiest, most entertaining comedies of the 30s, even with its tremolos and touches of heartbreak.' – *Pauline Kael, 70s*

♯ best picture; script; Gregory La Cava; Andrea Leeds

962
Stage Door

Life in a New York theatrical boarding house for girls.

The contrasting casting of the patrician Hepburn and the plebeian Rogers did much to ensure the success of this melodramatic, sharply comedic, always fascinating slice of stagey life in a New York theatrical boarding house for girls. The original Broadway hit was rewritten to accommodate its two stars: Rogers was then trying to move away from musicals, though she still played a street-wise dancer, and Hepburn was attempting to survive in films; fortunately, her role as a wealthy dilettante who wanted to try acting, was among her best, and most popular, performances. Apart from the two leads, the film was strongly cast, with Andrea Leeds remarkable as a suicidal young actress. Indeed, the performances alone make it worth preserving.

'More horrible than horror! More terrible than terror!'

Peeping Tom
GB   1959   109m   Eastmancolor
Anglo Amalgamated/Michael Powell

w Leo Marks d Michael Powell ph Otto Heller m Brian Easdale ad Arthur Lawrence ed Noreen Ackland
☆ Carl Boehm (Mark Lewis), Moira Shearer (Vivian), Anna Massey (Helen Stephens), Maxine Audley (Mrs. Stephens), Esmond Knight (Arthur Baden), Michael Goodliffe (Don Jarvis), Shirley Anne Field (Diane Ashley), Jack Watson (Inspector Gregg)

'Perhaps one would not be so disagreeably affected by this exercise in the lower regions of the psychopathic were it handled in a more bluntly debased fashion.' – *Dilys Powell*

'Of enormous and deserved reputation.' – *Time Out, 1982*

961
Peeping Tom

A film studio focus puller is obsessed by the lust to murder beautiful women and photograph the fear on their faces.

Michael Powell's forerunner of the slasher movie brought an abrupt stop to his career when it was reviled by audiences and critics on its first release. Its reputation has grown since. Yet its narrative, has a troubling quality about it. Like Hitchcock in some of his films, Powell seems to enjoy too much the humiliation of women. Part of the problem is the skill with which the film is made, forcing its audience to be implicated, as voyeurs, in the murders. There is no question that it is the work of a master director. The opening moments form a superb exposition of the film's theme, in which hardly a word is spoken from the first close-up of an eye opening wide to a movie camera's view of the murder of a prostitute and the revelation of the killer's identity as he returns to film the police removing the girl's body. Powell even finds a moment for a chilling joke. 'What paper are you from?' a policeman asks the cameraman. '*The Observer,*' the voyeur replies.

'The story of a family's ugly secret and the stark moment that thrust their private lives into public view!'

Written on the Wind
US   1956   99m   Technicolor
U-I (Albert Zugsmith)

w George Zuckerman *novel* Robert Wilder d Douglas Sirk ph Russell Metty m Frank Skinner ad Robert Clatworthy, Alexander Golitzen ed Russell Schoengarth
☆ Lauren Bacall (Lucy Moore Hadley), *Robert Stack* (Kyle Hadley), *Dorothy Malone* (Marylee Hadley), Rock Hudson (Mitch Wayne), Robert Keith (Jasper Hadley), Grant Williams (Biff Miley)
🏆 Dorothy Malone
⚲ title song (*m* Victor Young, *ly* Sammy Cahn); Robert Stack

960
Written on the Wind

A secretary marries her oil tycoon boss and finds herself the steadying force in a very rocky family.

Sirk's high-flying melodrama is the sheerest Hollywood moonshine. Its story is the stuff of which soap operas are made. It is full of marital upset and recriminations, drunken outbursts and the suggestion of adultery, all shot in vibrant, glossy colour and emphasizing its unreality by the obviousness of its studio setting. This is Texas as seen from a Hollywood back lot. You take it at its face value as a pulp romance, or regard it as a subversive comment on the horrors of American domestic and business life. Either way, it moves fast enough to be very entertaining.

'It was the look in her eyes that did it. How could he resist? How could he know it meant murder?'

The Woman in the Window
US   1944   95m   bw
International (Nunnally Johnson)

🔲 🎞

w Nunnally Johnson *novel Once Off Guard* by J. H. Wallis *d* Fritz Lang *ph* Milton Krasner *m* Arthur Lange, Hugo Friedhofer *ad* Duncan Cramer *ed* Gene Fowler Jnr, Marjorie Johnson

☆ Edward G. Robinson (Prof. Richard Wanley), Joan Bennett (Alice Reed), Raymond Massey (Frank Lalor), Dan Duryea (Heidt/Doorman), Edmund Breon (Dr. Michael Barkstone), Thomas Jackson (Inspector Jackson), Dorothy Peterson (Mrs. Wanley), Arthur Loft (Claude Mazard/Frank Howard)

'The accumulation of tiny details enlarged as though under a district attorney's magnifying glass gives reality a fantastic and anguishing appearance.' – *Jacques Bourgeois*

'In its rather artificial, club library style an effective and well made piece, absorbing, diverting and full of often painful suspense.' – *Richard Mallett, Punch*

'Art and Mammon, it seems to me, have been very prettily served.' – *Spectator*

♫ Arthur Lange, Hugo Friedhofer

Black Eyes
Italy   1987   117m   colour
Excelsior/RAI (Silvia D'Amico Bendico)

🔲 🎧

original title: *Oci Ciornie*
GB title: *Dark Eyes*
w Nikita Mikhalkov, Alexander Adabachian, Suso Cecchi d'Amico *d* Nikita Mikhalkov *ph* Franco di Giacomo *m* Francis Lai *pd* Mario Garbuglia, Alexander Adabachian *ad* Mario Garbuglia, Alexander Adabachian *ed* Enzo Meniconi

☆ Marcello Mastroianni (Romano), Silvana Mangano (Elisa, Romano's Wife), Marthe Keller (Tina, Romano's Mistress), Elena Sofonova (Anna Sergeyevna, Governor's Wife)

'The film effortlessly swings from farce to tenderness, love to betrayal, exuberance to poignancy without missing a beat.' – *Daily Variety*

♫ Marcello Mastroianni

959
The Woman in the Window

A grass widow professor befriends a girl who gets him involved with murder.

Fritz Lang's refreshingly intelligent little thriller was criticized at the time for a cop-out ending; this can now be seen as a decorative extra to a story which had already ended satisfactorily. It was a typical film noir: an engaging tale of a man who, left alone when his family go on holiday, briefly deviates from his respectable life and finds himself out of his depth. The novel ended with the professor's suicide; the studio changed it to a happier conclusion that does not spoil the drama that has gone before. Nunnally Johnson had written a funnier script than the one Lang made, since the director did not notice that the jokes were there. Lang concentrated on the moral dilemma of an honest man who is accidentally involved in a crime, and is then prepared to commit other crimes in order to protect his reputation. The film's ironic ending is an expression of the fears that keep him from temptation.

958
Black Eyes

At the turn of the century, an aged Italian recounts his lapses.

Marcello Mastroianni enjoyed one of his best roles as a penniless, indecisive, aging Italian count who has tried to escape his loveless marriage to a rich wife by going to spas and flirting with available women. He falls for a Russian, who is unhappily married, follows her home and proposes to her. But when he returns to his wife, he decides to forget about her and regrets it. A highly amusing star vehicle, it is based on stories by Chekhov, and, beneath the humour, reveals a tinge of melancholy in its diverting portrait of one of life's losers. Mastroianni had initiated the film by writing to Nikita Milkhalkov suggesting that they should work together. The character of the vacillating count resembled Mastroianni in some ways, as he acknowledged: 'somebody with constant fantasies, really a superficial person.' Yet he provides a portrait in depth that remains another triumph in his long and distinguished career.

The More the Merrier

US 1943 104m bw
Columbia (George Stevens)

▭▬ ▬ ◔ ◔

w Robert Russell, Frank Ross, Richard Flournoy, Lewis R. Foster d George Stevens ph Ted Tetzlaff m Leigh Harline md Morris Stoloff ad Lionel Banks, Rudolph Sternad ed Otto Meyer

☆ Jean Arthur (Connie Milligan), Joel McCrea (Joe Carter), Charles Coburn (Benjamin Dingle), Richard Gaines (Charles J. Pendergast), Bruce Bennett (Evans)

'The gayest comedy that has come from Hollywood in a long time. It has no more substance than a watermelon, but is equally delectable.' – Howard Barnes

'Farce, like melodrama, offers very special chances for accurate observation, but here accuracy is avoided ten times to one in favour of the easy burlesque or the easier idealization which drops the bottom out of farce. Every good moment frazzles or drowns.' – James Agee

● Garson Kanin has claimed to have written virtually all the script.
♟ Charles Coburn
♟ best picture; script; original story (Frank Ross, Robert Russell); George Stevens; Jean Arthur

957
The More the Merrier

In crowded Washington during World War II, a girl allows two men to share her apartment and falls in love with the younger one.

George Stevens's thoroughly amusing romantic comedy, with bright lines and situations, takes advantage of the problematic housing conditions in a crowded Washington during World War II. A woman rents half of her apartment to a crusty, elderly millionaire. He, in turn, rents half of his part to a young man army sergeant, who is in the city on special duty. The result is inevitable in a romantic movie, and as the crusty old gent intended, the two young people fall in love. There's a splendidly comic courtship on the apartment house's front steps, with McCrea attempting to seduce Jean Arthur while she prattles on about the advantages of her engagement to a mature, older bureaucrat.

Dodsworth

US 1936 101m bw
Samuel Goldwyn

▬ ◔ ◎

w Sidney Howard novel Sinclair Lewis d William Wyler ph Rudolph Maté m Alfred Newman ad Richard Day ed Daniel Mandell

☆ Walter Huston (Sam Dodsworth), Mary Astor (Edith Cortright), Ruth Chatterton (Fran Dodsworth), David Niven (Capt. Lockert), Paul Lukas (Arnold Iselin), Gregory Gaye (Kurt von Obersdorf), Maria Ouspenskaya (Baroness von Obersdorf), Odette Myrtil (Mme. Renee de Penable), Spring Byington (Matey Pearson), John Payne (Harry Howard)

'No one, I think, will fail to enjoy it, in spite of its too limited and personal plot, the sense it leaves behind of a very expensive, very contemporary, Bond Street vacuum flask.' – Graham Greene

'William Wyler has had the skill to execute it in cinematic terms, and a gifted cast has been able to bring the whole alive to our complete satisfaction.' – New York Times

'An offering of dignity and compelling power to provide you with a treat you can rarely experience in a picture house.' – Hollywood Spectator

♟ Richard Day
♟ best picture; Sidney Howard; William Wyler; Walter Huston; Maria Ouspenskaya

956
Dodsworth

An American businessman takes his wife on a tour of Europe, and their lives are changed.

Because he believed that you couldn't sell a middle-aged love story, Samuel Goldwyn turned down the rights to Sinclair Lewis's novel, only changing his mind when it became a Broadway hit. Huston repeats his sensitive stage role as a plain-speaking man who suffers his wife's foibles and affairs, but still loses her, and then unexpectedly finds love elsewhere, Wyler's meticulous direction gives fluidity and pace to the story, culminating in the moment when the wife's continental lover takes a letter from her husband, who has returned home, and sets it alight. Wyler's camera follows it as it flames, blows along a terrace and then turns to ashes.

The Black Swan

US 1942 85m Technicolor
TCF (Robert Bassler)

w Ben Hecht, Seton I. Miller *novel* Rafael Sabatini
d Henry King *ph* Leon Shamroy *m* Alfred Newman
ad James Basevi, Richard Day *ed* Barbara McLean
☆ Tyrone Power (James Waring), Maureen O'Hara
(Margaret Denby), *Laird Cregar* (Capt. Henry Morgan),
Thomas Mitchell (Tommy Blue), *George Sanders* (Capt.
Billy Leech), Anthony Quinn (Wogan), George Zucco (Lord
Denby), Edward Ashley (Roger Ingram)

'Performed by actors as though to the hokum
born.' – *Time*

'Battles between sailing ships, realistic sword
fights, assaults, abductions, tortures and love
making.' – *CEA Report*

🎖 Leon Shamroy
🎖 Alfred Newman

955
The Black Swan

Morgan the pirate is made governor of Jamaica and enlists the help of his old friends to rid the Caribbean of buccaneers.

Henry King, an underrated director, had worked often with Tyrone Power and knew how to get the best performance from him, not by forcing him to play a macho role, but by allowing him to relax so that his strength and grace became evident. This rousing adventure with comic asides is just what action hokum always aimed to be, with a spirited gallery of heroes and villains and an entertaining narrative taken at a spanking pace. The action hardly ever slackens, especially in the romantic sparring between the sword-wielding Power and Maureen O'Hara, whose gowns are cut as low as the censors would permit. The duels are not only fought with sabers: the piratical Thomas Mitchell and George Sanders make sure they steal every scene in which they appear.

Bombshell

US 1933 91m bw
MGM (Hunt Stromberg)

GB title and aka: *Blonde Bombshell*
w Jules Furthman, John Lee Mahin *play* Caroline Francke,
Mack Crane *d* Victor Fleming *ph* Chester Lyons, Hal
Rosson *ed* Margaret Booth
☆ Jean Harlow (Lola), Lee Tracy (Space), Frank Morgan
(Pops), Franchot Tone (Gifford Middleton), Pat O'Brien
(Brogan), Ivan Lebedeff (Marquis), Una Merkel (Mac), Ted
Healy (Junior), Isabel Jewell (Junior's Girl), C. Aubrey Smith
(Mr. Middleton), Louise Beavers (Loretta), Leonard Carey
(Winters), Mary Forbes (Mrs. Middleton)

'Bound to click and the best legitimate comedy in a
long time.' – *Variety*

954
Bombshell

A glamorous film star yearns for a new image.

With the immortal chat-up line of 'Your hair is like a field of daisies; I should like to run barefoot through your hair', Franchot Tone set the tone for this crackpot farce which, even by today's standards, moves at a fair clip and enabled Jean Harlow to give her best comedy performance as a glamorous, dumb blonde film star who yearns for a new image. Harlow made fun of the sexual allure she showed in *Red Dust* the previous year, and let her platinum blonde hair down in a wise-cracking, raunchy way. 'I ask you as one lady to another,' she says to a gossip columnist who is getting the lowdown on the star's supposed scandal, 'isn't that a load of clams?'

Bad Company

Bad Company
US   1972   92m   Technicolor
Paramount (Stanley R. Jaffe)
▬ ⓒ ⓐ
w David Newman, Robert Benton   *d* Robert Benton
ph Gordon Willis   *m* Harvey Schmidt   *ad* Robert Gundlach
ed Ralph Rosenblum
☆ Jeff Bridges (Jake Rumsey), Barry Brown (Drew Dixon), Jim Davis (Marshal), David Huddleston (Big Joe), John Savage (Loney)

953
Bad Company

During the Civil War, two youths on the run team up and become outlaws.

A successful attempt to recreate the feeling of a past time, by the writers of another criminal myth, *Bonnie and Clyde*. Drew (Barry Brown) is a God-fearing youth who intends to keep to the straight and narrow. Jake (Jeff Bridges) is an opportunist who plans to grab what he can while he can. Benton's and Newman's approach is far removed from the glamorous style in which outlaws are usually treated by Hollywood. The boys face a harsh world that provides little shelter or food, and where everyone they meet is tougher than they are, with the exception of a homesick settler who offers the gang his wife at a $1 a time. Benton directs this coming-of-age story, set in a recognizably ugly world, with leisurely aplomb.

Rome Express
GB   1932   94m   bw
Gaumont (Michael Balcon)
w Clifford Grey, Sidney Gilliat, Frank Vosper, Ralph Stock   *d* Walter Forde   *ph* Gunther Krampf   *ad* Andrew Mazzei
ed Frederick Y. Smith, Ian Dalrymple
☆ Conrad Veidt (Zurta), Gordon Harker (Tom Bishop), Esther Ralston (Asta Marvelle), Joan Barry (Mrs. Maxted), Harold Huth (Grant), Cedric Hardwicke (Alistair McBane), Donald Calthrop (Poole), Hugh Williams (Tony), Finlay Currie (Publicist), Frank Vosper (M. Jolif), Muriel Aked (Spinster), Eliot Makeham (Mills)

'A first class craftsman's job.' – *Basil Wright*

'Technically, and in a sense intellectually speaking, this film puts Forde into Class A1.' – *Cinema Quarterly*

● Remade 1948 as *Sleeping Car to Trieste*.

952
Rome Express

Thieves and blackmail victims are among the passengers on an express train.

This remains the prototype train thriller from which *The Lady Vanishes, Murder on the Orient Express* and a hundred others are all borrowed; it also spawned a myriad movies in which strangers are thrown together in dangerous situations. The passengers, who include several shady characters, become suspects when a murder is committed on the express from Paris to Rome. Technically it still works very well, though the script has begun to show its age and it is just a little faded as sheer entertainment. Built around the search for a stolen painting, the film is a skilful mix of comedy, romance and suspense. Forde made clever use of the enclosed environment of the train, on which all the action takes place, and the element of time, with the detective hurrying to solve the crime before the express steams into Rome.

Salaam Bombay!

India/France/GB 1988 114m colour
Mainline/Mirabai Films/NFDC/Cadrage/La SEPT/
Channel 4 (Mira Nair)
▣ ▤ ◎ ～ ◎ ◎ ♫
w Sooni Taraporevala d Mira Nair ph Sandi Sissel m L.
Subramaniam pd Mitch Epstein ed Barry Alexander
Brown
☆ Shafiq Syed (Krishna/Chaipau), Raghubir Yadav
(Chillum), Nana Patekar (Baba), Irshad Hasni, Aneeta
Kanwar (Rekha), Hansa Vithal (Manju)

'A notable debut.' – MFB

951
Salaam Bombay!

Street life in an Indian city as seen by a tea-boy abandoned by his mother.

Mira Nair offers a child's-eye view of street life in an Indian city among pimps, prostitutes, drug peddlers and addicts. Krishna, ten years old, is turned out of home by his angry mother and becomes just another one of Bombay's street children in a poignant, well-observed narrative of small treacheries and smaller hope. It is acted by a mainly amateur cast of street children, whose own experiences formed the basis of the script. The film was shot on the streets, aiding its authenticity, though its impact goes far beyond the documentary. Nair succeeds in her stated aim, to 'portray the reality of children who are denied a childhood, children who survive on the streets with resilience, humour, flamboyance and dignity.'

Pickpocket

France 1959 80m bw
Lux
▤
wd Robert Bresson ph Léonce-Henry Burel m Jean-
Bapiste Lully ed Raymond Lamy
☆ Martin Lassalle, Marika Green, Pierre Leymarie, Jean
Pelegri, Pierre Etaix, Kassagi, Dolly Scal, César Gattegno

'The style of the film is characteristic of the director. It is one of persistent concentration: the camera will not be deflected from its close stare at the silent face, the tense figure in the foreground. But this time the method defeats itself. In rejecting every irrelevant action, in ruthlessly refining away every decoration, Bresson has thrown away the motives as well.' – Dilys Powell

950
Pickpocket

A lonely, compulsive pickpocket is redeemed through love.

Bresson based this film on themes from Dostoevsky's *Crime and Punishment*. To give it authenticity, he shot the film on the streets of Paris, using lights rigged to car batteries. He also hired as consultant a noted pickpocket, which gives a reality to its scenes of thievery, particularly in a railway station. The result transcends that reality, to become an austere but moving and complex drama. As Bresson wrote in a note to himself, 'No art without transformation.' It is a study of a young man in the grip of an obsession, one that takes him into a lonely existence made bearable only by that moment when he steals and briefly comes alive. He finally recognizes that he can redeem himself only by allowing himself to be caught and is given a sign of his success through a loving gesture from the woman he abandoned: she kisses his hand.

The Devils

'Hell holds no surprises ... for them!'

The Devils

GB 1970 111m Technicolor Panavision
Warner/Russo (Robert H. Solo, Ken Russell)

wd Ken Russell *play* John Whiting *book* The Devils of Loudun by Aldous Huxley *ph* David Watkin *m* Peter Maxwell Davies *ad* Robert Cartwright

☆ Vanessa Redgrave, Oliver Reed, Dudley Sutton, Max Adrian, Gemma Jones, Murray Melvin, Michael Gothard, Graham Armitage

'Ken Russell doesn't report hysteria, he markets it.'
– New Yorker, 1976

'Russell's swirling multi-colored puddle ... made me glad that both Huxley and Whiting are dead, so that they are spared this farrago of witless exhibitionism.' – Stanley Kauffmann

'A garish glossary of sado-masochism ... a taste for visual sensation that makes scene after scene look like the masturbatory fantasies of a Roman Catholic boyhood.' – Alexander Walker

'A degenerate and despicable piece of art.'
– Charles Champlin, Los Angeles Times

An account of the apparent demoniacal possession of the 17th-century nuns of Loudun.

Ken Russell had Huxley's philosophical account and John Whiting's sardonic play to draw on in his version of the seemingly possessed Ursuline nuns of Loudun, who in 1632 worked themselves into a demonic frenzy that resulted in the torture and death by burning of a priest. This hysterical subject-matter gets an appropriately over-the-top treatment, with worm-eaten skulls, masturbating nuns and gibbering courtiers. It is a devastating study of sexual repression and erotic fantasy within a small, enclosed society, of superstition run rampant. Anachronisms, from Derek Jarman's modernist setting to some of Russell's odder jokes, force the audience to consider the present day implications of the story. Unjustly derided on release, it ranks among the best British movies of its time.

Shock Corridor

Shock Corridor

US 1963 101m bw (colour sequence)
Leon Fromkess/Sam Firks (Samuel Fuller)

wd Samuel Fuller *ph* Stanley Cortez *m* Paul Dunlap *ad* Eugene Lourie *ed* Jerome Thoms

☆ Peter Breck (Johnny Barrett), Constance Towers (Cathy), Gene Evans (Boden), James Best (Stuart), Hari Rhodes (Trent), Philip Ahn (Dr. Fong)

'A minor masterpiece'. – Derek Malcolm, Guardian

A journalist gets himself admitted to a mental asylum to solve the murder of an inmate.

Fuller was once defined as an authentic American primitive in critic Andrew Sarris's classification of directors, but he was something far more sophisticated: a tabloid journalist. A former crime reporter and pulp novelist, Fuller thrived on sensation. In this thriller he had a perfect vehicle for his talents. The film is a dizzying examination of madness and sanity, of an obsessive impersonation that becomes indistinguishable from what it pretends to be. Johnny Barrett, his anti-hero, is a journalist determined to get his story at whatever cost to himself or to others. He abandons all objectivity and moral scruples in his pursuit and succeeds only in losing himself, or his sense of self, in the process. Fuller's setting here is a dark, violent, claustrophobic space and a reflection of the wider world outside the asylum

Kühle Wampe

Germany 1932 73m bw
Prometheus/Praesens (George Hoellering)
aka: *Whither Germany?*
w Bertold Brecht, Ernst Ottwald *d* Slaten Dodow
ph Günther Krampf *m* Hanns Eisler, Josef Schmidt
ad C.P. Haacker, Robert Scharfenberg
☆ Hertha Thiele (Annie), Ernst Busch (Ballad Singer (voice)), Martha Wolter, Adolf Fischer (Genosse), Lili Schönborn, Max Sablotzki, Alfred Schaefer
● German authorities banned the film on its release as offending 'against the vital interests of the state' and as being 'a summons to violence and subversion'. Brecht, by lying, persuaded the censor to release it with a few minor cuts. He later wrote, 'Leaving the building, we did not conceal our high opinion of the censor. He had penetrated the essence of our artistic intentions with far greater sagacity than our most benevolent critics.'

947
Kühle Wampe

During the Depression in Berlin, a working-class family is forced to move to a shantytown on the outskirts of the city.

This is the only film in which Brecht was in control, as co-author and co-producer, working with a collective of like-minded collaborators. Even so, their financial backers withdrew before the film was finished. Set during the Depression in Berlin, it deals with the fate of unemployed workers, who discover that looking for work is itself a full-time, unpaid occupation. It follows a family that is made homeless and is forced to live in a shanty town. A powerful attack on capitalist brutality and working-class apathy, it also optimistically suggested that the hope of the future lay with the revolutionary young.

Force of Evil

US 1948 80m bw
MGM/Enterprise (Bob Roberts)
▧ ▤ ⌕ ⊚
w Abraham Polonsky, Ira Wolfert *novel Tucker's People* by Ira Wolfert *d* Abraham Polonsky *ph* George Barnes
m David Raksin *ad* Richard Day *ed* Art Seid
☆ John Garfield (Joe Morse), Thomas Gomez (Leo Morse), Beatrice Pearson (Doris Lowry), Roy Roberts (Ben Tucker), Marie Windsor (Edna Tucker), Howland Chamberlain (Freddy Bauer), Barry Kelley (Egan), Paul Fix (Bill Ficco)

946
Force of Evil

A lawyer is corrupted by the easy money provided by his clients, gangsters who are opposed by his brother in their plans to take over the city's numbers racket.

Polonsky's film noir is a bleak and powerful melodrama that is an attack on capitalism and monopolies, couched as a gangster movie. Highly stylized, with dialogue that rings true though it is eminently artificial, Polonsky creates a world of shades of grey, where even those doing an honest day's work are trapped in criminal activities. Garfield gives one of his best performances as the slick young lawyer who betrays those he loves. Polonsky would not direct another film for more than twenty years, for he was blacklisted in the 1950s during the House Committee on Un-American Activities' investigation of Hollywood. But he understood that he was in the business to make films, not to change the world, and created here a tough, thoughtful and potent entertainment.

Back to the Future

�*** US 1985 116m Technicolor
Universal/Steven Spielberg (Bob Gale, Neil Canton)
☷ ☷ ☷ ☷ ☷ ☷ ☷

w Robert Zemeckis, Bob Gale *d* Robert Zemeckis
ph Dean Cundey *m* Alan Silvestri *pd* Lawrence G. Paull
ad Todd Hallowell *ed* Arthur Schmidt, Harry Keramidas
☆ *Michael J. Fox* (Marty McFly), Christopher Lloyd (Dr Emmett Brown), Crispin Glover (George McFly), Lea Thompson (Lorraine Baines), Claudia Wells (Jennifer Parker), Thomas F. Wilson (Biff Tannen)

'Accelerates with wit, ideas, and infectious, wide-eyed wonder.' – *Variety*

● Eric Stoltz was originally cast as Marty McFly, but was replaced by Fox after five weeks' shooting.

♙ original screenplay; song ('The Power of Love'); sound

945
Back to the Future

With the help of a not-so-crazy scientist, a teenager goes back thirty years to make a man out of his dimwit father.

Robert Zemeckis has a lot of fun with the generation gap in his science-fiction fantasy, although it was absent from the movie's two sequels. The jokes are not just about the usual father and son relationship, but about a father in his teenaged years and his teenage son. The town has changed in thirty years – the cinema that was showing a Ronald Reagan movie in the 50s now screens porn – and so have youthful attitudes. The passing of time has given the film yet another dimension, as its present-day audience can also experience teenage life as it seemed in the mid 1980s.

Father Brown

GB 1954 91m bw
Columbia/Facet (Vivian A. Cox)
☷

US title: *The Detective*
w Thelma Schnee, Maurice Rapf, Robert Hamer story *The Blue Cross* by G. K. Chesterton *d* Robert Hamer *ph* Harry Waxman *m* Georges Auric *ed* Gordon Hales
☆ *Alec Guinness* (Fr. Brown), *Joan Greenwood* (Lady Warren), *Peter Finch* (Flambeau), Sidney James (Parkinson), *Cecil Parker* (The Bishop), *Bernard Lee* (Inspector Valentine), *Ernest Thesiger* (Vicomte), Marne Maitland (Maharajah)

'It has wit, elegance, and kindly humour – all somewhat rare commodities in the 1954 cinema.' – *Star*

● Maurice Rapf was not credited as one of the screenwriters at the time of the film's release as he was blacklisted.

944
Father Brown

A Catholic clergyman retrieves a priceless church cross from master thief Flambeau.

This delightfully eccentric comedy was based closely on G. K. Chesterton's early story of his Catholic detective. Guinness is perfectly cast as the nondescript priest who is as interested in saving souls as catching crooks. There is an underlying melancholy to the movie, for Father Brown's knowledge of the way the world works comes from the confessional, and it is that experience that enables him to solve crimes by putting himself in the mind of the criminal. Hamer's pointed direction and some delicious characterizations make for a thoroughly civilized entertainment.

Antonia's Line
Netherlands/Belgium/GB   1995   102m
Fujicolour
Guild/Antonia's Line/Bergen/Prime Time/Bard/NPS
(Hans de Weers)

wd Marleen Gorris *ph* Willy Stassen *m* Ilona Sekacz
ad Harry Ammerlaan *ed* Michiel Reichwein, Wim Louwrier
☆ Willeke van Ammelrooy (Antonia), Els Dottemans
(Danielle), Jan Decleir (Bas), Mil Seghers (Crooked Finger),
Marina de Graaf (DeeDee), Jan Steen (Loony Lips), Veerle
van Overloop (Therese), Dora van der Groen (Allegonde)

'A delightful, enjoyable and generous film.' – *Film Review*

♟ foreign language film

943
Antonia's Line

On her deathbed, an elderly woman recalls the events of her life and of those she gave a home to over a period of 40 years.

Marleen Gorris's feminist drama is a celebration of domestic and feminine virtues. It's a vivid, sprawling account that mixes reality with fantasy to heighten the story of love and survival. At one point, for instance, Antonia's mother gets up from her coffin to sing 'My Blue Heaven'. Men are not much in evidence, only appearing to discuss philosophy or father children before vanishing. It is one of those rare, humane films, following the cycle of life, that puts women's preoccupations at its centre. The women who inhabit it are busy discovering their own identities, as distinct from their familiar secondary roles as mothers, daughters or wives. Gorris positions their individuality within a community, as Antonia and her family gather like-minded or damaged people around them in an affirmation of living for oneself and others.

The Navigator: A Medieval Odyssey
Australia   1988   91m   colour/bw
Recorded Releasing/Arenafilm (John Maynard, Gary
Hannam)

w Vincent Ward, Kely Lyons, Geoff Chapple *d* Vincent
Ward *ph* Geoffrey Simpson *m* Davood A. Tabrizi *pd* Sally
Campbell *ad* Mike Becroft *ed* John Scott
☆ Bruce Lyons (Connor), Chris Haywood (Arno), Hamish
McFarlane (Griffin), Marshall Napier (Searle), Noel Appleby
(Ulf), Paul Livingstone (Martin), Sarah Pierse (Linnet), Mark
Wheatley (Tog 1), Tony Herbert (Tog 2)

'Rather modest in scale, but its themes are grand
and there's a grand passion behind its images.' –
Washington Post

942
The Navigator: A Medieval Odyssey

Medieval villagers go on a pilgrimage through a mine and emerge in the modern world.

Vincent Ward's visionary movie about the need for spirituality is an oddly disturbing fable of considerable originality. In Cumbria, urged on by a young boy's dream, medieval villagers, who are fearful of the Black Death, go on a pilgrimage through a mine and emerge in modern day New Zealand. The images carry the story: the medieval scenes are filmed in stark black and white; it is only when the pilgrims reach the modern world that the screen bursts into colour, emphasizing the shock of the new. The pilgrims experience both beauty and terror in the modern world before returning to their own time in a mysteriously ambiguous ending.

‘The nightmare world of a virgin's dreams becomes the screen's shocking reality!’

Repulsion
GB   1965   105m   bw
Compton/Tekli (Gene Gutowski)
🔲 ≡ ⊘
w Roman Polanski, Gerard Brach *d* Roman Polanski
ph Gilbert Taylor *m* Chico Hamilton *ad* Seamus Flannery
ed Alastair McIntyre
☆ *Catherine Deneuve* (Carol Ledoux), Ian Hendry (Michael), John Fraser (Colin), Patrick Wymark (Landlord), Yvonne Furneaux (Helen Ledoux)

‘An unashamedly ugly film, but as a lynx-eyed view of a crumbling mind it is a masterpiece of the macabre.’ – *Daily Mail*

941
Repulsion

A Belgian in London is driven by pressures into neurotic withdrawal; terrified above all by sex, she locks herself up in her gloomy flat and murders her boyfriend and landlord when they try to approach her.

Polanski's terrific psychological shocker concerns Carol, a beautiful, alienated Belgian manicurist, who is driven out of her mind in a gloomy London flat. A hallucinatory movie of possession, it relies on the sudden irruption of sound and images (walls cracking, hands groping from corridors) to convey her horror of sexuality, her fear of violation and her final slashing retaliation against the male sex. Clinically filmed, exploiting to the full Deneuve's glacial beauty, it remains one of the most chilling of horror movies. Polanski slowly tightens the tension, using distorted perspective to suggest Carol's increasing psychosis, and coolly observes her terror and the final disintegration of her personality.

My Life as a Dog
Sweden   1985   101m   Fujicolour
Svensk Filmindustri/Film-Teknik
🔲 ≡ ⊛ ⊘ ⊕ ⌒
original title: *Mitt Liv Som Hund*
w Lasse Hallström, Reidar Jonsson, Brasse Brännström, Per Berglund *novel* Reidar Jonsson *d* Lasse Hallström
ph Jörgen Persson, Rolf Lindström *m* Björn Isfält
ad Lasse Westfelt *ed* Christer Furubrand, Susanne Linnman
☆ Anton Glanzelius (Ingemar Johansson), Manfred Serner (Erik), Anki Lidén (His Mother), Tomas von Bromssen (Uncle Gunnar), Melinda Kinnaman (Saga), Ing-Marie Carlsson (Berit)
ℛ best director; best adapted screenplay

940
My Life as a Dog

12-year-old Ingemar learns to cope with his mother's illness and death, and his own propensity for getting into trouble, while staying with his aunt and uncle in the country.

By turns painful and funny, the film manages to achieve genuine charm while steering clear of sentimentality. The movie's episodic structure allows Ingemar scope to mix with village eccentrics and children as tough and sensitive as himself as he attempts to explore the point of sex and his own place in a confusing, adult universe. Lasse Hallström, whose best film this remains, coaxes a marvellous performance from the snub-nosed Anton Glanzelius, touching, funny and sad and none more so than when he decides he is a dog.

On Approval

GB   1943   80m   bw
(GFD)

w Clive Brook, Terence Young *play* Frederick Lonsdale
d Clive Brook *ph* C. Friese-Greene *m* William Alwyn
md Muir Mathieson *ad* Thomas Morahan *ed* Fergus
McDonell *cos* Cecil Beaton
☆ *Clive Brook* (George, Duke of Bristol), *Beatrice Lillie*
(Maria Wislack), *Googie Withers* (Helen Hale), *Roland
Culver* (Richard Halton), O. B. Clarence (Dr. Graham),
Lawrence Hanray (Parkes), Hay Petrie (Landlord)

'Totally diverting, highly cinematic.' – *NFT, 1974*

'There has probably never been a richer, funnier
anthology of late-Victorian mannerisms.' – *Time*

'I enjoyed it so thoroughly that I have to fight off
superlatives.' – *James Agee*

● Also filmed in 1930 by Tom Walls for Herbert Wilcox,
with Walls, Yvonne Arnaud, Winifred Shotter and Edmund
Breon.

939
On Approval

*In the 1890s, an English aristocrat tries out marriage to a wealthy
American.*

Frederick Lonsdale's long-running stage success was a witty well-con-
structed comedy about an Edwardian duke and an American heiress
who plan a chaperoned trial-marriage in a remote Scottish castle. The
film version sticks close to the original, although adding an amusing
dream sequence and setting it thirty years earlier, in the 1890s.
Beatrice Lillie gives her best screen performance, and Clive Brook's
acting is in that precise and seemingly effortless style that derived from
Gerald du Maurier. Deliberately old fashioned, it remains a sparkling
comedy of manners made even more piquant by careful casting and
mounting; a minor delight.

La Balance

France   1982   102m   colour
Les Films Ariane/Films A2 (Georges Dancigers,
Alexandre Mnouchkine)

w M. Fabiani, Bob Swaim *d* Bob Swaim *ph* Bernard
Ziztermann *m* Roland Bocquet *pd* Eric Moulard *ad* Eric
Moulard *ed* Françoise Javet
☆ Nathalie Baye (Nicole), Philipe Léotard (Dede), Richard
Berry (Palouzi), Maurice Ronet (Massina)

938
La Balance

*A pimp and his girlfriend are pressured by the police into becoming
informers.*

Director Bob Swaim, an American in Paris, brought the old Hollywood
gangster style to this thriller. Its moody, gritty approach meant that the
only difference between the cops and the crooks was that the police
were the more violent. Swaim gives proceedings a young, hip appeal,
allows the characters their individual idiosyncrasies, and keeps the
action fast and involving. Nathalie Baye and Philippe Léotard won best
actor awards as the ill-starred couple and the film, a box-office hit, was
voted the best of the year in France's César awards.

The Sign of the Cross
US   1932   123m   bw
Paramount (Cecil B. de Mille)

w Waldemar Young, Sidney Buchman *play* Wilson Barrett
d Cecil B. de Mille *ph* Karl Struss *m* Rudolph Kopp
ed Anne Bauchens
☆ Fredric March (Marcus Superbus), Elissa Landi (Mercia), *Charles Laughton* (Emperor Nero), *Claudette Colbert* (Empress Poppaea), Ian Keith (Tigellinus), Harry Beresford (Flavius), Arthur Hohl (Titus), Nat Pendleton (Strabo)

'De Mille's bang-them-on-the-head-with-wild-orgies-and-imperilled-virginity style is at its ripest.' – *New Yorker, 1976*

'Preposterous, but the laughter dies on the lips.' – *NFT, 1974*

'This slice of "history" has it all: Laughton's implicitly gay Nero fiddling away while an impressive miniature set burns, Colbert bathing up to her nipples in asses' milk, Christians and other unfortunates thrown to a fearsome menagerie, much suggestive slinking about in Mitchell Leisen's costumes, much general debauchery teetering between the sadistic and the erotic. Not for people with scruples.' – *Geoff Brown, Time Out, 1980*

♀ Karl Struss

937
The Sign of the Cross

A Roman officer is converted to Christianity.

De Mille had problems when he made this impressive film, based on a heavily theatrical play about a Roman officer who is converted to Christianity at the time of Nero. He was working under difficulties at Paramount, where the executives who backed him had just been sacked, and his budget was limited. He was forced to build a miniature set for Nero's Palace, and had cinematographer Karl Struss use a prism lens to double the size of the crowds of extras. The genuine horror of the arena, where lions and tigers mauled martyrs, contrasts with the debauched humour of the court. With exotic and erotic dancers, and Claudette Colbert bathing in asses' milk, he succeeded in conveying an atmosphere of opulence and decadence.

'Talk and die! Until now their lips were frozen with fear!'

They Won't Forget
US   1937   94m   bw
Warner (Mervyn Le Roy)
🇺🇸

w Robert Rossen, Aben Kandel *novel Death in the Deep South* by Ward Greene *d* Mervyn Le Roy *ph* Arthur Edeson, Warren Lynch *m* Adolph Deutsch *md* Leo F. Forbstein *ad* Robert Haas *ed* Thomas Richards
☆ Claude Rains (Andrew J. Griffin), Gloria Dickson (Sybil Hale), Edward Norris (Robert Paerry Hale), Otto Kruger (Michael Gleason), Allyn Joslyn (William P. Brock), Linda Perry (Imogene Mayfield), Elisha Cook Jnr (Joe Turner), Lana Turner (Mary Clay), Cy Kendall (Detective Laneart), Elizabeth Risdon (Mrs. Dale)

'Not only an honest picture, but an example of real movie-making.' – *Pare Lorenz*

936
They Won't Forget

The murder of a girl in a Southern town leads to a lynching.

A finely detailed social drama that is a classic of American realism. It is a fictional variation on the lynching in Georgia in 1915 of Leo Frank, a Jewish engineer who had been sentenced to life imprisonment for the murder of a 12-year-old girl. (In 1985 he was posthumously pardoned.) Le Roy's harrowing study of mob intolerance concerns the killing of a young girl in a small Southern town. A politically ambitious prosecutor decides that the murderer is the girl's teacher, who is a newcomer from the North, and proceeds accordingly, whipping the town into a crazed hysteria. A powerful indictment of intolerance, it was also notable for Claude Rains' performance as the prosecutor who needs a sensational case to aid him in his bid to become a senator. It also put Lana Turner on the way to stardom for her brief but seductive performance as the murdered girl.

A Private Conversation
USSR   1983   96m   colour
Contemporary/Mosfilm
original title: *Bez Svidetelei*
aka: *Without Witnesses*
w Nikita Mikhalkov, Sofia Prokofieva, Ramiz Fataliev *play* Sofia Prokofieva *d* Nikita Mikhalkov *ph* Pavel Lebeshev *m* Eduard Artemiev *ad* Alexander Adabashian, Igor Makarov, Alexander Samulekin *ed* Eleonora Praksina
☆ Mikhail Ulyanov, Irina Kupchenko

935
A Private Conversation

A Russian party hack visits his ex-wife for an evening of recrimination and raking over the past.

This two-character film, in a claustrophobic setting of a dingy flat, is an intimate drama by a director who more often works on a larger scale. Its examination of a failed marriage and a wasted life is a searing one, filmed with a passionate intensity, and excellently acted by the increasingly demonstrative Mikhail Ulyanov and Irina Kupchenko, as his more composed ex-wife. He is horrified to discover that she plans to marry one of his colleagues and threatens to tell their teenaged son that she is not his mother unless she calls off the wedding. She does as he demands, though there is a final twist that leaves her triumphant. Occasional extracts from Gluck's opera *Orpheus* suggest some parallels with the story of Orpheus and Eurydice, if only because of the ex-husband's desire not to completely lose his former wife.

Alias Nick Beal
US   1949   93m   bw
Paramount (Endre Bohem)
GB title: *The Contact Man*
w Jonathan Latimer *story* Mindret Lord *d* John Farrow
ph Lionel Lindon *m* Franz Waxman *ad* Hans Dreier, Franz Bachelin *ed* Eda Warren
☆ *Ray Milland* (Nick Beal), *Thomas Mitchell* (Joseph Foster), Audrey Totter (Donna Allen), George Macready (Rev. Thomas Gaylord), Fred Clark (Frankie Faulkner)

934
Alias Nick Beal

A politician is nearly corrupted by a mysterious stranger offering wealth and power.

A highly satisfactory modern version of *Faust*. The movie is done in gangster terms but not eschewing a supernatural explanation. Director John Farrow kept the film tight and suspenseful, and there are excellent performances from Ray Milland as the diabolical fog-shrouded visitor, Thomas Mitchell as the politician who realizes too late that he has sold his soul, and Audrey Trotter, smouldering as a femme fatale. A DVD release is long overdue.

Tobacco Road
US   1941   84m   bw
TCF (Darryl F. Zanuck)
w Nunnally Johnson *play* Jack Kirkland *novel* Erskine Caldwell *d* John Ford *ph* Arthur Miller *m* David Buttolph *ad* Richard Day, James Basevi *ed* Barbara McLean
☆ *Charley Grapewin* (Jeeter Lester), *Elizabeth Patterson* (Ada Lester), Dana Andrews (Dr. Tim), Gene Tierney (Ellie May Lester), *Marjorie Rambeau* (Sister Bessie), Ward Bond (Lov Bensey), William Tracy (Duke Lester), Zeffie Tilbury (Grandma Lester), Slim Summerville (Henry Peabody), Grant Mitchell (George Payne), Russell Simpson (Sheriff), Spencer Charters (Employee)

'The whole thing seems deranged.' – *Pauline Kael*

933
Tobacco Road

Poor whites in Georgia are turned off their land.

This bowdlerized version of a sensational book and play has superbly orchestrated farcical scenes separated by delightfully pictorial quieter moments: it isn't what was intended, but in its own way it's quite marvellous. Erskine Caldwell's novel had a sexual quality that could not survive the film censorship of the time. Ford relied on images of Gene Tierney looking sultry to convey eroticism and created a bucolic comedy of bad manners.

The Hot Rock

US 1972 105m DeLuxe Panavision
TCF (Hal Landers, Bobby Roberts)
▤ ◕ ⦿
GB title: *How to Steal a Diamond in Four Uneasy
Lessons*

w William Goldman *novel* Donald E. Westlake *d* Peter
Yates *ph* Ed Brown *m* Quincy Jones *ad* Bob Wrightman
ed Fred W. Berger, Frank P. Keller
☆ Robert Redford (Dortmunder), George Segal (Kelp),
Zero Mostel (Abe Greenberg), Paul Sand (Alan Greenberg),
Ron Leibman (Murch), Moses Gunn (Dr. Amusa), William
Redfield (Lt. Hoover)

'A funny, fast-paced, inventive and infinitely clever
crime comedy, almost as if *The French Connection*
had been remade as a piece of urban humour.'
– *Michael Korda*

932
The Hot Rock

Four crooks plan to rob the Brooklyn Museum of a priceless diamond.

It is refreshing to come across a film which hits its targets so precisely as Peter Yates's crime caper. Four crooks are hired to rob the Brooklyn Museum of a priceless and sacred diamond, and experience more problems than they anticipated. During their arrest, one of them swallows the diamond, causing further complications and frustrations. Together with highly skilled technical back-up, there are relaxed comic performances from Redford as the unflappable leader, Segal as his neurotic brother-in-law, Sand and Leibman as their sidekicks, and Mostel as an untrustworthy intruder.

One Hundred and One Dalmatians

👫 US 1961 79m Technicolor
Walt Disney
▤ ◉ ⦿

w Bill Peet *novel* Dodie Smith *d* Wolfgang Reitherman,
Hamilton S. Luske, Clyde Geronimi *m* George Bruns
ad Ken Anderson *ed* Roy M. Brewer Jr., Donald Halliday
☆ Featuring the voices of Rod Taylor, Cate Bauer, Betty
Lou Gerson, J. Pat O'Malley

'It has the freshness of the early short colour-
cartoons without the savagery which has often
disfigured the later feature-length stories.' – *Dilys
Powell*

931
One Hundred and One Dalmatians

The dogs of London help save puppies which are being stolen for their skins by a cruel villainess.

This charming animated movie, was the last of the Disney studio's really splendid feature cartoons until the 1990s. The old flexible style has been cleverly modernized and there is plenty of invention and detail in the story line. The London backgrounds are especially nicely judged. In the fur-clad Cruella De Vil, the animators, together with the voice of Betty Lou Gerson, created the most effective villainess since the wicked stepmother in *Snow White and the Seven Dwarfs*.

The Prize

US 1963 135m Metrocolor Panavision
MGM/Roxbury (Pandro S. Berman)

w *Ernest Lehman* novel *Irving Wallace* d *Mark Robson*
ph *William Daniels* m *Jerry Goldsmith* ad *George W.
Davis, Urie McCleary* ed *Adrienne Fazan*
☆ *Paul Newman* (Andrew Craig), *Elke Sommer* (Inger Lisa
Andersen), *Edward G. Robinson* (Dr. Max Stratman), *Diane
Baker* (Emily Stratman), *Kevin McCarthy* (Dr. John Garrett),
Leo G. Carroll (Count Bertil Jacobssen), *Micheline Presle*
(Dr. Denise Marceau)

'Suspense melodrama played for laughs. Trouble is
the basic comedy approach clashes with the
political-topical framework of the story.' – *Variety*

930
The Prize

*In Stockholm during the Nobel Prize awards, a drunken American
author stumbles on a spy plot.*

Mark Robson's thriller is a Hitchcock pastiche that works better than
most Hitchcocks: suspenseful, well characterized, fast moving and
funny from beginning to end. Newman deftly plays a role that, in a
Hitchcock movie, would have gone to Cary Grant, and Elke Sommer is
his blonde Swedish helpmeet. Only the Swedes were not amused,
protesting that it denigrated the Nobel Prize.

Only Two Can Play

GB 1962 106m bw
British Lion/Vale (Launder and Gilliat)

w *Bryan Forbes* novel *That Uncertain Feeling* by *Kingsley
Amis* d *Sidney Gilliat* ph *John Wilcox* m *Richard Rodney
Bennett* ad *Albert Witherick* ed *Thelma Connell*
☆ *Peter Sellers* (John Lewis), *Mai Zetterling* (Elizabeth
Gruffydd Williams), *Virginia Maskell* (Jean Lewis), Richard
Attenborough (Gareth Probert), Raymond Huntley (Vernon),
John Le Mesurier (Salter), *Kenneth Griffith* (Iaeun Jenkins)

'It has a kind of near-truth which is at once
hilarious and faintly macabre.' – *Dilys Powell*

929
Only Two Can Play

*A much-married assistant librarian in a Welsh town has an abortive
affair with a councillor's wife.*

Peter Sellers disliked this movie, even though it provided him with his
last good character performance. He tried to have Virginia Maskell
sacked, despite her fine acting as his downtrodden wife. Based on
Kingsley Amis's novel, it was a comedy of sexual mishaps in a Welsh
town. A well characterized and generally diverting comedy, it contains
many memorable sequences, notably Sellers attempting to make love
to Mai Zetterling in a car surrounded by cows.

The Job

Italy 1961 90m bw
24 Horses Films (Alberto Soffientini)
Ⓐ
original title: *Il Posto*
wd Ermanno Olmi *ph* Lamberto Caimi *ad* Ettore Lombardi *ed* Carla Colombo
☆ Sandro Panzeri (Domenico Cantoni), Loredana Detto (Antonietta Masetti)

'Rueful and funny and honest … the players have been encouraged not so much to act as to behave. Olmi stalks them like a naturalist, and the result is a small, unique and perfect achievement in film-making.' – *Penelope Houston, MFB*

928
The Job

A teenage boy gets his first job, and progresses from office boy to clerk when a senior man dies.

This social comedy, very simple and extremely effective, depends upon its appealing observation for its engaging effect. The narrative could hardly be more low-key. A teenage boy arrives in Milan in search of work. He is taken on as an office boy by a large corporation and, later, when a senior man dies, is elated to be promoted to clerk. Out of this, Olmi spins a miraculous movie, both funny and sad, since it is clear that the boy is facing a lifetime of being a clerk until he, too, dies and is replaced.

'She fell in love with the toughest guy on the toughest street in the world!'

San Francisco

US 1936 117m bw
MGM (John Emerson, Bernard Hyman)
🔳 🟰 ⓡ 🎧
w Anita Loos *story* Robert Hopkins *d* W. S. Van Dyke *ph* Oliver T. Marsh *m* Edward Ward *md* Herbert Stothart *ad* Harry McAfee, Arnold Gillespie, Cedric Gibbons *ed* Tom Held *montage* John Hoffman *title song* Bronislau Kaper
☆ Clark Gable (Blackie Norton), *Spencer Tracy* (Father Tim Mullin), *Jeanette MacDonald* (Mary Blake), *Jack Holt* (Jack Burley), *Jessie Ralph* (Maisie Burley), Ted Healy (Matt), Shirley Ross (Trixie), Al Shean (Professor), Harold Huber (Babe)

'Prodigally generous and completely satisfying.' – *Frank S. Nugent*

♟ best picture; Robert Hopkins; W. S. Van Dyke; Spencer Tracy

927
San Francisco

The loves and career problems of a Barbary Coast saloon proprietor climax in the 1906 earthquake.

'Earthquake! San Francisco! Gable! A dame! A priest! Can't you see it?' said MGM's ideas man Robert Hopkins at a story conference. They could, although Gable initially balked at the idea of working with the warbling Jeanette MacDonald. The result was an incisive, star-packed, superbly-handled melodrama. Gable has room to act the tough guy, Tracy plays the priest, and MacDonald sings arias from Gounod's *Faust* and Verdi's *La Traviata* as well as pop songs. It weaves in every kind of appeal and for a finale has some of the best special effects of its time as the city burns and crumbles.

Saboteur
US 1942 108m bw
Universal (Frank Lloyd, Jack H. Skirball)
▣ ▤ ◈ ◉ ◎

w Peter Viertel, Joan Harrison, Dorothy Parker *story* Alfred Hitchcock *d* Alfred Hitchcock *ph* Joseph Valentine *m* Frank Skinner *md* Charles Previn *ad* Jack Otterson *ed* Otto Ludwig
☆ Robert Cummings (Barry Kane), Priscilla Lane (Patricia Martin), Otto Kruger (Charles Tobin), Alan Baxter (Freeman), Alma Kruger (Mrs. Henrietta Sutton), *Norman Lloyd* (Frank Fry)

'It throws itself forward so rapidly that it allows slight opportunity for looking back.' – *New York Times*

'The drama of a nation stirred to action, of a people's growing realization of themselves and their responsibilities.' – *Motion Picture Herald*

● Hitchcock wanted for the three leading roles Gary Cooper, Barbara Stanwyck and Harry Carey, but all refused or were unavailable.

926
Saboteur

A war worker unjustly suspected of sabotage flees across the country and unmasks a spy ring.

Hitchcock's action thriller is a flawed work, but contains some splendid sequences. With its theme of a manhunt, it has some resemblance to *The 39 Steps*; it has a similar evil mastermind, and the hero finds himself on the run with a disbelieving young woman. A ballroom scene, with the gang of spies closing in, and a final chase and fight atop the Statue of Liberty, lift it out of the ordinary.

The Most Dangerous Game
US 1932 63m bw
(RKO)
▤ ◎

GB title: *The Hounds of Zaroff*
w James Creelman *story* Richard Connell *d* Ernest B. Schoedsack, Irving Pichel *ph* Henry Gerrard *m* Max Steiner *ed* Archie Marshek
☆ *Leslie Banks* (Count Zaroff), Joel McCrea (Bob Rainsford), Fay Wray (Eve Trowbridge), Robert Armstrong (Martin Trowbridge), Noble Johnson (Tartar Servant)

'Futile stab at horror film classification, ineffective as entertainment and minus cast names to compensate.' – *Variety*

925
The Most Dangerous Game

A mad hunter lures guests on to his island so that he can hunt them down like animals.

Richard Connell's story, has been filmed several times and copied much more often. Ernest B. Schoedsack's and Irving Pichel's original version is still the best, a dated, shivery melodrama with moments of horror and mystery and a splendidly photographed chase sequence. Schoedsack was an outdoors man, an explorer, and his use of actual locations rather than a studio set gives authenticity to the action, especially when the fugitives are hunted down by hounds.

'A Little Pig Goes a Long Way.'

Babe

ᴛᴛ Australia 1995 94m colour
Universal/Kennedy Miller (George Miller, Doug Mitchell, Bill Miller)

▭▭ ▇ ⊚ ⊚ ⊚ ⌒

w George Miller, Chris Noonan *novel The Sheep-Pig* by Dick King-Smith *d* Chris Noonan *ph* Andrew Lesnie *m* Nigel Westlake *pd* Roger Ford *ad* Colin Gibson *ed* Marcus D'Arcy, Jay Friedkin

☆ James Cromwell (Arthur Hoggett), Magda Szubanski (Esme Hoggett), Roscoe Lee Browne (Narrator) and also the voices of Christine Cavanaugh, Miriam Margolyes, Danny Mann, Hugo Weaving

'A dazzling family entertainment with enormous charm and utilizing breathtaking technical innovation.' – *Leonard Klady, Variety*

▮ visual effects
⚯ best picture; Chris Noonan; George Miller, Chris Noonan (screenplay adaptation); James Cromwell; Marcus D'Arcy, Jay Friedkin; Roger Ford

924
Babe

An orphaned piglet is adopted by a sheepdog and decides that he wants to grow up and follow in his mother's pawprints.

An orphaned piglet is adopted by a sheepdog in this almost irresistible children's film with a wide appeal. Talking animals can be a bore, but Noonan makes it seem natural in the movie's farm setting and the shift from live to animatronic creatures is seamless. From its charming and courteous piglet to its singing mice, it is delightful, witty, and clever, a pleasure all the way.

Midnight

US 1939 95m bw
Paramount (Arthur Hornblow Jnr)

▇

w Billy Wilder, Charles Brackett *story* Edwin Justus Mayer, Franz Schultz *d* Mitchell Leisen *ph* Charles Lang *m* Frederick Hollander *ad* Hans Dreier, Robert Usher *ed* Doane Harrison

☆ *Claudette Colbert* (Eve Peabody 'Baroness Czerny'), Don Ameche (Tibor Czerny), *John Barrymore* (George Flammarion), Francis Lederer (Jacques Picot), Mary Astor (Helene Flammarion), Elaine Barrie (Simone), Hedda Hopper (Stephanie), Rex O'Malley (Marcel)

'Leisen's masterpiece, one of the best comedies of the thirties.' – *John Baxter, 1968*

'One of the authentic delights of the thirties.' – *New Yorker, 1976*

'It has the elements of an American *La Règle du Jeu*.' – *John Gillett*

'Just about the best light comedy ever caught by the camera.' – *Motion Picture Daily*

923
Midnight

A girl stranded in Paris is hired by an aristocrat to seduce the gigolo paying unwelcome attention to his wife.

Given the opportunity to get away from insipid roles and play a wicked woman in DeMille's *The Sign of the Cross*, Claudette Colbert made the most of the new opportunities offered her. Here she gives a sparkling comic turn as a gold-digging shop-girl chased by a love-struck taxi driver, while being hired by an aristocrat to impersonate a countess. This sophisticated screwball comedy barely flags until a slightly disappointing ending; all the talents involved are in excellent form. Colbert took the role after Carole Lombard turned it down, a move that increased the film's budget but caused problems for the set designer, since she insisted on being filmed to show her left profile; the right side of her face is seen only in long shot. She also refused to do close-ups after 5 pm. But she added a touch of humanity to Wilder and Diamond's cynical script

The Good Earth
US 1937 138m bw
MGM (*Irving Thalberg*)
🇺🇸 ⊛~
w Talbot Jennings, Tess Schlesinger, Claudine West
play Owen and Donald Davis *novel* Pearl S. Buck
d Sidney Franklin *ph* Karl Freund *m* Herbert Stothart
ad Cedric Gibbons *ed* Basil Wrangell *montage* Slavko Vorkapich
☆ *Paul Muni* (Wang Lung), *Luise Rainer* (O-Lan), Walter Connolly (Uncle), Tilly Losch (Lotus), Jessie Ralph (Cuckoo), Charley Grapewin (Old Father), Keye Luke (Elder Son), Harold Huber (Cousin)

'A true technical achievement with names enough to send it across. But it's not going to be easy to get the three-million-dollar investment back. And if it does come back it's going to take a long time.' – *Variety*

'One of the superb visual adventures of the period.' – *John Baxter, 1968*

'Prestigious boredom, and it goes on for a very long time.' – *New Yorker, 1977*

👤 Karl Freund; Luise Rainer
♟ best picture; Sidney Franklin; Basil Wrangell

922
The Good Earth

A Chinese peasant grows rich but loses his beloved wife.

Louis B. Mayer, head of MGM, was concerned about the studio filming Pearl S. Buck's novel. Audiences won't go to see films about American farmers, he reasoned, so why should they be interested in Chinese ones? Irving Thalberg prevailed, believing that the story could capture the soul of China. The massive, well-meaning and fondly remembered production is historically valuable as a Hollywood prestige production of the thirties, despite its artificiality and undramatic second half. The star performances impress, and the final locust attack is as well done as it originally seemed.

Lovers and Other Strangers
US 1970 104m Metrocolor
ABC/David Susskind
🇺🇸 ⊛
w Renée Taylor, Joseph Bologna, David Zelag Goodman
d Cy Howard *ph* Andrew Laszlo *m* Fred Karlin *ed* David Bretherton, Sidney Katz
☆ *Gig Young* (Hal Henderson), *Anne Jackson* (Cathy), *Richard Castellano* (Frank Vecchio), Bonnie Bedelia (Susan Henderson), Michael Brandon (Mike Vecchio), *Beatrice Arthur* (Bea Vecchio), Robert Dishy (Jerry), Harry Guardino (Johnny), Diane Keaton (Joan), Cloris Leachman (Bernice), Anne Meara (Wilma), Marian Hailey (Brenda)

'An extremely engaging comedy.' – *Gillian Hartnoll*

👤 song 'For All We Know' (*m* Fred Karlin, *ly* Robb Wilson, Arthur James)
♟ script, Richard Castellano

921
Lovers and Other Strangers

After living together for eighteen months, Susan and Mike decide to get married, and find their parents have sex problems of their own.

A talented cast make the most of ample chances under firm directorial control in this deft romantic comedy. In a succession of individual episodes it charts the insecurities and problems of married love. Susan's father is having an affair with his wife's best friend, who expects him to marry her, while Mike's brother is thinking of leaving his wife and his parents' marriage has declined into an uneasy relationship. A pleasure to watch, it is wise, witty and well-acted.

The Happiest Days of Your Life

GB 1950 81m bw

British Lion/Individual (Frank Launder)

w Frank Launder, John Dighton *play* John Dighton *d* Frank Launder *ph* Stan Pavey *m* Mischa Spoliansky *ed* Oswald Hafenrichter

☆ *Alastair Sim* (Wetherby Pond), *Margaret Rutherford* (Miss Muriel Whitchurch), *Joyce Grenfell* (Miss Gossage), *Richard Wattis* (Arnold Billings), *Edward Rigby* (Rainbow), *Guy Middleton* (Victor Hyde-Brown), *Muriel Aked* (Miss Jezzard), John Bentley (Richard Tassell), Bernadette O'Farrell (Miss Harper)

'Absolutely first rate fun.' – *Richard Mallett, Punch*

'Launder couldn't have knocked another laugh out of the situation if he'd used a hockey stick.' – *Sunday Express*

'The best mixed comedy pairing since Groucho Marx and Margaret Dumont.' – *Sunday Chronicle*

920
The Happiest Days of Your Life

A ministry mistake billets a girls' school on a boys' school.

Alastair Sim, as headmaster of a boys' boarding school, is horrified when, during wartime, a girls' school, where Margaret Rutherford is headmistress, is sent to share his premises. The clash of these two titans of comic acting is a delight in a briskly handled version of a semi-classic postwar farce. It is very much a period piece, not only set during the Second World War but dating from a period when single sex schools were the norm. It still generates plenty of laughter with its expertly managed comedy, as when classrooms and sports fields change instantly from male to female and back again to placate two different visiting groups.

Random Harvest

US 1942 126m bw

MGM (Sidney Franklin)

w Claudine West, George Froeschel, Arthur Wimperis *novel* James Hilton *d* Mervyn Le Roy *ph* Joseph Ruttenberg *m* Herbert Stothart *ad* Cedric Gibbons, Randall Duell *ed* Harold F. Kress

☆ *Ronald Colman* (Charles Rainier), *Greer Garson* (Paula), Susan Peters (Kitty), Philip Dorn (Dr. Jonathan Benet), Reginald Owen ("Biffer"), Henry Travers (Dr. Sims), Margaret Wycherly (Mrs. Deventer), Bramwell Fletcher (Harrison), Arthur Margetson (Chetwynd)

'I would like to recommend this film to those who can stay interested in Ronald Colman's amnesia for two hours and who could with pleasure eat a bowl of Yardley's shaving soap for breakfast.' – *James Agee*

'A strangely empty film … its characters are creatures of fortune, not partisans in determining their own fates.' – *Bosley Crowther, New York Times*

♟ best picture; script; Mervyn Le Roy; Herbert Stothart; Ronald Colman; Susan Peters; art direction

919
Random Harvest

A World War I veteran loses all memory of his past.

A shell-shocked officer in the 1914–18 war escapes from an asylum, marries a music hall singer and is idyllically happy until a shock makes him remember that he is the head of a noble family. His wife, whom he does not now remember, dutifully becomes his secretary and years later another shock brings memory and happiness back. The story works remarkably well in this rather splendid, no holds barred, roses round the door romance in Hollywood's best style with incomparable stars. A triumph of the *Peg's Paper* syndrome, and hugely enjoyable because it is done so enthusiastically.

Nothing But the Best
GB   1964   99m   Eastmancolor
Anglo Amalgamated/Domino (David Deutsch)
👀

w Frederic Raphael *d* Clive Donner *ph* Nicolas Roeg
m Ron Grainer *ad* Reece Pemberton *ed* Fergus McDonell
☆ *Alan Bates* (Jimmy Brewster), *Denholm Elliott* (Charlie
Prince), Harry Andrews (Mr. Horton), Millicent Martin (Ann
Horton), Pauline Delany (Mrs. March)

'It is a film with a smooth, smiling, elegant fun,
witty but never concentrating on wit to the
detriment of tension; it makes a logical step-by-
step progression towards a climax which is
hilarious in a Stygian way without resort to the
usual bangabout.' – *Dilys Powell*

918
Nothing But the Best

An ambitious clerk learns to fight his way to the top by cheek and one-upmanship.

An entertaining comedy about Britain's class-ridden society. Jimmy, played with winning grace by Alan Bates, learns how to behave from his social betters and then makes it to the top by marrying the boss's daughter, with a little murder on the way. The sharp comedy of social aspirations is well-observed: Jimmy works as an estate agent, where facades can fool most of the customers most of the time. A witty script, tight direction and some excellent performances, notably Denholm Elliott's devastating upper-class layabout, ensure that this black comedy has lost none of its bite.

My Brilliant Career
Australia   1979   100m   Eastmancolor
NSW Film Corporation/Margaret Fink
🇺🇸 ©

w Eleanor Witcombe *novel* Miles Franklin *d* Gillian
Armstrong *ph* Don McAlpine *m* Nathan Waks
pd Luciana Arrighi *ed* Nicholas Beauman
☆ *Judy Davis* (Sybylla Melvyn), Sam Neill (Harry
Beecham), Wendy Hughes (Aunt Helen), Robert Grubb
(Frank Hawdon), Max Cullen (Mr. McSwat)

'Tasteful, slow, pictorial.' – *Pauline Kael*
🏆 Judy Davis

917
My Brilliant Career

The daughter of an Australian bush farmer at the turn of the century dreams of the world beyond and writes a memoir.

Despite discouragement from her parents, a poor Australian farm-girl grows up in the early 1900s with a determination to be a writer, even if it means abandoning the man she loves and accepting poverty and hardship. Miles Franklin's semi-autobiographical novel, written when she was a teenager, is turned into a tough-minded movie with feminist undertones by Gillian Armstrong. Judy Davis gives a strong performance as a woman who is not prepared to subjugate her individuality to others.

For Me and My Gal
US 1942 104m bw
MGM (Arthur Freed)

w Richard Sherman, Sid Silvers, Fred Finklehoffe *d* Busby Berkeley *ph* William Daniels *md* Georgie Stoll, Roger Edens *ad* Cedric Gibbons, Gabriel Scognamillo *ed* Ben Lewis

☆ *Judy Garland* (Jo Hayden), *Gene Kelly* (Harry Palmer), *George Murphy* (Jimmy K. Metcalf), Marta Eggerth (Eve Minard), Ben Blue (Sid Simms), Richard Quine (Danny Hayden), Stephen McNally (Mr. Waring)

'A touch of imagination and a deal more than a touch of energy.' – *The Times*

♫ 'Oh, You Beautiful Doll'; 'For Me and My Gal'; 'When You Wore a Tulip'; 'After You've Gone'; 'Till We Meet Again'; 'Ballin' the Jack'.

♕ Georgie Stoll, Roger Edens

916
For Me and My Gal

Just before World War I, a girl vaudevillian chooses between two partners.

A routine musical romance at the time of its production, this film now stands out because of its professional execution, its star value, and the fact that they don't make 'em like that any more. The story was a typical, corny backstage song and dance: three vaudeville performers – two men and a girl – quarrel, are split by the war and get together again, whereupon romance blossoms and their act triumphs. It was not a happy production: Kelly was at odds with the director and with Murphy, who had been forced to switch roles with Kelly at the last moment. But none of that showed in the film, which was full of verve, exciting dancing and joyous songs.

Autobus
France 1991 98m colour
Artificial Eye/Les Productions Lazennec/FR3/SGGC/
La Générale d'Images/Canal (Alain Rocca)
🔲 🎧
French title: *Aux yeux du monde*
wd Eric Rochant *ph* Pierre Novion *m* Gérard Torikian
pd Pascale Fenouillet *ad* Pascale Fenouillet *ed* Catherine
Quesemand
☆ Yvan Attal (Bruno Fournier), Kristin Scott-Thomas
(L'Institutrice), Marc Berman (Le Chauffeur), Charlotte
Gainsbourg (Juliette Mangin), Renan Mazeas (Sam)

'Slight and well-meaning, and less incisive than it
could be. But it is also much more appealing than
its rather whimsical premise would suggest.'
– *Verina Glaessner, Sight and Sound*

915
Autobus

*A frustrated and unemployed youth hijacks a bus full of schoolchildren
so that he can go to visit his girlfriend.*

Eric Rochant deals with a familiar theme but manages to avoid all the
conventional routes in this thriller. The trip goes wrong – the police are
alerted, the bus runs out of fuel, and along the way the youth is forced
to give a lift to a blind couple – but he begins to form a relationship
with the children's teacher and the driver. The movie turns into an
unexpected and uplifting vehicle that confounds expectations.

'Flesh to touch … Flesh to burn! Don't
keep the Wicker Man waiting!'
The Wicker Man
GB 1973 86m Eastmancolor
British Lion (Peter Snell)
🔲 ▦ ⊚ ⊚ 🎧
w Anthony Shaffer *d* Robin Hardy *ph* Harry Waxman
m Paul Giovanni *ad* Seamus Flannery *ed* Eric Boyd-
Perkins
☆ Edward Woodward (Sgt Howie), Britt Ekland (Willow),
Christopher Lee (Lord Summersisle), Ingrid Pitt (Librarian),
Diane Cilento (Miss Rose), Lindsay Kemp (Alder
MacGregor), Russell Waters (Harbour Master)

'An encouraging achievement for those who had
begun to despair of the British cinema.' – *David
McGillivray*

● The film also exists in other versions, the longest
running for 102m. It was also released on DVD in a
director's cut running for 99m.

914
The Wicker Man

*A policeman flies to a remote Scottish isle to investigate the death of a
child, and finds himself in the hands of diabolists.*

Anthony Shaffer's clever script gave an originality to this old-fashioned
but remarkably well made scare story, with effective shock moments.
Its setting was the unusual one of a remote Scottish isle, and it pitted a
rigid Presbyterian policeman from the mainland against the hedonistic
island pagans. There is uneven acting in some of the lesser roles, but
the movie rises to an impressive and horrific climax. The film was not
liked by British Lion who eventually released it in a cut version as part
of a double bill. Various versions of the film exist, and a restored 'director's cut' has been released on DVD.

Rebel Without a Cause
US 1955 111m Warnercolor
Cinemascope
Warner (David Weisbart)

⬛ ⬛ ▬ ◉〜 ◎ ◎ ◖

w Stewart Stern *story* Nicholas Ray *d* Nicholas Ray
ph Ernest Haller *m* Leonard Rosenman *ad* Malcolm Bert
ed William Ziegler
☆ *James Dean* (Jim), Natalie Wood (Judy), Jim Backus
(Jim's Father), Sal Mineo (Plato), Ann Doran (Jim's Mother),
Dennis Hopper (Goon)
♧ original story (Nicholas Ray); Natalie Wood; Sal Mineo

913
Rebel Without a Cause

The adolescent son of a well-to-do family gets into trouble with other kids and the police.

'Dean is beyond comprehension,' said Jack Warner when he first saw his studio's production of *Rebel Without a Cause*, which was the first film to suggest that juvenile violence is not necessarily bred in the slums. Now, of course, Dean's role as an unhappy youth in need of a strong father is more easily understood; it's his moody, slightly sullen charisma that still fascinates. The melodrama catapulted him to stardom as the prototype fifties rebel; the movie became an enormous success when it was released four days after his death. Director Nicholas Ray, temperamentally drawn to outcasts and loners, uses colour to suggest the garishness of youth and the CinemaScope screen to give a tragic dimension to his central trio of adolescents.

Straw Dogs
GB 1971 118m Eastmancolor
Talent Associates/Amerbroco (Daniel Melnick)

⬛ ▬ ◉〜 ◎ ◎

w David Zelag Goodman, Sam Peckinpah *novel The Siege
of Trencher's Farm* by Gordon M. Williams *d* Sam
Peckinpah *ph* John Coquillon *m* Jerry Fielding *pd* Ray
Simm *ad* Ken Bridgeman *ed* Paul Davies, Tony Lawson,
Roger Spottiswoode
☆ Dustin Hoffman (David Sumner), Susan George (Amy
Sumner), Peter Vaughan (Tom Hedden), David Warner
(Henry Niles), T. P. McKenna (Maj. Scott), Colin Welland
(Rev. Hood)

'Before the end you will have gasped and
shuddered through an orgy of detailed rape,
slaughter, arson and wanton destruction.' – *Cecil
Wilson, Daily Mail*

'A magnificent piece of red-raw, meaty
entertainment.' – *Ernest Betts, The People*

♧ Jerry Fielding

912
Straw Dogs

In a Cornish village, a mild American university researcher erupts into violence when taunted by drunken villagers who commit sustained assaults on himself and his wife.

Peckinpah's movie about a man redeemed by violence plays more like a horror movie than the psychological study he may have intended; perhaps it might have played better set in the wilder West rather than in the Cornish countryside, among the sort of degenerates who peopled the mining camp in *Ride the High Country*, with brothers eager to share their sibling's new bride. It is a better film than was suggested by the controversy at the time of its original release. There is well-sustained tension and release in the drama, though it shows Peckinpah at his most misogynistic.

'The great decade (1915–25) of the progress of motion picture art reaches its summit! A cast of 125,000!'

'The inspired love of the prince of Hur for the gentle lovely Esther!'

Ben-Hur
US   1925   170m approx (16 fps)   bw (colour sequence)   silent
MGM

w Bess Meredyth, Carey Wilson *novel* Lew Wallace *d* Fred Niblo *ph* Karl Struss, Clyde de Vinna, and others *ad* Horace Jackson, Ferdinand Pinney Earle *ed* Lloyd Nosler

☆ *Ramon Novarro* (Judah Ben-Hur), *Francis X. Bushman* (Messala), Carmel Myers (Iras), May McAvoy (Esther), Betty Bronson (Mary)

'Masterpiece of study and patience, a photodrama filled with artistry.' – *New York Times*

● To begin with, the film was directed by Charles Brabin and starred George Walsh. Both were replaced after Louis Mayer saw the first rushes. Previously filmed in 1907.

911
Ben-Hur

In the time of Christ, a Jew suffers mightily under the Romans.

The American silent screen's biggest epic has a sprightly quality lacking in its later, unimaginative remake, even though its director, William Wyler, was a production assistant on this version directed by Fred Niblo. Both films follow the pattern of Lew Wallace's novel. The film had a troubled production. Shooting began in Egypt and Italy, but the footage was unusable. The production was brought back to California with different leads. The sea battle and the chariot race, filmed with forty cameras, are its most famous and spectacular sequences.

The Bedford Incident
GB   1965   102m   bw
Columbia/Bedford Productions (James B. Harris)

w James Poe *novel* Mark Rascovich *d* James B. Harris *ph* Gilbert Taylor *m* Gerard Schurrmann *ed* John Jympson

☆ *Richard Widmark* (Capt. Eric Finlander, USN), *Sidney Poitier* (Ben Munceford), James MacArthur (Ens. Ralston), Eric Portman (Cmdr. Wolfgang Schrepke), Wally Cox (Sonarman, 2nd Class), Martin Balsam (Lt. Cmdr. Chester Potter), Phil Brown (Chief Pharmacist's Mate McKinley), Michael Kane (Cmdr. Allison), Gary Cockrell (Lt. Bascombe), Donald Sutherland (Pharmacist's Mate Nerny)

'Strong on virtues of a rather negative kind.' – *Penelope Houston*

910
The Bedford Incident

A ruthlessly efficient US destroyer captain in the Arctic chases a Russian submarine and accidentally fires an atomic weapon.

This film is a mixture of themes from *Dr Strangelove* and *The Caine Mutiny*. With its concern for the dangers of technological advance, its Cold War paranoia, and its portrait of men going to pieces under extreme pressure, it becomes very tense and forceful, with excellent acting. It was Poitier's first role with no reference to his colour.

Airplane

US   1980   88m   Metrocolor
Paramount/Howard W. Koch (Jon Davison)

wd Jim Abrahams, David and Jerry Zucker *ph* Joseph Biroc *m* Elmer Bernstein *pd* Ward Preston *ed* Patrick Kennedy

☆ Robert Stack (Kramer), Lloyd Bridges (McCroskey), Robert Hays (Ted Striker), Julie Hagerty (Elaine), Peter Graves (Capt. Oveur), Leslie Nielsen (Dr. Rumack), Lorna Patterson (Randy), Ethel Merman (Lt. Hurwitz), Kareem Abdul-Jabbar (Murdock)

'Parody may be the lowest form of humour, but few comedies in ages have rocked the laugh meter this hard.' – *Variety*

'It keeps going, like a dervish with skids on.' – *Derek Malcolm, Guardian*

'Proof that the cinema is alive and well and bursting with ingenuity.' – *David Hughes, Sunday Times*

'All pretty juvenile really, though the relentless pace and sheer poor taste make up for a lack of originality.' – *Time Out, 1984*

'Practically a satirical anthology of movie clichés … it compensates for its lack of original comic invention by its utter willingness to steal, beg, borrow and rewrite from anywhere.' – *Roger Ebert*

909
Airplane

A former pilot gets his nerve back when called upon to land a passenger plane because the crew all have food poisoning.

Arthur Hailey's play *Flight into Danger* and the film *Zero Hour*, from which it was made, get the zany parody treatment in this popular movie. The plot remains the same. Often very funny and occasionally very crude, the movie gains from Lloyd Bridges, Peter Graves and Leslie Nielsen, stalwarts of disaster movies, who all keep the straightest of faces through a myriad of gags.

'Sometimes there's a terrible penalty for telling the truth…'

The Great Lie

US   1941   107m   bw
Warner (Hal B. Wallis, Henry Blanke)

w Lenore Coffee *novel January Heights* by Polan Banks *d* Edmund Goulding *ph* Tony Gaudio *m* Max Steiner *ad* Carl Jules Weyl *ed* Ralph Dawson

☆ *Bette Davis* (Maggie Patterson), *Mary Astor* (Sandra Kovak), *George Brent* (Pete Van Allen), Lucile Watson (Aunt Ada), Hattie McDaniel (Violet), Grant Mitchell (Joshua Mason), Jerome Cowan (Jock Thompson)

👤 Mary Astor

908
The Great Lie

A determined girl loses the man she loves, believes him dead in a plane crash, and takes over the baby which his selfish wife does not want.

Bette Davis and Mary Astor spar wonderfully as the two bitchy female leads in this absurd story that becomes top flight entertainment with all concerned in cracking form. Davis was unhappy with the script, and the two of them rewrote it to bring out their conflict. The war is fought with clothes – Davis had twenty-two changes of costume and Astor eighteen – and words. Based on a best-selling novel, it was the stuff of melodrama. Its classical music trimmings, with the sound of a Tchaikovsky piano concerto, added the final Hollywood touch.

The Great McGinty
US   1940   83m   bw
Paramount (Paul Jones)

GB title: *Down Went McGinty*
wd Preston Sturges *ph* William C. Mellor *m* Frederick Hollander *ad* Hans Dreier, Earl Hedrick *ed* Hugh Bennett
☆ *Brian Donlevy* (Dan McGinty), *Akim Tamiroff* (The Boss), Muriel Angelus (Catherine McGinty), Louis Jean Heydt (Thompson), Arthur Hoyt (Mayor Tillinghast)

'This is his first directing job and where has he been all our lives? He has that sense of the incongruous which makes some of the best gaiety.' – *Otis Ferguson*

'The tough dialogue is matched by short, snappy scenes; the picture seems to have wasted no time, no money.' – *Gilbert Seldes*

'A director as adroit and inventive as any in the business … it starts like a five-alarm fire and never slackens pace for one moment until its unexpected conclusion.' – *Pare Lorentz*

'Sturges takes the success ethic and throws it in the face of the audience.' – *James Orsini*

'Capra with the gloves off.' – *Raymond Durgnat*

👤 script

907
The Great McGinty

A hobo and a crook have a hectic political career.

Preston Sturges's first film as a writer-director is an exhilarating satire on greed, fast-moving, witty and perfectly cast. During its making, he wrote many memos to the producer, both as a writer complaining about what the director was doing to his script, and as a director who was unhappy with his writer's work. The producer told him to consult himself, which he did with stimulating results. His story of a bum who made one mistake for one moment, trying to reform, skewers all the hustling and backstage manoeuvrings of politics.

Tampopo
Japan   1986   117m   colour   Panavision
Itami Productions/New Century Producers (Juzo Itami, Yashushi Tamaoki, Seigo Hosogoe)

wd Juzo Itami *ph* Masaki Tamura *m* Kinihiko Murai *ad* Takeo Kimura *ed* Akira Suzuki
☆ Tsutomu Yamazaki (Goro), Nobuko Miyamoto (Tampopo), Koji Yakuso (Man in White Suit), Ken Watanabe (Gun), Rikiya Yasouka (Pisuken)

906
Tampopo

Encouraged by a truck driver, a woman learns to become the best of noodle cooks.

A joyous comedy in celebration of food as nourishment, pleasure and aid to sexual enjoyment, contained within a parody of film genres. It begins with a crunching, munching cinema audience and ends with a baby happily suckling at his mother's breast. In between, Itami hijacks the plot of many a cowboy movie – this is the first noodle Western – as a lorry driver drives into town to show a widow how to run a successful noodle eaterie, and make a man of her son. An episodic movie, it veers off course to observe gourmet vagabonds, who eat the leftovers from the best restaurants, and a woman who can't resist squeezing super-market produce. Whatever inner demons possessed Itami to take his own life seven years later, they are not evident in this delicious bonbon.

'A perfectly swell motion picture!'

Born Yesterday
US 1950 103m bw
Columbia (S. Sylvan Simon)

w Albert Mannheimer *play* Garson Kanin *d* George
Cukor *ph* Joseph Walker *m* Frederick Hollander
ed Charles Nelson
☆ *Judy Holliday* (Billie Dawn), *Broderick Crawford* (Harry
Brock), William Holden (Paul Verrall), Howard St John (Jim
Devery)
● The original choices for the Judy Holliday role were Rita
Hayworth and Jean Parker (who had played it on tour).
🎭 Judy Holliday
🏆 best picture; Albert Mannheimer; George Cukor

The Mark of Zorro
US 1940 94m bw
TCF (Raymond Griffith)

w John Taintor Foote, Garrett Fort, Bess Meredyth
d Rouben Mamoulian *ph* Arthur Miller *m* Alfred Newman
ad Richard Day, Joseph C. Wright *ed* Robert Bischoff
☆ *Tyrone Power* (Zorro/Don Diego Vega), *Basil Rathbone*
(Capt. Esteban Pasquale), *J. Edward Bromberg* (Don Luis
Quintero), Linda Darnell (Lolita Quintero), Eugene Pallette
(Fra Felipe), Montagu Love (Don Alejandro Vega), Janet
Beecher (Senora Isabella Vega), Robert Lowery (Rodrigo)
● A Region 1 DVD release includes commentary by critic
Richard Schickel.
🏆 Alfred Newman

905
Born Yesterday

The ignorant ex-chorus girl mistress of a scrap iron tycoon takes English lessons, falls for her tutor, and politically outmanoeuvres her bewildered lover.

Judy Holliday could play a dumb blonde like no one else, which is why *Born Yesterday* made her a star in the role of the ignorant ex-chorus girl Billie Dawn not only on the Broadway stage but in the subsequent movie. Columbia head Harry Cohn wanted Rita Hayworth to play the part in the movie, but she had just married and wasn't interested. He tested at least ten other actresses for the role before agreeing to Holliday, who had made the part her own in its four year run on the stage. She is superb as the blonde mistress of a boorish scrap iron tycoon (modelled by Kanin on the blustering Cohn). As her director George Cukor noted, she was a great clown who could also move an audience.

904
The Mark of Zorro

After being educated in Spain, Diego de Vega returns to California and finds the country enslaved and his father half-corrupted by tyrants. Disguising himself as a masked bandit, he leads the country to expel the usurpers.

Mamoulian's action picture is splendid stuff for boys of all ages, with Tyrone Power in the role of the dandyish Diego de Vega and his dashing alter ego Zorro. The narrative could have been turned into the adventures of Robin Hood without much change. Power is relatively restrained in the role, especially when compared to Rathbone's rapier-waving villain, but Mamoulian's direction adds the necessary panache and an overwhelming pictorial sense, which makes it stand out as the finest of all adventures.

The League of Gentlemen
GB   1960   112m   bw
Rank/Allied Film Makers (Michael Relph)
▣ ▆ ◉

w Bryan Forbes *novel* John Boland *d* Basil Dearden
ph Arthur Ibbetson *m* Philip Green *ad* Peter Proud
ed John D. Guthridge
☆ *Jack Hawkins* (Hyde), Richard Attenborough (Edward Lexy), *Roger Livesey* (Mycroft), *Nigel Patrick* (Peter Graham Race), Bryan Forbes (Martin Porthill), Kieron Moore (Stevens), Terence Alexander (Rupert Rutland-Smith), *Norman Bird* (Frank Weaver), Robert Coote (Bunny Warren), Melissa Stribling (Peggy), Nanette Newman (Elizabeth), Gerald Harper (Capt. Saunders), Patrick Wymark (Wylie), David Lodge (C.S.M.), Doris Hare (Molly Weaver) and also Lydia Sherwood

903
The League of Gentlemen

An ex-army officer recruits high-class misfits with guilty secrets to help him in a bank robbery.

A delightfully handled comedy adventure, a caper movie from the days when crime did not pay. Jack Hawkins, whose voice had succumbed to throat cancer by the end of shooting, is commanding as a blackmailing officer and gentleman, and is matched by the terrific character actors who surround him. The planning of a £1m robbery and the actual heist are both suspenseful and funny, and a lighter ending would have made it an undoubted classic.

Get Carter
GB   1971   112m   Metrocolor
MGM/Mike Klinger
▣ ▆ ◉ ◎ ◯

wd Mike Hodges *novel* Jack's Return Home by Ted Lewis
ph Wolfgang Suschitzky *m* Roy Budd *ad* Roger King
ed John Trumper
☆ Michael Caine (Jack Carter), John Osborne (Cyril Kinnear), Ian Hendry (Eric Paice), Britt Ekland (Anna Fletcher)

'TV on the big screen – more sex, more violence, but no more attention to motivation or plot logic.' – *Arthur Knight*

'So calculatedly cool and soulless and nastily erotic that it seems to belong to a new era of virtuoso viciousness.' – *Pauline Kael*

'A cracking good movie.' – *Ken Russell*

902
Get Carter

A racketeer goes to Newcastle to avenge his brother's death at the hands of gangsters.

Mike Hodges's tough British thriller, has become a cult favourite. Moving through the movie's grubby, bleakly amoral environment, where violence is expected and sex has replaced affection, Caine remains coolly detached as a Raymond Chandler-reading, Cockney thug whose self-esteem puts him a rung above the provincial lowlifes he encounters.

Memories of Underdevelopment
Cuba 1968 104m bw
(Miguel Mendoza)
🇺🇸
original title: *Memorias De Subdesarollo*
wd Tomas Gutierrez Alea *novel* Edmundo Desnoes
ph Ramon F. Suarez *m* Leo Brouwer *ad* Julio Matilla
ed Nelson Rodríguez
☆ Sergio Corrieri (Sergio), Daisy Granados (Elena),
Eslinda Nuñez (Noemi), Omar Valdes, Rene de la Cruz,
Yolanda Far, Beatriz Pocnara (Laura)

'A film about alienation that is wise, sad, and often
funny, and that never slips into the bored and
boring attitudes that wreck Antonioni's later films'
– *Vincent Canby, New York Times*

901
Memories of Underdevelopment

In 1961, a blocked writer, left behind in Havana when his family moved to Miami, forms a relationship with a bird-brained actress.

Tomas Gutierrez Alea was the best filmmaker to appear in Cuba in the aftermath of revolution there. He views the social upheavals and the rise of the peasant class through the eyes of Sergio, a leisured intellectual whose family has left for Miami. Sergio remains behind, relying on his income as a landlord, and spending his time chasing young women. Alea is able to criticize both the pre- and post-Castro Cuba through this upper-class figure, using a variety of techniques and utilizing documentary footage.

'She always gets a part.'
Odishon
Japan 1999 115m colour
Metro Tartan/Omega (Akemi Suyama, Satoshi
Hukushima)
▭ ▆ ◉ ⊚
aka: *Audition*
w Daisuke Tengan *novel* Ryu Murakami *d* Takashi Miike
ph Hideo Yamamoto *m* Koji Endo *pd* Tatsuo Ozeki
ed Yasushi Shimamura
☆ Ryo Ishibashi (Shigeharu Aoyama), Eihi Shiina (Asami
Yamasaki), Jun Kunimura (Yoshikawa), Miyuki Matsuda
(Ryoko Aoyama), Ren Osugi (Shibata), Tetsu Sawaki
(Shigehiko Aoyama), Renji Ishibashi (Old Man)

'The best-disguised psychotronic splatter flick in
recent memory … a lethally poised Venus flytrap of
a movie.' – *Dennis Lim, Village Voice*

'The grimmest exploitation of sadistic violence I
have seen in months … pornographic.' –
Alexander Walker, London Evening Standard

900
Odishon

A middle-aged widower and TV producer auditions actresses as a means of finding a new wife, and gets more than he has bargained for.

Prolific Japanese director Takashi Miike is one of the most interesting of current filmmakers, turning out movies in many genres that push against the limits of cinema. This is one of his more restrained and classical films. A middle-aged widower and TV producer exploits the process of auditioning actresses to find a new wife. He chooses the wrong girl, who has already suffered at the hands of men. After a leisurely opening, Miike overturns expectations by developing a chilling, and ultimately extremely violent and gruesome drama. The tortured, hallucinatory finale is not easy to watch; there is no doubt, though, that his is an extraordinary talent.

'His only friend was his gun – his only refuge, a woman's heart!'

The Gunfighter
US   1950   84m   bw
TCF (Nunnally Johnson)
▣ ▤ ▥

w William Bowers, William Sellers d Henry King
ph Arthur Miller m Alfred Newman ad Richard Irvine, Lyle Wheeler ed Barbara McLean
☆ Gregory Peck (Jimmy Ringo), Helen Westcott (Peggy Walsh), Millard Mitchell (Sheriff Mark Strett), Jean Parker (Molly), Karl Malden (Mac), Skip Homeier (Hunt Bromley), Mae Marsh (Mrs. O'Brien)

'Preserves throughout a respectable level of intelligence and invention.' – *Lindsay Anderson*

'Not merely a good western, a good film.' – *Richard Mallett, Punch*

'The movie is done in cold, quiet tones of gray, and every object in it – faces, clothing, a table, the hero's heavy moustache – is given an air of uncompromising authenticity, suggesting those dim photographs of the nineteenth-century West …' – *Robert Warshow, The Immediate Experience*

♟ original story (William Bowers, André de Toth)

899
The Gunfighter

A gunfighter fails to shake off his past.

A gunfighter wants to quit his trade and settle down with his wife and child. His reputation precedes him; in every town, there is someone eager to make a reputation by killing him. He is chased by the three brothers of a would-be gunslinger he kills, and waits in a saloon for them to find him. Henry King's downbeat, moody, adult Western, which was set in a believable community, prefigured many later films, such as Peckinpah's *Ride the High Country*, about westerners who realize the changing world no longer has a place for them. It emphasized the isolation of a man with a gun on both sides of the law.

Melvin and Howard
US   1980   95m   Technicolor
Universal (Terry Nelson)
▤ ⊚

w Bo Goldman d Jonathan Demme ph Tak Fujimoto m Bruce Langhorne ad Richard Sawyer ed Craig McKay
☆ Paul Le Mat (Melvin Dummar), Jason Robards Jnr (Howard Hughes), Mary Steenburgen (Lynda Dummar), Elizabeth Cheshire (Darcy Dummar), Michael J. Pollard (Little Red), Gloria Grahame (Mrs. Sisk)

'An almost flawless act of sympathetic imagination … it's what might have happened if Jean Renoir had directed a comedy script by Preston Sturges.' – *New Yorker*

'Commercial American movie-making of a most expansive, entertaining kind.' – *Vincent Canby, New York Times*

♟ Bo Goldman; Mary Steenburgen
♟ Jason Robards Jnr (supporting actor)

898
Melvin and Howard

The life of a factory worker is changed when a man he picks up in the Nevada desert claims to be Howard Hughes.

In Demme's eccentric comedy, the hullabaloo that follows when Hughes leaves a fortune to the worker in his will has been compared to the work of Preston Sturges. And it does have much of Sturges's relish for unlikely small-town heroes, suddenly surrounded by the greedy and the venal. But it also has an agreeable style of its own. The American dream has rarely seemed so sweet and funny.

Bullitt
US 1968 113m Technicolor
Warner/Solar (Philip D'Antoni)
▭▭ ▭▭ ▬ ⌖ ⊕ ⊘ ⌒
w Harry Kleiner, Alan R. Trustman *novel Mute Witness* by
Robert L. Pike *d* Peter Yates *ph* William A. Fraker *m* Lalo
Schifrin *ad* Albert Brenner *ed* Frank P. Keller
☆ *Steve McQueen* (Bullitt), Jacqueline Bisset (Cathy),
Robert Vaughn (Chalmers), Don Gordon (Delgetti), Robert
Duvall (Weissberg), Simon Oakland (Capt. Bennett)

'It has energy, drive, impact, and above all, style.'
– Hollis Alpert

👤 Frank P. Keller

897
Bullitt

*A San Francisco police detective conceals the death of an underground
witness in his charge, and goes after the killers himself.*

Peter Yates's cop thriller will always be associated with Steve
McQueen's car chase over the hills of San Francisco, where the vehicle
takes off as the road dips, though there's also another exciting airport
chase, around moving planes at night. The film has a remarkable sense
of place, of everyday life going on around the propulsive action. The
plot is a familiar one, but McQueen's laconic presence gives it a feeling
of originality.

Black God, White Devil
Brazil 1964 110m bw
New Cinema/Copacabana (Luiz Augusto Mendes)
original title: *Deus e o Diabo na Terra do Sol*
w Glauber Rocha, Walter Lima Jnr *d* Glauber Rocha
ph Waldemar Lima *m* Villa-Lobos *ad* Glauber Rocha
ed L. Ririra
☆ Yona Magalhaes (Rosa), Geraldo Del Rey (Manuel),
Othon Bastos (Corsico), Mauricio Do Valle (Antonio Das
Mortes), Lidio Silva (Sebastiao)

'One is left wondering what a film so locked in its
own oppressive landscape can really communicate
to a European audience – other than the seduction
of alien violence and alien despair.' – *Penelope
Houston, Sight and Sound*

'The endless scenes of savage slaughter, ululating
cries and trudgings through arid landscape may
seem wilfully indulgent, as much exploitations as
explorations of a mentality Rocha believes must be
overcome.' – *Jan Dawson, MFB*

● The hired killer Antonio das Mortes became the
eponymous hero of a film Rocha made in 1969

896
Black God, White Devil

*A peasant follows the teachings of a fanatical prophet who preaches a
gospel of suffering and death and becomes an outlaw.*

Glauber Rocha, who died at the age of 42 in 1981, seems a forgotten
figure today, except in his home country of Brazil. None of his films are
available on video or DVD outside South America. Yet, as leader of the
Cinema Novo movement of the 60s, he was a director to be reckoned
with. *Black God, White Devil,* the film that brought him to worldwide
attention, retains its revolutionary power in its tale of a peasant, who
murders his corrupt landlord and joins the gang of a black prophet;
when the prophet dies and his followers are slaughtered by a hired
assassin, he becomes a bandit. Drawing on Brazilian myths and folk-
lore, it is a violent, angry movie about political liberation that deserves
to be seen.

Love
Hungary 1971 92m bw
Mafilm

original title: *Szerelem*
w Tibor Dery *d* Karoly Makk *ph* Janos Toth *m* Andras
Mihaly *ad* Jozsef Romvari *ed* Gyorgy Sivo
☆ Lili Darvas (Old Lady), Mari Torocsik (Luca), Ivan
Darvas (Janos), Erzsi Orsolya (Iren), Laszlo Mensaros
(Azorvos), Tibor Bitskey (Feri)

'Subtle, rich, reserved, even elegant, it is a beautiful
movie.' – *Roger Greenspun, New York Times*

895
Love

After her husband is jailed for his political opinions, a young woman cares for her dying mother-in-law.

An unsentimental film on a theme that could lend itself to mawkishness: a young woman, caring for her dying mother-in-law after her husband is jailed for his political opinions, reads letters purporting to be from her husband, telling the old woman that he is making good in America. The relationship between the two women, which is loving yet marked by personal differences, forms the basis of this touching movie. It was the last film made by Lili Darvas, the widow of dramatist Ferenc Molnar, who returned to Hungary after an absence of 30 years.

The Butterfly Murders
Hong Kong 1979 colour 'Scope
Ng See Yuen (Ng See Kin)

w Lam Fan *d* Tsui Hark *ph* Fun Chin Yu *ed* Zhixiong
Huang, David Wu
☆ Lau Siu Ming (Fang Hongye), Wong Shee Tong (Tian
Feng (as Shutang Huang)), Michelle (Green Shadow), Chan
Chi Chi (Lady Shen), Cheong Kwok Chu, Kuo Hung, Wong
Cheong, Kiu Fung

894
The Butterfly Murders

A wandering scholar, at a time of warring factions, solves the mystery of an aristocratic family apparently plagued by killer butterflies.

Many martial arts experts are summoned to a medieval castle to solve the problem of an aristocratic family in this visually splendid fantasy. The mystery is finally unravelled by a wandering scholar. Elaborately choreographed fight sequences take place in the castle's underground passages as one murder follows another. It is a movie of immense melodramatic style that marked the impressive start of Tsui Hark's directorial career.

Ordet
Denmark 1957 126m bw
Palladium (Carl Theodor Dreyer)

wd Carl Theodor Dreyer *ph* Henning Bendtsen *m* Poul Schierbeck
☆ Henrik Malberg, Emil Hass Christensen, Preben Lerdorff-Rye, Caj Kristensen
● It is available on Region 1 DVD as part of a four-disc set from Criterion, together with *Day of Wrath, Getrud*, and a 94m documentary *Carl Th. Dreyer – My Metier*.

893
Ordet

In a God-fearing village, a father and his three sons have various religious experiences.

Dreyer's ascetic, intellectual drama is an extraordinary work, very slow and austere but strangely compelling and difficult to dismiss. The drama deals with a collision of faith within a farming family who are part of a God-fearing community. One son believes he is Jesus, while another is an agnostic. It can be hard to take at times: Rye was encouraged by Dreyer to speak his lines in a high-pitched monotone. The final moments, though, are hair-raising, as, with the simplest means, Dreyer shows a convincing miracle of resurrection, a startling end to a film like no other.

La Femme Infidèle
France/Italy 1968 98m Eastmancolor
La Boëtie/Cinegay (André Génovès)

aka: *The Unfaithful Wife*
wd Claude Chabrol *ph* Jean Rabier *m* Pierre Jansen
ad Guy Littaye *ed* Jacques Gaillard
☆ Stéphane Audran (Helene Desvallees), Michel Bouquet (Charles Desvallees), Maurice Ronet (Victor Pegala)

'On any level, this bizarre murder framed by whiskies emerges as Chabrol's most flawless work to date.' – *Jan Dawson, MFB*

892
La Femme Infidèle

A middle-aged insurance broker, set in his ways, murders his wife's lover; when she suspects the truth, they are drawn closer together.

Chabrol's examination of marital infidelity and passion is an almost Buñuel-like black comedy, spare and quiet. With immaculate performances from Stéphane Audran as the wife and Michel Bouquet as the husband, it marries suspense and sophistication in a wholly satisfying manner.

Jubilee
GB   1978   104m   colour
Whaley-Malin/Megalovision
⬛ ⓔ ⓓ 🎧
w Derek Jarman and others *d* Derek Jarman *ph* Peter
Middleton *m* Brian Eno *ed* Nick Barnard, Tom Priestley
☆ Jenny Runacre (Queen Elizabeth I), Little Nell (Crabs),
Toyah Willcox (Mad), Jordan (Amyl Nitrite), Hermine
Demoriane (Chaos)

'One of the most intelligent and interesting films to
be made in Britain in a long time.' – *Scott Meek,
MFB*

891
Jubilee

*Queen Elizabeth I is transported by her astrologer into the latter part of
the 20th century, and is appalled by what she sees.*

Queen Elizabeth I is confronted by a post-apocalyptic world of girl
gangs and thuggish police, controlled by a power-crazed media mogul.
Jarman's *Jubilee* caught a punk moment in British culture and also
managed a warning for the future. His blackly comic movie began to
look more like a prophecy by the mid 1980s. It stands as a outrageous
dissection of modern urban life, about, as the media owner puts it, 'the
generation who forgot how to lead their lives'.

The Titfield Thunderbolt
👫   GB   1952   84m   Technicolor
Ealing (Michael Truman)
▦ ⓔ
w T. E. B. Clarke *d* Charles Crichton *ph* Douglas
Slocombe *m* Georges Auric *ad* C. P. Norman *ed* Seth
Holt
☆ *Stanley Holloway* (Valentine), *George Relph* (Rev.
Weech), John Gregson (Gordon), Godfrey Tearle (The
Bishop), *Edie Martin* (Emily), Naunton Wayne (Blakeworth),
Gabrielle Brune (Joan), Hugh Griffith (Dan), Sidney James
(Hawkins), Jack MacGowran (Vernon Crump), Ewan Roberts
(Alec Pearce), Reginald Beckwith (Coggett)

890
The Titfield Thunderbolt

*When a branch railway line is threatened with closure, the villagers take
it over as a private concern.*

A typical Ealing plot, of a small community fighting a big bureacracy,
was the subject of Charles Crichton's comedy, one of the last from the
studio. Undervalued on its release in the wake of other Ealing comedies, this now seems among the best of them as well as an immaculate
colour production showing the England that is no more; the script has
pace, the whole thing is brightly polished and the action works up to a
fine climactic frenzy.

Born on the Fourth of July
US 1989 144m DeLuxe Panavision
UIP/Ixtlan (A Kitman Ho, Oliver Stone)
▣ ▣ ▤ ◉ ⊘ ⊘ ⌢

w Oliver Stone, Ron Kovic *book* Ron Kovic *d* Oliver Stone *ph* Robert Richardson *m* John Williams *pd* Bruno Rubeo *ad* Victor Kempster, Richard L. Johnson *ed* David Brenner, Joe Hutshing
☆ Tom Cruise (Ron Kovic), Bryan Larkin (Young Ron), Raymond J. Barry (Mr. Kovic), Caroline Kava (Mrs. Kovic), Josh Evans (Tommy Kovic), Seth Allan (Young Tommy), Jamie Talisman (Jimmy Kovic), Sean Stone (Young Jimmy), Anne Bobby (Susanne Kovic), Jenna von Oy (Young Susanne)
♟ Oliver Stone; best film editing
♙ Tom Cruise; John Williams; best picture; best adapted screenplay; best cinematography

889
Born on the Fourth of July

A crippled Vietnam veteran joins the anti-war movement.

Oliver Stone's drama has little resemblance to other Vietnam movies, since it is about a different kind of heroism. Based on the life of Ron Kovic, a marine who returned from Vietnam paralysed from the waist down and confined to a wheelchair, it pushed Tom Cruise to give perhaps his best performance so far. Al Pacino had originally been set to star, but left when the financing collapsed three days before shooting was to start. It took another decade before Stone was able to make the film; the wait turned out to be worthwhile.

Bowling for Columbine
Canada/Germany/US 2002 123m DuArt
Momentum/Alliance Atlantis/Salter Street/Dog Eat Dog (Charles Bishop, Michael Donovan, Kathleen Glynn, Jim Czarnecki, Michael Moore)
▣ ▤ ⊘ ⊘

wd Michael Moore *ph* Brian Danitz, Michael McDonough *m* Jeff Gibbs *ed* Kurt Engfehr

'A rollicking, incendiary documentary that looks down the barrel of Americans' love affair with firearms.' – *Lisa Nesselson, Variety*

'Extremely serious without being solemn, passionate in a deliberately laid-back fashion and both hilarious and chilling.' – *Philip French, Observer*

'Sorting through the ideological debris, you realize that Mr Moore's case for disarming America has too much anger and not enough insight, and you begin to question his motives. A grand act of patriotic idealism begins to smell like a craving for controversial self-promotion thinly masked as crusading journalism.' – *Rex Reed, New York Observer*

♟ documentary

888
Bowling for Columbine

Documentary that examines America's attitudes to guns, beginning with the shooting rampage by students at Columbine high school.

Michael Moore's muckraking documentary examines America's attitudes to guns, beginning with the shooting rampage by students at Columbine high school, and asks why other countries, including Canada where guns are also ubiquitous, have much lower rates of murder. He doesn't find the answer, but his confrontational style does throw up even more interesting questions, such as why a bank would give away guns to new customers. Charlton Heston is cornered at one point and reduced to silence about his fervent presidency of the National Rifle Association. Moore's is a haphazard approach that goes off in different directions and doesn't always follow through on the matters it raises; but the matters it does raise are important and receive an airing that is at once funny and angry.

887

Call Me Madam

Call Me Madam
US 1953 114m Technicolor
TCF (Sol C. Siegel)

w Arthur Sheekman *play* Howard Lindsay, Russel Crouse
d Walter Lang *ph* Leon Shamroy *m/ly* Irving Berlin
md Alfred Newman *ch* Robert Alton *ad* John De Cuir, Lyle
Wheeler *ed* Robert Simpson
☆ *Ethel Merman* (Mrs. Sally Adams), *Donald O'Connor*
(Kenneth), *George Sanders* (Cosmo Constantine), *Vera-Ellen* (Princess Maria), Billy de Wolfe (Pemberton Maxwell),
Helmut Dantine (Prince Hugo), Walter Slezak (Tantinnin),
Steve Geray (Sebastian), Ludwig Stossel (Grand Duke)

'Good-tempered, warm, generous and about as
quiet as a massed brass band festival.' – *Dilys
Powell*

● Vera-Ellen's singing was dubbed by Carole Richards
♫ 'The Hostess with the Mostes'; 'Can You Use Any
Money Today?'; 'Marrying for Love'; 'It's a Lovely Day
Today'; 'That International Rag'; 'The Ocarina'; 'What Chance
Have I with Love?'; 'The Best Thing for You'; 'Something to
Dance About'; 'You're Just in Love'.
👤 Alfred Newman

A Washington hostess is appointed Ambassador to Lichtenberg and marries the foreign minister.

If for no other reason, this studio-bound but thoroughly lively transcription of Irving Berlin's last big success is worth cherishing for Ethel Merman's performance as the Washington 'hostess with the mostes', who is appointed Ambassador to Lichtenberg and marries the foreign minister. Other performers were also at their peak: George Sanders, who had been too frightened to appear in a Broadway musical, revealed an excellent baritone singing voice ('warm as toast,' was Merman's verdict), and O'Connor and Vera-Ellen danced well together.

886

Ghost World

'Accentuate the negative.'

Ghost World
US 2001 111m colour
United Artists/Granada/Jersey Shore (Lianne Halfon,
John Malkovich, Russel Smith)
▭ ▬ ◉ ◎ 🎧
w Daniel Clowes, Terry Zwigoff *comic book* Daniel Clowes
d Terry Zwigoff *ph* Affonso Beato *m* David Kitay
pd Edward T. McAvoy *ad* Alan E. Muraoka *ed* Carole
Kravetz *cos* Mary Zophres
☆ Thora Birch (Enid), Scarlett Johansson (Rebecca), Steve
Buscemi (Seymour), Brad Renfro (Josh), Illeana Douglas
(Roberta), Bob Balaban (Dad), Teri Garr (Maxine)

'A film like no other, an artful spellbinder that cuts
deep.' – *Peter Travers, Rolling Stone*

'One of the biggest disappointments of the
summer, though I would give it points for
projecting its own heart of darkness with apparent
conviction.' – *Andrew Sarris, New York Observer*

♟ Daniel Clowes, Terry Zwigoff (screenplay)

In an American suburb, two teenagers leave high school and feel like misfits in the adult world.

A witty, perceptive comedy of the confusions of adolescence, concerning two girls who leave their high school in a suburban town and feel alienated both from the adult world and the consumerist society devised for other teenagers. One eventually settles for a conventional life; the other leaves to discover a wider, less restricted world. Zwigoff observes the action from a distance, remaining scrupulously non-judgmental about the misfits, young and middle-aged, who populate his film and usually are invisible presences in the hurly-burly of life.

Samurai I: Musashi Miyamoto
Japan   1954   93m   colour
Toho (Kazuo Takimura)
▨ ▤ ⊚ ⊛
w Hiroshi Inagaki, Tokuhei Wakao play Hideji Hojo
novel Musashi by Eiji Yoshikawa d Hiroshi Inagaki
ph Jun Yasumoto m Ikuma Dan ad Makoto Sono, Kisaku
Ito ed Hideshi Ohi
☆ Toshiro Mifune (Takezo Musashi), Rentaro Mikuni
(Matahachi), Kuroemon Onoe (Takuan), Kaoru Yachigusa
(Otsu), Mariko Okada (Akemi), Mitsuko Mito (Oko), Eiko
Miyoshi (Osugi), Akihiko Hirata (Seijuro Yoshioka)
♟ foreign film

Samurai II: Duel at Ichijoji Temple
Japan   1955   103m   colour
Toho (Kazuo Takimura)
▨ ▤ ⊚ ⊛
w Hiroshi Inagaki, Tokuhei Wakao play Hideji Hojo
novel Musashi by Eiji Yoshikawa d Hiroshi Inagaki
ph Jun Yasumoto m Ikuma Dan ad Kisaku Ito, Makoto
Sono ed Hirokazu Iwashita
☆ Toshiro Mifune (Musashi Miyamoto), Koji Tsuruta
(Kojiro Sasaki), Kaoru Yachigusa (Otsu), Michiko Saga
(Omitsu), Mariko Okada (Akemi), Michiyo Kogure (Lady
Yoshino), Mitsuko Mito (Oko), Akihiko Hirata (Seijuro),
Daisuke Kato (Toji), Kuroemon Onoe (Takuan)

Samurai III: Duel at Ganryu Island
Japan   1956   104m   colour
Toho (Kazuo Takimura)
▨ ▤ ⊚ ⊛
w Hiroshi Inagaki, Tokuhei Wakao play Hideji Hojo
novel Eiji Yoshikawa d Hiroshi Inagaki, ph Kazuo
Yamada m Ikuma Dan ad Hiroshi Ueda, Kisaku Ito
ed Hirokazu Iwashita
☆ Toshiro Mifune (Musashi Miyamoto), Koji Tsuruta
(Kojiro Sasaki), Kaoru Yachigusa (Otsu), Michiko Saga
(Omitsu), Mariko Okada (Akemi), Takashi Shimura (Court
official)

885
Samurai Trilogy

Samurai I: Musashi Miyamoto

An ambitious young man goes in search of fame and fortune in a civil war, but returns home a sadder man before becoming pupil to a Buddhist monk.

Samurai II: Duel at Ichijoji Temple

A master swordsman learns that it is not enough to be strong; he also needs to learn humility and chivalry.

Samurai III: Duel at Ganryu Island

A warrior who has learned what it means to be a samurai is faced with a deadly opponent who kills for pleasure.

Hiroshi Inagaki's masterful trilogy is based on the life of a legendary swordsman Musashi Miyamoto (c 1584–1645), told in a high-romantic style, often beautifully composed. A story of love, betrayal and valour, it is also concerned with the moral education of a samurai. Musashi, a wild and ambitious youth, discovers his vocation as a pupil to a tough Buddhist monk, who teaches him discipline. In the second film, he realizes his need to learn humility and chivalry. After refusing both of the two women who love him, he is forced into a duel in which he is ambushed by 80 swordsmen. In the final episode, faced with a deadly opponent who kills for pleasure, he questions what qualities a warrior should possess. Although each film stands on its own, when seen in sequence they form an engrossing, action-filled, spiritual quest.

'Of what a boy did … what a girl did … of ecstasy and revenge!'

'The most shocking revenge a girl ever let one brother take on another!'

East of Eden
US 1955 115m Warnercolor
Cinemascope
Warner (Elia Kazan)
▣▣ ▣▣ ▤ ◕~ ◠
w Paul Osborn *novel* John Steinbeck *d* Elia Kazan *ph* Ted McCord *m* Leonard Rosenman *ad* James Basevi, Malcolm Bert *ed* Owen Marks
☆ *Raymond Massey* (Adam Trask), *James Dean* (Cal Trask), Julie Harris (Abra), Dick Davalos (Aron Trask), *Jo Van Fleet* (Kate), Burl Ives (Sam), Albert Dekker (Will)

'The first distinguished production in CinemaScope.' – *Eugene Archer*

♟ Jo Van Fleet
♟ Paul Osborn; Elia Kazan; James Dean

884
East of Eden

In a California farming valley in 1917 a wild adolescent rebels against his stern father and discovers that his mother, believed dead, runs a nearby brothel.

James Dean's first film role, as a farm boy, was close to his own upbringing, though Kazan at first thought he was too pale and under-nourished for the part. Steinbeck's Biblical story, or at least the part Kazan chose to film, could have been written for him. Kazan brilliantly uses CinemaScope to portray the vast, lush landscapes and moody interiors, and coaxes rousing performances from his cast.

The Pumpkin Eater
GB 1964 118m bw
Columbia/Romulus (James Woolf)
▤
w Harold Pinter *novel* Penelope Mortimer *d* Jack Clayton *ph* Oswald Morris *m* Georges Delerue *ad* Edward Marshall *ed* Jim Clark
☆ *Anne Bancroft* (Jo Armitage), *Peter Finch* (Jake Armitage), *James Mason* (Bob Conway), Maggie Smith (Philpot), Cedric Hardwicke (Mr. James, Jo's father), Richard Johnson (Giles), Eric Porter (Psychiatrist)

'There never was a film so rawly memorable.' – *Evening Standard*

'It is solid, serious, intelligent, stylish. It is also, for the most part, quite dead.' – *The Times*

'It plays like a house afire.' – *Time*

♟ Anne Bancroft
♟ Anne Bancroft; Oswald Morris

883
The Pumpkin Eater

A compulsive mother (of eight children) finds her third marriage rocking when she gets evidence of her husband's affairs.

Peter Finch gave one of his most sensitive performances as a womanizing writer in this raw drama. It struck a new note at the time, since it was told from the woman's point of view. His wife (Anne Bancroft at her best) begins to doubt their relationship when she gets evidence of her husband's affairs. As her problems increase – the death of her father, her sterilization, her attempted seduction by a man her husband has cuckolded – she withdraws from life. The movie's vivid kaleidoscope of characters are all quite recognizable as sixties Londoners.

Salvatore Giuliano

Italy 1961 125m bw
Lux/Vides/Galatea (Franco Cristaldi)
⊕

w Francesco Rosi, Suso Cecchi d'Amico, Enzo Provenzale, Franco Solinas *d* Francesco Rosi *ph* Gianni di Venanzo *m* Piero Piccioni *ad* Carlo Egidi, Sergio Canevari *ed* Mario Serandrei
☆ Frank Wolff (Gaspare Pisciotta), Salvo Randone (President of Viterbo Assize Court), Federico Zardi (Pisciotta's Defense Counsel)

'Epic reportage in the twentieth-century manner of a society reminiscent of some backward corner of the nineteenth century.' – *Peter John Dyer, MFB*

882
Salvatore Giuliano

The bullet-ridden body of key Sicilian Mafia leader Giuliano triggers flashbacks to his complex and brutal career.

Rosi takes a semi-documentary approach to the life and death of Sicilian Mafia leader Giuliano, who was shot to death in 1950. The film flashes back over his complex and brutal career, though Rosi's interest isn't so much in the man himself as in the political and economic forces that drove him to become a bandit and that led to his murder. Rosi's investigative approach was as factual as possible; he filmed the action where it actually happened; Giuliano's body lay in death precisely as he shows it. Vividly-made, it can at times be obscure, requiring some understanding of Sicily's politics and history. But Rosi's verisimilitude gives greater weight to his devastating portrait of a corrupt and violent society, where the rule of law no longer holds.

The Winslow Boy

🏃 GB 1948 117m bw
British Lion/London Films (Anatole de Grunwald)
📼 🎬

w Terence Rattigan, Anatole de Grunwald *play* Terence Rattigan *d* Anthony Asquith *ph* Frederick Young *m* William Alwyn *ed* Gerald Turney-Smith
☆ *Robert Donat* (Sir Robert Morton), *Cedric Hardwicke* (Arthur Winslow), *Margaret Leighton* (Catherine Winslow), *Frank Lawton* (John Watherstone), Jack Watling (Dickie Winslow), Basil Radford (Esmond Curry), Kathleen Harrison (Violet), Francis L. Sullivan (Attorney General), Marie Lohr (Grace Winslow), Neil North (Ronnie Winslow), Wilfrid Hyde-White (Wilkinson), Ernest Thesiger (Mr. Ridgeley-Pearce)

'Only a clod could see this film without excitement, laughter and some slight moisture about the eyes.' – *Daily Telegraph*

881
The Winslow Boy

A naval cadet is expelled for stealing a postal order; his father spends all he has on proving his innocence.

Terence Rattigan conceived his character-based legal drama as a movie, only turning it into a play after the idea had been turned down by the two men, de Grunwald and Asquith, who later filmed it. It's a highly enjoyable middle-class British entertainment, based on an actual case. The theme of unimportant people fighting for justice transferred perfectly to the screen, providing Donat, who had turned down the part in the play, with one of the best roles of his career as a probing barrister.

The Thief of Bagdad

US   1924   135m approx (24 fps)   bw
silent
Douglas Fairbanks

w Lotta Woods, Douglas Fairbanks d Raoul Walsh
ph Arthur Edeson m Mortimer Wilson ad William
Cameron Menzies ed William Nolan cos Mitchell Leisen
☆ Douglas Fairbanks (The Thief), Snitz Edwards (Evil
Associate of the Thief), Charles Belcher (The Holy Man),
Anna May Wong (The Mongol Slave), Julanne Johnston
(The Princess), Etta Lee (The Slave of the Sand Board),
Brandon Hurst (The Caliph), Sojin (The Mongol Prince)

'An entrancing picture, wholesome and compelling,
deliberate and beautiful, a feat of motion picture art
which has never been equalled.' – New York Times

'Here is magic. Here is beauty. Here is the answer
to cynics who give the motion picture no place in
the family of the arts … a work of rare genius.' –
James Quirk, Photoplay

880
The Thief of Bagdad

In old Bagdad, a thief uses magic to outwit the evil Caliph.

A celebrated silent version of the old fable of Aladdin. Fairbanks, in his role as producer, was influenced by Fritz Lang's epic German movies, and did his best to emulate them in this sprawling, episodic work in which he is at times almost overwhelmed by the elaborate Arabian Nights' sets and the special effects. He is at his most explosive and acrobatic in the film's early sequences, bounding and leaping with immense verve. Even though its camera tricks are a little timeworn now, it nevertheless maintains the air of a true classic by virtue of its leading performance and driving narrative energy.

'Keep the children home! And if you're squeamish, stay home with them!'

'The Depraved Must Die … Beware The Witchfinder!'

Witchfinder General
GB   1968   87m   Eastmancolor
Tigon/AIP (Arnold Miller, Philip Waddilove, Louis M. Heyward)
◨◨ ▬ ◉ ◔
US title: *The Conqueror Worm*
w Michael Reeves, Tom Baker *novel* Ronald Bassett
d Michael Reeves *ph* John Coquillon *m* Paul Ferris, Jim Morahan *ad* Jim Morahan *ed* Howard Lanning
☆ Vincent Price (Matthew Hopkins), Rupert Davies (John Lowes), Ian Ogilvy (Richard Marshall), Patrick Wymark (Oliver Cromwell), Hilary Dwyer (Sara), Wilfrid Brambell (Master Loach), Robert Russell (John Stearne), Nicky Henson (Trooper Swallow)

879
Witchfinder General

In 1645 a villainous lawyer finds it profitable to travel the country instigating witch hunts.

Michael Reeves's stylish and savage horror movie was based on the career of Matthew Hopkins, a lawyer who appointed himself as witchfinder general at the time of Oliver Cromwell and terrorised communities with his brutality and rapacity. Reeves was a fervent admirer of the work of Hollywood director Don Siegel and conceived it as a fast-moving action picture, much like a Western relocated to the flat, sky-dominated landscape of East Anglia. It is a story of betrayal and revenge, reflecting in its violence the bloody times in which it was set. Vincent Price's orotund performance as Hopkins tends to be over ripe (Reeves wanted Donald Pleasence for the role, but AIP insisted on an American star), but does not detract from the film's success. It is a lasting memorial to the precocious talent of Reeves, who died at the age of 24 from an overdose of barbiturates.

'With all my heart, I still love the man I killed!'

The Letter
US   1940   95m   bw
Warner (Robert Lord)
▬ ◔
w Howard Koch *story* W. Somerset Maugham *d* William Wyler *ph* Tony Gaudio *m* Max Steiner *ad* Carl Jules Weyl *ed* Warren Low
☆ *Bette Davis* (Leslie Crosbie), *Herbert Marshall* (Robert Crosbie), *James Stephenson* (Howard Joyce), *Sen Yung* (Ong Chi Seng), Frieda Inescort (Dorothy Joyce), Gale Sondergaard (Mrs. Hammond), Bruce Lester (John Withers), Tetsu Komai (Head Boy)

'The writing is taut and spare throughout … the unravelling of Maugham's story is masterly and the presentation visual and cinematic … the audience at the trade show did not move a finger.' – *James Agate*

● Herbert Marshall played the lover in the first version and the husband in the second.
♟ best picture; William Wyler; Tony Gaudio; Max Steiner; Bette Davis; James Stephenson; Warren Low

878
The Letter

A rubber plantation owner's wife kills a man in what seems to have been self-defence; but a letter from her proves it to have been a crime of passion, and becomes an instrument of blackmail.

Somerset Maugham's story was an unlikely subject for a forties film, given its subject matter. The mix of sex, murder and snobbery stayed, but censorship forced the addition of an infuriating moral ending. Even so, the excellent performances and presentation make this the closest approximation on film to reading a Maugham story of the Far East.

Laura
US 1944 85m bw
TCF (Otto Preminger)

w Jay Dratler, Samuel Hoffenstein, Betty Reinhardt *novel* Vera Caspary *d* Otto Preminger *ph* Joseph LaShelle *m* David Raksin *ad* Lyle Wheeler, Leland Fuller *ed* Louis Loeffler

☆ *Dana Andrews* (Mark McPherson), *Clifton Webb* (Waldo Lydecker), Gene Tierney (Laura Hunt), Judith Anderson (Ann Treadwell), *Vincent Price* (Shelby Carpenter), Dorothy Adams (Bessie Clary), James Flavin (McAvity)

'Everybody's favourite chic murder mystery.' – *New Yorker, 1977*

● Rouben Mamoulian directed some scenes before handing over to Preminger.
♟ Joseph LaShelle
♙ script; Otto Preminger; Clifton Webb; art direction

877

Laura

A beautiful girl is murdered … or is she? A cynical detective investigates.

Otto Preminger's mature *film noir* was a quiet, streamlined little murder mystery that brought a new adult approach to the genre. Preminger was originally hired as the producer; it was only when mogul Darryl Zanuck disliked footage shot by Rouben Mamoulian that he took over. Zanuck still had doubts about the finished picture until previews went well. The film grips from its opening line – 'I'll never forget this weekend, the weekend Laura died …' – and continues to hold attention through the many twists and turns of the plot. A small cast responds perfectly to a classically spare script, and in Clifton Webb a new star was born.

The Big Heat

A police detective's wife is killed by a bomb meant for himself; he quits his job to track down the gangsters responsible.

A dour, hard-boiled thriller about a detective, who quits his police job to track down the gangsters who killed his wife with a car bomb intended for himself, it was well-cast. Gloria Grahame played a tough dame – 'we're sisters under the mink,' she says to another embittered woman – and Glenn Ford gave one of his most typical performances as the uncompromising detective. Fritz Lang directed with great succinctness: in the film's most notorious scene, when Lee Marvin throws boiling coffee in the face of Grahame, he cuts not to her but to a close-up of his evil grin. Lang shot the film in four weeks, creating one of the best of his American movies.

'A hard cop and a soft dame!'
The Big Heat
US 1953 90m bw
Columbia (Robert Arthur)

w Sydney Boehm *novel* William P. McGivern *d* Fritz Lang *ph* Charles Lang *m* Arthur Morton *md* Mischa Bakaleinikoff *ad* Robert Peterson *ed* Charles Nelson
☆ Glenn Ford (Dave Bannion), Gloria Grahame (Debby Marsh), Alexander Scourby (Mike Lagana), Jocelyn Brando (Katie Bannion), Lee Marvin (Vince Stone), Jeanette Nolan (Bertha Duncan), Peter Whitney (Tierney)

'The main impression is of violence employed arbitrarily, mechanically and in the long run pointlessly.' – *Penelope Houston*

Withnail and I

In Britain's Sixties, two out-of-work actors settle in a dilapidated country cottage.

A deliberately seedy comedy which settles down as a study of character and contrives to be hard to forget. This semi-autobiographical movie of two unemployed actors evading responsibilities, or even washing-up, through the copious ingestion of drink and drugs has a boozy, melancholic nostalgia for the last gasp of the 1960s. It is a succession of comic set-pieces: confrontations with a variety of people, from a drunken Irishman to a middle-class tea-shop proprietor, who thwart their needs. It gets excellently judged performances from its cast, notably McGann, as the one who decides to grow up, and Richard E. Grant as an upper class anarchist on the point of disintegration.

'If you can't remember the 60's, …don't worry. Neither can they.'
Withnail and I
GB 1987 108m colour
Recorded Releasing/HandMade Films (Paul M. Heller)

wd Bruce Robinson *novel* Bruce Robinson *ph* Peter Hannan *m* David Dundas *pd* Michael Pickwoad *ad* Henry Harris *ed* Alan Strachan
☆ Richard E. Grant (Withnail), Paul McGann (Marwood), Richard Griffiths (Monty), Ralph Brown (Danny), Michael Elphick (Jake)

'The humor is both brutal and clever, and the acting uniformly excellent.' – *Variety*

'A sharply observed and beautifully acted slice of *nostalgie de la boue*.' – *Julian Petley, MFB*

'Movie-wise, there has never been anything like it – laugh-wise, love-wise, or otherwise-wise!'

The Apartment
US   1960   125m   bw   Panavision
UA/Mirisch (Billy Wilder)
⚫⚫ ▤ ⊜~ ⊚ ⊚

w Billy Wilder, I. A. L. Diamond *d* Billy Wilder *ph* Joseph LaShelle *m* Adolph Deutsch *ad* Alexander Trauner *ed* Daniel Mandell

☆ *Jack Lemmon* (C. C. Baxter), *Shirley MacLaine* (Miss Kubelik), *Fred MacMurray* (Jeff D. Sheldrake), Ray Walston (Joe Dobisch), Jack Kruschen (Dr Dreyfuss), Joan Shawlee (Sylvia), Edie Adams (Miss Olsen), David Lewis (Al Kirkeby)

'Without either style or taste, shifting gears between pathos and slapstick without any transition.' – *Dwight MacDonald*

'Billy Wilder directed this acrid story as if it were a comedy, which is a cheat, considering that it involves pimping and a suicide attempt and many shades of craven ethics.' – *New Yorker, 1980*

👤 picture; Billy Wilder, I. A. L. Diamond (as writers); Billy Wilder (as director)

👤 Joseph LaShelle; Jack Lemmon; Shirley MacLaine; Jack Kruschen; art direction; editing

🎜 picture; Jack Lemmon; Shirley MacLaine

874
The Apartment

A lonely, ambitious clerk rents out his apartment to philandering executives and finds that one of them is after his own girl.

The inspiration for Billy Wilder's agreeably mordant and cynical comedy came from David Lean's *Brief Encounter*, as Wilder wondered about the man who had lent his apartment to two married lovers. That thought became a satirical sidelight on the way that corporate life is at odds with morality. A lonely, ambitious clerk becomes a valued member of staff because he makes his apartment available to the company's philandering executives. Then he discovers that his boss is taking the elevator girl he loves to his apartment. There is a happy ending, with a typical Wilder sting in the tail: the clerk gets the girl but loses his job.

The Iron Giant

US 1999 86m Technicolor Celco Scope

Warner (Allison Abbate, Des McAnuff)

w Tim McCanlies *book The Iron Man* by Ted Hughes *d* Brad Bird *ph* Mark Dinicola *m* Michael Kamen *pd* Mark Whiting *ad* Alan Bodner *ed* Darren T. Holmes

☆ Featuring voices of: Jennifer Aniston, Eli Marienthal, Harry Connick Jnr, Vin Diesel, Christopher McDonald, James Gammon, Cloris Leachman, John Mahoney, M. Emmet Walsh

'An unalloyed success that works on several levels.' – *Variety*

'A modern classic.' – *Film Review*

● Despite critical plaudits, the movie did poorly at the box-office.

873
The Iron Giant

In 1957, a young boy tries to protect an iron giant from government officials who are convinced that it is an alien weapon and plan to destroy it.

An underrated animated story of pacifism and self-realization that is set in the 1950s, during the time of nuclear paranoia fed by the Cold War. A young boy tries to protect a giant robot that crash-lands on Earth, both from his pet-hating mother and a government agent who is convinced that it is an alien weapon. The movie doesn't try for Disney-styled cuteness, which is maybe why it was a comparative failure at the box-office. It remains an engaged and engaging fable, witty, well-made, excellently voiced, and a pleasure to watch.

'His passion captivated a woman. His courage inspired a country. His heart defied a king.'

Braveheart

US 1995 177m DeLuxe Panavision

TCF/Icon/Ladd (Mel Gibson, Alan Ladd Jnr, Bruce Davey)

w Randall Wallace *d* Mel Gibson *ph* John Toll *m* James Horner *pd* Tom Sanders *ad* Dan Dorrance *ed* Steven Rosenblum

☆ Mel Gibson (William Wallace), Sophie Marceau (Princess Isabelle), Patrick McGoohan (Longshanks, King Edward I), Catherine McCormack (Murron), Brendan Gleeson (Hamish), James Cosmo (Campbell), Alun Armstrong (Mornay), Angus Macfadyen (Robert the Bruce), Ian Bannen (The Leper)

'At last: a costume drama that wears its costumes with pride, a period drama that has the courage of its convictions.' – *Tom Shone, Sunday Times*

● The film took $168.5m at the box-office worldwide, according to *Variety*'s figures.

● Regions 1 and 2 DVDs include a commentary by Mel Gibson.

♟ best film; Mel Gibson (as director); John Toll; makeup; sound effects editing

♟ Randall Wallace; James Horner; Steven Rosenblum; costume design (Charles Knode); sound

872
Braveheart

William Wallace leads a Scottish rebellion against the claims of the English king, Edward I.

A stirring nationalistic epic, acted and directed with great verve; some of the history may be suspect, but the film creates a sense of myth with its sweep and passion. It was perhaps a surprising choice of subject for Gibson, though he seems to identify strongly with William Wallace. His own performance has emotional strength, and, as director, he handles the set piece battles with superb skill.

Paris, Texas

Paris, Texas
West Germany/France 1984 148m colour
Road Movies/Argos (Don Guest, Anatole Dauman)
▣ ▤ ▨ ▨ ▨ ◠
w Sam Shepard *d* Wim Wenders *ph* Robby Müller *m* Ry Cooder *ad* Kate Altman *ed* Peter Pryzgodda
☆ Harry Dean Stanton (Travis Clay Henderson), Dean Stockwell (Walt Henderson), Aurore Clement (Anne), Hunter Carson (Hunter), Nastassja Kinski (Jane), Bernhard Wicki (Dr. Ulmer)
● Filmed in English.
🏆 best director

871
Paris, Texas

After separating from his wife a man goes missing and is later found in the small town where he was born.

Wender's movie is about loneliness, loss and fantasy, about that gap between what is real and what is imagined, a place where love might be located. A man walks out of the desert who, four years before, had run from his wife and child and a marriage that had degenerated into jealous rages. He forms a tentative relationship with his seven-year-old son, who has been in the care of his brother and sister-in-law, and together they go in search of his wife. After re-uniting mother and son, he leaves again. The core of the film comes in the exchanges between Stanton and Kinski as they try to explain their marriage to each other, and can only express their isolation.

Kanal
Poland 1956 97m bw
Film Polski (Stanislaw Adler)
▣ ▤
aka: *They Loved Life*
w Jerzy Stawinski *novel Kloakerne* by Jerzy Stawinski
d Andrzej Wajda *ph* Jerzy Lipman *m* Jan Krenz
ad Roman Mann *ed* Halina Nawrocka
☆ Teresa Izewska (Daisy Stokrotka), Tadeusz Janczar (Corporal Korab), Emil Kariewicz (Madry), Wienczylaw Glinski (Lieutenant Zadra)

870
Kanal

In 1944, an anti-Nazi resistance group is trapped in a sewer.

There is no escape from the grim and suffocating realities of Wajda's excellent, if hard to watch, film of anti-Nazi partisans trapped in a Warsaw sewer in 1944. It is a tense and disturbing account of a heroic but futile resistance. In stark but beautiful images, Wajda makes it clear from the beginning that the group have no hope and that death is inevitable, though he allows brief moments of love and tenderness. References to Dante's *Inferno* seem right, for this is hell and we are in it.

'Fate raised her to fame – and killed the man she loved!'

A Star Is Born
US 1954 181m Technicolor
Cinemascope
Warner/Transcona (Sidney Luft)
▦ ▤ ◎. ◎ 🎧

w Moss Hart *d* George Cukor *ph* Sam Leavitt *md* Ray Heindorf *ad* Malcolm Bert, Gene Allen, Irene Sharaff ☆ *Judy Garland, James Mason*, Charles Bickford, Jack Carson, Tommy Noonan, Amanda Blake, Lucy Marlow

'Maintains a skilful balance between the musical and the tear jerker.' – *Penelope Houston*

'By far the best of all the films about life behind the cameras, the lights, the wind-machines, and the cocktail bars of Hollywood.' – *Dilys Powell*

● Cary Grant and Humphrey Bogart were both sought before James Mason was signed.
● Ronald Haver's book *A Star Is Born* (1988) is an account of the making of the film and its 1983 restoration.
🎵 'Born in a Trunk'; 'Gotta Have Me Go With You'; 'Here's What I'm Here For'; 'It's a New World'; 'Someone At Last'; 'The Man That Got Away'
♒ Ray Heindorf; song 'The Man that Got Away' (*m* Harold Arlen, *ly* Ira Gershwin); Judy Garland; James Mason; art direction

869
A Star Is Born

A young actress marries the ageing, alcoholic star who helps her to become a success.

It took twenty years before audiences could see this musical version of the 1937 movie as its director, George Cukor, intended. After its premiere, studio executives cut it by more than 40 minutes and destroyed the negative. It was not until 1983 that film historian Ronald Haver restored it to its original form. It enshrines Judy Garland's best and most heartfelt screen performance (one that mirrored her own unhappy life) as an actress whose career succeeds while that of her alcoholic husband, a famous actor, falters. Cukor found the limitations of CinemaScope a problem and, after a day of obeying the rule that everything had to be played on a level plane, did his best to ignore it. It is an uneven movie – the long 'Born in a Trunk' sequence is splendid Garland but does little but hold up the film – but an undeniably fascinating one.

Trilogy: On the Run, An Amazing Couple, After Life
France/Belgium 2002 colour
Metro Tartan/Agat/Entre Chien et Loup/RTBF/Rhône-Alps Cinema (Patrick Sobelman)
◉

d Lucas Belvaux *ph* Pierre Millon *m* Riccardo Del Fra *pd* Frederique Belvaux *ed* Ludo Troch, Valerie Loiseleux, Danielle Anezin
☆ Francois Morel (Alain Costes), Dominique Blanc (Agnes Manise), Gilbert Melki (Pascal Manise), Lucas Belvaux (Bruno Le Roux), Catherine Frot (Jeanne), Valerie Mairesse (Claire), Raphaele Godin (Louise)

'Belvaux's bold concept and accomplished execution mark his trilogy as one of contemporary European cinema's most interesting experiments.' – *David Stratton, Variety*

'The three build into a complex, rewarding assemblage, a daring experiment in narrative technique that is also an emotionally affecting, character-driven work of popular fiction.' – *Edward Lawrenson, Sight and Sound*

Seeing all three adds an extra layer of witty observation to each movie, demonstrating how the protagonists often misread each other's behaviour and make incorrect assumptions about their lives.

868
Trilogy: On the Run, An Amazing Couple, After Life

The lives of a former left-wing revolutionary, who is now a schoolteacher, a cop and his drug-addicted wife, and a lawyer and his suspicious wife, intertwine with surprising results.

Belvaux's three interlinked and contrasting films, which can be enjoyed in any order, form a fascinating and intriguing combination. All deal with the same group of characters, an escaped terrorist, his former revolutionary partner, who is now a schoolteacher, a harassed policeman and his drug-addicted wife, and a blandly successful lawyer and his edgy wife. *On the Run*, 114m, is a deft thriller centred on the terrorist; *An Amazing Couple*, 97m, is a clever farce of marital misunderstanding; and *After Life*, 120m, is a tense drama of the policeman's problems dealing with his wife's addiction. All the action happens simultaneously, so the behaviour of the characters takes on a different emphasis in each movie: what seems sinister in one becomes comic in another.

Lady Killer

US 1933 76m bw
Warner (Henry Blanke)

w Ben Markson *novel The Finger Man* by Rosalind Keating Shaffer *d* Roy del Ruth *ph* Tony Gaudio *md* Leo F. Forbstein *ad* Robert Haas *ed* George Amy

☆ *James Cagney* (Dan Quigley), Mae Clarke (Myra Gale), Leslie Fenton (Duke), Margaret Lindsay (Lois Underwood), Henry O'Neill (Ramick), Willard Robertson (Conroy), Raymond Hatton (Pete), Russell Hopton (Smiley)

'An all-time high in roughneck character work even for this rough-and-tumble star.' – *Variety*

'A kind of résumé of everything he has done to date in the movies.' – *New York Evening Post*

'Sprightly, more or less daring, thoroughly entertaining.' – *New York World Telegram*

867
Lady Killer

A cinema usher turns to crime, flees to Hollywood, and becomes a movie star.

James Cagney called this movie 'just another of those quick ones', meaning the speed at which it was made, rather than its hectic, slam-bang comic action. In *Lady Killer* he was teamed again with Mae Clarke. Cagney had squeezed half a grapefruit into her face in *The Public Enemy*; here he merely dragged her along the floor by her hair. Such melodramatic moments were few. The accent was on comedy, with the star at his energetic, arrogant best. Great fun.

'You may not like these people, nor pity them, but you'll never forget this picture!'

Dead End

US 1937 92m bw
Samuel Goldwyn

w Lillian Hellman *play* Sidney Kingsley *d* William Wyler *ph* Gregg Toland *m* Alfred Newman *ad* Richard Day *ed* Daniel Mandell

☆ Joel McCrea (Dave), Sylvia Sidney (Drina), *Humphrey Bogart* (Baby Face Martin), Wendy Barrie (Kay), Claire Trevor (Francie), Allen Jenkins (Hunk), *Marjorie Main* (Mrs. Martin), James Burke (Mulligan), Ward Bond (Doorman), *The Dead End Kids* (Billy Halop, Leo Gorcey, Bernard Punsley, Huntz Hall, Bobby Jordan, Gabriel Dell)

'Tense and accurate transcription, but sordid and depressing … in for a disappointing career.' – *Variety*

♔ best picture; Gregg Toland; Claire Trevor; Richard Day

866
Dead End

A slice of life in New York's east side, where slum kids and gangsters live in a river street next to a luxury apartment block.

A highly theatrical film of a highly theatrical play. The sensational play had been praised for its atmospheric stage design of a dirty tenement street, with ragged clothes hanging from lines, dirty mattresses slung over fire escapes, and filth clogging gutters. Wyler more or less preserved the single set. By sheer cinematic expertise he overcame the limitations of the script, much toned down by the censor who objected to the contrast between the lives of the poor and the rich, and the setting, which upset producer Sam Goldwyn because it was dirty. It is chiefly remembered, however, for introducing the Dead End Kids to a delighted world.

Mr Skeffington
US   1944   127m   bw
Warner (Julius J. and Philip G. Epstein)
■≡   ℚ~   ◌

w Julius J. and Philip G. Epstein *novel Elizabeth von Arnim d* Vincent Sherman *ph* Ernest Haller *m* Franz Waxman *ad* Robert Haas *ed* Ralph Dawson
☆ *Bette Davis* ("Fanny" Beatrice Trellis Skeffington), *Claude Rains* (Job Skeffington), Walter Abel (George Trellis), Richard Waring (Trippy Trellis), George Coulouris (Dr. Byles), John Alexander (Jim Conderley), Jerome Cowan (Edward Morrison)

'An endless woman's page dissertation on What To Do When Beauty Fades.' – *James Agee*

'To call the film a good one would be to exaggerate; but entertaining and interesting, I insist, it is.' – *Richard Mallett, Punch*

♟ Bette Davis; Claude Rains

865
Mr Skeffington

A selfish beauty finally turns to her discarded dull husband; when he is blind, he doesn't mind her faded looks.

A thoroughly enjoyable star melodrama that gave Bette Davis some problems. She had to appear as a great beauty, which was achieved by a hairdo that created that illusion, and as extremely feminine, which she managed by speaking in a higher voice than usual. She also had to age, which required a long makeup session before filming could begin. Warners hyped it on release as 'one of the finest motion pictures ever made – by anybody, anywhere'.

'The Film That Stunned A Nation!'

Hoop Dreams
US   1994   174m   colour
Feature/FineLine/Kartemquin/KCTA-TV (Fred Marx, Steve James, Peter Gilbert)
▭   ■≡   ℚ~   ◎   ◉   ◌

d Steve James *ph* Peter Gilbert *ed* Fred Marx, Steve James, Bill Haugse
☆ William Gates (Himself), Arthur Agee (Himself), Emma Gates (Herself, William's Mother), Curtis Gates (Himself, William's Brother), Sheila Agee (Herself, Arthur's Mother)

'Has the crackle and density of that elusive beast, the Great American Novel.' – *Geoff Brown, The Times*

'A prodigious achievement that conveys the fabric of modern American life, aspirations and, incidentally, sport in close-up.' – *Todd McCarthy, Variety*

♟ editing

864
Hoop Dreams

Two black teenagers pursue their hopes of becoming professional basketball players.

This riveting documentary makes redundant all the recent fictional accounts of basketball heroics; here is the real thing, a brilliant account of the conjunction and conflict of the American Dream and the realities of life, following its two protagonists and their families through four years of success and failure. The two youths win scholarships to a rich suburban school on their athletic ability. After a year, one is discarded by the school, causing financial problems to his family. The other is plagued with injuries. And so it goes, in an illuminating account, not only of the pressures of sport, but of American inner-city life.

The Young in Heart
US 1938 91m bw
David O. Selznick
▬ ◎

w Paul Osborn, Charles Bennett *novel The Gay Banditti* by I. A. R. Wylie *d* Richard Wallace *ph* Leon Shamroy *m* Franz Waxman *ad* Lyle Wheeler *ed* Hal C. Kern ☆ *Douglas Fairbanks Jnr* (Richard Carleton), *Janet Gaynor* (George-Ann Carleton), *Roland Young* (Col. Anthony "Sahib" Carleton), *Billie Burke* (Marmy Carleton), *Minnie Dupree* (Miss Ellen Fortune), Paulette Goddard (Leslie Saunders), Richard Carlson (Duncan McCrea), Henry Stephenson (Felix Amstruther)

'Sentimental drama, vastly touching and entertaining ... has everything to ensure box office success.' – *Variety*

'It comes as a gentle breeze in the hurricane of hurly burly comedies that have hurtled across the screen of late.' – *Motion Picture Herald*

● William Wright and Lewis Milestone were also involved in directing the movie.
♟ Leon Shamroy; Franz Waxman

863
The Young in Heart

A family of charming confidence tricksters move in on a rich old lady but she brings out the best in them.

David O. Selznick was pre-occupied with *Gone with the Wind* at the time this delightful movie was filmed, and did not interfere as much as he might have done; he still irritated English screenwriter Charles Bennett by discussing the script until the early hours of the morning and expecting Bennett to have the changes written by the time he arrived at the studio at noon. The late-night sessions paid off. The script is sharp and witty. Aided by Lyle Wheeler's inventive Art Deco sets and pacey direction, a perfect cast create an excellent, light-hearted, roguish, romantic comedy.

Adaptation
US 2002 115m DeLuxe
Columbia/Intermedia/Magnet/Clinica Estetico
(Edward Saxon, Vincent Landay, Jonathan Demme)
▥ ▬ ◎ ◎ ◠

w Charlie Kaufman, Donald Kaufman *book The Orchid Thief* by Susan Orlean *d* Spike Jonze *ph* Lance Acord *m* Carter Burwell *pd* KK Barrett *ad* Peter Andrus *ed* Eric Zumbrunnen *cos* Ann Roth ☆ *Nicolas Cage* (Charlie Kaufman/Donald Kaufman), *Meryl Streep* (Susan Orlean), *Chris Cooper* (John Laroche), Tilda Swinton (Valerie), Cara Seymour (Amelia), Brian Cox (Robert McKee), Judy Greer (Alice the Waitress), Maggie Gyllenhaal (Caroline)

'Screenwriting this smart, inventive, passionate and rip-roaringly funny is a rare species. It's magic.' – *Peter Travers, Rolling Stone*

'The trouble with experimental comedies is that it's often impossible to figure out how to end them. But at least this one is intricate fun before it blows itself up.' – *David Denby, New Yorker*

♟ Chris Cooper
♟ Nicolas Cage; Meryl Streep; Charlie Kaufman, Donald Kaufman
♟ Charlie Kaufman, Donald Kaufman

862
Adaptation

A screenwriter has problems turning a book about orchids into a Hollywood blockbuster.

Charlie Kaufman is one of the most interesting and inventive screenwriters of the present day. Here faced with trying to adapt an admired non-fiction book about a Florida orchid breeder, he instead creates what seems like a semi-autobiographical account of a neurotic screenwriter who can find no easy solution to his problems. He adds a sub-plot about a twin brother who happily churns out a script about a serial killer. It's a witty, playful movie about movie-making, with its blocked writer trying out various approaches to intractable material before relying on Hollywood clichés to get him through to the end. Stylish direction, from the equally quirky Spike Jonze, and expertly comic performances make it a joy.

Best Boy

US   1979   111m   colour   16mm
Ira Wohl

🎞 🇺🇸 🔍~ ◎

wd Ira Wohl *ph* Tom McDonough *ed* Ira Wohl

👤 best documentary

861
Best Boy

A documentary, shot by his cousin, of the problems of a mentally retarded 53-year-old man whose elderly parents are ailing.

Worried about his future, the parents of a mentally retarded man encourage him to become less dependent on their care. He ventures into the wider world and, when his father dies, moves to a residential home for others like himself. Made over a period of three years, this is a moving account of family relationships and the acceptance of change.

'She'll find a home in every heart! She'll reach the heart of every home!'

Mandy

👫   GB   1952   93m   bw
Ealing (Leslie Norman)

🎞 🇺🇸

US title: *The Crash of Silence*

w Nigel Balchin, Jack Whittingham *novel This Day Is Ours* by Hilda Lewis *d* Alexander Mackendrick *ph* Douglas Slocombe *m* William Alwyn *ed* Seth Holt

☆ *Jack Hawkins* (Searle), Terence Morgan (Harry), Phyllis Calvert (Christine), *Mandy Miller* (Mandy), Godfrey Tearle (Mr. Garland), Dorothy Alison (Miss Stockton)

'An extremely touching film, in spite of occasional obviousness in a plot never dull, and in spite of its subject never saccharine.' – *Dilys Powell*

860
Mandy

A little girl, born deaf, is sent to a special school.

Shooting on location in a school for the deaf and dumb in Manchester, Alexander Mackendrick took a very sympathetic, semi-documentary approach to this story. The core of the film, though, is the girl's search for her own identity in a world, and from a family, where she is often ignored, together with a subplot of her parents' disintegrating marriage, caused in part by her disability. Mandy Miller gives a remarkably convincing performance in the title role, though she did not last long as a new child star, and Jack Hawkins, who found making the film a help when he later lost his voice through throat cancer, is excellent as the awkward headmaster.

The Sixth Sense
US   1999   107m   Technicolor
Buena Vista/Hollywood/Spyglass (Frank Marshall,
Kathleen Kennedy, Barry Mendel)

🎬 🇺🇸 ⊙ ⊙ 🎧

wd M. Night Shyamalan *ph* Tak Fujimoto *m* James
Newton Howard *pd* Larry Fulton *ad* Philip Messina
ed Andrew Mondshein *sp* make-up fx: Stan Winston
Studio; visual fx: Dream Quest Images

☆ Bruce Willis (Malcolm Crowe), Toni Collette (Lynn
Sear), Olivia Williams (Anna Crowe), *Haley Joel Osment*
(Cole Sear), Donnie Wahlberg (Vincent Gray), Glenn
Fitzgerald (Sean), Mischa Barton (Kyra Collins), Trevor
Morgan (Tommy Tammisimo), Bruce Norris (Stanley
Cunningham)

'Moody, low-key and semi-pretentious effort is
ominous without being scary or suspenseful for
most of its running time.' – *Todd McCarthy, Variety*

'A preposterous piece of work.' – *Adam Mars-
Jones, Times*

● The film was a box-office success, taking more than
$276m at the US box-office, and earning Willis an estimated
$50m.

♟ picture; Haley Joel Osment; Toni Collette; M. Night
Shyamalan (as director); M. Night Shyamalan (as writer);
Andrew Mondshein

858
The Sixth Sense

*A child psychologist begins to treat a disturbed young boy, who can
see the dead.*

M. Night Shyamalan created something of a sensation with this film. It
was a spooky movie with a twist ending that changed the focus of what
had gone before. Both clever and disturbing, it maintained a haunting
atmosphere that kept its audience off-balance. It almost demanded to
be seen a second time to discover how well it stood up after the ending
was known. Much of its disquieting power came from Haley Joel
Osment's performance as the serious young boy.

The Cranes Are Flying

USSR　1957　94m　bw
Mosfilm
■　◎～　◎

original title: *Letyat Zhuravli*
w *Victor Rosov* d *Mikhail Kalatozov* ph *Sergei Urusevski*
ed M. Timofeyeva
☆ *Tatiana Samoilova* (Veronica), Alexei Batalov (Boris),
Vasili Merkuriev (Fyodor Ivanovich)

859
The Cranes Are Flying

When her lover goes to war, a girl refuses to believe later reports of his death even though she has suffered much, including marriage to a bully, in the interim.

A moving love story, it has most of the Hollywood production virtues plus an attention to detail and a realism which are wholly Russian. The film won the top prize at the 1958 Cannes Film Festival, a triumphant moment for director Mikhail Kalatozov, who had fallen out of favour in the early Thirties before being put in charge of Soviet film production in the mid Forties. Tatiana Samoilova as the impassioned woman who finally finds fulfilment, and Sergei Urusevski's brilliant cinematography, often using a hand-held camera, combine to make it an indelible experience.

'Altamont changed a lot of people's heads.'

Gimme Shelter

US　1970　90m　colour
Cinema 5 (Ronald Schneider)
◙◙　■　◎

d *Albert Maysles, David Maysles, Charlotte Zwerin*
☆ The Rolling Stones, Ike and Tina Turner, Jefferson Airplane, The Flying Burrito Brothers
● The Region 1 DVD includes commentary by Albert Maysles, Charlotte Zwerin and Stanley Goldstein.

857
Gimme Shelter

Documentary of the Rolling Stones' free concert at Altamont Speedway in December 1969, when a member of the audience was killed by Hell's Angels who had been hired as security for the event.

The documentary of the Rolling Stones' free concert at Altamont Speedway in December 1969 served as an epitaph for that euphoric time of peace and love that was epitomized by the Woodstock Festival. The two events were not that much separated in time, but while Woodstock seemed the climax of what had happened through the Sixties, Altamont was a harbinger of the 1970s. What began as an excellently photographed movie of a concert turned into something else when a black man in the audience was killed by Hell's Angels, who had been hired as security for the event. It threw a revealing light on the darker side of rock and the revolutionary fervour that once accompanied it.

England Made Me
GB 1972 100m Eastmancolor Panavision
Hemdale/Atlantic (Jack Levin)

w Desmond Cory, Peter Duffell *novel* Graham Greene
d Peter Duffell *ph* Ray Parslow *m* John Scott *ad* Peter
Young *ed* Malcolm Cooke

☆ *Peter Finch* (Eric Krogh), Michael York (Anthony
Farrant), Hildegarde Neil (Kate Farrant), *Michael Hordern* (F.
Minty), Joss Ackland (Haller)

856
England Made Me

In 1935 a sponging Englishman becomes involved through his sister with a German financier.

Graham Greene's novel about an incestuous love between a brother and sister was somewhat altered in Peter Duffel's lively, intelligent character melodrama. Though incest remains an ingredient, the film concentrated more on the political narrative, of how, in 1935, an immature, sponging Englishman becomes involved through his sister with a German financier. After rejecting Wolf Mankowitz's script, which had updated it to the 1970s, Duffel and screenwriter Desmond Cory set the action in Germany rather than Greene's Sweden, which gave extra point to its theme of political naivety and unrest, foreshadowing the later horrors of Nazism.

'There is nothing in the dark that isn't there in the light. Except fear.'

Cape Fear
US 1991 128m Technicolor Panavision
Universal/Amblin/Cappa/Tribeca (Barbara de Fina)

w Wesley Strick *novel* The Executioners by John D.
MacDonald *screenplay* James R. Webb *d* Martin
Scorsese *ph* Freddie Francis *m* Bernard Herrmann
md Elmer Bernstein *pd* Henry Bumstead *ad* Jack G.
Taylor Jr. *ed* Thelma Schoonmaker

☆ *Robert De Niro* (Max Cady), Nick Nolte (Sam Bowden),
Jessica Lange (Leigh Bowden), *Juliette Lewis* (Danielle
Bowden), Joe Don Baker (Claude Kersek), Robert Mitchum
(Lieutenant Elgart), Gregory Peck (Lee Heller), Martin
Balsam (Judge), Illeana Douglas (Lori Davis)

'A highly potent thriller that will strike fear into the hearts of a sizable public.' – *Variety*

'I'm glad I saw the film. I found it as gripping and offensive as Scorsese intended. But, apart from De Niro's transcendent performance, I'm not sure I'd want to see it again.' – *Ian Johnstone, Sunday Times*

• Gregory Peck, Robert Mitchum and Martin Balsam all featured in the 1962 version, as did Bernard Herrmann's score.

♟ Robert De Niro, Juliette Lewis

855
Cape Fear

A psychopathic ex-convict returns to threaten the family of the lawyer who unsuccessfully defended him on a charge of rape.

Martin Scorsese's underrated thriller is a remake of J. Lee-Thompson's 1961 movie. It is a grimly effective movie, filled with a sense of brooding menace and dealing with moral confusion. Nick Nolte's lawyer is a man involved in an adulterous affair, who arranges for his former client to be beaten up; there is a sexual tension between De Niro's violent Cady and the lawyer's wife and daughter. A tough and in some ways unpleasant movie, it is nevertheless undeniably unsettling for the right reasons.

La Baie des Anges

France 1962 85m bw CinemaScope
Sud-Pacifique (Paul-Edmond Decharme)
▬ ◎
GB title: *Bay of Angels*
wd Jacques Demy *ph* Jean Rabier *m* Michel Legrand
ed Anne-Marie Cotret
☆ *Jeanne Moreau* (Jackie), Claude Mann (Jean), Paul
Guers (Caron), Henri Nassiet (Jean's father)

'Immense lightness, speed and gaiety … stunning
visual texture.' – *Tom Milne, MFB*

'It's like a French attempt to purify, to get to the
essence of, a Warner's movie of the 30s.' – *Pauline
Kael*

854
La Baie des Anges

*A bank clerk who has had unexpected winnings at the Nice Casino falls
in love with a compulsive gambler.*

Demy is interested here in the nature of obsession. Jackie (a blonde
Jeanne Moreau) is obsessed with playing roulette, and Jean (the unobtrusive Claude Mann) is obsessed with Jackie. Utilizing many of the
cinema's most dazzling resources, the two win some, lose more and
perhaps decide that there is more to life than disposing of money to
casinos.

The Private Life of Sherlock Holmes

GB 1970 125m DeLuxe Panavision
UA/Phalanx/Mirisch/Sir Nigel (Billy Wilder)
▣ ▬ ▬ ◎~ ◎ ◎
w Billy Wilder, I. A. L. Diamond *d* Billy Wilder
ph Christopher Challis *m* Miklos Rozsa *ad* Alexander
Trauner *ed* Ernest Walter
☆ *Robert Stephens* (Sherlock Holmes), *Colin Blakely* (Dr.
John H. Watson), Genevieve Page (Gabrielle Valladon),
Clive Revill (Rogozhin), Christopher Lee (Mycroft Holmes),
Catherine Lacey (Old Lady), Stanley Holloway (1st
Gravedigger)

'Affectionately conceived and flawlessly executed.'
– *NFT, 1974*

'Wilder's least embittered film, and by far his most
moving. Great.' – *Time Out, 1984*

853
The Private Life of Sherlock Holmes

*A secret Watson manuscript reveals cases in which Sherlock Holmes
became involved with women.*

Billy Wilder had once tried to make a musical about Sherlock Holmes,
with Peter O'Toole as the detective and Peter Sellers as Dr Watson.
When that collapsed, he turned to this romantic drama. There were
problems from the start with the script and the finished film ran for
200 minutes, which the studio refused to release. After being chopped
about, what started as four episodes was reduced to two, one brightly
satirical and the other no more than a careful and discreet recreation,
with the occasional jocular aside, of the flavour of the stories themselves. Even so, it is a very civilized and pleasing entertainment.

The Dreamlife of Angels

France 1998 113m colour
Bagheera/Diaphana/France3 (François Marquis)
▣ ⊙ ⊙
original title: *La Vie Rêvée des Anges*
w Erick Zonca, Roger Bohbot *d* Erick Zonca *ph* Agnes
Godard *m* Yann Thiersen *pd* Jimmy Vansteenkiste
ad Jimmy Vansteenkiste *ed* Yannick Kergoat
☆ *Elodie Bouchez* (Isa), *Natacha Regnier* (Marie), Gregoire
Colin (Chriss), Jo Prestia (Fredo), Patrick Mercado (Charly)

'A passionate and unpretentious gem.' – *Film
Review*

● In France, it won the Prix Méliès as the best French film
of the year. Elodie Bouchez and Natacha Regnier were joint
winners of the best actress award at the 1998 Cannes Film
Festival.

852
The Dreamlife of Angels

*Two young women, trying to survive in Lille, form an uneasy friendship
with each other and with two bouncers at rock concerts.*

In this engrossing and frequently surprising narrative of French working-class life, its two protagonists have contrasting personalities: one
is happy to take life as it comes, the other strives for material success
and is prepared to marry a man she likes but does not love, but who
can offer her security. It's a movie about the tough choices life can
force upon people with few resources of their own, and how even
important and supportive relationships may not be enough for survival.
Erick Zonca's patient direction frames two exceptional, truthful performances by Elodie Bouchez and Natacha Regnier.

Damnation

Hungary 1988 116m bw
⊙
original title: *Kárhozat*
w Bela Tarr, Laszlo Krasznahorkai *d* Bela Tarr *ph* Gabor
Medvigy *m* Mihaly Vig *ad* Gyula Pauer *ed* Agnes
Hraniczky
☆ Miklos B. Szekely (Karrer), Vali Kerekes (The Singer),
Gyula Pauer (Willarsky), Hedi Temessy (Cloakroom
Attendant), Gyorgy Cserhalmi (Sebestyen)

'Technically brilliant but utterly dreary.' – *James
Christopher, Times*

851
Damnation

*Rejected by his married lover, an unemployed man plots to get her hus-
band out of the way so he can attempt to resume their affair.*

A bleak movie about a hopeless love affair, set in a desolate industrial
landscape. Tarr's films do not provide for easy viewing or optimism
about the human condition. As cable-cars chug to and from a mine, an
unemployed man lusts after his former mistress, a married singer in a
dingy bar, and arranges for her husband to become a drug courier so
that he can persuade her to resume their affair. An examination of
empty lives, this is existence reduced to its most basic components,
made bearable by Tarr's unyielding gaze that is able to conjure up, in
fog-shrouded black and white photography, unforgettable images.

'Here's the gay, glorious story of a war correspondent and a war ace ... a romance that could happen only in 1940!'

Arise My Love
US   1940   113m   bw
Paramount (Arthur Hornblow Jnr)
w Charles Brackett, Billy Wilder *d* Mitchell Leisen
ph Charles Lang *m* Victor Young *ad* Hans Dreier, Robert Usher *ed* Doane Harrison
☆ *Claudette Colbert* (Augusta Nash), *Ray Milland* (Tom Martin), *Walter Abel* (Mr Phillips) (Abel as the harassed editor comes out with his famous line, 'I'm not happy – I'm not happy at all.'), Dennis O'Keefe (Joe Shepard), George Zucco (Prison Governor), Dick Purcell (Pinky O'Connor), Frank Puglia (Fr. Jacinto), Esther Dale (Secretary)

'Against the background of European fisticuffs, Paramount brings forth a film of absorbing romantic interest, proving that love will find a way through the hazards of air raids, torpedo attacks and enemy invasions.' – *Variety*

● Joel McCrea was originally cast for the Milland role.
🎗 original story (Benjamin Glazer, John S. Toldy)
♟ Charles Lang; Victor Young; art direction

850
Arise My Love

American reporters in Europe and in love survive the Spanish Civil War, a wrathful editor in Paris and the sinking of the Athenia.

Mitchell Leisen's significant and stylish comedy melodrama was gleaned from the Twentieth Century's grimmest headlines. It bears the recognizable stamp of the great scriptwriting team of Charles Brackett and Billy Wilder, who were able to write about politics and love with equal passion. The tone is set by the opening minute: Ray Milland is marched out of his Spanish jail to face a firing squad; suddenly Claudette Colbert, whom he has never seen before, claims him as her husband and whisks him away. Despite this slick move from tragedy to comedy, Wilder was not happy with Leisen's direction; nevertheless, it remains a unique, sophisticated entertainment.

The Last Laugh
Germany   1924   73m approx (24 fps)   bw
silent
UFA
▬ 🔊 🔊 🔊
original title: *Der Letzte Mann*
w Carl Mayer *d* F. W. Murnau *ph* Karl Freund *ad* Robert Herlth, Walter Rohrig
☆ *Emil Jannings* (The Porter), Max Hiller (The Daughter's Fiance), Maly Delschaft (The Porter's Daughter), Hans Unterkirchen (Hotel Manager)

'A marvellous picture – marvellous in its simplicity, its economy of effect, its expressiveness, and its dramatic power.' – *Life*

● A German remake of 1955 had Hans Albers in the lead and was of no interest.

849
The Last Laugh

The old doorman of a luxury hotel is given the job of lavatory attendant but comes into a fortune and gets his revenge.

A bewhiskered Emil Jannings is at his best as the man who gets the last laugh in Murnau's entertaining, fully realized silent movie. The ironic anecdote is made important by its virtual abandonment of dialogue and whole-hearted adoption of the camera eye technique, which gives some thrilling dramatic effects. Karl Freund, the brilliant cinematographer, provides astonishingly mobile shots – the opening, which takes the spectator from a lift through the hotel's lobby to the revolving front door, was achieved by attaching the camera to a bicycle.

848

Fourteen Hours

Fourteen Hours
US   1951   92m   bw
TCF (Sol C. Siegel)
w John Paxton *article* Joel Sayre *d* Henry Hathaway
ph Joe MacDonald *m* Alfred Newman *ad* Lyle Wheeler,
Leland Fuller *ed* Dorothy Spencer
☆ Richard Basehart (Robert Cosick), Paul Douglas
(Dunnigan), Barbara Bel Geddes (Virginia), Grace Kelly
(Mrs. Fuller), Debra Paget (Ruth), Agnes Moorehead (Mrs.
Cosick), Robert Keith (Mr. Cosick), Howard da Silva (Lt.
Moksar), Jeffrey Hunter (Danny), Martin Gabel (Dr. Strauss),
Jeff Corey (Sgt. Farley).

'A model of craftsmanship in all departments.'
– *Penelope Houston*

'A highly enjoyable small scale picture, with a
strength immensely greater than its size would
suggest.' – *Richard Mallett, Punch*

Ω art direction

A man stands on the ledge of a tall building and threatens to jump.

Based on a true occurrence of a young man who stood on the ledge of
a tall building for fourteen hours before jumping to his death, Henry
Hathaway's film gave the story a happy ending. He shot Richard
Basehart's final death-plunge, but, deciding it was too grim, added a
scene where he falls into a net. First-class detail gives an impression of
realism to a documentary-styled drama. The interest is not confined to
the jumper, but also takes in his family and onlookers, whose lives are
changed by the event: a woman contemplating divorce (Grace Kelly in
her first screen role) decides to stay married; a young couple meet and
fall in love; others take bets on the outcome. A well-crafted, suspenseful film, it is a neglected minor classic.

847

Pickup on South Street

'How the law took a chance on a B-girl …
and won!'
Pickup on South Street
US   1953   80m   bw
TCF (Jules Schermer)
▆▆ ◉ ◎
wd Samuel Fuller *story* Dwight Taylor *ph* Joe MacDonald
m Leigh Harline *ad* Lyle R. Wheeler, George Patrick
ed Nick de Maggio
☆ Richard Widmark (Skip McCoy), Jean Peters (Candy),
Thelma Ritter (Moe), Richard Kiley (Joey), Murvyn Vye
(Captain Dan Tiger)
● Remade 1968 as *Capetown Affair*.
Ω Thelma Ritter

*A pickpocket steals a girl's wallet and finds himself up to his neck in
espionage.*

Samuel Fuller's thriller is ostensibly anti-Communist, though politics
play little part in this movie. Communism just made a convenient threat
for the outcasts, police-informers, petty crooks and prostitutes who
populate the film and gave them a reason for siding with America.
Fuller shows a gritty world where people are at the mercy of unexpected events, and suffer the consequences, Widmark here adds
another memorable turn to his collection of amoral criminals, and
Ritter is terrific as a world-weary informer.

French Can-Can

France/Italy 1955 105m Technicolor
Franco-London/Jolly (Louis Wipf)
🎬 🎞 🔍
w André-Paul Antoine d Jean Renoir ph Michel Kelber
m Georges Van Parys
☆ *Jean Gabin*, Françoise Arnoul, Maria Félix, Jean-Roger Caussimon, Edith Piaf, Patachou

846
French Can-Can

A new dance is created in a Paris night club.

Jean Renoir's exuberant film tells how the can-can was launched in a new Paris night club, the Moulin Rouge. It also deals with the sexual intrigues of its owner and the jealousies of his two mistresses, who discover that success as a performer does not guarantee personal happiness – that, indeed, the choice is between dancing and a contented private life, which was a theme explored a few years earlier in Michael Powell and Emeric Pressburger's *The Red Shoes*. Renoir provides a show business extravaganza, full of light and colour and glamour, with a little love on the side. It's a delirious celebration of the world of entertainment and of Paris of the late nineteenth century seen through a nostalgic, rose-coloured lens.

'She taught him good manners, he taught her bad ones.'

Sur Mes Lèvres

France 2001 118m colour
Pathé/Sedif/Cine b/France 2 (Jean-Louis Livi, Philippe Carcassonne)
🎬 🎞 🔍 🔍
GB and US title: *Read My Lips*
w Tonino Benacquista, Jacques Audiard d Jacques Audiard ph Mathieu Vadepied m Alexandre Desplat
ad Michel Barthelemy ed Juliette Welfling
☆ Vincent Cassel (Paul Angeli), Emmanuelle Devos (Carla Behm), Olivier Gourmet (Marchand), Olivia Bonamy (Annie), Olivier Perrier (Masson), Bernard Alane (Morel), Céline Samie (Josie Marchand), David Saracino (Richard Carambo)

'A breathless and rather audacious study in the sexiness of a nonsexual relationship.' – *David Denby, New Yorker*

'To be viewed and treasured for its extraordinary intelligence and originality as well as its lyrical variations on the game of love.' – *Andrew Sarris*

845
Sur Mes Lèvres

A deaf woman and a petty criminal become involved in corporate double-dealings.

Jacques Audiard's thriller has a touch of Hitchcock about it, as a hard-of-hearing secretary, who can lip-read, becomes involved with a petty criminal, whom she appoints as her assistant. The two exploit each other's abilities for their own gain. She advances in the firm and he uses her in a scam that takes them both into a corrupt double-crossing world of violence and a moment of self-realisation, when each discovers that the other makes them seem complete. Audiard's skilful direction also uses sound cleverly, to suggest the woman's deafness. It is an exceptional drama of the revenge of the unskilled and disadvantaged, who, trapped in an inconsiderate environment, are unexpectedly able to reveal their remarkable qualities.

'The gayest of mad musicals!'

'The dance-mad musical triumph of two continents!'

The Gay Divorcee
US   1934   107m   bw
RKO (Pandro S. Berman)
▣ ▤ ◎
GB title: *The Gay Divorce*
w George Marion Jnr, Dorothy Yost, Edward Kaufman *play* Dwight Taylor, J. Hartley Manners *musical comedy* Samuel Hoffenstein, Kenneth Webb, Cole Porter *d* Mark Sandrich *ph* David Abel *m/ly* various *md* Max Steiner *ad* Van Nest Polglase, Carroll Clark *ed* William Hamilton *sp* Vernon Walker

☆ *Fred Astaire* (Guy Holden), *Ginger Rogers* (Mimi Glossop), *Edward Everett Horton* (Egbert Fitzgerald), *Alice Brady* (Hortense Ditherwell), *Erik Rhodes* (Rodolfo Tonetti), *Eric Blore* (Waiter), Lillian Miles (Hotel Guest), Betty Grable (Hotel Guest)

'The plot is trivial French farce, but the dances are among the wittiest and most lyrical expressions of American romanticism on the screen.' – *New Yorker, 1977*

● 'Night and Day' was the only Cole Porter song to survive from the stage musical.

♪ song 'The Continental' (*m* Con Conrad, *ly* Herb Magidson)

♟ best picture; musical score (Ken Webb, Samuel Hoffenstein); art direction

844
The Gay Divorcee

A would-be divorcee in an English seaside hotel mistakes a dancer who loves her for a professional co-respondent.

Wildly and hilariously dated comedy musical with splendidly archaic comedy routines supporting Hollywood's great new dance team of Fred Astaire and Ginger Rogers in their first big success. Astaire, who had danced in the stage version with Claire Luce, did not want to work with Rogers again, and she was still hankering after a career as a dramatic actress. The plot is a forgettable one, of mistaken identity. Not much dancing, but the 17 minutes of 'The Continental' is a show-stopper with its three set piece dances from the two stars interspersed with the immaculate tap dancing of the chorus in snazzy black and white outfits.

☆ **Milos Forman**
Director ☆

1. Amarcord (Fellini)
2. American Graffiti (Lucas)
3. Citizen Kane (Welles)
4. City Lights (Chaplin)
5. The Deer Hunter (Cimino)
6. Les Enfants du Paradis (Carné)
7. Giant (Stevens)
8. The Godfather (Coppola)
9. Miracle in Milan (De Sica)
10. Raging Bull (Scorsese)

☆ **Jim Jarmusch**
Director ☆

1. L'Atalante (Vigo)
2. Tokyo Story (Ozu)
3. They Live by Night (N. Ray)
4. Bob le Flambeur (Melville)
5. Sunrise (Murnau)
6. The Cameraman (Sedgwick)
7. Mouchette (Bresson)
8. Seven Samurai (Kurosawa)
9. Broken Blossoms (Griffith)
10. Rome, Open City (Rossellini)

☆ **Norman Jewison**
Director ☆

1. Bicycle Thieves (De Sica)
2. The Bridge on the River Kwai (Lean)
3. Casablanca (Curtiz)
4. Citizen Kane (Welles)
5. City Lights (Chaplin)
6. 8 1/2 (Fellini)
7. The 400 Blows (Truffaut)
8. Gunga Din (Stevens)
9. Rashomon (Kurosawa)
10. The Wizard of Oz (Fleming)

Witness for the Prosecution

US 1957 114m bw
UA/Theme/Edward Small (Arthur Hornblow Jnr)

⬛ ▬ ◉⋍ ◎ ◎

w Billy Wilder, Harry Kurnitz *play* Agatha Christie *d* Billy Wilder *ph* Russell Harlan *m* Matty Melneck *ad* Alexander Trauner *ed* Daniel Mandell

☆ *Charles Laughton* (Sir Wilfrid Robarts), Tyrone Power (Leonard Stephen Vole), Marlene Dietrich (Christine Helm/Vole), John Williams (Brogan Moore), Henry Daniell (Mayhew), Elsa Lanchester (Miss Plimsoll), Norma Varden (Mrs. Emily French), Una O'Connor (Janet MacKenzie), Ian Wolfe (Carter)

'Inane, yet moderately entertaining.' – *Pauline Kael*

🏆 best picture; Billy Wilder; Charles Laughton; Elsa Lanchester; Daniel Mandell

843
Witness for the Prosecution

A convalescent QC takes on a murder defence and finds himself in a web of trickery.

Charles Laughton dominates this film as the convalescent QC. Agatha Christie loved what was done to her clever stage thriller, which was opened out and given more pace, but it is Laughton's performance as the fussy, monocled barrister that holds it together, snuffling and groaning and snapping out questions to the witnesses. Despite, or perhaps because of, being coached by Noel Coward, Dietrich makes an unconvincing Cockney. The artificiality of the thriller is condoned by smart dialogue and direction and a handful of surprises.

Berlin, Symphony of a Great City

Germany 1927 78m bw silent
Fox-Europa

◉

original title: *Berlin, die Symphonie einer Grosstadt*
w Walter Ruttman, Karl Freund, Carl Mayer *d* Walter Ruttman *ph* Reimar Kuntze, Robert Baberske, Laszlo Schäffer *m* Edmund Meisel *ad* Erich Kettelhut *ed* Walter Ruttman

842
Berlin, Symphony of a Great City

A documentary on a day in the life of a city.

Walter Ruttman's impression of the life of a city from dawn to midnight is expressed through cinematic montages, unusual camera angles and sequences, and set to music in this pioneering film. Much of the film was shot with hidden cameras to provide an unselfconscious expression of everyday activities. Ruttman, who had studied painting and architecture, began his career with abstract animations, and his concern for the rhythmic manipulation of images is evident here. A leader in the field of 'impressionistic' documentaries which later became much more familiar (*Rien que les Heures* did a similar job for Paris at around the same time), this still has moments of poetry that have seldom been equalled.

Sabotage
GB   1936   76m   bw
Gaumont British (Michael Balcon, Ivor Montagu)
US title: *A Woman Alone*
w Charles Bennett, Ian Hay, Helen Simpson, E. V. H.
Emmett *novel The Secret Agent* by Joseph Conrad
d *Alfred Hitchcock* ph Bernard Knowles *md* Louis Levy
ed Charles Frend
☆ *Oscar Homolka* (Karl Verloc), *Sylvia Sidney* (Sylvia
Verloc), John Loder (Sgt. Ted Spencer), Desmond Tester
(Steve), Joyce Barbour (Renee), Matthew Boulton (Supt.
Talbot)

'Tightly packed, economical, full of invention and
detail.' – *NFT, 1961*

'The cleverest picture Alfred Hitchcock has made
since the arrival of the talkies. It is also, to me, the
least likeable of them all ... Discreet directors don't
kill schoolboys and dogs in omnibuses. Believe me,
it isn't done.' – *C. A. Lejeune*

841
Sabotage

The proprietor of a small London cinema is a dangerous foreign agent.

Joseph Conrad's novel about an anarchist gang in London became an unattractively plotted but fascinatingly detailed Hitchcock suspenser. Screenwriters changed Conrad's secret agent to the proprietor of a small London cinema, which gave some effectively ironic counterpoint to the story. Hitchcock builds suspense, as a young boy, unknowingly carrying a bird cage that has a time-bomb concealed within it, dawdles on his way through London, eventually sitting on a bus next to an old lady with a puppy. Hitchcock came to regret the scene in which the bomb explodes, killing all the passengers, as it offended audiences. Yet it adds a suitably grim note to the movie's splendidly brooding melodramatic atmosphere.

'She brought a small town to its feet and a huge corporation to its knees.'
Erin Brockovich
US   2000   131m   CFI
Columbia TriStar/Universal/Jersey (Danny DeVito,
Michael Shamberg, Stacey Sher)
w *Susannah Grant* d *Steven Soderbergh* ph Ed Lachman
m Thomas Newman *pd* Phil Messina *ad* Christa Munro
ed Anne V. Coates *cos* Jeffrey Kurland
☆ *Julia Roberts* (Erin Brockovich), Albert Finney (Ed
Masry), Aaron Eckhart (George), Marg Helgenberger (Donna
Jensen), Cherry Jones (Pamela Duncan), Veanne Cox
(Theresa Dallavale), Conchata Ferrell (Brenda), Tracey
Walter (Charles Embry), Peter Coyote (Kurt Potter), Scotty
Leavenworth (Matthew), Gemmenne De la Pena (Katie),
Jamie Harrold (Scott)

'A movie that is both intensely funny and
emotionally satisfying.' – *Ian Nathan, Empire*

'An exhilarating tale about a woman discovering
her full potential and running with it.' – *Todd
McCarthy, Variety*

● Erin Brockovich herself appears briefly as a waitress in a coffee shop.
👤 Julia Roberts
🏆 picture; Steven Soderbergh; Susannah Grant; Albert Finney
🏆 Julia Roberts

840
Erin Brockovich

A working-class mother, who talks her way into a job in a law firm, organizes a winning investigation into industrial pollution that has devastated a community.

An unexpectedly lively and amusing movie of a heartening true story, one that gave Julia Roberts her best and most convincing role so far, as a feisty but vulnerable mother who refuses to be intimidated by anyone. The film sees her transformation from working-class single mother to the champion of victims of industrial pollution. Steven Soderbergh sets up the drama by his concentration on Roberts, whose own desperation allows her to identify with others whose problems are beyond their control. This may be ideal Hollywood feel-good material, but Soderbergh gives it more than just an upbeat feel; his approach is restrained and never sentimental, keeping his distance so that the performances and the scandal are what grab the attention.

'A murdered wife. A one-armed man. An obsessed detective. The chase begins.'

The Fugitive
US   1993   127m   Technicolor
Warner (Keith Barish, Arnold Kopelson)

w Jeb Stuart, David Twohy *story* David Twohy *based on characters created by Roy Huggins (for the TV series)* *d* Andrew Davis *ph* Michael Chapman *m* James Newton Howard *pd* Dennis Washington *ad* Charles Wood, Maher Ahmad *ed* Dennis Virkler, David Finfer, Dean Goodhill, Don Brochu, Richard Nord, Dov Hoenig
☆ Harrison Ford (Dr. Richard Kimble), *Tommy Lee Jones* (Deputy US Marshal Samuel Gerard), Sela Ward (Helen Kimble), Joe Pantoliano (Cosmo Renfro), Jeroen Krabbé (Dr. Charles Nichols), Andreas Katsulas (Sykes, "The One-Armed Man"), Julianne Moore (Dr. Ann Eastman)

'A remarkably successful Hollywood product, with a brilliantly contrived star double act pursuing different paths through the central plot.' – *Kim Newman, Sight and Sound*

● The TV series ran from 1963 to 1967 and starred David Janssen.
♟ Tommy Lee Jones
♟ best picture; Michael Chapman; James Newton Howard; editing; sound; sound effects editing

839
The Fugitive

A surgeon, unjustly accused of his wife's murder, goes on the run to find the real killer, while being hunted by a ruthless cop.

Andrew Davis's intense and exciting thriller is the only remake of a TV series to be anything more than an overblown exercise in nostalgia. There are many improbabilities in Dr Kimble's continued survival, from the opening thunderous train crash to his keeping only half a step ahead of his pursuers as he runs through sewers, makes impossible high dives, and fights on trains and rooftops. Yet it is filmed with such a visceral energy and skill that it remains compulsively watchable.

A Walk in the Sun
US 1946 117m bw
Lewis Milestone Productions
■ @~ ⊚

w Robert Rossen novel Harry Brown d Lewis Milestone
ph Russell Harlan m Fredric Efrem Rich ad Max Bertisch
ed Duncan Mansfield
☆ Dana Andrews (Sgt. Tyne), Richard Conte (Rivera),
Sterling Holloway (McWilliams), John Ireland (Windy),
George Tyne (Friedman), Herbert Rudley (Sgt. Porter),
Richard Benedict (Tranella), Norman Lloyd (Archimbeau),
Lloyd Bridges (Sgt. Ward), Huntz Hall (Carraway)

'Concerned with the individual rather than the
battlefield, the film is finely perceptive, exciting,
and very moving.' – Penelope Houston

'A swiftly overpowering piece of work.' – Bosley
Crowther

'A notable war film, if not the most notable war film
to come from America.' – Richard Winnington

'After nearly two hours one is sorry when it ends.'
– Richard Mallett, Punch

838
A Walk in the Sun

The exploits of a single army patrol during the Salerno landings of 1943, on one vital morning.

Lewis Milestone's vivid war film is sharply focused, following a single army patrol as they fight their way six miles to a farmhouse held by the Germans. Rossen's script captures the grunted dialogue of the soldiers, adding an ironic counterpoint through letters home that Windy (John Ireland) imagines writing. Keenly acted by its cast, who convey an intense camaraderie, it is one of the most mature of Hollywood's depictions of ordinary men in battle.

Alexander's Ragtime Band
US 1938 106m bw
TCF (Darryl F. Zanuck, Harry Joe Brown)
▣◌ ■ ⊚

w Kathryn Scola, Lamar Trotti, Richard Sherman d Henry
King ph Peverell Marley m/ly Irving Berlin md Alfred
Newman ad Bernard Herzbrun, Boris Leven ed Barbara
McLean
☆ Tyrone Power (Roger Grant), Alice Faye (Stella Kirby),
Don Ameche (Charlie Dwyer), Ethel Merman (Jerry Allen),
Jack Haley (Davey Lane), Jean Hersholt (Prof. Heinrich),
Helen Westley (Aunt Sophie), John Carradine (Taxi Driver),
Paul Hurst (Bill), Wally Vernon (Himself), Ruth Terry (Ruby),
Eddie Collins (Cpl. Collins), Douglas Fowley (Snapper),
Chick Chandler (Louie)

'A grand filmusical which stirs and thrills, finding
response in the American heart to memories of the
exciting, sentimental and patriotic moments of the
past quarter of a century.' – Variety

♫ 'Alexander's Ragtime Band'; 'Everybody's Doin' It';
'When the Midnight Choo-Choo Leaves for Alabam'; 'Oh,
How I Hate to Get Up in the Morning'; 'Say It with Music'; 'A
Pretty Girl Is Like a Melody'; 'Blue Skies'; 'What'll I Do';
'Easter Parade'; 'Heat Wave'.
♟ Alfred Newman
♟ picture; Irving Berlin (for original story); Irving Berlin
(for song, 'Now It Can Be Told'); art direction; editing

837
Alexander's Ragtime Band

Between 1911 and 1939, two songwriters vie for the affections of a rising musical comedy star.

Darryl Zanuck's liking for musical sagas, chronicling individuals across the decades, reached its ideal in this film that made great use of the songs of Irving Berlin, from his first big hit, *Alexander's Ragtime Band*, in 1911 to his successes of the 30s, such as *Heat Wave*. The narrative was a standard one, of two musicians in love with the same singer. Henry King's deft interweaving of the story and some 26 songs gave the movie a casual elegance and a verve that has not dated.

The Happy Time

US   1952   94m   bw
Columbia/Stanley Kramer (Earl Felton)

w Earl Felton *play* Samuel A. Taylor *d* Richard Fleischer *ph* Charles Lawton Jnr *m* Dimitri Tiomkin *pd* Rudolph Sternad *ad* Carl Anderson *ed* William Lyon
☆ *Charles Boyer* (Jacques Bonnard), *Louis Jourdan* (Uncle Desmonde), *Bobby Driscoll* (Bibi), Marsha Hunt (Susan Bonnard), Marcel Dalio (Grandpere Bonnard), Kurt Kasznar (Uncle Louis), Linda Christian (Mignonette Chappuis), Jeanette Nolan (Felice), Jack Raine (Mr. Frye), Richard Erdman (Alfred Grattin)

836
The Happy Time

Domestic misadventures of a family of French Canadians during the twenties.

This was Charles Boyer's last starring role in a major American production, playing with easy charm the father of a French-Canadian family during the early years of the last century. A story of domestic mishaps and a boy's coming of age, it remains a most agreeable film. The ill-fated Bobby Driscoll was ingratiating as the boy with adolescent sexual stirrings. Although Kurt Kasznar, repeating his Broadway stage performance, is fine as the boy's eccentric uncle, Zero Mostel might have been better – he was originally cast, but Harry Cohn, head of Columbia Pictures, vetoed him because Mostel had been blacklisted after appearing before the Un-American Activities Committee. Richard Fleischer, who directed with a light touch, correctly described the picture as 'about people, warm, human, alive, and funny'.

My Favorite Blonde

US   1942   78m   bw
Paramount (Paul Jones)
▤ ◉ ◉

w Don Hartman, Frank Butler, Melvin Frank, Norman Panama *d* Sidney Lanfield *ph* William Mellor *m* David Buttolph *ad* Hans Dreier, Robert Usher *ed* William Shea *cos* Edith Head
☆ *Bob Hope* (Larry Haines), *Madeleine Carroll* (Karen Bentley), *Gale Sondergaard* (Mme. Stephanie Runick), George Zucco (Dr. Hugo Streger), Lionel Royce (Karl), Walter Kingsford (Dr. Faber), Victor Varconi (Miller)
● Hope mad two further 'My Favorite' spy comedy thrillers: *My Favorite Brunette* (1947) and *My Favorite Spy* (1951).

835
My Favorite Blonde

A burlesque comic travelling by train helps a lady in distress and lives to regret it.

Bob Hope, as a burlesque comic, had one of his best roles in this smartly paced spy comedy thriller, even if he is occasionally upstaged by a penguin. The movie sometimes recalls Hitchcock in a lighter mood, helped by the casting of Madeleine Carroll, memorable in Hitchcock's *The 39 Steps*, as a British secret agent trying to evade pursuing Nazis. Hope is his usual slick, wisecracking self. 'Do you know how it feels to be followed and hounded and watched every second?' Carroll asks. 'I used to,' he replies, 'but now I pay cash for everything.' But, for once, he allows room for some genuine feeling and a believable romance.

The Paleface

♦♦ US 1948 91m Technicolor
Paramount (Robert L. Welch)
▤ ◎ ◉

w Edmund Hartmann, Frank Tashlin *d* Norman Z. McLeod
ph Ray Rennahan *m* Victor Young *ad* Hans Dreier, Earl
Hedrick *ed* Ellsworth Hoagland
☆ *Bob Hope* ('Painless' Peter Potter), *Jane Russell*
(Calamity Jane), Robert Armstrong (Terris), Iris Adrian
(Pepper), Robert Watson (Toby Preston), Jackie Searl
(Jasper Martin), Joe Vitale (Indian Scout), Clem Bevans
(Hank Billings), Charles Trowbridge (Gov. Johnson)
● Sequel: *Son of Paleface* (qv); remake, *The Shakiest Gun
in the West* (1968).
♫ song 'Buttons and Bows' (*m* Jay Livingston, *ly* Ray
Evans)

834
The Paleface

*Calamity Jane undertakes an undercover mission against desperadoes,
and marries a timid dentist as a cover.*

Bob Hope perfected his vain but craven persona in this splendid
comedy Western, his first Technicolor movie. The excellent comic
direction was by Norman Z. McLeod, a former animator who had
honed his craft directing the Marx Brothers, though screenwriter Frank
Tashlin thought he would have done better and went on to direct the
amusing sequel, *Son of Paleface*. The pairing of Hope and the voluptuous Russell ('Lumpy', as Hope called her off-screen), with a running
joke on the non-consummation of the marriage, created a comic
delight; Jay Livingston and Ray Evans's Oscar-winning song, 'Buttons
and Bows', added a little extra pleasure to the proceedings.

The Three Musketeers

♦♦ US 1948 125m Technicolor
MGM (Pandro S. Berman)
▦ ▤ ◎

w Robert Ardrey *novel* Alexandre Dumas *d* George
Sidney *ph* Robert Planck *m* Herbert Stothart *ad* Cedric
Gibbons, Malcolm Brown *ed* Robert J. Kern, George
Boemler
☆ *Gene Kelly* (D'Artagnan), Lana Turner (Charlotte de
Winter), June Allyson (Constance), Frank Morgan (Louis
XIII), Van Heflin (Athos), Angela Lansbury (Queen Anne),
Vincent Price (Richelieu), Keenan Wynn (Planchet), John
Sutton (George), Gig Young (Porthos), Robert Coote
(Aramis), Reginald Owen (De Treville), Ian Keith (De
Rochefort), Patricia Medina (Kitty)

'A heavy, rough-housing mess. As Lady de Winter,
Lana Turner sounds like a drive-in waitress
exchanging quips with hotrodders, and as
Richelieu, Vincent Price might be an especially
crooked used car dealer. Angela Lansbury wears
the crown of France as though she had won it at a
county fair.' – *New Yorker*, 1980

♟ Robert Planck
● Other versions of film: 1936 (Walter Abel as
D'Artagnan)1939 (with Don Ameche and the Ritz Brothers)
1977 (all-star international version with Michael York, Oliver
Reed, etc.).

833
The Three Musketeers

*High-spirited version of the famous story, with duels and fights pre-
sented like musical numbers.*

Gene Kelly drew inspiration from the swashbuckling of Douglas
Fairbanks for his role as D'Artagnan in this high-spirited version of
Alexandre Dumas's famous story. In trying to emulate Fairbanks's non-
chalant satisfaction at his own prowess, he achieved something new:
many of the action scenes were set to music, while the duels and fights
are choreographed like musical numbers, with Kelly's fencing seeming
an extension of his more usual dancing. There was a certain tension on
the set: Lana Turner originally refused the role of the wicked Charlotte
de Winter, while Angela Lansbury had fought for the part, and was disappointed to be playing Queen Anne. But it does not show in the finished film. Its vigour and inventiveness are a pleasure to behold.

I'm No Angel
US   1933   88m   bw
Paramount (William Le Baron)
▤   ◔   ◉

w *Mae West* d Wesley Ruggles *ph* Leo Tover
m/ly Harvey Brooks, Gladys Dubois *ad* Hans Dreier, Bernard Herzbrun *ed* Otho Lovering
☆ *Mae West* (Tira), Edward Arnold (Big Bill Barton), Cary Grant (Jack Clayton), Gregory Ratoff (Benny Pinkowitz), Ralf Harolde (Slick Wiley), Kent Taylor (Kirk Lawrence), Gertrude Michael (Alicia Hatton)

'The most freewheeling of all Mae's screen vehicles, and the most satisfying of the lot.' – *James Robert Parish*

'A quality of balance and proportion which only the finest films attain.' – *Views and Reviews*

832
I'm No Angel

A carnival dancer gets off a murder charge, moves into society and sues a man for breach of promise.

Mae West's most successful vehicle was credited with saving the fortunes of Paramount. Released before the Legion of Decency was formed, it also contains some of Mae's fruitiest lines. She insists, 'When I'm good, I'm very good, but when I'm bad, I'm better,' and warns a fortune-teller, 'You just tell me about my future. I know all about my past.' It remains a highly diverting side show with almost a laugh a minute; its star lived up to F. Scott Fitzgerald's description of her as 'the only Hollywood actress with an ironic edge and a comic spark'.

Boomerang!
US   1947   88m   bw
TCF (Louis de Rochemont)
w *Richard Murphy* d *Elia Kazan* ph Norbert Brodine
m David Buttolph *ad* Richard Day, Chester Gore
ed Harmon Jones
☆ *Dana Andrews* (Henry L. Harvey), Jane Wyatt (Mrs. Harvey), Lee J. Cobb (Chief Robinson), Cara Williams (Irene Nelson), Arthur Kennedy (John Waldron), Sam Levene (Woods), Taylor Holmes (Wade), Robert Keith (McCreery), Ed Begley (Harris)

'A study of integrity, beautifully developed by Dana Andrews against a background of political corruption and chicanery that is doubly shocking because of its documentary understatement.' – *Richard Winnington*

'For the first time in many a moon we are treated to a picture that gives a good example of a typical small American city – the people, their way of living, their mode of government, the petty politics practised, the power of the press.' – *Frank Ward, National Board of Review*

♟ Richard Murphy

831
Boomerang!

In a New England town, a clergyman is shot dead on the street. The DA prevents an innocent man from being convicted, but cannot track down the guilty party.

An incisive real-life thriller based on a true case. Using many of the actors he had worked with in the theatre, Kazan made this movie in an innovative documentary style that was much copied; justice is not seen to be done, though the murderer is known to the audience. A milestone movie of its kind, it also showed a young director gaining confidence in the craft of filmmaking.

Julia
US   1977   117m   Technicolor
TCF (Richard Roth)
🇺🇸 ⌕
w Alvin Sargent *book Pentimento* by Lillian Hellman
d Fred Zinnemann *ph* Douglas Slocombe *m* Georges
Delerue *pd* Carmen Dillon, Gene Callahan, Willy Holt
ed Walter Murch
☆ Jane Fonda (Lillian Hellman), Vanessa Redgrave
(Julia), Jason Robards Jnr (Dashiell Hammett), Maximilian
Schell (Johann), Hal Holbrook (Alan Campbell), Meryl
Streep (Anne Marie), Rosemary Murphy (Dorothy Parker),
Cathleen Nesbitt (Grandmother), Maurice Denham
(Undertaker)

'After a while it becomes apparent that Zinnemann
and Sargent are trafficking in too many quotations
and flashbacks because they can't find the core of
the material.' – *Pauline Kael*

👤 script; Vanessa Redgrave; Jason Robards Jnr
🏆 best picture; Fred Zinnemann; Douglas Slocombe;
Georges Delerue; Jane Fonda; Maximilian Schell
Ⓣ best picture; Alvin Sargent; Douglas Slocombe; Jane
Fonda

830
Julia

Lillian Hellman reflects on the fortunes of her friend Julia, filled with enthusiasm for European causes and finally killed by the Nazis.

Fred Zinnemann thought Lillian Hellman's apparently autobiographical story was 'brief, haunting and so gossamer-thin as to be almost transparent'. Set in the 1930s, it involved the relationship between wealthy Julia and Lillian, an aspiring writer when they first meet, and a successful playwright when Julia, who has become involved with the antifascist movement in Austria, asks her to smuggle money into Nazi Germany. When war breaks out, Lillian returns to America, and Julia is killed by the Nazis. (In reality, Zinnemann concluded the story was fiction, and the real 'Julia' was still alive.) Alvin Sargent filled out the story, Fonda, Redgrave and Robards fleshed out the characters, and the result was a thoughtful, elegant patchwork of thirties memories, a vehicle for actors and a subtle, self-effacing director.

The House on 92nd Street
US   1945   88m   bw
TCF (*Louis de Rochemont*)
w Barre Lyndon, Charles G. Booth, John Monks Jnr
d Henry Hathaway *ph* Norbert Brodine *m* David Buttolph
ad Lyle Wheeler, Lewis Creber *ed* Harmon Jones
☆ William Eythe (Bill Dietrich), Lloyd Nolan (Inspector
George A. Briggs), Signe Hasso (Elsa Gebhardt), *Leo G.
Carroll* (Col. Hammersohn), Gene Lockhart (Charles Ogden
Roper), Lydia St Clair (Johanna Schmedt), Harry Bellaver
(Max Coburg)

'Recommended entertainment for those who
believe that naive Americans are no match for wily
Europeans in the spy trade, and for those who just
like their movies to move.' – *Time*

'Imagine an issue of *The March of Time*. The hard
agglomeration of fact; the road drill style; the voice.
Prolong it to four times its usual length, throw in a
fictional climax, and there you have *The House on
92nd Street*.' – *William Whitebait, New Statesman*

👤 original story (Charles G. Booth)

829
The House on 92nd Street

During World War II in New York, the FBI routs Nazi spies after the atomic bomb formula.

A highly influential documentary-style 'now it can be told' spy drama, which borrowed the feel of its producer's *March of Time* series and applied them to a fairly true story set on genuine locations. A modicum of fictional mystery and suspense was added to the narrative of how, during World War II in New York, the FBI routed Nazi spies after the formula for the atomic bomb by the use of a double agent. Hathaway's desire for authenticity led him to use non-professional actors, including some FBI agents, though shooting it in the shadowy style of *film noir*.

The Scarlet Pimpernel

♔♔ GB 1934 98m bw
London Films (Alexander Korda)

w Robert E. Sherwood, Sam Berman, Arthur Wimperis, Lajos Biro *novel* Baroness Orczy *d* Harold Young *ph* Harold Rosson *m* Arthur Benjamin *ed* William Hornbeck
☆ *Leslie Howard* (Sir Percy Blakeney), *Merle Oberon* (Lady Marguerite Blakeney), *Raymond Massey* (Chauvelin), Nigel Bruce (The Prince of Wales), Bramwell Fletcher (The Priest), Anthony Bushell (Sir Andrew Ffoulkes), Joan Gardner (Suzanne de Tournay), Walter Rilla (Armand St. Just)

'Excellent British import that will do business.' – *Variety*

'One of the most romantic and durable of all swashbucklers.' – *New Yorker, 1976*

'A triumph for the British film world.' – *Sunday Times*

● Some scenes were directed by Alexander Korda, others by Rowland Brown, whom Korda replaced after a few days.
● The story was remade as *The Elusive Pimpernel*; in 1982 in a TV version starring Anthony Andrews, and in 1998 in a TV version starring Richard E. Grant. See also *The Return of the Scarlet Pimpernel*.

828
The Scarlet Pimpernel

In the early days of the French revolution, an apparently foppish Englishman leads a daring band in rescuing aristocrats from the guillotine.

In the justified hope of finding a transatlantic audience, Alexander Korda hired an American director, screenwriter, editor and cinematographer for Baroness Orczy's story. The director, Rowland V. Brown was replaced after a few days by another American, Harold Young, who achieved a first-class period adventure with a splendid and much imitated plot, strong characters, humour and a richly detailed historical background. Howard played fop and adventurer with style, and his game of wits with his French adversary (Raymond Massey as a lip-smacking villain) is much to be relished.

Stanley and Livingstone

US 1939 101m bw
TCF (Kenneth MacGowan)

w Philip Dunne, Julien Josephson *d* Henry King *ph* George Barnes *m* David Raksin, David Buttolph, Cyril Mockridge, Alfred Newman *ad* Thomas Little *ed* Barbara McLean
☆ *Spencer Tracy* (Henry M. Stanley), Cedric Hardwicke (Dr. David Livingstone), Richard Greene (Gareth Tyce), Nancy Kelly (Eve Kingsley), Walter Brennan (Jeff Slocum), Charles Coburn (Lord Tyce), Henry Hull (James Gordon Bennett), Henry Travers (John Kingsley), Miles Mander (Sir John Gresham), Holmes Herbert (Frederick Holcomb)

'Sound, worthy, interesting.' – *Richard Mallett, Punch*

'Most of the film consists of long shots of stand-ins moving across undistinguished scenery … Mr Tracy is always a human being, but Sir Cedric is an elocution lesson, a handclasp.' – *Graham Greene*

'Holds box office promise for socko biz … it's absorbing and adventurous drama.' – *Variety*

827
Stanley and Livingstone

An American journalist goes to Africa to find a lost Victorian explorer.

An adventurer meets an explorer ('Dr Livingstone, I presume?') in Darryl Zanuck's prestigious production about the journalist H. M. Stanley's search for the elusive British missionary, who had become lost to the outside world somewhere in Africa. Having found him, Stanley returned to London and was accused of lying before he was vindicated by news of Livingstone's death. From then on, the film departs from the facts, with Stanley returning to Africa to continue Livingstone's work. Spencer Tracy enjoyed the film for the chance it gave him to work with a great actor, Cedric Hardwicke. With the use of footage shot in Africa, Henry King creates the colonial atmosphere of the Victorian era and the genuine heroism of the time.

Speed
US 1994 115m DeLuxe Panavision
TCF (Mark Gordon)

w Graham Yost *d* Jan de Bont *ph* Andrzej Bartkowiak *m* Mike Mancina *pd* Jackson de Govia *ad* John R. Jensen *ed* John Wright

☆ Keanu Reeves (Jack Traven), Dennis Hopper (Howard Payne), Sandra Bullock (Annie), Joe Morton (Captain McMahon), Jeff Daniels (Harry), Alan Ruck (Stephens), Glenn Plummer (Jaguar Owner), Richard Lineback (Norwood), Beth Grant (Helen), Hawthorne James (Sam), Carlos Carrasco (Ortiz)

'A non-stop actioner that rarely pauses to take a breath. While highly derivative and mechanical in planning and execution, this high-octane thrillathon boasts more twists, turns and obstacles than the most hazardous video arcade road raceway.' – *Variety*

🯅 sound (Gregg Landaker, Steve Maslow, Bob Beemer, David R. R. MacMillan); sound effects editing (Stephen Hunter Flick)
🯅 editing
🯅 editing

826
Speed

A mad bomber attempts to hold a city to ransom by planting a bomb on a bus which will explode if the vehicle's speed drops below 50 mph.

Dennis Hopper perfected his performance as a psychopath in this fast, adrenalin-pumping action-packed thriller. Jan de Bont wracks up a high level of suspense. The movie works brilliantly well for the most part, even if the good guys cause more destruction than the bad. It goes off the rails towards the end, but otherwise supplies high-tech twists and thrills in a superior manner.

'Shriek And Shudder.'

'Graves Raided! Coffins Robbed! Corpses Carved! Midnight Murder! Body Blackmail! Stalking Ghouls! Mad Thrills Of Terror And Macabre Mystery!'

The Body Snatcher
US 1945 77m bw
RKO (Val Lewton)

w Philip MacDonald, Carlos Keith (Val Lewton) *story* R. L. Stevenson *d* Robert Wise *ph* Robert de Grasse *m* Roy Webb *ad* Walter E. Keller, Albert S. D'Agostino *ed* J.R. Whittredge

☆ *Henry Daniell* (Dr. MacFarlane), *Boris Karloff* (John Gray), Bela Lugosi (Joseph), Edith Atwater (Meg Camden), Russell Wade (Donald Fettes)

'A humane sincerity and a devotion to good cinema … However, most of the picture is more literary than lively.' – *Time*

825
The Body Snatcher

In 19th-century Edinburgh a doctor obtains 'specimens' from grave-robbers, and murder results when supplies run short.

This was the best of the horror-tinged thrillers produced by the inventive Val Lewton, whose films relied on atmosphere and suggestion rather than graphic terror. Based on Robert Louis Stevenson's story of an Edinburgh doctor who is driven to desperate action by the murderous grave robber he employs to provide him with corpses for his researches, the familiar theme is very imaginatively handled and well acted. Karloff gave one of the most sinister performances of his career, Daniell makes the most of a decent man driven to madness, and Bela Lugosi is effective in a minor role.

The Count of Monte Cristo

US   1934   114m   bw
Reliance (Edward Small)

w Philip Dunne, Dan Totheroh, Rowland V. Lee
novel Alexandre Dumas *d* Rowland V. Lee *ph* Peverell
Marley *m* Alfred Newman *ed* Grant Whytock
☆ *Robert Donat* (Edmond Dantes), Elissa Landi
(Mercedes), Louis Calhern (De Villefort, Jr.), Sidney
Blackmer (Mondego), Raymond Walburn (Danglars), O. P.
Heggie (Abbe Faria), William Farnum (Capt. Leclere)

'A near-perfect blend of thrilling action and grand
dialogue.' – *Variety*

● Remade in France in 1942, 1953 and 1961. Remade for
TV in 1976 with Richard Chamberlain.

824
The Count of Monte Cristo

After spending years in prison, Edmond Dantes escapes and avenges himself on those who framed him.

Alexandre Dumas's much-filmed story of the revenge of Edmond Dantes on the three men who had him falsely imprisoned for years, was turned by Rowland V. Lee into a classic swashbuckler, an engaging, large-scale, melodramatic adventure. The film was originally planned as a 'B' feature with a four week shooting schedule (the producer's company was aptly named after himself, 'Small Pictures'). Donat's film tests, trying out different make-up for the role, were so impressive that the budget was considerably increased. His performance is notably intelligent and romantic without falsity or exaggeration. The film as a whole is extremely well done with due attention to dialogue as well as action; a model of its kind and period.

'Gayest screen event of the year!'

One Hour with You

US   1932   84m   bw
Paramount (Ernst Lubitsch)

w *Samson Raphaelson play Only a Dream* by Lothar
Schmidt *d George Cukor, Ernst Lubitsch ph* Victor Milner
m Oscar Straus, Richard Whiting *ad* Hans Dreier
ed William Shea *ly* Leo Robin
☆ *Maurice Chevalier* (Dr. Andre Bertier), *Jeanette
MacDonald* (Colette Bertier), *Genevieve Tobin* (Mitzi
Olivier), *Roland Young* (Professor Olivier), Charles Ruggles
(Adolph), George Barbier (Police Commissioner)

'Sure fire if frothy screen fare, cinch b.o. at all
times.' – *Variety*

'A brand new form of musical entertainment … he
has mixed verse, spoken and sung, a smart and
satiric musical background, asides to the audience,
and sophisticated dialogue, as well as lilting and
delightful songs … The result is something so
delightful that it places the circle of golden leaves
jauntily upon the knowing head of Hollywood's
most original director.' – *Philadelphia Inquirer*

● A remake of Lubitsch's silent success *The Marriage
Circle*.
⚖ best picture

823
One Hour with You

The affairs of a philandering Parisian doctor.

Maurice Chevalier was never quite happy with his Hollywood films, disliking the way he was typecast as the typical Parisian lover, as he was here. He described this as 'still another film in the same genre with me in uniform, smiles and winks'. It was an accurate description of his role as a philandering French doctor, and one that teamed him again with Jeanette MacDonald. But the difference was that it was directed by Ernst Lubitsch at his most inventive. (George Cukor, the original director, was reduced to a bystander by Lubitsch after a couple of days and had to sue to get a screen credit.) It is a superbly handled comedy of manners, with an extremely capable cast. Unique entertainment of a kind which is, alas, no more.

'The first story of the double-fisted DA who tore apart the evil dynasty that peddled murder for a price!'

The Enforcer
US   1950   87m   bw
United States Pictures/Warner (Milton Sperling)
⬛ ⬛ 🇺🇸 🔍 ⊘
GB title: *Murder, Inc*
w Martin Rackin *d* Bretaigne Windust *ph* Robert Burks *m* David Buttolph *ad* Charles H. Clarke *ed* Fred Allen
☆ Humphrey Bogart (Martin Ferguson), *Everett Sloane* (Albert Mendoza), Zero Mostel (Big Babe Lazich), Ted de Corsia (Joseph Rico), Roy Roberts (Capt. Frank Nelson), King Donovan (Sgt. Whitlow)

'A tough, very slickly-made thriller with a host of fine character parts.' – *NFT, 1969*

'Absorbing and exciting, with little of the violence that so often disfigures films of this kind.' – *Richard Mallett, Punch*

'The first fifteen minutes is as powerful and rapid a sketch of tension as I can recall for seasons. The last fifteen might make Hitch weep with envy.' – *Observer*

● Raoul Walsh directed much of the film, uncredited.

822
The Enforcer

A crusading District Attorney tracks down the leader of a gang which murders for profit.

Bogart is cast as a crusading District Attorney in his final film for Warner Brothers. Told in flashback, after his star witness dies on the eve of the trail and he urgently reviews the evidence, Bogart gives a typically hard-bitten performance. This *film noir*, photographed in stark black and white by Robert Burks, was topical when first released, as a Senate committee was then investigating organized crime. An extremely suspenseful and well-characterized movie based on fact, it is one of the very best of its kind.

Les Enfants du Marais
France   1998   110m   colour   Panavision
UGC/Fechner/France2/Rhone-Alpes/KJB (Jean-Claude Bourlat)
⬛ ⊘
GB title: *Children of the Marshland*
w Sebastian Japrisot *novel* Georges Montforez *d* Jean Becker *ph* Jean-Marie Dreujou *m* Pierre Bachelet *ad* Therese Ripaud *ed* Jacques Witta *cos* Sylvie de Segonzac
☆ Jacques Villeret (Riton), Jacques Gamblin (Garris), Andre Dussollier (Amedée), Michel Serrault (Pépé), Isabelle Carré (Marie), Eric Cantona (Jo Sardi)

'The values celebrated seem stale and contrived rather than warm and vibrant.' – *Ginette Vincendeau, Sight and Sound*

821
Les Enfants du Marais

An old woman remembers life when she was young in the 1930s, living in a hut on the marshes in rural France.

Jean Becker's film is a charming, nostalgic recreation of a vanished time in rural France. It's not quite a pastoral idyll: a sense of melancholy and loss underlies its celebration of the enjoyment of friendship and the simple pleasures of life. Behind its small, enclosed world lie the traumatic effects of the First World War. With convincing performances from its central quartet – an odd-job man, his simple, feckless friend, a wealthy man who remembers his poor beginnings, and a middle-class dreamer – Becker conveys with style uncomplicated human truths.

Love on the Dole
GB   1941   100m   bw
British National (John Baxter)
⊡ ≣ ⊘
w Walter Greenwood, Barbara K. Emery, Rollo Gamble
novel Walter Greenwood *d* John Baxter *ph* James Wilson
m Richard Addinsell *ad* R. Holmes Paul *ed* Michael
Chorlton
☆ *Deborah Kerr* (Sally Hardcastle), Clifford Evans (Larry
Meath), *George Carney* (Mr. Hardcastle), Joyce Howard
(Helen Hawkins), Frank Cellier (Sam Grundy), Geoffrey
Hibbert (Harry Hardcastle), *Mary Merrall* (Mrs. Hardcastle),
Maire O'Neill (Mrs. Dorbell), *Marjorie Rhodes* (Mrs. Bull),
A. Bromley Davenport (Pawnbroker), Marie Ault (Mrs. Jilke),
Iris Vandeleur (Mrs. Nattle), Kenneth Griffith (Tom Hare)

820
Love on the Dole

Life among unemployed cotton workers in industrial Lancashire between the wars.

Walter Greenwood's classic novel was turned into an old-fashioned social melodrama, and can be seen as a precurser of the working-class kitchen-sink dramas of the 1960s. The narrative, based on Greenwood's own experiences in the slums of Salford, is vividly characterized, as a mill-girl sees the unemployed man she loves but cannot afford to marry, die from consumption, and gives herself to a rich bookie in the hope he will help her family to survive. Baxter spent five years arguing with the British censors, who felt the film was 'very coarse', before shooting this well-made adaptation that captures the threadbare ambience of the time, perhaps helped by the fact that it was itself a low-budget production.

49th Parallel
GB   1941   123m   bw
GFD/Ortus (John Sutro, Michael Powell)
⊡ ≣ ⊚ ⊘
US title: *The Invaders*
w Emeric Pressburger, Rodney Ackland *d* Michael Powell
ph F. A. Young *m* Ralph Vaughan Williams *ad* David
Rawnsley *ed* David Lean
☆ *Eric Portman* (Lt. Hirth), Laurence Olivier (Johnnie),
Anton Walbrook (Peter), *Leslie Howard* (Philip Armstrong
Scott), *Raymond Massey* (Andy Brock), Glynis Johns
(Anna), Niall MacGinnis (Vogel), Finlay Currie (Factor),
Raymond Lovell (Lt. Kuhnecke), John Chandos (Lohrmann)

'Some of the plotting and characterization look
rather rusty at this remove, but the sense of
landscape and figures passing through it remains
authoritatively dynamic.' – *Tony Rayns, Time Out,
1979*

'An admirable piece of work from every point of
view.' – *MFB*

♟ original story (Emeric Pressburger)
♟ best picture; script

819
49th Parallel

In Canada, five stranded U-boat men try to escape into the US.

This wartime propaganda piece must have been confusing at the time of its first release since the German group, though ruthless, are shown as brave and resourceful. Eric Portman, as their leader, gave a strong performance that made him a film actor to be reckoned with, and there is also an effective, smaller role, with a good death scene, from Laurence Olivier as a French Canadian who sacrifices himself for the good of the cause. An episodic movie, it develops some nice Hitchcockian touches along the way.

Folies Bergère

Folies Bergère
US 1935 84m bw
Twentieth Century (William Goetz, Raymond Griffith)
GB title: *The Man from the Folies Bergère*
w Bess Meredyth, Hal Long *play* *The Red Cat* by Rudolph
Lothar, Hans Adler *d* Roy del Ruth *ph* Barney McGill,
Peverell Marley *md* Alfred Newman *ch* Dave Gould
ad William Darling *ed* Allen McNeil, Sherman Todd
☆ *Maurice Chevalier* (Eugene Charlier/Fernand, the Baron
Cassini), Merle Oberon (Baroness Genevieve Cassini), Ann
Sothern (Mimi), Eric Blore (Francois)
● Remade as *That Night in Rio*, with Don Ameche, and *On
the Riviera*, with Danny Kaye.
👤 Dave Gould

818
Folies Bergère

A Parisian banker persuades a music-hall artist to impersonate him, but the wife and girlfriend become involved in the confusion.

Maurice Chevalier was tiring of Hollywood, and Hollywood of him, when he made this, his last US film for many years. His films seemed increasingly old-fashioned, as did the character he played, of a seductive Frenchman. This, however, was an excellent star vehicle in which he played two roles, that of a Parisian banker and the music-hall artist he persuades to impersonate him; the subsequent confusion involves the banker's wife and mistress. It had inventive Busby Berkeleyish numbers and some remarkably sexy dialogue to recommend it. The French language version was an improvement in one way: in France, the dancers of the Folies Bergère were bare breasted; in the American version they wore bras.

Cousin, Cousine
France 1975 95m Eastmancolor
Pomereu/Gaumont (Bertrand Javal)
🎞 ▬ ⌖
wd Jean-Charles Tacchella *ph* Georges Lendi *m* Gerard
Anfosso *ed* Agnès Guillemot
☆ Marie-France Pisier (Karine), Marie-Christine Barrault
(Marthe), Victor Lanoux (Ludovic), Guy Marchand (Pascal),
Ginette Garcin (Biju)

'One of those rare delights you want to see again and again just to share the sheer joy of living, zest for love, genuine affection, all-too-human absurdity, and pure happiness of all those delicious people on screen.' – *Judith Crist, Saturday Review*

🏆 best foreign film; script; Marie-Christine Barrault

817
Cousin, Cousine

Various furtive love affairs centre on a family wedding.

Jean-Charles Tacchella's sprightly satirical comedy is full of pleasing touches, mostly jibes at French bourgeois standards. It is also a celebration of the possibilities of romantic love. The attraction between Marthe and Ludovic, both married to unsatisfactory and promiscuous partners, is instant when they meet, though they postpone immediate consummation of their feelings to enjoy the pleasure they take in each other's existence. Set at two weddings and a funeral, Tacchella observes the hypocrisies of middle-class family relationships and celebrations with a beady eye, while allowing his two leading characters to charm with the contrasting honesty of their emotions.

Charley Varrick
US 1973 111m Technicolor Panavision
Universal (Don Siegel)

w Howard Rodman, Dean Riesner *novel The Looters* by John Reese *d* Don Siegel *ph* Michael Butler *m* Lalo Schifrin *ad* Fernando Carrere *ed* Frank Morriss
☆ *Walter Matthau* (Charley Varrick), Joe Don Baker (Molly), Felicia Farr (Sybil Fort), Andy Robinson (Harman Sullivan), John Vernon (Maynard Boyle), Sheree North (Jewell Everett), Norman Fell (Mr. Garfinkle)

'It proves there is nothing wrong with an auteur director that a good script can't cure.' – *Stanley Kauffmann*

'The narrative line is clean and direct, the characterizations economical and functional, and the triumph of intelligence gloriously satisfying.' – *Andrew Sarris*

🏆 Walter Matthau

816
Charley Varrick

A bank robber discovers he has stolen Mafia money, and devises a clever scheme to get himself off the hook.

A sharp, smart and well-observed thriller. Walter Matthau, its star, and director Don Siegel had conflicting ideas about the script – Matthau liked actions explained in advance, Siegel didn't. Siegel felt that Matthau's negative attitude, expressed to everyone, prevented the film becoming a success. Implausible it may be, but, astringently handled and agreeably set in Californian backlands, it is accomplished entertainment.

Bringing Out the Dead
US 1999 120m DeLuxe Panavision
Buena Vista/Paramount/Touchstone (Scott Rudin, Barbara De Fina)

w Paul Schrader *novel* Joe Connelly *d* Martin Scorsese *ph* Robert Richardson *m* Elmer Bernstein *pd* Dante Ferretti *ad* Robert Guerra *ed* Thelma Schoonmaker *sp* Industrial Light & Magic
☆ Nicolas Cage (Frank Pierce), Patricia Arquette (Mary Burke), John Goodman (Larry), Ving Rhames (Marcus), Tom Sizemore (Tom Wolls), Marc Anthony (Noel), Mary Beth Hurt (Nurse Constance), Cliff Curtis (Cy Coates), Nestor Serrano (Dr Hazmat), Aida Turturro (Nurse Crupp)

'An intense, volatile movie full of sorrow and wild, mordant humor.' – *Janet Maslin, New York Times*

'This is a work of bad imitation from an immature talent who thinks he's Martin Scorsese.' – *Cosmo Landesman, Sunday Times*

815
Bringing Out the Dead

In New York City, an overworked ambulance driver careers towards a breakdown over the unremitting horrors of his night shift.

Scorsese revisits familiar territory for him and his audience: a hellish city of low-life predators and hapless victims, an urban nightmare of dim alleys and garish streets inhabited by the dead and the dying. But his perspective has shifted from his customary petty gangsters and psychopaths to the good guys, however unbalanced they may seem. Despair is here tempered with humanity. As an ambulance driver's nerves frazzle, he is reminded that his suffering is self-inflicted: no one asked him to be a martyr. He knows, as does Scorsese, that it is necessary for someone to be a witness to suffering.

'He plucked from the gutter a faded rose and made an immortal masterpiece!'

The Life of Emile Zola
US   1937   116m   bw
Warner (Henry Blanke)
■ 📷

w Norman Reilly Raine *story* Heinz Herald and Geza Herczeg *d* William Dieterle *ph* Tony Gaudio *m* Max Steiner *ad* Anton Grot *ed* Warren Low
☆ *Paul Muni* (Emile Zola), *Joseph Schildkraut* (Capt. Alfred Dreyfus), Gale Sondergaard (Lucie Dreyfus), Gloria Holden (Alexandrine Zola), Donald Crisp (Maitre Labori), Erin O'Brien Moore (Nana), John Litel (Charpentier), Henry O'Neill (Col. Picquart), Morris Carnovsky (Anatole France), Ralph Morgan (Commander of Paris), Louis Calhern (Maj. Dort), Robert Barrat (Maj. Walsin-Esterhazy), Vladimir Sokoloff (Paul Cezanne), Harry Davenport (Chief of Staff), Robert Warwick (Maj. Henry) and also Walter Kingsford

'Destined to box office approval of the most substantial character. It is finely made and merits high rating as cinema art and significant recognition as major showmanship.' – *Variety*

'Rich, dignified, honest and strong, it is at once the finest historical film ever made and the greatest screen biography.' – *New York Times*

🏆 best picture; script; Joseph Schildkraut
🏅 original story; William Dieterle; Max Steiner; Paul Muni; Anton Grot

'They leap from the book and live!'

Little Women
👫 US   1933   115m   bw
RKO (David O. Selznick, Merian C. Cooper, Kenneth MacGowan)
▭ ■ 📷 〰

w Sarah Y. Mason, Victor Heerman *novel* Louisa May Alcott *d* George Cukor *ph* Henry Gerrard *m* Max Steiner *ad* Van Nest Polglase *ed* Jack Kitchin
☆ *Katharine Hepburn* (Jo), Paul Lukas (Prof. Fritz Bhaer), Joan Bennett (Amy), Frances Dee (Meg), Jean Parker (Beth), *Spring Byington* (Marmee), Edna May Oliver (Aunt March), Douglass Montgomery (Laurie), Henry Stephenson (Mr. Laurence), Samuel S. Hinds (Mr. March), John Lodge (Brooke), Nydia Westman (Mamie)

'If to put a book on the screen with all the effectiveness that sympathy and good taste and careful artifice can devise is to make a fine motion picture, then *Little Women* is a fine picture.' – *James Shelley Hamilton*

'One of the most satisfactory pictures I have ever seen.' – *E. V. Lucas, Punch*

'A reminder that emotions and vitality and truth can be evoked from lavender and lace as well as from machine guns and precision dances.' – *Thornton Delehanty, New York Post*

🏆 script
🏅 best picture; George Cukor
● Remade by MGM in 1949

814
The Life of Emile Zola

The French writer intervenes in the case of Alfred Dreyfus, condemned unjustly to Devil's Island.

The stylish direction and photography of this Hollywood biopic, coupled with Paul Muni's superb performance in the title role, have given it a lasting appeal. The narrative follows the standard Hollywood biographical format, of its protagonist going from rags to riches, before concentrating on the event that threatened Zola's fame and fortune: his championing of the case of Alfred Dreyfus, condemned unjustly to Devil's Island. Raine's script ignores the anti-semitism that lay behind the Dreyfus case, but gives full opportunity for Muni to exploit the complete range of his talents, as the bitter young writer, the successful author and angry campaigner and public conscience.

813
Little Women

The growing up of four sisters in pre-Civil War America.

George Cukor was startled when he first read Louisa May Alcott's novel, after David Selznick asked him to direct the film. He expected it to be sentimental, but discovered it had the qualities he brought to life in this adaptation: 'very strong-minded, full of character and a wonderful picture of New England family life.' It maintains the episodic nature of the book and is elevated by Hepburn as the tomboy Jo, a performance that also helped raise the acting of the others. It stands as a testament not only to a classic book, but a period of Hollywood's highest production values.

The Women

US 1939 132m bw (Technicolor sequence)
MGM (Hunt Stromberg)

▦ ◷ ◉

w Anita Loos, Jane Murfin *play* Clare Boothe *d* George
Cukor *ph* Oliver T. Marsh, Joseph Ruttenberg *m* Edward
Ward, David Snell *ad* Cedric Gibbons, Wade B. Rubottom
ed Robert J. Kern

☆ *Norma Shearer* (Mary Haines), Joan Crawford (Chrystal
Allen), *Rosalind Russell* (Sylvia Fowler), Mary Boland
(Countess DeLave), Paulette Goddard (Miriam Aarons),
Joan Fontaine (Peggy Day), Lucile Watson (Mrs.
Moorehead), Phyllis Povah (Edith Potter), Virginia Weidler
(Little Mary), Ruth Hussey (Miss Watts), Margaret Dumont
(Mrs. Wagstaff), Marjorie Main (Lucy), Hedda Hopper (Dolly
Dupuyster)

'Smash hit of solid proportions for extended runs
and heavy profits … a strong woman entry but still
has plenty of spicy lines and situations for the
men.' – *Variety*

'So marvellous that we believe every Hollywood
studio should make at least one thoroughly nasty
picture a year.' – *New York Times*

'Whether you go or not depends on whether you
can stand Miss Shearer with tears flowing steadily
in all directions at once, and such an endless damn
back fence of cats.' – *Otis Ferguson*

● Remade 1956 as *The Opposite Sex* (musicalized version).

The Little Foxes

US 1941 116m bw
Samuel Goldwyn

▭ ▬ ▦ ◷ ◉

w Lillian Hellman *play* Lillian Hellman *d* William Wyler
ph Gregg Toland *m* Meredith Willson *ad* Stephen
Goosson *ed* Daniel Mandell

☆ *Bette Davis* (Regina Hubbard Giddens), *Herbert
Marshall* (Horace Giddens), *Teresa Wright* (Alexandra
Giddens), Richard Carlson (David Hewitt), *Charles Dingle*
(Ben Hubbard), *Dan Duryea* (Leo Hubbard), *Carl Benton
Reid* (Oscar Hubbard), *Patricia Collinge* (Birdie Hubbard),
Jessica Grayson (Addie), Russell Hicks (William Marshall)

'One of the really beautiful jobs in the whole range
of movie making.' – *Otis Ferguson*

'No one knows better than Wyler when to shift the
camera's point of view, when to cut, or how to
relate the characters in one shot to those in the
next … you never have to wonder where you are in
a Wyler picture.' – *Arthur Knight*

♟ best picture; Lillian Hellman; William Wyler; Meredith
Willson; Bette Davis; Teresa Wright; Patricia Collinge;
Stephen Goosson; Daniel Mandell

812
The Women

A New York socialite gets a divorce but later thinks better of it.

George Cukor thought the point of *The Women* had been lost with
changing attitudes to sexual morality. '"Kept women" and marital
break-ups were big moral questions then. Now, of course, everybody
would be screwing everybody,' he told critic Gavin Lambert in 1973.
Yet the movie holds up remarkably well, despite the fact that censors
removed many of the funniest lines from the stage play. With Anita
Loos on hand to provide new jokes, this bitchy comedy drama, distinguished by an all-girl cast, is an over-generous slice of real theatre,
skilfully adapted, with rich sets, plenty of laughs, and some memorable
scenes between the fighting ladies.

811
The Little Foxes

*A family of schemers in post-Civil War days will stop at nothing to
outwit each other.*

William Wyler made a superb film of Lillian Hellman's brilliant play. It is
a study in greed, with Davis's Regina as the greediest and least good of
a decadent Southern family. Davis walked off the film for a time after
Wyler tried to make her performance softer and sexier. She is memorably chilling, and Wyler was more successful in coaxing the excellent
characterizations he wanted from the rest of the cast. The film is excellent to look at and listen to, with a compelling narrative line and memorable performances.

Bagdad Café

West Germany 1988 91m Eastmancolor
Mainline/Pelemele/Pro-Ject (Percy and Eleonore Adlon)

▣ ▤ ⊚ ⊚ ∩

aka: *Out of Rosenheim*

w Percy and Eleonore Adlon, Christopher Doherty *d* Percy Adlon *ph* Bernd Heinl *m* Bob Telson *ad* Bernt Amadeus Capra *ed* Norbert Herzner

☆ *Marianne Sägebrecht* (Jasmin Munchgstettner), Jack Palance (Rudi Cox), C. C. H. Pounder (Brenda), Christine Kaufmann (Debbie), Monica Calhoun (Phyllis), Darron Flagg (Sal Junior)

● The success of the film resulted in an American TV series starring Whoopi Goldberg.

🎵 song 'Calling You' (*m/ly* Bob Telson)

Bagdad Café

A middle-aged Bavarian woman, left stranded in the Mojave desert by her husband, transforms a seedy motel she stumbles across.

German director Percy Adlon ventured into the Mojave desert for his first English-language film, a high-spirited comedy. Left stranded by her husband after a row, a bulky, middle-aged Bavarian woman staggers out of the sun and into a rundown, seedy motel, run by an abrasive and harrassed woman with an idle husband and difficult children. The relationship between these two contrasting women provides much gentle wit and charm, as the German hausfrau works a transformation on the motel, its eccentric regulars and herself. Marianne Sägebrecht's performance, graceful and imperturbable, holds it all together wonderfully in this delightful collision between two cultures at a spot where the American dream had evaporated.

'One man … three women … one night!'

The Night of the Iguana

US 1964 125m bw
MGM/Seven Arts (Ray Stark)

▣ ▤ ⊚~

w Anthony Veiller *play* Tennessee Williams *d* John Huston *ph* Gabriel Figueroa *m* Benjamin Frankel *ad* Stephen Grimes *ed* Ralph Kemplen

☆ *Richard Burton* (Rev. T. Lawrence Shannon), Deborah Kerr (Hannah Jelkes), Ava Gardner (Maxine Faulk), Sue Lyon (Charlotte Goodall), *Grayson Hall* (Judith Fellowes), *Cyril Delevanti* (Nonno)

'Whatever poetry it had seems to have leaked out.' – *New Yorker, 1982*

🎵 Gabriel Figueroa; Grayson Hall

The Night of the Iguana

A disbarred clergyman becomes a travel courier in Mexico and is sexually desired by a teenage nymphomaniac, a middle-aged hotel owner and a frustrated itinerant artist.

John Huston fought with producer Ray Stark over making the picture in black and white, and won the argument. Later, he decided it would have been better in colour. But the monochrome cinematography of Gabriel Figueroa brilliantly coveys the hothouse atmosphere of Tennessee William's story of the disgraced, lusty priest who becomes an alcoholic travel courier in Mexico ('Tours of God's World Conducted by a Man of God'). Burton gives one of his best screen performances in his scenes with three contrasting women, Sue Lyon's teenage nymphomaniac, Deborah Kerr's frustrated artist and Ava Gardner's free spirited hotel owner. It is a sharp, funny picture with a touch of poetry.

'Things fall down. People look up. And when it rains, it pours.'

Magnolia
US 1999 188m DeLuxe Panavision
New Line/Ghoulardi (Joanne Sellar)
📼 ▬ ⊘ ⊙ ⌒
wd Paul Thomas Anderson *ph* Robert Elswit *m* John Brion *m/ly* Aimee Mann *pd* William Arnold, Mark Bridges *ed* Dylan Tichenor
☆ Jason Robards (Earl Partridge), Julianne Moore (Linda Partridge), *Tom Cruise* (Frank Mackey), Philip Seymour Hoffman (Phil Parma), *John C. Reilly* (Officer Jim Kurring), Melora Walters (Claudia Gator), Philip Baker Hall (Jimmy Gator), Melinda Dillon (Rose Gator), Jeremy Blackman (Stanley Spector), Michael Bowen (Rick Spector), William H. Macy (Donnie Smith), Emmanuel Johnson (Dixon)

‘May be self-regarding and pretentious, but there are some fiendishly clever moments.’ – *James Christopher, Times*

‘A remarkably inventive and audacious film that almost overcomes its flaws.’ – *Emanuel Levy, Variety*

♟ Tom Cruise; Paul Thomas Anderson; song ‘Save Me’ (m/l Aimee Mann)

808
Magnolia

In Los Angeles, the lives of various dysfunctional people coincidentally intertwine and interact.

Paul Thomas Anderson’s sprawling, episodic drama examines various unhappy, dysfunctional people. There’s a dying father, suffused with guilt, his hysterical wife, an estranged, misogynistic son, an unloved cop, a bullying father and his clever, timid son, and a dying games-show host and his estranged daughter. There is a moment, towards the end, that emphasizes Anderson’s manipulation of his characters: one begins to sing, and he cuts to another, and another, and another, and they are all singing the same song. Forgive him this, and the Biblical ending, and what is left is a clever, intense movie about relationships and the need for love among a group who never connect.

'The most beautiful love story ever told.'

Beauty and the Beast
👫 US 1991 85m Technicolor
Buena Vista/Walt Disney/Silver Screen Partners IV (Don Hahn)
📼 ▬ ⊛ ⊘ ⊙ ⌒
w Linda Woolverton *d* Gary Trousdale, Kirk Wise *m/ly* Alan Menken, Howard Ashman *ad* Brian McEntee *ed* John Carnochan
☆ Featuring the voices of Paige O’Hara, Robby Benson, Jerry Orbach, Angela Lansbury, Richard White, David Ogden Stiers, Jesse Corti, Rex Everhart, Bradley Michael Pierce, Jo Anne Worley, Kimmy Robertson

‘A lovely film that ranks with the best of Disney’s animated classics.’ – *Variety*

‘It’s got storytelling vigour and clarity, bright eclectic animation, and a frisky musical wit.’ – *New Yorker*

♟ Alan Menken; song ‘Beauty and the Beast’ (*m* Alan Menken, *ly* Howard Ashman)
♟ film; song ‘Belle’; song ‘Be Our Guest’; sound

807
Beauty and the Beast

A prince, turned into a beast by enchantment, is rescued by the love of a beautiful girl.

Disney’s excellent movie was the first indication for years that musicals were not entirely dead. The fairy tale had a lilting, singable score. Belle is a welcome improvement on the often bland Disney heroines of the past and there’s fun to be had from such individual characters as the candelabra Lumiere and Mrs Potts the teapot. There’s wit in the script and the animation, which is detailed without being fussy, with more than a touch of Busby Berkeley in the big production numbers. It is a classic of animation.

Carry On up the Khyber

GB   1968   88m   Eastmancolor
Rank/Adder (Peter Rogers)

⬛ ▦ ◎

w Talbot Rothwell d Gerald Thomas ph Alan Hume
m Eric Rogers ad Alex Vetchinsky ed Alfred Roome
☆ Sidney James (Sir Sidney Ruff-Diamond), Kenneth
Williams (Khazi of Kalabar), Charles Hawtrey (Pvt. James
Widdle), Joan Sims (Lady Ruff-Diamond), Roy Castle (Capt.
Keene), Bernard Bresslaw (Bungdit Din), Peter Butterworth
(The Missionary), Terry Scott (Sgt. Maj. MacNutt), Angela
Douglas (Princess Jelhi), Cardew Robinson (The Fakir),
Julian Holloway (Maj. Shorthouse), Peter Gilmore (Ginger)

'Continues to rely primarily on low-comedy visual
and verbal gag situations for its yocks.' – *Variety*

● The movie was filmed in Wales.

806
Carry On up the Khyber

A Scots regiment, the Third Foot and Mouth, fails to defend British interests in India.

Britain's long-running, low-budget series of Carry On movies reached its zenith with this wonderfully vulgar and ripe low comedy on an imperial theme. Set in India, though filmed in the mountains of Wales, its story is a glorious subversion of the many cinematic celebrations of Empire and Kipling (and if you've never kippled, this is the place to start). At the climax, Sir Sidney Ruff-Diamond and his guests display aplomb and stiff upper lips at dinner while the Burpas under the command of the Khazi of Kalabar attack the residency, and the air is filled with the sound of single entendres.

The Charge of the Light Brigade

US   1936   115m   bw
Warner (Hal B. Wallis, Sam Bischoff)

▦ ◎ 🎧

w Michel Jacoby, Rowland Leigh d Michael Curtiz
ph Sol Polito, Fred Jackman m Max Steiner md Leo
Forbstein ad John Hughes ed George Amy
☆ *Errol Flynn* (Major Geoffrey Vickers), Olivia de
Havilland (Elsa Campbell), Patric Knowles (Capt. Perry
Vickers), Donald Crisp (Col Campbell), David Niven (Capt.
Randall), Henry Stephenson (Sir Charles Macefield), Nigel
Bruce (Sir Benjamin Warrenton), *C. Henry Gordon* (Surat
Kahn), Spring Byington (Lady Octavia Warrenton), E. E.
Clive (Sir Humphrey Harcourt), Robert Barrat (Count Igor
Volonoff), J. Carrol Naish (Subahdar-Major Puran Singh)

'When the noble six hundred, lances level and
stirrups touching, pace, canter and, finally, charge
down the mile-long valley, with the enemy guns
tearing great holes in their ranks, you are a dead
stock if your pulses don't thunder and your heart
quicken perceptibly. This scene may be villainous
history, but it is magnificent cinema, timed, shot,
and cut with brilliance. It only cramps the patriotic
effect a trifle that the Union Jack, nine times out of
ten in the picture, is shown resolutely flying upside
down.' – *C. A. Lejeune*

♟ Max Steiner

805
The Charge of the Light Brigade

An army officer deliberately starts the Balaclava charge to even an old score with Surat Khan, who is on the other side.

Michael Curtiz's movie is magnificent, but it is not history. It is a travesty of the actual event, though allegedly 'based on the poem by Alfred Lord Tennyson'. Most of the invented story takes place in India, where a former ally, the warlord Surat Khan, massacres British captives, women and children. An army officer deliberately starts the charge at Balaclava to gain retribution against Khan, who is fighting with the Russians. As pure entertainment, it is a most superior slice of Hollywood hokum, with the actual charge being a moment of high excitement. The film set the seal on Errol Flynn's superstardom.

The Spiral Staircase
US   1945   83m   bw
RKO (Dore Schary)

w Mel Dinelli novel Some Must Watch by Ethel Lina White
d Robert Siodmak ph Nicholas Musuraca m Roy Webb
ad Albert S. D'Agostino, Jack Okey ed Harry Marker, Harry Gerstad
☆ Dorothy McGuire (Helen Capel), George Brent (Prof. Warren), Kent Smith (Dr. Parry), Ethel Barrymore (Mrs. Warren), Rhys Williams (Mr. Oates), Rhonda Fleming (Blanche), Gordon Oliver (Steve Warren), Sara Allgood (Nurse Barker), James Bell (Constable)

'A nice, cosy and well-sustained atmosphere of horror.' – C. A. Lejeune

☖ Ethel Barrymore
● Remade 1975

804
The Spiral Staircase

A small town in 1906 New England is terrorized by a psychopathic killer of deformed girls.

Robert Siodmak opens with the murder of a girl unable to defend herself in this creepy thriller. It is an archetypal old dark house thriller, superbly detailed and set during a most convincing thunderstorm. Dorothy McGuire's performance as a mute maid, scared that she will be the killer's next victim, is a moving one; her inability to speak adds a extra chill to the shadowy, psychological drama. Even though the identity of the villain is pretty obvious, this is a superior Hollywood product.

Will It Snow for Christmas?
France   1996   91m   colour
Artificial Eye/Ognon (Danny Lebigot)

original title: Y'Aura T'il de la Neige à Noël?
wd Sandrine Veysset ph Hélène Louvart m Henri Ancillotti ad Jacques Dubus ed Nelly Quettier
☆ Dominique Reymond (The Mother), Daniel Duval (The Father), Jessica Martinez (Jeanne), Alexandre Roger (Bruno), Xavier Colonna (Pierrot), Fanny Rochetin (Marie)

'If it does happen to snow for Christmas, make a snowman, slide down Ben Nevis on a tea tray, teach your grandma to ski, anything – just don't seek shelter in a cinema showing this miserable tale.' – Giala Murray, Empire

803
Will It Snow for Christmas?

In rural France, a married farmer's lover and their seven children scratch a bare living from the land.

Sandrine Veysset's film is a bleak, minimalist drama of poverty and maternal love. The film's slow rhythms are those of the seasons as the family undertake backbreaking work in the fields. The family is held together by the mother, tired, overworked and under-appreciated by the children's absentee and bullying father. But the life of the farm and the film resides in the children, in their spontaneity, resilience and affection for their mother. The result is a hypnotically unforgettable film.

Toy Story 2
US   1999   92m   Technicolor
Buena Vista/Walt Disney/Pixar (Helene Plotkin, Karen Robert Jackson)

w Andrew Stanton, Rita Hsiao, Doug Chamberlin, Chris Webb, John Lasseter, Pete Docter, Ash Brannon *d* John Lasseter, Lee Unkrich, Ash Brannon *ph* Sharon Calahan *m* Randy Newman *pd* William Cone, Jim Pearson *ad* Matt White *ed* Edie Bleiman, David Ian Salter, Lee Unkrich

☆ Featuring voices of: Tom Hanks, Tim Allen, Joan Cusack, Kelsey Grammer, Don Rickles, Jim Varney, Wallace Shawn, John Ratzenberger, Wayne Knight, John Morris, Laurie Metcalf

'It is not a sequel. It is an upgrade. It is a manufacturer's improvement of staggering ingenuity. It is a software refinement. It is a species leap, a higher order of being.' – *Peter Bradshaw, Guardian*

'A movie that is dazzlingly inventive in its graphic detail, tells an exciting, sophisticated story and raises complex ideas with clarity and wit.' – *Philip French, Observer*

♫ song 'When She Loved Me' (m/l Randy Newman)

802
Toy Story 2

A wicked toyshop owner steals the cowboy Woody so that he can complete a set of toys, rare collectables on a 50s TV show, and sell them to a Japanese museum.

John Lasseter and Pixar created a classic movie, the first feature to use computer animation, with *Toy Story* about the meeting of two toys, a cowboy and a spaceman. This sequel's narrative, lacking the darker impulses of the first film, is not as resonant, though it shows an advance in technique over the original. It is, though, a witty, brilliantly realized comedy of celebrity and obsolescence.

Sing As We Go

GB 1934 80m bw
ATP (Basil Dean)
w J. B. Priestley, Gordon Wellesley d Basil Dean
ph Robert G. Martin ad J. Elder Wills ed Thorold
Dickinson
☆ Gracie Fields (Gracie Platt), John Loder (Hugh
Phillips), Frank Pettingell (Murgatroyd Platt), Dorothy
Hyson (Phyllis Logan), Stanley Holloway (Policeman)

'We have an industrial north that is bigger than
Gracie Fields running around a Blackpool fun fair.'
– C. A. Lejeune

801
Sing As We Go

An unemployed mill-girl gets various holiday jobs in Blackpool.

You can almost smell the tripe and onions in this cheerful Gracie Fields' film, scripted by J. B. Priestley. The plot is a simple one – but it provided scope for Fields to show off her singing voice and display her comic timing in funny episodes. The finale, with the mill-girls returning to work while Gracie Fields leads them in a chorus of the title song, makes a heart-touching climax. It's a splendid, pawky star vehicle which, because it was filmed on location, is also the best picture we have of industrial Lancashire in the thirties. Great fun.

'See the sleepwalker, floating down the street, ripped from some nightmare! A street of misshapen houses with brooding windows, streaked by dagger strokes of light and darkened by blots of shadow! You will immediately feel the terror in the movements of that floating grotesque!'

The Cabinet of Dr Caligari

Germany 1919 90m approx (16 fps) bw
silent
Decla-Bioscop (Erich Pommer)
🎞 ▬ ✍ ◉ ◉
w Carl Mayer, Hans Janowitz d Robert Wiene ph Willy
Hameister ad Hermann Warm, Walter Röhrig, Walter
Reiman
☆ Werner Krauss, Conrad Veidt, Lil Dagover, Friedrich
Feher, Hans von Twardowski

'The first hundred shocks are the hardest.' – *New
York Evening Post, 1924*

● The film cost $18,000 to make.
● The Region 2 DVD release includes a commentary by
film scholar Mike Budd and an excerpt from *Genuine: A Tale
of a Vampire* (1920).
● Remade 1962 by Twentieth-Century-Fox.

800
The Cabinet of Dr Caligari

A fairground showman uses a somnambulist for purposes of murder and is finally revealed to be the director of a lunatic asylum; but the whole story is only the dream of a madman.

A film of immense influence on the dramatic art of cinema, with its odd angles, stylized sets and hypnotic acting. The sting in the tail was added by the producer, on the suggestion of Fritz Lang, who had intended to direct the film. The original screenwriters, the Czech poet Hans Janowitz and the Austrian playwright Carl Mayer, were dismayed by the alteration, which meant that the film no longer carried a revolutionary message about the madness of power. Their work, nevertheless, did bring about a change in cinema, opening the way to new approaches and experimentation.

Soldier of Orange

Netherlands   1977   colour
 (Rob Houwer)
◉ ◉

original title: *Soldaat Van Oranje*
w Gerard Soeteman, Paul Verhoeven, Kees Holierhoek
autobiography Erik Hazelhoff Roelfzema *d* Paul Verhoeven
ph Jost Vacano, Jan De Bont *m* Rogier Van Otterloo
ad Roland De Groot *ed* Jane Speer
☆ Rutger Hauer (Erik), Jeroen Krabbe (Gus), Peter Faber
(Will), Derek De Lint (Alex), Eddy Habbema (Robby), Lex
Van Delden (Nico), Edward Fox (Colonel Rafelli), Susan
Penhaligon (Susan), Andrea Domburh (Queen Wilhelmina),
Belinda Meuldijk (Esther)

'The physical production is impressive, but key plot
points are often too obscure for an action film so
full of boyish high spirits.' – *Vincent Canby, New
York Times*

'So crowded with character, adventure, intriguing
moral quandries and delightful humor that its two
and a half hours fly by without a lull.' – *Kevin
Thomas, Los Angeles Times*

• The Region 1 DVD release has commentary by
Verhoeven.

799
Soldier of Orange

*A group of university friends react in different ways after the Nazi inva-
sion of Holland.*

Verhoeven's sprawling epic of the Second World War concentrates on
the reaction of a group of university friends to the sudden and unexpected Nazi invasion of Holland. Some opt for the resistance, some
become collaborators, one joins the SS, and others try to keep out of
trouble. A suspenseful drama of loss, betrayal, ineffectual heroism and
national confusion, it is also study of a exuberant adventurer whose
naively romantic ideas of war are finally displaced by its grubby reality.

Yankee Doodle Dandy

US   1942   126m   bw
Warner (Hal B. Wallis, William Cagney)
▣ ▤ ◈ ◉ ◎
w Robert Buckner, Edmund Joseph *d* Michael Curtiz
ph James Wong Howe *m* Heinz Roemheld *md* Heinz
Roemheld, Ray Heindorf *ad* Carl Jules Weyl *ed* George
Amy *songs* George M. Cohan
☆ *James Cagney* (George M. Cohan), Joan Leslie (Mary),
Walter Huston (Jerry Cohan), Rosemary de Camp (Nellie
Cohan), Richard Whorf (Sam Harris), George Tobias (Dietz),
Jeanne Cagney (Josie Cohan), Irene Manning (Fay
Templeton), S. Z. Sakall (Schwab), George Barbier
(Erlanger), Frances Langford (Nora Bayes), Walter Catlett
(Manager), Eddie Foy Jnr (Eddie Foy)

'Possibly the most genial screen biography ever
made.' – *Time*

• Cohan wanted Fred Astaire to play him, but Jack Warner
insisted on Cagney for the role.
♫ 'Harrigan'; 'The Yankee Doodle Boy'; 'Give My Regards
to Broadway'; 'Oh, You Wonderful Girl'; 'Mary's a Grand Old
Name'; 'So Long, Mary'; 'You're a Grand Old Flag'; 'Over
There'.
♟ music direction; James Cagney
♟ best picture; original story (Robert Buckner); Michael
Curtiz; Walter Huston; George Amy

798
Yankee Doodle Dandy

The life story of dancing vaudevillian George M. Cohan.

James Cagney always regarded himself as a song-and-dance man,
however much Warner typecast him as a gangster. Here he gives a
marvellous, magnetic star performance as the dancing vaudevillian,
showman and patriotic songwriter George M. Cohan. He doesn't dance
so much as strut, a cocky, arrogant, stiff-legged swagger that can convince he is in a class with Astaire; he doesn't sing so much as talk, a
rhythmic chant that somehow gives a winning impetus to the melody.
The story, told in flashback to President Roosevelt, does not deviate
from the usual formula for such films, though Cohan stipulated that it
should include no love scenes. It is Cagney's dynamic performance
that makes it an outstanding showbiz biopic, with unassuming but
effective production.

Diner
US   1982   110m   Technicolor
MGM/SLM (Jerry Weintraub)
▦ ▤ ⬚~ ◎ ⌒
wd Barry Levinson *ph* Peter Sova *m* Bruce Brody, Ivan Kral *pd* Leon Harris *ad* Leon Harris *ed* Stu Linder
☆ Steve Guttenberg (Edward "Eddie" Simmons), Daniel Stern (Laurence "Shrevie" Schreiber), Mickey Rourke (Robert "Boogie" Shefteil), Kevin Bacon (Timothy Fenwick, Jr.), Timothy Daly (William "Billy" Howard), Ellen Barkin (Beth), Paul Reiser (Modell), Kathryn Dowling (Barbara), Michael Tucker (Bagel), Jessica James (Mrs. Simmons)

'A terrific movie – a gentle, lyrical, magically funny portrait of the games young men play to keep from growing up, and of the oddly childish society that encourages them.' – *Stephen Schiff*

⚐ original screenplay

797
Diner

In 1959, Baltimore college students congregate at their old meeting place and find themselves more occupied by adult problems than of yore.

Barry Levinson's character study of Baltimore college students, who congregate at their old meeting place and find themselves increasingly occupied by adult problems, was set in 1959, more than 20 years before it was made. It gave it even then a nostalgic quality, of life's potentials and likely disappointments. It is a little masterpiece of observation, for those with ears to hear, an attempt to define the meaning of life through an accumulation of detail. Levinson's oblique approach to his characters gives the dialogue an authenticity as the characters circle around the subject of their friendship and the future.

Phantom of the Opera
US   1925   94m (24 fps)   bw (Technicolor sequence)   silent
Universal
▦ ▤ ⬚~ ◎ ◎
w Raymond Schrock, Elliott Clawson *novel* Gaston Leroux *d* Rupert Julian *ph* Charles Van Enger, Virgil Miller *ad* Dan Hall *ed* Maurice Pivar
☆ Lon Chaney (The Phantom), Mary Philbin (Christine Daae), Norman Kerry (Raoul de Chagny), Gibson Gowland (Simon)

'The greatest inducement to nightmare that has yet been screened.' – *Variety*

● The chase was directed by Edward Sedgwick.
In 1930 an 89m talkie version was issued with approximately 35% dialogue which had been recorded by the surviving actors, and some new footage.
● The Region 1 two-disc ultimate edition includes both the original 1925 version and the 1929 restored v ersion, commentary by film historian Scott MacQueen, and the Carl Davis orchestral score.
● Remade in 1943 and 1989 in the US. Remade in Britain by Hammer in 1962.

796
Phantom of the Opera

A disfigured man in a mask abducts the prima donna of the Paris Opera House to his lair in the sewers below.

Rupert Julian, a New Zealand-born actor turned director, never made a better film than this first version of what was to become a much-filmed story. The melodramatic tale, owes its longevity to the impact the film had on audiences at the time and since. Its magnificent visual style was matched by the horror of Lon Chaney's skull-like appearance, which the audience see just before the heroine, so that they can share her terror. The film disappointed when it was first previewed and retakes were made to create an often splendid piece of Grand Guignol.

'The unforgettable film that proves love, family and imagination conquer all.'

Life Is Beautiful
Italy   1997   122m   colour
Buena Vista/Melampo (Elda Ferri, Gianluigi Braschi)
▭▭ ▤ ⊚ ⊚ ⌒
original title: *La Vita è Bella*
w Vincenzo Cerami, Roberto Benigni *d* Roberto Benigni
ph Tonino Delli Colli *m* Nicola Piovani *pd* Danilo Donati
ed Simona Paggi
☆ *Roberto Benigni* (Guido Orefice), Nicoletta Braschi
(Dora), Giustino Durano (Uncle), Sergio Bustric (Ferruccio
Orefice), Marisa Paredes (Dora's Mother), Horst Buchholz
(Dr. Lessing), Lydia Alfonsi (Guicciardini), Giuliana Lojodice
(Didactic Principal), Giorgio Cantarini (Giosue)

'One of the most unconvincing and self-
congratulatory movies ever made.' – *David Denby,
New Yorker*

● The film took in excess of $40m at the US box-office,
more than any other foreign-language film, and also
grossed more than $152m around the world.
● Benigni's concentration-camp number, 7397, was chosen
as a tribute to Charlie Chaplin, who wore the same number
in *The Great Dictator*.
♟ foreign-language film; Roberto Benigni (actor); Nicola
Piovani
♟ best picture; Roberto Benigni (director); Vincenzo
Cerami, Roberto Benigni (script); Simona Paggi
Ⓣ Roberto Benigni (actor)

795
Life Is Beautiful

During the Second World War, a Jewish bookshop owner, sent with his family to a concentration camp, protects his young son by pretending that they are in a holiday camp.

Roberto Benigni made a bold and brave film in which he also stars. Clowning, slapstick humour, and familial love, for all their affirmation of life, can seem an inappropriate response to the realities of the holocaust; but that, in part, is the point of the movie: laughter is inadequate when confronted by the true horrors of existence.

'Shinjo Ten No Amijima'
Double Suicide
Japan 1969 104m bw
Toho/Hyogensha/ATG

w Taeko Tomioka, Toru Takemitsu, Masahiro Shinoda *puppet play* Monzaemon Chikamatsu *d* Masahiro Shinoda *ph* Toichiro Narushima *m* Toru Takemitsu *ad* Kiyoshi Awazu
☆ Kichiemon Nakamura (Jihei), Shima Iwashita (Koharu/Osan), Hosei Kamatsu (Tahei), Yusuke Takita (Magoemon), Kamatari Fujiwara (Yamatoya Owner), Yoshi Kato (Gosaemon), Shizue Kawarazaki (Osan's Mother), Tokie Hidari (Osugi)

794
Double Suicide

In 18th-century Osaka, a married paper mechant and the courtesan he loves realize that they can only be together in death. After they run away together, he kills her and hangs himself.

Masahiro Shinoda's fascinating tragic drama of frustrated love was based on a bunraku puppet theatre piece written in 1720 by Chikamatsu, a revered figure in Japanese drama. The film opens with puppeteers, dressed from head to feet in black, getting the lifesize puppets ready, while the voice of Shinoda can be heard, talking of the film's final location. Although the film switches to live actors, the figures of the puppeteers remain and become involved in the story, set in 18th-century Osaka. The action takes place within an artificial setting, with scene changes often made by the puppeteers. The effect is theatrical and also suggests that its protagonists are manipulated by forces beyond their control.

Mary Poppins
👫 US 1964 139m Technicolor
Walt Disney (Bill Walsh)

w Bill Walsh, Don da Gradi *novel* P. L. Travers *d* Robert Stevenson *ph* Edward Colman *m/ly* Richard M. and Robert B. Sherman *md* Irwin Kostal *pd* Tony Walton *ad* Carroll Clark, William H. Tuntke *ed* Cotton Warburton *sp* Eustace Lycett, Peter Ellenshaw, Robert A. Mattey
☆ Julie Andrews (Mary Poppins), David Tomlinson (Mr. Banks), Glynis Johns (Mrs. Banks), Dick Van Dyke (Bert/Mr. Dawes, Sr.), Reginald Owen (Adm. Boom), Ed Wynn (Uncle Albert), Matthew Garber (Michael Banks), Karen Dotrice (Jane Banks), Hermione Baddeley (Ellen), Elsa Lanchester (Katie Nanna), Arthur Treacher (Constable Jones), Jane Darwell (The Bird Woman)

'A charming, imaginative and technically superb movie musical, sparkling with originality, melody and magical performances.' – *Judith Crist*

♫ 'Chim Chim Cheree'; 'Feed the Birds'; 'Fidelity Fiduciary Bank'; 'I Love to Laugh'; 'Jolly Holiday'; 'Let's Go Fly a Kite'; 'The Life I Lead'; 'The Perfect Nanny'; 'Sister Suffragette'; 'A Spoonful of Sugar'; 'Stay Awake'; 'Step in Time'; 'Supercalifragilisticexpialidocious'
🎖 Richard M. and Robert B. Sherman; Julie Andrews; song 'Chim Chim Cheree'; special visual effects; editing
🏆 best picture; script; Robert Stevenson; Edward Colman; Irwin Kostal; art direction
🏆 Julie Andrews

793
Mary Poppins

In Edwardian London a magical nanny teaches two slightly naughty children to make life enjoyable for themselves and others.

This is not a perfect musical, though it is among the best of the 60s. The narrative tends to wander in the second half, when Mary Poppins scarcely appears; there is also the problem of Dick Van Dyke's really lamentable attempt at a Cockney accent. But P. L. Travers' story does have the benefit of Julie Andrews. She demonstrates why she should have got the role that was denied her by Warner Brothers, as Eliza Doolittle in My Fair Lady, combining tough-mindedness with sheer niceness and singing with wonderful clarity. The flying sequences and the occasional mix of live action and cartoon adventures made it a very pleasant and effective entertainment for children of all ages, with plenty of brightness, charm and just plain fun.

Man Bites Dog

Belgium 1992 96m bw

Metro/Les Artistes Anonymes (Rémy Belvaux, André Bonzel, Benoît Poelvoorde)

⊡ ☰ ⌕ ⌒

original title: *C'est arrivé près de chez vous*

w Rémy Belvaux, André Bonzel, Benoît Poelvoorde, Vincent Tavier *d* Rémy Belvaux, André Bonzel, Benoît Poelvoorde *ph* André Bonzel *m* Jean-Marc Chenut *ed* Rémy Belvaux, Eric Dardill

☆ Benoît Poelvoorde (Ben), Jacqueline Poelvoorde-Pappaert (Ben's Mother), Nelly Pappaert (Ben's Grandmother), Jenny Drye (Jenny), Malou Madou (Malou), Willy Vandenbroeck (Boby)

'To encounter *Man Bites Dog* is to submit to a torrent of hilariously cruel humour, enacted without fuss or rancour, and inconceivably authentic.' – *Philip Strick, Sight and Sound*

'Offbeat, darkly hilarious … Violent yet trenchant, potential sleeper should attract a cult following and will look just right on video.' – *Variety*

'Carefully shaped to draw us in and repel us, to make us laugh and wipe the smiles off our faces. The most horrendous scenes are calculated to force us into asking how we can bear to watch such things.' – *Philip French, Observer*

792
Man Bites Dog

A documentary film crew begins by recording the activities of a motiveless serial killer and ends by helping him with his murders.

As so-called 'reality television' takes over small-screen entertainment, so this black comedy by Rémy Belvaux, André Bonzel and Benoît Poelvoorde seems ever more prescient. It makes some effective points about the relationship between voyeurism and exploitation. It is not an easy film to watch or enjoy, with its scenes of gang rape and brutality, but it is a remarkable, if sometimes repellent, feature, questioning not only an audience's pleasure in watching violence but also the obsessive intrusion of the media into private lives.

'Just ten tiny fingers and ten tiny toes … Trouble? Scandal? Gosh, nobody knows!'

Bachelor Mother

US 1939 82m bw

RKO (B. G. de Sylva)

⊡ ☰ ⌕

w Norman Krasna *story* Felix Jackson *d* Garson Kanin *ph* Robert de Grasse *m* Roy Webb *ad* Carroll Clark, Van Nest Polglase *ed* Henry Berman, Robert Wise

☆ *Ginger Rogers* (Polly Parrish), *David Niven* (David Merlin), *Charles Coburn* (J. B. Merlin), Frank Albertson (Freddie Miller), E. E. Clive (Butler), Ernest Truex (Investigator)

'Carries some rather spicy lines aimed at the adult trade, but broad enough in implication to catch the fancy of general audiences … a surprise laugh hit that will do biz generally and overcome hot weather box office lethargy.' – *Variety*

'An excellent comedy, beautifully done.' – *Richard Mallett, Punch*

'This is the way farce should be handled, with just enough conviction to season its extravagances.' – *New York Times*

● Remade as *Bundle of Joy*.

♫ Felix Jackson

791
Bachelor Mother

A shopgirl finds an abandoned baby and is thought to be its mother; the department store owner's son is then thought to be the father.

From this trite story of a shopgirl who marries the boss's son, Garson Kanin created a blithely-scripted comedy which has stood the test of time. It provided excellent roles for Charles Coburn as a besotted millionaire ('I don't care who the father is. I'm the grandfather', he insists), Ginger Rogers as the sharp-tongued, warmhearted girl, and David Niven as the confused son.

Public Enemy
US   1931   84m   bw
Warner
▭ ▤ ◲ ◎ ◉
GB title: *Enemies of the Public*
w Harvey Thew   *story* Kubec Glasmon, John Bright
d William Wellman   *ph* Dev Jennings   *m* David Mendoza
ad Max Parker   *ed* Ed McCormic k
☆ *James Cagney* (Tom Powers), Edward Woods (Matt Doyle), Jean Harlow (Gwen Allen), Joan Blondell (Mamie), Beryl Mercer (Ma Powers), Donald Cook (Mike Powers), Mae Clarke (Kitty), Leslie Fenton (Nails Nathan)

'Roughest, most powerful and best gang picture to date. So strong as to be repulsive in some aspects, plus a revolting climax. No strong cast names but a lot of merit.' – *Variety*

'The real power of *Public Enemy* lies in its vigorous and brutal assault on the nerves and in the stunning acting of James Cagney.' – *James Shelley Hamilton*

'What not many people know is that right up to two days before shooting started, I was going to play the good guy, the pal. Edward Woods played it in the end.' – *James Cagney*

♟ Kubec Glasmon, John Bright

790
Public Enemy

The rise and fall of two poor boys who turn to crime.

This early gangster film still has vivid and startling scenes and was most influential in the development of the urban American crime film. It also consolidated James Cagney's image as a star and tough guy; he began the picture in a secondary role, but soon took over the lead from Edward Woods. In its most celebrated scene, Cagney thrusts and twists half a grapefruit in Mae Clarke's face. Based on the lives of Al Capone's rivals, Hymie Weiss and Louis Altieri, it follows the progress of two slum boys, who begin as bootleggers, get too big for their boots, and wind up dead. The director, William Wellman, promised to make it a tougher picture than Warner's earlier gangster movie *Little Caesar* and succeeded, with a brutal joke at the end.

Friday the Thirteenth
GB   1933   84m   bw
Gainsborough (Michael Balcon)
w G. H. Moresby-White, Sidney Gilliat, Emlyn Williams
d Victor Saville   *ph* Charles Van Enger   *ad* Alfred Junge, Vetchinsky   *ed* R. E. Dearing
☆ Sonnie Hale (Alf), Cyril Smith (Fred), *Eliot Makeham* (Jackson), Ursula Jeans (Eileen Jackson), *Emlyn Williams* (Blake), Frank Lawton (Frank Parsons), Belle Chrystal (Mary), *Max Miller* (Joe), Alfred Drayton (Detective), Edmund Gwenn (Wakefield), Mary Jerrold (Flora Wakefield), Gordon Harker (Hamilton Briggs), *Robertson Hare* (Mr. Lightfoot), Martita Hunt (Agnes Lightfoot), Leonora Corbett (Dolly) and also Jessie Matthews, Ralph Richardson

789
Friday the Thirteenth

Several people are involved in a bus crash and we turn back the clock to see how they came to be there.

One of the best British movies of the 1930s, a compendium of comedy and drama that looked back to *The Bridge of San Luis Rey* and forward to the innumerable all-star films of the forties. It was, literally, an omnibus story, dealing in seven episodes with people involved in a horrendous bus crash in Piccadilly; it was not until the end that it was revealed which two passengers died. It featured a starry cast, with Jessie Matthews and Ralph Richardson as young lovers, Max Miller as a market trader about to be arrested for theft, Robertson Hare as a henpecked husband whose flirtation costs him dearly, and Emlyn Williams, responsible for the dialogue, as a blackmailer.

Thunder Rock

GB 1942 112m bw
Charter Films (John Boulting)
▣ ⊚

w Jeffrey Dell, Bernard Miles *play Robert Ardrey* d *Roy Boulting* ph Mutz Greenbaum (Max Greene) m Hans May ad Duncan Sutherland ed Roy Boulting
☆ *Michael Redgrave* (David Charleston), *Lilli Palmer* (Melanie Kurtz), *Barbara Mullen* (Ellen Kirby), *James Mason* (Streeter), *Frederick Valk* (Dr Kurtz), *Frederick Cooper* (Ted Briggs), *Finlay Currie* (Captain Joshua), *Sybilla Binder* (Anne-Marie)

'Boldly imaginative in theme and treatment.'
– *Sunday Express*

'More interesting technically than anything since *Citizen Kane*.' – *Manchester Guardian*

'If I thought it wouldn't keep too many people away, I'd call it a work of art.' – *Daily Express*

'What a stimulus to thought it is, this good, brave, outspoken, unfettered picture.' – *Observer*

788

Thunder Rock

A journalist disgusted with the world of the Thirties retires to a lighthouse on Lake Michigan and is haunted by the ghosts of immigrants drowned a century before.

Michael Redgrave achieved one of his best screen performances when he repeated his role in Robert Ardrey's stage play as journalist, David Charleston. There was also some excellent acting from the remainder of the cast in this subtle adaptation of an impressive and topical anti-isolationist drama. Roy Boulting's direction gave the somewhat static play a more cinematic feel. The script opened out the play by explaining that Charleston retired because no one paid any attention to his journalism warning of the rise of Fascism.

The Moon and Sixpence

US 1943 85m bw (colour sequence)
Albert Lewin/David L. Loew (Stanley Kramer)
▣

wd Albert Lewin *novel* W. Somerset Maugham *ph* John Seitz *m* Dimitri Tiomkin *ad* Gordon Willis *ed* Richard L. Van Enger
☆ *George Sanders* (Charles Strickland), *Herbert Marshall* (Geoffrey Wolfe), *Steve Geray* (Dirk Stroeve), *Doris Dudley* (Blanche Stroeve), *Elena Verdugo* (Ata), *Florence Bates* (Tiara Johnson), *Heather Thatcher* (Rose Waterford), *Eric Blore* (Captain Nichols), *Albert Basserman* (Dr Coutras)

'An admirable film until the end, when it lapses into Technicolor and techni-pathos.' – *James Agate*

♫ Dimitri Tiomkin

787

The Moon and Sixpence

A stockbroker leaves his wife and family, spends some selfish years painting in Paris and finally dies of leprosy on a South Sea island.

The life of Paul Gauguin was the basis for Somerset Maugham's elegant novel. Albert Lewin, a director with a literary style, made an excellent adaptation; it can seem a little stodgy in presentation now, although it is enlivened by Dimitri Tiomkin's score. The central character, Strickland's misogyny no longer plays well. 'I will probably beat you,' he says to the 14-year-old girl he marries in Tahiti. 'How else will I know you love me?' she replies. Sanders' chilling performance, as an artist whose only passion is for painting, made him famous, as well as, he claimed, giving him an off-screen reputation as an expert on women.

'He thought he had the world by the tail – till it exploded in his face with a bullet attached!'

All the King's Men
US 1949 109m bw
Columbia (Robert Rossen)
🔲 ▦ ▦ ◉ ◉ ◉
w Robert Rossen *novel* Robert Penn Warren *d* Robert Rossen *ph* Burnett Guffey *m* Louis Gruenberg *ad* Sturges Carne *ed* Robert Parrish, Al Clark
☆ *Broderick Crawford* (Willie Stark), *John Ireland* (Jack Burden), *Mercedes McCambridge* (Sadie Burke), *Joanne Dru* (Anne Stanton), John Derek (Tom Stark), Anne Seymour (Lucy Stark), Shepperd Strudwick (Adam Stanton)

> 'More conspicuous for scope and worthiness of intention than for inspiration.' – *Gavin Lambert*

> 'The film is like one of those lifeless digests, designed for people who cannot spare the time to read whole books. Perhaps that accounts for its popularity.' – *Lindsay Anderson*

> 'Broderick Crawford's Willie Stark might just make you feel better about the President you've got … By no means a great film, but it moves along.' – *Pauline Kael, New Yorker*

♟ picture; Broderick Crawford; Mercedes McCambridge
♟ Robert Rossen (as writer); Robert Rossen (as director); John Ireland; editing

'A town – a stranger – and the things he does to its people! Especially its women!'

Picnic
US 1955 113m Technicolor
Cinemascope
Columbia (Fred Kohlmar)
🔲 ▦ ▦ ◉ ◉ 🎧
w Daniel Taradash *play* William Inge *d* Joshua Logan *ph* James Wong Howe *m* George Duning *pd* Jo Mielziner *ad* William Flannery *ed* Charles Nelson, William A. Lyon
☆ *William Holden* (Hal Carter), Kim Novak (Madge Owens), Rosalind Russell (Rosemary Sydney), *Susan Strasberg* (Millie Owens), Arthur O'Connell (Howard Bevans), Cliff Robertson (Alan), Betty Field (Flo Owens), Verna Felton (Mrs. Helen Potts), Reta Shaw (Linda Sue Breckenridge)

> 'Mr Logan's idea of an outing in the corn country includes a choir of at least a hundred voices, a camera so alert that it can pick up the significance of the reflection of a Japanese lantern in a pool (futility, wistfulness, the general transience of life, as I get it) and a sound track let loose in the most formidable music I've heard in my time at the movies.' – *New Yorker*

♟ art direction; editing
♟ best picture; Joshua Logan; George Duning; Arthur O'Connell

786
All the King's Men

An honest man from a small town is elected mayor and then governor, but power corrupts him absolutely and he ruins his own life and those of his friends before being assassinated.

A rousing political melodrama, based on the hectic career of Huey Long, governor of Louisiana in the late Twenties and early Thirties, one of whose slogans was 'Every Man A King'. Willie Stark, the good old country boy turned populist demagogue and corrupt state governor, was optimistically called just a passing fad by writer-director Robert Rossen. In a dominating performance, Crawford embodies Stark's repugnance and appeal ('impudent, porcine and juvenile', as journalist A.J. Liebling once described Long) and his vitality carries the narrative through some clumsy moments to the shock ending of his assassination.

785
Picnic

A brawny wanderer causes sexual havoc one summer in a small American town.

This seminal melodrama set new directions for Hollywood. Generally quite compulsive despite some overacting, it illustrated a side of life that small-town movies, such as the Hardy family series, had never showed. William Inge had a talent for creating lonely, frustrated characters, and Kim Novak brought the right discontented quality to her role as a pretty young woman who does not like to be stared at. Having shaved his chest for his previous movie, *Love is a Many Splendored Thing*, Holden stayed shirtless here and conveyed a sexual magnetism.

'A comedy from the heart that goes for the throat.'

As Good as It Gets
US   1997   138m   Technicolor
Columbia TriStar/Gracie (James L. Brooks, Bridget Johnson, Kristi Zea)
▣ ▦ ⌖ ⓖ ⓦ ⌒
w Mark Andrus, James L. Brooks *d* James L. Brooks
ph John Bailey *m* Hans Zimmer *pd* Bill Brzeski
ad Philip Toolin *ed* Richard Marks
☆ *Jack Nicholson* (Melvin Udall), *Helen Hunt* (Carol Connelly), *Greg Kinnear* (Simon Bishop), Cuba Gooding Jnr (Frank Sachs), Skeet Ulrich (Vincent), Shirley Knight (Beverly), Yeardley Smith (Jackie), Lupe Ontiveros (Nora)

'A sporadically funny romantic comedy with all the dramatic plausibility and tonal consistency of a TV variety show.' – *Todd McCarthy, Variety*

👤 Jack Nicholson; Helen Hunt
🏆 Best picture; Greg Kinnear; Mark Andrus, James L. Brooks; Richard Marks; Hans Zimmer

784
As Good as It Gets

A misanthropic writer suffering from a obsessive-compulsive disorder learns to love again when he reluctantly involves himself in the lives of a neighbour and a waitress.

James L. Brooks' sour-toned comedy was well cast with Jack Nicholson as a misanthropic writer matched by Helen Hunt, an actress capable of holding her own with Nicholson's scene-stealing charisma. It was a clever matching of personalities and an original comedy of redemption. For all its occasional glibness and the ease with which problems are solved, it somehow worked; it convinced as long as the movie lasted.

State of the Union
US   1948   110m   bw
MGM/Liberty Films (Frank Capra)
▦ ⌖
GB title: *The World and His Wife*
w Anthony Veiller, Myles Connolly *play* Howard Lindsay, Russel Crouse *d* Frank Capra *ph* George J. Folsey
m Victor Young *ad* Cedric Gibbons, Urie McCleary
ed William Hornbeck
☆ *Spencer Tracy* (Grant Matthews), *Katharine Hepburn* (Mary Matthews), *Adolphe Menjou* (Jim Conover), *Van Johnson* (Spike McManus), Angela Lansbury (Kay Thorndyke), Lewis Stone (Sam Thorndyke), Howard Smith (Sam Parrish), Raymond Walburn (Judge Alexander), Charles Dingle (Bill Hardy)

'A triumphant film, marked all over by Frank Capra's artistry.' – *Howard Barnes*

783
State of the Union

An estranged wife rejoins her husband when he is running for president.

Presidential candidate Wendell Wilkie was the model for Howard Lindsay and Russel Crouse's stage comedy about a politically inexperienced man whose wife returns to him at the start of his campaign. Frank Capra was in decline as a director when he turned it into a film, but he had compensating star power in Katharine Hepburn, who replaced the demanding Claudette Colbert just before shooting began, Spencer Tracy and Angela Lansbury as the would-be president's tough young mistress. It is a brilliantly scripted political comedy which unfortunately goes soft at the end but offers stimulating entertainment most of the way.

My Man Godfrey
US   1936   90m   bw
Universal (Gregory La Cava)

w Morrie Ryskind, Eric Hatch, Gregory La Cava *d* Gregory La Cava *ph* Ted Tetzlaff *m* Charles Previn *ad* Charles D. Hall *ed* Ted J. Kent
☆ *Carole Lombard* (Irene Bullock), *William Powell* (Godfrey Parke), *Alice Brady* (Angelica Bullock), *Mischa Auer* (Carlo), Eugene Pallette (Alexander Bullock), Gail Patrick (Cornelia Bullock), Alan Mowbray (Tommy Gray), Jean Dixon (Molly, Maid)

'Entertaining (and huguely successful) screwball comedy.' – Pauline Kael

⚖ script; Gregory La Cava (as director); Carole Lombard; William Powell; Alice Brady; Mischa Auer
● Remade 1957.

782
My Man Godfrey

A zany millionaire family invite a tramp to be their butler and find he is richer than they are.

William Powell and Carole Lombard were recently divorced when they made this archetypal Depression concept; but there was an undeniable chemistry between them. His dapper charm and wry delivery of witty lines and her comic talents were wonderfully showcased in one of the best of the Thirties sophisticated screwball comedies. La Cava wrote new dialogue every day to keep the fun flowing and to deliver some satirical jabs at upper-class behaviour. As the father of the dizzy family says when he stands in the middle of a scavenger hunt in the Waldorf Astoria, 'All you need to start an asylum is an empty room and the right kind of people.'

I Married a Witch
US   1942   82m   bw
UA/Cinema Guild/René Clair

w Robert Pirosh, Marc Connelly *novel* The Passionate Witch by Thorne Smith *d* René Clair *ph* Ted Tetzlaff *m* Roy Webb *ad* Hans Dreier, Ernst Fegte *ed* Eda Warren
☆ *Fredric March* (Wallace Wooley), *Veronica Lake* (Jennifer), *Cecil Kellaway* (Daniel), *Robert Benchley* (Dr. Dudley White), Susan Hayward (Estelle Masterson), Elizabeth Patterson (Margaret), Robert Warwick (J.B. Masterson)

'A delightful sense of oddity and enchantment.' – New York World Telegram

⚖ Roy Webb

781
I Married a Witch

A Salem witch and her sorcerer father come back to haunt the descendant of the Puritan who had them burned.

French director René Clair, whose light touch had enlivened comedies in his homeland, found it difficult to get work in Hollywood until Preston Sturges persuaded Paramount to give him this opportunity. The result was a delightful romantic comedy fantasy which showed all concerned at the top of their form. Veronica Lake, as a blonde seductress who can slide up banisters, was matched against Susan Hayward, in splendid bitchy form as the snobbish fiancée of would-be politician Fredric March. It's Hollywood moonshine, impeccably distilled.

The Blue Lamp

GB   1949   84m   bw
Ealing (Michael Relph)

w *T. E. B. Clarke* d *Basil Dearden* ph Gordon Dines
md Ernest Irving ad Jim Morahan ed Peter Tanner
☆ *Jack Warner* (George Dixon), Jimmy Hanley (Andy Mitchell), Dirk Bogarde (Tom Riley), Meredith Edwards (PC Hughes), Robert Flemyng (Sgt. Roberts), Bernard Lee (Inspector Cherry), Patric Doonan (Spud), Peggy Evans (Diana Lewis), Gladys Henson (Mrs Dixon), Dora Bryan (Maisie)

'The mixture of coyness, patronage and naive theatricality which has vitiated British films for the last ten years.' – *Gavin Lambert*

'A soundly made crime thriller which would not be creating much of a stir if it were American.' – *Richard Mallett, Punch*

'It is not only foreigners who find the English policeman wonderful, and, in composing this tribute to him, the Ealing Studios are giving conscious expression to a general sentiment.' – *The Times Film Correspondent*

British picture

780
The Blue Lamp

A young man joins London's police force. The elderly copper who trains him is killed in a shootout, but the killer is apprehended.

In this seminal British police film, Basil Dearden wanted to show, in a realistic way, the new dangers that the police faced from a new breed of violent criminals, and shot the drama on London's streets. The film spawned not only a long line of semi-documentary imitations but also the twenty-year TV series *Dixon of Dock Green*, for which the shot PC, again played by Jack Warner, was happily revived. It was also notable for the performance of Bogarde as a swaggering young hoodlum. As an entertainment, it is pacy but dated; more importantly, it burnished the image of the British copper for generations.

The Awful Truth

US   1937   90m   bw
Columbia (Leo McCarey)

w Vina Delmar *play* Arthur Richman d *Leo McCarey* ph Joseph Walker md Morris Stoloff ad Lionel Banks, Stephen Goosson ed Al Clark
☆ *Irene Dunne* (Lucy Warriner), *Cary Grant* (Jerry Warriner), *Ralph Bellamy* (Daniel Leeson), Alexander D'Arcy (Armand Duvalle), Cecil Cunningham (Aunt Patsy), Molly Lamont (Barbara Vance), Esther Dale (Mrs. Leeson), Joyce Compton (Dixie Belle Lee/Toots Binswanger)

'Among the ingredients the raising powder is the important thing and out of the oven comes a frothy bit of stuff that leaves no taste in the mouth and is easy on the stomach.' – *Marion Fraser, World Film News*

• Remade 1953 as *Let's Do It Again*.
♨ Leo McCarey
♟ best picture; script; Irene Dunne; Ralph Bellamy; Al Clark
● Cary Grant and Irene Dunne were teamed twice more: *My Favorite Wife* (1940) and *Penny Serenade* (1941).

779
The Awful Truth

A divorcing couple endure various adventures which lead to reconciliation.

A classic screwball comedy of the thirties, in which a wealthy young divorced couple discover that they still love one another and foil each other's attempts to begin new relationships. It is a farce of loving hostilities that had been filmed twice before, and was remade in the Fifties, but never so successfully. Marked by a mixture of sophistication and farce and an irreverent approach to plot, it established both Dunne and Grant as among Hollywood's best comic actors.

A Slight Case of Murder
US 1938 85m bw
Warner (Sam Bischoff)

w Earl Baldwin, Joseph Schrank *play* Damon Runyon, Howard Lindsay *d* Lloyd Bacon *ph* Sid Hickox *m* M. K. Jerome, Jack Scholl *ad* Max Parker *ed* James Gibbon
☆ *Edward G. Robinson* (Remy Marco), Jane Bryan (Mary Marco), Willard Parker (Dick Whitewood), *Ruth Donnelly* (Mora Marco), Allen Jenkins (Mike), John Litel (Post), Harold Huber (Giuseppe), Edward Brophy (Lefty), Bobby Jordan (Douglas Fairbanks Rosenbloom)

'Nothing funnier has been produced by Hollywood for a long time … a mirthful and hilarious whimsy.' – *Variety*

'The complications crazily mount, sentiment never raises its ugly head, a long nose is made at violence and death.' – *Graham Greene*

● Remade 1953 as *Stop You're Killing Me*.

778
A Slight Case of Murder

When a beer baron tries to go legitimate his colleagues attempt to kill him, but end up shooting each other.

Damon Runyon's enjoyment of oddball underworld characters survives in Lloyd Bacon's raucous, black farce of a bootlegger, whose attempts to go legitimate are not helped by the four poker-playing corpses left in the bedroom of the house he has rented for a vacation. The bootlegger's wife is horrified that the owners didn't clean up the place before they left. And he has other problems to deal with, including a daughter who plans to marry a state trooper. There is pleasure to be got from Edward G. Robinson relishing the opportunity to make fun of his tough-guy image as a crook turned lawful brewer of undrinkable beer.

'Fear is the oxygen of blackmail. If Barrett was paying, others are. Find me one!'

Victim
GB 1961 100m bw
Rank/Allied Filmmakers/Parkway (Michael Relph)
▣ ▤ ◉ ◎

w Janet Green, John McCormick *d* Basil Dearden *ph* Otto Heller *m* Philip Green *ad* Alex Vetchinsky *ed* John D. Guthridge
☆ *Dirk Bogarde* (Melville Farr), Sylvia Syms (Laura Farr), John Barrie (Detective Inspector Harris), Norman Bird (Harold Doe), Peter McEnery (Jack Barrett), Anthony Nicholls (Lord Fullbrook), Dennis Price (Calloway), *Charles Lloyd Pack* (Henry), Derren Nesbitt (Sandy Youth), John Cairney (Bridie), Hilton Edwards (P.H.), Peter Copley (Paul Mandrake), Donald Churchill (Eddy Stone), Nigel Stock (Phip)

'Ingenious, moralistic, and moderately amusing.' – *Pauline Kael, 70s*

777
Victim

A barrister with homosexual inclinations tracks down a blackmailer despite the risk to his own reputation.

After Basil Dearden directed *Sapphire*, a successful thriller that was a plea for racial harmony, he was asked to make this film by the same husband-and-wife team of screenwriters, which was a plea for tolerance of homosexuality. With its vivid use of London locations and engrossing story, it is credited with changing the public perception of what John Trevelyan, secretary of the British Board of Film Censors, claimed in a letter to the makers was a subject that was 'shocking, distasteful and disgusting' to the majority of film-goers. Dirk Bogarde's anguished performance marked the start of his career as a serious actor.

776
Dear Diary

Dear Diary
Italy   1994   100m   colour
Artificial Eye/Sacher/Banfilm/La Sept/Canal (Angelo Barbagallo, Nanni Moretti, Nella Banfi)
🎬 🎞 🔊 🎧
original title: *Caro Diario*
wd Nanni Moretti *ph* Giuseppe Lanci *m* Nicola Piovani
pd Marta Maffucci *ed* Mirco Garrone
☆ Nanni Moretti (Himself), Jennifer Beals (Herself),
Alexandre Rockwell (Himself), Renato Carpentieri (Gerardo),
Antonio Neiwiller (Mayor of Stromboli)

'The film seems slight and a little slapdash until the final episode, when Moretti faces mortality with a deadpan humanism that, under the circumstances, is bracing, even heroic.' – *Time*

'Appearing to be about nothing very much, it manages to encompass an awful lot, and it would be a strange viewer who didn't, somewhere in the film, identify with its major concern, which is how to survive in an increasingly frustrating and impersonal world.' – *Derek Malcolm, Guardian*

A director films a diary of his everyday life and encounters.

Nanni Moretti bears out the prediction, made by François Truffaut in the late Fifties, that the future of cinema lay in confessional diaries. *Dear Diary* is precisely that: a filmed diary in three chapters. The first involves a trip around Rome on a scooter, a chance meeting with actress Jennifer Beals and a visit to the place where fellow director Pasolini was killed; the second is an island-hopping trip with a friend who stopped watching television in the Sixties but becomes obsessed by it again; the third involves hospital treatment for a form of cancer. It is a brilliant essay in autobiography, often bordering on the inconsequential but always interesting, full of charm and humour, which remains even when deepening into a confrontation with the likelihood of imminent death.

775
The Insider

'Ordinary Men Of Uncommon Courage Risk All To Speak Out ... And Change Everything.'

'Two Angry Men Driven To Tell The Truth ... Whatever The Cost'

The Insider
US   1999   158m   Technicolor   Super 35
Buena Vista/Touchstone/Forward Pass (Michael Mann, Pieter Jan Brugge)
🎬 🎞 ⓒ 🎧
w Eric Roth, Michael Mann *Vanity Fair article The Man Who Knew Too Much* by Marie Brenner *d* Michael Mann
ph Dante Spinotti *pd* Brian Morris *ad* Nancy Haigh
ed William Goldenberg, Paul Rubell, David Rosenbloom
☆ Al Pacino (Lowell Bergman), *Russell Crowe* (Jeffrey Wigand), *Christopher Plummer* (Mike Wallace), Diane Venora (Liane Wigand), Philip Baker Hall (Don Hewitt), Lindsay Crouse (Sharon Tiller), Debi Mazar (Debbie De Luca), Stephen Tobolowsky (Eric Kluster), Colm Feore (Richard Scruggs), Bruce McGill (Ron Motley), Gina Gershon (Helen Caperelli), Michael Gambon (Thomas Sandefur), Rip Torn (John Scanlon), Michael Moore (Himself), Wings Hauser (Tobacco Lawyer)

'An edge-of-your-seat, gut-churning thriller.' – *Newsweek*

⚲ picture; Russell Crowe; Michael Mann; script (Eric Roth, Michael Mann); Dante Spinotti; William Goldenberg, Paul Rubell, David Rosenbloom; sound (Andy Nelson, Doug Hemphill, Lee Orloff)

A TV producer persuades a former tobacco company scientist to expose the official denials that cigarettes are injurious to health, only to discover that his investigation will not be broadcast.

Michael Mann's true-life drama dealt with the way corporations and the media respond to unwelcome facts. Mann turns the scandal into a gripping drama. At its centre are two contrasting and terrific performances: Pacino as the investigative journalist, wheeling and dealing with consummate skill, and Crowe as the haggard, dumpy whistle-blower, an ordinary, principled man caught up in events beyond his control.

Ballad of a Soldier
USSR   1959   89m   bw
Mosfilm
▰ ☒ ◎
original title: *Ballada o Soldate*
w Valentin Yoshov, Grigori Chukrai   *d* Grigori Chukrai
ph Vladimir Nikolayev, Era Saveleva   *m* Mikhail Ziv
☆ Vladimir Ivashev (Alyosha), Sharma Prokhorenko
(Shura), Antonina Maximova (Alyosha's Mother)

'In an epoch when the entertainment in most
entertainment films is little more than offensive, its
persuasive charm is particularly welcome.' – *MFB*

Valentin Yoshov, Grigori Chukrai
best picture

774
Ballad of a Soldier

A soldier is granted four days' home leave before returning to be killed at the front.

Grigori Chukrai's film, set in wartime, is a lyrical tear-jerker most notable for its impeccably photographed detail of Russian domestic and everyday life. A young soldier is granted four days' home leave from the front for his apparent bravery in action. In the manner of a road movie, he travels by various means, meeting on his way people whose lives have been disrupted by the war. One is a girl, with whom he falls in love. After visiting his mother, he returns to be killed at the front. Its small-scale focus on the effect of war on individuals was, along with *The Cranes Are Flying*, a new and welcome venture in Soviet cinema.

'Not since *Gone with the Wind* has there been a great romantic epic like it!'

Reds
US   1981   196m   Technicolor
Paramount (Warren Beatty)
▱ ▰ ☒ ◠
w Warren Beatty, Trevor Griffiths   *d* Warren Beatty
ph Vittorio Storaro   *m* Stephen Sondheim   *pd* Richard
Sylbert   *ad* Simon Holland   *ed* Dede Allen, Craig McKay
☆ Warren Beatty (John Reed), Diane Keaton (Louise
Bryant), Edward Herrmann (Max Eastman), Jerzy Kosinski
(Grigory Zinoviev), Jack Nicholson (Eugene O'Neill),
Maureen Stapleton (Emma Goldman), Paul Sorvino (Louis
Fraina)

Warren Beatty (as director); Vittorio Storaro; Maureen Stapleton (supporting actress)
best picture; screenplay; editing (Dede Allen, Craig McKay); Warren Beatty (as actor); Diane Keaton; Jack Nicholson
best supporting actor (Jack Nicholson); best supporting actress (Maureen Stapleton)

773
Reds

The last years of John Reed, an American writer who after stormy romantic vicissitudes goes with his wife to Russia and writes Ten Days That Shook the World.

Warren Beatty's immensely ambitious film based on the last years of John Reed. It was long in gestation, long in shooting (240 days and 130 hours of exposed film), and longer than it perhaps should have been in the cinemas. But it is full of quality, an immensely detailed work that includes interviewed reminiscences with veteran radicals as well as a perceptive account of the involved and intense relationship between Reed and Louise Bryant.

The Music Man

The Music Man

US 1962 151m Technirama
Warner (Morton da Costa)

w Marion Hargrove *book* Meredith Willson *d* Morton da Costa *ph* Robert Burks *md* Ray Heindorf *ch* Onna White *ad* Paul Groesse *ed* William Ziegler *songs* Meredith Willson

☆ *Robert Preston* (Harold Hill), Shirley Jones (Marian Paroo), Buddy Hackett (Marcellus Washburn), *Hermione Gingold* (Eulalie MacKechnie Shinn), Pert Kelton (Mrs. Paroo), Paul Ford (Mayor Shinn)

'This is one of those triumphs that only a veteran performer can have; Preston's years of experience and his love of performing come together joyously.' – *Pauline Kael*

● Robert Preston, who originated the part on Broadway, was only offered the film role after Cary Grant had turned it down.

♫ 'Rock Island'; Iowa Stubborn'; 'Ya Got Trouble'; '76 Trombones'; 'Pick-a-Little, Talk-a-Little'; 'The Sadder But Wiser Girl'; 'Wells Fargo'; 'Will I Ever Tell You?'; 'It's You'; 'Being in Love'; 'Till There Was You'

♟ Ray Heindorf
♟ best picture

772
The Music Man

A confidence trickster persuades a small-town council to start a boys' band, with himself as the agent for all the expenses.

Morton Da Costas's transference to the screen of a hit Broadway musical was thoroughly invigorating, with splendid period atmosphere. Robert Preston brilliantly repeats his brashly charming stage performance. His sheer exuberance is infectious, even if the film's style leans towards the stagey. Meredith Willson's music, with its brass band and barbershop quartet, superbly conveys the nostalgic, communal small-town values of the time.

Zelig

US 1983 79m bw/colour
Orion/Rollins-Joffe (Robert Greenhut)

wd Woody Allen *ph* Gordon Willis *m* Dick Hyman *pd* Mel Bourne *ad* Speed Hopkins *ed* Susan E. Morse

☆ Woody Allen (Leonard Zelig), Mia Farrow (Dr Eudora Fletcher), John Buckwater (Dr Sindell), Marvin Chatinover (Glandular Diagnosis Doctor), Stanley Swerdlow (Mexican Food Doctor), Paul Nevens (Dr. Birsky), Howard Erskine (Hypodermic Doctor)

'We can all admire the brilliance and economy with which it is made. But is it funny enough? I take leave to doubt it.' – *Derek Malcolm, Guardian*

'*Citizen Kane* miraculously transformed into side-splitting comedy.' – *New York Times*

'The movie is a technical masterpiece, but in artistic and comic terms, only pretty good.' – *Roger Ebert*

♟ cinematography; costume design

771
Zelig

A parody documentary tracing a chameleon-like nonentity who contrives to have been associated with all the major events of the 20th century.

Woody Allen's use of technical trickery gave an added dimension to his psuedo-documentary styled comedy. Zelig is a man so insistent on being liked that he takes on the personality of those he meets, an ability that turns him into a celebrity in his own right. But fame, as in Allen's *Stardust Memories*, brings only unhappiness and emptiness. In the end, he is redeemed by love. There was considerable amusement in putting Allen in pictorial association with Hitler, Roosevelt and Eugene O'Neill. In all, an after-dinner treat for the intellectuals.

Blue Collar
US 1978 114m Technicolor
Universal/TAT (Don Guest)
🎬 ▦ ⊛ ◉ ♫

w Paul Schrader, Leonard Schrader *d* Paul Schrader
ph Bobby Byrne *m* Jack Nitzsche *ed* Tom Rolf
☆ Richard Pryor (Zeke Brown), Harvey Keitel (Jerry
Bartowski), Yaphet Kotto (Smokey), Ed Begley Jnr (Bobby
Joe), Harry Bellaver (Eddie Johnson), George Memmoli
(Jenkins), Lucy Saroyan (Arlene Bartowski), Lane Smith
(Clarence Hill)

'This is Schrader's first directing job and the best
elements in the script fit his ability like a role
tailored for an actor. His work is easy and quick,
imaginative but not ostentatious.' – *Stanley
Kauffmann*

770
Blue Collar

*Three car factory workers try to improve their lot by unionization and
robbery.*

Paul Schrader's salty, rough but impressively realistic modern drama is
a belated American equivalent of *Saturday Night and Sunday Morning*.
A film about endemic corruption, it takes an ironic view of the
American Dream. Discovering that their union is exploiting them in
much the same way as their employer, the hard-up trio take desperate
action that threatens their survival. Despite a troubled production – the
three leads quarrelled bitterly off-screen – the film works as a study in
alienation and betrayal, with a suitably downbeat ending.

Quiet Wedding
GB 1940 80m bw
Paramount/Conqueror (Paul Soskin)
w *Terence Rattigan, Anatole de Grunwald* play *Esther
McCracken d Anthony Asquith ph* Bernard Knowles
m Nicholas Brodszky *ad* Paul Sheriff *ed* Reginald Beck
☆ Margaret Lockwood (Janet Royd), Derek Farr (Dallas
Chaytor), *A. E. Matthews* (Arthur Royd), *Marjorie Fielding*
(Mildred Royd), *Athene Seyler* (Aunt Mary), *Peggy Ashcroft*
(Flower Lisle), Margaretta Scott (Marcia Royd), Frank Cellier
(Mr. Chaytor), Roland Culver (Boofy Ponsonby), Jean
Cadell (Aunt Florence), David Tomlinson (John Royd),
Bernard Miles (PC)

'A completely unpretentious and charming film, the
components of which are as delicately balanced as
the mechanism of a watch.' – *New York Times*

'No subtlety of glance, movement or dialogue has
been missed, no possible highlight omitted.' – *MFB*

● Production was halted five times when bombs fell on the
studio.
● Remade as *Happy is the Bride*.

769
Quiet Wedding

Middle-class wedding preparations are complicated by family guests.

Esther McCracken's semi-classic stage comedy, set in a country house,
was filmed at an inauspicious time, during the London Blitz, with filming being frequently interrupted by German air raids. There is no trace
of worry in the polished result, a gentle drama of middle-class wedding
preparations being complicated by family guests until the groom
decides to escape by kidnapping his bride-to-be. It was admirably
filmed, with a splendid cast in excellent, subtle performances.

The Asthenic Syndrome

Russia 1989 153m bw/Fujicolor
Odessa Film Studio
original title: *Asteniceskij Sindrom*
w Kira Muratova, Sergei Popov, Alexander Tschernych
d Kira Muratova *ph* Vladimir Pankov *ed* Vladimir Olinik
☆ Olga Antonova (Natasha), Sergei Popov (Nikolai),
Galina Zakhrudayeva (Masha)
● The film was banned on its release, and was only seen in Russia after it won the Special Jury Prize at the Berlin Film Festival in 1990.

768

The Asthenic Syndrome

A bleak tale of a woman who cannot come to terms with her bereavement turns out to be a film within the film; the real story is of modern-day Moscow and events centring around a narcoleptic teacher.

The film opens with a chorus of three old ladies chanting, 'In my childhood and youth I thought that if everybody read Leo Tolstoy carefully they would understand absolutely everything and would become very kind and wise.' The sombre reality that follows reveals the obverse of what the old ladies had been led to expect when young: a society of uncaring and hostile people who will not wake up to their condition. It is also witty, structurally bold and harshly ironic.

'Inside every one of us is a special talent waiting to come out. The trick is finding it.'

Billy Elliot

GB 2000 111m colour
UIP/Working Title/BBC/Arts Council/Tiger Aspect/
WT2 (Greg Brenman, Jon Finn)
▣ ▤ ⊚ ⊚ ⌾
w Lee Hall *d* Stephen Daldry *ph* Brian Tufano
m Stephen Warbeck *pd* Maria Djurkovic *ad* Adam O'Neill
ed John Wilson *ch* Peter Darling
☆ *Julie Walters* (Mrs Wilkinson), *Gary Lewis* (Dad), *Jamie Bell* (Billy), Jamie Draven (Tony), Jean Heywood (Grandmother), Stuart Wells (Michael), Nicola Blackwell (Debbie)

'Has a feel-good factor that registers off the scale.' – Allan Hunter, Screen International

'The first genuinely exhilarating Brit flick of the new millennium, a no-holds-barred triumph.' – Caroline Westbrook, Empire

♙ Stephen Daldry; Lee Hall; Julie Walters
♆ British film; Jamie Bell; Julie Walters

767

Billy Elliot

In a Durham village during a year-long strike in 1984, an eleven-year-old miner's son defies his father by learning ballet rather than boxing.

Strong performances added grit to this ingratiating, uplifting, drama. Set against the year-long miner's strike in 1984, it gained from Jamie Bell's energetic performance as the boy, dancing with joy down a cobbled street, and from Julie Walters as his chain-smoking, down-to-earth teacher. It was deftly enough directed to disguise the manipulative nature of its narrative, though its feel-good ending felt a cheat. But realism wasn't the point, for all the film's authentic setting; it is an expertly presented parable about making dreams come true, and it is not surprising that it has been turned into a stage musical.

Sitting Pretty
US 1948 84m bw
TCF (Samuel G. Engel)

w F. Hugh Herbert *novel Belvedere* by Gwen Davenport
d Walter Lang *ph* Norbert Brodine *m* Alfred Newman
ad Leland Fuller, Lyle Wheeler *ed* Harmon Jones
☆ *Clifton Webb* (Lynn Belvedere), Robert Young (Harry),
Maureen O'Hara (Tracey), *Richard Haydn* (Mr. Appleton),
Louise Allbritton (Edna Philby), Ed Begley (Hammond),
Randy Stuart (Peggy), Larry Olsen (Larry)
♟ Clifton Webb

766
Sitting Pretty

A young couple acquire a most unusual male baby sitter, a self-styled genius who sets the neighbourhood on its ears by writing a novel about it.

An unexpected, very funny comedy that entrenched Clifton Webb as one of Hollywood's great characters. The humour lies in the contrast between Webb's dignified child-despising fusspot and his methods of dealing with problems: he cures a baby who flicks food around the breakfast table by upending a bowl of porridge on the child's head. Robert Young and Maureen O'Hara bring high spirits to the young couple and Richard Haydn is splendid as a snobby gossip.

Billy Elliot

129

Anne and Muriel

France 1971 108m Eastmancolor
Gala/Les Films du Carrosse/Cinetel (Marcel Berbert)
📖 ≣ ⊘ ⊘
original title: *Les Deux Anglaises et le Continent*
w François Truffaut, Jean Gruault *novel* Henri-Pierre
Roche *d* François Truffaut *ph* Nestor Almendros
m Georges Delerue *ad* Michel de Broin *ed* Yann Dedet
☆ Jean-Pierre Léaud (Claude Roc), Kika Markham (Anne
Brown), Stacey Tendeter (Muriel Brown), Sylvia Marriott
(Mrs. Brown), Marie Mansart (Madame Roc), Philippe
Léotard (Diurka), Irene Tunc (Ruta)

765
Anne and Muriel

A French writer falls in love with two English sisters.

As in *Jules et Jim*, Truffaut provided an elegant variation on the eternal love triangle in this literary story. His inspiration came from the only other novel by the same writer, Henri-Pierre Roche, which was also semi-autobiographical. The story mirrored Truffaut's own experience: he had been in love with two sisters, Françoise Dorleac, who died, and Catherine Deneuve, whose relationship with him had just ended. A powerful and painful drama of unrequited emotions, it was a commercial failure and Truffaut was unhappy that it was cut ('massacred, amputated and truncated,' as he put it) from its original length of 132m. It is the most beautiful of his films, with Almendros' photography conjuring the colours of the French Impressionists and bringing to it a wonderful sense of the period of the *belle epoque*.

'Thrills for a thousand movies plundered for one mighty show!'

'Romance aflame through dangerous days and nights of terror! In a land where anything can happen – most of all to a beautiful girl alone!'

Gunga Din

👥 US 1939 117m bw
RKO (George Stevens)
≣ ⊘
w Joel Sayre, Fred Guiol, Ben Hecht, Charles MacArthur
poem Rudyard Kipling *d* George Stevens *ph* Joseph H.
August *m* Alfred Newman *ad* Van Nest Polglase
ed Henry Berman, John Lockert
☆ *Cary Grant* (Sgt. Cutter), *Victor McLaglen* (Sgt.
MacChesney), *Douglas Fairbanks Jnr* (Sgt. Ballantine), *Sam
Jaffe* (Gunga Din), Eduardo Ciannelli (Guru), Joan Fontaine
(Emmy Stebbins), Montagu Love (Col. Weed), Robert Coote
(Higginbotham), Cecil Kellaway (Mr. Stebbins), Abner
Biberman (Chota), Lumsden Hare (Maj. Mitchell)

'One of the most enjoyable nonsense-adventure movies of all time.' – *Pauline Kael, 1968*

'Bravura is the exact word for the performances, and Stevens' composition and cutting of the fight sequences is particularly stunning.' – *NFT, 1973*

● Howard Hawks was replaced as director by George Stevens.

764
Gunga Din

Three cheerful army veterans meet adventure on the North-West Frontier.

Kipling's original story provided little more than a title for this rousing period actioner with comedy asides. Ben Hecht and Charles MacArthur concocted a script that took characters from Kipling's *Soldiers Three*, added a flavour of *The Three Musketeers*, and borrowed the ending from their *The Front Page*. Set in India's North-West Frontier, it tells of the adventures of two soldiers of the Royal Engineers, who try to prevent their friend from marrying and leaving the army. The cheerful veterans are captured after uncovering plans by an Indian cult to kill British troops, before escaping and capturing the cult's leader. Douglas Fairbanks Jnr claimed that the film was a satirical attack on Hitler, but it seems too light-hearted for that. Cary Grant, playing a dashing Cockney sergeant, regarded it as among his favourite films. It is one of the most entertaining of its kind ever made.

The Day of the Jackal

GB/France   1973   142m   Technicolor
Universal/Warwick/Universal France (John Woolf,
David Deutsch)

⬤⬤ ▤ ⊚ ⊚ ⊚

w Kenneth Ross *novel* Frederick Forsyth *d* Fred
Zinnemann *ph* Jean Tournier *m* Georges Delerue
ad Ernest Archer, Willy Holt *ed* Ralph Kemplen
☆ *Edward Fox* ('The Jackal'), Michel Lonsdale (Lebel),
Alan Badel (The Minister), Eric Porter (Colonel Rodin), Cyril
Cusack (Gunsmith), Delphine Seyrig (Colette), Donald
Sinden (Mallinson), Tony Britton (Inspector Thomas),
Timothy West (Berthier), Olga Georges-Picot (Denise),
Barrie Ingham (St. Clair), Maurice Denham (General
Colbert), Anton Rodgers (Bernard)

'Before *Jackal* is five minutes old, you know it's just
going to be told professionally, with no flavour and
no zest.' – *Stanley Kauffmann*

'All plot, with scarcely a character in sight.'
– *Michael Billington, Illustrated London News*

'A better than average thriller for those who haven't
read the book.' – *Judith Crist*

'A rare lesson in film-making in the good old grand
manner.' – *Basil Wright, 1972*

⚱ Ralph Kemplen

763

The Day of the Jackal

*British and French police combine to prevent an OAS assassination
attempt on General de Gaulle by use of a professional killer.*

Fred Zinnemann's thriller is an incisive, observant and extremely professional piece of work, based on a rather clinical bestseller. Following both the killer's elaborate preparations, from arranging false papers to obtaining a special gun, and the police's increasingly desperate search for the unknown assassin, it combines a nicely ironic approach with a breathless pace.

Coal Miner's Daughter

US   1980   124m   Technicolor
Universal (Bob Larson)

⬤⬤ ▤ ⊚ ⊚ ⊚ ♫

w Tom Rickman *d* Michael Apted *ph* Ralf D. Bode
md Owen Bradley *pd* John W. Corso *ed* Arthur Schmidt
☆ *Sissy Spacek* (Loretta), Tommy Lee Jones (Doolittle
Lynn), Levon Helm (Ted Webb), Jennifer Beasley (Peggy
Lynn), Phyllis Boyens (Clara Webb)
● A Region 1 DVD has commentary by Sissy Spacek and
Michael Apted.
♟ Sissy Spacek
⚱ best picture; Tom Rickman; Ralf D. Bode; editing (Arthur
Schmidt); art direction (John W. Corso, John M. Dwyer)

762

Coal Miner's Daughter

The wife of a Kentucky hillbilly becomes a star of country music.

Based on the life of the country and western singer Loretta Lynn, the wife of a Kentucky hillbilly who became a star, Michael Apted's film follows the familiar trajectory of showbusiness stories: gradual success, stardom, nervous breakdown, reconciliation. It is mainly notable for its depiction of backwoods Kentucky and the performance of Sissy Spacek in the title role, who provides an utterly convincing Loretta Lynn, from her nervous beginnings to her confident stardom. Apted directs sympathetically, providing a more accurate picture of individuals surprised by success than Hollywood's usual sanitized biographies.

'Three urban hombres heading west, seeking adventure, craving excitement ... and longing for room service.'

City Slickers
US   1991   114m   CFI color
First Independent/Castle Rock/Nelson/Face (Irby Smith)
▄ ▆ ◎ ◉ ◉ ◠

w Lowell Ganz, Babaloo Mandel d Ron Underwood
ph Dean Semler m Marc Shaiman, Hummie Mann
pd Lawrence G. Paull ad Mark Mansbridge ed O. Nicholas Brown
☆ Billy Crystal (Mitch Robbins), Daniel Stern (Phil Berquist), Bruno Kirby (Ed Furillo), Patricia Wettig (Barbara Robbins), Helen Slater (Bonnie Rayburn), Jack Palance (Curly), Josh Mostel (Barry Shalowitz), David Paymer (Ira Shalowitz), Noble Willingham (Clay Stone)

'A deft blend of wry humour and warmth (albeit with a little too much *thirty-something*-esque angst for its own good).' – *Variety*

🏆 Jack Palance

761
City Slickers

Three friends, all facing midlife crises, decide to spend their vacation on a cattle drive.

Three white-collar workers, all facing midlife crises, spend their vacation on a dude ranch and take part in a cattle drive in this witty and engaging comedy. There are some affectionate parodies of moments from such classic Westerns as *Red River*, and the theme from *The Magnificent Seven* underscores their hapless antics on horseback. The difference between the reality of cowboy life they experience and their fantasies is emphasized by casting Jack Palance, memorable as the bad guy in *Shane*, as their leathery mentor.

Blithe Spirit
GB   1945   96m   Technicolor
Two Cities/Cineguild (Anthony Havelock-Allan)
▄ ▆ ◉ ◉

w Noël Coward play Noël Coward scenario David Lean, Anthony Havelock-Allan, Ronald Neame d David Lean
ph Ronald Neame m Richard Addinsell ad C.P. Norman
ed Jack Harris
☆ Rex Harrison (Charles Condomine), Kay Hammond (Elvira), Constance Cummings (Ruth Condomine), Margaret Rutherford (Madame Arcati), Hugh Wakefield (Dr. Bradman), Joyce Carey (Mrs. Bradman), Jacqueline Clark (Edith)

'Ninety minutes of concentrated, cultivated fun.' – C. A. Lejeune

● After seeing this, Noël Coward reputedly told Rex Harrison: 'After me, you're the best light comedian in the world.'

760
Blithe Spirit

A cynical novelist's second marriage is disturbed when the playful ghost of his first wife materializes during a séance.

Direction and acting carefully preserve a comedy which on its first West End appearance in 1941 achieved instant classic status. Lean was a reluctant director of it, because he did not feel at home with light comedy. He also thought the plot was totally unreal. The film is virtually stolen by Margaret Rutherford as an eccentric medium (though Coward had not liked her performance in either medium. 'Amateur', he hissed after first seeing her). If Lean wasn't at home in this kind of comedy, Rex Harrison certainly was. The repartee scarcely dates, and altogether this is a most polished job of film-making.

'He's dynamite with a gun or a girl.'

This Gun for Hire
US 1942 81m bw
Paramount (Richard M. Blumenthal)

▬ ⊛~ ◎ ⌒

w Albert Maltz, W. R. Burnett *novel* A Gun for Sale by
Graham Greene d Frank Tuttle ph John Seitz m David
Buttolph *ad* Hans Dreier *ed* Archie Marshek
☆ *Alan Ladd* (Philip Raven), *Veronica Lake* (Ellen
Graham), Robert Preston (Michael Crane), *Laird Cregar*
(Willard Gates), Tully Marshall (Alvin Brewster), Mikhail
Rasumny (Slukey), Marc Lawrence (Tommy)
● It was remade, less effectively, as a TV movie in 1991,
directed by Lou Antonio and starring Robert Wagner.

759
This Gun for Hire

A professional killer becomes involved in a fifth columnist plot.

An efficient Americanization of one of its author's more sombre enter-
tainments. The novel was one of Greene's most cinematic stories, told
in a sequence of short scenes, which translated well to the screen,
even if much of the subtlety of the original was lost, and the character
of the gunman was softened to suit Alan Ladd. The melodrama has an
authentic edge and strangeness to it, and it established the star images
of both Ladd and Lake, as well as being oddly downbeat for a
Hollywood product of a jingoistic time.

Marathon Man
US 1976 126m Metrocolor
Paramount (Robert Evans, Sidney Beckerman)

▭ ▬ ⊛~ ◎ ◎

w William Goldman *novel* William Goldman *d John
Schlesinger ph Conrad Hall m* Michael Small
pd Richard MacDonald *ad* Jack DeShields *ed* Jim Clark
☆ Dustin Hoffman (Babe Levy), *Laurence Olivier* (Szell),
Roy Scheider (Doc Levy), William Devane (Janeway),
Marthe Keller (Elsa), Fritz Weaver (Prof. Biesenthal), Marc
Lawrence (Erhard)

'A film of such rich texture and density in its
construction, so fascinatingly complex in its
unfolding, so engrossing in its personalities, and
so powerful in its performance and pace that the
seduction of the senses has physical force.'
– *Judith Crist, Saturday Review*

'If at the film's end, you have followed the series of
double and triple crosses, braved the torture
scenes, and still don't know what it was about,
you're bound to have company.' – *Paul Coleman,
Film Information*

'A Jewish revenge fantasy.' – *Pauline Kael*

'He has made a most elegant, bizarre, rococo
melodrama out of material which, when you think
about it, makes hardly any sense at all.' – *Vincent
Canby, New York Times*

⚥ Laurence Olivier

758
Marathon Man

*A vicious Nazi returns from Uruguay to New York in search of dia-
monds which had been kept for him by his now-dead brother, and is
outwitted by the young brother of an American agent he has killed.*

John Schlesinger's complex mystery thriller has become famous for
one scene, in which Laurence Olivier, as an ex-Nazi and dentist, ties
down Dustin Hoffman, an innocent who gets caught up in an espionage
plot, and tortures him by drilling his teeth. Olivier, in one of his best
latter-day screen performances, was able to use to advantage what he
regarded as a disfigurement, his scarred, thin upper lip, which gave
him a hardened appearance. The film has more than thrills to offer in its
labyrinthine story. Underpinning the action are meditations on freedom,
McCarthyism and Fascism, before it finally settles down to being a
simple shocker with a nick-of-time climax. The presentation is dazzling.

'The true story of a girl who took on all of Texas … and almost won.'

Sugarland Express
US   1974   110m   Technicolor   Panavision
Universal (Richard Zanuck, David Brown)
▬ &. ⌕
w Hal Barwood, Matthew Robbins *d* *Steven Spielberg*
ph Vilmos Zsigmond *m* John Williams *ad* Joe Alves
ed Edward Abroms, Verna Fields
☆ Goldie Hawn (Lou Jean Poplin), Ben Johnson (Capt. Tanner), Michael Sacks (Officer Slide), William Atherton (Clovis Poplin)

'*Ace in the Hole* meets *Vanishing Point*.' – *Sight and Sound*

757
Sugarland Express

A criminal couple goes on the run and becomes a media sensation.

Steven Spielberg's movie of a chase through Texas is comedy with a bitter aftertaste, very stylishly handled. A convict's wife persuades him to escape because their baby is being adopted. They hijack a patrol car, take the cop hostage, and career through the state, inadvertently leaving behind them a trail of destruction, while becoming media sensations, cheered on their way by sympathetic spectators. Based on a real happening in the late Sixties, it engenders an atmosphere of excess as more than a hundred police cars join the chase, and the naive couple behaves as if they are out for an afternoon's drive in the country. There is only one way for the story to end, but even so the sudden tragedy shocks.

'The story of a family on the edge and a man who brought them back.'

Ulee's Gold
US   1997   111m   DuArt
Orion/Jonathan Demme/Nunez/Gowan/Clinica Estetico
▦ ▬ &. ⌕
wd Victor Nuñez *ph* Virgil Marcus Mirano *m* Charles Engstrom *pd* Robert 'Pat' Garner *ad* Debbie Devilla
ed Victor Nuñez
☆ *Peter Fonda* (Ulee Jackson), Patricia Richardson (Connie Hope), Jessica Biel (Casey Jackson), J. Kenneth Campbell (Sheriff Bill Floyd), Christine Dunford (Helen Jackson), Steven Flynn (Eddie Flowers), Dewey Weber (Ferris Dooley)

'Nuñez achieves a rare, and rarely earned, emotional depth that rewards the moderate demands he makes on contemporary viewers' short attention spans.' – *Todd McCarthy, Variety*

⚜ Peter Fonda

756
Ulee's Gold

A bee-keeper, a middle-aged widower with family problems, is threatened by two hoodlums, associates of his jailed son and his drug-addicted wife.

Victor Nuñez's slow-moving drama deals with a bee-keeper, a middle-aged widowed Vietnam veteran with domestic problems, who is victimized by two hoodlums, who are closely connected with his wife, a drug addict, and son, who is in jail. It builds inexorably to a compelling, emotionally satisfying peak. Peter Fonda gives his best performance for a director that he found the most generous and exacting of his career. Fonda's Ulee finds redemption by applying to other people the understanding he has made with the bees: he takes care of them, they take care of him.

Hue and Cry

Hue and Cry
GB 1946 82m bw
Ealing (Michael Balcon)

w T. E. B. Clarke *d* Charles Crichton *ph* Douglas Slocombe, John Seaholme *m* Georges Auric *ed* Charles Hasse

☆ Alastair Sim (Felix H. Wilkinson), Jack Warner (Nightingale), Harry Fowler (Joe Kirby), Valerie White (Rhona), Frederick Piper (Mr Kirby), Jack Lambert (Ford), Joan Dowling (Clarry), Douglas Barr (Alec), Stanley Escane (Boy), Vida Hope (Mrs Kirby), Ian Dawson (Norman), Gerald Fox (Dicky), Bruce Belfrage (BBC Announcer)

'Refreshing, bloodtingling and disarming.'
– *Richard Winnington*

755
Hue and Cry

East End boys discover that their favourite boys' paper is being used by crooks to pass information.

The first 'Ealing comedy' uses vivid London locations as background for a sturdy comic plot with a climax in which the criminals are rounded up by thousands of boys swarming over dockland. It laid the groundwork for the studio's very British comedies that followed it, by putting odd happenings within a realistic setting. It is a film of considerable charm, with the vitality of its young cast matched by expert adult performances from Alastair Sim, as a child-hating writer of kid's stories, and Jack Warner as a Cockney crook.

'Are You Ready To Play?'

The Game
US 1997 128m Technicolor Panavision
Polygram/Propaganda (Steve Golin, Cean Chaffin)

w John Brancato, Michael Ferris *d* David Fincher *ph* Harris Savides *m* Howard Shore *pd* Jeffrey Beecroft *ad* Jim Murakami *ed* James Haygood

☆ Michael Douglas (Nicholas Van Orton), Sean Penn (Conrad), Deborah Kara Unger (Christine), James Rebhorn (Jim Feingold), Peter Donat (Samuel Sutherland), Carroll Baker (Ilsa), Anna Katarina (Elizabeth), Armin Mueller-Stahl (Anson Baer)

'A high-toned mind-game of a movie.' – *Variety*

754
The Game

A middle-aged workaholic millionaire is, for his birthday, given a gift that casts him as a participant in a mysterious game that turns his life upside down.

David Fincher's high-energy thriller plunges its protagonist Michael Douglas, and the audience, into a world where nothing is to be trusted. Fincher maintains a dark and deadly atmosphere, heavy with paranoia. The plot climaxes with a clever twist as Douglas, finding himself renewed by his struggles to survive the sudden chaos that surrounds him, discovers he has been set up as a pawn in an elaborate, mysterious game.

The Golem

The Golem
Germany 1920 75m approx bw silent
UFA
▭ ▬ ⊚ ⊘
w Paul Wegener, Henrik Galeen *d* Paul Wegener, Carl Boese *ph* Karl Freund, Guido Seeber *ad* Hans Poelzig
☆ Paul Wegener (The Golem), Albert Steinruck (Rabbi Loew), Ernst Deutsch (Famulus)

753
The Golem

In 16th-century Prague a Jewish rabbi constructs a man of clay to defend his people against a pogrom.

There have been several versions of this story, but this is by far the best. Its splendid sets, performances and certain scenes are all clearly influential on later Hollywood films, especially *Frankenstein*. Paul Wegener had filmed the story twice before in modern-day settings. This version takes the story back to its origins and is not without pathos in its depiction of the creature's unfulfilled desire to be human; as novelist Arnold Zweig put it, 'there it stands, in perplexity and anguish, unable to grasp what is before it; and the hour goes by.'

The Fencing Master

The Fencing Master
Spain 1992 88m colour
Mayfair/Majestic/Origen/Altube Filmeak/ICAA
(Antonio Cardenal, Pedro Olea)
▭ ▬
original title: *El Maestro de Esgrima*
w Antonio Larreta, Francisco Prada, Arturo Pérez Reverte, Pedro Olea *novel* Arturo Pérez Reverte *d* Pedro Olea *ph* Alfredo Mayo *m* José Nieto *ad* Luis Valles *ed* José Salcedo
☆ *Omero Antonutti* (Don Jaime Astarloa), *Assumpta Serna* (Adela de Otero), Joaquim de Almeida (Luis de Ayala), José Luis Lopez Vázquez (Jenaro Campillo), Alberto Closas (Álvaro Salanova), Miguel Rellán (Agapito Cárceles)

'Stellar performances ... a distinguished and literate script, fine plot development and accomplished direction and lensing.' – *Variety*

'A deeply romantic Spanish thriller with two performances at its centre that do more than catch the eye. At times they catch the breath.' – *Derek Malcolm, Guardian*

752
The Fencing Master

In Madrid in the 1860s, at a time of extreme political upheaval, a fencing master becomes involved with a beautiful woman and finds himself caught up in a situation he does not understand.

The Spanish director Pedro Olea began making films in the 1960s and suffered from censorship during and immediately after Franco's dictatorship, which may explain why this, his masterpiece, an elegant, erotically-charged melodrama of love, loyalty and mystery, is of more recent date. It is graced by two subtly effective performances from Omero Antonutti, as the teacher of a moribund art, and Assumpta Serna as his *femme fatale*.

An American Werewolf in London
GB   1981   97m   Technicolor
Polygram/Lycanthrope (Peter Guber, Jon Peters)
▭ ▤   ◎~   ◎   ◎

wd John Landis *ph* Robert Paynter *m* Elmer Bernstein
ad Leslie Dilley *ed* Malcolm Campbell *sp Effects
Associates, Rick Baker*
☆ David Naughton (David Kessler), Jenny Agutter (Alex
Price), Griffin Dunne (Jack Goodman), John Woodvine (Dr.
Hirsch), Lila Kaye (Barmaid), Brian Glover (Chess Player)

'The gear changes of tone and pace make for a very
jerkily driven vehicle.' – *Sunday Times*

'Seems curiously unfinished, as though Landis
spent all his energy on spectacular set-pieces and
then didn't want to bother with things like
transitions, character development, or an ending.'
– *Roger Ebert*

751

An American Werewolf in London

Two American tourists are bitten by a werewolf.

A curious but oddly endearing mixture of horror film and spoof, of
comedy and shock, with everything grist to its mill, including tourist
Britain and the wedding of Prince Charles. John Landis wrote a witty
script about two American backpackers who are attacked by a werewolf on the Yorkshire moors. The survivor is horrified to discover that
at full moon, he, too, becomes a werewolf. The mix of horror and black
humour works well, especially when the werewolf meets his undead,
decaying victims in a Soho porn cinema. Rick Baker's special effects of
the change from man to wolf are notable, and signalled new developments in this field.

☆ **Joe Dante**
Director ☆

1. Citizen Kane (Welles)
2. City Lights (Chaplin)
3. 8 1/2 (Fellini)
4. Les Enfants du Paradis (Carné)
5. The Dead (Brakhage)
6. Rashomon (Kurosawa)
7. Psycho (Hitchcock)
8. Raging Bull (Scorsese)
9. The Searchers (Ford)
10. Once Upon a Time in the West (Leone)

☆ **Sam Mendes**
Producer, Director ☆

1. Citizen Kane (Welles)
2. Fanny and Alexander (Bergman)
3. The Godfather Part II (Coppola)
4. The Piano (Campion)
5. The Red Shoes (Powell, Pressburger)
6. Sunset Blvd. (Wilder)
7. 2001: A Space Odyssey (Kubrick)
8. Taxi Driver (Scorsese)
9. Vertigo (Hitchcock)
10. The Wizard of Oz (Fleming)

☆ **Michael Mann**
Producer, Director ☆

1. Apocalypse Now (Coppola)
2. Battleship Potemkin (Eisenstein)
3. Citizen Kane (Welles)
4. Dr. Strangelove (Kubrick)
5. Faust (Murnau)
6. Last Year at Marienbad (Resnais)
7. My Darling Clementine (Ford)
8. The Passion of Joan of Arc (Dreyer)
9. Raging Bull (Scorsese)
10 The Wild Bunch (Peckinpah)

Showboat

Showboat
US 1936 110m bw
Universal (Carl Laemmle Jnr)
▪️ ◎

w Oscar Hammerstein II *book* Oscar Hammerstein II for the Broadway musical *novel* Edna Ferber *d* James Whale *ph* John Mescall *m/ly* Jerome Kern, Oscar Hammerstein II *md* Victor Baravalle *ch* LeRoy Prinz *ad* Charles D. Hall *ed* Ted J. Kent, Bernard W. Burton
☆ *Irene Dunne* (Magnolia Hawks), *Allan Jones* (Gaylord Ravenal), *Helen Morgan* (Julie), *Paul Robeson* (Joe), *Charles Winninger* (Capt. Andy Hawks), *Hattie McDaniel* (Queenie, Joe's Wife), Donald Cook (Steve), Sammy White (Frank Schultz)

'For three quarters of its length, good entertainment: sentimental, literary, but oddly appealing.' – *Graham Greene*

● A primitive version of *Showboat* was made in 1929, which was part-talkie with synchronized sound for the silent sequences. Once thought lost, it survives in a version that lacks some of its sound. Directed by Harry Pollard, it starred Laura La Plante and Joseph Schildkraut. Remade by MGM in 1951.
● Before Allan Jones was cast, Walter Pidgeon, Robert Taylor, John Boles, Fredric March and Nelson Eddy were all considered.
♫ 'I Have the Room Above Her'; 'Ah Still Suits Me'; 'Gallavantin' Around'; 'Cotton Blossom'; 'Where's The Mate For Me?'; 'Make Believe'; 'Ol' Man River'; 'Can't Help Lovin' Dat Man'; 'You Are Love'; 'Bill'; 'Goodbye My Lady Love'; 'After the Ball'.

750
Showboat

Lives and loves of the personnel on an old-time Mississippi showboat.

Great style and excellent performances mark this version of Jerome Kern's operetta. There are two moments in themselves that make it a classic: Paul Robeson singing 'Ol' Man River' as the camera pans around him, moves into a close-up and dissolves to a montage of work on the river, and Helen Morgan's poignant love song 'Bill', which she sang in the original Broadway production. It also has the excellent Charles Winninger as Cap'n Andy, another member of the Broadway show, who had actually worked on a showboat. Whale's approach did not go down well with some of the cast, who were more used to the theatre, but his insistence on realism has helped to give the film a timeless quality.

Ivan the Terrible

Ivan the Terrible
USSR 1942 100m bw some Agfacolor in part two
Mosfilm .
▪️ ▪️ ◎ ◉ ◉ ◖
original title: *Ivan Groznyi*
ph Edouard Tissé (exteriors), Andrei Moskvin (interiors) *m* Sergei Prokofiev *ad* Isaac Shpinel, L. Naumova *wd/ed* Sergei Eisenstein
☆ Nikolai Cherkassov, Ludmilla Tselikovskaya, Serafima Birman

'A visual opera, with all of opera's proper disregard of prose-level reality … an extraordinarily bold experiment, fascinating and beautiful to look at.' – *James Agee*

749
Ivan the Terrible

The life of a 16th-century tsar.

Eisenstein's film was intended to be in three parts, detailing Ivan's early years, his romance and his struggle with the Boyars. Only two parts were finished and the second (released in 1946 and also known as *The Boyars' Plot*) is not up to the standard of part one. Eisenstein's style had changed. The swift-cutting montage of *Battleship Potemkin* had given way to a more stately approach, influenced here by Russian religious art. The plot is by the way; the film overflows with grim, gloomy and superbly composed images and the coronation sequence alone is a masterpiece of cinema.

The Nightmare Before Christmas

♦♦ US 1993 75m Technicolor
Buena Vista/Touchstone (Tim Burton, Denise Di Novi)
▭ ▬ ◉ ⊚ ◌ ⌂
aka: *Tim Burton's The Nightmare Before Christmas*
w Caroline Thompson, Michael McDowell *story* Tim
Burton *d* Henry Selick *ph* Pete Kozachik *m/ly* Danny
Elfman *ad* Deane Taylor *ed* Stan Webb *sp* Pete Kozachik,
Eric Leighton, Ariel Velasco Shaw, Gordon Baker
☆ Featuring the voices of Danny Elfman, Chris Sarandon,
Catherine O'Hara, William Hickey, Glenn Shadix, Paul
Reubens

'The dazzling techniques employed here create a
striking look that has never been seen in such a
sustained form before, making this a unique curio
that will appeal to kids and film enthusiasts alike.' –
Variety

'An animated fun-house for eeek freaks of all ages.'
– *Peter Travers, Rolling Stone*

'It displays more inventiveness than some studios
can manage in an entire year.' – *Kenneth Turan,
Los Angeles Times*

● Regions 1 and 2 special edition includes commentary by
Henry Selick and two short films, *Vincent* and
Frankenweenie.
♟ visual effects

Woman of the Year

US 1942 114m bw
MGM (Joseph L. Mankiewicz)
▭ ▬ ◉ ⊚
w Ring Lardner Jnr, Michael Kanin *d* George Stevens
ph Joseph Ruttenberg *m* Franz Waxman *ad* Randall
Duell, Cedric Gibbons *ed* Frank Sullivan
☆ *Spencer Tracy* (Sam Craig), *Katharine Hepburn* (Tess
Harding), Fay Bainter (Ellen Whitcomb), Reginald Owen
(Clayton), William Bendix (Pinkie Peters), Dan Tobin
(Gerald), Minor Watson (William Harding), Roscoe Karns
(Phil Whittaker)

'Between them they have enough charm to keep
any ball rolling.' – *William Whitebait*

♟ script
♟ Katharine Hepburn

748
The Nightmare Before Christmas

Jack Skellington, Pumpkin King of Halloween Town, tries to take over Christmas as well.

Henry Selick's superbly animated musical used an old-fashioned stop-motion technique with models to achieve a modern fairy tale. The method gives a three-dimensional quality to its imaginary landscape and characters dreamed up by Tim Burton, an artist with a liking for oddity and the macabre. Small children may not warm to its quirky humour, but as they grow more mature they will appreciate the film's diabolical jokes and visual richness.

747
Woman of the Year

A sports columnist marries a lady politician; they have nothing in common but love.

It was at the first meeting of the two stars that Katharine Hepburn remarked, 'I'm afraid I'm a bit tall for Mr Tracy', and the producer, Joseph Mankiewicz replied, 'Don't worry, he'll cut you down to size'. It is the sort of snappy dialogue that also featured in this comedy. He refers to her as the 'Calamity Jane of the international set'; she regards him as 'an ostrich with amnesia'. A simple, effective, mildly sophisticated movie, it allowed its two splendid stars to do their thing to the general benefit. The ending was changed by Mankiewicz, despite objections from the screenwriters, so that Hepburn was shown as unable to make a simple breakfast for her husband, a scene which is said to have endeared the movie to its female audience.

The Picture of Dorian Gray

US   1945   110m   bw   (Technicolor inserts)
MGM (Pandro S. Berman)

wd *Albert Lewin* novel Oscar Wilde *ph* Harry Stradling
m Herbert Stothart *ad* Cedric Gibbons, Hans Peters
ed Ferris Webster
☆ *George Sanders* (Lord Henry Wotton), *Hurd Hatfield*
(Dorian Gray), Donna Reed (Gladys Hallward), Angela
Lansbury (Sybil Vane), Peter Lawford (David Stone)

'Respectful, earnest, and, I'm afraid, dead.'
– *James Agee*

'Loving and practised hands have really improved
Wilde's original, cutting down the epigrammatic
flow … and rooting out all the preciousness which
gets in the way of the melodrama.' – *Richard
Winnington*

🏆 Harry Stradling
🏆 Angela Lansbury; art direction

746
The Picture of Dorian Gray

*A Victorian gentleman keeps a picture of himself in the attic, that
shows his age and depravity while he stays eternally young.*

Albert Lewin, a man drawn to literary subjects, was the ideal director
for Oscar's Wilde's story. In George Sanders, he had the ideal lead to
utter such Wildean epigrams as, 'When a man says he has exhausted
life, you may be sure that life has exhausted him.' An elegant variation
on *Dr Jekyll and Mr Hyde*, it was presented in a portentous style that
suited the subject admirably.

'A White Hot Night of Hate!'

Assault on Precinct 13

US   1976   91m   Metrocolor   Panavision
CKK (Joseph Kaufman)

wd *John Carpenter* *ph* Douglas Knapp *m* John Carpenter
ad Tommy Wallace *ed* John T. Chance (John Carpenter)
☆ Austin Stoker (Bishop), Darwin Joston (Wilson), Laurie
Zimmer (Leigh), Martin West (Lawson), Tony Burton
(Wells), Nancy Loomis (Julie)

'One of the most effective exploitation movies of
the last ten years … Carpenter scrupulously avoids
any overt socio-political pretensions, playing
instead for laughs and suspense in perfectly
balanced proportions.' – *Time Out*

745
Assault on Precinct 13

Gang members on a vendetta attack a police station.

John Carpenter's violent movie was in some ways a throwback to the
movies of the 1940s and 50s, but updated to fit modern sensibilities. It
was an urban Western, with members of a Los Angeles gang on a
vendetta attacking a police station in much the same way that, once
upon a time, Indians on the rampage lay siege to an isolated home-
stead, or a sheriff and his friends held off outlaws in Howard Hawks'
Rio Bravo. The conflicts that take place here are not a simple matter of
good versus bad, giving a certain moral complexity to the fast-paced,
exciting and often funny action.

Boys Don't Cry
US   1999   118m   DeLuxe
TCF/Killer Films (Jeffrey Sharp, John Hart, Eva Kolodner, Christine Vachon)
▣ ▤ ⊚ ⊘ ⌒

w Kimberly Peirce, Andy Bienen *d* *Kimberly Peirce*
ph Jim Denault *m* Nathan Larson *pd* Michael Shaw
ed Lee Percy, Tracy Granger
☆ *Hilary Swank* (Brandon Teena), *Chloe Sevigny* (Lana), Peter Sarsgaard (John), Brendan Sexton III (Tom), Alison Folland (Kate), Alicia Goranson (Candace), Matt McGrath (Lonny), Rob Campbell (Brian), Jeannetta Arnette (Lana's Mom)

'Audacious, accomplished pic should play well with open minded viewers seeking edgy, mature fare.' – *Emanuel Levy, Variety*

'A delicately conceived, fearless movie.' – *David Denby, New Yorker*

'Scorches the screen like a prairie fire.' – *J. Hoberman, Village Voice*

🯆 Hilary Swank
🯆 Chloe Sevigny

744
Boys Don't Cry

In Nebraska in the early Nineties, a girl decides to live as a boy.

Kimberly Peirce's film treated as tragedy a subject – cross-dressing – that has usually been an opportunity for cinematic comedy. Based on a true story and a re-working of a short film Peirce made four years earlier, this gains from a heartfelt performance from Hilary Swank as the gender-bending woman who makes a better man than the insecure petty criminals whom she upstages and outrages. It is an abrasive, jolting drama of shock and outrage, more disturbing than the grisliest horror movie because, based on fact, it exposes a desperation at the heart of America.

Smile
US   1975   113m   DeLuxe
UA (Michael Ritchie)
▬   ⊚~ ⊘

w Jerry Belson *d* Michael Ritchie *ph* Conrad Hall
m various *ed* Richard A. Harris
☆ Bruce Dern ("Big Bob" Freelander), Barbara Feldon (Brenda DiCarlo), Michael Kidd (Tommy French), Geoffrey Lewis (Wilson Shears), Nicholas Pryor (Andy DiCarlo)

'A beady, precise, technically skilful movie.' – *Michael Billington, Illustrated London News*

743
Smile

A bird's-eye view of the Young Miss America pageant in a small California town.

Michael Ritchie's film is highly polished fun. It is a witty series of vignettes in the form of a drama-documentary or satirical mosaic. What is remarkable is that this exposure of the rancid nature of the beauty parade and its soulless, upbeat, ever-smiling organizers manages somehow to be also warm-hearted and good natured, which finally makes it all the more devastating.

Gregory's Girl
GB 1980 91m colour
Lake/NFFC/STV (Davina Belling, Clive Parsons)

wd Bill Forsyth *ph* Michael Coulter *m* Colin Tully
ad Adrienne Coulter *ed* John Gow
☆ Gordon John Sinclair (later John Gordon Sinclair)
(Gregory), Dee Hepburn (Dorothy), Jake D'Arcy (Phil
Menzies), Claire Grogan (Susan)
🏆 best script

742
Gregory's Girl

In a Scottish new town, a school footballer becomes aware of sex.

Bill Forsyth, the talented Scottish director whose career suffered when he went to Hollywood and seemed to come to a halt in the final years of the last century, enjoyed a deserved world-wide success with this, his second film, about a daydreaming schoolboy falling for the beautiful girl who replaces him as centre-forward in the school's football team; eventually he finds greater success with other girls. It is a curiously diverting comedy, peopled by dreamers, from the cake-loving headmaster to Gregory's hapless friends; only the girls seem in control of the difficulties of negotiating any relationship with the opposite sex.

Night of the Demon

GB 1957 87m bw
Columbia/Sabre (Frank Bevis)
📷 ▬ ◐ ◎
US title: *Curse of the Demon*
w *Charles Bennett, Hal E. Chester* story *Casting the Runes*
by *M. R. James* d *Jacques Tourneur* ph *Ted Scaife*
m *Clifton Parker* ad *Ken Adam* ed *Michael Gordon*
☆ Dana Andrews (John Holden), Peggy Cummins
(Joanna Harrington), *Niall MacGinnis* (Dr. Karswell), *Athene
Seyler* (Mrs. Karswell), Brian Wilde (Rand Hobart), Maurice
Denham (Prof. Harrington), Ewan Roberts (Lloyd
Williamson), Liam Redmond (Mark O'Brien), Reginald
Beckwith (Mr. Meek)
● A Region 1 DVD release includes both the UK release
and the shorter US version, *Curse of the Demon*.

741
Night of the Demon

An occultist despatches his enemies by raising a giant medieval devil.

Jacques Tourneur's supernatural thriller is intelligently scripted and he makes good use of its British setting. The opening, with a man being chased through a dark wood, sets a tone of unease that is maintained throughout as a professor of psychology (Dana Andrews) comes to realize that an otherworldly evil force exists and his life is in danger. There are, unfortunately, pallid performances from the leads, but Tourneur achieves several frightening and memorable sequences in the best Hitchcock manner.

Major Barbara

GB 1941 121m bw
Gabriel Pascal
▬

w Anatole de Grunwald, Gabriel Pascal *play Bernard Shaw*
d *Gabriel Pascal, Harold French, David Lean* ph *Ronald
Neame* m *William Walton* ad *Vincent Korda, John Bryan*
ed *Charles Frend* cos *Cecil Beaton*
☆ *Wendy Hiller* (Maj. Barbara Undershaft), *Rex Harrison*
(Adolphus Cusins), *Robert Morley* (Andrew Undershaft),
Robert Newton (Bill Walker), *Marie Lohr* (Lady Brittomart),
Emlyn Williams (Snobby Price), Sybil Thorndike (The
General), Deborah Kerr (Jenny Hill), David Tree (Charles
Lomax), Felix Aylmer (James), Penelope Dudley Ward
(Sarah Undershaft), Walter Hudd (Stephen Undershaft),
Marie Ault (Rummy Mitchens), Donald Calthrop (Peter
Shirley)

'Shaw's ebullience provides an unslackening fount
of energy … his all-star cast of characters are
outspoken as no one else is in films except the
Marx Brothers.' – *William Whitebait*

'To call it a manifest triumph would be an arrant
stinginess with words.' – *New York Times*

740
Major Barbara

The daughter of an armaments millionaire joins the Salvation Army but resigns when it accepts her father's donation.

Bernard Shaw guarded the screen rights of his plays most scrupulously until he met Gabriel Pascal, a man whose main talent lay in persuading him to part with the rights for a pittance. It was not a deal that improved Shaw's transition to the screen, but, on this occasion, Pascal had the help of the more-than-competent Harold French and an impeccable cast. Shaw's drama contrasts two religious beliefs followed by an armaments millionaire and his daughter. The daughter joins the Salvation Army but resigns when it accepts a donation from her father, who believes in self-reliance and regards poverty as the worst of crimes. In this stagey but compulsive and witty version, there is some gorgeous acting (and overacting).

The Cameraman

US 1928 78m approx (24 fps) bw silent
MGM (Lawrence Weingarten)

w Clyde Bruckman, Lex Lipton, Richard Schayer *d* Edward Sedgwick *ph* Elgin Lessley, Reggie Manning *ad* Fred Gabourie *ed* Hugh Wynn

☆ Buster Keaton (Buster), Marceline Day (Sally), Harry Gribbon (Cop), Harold Goodwin (Stagg)

● The film was remade in 1948 for Red Skelton as *Watch the Birdie*, with Keaton supervising the gags but sadly getting no credit.

739
The Cameraman

In order to woo the object of his affection, a street photographer becomes a newsreel cameraman.

Buster Keaton's change in working methods after he signed with MGM, the first time he had given up control over his artistic freedom, was to have disastrous effects on his comedy. With this, his first film for the studio, he was able to ignore producer Lawrence Weingarten and make a charming and hilarious farce of errors under the direction of Edward Sedgwick, who, like him, had begun in vaudeville. Keaton plays a street photographer who becomes a newsreel cameraman in order to woo a secretary of a news organization. His amateur film, accidently double-exposed, includes shots of battleships sailing up Broadway. The best scene comes when he and a short, fat man attempt to change into their swimming costumes in the same cramped cubicle, with their clothes becoming inextricably tangled. For years after, MGM screened the film to new writers to demonstrate a perfectly constructed comedy.

Stormy Weather

US 1943 77m bw
TCF (Irving Mills)

w Frederick Jackson, Ted Koehler *d* Andrew Stone *ph* Leon Shamroy, Fred Sersen *md* Benny Carter *ch* Clarence Robinson *ad* Joseph C. Wright, James Basevi *ed* James B. Clark

☆ *Bill Robinson* (Corky), *Lena Horne* (Selina Rogers), *Fats Waller* (Himself), *Ada Brown* (Ada), *Cab Calloway* (Himself), Katherine Dunham and her Dancers (Themselves), Eddie Anderson, Flournoy Miller (Miller), *The Nicholas Brothers* (Themselves), Dooley Wilson (Gabe)

'A first-rate show, a spirited divertissement … a joy to the ear.' – *New York Times*

♫ 'There's No Two Ways about Love'; 'That Ain't Right'; 'Ain't Misbehavin''; 'Diga Diga Doo'; 'I Can't Give You Anything but Love'; 'Geechee Joe'; 'Stormy Weather'; 'My, My, Ain't That Somethin'?'

738
Stormy Weather

A backstage success story lightly based on the career of Bill Robinson.

This backstage success story was virtually a high-speed revue with all-black talent. And what talent! It is good to see Robinson himself, in his last screen performance, in more suitable company than Shirley Temple. Lena Horne sings the title song, which is also danced by Katherine Dunham and her troupe, the zoot-suited Cab Calloway performs some novelty numbers, Benny Carter and other excellent jazz players can be glimpsed, and Fats Waller steals the film with his exuberant playing and humour.

The Big Country

US   1958   165m   Technicolor   Technirama
UA/Anthony/Worldwide (William Wyler, Gregory Peck)

w James R. Webb, Sy Bartlett, Robert Wilder *novel* Donald Hamilton *d* William Wyler *ph* Franz Planer *m* Jerome Moross *ed* John Faure, Robert Belcher

☆ *Gregory Peck* (James McKay), Jean Simmons (Julie Maragon), Charlton Heston (Steve Leech), Carroll Baker (Patricia Terrill), *Burl Ives* (Rufus Hannassey), *Charles Bickford* (Maj. Henry Terrill), Alfonso Bedoya (Ramon), Chuck Connors (Buck Hannassey)

'Has, in fact, most of the elements one asks for in the Western. Especially it has a feeling of size and space ... Yet something, I think, is missing: the romantic heart.' – *Dilys Powell*

♟ Burl Ives
♟ Jerome Moross

737

The Big Country

The Terrills and the Hannasseys feud over water rights, and peace is brought about only with the deaths of the family heads.

William Wyler's big-scale Western was, as Peck pointed out, an anti-macho Western, in which the hero questioned the unwritten rule that 'a man's gotta do what a man's gotta do', refusing to fight when publicly challenged (though later he proves he is a man by fighting in private). The production was troubled: it took seven writers to produce a script, Bickford was as cantankerous as the character he played, and Wyler and Peck, its production partnership, were not speaking by the end. Perhaps because of the internecine battles, the film can be seen as an allegory of the Cold War, and is all very fluent, star-laden and easy to watch.

Yol

Switzerland   1982   114m   Fujicolor
Cactus/Maran/Antenne 2/Swiss Television/Güney (Edi Hubschmid, K. L. Puldi)

w Yilmaz Güney *d* Serif Gören *ph* Erdogan Engin *m* Sebastian Argol *ed* Yilmaz Güney, Elisabeth Waelchli
☆ Tarik Akan (Seyit Ali), Halil Ergün (Mehmet Salih), Necmettin Cobanoglu (Omer), Serif Sezer (Zine)
● It was a joint winner of the Palme d'Or for best film at the Cannes Film Festival in 1982.

736

Yol

Five convicts are released on a week's leave, and their various circumstances lead them to tragedy.

A rewarding, if occasionally heavy-going epic, *Yol* was one of the few Turkish films to be seen outside that country. It was written by Yilmaz Güney and masterminded by him while in prison for his left-wing political activities. Güney, the son of Kurdish peasants, escaped in time to edit the film, lost his Turkish citizenship as a result, and died from cancer at the age of 47 after completing one further film. Serif Gören's direction makes its point in a sequence of harsh images of repression. This is Güney's lasting memorial, a saga of man's inhumanity to man during a time of political unrest and military intervention in Turkey.

The Niebelungen
Germany   1924   bw   silent
Decla-Bioscop (Erich Pommer)

Part 1: *Siegfried*, 115m approx (24 fps)
Part 2: *Kriemheld's Revenge*, 125m approx (24 fps)
w Thea von Harbou *d* Fritz Lang *ph* Carl Hoffman,
Günther Rittau *ad* Otto Hunte, Karl Vollbrecht, Erich
Kettelhut *ed* Fritz Lang
☆ Paul Richter (Siegfried), Marguerite Schön (Kriemhild),
Theodor Loos (Gunther), Hannah Ralph (Brunhilde), Rudolf
Klein-Rogge (Attila, King of the Huns)
● A Region 1 two-disc DVD release features the original
1924 orchestral score and footage of Fritz Lang on the set.

735
The Niebelungen

An epic re-telling of the saga of Siegfried the dragon-killer.

This was the silent cinema's *The Lord of the Rings*, a vast, nationalistic epic set in a Germanic fantasy world. Lang's film drew on Richard Wagner's opera as well as the medieval saga of Siegfried, who killed a dragon and slayed a dwarf-king on his way to woo and marry Kriemhild, a princess of Burgundy; he upsets the fierce Brunhilde, Queen of Iceland, who arranges his death; Kriemhild then marries Attila the Hun and exacts her revenge with a mass slaughter of her enemies. Lang transformed the legends into a slow, chilling, awe-inspiring sequence of films, conceived as a tribute to the German nation. The fact that they were among Hitler's favourite viewing should not be held against them.

Man of Marble
Poland   1977   165m   colour
PRF/Zespol X (Andrzej Wajda)

original title: *Czlowiek Z Marmur*
w Aleksander Scibor-Rylski *d* Andrzej Wajda *ph* Edward
Klosinski *m* Andrzej Korzinski
☆ Jerzy Radziwilowicz (Mateusz Birkut/Maciej Jomczyk),
Krystyna Janda (Agnieszko), Michael Tarkowski (Michael
Tarkowski), Tadeusz Lomnicki (Jerzy Burski))

Man of Iron
Poland   1981   152m   colour/bw
PRF/Filmowy X

original title: *Czowiek Z Zelaza*
w Aleksander Scibor-Rylski *d* Andrzej Wajda *ph* Edward
Klosinski *m* Andrzej Korzynski
☆ Jerzy Radziwilowicz (Mateusz Birkut/Maciej Jomczyk),
Krystyna Janda (Agnieszka), Marian Opania (Winkel)
♟ best foreign film

734
Man of Marble/Man of Iron

Young film makers gather material on a political hero of the Fifties.

The first of two political dramas directed by Andrzej Wajda, both key films in the history of Polish cinema. *Men of Marble* is an extended drama in the style of *Citizen Kane* but with much more relavence to contemporary history. It depicts the rise and fall of a working-class hero, who is first praised and then destroyed by the state. The stirring companion piece *Man of Iron* deals with the events of 1980 and the rise of Solidarity in Poland, as seen through the eyes of a strike leader. Based on the career of Lech Walesa, who also appeared in a brief role in the movie, it is as honest a piece of history as one is likely to get from a so-called fiction film.

The Ox-Bow Incident
US   1943   75m   bw
TCF (Lamar Trotti)
🇺🇸 ⊙~ ⊙
GB title: *Strange Incident*
w Lamar Trotti *novel* Walter Van Tilburg Clark *d* William
Wellman *ph* Arthur Miller *m* Cyril Mockridge *ad* James
Basevi, Richard Day *ed* Allen McNeil
☆ *Henry Fonda* (Gil Carter), Henry Morgan (Art Croft),
Jane Darwell (Jenny Grier), Anthony Quinn (Juan
Martinez/Francisco Morez), Dana Andrews (Donald Martin),
Mary Beth Hughes (Rose Mapen/Rose Swanson), William
Eythe (Gerald Tetley), Harry Davenport (Arthur Davies),
Frank Conroy (Maj. Tetley)

'Realism that is as sharp and cold as a knife.'
– *Frank S. Nugent, New York Times*

'Very firm, respectable, and sympathetic; but I still
think it suffers from *rigor artis*.' – *James Agee*

🏆 best picture

733

The Ox-Bow Incident

A cowboy is unable to prevent three wandering travellers being unjustly lynched for murder.

Wellman's Western is one of the most uncompromising ever filmed, though it can also be seen as a warning against fascism, which was the original intention of Clark's novel. It is a harsh story: a cowboy unsuccessfully strives to prevent three wandering travellers being unjustly accused and subsequently lynched for the murder of a rancher. After the townspeople, urged on by a bigoted former army officer, have hanged the men, they discover that the rancher is alive and well. Wellman emphasizes the bleakness of the narrative by shooting much of it at night, in claustrophobic darkness. The movie, never popular because of its depressing nature, retains its power as an indictment of mob violence.

☆ **Charles Gant**,
Film Editor ☆

1. A Place In The Sun (George Stevens)
2. Chinatown (Polanski)
3. Safe (Haynes)
4. Festen (aka The Celebration) (Vinterberg)
5. William Shakespeare's Romeo and Juliet (Luhrmann)
6. The Thin Red Line (Malick)
7. One Flew Over The Cuckoo's Nest (Foreman)
8. Fargo (Coen)
9. Pulp Fiction (Tarantino)
10. The Night Of The Hunter (Laughton)

☆ **Richard Linklater**
Director ☆

1. Some Came Running (Minnelli)
2. Pickpocket (Bresson)
3. 2001: A Space Odyssey (Kubrick)
4. GoodFellas (Scorsese)
5. La Maman et la Putain (Eustache)
6. Los Olvidados (Buñuel)
7. In a Year with Thirteen Moons (Fassbinder)
8. Citizen Kane (Welles)
9. Fanny and Alexander (Bergman)
10. Carmen Jones (Preminger)

☆ **Lukas Moodysson**
Director ☆

1. Bicycle Thieves (De Sica)
2. Fanny and Alexander (Bergman)
3. Gummo (Korine)
4. La Haine (Kassovitz)
5. 'america (Amelio)
6. The Last Picture Show (Bogdanovich)
7. Mirror (Tarkovsky)
8. On the Waterfront (Kazan)
9. Riff-Raff (Loach)
10. Secrets & Lies (Leigh)
11. Where Is My Friend's House? (Kiarostami)

'A Comedy Of Families, A Chip Shop ...
And A Very Randy Dog.'

East is East
GB   1999   96m   DeLuxe
FilmFour/Assassin/BBC (Leslee Udwin)
⌷⌷ ☰ ⊘ ⊘

w Ayub Khan-Din *play* Ayub Khan-Din *d* Damien
O'Donnell *ph* Brian Tufano *m* Deborah Mollison *pd* Tom
Conroy *ad* Henry Harris *ed* Michael Parker
☆ *Om Puri* (George Khan), Linda Bassett (Ella Khan),
Jordan Routledge (Sajid Khan), Archie Panjabi (Meenah
Khan), Emil Marwa (Maneer Khan), Chris Bisson (Saleem
Khan), Jimi Mistry (Tariq Khan), Raji James (Abdul Khan),
Ian Aspinall (Nazir Khan), Lesley Nicol (Auntie Annie), Gary
Damer (Earnest Moorhouse), John Bardon (Mr.
Moorhouse), Emma Rydal (Stella Moorhouse), Ruth Jones
(Peggy)
● It is the most successful fully-funded British film so far.
Ⓣ British film

732
East is East

The children of a strict Pakistani father, who is married to an English woman, rebel when he arranges marriages for them.

An often broad but always enjoyable comedy that, in Ayub Khan-Din's screenplay, pits mixed-race Manchester-born children against their strict Pakistani father. The sons are on the other side of a generation and culture gap to their father, with their English mother trying to keep the peace between them. Om Puri's excellent performance as the father is evidence enough that paternal attitudes have little to do with nationality. For all its use of stereotypical characters and situations, this is a comedy of misunderstanding that manages to be truthful about family relationships and racial attitudes.

The Defiant Ones
US   1958   96m   bw
UA/Stanley Kramer
⌷⌷ ☰ ⊘↝ ⊘ ⊘

w Nathan E. Douglas (Nedrick Young), Harold Jacob Smith
d Stanley Kramer *ph* Sam Leavitt *m* Ernest Gold
ed Frederic Knudtson
☆ Tony Curtis (John 'Joker' Jackson), Sidney Poitier
(Noah Cullen), Theodore Bikel (Sheriff Max Miller), Charles
McGraw (Capt. Frank Gibbons), Lon Chaney Jnr (Big Sam),
King Donovan (Sally), Claude Akins (Mack), Lawrence
Dobkin (Editor), Whit Bissel (Lou Gans)l, Carl 'Alfalfa'
Switzer (Angus), Cara Williams (The woman)

'Probably Kramer's best picture. The subject matter
is relatively simple, though "powerful"; the action
is exciting; the acting is good. But the singleness of
purpose behind it all is a little offensive.' – *Pauline
Kael*

● Nathan E. Douglas was a pseudonym for the blacklisted
writer Nedrick Young.
🖥 Nathan E. Douglas, Harold Jacob Smith; Sam Leavitt
🏆 picture; Stanley Kramer; Tony Curtis; Sidney Poitier;
Theodore Bikel; Cara Williams; editing
Ⓣ Sidney Poitier

731
The Defiant Ones

Handcuffed together, a black convict and a white racist escape their captors and go on the run.

Stanley Kramer dealt with the subject of racism in several films. including *Home of the Brave*, *Pressure Point* and *Guess Who's Coming to Dinner*. Here he takes the most direct approach possible. by having a black and a white convict escape from a chain gang, still linked together but hating each other. Fortunately, he made this schematic melodrama into an exciting, suspenseful chase, as, hunted down by a posse with dogs, the two breast swollen rivers and race through woods and swamps. Through the rigours of their flight, they learn to respect one another: through knowledge comes acceptance.

Shadow of a Doubt

US 1943 108m bw
Universal (Jack H. Skirball)
🇺🇸 ◎~

w Thornton Wilder, Sally Benson, Alma Reville
story Gordon McDonell d Alfred Hitchcock ph Joe
Valentine m Dimitri Tiomkin ad Robert Boyle, John B.
Goodman ed Milton Carruth
☆ Joseph Cotten (Uncle Charlie), Teresa Wright (Young
Charlie), Hume Cronyn (Herbie Hawkins), Macdonald Carey
(Jack Graham), Patricia Collinge (Emma Newton), Henry
Travers (Joseph Newton), Wallace Ford (Fred Saunders)

'Some clever observation of rabbity white-collar life
which, in spite of a specious sweetness, is the best
since It's a Gift.' – James Agee

● Remade in 1959 as Step Down to Terror, with Charles
Drake.
● A lacklustre TV version was made in 1991, starring Mark
Harmon and directed by Karen Arthur.
● Hitchcock makes his cameo appearance on a train
playing cards.
♟ original story.

730
Shadow of a Doubt

A favourite uncle comes to visit his family in a small Californian town. He is actually on the run from police, who know him as the Merry Widow Murderer.

Hitchcock's quietest film is memorable chiefly for its depiction of small-town life in California. Its authentic atmosphere owes much to the writing of Thornton Wilder, whose classic play *Our Town* detailed such everyday matters. Hitchcock keeps the suspense moving slowly but surely, illustrating the point that, as he told François Truffaut, 'villains are not all black and heroes are not all white; there are greys everywhere.'

'Seven deadly sins. Seven ways to die.'

Seven

US 1995 127m DeLuxe Panavision
Entertainment/New Line (Arnold Kopelson, Phyllis
Carlyle)
📼 📼 🇺🇸 ◎~ ⊚ ◉ ⌖

w Andrew Kevin Walker d David Fincher ph Darius
Khondji m Howard Shore pd Arthur Max ad Gary
Wissner ed Richard Francis-Bruce
☆ Brad Pitt (Detective David Mills), Morgan Freeman
(Lieutenant William Somerset), Richard Roundtree (Talbot),
R. Lee Ermey (Police Captain), John C. McGinley
(California), Julie Araskog (Mrs. Gould), Kevin Spacey
(John Doe), Gwyneth Paltrow (Tracy)

'Dark, grim and terrific ... this weirdly off-kilter
suspenser goes well beyond the usual police
procedural or killer-on-the-rampage yarn.' – Todd
McCarthy, Variety

♟ Richard Francis-Bruce

729
Seven

A detective nearing retirement and his temperamental young replacement track down a serial killer who is working his way through the seven deadly sins.

David Fincher's tense, involving thriller rises above the somewhat predictable schematics of its screenplay. In its dark journey to a surprisingly downbeat conclusion, the film depicts the city as a paradise lost, and its inhabitants as mostly beyond redemption. Morgan Freeman, as the grizzled detective, and Brad Pitt, as his brash sidekick, play off one another with great skill, while Fincher creates an effectively dingy setting in which corruption can flourish.

The Damned

West Germany/Italy 1969 164m
Eastmancolor
Praesidens/Pegaso
◧ ▤ ◐ ♫ ⌒
original title: *Götterdämmerung*
aka: *Le Caduta Degli Dei*
w Nicola Badalucco, Enrico Medioli, Luchino Visconti
d Luchino Visconti *ph* Armando Nannuzzi, Pasquale de
Santis *m* Maurice Jarre *ad* Enzo del Prato, Pasquale
Romano *ed* Ruggero Mastroianni
☆ Dirk Bogarde (Friedrich Bruckmann), Ingrid Thulin
(Baroness Sophie von Essenbeck), Helmut Berger (Martin
von Essenbeck), Renaud Verley (Gunther von Essenbeck),
Helmut Griem (Aschenbach), René Kolldehoff (Baron
Konstantin von Essenbeck), Albrecht Schönhals (Baron
Joachim von Essenbeck), Umberto Orsini (Herbert
Thallman)

'One is left lamenting that such a quondam master
of realism as Visconti is making his films look like
operas from which the score has been inexplicably
removed.' – *MFB*

'The ludicrous flailings of puny puppets in
inscrutable wooden frenzies.' – *John Simon*

♟ script

728
The Damned

A family of German industrialists divides and destroys itself under Nazi influence.

Visconti, a director of many operas, brought a Wagnerian touch to this drama. Its exaggerated colour and make-up to match the rotting theme can make it rather a strain to watch, but it is a strongly acted drama of a power struggle in which the participants are prepared not only to betray, but to kill, one another. Visconti uses sexual transgression as a sign of Fascism, while revealing, within the microcosm of a family, the complicity of the upper middle-classes in the rise of Hitler, a man for whom they had contempt.

'The greatest fairy tale never told.'
Shrek
♈ US 2001 89m Technicolor
DreamWorks/PDI (Aron Warner, John H. Williams,
Jeffrey Katzenberg)
◧ ▤ ◐ ◎ ⌒
w Ted Elliott, Terry Rossio, Joe Stillman, Roger S. H.
Schulman *book* William Steig *additional dialogue* Cody
Cameron, Chris Miller, Conrad Vernon *d* Andrew
Adamson, Vicky Jenson *m* Harry Gregson-Williams, John
Powell *pd* James Hegedus *ad* Guillaume Aretos, Douglas
Rogers *ed* Sim Evan-Jones
☆ Mike Myers (Shrek), Eddie Murphy (Donkey), Cameron
Diaz (Princess Fiona), John Lithgow (Lord Farquaad),
Vincent Cassel (Monsieur Hood)

'An instant animated classic … It offers
entertainment equally to viewers from 4 to 104.'
– *Todd McCarthy, Variety*

⚱ animated feature film
♟ Ted Elliott, Terry Rossio, Joe Stillman, Roger S. H.
Schulman
Ⓣ Ted Elliott, Terry Rossio, Joe Stillman, Roger S. H.
Schulman

727
Shrek

When his swamp is occupied by exiled fairy-tale characters, an ugly, green ogre agrees to rescue a princess in return for being left alone, and falls in love with her.

This, like *Toy Story*, was a film, using slick computer-generated animation, that seemed to spell the end, in America at least, of hand-drawn animation in the style of the classic Disney movies. Eddie Murphy is in exceptional, motor-mouth form as Donkey (reminiscent of Robin Williams' turn as the genie in Disney's *Aladdin*). It was both clever and witty, managing to be true to the conventions of fairy tales and to make fun of them, mainly at the expense of Disney's approach to traditional stories. The result had charm and was as polished as its gleaming animations.

Dracula

'Who will be his bride tonight?'

Dracula
GB   1958   82m   Technicolor
Rank/Hammer (Anthony Hinds)
US title: *Horror of Dracula*
w Jimmy Sangster *novel* Bram Stoker *d* Terence Fisher
ph Jack Asher *m* James Bernard *ad* Bernard Robinson
ed James Needs, Bill Lenny
☆ *Peter Cushing* (Van Helsing), *Christopher Lee*
(Dracula), Melissa Stribling (Mina Holmwood), Carol Marsh
(Lucy), Michael Gough (Arthur Holmwood), John Van
Eyssen (Jonathan Harker), Valerie Gaunt (Vampire Woman),
Miles Malleson (Marx, the Undertaker)

A vampire hunter sets out to destroy Count Dracula.

Terence Fisher's remake of *Dracula* was the best of the horror movies made by the British company Hammer Films, as well as the most faithful to the original story. It played down some of the supernatural aspects, such as Dracula turning into a bat, for reasons of expense, and concentrates on the set pieces of Stoker's novel. Decor and colour were well used, and the leading performances are striking. Christopher Lee gets his teeth into the role of Dracula, bringing to it a seductive panache, and Peter Cushing gives a puritanical intensity to the vampire's adversary, Van Helsing.

The Treasure of the Sierra Madre

'Greed, gold and gunplay on a Mexican mountain of malice!'

'The nearer they got to their treasure, the further they got from the law!'

The Treasure of the Sierra Madre
US   1948   126m   bw
Warner (Henry Blanke)
wd John Huston *novel* B. Traven *ph* Ted McCord *m* Max
Steiner *md* Leo F. Forbstein
☆ Humphrey Bogart, *Walter Huston*, Tim Holt, Alfonso
Bedoya, John Huston, Bruce Bennett, Barton MacLane

'This bitter fable is told with cinematic integrity and considerable skill.' – *Henry Hart*

'The faces of the men, in close-up or in a group, achieve a kind of formal pattern and always dominate the screen.' – *Peter Ericsson*

'One of the very few movies made since 1927 which I am sure will stand up in the memory and esteem of qualified people alongside the best of the silent movies.' – *James Agee*

🏆 John Huston (as writer and director); Walter Huston
♟ best picture
● Father and son, Walter and John Huston both received oscars.

Three gold prospectors come to grief through greed.

John Huston's fable has its faults, being too studio-bound for an outdoor movie set in Mexico, but it is engaging for all that. The toothless Walter Huston's triumphant dance when he realizes that they have struck gold, would alone make it memorable. Bogart gives one of his better performances, as the mean-spirited, unshaven, down-at-heel Fred C. Dobbs, whose paranoia gets the better of him, and Huston, aided by having on hand the reclusive author B. Traven, captures well the feverish atmosphere and the divisive interplay between the contrasting trio of prospectors.

The Nun's Story

'Filmed in Belgium, Italy, Africa … and mostly in the conscience of a beautiful young girl!'

The Nun's Story
US   1959   151m   Technicolor
Warner (Henry Blanke)
📷 ▦ ◷ 🎧
w *Robert Anderson* book *Kathryn C. Hulme* d *Fred Zinnemann* ph *Franz Planer* m *Franz Waxman* ad *Alexander Trauner* ed *Walter Thompson*
☆ *Audrey Hepburn* (Sister Luke/Gabrielle Van Der Mal), *Peter Finch* (Dr. Fortunati), Edith Evans (Mother Emmanuel Superior General), Peggy Ashcroft (Mother Mathilde), Dean Jagger (Dr. Van Der Mal), Mildred Dunnock (Sister Margharita), Patricia Collinge (Sister William), Beatrice Straight (Mother Christophe)

'A major directorial achievement … the best study of the religious life ever made in the American cinema.' – *Albert Johnson, Film Quarterly*

⚨ picture; Robert Anderson; Fred Zinnemann; Franz Planer; Franz Waxman; Audrey Hepburn; editing
🎭 Audrey Hepburn

A Belgian girl joins a strict order, endures hardship in the Congo, and finally returns to ordinary life.

Audrey Hepburn was the reason Warner Brothers agreed to finance this story. She gave one of her finest performances in the role that, as she said, suited her nature, showing a delicate and vulnerable sensitivity that was best brought out by her scenes with Peter Finch as a worldly, overworked, perceptive doctor. The fascinating early sequences of convent routine are more interesting than the African adventures, but this is a careful, composed and impressive film with little Hollywood exaggeration.

The Matrix

'Believe the unbelievable.'

The Matrix
US/Australia   1999   136m   Technicolor
Panavision
Warner/Village Roadshow/Groucho II (Joel Silver)
📷 ▦ ◷ ⊘ 🎧
wd *Andy Wachowski, Larry Wachowski* ph *Bill Pope* m *Don Davis* pd *Owen Paterson* ed *Zach Staenberg* sp *Geoffrey Darrow; Bob McCarron; Makeup Effects Group Studio*
☆ Keanu Reeves (Neo), Laurence Fishburne (Morpheus), Carrie-Anne Moss (Trinity), Hugo Weaving (Agent Smith), Gloria Foster (Oracle), Joe Pantoliano (Cypher), Marcus Chong (Tank), Paul Goddard (Agent Brown), Robert Taylor (Agent Jones), Julian Arahanga (Apoc), Matt Doran (Mouse), Belinda McClory (Switch), Anthony Ray Parker (Dozer)

'A dazzingly nifty slice of sci-fi cool.' – *Empire*

● Yuen Wo-Ping was responsible for the kung fu choreography.
● The film cost $60m to make and grossed $475m at cinemas around the world.
⚨ Zach Staenberg; sound (John Reitz, Gregg Rudloff, David Campbell, David Lee); sound effects editing (Dane A. Davis); visual effects (John Gaeta, Janek Sirrs, Steve Courtley, Jon Thum)
🎭 special visual effects; sound

An insignificant worker turns out to be the promised leader who fights against the Matrix, an artificial intelligence that controls the world and consumes its inhabitants.

A film that became a phenomenon, both for the philosophical framework of its science-fiction story, of an average man who may be the saviour of humanity, and for its spectacular special effects and battles that owed much to Hong Kong action films. Its theme resonated with current scientific speculation of a world controlled by the Matrix, an artificial intelligence that condemns the human inhabitants to live in a virtual reality. Slick design and the speed and vitality of its narrative swept away its deficiencies, particularly its derivative plot that drew on so many science-fiction clichés and conventions.

The Matrix

Interrogation

Poland 1982 120m colour
Gala/Zespol Filmowy 'X' (Tadeusz Drewno)
original title: *Przesluchanie*
wd Ryszard Bugajski *ph* Jacek Petrycki *pd* Janusz
Sosnowski *ed* Katarzyna Maciejko
☆ Krystyna Janda (Antonia Dziwisz), Adam Ferency
(Morawsky), Janusz Gajos (Zawada), Agnieszka Holland
(Witowska), Anna Romantowska (Miroslawa "Mira"
Szejnert), Bozena Dykiel (Honorata), Olgierda Lukaszewicza
(Konstanty Dziwisz), Tomasz Dedek

722
Interrogation

*In the 1950s, a fun-loving singer is arrested, questioned and tortured
by the secret police.*

Made in 1982, Ryszard Bugajski's film was banned by the authorities
and not released for eight years. It is harrowing, but uplifting in its
depiction of an unquenchable human spirit. A singer is pressured to
confess to invented crimes and treated as expendable, but refuses to
submit. Krystyna Janda won the award for best actress at the Cannes
Film Festival in 1990 for her riveting performance. By the time the film
was shown there, the director had moved to Canada; since his return to
Poland in the mid 1990s he has worked in television.

Delicatessen
France   1990   99m   colour
Electric/Constellation/UGC/Hachette Première
(Claudie Ossard)
⊕ ▤ ⊗ ◠
wd Jean-Pierre Jeunet, Marc Caro   *ph* Darius Khondji
m Carlos D'Alessio   *ad* Marc Caro   *ed* Hervé Schneid
☆ Dominique Pinon (Louison), Marie-Laure Dougnac
(Julie Clapet), Jean-Claude Dreyfus (The Butcher), Karin
Viard (Miss Plusse), Ticky Holgado (Mr. Tapioca), Anne-
Marie Pisani (Mrs. Tapioca), Jacques Mathou (Roger Kube)

'Beautifully textured, cleverly scripted and eerily
shot … a zany little film that should get terrific
word of mouth.' – *Variety*

'An impressive achievement and extremely funny.'
– *Philip French, Observer*

721
Delicatessen

In a decaying city of the future, a butcher, who flourishes by killing his workers and selling their flesh, is attacked by underground vegetarian terrorists.

A prime example of the cinema of the absurd: a woman tries to kill herself with the aid of a sewing machine activated by a front door bell, a scarf and a lamp, while sitting in a tub of water; and a man breeds frogs and snails in his waterlogged flat to provide himself with food; a clown and a woman play a rooftop duet on a cello and musical saw. Set in a decaying, hungry city of the future, where a butcher flourishes by killing his workers and selling their flesh, this is an exuberant, witty, black comedy that maintains a cartoon-like quality, filmed in orange- and blue-tinged light. Sound is used to marvellous effect: the creaking of bed springs as the butcher makes love sets up a rhythm that infects the household, from a woman beating carpets to a boy pumping a bike in a symphony of rattles.

'Everyone Wants To Kiss The Bride …
Except The Groom.'
The Wedding Banquet
Taiwan/US   1993   108m   DuArt
Mainline/Central Motion Picture/Good Machine (Ang
Lee, Ted Hope, James Schamus)
⊕ ▤ ⊗ ◠
original title: *Xiyan*
w Ang Lee, Neil Peng, James Schamus   *d* Ang Lee
ph Jong Lin   *m* Mader   *pd* Steve Rosenzweig   *ad* Rachel
Weinzimer   *ed* Tim Squyres
☆ Mitchell Lichtenstein (Simon), Winston Chao (Wai
Tung), May Chin (Wei-Wei), Sihung Lung (Mr. Gao), Ah-
Leh Gua (Mrs. Gao), Dion Birney (Andrew), Jeanne Kuo
Chang (Wai Tung's Secretary)

'Canny mix of feelgood elements and ethnic color.'
– *Variety*

'A wish-fulfilment fantasy on a par with the equally
crowd-pleasing *Strictly Ballroom*.' – *Tony Rayns,
Sight and Sound*

🏆 best foreign-language film

720
The Wedding Banquet

A homosexual American-Taiwanese businessman has to conceal his sexual preferences and his lover when his staid mother and father arrive in New York to celebrate his arranged marriage to a Chinese woman.

Ang Lee came to international attention with his delightful film of an American-Taiwanese businessman, who, in his attempt to hide his homosexuality from his parents, enters a marraige of convenience with a Chinese woman. His parents complicate matters by coming to New York to celbrate the happy occasion. The comedy came from its shrewd observation of culture clashes, racial and generational differences and the problems of living up to your parents' expectations. It made light of situations without concealing their truth and occasional pain.

'Sometimes good people do evil things.'

A Simple Plan
US   1998   120m   colour
Paramount/Mutual/Savoy (James Jacks,
AdamSchroeder)
▣ ▤ ◉ ◠
w Scott B.Smith *novel* Scott B. Smith *d* *Sam Raimi*
ph Alar Kivilo *m* *Danny Elfman* *pd* Patrizia von
Brandenstein *ad* James Truesdale *ed* Arthur Coburn, Eric
L. Beason
☆ Bill Paxton (Hank Mitchell), *Billy Bob Thornton* (Jacob
Mitchell), Bridget Fonda (Sarah Mitchell), Brent Briscoe
(Lou Chambers), Gary Cole (Baxter), Becky Ann Baker
(Nancy), Chelcie Ross (Carl), Jack Walsh (Mr. Pederson)

'Marvellously nuanced and beautifully acted.'
– *Andrew Sarris*

⚖ Billy Bob Thornton; Scott B. Smith

719
A Simple Plan

Three friends fall out after they discover a hoard of stolen money.

Sam Raimi's deft, chilling movie dealt with three friends who stumble across a bag containing $4.4m dollars in a crashed plane outside a small Minnesota town, and decide to keep the money. It's a thriller of corruption, charting an inexorable slide from integrity to betrayal and worse. Danny Elfman's music underscores the unease that pervades the film, as friendships crumble and greed takes over. What gives this morality tale an extra force is the quality of its acting. Bill Paxton as a man who knows better than he acts, Bridget Fonda as his pregnant wife, Bily Bob Thornton's dim-witted brother, and Brent Briscoe as their easy-going friend all give pitch-perfect performances, involving the audience in their inevitable tragedies.

Crimes and Misdemeanors
US   1989   104m   DeLuxe
Rank/Orion (Robert Greenhut)
▣ ▤ ◔ ◉ ◉
wd *Woody Allen* *ph* Sven Nykvist *md* Joe Malin
pd Santo Loquasto *ad* Speed Hopkins *ed* Susan E. Morse
☆ Caroline Aaron (Barbara), Alan Alda (Lester), Woody
Allen (Cliff Stern), Claire Bloom (Miriam Rosenthal), Mia
Farrow (Halley Reed), Joanna Gleason (Wendy Stern),
Anjelica Huston (Dolores Paley), Martin Landau (Judah
Rosenthal), Jenny Nichols (Jenny), Jerry Orbach (Jack
Rosenthal)
⚖ best director; best original screenplay; Martin Landau

718
Crimes and Misdemeanors

Brothers-in-law deal with marital crises.

Two interlinked stories, one comic, the other tragic, form a winning combination in Woody Allen's film. Judah's (Martin Landau) mistress threatens to tell his wife of their affair. Documentary film-maker Clifford (Woody Allen) has a marriage on the rocks but also is hired to shoot a film on another brother-in-law, a TV producer, whom he despises. The collision of the two stories in which Judah solves his problem through murder and Clifford by making a satirical documentary, provides a subtly intriguing view of marriage, family relationships and the place of conscience and guilt within them.

'They're Deserters, Rebels And Thieves. But In The Nicest Possible Way.'

'It's Good To Be King.'

Three Kings
US 1999 115m Technicolor Panavision
Warner/Village Roadshow/Village-A.M Film/Coast Ridge/Atlas (Charles Roven, Paul Junger Witt, Edward L. McDonnell)

▣ ▤ ⊚ ⊚ ⌒

wd David O. Russell *story* John Ridley *ph* Newton Thomas Sigel *m* Carter Burwell *pd* Catherine Hardwicke *ad* Jann K. Engel, Derek R. Hill *ed* Robert K. Lambert
☆ George Clooney (Archie Gates), Mark Wahlberg (Troy Barlow), Ice Cube (Chief Elgin), Spike Jonze (Conrad Vig), Jamie Kennedy (Walter Wogaman), Mykelti Williamson (Colonel Horn), Cliff Curtis (Amir Abdulah), Said Taghmaoui (Captain Said), Judy Greer (Cathy Daitch), Liz Stauber (Debbie Barlow)

'That most unusual of sights, the grown up, intelligent Hollywood war film.' – *Times*

'There are many clever touches, but there's something tamely conventional at the film's core.' – *Janet Maslin, New York Times*

● Regions 1 and 2 DVDs include commentary by David O. Russell, and by Chuck Roven and Ed McDonnell.

717
Three Kings

As the Gulf War ends in 1991, a group of US soldiers attempt to steal Saddam Hussein's hoard of gold, buried behind Iraqi lines.

An ironic, blackly humorous drama that manages to take seriously the messy mechanics of war while staying within most of the conventions of a caper movie. George Clooney gives an edgier, angrier performance than usual (perhaps because he and the director exchanged blows during filming), playing an opportunistic Major. The movie zigzags between moral outrage and slam-bang action; some sequences add unsettling photographic effects to the genre, showing in detail the effect bullets have on the human body.

La Terra Trema
Italy 1948 160m bw
Universalia

▣ ⊚ ⊚

wd Luchino Visconti *ph* G. R. Aldo *m* Luchino Visconti, Willy Ferrero *ed* Mario Serandrei
☆ Luchino Visconti (Narrator), Antonio Pietrangeli (Narrator)
● The cast was drawn from the inhabitants of Aci Trezza, Sicily.

716
La Terra Trema

The life of a Sicilian fisherman and his family.

Visconti's semi-documentary was a key film in the postwar neo-realist renaissance of Italian cinema. The Catholic censorship board classified it as 'for adults with reservations', the reservations being the Church's dislike of its socialist viewpoint of the exploitation of the fishermen by the men who owned their boats. Using non-professional actors and working without a script, he made a carefully composed work that, in its concentration on a particular family, also revealed wider truths about the particular problems of Sicily, which was poor, isolated and corrupt. The film was a commercial disaster: even the Italians couldn't understand the local accents. It was the only part completed of what Visconti had planned as a trilogy about the exploited.

Le Fils

Le Fils
Belgium/France   2002   103m   colour
Artificial Eye/Films du Fleuve/Archipel35/RTBF (Jean-Pierre and Luc Dardenne, Denis Freyd)
🎞 ▦ ⊚ ⊚
aka: *The Son*
wd Jean-Pierre Dardenne, Luc Dardenne *ph* Alain Marcoen *pd* Igor Gabriel *ed* Marie-Helene Dozo
☆ Olivier Gourmet (Olivier), Morgan Marinne (Francis), Isabella Soupart (Magali)

'The ability to conceive a compact drama on this huge subject and to embody it as perfectly as they have done, added to what they have already accomplished, puts Jean-Pierre and Luc Dardenne among the premier film artists of our time.'
– *Stanley Kaufmann, New Republic*

'It is as assured and flawless a telling of sadness and joy as I have ever seen.' – *Roger Ebert, Chicago Sun-Times*

715
Le Fils

A carpentry teacher at a vocational training school for delinquent boys takes as a pupil the youth who killed his young son.

Jean-Pierre and Luc Dardenne brought a concentration on the ordinary rituals of life to their extraordinary story. It is a simple, deeply affecting drama of loss and forgiveness, involving individuals who are defined by their work and the respect they bring to it. Olivier Gourmet as the teacher won the best actor award at the Cannes Film Festival for his quietly commanding performance; his nondescript face, filmed in close-up, dominates the film, giving little hint of the motive for his behaviour.

'This time the whole world is watching…'
Woodstock
US   1970   184m   Technicolor
Warner/Wadleigh-Maurice (Bob Maurice)
🎞 🎞 ▦ ⊚ ⊚ ⊚ 🎧
d Michael Wadleigh *ph* Michael Wadleigh and others
ed Thelma Schoonmaker, Martin Scorsese
☆ Joan Baez, Canned Heat, Joe Cocker, Country Joe and The Fish, Crosby, Stills, Nash & Young, Arlo Guthrie, Richie Havens, Jimi Hendrix, Santana, John Sebastian, Sha-Na-Na, Sly & The Family Stone, Ten Years After and also The Who

'A joyous, volcanic new film that will make those who missed the festival feel as if they were there. But *Woodstock* is far more than a sound-and-light souvenir of a long weekend concert. Purely as a piece of cinema, it is one of the finest documentaries ever made in the U.S.' – *Time*

'What is distressing about most of the performers at this mammoth mud-in, apart from their obvious lack of musical talent, is, in most cases, their equally obvious hostility. I mean not just laudable hostility to the war, but also profound neurotic hostility.' – *John Simon*

• A 'director's cut' lasting 220m was released in cinemas and on video in 1994.
👤 best documentary

714
Woodstock

A documentary on the three-day festival ('of peace, music … and love') that attracted an audience of around 500,000 young people.

This is a definitive moment of the 1960s, with the mood and music brilliantly captured on film in this documentary of the three-day festival. To make it took a team of 20 cameramen, who shot 120 hours of film, as well as eight camera assistants, 20 sound-men and engineers, six still photographers and 30 production assistants. Using a split-screen, it captured many iconic performers of the era, including the music of Crosby, Stills, Nash and Young, Country Joe McDonald's anti-Vietnam anthem 'I-Feel-Like-I'm-Fixin'-to-Die Rag' and Jimi Hendrix's wailing improvisation on 'the 'Star-Spangled Banner'.

The Silence of the Lambs

US 1990 118m Technicolor Panavision
Rank/Orion/Strong Heart/Demme (Edward Saxon, Kenneth Utt, Ron Bozman)

w Ted Tally *novel* Thomas Harris *d* Jonathan Demme *ph* Tak Fujimoto *m* Howard Shore *pd* Kristi Zea *ad* Tim Galvin *ed* Craig McKay

☆ *Jodie Foster* (Clarice Starling), *Anthony Hopkins* (Dr. Hannibal Lecter), Scott Glenn (Jack Crawford), Ted Levine (Jame Gumb), Anthony Heald (Dr. Frederick Chilton), Lawrence A. Bonney (FBI Instructor), Kasi Lemmons (Ardelia Mapp), Lawrence J. Wrentz (Agent Burroughs), Frankie Faison (Barney), Roger Corman (FBI Director Hayden Burke)

'A mesmerizing thriller that will grip audiences from first scene to last.' – *Variety*

'An exceptionally good film, perhaps this fine director's best, in which the horror genre is elevated into the kind of cinema that can at least be argued about as a treatise for its unsettling times.' – *Derek Malcolm, Guardian*

● It was followed by *Hannibal* in 2001 and *Red Dragon (qqv)* in 2002. An earlier version of *Red Dragon* was made in 1986 as *Manhunter (qv)*.

film; Jonathan Demme; Anthony Hopkins; Jodie Foster; Ted Tally

editing; sound

Anthony Hopkins; Jodie Foster

713
The Silence of the Lambs

An FBI agent seeks the help of one serial killer in order to catch another.

This is a tense, exciting and sometimes gruesome thriller about a young female FBI agent who seeks the aid of an imprisoned serial killer to track down another mass murderer. It is suspenseful enough to make you overlook its essential absurdities. Hopkins plays the role of the devious murderer and psychiatrist, Hannibal 'The Cannibal' Lecter, with lip-smacking relish. Jodie Foster's introverted agent brings an ordinariness to the surrounding gothic grotesquery that enables audiences to experience through her both the evil and the fascination of Lecter's arrogant and sophisticated distaste for social norms.

Late Spring

Japan 1949 108m bw
Shochiku

original title: *Banshun*

w Yasujiro Ozu, Kogo Noda *novel* Kazuo Hirotsu *d* Yasujiro Ozu *ph* Yuharu Atsuta *m* Senji Ito *ad* Tatsuo Hamada *ed* Yoshiyasu Hamamura

☆ Chishu Ryu (Shukichi), Setsuko Hara (Noriko), Haruko Sugimura (Masa Taguchi), Yumeji Tsukioka (Aya Kitagawa), Jun Osami (Shuichi Hattori), Masao Mishima (Jo Onodera)

712
Late Spring

A widower announces his intention of re-marrying in order to persuade his daughter to marry and leave home.

This was the first of Ozu's films to deal with the matter of his greatest works: a conflict within a middle-class family. The style is simple, pared-down, with little camera movement and the action observed from a low viewpoint so that the concentration is on character. A study in domestic discord and the acceptance of whatever life has to offer, it ends with the widower, who had no real intention of marrying again, sitting down and, peeling an apple with great concentration, left alone and reconciled to the ending of his life.

'There are three sides to this love story!'

Kramer versus Kramer
US 1979 105m Technicolor
Columbia/Stanley Jaffe (Richard C. Fischoff)
📷 ▬ ⌕ ⊚ ⊙ ◯
wd Robert Benton *novel* Avery Corman *ph* Nestor
Almendros *md* Erma E. Levin *pd* Paul Sylbert *ed* Jerry
Greenberg
☆ *Dustin Hoffman* (Ted Kramer), *Justin Henry* (Billy
Kramer), Meryl Streep (Joanna Kramer), Jane Alexander
(Margaret Phelps), Howard Duff (John Shaunessy)

'Pastel colours, a cute kid and a good script made
this one of the most undeserved successes of the
year: wall-to-wall sentiment.' – *Time Out*

🏆 best picture; Robert Benton (as director); Dustin
Hoffman; Meryl Streep; screenplay adapted from another
medium
🏆 Justin Henry; Jane Alexander; Nestor Almendros; editing

711
Kramer versus Kramer

A divorced advertising executive gets temporary custody of his seven-year-old son.

Robert Benton's film was a new-fashioned tearjerker, with its battle between a divorcing husband and wife over the custody of their seven-year-old son. It was also a contest between Dustin Hoffman and Meryl Streep to see who could out-act the other. Hoffman had the advantage here, since he had the better lines and bigger scenes. That may have been because he originally refused the role as he thought the novel was no more than a soap opera, only agreeing to star after the script had been rewritten to his satisfaction. The well-made film charts his painful progress from workaholic advertising executive to a devoted father in an open-minded movie that is still catnip to emotion-starved audiences.

The Court Jester
👫 US 1955 101m Technicolor
Vistavision
Paramount/Dena (Melvin Frank, Norman Panama)
📷 ▬ ⌕ ◯
wd Norman Panama, Melvin Frank *ph* Ray June
m/ly Sylvia Fine, Sammy Cahn *ad* Hal Pereira, Roland
Anderson *ed* Tom McAdoo
☆ *Danny Kaye* (Hubert Hawkins), Glynis Johns (Maid
Jean), *Basil Rathbone* (Sir Ravenhurst), Cecil Parker (King
Roderick), *Mildred Natwick* (Griselda), Angela Lansbury
(Princess Gwendolyn), Edward Ashley (Black Fox), Robert
Middleton (Sir Griswold), Michael Pate (Sir Locksley), Alan
Napier (Sir Brockhurst)

'Costumed swashbucklers undergo a happy
spoofing.' – *Variety*

710
The Court Jester

Opposition to a tyrannical king is provided by the Fox, but it is one of the rebel's meekest men who, posing as a jester, defeats the usurper.

Danny Kaye's most delightful vehicle, this romp has good tunes, a witty script and lively action, not to mention an exceptional cast. Set in medieval England (or, rather, a familiar Hollywood version of that time and place) and surrounded by expert comic actors, Kaye makes fun of such swashbuckling movies as Errol Flynn's *The Adventures of Robin Hood*. It includes the classic 'chalice from the palace' routine, written by Norman Panama, that remains one of cinema's great comic set pieces.

One Eyed Jacks
US 1961 141m Technicolor Vistavision
Paramount/Pennebaker (Frank P. Rosenberg)
🎞 🏳 ⌕ ⊚ ⊚ ⌂
w Guy Trosper, Calder Willingham *novel The Authentic Death of Hendry Jones* by Charles Neider *d* Marlon Brando *ph* Charles Lang Jnr *m* Hugo Friedhofer
☆ Marlon Brando (Rio), Karl Malden (Sheriff Dad Longworth), Pina Pellicer (Louisa), Katy Jurado (Marian Longworth), Slim Pickens (Deputy Lon Dedrick), Ben Johnson (Bob Amory), Timothy Carey (Howard Tetley), Elisha Cook Jnr (Carvey)

'This is not the ordinary Western; not the ordinary good Western; not even the ordinary extraordinary Western … The figures and the background, the colour and the movement repeatedly unite in compositions of mesmerizing beauty.' – *Dilys Powell*

'The picture is of variable quality: it has some visual grandeur; it also has some bizarrely brutal scenes. It isn't clear why Brando made this peculiarly masochistic revenge fantasy, or whether he hoped for something quite different from what he finished with.' – *Pauline Kael*

⛹ Charles Lang Jnr

709
One Eyed Jacks

An outlaw has a running battle with an old friend.

Brando's moody, romantic Western, a story of betrayal and revenge, was a project he took very seriously, possibly because he and the bank robber he played had many characteristics in common, from vanity to a naive regard for honour, even among thieves. The film's style partly derives from two men who were fired during its production: Sam Peckinpah, as writer, and Stanley Kubrick, as director. The extravagant movie has the defining violence of the former and something of the lyrical qualities of the latter. Unusually for a Western, the main setting was the beaches of California, where the sea became a participant in the action. The few who saw a three-hour cut thought it a masterpiece. Paramount cut it further and destroyed all the out takes. Even with the happier ending the studio forced upon Brando, he offers a fascinating character study in a glorious landscape.

Greed
US 1924 110m (24 fps) bw silent
MGM/Goldwyn Company (Erich von Stroheim, Irving Thalberg)
🎞 🏳 ⌕
wd Erich von Stroheim *novel McTeague* by Frank Norris *ph* Ben Reynolds, William Daniels *ad* Richard Day, Cedric Gibbons, Erich von Stroheim *ed* Erich Von Stroheim, Rex Ingram, June Mathis, Jos W. Farnham
☆ Gibson Gowland (McTeague), Zasu Pitts (Trina Sieppe), *Jean Hersholt* (Marcus Schuler), Chester Conklin (Mr. Sieppe), Dale Fuller (Maria)

'The end leaves one with an appalling sense of human waste, of futility, of the drabness and cruelty of lives stifled by genteel poverty. Every character in the film is overwhelmed by it.' – *Gavin Lambert*

'Nothing more morbid and senseless, from a commercial picture standpoint, has been seen on the screen for a long time … Never has there been a more out-and-out box-office flop.' – *Variety*

● In 1972 Herman G. Weinberg published a complete screenplay with 400 stills.
● The original length at the première is said to have been 420m. A restored version by Rick Schmidlin was shown in 1999 that ran for 239m and used production stills to flesh out the story.

708
Greed

An ex-miner dentist kills his avaricious wife. Later in Death Valley, he also kills her lover, but is bound to him by handcuffs.

This much-discussed film is often cited as its director's greatest folly: the original version ran eight hours. Re-edited by June Mathis (after which MGM burnt all the cut footage), it retains considerable power sequence by sequence, but is necessarily disjointed in development. What remains surprising is that it was ever released, least of all by MGM, the glossiest of studios, given its subject matter. Stroheim called the butchered version of another of his films 'the skeleton of my dead child'. *Greed*, whatever its shortcomings in its available versions, has flesh enough to be an engrossing study of a money-obsessed society and the individuals struggling within it.

Mother
USSR   1926   90m approx (24 fps)   bw
silent
Mezhrabpom-Russ
▰ ⊘
original title: *Mat*
w N. Zarkhi, V. I. Pudovkin *novel* Maxim Gorky *d* V. I.
Pudovkin *ph* A. Golovnia *ad* Sergei Kozlovsky
☆ Vera Baranovskaya (Niovna-Vlasova, the Mother),
Nikolai Batalov (Pavel Vlasov), Ivan Koval-Samborsky
(Strike organiser), Anna Zemtsova (Revolutionary)
● Other versions appeared in 1920 and ({KW}d{/KW}Mark
Donskoi) 1955

707
Mother

A mother incriminates her strike-breaking son but realizes her error.

Vsevolod Pudovkin was the oldest of the first generation of Russian directors that also included Dovzhenko and Eisenstein; this was his first great work, a free adaptation of Gorky's novel, which is a propagandist social melodrama that is also brilliantly conceived and edited. Pudovkin once wrote, 'an artist must seek a large and *poetic* significance in the world around him'. He achieves that here with a lyrical, rhythmically conceived film that accelerates into tragedy, with sequences matching those of Eisenstein.

☆ **Christopher Tilly**, Contributing Editor, *Hotdog Magazine* ☆

1. Back To The Future (Zemeckis)
   Represents everything that's great in film – a wonderful story, spot-on casting and a director who knows exactly how to keep the audience on their toes. It also has the best example of cause and effect in the movies – every scene, every prop and just about every line is there for a reason in one of the tightest scripts ever written.
2. The Godfather (Coppola)
3. Donnie Darko (Kelly)
   A brilliant, confusing and unforgettable tale of time travel, first love, madness and a giant bunny called Frank, Donnie Darko is the film that the word "cult" was created for.
4. It's A Wonderful Life (Capra)
5. GoodFellas (Scorsese
6. Swingers (Liman)
7. The Usual Suspects (Singer)
8. Die Hard (McTiernan)
9. City Of God (Meirelles, Lund)
10. Caddyshack (Ramis)

Scrooge

GB 1951 86m bw

Renown (Brian Desmond Hurst)

US title: *A Christmas Carol*

w Noel Langley d Brian Desmond Hurst ph C. Pennington-Richards m Richard Addinsell ad Ralph Brinton ed Clive Donner

☆ *Alastair Sim* (Scrooge), Mervyn Johns (Bob Cratchit), Kathleen Harrison (Mrs. Dilber), Jack Warner (Mr. Jorkins), Michael Hordern (Jacob Marley), Hermione Baddeley (Mrs. Cratchit), George Cole (Scrooge as Young Man), Miles Malleson (Old Joe)

- First made in 1933 with Seymour Hicks.
- Remade 1970 as a musical version with Albert Finney.

706

Scrooge

A miser discovers the error of his ways after being haunted by the ghosts of his past, present and future life.

Alastair Sim brought to the fore the slightly sinister side of his more usual bonhomie as Scrooge in what still survives as the best version of Dickens' *A Christmas Carol*. It gives weight to his younger self and the events that turned him into a miser. Sim's gradual transformation from skinflint to benevolence is a joy to behold. The art direction, pace and general handling are as good as can be.

Closely Observed Trains

Czechoslovakia 1966 92m bw
Ceskoslovensky Film (Zdenek Oves)
▦ ▤ ◎ ⌾ ◎

wd *Jiri Menzel* novel Bohumil Hrabal *ph* Jaromir Sofr
m Jiri Pavlik *ad* Oldrich Bosak *ed* Jirina Lukesova
☆ Vaclav Neckar (Trainee Milos Hrma), Jitka Bendova
(Conductor Masa), Vladimir Valenta (Stationmaster Max),
Josef Somr (Train Dispatcher Hubicka)

'Like Forman, Menzel seems incapable of being
unkind to anybody.' – *Tom Milne*

'The director has made extraordinarily effective use
of the solitude which the characters share.' – *Dilys
Powell*

🏆 best foreign film

705
Closely Observed Trains

*During World War II, an apprentice railway guard at a country station
falls in love and becomes a saboteur.*

Set in World War II, Jiri Menzel's comedy is warm and charming. Its
disconcerting downbeat ending comes as a shock after an amusing
detail of station life in a slackers' paradise, removed from the horrors
of the war. 'My one desire is to stand on a platform and avoid hard
work while others slave,' says the apprentice, whose preoccupation,
like his elders, is for sexual adventure. The final moments, though,
show that resistance to totalitarian regimes can come from unexpected
causes, as well as being a salutary reminder of the uncertainty of life.

'The strangest love a woman has ever known
… a livid face bent over her in the ghostly mist!'

Dracula

US 1931 84m bw
Universal (Carl Laemmle Jnr)
▤ ◎ ⌾ ◎

w Garrett Fort *play* Hamilton Deane, John Balderston
novel *Bram Stoker* d *Tod Browning* ph *Karl Freund*
m Tchaikovsky *ad* Charles D. Hall *ed* Milton Carruth,
Maurice Pivar
☆ *Bela Lugosi* (Count Dracula), Helen Chandler (Mina
Seward), David Manners (Jonathan Harker), *Dwight Frye*
(Renfield), *Edward Van Sloan* (Dr. Van Helsing)

'… a sublimated ghost story related with all
surface seriousness and above all with a
remarkably effective background of creepy
atmosphere.' – *Variety*

'A too literal adaptation of the play (*not* the book)'.
– *William K. Everson*

'The mistiest parts are the best; when the lights go
up the interest goes down.' – *Ivan Butler*

'It'll chill you and fill you with fears. You'll find it
creepy and cruel and crazed.' – *New York Daily
News*

● Later advertising variations concentrated on the horror
element: 'In all the annals of living horror, one name stands
out as the epitome of evil! So evil, so fantastic, so degrading
you'll wonder if it isn't all a nightmare! Innocent girls lured
to a fate truly worse than death!'

704
Dracula

A Transylvanian vampire count gets his come-uppance in Yorkshire.

A film that has much to answer for: it started its star and its studio on
horror careers and launched innumerable sequels to its story of the
downfall of an aristocratic Transylvanian vampire (a figure partly based
by author Bram Stoker on his employer, actor Sir Henry Beerbohm
Tree). In itself, after two eerie reels, it becomes a pedantic and slow
transcription of a stage adaptation, and its climax takes place offscreen.
But for all kinds of reasons it remains full of interest. The recent avail-
ability on DVD of a contemporary Spanish version, directed by George
Melford and Enrique Tovar Avalos, working by night on the same sets,
confirms its technical superiority, with its greater fluidity of camera
movement, over Browning's film. What it lacks, however, is the extraordinarily charismatic performance of Lugosi as the Count, who, with his
curiously accented, sinister lisp and glittering eyes, remains the definitive vampire.

'In Havana, music isn't a pastime… it's a way of life.'

Buena Vista Social Club
Germany   1998   105m   colour
Film Four/Road Movies/Kintop/Arte/ICAIC (Ulrich Felsberg, Deepak Nayar)
▣ ▤ ◉ ◎

d Wim Wenders *ph* Joerg Widmer, Robby Mueller, Lisa Renzler *ed* Brian Johnson
☆ Ry Cooder, Compay Segundo, Ruben Gonzalez, Ibrahim Ferrer, Eliades Ochoa, Omara Portuondo, Manuel 'Guajiro' Mirabal, Orlando 'Cachaito' Lopez, Barbarito Torres, Manuel 'Puntillita' Licea, Raul Planes, Felix Valoy, Maceo Rodriguez, Richard Eques, Joaquim Cooder

'A film of ineffable sweetness and glorious music, which puts the shallow, affectless popular culture of our prosperous west to shame.' – *Peter Bradshaw, Guardian*

🔊 documentary

703
Buena Vista Social Club

A documentary on the joys of Cuban music and musicians.

Wim Wender's affectionate documentary tracked a forgotten generation of now elderly Cuban musicians, who were brought back into the limelight by guitarist Ry Cooder for a best-selling record album. It is a charming account of some exceptional players experiencing a late flowering; their enjoyment of life is reflected in the liltingly rhythmic style of music they developed that draws on Cuban folksong and peasant life. The energetic, 90-year-old Compay Segundo slyly steals the show with his reminiscences and vocals. It is a celebration not only of music-making and collaborative effort but of the irrepressible individuality that living long can bestow.

Farewell My Lovely
US   1975   95m   Technicolor
Avco Embassy/Elliott Kastner/ITC (George Pappas, Jerry Bruckheimer)
▣ ▤ ◉ ◎

w David Zelag Goodman *novel* Raymond Chandler *d* Dick Richards *ph* John A. Alonzo *m* David Shire *pd* Dean Tavoularis *ad* Angelo Graham *ed* Joel Cox, Walter Thompson
☆ Robert Mitchum (Philip Marlowe), Charlotte Rampling (Mrs. Velma Grayle), John Ireland (Lt. Nulty), Sylvia Miles (Mrs. Jessie Florian), Anthony Zerbe (Laird Burnette), Jack O'Halloran (Moose Malloy), Kate Murtagh (Frances Amthor)

'A moody, bluesy, boozy recreation of Marlowe's tacky, neon-flashed Los Angeles of the early Forties.' – *Judith Crist*

'A delicious remake with a nice, smoky 1940s atmosphere.' – *Michael Billington, Illustrated London News*

🔊 Sylvia Miles

702
Farewell My Lovely

A private eye realizes that two separate cases he is working on concern the same woman.

Robert Mitchum is in excellent form as a world-weary Phillip Marlowe is this sharp remake of the 1944 movie, in which the plot has been slightly rewritten but tightened. Chandler's novel is done with great atmospheric detail of the seedy side of 1940s Los Angeles. Mitchum's rumpled and slightly puffy appearance were perfectly in character, though he was not happy with Richards' constant rewriting of the script or his approach, claiming that, 'he was a fine still photographer. I think, though, that moving objects confused him a little.' Mitchum didn't move much, which may be why this is still one of the best detective movies made.

Crossfire
US   1947   86m   bw
RKO (Adrian Scott)

w *John Paxton* novel *The Brick Foxhole* by Richard Brooks
d *Edward Dmytryk* ph J. Roy Hunt m Roy Webb
ad Albert D'Agostino, Alfred Herman ed Harry Gerstad
☆ *Robert Young* (Finlay), Robert Mitchum (Keeley), *Robert Ryan* (Montgomery), Gloria Grahame (Ginny), *Paul Kelly* (The Man), Sam Levene (Joseph Samuels), Jacqueline White (Mary Mitchell), Steve Brodie (Floyd)

'Another murder story that holds its own with any on the basis of suspense and speed.' – *Richard Winnington*

⚖ best picture; John Paxton; Edward Dmytryk; Robert Ryan; Gloria Grahame

701
Crossfire

A Jew is murdered in a Washington hotel, and three soldiers are suspected.

Edward Dmytryk's film was the first from Hollywood to hit out at racial bigotry (though Richard Brooks' novel, on which it is based, dealt with the killing of a homosexual. There were some prejudices Hollywood was not then prepared to recognize). A tense, talky thriller, it was shot entirely at night, with pretty full expressionist use of camera technique, and is notable for its style, acting and experimentation.

Seven Days in May
US   1964   120m   bw
Seven Arts/Joel/John Frankenheimer (Edward Lewis)

w *Rod Serling* novel Fletcher Knebel, Charles W. Bailey II
d *John Frankenheimer* ph Ellsworth Fredericks m Jerry Goldsmith ad Cary Odell ed Ferris Webster
☆ *Kirk Douglas* (Col. Martin "Jiggs" Casey), Burt Lancaster (Gen. James M. Scott), *Fredric March* (President Jordan Lyman), Ava Gardner (Eleanor Holbrook), Martin Balsam (Paul Girard), *Edmond O'Brien* (Sen. Raymond Clark), George Macready (Christopher Todd), John Houseman (Adm. Barnswell)

'A political thriller which grips from start to finish.' – *Penelope Houston*

'It is to be enjoyed without feelings of guilt, there should be more movies like it, and there is nothing first class about it.' – *John Simon*

'In the best tradition of the suspense thriller, with the ultimate thrill our awareness of its actual potential.' – *Judith Crist*

'An entertainment, in Graham Greene's sense of the word, and an intelligent one.' – *MFB*

● In 1994, it was remade as a TV movie, *The Enemy Within*, starring Forest Whitaker and Sam Waterston.
⚖ Edmond O'Brien

700
Seven Days in May

An American general's aide discovers that his boss intends a military takeover because he considers the president's pacifism traitorous.

It was not long after President Eisenhower had warned of the potential dangers posed by the military-industrial complex of the day that this topical thriller put forward a scenario in which a popular and influential general attempted a coup to remove the US president for a treasonable act in signing a nuclear disarmament treaty with the Soviet Union. John Frankenheimer's direction made it an absorbing political drama, with the highlight being the confrontation between two different kinds of patriot, Burt Lancaster's conservative general and Fredric March's liberal president. It was stimulating entertainment.

Fail Safe

'It will have you sitting on the brink of eternity!'

Fail Safe
US 1964 111m bw
Columbia/Max E. Youngstein/Sidney Lumet
■ &⚲ ⊚

w Walter Bernstein *novel* Eugene Burdick, Harvey Wheeler *d* Sidney Lumet *ph* Gerald Hirschfeld *m* none *ad* Albert Brenner *ed* Ralph Rosenblum
☆ *Henry Fonda* (The President), Walter Matthau (Groeteschele), Dan O'Herlihy (Gen. Black), Frank Overton (Gen. Bogan), Fritz Weaver (Col. Cascio), Edward Binns (Col. Grady), Larry Hagman (Buck), Russell Collins (Knapp)

When an American atomic bomber is programmed by accident to bomb Moscow, the president must destroy New York in retaliation.

A film that is the obverse of the contemporaneous *Dr Strangelove*, which treated the same plot as black comedy: an American atomic bomber is accidentally set to destroy Moscow and the president has to destroy New York in retaliation. The details here, in this deadly earnest melodrama, are both terrifying and convincing: the surviving American pilot ignores orders to turn back his plane from the president and his wife because his training has been to ignore such commands. Fonda, as the embattled and increasingly frustrated president gives a finely nuanced performance.

Elizabeth

'Declared Illegitimate Aged 3. Tried For Treason Aged 21. Crowned Queen Aged 25.'

'Absolute Power Demands Absolute Loyalty.'

Elizabeth
GB 1998 121m colour
Polygram/Channel 4/Working Title (Alison Owen, Eric Fellner, Tim Bevan)
▣ ■ &⚲ ⊚ ⊚ ⌒

w Michael Hirst *d* Shekhar Kapur *ph* Remi Adefarasin *m* David Hirschfelder *pd* John Myhre *ad* Lucy Richardson *ed* Jill Bilcock
☆ *Cate Blanchett* (Elizabeth I), *Geoffrey Rush* (Sir Francis Walsingham), Christopher Eccleston (Duke of Norfolk), Joseph Fiennes (Robert Dudley, Earl of Leicester), Richard Attenborough (Sir William Cecil), Fanny Ardant (Mary of Guise), Kathy Burke (Queen Mary Tudor), Eric Cantona (Monsieur de Foix), James Frain (Alvaro de la Quadra), Vincent Cassel (Duc d'Anjou), Daniel Craig (John Ballard), John Gielgud (The Pope), Angus Deayton (Waad, Chancellor of the Exchequer), Edward Hardwicke (Earl of Arundel), Terence Rigby (Bishop Gardiner)

'A horror film masquerading as a historical pageant.' – *David Denby, New Yorker*

⚲ Jenny Shircore (make-up)
⚖ best picture; Cate Blanchett; Remi Adefarasin; David Hirschfelder; John Myhre; Alexandre Byrne (costumes)
⬡ best British film; Cate Blanchett; Remi Adefarasin; David Hirschfelder; Jenny Shircore (make-up)

Amid plots and counter-plots, the hatred of her Catholic sister, Queen Mary, and the loss of her lover, Elizabeth survives to become absolute ruler of England.

Shekhar Kapur brought a iconoclastic spirit to the period movie in this drama of how Elizabeth I survived to become absolute ruler of England, despite plots and counter-plots, the hatred of her sister, and the loss of her lover. He created a fast-moving drama which, while it rearranges historical events, seems accurate in spirit to the political upheavals of the time. Against the background of religious persecution and overweening ambitions, it charted Elizabeth's emotional life, as she moved from frightened and passionate girl to a frightening and passionless queen.

'What We Do In Life Echoes In Eternity.'

Gladiator
US 2000 154m Technicolor Panavision
Universal/DreamWorks/Scott Free (Douglas Wick,
David Franzoni, Branko Lustig)

w David Franzoni, John Logan, William Nicholson
d *Ridley Scott* ph *John Mathieson* m Hans Zimmer, Lisa
Gerrard pd *Arthur Max* ed Pietro Scalia sp John Nelson,
Neil Corbould, Tim Burke, Rob Harvey; Mill Film cos Janty
Yates

☆ *Russell Crowe* (Maximus), Joaquin Phoenix
(Commodus), Connie Nielsen (Lucilla), *Oliver Reed*
(Proximo), Derek Jacobi (Gracchus), Djimon Hounsou
(Juba), Richard Harris (Marcus Aurelius), David Schofield
(Falco), John Shrapnel (Gaius), Tomas Arana (Quintus), Ralf
Moeller (Hagen), Spencer Treat Clark (Lucius), David
Hemmings (Cassius)

● The film cost $100m to make and took $449m at the box
office world wide.

👤 picture; Russell Crowe; Janty Yates; sound (Scott Millan,
Bob Beemer, Ken Weston) ; visual effects (John Nelson, Neil
Corbould, Tim Burke, Rob Harvey)

♗ Ridley Scott; Joaquin Phoenix; John Mathieson; Pietro
Scalia; script (David Franzoni, John Logan, William
Nicholson); art direction (Arthur Max, Crispian Sallis); Hans
Zimmer

🎬 film; John Mathieson; Arthur Max; Pietro Scalia

697
Gladiator

Condemned to die by a power-mad Emperor, a Roman general escapes to become a slave and a gladiator before he gains an opportunity for vengeance.

Ridley Scott re-invigorated a moribund genre with this epic movie of a Roman general who, condemned to die with his wife and son by a power-mad Emperor, escapes to become a slave and a gladiator before he gains an opportunity for vengeance. It is a lavish, spectacular, action-packed drama, though in contrast to its predecessors it is some-what glum in its approach; in its attempt at a tragic dimension, it eschews the camp decadence and fun of previous excursions into ancient Rome. Its compensations are the exciting set pieces, excellent acting, and the pleasure of matching its imperial theme of Rome as the light of the world to present day political realities.

Our Hospitality

US 1923 70m approx (24 fps) bw silent
Metro/Buster Keaton (Joseph M. Schenck)

w Jean Havez, Joseph Mitchell, Clyde Bruckman *d* Buster Keaton, Jack Blystone *ph* Elgin Lessley, Gordon Jennings *ad* Fred Gabourie
☆ *Buster Keaton* (William McKay), Natalie Talmadge (Virginia Canfield), Joe Keaton (Lem Doolittle), Buster Keaton Jnr (William McKay as a Baby)

'A novelty mélange of dramatics, low comedy, laughs and thrills ... one of the best comedies ever produced.' – *Variety*

696
Our Hospitality

Around 1830, a Southerner returns home to claim his bride and finds himself in the middle of a blood feud.

Buster Keaton used to comic effect the legendary feud between the Hatfields of West Virginia and the McCoys of Kentucky that escalated when a Hatfield tried to elope with a McCoy. He moved the story back in time so that he could include a splendid ancient train resembling George Stevenson's original Rocket. Keaton's acrobatic stunt to rescue the heroine from drowning gave him problems: the safety wire that held him to a large log broke and he was nearly crushed by it, and swept over a high waterfall. He plays a Southerner who visits the home of his intended bride and discovers that she is a member of the clan who killed his father. They want to kill him, too, but can't do so as long as he remains under their roof. It is a charming, rather than hilarious, comedy.

Hellzapoppin

US 1942 84m bw
Universal/Mayfair (Glenn Tryon, Alex Gottlieb)

w Nat Perrin, Warren Wilson *d* H. C. Potter *ph* Woody Bredell *m* Frank Skinner *md* Charles Previn *ed* Milton Carruth
☆ *Ole Olsen* (Ole), *Chic Johnson* (Chic), *Hugh Herbert* (Detective Quimby), *Martha Raye* (Betty Johnson), *Mischa Auer* (Pepi), Robert Paige (Jeff Hunter), Jane Frazee (Kitty Rand), Shemp Howard (Louie), Elisha Cook Jnr (Assistant Director), Richard Lane (Director)

'Alive with good gags, mechanical surprise effects, and novelty touches.' – *CEA Report*

● The Frankenstein monster and Man Who Falls into Pool were played by Dale Van Sickel.

695
Hellzapoppin

Two incompetent comics make a picture.

Of the eight films that the comic vaudeville duo of Olsen & Johnson made in the 1930s and 40s, this is the only one to still be of interest. A zany modification of a smash burlesque revue, the crazy gags are toned down and a romantic interest is added (and tentatively sent up). A mix of non-sequiturs, slapstick, running jokes, quick-fire gags and some moments of jazz and athletic dancing, the result is patchy but often hilarious, and the whole is a handy consensus of Forties humour and pop music.

From Here to Eternity
US   1953   118m   bw
Columbia (Buddy Adler)

w Daniel Taradash *novel* James Jones *d* Fred Zinnemann
ph Burnett Guffey *m* George Duning *ad* Cary Odell
ed William Lyon
☆ Burt Lancaster (Sgt. Milton Warden), Deborah Kerr
(Karen Holmes), *Frank Sinatra* (Angelo Maggio), Donna
Reed (Alma Lorene), Ernest Borgnine (Sgt. "Fatso" Judson),
Montgomery Clift (Robert E. Lee Prewitt), Philip Ober (Capt.
Dana Holmes), Mickey Shaughnessy (Sgt. Leva)

'This is not a theme which one would expect
Zinnemann to approach in the hopeful, sympathetic
mood of his earlier films; but neither could one
expect the negative shrug of indifference with
which he seems to have surrendered to its
hysteria.' – *Karel Reisz, Sight and Sound*

● The story was remade for TV in 1979 as a six-hour mini-
series.
● Frank Sinatra got his key role after Eli Wallach dropped
out.
🏆 best picture; Daniel Taradash; Fred Zinnemann; Burnett
Guffey; Frank Sinatra; Donna Reed; William Lyon
🏆 George Duning; Burt Lancaster; Deborah Kerr;
Montgomery Clift

694
From Here to Eternity

Life in a Honolulu barracks at the time of Pearl Harbor.

James Jones' sprawling, critical novel of army life in a Honolulu barracks
up to the time of Pearl Harbor had to be considerably cleaned up
before it could be filmed. The Pentagon insisted on changes to the
script before they would provide assistance, and the censors were
unhappy at its suggestion of marital infidelity. They forced a cut in the
film's most famous scene, of Burt Lancaster and Deborah Kerr rolling
together in the surf as they make love. Montgomery Clift gave one of
his best performances as a loner and Frank Sinatra, as a rebellious
soldier who suffers brutal punishment, was established as an acting
force. Zinnemann directed with style, making light of the problem the
two actors gave him in their scenes together: Sinatra was best on the
first take, Clift needed many tries to get the performance he wanted.

Lamerica
Italy/France   1994   125m   colour
Cinemascope
CGG Tiger/Arena (Mario and Vittorio Cecchi Gori)

w Gianni Amelio, Andrea Porporati, Alessandro Sermoneta
d *Gianni Amelio* *ph* *Luca Bigazzi* *m* Franco Piersanti
ad Giuseppe M. Gaudino *ed* Simona Paggi
☆ *Enrico Lo Verso* (Gino), Michele Placido (Fiore),
Carmelo di Mazzarelli (Spiro), Piro Milkani (Selimi)

'Its evangelical sincerity and the sweeping emotion
of its finale could win the director new admirers
abroad.' – *Variety*

● The film won a Felix as European film of the year in
1994.

693
Lamerica

Two Italian con men come unstuck when they go to Albania to get rich quick.

Gianni Amelio was true to the traditions of Italian neo-realism in his
study of Albania just after the fall of communism and of its relationship
with nearby, wealthy Italy, which seems the land of plenty to the dispossessed Albanians. His approach is documentary, and he used
mainly non-professional actors for a story of two Italian con men, who
come unstuck when they go to Albania to take advantage of a period of
confusion and get rich quick. It is a powerful and bleak drama of
appalling poverty and despair, and of the humanity that somehow survives in the direst situations.

The Man Who Wasn't There
US   2001   116m   DeLuxe/bw
Entertainment/USA/Working Title/Gramercy (Ethan Coen)
🔲 ▤ ⊚ ⊚ ⌒
w Joel Coen, Ethan Coen *d* Joel Coen *ph* Roger Deakins
m Carter Burwell *pd* Dennis Gassner *ad* Chris Gorak
ed Roderick Jaynes, Tricia Cooke *cos* Mary Zophres
☆ Billy Bob Thornton (Ed Crane), Frances McDormand (Doris Crane), Michael Badalucco (Frank), James Gandolfini (Big Dave), Katherine Borowitz (Ann Nirdlinger), Jon Polito (Creighton Tolliver), Scarlett Johansson (Birdy Abundas), Richard Jenkins (Walter Abundas), Tony Shalhoub (Freddy Riedenschneider), Adam Alexi-Malle (Carcanogues)

'Steadily engrossing and devilishly funny, and, oh brother, does it look sharp.' – *Peter Travers, Rolling Stone*

'A work of finely fabricated art. For much of its length it gives enormous pleasure of a kind that comes from observing events interlocking inexorably.' – *Alexander Walker, London Evening Standard*

⚖ Roger Deakins
🏆 Roger Deakins

692
The Man Who Wasn't There

In the late 1940s, an insignificant, small-town barber turned blackmailer finds himself in a situation he cannot control.

The Coen Brothers' stylish, stylized, highly polished, and leisurely thriller is the story of a small-town barber turned blackmailer, who comes close to being invisible: both socially insignificant and so anonymous and withdrawn that, despite his occupation, he has little interaction with the world. Yet he becomes the still centre of events and a situation that he cannot control in his desire to attain a recognizable identity as a successful businessman. Impeccably written, photographed and acted, it is in the great tradition of *film noir*, in which the guilty are undone by their own failures of character.

'His thrilling, exciting, romantic youth … wrestling, fighting, telling funny stories, falling in love! A picture stirring with its drama, romance, action, emotion!'

Young Mr Lincoln
US   1939   100m   bw
TCF (Kenneth MacGowan)
▤ ⊚
w Lamar Trotti *d* John Ford *ph* Bert Glennon *m* Alfred Newman *ad* Richard Day, Mark-Lee Kirk *ed* Walter Thompson
☆ Henry Fonda (Abraham Lincoln), Alice Brady (Abigail Clay), Marjorie Weaver (Mary Todd), Arleen Whelan (Hannah Clay), Eddie Collins (Efe Turner), Richard Cromwell (Matt Clay), Donald Meek (John Felder), Eddie Quillan (Adam Clay), Spencer Charters (Judge Herbert A. Bell)

'A dignified saga of early Lincolniana, paced rather slowly … lack of romantic interest is one of the prime factors which deter the film from interpreting itself into big box office.' – *Variety*

'In spite of the excitements of a murder, a near-lynching and a crackerjack trial, it remains a character study.' – *New York Sun*

'One of John Ford's most memorable films.' – *Pauline Kael, 70s*

⚖ Lamar Trotti

691
Young Mr Lincoln

Abraham Lincoln as a young country lawyer stops a lynching and proves a young man innocent of murder.

Henry Fonda was reluctant to play Lincoln until John Ford pointed out that he wasn't being asked to act the part of a president but 'a jack-legged lawyer, a gawky kid still wet behind the ears who rides a mule because he can't afford a horse.' Lamar Trotti's sensitive script portrayed Lincoln as a country lawyer who stops a lynching and proves a young man innocent of murder. Ford took the story at a gentle pace that allowed room for period atmosphere. He printed only one take so that Darryl Zanuck, a notorious editor who liked to add pace to Twentieth Century Fox's movies, was unable to alter it. Despite the second-feature courtroom twists, this is a marvellous old-fashioned entertainment with its heart in the right place.

The Big Chill
US   1983   105m   Metrocolor
Columbia/Carson Productions (Michael Shamberg)
📺 ▤ ⊙ ⊚ ⊚ 🎧
w Lawrence Kasdan, Barbara Benedek *d* Lawrence Kasdan
ph John Bailey *m* various *pd* Ida Random *ed* Carol Littleton
☆ Tom Berenger (Sam), Glenn Close (Sarah), Jeff Goldblum (Michael), William Hurt (Nick), Kevin Kline (Harold), Mary Kay Place (Meg), Meg Tilly (Chloe), JoBeth Williams (Karen), Don Galloway (Richard)

'The final impression left is of a collage of small relishable moments.' – *Kim Newman, MFB*

'An entertainment in which humour and sentiment are finely balanced and profundities are artfully skirted.' – *Sight and Sound*

'A splendid technical exercise … but there's no pay-off and it doesn't lead anywhere.' – *Roger Ebert*

♟ best picture; Glenn Close; screenplay

690
The Big Chill

University contemporaries try to comfort each other after the death of a friend.

Seven contemporaries at the University of Michigan try to comfort each other after the suicide of a friend in Lawrence Kasdan's wry satirical comedy. The approach of middle-age has brought change to most of them: a would-be novelist has become a celebrity journalist, a lawyer has gone from representing the poor to working for a large corporation, an actor is a success on a TV show that embarrasses him, and a Vietnam veteran and psychologist is now a drug-fuelled drifter. As they talk, drink and smoke the weekend away, they relive the past and make decisions about the future. In its witty lament for lost idealism and the shattering of youthful dreams, it encapsulates the experience of a generation.

☆ **Jim Jarmusch**
Director ☆

1. L'Atalante (Vigo)
2. Tokyo Story (Ozu)
3. They Live by Night (N. Ray)
4. Bob le Flambeur (Melville)
5. Sunrise (Murnau)
6. The Cameraman (Sedgwick)
7. Mouchette (Bresson)
8. Seven Samurai (Kurosawa)
9. Broken Blossoms (Griffith)
10. Rome, Open City (Rossellini)

☆ **Bernardo Bertolucci**
Director ☆

1. La Règle du Jeu (Renoir)
2. Sansho Dayu (Mizoguchi)
3. Germany Year Zero (Rossellini)
4. À Bout de Souffle (Godard)
5. Stagecoach (Ford)
6. Blue Velvet (Lynch)
7. City Lights (Chaplin)
8. Marnie (Hitchcock)
9. Accattone (Pasolini)
10. Touch of Evil (Welles)

☆ **John Boorman**
Director ☆

1. Seven Samurai (Kurosawa)
2. The Seventh Seal (Bergman)
3. 8½ (Fellini)
4. That Obscure Object of Desire (Buñuel)
5. Dr. Strangelove (Kubrick)
6. Citizen Kane (Welles)
7. Sunset Blvd. (Wilder)
8. Solaris (Tarkovsky)
9. La Roue (Gance)
10. The Birth of a Nation (Griffith)

The Ruling Class
GB 1972 155m DeLuxe
Keep Films (Jules Buck, Jack Hawkins)

w Peter Barnes *play* Peter Barnes *d* Peter Medak *ph* Ken Hodges *m* John Cameron *ed* Ray Lovejoy

☆ Peter O'Toole (Jack, 14th Earl of Gurney), Harry Andrews (13th Earl of Gurney), *Arthur Lowe* (Tucker), *Alastair Sim* (Bishop Lampton), Coral Browne (Lady Claire Gurney), Michael Bryant (Dr. Herder)

'This irritating and unsatisfying film is worth being irritated and unsatisfied by.' – *Stanley Kauffmann*

♧ Peter O'Toole

689
The Ruling Class

The fetishistic Earl of Gurney is succeeded by his mad son Jack who believes he is God.

Peter Barnes, one of Britain's best playwrights of the last century, was an admirer of Ben Jonson and wrote savage comedies in a similar vein, holding up the society of his time to moral scrutiny. The film has not quite the bravura of the original stage production, but is a substantial work. O'Toole provides an enjoyably over-the-top performance as a peer who is regarded as mad when he believes he is Jesus Christ, but is seen as sane after he decides he is Jack the Ripper. Barnes' mocking attack on the British establishment is grounded in the lack of love he perceives in its attitudes and bizarre rituals, social and sexual. The Earl of Gurney's gentle lunacy is lost when he is confronted by another madman representing the vengeful God of the Old Testament. But in his new persona as the Ripper, he is able to take advantage of his social standing to get away with murder. It is a bracing, uncompromising comedy of a kind rarely found on film.

The Bachelor Party

US 1957 93m bw
UA/Norma (Harold Hecht)

📼 🟰 ⊚

w Paddy Chayefsky *TV play* Paddy Chayefsky *d* Delbert Mann *ph* Joseph LaShelle *m* Alex North *ed* William B. Murphy

☆ *Don Murray* (Charlie Samson), *E. G. Marshall* (Walter), *Jack Warden* (Eddie), Philip Abbott (Arnold), Larry Blyden (Kenneth), Patricia Smith (Helen Samson), Carolyn Jones (The Existentialist)

♟ Carolyn Jones

688
The Bachelor Party

As New York book-keepers drink at a premaritial party for one of their friends, merriment gives way to despair.

New York book-keepers throw a wedding eve party for one of their fellows, but drink only brings to the fore their own private despairs, in this brilliantly observed social study of New York life at its least attractive. The acting matches the incisiveness of the script, from Philip Abbot's shy bachelor, Don Murray's married man who is tempted to stray, E.G. Marshall's middle-aged swinger consumed with self-loathing, to Carolyn Jones as a needy, love-starved woman. Paddy Chayefsky's tart dialogue catches the underlying despair of relationships in crisis.

Five Graves to Cairo

US 1943 96m bw
Paramount (Charles Brackett)

🟰

w Charles Brackett, Billy Wilder *play* Lajos Biro *d* Billy Wilder *ph* John Seitz *m* Miklos Rozsa *ad* Hans Dreier, Ernst Fegte *ed* Doane Harrison

☆ Franchot Tone (John J. Bramble), Anne Baxter (Mouche), *Erich von Stroheim* (Rommel), Akim Tamiroff (Farid), Peter Van Eyck (Lt. Schwegler), Miles Mander (British Colonel)

'Von Stroheim has all the other movie Huns backed completely off the screen.' – *Variety*

'Billy Wilder must have had something a little grander in mind: the cleverness lacks lustre.' – *New Yorker, 1978*

'A fabulous film fable, but it has been executed with enough finesse to make it a rather exciting pipe dream.' – *Howard Barnes, New York Herald Tribune*

● Locations representing the African desert include California's Salton Sea and Yuma, Arizona.

♟ John Seitz; art direction; editing

687
Five Graves to Cairo

During the North Africa campaign, British spies try to destroy Rommel's secret supply dumps.

Billy Wilder's intriguing melodrama dealt with British spies trying to destroy Rommel's secret supply dumps during the North Africa campaign of World War II. Set in a desert hotel, it was a notable example of Hollywood's ability to snatch polished drama from the headlines. Franchot Tone plays a lone British survivor who impersonates a waiter at the hotel that Rommel takes over; his task is to get back to British lines with information on where the Germans have hidden supplies of petrol and ammunition in the desert. Erich von Stroheim, as Rommel, maintained his belief in realism that had bankrupted his own career as a director. He insisted that the Leica cameras he carried should be loaded with film, claiming that the audience would feel it if they were empty.

A Fistful of Dollars
Italy/Germany/Spain   1964   100m
Techniscope
UA/Jolly/Constantin/Ocean (Arrigo Colombo, Georgio Papi)
🎬 ▦ ◎ ⊚ ◎ 🎧
original title: *Per un Pugno di Dollari*
w Sergio Leone, Duccio Tessari *d* Sergio Leone
ph Massimo Dallamano *m* Ennio Morricone *ed* Roberto Cinquini
☆ *Clint Eastwood* (The Man with No Name), Gian Maria Volonte (Ramon Rojo), Marianne Koch (Marisol), Wolfgang Lukschy (John Baxter)

'A film with no purpose beyond its ninety-five-minute Technicolor close-up portrayals of men being shot, gouged, burned, beaten and stomped to death.' – *Judith Crist*

● Direct sequels by Leone, apart from numerous imitations, are *For a Few Dollars More* and *The Good, the Bad and the Ugly*.

686
A Fistful of Dollars

A brutal and avenging stranger cleans up a Mexican border town.

A film with much to answer for: it began the craze for 'spaghetti Westerns', took its director to Hollywood, and made a TV cowboy into a world star. Leone, using Akira Kurosawa's *Yojimbo* for inspiration, turned the Western into a brutal baroque opera, a violent clash between individuals, orchestrated to Ennio Morricone's spare and haunting score. Leone's tale of an avenging stranger, violent and mysterious, who cleans up a Mexican border town was notable for its near-anonymous, laconic hero – what Leone called a violent, uncomplicated man – played in a stone-faced style by Eastwood.

'Reading. Writing. Revenge.'
Election
US   1999   103m   DeLuxe   Super 35
Paramount/MTV/Bonafide (Albert Berger, Ron Yerxa, David Gale, Keith Samples)
🎬 ▦ ⊚ ◎ 🎧
w Alexander Payne, Jim Taylor *novel* Tom Perrotta
d Alexander Payne *ph* James Glennon *m* Rolfe Kent
pd Jane Ann Stewart *ed* Kevin Tent
☆ Matthew Broderick (Jim McAllister), *Reese Witherspoon* (Tracy Flick), Chris Klein (Paul Metzler), Jessica Campbell (Tammy Metzler), Mark Harelik (Dave Novotny), Phil Reeves (Walt Hendricks), Molly Hagan (Diane McAllister), Delaney Driscoll (Linda Novotny), Colleen Camp (Judith R. Flick)

'If Billy Wilder had been assigned to make a teen comedy, he might well have come up with a film as sour and witty as this.' – *Geoffrey Macnab, Sight and Sound*

'Pertinent, fiendishly funny … A modern classic.' – *Peter Bradshaw, Guardian*

𝄐 script (Alexander Payne, Jim Taylor)

685
Election

The star pupil at a Midwestern high school is determined to become president of the student government but a discontented teacher is determined to prevent her doing so.

Alexander Payne's witty, inventive satire reduces politics to its lowest common denominator, an election to become president of the student government at a Midwestern high school. The school's star pupil is determined to win; a disgruntled teacher is equally determined that she should fail. The ever-smiling Reese Witherspoon is wonderful as the all-American girl on her ruthless way to the top. With its undercurrent of scandalous sex, dirty tricks and vote rigging, the film makes telling points about the underhand methods involved in all kinds of power struggles.

The Thin Man
US   1934   93m   bw
MGM/Cosmopolitan (Hunt Stromberg)

w Frances Goodrich, Albert Hackett *novel* Dashiell Hammett *d* W. S. Van Dyke *ph* James Wong Howe *m* William Axt *ad* Cedric Gibbons, David Townsend *ed* Robert J. Kern

☆ *William Powell* (Nick Charles), *Myrna Loy* (Nora Charles), Maureen O'Sullivan (Dorothy Wynant), Nat Pendleton (Lt. John Guild), Minna Gombell (Mimi Wynant), Edward Ellis (Clyde Wynant), Porter Hall (MacCauley), Henry Wadsworth (Tommy), William Henry (Gilbert Wynant), Harold Huber (Nunheim), Cesar Romero (Chris Jorgenson), Edward Brophy (Joe Morelli)

'A strange mixture of excitement, quips and hard-boiled sentiment … full of the special touches that can come from nowhere but the studio, that really make the feet a movie walks on.' – *Otis Ferguson*

● Sequels, on the whole of descending merit, included the following, all made at MGM with the same star duo: 1936: *After the Thin Man* (■, ◐~; 110m). 1939: *Another Thin Man* (■, ◐~; 102m). 1941: *Shadow of the Thin Man* (■, ◐~; 97m). 1944: *The Thin Man Goes Home* (■* ◐~; 100m). 1947: *Song of the Thin Man* (■, ◐~; 86m).
♟ best picture; script; W. S. Van Dyke; William Powell

684
The Thin Man

In New York over Christmas, a tipsy detective with his wife and dog solve the murder of an eccentric inventor.

William Powell and Myrna Loy formed one of the great Hollywood teamings as a tipsy detective and his witty wife. This, the first in their series of thrillers, in which they solve the murder of an eccentric inventor, showed a wisecracking, affectionate, married relationship almost for the first time. It set a sparkling comedy career for two stars previously known for heavy drama. The quick-moving, alternately comic and suspenseful mystery drama was developed in brief scenes and fast wipes. If heavy drinking no longer seems as amusing as it did, the wit and the couple's sophisticated relationship keep the film very much alive.

Wuthering Heights
US   1939   104m   bw
Samuel Goldwyn

w Ben Hecht, Charles MacArthur *novel* Emily Brontë *d* William Wyler *ph* Gregg Toland *m* Alfred Newman *ad* James Basevi *ed* Daniel Mandell

☆ *Laurence Olivier* (Heathcliff), *Merle Oberon* (Cathy Linton), David Niven (Edgar Linton), Hugh Williams (Hindley Earnshaw), Flora Robson (Ellen Dean), Geraldine Fitzgerald (Isabella Linton), Donald Crisp (Dr. Kenneth), Leo G. Carroll (Joseph), Cecil Kellaway (Mr. Earnshaw), *Miles Mander* (Lockwood)

'Sombre dramatic tragedy, productionally fine, but with limited appeal.' – *Variety*

'Unquestionably one of the most distinguished pictures of the year.' – *Frank S. Nugent, New York Times*

'A strong and sombre film, poetically written as the novel not always was, sinister and wild as it was meant to be, far more compact dramatically than Miss Brontë had made it.' – *Richard Mallett, Punch*

♟ Gregg Toland
♟ best picture; script; William Wyler; Alfred Newman; Laurence Olivier; Geraldine Fitzgerald; art direction

683
Wuthering Heights

The daughter of an unhappy middle-class Yorkshire family falls passionately in love with a gypsy who has been brought up with her.

Despite an American script and settings, this wildly romantic film makes a good stab at capturing the power of at least the first half of a classic Victorian novel, about the passionate love between the daughter of an unhappy middle-class Yorkshire family and a gypsy who has been brought up by them. Wyler directed with his usual fluid and perfectionist style, and his favourite cinematographer, Gregg Toland, created some ravishing images. Olivier's vitality enlivens the scenes with the no-more-than-adequate Merle Oberon. Wyler refused to shoot the ending Goldwyn wanted, of Cathy and Heathcliff re-united after death, so Goldwyn had H.C. Potter film from the back doubles of Olivier and Oberon walking along a path, superimposed in the sky. In all respects it is a superb Hollywood production of its day.

War and Peace
USSR 1967 507m Sovcolor 'Scope 70mm
Mosfilm
🎞️ 🎬 ◎
original title: *Vojna i Mir*
w Sergei Bondarchuk, Vasili Solovyov *novel* Leo Tolstoy *d* Sergei Bondarchuk *ph* Anatoli Petritsky *m* Vyacheslav Ovchinnikov *pd* Mikhail Bogdanov, Gennadi Myasnikov *ad* Gennadiy Myasnikov, Mikhail Bogdanov *ed* Tatyana Likhachyova
☆ Lyudmila Savelyeva (Natasha Rostova), Sergei Bondarchuk (Pierre Bezuhov), Vyacheslav Tikhonov (Prince Andrey Bolkonsky), Gennadi Ivanov (Narrator), Irina Gubanova (Sonya), Antonina Shuranova (Princess Maria)

'It has a cumulative force which overcomes some of its academic and posey qualities.' – *Variety*

● The film was five years in production and cost between $50m and $70m.
● A Region 1 five-disc special edition DVD release includes documentaries on Bondarchuk and Tolstoy.
👤 best foreign film

682
War and Peace

An immensely long Russian version which includes some some of the most spectacular battle scenes ever filmed.

Sergei Bondarchuk's long, involved epic punctiliously follows Leo Tolstoy's novel chronicling the lives of several Russian families and their tangled love affairs during the Napoleonic wars and the invasion of Russia. The film, which took five years to make, is a treat for the eyes throughout, with some of the most magnificently spectacular battle scenes ever filmed, using some effective aerial shots to provide an overview of the action. A dubbed version running for 357m was released in the US in 1969.

Los Olvidados
Mexico 1951 88m bw
Utramar/Oscar Dancigers
🎬 ◎
aka: *The Young and the Damned*
w Luis Buñuel, Luis Alcoriza, Oscar Dancigers *d* Luis Buñuel *ph* Gabriel Figueroa *m* Gustavo Pitaluga *ed* Carlos Savage
☆ Alfonso Mejia (Pedro), Miguel Inclan (The Blind Man), Estela Inda (The Mother), Roberto Cobo (Jaibo)

'I shall not put *Los Olvidados* among the films I have most enjoyed; but I am far from sure that it should not go among the monuments of the cinema.' – *Dilys Powell*

681
Los Olvidados

A good boy is corrupted by young thugs in Mexico City's slums, and both he and his tormentor die violently.

Luis Buñuel became a citizen of Mexico in 1949 and was to direct some twenty films there. They were made under difficult circumstances and were, he admitted, uneven in quality. This is among the best of them, a sober and penetrating analysis of social conditions leading to violence in the slums of Mexico City. He focused on Pedro, a good boy who becomes contaminated by the young thugs around him. Jaibo, an older boy who becomes the gang leader and the lover of Pedro's mother, kills him before being killed himself. It is a harsh film about brutal conditions: the young delinquents tip a legless beggar out of his cart and torment a blind man. It is Buñuel's tragic masterpiece, though it is a pity he could not afford a surrealist shot he wanted, of the delinquents running past a half-completed building with a symphony orchestra playing soundlessly on the scaffolding.

'The time to hide is over.'

The Hours
US   2002   114m   DeLuxe
Buena Vista/Paramount/Miramax (Scott Rudin, Robert Fox)
📼 ■ ⊚ ⊚ ⌒
w David Hare *novel* Michael Cunningham *d* Stephen Daldry *ph* Seamus McGarvey *m* Philip Glass *pd* Maria Djurkovic *ad* Mark Raggett *ed* Peter Boyle *cos* Ann Roth
☆ Meryl Streep (Clarissa Vaughan), Julianne Moore (Laura Brown), Nicole Kidman (Virginia Woolf), Ed Harris (Richard Brown), Toni Collette (Kitty), Claire Danes (Julia Vaughan), Jeff Daniels (Louis Waters), Stephen Dillane (Leonard Woolf)

'A moving, somewhat depressing film that demands and rewards attention.' – *Philip French, Observer*

'A grim and uninvolving film, for which Philip Glass unwittingly provides the perfect score – tuneless, oppressive, droning, painfully self-important.' – *Richard Shickel, Time*

● The DVD release includes audio commentary by Daldry and Cunningham, and by Meryl Streep, Julianne Moore and Nicole Kidman.
♟ Nicole Kidman
♟ picture; David Hare; Stephen Daldry; Ed Harris; Julianne Moore; Philip Glass; Peter Boyle; Ann Roth
♟ Nicole Kidman; Philip Glass

Spirited Away
♟♟ Japan   2001   125m   Technicolor
Optimum/Tokuma Shoten/Studio Ghibli/NipponTV/Dentsu/Buena Vista/Tohokushinsha/Mitsubishi (Toshio Suzuki)
📼 ■ ⊚ ⊚ ⌒
original title: *Sen to Chihiro – No Kamikakushi*
wd Hayao Miyazaki *m* Joe Hisaishi *ad* Yoji Takeshige *ed* Takeshi Seyama
☆ voices of: Rumi Hiiragi (Chihiro), Miyu Irino (Haku), Mari Natsuki (Yubaba/Zeniba), Takashi Naito (Akio), Yasuko Sawaguchi (Yugo)

'A work of unparalleled genius.' – *Jason Solomons, Times*

'This uninspired story … is clumsy in execution and lacks the complexity to sustain a film of two hours.' – *Cosmo Landesman, Sunday Times*

● The movie was released in two versions, one subtitled and the other dubbed into English. Both versions are on the DVD release.
● It shared the Golden Bear award at the Berlin Film Festival in 2002.
♟ animated feature

680
The Hours

In three different eras, three women contemplate their choices, their lives and death.

A deft, engrossing film about three women contemplating their lives and the possibilities of death in three different eras. It is built around the suicide of Virginia Woolf and the themes of her novel *Mrs Dalloway*, in which the life of her heroine is contrasted with that of other women and a suicidal poet. Woolf's book connects with two women: one is an unhappy housewife in the Fifties, the other a woman caring for a former lover, a homosexual poet dying of AIDS. The events of the film echo those of the novel so that it becomes a multi-layered, deeply affecting account of the choices people make in their lives and the consequences of them.

679
Spirited Away

Moving to a new town with her family, a melencholy young girl is stranded in a bathhouse occupied by gods and spirits.

While American animated films have wholeheartedly embraced computer-generated imagery, with some stunning results, Japanese *anime* has shown that there are still many unexplored possibilities in a traditional hand-drawn approach. Hayao Miyazaki is the acknowledged master of the form, though, as with other Japanese movies, his narratives can be confusing to Western minds. But this is, for the most part, easy and enjoyable to follow: moving to a new town with her parents, an unhappy girl finds herself stranded in a bathhouse occupied by gods and spirits, where she has to work her way to freedom. The gods may seem bizarre, but the girl's discovery of self-reliance bridges cultures. When the story does stray into strange metaphysics, the quality of the animation provides marvels enough.

A Self-Made Hero

France 1995 106m colour
Artificial Eye/Alicélo/Lumière/France 3/M6/Initial
(Patrick Godeau)

original title: *Un Héros Très Discret*
w Alain Le Henry, Jacques Audiard *novel* Jean-François Deniau *d* Jacques Audiard *ph* Jean-Marc Fabre *m* Alexandre Desplat *ad* Michel Vandestien *ed* Juliette Welfling
☆ Mathieu Kassovitz (Albert Dehousse), Anouk Grinberg (Servane), Sandrine Kiberlain (Yvette), Jean-Louis Trintignant (Albert, Present), Albert Dupontel (Dionnet), Nadia Barentin (Madame Louvier/Madame Revuz/The General's Wife), Bernard Bloch (Ernst)

'Half comic and half in deadly earnest – a political film seemingly determined to cause offence by questioning both orthodox history and those who made it.' – *Derek Malcolm, Guardian*

678
A Self-Made Hero

After the liberation of France, a cowardly and foolish fantasist reinvents himself as a hero of the Resistance.

A sharply political comedy of assumed identity and innocence – imagine a cross between *Candide* and *The Captain of Kopenick* or *The Government Inspector* – which casts a beady and entertaining eye over French attitudes to the recent past. Jacques Audiard presents a cowardly and simple-minded fantasist who creates a new identity, presenting himself as a hero of the Resistance after the liberation of France, a confused period when truth was often buried. Mathieu Kassovitz gives a sympathetic performance as the fantasist whose confession of his deception is conveniently ignored.

Fat City

US 1972 96m Eastmancolor
Columbia/Rastar (Ray Stark)

w Leonard Gardner *novel* Leonard Gardner *d* John Huston *ph* Conrad Hall *md* Marvin Hamlisch *pd* Richard Sylbert *ed* Margaret Booth
☆ Stacy Keach (Billy Tully), Jeff Bridges (Ernie Munger), Susan Tyrrell (Oma), Candy Clark (Faye)

'Huston has confronted a piece of material and a milieu perfectly suited to his insights and talents. The result is his best film in years and one of the best he has ever done: a lean, compassionate, detailed, raucous, sad, strong look at some losers and survivors on the side streets of small-city Middle America.' – *Charles Champlin*

♟ Susan Tyrrell

677
Fat City

In a small Californian town, a has-been boxer tries to recover his success, but loses his self-respect and becomes a hobo.

John Huston's *Fat City* is one of the best boxing movies there is, dealing not with champions but with the small-time fighters, whose hopes of success have long faded as they continue to dream and go through the motions: in a small Californian town, a has-been boxer tries to get back to the top, but loses his self respect and becomes a hobo. It is a character-driven film and gets a fine central performance from Stacy Keach, an actor who has rarely had the film roles he deserved, and from Jeff Bridges, as a young hopeful with no future. Huston's own description of the film is an accurate one: 'a fine picture, no question – well conceived, well acted, made with deep love and considerable understanding.'

Butcher Boy

Ireland/US 1997 110m Technicolor
Warner/Geffen (Redmond Morris, Stephen Woolley)

w Neil Jordan, Patrick McCabe *novel* Patrick McCabe
d Neil Jordan *ph* Adrian Biddle *m* Elliot Goldenthal
pd Anthony Pratt *ad* Anna Rackard *ed* Tony Lawson
☆ Stephen Rea (Benny Brady, "Da"), Fiona Shaw (Mrs.
Nugent), *Eamonn Owens* (Francie Brady), Alan Boyle (Joe
Purcell), Brendan Gleeson (Father Bubbles), Milo O'Shea
(Father Sullivan), Ian Hart (Uncle Alo), Sinead O'Connor
(Our Lady/Colleen), Patrick McCabe (Jimmy-the-Skite)

'A heart-wrenching black comedy.' – *Paddy Barrett,
Screen International*

'Grips like *The 400 Blows* crossed with *A Clockwork
Orange*.' – *Alexander Walker*

676
Butcher Boy

*In the early 1960s, an Irish boy from a troubled family background grows up to
be a murderer.*

Sustained by a superb performance in the title role from Eamonn
Owens, this is a bleak, dark drama of alienation and despair, shot
through with gallows humour. Patrick McCabe's story of an Irish boy,
with an alcoholic father and suicidal mother, who grows up to be a
murderer in the early 1960s, is directed by Neil Jordan with great
attention to detail. He slightly skews the setting and performances to
provide a particular atmosphere of unease, topped by the vision of
Sinead O'Connor as the Virgin Mary.

Rosetta

Belgium/France 1999 94m colour
Artificial Eye/Les Films du Fleuve/RTBF/ARP (Luc and
Jean-Pierre Dardenne, Michele and Laurent Petin)

wd Luc and Jean-Pierre Dardenne *ph* Alain Marcoen
m Jean-Pierre Cocco *ad* Igor Gabriel *ed* Marie-Hélène
Dozo
☆ *Emilie Dequenne* (Rosetta), Fabrizio Rongione (Riquet),
Anne Yernaux (Rosetta's mother), Olivier Gourmet (Boss)

'A stunning and remarkable achievement … It is a
film whose grace and lyricism has earned it,
simply, the status of classic: something of real
greatness.' – *Peter Bradshaw, Guardian*

'An unforgiving piece of hard-boiled cinéma-vérité
… desperately moving and desperately
depressing.' – *James Christopher, Times*

● At the 1999 Cannes Film Festival, the film won the
Palme d'Or , and Emilie Dequenne was awarded the prize for
best actress.
● A Region 2 collector's edition two-disc DVD includes an
interview with Luc & Jean-Pierre Dardenne, and their feature
film *La Promesse*.

675
Rosetta

*In a Belgian industrial town, a young unemployed woman, living on a caravan
site with her alcoholic mother, dreams of leading a normal life.*

The Belgian filmmakers Luc and Jean-Pierre Dardenne created an
intense, gritty drama that concentrated almost entirely on a young
woman's desperate search for some small acceptance from a hostile
world. It gained immeasurably from its unforced central performance
from Emilie Dequenne as a woman who lives on a caravan site with her
alcoholic mother while looking for work in an industrial town and
dreaming of leading a normal life. The film offers little hope for her. At
night she holds a conversation with herself that begins, 'Your name is
Rosetta. My name is Rosetta. You found a job. I found a job. You've got
a friend. I've got a friend. You have a normal life. I have a normal life.'
There is no job. She betrays the only person who seemed a friend.
There is no life.

The Way Ahead
GB 1944 115m bw
GFD/Two Cities (John Sutro, Norman Walker)
📹 ≣ ⊚ ⊛
US title: *Immortal Battalion*
w Eric Ambler, Peter Ustinov *d* Carol Reed *ph* Guy Green
m William Alwyn *ad* David Rawnsley *ed* Fergus
McDonell

☆ *David Niven* (Lt. Jim Perry), *Stanley Holloway* (Brewer),
Raymond Huntley (Davenport), *William Hartnell* (Sgt.
Fletcher), James Donald (Lloyd), John Laurie (Luke), Leslie
Dwyer (Beck), Hugh Burden (Parsons), Jimmy Hanley
(Stainer), Renée Asherson (Marjorie Gillingham), Penelope
Dudley Ward (Mrs. Perry), Reginald Tate (Commanding
Officer), Leo Genn (Company Commander), Mary Jerrold
(Mrs. Gillingham), Peter Ustinov (Rispoli)

'Is to be admired and recommended for its
direction, its writing and its playing.' – *Dilys Powell*

674
The Way Ahead

The lives of a platoon of new recruits during World War II.

Carol Reed's memorable semi-documentary grew out of a training film
he made, showing the adventures of a platoon of raw recruits during
World War II. At the time, the Army felt that they were losing out to the
other two services, who had each been the subject of a successful film:
In Which We Serve, about the navy, and *One of Our Aircraft is Missing*, about
the RAF. Major David Niven became the film's star. Private Peter
Ustinov, the screenwriter, knew at first hand the life of a new recruit (he
was made an honorary civilian during filming so he could mix freely
with the officers). It succeeds in being both convincing propaganda
and an entertaining and engrossing film, humorous and touching in
showing the process of turning civilians into soldiers.

'Life's greatest adventure is finding your
place in the Circle of Life.'
The Lion King
🚸 US 1994 88m Technicolor
Buena Vista/Walt Disney (Don Hahn)
📹 ≣ ⊛⊙ ⊚ ⊛ ∩
w Irene Mecchi, Jonathan Roberts, Linda Woolverton
d Roger Allers, Rob Minkoff *m* Hans Zimmer, Lebo M
m/ly Elton John, Tim Rice *pd* Chris Sanders
☆ Featuring the voices of Matthew Broderick, Rowan
Atkinson, Niketa Calame, Jim Cummings, Whoopi
Goldberg, Jeremy Irons, Robert Guillaume, James Earl
Jones, Cheech Marin, Jonathan Taylor Thomas

'*Bambi*, but with carnivores ... The animation,
computer-assisted in some of the more elaborate
sequences, is sometimes impressive, but rarely
impressive enough to overcome a certain
impersonality – a stubborn mechanical coldness.'
– *Terrence Rafferty, New Yorker*

● The film was the biggest earner of 1994 in the US, taking
$298.9m at the box office. Its plot reportedly resembles that
of *Jungle Taitei* (aka *Jungle Emperor*), a Japanese animated
series made in the 60s.
🏆 Hans Zimmer; song 'Can You Feel the Love Tonight' (*m*
Elton John, *ly* Tim Rice)
♫ songs 'Circle of Life', 'Hakuna Matata'

673
The Lion King

*A lion cub, exiled by his evil uncle, grows up happy and carefree but realizes
that he must fight to reclaim his royal destiny.*

With this vivid example of classic animation, Disney returned to a
theme that had first surfaced in *Bambi*: the cycle of life and the growth
from birth to maturity of an animal destined to be ruler of its world. Its
difference is that the lion cub does not come into his inheritance easily.
Exiled by his evil uncle, he grows up enjoying the easy life, but is persuaded that he must fight to restore himself to his rightful place as
king. Despite an occasional preachy tone, it is an entertaining drama
with some stunning moments.

The Watchmaker of St Paul
France   1973   105m   Eastmancolor
Lira (Raymond Danon)
◙ ▤ ⊚ ⊚
original title: *L'Horloger de St Paul*
w Jean Aurenche, Pierre Bost, Bertrand Tavernier
novel L'Horloger d'Everton by Georges Simenon
d Bertrand Tavernier *ph* Pierre William Glenn *m* Philippe
Sarde *ad* Jean Mandareux *ed* Armand Psenny
☆ Philippe Noiret (Michel Descombes), Jean Rochefort
(Commissioner Guiboud), Sylvain Rougerie (Bernard
Descombes), Christine Pascal (Liliane Terrini)

672
The Watchmaker of St Paul

A watchmaker's quiet life is ruined when he learns that his son is wanted for murder.

Bertrand Tavernier's political thriller provides magnificent opportunities for excellent performances from Philip Noiret as a watchmaker, whose tranquil life is shattered when he learns that his teenage son has killed a security guard and is on the run with his girlfriend, and Jean Rochefort as the police inspector in charge of the investigation. Against a background of political manoeuverings, since the boy has murdered a former paratrooper with right wing connections, the two men form a tentative friendship before acknowledging that they have little in common. A remarkable character drama, it offers a revealing study in shifting relationships.

'It happens in the best of families.'

Now Voyager
US   1942   117m   bw
Warner (Hal B. Wallis)

📽 🖿 🗪 ◎ 🎧

w Casey Robinson *novel* Olive Higgins Prouty *d* Irving
Rapper *ph* Sol Polito *m* Max Steiner *ad* Robert Haas
ed Warren Low
☆ *Bette Davis* (Charlotte Vale), *Claude Rains* (Dr. Jaquith),
Paul Henreid (Jerry D. Durrance), Gladys Cooper (Mrs.
Henry Windle Vale), John Loder (Elliott Livingston), Bonita
Granville (June Vale), Ilka Chase (Lisa Vale), Lee Patrick
("Deb" McIntyre), Charles Drake (Leslie Trotter), Franklin
Pangborn (Mr. Thompson), Janis Wilson (Tina Durrance)

'If it were better, it might not work at all. This way,
it's a crummy classic.' – *New Yorker, 1977*

🏃 Max Steiner
🏋 Bette Davis; Gladys Cooper

671
Now Voyager

A dowdy frustrated spinster takes the psychiatric cure and begins a doomed love affair.

Bette Davis gave one of her best performances as a dowdy frustrated spinster – 'my ugly duckling,' as her domineering mother describes her – who, after treatment from a psychiatrist, discovers that she can be glamorous and embarks on a doomed love affair with a married man. The moment when Paul Henreid puts two cigarettes between his lips, lights them and hands one to Bette Davis, establishing their intimacy, has become one of romantic cinema's iconic scenes. Gladys Cooper adds venomous bite to her portrayal of the mother who insists on making all the right decisions for her daughter. The basically soggy script still gets by through the romantic magic of its stars, who were all at their best; and suffering in mink went over very big in wartime. Even now, it is hard to resist.

Vagabonde
France   1985   104m   colour
Cine-Tamaris/A2/Ministère de la Culture

🖿 🗪 ◎

French title: *Sans Toit ni Loi*
aka: *Vagabond*
wd Agnès Varda *ph* Patrick Blossier *m* Joanna
Bruzdowicz *ed* Agnès Varda, Patricia Mazuy
☆ Sandrine Bonnaire (Mona), Macha Meril (Madame
Landier), Stéphane Freiss (Mme Landier), Laurence
Cortadellas (Elaine), Marthe Jarnais (Tante Lydie), Yolande
Moreau (Yolande), Joel Fosse (Paulo)
● It won the Golden Lion award for best film at the Venice
Film Festival in 1985.

670
Vagabonde

After a young woman is found frozen to death in a ditch, people tell of their experiences of her in the last weeks of her life and of how she abandoned conventional living to become a tramp.

There is an enigma at the centre of Agnès Varda's disturbingly chill movie that reconstructs the life of a young woman who is found frozen to death in a ditch. Those she met as she hitch-hiked around the south of France recall the impression she made on them. They range from a lorry driver to farming couple, a nun, a man she lived with for a time in a deserted chateau, and a wealthy, blind woman. As different aspects of her character emerge, she remains largely unknown, as someone who may have found what she was looking for in death. It is a gripping account of the accidental collisions of people's lives, and the changes they cause.

'His Majesty was all powerful and all knowing. But he wasn't quite all there.'

'First he lost America. Now he's losing his mind.'

The Madness of King George
GB   1994   107m   Technicolor
Rank/Samuel Goldwyn/Channel 4/Close Call
(Stephen Evans, David Parfitt)
⬤⬤ ⬤⬤ ▬ 🞰 ◉ ◉ ◉ ◎
w Alan Bennett *play The Madness of George III* by Alan Bennett
d Nicholas Hytner *ph* Andrew Dunn *m* George Fenton,
Handel *pd* Ken Adam *ad* Martin Childs *ed* Tariq Anwar
☆ *Nigel Hawthorne* (King George III), *Helen Mirren*
(Queen Charlotte), Ian Holm (Willis), Amanda Donohoe
(Lady Pembroke), Rupert Graves (Greville), Rupert Everett
(The Prince of Wales), Jim Carter (Fox), Geoffrey Palmer
(Warren), John Wood (Thurlow), Jeremy Child (Black Rod),
Cyril Shaps (Pepys)
● The title of the play, *The Madness of George III*, was not
used in case audiences thought it was the third film in a
series (just as audiences are said to have come out of *Henry
V* regretting that they had missed the first four films).
🯅 Ken Adam
🯄 Nigel Hawthorne; Helen Mirren; Alan Bennett
🯇 best British picture; Nigel Hawthorne

669
The Madness of King George

In the 1780s, King George III's behaviour becomes more and more eccentric and unbalanced until he is diagnosed as mad and comes close to losing his power.

The point, or pointlessness, of the monarchy is obliquely questioned in this entertaining drama of the eccentricities of royalty – specifically the behaviour of King George III, which became more and more unbalanced in the 1780s until he was diagnosed as mad and came close to losing his power. (Bennett speculates that the King's problem may have been caused by the illness porphyria.) Directed with a sense of pace and an excellent eye for the inequalities of society, even within palaces, it gains immeasurably by the superb performance of Hawthorne in the title role, honed by his having played it so often on the stage.

'Where the game is never over.'

House of Games
US   1987   102m   Du Art Color
Filmhaus/Orion (Michael Hausman)

wd David Mamet *ph* Juan Ruiz Anchia *m* Alaric Jans
pd Michael Merritt *ed* Trudy Ship
☆ Lindsay Crouse (Dr. Margaret Ford), Joe Mantegna
(Mike), Mike Nussbaum (Joey), Lilia Skala (Dr. Littauer)

'It arrived with the shock of the new: I saw it and
was in the presence of a new style, a distinctive
voice.' – Roger Ebert

668
House of Games

A psychiatrist becomes involved with a confidence trickster.

The respected Broadway playwright David Mamet made his stylish directorial debut with a film that was both a confidence trick and about a confidence trickster who becomes involved with an inquisitive psychiatrist. She wants a gambler to give up his threat to kill one of her patients who owes him money; he agrees if she will help him win a poker game against a wealthy Texan. She is intrigued by a world far removed from her own, but, for all her understanding of people, is an innocent astray in a dangerous jungle. As her education unfolds, Mamet plays dazzling tricks with an audience's expectations.

'She Came To Venice As a Tourist – And
Went Home a Woman!'

Summertime
US   1955   99m   Eastmancolor
London Films/Lopert Productions (Ilya Lopert)

GB title: *Summer Madness*
w David Lean, H. E. Bates *play* The Time of the Cuckoo by
Arthur Laurents *d* David Lean *ph* Jack Hildyard
m Sandro Cicognini *ad* Vincent Korda *ed* Peter Taylor
☆ *Katharine Hepburn* (Jane Hudson), Rossano Brazzi
(Renato Di Rossi), Isa Miranda (Signora Fiorina), Darren
McGavin (Eddie Jaeger), Mari Aldon (Phyl Jaeger), André
Morell (Englishman)

'The eye is endlessly ravished.' – *Dilys Powell*

⚖ David Lean; Katharine Hepburn

667
Summertime

An American spinster has a holiday in Venice and falls in love.

A delightful, sympathetic travelogue with dramatic asides, this was great to look at and hinged on a single, superb performance by Katharine Hepburn as an American spinster who holidays in Venice and becomes romantically involved. Hepburn spent much time in the 1950s playing spinsters who fall for a seductive stranger, who, in this instance, was a married man. When she returned to America, she had only the memory of the brief affair to warm her life. Hepburn's perfect performance as a lonely woman seemed to chime with her own mood. 'Being an actor is such a humiliating experience,' she said at the time. 'As you get older, it becomes more humiliating because you've got less to sell.'

'Mightier than Broadway ever beheld.'

'Most important entertainment event since Warner Bros gave you Vitaphone!'

42nd Street
US   1933   89m   bw
Warner (Hal B. Wallis)
▣ ▤ ◉~ ◎

w *James Seymour, Rian James* novel *Bradford Ropes* d *Lloyd Bacon* ph *Sol Polito* m/ly *Al Dubin, Harry Warren* ch *Busby Berkeley* ad *Jack Okey* ed *Thomas Pratt*
☆ *Warner Baxter* (Julian Marsh), *Ruby Keeler* (Peggy Sawyer), *Bebe Daniels* (Dorothy Brock), George Brent (Pat Denning), Una Merkel (Lorraine Fleming), Guy Kibbee (Abner Dillon), Dick Powell (Billy Lawler), *Ginger Rogers* (Anytime Annie), *Ned Sparks* (Thomas Barry), George E. Stone (Andy Lee), Allen Jenkins (Mac Elory)

'The story has been copied a hundred times since, but never has the backstage atmosphere been so honestly and felicitously caught.' – *John Huntley, 1966*

'It gave new life to the clichés that have kept parodists happy.' – *New Yorker, 1977*

♫ 'Forty-Second Street'; 'It Must Be June'; 'Shuffle Off to Buffalo'; 'Young and Healthy'; 'You're Getting to Be a Habit with Me'
♕ best picture

Bob le Flambeur
France   1956   95m   bw
Jenner/Cyme/Play Art/OG
▣ ▤ ◎ ◎

w *Auguste Le Breton, Jean-Pierre Melville* d *Jean-Pierre Melville* ph *Henri Decae* m *Eddie Barclay, Jean Boyer* ad *Jean-Pierre Melville, Bouxin* ed *Monique Bonnot*
☆ Roger Duchesne (Bob), Isabelle Corey (Anne), Daniel Cauchy (Paolo), Howard Vernon (McKimmie), Guy Decomble (Inspector Ledru), Claude Cerval (Jean)

'Its dark-toned cinematography by Henri Decae still packs a wallop, and the screenplay has a refreshing sense of humor, reflecting Melville's concept of the picture as less a straightforward cops-and-robbers story than a scruffy comedy of manners.' – *David Sterrit, Christian Science Monitor*

● It was remade by Neil Jordan in 2002 as *The Good Thief*.

666
42nd Street

An ailing Broadway producer struggles while rehearsing a show but achieves a dazzling open night.

The archetypal Hollywood putting-on-a-show musical in which a Broadway musical producer has troubles during rehearsal but reaches a successful opening night. The leading lady is indisposed and a chorus girl is told to get out there and come back a star. The clichés are written and performed with great zest; the dialogue crackles ('Not "Anytime Annie"? Say, who could forget her? She only said "no" once, and then she didn't hear the question'); the atmosphere is convincing, and the numbers, when they come, are dazzlers, thanks to Busby Berkeley's inspired and inventive kaleidoscopic choreography. Made at the time of the Depression, it offered glamour and a hope for a happier future.

665
Bob le Flambeur

An ageing, compulsive gambler and former gangster plans one last heist: to rob a casino.

A gangster movie that is one of a kind: elegiac and nostalgic, it is less concerned with crime than with character. Its hero, Bob le Flambeur, is an ageing gambler. A creature of crepuscular dawns, he has no illusions about himself – 'a fine hoodlum face,' he remarks, seeing himself in a mirror. He retains old-fashioned notions about romance and honour among thieves. Planning one last robbery at the casino that has bankrupted him, he almost accepts that it is bound to go wrong. Melville deliberately avoids the big moments, such as the race on which Bob bets all, to concentrate on a melancholy portrait of the last of his kind, cruising the seedier parts of Paris, the Pigalle and Montmartre. All are captured with enormous affection.

The Roaring Twenties
US 1939 106m bw
Warner (Hal B. Wallis)
🎬 ■ 🔍 ⊘

w Jerry Wald, Richard Macaulay, Robert Rossen
story Mark Hellinger d Raoul Walsh, Anatole Litvak
ph Ernest Haller m Heinz Roemheld ad Max Parker
ed Jack Killifer
☆ James Cagney (Eddie Bartlett), Humphrey Bogart
(George Hally), Priscilla Lane (Jean Sherman), Jeffrey Lynn
(Lloyd Hart), Gladys George (Panama Smith), Frank
McHugh (Danny Green), Paul Kelly (Nick Brown), Elizabeth
Risdon (Mrs. Sherman)

'Story and dialog are good. Raoul Walsh turns in a fine directorial job; the performances are uniformly excellent.' – *Variety*

● The James Cagney character was based on Larry Fay, who was Texas Guinan's partner, and Gladys George is clearly Guinan herself.
● Walsh replaced Litvak as director during filming.

664
The Roaring Twenties

A World War I veteran returns to New York, innocently becomes involved in bootlegging, builds up an empire and dies in a gang war.

James Cagney and Humphrey Bogart squared up to each other as rival gangsters in one of the last, and perhaps the best, of the Warner gangster cycle. Cagney played a veteran, who after returning to New York after World War I builds up a bootlegging empire, only to meet his end in a gang war. Bogart was his former partner turned nemesis. Raoul Walsh, who replaced Anatol Litvak as director, uses a fluid documentary approach, based on the life of a New York gangster Larry Fay. The dialogue crackles with the idiom of tough talking hoodlums – 'you came into this racket with your eyes open. You learned a lot and you know a lot. If any of it gets out, you go out with your eyes open, only this time, they'll have pennies on them.' Despite the familiar plot line, stars and studio were in cracking form.

Zazie dans le Métro
France 1960 88m Eastmancolor
Nouvelles Editions (Irène Leriche)
🎬 ■

wd Louis Malle novel Raymond Queneau ph Henri Raichi
m Fiorenzo Capri ad Bernard Evein ed Kenout Peltier
☆ Catherine Demongeot (Zazie), Philippe Noiret (Uncle
Gabriel), Vittorio Caprioli (Trouscaillon), Hubert Deschamps
(Turandot), Carla Marlier (Albertine), Annie Fratellini (Mado)

'There is something not quite innocent or healthy about this film.' – *Bosley Crowther*

663
Zazie dans le Métro

A naughty little girl spends a day in Paris and causes chaos.

A foul-mouthed, mischievous ten-year-old girl has a day in Paris and causes chaos in Louis Malle's inventive little comedy which almost turns into a French *Hellzapoppin*, with everybody chasing or fighting everybody else. Malle achieves a visual equivalent to Raymond Queneau's pun-filled, allusive prose in the original novel, quoting from dozens of other films, including the Marx Brothers and *Hiroshima, Mon Amour*. After thirty-six hours of insane and surreal escapades, in a normal world where adults say one thing and do another, Zazie is reunited with her mother, who asks her what she has done. Says Zazie, 'I've grown older.' But this is a movie to make audiences feel young and irresponsible again.

Une Partie de Campagne

France 1936 40m bw
Pantheon/Pierre Braunberger
▣ ◉

aka: *A Day in the Country*

wd Jean Renoir *story* Guy de Maupassant *ph* Claude Renoir, Jean Bourgoin *m* Joseph Kosma *ad* Robert Gys *ed* Marinette Cadix, Marguerite Renoir

☆ Sylvia Bataille (Henriette Dufour), Georges Darnoul (Henri), Jane Marken (Mme. Juliette Dufour), Paul Temps (Anatole)

'Nothing can tarnish the intense lyrical simplicity underlaid with an aching irony and made almost unbearable by the yearning musical score of Kosma. This is everybody's lost love.' – *Richard Winnington*

A Tree Grows in Brooklyn

US 1945 128m bw
TCF (Louis D. Lighton)
▤ ◔ ◉

w Tess Slesinger, Frank Davis *novel* Betty Smith *d* Elia Kazan *ph* Leon Shamroy *m* Alfred Newman *ad* Lyle Wheeler *ed* Dorothy Spencer

☆ Peggy Ann Garner (Francie Nolan), James Dunn (Johnny Nolan), Dorothy McGuire (Katie), Joan Blondell (Aunt Sissy), Lloyd Nolan (McShane), Ted Donaldson (Neeley Nolan), James Gleason (McGarrity), Ruth Nelson (Miss McDonough), John Alexander (Steve Edwards), Adeline de Walt Reynolds (Mrs. Waters), Charles Halton (Mr. Barker)

'He tells a maximum amount of story with a minimum of film. Little touches of humour and human understanding crop up throughout.' – *Frank Ward, NBR*

'An artistically satisfying and emotionally quickening tearjerker.' – *Kine Weekly*

'Its drabness is softened by a glow of love and hope.' – *Picture Show*

🧍 James Dunn; Peggy Ann Garner (Special Award as outstanding child actress)
𝄐 script

662
Une Partie de Campagne

Around 1880, a Parisian tradesman and his family picnic one Sunday in the country, and one of the daughters falls in love.

Jean Renoir never quite finished this film. He quarreled with his leading actress and ran out of money before it was finished, though what remains forms a whole. Based on a story by Guy de Maupassant, it tells of a young girl who goes with her parents on a Sunday outing to the country. She is engaged to be married to an uninteresting boy who works in her father's shop. They stop for lunch at an inn, where the mother and daughter lightheartedly agree to an outing on the river with two young men. The girl falls in love with one of them, but a thunderstorm ends their meeting. Made in the landscape painted by Renoir's father, the film is like an impressionist picture come to life, graced by a seductive performance from Sylvia Bataille as the girl who will never again experience such a moment of love.

661
A Tree Grows in Brooklyn

At the turn of the last century, a New York, Irish family struggle to survivie poverty and the actions of an alcoholic father.

In casting this film about life for an Irish family in New York's teeming slums at the turn of the last century, Eliza Kazan, who was directing his first film, looked for an actor with the same characteristics as its charming, drunken father and found him in James Dunn an alcoholic who had never fulfilled his promise. (Dunn stopped drinking during filming). With child star Peggy Ann Garner as the daughter who loved him, Kazan was unhappy with the result, regarding it as 'poverty all cleaned up'. Yet it is a superbly-detailed studio production of the type they don't make any more: a family drama with interest for everybody.

A Taste of Cherry

Iran   1997   98m   colour
Artificial Eye/Abbas Kiarostami
◲ ▤ ◉
original title: *Ta'm e Guilass*
wd Abbas Kiarostami *ph* Homayon Payvar *ad* Hassan Yekta Panah *ed* Abbas Kiarostami
☆ Homayon Ershadi (Mr. Badii), Abdol Hossain Bagheri (Taxidermist)

'Filmed with the piercing intensity of a parable.'
– *Variety*

660
A Taste of Cherry

In Tehran, a middle-aged man who plans to kill himself, seeks someone to bury him.

Iranian director Abbas Kiarostami has become one of the most interesting and talented of current directors, with a sequence of films that were all made cheaply, in which he often uses non-professionals to act out events from their own lives. Here the situation is fictional: in Tehran, a middle-aged man who, ahead of his plan to kill himself, first tries to find someone who will bury him. It is a teasing meditation on death and the simpler joys of life, told in a series of episodic meetings that never reach a conclusion; what matters is the journey, not the destination.

Daisies

Daisies

Czechoslovakia   1966   80m   colour
Bohumil Smida (Lasislav Fikar)
▣▣

original title: *Sedmikrásky*

w Ester Krumbachova, Vera Chytilova *d* Vera Chytilova
ph Jaroslav Kucera *pd* Ester Krumbachova *ed* Miroslav Hajek

☆ Jitka Cerhova (Marie I), Ivana Karbanova (Marie II),
Julius Albert (Man about Town)

'What makes this film particularly distasteful is its idiot yearning for Western beatnikdom, its slobbering (and, I suspect, lesbian) adulation of its ghastly heroines.' – *John Simon*

659
Daisies

Bored by their lives, two girls go in search of decadence.

Vera Chytilova's witty, playful, visually exuberant attack on conformity and a materialistic society was banned for a time by the Czech authorities. Its two heroines, seeking to inject some excitement and decadence into their boring lives, ultimately find their experiences no more interesting and discover that happiness is illusory, even when swinging on a chandelier. After a final scene, in which the two destroy a banquet, an end title dedicates the film to those who 'become bitter over trampled-down lettuce only'. It was this wider feeling of subversion that led to the film being banned, but still gives it a vitality today.

Wise Blood

US/Germany   1979   108m   colour
Artificial Eye/Anthea/Ithaca (Michael Fitzgerald, Kathy Fitzgerald)
▣

w Benedict Fitzgerald *novel* Flannery O'Connor *d* John Huston *ph* Gerry Fisher *m* Alex North *ad* Sally Fitzgerald *ed* Roberto Silvi

☆ Brad Dourif (Hazel Motes), Ned Beatty (Hoover Shoates), Harry Dean Stanton (Asa Hawks), Daniel Shor (Enoch Emery), Amy Wright (Sabbath Lily), John Huston (Grandfather)

'So eccentric, so funny, so surprising and haunting.' – *Vincent Canby, New York Times*

658
Wise Blood

In the deep South, a war veteran with no beliefs becomes a travelling preacher.

This Southern Gothic tale was one of John Huston's more extraordinary films, peopled by misfits, con men and frustrated women. It followed the career of an obsessive army veteran who returns to his hometown to start a new religion, the 'Church of the Truth Without Christ'. His enterprise attracts those who wish to make money out of it, as well as rival preachers, including a fake blind prophet. As his career spirals downward into madness, he becomes self-destructive. Huston gathered a cast of excellent character actors as well as using non-professionals in smaller parts to create a grotesquely comic and despairing account of a fall from grace.

Empire of the Sun

US 1987 152m Technicolor
Robert Shapiro/Amblin (Steven Spielberg, Kathleen Kennedy, Frank Marshall)
🎬 ▦ 🎞 🎧
w Tom Stoppard *novel* J. G. Ballard *d* Steven Spielberg *ph* Allen Daviau *m* John Williams *pd* Norman Reynolds *ad* Charles Bishop, Maurice Fowler, Fred Hole, Norman Dorme, Huang Qia Gui *ed* Michael Kahn
☆ Christian Bale (Jim Graham), John Malkovich (Basie), Miranda Richardson (Mrs. Victor), Nigel Havers (Dr. Rawlins), Joe Pantoliano (Frank Demerest)

'A masterpiece of popular cinema.' – *MFB*

🏆 Allen Daviau; editing; Norman Reynolds; John Williams; costumes (Bob Ringwood); sound
🏆 Allen Daviau; John Williams

657
Empire of the Sun

Semi-autobiographical story of an 11-year-old English boy's experience in a Japanese internment camp.

Steven Spielberg's intelligent and thought-provoking movie is a sprawling epic of a semi-autobiographical story about an 11-year-old English boy learning to grow up in a Japanese internment camp during World War II. The themes of the loss of childhood innocence through the experience of war, and the confusion as to what constitutes reality, obviously resonated with the director, who has dealt with similar matters in *Close Encounters of the Third Kind* and *ET the Extra-Terrestrial*. Bale gives an extraordinarily believable performance as the fatherless boy who seeks role models in the camp and finds only a freebooting capitalist who knows the price of everything.

'Hope & vengeance. Tragedy & love.'

'The greatest love story the world has ever known.'

William Shakespeare's Romeo and Juliet

US 1996 120m DeLuxe Panavision
TCF/Bazmark (Gabriella Martinelli, Baz Luhrmann)
🎬 ▦ 🎞 🎧 🎧 🎧
w Craig Pearce, Baz Luhrmann *play* William Shakespeare *d* Baz Luhrmann *ph* Donald McAlpine *m* Nellee Hooper, Craig Armstrong, Marius de Vries *pd* Catherine Martin *ad* Doug Hardwick *ed* Jill Bilcock
☆ Leonardo DiCaprio (Romeo), Claire Danes (Juliet), Brian Dennehy (Ted Montague), John Leguizamo (Tybalt), Pete Postlethwaite (Father Laurence), Paul Sorvino (Fulgencio Capulet), Diane Venora (Gloria Capulet)

'Will undoubtedly do for Shakespeare what *Strictly Ballroom* did for ballroom dancing and make it fresh, vibrant and hot, hot, hot for a whole generation new to the Bard.' – *Marianne Gray, Film Review*

'Luhrmann has produced a splendid rock video.' – *Mark Steyn, Spectator*

● Leonardo DiCaprio won the best actor award at the Berlin Film Festival in 1997.
🏆 Catherine Martin
🏆 Baz Luhrmann; Catherine Martin; Nellee Hooper; screenplay

656
William Shakespeare's Romeo and Juliet

In modern-day Verona Beach, two young lovers suffer from family opposition to their affair.

Baz Luhrmann made an exuberantly witty film of Shakespeare's play about young star-crossed lovers who meet family opposition to their romance. It was a modern-day version, set in Verona Beach, where for once the language and the setting match: the weapons toted by its hoodlum cast may be guns, but they bear trademarks such as 'Sword' and 'Dagger'. The poetry of the play tends to get lost in the ethnic mix and loud rock accompaniment, and it dazzles the eye rather than the ear, with its vivid, kitsch settings, but the updating has been thought through with an invigorating invention that sweeps objections aside.

'A completely new experience between men and women!'

'I was afraid I was gonna die … now I'm afraid I'm gonna live!'

The Men
US   1950   85m   bw
Stanley Kramer
◉◉ ▤ ⊙⌁ ⊚
reissue title: *Battle Stripe*
w Carl Foreman *d* Fred Zinnemann *ph* Robert de Grasse *m* Dimitri Tiomkin *pd* Edward G. Boyle *ed* Harry Gerstad
☆ *Marlon Brando* (Ken), *Teresa Wright* (Ellen), *Everett Sloane* (Dr. Brock), Jack Webb (Norm), Howard St John (Ellen's Father)

'Don't be misled into feeling that to see this film is merely a duty; it is, simply, an experience worth having.' – *Richard Mallett, Punch*

'As a bold, brave motion picture, *The Men* is to be applauded; but it would be a mistake to imagine that noble intentions and the courage to speak in hitherto unmentionable medical jargon necessarily make great films.' – *Margaret Hinxman*

♟ Carl Foreman

Women in Love
GB   1969   130m   DeLuxe
UA/Brandywine (Larry Kramer)
◉◉ ▤ ⊙⌁ ⊚ ⊚
w Larry Kramer *novel* D. H. Lawrence *d* Ken Russell *ph* Billy Williams *m* Georges Delerue *ad* Ken Jones *ed* Michael Bradsell
☆ *Glenda Jackson* (Gudrun Brangwen), Jennie Linden (Ursula Brangwen), Alan Bates (Rupert Birkin), Oliver Reed (Gerald Crich), Michael Gough (Tom Brangwen), Alan Webb (Thomas Crich)

'They should take all the pretentious dialogue off the soundtrack and call it *Women in Heat*.' – *Rex Reed*

'Two-thirds success, one-third ambitious failure.' – *Michael Billington, Illustrated London News*

● A Region 1 DVD has commentary by Ken Russell and Larry Kramer.
♟ Glenda Jackson
♟ Larry Kramer; Ken Russell; Billy Williams

655
The Men

Paraplegic war veterans are prepared for civilian life; the fiancée of one of them helps overcome his problems.

Marlon Brando's first Hollywood movie was set in a hospital ward of paraplegic war veterans being prepared for civilian life. He played a crippled soldier whose fiancée helps him to overcome his problems. A vivid semi-documentary melodrama that included actual paraplegics among its actors, it was rather shocking at the time in its no-holds-barred treatment of sexual problems. It retains its interest not only for Brando's intense, wheel-chair bound performance as a soldier who moves from despair to acceptance, but for Fred Zinnemann's careful, low key direction.

654
Women in Love

Two girls have their first sexual encounters in the Midlands during the Twenties.

Ken Russell's film tends to be first remembered for its naked wrestling scene between Alan Bates and Oliver Reed. It is memorable for other reasons: with its excellent period detail, it is a fascinating account of D. H. Lawrence's novel of two sisters in a Midlands colliery town and the men with whom they become sexually involved. The film refracts the characters and Lawrence's view of two kinds of love and the need for spiritual regeneration through Russell's own slightly mocking sensibility.

Those Wonderful Movie Cranks

Czechoslovakia 1978 88m colour
Barrandov (Jan Suster)
original title: *Bajecni Muzi S Klikou*
w Oldrich Vlcek, Jiri Menzel *d* Jiri Menzel *ph* Jaromir
Sofr *m* Jiri Sust
☆ Rudolf Hrusinsky (Pasparte), Vlasta Fabianova (Emílie
Kolárová-Mladá), Blazena Holisova (Evzenie)

653
Those Wonderful Movie Cranks

A travelling conjuror at the turn of the century introduces short cinema films into his act, and meanwhile solves his woman trouble.

Czech director Jiri Menzel's charming, melancholy comedy celebrated the 80th anniversary of his country's cinema with a story of a travelling conjuror at the turn of the century, who introduces short cinema films into his act and solves his woman trouble. He also starts a local cinema industry, instead of relying on imported films, by persuading a famous actress to appear before the camera, and plans to open a proper cinema. It is a film that adds a little to art as well as to history.

Cabaret Balkan

France/Greece/Macedonia/Turkey /Yugoslavia
1998 102m colour
Macht/Ticket/Vans/Stefi/Mine/Gradski/Canal+
(Antoine De Clermont-Tonnerre, Goran Paskaljevic)
👓 ▤
original title: *Bure Baruta*
w Dejan Dukovski, Goran Paskaljevic, Filip David, Zoran
Andric *play Bure Baruta* by Dejan Dukovski *d* Goran
Paskaljevic *ph* Milan Spasic *m* Zoran Simjanovic
ad Milenko Jeremic *ed* Petar Putnikovic *cos* Zora
Mojsilovic-Popovic
☆ Aleksandar Bercek (Dimitri), Vojislav Brajovic (Topi),
Bogdan Diklic (Jovan), Nebojsa Glogovac (Taxi Driver),
Mirjana Jokovic (Ana), Mirjana Karanovic (Natalia), Miki
Manojlovic (Michael), Toni Mihajlovski (George), Nebojsa
Milovanovic (Bosnian Serb Son), Dragan Nikolic, Lazar
Ristovski (Boxer), Nikola Ristanovski, Ana Sofrenovic,
Sergej Trifunovic (Young Man)

'Presents a devastating vision of a war-torn country
in which the basic laws of civilized behavior have
eroded in a climate of all-consuming suspicion,
hatred and vengeance.' – *Stephen Holden, New York
Times*

652
Cabaret Balkan

The lives of many people intersect during one night in Belgrade, with tragic and comic results.

Goran Paskaljevic has made a war film, though it is set in the city of Belgrade, miles away from any front line. The action reflects the civil war that destroyed Yugoslavia; it reveals a city of casual violence and desperation, where everyday life can suddenly turn ominous and threatening. As the title suggests, it is a series of ironic acts, with various people's lives interacting after a car crashes into a taxicab. A man returns in search of the lover he left behind and is bested by a rival he regards with contempt; two friends admit they betrayed one other; strangers meet on a train and blow themselves up; a man buys a drink for a crippled cop before admitting that he was responsible, in revenge for a beating the cop gave him; they leave the bar arm in arm. It is a harsh, blackly comic entertainment.

Happiness

US 1998 139m DuArt
October/Good Machine/Killer Films (Ted Hope, Christine Vachon)

▣ ▤ ⊘ ⊚

wd Todd Solondz *ph* Maryse Alberti *m* Robbie Kondor
pd Therese Deprez *ad* John Bruce *ed* Alan Oxman
☆ Jane Adams (Joy Jordan), Dylan Baker (Bill Maplewood), Lara Flynn Boyle (Helen Jordan), Ben Gazzara (Lenny Jordan), Jared Harris (Vlad), Philip Seymour Hoffman (Allen), Jon Lovitz (Andy Kornbluth), Marla Maples (Ann Chambeau), Cynthia Stevenson (Trish Maplewood), Elizabeth Ashley (Diane Freed), Louise Lasser (Mona Jordan)

'A disturbing black comedy that, at bottom, is about all the trouble sex causes people … Controversy and critical support will create want-see among discerning and adventurous specialty audiences, but breakout to a wider public will be difficult.' – *Todd McCarthy, Variety*

The Adventures of Robinson Crusoe

Mexico 1953 89m Pathécolor
Tepeyac (Oscar Dancigers, Henry F. Ehrlich)

▤ ⊚ ♫

w Luis Buñuel, Phillip Ansell Roll (Hugo Butler)
novel Daniel Defoe *d* Luis Buñuel *ph* Alex Phillips
m Anthony Collins
☆ *Dan O'Herlihy* (Robinson Crusoe), Jaime Fernandez (Friday)

'A film of which the purity, the tense poetic style, evokes a kind of wonder.' – *Gavin Lambert*

'Free of that deadly solicitude which usually kills off classics.' – *New Yorker, 1977*

● Hugo Butler used the pseudonym of Roll because he was blacklisted at the time.
● The Region 1 DVD release includes an audio interview with O'Herlihy.
♟ Dan O'Herlihy

651
Happiness

A group of suburbanites seek fulfilment, only to find disappointment.

Todd Solondz was one of the most interesting directors to emerge in the 1990s with this bleak drama of a group of American suburbanites, who seek, but do not find, fulfilment. His protagonists on the unsuccessful pursuit of happiness discover the joylessness of sex and the damage that people can do to one another in unsatisfactory relationships. The film focuses on three sisters, who are equally unhappy in different ways. One lives with her parents, who are separating; one is married to a psychiatrist who is also a child molester; the third invites around the sender of an obscene phone call. At times the film verges on the misanthropic, but is redeemed by a cutting wit and a curious sympathy for its misfits.

650
The Adventures of Robinson Crusoe

A 17th-century mariner is shipwrecked on an uninhabited tropical island.

Daniel Defoe's story of a 17th-century shipwrecked mariner is given a fascinating treatment by Luis Buñuel in his only English-language film. O'Herlihy is the only character on screen until the belated arrival of Friday and the escape to civilization. Buñuel turns the adventure story into a questioning of moral absolutes and a satire on colonialism: Crusoe, a survivor from a slave-ship, is unable at first to do the simplest tasks for himself; when he first rescues Friday, he treats him as a slave, putting him in chains before allowing him some freedom. Luis Buñuel's treatment is subtle and compelling, with only the colour unsatisfactory.

Sunshine State
US 2002 141m CFI
Columbia/Sony Classics/Anarchists' Convention
(Maggie Renzi)
📷 ▣ 📀 ◉ 🎧
wd John Sayles *ph* Patrick Cady *m* Mason Daring
pd Mark Ricker *ed* John Sayles
☆ Edie Falco (Marly Temple), Angela Bassett (Desiree Perry), Jane Alexander (Delia Temple), Ralph Waite (Furman Temple), James McDaniel (Reggie), Timothy Hutton (Jack Meadows), Mary Alice (Eunice Stokes), Bill Cobbs (Dr. Lloyd), Mary Steenburgen (Francine Pickney), Miguel Ferrer (Lester)

'If there's a more acute film about 'community' in America, it's yet to be made.' – *James Christopher, Times*

'You can feel the heat that ignites this gripping tale, and the humor and humanity that root it in feeling.' – *Peter Travers, Rolling Stone*

● Region 1 and 2 DVDs include commentary by John Sayles.

649
Sunshine State

Residents of a small Florida seaside town resist attempts by property companies to redevelop the town.

John Sayles' ensemble film is a sprawling account of some unsatisfactory lives, of dreams gone wrong and futures to be avoided. It is set in a small Florida seaside town, where the residents have mainly come to an accommodation with their failures, but now face up to change, which is orchestrated by property companies that want to redevelop the town. In concentrating on the lives of two families, one white, one black, it also manages to reflect the problems and momentary pleasures of a larger society.

Ship of Fools
US 1965 150m bw
Columbia/Stanley Kramer
▣ 📀～ ◉
w Abby Mann *novel* Katherine Anne Porter *d* Stanley Kramer *ph* Ernest Laszlo *m* Ernest Gold *ed* Robert C. Jones
☆ *Vivien Leigh* (Mary Treadwell), *Simone Signoret* (La Condesa), *Oskar Werner* (Dr. Schumann), *Heinz Ruhmann* (Lowenthal), José Ferrer (Rieber), Lee Marvin (Tenny), Elizabeth Ashley (Jenny), *Michael Dunn* (Glocken), George Segal (David), Jose Greco (Pepe), Charles Korvin (Capt. Thiele), Alf Kjellin (Freytag), Werner Klemperer (Lt. Heebner), John Wengraf (Graf), Lilia Skala (Frau Hutten) and also Karen Verne

'When you're not being hit over the head with the symbolism, you're being punched in the stomach by would-be inventive camera work while the music score unremittingly fills your nostrils with acrid exhalations.' – *John Simon*

'There is such wealth of reflection upon the human condition, so subtle an orchestration of the elements of love and hate, that it is not fair to tag this with the label of any other film.' – *New York Times*

🏆 Ernest Laszlo
🏆 best picture; Abby Mann; Simone Signoret; Oskar Werner; Michael Dunn

648
Ship of Fools

In 1933, a German liner leaves Vera Cruz for Bremerhaven with a mixed bag of passengers.

Grand Hotel with its passengers all at sea is what screenwriter Abby Mann and director Stanley Kramer provided in this adaptation of a best-selling novel about a group of passengers sailing from Vera Cruz to Bremerhaven. They include an alcoholic, middle-aged Southern belle who falls for a coarse Texan, a Nazi braggart, a jolly Jew, and a political exile who has a brief affair with the ship's doctor; sensitively acted by Simone Signoret and Oscar Werner, the two give the drama a greater depth. Capable direction, other memorable performances and a bravura finale erase memories of padding and symbolic pretensions. It is an ambitious, serious, quite fascinating slice-of-life shipboard multi-melodrama.

Pixote
Brazil   1981   127m   colour
Palace/Embrafilme
🎞 ▤ ⊘

w Hector Babenco, Jorge Duran *novel Infancia dos Mortos* by José Louzeiro *d Hector Babenco ph* Rodolfo Sanches *m* John Neschling *ad* Clovis Bueno *ed* Luiz Elias
☆ Fernando Ramos da Silva (Pixote), Jorge Julião (Lilica), Gilberto Moura (Dito), Edilson Lino (Chico), Zenildo Oliveira Santos (Fumaca), Claudio Bernardo (Garatao), Marilia Pera (Sueli), José Nilson Dos Santos (Diego)
● Fernando Ramos da Silva, who played Pixote, had roles in two subsequent films, but his career was limited as he could neither read nor write. He became involved in petty crime and, at the age of 19, was shot dead in his home by police.

647
Pixote

A 10-year-old living on the streets of São Paulo tries to survive by pimping, drug-dealing and murder.

Hector Babenco's grim and sensational exposé of the life of abandoned children on the streets of São Paulo used actual homeless children to add to its reality. It focused on the life of a 10-year-old illiterate, street-wise boy who, like his companions, tried to get by living a life of degradation, crime and corruption, fuelled by drug-dealing, murder and prostitution. Rounded up for no particular reason by the police, he and others are sent to a reformatory, which turns out to be as harsh as the street, to which they return, but that, too, offers no respite, hope or redemption. It is a pain-filled pitiless film about pitiful lives, one of the best to come out of Brazil.

'I want a man ... not a human punch bag?'
The Set Up
US   1949   72m   bw
RKO (Richard Goldstone)
▤ ⊘ ⊘

w Art Cohn *poem* Joseph Moncure March *d Robert Wise ph* Milton Krasner *md* Constantin Bakaleinikoff *ad* Albert S. D'Agostino, Jack Okey *ed* Roland Gross
☆ *Robert Ryan* (Bill "Stoker" Thompson), Audrey Totter (Julie), George Tobias (Tiny), Alan Baxter (Little Boy), Wallace Ford (Gus), Percy Helton (Red)

646
The Set Up

An ageing boxer is unknowlingly set-up to loose his last fight. He refuses to throw the fight unaware that the consequence of his victory could cost him his life.

One of the most brilliant little *films noirs* of the late Forties, this takes place entirely at night, in a seedy dressing-room and a small-town ring. A boxer reaching the end of his career refuses to throw his last fight, which has been fixed by his dishonest manager, and is beaten up by gangsters. Although thoroughly studio-bound, it evokes a brilliant feeling for time and place. Robert Ryan conveys well the toughness and weariness of a boxer who knows he is on the way down but still retains his pride, even though he realizes the consequences of his quixotic gesture. The boxing scenes are intense and there are some excellent performances by supporting actors. Photography, direction, editing, acting are all of a piece. Martin Scorsese has acknowledged it as an influence on his *Raging Bull*.

The Pajama Game

US 1957 101m Warnercolor
Warner/George Abbott

w George Abbott, Richard Bissell book Seven and a Half Cents by Richard Bissell d Stanley Donen ph Harry Stradling m Buddy Bregman m/ly Richard Adler, Jerry Ross ch Bob Fosse ad Malcolm C. Bert ed William Ziegler

☆ Doris Day (Kate "Babe" Williams), John Raitt (Sid Sorokin), Eddie Foy Jnr (Vernon Hines), Reta Shaw (Mabel), Carol Haney (Gladys Hotchkiss)

'Unspoilt, splendidly performed and to my mind immensely enjoyable.' – Dilys Powell

♫ 'The Pajama Game'; 'Racing with the Clock'; 'I'm Not At All in Love'; 'I'll Be Jealous Again'; 'Hey There'; 'Once a Year Day'; 'Small Talk'; 'There Once Was a Man'; 'Steam Heat'; 'Hernando's Hideaway'; 'Seven and a Half Cents'

645

The Pajama Game

Workers in a pyjama factory are in conflict with the management over salary, but their lady negotiator falls for the new boss.

Union troubles in the Sleep Tite Pajama factory seemed an unlikely subject for a musical, even when there was romance at steam heat. This tale of workers demanding a pay rise while their lady negotiator falls for the new boss was a brilliantly conceived work. John Raitt and Doris Day made a romantic couple to sing about, and Carol Haney, in her moment of stardom before her early death, repeated her show-stopping 'Steam Heat' routine from the Broadway show, choreographed with great bowler-hatted panache by Bob Fosse. Stanley Donen's direction effectively concealed its Broadway origins, turning it into an expert, fast-moving, hard-hitting piece of modern musical cinema.

'A love story every woman would die a thousand deaths to live!'

Jane Eyre

US 1943 96m bw
TCF (William Goetz)

w Aldous Huxley, Robert Stevenson, John Houseman d Robert Stevenson ph George Barnes m Bernard Herrmann ad Wiard B. Ihnen, James Basevi ed Walter Thompson sp Fred Sersen

☆ Joan Fontaine (Jane Eyre), Orson Welles (Edward Rochester), Margaret O'Brien (Adele), Henry Daniell (Brockelhurst), John Sutton (Dr. Rivers), Agnes Moorehead (Mrs. Reed), Elizabeth Taylor (Helen Burns), Peggy Ann Garner (Jane as a Child), Sara Allgood (Bessie), Aubrey Mather (Col. Dent), Hillary Brooke (Blanche), Edith Barrett (Mrs. Fairfax), Ethel Griffies (Grace Poole), Barbara Everest (Lady Ingraham), John Abbott (Mason)

'A careful and tame production, a sadly vanilla-flavoured Joan Fontaine, and Orson Welles treating himself to broad operatic sculpturings of body, cloak and diction, his eyes glinting in the Rembrandt gloom at every chance, like side orders of jelly.' – James Agee

'The essentials are still there; and the non-essentials, such as the gloom, the shadows, the ground mist, the rain and the storms, have been expanded and redoubled and magnified to fill up the gaps.' – Richard Mallett, Punch

644

Jane Eyre

In Victorian times, a harshly treated orphan girl becomes governess in a mysterious Yorkshire mansion with a brooding master.

A sharply paced, reasonably faithful and superbly staged Hollywood version of Charlotte Brontë's Victorian romantic novel of an orphan girl deprived of love and compassion, who becomes governess to Edward Rochester, the brooding master of a Yorkshire mansion with a dark past. Joan Fontaine's meek Jane made a good foil to Orson Welles's operatic Rochester, a man of grand gestures and bigger secrets. Welles himself had to be restrained from taking over the film entirely. Robert Stevenson's direction, full of storm and shadows, created a visual equivalent of the couple's dark romance.

'Desire Is A Danger Zone.'

The Crying Game

GB   1992   112m   Metrocolor   Panavision
Palace/Channel 4/Eurotrustees/NDF/British Screen
(Stephen Woolley)

🎞 ▬ 🎧 ◉ ଋ

wd Neil Jordan *ph* Ian Wilson *m* Anne Dudley *pd* Jim
Clay *ad* Chris Seagers *ed* Kant Pan

☆ *Stephen Rea* (Fergus), *Miranda Richardson* (Jude),
Forest Whitaker (Jody), *Jim Broadbent* (Col), Ralph Brown
(Dave), Adrian Dunbar (Maguire), *Jaye Davidson* (Dil), Tony
Slattery (Deveroux)

'An astonishingly good and daring film.' – *Variety*

'Every so often, a "little" film hits the collective
heart. *The Crying Game* is one of these, because it
shows that a man is never so naked as when he
reveals his secret self.' – *Richard Corliss, Time*

👤 Neil Jordan (as writer)
🏆 best picture; Neil Jordan (as director); Kant Pan; Stephen
Rea; Jaye Davidson

643
The Crying Game

In London, an IRA gunman falls for the lover of a dead black British soldier.

In Neil Jordan's thriller, things are never as straightforward as they seem: a man is betrayed by his lover and saved by the person who should hate him; an IRA gunman befriends his hostage, a black British soldier, despite knowing that he will be ordered to kill him; the person both of them loved is changed from girl to boy and back again. The heart of this intriguing drama is set in London, where the IRA man falls for the lover of the dead solider. Stephen Rea's dour gunman discovers that his own reality is far from the one he has invented for himself, in contrast to Jaye Davidson's Dil, his black lover, who has constructed a fitting personality. The twist and turns of the plot parallel the emotional discoveries of the characters, as Jordan delivers a complex and brilliantly successful examination of matters of identity and gender.

'Two men chasing dreams of glory!'

Chariots of Fire
GB   1981   121m   colour
TCF/Allied Stars/Enigma (David Puttnam)

w Colin Welland   *d* Hugh Hudson   *ph* David Watkin *m* Vangelis   *ad* Roger Hall, Jonathan Amberston, Len Huntingford, Andrew Sanders, Anna Ridley   *ed* Terry Rawlings   *cos* Milena Canonero
☆ *Ben Cross* (Harold Abrahams), *Ian Charleson* (Eric Liddell), Nigel Havers (Lord Andrew Lindsay), Nicholas Farrell (Aubrey Montague), Daniel Gerroll (Henry Stallard), Cheryl Campbell (Jennie Liddell), Alice Krige (Sybil Gordon), John Gielgud (Master of Trinity), Lindsay Anderson (Master of Caius), Nigel Davenport (Lord Birkenhead), *Ian Holm* (Sam Mussabini), Patrick Magee (Lord Cadogan)

'The whole contradictory bundle is unexpectedly watchable.' – *Jo Imeson, MFB*

'A piece of technological lyricism held together by the glue of simple-minded heroic sentiment.' – *Pauline Kael*

'A hymn to the human spirit as if scored by Barry Manilow.' – *Richard Corliss, Film Comment*

🏆 best picture; Colin Welland; Vangelis; Milena Canonero
🏆 Hugh Hudson; Terry Rawlings; Ian Holm
🏆 best picture; Ian Holm; Milena Canonero

642
Chariots of Fire

Two athletes, a Jew and a devout Christian Scotsman, run for Britain in the 1924 Paris Olympics and face the difficulties and prejudice that beset them.

Hugh Hudson made a quintessentially British film, lyrical in style, slightly eccentric in content about two athletes, a Jew and a Scotsman running for Britain in the 1924 Paris Olympics. It is a film of subtle qualities, rather like those of a BBC classic serial. Colin Welland's script fleshes out the particular characters of the two: Abrahams suffering racial prejudice at Cambridge, and Liddell's devout Christianity preventing him from racing on a Sunday. Ben Cross and Ian Charleson add depth to the two men by the power of their performances. Hudson's excellent direction captures the excitement of the races, using slow motion to great effect, particularly when underscored by Vangelis' emotional music. It is full of pleasant romantic touches and sharp glimpses of the wider issues involved.

'The black shadows of the past bred this half-man, half-demon!'

Son of Frankenstein
US   1939   99m   bw
Universal (Rowland V. Lee)

w Willis Cooper   *d* Rowland V. Lee   *ph* George Robinson *m* Frank Skinner   *ad* Jack Otterson   *ed* Ted J. Kent
☆ *Basil Rathbone* (Baron Wolf von Frankenstein), *Boris Karloff* (The Monster), *Bela Lugosi* (Ygor), *Lionel Atwill* (Inspector Krogh), Josephine Hutchinson (Elsa von Frankenstein), Donnie Dunagan (Peter von Frankenstein), Emma Dunn (Amelia), *Edgar Norton* (Thomas Benson), Lawrence Grant (Burgomaster)

'Rather strong material for the top keys, picture will still garner plenty of bookings in the secondary first runs along the main stem.' – *Variety*

'The slickness of production gives a kind of refinement to the horrific moments and a subtlety to the suspense.' – *Film Weekly*

641
Son of Frankenstein

The old baron's son comes home and starts to dabble, with the help of a broken-necked and vindictive shepherd.

A handsomely mounted sequel to *Bride of Frankenstein* and the last of the classic trio of movies, in which Frankenstein's son returns home to claim his inheritance, the old baron's castle. Upon discovering the monster is still alive he creates havoc with the help of a crooked shepherd, Ygor. Karloff's monster is less interesting, but there are plenty of other diversions, including Lionel Atwill's police chief, with a false arm to replace the one he lost to the monster, and the splendid if impractical sets. It was this movie more than any other that formed the basis for Mel Brooks' parody *Young Frankenstein*.

The Talk of the Town
US   1942   118m   bw
Columbia (George Stevens, Fred Guiol)

w Irwin Shaw, Sidney Buchman d George Stevens ph Ted Tetzlaff m Frederick Hollander ad Lionel Banks, Rudolph Sternad ed Otto Meyer

☆ Ronald Colman (Michael Lightcap), Cary Grant (Leopold Dilg), Jean Arthur (Nora Shelley), Edgar Buchanan (Sam Yates), Glenda Farrell (Regina Bush), Charles Dingle (Andrew Holmes), Emma Dunn (Mrs. Shelley), Rex Ingram (Tilney)

'I can't take my lynching so lightly, even in a screwball. Still, I am all for this kind of comedy and for players like Arthur and Grant, who can mug more amusingly than most scriptwriters can write.' – Manny Farber

● Two endings were filmed: the eventual choice of mate for Miss Arthur was determined by audience reaction at previews.

♟ best picture; original story (Sidney Harmon); script; Ted Tetzlaff; Frederick Hollander; art direction; Otto Meyer

640
The Talk of the Town

A girl loves both a suspected murderer and the lawyer who defends him.

George Stevens brought together a splendid collection of talent for this unusually entertaining mixture of comedy and drama. Irwin Shaw and the left-leaning Sidney Buchman (who was later blacklisted) wrote an intriguing variation on the usual love triangle, as Leopold Dilg, on trial for murder and arson, and his tragic defence lawyer vie for the affection of the same woman, while she develops feelings for them both. The theme allowed for discussions of more than sexual attraction, as it explored questions of justice and law and order. It had three delightful and sympathetic stars. Cary Grant played against his more usual role as an anarchist factory worker and street corner orator sentenced to death for arson and murder. Ronald Coleman was effective as a principled lawyer, and Jean Arthur was charming as the woman in the middle. Stevens shot two endings and previewed them to decide which of the men wins her, deciding in favour of the one who was the bigger star.

The Thin Red Line
US   1998   170m   Technicolor   Panavision
TCF/Fox 2000/Phoenix (Robert Michael Geisler, John Roberdeau, Grant Hill)

wd Terrence Malick novel James Jones ph John Toll m Hans Zimmer pd Jack Fisk ad Ian Gracy ed Billy Weber, Leslie Jones, Saar Klein

☆ Sean Penn (First Sergeant Welsh), Adrien Brody (Corporal Fife), Jim Caviezel (Pvt. Witt), Ben Chaplin (Bell), George Clooney (Bosche), John Cusack (Gaff), Woody Harrelson (Keck), Elias Koteas (Captain "Bugger" Staros), Jared Leto (Whyte), Dash Mihok (Doll), Tim Blake Nelson (Tills), Nick Nolte (Colonel Tall), John C. Reilly (Storm), Larry Romano (Mazzi), John Savage (McCron) and also John Travolta, Arie Verveen, Miranda Otto

'A complex, highly talented work marked by intellectual and philosophical ambitions that will captivate some critics and serious viewers as well as by an abstract nature, emotional remoteness and lack of dramatic focus that will frustrate mainstream audiences.' – Todd McCarthy, Variety

♟ best picture; Terrence Malick (as director and writer); John Toll; Hans Zimmer; Billy Weber, Leslie Jones, Saar Klein; sound

639
The Thin Red Line

During World War II, an American platoon undertakes an impossible assault against Japanese troops.

Terrence Malick's ruminative war movie is set in 1943, when a group of American soldiers, fighting the Japanese on Guadalcanal, are ordered by a gung ho colonel to take a heavily defended position. Malick uses voice-over to provide the views of his various and varied soldiers as they prepare for the forthcoming battle and recall the home life that they are unlikely to experience again. At the centre is the figure of Nick Nolte's colonel, isolated from feeling by his determination to succeed, whatever the cost to his men. When they go into battle, it is in a lush and beautiful landscape that is soon scarred by their weaponry. War here becomes an aberration, an intrusion on a natural paradise.

A Star Is Born

US 1937 111m Technicolor
David O. Selznick

w Dorothy Parker, Alan Campbell, Robert Carson
story William A. Wellman, based partly on 'What Price
Hollywood' (1932) (qv) d William A. Wellman ph W.
Howard Greene m Max Steiner ad Lyle Wheeler
ed James E. Newcom

☆ Janet Gaynor (Esther Blodgett/Vicki Lester), Fredric
March (Norman Maine), Adolphe Menjou (Oliver Niles),
Lionel Stander (Libby), Andy Devine (Danny McGuire), May
Robson (Lettie), Owen Moore (Casey Burke), Franklin
Pangborn (Billy Moon)

'One of those rare ones which everyone will want
to see and talk about … disproves the tradition that
good pictures can't be made with a Hollywood
background.' – Variety

'The first colour job that gets close to what colour
must eventually come to: it keeps the thing in its
place, underlining the mood and situation of the
story rather than dimming everything else out in an
iridescent razzle-dazzle.' – Otis Ferguson

🎞 original story; Special Award to W. Howard Greene for
colour photography
🏆 best picture; script; William A. Wellman; Janet Gaynor;
Fredric March

638
A Star Is Born

A young actress meets Hollywood success and marries a famous lead-ing man, whose star wanes as hers shines brighter.

An abrasive, romantic melodrama which is also one of the most accu-rate studies of Hollywood ever put on film. This much-filmed story began life as *What Price Hollywood?*, filmed in 1932 and written, like this new version, by Dorothy Parker and Alan Campbell. It captured the way Hollywood could manufacture stars and discard the old in favour of the new. There were standout performances from Fredric March as a actor who turns to drink as his public deserts him, and from Lionel Stander as a tough publicist, who has seen it all before. As he might well have done: Selznick's lawyers wrote a twenty page memo listing similarities to real people, including the marriages of Frank Fay and Barbara Stanwyck and of John Gilbert and Virginia Bruce.

Metropolitan

US 1989 98m DuArt
Mainline/Westerly Film-Video/Allagash Films (Whit
Stillman)

wd Whit Stillman ph John Thomas m Mark Suozzo, Tom
Judson ed Christopher Tellefsen

☆ Carolyn Farina (Audrey Rouget), Edward Clements
(Tom Townsend), Christopher Eigeman (Nick Smith), Taylor
Nichols (Charlie Black), Allison Rutledge-Parisi (Jane
Clarke), Dylan Hundley (Sally Fowler), Isabel Gillies
(Cynthia McClean), Bryan Leder (Fred Neff), Will Kempe
(Rick Von Sloneker)

'A cast of attractive young newcomers plays out
this ironic, arch, gently mocking and refreshingly
original comedy with confident style.' – David
Robinson, The Times

🏆 best original screenplay

637
Metropolitan

A left-wing student becomes a member of a group of rich young people intent on having a good time.

Whit Stillman's debut as a director (and still his best work) was this witty, stylish conversation piece, set in Manhattan, about a group of young upper-class friends who meet to discuss and enjoy their common social interests with every intention of living life to the full. Tom Edwards, a fellow student, but chivalrous and left-wing, is invited to join the camaraderie. Tom (Edward Clements) goes along with the charade because he is attracted to one of the women, though he real-izes his error in time and chases after his true love. Without malice, Stillman exposes not only the group's determined frivolity, but their concerns over being unable to take life more seriously.

'It's about three decent people. They will break your heart!'

Sunday, Bloody Sunday
GB   1971   110m   DeLuxe
UA/Vectia (Joseph Janni)
▣   ▨   ◉

w Penelope Gilliatt d John Schlesinger ph Billy Williams m Ron Geesin pd Luciana Arrighi ad Norman Dorme ed Richard Marden

☆ Glenda Jackson (Alex Greville), Peter Finch (Dr. Daniel Hirsh), Murray Head (Bob Elkin), Peggy Ashcroft (Mrs. Greville), Maurice Denham (Mr. Greville), Vivian Pickles (Alva Hodson), Frank Windsor (Bill Hodson), Tony Britton (George Harding), Harold Goldblatt (Daniel's Father)

'This is not a story about the loss of love, but about its absence.' – Roger Ebert

● Ian Bannen was originally cast as Dr Hirsh, but developed viral pneumonia after shooting began and had to be replaced by Peter Finch.
♟ Penelope Gilliatt; John Schlesinger; Glenda Jackson; Peter Finch
♕ best picture; John Schlesinger; Peter Finch; Glenda Jackson

636
Sunday, Bloody Sunday

A young designer shares his sexual favours equally between two lovers of different sexes, a Jewish doctor and a lady executive.

John Schlesinger's film is semi-autobiographical. Bob Elkins is a young artist who is having simultaneous affairs with two consenting lovers, a male Jewish doctor and a divorced professional woman who are both aware of, but turn a blind eye to, the other's existence. With Peter Finch acting with an openness and sensitivity as Schlesinger's alter ego, it was a stylishly made character study with melodramatic leanings. It was at times rather self-conscious about its risky subject (when it came to film the scene where Peter Finch and Murray Head kiss, the cameraman asked Schlesinger, 'John, is this really necessary?'). But, scene by scene, it was both adult and absorbing, with an overpowering mass of sociological detail about the way we lived then.

Meet John Doe
US   1941   123m   bw
Liberty Films (Frank Capra)
▣▣   ▣   ▨   ◉   ◉

w Robert Riskin d Frank Capra ph George Barnes m Dimitri Tiomkin ad Stephen Goosson ed Daniel Mandell

☆ Gary Cooper ("John Doe"/Long John Willoughby), Barbara Stanwyck (Ann Mitchell), Edward Arnold (D.B. Norton), Walter Brennan (Colonel), James Gleason (Henry Connell), Spring Byington (Mrs. Mitchell), Gene Lockhart (Mayor Lovett), Rod la Rocque (Ted Sheldon), Irving Bacon (Beany), Regis Toomey (Bert Hansen), Ann Doran (Mrs. Hansen), Warren Hymer (Angelface), Andrew Tombes (Spencer)

'Capra is as skilled as ever in keeping things moving along briskly and dramatically.' – National Board of Review

'The meanings were so distorted that the original authors sued … It starts out in the confident Capra manner, but with a darker tone; by the end, you feel puzzled and cheated.' – Pauline Kael, 70s

♟ original story (Richard Connell, Robert Presnell)

635
Meet John Doe

A tramp is hired to embody the common man in a phony political drive, and almost commits suicide.

Frank Capra's movie was intended as a satire on empty political rhetoric: Willoughby, a man of limited means, agrees to impersonate 'John Doe' in a newspaper publicity stunt, in which he threatens to commit suicide to protest 'slimy politics'; when he discovers that he is being used by a power-hungry media tycoon, he decides to kill himself, but doesn't. The problem with the film is that its hero is amoral, even when played by Gary Cooper, so there's no sincere centre to the action. But it is a vividly staged extravaganza with high spots outnumbering low.

634
Maxim Gorky Trilogy

Orphan Gorky is raised by his grandparents, and becomes a ship's cook and a painter before going on to university.

Based on the autobiography of the Russian novelist and playwright Maxim Gorky, the simple and direct story of his adolescence is told in three beautifully made films: *The Childhood of Maxim Gorky* (1938, 101m), *Out in the World* (1939, 98m), *My Universities* (1940, 104m). The style is episodic, providing a finely detailed portrait of the hard upbringing of Gorky amid poverty, hardship and exploitation in the lower depths of 19th-century Czarist Russia. Though the telling begins to drag in the final film, it remains one of the great achievements of Russian cinema.

633
The Informer

An IRA informer awaits his inevitable death at the hands of his former comrades.

John Ford worked with a tedious plot of a simple-minded hanger-on who betrays an IRA leader and is hounded by fellow rebels and his own conscience. But he turned it into brilliant cinema by full-blooded acting and a highly stylized yet brilliantly effective *mise en scène* which never attempts reality; Dublin was made from painted canvas, and shot as a place of shadows and fog. Ford himself thought it lacked humour, which it does. But humour would have destroyed the tension of the situation, of a traitor who knows that he will be killed by his former comrades. Victor McLaglen forsook his usual macho heartiness to give his finest performance as the unthinking, brutish informer, tortured by guilt.

.

'There is something in the air. It might be love … but it isn't'

Strictly Ballroom
Australia 1992 94m Eastmancolor
Rank/M&A/Australian Film Finance Corp (Tristam Miall)

⚆ ▤ ▨ ◉ ◎ ♫

w Baz Luhrmann, Craig Pearce *play* N.I.D.A. stage production devised by its original cast *story* Baz Luhrmann, Andrew Bovell *d* Baz Luhrmann *ph* Steve Mason *m* David Hirschfelder *ch* John 'Cha Cha' O'Connell, Paul Mercurio *pd* Catherine Martin *ed* Jill Bilcock

☆ *Paul Mercurio* (Scott Hastings), Tara Morice (Fran), Bill Hunter (Barry Fife), Pat Thomson (Shirley Hastings), Gia Carides (Liz Holt), Peter Whitford (Les Kendall), Barry Otto (Doug Hastings), John Hannan (Ken Railings), Sonia Kruger (Tina Sparkle), Kris McQuade (Charm Leachman), Antonio Vargas (Rico), Armonia Benedito (Ya Ya)

'Bright, breezy and immensely likable musical-comedy.' – *Variety*

Ⓣ David Hirschfelder; Catherine Martin

632
Strictly Ballroom

A ballroom dancer offends his rivals by his unorthodox approach.

Australian director Baz Luhrmann first reached an international audience with this exuberant romance about a would-be champion ballroom dancer who, after incurring the wrath of the establishment by improvising his own steps, searches for a new partner in tune with his ideas. It had charm and wit, as well as a flashing performance from Paul Mercurio as its hero. Luhrmann's direction took this curious subculture seriously when the dancing began and pointed up the absurdity elsewhere. His stylized approach and use of often lurid colours emphasized the obsessive nature of a tiny world, which was inhabited by people who, outside its confines, would seem highly eccentric; within it, though, they are regarded as normal. It made for a delightful waltz across a crowded dance-floor.

She Done Him Wrong
US 1933 68m bw
Paramount (William Le Baron)

▤ ▨

w Mae West *play* Diamond Lil by Mae West (with help on the scenario from Harry Thew, John Bright) *d* Lowell Sherman *ph* Charles Lang *ad* Robert Usher *ed* Al Hall *songs* Ralph Rainger (m), Leo Robin (ly)

☆ *Mae West* (Lady Lou), *Cary Grant* (Capt. Cummings), Owen Moore (Chick Clark), Gilbert Roland (Serge Stanieff), Noah Beery (Gus Jordan), David Landau (Dan Flynn), Rafaela Ottiano (Russian Rita), Rochelle Hudson (Sally Glynn), Dewey Robinson (Spider Kane)

'Only alternative to a strong drawing cast, nowadays if a picture wants business, is strong entertainment. This one has neither.' – *Variety*

♫ 'Easy Rider'; 'Mazie'; 'A Guy What Takes His Time'; 'Frankie and Johnnie'
♙ best picture

631
She Done Him Wrong

A lady saloon keeper of the Gay Nineties falls for the undercover cop who is after her.

Based on her Broadway play that Hollywood studios had promised would never be filmed, this is as near to undiluted Mae West as Hollywood ever came: fast, funny, melodramatic and pretty sexy. Paramount changed the name of West's character from the original Diamond Lil to Lady Lou, though she still announces herself as 'one of the finest women who ever walked the streets.' West, who plays a raunchy saloon keeper, dominates every scene with a bawdily suggestive performance. At the time of its first release, the film caused a sensation and roused the ire of other studios by its sexual frankness. Paramount were forced to cut to a minimum West's song 'A Guy What Takes His Time', which lost its seeming innocence the way she sang it. A very atmospheric and well-made movie, it is still a joy.

Rocky
US   1976   119m   Technicolor
UA/Chartoff-Winkler (Gene Kirkwood)

w Sylvester Stallone *d* John G. Avildsen *ph* James Crabe *m* Bill Conti *pd* Bill Cassidy *ad* James H. Spencer *ed* Scott Conrad, Richard Halsey
☆ *Sylvester Stallone* (Rocky Balboa), Burgess Meredith (Mickey), Talia Shire (Adrian), Burt Young (Paulie), Carl Weathers (Apollo Creed), Thayer David (Miles Jergens)
● Regions 1 and 2 DVD releases include commentary by John Avildsen, producer and cast.
🏆 best picture; John G. Avildsen
☆ Sylvester Stallone (as writer); song 'Gonna Fly Now' (*m* Bill Conti, *ly* Carol Connors, Ayn Robbins); Sylvester Stallone (as actor); Burgess Meredith; Talia Shire; Burt Young

630
Rocky

A slightly dimwitted Philadelphia boxer makes good.

Sylvester Stallone's working-class small-time boxer who proves he can go the distance obviously chimed with the public, since seemingly endless sequels followed. It was a variation on the familiar American Dream, of optimism and effort ensuring success (Carl Weathers' heavyweight champ spells it out: 'If history proves one thing, American history proves that everybody's got a chance to win'). A feel-good movie, which was reminiscent of *Marty* in its romance between two misfits and of many other boxing sagas in its fight scenes, it was a pleasantly old-fashioned comedy-drama with the sense to have Rocky defeated but unbowed in his shot at the world championship. It was an ending that made it a knockout success.

Grave of the Fireflies
Japan   1988   93m   colour
Stufio Ghibli (Toru Hara)

original title: *Hotaru no haka*
wd Isao Takahata *story* Akiyuki Nosaka *ph* Nobuo Koyama *m* Michio Mamiya *pd* Ryoichi Sato *ad* Nizo Yamamoto *character design* Yoshi Fumi Kondo
☆ voices of: Tsutomu Tatsumi (Seita), Ayano Shiraishi (Setsuko), Yoshiko Shinohara (Mother), Akemi Yamaguchi (Aunt)

'It belongs on any list of the greatest war films ever made.' – *Roger Ebert*

● The Region 1 DVD release includes subtitled and American dubbed versions.

629
Grave of the Fireflies

The story of a young brother and sister and their ill-fated fight for survival, alone in wartime Japan, 1945.

Based on a semi-autobiographical novel by Akiyuki Nosaka, who saw his sister starve to death, Isao Takahata's animated film is set towards the end of World War II, just before Japan's surrender. After their mother is killed and their home destroyed in a bombing raid, a Japanese boy and his young sister try to survive on their own, and fail. It is a story told by the dead boy, of a struggle for survival and a breakdown of community. The bombs that fall from the sky resemble the fireflies that give them pleasure as they shelter at night, and their lives are as evanescent. Beautifully animated in a stylized way and told with restraint, the film packs a powerful emotional punch.

The Man with the Movie Camera
USSR   1928   60m approx   bw   silent
VUFKU
▣ ▤ ⊚ ⊘
original title: *Chelovek sKinoapparatom*
ph *Mikhail Kaufman* wd/ed *Dziga Vertov*
● A special edition DVD was released in 2002 with a new score composed by Michael Nyman.

628

The Man with the Movie Camera

A 'camera eye' documentary without any plot, showing, through a succession of street and interior scenes, all the tricks of which the instrument is capable; it takes a bow at the end.

A groundbreaking documentary that is a camera-eye view of everyday life in the Soviet Union in the late Twenties, and which still retains much of its force. Vertov used every trick at his disposal, from split screen to slow motion and freeze frames to give life to his images – and then combined them with his individual style of editing that sometimes matched his directorial pseudonym, which can be translated as 'spinning top'. His film reflects the realities of life as he found them through his lens. As he wrote, 'I am a mechanical eye. I, a machine, am showing you a world, the likes of which only I can see.'

☆ **Quentin Tarantino**
Director ☆

1. The Good, the Bad and the Ugly (Leone)
2. Rio Bravo (Hawks)
3. Taxi Driver (Scorsese)
4. His Girl Friday (Hawks)
5. Rolling Thunder (Flynn)
6. They All Laughed (Bogdanovich)
7. The Great Escape (Sturges)
8. Carrie (De Palma)
9. Coffy (Hill)
10. Dazed and Confused (Linklater)
11. Five Fingers of Death (Chang)
12. Hi Diddle Diddle (Stone)

☆ **Ken Loach**
Director ☆

1. À Bout de Souffle (Godard)
2. The Battle of Algiers (Pontecorvo)
3. A Blonde in Love (Forman)
4. Bicycle Thieves (De Sica)
5. Closely Observed Trains (Menzel)
6. Fireman's Ball (Forman)
7. Jules et Jim (Truffaut)
8. La Règle du Jeu (Renoir)
9. The Tree of the Wooden Clogs (Olmi)
10. Wild Strawberries (Bergman)

☆ **Paul Verhoeven**
Director ☆

1. La Dolce Vita (Fellini)
2. Ivan the Terrible, Part II (Eisenstein)
3. Lawrence of Arabia (Lean)
4. Rashomon (Kurosawa)
5. Vertigo (Hitchcock)
6. The Seventh Seal (Bergman)
7. La Règle du Jeu (Renoir)
8. Metropolis (Lang)
9. Los Olvidados (Buñuel)
10. Some Like It Hot (Wilder)

Comrades
GB   1987   180m   colour
Curzon/Skreba/National Film Finance (Simon Relph)
wd Bill Douglas *ph* Gale Tattersall *m* Hans Werner Henze,
David Graham *pd* Michael Pickwoad *ad* Derrick Chetwyn,
Henry Harris *ed* Mick Audsley
☆ Robin Soans (George Loveless), William Gammara
(James Loveless), Stephen Bateman (Old Tom Stanfield),
Philip Davis (Young Stanfield), Jeremy Flynn (Brine), Keith
Allen (James Hammett), Alex Norton (Lanternist/Sgt.
Bell/Diorama Showman/Laughing Cava), Michael Clark
(Sailor), Arthur Dignam (Fop), James Fox (Norfolk), John
Hargreaves (Convict), Michael Hordern (Mr. Pitt), Freddie
Jones (Vicar), Vanessa Redgrave (Mrs. Carlyle), Robert
Stephens (Frampton) and also Murray Melvin, Barbara
Windsor, Imelda Staunton

627
Comrades

In the 1830s six Dorset farm labourers who form a union to campaign against low wages are tried and transported to Australia as criminals.

It was at the time that the union-bashing Margaret Thatcher was elected as the Conservative Prime Minister that Bill Douglas began work on his film based on the true story of the Tolpuddle Martyrs in the 1830s, whose fight to receive fair wages resulted in expulsion. Subtitled 'a lanternist's account', with its incidental focus on the early forms of optical entertainment, it is a flawed masterpiece: too long and too preachy, yet its qualities outweigh these defects. It recreates with imaginative intensity the period and the belief in the importance of community through character and imagery.

One False Move
US   1992   105m   colour
Metro/I.R.S. Media (Jesse Beaton, Ben Myron)
◧ ▬ ◎ ◎ ◎
w Billy Bob Thornton, Tom Epperson d Carl Franklin
ph James L. Carter m Peter Haycock, Derek Holt pd Gary
T. New ad Dana Torrey ed Carole Kravetz
☆ Bill Paxton (Dale "Hurricane" Dixon), Cynda Williams
(Fantasia/Lila), Billy Bob Thornton (Ray Malcolm), Michael
Beach (Pluto), Jim Metzler (Dud Cole), Earl Billings
(McFeely), Natalie Canerday (Cherylann)

'Gives film buffs that special jolt they're always looking for.' – *Jami Bernard, New York Post*

'A crime film that lifts you up and carries you along in an ominously rising tide of tension, building to an emotional pay-off of amazing power.' – *Roger Ebert*

626
One False Move

Two runaway killers make for a small town, where the police are expecting them.

A lot of bodies litter the path of two killers, who go on the run from Los Angeles with their black girlfriend, heading for a small town in Alabama, where the local police chief and two big city detectives are already waiting for them. It's a film filled with tension, not only involving the two murderers and those they deal with along the way, but between the modest police chief and the LA detectives who look down on him, though it is his local knowledge that will crack the case. Carl Franklin directed a tough, complex, suspenseful thriller-cum-road movie that also found room to concern itself with relationships and racism. It is an often brutal film, but its power comes from elsewhere – in the fate that binds together the lives of the police chief and the black woman, who both seek their own moment of redemption, one true move.

'Wild longings … fierce desires he could not name … for an interlude of stolen love! To one woman he gave his memories – to another he gave his dreams!'

Intermezzo
US   1939   69m   bw
David O. Selznick
◧ ▬ ◎ ◎ ◎
GB title: *Escape to Happiness*
w George O'Neil original scenario Gosta Stevens, Gustav
Molander d Gregory Ratoff ph Gregg Toland m Lou
Forbes ad Lyle Wheeler ed Hal C. Kern, Francis D. Lyon
☆ Leslie Howard (Holger Brandt), Ingrid Bergman (Anita
Hoffman), John Halliday (Thomas Stenborg), Edna Best
(Margit Brandt), Cecil Kellaway (Charles Moler)
● Harry Stradling was replaced as cinematographer
because Selznick thought he was not capturing Bergman's
beauty.
♫ Lou Forbes

625
Intermezzo

A renowned, married violinist has an affair with his musical protégée.

Ingrid Bergman first made *Intermezzo* in 1936, when it was a Swedish film and she was a local star hardly known to the outside world. Her performance brought her the beginnings of international fame and a remake of the film in Hollywood. It is an archetypal cinema love story. William Wyler was to have directed it, but he quarreled with the producer, David Selznick, on the first day and was replaced. Gregory Ratoff was not in Wyler class, but he managed well (though Wyler thought he missed every point in every scene). Bergman captivated the hard-to-please Graham Greene, who thought her performance 'doesn't give the effect of acting at all but to living'. It is quite perfect in its brief, sentimental way.

Poil de Carotte
France   1932   94m   bw
Legrand Majestic/Marcel Vandal-Charles Delac
🇺🇸
aka: *The Redhead*
wd Julien Duvivier *story* Jules Renard *ph* Armand
Thirard *m* Alexandre Tansman *ed* Marthe Poncin
☆ *Harry Baur* (M. Lepic), *Robert Lynen* (Francois, "Poil de
Carotte"), Catherine Fonteney (Mme. Lepic), Louis Gouthier
(Uncle), Simone Aubry (Ernestine Lepic), Maxime Fromiot
(Felix Lepic), Colette Segall (Mathilde), Christiane Dor
(Annette)
● The British censors banned the film for a time and in
America it was restricted to adult audiences. Duvivier had
made a silent version of the story in 1925. There were less
successful remakes by Paul Mesnier in 1951 and Henri
Graziani in 1973.

624
Poil de Carotte

A red-haired boy, neglected by his father and tormented by his mother, attempts suicide.

Julien Duvivier, the French director whose long career took him to Hollywood in the 1940s, first made a silent movie of this story. He returned to the subject in what became his personal favourite, a moving and unsentimental account of childhood, notable for the performances of Baur, one of the greatest of French screen actors, and Lynen as father and son, who are eventually reconciled to each other. (Tragically, both were killed by the Nazis during World War II for their involvement in the French Resistance).

Quai des Brumes
France   1938   89m   bw
Rabinovitch
📼 🇺🇸 ⊚ ⊚ 🎧
US title: *Port of Shadows*
w Jacques Prévert *novel* Pierre MacOrlan *d* Marcel
Carné *ph* Eugen Schüfftan *m* Maurice Jaubert
ad Alexander Trauner *ed* René Le Hénaff
☆ *Jean Gabin* (Jean), *Michèle Morgan* (Nelly), *Michel
Simon* (Zabel), *Pierre Brasseur* (Lucien Laugardier)

'Unity of space, time and action give the film a classical finish.' – *Georges Sadoul*

'The sort of powerful and joyless film that the French do so well – a study in foetid atmosphere, in which the one beauty is its uncompromising honesty.' – *C. A. Lejeune*

● The plot was in fact almost identical with that of *Pépé le Moko*. The romantic pessimism of these films, plus *Le Jour Se Lève*, so suited the mood of France that Vichy officials later said: 'If we have lost the war it is because of *Quai des Brumes*.'

623
Quai des Brumes

An army deserter rescues a girl from crooks but is killed before they can escape.

An artificial, set-bound, but at the time wholly persuasive melodrama which became one of the archetypal French films of the Thirties, its doomed lovers syndrome not being picked up by Hollywood until after World War II. The story, which unfolds around a fog-shrouded dockside, with its downbeat, anti-military approach led the Vichy government of the time to claim it had contributed to the wartime defeat of France; now it merely adds to the glories of French cinema.

'All it takes is a little confidence!'

The Sting
US   1973   129m   Technicolor
Universal/Richard Zanuck, David Brown (Tony Bill,
Michael S. Phillips)
📷 🎬 🔍 📀 🎧
w David S. Ward *d* George Roy Hill *ph* Robert Surtees
m Scott Joplin (arranged by Marvin Hamlisch) *ad* Henry
Bumstead *ed* William Reynolds
☆ Paul Newman (Henry Gondorff/Mr. Shaw), *Robert
Redford* (Johnny Hooker/Kelly), Robert Shaw (Doyle
Lonnegan), Charles Durning (Lt. William Snyder), Ray
Walston (J.J. Singleton), Eileen Brennan (Billie)

'A visually claustrophobic, mechanically plotted
movie that's meant to be a roguishly charming
entertainment.' – *New Yorker*

'It demonstrates what can happen when a gifted
young screenwriter has the good fortune to fall
among professionals his second time out.' – *Judith
Crist*

'A testament to the value of blue eyes and bright
smiles.' – *Les Keyser, Hollywood in the Seventies*

🏆 best picture; David S. Ward; George Roy Hill; Marvin
Hamlisch
🏅 Robert Surtees; Robert Redford

622
The Sting

In Thirties Chicago, two con men stage an elaborate revenge on a big-time gangster responsible for the death of a friend.

This is a bright, likeable comedy suspenser. There is always great pleasure to be derived from watching professionals at work, and here there are two charismatic actors in Redford and Newman, who give well-judged performances, playing two tricksters at the top of their game. With a soundtrack of infectious ragtime music, Robert Surtees' elegant camerawork that captured the flavour of the period, and direction which made the complex scam easy to follow, this was a demonstration of Hollywood film-making at its most accomplished.

'Roxanne drives her mother crazy.
Maurice never speaks to his niece.
Cynthia has a shock for her family.
Monica can't talk to her husband.
Hortense has never met her mother.'

Secrets and Lies
GB   1995   141m   Metrocolor
Film Four/CiBy 2000/Thin Man/Channel 4 (Simon
Channing-Williams)
📷 📷 🎬 🔍 📀 📀
wd Mike Leigh *ph* Dick Pope *m* Andrew Dickson
pd Alison Chitty *ed* Jon Gregory
☆ *Timothy Spall* (Maurice), Phyllis Logan (Monica),
Brenda Blethyn (Cynthia), Claire Rushbrook (Roxanne),
Marianne Jean-Baptiste (Hortense), Elizabeth Berrington
(Jane), Michele Austin (Dionne), Lee Ross (Paul)

'A beautifully constructed sentimental melodrama,
with none of the rough edges that Mike Leigh has
insisted on in the past. The only mystery is that
Leigh should have come up with so classic a
humanist product after proclaiming for so long that
things could never be so simple.' – *Adam Mars-
Jones, Independent*

● It won the Palme d'Or, and Brenda Blethyn received the
best actress award, at the Cannes Film Festival in 1996.
🏅 best picture; Mike Leigh (as writer and director); Brenda
Blethyn; Marianne Jean-Baptiste
🏆 best British film; Mike Leigh (as writer); Brenda
Blethyn

621
Secrets and Lies

A successful black woman goes in search of her real mother.

Mike Leigh's portrait of a family finding redemption through the sharing of its secrets concerned a successful black woman, who goes in search of her real mother, and discovers that she is white, unmarried and working-class. The emphasis is on a tight-knit, if unravelling, group that looks inward for comfort and succour. Surprisingly, Leigh does not investigate racial attitudes, leaving a great deal unsaid. His treatment of a family that has buried truths about themselves and others is nevertheless sensitively handled, allowing room for some moving performances, particularly in the early confrontations between Brenda Blethyn and Marianne Jean-Baptiste as mother and unacknowledged daughter.

'Schmidt Happens.'

About Schmidt
US   2002   125m   DeLuxe
Entertainment/New Line (Michael Gittes, Harry
Besman)
▣ ▤ ◉ ◉ ◎

w Alexander Payne, Jim Taylor *novel* Louis Begley
d Alexander Payne *ph* James Glennon *m* Rolfe Kent
pd Jane Ann Stewart *ad* Tim Kirkpatrick, Pat Tagliaferro
ed Kevin Tent
☆ *Jack Nicholson* (Warren Schmidt), Hope Davis
(Jeannie), Dermot Mulroney (Randall Hertzel), Kathy Bates
(Roberta Hertzel), Len Cariou (Ray), Howard Hesseman
(Larry), June Squibb (Helen Schmidt)

'The power of this great movie – part comedy, part
tragedy, part satire, mostly masterpiece – is in the
details.' – *Lisa Schwarzbaum, Entertainment
Weekly*

'Sublimely funny and exquisitely sad, this might
just turn out to be an American classic.' – *Peter
Bradshaw, Guardian*

'Doesn't bring us deeply into the lives of its people
because it's too busy trying to feel superior to
them.' – *Peter Rainer, New York*

☒ Jack Nicholson; Kathy Bates

620
About Schmidt

A retired and suddenly-widowed actuary experiences a late-life crisis.

Jack Nicholson gives one of his best, and most restrained, performances in years as Warren Schmidt, a man in his Sixties who has just
entered retirement and recently lost his wife. Forced to confront the
stark reality of his life head-on, he is compelled to deal with the crisis
of an empty and uncertain future. He attempts to overcome his desperation and loneliness by getting behind the wheel of his large
Winnebago and driving across country to visit his daughter, who is
about to marry a man he regards as a fool. At once affecting and funny,
slyly observant and celebratory, this dark, comic look at old age gains
immeasurably from Nicholson's contained performance; he holds back
on his usual mannerisms to suggest the confusions and decencies of a
man who has lost his place in the world.

'All assassins live beyond the law. Only
one follows the code.'

Ghost Dog: The Way of the Samurai
US/Japan/France/Germany   1999   116m
DeLuxe
Film4/JVC/Bac Films/Canal+/Pandora/ARD/Degeto/
Plywood (Richard Guay, Jim Jarmusch)
▣ ▤ ◉ ◉ ◎

wd Jim Jarmusch *ph* Robby Muller *m* RZA *pd* Ted
Berner *ad* Mario Ventenilla *ed* Jay Rabinowitz
☆ Forest Whitaker (Ghost Dog), John Tormey (Louie),
Cliff Gorman (Sonny Valerio), Henry Silva (Vargo), Isaach
de Bankolé (Raymond), Tricia Vessey (Louise Vargo), Victor
Argo (Vinny), Gene Ruffini (Old Consigliere), Richard
Portnow (Handsome Frank), Camille Winbush (Pearline)

'A playful but exceedingly wispy piece of doodling.'
– *Todd McCarthy, Variety*

619
Ghost Dog: The Way of the Samurai

*An American assassin tries to live his life as if he were a Japanese
warrior.*

With modern business executives following the precepts laid down by
Sun Tzu in *The Art of War*, the most ancient of military treatises, it is
perhaps not so surprising to find the hitman of Jim Jarmusch's slyly
comic movie living his life according to the code of *bushido*, the way of
life for samurai warriors that emphasized loyalty, modesty, fearless-
ness and self-sacrifice. A reclusive pigeon-fancier when he is not
shooting people, he becomes a target for assassination after killing a
member of a Mafia gang, who live by a different code of honour.
Despite its high body count among those who settle arguments with
guns, this is a disarming movie that is also concerned with obstacles to
understanding. Forest Whitaker's Ghost Dog has his closest relationship with Isaach de Bankolé's ice cream seller because neither understands the other's language.

Panic in the Streets

US 1950 96m bw
TCF (Sol C. Siegel)

w Richard Murphy, Edward and Edna Anhalt *d* Elia Kazan
ph Joe MacDonald *m* Alfred Newman *ad* Lyle Wheeler,
Maurice Ransford *ed* Harmon Jones
☆ *Richard Widmark* (Clinton Reed), *Jack Palance*
(Blackie), Paul Douglas (Police Capt. Tom Warren), Barbara
Bel Geddes (Nancy Reed), Zero Mostel (Raymond Fitch)

'Elia Kazan directs this tough and unique story with
the speed, imagination and ruthlessness that it
needs.' – *Milton Shulman*

'A model of what an action story should be …
every department is admirably handled.' – *Richard
Mallett, Punch*

👤 original story (Edward and Edna Anhalt)

618
Panic in the Streets

*On the New Orleans waterfront, public health officials seek two killers
who are carriers of bubonic plague.*

Elia Kazan had been unhappy with his first Hollywood films; when,
taking a break on his own, he hitchhiked into the countryside, he knew
why: the studio's soundstages could not capture the feeling of being
outside, in the wind and open air. He insisted on using actual locations
for this film, which is set on the grubby New Orleans waterfront. It was
the first film he enjoyed making, and it showed in the freedom he
brought to camera set-up and movement and in the assured performances. There is tension in the narrative itself, as Widmark, as a public
health official faced with police stubbornness, goes into a shadowy
world in a race against time to find the killers before they can infect the
city.

Rabbit-Proof Fence
Australia/GB   2002   94m   Atlab   Panavision
Buena Vista/AFFC/Hanway (Phillip Noyce, Christine Olsen, John Winter)

w Christine Olsen *book* Follow the Rabbit-Proof Fence by Doris Pilkington Garimara *d* Phillip Noyce *ph* Christopher Doyle *m* Peter Gabriel *pd* Roger Ford *ad* Laurie Faen *ed* John Scott, Veronika Jenet

☆ Everlyn Sampi (Molly Craig), Tianna Sansbury (Daisy Craig), Laura Monaghan (Gracie Fields), David Gulpilil (Moodoo), Kenneth Branagh (A. O. Neville), Deborah Mailman (Mavis), Jason Clarke (Constable Riggs), Ningali Lawford (Molly's Mother)

'Bold in concept and inspirational in intent.' – David Stratton, Variety

'It has real beauty and feeling.' – Anthony Quinn, Independent

• Regions 1 and 2 DVD releases include commentary by Phillip Noyce with Peter Gabriel, Kenneth Branagh, Christine Olsen and Doris Pilkington Garimara.

617
Rabbit-Proof Fence

In the early 1930s, three young girls of mixed race escape after they are taken away from their aboriginal mother and sent to a government camp to be trained as servants for whites.

In returning from Hollywood to make a film in his Australian homeland, Phillip Noyce took a true story of how, in the early 1930s, three mixed race girls attempt an epic journey home after having been snatched from their mothers and sent to a special government camp and trained as servants to be integrated into white society. Molly Craig leads her younger sisiter and cousin on foot over a distance of 1,500 miles along the rabbit-proof fence in Australia's outback. Shot against a spare desert landscape that emphasizes the empty vastness of the country; it is both an exciting chase film and a startling insight into the human cost of an Australian government policy that continued until the 1970s.

Saturday Night Fever
US   1977   119m   Movielab
Paramount/Robert Stigwood (Milt Felsen)

w Norman Wexler *story* Nik Cohn *d* John Badham *ph* Ralf D. Bode *m* David Shire *ch* Lester Wilson (Lorraine Fields) *pd* Charles Bailey *ed* David Rawlins *songs* Barry, Robin and Maurice Gibb (and others), performed by the Bee Gees

☆ John Travolta (Tony Manero), Karen Lynn Gorney (Stephanie), Barry Miller (Bobby C.), Joseph Cali (Joey), Paul Pape (Double J.), Bruce Ornstein (Gus)

'A stylish piece of contemporary anthropology, an urban safari into darkest America, a field study of the mystery cults among the young braves and squaws growing up in North Brooklyn.' – Alan Brien, Sunday Times

• Regions 1 and 2 DVDs include a commentary by John Badham.
• John Avildsen was sacked as director just before shooting began, on the day he was nominated for an Oscar, which he later won, for Rocky.
⚖ John Travolta

616
Saturday Night Fever

Italian roughnecks in Brooklyn live for their Saturday night disco dancing, and one of them falls in love with a girl who makes him realize there are better things in life.

According to journalist Nik Cohn in the magazine feature that sparked this tough, foul-mouthed, fast-paced, all disco dancing slice of life, the young played safe and had dull jobs until on a Saturday, 'it's one great moment of release, it explodes'. No actor could have been more explosive than John Travolta, as the smart-suited Brooklyn boy Tony Manero, strutting his stuff on the dance floor. Teamed with a tender romance, when he falls in love with a girl who makes him realize there is more to life than disco dancing, the film's slick direction, fast editing and exciting dance numbers gave it an irresistible, propulsive energy.

The Tragedy of a Ridiculous Man
Italy 1981 116m Technicolor
Warner/Ladd Company (Giovanni Bertolucci)
🇺🇸
original title: *La Tragedia Di Un Uomo Ridicolo*
wd Bernardo Bertolucci *ph* Carlo Di Palma *m* Ennio
Morricone *pd* Gianni Silvestri *ed* Gabriella Cristani
☆ Ugo Tognazzi (Primo), Anouk Aimee (Barbara), Laura
Morante (Laura), Victor Cavallo (Adelfo), Olympia Carlisi
(Chiromant), Riccardo Tognazzi (Giovanni), Vittorio Caprioli
(Marshal)

615
The Tragedy of a Ridiculous Man

A dairy farmer is faced with losing his livelihood in order to pay a ransom demanded by terrorists who have kidnapped his son.

Bertolucci's film was an engrossing, low-key study of contemporary terrorism and individual responsibility. It is a film of confused motives: the father comes to believe that his son may be colluding with his kidnappers, and realizes he knows little about his life. Bertolucci's refusal to explain everything alienated many audiences; by leaving the film open-ended, he forced his audiences to think through the consequences of the protagonists' actions and the kidnappers' attitude of treating people as commodities.

Aranyer Din Ratri
India 1969 115m bw
Contemporary/Priya (Nepal Dutta, Ashim Dutta)
GB and US title: *Days and Nights in the Forest*
wd Satyajit Ray *novel* Sunil Ganguli *ph* Soumendu Roy,
Purnendu Bose *m* Satyajit Ray *ad* Bansi Chandragupta
ed Dulal Dutta
☆ Soumitra Chatterjee (Ashim), Subhendu Chatterjee
(Sanjoy), Samit Bhanja (Hari), Rabi Ghose (Shekhar), Pahari
Sanyal (Sadashiv Tripathi), Sarmila Tagore (Aparna), Kaveri
Bose (Jaya), Simi Garewal (Duli), Aparna Sen (Hari's former
lover)

'One would rate this lucid, ironic and superlatively
graceful film among the very best of his work.'
– *Penelope Huston, MFB*

'A major film by one of the great film artists.'
– *Pauline Kael*

'Pretentious, short on plot but striving to be long
on character, stylistically awkward as a sign of
sincere emotions, and all of it held together by a
title that is more poetic than anything in the movie
itself.' – *William Paul, Village Voice*

614
Aranyer Din Ratri

A group of friends leave Calcutta to spend a few days in the country.

There is an underlying seriousness to Ray's episodic comedy. Its four young, middle-class idlers are forced to re-examine their lives in an unfamiliar and untamed environment. Ray thought of it as a specifically Bengali film, though in many ways it is his most accessible work; its young, seemingly rootless men do not seem far removed from their western counterparts in their blunted responses to the world around them. There is not a word, gesture or moment out of place in the film.

Safety Last
US 1923 70m (24 fps) bw silent
Harold Lloyd

w Harold Lloyd, Sam Taylor, Tim Whelan, Hal Roach
d Sam Taylor, Fred Newmeyer ph Walter Lundin ad Fred
Guiol ed T.J. Crizer
☆ *Harold Lloyd* (Harold, The Boy), Mildred Davis
(Mildred, The Girl), Noah Young (The Law)

613
Safety Last

A small-town boy goes to the big city and to impress his girlfriend enters a contest to climb a skyscraper.

Harold Lloyd was the master of daredevil comedy, that meticulous mix of humour and suspense, and nowhere did he demonstrate it so marvellously as in *Safety Last*. The movie contains the iconic image of Lloyd, desperately hanging from the minute-hand of a store clock, high above a Los Angeles street. A moment later, the clock face breaks, and he dangles even more precariously. The actual narrative here is a stock one, of small-town boy trying to make it in the big city to impress his girlfriend. What matters are the sight gags, wonderfully worked out so that one follows inevitably from another, climaxing in Lloyd's often impeded climb up the outside of a twelve-story building. It remains a high-point of comic invention.

The Best Intentions
Sweden 1992 181m colour
Artificial Eye/STV1/ZDF/Channel 4/RAIDU/La Sept/
DR/YLE 2/NRK/RUV (Lars Bjälkeskog)

original title: *Den Goda Viljan*
w Ingmar Bergman d Bille August ph Jörgen Persson
m Stefan Nilsson pd Anna Asp ed Janus Billeskov
Jansen
☆ Samuel Fröler (Henrik Bergman), *Pernilla August* (Anna
Akerblom-Bergman), Max von Sydow (Johan Akerblom,
Anna's Father), Ghita Norby (Karin Akerblom, Anna's
Mother), Lennart Hjulström (Nordenson, Landowner and
Owner of the Works), Mona Malm (Alma Bergman, Henrik's
Mother), Lena Endre (Frida Strandberg, Henrik's First
Fiancee), Keve Hjelm (Fredrik Bergman, Henrik's Paternal
Grandfather)

'The picture is uniformly well acted, has a wonderful feeling for the distinct Scandinavian seasons, and re-creates social occasions with an acute moral edge.' – *Philip French, Observer*

'Ingmar Bergman may have officially retired from film direction, but his genius marches on.' – *Geoff Brown, The Times*

● At the 1992 Cannes Film Festival, the film won the Palme D'Or for best film and Pernilla August the award for best actress.

612
The Best Intentions

In Sweden in the early 1900s, a priest overcomes parental objections to marry a nurse, but their union is a troubled one.

Ingmar Bergman's semi-autobiographical, sharply observed account of the early years of his parents' marriage, ending just before his birth, was turned into a wonderfully observed film by Danish director Bille August, who added his individual, nostalgic touch. The setting is Sweden in the early 1900s. The marriage is a troubled one: she comes from a lively, wealthy family and is used to the pleasures of the city; he is an emotionally repressed, rigidly religious man. They begin their life together in a mining town in the bleak and inhospitable north. Their adjustment to one another is a painful process, in which they come to terms with their own, and their partner's, inadequacies. Dominated by Pernilla August's performance of wrenching emotional power as the wife, this fascinating study of a lasting relationship lays bare the limits of love.

The Opposite of Sex
US   1998   105m   Foto-Kem
Sony/Rysher (David Kirkpatrick, Michael Besman)
▣ ▬ ⊚ ⊚ ◠
wd Don Roos ph Hubert Taczanowski *m* Mason Daring
pd Michael Clausen *ed* David Codron
☆ *Christina Ricci* (Dedee Truitt), Martin Donovan (Bill Truitt), *Lisa Kudrow* (Lucia Dalury), Lyle Lovett (Sheriff Carl Tippett), Johnny Galecki (Jason Bock), Ivan Sergei (Matt Mateo)

'A delight on every conceivable level.' – *Andy Medhurst, Sight and Sound*

● Region 1 and 2 DVD releases include commentary by Don Roos.

611
The Opposite of Sex

A teenager runs away from home, seduces her gay brother's boyfriend, and runs off with him to LA.

Don Roos, who began as a screenwriter of conventional movies (*Single White Female*, *Love Field*) wrote something far more idiosyncratic for his debut as a director: a tough, tart, smart movie that made fun of the usual rites-of-passage stories. It featured a pregnant teenager, who ran away from home, seduced her gay brother's boyfriend, and took off with him to LA. It had enough twists in its plot to provide a continual surprise. Christina Ricci was wickedly witty as the young runaway, who commented on the action and warned, 'If you think I'm just plucky and scrappy and all I need is love, you're in over your head.' Her narration almost subverted the film itself and certainly played havoc with an audience's expectations.

☆ **Cameron Crowe**
Writer, Producer, Director ☆

1. The Apartment (Wilder)
2. La Règle du Jeu (Renoir)
3. La Dolce Vita (Fellini)
4. Manhattan (Allen)
5. The Best Years of Our Lives (Wyler)
6. To Kill a Mockingbird (Mulligan)
7. Harold and Maude (Ashby)
8. Pulp Fiction (Tarantino)
9. Quadrophenia (Roddam)
10. Ninotchka (Lubitsch)

☆ **George A. Romero**
Director ☆

1. The Brothers Karamazov (Brooks)
2. Casablanca (Curtiz)
3. Dr. Strangelove (Kubrick)
4. High Noon (Zinnemann)
5. King Solomon's Mines (Bennett)
6. North by Northwest (Hitchcock)
7. The Quiet Man (Ford)
8. Repulsion (Polanski)
9. Touch of Evil (Welles)
10. The Tales of Hoffmann (Powell, Pressburger)

☆ **Roger Ebert**
Film Editor☆

1. Aguirre, Wrath of God (Herzog)
2. Apocalypse Now (Coppola)
3. Citizen Kane (Welles)
4. Dekalog (Kieslowski)
5. La dolce vita (Fellini)
6. The General (Keaton)
7. Raging Bull (Scorsese)
8. 2001: A Space Odyssey (Kubrick)
9. Tokyo Story (Ozu)
10. Vertigo (Hitchcock)

Loves of a Blonde

Czechoslovakia　1965　82m　bw
Barrandov Studios

⬚⬚ ▬ ℚ ⌇ ⌀

original title: *Lasky Jedne Plavovlasky*
aka: *A Blonde in Love*
w Milos Forman, Jaroslav Papousek, Ivan Passer　*d* Milos Forman　*ph* Miroslav Ondricek　*m* Evzen Illin　*ad* Karel Cerny　*ed* Miroslav Hajek
☆ Hanna Brejchova (Andula), Vladimir Pucholt (Milda), Vladimír Mensík (Vacivsky), Ivan Kheil (Manas), Jiri Hruby (Burda)

'It depends on an instinctive sense of timing and a consistent vision of life and people.' – *Georges Sadoul*

♟ best foreign film

610

Loves of a Blonde

A factory girl falls for a visiting musician but meets suspicion from his family when she pursues him.

Milos Forman based his delightful, bittersweet film on his memory of picking up in Prague a girl he saw dragging a battered suitcase. 'She was lost, but she didn't seem to mind very much,' he wrote in his memoir. Living in a town with few eligible men, she had had a brief affair with a visitor and had come to Prague to find him, only to discover that he had given her a false address. Here, the factory girl finds her man, but meets with suspicion from his family when she pursues him and, like the girl Forman met, returns home alone. There is still a tremendous sweetness and freshness about this telling anecdote of disappointed love.

The Producers

US 1968 88m Pathécolor
Avco/Springtime/Crossbow (Sidney Glazier)
🎬 ▦ 📷 ◎ 🎧
wd Mel Brooks *ph* Joseph Coffey *m* John Morris
ch Alan Johnson *ad* Charles Rosen *ed* Ralph
Rosenbloom
☆ Zero Mostel (Max Bialystock), Gene Wilder (Leo
Bloom), Kenneth Mars (Franz Liebkind), Estelle Winwood
(Old Lady), Renee Taylor (Eva Braun), Dick Shawn (Lorenzo
St. Du Bois)

'One of the funniest movies ever made.' – *Roger
Ebert*

'An almost flawless triumph of bad taste,
unredeemed by wit or style.' – *Arthur Schlesinger
Jnr*

'Over and over again promising ideas are killed off,
either by over-exposure or bad timing.' – *Tom
Milne*

♟ Mel Brooks (as writer)
♟ Gene Wilder

609
The Producers

*A Broadway producer seduces elderly widows to obtain finance for his
new play, sells 25,000 per cent in the expectation that it will flop, and is
horrified when it succeeds.*

Mel Brooks's showbiz comedy had good, vulgar fun at the expense of a
Broadway producer, who, with his timid accountant Leo Bloom, scams
rich old ladies into financing what he hopes will be a flop. He enthusiastically embraces bad taste with a terrible musical entitled *Springtime
for Hitler*, complete with goose-stepping chorus girls. Zero Mostel as
the wheedling producer and Gene Wilder as his neurotic accountant
give it more class than it probably deserves.

Taking Off

US 1971 92m Movielab
Universal (Alfred W. Crown, Michael Hausman)
w Milos Forman, John Guare, Jean-Claude Carrière, John
Klein *d* Milos Forman *ph* Miroslav Ondricek *ad* Robert
Wightman *ed* John Carter
☆ Lynn Carlin (Lynn Tyne), Buck Henry (Larry Tyne),
Linnea Heacock (Jeannie Tyne), Georgia Engel (Margot),
Tony Harvey (Tony), Audra Lindley (Ann)

608
Taking Off

*Suburban parents seek their errant daughter among the hippies, and
gradually lose their own inhibitions.*

Milos Forman's first American movie is one he came to think of as his
last Czech film, just made in English and shot in New York. He had
planned to make a film of the musical *Hair* (something that did not
happen until 1979) and, when that project fell through, he turned to
something that kept the same hippie sensibility, but that also concerned
an older generation. The film switches between the parents and actual
auditions for singers in New York's East Village, filmed in a documentary style. It has a looseness and sweetness about it that is more like
his Czech films than his later American movies, an outsider's view of
another culture.

The Phantom of Liberty

France 1974 104m Eastmancolor
Fox-Rank/Greenwich (Serge Silberman)

original title: *Le Fantôme de la Liberté*
w Luis Buñuel, Jean-Claude Carrière *d* Luis Buñuel
ph Edmond Richard *ad* Pierre Guffroy *ed* Hélène
Plemiannikov
☆ Monica Vitti (Mme. Foucauld), Jean-Claude Brialy (M.
Foucauld), Michel Piccoli (2nd Prefect of Police), Jean
Rochefort (M. Legendre), Adolfo Celi (Dr. Pasolini), Michel
Lonsdale (Jean Bermans), Adriana Asti (Woman in
Black/Prefect's Sister), Bernard Verley (Captain of
Dragoons), Maxence Mailfort (Lt. of Dragoons), Muni
(Foucauld's Nanny), Philippe Brigaud (Sinister Stranger)

'A magnificent film … one of Buñuel's
masterpieces.' – *Tom Milne, Sight and Sound*

'Buñuel has a great spare, tonic style, but the
domesticated surrealism of this picture has no
sting and no after-effect. The film drifts out of your
head before it's over.' – *Pauline Kael, New Yorker*

607
The Phantom of Liberty

A group of individuals experience a series of odd happenings.

Luis Buñuel's satire of middle-class hypocrisies presents surrealist episodes in the lives of various loosely linked individuals that range from a firing squad in 1808 and a fox hunt with tanks to events in modern-day Paris. There, a dead woman phones her brother to offer him consolation and the police prepare to suppress a revolt. No one behaves quite as expected: a middle-class couple is titillated by looking at postcards of ancient monuments, priests play cards for religious relics and guests commune with one another in a row of toilets but regard eating as something shameful and done in private. It is often funny, but sometimes no more than bizarre, although you keep watching just to see what happens next. It was an example of Buñuel's belief that 'the crucial imperative is to avoid boredom at all costs.'

The Good, the Bad and the Ugly

Italy 1966 180m Techniscope
PEA (Alberto Grimaldi)

original title: *Il Buono, il Brutto, il Cattivo*
w Age Scarpelli, Luciano Vincenzoni, Sergio Leone
d Sergio Leone *ph* Tonino delli Colli *m* Ennio Morricone
ad Carlo Simi *ed* Eugenio Alabiso, Nino Baragli
☆ Clint Eastwood (Joe), Eli Wallach (Tuco), Lee Van Cleef
(Setenza), Luigi Pistilli (Father Pablo Ramirez), Rada
Rassimov (Maria), Antonio Casas (Stevens)

'The most expensive, pious and repellent movie in
the history of its peculiar genre.' – *Renata Adler,
New York Times*

'A curious amalgam of the visually striking, the
dramatically feeble and the offensively sadistic.'
– *Variety*

● The US DVD release included reinstated scenes from the
Italian version that had been cut from the film on its
American cinema release.

606
The Good, the Bad and the Ugly

During the American Civil War, three men seek hidden loot.

Sergio Leone had a bigger budget for this, the final film in his Dollars Western trilogy, and spent it on spectacle, re-fighting the American Civil War while three drifters go in search of Confederate gold. Its trio of American stars were well-contrasted: the laid back Clint Eastwood setting off the exuberant, over-the-top Eli Wallach as his Mexican partner, with Lee Van Cleef grinning evilly as the conscienceless bad guy, who slaughters indiscriminately. Leone took time over getting what he wanted – both while shooting and in the film's three hour running time – so much so that Eastwood thought he was trying to match David Lean's epics; he certainly had one of the great Italian cinematographers to help him achieve an often painterly look. The result is an operatic Western, the genre at its most hyperbolic, with splendid set pieces, including the final shoot out in an arena-like cemetery.

The Good, the Bad and the Ugly

Germinal

France/Italy   1993   158m   colour
Panavision
AMLF/Renn/France 2/DD/Alternative Films/Nuova
Artisti (Claude Berri)

▭ ▤ ◎ ◌

w Claude Berri, Arlette Langmann *novel* Emile Zola
d Claude Berri *ph* Yves Angelo *m* Jean-Louis Roques
ad Thanh At Hoang, Christian Marti *ed* Hervé de Luze
☆ Gérard Depardieu (Maheu), *Miou-Miou* (Maheude),
Renaud (Etienne Lantier), Jean Carmet (Bonnemort), Judith
Henry (Catherine Maheu), Jean-Roger Milo (Chaval),
Laurent Terzieff (Souvarine)

'One of those truly great examples of European
filmmaking, a monumental statement of a movie
about the fundamental struggles for life, love,
freedom and the pursuit of even the most fragile
happiness.' – *Phillipa Bloom, Empire*

'Strangely flat and matter-of-fact, this earnest
depiction of class struggle will be a struggle for
many viewers as well.' – *Variety*

● It was the most expensive film so far made in France, at a
cost of 172m francs ($30m).

605
Germinal

*In the 1870s, an unemployed railroad engineer finds work as a miner
and joins a strike against poverty and appalling working conditions; the
result is tragedy as the workers are starved, soldiers are called in, and
the mine is sabotaged.*

Emile Zola's novel, set in the 1870s, about the condition of near slavery
suffered by France's coal miners, was based on his own observations
of the striking workers. He brought the matter to the attention of a
wider public with his powerful story. Claude Berri's detailed and sweep-
ingly epic evocation of the novel is an impassioned portrait of exploitation and a plea for a more just society. It retains much of the force of
the original.

Room at the Top
GB   1958   117m   bw
Remus (John and James Woolf)
📽 ▤ ⊙ ⊙

w Neil Paterson *novel* John Braine *d* Jack Clayton
ph Freddie Francis *m* Mario Nascimbene *ad* Ralph
Brinton *ed* Ralph Kemplen
☆ Laurence Harvey (Joe Lampton), *Simone Signoret*
(Alice Aisgill), Heather Sears (Susan Brown), Donald Wolfit
(Mr. Brown), Ambrosine Philpotts (Mrs. Brown), Donald
Houston (Charles Soames), Raymond Huntley (Mr.
Hoylake), John Westbrook (Jack Wales), Allan Cuthbertson
(George Aisgill), Hermione Baddeley (Elspeth), Mary Peach
(June Samson)

'A drama of human drives and torments told with
maturity and precision.' – *Stanley Kauffmann*

♟ Neil Paterson; Simone Signoret
♟ picture; Jack Clayton; Laurence Harvey; Hermione
Baddeley
🏆 film; British film; Simone Signoret

604
Room at the Top

An ambitious young clerk causes the death of his real love but manages to marry into a rich family.

John Braine's novel about an ruthless young clerk who gets to the top by foul means was a harbinger of a shift in British culture towards working-class subjects that, in theatre and cinema, also brought to the front working class actors. The film version that followed eighteen months later was claimed as the first British film to take sex seriously, and the first to show the industrial north as it really was. It had an attack and a social awareness that was new, even though its gritty qualities were soon to look tame alongside Karel Reisz's *Saturday Night and Sunday Morning* a year later. Despite the miscasting of Laurence Harvey (the acting honours went to the intense Simone Signoret as the mistress he abandons), scene for scene this melodrama is vivid and entertaining.

Run Lola Run
Germany   1998   80m   colour
Columbia TriStar/Bavaria/German Independents/X
Filme/ (Stefan Arndt)
📽 ▤ ⊙ ⊙ 🎧
original title: *Lola Rennt*
wd Tom Tykwer *ph* Frank Griebe *m* Tom Tykwer, Johnny
Klimek, Reinhold Hei *ad* Alexander Manasse *ed* Mathilde
Bonnefoy
☆ Franka Potente (Lola), Moritz Bleibtreu (Manni), Herbert
Knaup (Lola's Father), Armin Rohde (Mr Schuster), Joachim
Krol (Nortbert von Au), Nina Petri (Jutta Hansen), Heino
Ferch (Ronnie)

'That Tykwer maintains our flow of empathy while
demonstrating and exploiting the potential of
interactive cinema manqué is, in itself, an awesome
achievement.' – *Richard Falcon, Sight and Sound*

'This stylish, hugely likeable bit of adrenaline-
pumped Euro-nonsense should shatter the illusions
of those convinced that all subtitled fare is musty,
wordy and dull.' – *Caroline Westbrook, Empire*

603
Run Lola Run

A girl has 20 minutes in which to save her boyfriend from death, after he loses a bag of money belonging to a drug dealer.

Franka Potente became an international star playing Lola in this exhilarating, speedy thriller. The narrative provides three alternative versions of events, depending on tiny incidents which precipitate different consequences; it is a witty demonstration of the vagaries of cause and effect and the unpredictability of life.

Tango
France 1993 90m colour
Cinea/Hachette Premiere/TF1/Zoulou (Henri Brichetti)
🎬 🎧
w Patrice Leconte, Patrick Dewolf *d* Patrice Leconte
ph Eduardo Serra *m* Angelique and Jean-Claude Nachon
ad Ivan Maussion *ed* Genevieve Winding
☆ *Philippe Noiret* (L'Elégant), *Richard Bohringer* (Vincent Baraduc), Thierry Lhermitte (Paul), Miou Miou (Marie), Judith Godreche (Madeleine), Carole Bouquet (Female Guest), Jean Rochefort (Bellhop)

'A deliciously dark comedy.' – *Variety*

602
Tango

A woman-hating judge arranges the murder of his nephew's wife by a husband he acquitted of killing his wife and her lover.

Patrice Leconte's outrageous black comedy is a witty examination of masculine and feminine attitudes to life and love, with infidelity, and its often fatal consequences, being treated as a joke the sexes play on one another. The masculine trio of Noiret, Bohringer and Lhermitte play their parts with gusto that does not hide their underlying melancholy, and Jean Rochefort provides a memorable moment as a cuckolded bell hop. Style and sprightly acting carry the day.

Private's Progress
GB 1956 97m bw
British Lion/Charter (Roy Boulting)
🎬 📺 ⊚
w Frank Harvey, John Boulting *novel* Alan Hackney
d John Boulting *ph* Eric Cross *m* John Addison
ad Allan Harris *ed* Anthony Harvey
☆ *Ian Carmichael* (Stanley Windrush), Terry-Thomas (Maj. Hitchcock), Richard Attenborough (Pvt. Cox), *Dennis Price* (Brigadier Bertram Tracepurcel), Peter Jones (Egan), William Hartnell (Sgt. Sutton), Thorley Walters (Capt. Bootle), Ian Bannen (Pvt. Horrocks), Jill Adams (Prudence Greenslade), Victor Maddern (Pvt. George Blake), Kenneth Griffith (Pvt. Dai Jones), Miles Malleson (Mr. Windrush), *John Le Mesurier* (Psychiatrist)

601
Private's Progress

An extremely innocent young national serviceman is taught a few army dodges and becomes a dupe for art thieves.

The Boulting Brothers' celebrated army farce had satirical pretensions. The film makes fun of the officer class, showing them as either incompetent or crooked; their success depends on those they regard as the lower orders obeying their commands. Ian Carmichael dithers wonderfully as the middle-class sucker. There is a savagery beneath the fun. Raymond Durgnant, a perceptive critic of British movies, pointed out that the Boultings' satire is a flip side of a painfully disappointed earnestness. When it was released, the movie had something to make everyone in Britain laugh, and it has not yet lost its humour.

The Story of Qiu Ju

China/Hong Kong   1992   100m   colour
Sil-Metropole/Beijing Film Academy Youth Film Studio
(Ma Fung Kwok)
▣ ◫ ▦ ▨ ◉

w Liu Heng *novel* Chen Yuanbin *d* Zhang Yimou *ph* Chi
Xiaoning, Yu Xiaoqun *m* Zhao Jiping *ad* Cao Jiuping
ed Du Yuan
☆ Gong Li (Wan Qiu Ju), Lei Laosheng (Wan Shantung,
Village Head), Liu Peiqi (Wan Qing Lai, Husband), Yang
Liuchun (Meizi)

'This simple, repetitive tale has a mesmerizing
quality able to hook audiences from beginning to
end.' – *Variety*

● The film won the Golden Lion award for best film and
Gong Li won the award for best actress at the 1992 Venice
Film Festival.

600
The Story of Qiu Ju

*The pregnant wife of a peasant appeals to higher authorities to force
the village headman to apologize for injuring her husband.*

Zhang Yimou's film was less flamboyant than his usual approach,
using a documentary method to tell the story of a pregnant woman's
determination that principles must be upheld whatever the cost. The
narrative was consciously designed to appease the authorities who had
banned his first two films: the pregnant wife of a peasant appeals to
higher authorities to force the village headman to apologize for injuring
her husband. Whatever compromises were made, the film presents a
beautifully detailed and authentic account of Chinese village life and
attitudes.

'Three centuries in the making!'
A Midsummer Night's Dream

👫   US   1935   133m   bw
Warner (Max Reinhardt)
▦ ▨ ◉

w Charles Kenyon, Mary McCall Jnr *play* William
Shakespeare *d* Max Reinhardt, William Dieterle *ph* Hal
Mohr, Fred Jackman, Byron Haskin, H. F. Koenekamp
m Mendelssohn *md* Erich Wolfgang Korngold
ch Bronislawa Nijinska *ad* Anton Grot *ed* Ralph Dawson
☆ *James Cagney* (Bottom), Dick Powell (Lysander), Jean
Muir (Helena), Ross Alexander (Demetrius), Olivia de
Havilland (Hermia), Joe E. Brown (Flute), Hugh Herbert
(Snout), Arthur Treacher (Ninny's Tomb), Frank McHugh
(Quince), Otis Harlan (Starveling), Dewey Robinson (Snug),
Victor Jory (Oberon), Verree Teasdale (Hippolyta, Queen of
the Amazons), *Mickey Rooney* (Puck), Anita Louise (Titania)
and also Grant Mitchell, Ian Hunter, Hobart Cavanaugh

'The publicity push behind the film is tremendous –
it is going to be a success or everyone at Warner
Brothers is going to get fired.' – *Robert Forsythe*

'Its worst contradiction lies in the way Warners first
ordered up a whole batch of foreign and high-
sounding names to handle music, dances, general
production – and then turned around and handed
them empty vessels for actors.' – *Otis Ferguson*

👤 photography; editing
👤 best picture

599
A Midsummer Night's Dream

*The love lives of two Athenian couples are complicated by the fairies,
but all ends happily.*

The great Austrian director Max Reinhardt influenced cinema mainly in
a secondhand way, through the members of his theatre companies
who went on to work in films, including the directors William Dieterle,
Ernst Lubitsch, F. W. Murnau and Paul Wegener. After the Nazis came
to power, he moved to America and signed a seven-year contract with
Warner Brothers. The deal was abruptly ended by the failure of his version of Shakespeare's comedy, of two pairs of lovers who sort out their
problems with fairy help at midnight in the woods of Athens. Based on
his Broadway production, this spectacular and super-glamorous
Hollywood adaptation is never less than fascinating The humour of
James Cagney's boastful Bottom and his friends rehearsing their amateur dramatics survives surprisingly well, and Mickey Rooney makes a
wonderfully mischievous Puck. Much of it comes off, and visually the
production is a treat.

L'Invitation
Switzerland/France   1973   100m   colour
Groupe 5/Television Suisse/Citel Films/Planfilm

🏳️
w Claude Goretta, Michel Viala *d* Claude Goretta *ph* Jean
Zeller *m* Patrick Moraz *ad* Yanko Hodjis *ed* Joelle Van
Effenterre
☆ Jean-Luc Bideau (Maurice), Jean Champion (Alfred),
Corinne Coderey (Simone), Pierre Collet (Pierre), Neige
Dolsky (Emma), Jacques Rispal (Rene), Michel Robin
(Remy), Rosine Rochette (Helene), François Simon (Emile),
Cecile Vassort (Aline)

598
L'Invitation

Following his mother's death, a middle-aged bachelor buys a country house and invites his office colleagues to a party.

Swiss director Claude Goretta's gentle comedy of manners is full of sharp observation of social types, as, following the death of his mother, a middle-aged bachelor buys a grand home in the country and invites his office colleagues to a garden party. As the afternoon wears on, inhibitions are relaxed and it requires all the tact of François Simon's butler, hired for the occasion, to maintain decorum. This delightful film won a special Jury Prize at the Cannes Film Festival.

Knife in the Water
Poland   1962   94m   bw
ZRF Kamera (Stanislaw Zylewicz)
🎞️ 🏳️ 🔍 ⊚ ⊚ 🎧
original title: *Noz w Wodzie*
w Jerzy Skolimowski, Roman Polanski, Jakub Goldberg
d Roman Polanski ph Jerzy Lipman *m* Krzystof Komeda
☆ Leon Niemczyk (Andrzej), Jolanta Umecka (Christine),
Zygmunt Malanowicz (The Young Man)

'Has all the virtues of an intensely psychological,
sardonically probing modern novel.' – *John Simon*

⚖ best foreign film

597
Knife in the Water

A young couple ask a hitchhiker to spend a weekend on their yacht, and regret it.

This is Polanski's first, and last, feature made in Poland. A couple regret inviting a weekend guest to their yacht. The film gradually turns into a drama in which the sex and violence hover beneath the surface. The two men compete for the woman's attention and the situation is exacerbated by a storm that forces them all into the boat's enclosed space below deck. Polanski's detached approach and his use of close-ups –– an inevitable result of the cramped room in which the camera could operate – adds an extra layer of unease to this deft and troubling psychological thriller.

'Five Good Reasons To Stay Single.'

Four Weddings and a Funeral

GB 1994 117m Eastmancolor
Rank/Polygram/Channel 4/Working Title (Duncan Kenworthy)

▣ ▤ ⊚ ⊚ ⌂

w Richard Curtis d Mike Newell ph Michael Coulter
m Richard Rodney Bennett pd Maggie Gray ed Jon Gregory

☆ Hugh Grant (Charles), Andie MacDowell (Carrie), Kristin Scott Thomas (Fiona), Simon Callow (Gareth), James Flett (Tom), David Bower (David), Charlotte Coleman (Scarlett), John Hannah (Matthew), Anna Chancellor (Henrietta), Robert Lang (Lord Hibbott), Jeremy Kemp (Sir John Delaney), Rosalie Crutchley (Mrs. Beaumont), Rowan Atkinson (Father Gerald)

'Old-fashioned in its essence, and highly conservative: there will certainly be some British viewers who find the languid mating rites of the moneyed upper-middle-classes less than compulsive.' – Sheila Johnston, Independent

● The film is the most successful British movie so far, having taken more than £130m at the box-office worldwide. Its British video release was available for sale for five weeks only.
● Following the recitation of one of his poems in the film, a slim paperback of love poems by W. H. Auden became a best-seller.

Ω picture; Richard Curtis
♛ film; Mike Newell; Hugh Grant; Kristin Scott Thomas

Atlantic City

Canada/France 1981 105m colour
Cine-Neighbour/Selta Films (Denis Heroux)

▣ ▤ ⊚~ ⊚ ⊚ ⌂

w John Guare d Louis Malle ph Richard Ciupka
m Michel Legrand pd Anne Pritchard ed Suzanne Baron
☆ Burt Lancaster (Lou), Susan Sarandon (Sally), Kate Reid (Grace), Michel Piccoli (Joseph), Hollis McLaren (Chrissie)

Ω best picture; John Guare; Burt Lancaster; Susan Sarandon; Louis Malle
♛ best direction; Burt Lancaster

596
Four Weddings and a Funeral

A confirmed bachelor chases the woman of his dreams from one wedding to another.

Mike Newell's comedy did much to create the persona that Hugh Grant has never been able to shake off since; that of a hesitant, floppy-haired charmer and the ideal lead for a modern British romantic comedy. As a confirmed bachelor who meets the woman of his dreams at the first of the weddings in the title, and spends the remainder chasing her, he gives a perfectly judged, shyly ingratiating performance. He is surrounded by an excellent comic cast of characters who inhabit the film's five public episodes, adding moments of joy and sadness to the proceedings.

595
Atlantic City

Small-time crooks congregate round Atlantic City's new casinos.

Louis Malle, who had left his native France in search of fresh inspiration, thought of Atlantic City, then attempting to transform itself into another Las Vegas, as a microcosm of America. Burt Lancaster was pleased to take the role of an aging small-time crook in this elegiac character drama because it gave him the chance to play against his familiar, powerful screen image. Lancaster, though, was unhappy with the ending, in which Susan Sarandon's waitress walks out on him. 'It was inconceivable to him that a woman would leave after spending a night with him,' Malle recalled. Though sometimes it is too understated for its own good, the film often achieves the mood it seeks and allows for some rich characterizations from Lancaster as the loser revitalized by murder, Kate Reid as his elderly harridan of a lover, and Sarandon as the woman who got away.

'There is no such thing as the simple truth.'

The Sweet Hereafter
Canada 1997 112m colour Panavision
Electric/Speaking Parts/Alliance/Ego (Camelia Frieberg, Atom Egoyan)

wd Atom Egoyan *novel* Russell Banks *ph* Paul Sarossy *m* Mychael Danna *pd* Philip Barker *ad* Kathleen Climie *ed* Susan Shipton
☆ Ian Holm (Mitchell Stephens), Maury Chaykin (Wendell Walker), Gabrielle Rose (Dolores Driscoll), Peter Donaldson (Schwartz), Bruce Greenwood (Billy Ansell), David Hemblen (Abbott Driscoll), Brooke Johnson (Mary Burnell), Arsinée Khanjian (Wanda Otto)

'The cumulative impact is, by this director's standards, disappointingly uni-dimensional and almost banal.' – *Sheila Johnston, Screen International*

'A film of great scrupulousness and restraint, with few false notes.' – *Richard Williams, Guardian*

⚲ Atom Egoyan (as director and as writer)

594
The Sweet Hereafter

A lawyer seeks to represent parents grieving over the death of their children.

A lawyer arrives in a small town to persuade parents, who are grieving over the deaths of 14 children killed in a school bus accident, to let him represent them in an action against the bus company. In a complex and compelling retelling of a tragic event that flashes back and forward in time, Atom Egoyan, in his adaptation of Russell Banks' novel, details the inner life of the town and the way one person's existence links and affects another's, so that a sense of community prevails. But it is one riven by betrayals and secret lusts, adulterous and incestuous affairs. The town comes together only in its decision not to hire the lawyer, a man whose troubles echo their own. Their refusal points the way to a possibly happier future. Egoyan, adapting for the first time the work of another writer, has created a moving portrayal of accident, grief and understanding.

'There's Only One Thing Stranger Than What's Going On Inside His Head. What's Going On Outside.'

'Between Heaven and Hell there's always Hollywood.'

Barton Fink
US 1991 116m colour
Rank/Circle (Ethan Coen)

w Ethan and Joel Coen *d* Joel Coen *ph* Roger Deakins *m* Carter Burwell *pd* Dennis Gassner *ad* Bob Goldstein, Leslie McDonald *ed* Roderick Jaynes
☆ John Turturro (Barton Fink), John Goodman (Charlie Meadows), Judy Davis (Audrey Taylor), Michael Lerner (Jack Lipnick), John Mahoney (W.P. Mayhew), Tony Shalhoub (Ben Geisler), Jon Polito (Lou Breeze), Steve Buscemi (Chet)

'Scene after scene is filled with a ferocious strength and humour.' – *Variety*

● The film took an unprecedented three prizes at the 1991 Cannes Film Festival: Palme d'Or for best film, best actor (John Turturro) and best director.
⚲ Michael Lerner; Dennis Gassner

593
Barton Fink

An intellectual, left-wing playwright goes to work in Hollywood, where he is told to write a wrestling picture for Wallace Beery.

The Coen brothers' Hollywood film is built around a writer who most resembles Clifford Odets, the left-wing playwright who had mixed feelings about working as a screenwriter. When, in the 1940s, the intellectual Barton Fink arrives in Hollywood, he, of course, is ordered to write a wrestling picture for Wallace Beery. The comedy gives way to something darker and more disturbing from the halfway mark, as Fink develops writer's block and a fellow guest in his hotel, an insurance salesman, becomes unhinged. The genial satire turns into a dizzying trip inside two disordered minds, as if what was happening in Europe at that time was seeping into their consciousness. It is a curious movie, but a satisfying one.

Sense and Sensibility

GB/US 1995 136m Technicolor
Columbia/Mirage (Lindsay Doran)

⊞ ⊞ ▤ ⊛ ⊘ ⊘ 🎧

w *Emma Thompson* novel Jane Austen d *Ang Lee*
ph Michael Coulter m Patrick Doyle pd Luciana Arrighi
ad Philip Elton ed Tim Squyres

☆ Emma Thompson (Elinor Dashwood), Alan Rickman
(Colonel Brandon), *Kate Winslet* (Marianne Dashwood),
Hugh Grant (Edward Ferrars), James Flett (John Dashwood),
Harriet Walter (Fanny Dashwood), Gemma Jones (Mrs.
Dashwood), Elizabeth Spriggs (Mrs. Jennings), Robert
Hardy (Sir John Middleton), Greg Wise (John Willoughby),
Hugh Laurie (Mr. Palmer), Imelda Staunton (Charlotte
Palmer), Imogen Stubbs (Lucy Steele), Emile François
(Margaret Dashwood)

'Luminously brings to life Austen's vision of the
dance of the sexes. The final romantic epiphany is
a stunner, at once rapturous and funny.' – *Owen
Gleiberman, Entertainment Weekly*

● It won the Golden Bear as the best film at the 1996 Berlin
Film Festival.
● Regions 1 and 2 DVD releases include commentary by
Emma Thompson and Lindsay Doran, and by Ang Lee and
James Schamus, and deleted scenes.
🎙 Emma Thompson (adapted screenplay)
👤 best picture; Emma Thompson (as actress); Kate
Winslet; Michael Coulter; Patrick Doyle; costume design
(Jenny Beavan, John Bright)
🏆 best film; Emma Thompson (as actress); Kate Winslet

592
Sense and Sensibility

Two sisters lose their fortune but still hope to find husbands.

The Taiwanese-born director Ang Lee was a surprising choice to direct
an 18th-century English novel by Jane Austen, about two sisters who
hope for suitable husbands when they and their widowed mother lose
their home and money and are forced to move into a small cottage. The
result, though, was a high-spirited romance that is a joy to watch;
Emma Thompson's casting as Elinor (who is a 19-year-old in the book)
slightly undermines Austen's intent, but does not reduce the pleasure
the film provides; her sprightly, slightly feminist screenplay gave Lee
the opportunity to direct an affectionate and ironic look back at love.

This Sporting Life

GB 1963 134m bw
Rank/Independent Artists (Karel Reisz)

⊞ ▤ ⊘ ⊘

w David Storey novel David Storey d *Lindsay Anderson*
ph Denys Coop m Roberto Gerhard ad Alan Withy
ed Peter Taylor

☆ *Richard Harris* (Frank Machin), *Rachel Roberts* (Mrs.
Hammond), Alan Badel (Weaver), William Hartnell
(Johnson), Colin Blakely (Maurice Braithwaite), Vanda
Godsell (Mrs. Weaver), Arthur Lowe (Slomer)

'Translates the confusions and unrequited longings
of the angry young men and women of our time
into memorable universal truths.' – *New York
Times*

👤 Richard Harris; Rachel Roberts
🏆 Rachel Roberts

591
This Sporting Life

*A tough miner becomes a successful rugby player, but his inner crude-
ness and violence keep contentment at bay.*

A landmark British film that brought together remarkable talents in full
command of their abilities. Although it was Lindsay Anderson's first
feature film, he had worked successfully as a theatre director. He said
of David Storey, 'he seeks to penetrate the soul; yet he never forgets
the relevance of the social world in which souls meet, conflict and
struggle.' Anderson found another person who shared his and Storey's
views in Richard Harris, who gives an intense and sensitive performance as a tough miner who becomes a successful rugby league player,
but is destroyed by his inner violence and lack of tenderness. Rachel
Roberts matched his intensity as the landlady with whom he has a desperate affair. It is among the most impressive films of the British new
wave of the 1960s.

'The Immortal Lovers All The World Loves!'

The Prisoner of Zenda

👥 US 1937 101m bw
David O. Selznick

w John Balderston, Wells Root, Donald Ogden Stewart novel Anthony Hope d John Cromwell ph James Wong Howe m Alfred Newman ad Lyle Wheeler ed Hal C. Kern, James E. Newcom

☆ Ronald Colman (Rudolph Rassendyl/King Rudolf V), Douglas Fairbanks Jnr (Rupert of Hentzau), Madeleine Carroll (Princess Flavia), David Niven (Capt. Fritz von Tarlenheim), Raymond Massey (Black Michael), Mary Astor (Antoinette De Mauban), C. Aubrey Smith (Col. Zapt), Byron Foulger (Johann), Montagu Love (Detchard)

'The most pleasing film that has come along in ages.' – New York Times

'One of those rare movies that seem, by some magic trick, to become more fascinating and beguiling with each passing year.' – John Cutts, 1971

- Previously filmed in 1913 and 1922.
- Remade in 1952 and 1979
- Alfred Newman; Lyle Wheeler

590
The Prisoner of Zenda

In Ruritania, an Englishman saves the day by taking the place of a kidnapped king.

A splendid schoolboy adventure story is perfectly transferred to the screen in this exhilarating swashbuckler, in which an Englishman on holiday in Ruritania finds himself helping to defeat a rebel plot by impersonating the kidnapped king at his coronation. He falls for the king's fiancee and is caught up in court intrigue. Raymond Massey, as the king's illegitimate half-brother, was an almost sympathetic villain, David Niven gave a star-making performance as a loyal friend, Ronald Colman was at his dashing best with sword and repartee and Douglas Fairbanks Jnr stole several scenes as the dastardly Rupert of Hentzau. This is among the most entertaining films to come out of Hollywood.

The Best Man

US 1964 104m bw
UA/Stuart Millar, Lawrence Turman

w Gore Vidal play Gore Vidal d Franklin Schaffner ph Haskell Wexler m Mort Lindsey ed Robert Swink

☆ Henry Fonda (William Russell), Cliff Robertson (Joe Cantwell), Lee Tracy (Art Hockstader), Margaret Leighton (Alice Russell), Edie Adams (Mabel Cantwell), Kevin McCarthy (Dick Jensen), Shelley Berman (Sheldon Bascomb), Ann Sothern (Mrs. Gamadge), Gene Raymond (Dan Cantwell), Mahalia Jackson (Herself)

'A fine opportunity to watch pros at work in a hard-hitting and cogent drama that seems to become more topical and have more relevance with each showing.' – Judith Crist

'Some of the wittiest lines since Strangelove ... the acting fairly crackled with authenticity.' – Isabel Quigly

'You are left gasping at its sheer professionalism.' – Evening News

- This was Oscar-nominated Lee Tracy's last screen role.
- Lee Tracy

589
The Best Man

Two contenders for a presidential nomination seek the support of the dying ex-president.

Gore Vidal adapted his incisive play for the screen about political rivals vying for favour. Frank Capra was going to make the movie version, but Vidal, who found him 'deeply reactionary', managed to get him removed from the project. Schaffner was a more sympathetic director. Ingeniously adapted on a low budget, it was a brilliant political melodrama with splendid dramatic scenes, good convention detail and memorable performances.

Dangerous Liaisons
US 1988 120m Eastmancolor
Warner/Lorimar/NFH (Norma Heyman, Hank Moonjean)
⬛ ▦ ⬙ ⊚ ⊙ ⌒

w Christopher Hampton *play* Christopher Hampton *novel* Choderlos de Laclos *d* Stephen Frears *ph* Philippe Rousselot *m* George Fenton *pd* Stuart Craig *ed* Mick Audsley
☆ Glenn Close (Marquise de Merteuil), John Malkovich (Vicomte de Valmont), Michelle Pfeiffer (Madame de Tourvel), Swoosie Kurtz (Madame de Volanges), Keanu Reeves (Chevalier Danceny), Mildred Natwick (Madame de Rosemonde), Uma Thurman (Cecile de Volanges)

'Beautifully acted (by Glenn Close in particular), elegantly phrased, carefully shot on location in an appropriate selection of chateaux, directed with a limpidly formalised serenity, it's a handsome and intelligent piece of work.' – *Tom Milne, MFB*

🯅 Christopher Hampton; Stuart Craig
🯄 best picture; Glenn Close; Michelle Pfeiffer; George Fenton
🯃 adapted screenplay; Michelle Pfeiffer

588
Dangerous Liaisons

Two jaded French aristocrats play games of sexual politics.

Like the protagonists in this cool dissection of sexual feeling, Stephen Frears inveigles us to observe and marvel at the intrigues of lovers, seducing with his masterly command of cinematic technique. At a time just before the French revolution, an aristocratic libertine (Glenn Close), jealous that her young lover has left her for a virginal girl, asks the Viscomte de Valmont (John Malkovich) to seduce her. He also plans to persuade into his bed the devout Madame de Tourvel (Michelle Pfeiffer), and then makes the mistake of falling in love with her. In this elegant tragi-comedy of sexual manners, these two jaded cynics, who ruin the lives of others as an erotic game, destroy themselves by momentarily yielding to true emotions.

Casino
US 1995 178m Technicolor Super 35
Universal/Syalis/Legende/De Fina/Cappa (Barbara de Fina)
⬛ ▦ ⬙ ⊚ ⊙ ⌒

w Nicholas Pileggi, Martin Scorsese *book* Nicholas Pileggi *d* Martin Scorsese *ph* Robert Richardson *pd* Dante Ferretti *ad* Jack G. Taylor Jr. *ed* Thelma Schoonmaker
☆ Robert DeNiro (Sam 'Ace' Rothstein), Sharon Stone (Ginger McKenna), Joe Pesci (Nicky Santoro), James Woods (Lester Diamond), Don Rickles (Billy Sherbert), Alan King (Andy Stone), Kevin Pollak (Phillip Green), L. Q. Jones (Pat Webb), Dick Smothers (Senator)

'I simply can't see any urgent reason for *Casino* to exist. Scorsese has always been a master of camera movement, but here the camera is just going through the motions.' – *Tom Shone, Sunday Times*

'It doesn't seem too much to ask, in exchange for three hours of our lives, to be offered an emotion less tainted than watching nasty people fall foul of one another.' – *Adam Mars-Jones, Independent*

'A must-see for cinema-savvy audiences.' – *Variety*

🯄 Sharon Stone

587
Casino

A gambler who is put in charge of a Las Vegas casino by the Mafia runs into trouble.

A deft and involving depiction of the inescapable corruption of the spirit that begins in a leisurely, documentary style before focusing on individuals as flawed as the system they operate, and as expendable as the chips they bet. DeNiro plays a gambler who is put in charge of a Las Vegas casino by the Mafia and gets into trouble when he tries to run the business honestly. His downfall, and that of the mob, is brought about by the call-girl he marries, and by his childhood friend, a vicious crook who kills on impulse. Scorsese's intriguing film evokes a past historical era and ethos of a city built on greed.

'He's got to face a gunfight once more to live up to his legend once more. To win just one more time.'

The Shootist
US   1976   100m   Technicolor   Panavision
Paramount/Frankovich-Self
▭ ▰ ◎ ◎ ◎ ◠
w *Miles Hood Swarthout, Scott Hale* *novel* Glendon Swarthout   *d* *Don Siegel*   *ph* Bruce Surtees   *m* Elmer Bernstein   *ed* Douglas Stewart
☆ *John Wayne* (John Bernard Books), Lauren Bacall (Bond Rogers), James Stewart (Dr. Hostetler), Ron Howard (Gillom Rogers), Bill McKinney (Cobb), Richard Boone (Sweeney), John Carradine (Beckum), Scatman Crothers (Moses), Harry Morgan (Marshall Thibido), Hugh O'Brian (Pulford), Sheree North (Serepta)

'Just when it seemed that the Western was an endangered species, due for extinction because it had repeated itself too many times, Wayne and Siegel have managed to validate it once more.' – *Arthur Knight*

'Watching this film is like taking a tour of Hollywood legends.' – *Frank Rich*

586
The Shootist

In 1901, a dying ex-gunfighter arrives in a small town to set his affairs in order.

This was John Wayne's valedictory Western, his farewell to the genre and to cinema. The story of a dying ex-gunfighter who arrives in a small town in 1901 to set his affairs in order, reflected Wayne's own life: like J. B. Books, he was dying of cancer. At the start of the film come glimpses of a younger Wayne in action, with moments from *Red River*, *Rio Bravo* and *El Dorado*. What follows is an impressive melodrama, very well written and acted all round by a splendid cast, solidly entertaining and thoughtful.

'I can't go on *live*! I'm a movie star, not an actor!'

My Favorite Year
US   1982   92m   Metrocolor
MGM-UA/Brooksfilms/Michael Gruskoff
▭ ▰ ◎ ◎
w Norman Steinberg, Dennis Palumbo   *d* Richard Benjamin   *ph* Gerald Hirschfeld   *m* Ralph Burns   *pd* Charles Rosen   *ed* Richard Chew
☆ *Peter O'Toole* (Alan Swann), Mark Linn-Baker (Benjy Stone), Jessica Harper (K.C. Downing), Joseph Bologna (King Kaiser), Bill Macy (Sy Benson), Lainie Kazan (Belle Carroca), Lou Jacobi (Uncle Morty), Cameron Mitchell (Karl Rojeck)

'A field day for a wonderful bunch of actors.' – *Variety*

● A Region 1 DVD release includes commentary by Richard Benjamin.
Ω Peter O'Toole

585
My Favorite Year

In 1954, a legendary Hollywood star noted for wine and women is unwisely invited to star in a television series.

Peter O'Toole is a sprightly presence as a swashbuckling star in this good-humoured and well-researched romp. The legendary Hollywood name, noted for wine and women, who is unwisely invited to star in a television series is not too far removed from Errol Flynn, though the old film clips shown are O'Toole's own. The comedy stems from the notion that O'Toole's Alan Swann is a man who regards his life as a widescreen Technicolor epic. 'That was a movie. This is real life,' explains the man dedicated to keeping Swann sober as the star prepares to carry out a stunt from one of his period films. 'What's the difference?' comes the reply.

The Quiet Man

US   1952   129m   Technicolor
Republic/Argosy (John Ford, Merian C. Cooper)

w Frank Nugent story Maurice Walsh d John Ford
ph Winton C. Hoch, Archie Stout m Victor Young
ad Frank Hotaling ed Jack Murray
☆ John Wayne (Sean Thornton), Maureen O'Hara (Mary Kate Danaher), Barry Fitzgerald (Michaeleen Flynn), Victor McLaglen (Red Will Danaher), Ward Bond (Fr. Peter Lonergan), Mildred Natwick (Mrs. Sarah Tillane), Francis Ford (Dan Tobin), Arthur Shields (Rev. Cyril Playfair), Eileen Crowe (Mrs. Elizabeth Playfair), Sean McClory (Owen Glynn), Jack MacGowran (Feeney)

'Ford's art and artifice … are employed to reveal a way of life – stable, rooted, honourable, purposeful in nature's way, and thereby rhythmic. Everyone is an individual, yet everyone and everything has a place.' – Henry Hart, Films in Review

● A Region 1 collector's edition DVD release has commentary by Maureen O'Hara and a documentary on the making of the film.
🎬 John Ford; Winton C. Hoch, Archie Stout
🏆 best picture; Frank Nugent; Victor McLaglen

584
The Quiet Man

An Irish fighter returns home to find a wife.

John Ford's comedy was Irish as can be, with everything but leprechauns and the Blarney Stone on hand. It was an Irish village version of *The Taming of the Shrew*, the tamer being an ex-boxer retired to the land of his fathers and in need of a wife. Despite some poor sets, the film has a gay swing to it, with much brawling vigour and broad comedy, while the actors all give of their roistering best. John Wayne's tough guy is matched by the pugnacity of Maureen O'Hara's fiery woman, who does not intend to be an easy conquest. Ford had wanted to make the film for ten years and returned to his father's native Galway to do it. He was eager to try his hand at a mature love story, one that featured equally matched adults. The result was a triumph.

'Destiny cannot be denied.'

Lovers of the Arctic Circle

Spain/France   1998   108m   colour   Super 35
Metro Tartan/Alicia/Bailando en la Luna/Sogetel (Fernando Bovaira, Enrique Lopez Lavinge)

original title: *Los Amantes del Circulo Polar*
wd Julio Medem ph Gonzalo F. Berridi m Alberto Iglesias
pd Satur Udarreta, Karmele Soler, Estibaliz Markiegi, Itziar Arrieta ed Ivan Aledo
☆ Najwa Nimri (Ana), Fele Martinez (Otto), Nancho Nova (Alvaro), Maru Valdivieslo (Olga), Peru Medem (Otto as a child), Sara Valiente (Ana as a child), Victor Hugo Oliveira (Adolescent Otto), Kristel Diaz (Adolescent Ana), Pep Munné (Javier)

'It never loses the air of a dispassionate exercise, arranged by its creator according to an oppressively rigid pattern of his own.' – Edward Porter, Sunday Times

583
Lovers of the Arctic Circle

Two childhood lovers' attempts to meet again are continually frustrated.

There is a poignancy about Julio Medem's charmingly romantic tale of loves lost and won, in which the lives of a man and a woman interlock from their first meeting in childhood; but their later attempts to meet fail, though they are often unknowingly close to one another. It is an unusual, lyrical movie about predestination, and the way one life links unexpectedly with another. The protagonists, whose names – Otto, Ana – can be read backwards as well as forwards, have lives that rotate around one other and reach a kind of fulfillment in a place where the sun circles the sky, but never sets. It is, in part, an exercise in pattern-making by Medem, but he invests his drama with genuine emotion so that their inconclusive affair seems not arbitrary, but inevitable.

Meet Me in St Louis

👥 US 1944 113m Technicolor
MGM (Arthur Freed)
🎞 ▬ 🔍 Ⓖ Ⓟ 🎧

w Irving Brecher, Fred Finklehoffe *novel* Sally Benson
d Vincente Minnelli *ph* George Folsey *md* Georgie Stoll
ad Lemuel Ayers, Cedric Gibbons *ed* Albert Akst
☆ *Judy Garland* (Esther Smith), *Margaret O'Brien* ('Tootie' Smith), Tom Drake (John Truett), Leon Ames (Mr Alonzo Smith), Mary Astor (Mrs Anne Smith), Lucille Bremer (Rose Smith), June Lockhart (Lucille Ballard), *Harry Davenport* (Grandpa), Marjorie Main, Joan Carroll, Hugh Marlowe, Robert Sully, Chill Wills

'A family group framed in velvet and tinsel … it has everything a romantic musical should have.'
– *Dilys Powell, 1955*

'A charming picture. There is much more in it than meets the ear.' – *C. A. Lejeune*

🎵 'Meet Me in St Louis'; 'The Boy Next Door'; 'Under the Bamboo Tree'; 'The Trolley Song'; 'You and I'; 'Have Yourself a Merry Little Christmas'
🎖 script; George Folsey; Georgie Stoll; song 'The Trolley Song' (*m/ly* Ralph Blane, Hugh Martin)

582
Meet Me in St Louis

Scenes in the life of an affectionate family at the turn of the last century.

An evergreen, nostalgic musical about affectionate family life in St Louis, with a setting inspired by the paintings of Thomas Eakins. It uses an effective sense of the passing of four seasons, from the summer of 1903 to the spring of 1904, as four daughters oppose their father's wish to move to New York. The first great production of Arthur Freed's unit at MGM, it was innovative in its lack of big production numbers, with songs and action integrated. The production was a bumpy one: Judy Garland was tired of playing teenagers, found Minnelli at first impossible to work with (though she married him a year later) and, after a failed affair, disliked Ted Drake, her love interest. Scenes of the vulnerability of its domestic harmony, Garland's nervy performance, and Margaret O'Brien, the best of all the child stars, as her morbid sister, add the necessary spice to the sweetness.

☆ **Catherine Breillat**
Director, Writer ☆

1. Ai no corrida (Oshima)
2. Sawdust and Tinsel (Bergman)
3. Baby Doll (Kazan)
4. Lost Highway (Lynch)
5. Vertigo (Hitchcock)
6. Salò (Pasolini)
7. L'Avventura (Antonioni)
8. Ordet (Dreyer)
9. Lancelot du Lac (Bresson)
10. Ten (Kiarostami)

☆ **Gurinder Chadha**
Director ☆

1. Tokyo Story (Ozu)
2. Bicycle Thieves (De Sica)
3. Kes (Loach)
4. West Side Story (Wise)
5. Baiju Bawra (Bhatt)
6. Raining Stones (Loach)
7. William Shakespeare's Romeo and Juliet (Luhrmann)
8. Purab Aur Pachim (Kumar)
9. Up the Junction (Loach)
10. Car Wash (Schultz)

☆ **Roger Corman**
Producer ☆

1. Potemkin (Eisenstein)
2. Citizen Kane (Welles)
3. The Seventh Seal (Bergman)
4. Lawrence of Arabia (Lean)
5. The Godfather (Coppola)
6. The Grapes of Wrath (Ford)
7. Shane (Stevens)
8. On the Waterfront (Kazan)
9. Star Wars (Lucas)
10. The Cabinet of Dr. Caligari (Wiene)
11. Tokyo Story (Ozu)

Saving Private Ryan
US   1998   169m   Technicolor
Paramount/Amblin/Mutual (Steven Spielberg, Ian
Bryce, Mark Gordon, Gary Levinsohn)
◙ ▬ ◎ ⌕ ◉ ◎ ⌂

w Robert Rodat *d* Steven Spielberg *ph* Janusz Kaminski
m John Williams *pd* Tom Sanders *ad* Alan Tomkins, Tom
Brown, Daniel T. Dorrance, Ricky Eyres, Chris Seagers
ed Michael Kahn

☆ Tom Hanks (Captain Miller), Edward Burns (Private
Reiben), Tom Sizemore (Sergeant Horvath), Jeremy Davies
(Corporal Upham), Vin Diesel (Private Caparzo), Adam
Goldberg (Private Mellish), Barry Pepper (Private Jackson),
Giovanni Ribisi (T/4 Medic Wade), Matt Damon (Private
Ryan), Dennis Farina (Lieutenant Colonel Anderson), Ted
Danson (Captain Hamill), Harve Presnell (General
Marshall), Harrison Young (Ryan as Old Man)

'As powerful, devastating, memorable and moving
as movies get.' – *Ian Freer, Empire*

'One of the greatest war movies ever made.'
– *James Cameron-Wilson, Film Review*

● The film took more than $460m at the box-office
worldwide.
👤 Steven Spielberg; Janusz Kaminski; Michael Kahn;
sound; sound effects editing
🏆 best picture; Tom Hanks; Robert Rodat; John Williams;
Tom Sanders; make-up
🏆 visual effects; sound

581
Saving Private Ryan

*Eight soldiers are sent on a mission to bring back a private from
behind enemy lines.*

In his drama of the D-Day landings and its aftermath, Steven Spielberg
provides a virtuoso demonstration of the director's art in his staging of
two battles, the opening sequence on the Omaha beach and a later one
in a ruined town. They go beyond naturalism, into a hyperkinetic world
of blood and bullets. Spielberg heightens the reality of war to create the
terrifying equivalent of its effect on its participants. In between, though,
the film settles for a standard platoon-in-peril routine, as after surviving the battle on the beaches, eight soldiers are sent on a special mission to bring back a private, the only survivor of four brothers, who is
stranded somewhere behind enemy lines. Tom Hanks' Captain, confidently leading his men he knows not where, carries the film through
these more conventional moments so that it remains an astonishing
tour de force on the appalling nature of armed conflict and the courage
of those involved in its horrors.

Scenes from a Marriage

Sweden 1973 168m colour
Cinematograph (Ingmar Bergman)
📽 ▤ ⊚ ⊛

original title: *Scener Ur Ett äktenskap*

wd Ingmar Bergman *ph* Sven Nykvist *m* none *ad* Björn Thulin *ed* Siv Lundgren

☆ *Liv Ullmann* (Marianne), *Erland Josephson* (Johan), Bibi Andersson (Katarina), Jan Malmsjö (Peter), Gunnel Lindblom (Eva), Anita Wall (Mrs. Palm)

'Shows how habit and conciliatory effort erode communication. But it is ultimately an optimistic film, suggesting that beyond the hell of a return to zero, the knowledge of one's absolute separateness from others can lead through despair to a glowing fulfilment.' – *Jan Dawson, MFB*

580
Scenes from a Marriage

Over a decade a divorced couple dissect what went wrong with their marriage.

Ingmar Bergman edited his film from six 50-minute episodes made for television, dealing with the breakdown of a marriage after ten years; over the next ten years, the former husband and wife continue to meet. The structure of the original remains, with each episode given its own title, moving from *Innocence and Panic*, with an apparently happy marriage on display, to *In the Middle of the Night in a Dark House Somewhere in the World*, with the couple by now remarried to others, but seeking solace with each other. The time-span gives the characters room to develop: the husband from complacency to wry understanding, the wife from subservience to individuality. It is an unsparing and detailed examination of a relationship, marked more by pain than pleasure, but reaching a hopeful conclusion; it is also, despite its claustrophobic style, of a succession of close-ups of talking heads, riveting cinema.

A Private Function

GB 1984 94m colour
Handmade (Mark Shivas)
📽 ▤ ⊚ ⊛

w Alan Bennett *d* Malcolm Mowbray *ph* Tony Pierce-Roberts *m* John Du Prez *pd* Stuart Walker *ad* Michael Porter, Judith Lang *ed* Barrie Vince

☆ Michael Palin (Gilbert Chilvers), Maggie Smith (Joyce Chilvers), *Denholm Elliott* (Dr. Swaby), Richard Griffiths (Allardyce), Tony Haygarth (Sutcliff), *Liz Smith* (Mother), John Normington (Lockwood)

'A comedy of immense if often scatalogical charm.' – *Vincent Canby*

Ⓣ Maggie Smith; Liz Smith (supporting actress); Denholm Elliott (supporting actor)

579
A Private Function

In 1947 Yorkshire, a family secretly fatten an unlicensed pig.

Alan Bennett's sharply-detailed comedy of greed and social climbing, set in the austerity of 1947 Britain, centred around a Yorkshire chiropodist who kidnaps and secretly fattens an unlicensed pig, which was being kept by the town's leading citizens for a special civic dinner. It is a class-conscious farce, with Michael Palin's timid chiropodist contrasted with Denholm Elliott's snobbish doctor, who refers to him as 'a silly little bunion-clipping pillock'. There are performances to delight in from Palin and Maggie Smith as a child-hating, social-climbing wife, while the rationing restrictions on food are allied with attitudes to sex and to social acceptance; it is the prospect of a feast that brings with it a wider sense of community.

'Five charming sisters on the gayest, merriest manhunt that ever snared a bewildered bachelor! Girls! take a lesson from these husband hunters!'

Pride and Prejudice
US 1940 116m bw
MGM (Hunt Stromberg)

w Aldous Huxley, Jane Murfin *play* Helen Jerome *novel* Jane Austen *d* Robert Z. Leonard *ph* Karl Freund *m* Herbert Stothart *ad* Cedric Gibbons, Paul Groesse *ed* Robert J. Kern

☆ *Laurence Olivier* (Mr. Darcy), *Greer Garson* (Elizabeth Bennet), *Edmund Gwenn* (Mr. Bennet), *Mary Boland* (Mrs. Bennet), *Melville Cooper* (Mr. Collins), *Edna May Oliver* (Lady Catherine de Bourgh), Karen Morley (Charlotte Lucas), Frieda Inescort (Miss Caroline Bingley), Bruce Lester (Mr. Bingley), Edward Ashley (Mr. Wickham), Ann Rutherford (Lydia Bennet), Maureen O'Sullivan (Jane Bennet), E. E. Clive (Sir William Lucas), Heather Angel (Kitty Bennet), Marsha Hunt (Mary Bennet)

'The most deliciously pert comedy of old manners, the most crisp and crackling satire in costume that we can remember ever having seen on the screen.' – *Bosley Crowther*

● Norma Shearer and Robert Donat had been the first choices for the stars, with George Cukor directing.
🏆 art direction

578
Pride and Prejudice

An opinionated young lady of the early 19th century wins herself a rich husband she had at first despised for his pride.

Jane Austen's splendid romantic comedy was blessed with an excellent cast. Aldous Huxley, an incongruous figure among Hollywood screenwriters, was involved with the script, based on Helen Jerome's play rather than Austen's novel. He was not happy with the work, writing, 'the insistence upon the story, as opposed to the diffuse irony with which the story is designed to contain, is a major falsification.' The result, nevertheless, was full of pleasurable moments, with Laurence Olivier's performance as Darcy adding that note of irony which lifted it above the mundane.

Pretty Village Pretty Flame
Serbia 1996 129m colour 'Scope
Guild Pathé/Cobra/RTV/MCRC (Goran Bjelogrlic, Dragan Bjelogrlic, Nikola Kojo, Milko Josifov)

original title: *Lepa Sela Lepo Gore*
w Vanja Bulic, Srdan Dragojevic, Nikola Pejakovic *d* Srdan Dragojevic *ph* Dusan Joksimovic *m* Aleksandar Sasa Habic *pd* Milenko Jeremic *ed* Petar Markovic

☆ Dragan Bjelogrlic (Milan), Nikola Kojo (Velja), Dragan Maksimovic (Petar), Velimir Bata Zivojlinovic (Gvozden), Zoran Cvijanovic (Brzi), Milorad Mandic (Gavra), Dragan Petrovic (Laza)

'It's enough to know this one has plenty of action, a witty script, buckets of blood, a couple of sex scenes and is pretty darned good.' – *Jake Hamilton, Empire*

577
Pretty Village Pretty Flame

Two friends from boyhood, one Serbian, the other Muslim, find themselves on opposite sides in a civil war.

This is an angry, bitter film, about the madness of the conflict that overwhelmed Yugoslavia, from Srdan Dragojevic, who trained, and was born, in Belgrade. It shifts back and forth in time to illumine the lives of those caught up in the craziness, focusing on two boyhood friends who find themselves on opposing sides in the civil war. Much of the action takes place in a tunnel, where a Muslim army besieges a small Serbian force, which is led by a Communist who recalls with nostalgia the time of Tito. It is a despairing account of long buried grievances overcoming reasoned responses, containing a damning portrait of a vicious profiteer of hatred, who bears the same name as the Serbian leader Slobodan Milosevic.

Once Were Warriors

New Zealand 1994 103m Eastmancolor
Entertainment/Communicado/NZFC/Avalon/New
Zealand On Air (Robin Scholes)

◧ ▤ ◕ ◉ ◉ ◌

w Riwia Brown *novel* Alan Duff *d* Lee Tamahori
ph Stuart Dryburgh *m* Murray Grindley, Murray McNabb
pd Michael Kane *ad* Shayne Radford *ed* Michael Horton
☆ *Rena Owen* (Beth Heke), *Temuera Morrison* (Jake
Heke), Mamaengaroa Kerr-Bell (Grace Heke), Julian
Arahanga (Nig Heke), Taungaroa Emile (Boogie Heke),
Rachael Morris (Polly Heke), Joseph Kairau (Huata Heke),
Clifford Curtis (Bully)

'Unflinchingly scans the domestic tragedy which
can be found in any culture where hope is a luxury
no one can afford.' – *Time*

'It's certainly operatic in style and melodramatic in
concept. It shouldn't work as well as it does. But by
flinging caution to the winds, it winds up mightily
effective.' – *Derek Malcolm, Guardian*

● It took more money at the New Zealand box-office than
any other film so far.
● A sequel *What Becomes of the Broken-Hearted?*
followed in 1999.
● A Region 1 DVD release includes commentary by Lee
Tamahori.

576
Once Were Warriors

In Auckland, a Maori mother struggles to raise her family against the odds.

Lee Tamahori's emotionally powerful portrait of a dysfunctional urban Maori family brought to screen a people not seen before. It showed a Maori mother attempting to bring up her children, who included a bookish daughter and a son attracted to street gangs, while trying to cope with her unemployed, heavy-drinking and violent husband. It was an often disturbing drama of the dispossessed, making its points with sledgehammer force, but also giving a place to the tenderness and pride that existed within a family forced to the edge of society. It was enhanced by the superb performances of Rena Owen as the mother and Temuera Morrison as a loving, but brutal, husband.

Mr Blandings Builds His Dream House

US 1948 84m bw
RKO (Norman Panama, Melvin Frank)

◧ ▤ ◕ ◌

w Norman Panama, Melvin Frank *novel* Eric Hodgins
d H. C. Potter *ph* James Wong Howe *m* Leigh Harline
md Constantin Bakaleinikoff *ad* Albert S. D'Agostino,
Carroll Clark *ed* Harry Marker
☆ *Cary Grant* (Jim Blandings), *Myrna Loy* (Muriel
Blandings), *Melvyn Douglas* (Bill Cole), *Reginald Denny*
(Simms), Louise Beavers (Gussie), Ian Wolfe (Smith), Harry
Shannon (Tesander), Nestor Paiva (Joe Apollonio), Jason
Robards (John Retch), Lex Barker (Carpenter Foreman)

'A bulls-eye for middle-class middlebrows.'
– *James Agee*

'I loved it. That was really a pleasure to make.'
– *H. C. Potter, 1973*

575
Mr Blandings Builds His Dream House

A New York advertising man longs to live in the Connecticut country-side, but finds the way to rural satisfaction is hard.

A comedy that skewers the dream of city dwellers to leave their cramped apartments and move to large houses in the country. Cary Grant brings an amusing bewilderment to the role of a New York advertising man who finds that change is difficult. He buys an old house and begins to renovate it, then discovers the only way to save it is to destroy it and start again. Myrna Loy's sharp comic timing matches Grant's, as a wife who knows how she wants each room to look but has trouble explaining that to the decorators, who sum up her delicate, matching colour schemes as ' Red, green, blue, yellow, white… Correct!' The film was remade as the less successful *The Money Pit* in 1987 and under its original title in 2005.

Out of Sight
US   1998   123m   DeLuxe
Universal/Jersey (Danny de Vito, Michael Shamberg, Stacey Sher)
▣ ▤ ◎ ◎ ◎ ⌒
w Scott Frank *novel* Elmore Leonard *d* Steven Soderbergh *ph* Elliot Davis *m* Cliff Martinez *pd* Gary Frutkoff *ad* Phil Messina *ed* Anne V. Coates
☆ George Clooney (Jack Foley), Jennifer Lopez (Karen Sisco), Vingh Rhames (Buddy Bragg), Don Cheadle (Maurice (Snoopy) Miller), Dennis Farina (Marshall Sisco), Albert Brooks (Richard Ripley)

'There's no getting away with the simplicity of its success – great script based on a good book, good actors working with great characters, a great director empowered to be great again.' – *Ian Nathan, Empire*

● Region 1 and 2 DVD releases include commentary by Steven Soderbergh and Scott Frank.
♟ Scott Frank; Anne V. Coates

574
Out of Sight

A bank robber and a federal marshal fall for each other, despite being on opposite sides of the law.

A thriller disguised as a romantic comedy, acted and directed with the necessary light touch. George Clooney plays a bank robber who kidnaps a federal marshal (Jennifer Lopez); they begin to fall for each other, despite being on opposite sides of the law. Clooney brings vulnerability to his role as a veteran crook wondering if it is too late to go straight after one more heist, and Lopez has a naturalness not seen before or since. Elmore Leonard plots his novels with the intricate mathematical precision of a farce. Within this machine-like interlocking, Soderbergh allows room for romance to flower, while dazzling with his technical expertise in orchestrating the flash forwards and back with which he gives impetus to the absorbing story.

The Wind
US   1928   75m   bw
MGM
▤ ◎
w Frances Marion *novel* Dorothy Scarborough *d* Victor Sjostrom *ph* John Arnold *ed* Conrad A. Nervig
☆ *Lillian Gish* (Letty), Lars Hanson (Lige), Montagu Love (Roddy Wirt), Dorothy Cummings (Cora)

'So penetrating is the atmosphere that one can almost feel the wind itself and taste the endless dust.' – *Georges Sadoul*

'Unrelieved by the ghost of a smile … but its relentlessness is gripping … a fine and dignified achievement.' – *Pictureplay*

● New version by Thames Silents 1984.

573
The Wind

A sheltered Virginia girl goes to live on the rough and windy Texas prairie, marries a man she does not love and kills a would-be rapist.

In her last silent film, Lillian Gish gave one of her best performances under the worst conditions of her career, as a sheltered Virginia girl who goes to live on the rough and windy Texas prairie, marries a man she doesn't love and kills a would-be rapist. The central character is the wind, and she found herself having sand blown at her by eight airplane propellers while sulphur pots were used to suggest a sandstorm's murk. A psychological melodrama of a woman being driven mad by masculine desire, the film was given a stunning visual quality by director Victor Sjostrom and cinematographer John Arnold. MGM imposed on it a happy ending, which caused Sjostrom to leave Hollywood and return to his native Sweden.

'The closer you are to death. The more you realize you are alive.'

Touching the Void
GB/US 2003 106m colour
Pathé/Film4/Film Council/Darlow Smithson
▭ ▤ ◉ ◉

book Joe Simpson *d* Kevin Macdonald *ph* Mike Eley
m Alex Heffes *ad* Patrick Bill *ed* Justine Wright
☆ Brendan Mackey (Joe Simpson), Nicholas Aaron (Simon Yates), Ollie Ryall (Richard Hawking), Joe Simpson (as himself), Simon Yates (as himself), Richard Hawking (as himself)

'A gripping testament to survival in the face of unimaginably harsh odds, and won't be quickly forgotten.' – *Anthony Quinn, Independent*

'Compelling stuff, but there is something deeply distracting in the use of recreated material.' – *David Kehr, New York Times*

🇹 British film

572
Touching the Void

Two mountaineers recall the disastrous accident during a dangerous climb in Peru in 1985 that left one of them for dead.

Kevin Macdonald used a fascinating mix of documentary, commentary and actors in a brilliant re-creation of a mountaineering classic. While actors play them in a beautiful, icy, mountainous landscape, Joe Simpson and Simon Yates recall a disastrous accident in 1985, during a dangerous climb in Peru. It left Simpson dangling over the side of the mountain with a broken leg, and Yates unable to help. Eventually, Yates felt he had no option but to cut the rope that joined them, believing that his action would kill his companion, if he were not already dead. Simpson somehow survived and, despite his injuries, made his way back to the base camp. Macdonald's re-creation is more tense and frightening than any horror movie, giving a real sense of the terror felt by both men. It is less about climbing than the survival of the human spirit.

The Ghost Goes West
GB 1935 85m bw
London Films (Alexander Korda)
▭ ▤ ◉

w Robert E. Sherwood, Geoffrey Kerr *story* Eric Keown
d René Clair *ph* Harold Rosson *m* Mischa Spoliansky
ed Harold Earle-Fishbacher, Henry Cornelius
☆ Robert Donat (Murdoch/Donald Glourie), Jean Parker (Peggy Martin), Eugene Pallette (Joe Martin), Elsa Lanchester (Lady Shepperton), Ralph Bunker (Ed Bigelow), Patricia Hilliard (Shepherdess), Morton Selten (Gavin Glourie)

'Fine business likely in the keys, but not for the tanks.' – *Variety*

'Although the film is not cast in the fluid, rapidly paced style of Clair's typical work, it has a sly wit and an adroitness of manner that make it delightful.' – *André Sennwald, New York Times*

'It is typical of the British film industry that M. René Clair should be brought to this country to direct a Scottish film full of what must to him be rather incomprehensible jokes about whisky and bagpipes, humorous fantasy without any social significance, realistic observation, or genuine satire.' – *Graham Greene*

571
The Ghost Goes West

When a millionaire buys a Scottish castle and transports it stone by stone to America, the castle ghost goes too.

Robert Donat gave a splendid star performance in this amusing whimsy about a ghost who haunts a Scottish castle; when a millionaire buys it and transports it stone by stone to America, the ghost goes too. Donat played both the ghost and its present day descendant, while there was a sprightly on-screen romance between him and Jean Arthur, as the millionaire's daughter. René Clair directed with a light touch and an attention to detail. As Donat said, 'no finer choice could have been made.'

The People vs. Larry Flynt
US 1996 130m Technicolor Panavision
Columbia TriStar/Ixtlan/Phoenix (Oliver Stone, Janet Yang, Michael Hausman)

▣ ▤ ◎⌣ ◎ ◎ ◠

w Scott Alexander, Larry Karaszewski *d* Miloš Forman *ph* Philippe Rousselot *m* Thomas Newman *pd* Patrizia von Brandenstein *ad* Shawn Hausman, James Nezda *ed* Christopher Tellefsen

☆ *Woody Harrelson* (Larry Flynt), *Courtney Love* (Althea Leasure), *Edward Norton* (Isaacman), James Cromwell (Charles Keating), Crispin Glover (Arlo), James Carville (Simon Leis), Brett Harrelson (Jimmy Flynt), Donna Hanover (Ruth Carter Stapleton)

'That Forman has found the raucous, satirical side of Larry Flynt's story doesn't surprise us; that he has uncovered its pathos, and something that could even be considered its patriotism, is a stunning achievement.' – *David Ansen, Newsweek*

● Larry Flynt himself appears as the judge who sentenced him early in his career to 25 years' imprisonment on charges of obscenity and links to organized crime.
● Regions 1 and 2 special edition DVDs include commentary by Woody Harrelson, Edward Norton and Courtney Love, Scott Alexander and Larry Karaszewski.
♟ Milos Forman; Woody Harrelson

570
The People vs. Larry Flynt

A poor Kentucky boy becomes a successful publisher of porn magazines, and takes his fight to protect his business and freedom of speech to the Supreme Court.

There is an irony at the heart of this witty movie, which is a biopic of a successful pornographer, a poor Kentucky boy who grew up to publish *Hustler* magazine and inadvertently became the champion of freedom of speech by taking his fight to protect his business to the Supreme Court. It is an engaging portrait of the extremes and excesses – sexual, religious, judicial and political – of modern American society. Woody Harrelson's performance both comments on, and delights in, Larry Flynt's vulgarity and tastelessness, and Courtney Love is convincing as the stripper who married him. Miloš Forman had the benefit of being an observant outsider, and his direction has the light, comic touch of his Czech films.

'The greatest comedy ever made!'

The Great Race
🕂 US 1965 163m Technicolor Super Panavision
Warner/Patricia/Jalem/Reynard (Martin Jurow)

▣ ▤ ◎⌣ ◎ ◠

w Arthur Ross *d* Blake Edwards *ph* Russell Harlan *m* Henry Mancini *pd* Fernando Carrere *ed* Ralph E. Winters

☆ *Jack Lemmon* (Prof. Fate), *Tony Curtis* (The Great Leslie), *Peter Falk* (Max), *Natalie Wood* (Maggie DuBois), George Macready (Gen. Kuhster), Ross Martin (Baron Rolfe Von Stuppe), Vivian Vance (Hester Goodbody), Dorothy Provine (Lily Olay)

'The most expensive comedy ever filmed; but there the superlatives end: it is not exactly the worst.' – *Time*

♟ Russell Harlan; song 'The Sweetheart Tree' (*m* Henry Mancini, *ly* Johnny Mercer)

569
The Great Race

In 1908, The Great Leslie and Professor Fate are favourites in the first New York to Paris car race.

Thia elaborate comedy spectacular has many good moments about the first New York to Paris car race in 1908, when The Great Leslie (Tony Curtis) and the villainous Professor Fate (Jack Lemmon) are leading contenders. During filming, Curtis clashed with Lemmon and Natalie Wood, who played a seductive journalist (Blake Edwards said the party at the end of the film would be quite an occasion, 'Natalie and Tony are going to set each other on fire'). But the set pieces worked well, notably the early disasters, a Western saloon brawl, and a custard pie fight. Elsewhere, there was more evidence of an oversize budget than of wit or finesse, and the entire *Prisoner of Zenda* spoof could have been omitted. But it is full of excellent production detail and general good humour.

Doctor Mabuse the Gambler

Germany   1922   101m (24 fps)   bw   silent
UFA (Erich Pommer)
📽 ▀ ⓢ ⓦ
original title: *Doktor Mabuse, der Spieler*
w Thea von Harbou, Fritz Lang *novel* Norbert Jacques
d Fritz Lang *ph* Carl Hoffman *ad* Otto Hunte, Stahl-Urach,
Erich Kettelhut, Karl Vollbrecht
☆ Rudolf Klein-Rogge (Dr. Mabuse), Alfred Abel (Graf
Told), Gertrude Welcker (Graefin Told), Lil Dagover, Paul
Richter (Edgar Hull)
● Originally issued in Germany in two parts, *Der Grosse
Spieler* and *Inferno*, adding up to a much longer running
time.
● Sequels were, *The Testament of Dr Mabuse* and *The
Thousand Eyes of Dr Mabuse*.

568
Doctor Mabuse the Gambler

A criminal mastermind uses hypnotism and blackmail in his efforts to obtain world domination, but when finally cornered is discovered to be a raving maniac.

Doctor Mabuse is a real wallow in German post-war depression and melodrama, in the form of a Fu Manchu/Moriarty type thriller. Fritz Lang later claimed that the film was in part inspired by Al Capone, and it ends with a spectacular shoot-out between police and gangsters. For its time, it was an astounding film with political implications. Rudolf Klein-Rogge, who played Mabuse, regarded him as 'a symptom of a Europe that was falling apart'; he could also be seen as a foreshadowing of Hitler's rise to power.

The Palm Beach Story

US   1942   88m   bw
Paramount (Paul Jones)
▀ ⓠ ⓦ
wd Preston Sturges *ph* Victor Milner *m* Victor Young
ad Hans Dreier, Ernst Fegte *ed* Stuart Gilmore
☆ *Claudette Colbert* (Gerry Jeffers), *Joel McCrea* (Tom
Jeffers), *Rudy Vallee* (J.D. Hackensacker III), Mary Astor
(Princess Centimillia), Sig Arno (Toto), Robert Warwick (Mr.
Hinch), Torben Meyer (Dr. Kluck), Jimmy Conlin (Mr.
Asweld), William Demarest (Member of Ale and Quail Club),
Jack Norton (Member of Ale and Quail Club), Robert Greig
(Member of Ale and Quail Club), Roscoe Ates (Member of
Ale and Quail Club), Chester Conklin (Member of Ale and
Quail Club), Franklin Pangborn (Manager), Alan Bridge
(Conductor) and also *Robert Dudley*

'Surprises and delights as though nothing of the
kind had been known before … farce and
tenderness are combined without a fault.' –
William Whitebait

'Minus even a hint of the war … packed with
delightful absurdities.' – *Variety*

567
The Palm Beach Story

The wife of an engineer goes to Florida to get herself a millionaire.

Preston Sturges was at his most brilliant if uncontrolled in his flighty comedy about the wife of a penurious engineer who takes off for Florida to set her sights on a millionaire. Inconsequential in itself, it is decorated with zany scenes, characters and touches. Sturges was amused by the irresponsible rich ('millionaires are fun,' he once wrote). At the same time he insisted that it was sex, rather than money, that makes the world go round. As Gerry (Claudette Colbert) tells Tom (Joel McCrea), 'You have no idea what a long-legged girl can do without doing anything.'

Journey into Fear
US 1942 71m bw
RKO (Orson Welles)
🟦 🔍~

w *Joseph Cotten, Orson Welles* novel *Eric Ambler*
d *Norman Foster (and Orson Welles)* ph *Karl Struss*
m *Roy Webb* md *Constantin Bakaleinikoff* ad *Albert S. D'Agostino, Mark-Lee Kirk* ed *Mark Robson*
☆ *Joseph Cotten* (Graham), Dolores del Rio (Josette), Jack Moss (Banat), Orson Welles (Col. Haki), Ruth Warrick (Stephanie), Agnes Moorehead (Mme. Mathews)

'Brilliant atmosphere, the nightmare of pursuit, eccentric encounters on the way, and when the shock comes it leaps at eye and ear.' – *William Whitebait*

● A 1976 remake, much heralded, was for obscure legal reasons hardly seen. Directed by Daniel Mann for New World, it starred Zero Mostel, Shelley Winters, Stanley Holloway, Vincent Price, Donald Pleasence, Sam Waterston, Joseph Wiseman, Scott Marlowe and Yvette Mimieux.

566
Journey into Fear

A munitions expert finds himself in danger from assassins in Istanbul and has to be smuggled home.

A highly enjoyable impressionist melodrama that might have been even better without studio interference. Welles wrote the script with Joseph Cotten while they were making *The Magnificent Ambersons*, but left the directing to another friend, Norman Foster. Welles was away when most of it was shot, only returning at the end to try to salvage it after RKO cut it to shreds in post-production ('run through a broken lawn-mower,' said Welles), removing all the atmospheric touches to concentrate on a mundane story of the smuggling out of Istanbul of a munitions expert in danger from assassins. Welles shot extra scenes with Cotten, and the film is full of his touches and excesses.

'Sometimes love isn't enough.'
Lantana
Australia/Germany 2001 121m Technicolor Panavision
Winchester/AFFC/MPB (Jan Chapman)
🔲 🟦 🔍 🎧

w *Andrew Bovell* play *Speaking in Tongues* by Andrew Bovell d *Ray Lawrence* ph *Mandy Walker* m *Paul Kelly* pd *Kim Buddee* ed *Karl Sodersten*
☆ Anthony LaPaglia (Leon Zat), Geoffrey Rush (John Knox), Barbara Hershey (Dr Valerie Somers), Kerry Armstrong (Sonja Zat), Rachael Blake (Jane O'May), Vince Colosimo (Nik D'Amato), Daniela Farinacci (Paula D'Amato), Peter Phelps (Patrick Phelan)

'Elegant but never overstated, sinister but never coldhearted, this is a note-perfect masterwork on a modest, human scale.' – *Andrew O'Hehir, Salon.com*

'It was subtle, really interesting, and it also possessed a word I would use with great care: integrity.' – *Harold Pinter*

565
Lantana

In Sydney, a policeman investigates the disappearance of a psychiatrist and uncovers guilty secrets.

Ray Lawrence, an Australian director of commercials making his second feature in sixteen years, managed a tense exploration of prickly relationships in this film of an unhappily married Sydney policeman investigating the disappearance of a psychiatrist, and uncovering guilty secrets in several lives. A well-crafted and -acted movie, it is less a murder mystery than an examination of messy lives, providing both suspense and insight into modern manners and customs. The film's title is taken from the name of a thorny, tropical shrub that has grown out of control, as have the emotions of the unusual suspects in this thriller.

Our Relations

Our Relations
US   1936   65m   bw
Hal Roach/Stan Laurel Productions

w Richard Connell, Felix Adler, Charles Rogers, Jack Jevne
story The Money Box by W. W. Jacobs d Harry Lachman
ph Rudolph Maté ad William Stevens, Arthur I. Royce
ed Bert Jordan
☆ Stan Laurel (Himself/Alfie Laurel), Oliver Hardy
(Himself/Bert Hardy), James Finlayson (Finn, the Chief
Engineer), Alan Hale (Joe Groagan, the Waiter), Sidney Toler
(Captain of the S.S. Periwinkle), Daphne Pollard (Mrs.
Daphne Hardy), Iris Adrian (Alice, the Beer Garden Girl),
Noel Madison (Gangster), Ralf Harolde (Gangster), Arthur
Housman (Inebriated Stroller)

564
Our Relations

Two sailors get mixed up with their long-lost twin brothers.

This fast-moving comedy contains some of Laurel and Hardy's most polished work. It is also their most satisfying production, in which two sailors, the black sheep of their family, are entrusted with a diamond ring and get mistaken for their long lost and happily married twin brothers. A little inspiration was provided by Shakespeare's classic play about twins *The Comedy of Errors*. There may be a little too much plot, which doesn't allow the pair time for leisurely comedy, but there are some hilarious moments of inspired comedy, including a routine where they teeter on the edge of the waterfront after gangsters encase their feet in bowls of cement.

Zamani Baraye Masti Asbha

Zamani Baraye Masti Asbha
Iran   2000   80m   colour
Porter Frith/B.H. (Bahman Ghobadi)

GB title: A Time for Drunken Horses
wd Bahman Ghobadi ph Saed Nikzat m Hossein Alizadeh
ed Samad Tavazoi
☆ Amaneh Ekhtiar-Dini, Madi Ekhtiar-Dini, Ayoub
Ahmadi, Rouvin Younessi, Nezhad Ekhtiar-Dini

'The film carries a searing emotional charge.'
– Geoffrey Macnab, Sight and Sound

563
Zamani Baraye Masti Asbha

A young Kurdish orphan joins a group of smugglers in order to raise money for treatment for his dying and disabled brother.

Bahman Ghobadi's harsh, moving documentary-style feature shows the life of a young Kurdish orphan whose only means of raising the money to treat his dying brother is to join a group of smugglers. This is life lived at the extreme of hardship and poverty – the title refers to the alcohol-laced water given to the mules in order that they can cope with the snow-bound journeys – told without sentimentality and using non-professional actors. Ghobadi's camera captures the terrible beauty of the mountainous landscape, thigh-deep in snow, and the terrifying predicament of the orphaned children, whose heartbreaking care and affection for one another will not be sufficient for their survival.

'Oh, my God ... that's my daughter.'

Hardcore
US   1979   108m   Metrocolor
Columbia/A-Team (John Milius)
▤ ◉~ ⊘
GB title: *The Hardcore Life*
wd Paul Schrader *ph* Michael Chapman *m* Jack Nitzsche
ad Edwin O'Donovan *ed* Tom Rolf
☆ *George C. Scott* (Jake Van Dorn), Peter Boyle (Andy
Mast), Season Hubley (Niki), Dick Sargent (Wes DeJong),
Leonard Gaines (Ramada)

'Flawed and uneven, it contains moments of pure
revelation.' – *Roger Ebert*

562
Hardcore

A father goes in search of his daughter, who has become a porn actress.

An intense and solemn treatment of a situation that could have gone over the top, and very nearly does: a religious man from Michigan journeys to California in search of his daughter, who has taken to appearing in porno films. The acting saves it, notably George Scott's fervent Calvinist who is forced for the first time to defend and examine his beliefs, and Season Hubley, as a prostitute he meets along the way, who shares his contempt for sex.

The Nasty Girl
West Germany   1990   92m   Eastmancolor
Mainline/Sentana/ZDF
▧ ▤ ◉~ ⊘
original title: *Das Schreckliche Mädchen*
wd Michael Verhoeven *ph* Axel de Roche *m* Mike
Hertung, Elmar Schloter, Billy Gorlt, Lydie Auvray
ad Hubert Popp *ed* Barbara Hennings
☆ Lena Stolze (Sonja), Monika Baumgartner (Maria),
Michael Gahr (Paul Rosenberger), Fred Stillkrauth (Uncle),
Elisabeth Bertram (Grandmother), Robert Giggenbach
(Martin), Karin Thaler (Nina), Hans-Reinhard Muller (Dr.
Juckenack)

'The story itself is fascinating, but the style seems
to add another tone, a level of irony that is
somehow confusing.' – *Roger Ebert*

'Energetic, black-comic celebration of a gutsy gal
news-gatherer and the high cost of digging for
truth.' – *Rita Kempley, Washington Post*

♟ best foreign film
♛ best foreign film

561
The Nasty Girl

Despite local hostility, a girl researches into events in her home town during the Nazi regime.

Michael Verhoeven's film uses a documentary approach to his social satire about a young German woman who takes it on herself to discover the truth about her home town and its role in the Holocaust. The style is almost light-hearted, often witty and exuberant in its use of images, but the content is more serious. It deals perceptively with a collective amnesia about the war and a refusal to open up historical archives to discover buried truths.

'I'm decent, I tell ya! Nobody's got the right to call me names!'

'The picture Hollywood said could never be made!'

Of Mice and Men
US   1939   107m   bw
Hal Roach (Lewis Milestone)
▬   ⦿

w Eugene Solow *novel* John Steinbeck *d* Lewis Milestone *ph* Norbert Brodine *m* Aaron Copland *ad* Nicolai Remisoff *ed* Bert Jordan
☆ *Burgess Meredith* (George), *Lon Chaney Jnr* (Lennie), *Betty Field* (Mae), Charles Bickford (Slim), Roman Bohnen (Candy), Bob Steele (Curley), Noah Beery Jnr (Whit)

'The film is excellently acted by everyone … there are, mercifully, no stars to intrude their tedious flat personalities into this picture of life. It is a picture which, for all its grief, is not depressing; and if it should be said that this is no time for adding to one's own melancholy, let me reply that it is sometimes well not to lose from sight the individual pity of the lives of men.' – *Dilys Powell*

⚖ best picture; Aaron Copland

560
Of Mice and Men

An itinerant worker looks after his mentally retarded cousin, a giant who doesn't know his own strength.

Lewis Milestone made a sensitive film of John Steinbeck's classic novella set in America during the Great Depression. He was as alert to the landscape these two drifters move through as to the strengths and weaknesses of the individuals caught up in events they cannot control. The acting could not be bettered. Lon Chaney Jnr gave the best performance of his career as the huge and simple-minded Lennie who inadvertently kills the things he loves. Burgess Meredith wonderfully conveyed the dreamer as well as the protective friend, and Betty Field was convincing as a bored, rustic flirt. They are people ill-matched for the tragedy that befalls them, which is what gives the story its universal appeal. Steinbeck approved; he thought Milestone and the others had done 'a beautiful job'.

'Six sticks of dynamite that blasted his way to freedom … and awoke America's conscience!'

I am a Fugitive from a Chain Gang
US   1932   90m   bw
Warner (Hal B. Wallis)
▬   ⦿~

w Howard J. Green, Brown Holmes *book* Robert E. Burns *d* Mervyn LeRoy *ph* Sol Polito *m* Bernhard Kaun *ad* Jack Okey *ed* William Holmes
☆ *Paul Muni* (James Allen), Glenda Farrell (Marie Woods), Helen Vinson (Helen), Preston Foster (Pete), Allen Jenkins (Barney Sykes), Edward J. Macnamara (Warden), Berton Churchill (Judge), Edward Ellis (Bomber Wells)

'A picture with guts … everything about it is technically 100 per cent … shy on romantic angles, but should get nice money all over.' – *Variety*

'To be enthusiastically commended for its courage, artistic sincerity, dramatic vigour, high entertainment concept and social message.' – *Wilton A. Barrett*

'I quarrel with the production not because it is savage and horrible, but because each step in an inevitable tragedy is taken clumsily, and because each character responsible for the hero's doom is shown more as a caricature than as a person.' – *Pare Lorentz*

⚖ best picture; Paul Muni

559
I am a Fugitive from a Chain Gang

An innocent man is convicted and after brutal treatment with the chain gang becomes a vicious criminal on the run.

Made in a semi-documentary manner, this horrifying story of a man's imprisonment and subsequent escape was a milestone in Hollywood history. Based on a true story, the film succeeded by what it didn't show: when James Allen (Paul Muni) is flogged by the guards, director Mervyn LeRoy filmed only the shadow of the beating on a wall, intercut with other prisoners' shocked faces. The film was effective in getting changes made to the chain gang system in Georgia. It is still a compelling piece of shock entertainment.

'Somewhere in the universe, there must be something better than man!'

Planet of the Apes
US   1968   119m   DeLuxe
Panavision
TCF/Apjac (Mort Abrahams)

w Michael Wilson, Rod Serling *novel Monkey Planet* by Pierre Boulle *d* Franklin Schaffner *ph* Leon Shamroy *m* Jerry Goldsmith *ad* William Creber, Jack Martin Smith *ed* Hugh S. Fowler *sp* L.B. Abbott, John Chambers, Art Cruickshank, Emil Kosa Jnr
☆ Charlton Heston (George Taylor), Roddy McDowall (Cornelius), *Kim Hunter* (Dr. Zira), Maurice Evans (Dr. Zaius), James Whitmore (President of the Assembly), James Daly (Honorius), Linda Harrison (Nova)

'One of the most telling science fiction films to date.' – Tom Milne

● Sequels were: *Beneath the Planet of the Apes* (1961), *Escape from the Planet of the Apes* (1970), *Conquest of the Planet of the Apes*, and *Battle for the Planet of the Apes* (1973).
● John Chambers was awarded an honorary Oscar for 'outstanding make-up achievement'.
👤 make-up (John Chambers)
Jerry Goldsmith; costumes (Morton Haack)

558
Planet of the Apes

Astronauts crash-land on a planet where apes are the ruling species and men are beasts.

This is stylish, thoughtful science-fiction that starts and finishes splendidly. Caught in a time warp, astronauts discover a planet where orangoutangs, gorillas and chimpanzees are the intelligent species and men are inarticulate animals, to be enslaved or hunted down. The ape make-up seemed great at the time, as did the performances of those actors encased within it. Leon Shamroy's cinematography creates a world that manages to seem both alien and familiar. It is only at the very end of the film, when George Taylor (Charlton Heston) see a half-buried Statue of Liberty – one of science-fiction cinema's iconic images – that he realizes that he is on his home planet in a distant future. Within a movie of exciting action, Franklin Schaffner has made a witty and provocative satire on man's arrogant and destructive nature.

An Italian Straw Hat
France   1927   74m (24 fps)   bw   silent
Albatross
original title: *Un Chapeau de Paille d'Italie*
wd René Clair *play* Eugène Labiche *ph* Maurice Desfassiaux, Nicolas Roudakoff *ad* Lazare Meerson
☆ Albert Préjean (Fadinard), Olga Tschekowa (Anais), Marise Maia (Helene), Alice Tissot (A Cousin)

'The very springtime of screen comedy.' – *Tatler*

'One of the funniest films ever made.' – *Tribune*, 1945

'Still one of the funniest films in the world.' – *Sunday Times*, 1948

557
An Italian Straw Hat

A bridegroom runs into marital difficulties after his horse eats the straw hat of a woman who is enjoying an adulterous relationship.

René Clair's very influential and still amusing work concerns the complications that ensue when a man on his way to be married allows his horse to eat a lady's straw hat; her escort, a soldier, demands that it be replaced lest her husband finds out. The couple hides at his house while he attempts to buy a hat and get married, neither task proving easy as complications arise. At one point he finds himself discussing his problem with the woman's jealous husband. It is a lively but gentle comedy of errors, a stage bedroom farce expanded for the screen and filled with visual gags. Albert Préjean, who was to be a regular in Clair's later films, is at his best as the bridegroom.

'There is no conspiracy. Just twelve people dead.'

The Parallax View
US 1974 102m Technicolor Panavision
Paramount/Gus/Harbour/Doubleday (Alan J. Pakula)
🎬 ◎

w David Giler, Lorenzo Semple Jnr *novel* Loren Singer
d Alan J. Pakula *ph* Gordon Willis *m* Michael Small
pd George Jenkins *ad* George Jenkins *ed* Jack Wheeler
☆ Warren Beatty (Joseph Frady), Paula Prentiss (Lee Carter), William Daniels (Austin Tucker), Hume Cronyn (Editor Edgar Rintels), Walter McGinn (Parallax Agent Jack Younger)

'Pakula at his best ... the test sequence is one of the most celebrated, manipulating the audience as it bombards Beatty's psyche.' – *Les Keyser, Hollywood in the Seventies*

'It is terribly important to give an audience a lot of things they may not get as well as those they will, so that finally the film does take on a texture and is not just simplistic communication.' – *Alan J. Pakula*

556
The Parallax View

Witnesses to a political assassination are systematically killed, despite the efforts of a crusading journalist.

Alan J. Pakula's stylish, persuasive political thriller shares the same paranoia that fuelled John Frankenheimer's *The Manchurian Candidate* a decade earlier: something is rotten in the government of the country. Warren Beatty plays a crusading journalist who finds himself at the centre of a conspiracy, unable to prevent a series of politically-motivated murders. In a tense, dizzyingly constructed movie, Beatty's journalist-hero imagines that he is getting ever closer to finding out the truth; instead, he is being encouraged to walk into a trap. There is even a downbeat ending; the villains win.

'A salesman's got to dream – it comes with the territory!'

'One mistake – seen by his son – unleashes with overwhelming power the great drama of our day!'

Death of a Salesman
US 1951 112m bw
Columbia (Stanley Kramer)
w Stanley Roberts *play* Arthur Miller *d* Laslo Benedek
ph Franz Planer *m* Alex North *md* Morris Stoloff
pd Rudolph Sternad *ad* Cary Odell *ed* William Lyon, Harry Gerstad
☆ *Fredric March* (Willy Loman), *Kevin McCarthy* (Biff), Cameron Mitchell (Happy), Mildred Dunnock (Linda Loman), Howard Smith (Charley), Royal Beal (Ben), Jesse White (Stanley)

'Its time shifts with light, which were poetic in the theatre, seemed shabby in a medium that can dissolve time and space so easily.' – *Stanley Kauffmann*

● Remade for TV in 1985 with Dustin Hoffman repeating his performance on Broadway.
♗ Franz Planer; Alex North; Fredric March; Kevin McCarthy; Mildred Dunnock

555
Death of a Salesman

A salesman faces up to the consequences of his failure in life.

Arthur Miller's classic play of an ageing travelling salesman, who recognizes the emptiness of his life and commits suicide, was well transferred to the screen. Fredric March provides an anguished performance in the title role (though producer Stanley Kramer thought there was something emotionally wrong with his acting) and Mildred Dunnock brilliantly repeats her stage role as his suffering wife. Stage conventions and tricks were cleverly adapted to cinematic use, especially when its tragic protagonist walks from the present into the past and back again.

'Pick up the pieces, folks, Jimmy's in action again!'

White Heat
US   1949   114m   bw
Warner (Louis F. Edelman)
⊞ ▤ ◎~

w Ivan Goff, Ben Roberts *story* Virginia Kellogg *d Raoul Walsh ph* Sid Hickox *m* Max Steiner *ad* Edward Carrere *ed* Owen Marks
☆ *James Cagney* (Arthur Cody Jarrett), Edmond O'Brien (Hank Fallon/Vic Pardo), *Margaret Wycherly* (Ma Jarrett), Virginia Mayo (Verna Jarrett), Steve Cochran (Big Ed Somers), John Archer (Phillip Evans)

'The most gruesome aggregation of brutalities ever presented under the guise of entertainment.' – *Cue*

'In the hurtling tabloid traditions of the gangster movies of the Thirties, but its matter-of-fact violence is a new post-war style.' – *Time*

'A wild and exciting picture of mayhem and madness.' – *Life*

● Just before his death, Cagney comes out with his famous line, 'Made it Ma! Top of the world!'.
⚨ Virginia Kellogg

554
White Heat

A violent, mother-fixated gangster gets his come-uppance when a government agent is infiltrated into his gang.

This searing melodrama reintroduced the old Cagney and then some: spellbinding suspense sequences complemented his vivid and hypnotic performance as a fast-talking, ruthless mobster. The film was based on the real life criminal Ma Barker and her gang, and Cagney played his part gleefully, sitting on his mother's lap to seek comfort for his headache in a scene that still startles. Whereas Cagney's earlier gangsters had poverty as an excuse for their crimes, this time around he is a psychopath, impure and not so simple; a mad killer who enjoys it, chewing on a chicken leg and cracking one-liners as he murders, in a style that later became an expected part of action movies.

'The Most Exciting Story Of The World's Most Exciting City!'

The Naked City
US   1948   96m   bw
Universal (Mark Hellinger)
▤ ◎

w Malvin Wald, Albert Maltz *d* Jules Dassin *ph* William Daniels *m* Frank Skinner, Miklos Rozsa *md* Milton Schwarzwald *ad* John DeCuir *ed* Paul Weatherwax
☆ *Barry Fitzgerald* (Lt. Dan Muldoon), *Don Taylor* (Jimmy Halloran), Howard Duff (Frank Niles), Dorothy Hart (Ruth Morrison), Ted de Corsia (Garzah), Adelaide Klein (Mrs. Batory)
● Made as a television series from 1958–1962.
⚨ William Daniels; Paul Weatherwax
⚨ original story (Malvin Wald)

553
The Naked City

New York police track down a killer.

A highly influential documentary thriller which, shot on location in New York, claimed to be giving an impression of real city life, as the NYPD hunt for a murderer through the teeming city streets. Actually its real mission was to tell an ordinary murder tale with an impressive accumulation of detail and humour. The narrator's last words became a cliché: 'There are eight million stories in the naked city. This has been one of them.' The film's shadowy style, brilliantly captured by cinematographer William Daniels, derived from a book by Weegee (aka Arthur Fellig), a news photographer noted for his often snatched and sensational night-time photographs, taken by flashlight on the streets of the city, of fires, gangsters, suicides and murder victims.

The Innocent

Italy 1976 125m colour Technovision
Rizzoli (Giovanni Bertolucci)

original title: *Innocente*
aka: *The Intruder*
w Suso Cecchi D'Amico, Luchino Visconti, Enrico Medioli
novel Gabriele d'Annunzio *d* Luchino Visconti
ph Pasqualino De Santis *m* Chopin, Liszt, Mozart, Gluck
ad Mario Garbuglia *ed* Ruggero Mastroianni
☆ Giancarlo Giannini (Tullio Hermil), Laura Antonelli
(Guiliana), Jennifer O'Neill (Teresa Raffo), Rina Morelli
(Tullio's Mother), Didier Haudepin (Federico Hermil),
Massimo Girotti (Count Stefano Egano), Marie Dubois (The
Princess)

'An outstanding example of what Hemingway
would have called grace under pressure.' – *Sight
and Sound*

'The protagonist is meant to be an atheist hero, a
brave anarch who pays the price for his amorality.
But he comes out only a sordid, spoiled sensualist
swine, with no kind of depth, so this story has no
involvement for the viewer.' – *Stanley Kauffmann*

• Visconti had wanted Alain Delon and Romy Schneider
for the two leads. He directed the film from a wheelchair and
died just before its release.

552
The Innocent

In fin-de-siècle Rome, an affair leads to the breakdown of a marriage.

Visconti's final film, made just before he died, when he was in great
pain and confined to a wheelchair, is an elegant account of decadence
and sexual politics that subverts the intentions of the novel on which it
is based. Set in Italy in the 1890s, it tells the story of a Sicilian aristocrat who, though quick to keep his wife informed of his own affair,
takes a terrible revenge when he discovers she also has a lover. In
Gabriele d'Annunzio's book, the aristocrat was a hero; here he is more
of a victim.

The Asphalt Jungle

US 1950 112m bw
MGM (Arthur Hornblow Jnr)

w Ben Maddow, John Huston *novel* W. R. Burnett *d John
Huston ph* Harold Rosson *m* Miklos Rozsa *ad* Randall
Duell, Cedric Gibbons *ed* George Boemler
☆ Sterling Hayden (Dix Handley), Louis Calhern (Alonzo
D Emmerich), *Sam Jaffe* (Doc Erwin Riedenschneider), Jean
Hagen (Doll Conovan), James Whitmore (Gus Minissi),
John McIntire (Police Commissioner Hardy), Marc
Lawrence (Cobby), Marilyn Monroe (Angela Phinlay), Barry
Kelley (Lt Ditrich)

'Where this film excels is in the fluency of its
narration, the sharpness of its observation of
character and the excitement of its human
groupings.' – *Dilys Powell*

'That Asphalt Pavement thing is full of nasty, ugly
people doing nasty things. I wouldn't walk across
the room to see a thing like that.' – *Louis B. Mayer
(who was head of the studio which made it)*

• Apart from imitations, the film has been directly remade
as *The Badlanders, Cairo* and *A Cool Breeze* (qqv).
⚥ Ben Maddow, John Huston (writers); John Huston (as
director); Harold Rosson; Sam Jaffe

551
The Asphalt Jungle

*An elderly crook comes out of prison and assembles a gang for one
last robbery.*

The plot is now an over-used one, but this was probably the very first
film to show a 'caper' from the criminals point of view, and is considered by many to be the definitive heist movie. It is a clever character
study rather than a thriller, extremely well executed and indeed generally irreproachable. Its theme is made explicit by Louis Calhern as a
crooked lawyer: 'Crime is only a left-handed form of human endeavour.'
An uncredited Marilyn Monroe's small scene as the lawyer's mistress,
which she always thought was one of her best performances, established her as someone to watch. MGM executive Dore Schary regretted
ever after that he let her leave the studio to go to Twentieth Century
Fox.

Odd Man Out

GB   1946   115m   bw
GFD/Two Cities (Carol Reed)

US title: *Gang War*

w F. L. Green, R. C. Sherriff   *novel* F. L. Green   *d* Carol
Reed   *ph* Robert Krasker   *m* William Alwyn   *ad* Roger
Furse   *ed* Fergus McDonnell
☆ *James Mason* (Johnny), *Robert Newton* (Lukey),
Kathleen Ryan (Kathleen), *F. J. McCormick* (Shell), Cyril
Cusack (Pat), Robert Beatty (Dennis), Fay Compton (Rosie),
Dan O'Herlihy (Nolan), Denis O'Dea (Head Constable),
Maureen Delany (Theresa), Joseph Tomelty (Carby), William
Hartnell (Barman), Beryl Measor (Maudie)

'The story seems to ramify too much, to go on too
long, and at its unluckiest to go arty. Yet detail by
detail *Odd Man Out* is made with great skill and
imaginativeness and with a depth of ardour that is
very rare.' – *James Agee*

'Quite simply the most imaginative film yet
produced in England, comparable with *Quai des
Brumes* and *Le Jour se Lève*.' – *William Whitebait,
New Statesman*

🎞 Fergus McDonnell
🏆 British picture

550
Odd Man Out

*In Belfast, a wounded IRA gunman is helped and hindered by a variety
of people.*

Shot by Robert Krasker in the style of a *film noir*, all shadows against
pools of light, Carol Reed's superbly crafted drama had as its central
character an IRA gunman, wounded and on the run in Belfast. As the
fugitive killer, James Mason had to convey his emotional state without
the aid of much dialogue. Reed had Krasker photograph him from low
angles to suggest a heroic figure; it was done without endorsing his
ideology. Indeed, neither Belfast nor the IRA are ever identified during
the unfolding tragedy. Despite its subject matter, Reed avoided politics,
turning the movie into a dramatic character study, visually and emotionally memorable.

'Boy Makes Girl Make Fool Of New York.'

Nothing Sacred

US   1937   77m   Technicolor
David O. Selznick

w Ben Hecht   *story* Letter to the Editor by James H. Street
d William Wellman   *ph* W. Howard Greene   *m* Oscar
Levant   *ad* Lyle Wheeler   *ed* James E. Newcom
☆ *Carole Lombard* (Hazel Flagg), *Fredric March* (Wally
Cook), *Walter Connolly* (Oliver Stone), Charles Winninger
(Dr. Enoch Downer), Sig Rumann (Dr. Emile Egglehoffer),
Frank Fay (MC), Maxie Rosenbloom (Max Levinsky),
Margaret Hamilton (Drug Store Lady), Hedda Hopper
(Dowager), Monty Woolley (Dr. Vunch), Hattie McDaniel
(Mrs. Walker), Olin Howland (Baggage Man), John Qualen
(Swedish Fireman)

'Hit comedy ... will be one of the big grossers of
the year.' – *Variety*

'Because it does hold up a mirror, even though a
distorting mirror, to a very real world of ballyhoo
and cheap sensationalism, the pleasure to be
obtained from it is something more than the usual
mulish guffaw.' – *Spectator*

● Refashioned in 1953 as a stage musical, *Hazel Flagg*,
with Jule Styne; this in turn became a Martin and Lewis
comedy *Living It Up* (Jerry Lewis in the Carole Lombard
part).

549
Nothing Sacred

*A girl thought to be dying of a rare disease is built up by the press into
a national heroine; but the diagnosis was wrong.*

Hollywood's most bitter and hilarious satire, with crazy comedy elements and superb wisecracks. Written by a former journalist, Ben
Hecht, it made fun of newspapers and their liking for a sob-story, with
Carole Lombard playing the small town girl who, apparently dying of
radium poisoning, sparks a media frenzy that grips the nation. The
movie's titles showed the stars as puppets, and they manipulate each
other. Even children are not cute here; when Fredric March's reporter
visits a Vermont town, a small child bites his leg. It remains a historical
monument of screen comedy, though its freshness at the time cannot
now be recaptured.

'The funniest, fastest honeymoon ever screened!'

My Favorite Wife
US   1940   88m   bw
RKO (Leo McCarey)
▬   ⊗.   ⊚   ⊚

w Sam and Bella Spewack, Leo McCarey d Garson Kanin
ph Rudolph Maté m Roy Webb ad Van Nest Polglase
ed Robert Wise
☆ Cary Grant (Nick Arden), Irene Dunne (Ellen Arden), Randolph Scott (Stephen Burkett), Gail Patrick (Bianca), Ann Shoemaker (Ma), Donald MacBride (Hotel Clerk)

'One of those comedies with a glow on it.' – Otis Ferguson

● Other variations (qv): Too Many Husbands, Our Wife, Three for the Show, Move Over Darling.
♟ story; Roy Webb; art direction

548
My Favorite Wife

A female explorer returns after several shipwrecked years to find that her husband has married again.

A well-worn plot is given a bright new twist: a woman returns from years lost at sea to find that her children no longer recognize her – and her husband has a new wife. Leo McCarey, who co-scripted and was directing until a drunken car crash put him out of action, re-worked some of the jokes from his *The Awful Truth* of three years earlier, which also starred Irene Dunne and Cary Grant as a couple who were unhappy together and unhappier apart. The censors objected to its 'general offensive sex suggestiveness', but much of the fun survives, including the final fade-out when Ellen (Irene Dunne) tells Nick (Cary Grant) that he cannot share her bed until the annulment of his second marriage comes through in sixty days, which will be around Christmas time. Grant leaves, only to reappear dressed as Santa Claus.

'New songs and old favourites sung by Mr Jolson during the action of the story on the Vitaphone!'

The Jazz Singer
US   1927   89m   bw
👓   ▬   ⊗.   ◠

w Alfred A. Cohn play Samson Raphaelson d Alan Crosland ph Hal Mohr md Louis Silvers ed Harold McCord
☆ Al Jolson (Jakie Rabinowitz/Jack Robin), May McAvoy (Mary Dale), Warner Oland (Cantor Rabinowitz), Eugenie Besserer (Sara Rabinowitz), Otto Lederer (Moishe Yudelson)

'The Jazz Singer definitely establishes the fact that talking pictures are imminent. Everyone in Hollywood can rise up and declare that they are not, and it will not alter the fact. If I were an actor with a squeaky voice I would worry.' – Welford Beaton, The Film Spectator

♪ 'Blue Skies'; 'Mother I Still Have You'; 'My Mammy'; 'Toot Toot Tootsie Goodbye'; 'Dirty Hands Dirty Face'
♟ Special Award to Warner for producing 'the pioneer outstanding talking picture'
♟ Alfred A. Cohn

547
The Jazz Singer

A cantor's son makes it big in show business.

Al Jolson's ad-libbing, 'Wait a minute, wait a minute. You ain't heard nothin' yet!', was a sensational moment in this archetypal Jewish weepie which became of interest as the first talkie film (songs and a few fragments of speech) and in its way, surprisingly, is not half bad. The title was a misnomer, since Jolson's singing is of a kind that is far removed from jazz, with him appearing in blackface. The film has been remade twice, in 1952 with Danny Thomas and 1980 with Neil Diamond. But it is this historically important version that remains the best. Jolson's over-enthusiastic sentimentality can be hard to take, yet his vitality and sheer exuberance as a performer keeps alive the movie's classic status.

Nixon

US 1995 192m Technicolor Panavision
Entertainment/Illusion/Cinergi (Clayton Townsend,
Oliver Stone, Andrew G. Vajna)

⊞ ⊞ ▤ ⊛ ⊚ ⊚ ⌒

w Stephen J. Rivele, Christopher Wilkinson, Oliver Stone
d Oliver Stone *ph* Robert Richardson *m* John Williams
pd Victor Kempster *ad* Richard Mays, Donald Woodruff,
Margery Zweizig *ed* Brian Berdan, Hank Corwin
☆ *Anthony Hopkins* (Nixon), *Joan Allen* (Pat Nixon),
Powers Boothe (Alexander Haig), Ed Harris (E. Howard
Hunt), E. G. Marshall (John Mitchell), David Paymer (Ron
Ziegler), David Hyde Pierce (John Dean), Paul Sorvino
(Henry Kissinger), J. T. Walsh (John Erlichman), James
Woods (H. R. Haldeman), Mary Steenburgen (Hannah
Nixon)

'Inescapably interesting due to the parade of recent
history on view, but it finally emerges as an
honorable, and rather too strenuous, failure.'
– Todd McCarthy, Variety

'Achieves the dubious distinction of being a film
about Nixon that is actually more paranoid than
Nixon was.' – Tom Shone, Sunday Times

● A Region 1 collector's edition two-disc set includes
commentary by Oliver Stone.
⚝ Anthony Hopkins, Joan Allen; John Williams; screenplay

546
Nixon

As the Watergate cover-up begins to unravel, Richard Nixon recalls his past, from his Quaker childhood to his marriage and the triumphs of his political career.

Oliver Stone's boldly conceived film on the nature of power and its corrupting influence attempted to cast Nixon as the protagonist of a tragedy in a Shakespearean mould – like Macbeth, he clambered over the dead bodies of others to seize power and to retain it. While the film failed to show that Nixon had sufficient stature to qualify as a tragic hero, it did provide a fascinating portrait of a flawed and envious man, who sought support from dubious allies and was brought down by his own failings. Anthony Hopkins was utterly convincing in the title role.

Ermo

China/Hong Kong 1994 98m colour
ICA/Ocean/Shanghai Studio (Jimmy Tan, Chen
Kunming)

▤ *w* Lang Yun *story* Xu Baoqi *d* Zhou Xiaowen *ph* Lu
Gengxin *m* Zhoi Xiaowen *ad* Zhang Daqian *ed* Zhong
Furong
☆ Ailiya (Ermo), Liu Peiqi (Xiazi, Blindman), Ge Zhijun
(Village Chief, Ermo's Husband), Zhang Haiyan (Fatwoman,
Xiazi's Wife), Zan Zhenguo (Huzi, Ermo's Son)

'A lively, constantly diverting film: it has amusing,
colourful characters, a generous dash of humour
and not a jot of sentimentality.' – Independent

545
Ermo

A wife with an elderly and impotent husband works hard in order to buy a big-screen television set to impress the neighbours.

One of China's leading Fifth Generation filmmakers, who began directing in the 1980s, Zhou Xiaowen's scathing comedy of village and peasant life centres on Ermo, a noodle maker consumed by dreams of owning the biggest television in her village. Ermo becomes so obsessive in her desire to earn more money that she leaves her village to work in town and endangers her health. In part a satire on Western consumerism, it also points out the dangers of getting what you wish for, and asks some tough questions on what gives meaning and purpose to a person's existence.

Night Train to Munich

GB 1940 93m bw
TCF (Edward Black)

aka: *Gestapo*
aka: *Night Train*

w Frank Launder, Sidney Gilliat novel *Report on a Fugitive* by Gordon Wellesley d Carol Reed ph Otto Kanturek m Charles Williams md Louis Levy ad Vetchinsky ed R. E. Dearing

☆ Margaret Lockwood (Anna Bomasch), *Rex Harrison* (Gus Bennett), *Basil Radford* (Charters), *Naunton Wayne* (Caldicott), Paul Henreid (Karl Marsen), Keneth Kent (Controller), Felix Aylmer (Dr. John Fredericks), Roland Culver (Roberts), *Eliot Makeham* (Schwab), *Raymond Huntley* (Kampenfeldt), Wyndham Goldie (Dryton), Billy Russell (Adolph Hitler)

'A very nice triumph of skill and maturity in films, and thus a pleasure to have.' – *Otis Ferguson*

♟ Gordon Wellesley

544
Night Train to Munich

A British agent poses as a Nazi in order to save a Czech inventor.

Carol Reed's first-rate comedy thriller was obviously inspired by the success of Hitchcock's *The Lady Vanishes* and provided much the same measure of thrills and laughs. It once again had Margaret Lockwood as the star, and featured the comedy of the little Englanders Charters and Caldicott, played by Basil Radford and Naunton Wayne. Rex Harrison replaced Hitchcock's other star, Michael Redgrave, who was busy in the theatre, as the British Secret Service agent charged with rescuing the Czech scientist from the Gestapo. It was a wartime morale booster, in which British humour triumphed over German efficiency.

'Titanic… The greatest sea drama in living memory told as it really happened!'

A Night to Remember

GB 1958 123m bw
Rank (William Macquitty)

w Eric Ambler book Walter Lord d Roy Ward Baker ph Geoffrey Unsworth m William Alwyn ad Alex Vetchinsky ed Sidney Havers

☆ Kenneth More (Herbert Lightoller), Honor Blackman (Mrs. Lucas), Michael Goodliffe (Thomas Andrews), David McCallum (Bride), George Rose (Joughin), Anthony Bushell (Capt. Rostron), Ralph Michael (Yates), John Cairney (Murphy), Kenneth Griffith (Phillips), Frank Lawton (Chairman), Michael Bryant (Moody)

'A worthy, long-drawn-out documentary, with noticeably more honesty about human nature than most films, but little shape or style.' – *Kenneth Cavender*

'As fine and convincing an enactment as anyone could wish–or expect.' – *Bosley Crowther, New York Times*

543

A Night to Remember

The story of the 1912 sea disaster when the Titanic struck an iceberg.

This remains the best, and the most accurate film, about the sinking in 1912 of the supposedly unsinkable Titanic. Roy Ward Baker treats it like a documentary, sticking to the facts and bringing to life the passengers and crew. It was a major enterprise that featured hundreds of cameos, none discernibly more important than any other. On this account the film seems alternately stiff and flabby as narrative, but there is much to enjoy and admire along the way, though the sense of awe is dissipated by the final model shots.

'The Greatest Actress Of The Screen ...
In The Greatest Romance Of The South!'

Jezebel
US   1938   104m   bw
Warner (Henry Blanke)

w Clements Ripley, Abem Finkel, John Huston *play* Owen Davis Snr *d* William Wyler *ph* Ernest Haller *m* Max Steiner *ad* Robert Haas *ed* Warren Low

☆ *Bette Davis* (Julie Morrison), Henry Fonda (Preston Dillard), George Brent (Buck Cantrell), Margaret Lindsay (Amy Bradford Dillard), Fay Bainter (Aunt Belle Massey), Richard Cromwell (Ted Dillard), Donald Crisp (Dr. Livingstone), Henry O'Neill (Gen. Theopholus Bogardus), John Litel (Jean LeCour), Spring Byington (Mrs. Kendrick), Eddie Anderson (Gros Bat), Gordon Oliver (Dick Allen), Irving Pichel (Huger)

'Its excellences come from many sources – good plotting and writing, a director and photographer who know how to make the thing flow along with dramatic pictorial effect, and a cast that makes its story a record of living people.' – *James Shelley Hamilton, National Board of Review*

'Without the zing Davis gave it, it would have looked very mossy indeed.' – *Pauline Kael, 1968*

♟ Bette Davis; Fay Bainter
♟ best picture; Ernest Haller; Max Steiner

Here Comes Mr Jordan
US   1941   93m   bw
Columbia (Everett Riskin)

w Seton I. Miller, Sidney Buchman *play Halfway to Heaven* by Harry Segall *d* Alexander Hall *ph* Joseph Walker *m* Frederick Hollander *md* Morris Stoloff *ad* Lionel Banks *ed* Viola Lawrence

☆ Robert Montgomery (Joe Pendleton), Evelyn Keyes (Bette Logan), Rita Johnson (Julia Farnsworth), *Claude Rains* (Mr. Jordan), *James Gleason* (Max Corkle), *Edward Everett Horton* (Messenger No. 7013), John Emery (Tony Abbott), *Donald MacBride* (Inspector Williams), Halliwell Hobbes (Sisk), Don Costello (Lefty)

'There is something about this original, so sweet-spirited and earnest that it transcends its plot devices and shines through its comedic asides to become a true morality play without once becoming either preachy or mawkish.' – *Kit Parker catalogue, 1980*

'Audiences loved this chunk of whimsy ... the slickly hammy Rains gives Mr Jordan a sinister gloss, as if he were involved in some heavenly racket, like smuggling Chinese.' – *Pauline Kael, 70s*

● Remade 1978 as *Heaven Can Wait*.
♟ original story (Harry Segall); script
♟ best picture; Alexander Hall; Joseph Walker; Robert Montgomery; James Gleason

---

542
Jezebel

Before the Civil War, a Southern belle stirs up trouble among the menfolk by her wilfulness and spite, but atones when a plague strikes.

This superb star melodrama was tossed to Bette Davis in compensation for losing *Gone with the Wind* and also to cash in on the publicity surrounding that film by quickly bringing out a similar story. The Southern belle became one of her defining roles, but Davis was worked hard on set: the perfectionist director made her do forty-seven takes of one scene (when she saw them all, she realized that he was right). The film's dramatic centre-piece is the Mardi Gras Ball, where all the unmarried girls are dressed in white, except for Davis who breaks convention by wearing a red gown. Under Wyler's direction, Ernest Haller's camera swoops around the ballroom to focus on the isolated, dancing figures of her and her escort as the others all leave the floor.

541
Here Comes Mr Jordan

A man who died too soon is sent back to find a new body in which to live his life.

This weird heavenly fantasy had many imitations, including *Angel on My Shoulder*, *Down to Earth*, *A Guy Named Joe*, *Heaven Only Knows*, *The Horn Blows at Midnight* and *That's the Spirit*. Here, a prizefighter who is also an amateur saxophonist crashes in his private plane and goes to heaven by mistake; he was supposed to survive and live another forty years. Unfortunately, when he returns for his body it has been cremated, so he has to find another, recently deceased. The story succeeded because of its novelty and because heaven in wartime was a comforting vision. As a movie taken on its own merits, it suffers from illogicalities, but scene for scene there is enough firmness and control to make it memorable and the performances still delight.

Kolya
Czech Republic/France/GB   1996   105m   colour
Buena Vista/Portobello/Ceska Televize/Biograf Jan Sverák

📽 ▦ ≋ ⊗ ◉ ⌒

w Zdenek Sverák *idea* Pavel Taussig *d* Jan Sverák *ph* Vladimir Smutny *m* Ondrej Soukup *ed* Alois Visárek
☆ Zdenek Sverák (Frantisek Louka), Andrej Chalimon (Kolya), Libuse Safránková (Klara), Ondrej Vetchy (Mr. Broz), Stella Zázvorková (Mother), Ladislav Smoljak (Mr. Houdek), Irina Livanova (Nadezda)

'Balances heart-warming sentiment with gentle humor and observations that strike universal chords.' – *David Rooney, Variety*

👤 foreign film

540
Kolya

In Prague, a penniless musician marries a Russian woman in exchange for cash, but finds that the transaction leaves him with her five-year-old son.

This is a film that begins on a note of quiet desperation and ends with a feeling of hope as the Berlin Wall comes down and the people of Prague celebrate a new freedom. The political events are a backdrop to a charming, tough-minded drama of people trying to get by within a system that leaves them little room for manoeuvre. Louka is a poor musician, sacked from the symphony orchestra, who scrapes a living playing at funerals. In return for money, he marries a Russian woman who needs Czech papers. She then disappears, leaving him to care for Kolya, her five-year-old son. Zdenek Sverák, the star and writer, and his director son Jan have contrived a comic and affectionate film that can make fun of officialdom while being unsentimental on the matter of love.

The Narrow Margin
US   1952   70m   bw
RKO (Stanley Rubin)

≋ ⊗

w Earl Fenton *d* Richard Fleischer *ph* George E. Diskant *ad* Albert D'Agostino, Jack Okey *ed* Robert Swink
☆ *Charles McGraw* (Walter Brown), *Marie Windsor* (Mrs. Neall), Jacqueline White (Ann Sinclair), Queenie Leonard (Mrs. Troll)

'A taut, breathlessly fast and highly suspenseful "sleeper" par excellence.' – *Time Out, 1986*

● Remade in 1990 with Gene Hackman.
👤 original story (Martin Goldsmith, Jack Leonard)

539
The Narrow Margin

Police try to guard a prosecution witness on a train from Chicago to Los Angeles.

A tight little thriller, this takes every advantage of its setting, with the action confined to an express train racing across America. It was a low budget movie, shot in thirteen days, but not a second was wasted, either in making it or in what was shown on the screen. Howard Hughes, then running RKO, was so impressed with it he kept it in his projection booth for a year and wanted to remake it as a much bigger budget movie with Robert Mitchum starring in the role played by Charles McGraw. Fortunately, he changed his mind. It is basically a 'B' movie, but its suspense and twisting plot provide more satisfaction than many a top feature.

Nada

France/Italy 1974 134m Eastmancolor
Academy/Connoisseur/Verona/Films La Boétie (André
Génovès)

■■ ⊘

w Jean-Patrick Manchette *novel* Jean-Patrick Manchette
d Claude Chabrol *ph* Jean Rabier *m* Pierre Jansen
ad Guy Littaye *ed* Jacques Gaillard
☆ Fabio Testi (Diaz), Michel Duchaussoy (Treuffais),
Maurice Garrel (Epaulard), Michel Aumont (Inspector
Goemond), Lou Castel (D'Arey), Didier Kaminka (Meyer),
Lyle Joyce (Ambassador Richard Poindexter), Viviane
Romance (Gabrielle)

'Chabrol's most profoundly cynical film to date …
he lays bare the cause-and-effect mechanism of
terrorism.' – *Jan Dawson, MFB*

538
Nada

*A tough policeman tracks down a group of anarchists who kidnap the
American Ambassador in Paris.*

Claude Chabrol's bleak and violent thriller, expertly made, does not take
sides in its account of the agents of the state hunting for members of
the activist group Nada. It is difficult to tell the good guys from the bad.
The terrorists, a motley crew of drifters, dreamers and an alcoholic, are
irresponsible in their actions. The police are unthinking in their
response. Neither side demonstrates a belief in the value of individual
human lives. The intellectual among the anarchists claims that 'leftist
terrorism and state terrorism are the twin jaws of the same trap', and
Chabrol, cynically, seems to agree.

My Learned Friend

GB 1943 76m bw
Ealing (Michael Balcon)

⊘

w John Dighton, Angus MacPhail *d* Basil Dearden, Will
Hay *ph* Wilkie Cooper *m* Ernest Irving *ad* Michael Relph
ed Charles Hasse
☆ *Will Hay* (William Fitch), *Claude Hulbert* (Claude
Babbington), *Mervyn Johns* (Grimshaw), Ernest Thesiger
(Ferris), Charles Victor ('Safety' Wilson), Lloyd Pearson
(Col. Chudleigh), Maudie Edwards (Aladdin), G. H.
Mulcaster (Dr. Scudamore), Gibb McLaughlin (Butler)
● The Big Ben sequence must surely have been the
inspiration for the climax of the 1978 version of *The 39
Steps* with Robert Powell.

537
My Learned Friend

*A shady lawyer is last on a mad ex-convict's murder list of those who
helped get him convicted.*

Will Hay was without his frequent comic companions Moore Marriott
and Graham Moffatt when he made this madcap black farce, playing a
barrister targeted by an escaped convict. He had, though, an excellent
cast of character actors, including the dithering Claude Hulbert, to add
to the amusement. Plot-packed and generally hilarious, it was the star's
last vehicle, but one of his best, with superbly timed sequences during
a pantomime and on the face of Big Ben, when he hangs from the
minute hand to prevent the clock from striking 12 noon and triggering
a bomb.

My Learned Friend

Miracle on 34th Street

US 1947 94m bw
TCF (William Perlberg)

GB title: *The Big Heart*

wd George Seaton *story* Valentine Davies *ph* Charles
Clarke, Lloyd Ahern *m* Cyril Mockridge *ad* Richard Day,
Richard Irvine *ed* Robert Simpson

☆ *Edmund Gwenn* (Kris Kringle), Maureen O'Hara (Doris
Walker), John Payne (Fred Gailey), Natalie Wood (Susan
Walker), Gene Lockhart (Judge Henry X. Harper), Porter Hall
(Mr. Sawyer), William Frawley (Charles Halloran), Jerome
Cowan (Thomas Mara), Thelma Ritter (Mother)

'Altogether wholesome, stimulating and enjoyable.'
– *Motion Picture Herald*

● Remade for TV in 1973. Remade in 1994 with Richard
Attenborough.

👤 George Seaton (as writer); Valentine Davies; Edmund
Gwenn

♟ best picture

536
Miracle on 34th Street

A department store Santa Claus claims to be the real thing.

This mainly charming comedy fantasy quickly became an American
classic. Edmund Gwenn's jolly Kris Kringle persuades a store executive
and her daughter of the power of imagination and the importance of
belief. It does suffer from a few dull romantic stretches, but the court
hearing in which Gwenn's sanity is tested is a comic and sentimental
highlight.

The Way to the Stars

GB   1945   109m   bw
Two Cities (Anatole de Grunwald)

US title: *Johnny in the Clouds*

w *Terence Rattigan, Anatole de Grunwald* poem *John Pudney* d *Anthony Asquith* ph Derick Williams m Nicholas Brodszky ad Carmen Dillon ed Fergus McDonell

☆ *John Mills* (Peter Penrose), *Rosamund John* (Miss Toddy Todd), *Michael Redgrave* (David Archdale), *Douglass Montgomery* (Johnny Hollis), Basil Radford (Tiny Williams), Stanley Holloway (Palmer), Joyce Carey (Miss Winterton), Renée Asherson (Iris Winterton), Felix Aylmer (Rev. Charles Moss), Bonar Colleano (Joe Friselli), Trevor Howard (Squadron Leader Carter), Jean Simmons (Singer)

'Not for a long time have I seen a film so satisfying, so memorable, or so successful in evoking the precise mood and atmosphere of the recent past.' – *Richard Mallett, Punch*

'Humour, humanity, and not a sign of mawkishness … a classic opening sequence, with the camera wandering through an abandoned air base, peering in at each detail in the nissen huts, the sleeping quarters, the canteens, noting all the time a procession of objects each of which will have its own special significance in the action of the film.' – *Basil Wright, 1972*

The Candidate

US   1972   110m   Technicolor
Warner/Redford-Ritchie (Walter Coblenz)

w Jeremy Larner d *Michael Ritchie* ph Victor J. Kemper m John Rubinstein ed Robert Estrin, Richard A. Harris

☆ *Robert Redford* (Bill McKay), Peter Boyle (Luck), *Don Porter* (Sen. Crocker Jarmon), Allen Garfield (Howard Klein), Karen Carlson (Nancy McKay), Quinn Redeker (Rich Jenkin), Morgan Upton (Henderson), *Melvyn Douglas* (John J. McKay)

'Decent entertainment … it is never boring, but it is never enlarging, informationally or emotionally or thematically.' – *Stanley Kauffmann*

🎬 Jeremy Larner

535
The Way to the Stars

World War II as seen by the guests at a small hotel near an airfield.

This is one of the few films to rely for much of its emotional impact on a poem, written by John Pudney which was no more than twelve lines long and began, 'Do not despair/For Johnny-head-in-air/He sleeps as sound/As Johnny underground'. Set in a hotel where the guests mingle with British and American airmen, it was one of the few films which accurately captured the atmosphere of World War II in Britain. A generally delightful comedy drama, it was suffused with a tragic atmosphere.

534
The Candidate

A young Californian lawyer is persuaded to run for senator; in succeeding, he alienates his wife and obscures his real opinions.

Michael Ritchie's film, put together in a slightly scrappy but finally persuasive style, joins a select band of rousing, doubting American political films. Robert Redford uses his glamour to good effect as the young Californian lawyer striving to retain his integrity on the campaign trail. His corruption is a gradual one: he begins by voicing his own strongly-held views, but as his advisers and publicity men take over, rewriting his speeches and coaching him in his responses, he becomes just another product to be marketed to the masses.

'Everything is in its proper place – except the past!'

Ordinary People
US   1980   124m   Technicolor
Paramount/Wildwood (Ronald L. Schwary)
🎞 ▤ ◕ ◉ ◎
w *Alvin Sargent* novel Judith Guest d *Robert Redford*
ph John Bailey m Marvin Hamlisch ad Phillip Bennett, J. Michael Riva ed Jeff Kanew
☆ Donald Sutherland (Calvin), *Mary Tyler Moore* (Beth), *Timothy Hutton* (Conrad), Judd Hirsch (Berger), Elizabeth McGovern (Jeannine), M. Emmet Walsh (Swim Coach)

'This is an academic exercise in catharsis: it's earnest, it means to improve people, and it lasts a lifetime.' – *New Yorker*

👤 best film; Alvin Sargent; Robert Redford; Timothy Hutton
👤 Mary Tyler Moore; Judd Hirsch (supporting actor)

533
Ordinary People

The eldest son of a well-heeled American family is drowned, and the survivors take stock and indulge in recriminations.

This is an actor's piece which, on that level, succeeds very well, and accurately pins down a certain species of modern American family, that of a privileged and successful lawyer and his organizing wife. Robert Redford, in Alvin Sargent's adaptation of Judith Guest's best-seller, examines them at a crucial moment following the death by drowning of their eldest son; the others take stock and indulge in recriminations. The most affected is Conrad (Timothy Hutton), the younger son who attempted suicide and upsets his mother by bleeding over the bathroom rug. The disintegration of an apparent domestic harmony is observed by Redford at a little distance that provides the cast with room for some immaculate performances.

Occupe-Toi d'Amélie
France   1949   95m   bw
Lux (Louis Wipf)
aka: *Keep an Eye on Amelia*
w *Jean Aurenche, Pierre Bost* play Georges Feydeau
d *Claude Autant-Lara* ph André Bac m René Cloërc
pd Max Douy ed Madeleine Gug
☆ *Danielle Darrieux, Jean Desailly*, Bourvil, Carette, Grégoire Aslan

'Even those who do not respond to the artificialities of French vaudeville will admire the ingenuity and elegance of treatment.' – *Gavin Lambert, MFB*

'Most people, I think, could see it with considerable enjoyment even twice on the same evening.' – *Richard Mallett, Punch*

532
Occupe-Toi d'Amélie

In Paris, a playboy's mistress takes part in a mock marriage with his friend and discovers that the ceremony was real.

Georges Feydeau remains the greatest writer of farces and this is perhaps his best work, given a hilarious and superbly stylized adaptation: a Parisian cocotte agrees to go through a mock marriage ceremony with her lover's best friend to fool his uncle, but the ceremony turns out to be real. The director, Claude Autant-Lara, acknowledges the theatrical nature of this period boulevard comedy by beginning it as a play in a theatre before an audience; but gradually cinema technique takes over. Acting, timing and editing are all impeccable, and the production stands as a model of how such things should be done.

The Red Circle

France/Italy 1970 102m colour
Corona (Robert Dorfmann)
📺 ▦ ◉ ⊘
original title: *Le Cercle Rouge*
wd Jean-Pierre Melville *ph* Henri Decae *m* Eric de
Marsan *ad* Theo Meurisse *ed* Marie-Sophie Dubus
☆ Alain Delon (Corey), André Bourvil (Le Commissaire
Mattei), Gian-Maria Volonte (Vogel), Yves Montand
(Jansen), Paul Crauchet (Le Receleur), François Périer
(Santi)
● A restored version running for 140m was released in
2003.

531
The Red Circle

*Three men join forces to rob a jewellery store with a sophisticated
security system.*

Jean-Pierre Melville was the most American of French directors, who
made the most French of gangster movies. This dark, grim thriller dealt
with an ex-convict who teamed up with a criminal on the run and a
former police marksman to steal jewels from a shop equipped with a
high-tech security system. A thriller with a downbeat ending, it was
enlivened by the central set-piece of the robbery itself, though it was
the matter of honour among thieves that Melville wanted to explore.
The three are all hunted men in one way or another and accept their
fate with a cool indifference; it is this insouciance, common to many of
Melville's heroes, that makes them undeniably and stylishly French.

All That Jazz

US 1979 123m Technicolor
COL/TCF (Robert Alan Aurthur, Daniel Melnick)
📺 ▦ ◎ ◉ ⊘ ♫
w Robert Alan Aurthur, Bob Fosse *d* Bob Fosse
ph Giuseppe Rotunno *m* Ralph Burns *pd* Philip
Rosenberg, Tony Walton *ed* Alan Heim
☆ *Roy Scheider* (Joe Gideon), Jessica Lange (Angelique),
Ann Reinking (Kate Jagger), Leland Palmer (Audrey Paris),
Ben Vereen (O'Connor Flood), Cliff Gorman (David
Newman)

'Egomaniacal, wonderfully choreographed, often
compelling ... more an art item than a broad
commercial prospect.' – *Variety*

'An improbable mixture of crass gags, song 'n'
dance routines and open heart surgery. Not for the
squeamish.' – *Time Out*

'By the end I felt I'd learned more about Fosse than
I actually cared to know.' – *Daily Mail*

'High cholesterol hokum. Enjoyable, but probably
not good for you.' – *Pauline Kael, New Yorker*

♟ art direction; editing; musical adaptation; costume
design (Albert Wolsky)
♟ picture; Bob Fosse; Roy Scheider; Giuseppe Rotunno;
script
♙ cinematography; editing; sound

530
All That Jazz

*A stage musical director pushes himself too hard, and dies of a surfeit
of wine, women and work.*

Bob Fosse's semi-autobiographical, dancing meditation on death is an
extraordinary display of egocentricity, a dazzling multi-million dollar
confessional tracing the highs and lows of his own life. The self-indulgent, tragi-comic extravaganza comes complete with heart operations,
a recurring angel of death and some typically dazzling choreography.
The flashes of brilliant talent make it a must for Fosse fans and all
those who love show business pizzazz.

Moonlighting
GB   1982   97m   colour
Michael White/Channel 4 (Mark Shivas, Jerzy Skolimowski)

wd Jerzy Skolimowski *ph* Tony Pierce Roberts *m* Stanley Myers *pd* Tony Woollard *ed* Barrie Vince
☆ Jeremy Irons (Nowak), Eugene Lipinski (Banaszak), Jiri Stanislaw (Wolski), Eugeniusz Haczkiewicz (Kudaj)

529
Moonlighting

In 1981, four Polish building workers arrive in London to renovate a house for their boss and make a quick profit. The scheme is somewhat upset by the news of martial law at home …

The Polish-born director Jerzy Skolimowski based this intriguing, ironic drama on his own experiences of exile and adjustment to other cultures. It is a sharp political parable that makes its points through the comedy of survival. Skolimowski used as a location his own London house, which he had just finished renovating with some Polish workmen and had to dirty again for the film ('If I follow my own experience I can control it in a way I couldn't if I filmed somewhere else,' he told me at the time. 'It is very difficult to transform the imagination').

'Today, only a handful of people know what it means … Soon you will know.'
The China Syndrome
US   1979   122m   Metrocolor
Columbia/IPC (Michael Douglas)

w Mike Gray, T. A. Cook, James Bridges *d* James Bridges *ph* James Crabe *m* various *pd* George Jenkins *ad* George Jenkins *ed* David Rawlins
☆ Jane Fonda (Kimberly Wells), *Jack Lemmon* (Jack Godell), Michael Douglas (Richard Adams), Scott Brady (Herman DeYoung), Peter Donat (Don Jacovich), James Hampton (Bill Gibson)

'The performances are so good, and the screen so bombarded with both action and informative images … that it's only with considerable hindsight that one recovers sufficient breath to reproach the script with the occasional glib symmetry.' – *Jan Dawson, MFB*

Jack Lemmon, Jane Fonda; script
Jack Lemmon; Jane Fonda

528
The China Syndrome

The controller of a nuclear power plant discovers an operational flaw which could lead to disaster, but the unscrupulous authorities want to cover it up.

Jack Lemmon, as the controller of the nuclear power plant and Jane Fonda as a TV reporter both give superb performances in James Bridges' melodramatic, paranoid and topical thriller-with-a-moral, in which they discover that truth is a luxury neither can afford. Bridges maintains a high level of suspense, Lemmon's anguished face and haunted eyes make dialogue unnecessary, while Fonda's characterization moves from self-absorbed ambition to frantic resolve. It is absorbingly done in the old style.

Nosferatu

Germany 1921 72m approx (24 fps) bw
Prana

⬚ ▦ ◉ ⊚ ⊚ 🎧

w Henrik Galeen *d* *F. W. Murnau* *ph* Fritz Arno Wagner
ad Albin Grau

☆ *Max Schreck* (Count Orlok, Nosferatu the Vampire),
Gustav von Wangenheim (Thomas Hutter), Greta Schröder
(Ellen), Alexander Granach (Knock)

> 'The film is in awe of its material. It seems to really
> believe in vampires.' – *Roger Ebert, Chicago Sun-
> Times*

> 'A concentrated essay in horror fantasy, full of
> weird, macabre camera effects.' – *Pauline Kael*

• Remade in 1974 with Klaus Kinski

527
Nosferatu

Count Dracula travels to Bremen and is destroyed by sunlight.

F. W. Murnau made an unofficial treatment of Bram Stoker's novel about Dracula, with a terrifying count and several splendid moments. Max Schreck as the vampire is far removed from the suave Hollywood version incarnated by Bela Lugosi. He is a wizened, bat-eared, long-fanged, clawed creature who looks as though he has just crawled out of a rotting grave. (In 2000, Willem Dafoe played Schreck as an actual vampire in *Shadow of a Vampire*, a fantasy about the making of *Nosferatu*). Murnau's shadowy setting enhances the film's sense of dread, of vampirism as a contagious plague. Its success took its director to Hollywood to direct his masterpiece *Sunrise*.

Doctor No

🏃 GB 1962 111m Technicolor
UA/Eon (Harry Saltzman, Albert R. Broccoli)

⬚ ⬚ ▦ ◉ ⊚ ⊚ 🎧

w Richard Maibaum, Johanna Harwood, Berkely Mather
novel Ian Fleming *d* Terence Young *ph* Ted Moore
m Monty Norman *ad* Syd Cain *ed* Peter Hunt

☆ *Sean Connery* (James Bond), *Ursula Andress* (Honey),
Jack Lord (Felix Leiter), Joseph Wiseman (Dr. No), John
Kitzmiller (Quarrel), Bernard Lee ('M'), Lois Maxwell (Miss
Moneypenny), Zena Marshall (Miss Taro), Eunice Gayson
(Sylvia), Anthony Dawson (Prof. Dent)

526
Doctor No

A British secret service agent foils a master criminal operating in the West Indies.

The first of the phenomenally successful James Bond movies, which mixed sex, violence and campy humour against expensive sets and exotic locales. Toned down from the original novels, they expressed a number of sixties attitudes, and have proved an unstoppable box-office attraction. If not quite the best, the first set a high standard and provided an outline of plot that has been used ever since: a British Secret Service agent foils a master criminal who plans to hold the world to ransom. Ursula Andress provides an iconic cinematic moment as she emerges from the sea in a white bikini, and Connery, while not the Bond of Fleming's novels, brings strength and humour to the role without falling into the self-parody of the later instalments of the series.

Ginger and Fred

Italy/France/West Germany   1986   126m
colour
PEA/Revcom/Stella/RAI (Alberto Grimaldi)

w Federico Fellini, Tonino Guerra, Tullio Pinelli d Federico
Fellini ph Tonino Delli Colli, Ennio Guarnieri m Nicola
Piovani pd Dante Ferretti ad Nazzareno Piani ed Ugo De
Rossi, Ruggero Mastroianni, Nino Baragli
☆ Giulietta Masina (Amelia Bonetti/Ginger), Marcello
Mastroianni (Pippo Botticella/Fred), Franco Fabrizi (Show
Host), Frederick von Ledebur (Admiral Aulenti)

525
Ginger and Fred

Two dancers are brought out of retirement to appear on a TV show.

An ageing pair of dancers who used to imitate the dance routines of Fred Astaire and Ginger Rogers, are the centrepoint of Federico Fellini's melancholy comedy. The couple are impersonated by Fellini's favourite actors, his wife, Giulietta Masina, and Marcello Mastroianni, who is the image of Fellini himself as 'Fred'. She is all smiles, professionalism and tolerance of the odd collection of television misfits she finds herself among; he is scornful of the TV-watching public, but glad to perform, however hesitantly, one more time. This is almost the director's farewell to films, a short, final flourish of magic before he put away his dancing shoes.

My Name Is Joe

GB/Germany   1998   105m   colour
Parallax/Road Movies (Rebecca O'Brien)

w Paul Laverty d Ken Loach ph Barry Ackroyd
m George Fenton pd Martin Johnson ad Fergus Clegg
ed Jonathan Morris
☆ Peter Mullan (Joe Kavanagh), Louise Goodall (Sarah
Downie), David McKay (Liam), Annemarie Kennedy
(Sabine), David Hayman (McGowan), Gary Lewis (Shanks),
Lorraine McIntosh (Maggie)

'Ken Loach works very near the top of his form, his
angrily unblinkered vision of life at the rough end of
modern Britain tempered with humanity, humour
and a storyline that could almost come from a
classic screwball romantic comedy.' – *Kim
Newman, Empire*

● Peter Mullan won the best actor award at the Cannes
Film Festival of 1998.
● The film was subtitled for American audiences.

524
My Name Is Joe

A ex-alcoholic Scot is caught between aiding a friend and losing woman he loves.

Ken Loach's drama of Glaswegian working-class life is a grimly compassionate account of Joe Kavanagh, a reformed alcoholic who ruins his developing relationship with a nurse when he agrees to carry drugs for a local gangster in order to help a friend stay out of trouble. Loach's careful, low key direction captures the atmosphere of the city's slums and the problematic lives of those trapped within them. He deals with deprivation and the desperation of poverty. There is hardly a glimmer of hope here, as violence and tragedy threatens to overwhelm them all; only the energy of Peter Mullan's Joe offers any optimism for the future.

Mr Deeds Goes to Town

US 1936 118m bw
Columbia (Frank Capra)

w *Robert Riskin* story *Opera Hat* by Clarence Budington Kelland *d* Frank Capra *ph* Joseph Walker *m* Adolph Deutsch *md* Howard Jackson *ad* Stephen Goosson *ed* Gene Havlick

☆ *Gary Cooper* (Longfellow Deeds), Jean Arthur (Babe Bennett), Raymond Walburn (Walter), Lionel Stander (Cornelius Cobb), Walter Catlett (Morrow), George Bancroft (MacWade), Douglass Dumbrille (John Cedar), H. B. Warner (Judge Walker), Ruth Donnelly (Mabel Dawson), *Margaret Seddon* (Jane Faulkner), *Margaret McWade* (Amy Faulkner)

'I have an uneasy feeling he's on his way out. He's started to make pictures about themes instead of people.' – *Alistair Cooke*

'A comedy quite unmatched on the screen.' – *Graham Greene*

'The film culminates in a courtroom sequence that introduced the word "pixilated" to just about every American home, and set people to examining each other's casual scribbles or sketches – their "doodles".' – *Pauline Kael, 70s*

🏆 Frank Capra
♟ best picture; Robert Riskin; Gary Cooper

'Beware The Night!'
The Old Dark House

US 1932 71m bw
Universal (Carl Laemmle Jnr)

w Benn W. Levy, R. C. Sherriff novel *Benighted* by J. B. Priestley *d* James Whale *ph* Arthur Edeson *ad* Charles D. Hall *ed* Clarence Kolster

☆ *Melvyn Douglas* (Roger Penderell), *Charles Laughton* (Sir William Porterhouse), *Raymond Massey* (Philip Waverton), *Boris Karloff* (Morgan), *Ernest Thesiger* (Horace Femm), *Eva Moore* (Rebecca Femm), Gloria Stuart (Margaret Waverton), Lillian Bond (Gladys DuCane), Brember Wills (Saul Femm), John Dudgeon (Elspeth Dudgeon) (Sir Roderick Femm)

'Somewhat inane, it's a cinch for trick ballyhooing. Better for the nabes than the big keys.' – *Variety*

'Each threat as it appears is revealed to be burlap and poster paint … despite storm, attempted rape and a remarkable final chase, the film is basically a confidence trick worked with cynical humour by a brilliant technician.' – *John Baxter, 1968*

'Basically a *jeu d'esprit* in which comedy of manners is edged into tragedy of horrors, the film never puts a foot wrong.' – *Tom Milne, MFB, 1978*

● The Region 1 DVD release includes commentary by Gloria Stuart and by James Whale's biographer James Curtis.
● Remade by Hammer in 1962.

523
Mr Deeds Goes to Town

A honest man finds that inherited wealth can be an embarrassment.

In Frank Capra's Depression-era comedy, a small-town poet inherits a vast fortune and sets New York on its heels by his honesty. Longfellow Deeds (Gary Cooper) is a man who does not need the millions though for a time he enjoys the rich life. After a penniless farmer wants to kill him because of his lavish living, he decides to give away most of his money to help others, and is thought to be insane. Robert Riskin's populist screenplay makes it clear, in words given to Cooper, that the rich have responsibilities to others. It is warm, funny and sentimental; the good intentions conquer all. Jean Arthur, as the journalist who comes to love Deeds, gave a star performance. And Cooper brings to the role his air of incorruptibility and unshakeable integrity that did much to elevate this depression-era drama into a film for the ages.

522
The Old Dark House

On a dark and stormy night, travellers seek shelter among a mad Welsh family.

A marvellous horror comedy filled with superb grotesques and memorable lines, which is closely based on J. B. Priestley's novel of stranded travellers taking refuge in the house of a Welsh family of eccentrics, who are waited on by a thuggish, mute butler. The bedridden patriarch of the family, played by a bearded Elsbeth Dudgeon, tells them that his three elderly children are all mad and one is a pyromaniac. The first appearance of the wizened Ernest Thesiger, disdainfully throwing flowers on the fire, emphasizes their oddity, as does Brember Wills' appearance at the film's climax as a mild-appearing, but mad-eyed, killer. The film omits the book's more thoughtful moments, for Priestley had been trying to write a novel of ideas, a thriller with psychological depth that exposed the follies of still prevalent Edwardian attitudes. Instead, under James Whale's direction, it became a macabre romp that is a stylist's and connoisseur's treat.

Green for Danger

GB   1946   93m   bw
Rank/Individual (Frank Launder, Sidney Gilliat)
■ ⓠ

w Sidney Gilliat, Claud Guerney novel Christianna Brand *d* Sidney Gilliat *ph* Wilkie Cooper *m* William Alwyn *pd* Peter Proud *ed* Thelma Myers
☆ *Alastair Sim* (Inspector Cockrill), *Sally Gray* (Nurse Linley), *Rosamund John* (Nurse Sanson), *Trevor Howard* (Dr Barnes), *Leo Genn* (Mr Eden), *Megs Jenkins* (Nurse Woods), *Judy Campbell* (Sister Bates), Ronald Adam (Dr White), *Moore Marriott* (Joseph Higgins), George Woodbridge (Det Sgt Hendricks)

'Slick, witty and consistently entertaining.' – *Daily Telegraph*

'Launder and Gilliat have told an exciting story excitingly.' – *Times*

521
Green for Danger

A mysterious murderer strikes on the operating table at a wartime emergency hospital.

Alastair Sim is in excellent, witty form as a detective who takes great pleasure in investigating murders. After gathering his five suspects together in a hospital office, he jauntily tells them, 'Four of you are in mortal danger from the fifth.' As people die on the operating table of a wartime emergency hospital, he ferrets out the secret intrigues of doctors and nurses while his own dignity suffers from a few pratfalls. It is a clever amalgam of jokes and suspense, with occasional shocks, that makes a diverting entertainment.

Harvey

👫 US   1950   104m   bw
U-I (John Beck)
▣ ■ ⓠ ⓖ ⓐ

w Mary Chase (with Oscar Brodney) play Mary Chase *d* Henry Koster *ph* William Daniels *m* Frank Skinner *ad* Bernard Herzbrun, Nathan Juran *ed* Ralph Dawson
☆ *James Stewart* (Elwood P. Dowd), *Josephine Hull* (Veta Louise Simmons), *Victoria Horne* (Myrtle Mae), Peggy Dow (Miss Kelly), *Cecil Kellaway* (Dr. Chumley), Charles Drake (Dr. Sanderson), *Jesse White* (Wilson), Nana Bryant (Mrs. Chumley), Wallace Ford (Lofgren)
🏆 Josephine Hull
🏆 James Stewart

520
Harvey

A middle-aged drunk has an imaginary white rabbit as his friend, and his sister tries to have him certified.

An amiably batty play with splendid lines is here transferred virtually intact to the screen. It survives superbly thanks to understanding by all concerned. Cinematographer William Daniels always framed Stewart to leave enough room for an invisible rabbit. The star, though, was as yet too young for a role which he later made his own; he always was at his best in monologues. Stewart was glad to return to the role on television in the 1970s, and more than once on the stage; he thought he was 'a little too cute-cute' in the film, but it is an engaging and very likeable performance.

'The things I do for England!'

The Private Life of Henry VIII
GB 1933 97m bw
London Films (Alexander Korda)

w Lajos Biro, Arthur Wimperis d Alexander Korda
ph Georges Périnal m Kurt Schroeder ad Vincent Korda
ed Harold Young, Stephen Harrison
☆ Charles Laughton (Henry VIII), Elsa Lanchester (Anne of Cleves), Robert Donat (Thomas Culpepper), Merle Oberon (Anne Boleyn), Binnie Barnes (Katherine Howard), Franklin Dyall (Thomas Cromwell), Miles Mander (Wriothesley), Wendy Barrie (Jane Seymour), Claud Allister (Cornell), Everley Gregg (Catherine Parr)

'Among the best anywhere and by far the top British picture … figures a sock entry, especially for the best houses.' – Variety

👤 Charles Laughton
🏆 best picture

519
The Private Life of Henry VIII

How Henry beheaded his second wife and acquired four more.

Alexander Korda's production and Charles Laughton's Oscar-winning performance gained an international audience for this British film about Henry VIII's brash, bawdy matrimonial adventures. It never was a perfect film, but certain scenes are very funny and its sheer sauciness established the possibility of British films making money abroad, as well as starting several star careers. It is Laughton's acting that keeps the film alive; it is a rounded, fully human portrait of a uncomplicated, extrovert man of large appetites.

'Let's go to work.'

Reservoir Dogs
US 1991 99m colour
Rank/Live America/Dog Eat Dog (Lawrence Bender)

wd Quentin Tarantino ph Andrzej Sekula pd David Wasco
ed Sally Menks
☆ Harvey Keitel (Mr. White/Larry), Tim Roth (Mr. Orange/Freddy), Michael Madsen (Mr. Blonde/Vic), Chris Penn (Nice Guy Eddie), Steve Buscemi (Mr. Pink), Lawrence Tierney (Joe Cabot), Randy Brooks (Holdaway), Kirk Baltz (Marvin Nash), Eddie Bunker (Mr. Blue), Quentin Tarantino (Mr. Brown)

'An astute mix of wit and cynicism which washes down its melodramatic excesses with sly satire on the blood-and-guts elements of the crime movie, this is a film of considerable acuity and power.' – Kim Newman, Sight and Sound

'No one should go to see Reservoir Dogs without prior thought. But what they will see is a riveting treatment on the theme of betrayal set in an urban wasteland that murders hope and makes redemption virtually impossible.' – Derek Malcolm, Guardian

● Quentin Tarantino has acknowledged that the film was influenced by Hong Kong director Ringo Lam's City on Fire, as well as by Stanley Kubrick's The Killing and Joseph Sargent's The Taking of Pelham 123.

518
Reservoir Dogs

While one of their number bleeds to death after a bungled robbery, the rest of the gang, hiding out in a warehouse, try to discover what went wrong.

A brilliant, if sometimes repellent and notably violent gangster movie that is also a tense and exciting examination of male egos on a collision course. The gang of robbers are all strangers, chosen for the robbery by the tough crime boss Joe Cabot (Lawrence Tierney), but they show shifting loyalties as they form alliances and their disputes become angry. Quentin Tarantino, in his debut movie, showed a mastery of popular culture and a sure understanding of the genre.

Before the Rain

GB/France/Macedonia   1994   113m
Eastmancolor
Electric/Aim/Noe/Vardar (Judy Counihan, Cedomir Kolar, Sam Taylor, Cat Villiers)

⬚ ▦ ⌒

original title: *Pred Dozdot*

wd Milcho Manchevski *ph* Manuel Teran *m* Anastasia *pd* Sharon Lamofsky, David Munns *ed* Nicolas Gaster
☆ Katrin Cartlidge (Anne), Rade Serbedzija (Aleksandar), Gregoire Colin (Kiril), Labina Mitevska (Zamira), Jay Villiers (Nick), Silvija Stojanovska (Hana), Phyllida Law (Anne's Mother)

'Dense with threat and tense with the possibility of its release.' – *Tom Shone, Sunday Times*

⚲ best foreign film

517
Before the Rain

A man experiences the fatal effect of civil war on his village when he returns home to Macedonia.

In Milcho Manchevski's gripping drama three separate stories intertwine: a young monk shelters from bandits an Albanian Muslim girl; a gunman in a London restaurant kills the husband of a woman who was about to ask for a divorce; an expatriate Macedonian photographer leaves his pregnant English lover in London to return to his homeland. As his country is caught in the conflict that has destroyed Yugoslavia, he witnesses the effects of the civil war on the village where he grew up and attempts to settle a dispute between Christians and Muslims. The connections between the stories, and the way each leads forward and back to the other, is not evident until the final moments. The construction mirrors the circle of violence the film depicts, with its characters mired in unthinking hate.

The Garden of the Finzi-Continis

Italy/West Germany   1970   95m
Eastmancolor
Documento Film/CCC Filmkunst (Gianni Hecht Lucari, Arthur Cohn)

▦ ⚲~ ⊘ ⌒

w Tullio Pinelli, Valerio Zurlini, Franco Brusati, Ugo Pirro, Vittorio Bonicelli, Alain Katz *novel* Giorgio Bassani *d* Vittorio de Sica *ph* Ennio Guarnieri *m* Manuel de Sica *ad* Giancarlo Bartolini Salimbeni *ed* Adriana Novelli
☆ *Dominique Sanda* (Micol), Lino Capolicchio (Giorgio), Helmut Berger (Alberto), Romolo Valli (Giorgio's Father), Fabio Testi (Malnate)

'I lived through the period. The same feelings I experienced in life, I transposed to the picture: that is the definition of the artist.' – *Vittorio de Sica*

'This extraordinary film, with its melancholy glamour, is perhaps the only one that records the halfhearted anti-Jewish measures of the Mussolini period.' – *New Yorker*

⚱ best foreign film
⚲ script

516
The Garden of the Finzi-Continis

In 1938, a family of wealthy Italian Jews sees its world collapse, with a concentration camp as the next destination.

Giorgio Bassani, on whose autobiographical novel the film was based, was unhappy with the result, although it is difficult to see why. De Sica made a dreamlike, poignant, and very beautiful film. The Finzi-Contini family ignore Italy's increasing anti-semitism, retreating into the private world of their estate, where they and their friends can take shelter from the Fascists' persecution. When war comes, they are rounded up, bound for the concentration camps. De Sica's restrained approach conjures a nostalgia, not only for what has been destroyed, but for what might have been in a better world.

Shine
Australia/GB   1996   105m   Cinevex
Buena Vista/AFFC/Momentum/SAFC/Film Victoria
(Jane Scott)
🎞 ▦ ⊚~ ⊚ ⊚ ⌒

w Jan Sardi *story* Scott Hicks *d* Scott Hicks *ph* Geoffrey
Simpson *m* David Hirschfelder *pd* Vicki Niehus *ed* Pip
Karmel
☆ *Geoffrey Rush* (David as an Adult), *Armin Mueller-Stahl* (Peter), *Noah Taylor* (David as a Young Man), Lynn
Redgrave (Gillian), Googie Withers (Katharine Susannah
Prichard), Sonia Todd (Sylvia), Nicholas Bell (Ben Rosen),
John Gielgud (Cecil Parkes), Chris Haywood (Sam)

> 'A throwback to the best of old-fashioned
> Hollywood movies, able to move an audience
> without insulting it in the process.' – *Kenneth
> Turan, Los Angeles Times*

● The film is based on the life of pianist David Helfgott,
who embarked on an international concert tour following the
film's release, and also played at the Oscars award ceremony
in 1997.
● It won nine Australian Film Institute awards, including
best picture, best director, best actor (Geoffrey Rush) and
best original screenplay.
🏃 Geoffrey Rush
♟ best picture; Scott Hicks (as director and writer); Jan
Sardi; Armin Mueller-Stahl; David Hirschfelder; Pip Karmel
🏆 Geoffrey Rush

515
Shine

A promising classical pianist, dominated by his anxious and repressive father, suffers a mental breakdown, from which he is eventually rescued by an unexpected love.

A moving, superbly acted drama of tragedy and redemption that brilliantly evoked a man's alienation from his roots and his disintegration, as well as his re-emergence into the world. It was based on the true story of David Helfgott. Geoffrey Rush, in his first film role, was extraordinary as the troubled Helfgott, given to sudden manic bursts of energy, and Noah Taylor, as the young, inarticulate David, and Armin Mueller-Stahl, as the crushing father, a survivor from a Nazi concentration camp, were no less fine.

'China, 1920's. One master, four wives …
One fate.'

Raise the Red Lantern
Hong Kong   1991   125m   Eastmancolor
Palace/Era/China Film (Chiu Fu-Sheng)
🎞 ▦ ⊚~ ⌒

original title: *Dahong Denglong Gaogao Gua*
w Ni Zhen *story* Su Tong *d* Zhang Yimou *ph* Zhao Fei
m Zhao Jiping *ad* Cao Jiuping, Dong Huamiao *ed* Du
Yuan
☆ Gong Li (Songlian), Ma Jingwu (Master Chen Zuoqian),
He Caifei (Meishan), Cao Cuifeng (Zhuoyun), Jin Shuyuan
(Yuru), Kong Li (Yan'er), Ding Weimin (Mother Song), Cui
Zhigang (Doctor Gao), Chu Xiao (Feipu)
♟ best foreign film
🏆 best foreign film

514
Raise the Red Lantern

A young woman, who has become the fourth wife of a rich merchant, finds herself in competition with his other wives for her husband's favour.

Zhang Yimou's film is a cool study of sexual politics. It is an enclosed world where betrayal is the only possible action, and a decomposing body in a tower is evidence of what happens to a wife who transgresses. No doubt this account of the subjugation of women can be read as having wider political implications; as a melodrama of the descent into madness of an educated woman, it is always fascinating.

Mine Own Executioner
GB   1947   108m   bw
London Films (Anthony Kimmins, Jack Kitchin)

🏴

w Nigel Balchin *novel* Nigel Balchin *d* Anthony Kimmins
ph Wilkie Cooper *m* Benjamin Frankel *ad* William C.
Andrews *ed* Richard Best

☆ *Burgess Meredith* (Felix Milne), Kieron Moore (Adam
Lucian), Dulcie Gray (Patricia Milne), Barbara White (Molly
Lucian), Christine Norden (Barbara Edge), Michael Shepley
(Peter Edge), Walter Fitzgerald (Dr. Norris Pile), John Laurie
(Dr. James Garsten), Clive Morton (Robert Paston)

'The first psychoanalytical film that a grown-up can
sit through without squirming.' – *Richard
Winnington*

'One feels invigorated by having seen and
understood other people's lives.' – *Daily Worker*

513

Mine Own Executioner

A lay psychiatrist undertakes the care of a mentally disturbed war veteran, but fails to prevent him from murdering his wife.

When this film first appeared it seemed like the first adult drama featuring sophisticated people to emerge from a British studio. Time and television may have blunted its impact, but it remains a well-told suspense melodrama with memorable characters. Burgess Meredith is convincing as the psychiatrist who treats his own wife badly while beginning an extra-marital affair.

'Based on a private diary of Catherine the
Great!'

'The screen's reigning beauty in a wild
pageant of barbaric splendour!'

'A cavalcade of fury led by a woman of
fire!'

The Scarlet Empress
US   1934   109m   bw
Paramount
📷 🎞 ⊚

w Manuel Komroff *d* Josef von Sternberg *ph* Bert
Glennon *md* W. Franke Harling, John M. Leipold, Milan
Roder *ad* Hans Dreier, Peter Ballbusch, Richard Kollorsz
ed Josef von Sternberg *cos* Travis Banton

☆ *Marlene Dietrich* (Sophia Frederica), *John Lodge*
(Count Alexei), *Sam Jaffe* (Grand Duke Peter), Louise
Dresser (Empress Elizabeth), C. Aubrey Smith (Prince
August), Gavin Gordon (Gregory Orloff), Jameson Thomas
(Lt. Ostvyn)

'She's photographed behind veils and fishnets,
while dwarfs slither about and bells ring and
everybody tries to look degenerate.' – *New Yorker,
1975*

'A ponderous, strangely beautiful, lengthy and
frequently wearying production.' – *Mordaunt Hall,
New York Times*

● 'Catherine the Great', an Alexander Korda production with
Elisabeth Bergner, was released at the same time.

512

The Scarlet Empress

A fantasia on the love life of Catherine the Great.

Josef von Sternberg's film was a marvellous, overwhelming, dramatically insubstantial but pictorially brilliant homage to its star. Sternberg called it 'a relentless excursion into style'. In his baroque, mad imaginings, it resembles no other film. The sets had huge, heavy doors with handles six feet off the ground, and sculptures loomed from every corner, dwarfing the cast. Even Dietrich thought he was overdoing it, though she was serene at its centre, swathed in white furs, or wearing an enormous hooped, mink-trimmed costume and tall fur hat. It was not to everyone's taste, but remains a film to remember.

Ai No Corrida

France/Japan 1976 105m Eastmancolor
Argos/Oshima/Shibata (Anatole Dauman)

French title: *L'Empire des Sens*
aka: *Empire of the Passions; In the Realm of the Senses*

wd Nagisa Oshima *ph* Hideo Ito *m* Minoru Miki
☆ Tatsuya Fuji, Eiko Matsuda, Aoi Nakajima, Meika Seri

'By the final sequence, we are all implicated in the continuing social system which makes such love impossible. It is not Sade, but the censor in all of us who ultimately wields the knife.' – *Jan Dawson, MFB*

● The film was not given a certificate by the BBFC or a cinema release in Britain until 1991, although it had been shown in cinema clubs.

511
Ai No Corrida

A sexually complicated servant girl has an intense affair with the master of the house, and finally murders and mutilates him.

A sexually explicit film about sexual obsession, the movie was condemned as pornographic and banned in many countries on its first release. Oshima is not interested in the mechanics of sex, even when he shows them. He is more concerned with its context: the affair's tragic outcome, and the fact that its two insatiable lovers ignore servants and onlookers in their desire. The movie is based on a famous murder that was also filmed a year before by Noboru Tanaka: in 1936, Abe Sada, a servant, killed her lover and castrated him so that she could keep a piece of him with her. The action takes place at a time of political unrest, only briefly glimpsed in the movie, but suggesting that ignoring the wider world in search of personal, sexual liberation is, literally, a dead end.

From Russia with Love

GB 1963 118m Technicolor
UA/Eon (Harry Saltzman, Albert Broccoli)

w Richard Maibaum, Johanna Harwood *novel* Ian Fleming
d Terence Young *ph* Ted Moore *m* John Barry *ad* Syd Cain *ed* Peter Hunt *titles* Robert Brownjohn
☆ *Sean Connery* (James Bond), *Robert Shaw* (Red Grant), *Pedro Armendariz* (Kerim Bey), Daniela Bianchi (Tatiana Romanova), *Lotte Lenya* (Rosa Klebb), Bernard Lee ('M'), Eunice Gayson (Sylvia), Lois Maxwell (Miss Moneypenny)
Ⓣ Ted Moore

510
From Russia with Love

James Bond is lured into a deadly trap by an international spy ring.

This second Bond adventure is one of the best, in which 007 faces murder from a Russian spy, who joins an international crime organization and develops a plan to steal a coding machine. With Istanbul and Venice for backdrops, and climaxes involving a speeding train and a helicopter, it is arrant nonsense with tongue in cheek, on a big budget. Chosen as the follow-up to the first movie because the novel was one of President Kennedy's favourites, it demonstrated how well Sean Connery inhabited the role of the unflappable and sophisticated 007 and matched him against two superb villains in Robert Shaw's talkative assassin and Lotte Lenya's vicious killer with deadly, poison-tipped stiletto shoes.

The Kid Brother

👥 US 1927 83m bw silent
Paramount/Lloyd (Harold Lloyd)

w John Grey, Tom Crizer, Ted Wilde *d* Ted Wilde, J. A. Howe, Lewis Milestone *ph* Walter Lundin, Henry N. Kohler *ad* Liell K. Vedder *ed* Allen McNeil

☆ *Harold Lloyd* (Harold Hickory), Jobyna Ralston (Mary Powers), Walter James (Jim Hickory), Leo Willis (Leo Hickory), Olin Francis (Olin Hickory), Constantine Romanoff (Sandoni)

'As gaggy a gag picture as he has ever done.' – *Variety*

'Perfect.' – *New York Times*

509
The Kid Brother

The youngest son in the family proves that he is more than the house-hold drudge.

A lively, slapstick comedy with the star at his considerable best. Harold Lloyd was the intelligent but bashful and puny son of a tough sheriff, who proved his worth after his father was wrongly accused of stealing the town's money. It is Lloyd's best constructed comedy; the jokes flow from the narrative situations rather than being tacked on and, for once, Lloyd does no dangerous stunts, other than climbing a tall tree so he can keep in sight the girl he loves.

'A raging torrent of emotion that even nature can't control!'

Niagara
US   1952   89m   Technicolor
TCF (Charles Brackett)

w Charles Brackett, Walter Reisch, Richard Breen *d* Henry Hathaway *ph* Joe MacDonald *m* Sol Kaplan *ad* Maurice Ransford, Lyle Wheeler *ed* Barbara McLean
☆ *Joseph Cotten* (George Loomis), Jean Peters (Polly Cutler), *Marilyn Monroe* (Rose Loomis), Don Wilson (Mr. Kettering), Casey Adams

'The story is most imaginatively treated, the production values are excellent.' – *CEA Film Report*

'Seen from any angle, the Falls and Miss Monroe leave little to be desired.' – *New York Times*

'A masterly example of fluid screen narrative.' – *Charles Higham*

'It would have turned out a much better picture if James Mason had played the husband as I wanted. He has that intensity, that neurotic edge. He was all set to do it, but his daughter Portland said she was sick of seeing him die in his pictures.' – *Henry Hathaway*

'This isn't a good movie but it's compellingly tawdry and nasty … the only movie that explored the mean, unsavoury potential of Marilyn Monroe's cuddly, infantile perversity.' – *Pauline Kael, 70s*

Diary for My Children
Hungary   1982   107m   bw
Artificial Eye/Mafilm/Hungarofilm
original title: *Napló Gyermekeimnek*
w Márta Mészáros, Balàzs Fakan, András Szeredás *d* Márta Mészáros *ph* Miklós Jancsó Jnr *m* Zsolt Döme *ed* Eva Karmento
☆ Zsuzsa Czinkóczi (Juli), Anna Polony (Magda), Jan Nowicki (Janos/Juli's Father), Mari Szémes (Grandma), Pàl Zolnay (Grandpa)

508
Niagara

While visiting Niagara Falls, a faithless wife is plotting to murder her husband, but he turns the tables.

This was an excellent suspenser in the best Hitchcock class, with breathtaking locations. In this *film noir*, Marilyn Monroe (in her first staring role) was not in the classic tradition of a *femme fatale*, but was already being used as a sex-object by Joseph Cotten's husband, by the director, who put much emphasis on her wiggly walk, and the audience.

507
Diary for My Children

An orphan, returning to Budapest in 1947, recalls her happy childhood while dealing with a less enjoyable present.

The Hungarian director Márta Mészáros used her own life as a basis for an enthralling film. As a small child she moved to the Soviet Union with her family. When she was seven, her father, a sculptor, was arrested, jailed and executed. After her mother died a few years later, she moved back to Hungary. Its account of three generations of a family encapsulates the modern history of Hungary. Withheld from the West for two years, it won a special jury prize at the Cannes Film Festival in 1984.

Mother and Son

Russia/Germany 1997 71m colour
Zero/O-Film/Severnij Fond/Lenfilm

▣ ▤ ⊘

original title: *Mat i syn*
w Yuri Arabov *d* Alexandr Sokurov *ph* Alexei Yodorov
m Mikhail Ivanovich Glinka, Otmar Nussio *ad* Vera
Zelinskaya *ed* Leda Semyonova
☆ Gudrun Geyer (Mother), Alexei Ananishov (Son)

'Its majestic, affective power makes most of
cinema seem trivial, raucous, faked.' – *Julian
Graffy, Sight and Sound*

506
Mother and Son

In a large house near the sea, a son tends his dying mother.

Alexandr Sokurov's bold film has little dialogue, the actors are not professional, and it has no action in the conventional sense. Sokurov and cinematographer Alexei Yodorov use mirrors, coloured glass filter and distorted images to create a fractured dreamlike world, influenced by the mysterious paintings of the German landscape artist Caspar David Friedrich. The result is a gently lyrical film about love and the immanence of death, and the beauty of the natural world that maintains a hushed and hypnotic hold.

Tillsammans

Sweden/Denmark/Italy 2000 106m colour
Metrodome/Memfis/Film i Vast/SVT/Zentropa/Keyfilms
Roma (Lars Jonsson)

▣ ⊘ ⊘

GB and US title: *Together*
wd Lukas Moodysson *ph* Ulf Brantas *ad* Carl Johan de
Geer *ed* Michal Leszczylowski, Fredrik Abrahamsen
☆ Lisa Lindgren (Elisabeth), Mikael Nyqvist (Rolf), Gustaf
Hammarsten (Goran), Anja Lundqvist (Lena), Jessica
Liedberg (Anna), Ola Norell (Lasse), Shanti Roney (Klas),
Sam Kessel (Stefan)

'A funny, graceful and immensely good-natured
work.' – *David Kehr, New York Times*

505
Tillsammans

In the mid Seventies, a mother leaves her abusive husband and moves into a disorganized, vegetarian commune with her two children.

Swedish director Lukas Moodysson's second feature, set in the mid-1970s, was a delightful comedy. Elisabeth (Lisa Lindgren) joining her cuckolded brother and his girlfriend and other couples, whose reasons for joining range from political commitment to sexual identity. The film explored the problems of living together and apart, and was told with a warm-hearted tolerance and keen observation.

'I'm going to run the whole works. There's only one law: do it first, do it yourself, and keep doing it!'

Scarface
US   1932   99m   bw
Howard Hughes
⊞ ⊞ ▤ ◉ ◉
aka: *The Shame of a Nation*
w Ben Hecht, Seton I. Miller, John Lee Mahin, W. R. Burnett, Fred Pasley *novel* Armitage Trail *d* Howard Hawks *ph* Lee Garmes, L. W. O'Connell *m* Adolph Tandler, Gus Arnheim *ed* Edward Curtiss
☆ *Paul Muni* (Tony Camonte), *Ann Dvorak* (Cesca Camonte), *George Raft* (Guino Rinaldo), Boris Karloff (Gaffney), Osgood Perkins (Johnny Lovo), Karen Morley (Poppy), C. Henry Gordon (Inspector Guarino), Vince Barnett (Angelo), Henry Armetta (Pietro), Edwin Maxwell (Commissioner)

'More brutal, more cruel, more wholesale than any of its predecessors.' – *James Shelley Hamilton*

'Because it was so close to the actual events, it possesses a kind of newsreel quality which cannot be recaptured or imitated. It vibrates with the impact of things that were real and deeply felt.' – *National Film Theatre programme, 1961*

● On original release, added scenes showed Tony tried, convicted and hanged, though since Muni is never seen, it appears that they were an afterthought made when he was not available.

504
Scarface

The life and death of a Chicago gangster of the Twenties.

Obviously modelled on the life and death of Chicago gangster Al Capone, with an incestuous sister thrown in, this was perhaps the most vivid film of the gangster cycle, and its revelling in its own sins was not obscured by the subtitle, *The Shame of a Nation*. Howard Hawks saw it as a modern-day version of the Borgia family of 15th-century Italy. Paul Muni and George Raft made an excellent tough-guy pairing in a violent, fast-moving drama that showed the director at his masculine best.

Raiders of the Lost Ark
🕇🕇   US   1981   115m   Metrocolor
Panavision
Paramount/Lucasfilm (Frank Marshall)
⊞ ⊞ ▤ ◉ ◉ 🎧
w Lawrence Kasdan *d* Steven Spielberg *ph* Douglas Slocombe *m* John Williams *pd* Norman Reynolds *ad* Leslie Dilley *ed* Michael Kahn
☆ Harrison Ford (Indiana Jones), Karen Allen (Marion Ravenwood), Ronald Lacey (Toht), Paul Freeman (Belloq), John Rhys-Davies (Sallah), Denholm Elliott (Brody), Wolf Kahler (Dietrich), Anthony Higgins (Gobler), Alfred Molina (Satipo)

'An out of body experience, a movie of glorious imagination and breakneck speed that grabs you in the first shot, hurtles you through a series of incredible adventures, and deposits you back in reality two hours later – breathless, dizzy, wrung-out, and with a silly grin on your face.' – *Roger Ebert*

● Tom Selleck was the first choice for the lead, but was tied up with his TV series *Magnum*.
● It was followed by two sequels: *Indiana Jones and the Temple of Doom* and *Indiana Jones and the Last Crusade*.
👤 editing (Michael Kahn); visual effects
🏆 best picture; Steven Spielberg; Douglas Slocombe; John Williams
🏆 Norman Reynolds

503
Raiders of the Lost Ark

In the Thirties, an American archaeologist and explorer beats the Nazis to a priceless artefact, the magical box containing fragments of the stones on which God wrote his laws.

Commercially very successful, the film is a throwback to Saturday morning serials of three generations ago. Spielberg directed an ingeniously detailed fast-paced story, with an equally quick-witted and -moving hero at its centre – 'either he's chasing them, or they're chasing him,' as George Lucas put it. It cleverly opens with what might have been the climax of any other film, with Indiana Jones escaping booby-traps and being chased by a giant boulder, and then goes on to top it. It is brilliantly conceived juvenile fun.

Field of Dreams

👫 US 1989 106m DeLuxe
Guild/Universal/Carolco (Lawrence Gordon, Charles Gordon)

wd Phil Alden Robinson *book* Shoeless Joe by W. P. Kinsella *ph* John Lindley *m* James Horner *pd* Dennis Gassner *ad* Leslie McDonald *ed* Ian Crafford

☆ Kevin Costner (Ray Kinsella), Amy Madigan (Annie Kinsella), James Earl Jones (Terence Mann), Timothy Busfield (Mark), Ray Liotta (Shoeless Joe Jackson), Burt Lancaster (Dr. 'Moonlight' Graham), Gaby Hoffman (Karin Kinsella), Frank Whaley (Archie Graham), Dwier Brown (John Kinsella)

🏆 best film; best adapted screenplay; best original score

502
Field of Dreams

A farmer builds a baseball pitch to summon the ghosts of past players.

Phil Alden Robinson's gentle fantasy has a great deal of charm. The narrative is occasionally clumsy, for it involves not only ghosts, but time travel, when Kevin Costner's restless farmer returns to the 1970s to meet a dead, one-time player who regrets never having confronted a major league pitcher. It also requires a little extra effort for audiences to whom baseball is not a normal part of sporting life. It is, any way, not about sport so much as dreams and dreaming, of innocence and pleasure, of dealing with regrets and enjoying the moment.

Milou in May

France/Italy   1989   108m   colour
Gala/Nouvelles Editions de Films/TFI/Ellepi Film
(Jean-Yves Asselin)
📷 🎬 ♫
original title: Milou en Mai
US title: May Fools
w Louis Malle, Jean-Claude Carrière *d* Louis Malle *ph*
Renato Berta *m* Stéphane Grappelli *ed* Emmanuelle
Castro
☆ Michel Piccoli (Milou), Miou-Miou (Camille), Michel
Duchaussoy (Georges), Dominique Blanc (Claire), Harriet
Walter (Lily), Bruno Carette (Grimaldi), François Berléand
(Daniel), Martine Gautier (Adele), Paulette Dubost (Mme.
Vieuzac)

'A film of Chekhovian generosity that never strays
into sentimentality or cynicism.' – Philip French,
Observer

501
Milou in May

Following the death of his mother, a 60-year-old man invites her relatives to the funeral.

Louis Malle's warm, well-observed study of family relationships came out of his wish to make an ensemble film as well as his liking for the plays of Chekhov. The time was the spring of 1968, when France seemed on the brink of a revolution and there were riots in Paris. The group relive their past, rekindle old disagreements with others, and contemplate an uncertain future. With an excellent cast who related to one another as if they were really one family, Malle provides some surprises in his depiction of group dynamics as well as showing a change in social conditions and aspirations. The drama is accentuated by the mainly improvised score of jazz violinist Stéphane Grappelli.

Chimes at Midnight

Spain/Switzerland   1966   119m   bw
Internacional Films Española/Alpine (Alessandro
Tasca)
🎬 ♫
aka: *Falstaff*
wd Orson Welles *ph* Edmond Richard *m* Angelo
Francesco Lavagnino *pd* Gustavo Quintano *ad* Mariano
Erdorza, Jose Antonio de la Guerra *ed* Fritz Mueller
☆ Orson Welles (Falstaff), Keith Baxter (Prince Hal), John
Gielgud (Henry IV), Margaret Rutherford (Mistress Quickly),
Jeanne Moreau (Doll Tearsheet), Norman Rodway (Henry
Percy), Alan Webb (Justice Shallow), Marina Vlady, Tony
Beckley, Fernando Rey, Michael Aldridge

'One of Orson Welles' best and least-seen movies
… The film is a near-masterpiece.' – *New Yorker*

'Ridiculous is the word for the whole enterprise –
not funny and certainly not moving.' – *John Simon*

'A testament to the enduring genius of Orson
Welles as screenwriter, director and actor … does
justice to Shakespeare, to cinema and to his own
great talents.' – *Judith Crist*

500
Chimes at Midnight

Prince Hal becomes King Henry V and rejects his old friend Falstaff.

Orson Welles adaptation of several of Shakespeare's plays to tell the story of Falstaff – and who better to play him than Welles? – is notable for its elegiac quality, a lament for a simpler, better, lost England. The production, as was the way with the improvident director, was filmed over a long period in the brief moments when money was available; doubles had to be used in long shots and cardboard cutouts stood in for extras in one crowd scene. Welles somehow gave it all a unity, possibly because he tried it out on stage first. It is the best of his Shakespearean adaptations and a fine film in its own right.

Charlie Bubbles

GB 1968 91m Technicolor
Universal/ Memorial (Michael Medwin, George Pitcher)

w Shelagh Delaney *d* Albert Finney *ph* Peter Suschitzky
m Mischa Donat *ad* Edward Marshall *ed* Fergus McDonell

☆ *Albert Finney* (Charlie Bubbles), Billie Whitelaw (Lottie Bubbles), Liza Minnelli (Eliza), Colin Blakely (Smokey Pickles), Timothy Garland (Jack Bubbles), Diana Coupland (Maud), Alan Lake (Airman), Yootha Joyce (Woman in Cafe), Joe Gladwin (Hotel Waiter)

'A modest thing, but like all good work in minor keys it has a way of haunting the memory.' – *Richard Schickel*

'The supreme deadweight is Liza Minnelli, whose screen debut proves easily the most inauspicious since Turhan Bey's.' – *John Simon*

🇹 Billie Whitelaw

499
Charlie Bubbles

A successful novelist loathes the pointlessness of the good life and tries unsuccessfully to return to his Northern, working-class background.

In Albert Finney's directorial debut (with Stephen Frears as his assistant), Finney extracts a perfect performance from Albert Finney, actor. It was a subject its writer and star knew at first hand, both going from a Northern, working-class background to success. A little arid and slow in its early stages, and with an extraordinary end (our hero escapes by air balloon), this is nevertheless a fascinating, fragmentary character study with a host of wry comedy touches and nimbly sketched characters; in its unassuming way it indicts many of the attitudes people lived by in the Sixties.

My American Uncle

France 1980 126m Eastmancolor
Andrea Films/TFI (Philippe Dussart)
ⓒ ⓡ

original title: *Mon Oncle Américain*

w Jean Gruault *books* Henri Laborit *d* Alain Resnais
ph Sacha Vierny *m* Arié Dzierlatka *ed* Albert Jurgenson
☆ Gérard Depardieu (Rene Ragueneau), Nicole Garcia (Janine Garnier), Roger Pierre (Jean Le Gall), Henri Laborit (Himself)

'Fine, funny new French comedy … immensely good-humored and witty.' – *Vincent Canby*

🔍 screenplay

498
My American Uncle

Professor Henri Laborit explains the lives of two men and a woman in terms of animal behaviour.

A fascinatingly assembled but basically pessimistic dissection of human life, in Alain Resnais' most meticulous style. It sprang from an abortive documentary that he planned on Professor Henri Laborit, a well-known behavioural scientist. Instead, he made a fictional film on the lives of two men and a woman, with Professor Laborit providing a commentary on their actions in the light of his theories of animal behaviour. The American uncle is the piece of good luck that may be just around the corner (but probably is not).

A Room with a View

GB   1985   115m   colour

Merchant Ivory/Goldcrest (Ismail Merchant)

📽 ▤ 🎞 ⊚ ⊚ 🎧

w Ruth Prawer Jhabvala *novel* E. M. Forster *d* James Ivory *ph* Tony Pierce-Roberts *m* Richard Robbins *pd* Gianna Quaranta, Brian Ackland-Snow *ed* Humphrey Dixon

☆ Maggie Smith (Charlotte Bartlett), Denholm Elliott (Mr. Emerson), Helena Bonham Carter (Lucy Honeychurch), Julian Sands (George Emerson), Daniel Day-Lewis (Cecil Vyse), Simon Callow (Rev. Beebe), Judi Dench (Miss Lavish), Rosemary Leach (Mrs. Honeychurch), Rupert Graves (Freddy Honeychurch)

'Quality-starved filmgoers will welcome it.' – *Variety*

👤 art direction; adapted screenplay; costumes (Jenny Beavan, John Bright)

🏆 James Ivory as director; Tony Pierce-Roberts; best picture; Maggie Smith; Denholm Elliott

Ⓣ best picture; production design; Maggie Smith; Judi Dench

497
A Room with a View

An innocent Edwardian girl travelling in Italy has her eyes opened to real life and romance.

E. M. Forster's novel provided opportunities for excellent acting from the talented cast assembled by director James Ivory. Maggie Smith, Denholm Elliott, Judy Dench and Daniel Day-Lewis bring their characters to vital life amid the gorgeous Italian countryside and the elegance of Florence. There is pleasure in the romance and humour in the observation of the English abroad, as well as a careful delineation of class between the would-be lovers, Julian Sands' slightly common George and Helena Bonham Carter's aristocratic Lucy. It is charming, civilized entertainment.

Cyrano de Bergerac

France   1990   138m   colour

Hachette Première/Camera One/Films A2/D.D. Productions/UGC (Rene Cleitman, Michael Seydoux)

📽 📽 🎞 ⊚ ⊚ 🎧

w Jean-Paul Rappeneau, Jean-Claude Carrière *play* Edmond Rostand *d* Jean-Paul Rappeneau *ph* Pierre Lhomme *m* Jean-Claude Petit *ad* Ezio Frigerio *ed* Noëlle Boisson

☆ *Gérard Depardieu* (Cyrano de Bergerac), Anne Brochet (Roxane), Vincent Perez (Christian de Neuvillette), Jacques Weber (Count DeGuiche), Roland Bertin (Ragueneau), Philippe Morier-Genoud (Le Bret), Philippe Volter (Viscount of Valvert), Pierre Maguelon (Carbon de Castel-Jaloux)

'A near-perfect balance of verbal and visual flamboyance.' – *Variety*

'Cyrano? Bravo!' – *Le Monde*

👤 Gérard Depardieu; best foreign film; best art direction; best costume design; best make-up

Ⓣ Pierre Lhomme; Jean-Claude Petit

• Previously filmed in 1950.

496
Cyrano de Bergerac

A dashing soldier and noted duellist, handicapped by his long nose, helps a handsome friend make love to the woman he adores from afar.

An exuberant version of the romantic French classic. Depardieu gives an appropriately larger-than-life performance as the love-struck poet and swordsman, one that mixes a swaggering panache with an underlying melancholy, as one moment he defeats a hundred assassins, and at another watches his friend claim a lover's kiss that should have been his; his death scene is one of immense bravura. The English subtitles are in a rhyming translation by Anthony Burgess, following Rostand's rhyming couplets that have been retained here, but can be a distraction from the action.

The Man Who Came to Dinner

US   1941   112m   bw

Warner (Jack Saper, Jerry Wald)

■   @~

w Julius J. and Philip G. Epstein play George S. Kaufman, Moss Hart d William Keighley ph Tony Gaudio m Frederick Hollander ad Robert Haas ed Jack Killifer

☆ Monty Woolley (Sheridan Whiteside), Bette Davis (Maggie Cutler), Ann Sheridan (Lorraine Sheldon), Jimmy Durante (Banjo (spoofing Harpo Marx)), Reginald Gardiner (Beverly Carlton (spoofing Noël Coward)), Richard Travis (Bert Jefferson), Billie Burke (Mrs Stanley), Grant Mitchell (Ernest Stanley), Ruth Vivian (Harriett Stanley), Mary Wickes (Miss Preen), George Barbier (Dr. Bradley), Elisabeth Fraser (June Stanley)

● There are many references made in the film eg.; 'Winston Churchill', 'The Hound of the Baskervilles', 'The Duke of Windsor', 'Winnie the Pooh', 'Cary Grant', 'H. G. Wells'.

495
The Man Who Came to Dinner

An acid-tongued radio celebrity breaks his hip while on a lecture tour, and terrorizes the inhabitants of the suburban home where he must stay for several weeks.

A comic delight that has outlasted Alexander Woollcott, the man it maliciously caricatures. Woollcott, author and wit, was often mocked by his contemporaries. ('What is so rare as a Woollcott first edition?' he once asked. 'A Woollcott second edition,' came the reply.) The work's inspiration was a visit Woollcott had made to co-author Moss Hart, writing in Hart's guest book when he left, 'I had one of the most unpleasant times I ever spent.' With other characters based on Noel Coward and Harpo Marx, it provides more than a laugh a minute, especially for those old enough to understand all the references.

'Fateful Fascination! Electric Tension!'

'The screen's top romantic stars in a melodramatic masterpiece!'

Notorious

US   1946   101m   bw

RKO (Alfred Hitchcock)

■   @~   ⊚   ⊙   ⌒

w Ben Hecht d Alfred Hitchcock ph Ted Tetzlaff m Roy Webb ad Albert D. D'Agostino, Carroll Clark ed Theron Warth

☆ Cary Grant (Devlin), Ingrid Bergman (Alicia Huberman), Claude Rains (Alexander Sebastian), Louis Calhern (Paul Prescott), Leopoldine Konstantin (Mme. Sebastian), Reinhold Schünzel (Dr. Anderson)

'Velvet smooth in dramatic action, sharp and sure in its characters, and heavily charged with the intensity of warm emotional appeal.' – Bosley Crowther

'The suspense is terrific.' – New Yorker, 1976

'A film in the supercharged American idiom which made Casablanca popular.' – Hermione Rich Isaacs, Theatre Arts

● A Region 1 DVD release has commentary by Hitchcock scholar Marian Keane and Rudy Behlmer.
● Hitchcock makes a cameo appearance drinking chapagne at a party.
♟ Ben Hecht; Claude Rains

494
Notorious

In Rio, a notorious lady marries a Nazi renegade to help the US government but finds herself falling in love with her contact.

A superb romantic suspenser that contains some of Hitchcock's best work. Ingrid Bergman and Cary Grant play well together and Claude Rains is one of Hitchcock's best villains; a spy who is also a sympathetic character. A film of a woman redeemed by love, it is made complex by its series of misunderstandings, and no one is quite what they seem; when Bergman and Grant kiss outside a wine-cellar that holds a deadly secret, it is not out of passion but to hide another truth.

'In war, the most powerful weapon is seduction.'

The Quiet American
US/Germany   2002   101m   Atlab
Panavision
Buena Vista/Mirage/Saga/IMF (William Horberg, Staffan Ahrenberg)
🎞 ▦ ⊚ ⌒
w Christopher Hampton, Robert Schenkkan *d* Phillip Noyce *ph* Christopher Doyle *m* Craig Armstrong *pd* Roger Ford *ad* Ian Gracie *ed* John Scott *cos* Norma Moriceau
☆ *Michael Caine* (Thomas Fowler), Brendan Fraser (Alden Pyle), Do Thi Hai Yen (Phuong), Rade Sherbedgia (Inspector Vigot), Tzi Ma (Hinh), Robert Stanton (Joe Tunney), Holmes Osborne (Bill Granger), Pham Thi Mai Hoa (Phuong's Sister), Quang Hai (The General)

'Greene's lifelong concern with moral ambiguity gives this film a texture and complexity that movies don't usually achieve.' – *Kenneth Turan, Los Angeles Times*

'Reveals itself to be not so much a historical allegory as an *Iliad* of the heart. It's sad and smart and beautiful and true.' – *Shawn Levy, Oregonian*

493
The Quiet American

In Vietnam in the early Fifties, a tired and cynical British journalist and an idealistic American agent clash over love and politics.

Unlike the earlier version of Graham Greene's novel, filmed by Joseph Mankiewicz in 1957, Phillip Noyce was true to the spirit and the story of the original. Its subject matter, of a disastrous meddling by a foreign power in the affairs of another country, seemed more than ever relevant. It superbly captured an account of political and personal betrayal, the danger of do-gooders and the corruption of spirit that weariness with the world can bring.

Onibaba
Japan   1964   104m   bw   Tohoscope
Kindai Eiga Kyokai/Tokyo Eiga
🎞 ▦ ⊚
aka: *The Hole*
wd Kaneto Shindo *ph* Kiyomi Juroda *m* Hikaru Hayashi *ad* Kaneto Shindo *ed* Kazuo Enoko
☆ Nobuko Otowa (The Mother), Jitsuko Yoshimura (The Daughter-in-Law), Kei Sato (Hachi, the Farmer)

'The film is the most ardent and unflinching celebration of sex. It shows with equal faithfulness the ecstasies of its fulfilment and the agonies of its frustration.' – *John Simon*

492
Onibaba

In sixteenth century Japan, two peasant women eke out a living by killing lost samurai.

There is no other film quite like Kaneto Shindo's medieval horror story about a starving mother and daughter who live on a remote marshy plain and kill stray samurai so that they can sell their armour. When the daughter takes as a lover a farmer who has returned from the war, the mother becomes jealous and tries to end the romance by pretending to be a demon. Shindo's previous films had been concerned with social realism. Here, for the first time, he mixes eroticism with violence and nastiness. In one shocking scene, a stranger arrives at the women's hut wearing a devil mask to hide, he says, his exceptional beauty; when the mother kills him and removes his mask, she finds a face of rotting flesh. Filmed in a desolate space, where tall reeds move and rustle restlessly in the wind, this strange, compelling piece remains, perhaps mercifully, unique.

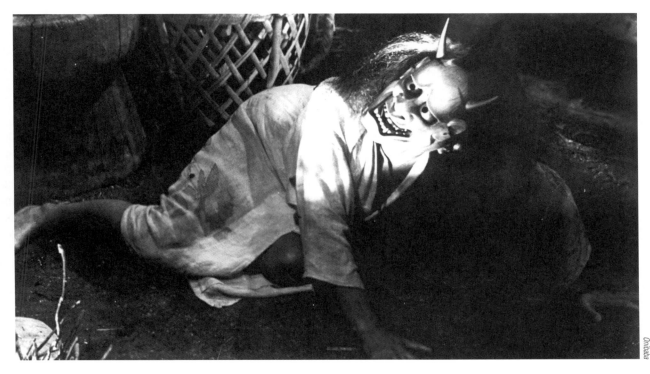

Onibaba

The Man Who Knew Too Much
GB 1934 84m bw
GFD/Gaumont British (Ivor Montagu)

w A. R. Rawlinson, Charles Bennett, D. B. Wyndham Lewis,
Edwin Greenwood, Emlyn Williams *d* Alfred Hitchcock
ph Curt Courant *m* Arthur Benjamin *ad* Alfred Junge,
Peter Proud *ed* Hugh Stewart
☆ *Leslie Banks* (Bob Lawrence), Edna Best (Jill
Lawrence), *Peter Lorre* (Abbott), Nova Pilbeam (Betty
Lawrence), Frank Vosper (Ramon Levine), Hugh Wakefield
(Clive), Pierre Fresnay (Louis Bernard)

'A natural and easy production that runs smoothly
and has the hallmark of sincerity.' – *Variety*

'The film's mainstay is its refined sense of the
incongruous.' – *Peter John Dyer, 1964*

● Remade in Hollywood in 1956.

491
The Man Who Knew Too Much

A child is kidnapped by spies to ensure her father's silence, but he springs into action.

Hitchcock based the ending of this splendid early film on the Sidney Street siege which took place in London in the early 1900s, when police surrounded a house in which anarchists had taken refuge. It has several memorable sequences involving a dentist, an East End mission and the Albert Hall. All very stagey by today's standards, but much more fun than Hitchcock's expensive American remake.

'He thought that magic only existed in books, and then he met her.'

Shadowlands
GB 1993 131m colour Scope
UIP/Showlands/Spelling/Pirce/Savoy (Richard Attenborough, Brian Eastman)
▦ ▤ ◎⌐ ⊚ ⊕

w William Nicholson *play* William Nicholson *d* Richard Attenborough *ph* Roger Pratt *m* George Fenton *pd* Stuart Craig *ad* Michael Lamont *ed* Lesley Walker
☆ *Anthony Hopkins* (Jack Lewis), *Debra Winger* (Joy Gresham), John Wood (Christopher Riley), Edward Hardwicke (Warnie Lewis), Joseph Mazzello (Douglas Gresham), Julian Fellowes (Desmond Arding), Roddy Maude-Roxby (Arnold Dopliss), Michael Denison ('Harry' Harrington), Peter Firth (Dr. Craig)

'Reticent is the word for Richard Attenborough's film version. But that's a virtue, not a defect, when the setting is English academia (no one has more persuasively captured its manners) and your subject is mortality.' – *Richard Corliss, Time*

'A beautifully crafted movie that gleams like a newly-made antique.' – *Philip French, Observer*

• William Nicholson first wrote the story as a play for BBC TV and then adapted it for the stage before it became a film. Despite Hopkins's Welsh accent, Lewis was an Ulsterman, born in Belfast.
⚖ Debra Winger; William Nicholson

Love Affair
US 1939 89m bw
RKO (Leo McCarey)
▤ ◎

w Delmer Daves, Donald Ogden Stewart *story* Mildred Cram, Leo McCarey *d* Leo McCarey *ph* Rudolph Maté *m* Roy Webb *ad* Van Nest Polglase, Al Herman *ed* Edward Dmytryk, George Hively
☆ *Charles Boyer* (Michel Marnet), *Irene Dunne* (Terry McKay), *Maria Ouspenskaya* (Grandmother Janou), Lee Bowman (Kenneth Bradley), Astrid Allwyn (Lois Clarke), Maurice Moscovich (Maurice Cobert)

'Production is of grade A quality … its b.o. chances look good.' – *Variety*

'Those excited over the mastery of form already achieved in pictures, will like to follow this demonstration of the qualities of technique and imagination the films must always have and keep on recruiting to their service … Clichés of situation and attitude are lifted almost beyond recognition by a morning freshness of eye for each small thing around.' – *Otis Ferguson*

• Remade as *An Affair to Remember* .
⚖ best picture; original story; Irene Dunne; Maria Ouspenskaya; art direction; song 'Wishing' (*m/ly* Buddy de Sylva)

490
Shadowlands

An Oxford academic enters into a marraige of convenience.

Richard Attenborough's small scale film packs a considerable emotional punch in a true story: the emotionally repressed C. S. Lewis, Oxford don and famous writer of children's books and works of popular theology, enters into a marriage of convenience with an American woman, whom he grows to love, only to learn that she has terminal cancer. It is impeccably acted, with Anthony Hopkins as a buttoned-up academic and Debra Winger as the life-affirming woman who shakes him out of his routine. It is a moving account of emotional risk, and the pain and joy it can bring.

489
Love Affair

On a transatlantic crossing, a European man of the world meets a New York girl, but their romance is flawed by misunderstanding and physical accident.

This was Charles Boyer's favourite of the films he made in America, because of its almost perfect execution. It is the essence of a Hollywood love affair. Leo McCarey fashioned the role for Boyer and he and Irene Dunne made an elegant couple so that the film became one of the most fondly remembered films of the Thirties, perhaps because of the easy comedy sense of the first half.

The Long Day Closes

GB   1992   85m   colour
Mayfair/Palace/Film Four/BFI (Olivia Stewart)

wd Terence Davies *ph* Michael Coulter *md* Robert Lockhart *pd* Christopher Hobbs *ad* Kave Naylor *ed* William Diver

☆ Marjorie Yates (Mother), Leigh McCormack (Bud), Anthony Watson (Kevin), Nicholas Lamont (John), Ayse Owens (Helen), Tina Malone (Edna), Jimmy Wilde (Curly), Robin Polley (Mr. Nicholls)

'A technically elaborate, dryly witty mood piece.' – *Variety*

'A warm and oddly moving experience.' – *Empire*

'Davies' best film yet testifies to the vigour and flexibility of cinematic realisms.' – *Raymond Durgnat, Sight and Sound*

488
The Long Day Closes

A man remembers growing up in working-class Liverpool of the mid-1950s as a solitary, movie-obsessed 11-year-old.

Terence Davies' film is based on his own memories and is an atmospheric, understated, nostalgic movie, though not regretting the gap between its adult narrator and its undersized introverted boy, who is a misfit within his own family. It presents the past recalled with great exactness, from the pleasures at home of listening to his mother and her friends gossiping to the horrors of school with its bullying and unsympathetic teachers. A remarkable film in many ways, it deals in an individual manner with emotional repression and the release offered by the cinema.

Umberto D

Italy   1952   89m   bw
Dear Films

w Cesare Zavattini, Vittorio de Sica *d* Vittorio de Sica *ph* G. R. Aldo *m* Alessandro Cicognini *ed* Eraldo di Roma
☆ *Carlo Battisti* (Umberto Domenico Ferrari), Maria Pia Casilio (Maria), Lina Gennari (Landlady)

'There isn't a minute of banality in this simple, direct film.' – *New Yorker*

⚖ Cesare Zavattini (original story)

487
Umberto D

A retired civil servant can barely afford his rent but will not part with his dog.

Vittorio de Sica's neo-realism drama is in the same mould as *Bicycle Thieves*. Using non-professional actors, it is a downbeat, immensely moving study of old age in a society that fails to provide for it. There is a remarkable performance in the title role from Carlo Battisti, a university professor who had never acted before. It is a low-key study in loneliness, as he attempts to placate his angry landlady, who takes the opportunity of his hospital stay to throw his dog on to the street and tear down the wall of his room. Neither he nor the director play for the audience's sympathy: he is a sometimes petulant old man, who has nothing left but his pride and his dog, and de Sica's austere direction is devoid of sentimentality.

'You'll never laugh as long and as loud again as long as you live! The laughs come so fast and so furious you'll wish it would end before you collapse!'

Modern Times
US   1936   87m   bw
Charles Chaplin
wd Charles Chaplin *ph* Rollie Totheroh, Ira Morgan *m* Charles Chaplin *ad* Charles D. Hall, J. Russell Spencer
☆ *Charles Chaplin* (A Worker), *Paulette Goddard* (Gamine), Henry Bergman (Gamine), Chester Conklin (Mechanic), Tiny Sandford (Big Bill/Worker)

'A natural for the world market … box office with a capital B.' – *Variety*

'A feature picture made out of several one- and two-reel shorts, proposed titles being *The Shop, The Jailbird, The Singing Waiter*.' – *Otis Ferguson*

486
Modern Times

An assembly-line worker goes berserk but can't get another job.

Chaplin's satire was a silent comedy produced in the middle of the sound period. He had tried out some sound tests for the film, but decided to stick to his familiar style of comedy, in an episodic movie that follows him from the factory, where he causes chaos, to prison, falling in love with a girl of the streets, working as a night watchman of a department store, where he roller-skates round the place, and as a singing waiter before he and the girl set off in search of work and happiness. Flashes of genius alternate with sentimental sequences.

The Ploughman's Lunch
GB   1983   107m   colour
Goldcrest/Greenpoint/AC & D (Simon Relph, Ann Scott)
w Ian McEwan *d* Richard Eyre *ph* Clive Tickner *m* Dominic Muldowney *pd* Luciana Arrighi *ad* Michael Pickwoad *ed* David Martin
☆ Jonathan Pryce (James Penfield), Tim Curry (Jeremy Hancock), Rosemary Harris (Ann Barrington), Frank Finlay (Matthew Fox), Charlie Dore (Susan Barrington), David de Keyser (Gold), Nat Jackley (Mr. Penfield)

'You don't have to agree with it, but you can't ignore it.' – *Daily Mail*

'It quietly and persuasively suggests that we get precisely the media we deserve.' – *Guardian*

485
The Ploughman's Lunch

Media people find their cynicism deepened after the Falklands War.

Richard Eyre's overtly political film is about personal betrayal in the wake of the Falkands War. Its central figure is a journalist who is willing to ditch his political convictions in order to advance his career and get the woman he desires into his bed. The film's title is ironic, for what pubs serve as a ploughman's lunch is not, it points out, a traditional English meal but the coinage of some advertising man in the 1960s. The film's condemnation of political life as ersatz was tough and timely.

In Cold Blood

US 1967 134m bw Panavision
Columbia/Richard Brooks

■ ☜ ◉ ◉

wd Richard Brooks *book* Truman Capote *ph* Conrad Hall
m Quincy Jones *ad* Robert Boyle *ed* Peter Zinner
☆ Robert Blake (Perry Smith), Scott Wilson (Dick
Hickock), John Forsythe (Alvin Dewey), Paul Stewart
(Reporter), Gerald S. O'Loughlin (Harold Nye), Jeff Corey
(Hickock's Father)

'It marks a slight step up for its director, best
remembered for reducing *Lord Jim* to Pablum and
The Brothers Karamazov to pulp.' – *John Simon*

● It was remade as an 180m TV mini-series in 1990,
directed by Jonathan Kaplan and starring Anthony Edwards
and Eric Roberts.
Ω Richard Brooks (as writer); Richard Brooks (as director);
Conrad Hall; Quincy Jones

484

In Cold Blood

*An account of a real-life crime in which an entire family was brutally
murdered by wandering gunmen.*

Truman Capote's 'non-fiction novel' was made into an absorbing,
documentary-style movie that concentrated on the subsequent execution of the killers five years later, rather than on the ordinary, everyday
family they murdered for $43, a radio and binoculars. The fatal colli-
sion between the murdered family and two rootless drifters from dysfunctional homes is given an ironic weight in this detailed
reconstruction of a haphazard tragedy.

City of Hope

US 1991 130m DuArt Panavision
Mainline/Esperanza

▣ ■ ☜

wd John Sayles *ph* Robert Richardson *m* Mason Daring
pd Dan Bishop, Dianna Freas *ad* Charles B. Plummer
ed John Sayles
☆ Vincent Spano (Nick Rinaldi), Joe Morton (Wynn), Tony
Lo Bianco (Joe Rinaldi), Barbara Williams (Angela), Stephen
Mendillo (Yoyo), Chris Cooper (Riggs), Charlie Yanko
(Stavros), Jace Alexander (Bobby), Todd Graff (Zip), Scott
Tiler (Vinnie), John Sayles (Carl), Frankie Faison (Levonne),
Gloria Foster (Jeanette), Tom Wright (Malik)

'A major film, suggesting that Sayles might
become as significant a film-maker for the Nineties
as Altman was for the Seventies.' – *Kim Newman,
Sight and Sound*

'Epic, masterly, urgent, adult and unforgettable. Put
simply – which is grossly unfair to its complexity –
it is *Bonfire of the Vanities* without the vanities.'
– *Alexander Walker, London Evening Standard*

'It plays as if it were still on the drawing board.'
– *Michael Sragow, New Yorker*

483

City of Hope

*Corruption and crime in Hudson City, New Jersey touch the lives of
locals, from building contractors and petty thieves to the mayor.*

John Sayles' complex and engrossing film has a narrative style that
brings to busy life a whole community. What links them is chicanery of
one kind and another; self-interest is everyone's motivation and guilt is
the lever used to persuade others into action. Those that suffer most,
though, are the ones with no power: the black kids on the streets, and
the squatters in a slum tenement.

'Loyalty Without Question. Friendship Without Equal.'

Mrs Brown
GB   1997   103m   colour
Miramax/Ecosse (Sarah Curtis)
🎞 ▤ ⚲ ⊚ ⊚ 🎧

w Jeremy Brock *d* John Madden *ph* Richard Greatrex
m Stephen Warbeck *pd* Martin Childs *ad* Charlotte Watts
ed Robin Sales
☆ *Judi Dench* (Queen Victoria), *Billy Connolly* (John Brown), *Geoffrey Palmer* (Henry Ponsonby), *Anthony Sher* (Disraeli), Gerald Butler (Archie Brown), Richard Pasco (Doctor Jenner), David Westhead (Bertie, Prince of Wales)

'Possesses resonances that are rich, complex and instructive.' – *Richard Williams, Guardian*

● Executive producer Douglas Rae conceived the film in the Sixties and originally planned to cast Sean Connery in the role of John Brown, but the film was then abandoned when he learned that the Royal Family was not happy with the project.
♟ Judi Dench; make-up
👒 Judi Dench; Deidre Clancy (costumes)

482
Mrs Brown

Faithful Scottish servant John Brown lifts Queen Victoria out of her funereal gloom, arousing the jealousy of her other household staff.

The curiously close relationship between Queen Victoria and her faithful Scottish servant John Brown is the intriguing subject of John Madden's absorbing and deftly directed film. Judi Dench as the Queen and Billy Connolly as Brown are both excellent, Geoffrey Palmer is fine as a concerned official and Anthony Sher contributes a telling cameo as Disraeli. Madden skirts round the precise nature of their relationship implied in the title, but does raise some still vital questions about the point and purpose of the monarchy.

Dayereh
Iran/Italy/Switzerland   2000   90m   colour
Artificial Eye/Mikado/Lumiere/Jafar Panahi
🎞 ▤ ⊚ ⊚
aka: *The Circle*
w Kambozia Partovi *d* Jafar Panahi *ph* Bahram Badakhshani *ad* Iraj Raminfar *ed* Jafar Panahi
☆ Maryiam Parvin (Arezou), Nargess Mamizadeh (Nargess), Fereshteh Sadr Orafai (Pari), Monir Arab (Ticket seller), Elham Saboktakin (Nurse), Fatemeh Naghavi (Mother), Mojgan Faramarzi (Prostitute)

'Whatever its political significance, this is a dark, sustained, and wrenching film.' – *J. Hoberman, Village Voice*

'A compelling, humane and deeply serious film.' – *Peter Bradshaw, Guardian*

● It won the Golden Lion at the Venice Film Festival in 2000.

481
Dayereh

In Teheran, women attempt to cope in a society where men make the law.

Iranian cinema has blossomed in the last few years and Jafar Panahi's film shows why, for it exposes to view real problems and conflicts within a society. Here, it is the arbitrary subjugation of women: in Teheran, various women attempt to cope in a society where men rule: a wife is distraught at having given birth to a girl, certain that her husband will divorce her for not producing a son; three paroled prisoners discover that their passes will not prevent them being re-arrested; and a mother abandons her daughter in the hope that she will be taken in by others and have a better life. It is an urgent, understated drama with a documentary feel, and it derives its considerable power from such a matter-of-fact, non-histrionic approach.

Husbands and Wives

US 1992 108m DuArt
Columbia TriStar/TriStar (Jack Rollins, Charles H. Joffe)

wd Woody Allen *ph* Carlo Di Palma *pd* Santo Loquasto *ad* Speed Hopkins *ed* Susan E. Morse
☆ Woody Allen (Gabe Roth), *Judy Davis* (Sally), Mia Farrow (Judy Roth), Juliette Lewis (Rain), Liam Neeson (Michael), Blythe Danner (Rain's Mother), Sydney Pollack (Jack), Lysette Anthony (Sam)

'The thing that moviegoers will realize decades hence is that *Husbands and Wives* is a damn fine film.' – *Richard Corliss, Time*

'Rich in characterisation, waspishly witty and profound in its observations about the frailty and fallibilities of modern marriage.' – *Ian Johnstone, Sunday Times*

Judy Davis; Woody Allen (as writer)
original screenplay

480
Husbands and Wives

A couple begin to question their marriage after their friends separate and find new partners.

This is one of Woody Allen's best films on the matter of marriage through the experiences of two couples: after their best friends announce that they are splitting up, a writer and his wife decide to separate; she is attracted to a colleague at work and he becomes infatuated with a young student. Allen has created a clever and insightful examination of the insecurities and often self-destructive behaviour of couples, who here yearn for a freedom from each other, though they sense that it will not improve their lives. Allen explores attitudes to love not only through narrative but with interviews to camera in which the protagonists comment on their relationships and those of their friends. Carlo Di Palma's nervy, hand-held camera work adds an unneeded neurotic tinge to the action, which is unstable enough without his contribution.

A Day in the Death of Joe Egg

GB 1971 106m Eastmancolor
Columbia/Domino (David Deutsch)

w Peter Nichols *play* Peter Nichols *d* Peter Medak *ph* Ken Hodges *m* Elgar *ad* Ted Tester *ed* Ray Lovejoy
☆ *Alan Bates* (Bri), *Janet Suzman* (Sheila), Peter Bowles (Freddie), Sheila Gish (Pam), *Joan Hickson* (Grace)

'It's unsatisfying, and it's not to be missed.' – *Stanley Kauffmann*

479
A Day in the Death of Joe Egg

A teacher and his wife are frustrated by their own inability to cope with the problem of their spastic daughter.

Peter Nichols wrote the play out of personal experience and Peter Medak's film is notable for the performances of Alan Bates as the increasingly unhappy father of a child he calls 'Joe Egg' in order to give her a personality she lacks, and Janet Suzman, as his beleaguered wife. Humour and fantasy sequences leaven the gloom of a work that deals obliquely with the moral dilemmas of euthanasia.

Innocents with Dirty Hands

Innocents with Dirty Hands
France/West Germany/Italy 1975 125m
Eastmancolor
Fox-Rank/Films la Boétie/Terra/Juppiter (André Génovès)
▣ ▤ ⦿
original title: *Les Innocents aux Mains Sales*
wd Claude Chabrol *novel* The Damned Innocents by Richard Neely *ph* Jean Rabier *m* Pierre Jansen *ad* Guy Littaye *ed* Jacques Gaillard
☆ Romy Schneider (Julie), Rod Steiger (Louis), Paolo Giusti (Jeff), Jean Rochefort (Legal), François Maistre (Lamy), Pierre Santini (Villon), François Perrot (Thorent)

'One of cinema's most enjoyable charades.'
– Richard Combs, MFB

478
Innocents with Dirty Hands

A married couple plot to kill one another.

Claude Chabrol's enjoyable, teasing thriller keeps its audience, as well as its characters, guessing as one double-cross quickly follows upon another. The plot keeps thickening as an unhappy wife and her new young lover decide to kill her alcoholic and impotent husband, but he is aware of their plan and intends to use it for his own purposes. Chabrol has everyone off-balance throughout and keeps up his sleight of hand trickery with an ambiguous ending. Romy Schneider alternates winningly between guilt and fear as she finds herself trapped in relationships with two untrustworthy men, while their identities begin to disintegrate and merge. The result is not to be taken too seriously by onlookers, who can sit back and enjoy the fatal games people play.

Les Misérables

Les Misérables
France 1995 177m colour Super 35
Warner/Films 13/TF1/Canal (Claude Lelouch)
▣ ▤
wd Claude Lelouch *novel* Victor Hugo *ph* Claude Lelouch, Philippe Pavans de Ceccatty *m* Francis Lai, Didier Barbelivien, Philippe Servain, Erik Berchot, Michel Legrand *ad* Jacques Bufnoir *ed* Hélène de Luze
☆ Jean-Paul Belmondo (Henri Fortin/Jean Valjean/Roger Fortin), Michel Boujenah (Andre Ziman), Alessandra Martines (Elise Ziman), Annie Girardot (Farmer Woman), Philippe Leotard (Farmer), Clementine Celarie (Catherine/Fantine), Rufus (Thenardier Father and Son), Ticky Holgado (The Kind Hoodlum)

'Hugely ambitious in both theme and scope and brimming with sheer delight in the medium.'
– Derek Elley, Variety

'A righteous, passionate and witty soap opera.'
– Sarah Kerr, New Yorker

477
Les Misérables

A former boxing champion who helps a Jewish couple during the Nazi occupation of France finds that his life begins to resemble that of Jean Valjean, the hero of Victor Hugo's novel.

An engrossing, intriguing, emotionally satisfying drama that both echoes and dramatizes Hugo's epic. Claude Lelouch's direction reveals the timelessness of the story and the changes that time and circumstance might have made to its characters. Belmondo, in a fine performance as Henri Fortin, the boxer turned truck driver, takes a Jewish refugee couple to safety in Switzerland, while their young daughter reads Hugo's novel to him on the road. Lelouch cuts from a re-creation of Hugo's original to the lives of Fortin and his father with masterly skill, revealing patterns of repetition between the different times and people, who are caught up in similarly dramatic circumstances. It is a heartening study of survival and generosity.

Woman of the Dunes
Japan   1964   127m   bw
Teshigahara (Kiichi Ichikawa)
📽 ▤ ◉ 🎧
original title: *Suna no Onna*
US title: *Woman in the Dunes*
w Kobo Abe *d* Hiroshi Teshigahara *ph* Hiroshi Segawa
m Toru Takemitsu *ad* Masao Yamazaki, Toutetsu Hirakawa
ed F. Susui
☆ Eiji Okada (The man), Kyoko Kishoda (The woman)

'Teasingly opaque, broodingly erotic.' – *MFB*

Ω Hiroshi Teshigahara; best foreign film

476
Woman of the Dunes

A man becomes trapped in a vast sand pit by villagers.

Kobo Abe's surreal melodrama was a study of an entomologist on a deserted beach, who found an attractive young widow living in a shack at the bottom of a huge pit. Her task was to shovel sand into buckets for the nearby villagers to remove so that they would not be overwhelmed by the shifting sands; her digging also prevented her own shack from being buried. He spends the night with her, discovers in the morning that he can not escape, and finally does not want to. Hiroshi Teshigahara's direction was all moving sand and picturesque angles, using deep focus to emphasize the story's symbolic aspects. It can be taken as an allegory of the difficulties of life within an official and officious society. But it can also be enjoyed for its curious story, strange atmosphere and incisive acting.

L'Avventura
Italy/France   1960   145m   bw
Cino del Duca/PCE/Lyre (Amato Pennasilico)
🎧
w Michelangelo Antonioni, Elio Bartolini, Tonino Guerra
d Michelangelo Antonioni *ph* Aldo Scavarda *m* Giovanni
Fusco *ad* Piero Poletto *ed* Eraldo da Roma
☆ Monica Vitti (Claudia), Lea Massari (Anna), Gabriele
Ferzetti (Sandro), Dominique Blanchar (Giulia), James
Addams (Corrado), Lelio Luttazi (Raimondo)

'A film of complete maturity, sincerity and creative intuition.' – *Peter John Dyer, MFB*

475
L'Avventura

Young people on a yachting holiday go ashore on a volcanic island. One of them disappears; this affects the lives of the others, but she is never found.

Antonioni's film was greeted with cheers and jeers on its first showing, and that reaction has hardly abated since. His story was deliberately mysterious. His interest is not in what happened to the missing girl. His concern is how it changed the girl's fiance and one of her friends, who during their search become attracted to one another. Antonioni developed a new approach to cinema with this film. Shot with great precision against a volcanic landscape, it is a devastating portrait of a particular, directionless society, of modern alienation.

'I can smile … and murder while I smile.'

Richard III
GB   1995   105m   Technicolor
UA/British Screen/First Look (Liza Katselas Pare,
Stephen Bayly)

▣ ▭ ◉ ⊘ ∩

w Ian McKellen *play* William Shakespeare *stage
production* Richard Eyre *d* Richard Loncraine *ph* Peter
Biziou *m* Trevor Jones *pd* Tony Burrough *ad* Richard
Bridgland, Choi Ho Man *ed* Paul Green

☆ Ian McKellen (Richard III), Annette Bening (Queen
Elizabeth), Jim Broadbent (Buckingham), Robert Downey
Jnr (Earl Rivers), Nigel Hawthorne (Clarence), Kristin Scott
Thomas (Lady Anne), Maggie Smith (The Duchess of York),
John Wood (King Edward IV), Adrian Dunbar (Corporal
James Tyrell), Dominic West (Richmond)

> 'A superb political thriller in an England that is a
> subtly distorting mirror of reality – or a reality
> adjacent to our own.' – *Peter Holland, TLS*

> 'A fast, exuberant, violent ride.' – *Variety*

⚖ Tony Burrough; costume design (Shuna Harwood)

474
Richard III

In a fascist England of the 1930s, the king's younger brother murders his way to the throne and attempts to hold it as civil war rages.

Richard Loncraine and Ian McKellen's updating of Shakespeare's play turned it into fast-moving, pared-down thriller. It remained true to much of Shakespeare's poetry, while concentrating on political manoeuvre and successfully translating the action to a disturbing period; this is England as it almost might have been. The filming is bold; there is no dialogue spoken for the first nine minutes of exposition, and when McKellen gives his first speech, much of it is delivered in a urinal. He also inveigles the audience into becoming his co-conspirators, fascinated spectators of his seductive performance.

Last Exit to Brooklyn
West Germany   1989   98m   colour
Guild/Neue Constantin Film Produktion/Bavaria Film/
Allied Filmmakers (Bernd Eichinger)

▣ ▭ ◉ ⊘ ∩

w Desmond Nakano *novel* Hubert Selby Jnr *d* Uli Edel
ph Stefan Czapsky *m* Mark Knopfler *pd* David Chapman
ad Mark Haak *ed* Peter Przygodda

☆ Stephen Lang (Harry Black), Jennifer Jason Leigh
(Tralala), Burt Young (Big Joe), Peter Dobson (Vinnie),
Christopher Murney (Paulie), Jerry Orbach (Boyce), Alexis
Arquette (Georgette)

> 'Edel surprisingly has managed to capture exactly
> the horrified yet tender tone of Selby's book.'
> – *MFB*

473
Last Exit to Brooklyn

Striking workers and their families and a prostitute lead thwarted lives in Brooklyn in the early 1950s.

Uli Edel's film is true to the spirit of Hubert Selby's grim, but compassionate, low-life novel. Photographed by Stefan Czapsky in a way that brings out the seedy grubbiness of the locale, with Mark Knopfler's excellent musical accompaniment, and fine ensemble acting, Edel shows the locale as the hellish place it is, while allowing its inhabitants moments of tenderness amid the unremitting brutality that bears down upon them all.

'A Story from the Spanish Civil War.'

Land and Freedom
GB/Germany/Spain   1995   110m   colour
Artificial Eye/Parallax/Messidor/Road Movies
(Rebecca O'Brien)
🔳 ▦ ◎~
w Jim Allen *d* Ken Loach *ph* Barry Ackroyd *m* George
Fenton *pd* Martin Johnson *ed* Jonathan Morris
☆ *Ian Hart* (David Carne), *Rosana Pastor* (Blanca), Iciar
Bollain (Maite), Tom Gilroy (Gene Lawrence), Marc Martinez
(Vidal), Frederic Pierrot (Bernard), Suzanne Maddock (Kim)

'Direct, passionate and formidably informed by
political conviction.' – *Derek Malcolm, Guardian*

'Ken Loach's real triumph is to get the viewer
rooting for characters in a conflict that, for most, is
as remote as the Trojan War.' – *John Hopewell,
Variety*

472
Land and Freedom

*An unemployed Liverpudlian Communist goes to fight in the Spanish
Civil War.*

An engrossing and passionate Orwellian account of the Spanish Civil
War, as experienced on an individual level by an unemployed
Liverpudlian Communist, who fights on the side of the socialist POUM;
he discovers that the activities of the Stalinist Republican forces and
Communists in suppressing other left-wing groups will give victory to
the Fascists. Ken Loach frames the narrative with a death in present-
day Liverpool, to point up the contemporary relevance of its story of a
revolution betrayed.

☆ **Alan Morrison** Contributing Editor, *Empire Magazine* ☆

1. The Godfather Part 2 (Coppola)
   Coppola's operatic sequel isn't the simple continuation of Michael Corleone's story coupled with flashbacks chronicling
   Don Vito's rise to power. It's the simultaneous portrait of a father and son in the process of selling their souls, and the
   history of an immigrant culture slowly discovering the violent underbelly of the American Dream.
2. The Deer Hunter (Cimino)
   Before, during, and after. The wedding, the war, and the return home. The workers, the soldiers, and the casualties. It's
   only because Cimino spends so long setting up the relationships between the characters in the workplace, at the marriage
   celebration and in the mountains, that we register the devastating effect Vietnam has had on blue collar America.
3. La Grande Illusion (Renoir)
   Jean Renoir's plea for peace and an end to all wars is cinema's greatest statement on common humanity. An intensely
   moving elegy to a dying age of honour and friendship, its message hasn't diminished one iota over the decades.
4. The Godfather (Coppola)
5. The Lord of the Rings: The Fellowship of The Ring (Jackson)
6. Bicycle Thieves (De Sica)
7. Pather Panchali (Ray)
8. The Seven Samurai (Kurosawa)
9. Three Colours Blue (Kieslowski)
10. Trainspotting (Boyle)

Blade Runner

US 1982 117m Technicolor Panavision
Warner/Ladd/Blade Runner Partnership (Michael Deeley, Ridley Scott)

w Hampton Fancher, David Peoples *novel Do Androids Dream of Electric Sheep?* by Philip K. Dick *d* Ridley Scott *ph* Jordan Cronenweth *m* Vangelis *pd* Lawrence G. Paull *ad* David L. Snyder *ed* Terry Rawlings
☆ Harrison Ford (Rick Deckard), Rutger Hauer (Roy Batty), Sean Young (Rachael), Edward James Olmos (Gaff), M. Emmet Walsh (Bryant), Daryl Hannah (Pris)

'A richly detailed and visually overwhelming trip to 2019, which sticks with you like a recurrent nightmare.' – *Sunday Times*

'Glitteringly and atmospherically designed; but ultimately mechanics win out over philosophizing.' – *Sight and Sound*

● Ridley Scott's original cut of the film, which dispenses for the most part with the voice-over narration and has a different ending, was shown to general critical approval in 1991 and also released on video and DVD.
⚨ art direction; visual effects (Douglas Trumbull, Richard Yuricich, David Dryer)
Ⓣ Jordan Cronenweth; Lawrence G. Paull

471
Blade Runner

Los Angeles, AD 2019; a licensed-to-kill policeman tracks down and destroys a group of intelligent robots who have hijacked a space shuttle and returned to Earth.

A cult film *par excellence*, and notable for its exceptional production design of a future Los Angeles, which has become a mix of high-tech buildings surrounded by seedy street life under lowering clouds and incessant acid rain. Almost incidental to the atmosphere is the story, from the paranoid science fiction writer Philip K. Dick. Scott's director's cut dispensed with the voice-over narration of the original release and changed the ending. An enigmatic quality to the film and much brooding symbolism has resulted in endless exegeses of its meaning, though it is possibly best enjoyed as a brilliantly dystopian vision of the near future.

Klute

US 1971 114m Technicolor Panavision
Warner (Alan J. Pakula)

w Andy K. Lewis, Dave Lewis *d* Alan J. Pakula *ph* Gordon
Willis *m* Michael Small *ad* George Jenkins *ed* Carl
Lerner
☆ Jane Fonda (Bree Daniels), Donald Sutherland (John
Klute), Charles Cioffi (Peter Cable), Roy Scheider (Frank
Ligourin), Rita Gam (Trina)
♟ Jane Fonda
♟ Andy K. Lewis, Dave Lewis

470
Klute

A policeman leaves the force to investigate the disappearance of a research scientist, and takes up with a call girl who is involved.

Jane Fonda was never better than here, as a psychologically vulnerable call girl. She is someone searching for a simpler way of life, while enjoying the money and the power over men that her job gives her. Gordon Willis' cinematography emphasizes her lonely instability, isolating her and others in pools of light, surrounded by shadows that could conceal anything. Alan J. Pakula's excellent adult thriller gives attention to detail and puts the emphasis on character. He explores urban alienation and the fragility of the family with a voyeuristic intensity.

'1978. The US Government Waged A War Against Organised Crime. One Man Was Left Behind The Lines.'

Donnie Brasco

US 1997 126m Technicolor Panavision
Entertainment/Mandalay/Baltimore (Mark Johnson,
Barry Levinson, Louis DiGiaimo, Gail Mutrux)

w Paul Attanasio *book* Joseph D. Pistone with Richard
Woodley *d* Mike Newell *ph* Peter Sova *m* Patrick Doyle
pd Donald Graham Burt *ad* Jefferson Sage *ed* Jon
Gregory
☆ *Al Pacino* (Lefty Ruggiero), *Johnny Depp* (Donnie
Brasco/Joe Pistone), Michael Madsen (Sonny Black), Bruno
Kirby (Nicky), James Russo (Paulie), Anne Heche (Maggie
Pistone), Zeljko Ivanek (Tim Curley), Gerry Becker (Dean
Blandford), Zach Grenier (Dr. Berger)

'One of the best gangster movies you'll see this year, bursting with tension and filled with rewarding moments.' – *John Patterson, Neon*

♟ Paul Attanasio

469
Donnie Brasco

After he successfully infiltrates the Mafia, an undercover agent for the FBI finds himself torn between duty and friendship for the gangster who vouched for him.

A Mafia movie, based on a true story, that takes an almost academic interest in the rituals and manners of gangsters. Mike Newell's movie deals with the moral dilemma of an undercover agent for the FBI. It is concerned less with the gang members' actions than their characters, which gives it an effectively tragic intensity as two different sets of loyalties collide. Al Pacino and Johnny Depp, as respectively the teacher and the pupil of Mafia behaviour, are both at their best in conveying a close friendship based on betrayal.

'So daring – so tender – so human – so true – that everyone in love will want to see it!'

Holiday
US   1938   93m   bw
Columbia (Everett Riskin)
▭▭ ▭▭ ⌕~ ⊙
GB titles: *Free to Live*
aka: *Unconventional Linda*
w Donald Ogden Stewart *d* George Cukor *ph* Franz Planer *m* Sidney Cutner *ad* Stephen Goosson, Lionel Banks *ed* Otto Meyer, Al Clark
☆ *Katharine Hepburn* (Linda Seton), *Cary Grant* (Johnny Case), Doris Nolan (Julia Seton), *Edward Everett Horton* (Nick Potter), *Ruth Donnelly*, *Lew Ayres* (Ned Seton), Henry Kolker (Edward Seton), Binnie Barnes (Laura Cram)

'Corking comedy … exhibitors will pencil in some extra days.' – *Variety*

'I suppose actually it is a neat and sometimes elegant job, but under its surface of too much brightness and too many words it seems so deadly bored and weary. Hell, save your money and yawn at home.' – *Otis Ferguson*

'Played with the greatest cheerfulness and a winning skill.' – *Brooklyn Daily Eagle*

♟ art direction

468
Holiday

A man becomes engaged to a millionaire's daughter but discovers that he loves her unconventional sister.

Katharine Hepburn had begun her stage career as an understudy to the star of this Broadway success, and so was eager to play the leading role, of a millionaire's unconventional daughter; she runs off with her sister's fiance, a man who wants to enjoy life rather than make money. It had been filmed eight years earlier, but this elegant, highly successful remake was subtly devised to make the very most of the lines and performances. Cary Grant, who was cast opposite her, always brought out the best in Hepburn, and surprises by making a sudden back-flip in mid-conversation. Horton, incidentally, played the same role in both versions.

Farewell My Lovely
US   1944   95m   bw
RKO (Adrian Scott)
▭▭ ▭▭ ⌕~
aka: *Murder My Sweet*
w John Paxton *novel* Raymond Chandler *d* Edward Dmytryk *ph* Harry J. Wild *m* Roy Webb *ad* Carroll Clark, Albert S. D'Agostino *ed* Joseph Noriega
☆ *Dick Powell* (Philip Marlowe), Claire Trevor (Velma/Mrs. Grayle), Anne Shirley (Ann), *Mike Mazurki* (Moose Malloy), Otto Kruger (Amthor), Miles Mander (Mr. Grayle), Douglas Walton (Marriott), Ralf Harolde (Dr. Sonderborg), Don Douglas (Lt. Randall), Esther Howard (Mrs. Florian)

'A nasty, draggled bit of dirty work, accurately observed.' – *C. A. Lejeune*

● Remade in 1975 with Robert Mitchum.

467
Farewell My Lovely

A private eye searches for an ex-convict's missing girlfriend.

Raymond Chandler's thriller became a revolutionary crime film; it was the first to depict the genuinely seedy milieu suggested by his book. It also brought a total change of direction for Dick Powell, a baby-faced crooner who suddenly became a tough guy. One of the first *films noirs* of the mid-Forties, with its depiction of a corrupt and paranoid society, it is a minor masterpiece of expressionist film making.

Heavenly Creatures
New Zealand 1994 98m Eastmancolor Super 35
Buena Vista/Wingnut/Fontana/NZFC (Jim Booth)

w Frances Walsh, Peter Jackson *d* Peter Jackson *ph* Alun Bollinger *m* Peter Dasent *pd* Grant Major *ad* Jill Cormack *ed* Jamie Selkirk

☆ Melanie Lynskey (Pauline Parker), Kate Winslet (Juliet Hulme), Sarah Peirse (Honora Parker), Diana Kent (Hilda Hulme), Clive Merrison (Henry Hulme), Simon O'Connor (Herbert Rieper), Jed Brophy (John/Nicholas)

'The sad creatures who Pauline and Juliet must have been in real life are alchemized into figures of horror and beauty. They become the stuff of thrilling popular art.' – *Richard Corliss, Time*

'A striking addition to the cinema of *folie à deux*, the madness for two that is either a perversion of true love or its purest manifestation.' – *Adam Mars-Jones, Independent*

● The real-life Juliet now lives in Scotland and writes mystery novels set in Victorian times under the name of Anne Perry.
♫ Frances Walsh, Peter Jackson (screenplay)

466
Heavenly Creatures

In New Zealand, two schoolgirls, who form a close relationship, based on a shared fantasy world, decide to kill the mother of one of them to prevent their separation.

Before Peter Jackson went on to international acclaim for his *The Lord of the Rings* trilogy, he attracted attention for this chilling, sensitively directed tale. Based on a true story, the film brought out the dangerous mixture of fantasy and reality that precipitated a tragic and violent death. It was a considerable achievement and an unexpected advance from a director hitherto known for slapdash, gore-filled horror movies such as *Braindead*.

Lenny

Lenny
US   1974   111m   bw
UA (Marvin Worth)

w Julian Barry *play* Julian Barry *d* Bob Fosse *ph* Bruce Surtees *md* Ralph Burns *pd* Joel Schiller *ed* Alan Heim
☆ *Dustin Hoffman* (Lenny Bruce), Valerie Perrine (Honey Bruce), Jan Miner (Sally Marr), Stanley Beck (Artie Silver), Gary Morton (Sherman Hart)

'For audiences who want to believe that Lenny Bruce was a saintly gadfly who was martyred for having lived before his time.' – *New Yorker*

♟ best picture; Julian Barry; Bob Fosse; Bruce Surtees; Dustin Hoffman; Valerie Perrine
Ⓣ Valerie Perrine

465
Lenny

The career of outspoken comedian Lenny Bruce and his struggles with the law.

Bob Fosse, with his razzle-dazzle style of upbeat showbusiness panache was a surprising choice to direct a film about the life of Lenny Bruce, a stand-up comic who worked in seedy clubs delivering outrageous, vitriolic monologues, spiced with obscenity, and died of a drug overdose. Hoffman had much of the same energy as Bruce and, without offering an impersonation, captured something of the satirist's paranoid manner. Fosse shot on location to give it a reality while keeping an emotional distance from the story. The result is filmically extremely clever, but often emotionally hollow.

'The secrets of a street you know.'

It Always Rains on Sunday
GB   1947   92m   bw
Ealing (Henry Cornelius)
w *Angus MacPhail, Robert Hamer, Henry Cornelius novel* Arthur La Bern *d* Robert Hamer *ph* Douglas Slocombe *m* Georges Auric *ad* Duncan Sutherland *ed* Michael Truman
☆ Googie Withers (Rose Sandigate), John McCallum (Tommy Swann), Jack Warner (Detective Sgt. Fothergill), Edward Chapman (George Sandigate), Susan Shaw (Vi Sandigate), Sydney Tafler (Morry Hyams)

'Let me pay it the simplest of compliments and say that it has the persuasiveness of an exciting story professionally told.' – *Sunday Times*

464
It Always Rains on Sunday

An escaped convict takes refuge in his married mistress's house in East London.

Robert Hamer's influential slumland melodrama may now be dated – the stuff of every other television play – but at the time it was electrifyingly vivid and very well done. An authentic look at postwar working-class life, with many Londoners in the cast, was brought to the screen. The married mistress is a housewife and former barmaid, burdened with a dull husband and two rebellious stepchildren, whose feelings for him are momentarily, and disastrously, rekindled. Ending with a gripping chase sequence, it is a film that can still hold an audience.

Lost Horizon

↟ US 1937 130m bw
Columbia (Frank Capra)
⬓ ▤ ⌕ ⌖ ⌾ ⌒

w *Robert Riskin* novel *James Hilton* d *Frank Capra*
ph *Joseph Walker* m *Dimitri Tiomkin* ad *Stephen Goosson* ed *Gene Havlick, Gene Milford*
☆ *Ronald Colman* (Robert Conway), *H. B. Warner* (Chang), *Thomas Mitchell* (Henry Barnard), *Edward Everett Horton* (Alexander P. Lovett), *Sam Jaffe* (High Lama), *Isabel Jewell* (Gloria Stone), *Jane Wyatt* (Sondra), *Margo* (Maria), *John Howard* (George Conway)

> 'One of the most impressive of all Thirties films, a splendid fantasy which, physically and emotionally, lets out all the stops.' – *John Baxter, 1968*

> 'One is reminded of a British critic's comment on Mary of Scotland, "the inaccuracies must have involved tremendous research".' – *Robert Stebbins*

> 'If the long dull ethical sequences had been cut to the bone there would have been plenty of room for the real story: the shock of western crudity and injustice on a man returned from a more gentle and beautiful way of life.' – *Graham Greene*

● A 1943 reissue trimmed down the negative still further, to 109 minutes; but in 1979 the American Film Institute restored a print of the original length.
● Remade as a musical in 1973
♟ Stephen Goosson
♟ best picture; Dimitri Tiomkin; H. B. Warner

Decline of the American Empire

Canada 1986 101m colour
Malofilm/National Film Board Of Canada (Rene Malo, Roger Frappier)
⬓ ▤ ⌖ ⌾

original title: *Le Déclin de l'Empire Américain*
wd *Denys Arcand* ph *Guy Dufaux* md *François Dompierre*, based on themes by Handel ad *Gaudeline Sauriol* ed *Monique Forcier*
☆ *Dorothée Berryman* (Louise), *Louise Portal* (Diane), *Pierre Curzi* (Pierre), *Rémy Girard* (Remy), *Yves Jacques* (Claude), *Genevieve Rioux* (Danielle), *Daniel Briere* (Alain), *Gabriel Arcand* (Mario)

> 'Arcand isn't out to expose these people as spiritually empty; he's trying to present a truthful look at how they live. There's nothing weighty in his approach; it's a lovely, very unassuming picture, yet there is enough drama so that by the end a subtle shift in all the relationships is necessary.' – *New Yorker*

♟ foreign film

463
Lost Horizon

Escaping from a Chinese revolution, four people are kidnapped by plane and taken to an idyllic civilization in a Tibetan valley, where the weather is always kind and men are not only gentle to each other but live to a very advanced age.

A much re-cut romantic adventure which leaves out some of the emphasis of James Hilton's Utopian novel set in the fantasy world of Shangri La far removed from normal civilization. The film stands up pretty well on its own, at least as a supreme example of Hollywood moonshine, with perfect casting, direction and music. If the design has a touch of Ziegfeld, that is Hollywood.

462
Decline of the American Empire

A group of intellectuals discuss their attitudes to gender, sex and love.

Denys Arcand's witty, perceptive conversation piece won the Film Critics' award at the Cannes Film Festival in 1986. Four men, all history professors, discuss their attitude to sex while preparing a meal at which they'll be joined by four women who spend time at a health club, also talking about their feelings towards men, fidelity and adultery. At the subsequent meal, the evening is spoiled when one of the woman, who is unmarried, reveals that she has had affairs with two of the men, who are both married. The battle of the sexes here results in a no-win situation for the assembled company, for whom sex is a consolation, but the talk is good. In 2003, Arcand's film *The Barbarian Invasions* dealt with many of the same group 18 years on.

Goodbye Mr Chips

GB   1939   114m   bw

MGM (Victor Saville)

🔲 🇬🇧 🔍 ✏️ ◎

w R. C. Sherriff, Claudine West, Eric Maschwitz
novel James Hilton *d* Sam Wood *ph* Frederick A. Young
m Richard Addinsell *ad* Alfred Junge *ed* Charles Frend
☆ *Robert Donat* (Charles Chipping), *Greer Garson*
(Katherine Ellis), *Paul Henreid* (Max Staefel), Lyn Harding
(Dr. Wetherby), Austin Trevor (Ralston), Terry Kilburn
(John/Peter Colley), John Mills (Peter Colley as a young
man), Milton Rosmer (Charteris), Judith Furse (Flora)

''The whole picture has an assurance, bears a glow
of popularity like the face of a successful candidate
on election day. And it is wrong to despise
popularity in the cinema.' – *Graham Greene*

'The picture has no difficulty in using two hours to
retell a story that was scarcely above short story
length. *Mr Chips* is worth its time.' – *New York
Times*

'The novel became an American best seller when
that old sentimentalist Alexander Woollcott touted
it on the radio … the movie clogs the nose more
than necessary.' – *Pauline Kael, 70s*

● Remade as a musical in 1969.
♟ Robert Donat
🏆 best picture; script; Sam Wood; Greer Garson; editing

461
Goodbye Mr Chips

The life of a shy schoolmaster from his first job to his death.

Robert Donat's most famous role was a shy schoolmaster in this sentimental romance in MGM's best style. Donat, who was then in his early
thirties, provided a virtuoso exhibition of acting; he was seen at the
ages of twenty-four, forty, sixty-four and eighty-three. He played a man
redeemed by marriage (to Greer Garson, in her first screen performance as Katherine), and his middle-aged Chips is notable for its deliberate banality. The film has become a long-standing favourite for its
performances and humour; but the production seems slightly unsatisfactory, perhaps because the accomplished Sam Wood, the most
American of directors, was not at home in the atmosphere of an
English public school.

Newsfront

Australia   1978   110m   colour/bw

Palm Beach Productions (David Elfick)

🇦🇺 🔍

wd Phillip Noyce, from a concept by David Elfick
ph Vincent Monton *pd* Lissa Coote *ad* Lawrence
Eastwood *ed* John Scott
☆ Bill Hunter (Len Maguire), Wendy Hughes (Amy
McKenzie), Gerard Kennedy (Frank Maguire), Chris
Haywood (Chris Hewett)

460
Newsfront

*In the Fifties, rival news teams battle to get the best shots for cinema
newsreels.*

Phillip Noyce's film was a lively tribute to the newsreel cameramen of
the late 1940s and mid 1950s, as seen through the rivalry between two
fraternal top cameramen. Their lives are seen against the shifting social
and political scene, with actual newsreel footage of the time being cut
into re-creations of the events. Len (Bill Hunter), a man with fierce loyalty to Australia, is contrasted with his brother Frank (Gerard Kennedy),
who hopes to go to work in Hollywood and is regarded as selling out.
(It is, of course, what many Australian talents were to do a little later.)
Its crisp, witty dialogue help to make it an enjoyably nostalgic history
lesson.

Olympische Spiele

Germany   1936   225m   bw
Leni Riefenstahl

d Leni Riefenstahl *ph* Hans Ertl, Walter Franz and 42 others *m* Herbert Windt *ed* Leni Riefenstahl *assistant* Walter Ruttman

'Here is the camera doing superbly what only the camera can do: refashioning the rhythms of the visible; of the moment seen.' – *Dilys Powell*

● Part 1 runs to 118m, and Part 2 to 107m.

459
Olympische Spiele

An account of the Berlin Olympic Games.

This magnificent film is in no sense a mere reporting of an event. Camera movement, photography and editing combine with music to make it an experience truly olympian, especially in the introductory symbolic sequence suggesting the birth of the games. It was also, dangerously, a hymn to Nazi strength.

'When she was good she was very very good. When she was bad, she was…'

Darling

GB   1965   127m   bw
Anglo-Amalgamated/Vic/Appia (Joseph Janni, Victor Lyndon)

w Frederic Raphael *d* John Schlesinger *ph* Ken Higgins *m* John Dankworth *pd* Ray Simm *ed* James B. Clark ☆ Julie Christie (Diana Scott), Dirk Bogarde (Robert Gold), Laurence Harvey (Miles Brand), Roland Curram (Malcolm), Alex Scott (Sean Martin), Basil Henson (Alec Prosser-Jones), Pauline Yates (Estelle Gold)

'As empty of meaning and mind as the empty life it's exposing.' – *Pauline Kael*

'A cool, clear and devastating look at the glossy success set.' – *Judith Crist*

🏆 Frederic Raphael; Julie Christie
🏆 best picture; John Schlesinger
🏆 Frederic Raphael; Ray Simm; Dirk Bogarde; Julie Christie

458
Darling

An ambitious young woman deserts her journalist mentor for a company director, an effeminate photographer and an Italian prince.

John Schlesinger's influential and fashionable film, done with high style, helped to create the image of swinging London, due not only to the setting of the film but also to the performance of Julie Christie. In retrospect, Christie disliked the fact that the film showed a woman who behaved as she wanted and is punished for it; she wished she had portrayed the character's selfishness as worthwhile. It is a film of its time that captures a particular moment in history with clarity and insight.

Intruder in the Dust

US 1949 87m bw
MGM (Clarence Brown)

🇺🇸

w Ben Maddow *novel* William Faulkner *d* Clarence Brown *ph* Robert Surtees *m* Adolph Deutsch *ad* Cedric Gibbons, Randall Duell *ed* Robert J. Kern

☆ *Juano Hernandez* (Lucas Beauchamp), *Elizabeth Patterson* (Miss Habersham), David Brian (John Gavin Stevens), Claude Jarman Jnr (Chick Mallison), *Porter Hall* (Nub Gowrie), Will Geer (Sheriff Hampton)

'It is surely the years of range and experience which have given him a control of the medium so calm, sure and – apparently – easy that he can make a complex story seem simple and straightforward.' – *Pauline Kael*

'A really good movie that is also and incidentally the first honestly worked out "racial" film I have seen.' – *Richard Winnington*

'An example of gripping film craftsmanship.' – *News of the World*

457
Intruder in the Dust

In a Southern town, a boy and an old lady solve a mystery and prevent a black man from being lynched.

Clarence Brown's account of racism, from William Faulkner's novel is an excellent character drama; it also offers vivid local colour, a murder puzzle and social comment. It was one of the first productions from MGM's new production head, the liberal Dore Schary, after Louis B. Mayer had turned down filming the story. Brown directs in a documentary style that is far removed from MGM's usual glossy approach, confronting the subject of racial prejudice without compromise.

Dinner at Eight

US 1933 113m bw
MGM (David O. Selznick)

◼◼ 🇺🇸 🔍

w Frances Marion, Herman J. Mankiewicz *play* George S. Kaufman, Edna Ferber *d* George Cukor *ph* William Daniels *m* William Axt *ad* Hobe Irwin, Fredric Hope *ed* Ben Lewis

☆ *Marie Dressler* (Carlotta Vance), John Barrymore (Larry Renault), Lionel Barrymore (Oliver Jordan), Billie Burke (Mrs. Oliver Jordan), Wallace Beery (Dan Packard), *Jean Harlow* (Kitty Packard), Lee Tracy (Max Kane), Edmund Lowe (Dr. Wayne Talbot), Madge Evans (Mrs. Wayne Talbot), Jean Hersholt (Joe Stengel), Karen Morley (Mrs. Wayne Talbot), Louise Closser Hale (Hattie Loomis), Phillips Holmes (Ernest DeGraff), May Robson (Mrs. Wendel), Grant Mitchell (Ed Loomis) and also Elizabeth Patterson

'Marquee speaks for itself. It spells money, and couldn't very well be otherwise.' – *Variety*

456
Dinner at Eight

Guests at a society dinner party all find themselves in dramatic circumstances.

It was Edna Ferber's idea to write a play about the hypocrisy of fashionable social happenings by showing the unpleasant truths that lurked behind an elegant dinner party. Her collaboration with George Kaufman was a hit on Broadway. David Selznick saw it as another *Grand Hotel*, cast it with stars and had it rewritten to give it a happy ending, although the social satire remains; the dinner guests are unhappy or fraudulent or both. It retained an astringent quality, and included comic performances from Jean Harlow, John Barrymore and Marie Dressler that match their best.

Pulp Fiction
US 1994 153m DeLuxe Panavision
Buena Vista/Miramax/A Band Apart/Jersey (Lawrence Bender)

⬚⬚ ⬚⬚ ▬ ⬚~ ⊙ ⊚ ⌒

w Quentin Tarantino, Roger Avary d Quentin Tarantino
ph Andrzej Sekula pd David Wasco ad Charles Collum
ed Sally Menke
☆ John Travolta (Vincent Vega), Samuel L. Jackson (Jules Winfield), Uma Thurman (Mia Wallace), Harvey Keitel (The Wolf), Tim Roth (Pumpkin), Amanda Plummer (Honey Bunny), Ving Rhames (Marsellus Wallace), Maria de Madeiros (Fabienne), Eric Stoltz (Lance), Rosanna Arquette (Jody), Christopher Walken (Captain Koons), Bruce Willis (Butch Coolidge)

'Tarantino's adrenaline rush of an American melodrama is a brash dare to Hollywood filmmakers in their current slough of timidity. Let's see, he says, if you can be this smart about going this far.' – Time

● In a poll conducted by the Sunday Times in April 1995, its readers voted it the seventh-best film of all time, and Tarantino the seventh-best director, ahead of Martin Scorsese, Orson Welles and Stanley Kubrick but behind David Lean, Alfred Hitchcock, Michael Curtiz, Billy Wilder and Francis Ford Coppola.
♟ Quentin Tarantino, Roger Avary (screenplay)
♙ best picture; Quentin Tarantino; John Travolta; Samuel L. Jackson; film editing
Ⓣ Quentin Tarantino, Roger Avary; Samuel L. Jackson

'The Screen's All-Time Classic Of Suspense!'
The Killers
US 1946 105m bw
U-I (Mark Hellinger)
⬚⬚ ▬ ⊚
TV title: A Man Alone
w Anthony Veiller story Ernest Hemingway d Robert Siodmak ph Elwood Bredell m Miklos Rozsa ad Martin Obzina, Jack Otterson ed Arthur Hilton
☆ Burt Lancaster (Swede), Edmond O'Brien (Jim Reardon), Ava Gardner (Kitty Collins), Albert Dekker (Big Jim Colfax), Sam Levene (Lt. Sam Lubinsky), John Miljan (Jake), Virginia Christine (Lilly Lubinsky), Vince Barnett (Charleston), Charles D. Brown (Packy Robinson), Donald MacBride (Kenyon), Phil Brown (Nick Adams), Charles McGraw (Al), William Conrad (Max)

'Seldom does a melodrama maintain the high tension that distinguishes this one.' – Variety

'There is nothing unique or even valuable about the picture, but energy combined with attention to form and detail doesn't turn up every day; neither does good entertainment.' – James Agee

● John Huston contributed to the script but is not credited.
● The Killers marked Burt Lancaster's screen debut.
● Remade in 1964.
♙ Anthony Veiller; Robert Siodmak; Miklos Rozsa; Arthur Hilton

455
Pulp Fiction

Four interlocking stories with unexpected twists involve a gangster, his two hitmen, his wife, a mysterious briefcase, and a boxer who refuses to throw a fight after being paid to do so.

Quentin Tarantino's film was a clever, witty and violent celebration of junk culture. These familiar stories drew rather too heavily on past thrillers, such as *Kiss Me Deadly*. What gave them a new interest was the intricate way they were told, and the fact that they were blessed with some excellent performances, crackling with menace.

454
The Killers

In a small sleazy town, a gangster waits for two assassins to kill him, and we later find out why.

Robert Siodmak's hard-boiled *film noir* was based on a short story by Ernest Hemingway. An elaborate tale of cross and double-cross, stunningly executed, it is told in flashback as an insurance investigator uncovers the history of a man who did not resist death and, discovering that there is a large stash of stolen money involved, goes looking for it. Ava Gardner is a seductive femme fatale whose cool self-interest destroys two men. In her autobiography, she writes that Hemingway liked the film and would show it to his guests – 'he'd usually fall asleep after the first reel, which made sense, because that first reel was the only part of the movie that was really taken from what he wrote.' He must be the only person to have ever slept through this thriller.

'A storm of fear and fury in the sizzling Florida keys!'

Key Largo
US   1948   101m   bw
Warner (Jerry Wald)
🔲 🔳 ⊕~ ⊕ ⊕

w *Richard Brooks, John Huston* play Maxwell Anderson
d *John Huston* ph Karl Freund m Max Steiner ad Leo K. Kuter ed Rudi Fehr
☆ *Humphrey Bogart* (Frank McCloud), *Lauren Bacall* (Nora Temple), *Claire Trevor* (Gaye Dawn), *Edward G. Robinson* (Johnny Rocco), *Lionel Barrymore* (James Temple), Thomas Gomez (Curley), Marc Lawrence (Ziggy)

'It's a confidently directed, handsomely shot movie, and the cast go at it as if the nonsense about gangsters and human dignity were high drama.' – *New Yorker, 1977*

'A completely empty, synthetic work.' – *Gavin Lambert*

👤 Claire Trevor

453
Key Largo

A returning war veteran fights gangsters on the Florida keys.

A moody melodrama on similar lines to *To Have and Have Not*, it summed up the post-war mood of despair, allowed several good acting performances, and built up to a pretty good action climax. Edward G. Robinson, first seen smoking a cigar in the bath (looking 'like a crustacean with its shell off', according to Huston), was a cowardly gangster who refused to let guests leave an isolated Florida hotel. Bogart, as a returning war hero, was in a disillusioned mood, unwilling to risk his life again and taking the view that a gangster was not worth dying for. There is a great deal of talk and the action is confined to a few rooms until the final showdown, but Huston's direction kept the tension high.

'Doyle is bad news ... but a good cop!'

The French Connection
US   1971   104m   DeLuxe
TCF/Philip D'Antoni
🔲 🇺🇸 ⊕~ ⊕ ⊕

w *Ernest Tidyman* book Robin Moore d *William Friedkin*
ph Owen Roizman m Don Ellis ad Ben Kazaskow
ed Jerry Greenberg
☆ *Gene Hackman* (Jimmy 'Popeye' Doyle), Roy Scheider (Buddy Russo), *Fernando Rey* (Alain Charnier), Tony Lo Bianco (Sal Boca), Marcel Bozzufi (Pierre Nicoli)

'The only thing this movie believes in is giving the audience jolts, and you can feel the raw, primitive responses in the theater.' – *Pauline Kael, New Yorker*

'A film of almost incredible suspense.' – *Roger Greenspun, New York Times*

● A Regions 1 and 2 two-disc DVD set includes commentaries by William Friedkin, Gene Hackman and Roy Scheider
👤 best picture; Ernest Tidyman; William Friedkin; Gene Hackman
👤 Owen Roizman; Roy Scheider
👤 Gene Hackman

452
The French Connection

New York police track down a consignment of drugs entering the country in a car.

A lively semi-documentary based on the true exploits of two tough cops who track down a gang that is bringing cocaine into New York from France. Although there were many fictional elements added to the story, it has an authentic feel for the drudgery of police work and for the seamy side of the city. Most memorable is the ten-minute car chase after a killer on a subway train, which was added at the insistence of producer Philip D'Antoni, who was still enjoying the praise for the car chase in his previous production, *Bullitt*. As the two cops who do not mind breaking a few rules to put villains away, Gene Hackman and Roy Scheider formed a convincingly uneasy but co-operative relationship.

Shakespeare in Love
US   1998   113m   DeLuxe
UIP/Miramax/Universal/Bedford Falls (David Parfitt, Donna Gigliotti, Harvey Weinstein, Edward Zwick, Mark Norman)

w Marc Norman, Tom Stoppard *d* John Madden
ph Richard Greatrex *m* Stephen Warbeck *pd* Martin Childs *ad* Steve Lawrence *ed* David Gamble
☆ *Gwyneth Paltrow* (Viola De Lesseps), Joseph Fiennes (Will Shakespeare), *Geoffrey Rush* (Philip Henslowe), Colin Firth (Lord Wessex), Ben Affleck (Ned Alleyn), *Judi Dench* (Queen Elizabeth), Rupert Everett (Christopher Marlowe), Simon Callow (Tilney, Master of the Revels), Jim Carter (Ralph Bashford), Martin Clunes (Richard Burbage), Antony Sher (Dr. Moth), Imelda Staunton (Nurse), Tom Wilkinson (Hugh Fennyman), Mark Williams (Wabash)

'A ripely emotional comedy fantasia.' – *David Denby, New Yorker*

● Daniel Day-Lewis and Julia Roberts were the first choices for the roles played by Joseph Fiennes and Gwyneth Paltrow.

♦ best picture; Gwyneth Paltrow; Judi Dench; Marc Norman, Tom Stoppard; Stephen Warbeck; Martin Childs; Sandy Powell (costumes)

♢ John Madden; Geoffrey Rush; Richard Greatrex; David Gamble; make-up; sound

♘ best film; Judi Dench; Geoffrey Rush; David Gamble

451
Shakespeare in Love

Shakespeare is inspired by his infatuation with an aristocratic woman who is in love with the theatre.

If movies be the food of love, then there is an excess of it in this delightful romantic fantasy of Shakespeare, suffering writer's block over his new work, *Romeo and Ethel, the Pirate's Daughter*; his writing becomes inspired when he falls in love with a cross-dressing heiress. It is a clever romp that makes witty use of theatrical conventions and Shakespeare's own works, turning *Romeo and Juliet* into a new narrative of star-crossed lovers. It provides the pleasures of period movies, including a little swashbuckling, a vigorous re-creation of Tudor England and its hierarchical society, and some more modern jokes – 'I had that Christopher Marlowe in my boat once,' mutters a Thames ferryman, the Elizabethan equivalent of a taxi-driver. It is glorious fun with a purpose, for the film is not only in love with love, but with the power and passion of theatre and art.

Burnt by the Sun

Russia/France 1994 134m colour
Studio Trite/Camera One (Nikita Mikhalkov, Michel Seydoux)

original title: *Utomlennye Solntsem*

w Nikita Mikhalkov, Rustam Ibragimbekov *d* Nikita Mikhalkov *ph* Vilen Kaliuta *m* Eduard Artemiev *ad* Aleksandr Samuelekin, Vladimir Aronin *ed* Enzo Meniconi, Joëlle Hache
☆ Nikita Mikhalkov (Serguei Petrovitch Kotov), Oleg Menchikov (Dimitri (Mitia)), Ingeborga Dapkunaité (Maroussia), Nadya Mikhalkov (Nadia), Viacheslav Tikhonov (Vsevolod Konstantinovich), Svetlana Kriuchkova (Mokhova), Vladimir Ilyin (Kirik)

'The acting is excellent and the direction sympathetic to it, so that the whole glimmers in the mind's eye in a totally different way to anything the American cinema seems capable of at the moment.' – *Derek Malcolm, Guardian*

'Surely the most charming movie about the horrors of totalitarianism ever made.' – *Tom Shone, Sunday Times*

● The film shared the Grand Prix at the Cannes Film Festival in 1995. It is dedicated to 'everyone who was burnt by the sun of Revolution'.

450
Burnt by the Sun

In rural Russia in the Stalinist mid-Thirties, an ageing military hero of the Revolution is betrayed by a former acquaintance, his wife's old boyfriend, who is a turncoat White Russian now working for the secret police.

There is more than a touch of Chekhov about this rural evocation of Stalinist Russia, as unthinking brutality darkens a summer landscape and a country house party. It evokes an ambiguous time in its melancholy tale. In this complex and tragic story, the final image is of a hot air balloon, which carries a huge portrait of Stalin, rising up to dominate the landscape.

Heaven Can Wait

US 1943 112m Technicolor
TCF (Ernst Lubitsch)

w Samson Raphaelson *play Birthday* by Lazlo Bus-Fekete *d* Ernst Lubitsch *ph* Edward Cronjager *m* Alfred Newman *ad* James Basevi, Leland Fuller *ed* Dorothy Spencer
☆ *Don Ameche* (Henry Van Cleve), Gene Tierney (Martha), *Laird Cregar* (His Excellency), *Charles Coburn* (Hugo Van Cleve), *Marjorie Main* (Mrs. Strabel), Eugene Pallette (Mr. Strabel), Allyn Joslyn (Albert Van Cleve), Spring Byington (Bertha Van Cleve), Signe Hasso (Mademoiselle), Louis Calhern (Randolph Van Cleve)

'It was so good I half believed Lubitsch could still do as well as he ever did, given half a chance.' – *James Agee*

⌘ best picture; Ernst Lubitsch; Edward Cronjager

449
Heaven Can Wait

On arrival in Hades, an elderly playboy reports his peccadilloes to Satan, who sends him Upstairs.

You cannot keep a good sinner down was the message of Ernst Lubitsch's charming period piece with fantasy bookends and warm performances from Don Ameche and Gene Tierney. The essence of the comedy is its evocation of American society in the 1890s, and in its director's waspish way with a funny scene. It was Lubitsch's first film in Technicolor and, as his way with decor and, indeed, actors, he went for restraint and elegance.

'A magician's spell, the innocence of young love and a dream of revenge unite to create a tempest.'

Prospero's Books
Netherlands/France/Italy 1991 120m colour
Palace/Allarts/Cinea/Camera One/Penta/Elsevier
Vendex/Film Four/VPRO/Canal Plus/NHK (Kees
Kasander, Denis Wigman)
▣ ▤ ▦ ◠
wd Peter Greenaway *play The Tempest* by William
Shakespeare *ph* Sacha Vierny *m* Michael Nyman *pd* Ben
van Os, Jan Roelfs *ed* Marina Bodbyl
☆ John Gielgud (Prospero), Michael Clark (Caliban),
Michel Blanc (Alonso), Erland Josephson (Gonzalo),
Isabelle Pasco (Miranda), Tom Bell (Antonio), Kenneth
Cranham (Sebastian), Mark Rylance (Ferdinand), Gérard
Thoolen (Adrian), Pierre Bokma (Francisco), Michiel
Romeyn (Stephano)

'An intellectually and erotically rampaging
meditation on the arrogance and value of the
artistic process.' – *Variety*

'A remarkable feast, taking in the video revolution
at one level and a highly literate interpretation of
Shakespeare at another. Nothing quite like it has
been seen before, let alone from a British director.'
– *Derek Malcolm, Guardian*

448
Prospero's Books

Abandoned with his daughter on an island, the former Duke of Milan invokes a storm to wreck the ship carrying those who betrayed him and so regain his dukedom.

One of John Gielgud's greatest roles was as Shakespeare's Prospero, the desposed Duke of Milan. If for nothing else, this would be invaluable for preserving Gielgud's speaking of the magical verse. In fact, he speaks almost the entire play in a free and exuberant adaptation that turns it into a visual masterpiece. Peter Greenaway uses the techniques of High Definition Television and computer technology to create dense, rich, bookish images that demand more than one viewing to fully appreciate.

Those Who Love Me Can Take The Train
France 1998 122m colour Panavision
Artificial Eye/Telema/Canal+/France 2/France 3/Azor
(Charles Gassot)
▣ ▤ ◉ ◉
original title: *Ceux Qui M'aiment Prendront le Train*
w Danièle Thompson, Patrice Chéreau, Pierre Trividic
d Patrice Chéreau *ph* Eric Gautier *ad* Richard Peduzzi,
Sylvain Chauvelot *ed* François Gedigier *cos* Caroline de
Vivaise
☆ Pascal Greggory (François), Jean-Louis Trintignant
(Lucien/Jean-Baptiste), Valeria Bruni-Tedeschi (Claire),
Charles Berling (Jean-Marie), Bruno Todeschini (Louis),
Sylvain Jacques (Bruno), Vincent Perez (Viviane), Roschdy
Zem (Thierry), Dominique Blanc (Catherine), Nathan Cogan
(Sami), Marie Daems (Lucie)

'Technically acute, dramatically dense, utterly
compelling.' – *David Parkinson, Empire*

'Cinematically vivid and emotionally draining
ensembler that makes the average Woody Allen
film seem like a picnic for the well-adjusted.' – *Lisa
Nesselson, Variety*

447
Those Who Love Me Can Take The Train

Mourners ponder their personal problems on the train journey from Paris to Limoges, and at the funeral of a bisexual painter who influenced their lives in one way or another.

Patrice Chéreau's study of a group of mourners is brilliantly choreographed. Eric Gautier used a hand-held camera to get close to a disparate group united mainly by their capacity for emotional outbursts. The performances match the intensity of the director's style.

Utu
New Zealand   1983   118m   Fujicolour
Glitteron (Geoff Murphy, Don Blakeney)
📺 ▦ ⓢ 🎧
w Geoff Murphy, Keith Aberdein d Geoff Murphy
ph Graeme Cowley m John Charles pd Ron Highfield
ad Rick Kofoed ed Michael Horton, Ian John
☆ Anzac Wallace (Te Wheke), Bruno Lawrence
(Williamson), Wi Kuki Kaa (Wiremu), Kelly Johnson (Lt.
Scott), Tim Elliott (Col. Elliot), Tanya Bristowe (Kura), Ilona
Rodgers (Emily), Merata Mita (Matu), Tom Polan (Puni)

446
Utu

In New Zealand in the 1870s, a Maori, whose family is massacred by the army, and a farmer, whose wife is killed by the Maoris, are both obsessed by revenge.

New Zealand director Geoff Murphy's powerful and absorbing drama of imperialist and colonial attitudes is set against wild, open spaces of the country in the 1870s. On one side is Te Wheke (Anzac Wallace), a Maori scout whose family is massacred by the army and takes a vow of vengeance against all white people. On the other is Lieutenant James Scott (Kelly Johnson), a New Zealand-born army officer, who has fought against the Boers in South Africa, and Williamson (Bruno Lawrence), a farmer whose wife has been killed by the Maoris. Eventually Te Wheke is captured and immediately tried, which is shown in a series of flash forwards during the action. It is a complex and intriguing film that raises questions about profound cultural differences.

'A love caught in the fire of revolution!'
Doctor Zhivago
US   1965   192m   Metrocolor   Panavision 70
MGM/David Lean/Carlo Ponti
📺 📺 ▦ ⓠ ⓢ ⓢ 🎧
w Robert Bolt novel Boris Pasternak d David Lean
ph Frederick A. Young m Maurice Jarre pd John Box
ad Gil Parrondo, Terence Marsh ed Norman Savage
☆ Omar Sharif (Yuri Zhivago), Julie Christie (Larissa
'Lara' Guishar), Rod Steiger (Viktor Komarovsky), Alec
Guinness (Yevgrav Zhivago), Rita Tushingham (The Girl),
Ralph Richardson (Alexander Gromeko), Tom Courtenay
(Pasha Antipov/Strelnikoff), Geraldine Chaplin (Tonya
Gromeko), Siobhan McKenna (Anna Gromeko), Noel
Willman (Razin), Geoffrey Keen (Prof. Boris Kurt), Adrienne
Corri (Amelia Guishar)

'A long haul along the road of synthetic lyricism.'
– MFB

'David Lean's *Doctor Zhivago* does for snow what his *Lawrence of Arabia* did for sand.' – *John Simon*

'It isn't shoddy (except for the music); it isn't soap opera; it's stately, respectable, and dead. Neither the contemplative Zhivago nor the flow of events is intelligible, and what is worse, they seem unrelated to each other.' – *Pauline Kael*

● The film was shot in Spain and Finland.
♟ Robert Bolt; Frederick A. Young; Maurice Jarre
♟ best picture; David Lean; Tom Courtenay

445
Doctor Zhivago

A Moscow doctor is caught up in World War I, exiled for writing poetry, forced into partisan service and separated from his only love.

This is a beautifully photographed and meticulously directed epic romance. David Lean, who thought the novel was 'somehow all our lives', set out to make a film with universal appeal. His concern was that the audience should not condemn Zhivago's adulterous romance. In the process, the novel was so reduced that it became a collection of expensive set-pieces when not in thrall to Julie Christie. The politics, and the pivotal importance of the Russian revolution, were downplayed in favour of love on a grand scale.

Doctor Zhivago

The Last Seduction
US   1994   110m   CFI color
ITC (Jonathan Shestack)
▣ ▤ ⊚~ ⊚ ⊚ ⌾

w Steve Barancik *d* John Dahl *ph* Jeffrey Jur *m* Joseph
Vitarelli *pd* Linda Pearl *ad* Dina Lipton *ed* Eric L. Beason
☆ *Linda Fiorentino* (Bridget Gregory), Peter Berg (Mike
Swale), J. T. Walsh (Frank Griffith), Bill Nunn (Harlan), Bill
Pullman (Clay Gregory)

'Funny, sexy and so intricately plotted that you are
never quite sure what is going to happen next.'
– *Derek Malcolm, Guardian*

'Erotically ravenous, exceptionally witty, and
impressively knowledgeable about all the dirty
deals and low maneuvers that keep a corrupt world
going.' – *David Denby, New York*

444

The Last Seduction

*A tough, manipulative New York woman leaves her husband, taking
with her a million dollars he made on a drug deal.*

John Dahl revamped in virtuoso fashion the *film noir* genre. The film
had a clever, tightly written, witty script, taut direction and a splendidly
tart performance from Linda Fiorentino. Tough and selfish, she uses
her considerable sex-appeal to get rich quick and never be poor again;
even her lawyer thinks of her as 'a self-serving bitch'. It is a clever, cynical thriller that, like its central character, makes up its own rules as it
speeds along.

The Sound of Music

♔♔ US 1965 172m DeLuxe Todd-AO
TCF/Argyle (Robert Wise)
▦▦ ▦▦ ▤ ◕ ◉ ◉ ⌂

w Ernest Lehman *book* Howard Lindsay, Russel Crouse
d Robert Wise *ph* Ted McCord *m/ly* Richard Rodgers,
Oscar Hammerstein II *md* Irwin Kostal *pd* Boris Leven
ed William Reynolds

☆ *Julie Andrews* (Maria), *Christopher Plummer* (Capt.
Von Trapp), Richard Haydn (Max Detweiler), Eleanor Parker
(The Baroness), *Peggy Wood* (Mother Abbess), Anna Lee
(Sister Margaretta), Marni Nixon (Sister Sophia)

'The success of a movie like *The Sound of Music*
makes it even more difficult for anyone to try to do
anything worth doing, anything relevant to the
modern world, anything inventive or expressive.'
– Pauline Kael, New Yorker

'… sufficient warning to those allergic to singing
nuns and sweetly innocent children.' – John Gillett

● Christopher Plummer's singing was dubbed by Bill Lee,
and Peggy Wood's by Margery McKay.
♫ 'The Sound of Music'; 'Morning Hymn'; 'Alleluia';
'Maria'; 'I Have Confidence In Me'; 'Sixteen Going on
Seventeen'; 'My Favorite Things'; 'Do-Re-Mi'; 'The Lonely
Goatherd'; 'Edelweiss'; 'So Long Farewell'; 'Climb Every
Mountain'; 'Something Good'
♟ best picture; Robert Wise; Irwin Kostal
♟ Ted McCord; Julie Andrews; Peggy Wood

443
The Sound of Music

*In 1938 Austria, a trainee nun becomes governess to the Trapp family,
falls in love with the widower father, and helps them all escape from
the Nazis.*

A phenomenally successful musical that has become something of a
cult, with performances where the audience sings along with the cast.
It is a very handsome version of an enjoyably old-fashioned stage
musical. There are splendid tunes and excellent performances from the
stars. Julie Andrews' straightforward sincerity cuts through the sentimentality of the story to give it mass appeal.

Werckmeister Harmonies

Hungary/Germany/France 2000 145m bw
Goess/Von Vietinghoff/13 (Miklos Szita, Franz Goess)
▤ ⊘

w Laszlo Krasznahorkai, Bela Tarr novel The Melancholy of Resistance by Laszlo Krasznahorkai d Bela Tarr ph Gabor Medvigy m Mihaly Vig ed Agnes Hranitzky
☆ Lars Rudolph (Janos Valuska), Peter Fitz (Gyorgy Eszter), Hanna Schygulla (Tunde Eszter), Janos Derzi (Man In the Broadcloth Coat), Djoko Rossich (Man in the Western Boots)

'As challenging as movies come, alluding to everything from philosopher Thomas Hobbes to the history of Western music.' – David Sterrit, Christian Science Monitor

'If genius is close to madness, then Tarr's genius – because genius has to be what it is – is closer to autism, a kind of untrained savant touch for compelling imagery. Famously unschooled in European cinema, he has developed his own vernacular language of movie-making.' – Peter Bradshaw, Guardian

● The title refers to Andreas Werckmeister (1645-1706), who devised a method of musical tuning that was a closed 12-tone system.
● The two-disc Region 2 release includes an earlier feature Damnation (qv).

442
Werckmeister Harmonies

Unrest leads to violence and political oppression in a small, bleak Hungarian town when a circus arrives, putting on show a dead whale.

Bela Tarr is one of the most enigmatic of directors, approaching his subjects obliquely. The extraordinary opening sequence here shows a man trying to demonstrate the movement of the planets by getting the drunks at closing time in the pub to whirl around each other until they collapse. Order soon disappears from the small, bleak Hungarian town. This mysterious film is shot in a series of long takes, and shadowy black and white images, that convey a sense of growing dread. It may be a fable of the end of Communism, of intellectual apathy and political opportunism, but once seen it will never be forgotten.

The Blue Kite

China/Japan 1993 138m colour
Longwick/Beijing Film Studio
◧ ▤ ♫

original title: Lan Fengzheng
w Xiao Mao d Tian Zhuangzhuang ph Hou Yong m Yoshihide Otomo ad Zhang Xiande ed Qian Lengleng
☆ Zhang Wenyao (Tietou, as a child), Chen Xiaoman (Tietou, as a teenager), Lu Piping (Mum (Chen Shujuan)), Pu Quanxin (Dad (Lin Shaolong)), Li Xuejian (Uncle Li (Li Guodong)), Guo Baochang (Stepfather (Lao Wu)), Zhong Ping (Chen Shusheng), Chu Qhuangzhong (Chen Shuyan), Song Xiaoying (Sis), Zhang Hong (Zhu Ying)

'Major surprise of the movie is that, despite a story and multi-character cast that looks more fitted to a mini-series, it works on a simple emotional level as a feature film. Characters emerge as real people rather than political stereotypes.' – Variety

● The film had a troubled production with interference from Chinese officials, who forbade a print to leave the country for post-production work. The film was finished from the director's script and notes after a print was smuggled out of the country. In a statement made at the 1993 Cannes Film Festival the director said, 'The stories in the film are real, and they are related with total sincerity. What worries me is that it is precisely a fear of reality that has led to the ban on such stories being told.' It has not been shown in China, and in April 1994 Tian Zhuangzhuang was one of seven film directors banned from making films in mainland China.

441
The Blue Kite

A boy recalls his mother's three marriages and the troubles that beset his family life during the 1950s and 1960s, a time of political upheaval during China's Great Leap Forward and the Cultural Revolution inspired by the Red Guards.

Tian Zhuangzhuang's film is one of the few to deal with China's Cultural Revolution, inspired by the Red Guards, that damaged or destroyed artists and intellectuals. He, too, had a hard job finishing the film and getting it shown because of official opposition. It is a story told in recollection. A gripping, though often depressing, domestic drama seen against the ideological upheavals that made a hero of one period a villain of the next, it has warmth and humour in the telling; but the story is one of personal tragedy.

Alice

👣 GB/Switzerland/West Germany 1988
85m Eastmancolor
Condor-Hessisches/SRG/Film Four (Peter-Christian Fueter)

📼 ◎~ ◎ ◎

original title: *Neco z Alenky*
wd Jan Svankmajer *novel* *Alice in Wonderland* by Lewis Carroll *ph* Svatoluk Maly *ad* Eva Svankmerova, Jiri Blaha *ed* Marie Drvotova
☆ Kristyna Kohoutova (Alice)

'A film for children of a certain kind, for the quiet solitary ones who spend hours in conversation with their dolls; who invest the smallest cast-off objects with secret significance.' – *Terrence Rafferty, New Yorker*

440
Alice

A young girl follows a rabbit through a broken glass case into Wonderland.

Jan Svankmajer, the great Czech animator, has made only a couple of full-length films, preferring to create brilliantly strange short films, often using clay figures. In his version of Lewis Carroll's quirky masterpiece, Svankmajer has created a free, sometimes disturbing interpretation with surrealist overtones. Its mix of live actors and animation comes closer than any other to conjuring the curious atmosphere of the original.

'Nobody ever won a war by dying for his country. He won it by making the other poor dumb bastard die for his country!'

Patton

US 1969 171m DeLuxe Dimension 150
TCF (Frank McCarthy)

📼 ▬ ◎~ ◎ ◎ 🎧

GB title: *Patton – Lust for Glory*
w Francis Ford Coppola, Edmund H. North *d* Franklin Schaffner *ph* Fred Koenekamp *m* Jerry Goldsmith *ad* Urie McCleary, Gil Parrondo *ed* Hugh S. Fowler
☆ George C. Scott (Gen. George S. Patton Jr.), Karl Malden (Gen. Omar N. Bradley), Michael Bates (Field Marshal Sir Bernard Law Montgomery), Stephen Young (Capt. Chester B. Hansen), Michael Strong (Brig. Gen. Hobart Carver), Frank Latimore (Lt. Col. Henry Davenport)

'Here is an actor so totally immersed in his part that he almost makes you believe he is the man himself.' – *John Gillett*

🏆 best picture; script; Franklin Schaffner; George C. Scott; art direction; editing; sound (Douglas Williams, Don Bassman)
👤 Fred Koenekamp; Jerry Goldsmith; special visual effects

439
Patton

World War II adventures of an aggressive American general.

One of the most commanding and physically intimidating of actors, George C. Scott was ideally suited to play the aggressive American General Patton during his career in World War II. It is a brilliantly handled character study. A tough disciplinarian, Patton found himself frustrated by allied commanders and politicians, violently disputing their views, an attitude that finally left him disgraced, dismissed and bitter. Scott's performance is among the greatest in cinema history, full of fine nuances of behaviour when the role could so easily have been played on one note. As a piece of film-making, this is hard to beat.

'The story that will live … as long as there is love!'

Letter from an Unknown Woman
US   1948   89m   bw
Universal/Rampart (John Houseman)
📽 ▦ ⊙

w Howard Koch *novel* Stefan Zweig *d* Max Ophüls *ph* Franz Planer *m* Daniele Amfitheatrof *ad* Alexander Golitzen *ed* Ted J. Kent

☆ *Joan Fontaine* (Lisa Berndle), Louis Jourdan (Stefan Brand), Mady Christians (Frau Berndle), Art Smith (John), Marcel Journet (Johann Stauffer)

'A film full of snow, sleigh bells, lights gleaming in ornamental gardens and trysts at night.' – *Charles Higham, 1972*

'It is fascinating to watch the sure deft means by which Ophuls sidetracks seemingly inevitable clichés and holds on to a shadowy, tender mood, half buried in the past. Here is a fragile filmic charm that is not often or easily accomplished.' – *Richard Winnington*

'Film narrative of a most skilled order.' – *William Whitebait*

'Probably the toniest "woman's picture" ever made.' – *Pauline Kael, 70s*

438
Letter from an Unknown Woman

A woman wastes her life in unrequited love for a rakish pianist.

This is a superior 'woman's picture' which gave Max Ophuls his best chance in America to recreate his beloved Vienna of long ago. The woman's letter is written on her deathbed and ends, 'if only you could have recognized what was always yours, could have found what was never lost'. It is read by the pianist, who has dissipated his talent, while he waits for dawn and a duel with the woman's husband, and tries to remember her. It is a swooningly romantic story, elegantly filmed and showing Hollywood production magic at its best.

Amarcord
Italy/France   1973   123m   Technicolor
FC Produzione/PECF (Franco Cristaldi)
▦ ⊙ ⌒

w Federico Fellini, Tonino Guerra *d* Federico Fellini *ph* Giuseppe Rotunno *m* Nino Rota *ad* Danilo Donati *ed* Ruggero Mastroianni

☆ Pupella Maggio (Miranda Biondi, Titta's Mother), Magali Noel (Gradisca), Armando Brancia (Aurelio Biondi, Titta's Father), Ciccio Ingrassia (Uncle Teo)

'A rich surface texture and a sense of exuberant melancholia.' – *Michael Billington, Illustrated London News*

'Peaks of invention separated by raucous valleys of low comedy.' – *Sight and Sound*

'Some idea of attitudes within the film business may be conveyed by the fact that this witty, tender, humane, marvellously photographed picture has been booked into a cinema with 132 seats.' – *Benny Green, Punch*

'Hitchcock once said that he wanted to play his audiences like a piano. Fellini requires the entire orchestra.' – *Roger Ebert*

🏆 foreign film
⚐ script; direction

437
Amarcord

Memories of a small Italian town during the fascist period.

Fellini chose his title (which translates as 'I remember') with care, for his film is about memory. It was his farewell to the ghosts of his past. The film, which begins and ends at springtime, is an episodic succession of seasonal events in a provincial setting that circumscribed individual freedom. If there is a feeling of unreality about it, such as the dazzling image of a great liner that is obviously fake, then that is deliberate. It is a bizarre, intriguing mixture of fact, fantasy and obscurity, pleasing to watch.

Felicia's Journey

GB/Canada 1999 116m DeLuxe
Panavision
Icon/Marquis/Screen Ventures XLIII

⊡ ▤ ⊚ ⊘ ⌕

wd Atom Egoyan *novel* William Trevor *ph* Paul Sarossy
m Mychael Danna *pd* Jim Clay *ed* Susan Shipton
cos Sandy Powell

☆ *Bob Hoskins* (Hilditch), Elaine Cassidy (Felicia),
Arsinee Khanjian (Gala), Peter McDonald (Johnny), Gerard
McSorley (Felicia's Father), Brid Brennan (Mrs Lysaght),
Danny Turner (Young Hilditch), Claire Benedict (Miss
Calligary)

'An altogether amazing work; it creates a world and
then leaves it with you, what's more, in a manner
that you might find difficult to forget.' – *Andrew
O'Hagan, Daily Telegraph*

'Very well-made, but cold and hollow at its core.'
– *Stephen Farber, Movieline*

436
Felicia's Journey

*Searching for the English father of her unborn child, an Irish girl is
offered a place to stay by a middle-aged man with murder on his mind.*

Atom Egoyan journeys into the chill banality of the mind of a serial
killer in this melancholy drama of a pregnant Irish girl's search for the
father of her child. She comes to England not knowing and is taken in
by a middle-aged catering manager who lives alone in the family house
once occupied by his mother, a TV cook. Both the dull, suburban
would-be killer and his naive victim recognize a similarity in each other,
both fearful people who seem at home with one another. A bleak drama
of the unloved searching for redemption, it provides an unsettling
insight into the motivations of a mass murderer.

'The year's most revealing comedy.'

The Full Monty

GB/US 1997 91m Metrocolor
TCF/Redwave (Uberto Pasolini)

⊡ ▤ ⊚ ⊘ ⌕

w Simon Beaufoy *d* Peter Cattaneo *ph* John de Borman
m Anne Dudley *pd* Max Gottlieb *ed* David Freeman, Nick
More

☆ Robert Carlyle (Gaz), Tom Wilkinson (Gerald), Mark
Addy (Dave), Lesley Sharp (Jean), Emily Woof (Mandy),
Steve Huison (Lomper), Paul Barber (Horse), Hugo Speer
(Guy), Deirdre Costello

● The film cost $3.5m and grossed $35m in the US, and
another $132m elsewhere. It was, briefly, the biggest-
grossing film at the British box-office, and is now second
only to *Titanic*.
● Two origins are given for the title phrase. 'Monty' was the
nickname given to Field Marshal Montgomery. The Full
Monty is either slang to describe the three-piece suits
provided to soldiers on demobilization at the end of the
Second World War, or to the Field Marshal's insistence on
being served with a full English breakfast on the battlefield.
● The story was turned into a Broadway musical, with the
action relocated to Buffalo, N.Y., in 2000.
🕴 Anne Dudley
♟ picture; Peter Cattaneo; Simon Beaufoy
🏆 film; Robert Carlyle; Tom Wilkinson

435
The Full Monty

*A group of unemployed Sheffield steelworkers decide to become male
strippers in order to raise some money.*

Set in a declining industrial city, this was a clever, enjoyable comedy.
Its scenes of audition and rehearsal for the troupe were funny, but elsewhere it let the men's pain show through; the worker's upwardly mobile
former foreman, who coached them in their routine, was unable to face
telling his wife that he had lost his job. About salvaging self-respect
and baring all, emotionally as well as physically, the film struck a chord
not only in Britain, but around the world and was also transformed into
a Broadway musical.

La Chinoise

France   1967   95m   Eastmancolor
Fair Enterprises/Productions de la Guéville/Parc/
Simar/Anouchka/Athos

wd Jean-Luc Godard *ph* Raoul Coutard *m* Karl-Heinz
Stockhausen *ed* Agnès Guillemot, Delphine Desfons
☆ Anne Wiazemsky (Veronique), Jean-Pierre Léaud
(Guillaume), Michel Sémeniako (Henry), Lex de Brujin
(Kirilov), Juliet Berto (Yvonne), Omar Diop (Comrade X),
Francis Jeanson (Himself)

'The movie is like a speed-freak's anticipatory
vision of the political horrors to come; it's
amazing.' – *Pauline Kael*

'A piece of mitigated trash … Godard, his material,
his pretentiousness and undisciplined garrulity, are
boring when not exasperating.' – *John Simon*

434
La Chinoise

In 1967, five Parisian Maoist revolutionaries debate the best ways of achieving the end of the capitalist system, from closing the universities to acting Brecht, and decide that terrorism is the way forward.

With hindsight, it is clear that Godard made a prophetic movie of the student politics that shook Paris a year later. He mixes a documentary and a fictional approach, with on-screen interviews as well as confrontations between the characters. It did signal Godard's increasing dissatisfaction with conventional cinema, which led him into less accessible experiments from 1968, but it is still a troubling and wittily intriguing film in its search for new means of cinematic expression.

Last Tango in Paris

Last Tango in Paris
France/Italy/US 1972 129m Technicolor
Les Artistes Associés/PEA/UA (Alberto Grimaldi)

w Bernardo Bertolucci, Franco Arcalli *d* Bernardo Bertolucci *ph* Vittorio Storaro *m* Gato Barbieri *ad* Ferdinando Scarfiotti *ed* Franco Arcalli, Roberto Perpignani

☆ Marlon Brando (Paul), Maria Schneider (Jeanne), Jean-Pierre Léaud (Tom), Massimo Girotti (Marcel), Veronica Lazare (Rosa), Maria Michi (Rosa's mother), Gitt Magrini (Jeanne's mother)

'An intense meditation on the realization of mortality.' – *Sight and Sound*

'The most powerfully erotic movie ever made.' – *Pauline Kael*

♘ Bernardo Bertolucci (as director); Marlon Brando

433

Last Tango in Paris

A middle-aged man and a young French girl have a doomed love affair.

When Bertolucci first met Brando to talk about this film, he said 'Let's talk about ourselves – our lives, our loves, about sex. That's what the film is going to be about.' And much of it was. Its central situation involved anonymous sex: a middle-aged hotel owner, who is lonely and in despair, becomes infatuated with a young French girl and spends three sex-filled days in an apartment with her. It is when he wants to know her better that tragedy ensues. With both Marlon Brando and Maria Schneider improvising their roles, it became a revelatory film on a personal level. Brando indulged in what seemed to be autobiographical reminiscences, and later thought the film was a violation of his inner self. It provided an extra level of fascination to a cool examination of how power shifts from one partner to another in a sexual relationship.

The Miracle of Morgan's Creek

The Miracle of Morgan's Creek
US 1943 99m bw
Paramount (Preston Sturges)

wd Preston Sturges *ph* John Seitz *m* Leo Shuken, Charles Bradshaw *ad* Hans Dreier, Ernst Fegte *ed* Stuart Gilmore

☆ Betty Hutton (Trudy Kockenlocker), Eddie Bracken (Norval Jones), William Demarest (Officer Kockenlocker), Diana Lynn (Emmy Kockenlocker), Porter Hall (Justice of the Peace), Akim Tamiroff (The Boss), Brian Donlevy (Governor McGinty), Alan Bridge (Mr. Johnson)

'Like taking a nun on a roller coaster.' – *James Agee*

'This film moves in a fantastic and irreverent whirl of slapstick, nonsense, farce, sentiment, satire, romance, melodrama – is there any ingredient of dramatic entertainment except maybe tragedy and grand opera that hasn't been tossed into it?' – *National Board of Review*

'Bad taste, or no bad taste, I thoroughly enjoyed it.' – *Richard Mallett, Punch*

♘ Preston Sturges (as writer)

432

The Miracle of Morgan's Creek

Chaos results when a stuttering hayseed tries to help a girl accidentally pregnant by a soldier she met hazily at a dance.

Preston Sturges's comedy is a weird and wonderful one-man assault on the Hays Office and sundry other American institutions such as motherhood and politics, with great performances from Eddie Bracken as the hayseed, Betty Hutton as the pregnant girl as well as the usual Sturges repertory company. It is an indescribable, tasteless, roaringly funny mêlée, as unexpected at the time as it was effective, like a kick in the pants to all other film comedies.

I'm All Right Jack
GB   1959   104m   bw
British Lion/Charter (Roy Boulting)

w Frank Harvey, John Boulting, Alan Hackney
novel Private Life by Alan Hackney *d* John Boulting
ph Max Greene *m* Ken Hare *ed* Anthony Harvey
☆ *Ian Carmichael* (Stanley Windrush), *Peter Sellers* (Fred
Kite), Irene Handl (Mrs. Kite), Richard Attenborough (Sidney
de Vere Cox), *Terry-Thomas* (Maj. Hitchcock), Dennis Price
(Bertram Tracepurcel), Margaret Rutherford (Aunt Dolly), Liz
Fraser (Cynthia Kite), *John Le Mesurier* (Waters), Sam Kydd
(Shop Steward)
Ⓣ Peter Sellers; screenplay

431
I'm All Right Jack

*A world-innocent graduate takes a job in industry; by starting ⌐
bottom he provokes a national strike.*

The Boulting Brothers' satirical farce managed to hit most of its wid⌐
spread targets and found corruption in high, low and middle places.
Ian Carmichael was suitably innocent as a graduate who takes a job in
industry but it was mainly memorable for Peter Sellers as a pompous,
inarticulate shop steward, a terror in the workplace and terrorized in
his own home by his wife and daughter. It was a richly comic performance in a film that provided a not inaccurate picture of aspects of
British life in the Fifties.

The Assault
Netherlands   1986   148m   colour
Cannon (Fons Rademakers)

original title: De Aanslag
w Gerard Soeteman *novel* Harry Mulisch *d* Fons
Rademakers *ph* Their Van Der Sande *m* Jurriaan
Andriessen *ad* Dorus van der Linden *ed* Kees Linthorst
☆ Derek de Lint (Anton Steenwijk), Marc Van Uchelen
(Anton as a Boy), Monique Van de Ven (Truus Coster/Saskia
de Graaff), John Kraaykamp (Cor Takes), Huub Van Der
Lubbe (Fake Ploeg/His Father), Elly Weller (Mrs. Beumer),
Ina Van Der Molen (Karin Korteweg)
🏆 best foreign film

430
The Assault

*An adult is forced to recall the traumatic events of his childhood, when
he saw his family murdered by the Nazis.*

A Dutch doctor is forced to recall the horrors of the past, in Fons
Rademakers' thriller. As the past is recalled during times of post-war
political protest by those who were witnesses to the killings, a picture
emerges of the lasting effects of the war. The film is in part a gripping
story and part an indictment of those who would forget the past, and is
wholly watchable and unforgettable.

429

Ninotchka

A Paris playboy falls for a communist emissary sent to sell some crown jewels.

A sparkling comedy on a theme which has been frequently explored. The film is blithe satire about communism meeting capitalism. Its delicate pointing and hilarious character comedy sustain this version perfectly until the last half hour, when it certainly sags; but it remains a favourite Hollywood example of this genre. It was Garbo's favourite part. 'It was nice to make people laugh after so many tears,' she told Billy Wilder, who was one of its scriptwriters.

alter Reisch
rnst Lubitsch *ph* William
ymann *ad* Cedric Gibbons, Randall
Ruggiero

Garbo (Lena Yakushova, 'Ninotchka'), *Melvyn Douglas* (Count Leon Dolga), *Sig Rumann* (Michael Ironoff), *Alexander Granach* (Kopalski), *Felix Bressart* (Buljanoff), *Ina Claire* (Grand Duchess Swana), *Bela Lugosi* (Commissar Razinin)

'High calibre entertainment for adult audiences, and a top attraction for the key de-luxers.' – *Variety*

'The Lubitsch style, in which much was made of subtleties – glances, finger movements, raised eyebrows – has disappeared. Instead we have a hard, brightly lit, cynical comedy with the wisecrack completely in control.' – *John Baxter, 1968*

● Remade in 1957 as a musical, *Silk Stockings*.
● William Powell and Robert Montgomery were formerly considered for the Melvyn Douglas role.
♗ best picture; script; story; Greta Garbo

La Ronde

France 1950 100m bw
Sacha Gordine
◧ ▣

w Jacques Natanson, Max Ophüls *novel* Arthur Schnitzler
d Max Ophüls *ph* Christian Matras *m* Oscar Straus
ad Marpaux, M. Frederix, Jean d'Eaubonne *ed* Leonide
Azar, S. Rondeau
☆ *Anton Walbrook* (Master of Ceremonies), Simone
Signoret (Leocadie, the Prostitute), Serge Reggiani (Franz,
the Soldier), Simone Simon (Marie, the Chambermaid),
Daniel Gélin (Alfred, the Young Man), Danielle Darrieux
(Emma Breitkopf, the Married Lady), Fernand Gravey
(Charles, the Husband), Odette Joyeux (The Grisette), Jean-
Louis Barrault (Robert Kuhlenkampf, the Poet), Isa Miranda
(The Actress), Gérard Philipe (The Count)

'One of the most civilized films to have come from
Europe in a long time.' – *Gavin Lambert, MFB*

'A film that drags on and on by what seems like
geometric progression.' – *John Simon, 1968*

● Remade in 1964, where it was set in Paris.
♟ Jacques Natanson, Max Ophuls (script)
♆ film

428
La Ronde

In 1900 Vienna, an elegant compere shows that love is a merry-go-round.

Max Ophüls' superb stylized comedy is a carousel of love and desire: in
fin-de-siècle Vienna, prostitute meets soldier meets housemaid meets
master meets married woman meets husband meets midinette meets
poet meets actress meets officer meets prostitute meets soldier …
It has all the ingredients of a classic; a fine cast, subtle jokes, rich
decor and fluent direction, not to mention a haunting theme tune. Its
subject may be sexual allure and the discovery that most of the pleasure comes from the anticipation of love rather than its consummation,
but Ophüls' treatment is deliciously delicate and light-hearted.
Nevertheless, it was banned in parts of America as immoral, released
there in a cut version and not seen in its original form until the late
1960s.

The Front Page

US 1931 101m bw
Howard Hughes
▣ ⊚

w Bartlett Cormack, Charles Lederer *play* Charles
MacArthur, Ben Hecht *d* Lewis Milestone *ph* Glen
MacWilliams
☆ *Adolphe Menjou* (Walter Burns), *Pat O'Brien* (Hildy
Johnson), Mary Brian (Peggy), Edward Everett Horton
(Bensinger), Walter Catlett (Murphy), George E. Stone (Earl
Williams), Mae Clarke (Molly), Slim Summerville (Pincus),
Matt Moore (Kruger), Frank McHugh (McCue)

'Sure money-getter … it will universally entertain
and please.' – *Variety*

'The most riproaring movie that ever came out of
Hollywood.' – *Pare Lorentz*

'It excelled most of the films of its day by sheer
treatment. The speedy delivery of lines and
business and the re-emphasis upon cutting as a
prime structural element made the film a model of
mobility for confused directors who did not know
yet how to handle sound.' – *Lewis Jacobs, The
Rise of the American Film*

● Remade in 1940 as *His Girl Friday* , in 1974 by Billy
Wilder and in 1988 as *Switching Channels*.
♟ best picture; Lewis Milestone; Adolphe Menjou

427
The Front Page

*Chicago's top reporter is prevented from quitting his job by his wily
editor.*

Ben Hecht and Charles MacArthur's much filmed classic comedy-
drama of Chicago newspaper life was turned into a brilliant early talkie
under Lewis Milestone's precise direction. It perfectly transferred into
screen terms the story of a reporter who wanted to retire and marry,
but was tricked by his scheming editor into covering one last story. It
was based on MacArthur's own experiences working for editor Walter
Howey on the *Chicago Examiner*, a period of political chicanery and
exuberant journalism that is reflected in the film. Adolphe Menjou, as
editor, and Pat O'Brien, as reporter, make the most of the slick, wisecracking dialogue and their love-hate relationship. Superficially a shade
primitive now, its essential power remains.

Thelma and Louise
US   1991   129m   DeLuxe   Panavision
UIP/Pathé Entertainment (Ridley Scott, Mimi Polk)

w Callie Khouri *d* Ridley Scott *ph* Adrian Biddle *m* Hans Zimmer *pd* Norris Spencer *ad* Lisa Dean *ed* Thom Noble ☆ *Susan Sarandon* (Louise), *Geena Davis* (Thelma), Harvey Keitel (Hal), Michael Madsen (Jimmy), Christopher McDonald (Darryl), Stephen Tobolowsky (Max), Brad Pitt (J.D.)

'An exhilarating feminist movie … that's designed to appeal to the outlaw lurking in all of us.' – *Philip French, Observer*

'The first important American movie to plop two women in a car and send them careering down open Western roads with the cops in wheel-spinning pursuit. And it is the first to use sexism as the motivating force for their misdeeds.' – *Richard Schickel, Time*

● Regions 1 and 2 special edition DVD releases include commentary by the director, and by Geena Davis and Callie Khouri.

♟ Callie Khouri
♟ Ridley Scott; Geena Davis; Susan Sarandon; Adrian Biddle; editing

426
Thelma and Louise

Two women, off together on a weekend spree, go on the run after one of them kills a man who tries to rape the other.

A timely, exuberant and off-beat feminist road movie, it manages to say something interesting about the relationship between the sexes and gets two contrasting and effective performances from Susan Sarandon and Geena Davis as the two women who are determined never to look back.

Gaslight
GB   1940   88m   bw
British National (John Corfield)

US title: *Angel Street*
w A. R. Rawlinson, Bridget Boland *play* Patrick Hamilton *d* Thorold Dickinson *ph* Bernard Knowles *m* Richard Addinsell *ed* Sidney Cole ☆ *Anton Walbrook* (Paul Mallen), *Diana Wynyard* (Bella Mallen), *Frank Pettingell* (Rough), Cathleen Cordell (Nancy), Robert Newton (Vincent Ullswater), Jimmy Hanley (Cobb)

'For one who has seen the stage play, much of the tension is destroyed by the insistence on explaining everything rather than hinting at it.' – *Dilys Powell*

'The electric sense of tension and mid-Victorian atmosphere are entirely cinematic.' – *Sequence, 1950*

● The Region 1 DVD release includes both the British and the Hollywood versions.

425
Gaslight

A Victorian schizophrenic drives his wife insane when she seems likely to stumble on his guilty secret of an old murder and hidden rubies.

A modest but absolutely effective film version of a superb piece of suspense theatre. There have been two films of Patrick Hamilton's thriller. This was the first; when MGM remade it to lesser effect in Hollywood in 1944 with a bigger budget and starring Ingrid Bergman and Charles Boyer, the studio ordered that the negative should be destroyed. Fortunately, the film somehow survived, and can still strike a chill.

Jesus of Montreal
Canada/France   1989   120m   colour
Max Films/Gérard Mital Productions/NFB Canada
(Roger Frappier, Pierre Gendron)
▣ ▤ ◍ ◎ ◎
original title: *Jésus de Montréal*
wd Denys Arcand *ph* Guy Dufaux *m* Yves Laferrière,
François Dompierre, Jean-Marie Benoît *ad* François
Seguin *ed* Isabelle Dedieu
☆ Lothaire Bluteau (Daniel), Catherine Wilkening
(Mireille), Johanne-Marie Tremblay (Constance), Rémy
Girard (Martin), Robert Lepage (Rene), Gilles Pelletier (Fr.
Leclerc), Yves Jacques (Richard Cardinal)

'Arcand is a master of tone, a sympathetic director
of actors, and an unsanctimonious moralist, who
locates his fable within a well-observed society.'
– *Philip French, Observer*

⚖ best foreign film

424
Jesus of Montreal

An actor, chosen to play Christ in a religious play, finds himself in conflict with the church authorities.

Denys Arcand's modern morality play gains immeasurably from Lothaire Bluteau, who has the gentle, suffering appearance, and also the inner anger, for a Christ-like figure. The film, driven by a passionate irony, is surprisingly effective despite sometimes forced parallels between the actor's experience and those of Jesus. While the focus of the film is the itinerant life of actors, it makes the point that religion can be used to justify any behaviour.

Cleo From 5 to 7
France/Italy   1961   90m   bw/colour
Rome/Paris (Bruno Drigo)
▣ ▤ ◎
original title: *Cleo de 5 à 7*
wd Agnès Varda *ph* Jean Rabier *m* Michel Legrand
ad Bernard Evein *ed* Jeanne Verneau
☆ Corinne Marchand (Cleo), Antoine Bourseiller
(Antoine), Dorothée Blanck (Dorothee), Michel Legrand
(Bob, the Pianist)

423
Cleo From 5 to 7

A girl waiting for the result of a medical examination wanders around Paris thinking she has cancer.

An impressively handled character sketch with gratifying attention to detail, Agnès Varda's drama concerns two hours in the life of a singer. Much depends upon the performance of Corinne Marchand as Cleo; she is convincing as the self-absorbed beauty who seems without many inner resources; in her journey through the streets of the city, she gains awareness of a wider world outside herself; as a fortune teller pointed out at the beginning of her wanderings, the number 13 tarot card she turns up does not mean death, but transformation.

'Rich is their humor! Deep are their passions! Reckless are their lives! Mighty is their story!'

'"What are you? A man or a saint? I don't want him, I want you!" Her desire scorched both their lives with the vicious breath of scandal!'

How Green Was My Valley
👫 US 1941 118m bw
TCF (Darryl F. Zanuck)
▭ ▬ ▨ ◉ ◉ ◠

w Philip Dunne *novel* Richard Llewellyn *d* John Ford *ph* Arthur Miller *m* Alfred Newman *ad* Richard Day, Nathan Juran *ed* James B. Clark
☆ Walter Pidgeon (Mr. Gruffydd), Maureen O'Hara (Angharad), Roddy McDowall (Huw Morgan), Donald Crisp (Mr. Morgan), Sara Allgood (Mrs. Morgan), Anna Lee (Bronwyn), John Loder (Ianto Morgan), Barry Fitzgerald (Cyfurtha), Patric Knowles (Ivor Morgan), Morton Lowry (Mr. Jonas), Arthur Shields (Parry), Frederic Worlock (Dr. Richards)
● The elaborate village set was used again two years later for the war movie, *The Moon is Down.*
♟ best picture; John Ford; Arthur Miller; Donald Crisp; art direction
♟ Philip Dunne; Alfred Newman; Sara Allgood; James B. Clark

Genevieve
👫 GB . 1953 86m Technicolor
GFD/Sirius (Henry Cornelius)
▭ ▬ ▨ ◉

w William Rose *d* Henry Cornelius *ph* Christopher Challis *m* Larry Adler (who also played it) *md* Muir Mathieson *ad* Michael Stringer *ed* Clive Donner
☆ Dinah Sheridan (Wendy McKim), John Gregson (Alan McKim), Kay Kendall (Rosalind Peters), Kenneth More (Ambrose Claverhouse), Geoffrey Keen (1st Speed Cop), Joyce Grenfell (Hotel Proprietress), Reginald Beckwith (J.C. Callahan), Arthur Wontner (Elderly Gentleman)

'One of the best things to have happened to British films over the last five years.' – *Gavin Lambert*

'One of the funniest farce-comedies in years.' – *Bosley Crowther*

● On American prints, Muir Mathieson was credited as the composer and with the Oscar nomination rather than Larry Adler, who was blacklisted at the time.
♟ William Rose; Larry Adler
♟ British film

422
How Green Was My Valley

Memories of childhood in a Welsh mining village.

Richard Llewellyn's novel became a prettified and unconvincing but dramatically very effective tearjerker in the hands of the Irish-American John Ford. He ignored the book's political content to concentrate on its depiction of family life. William Wyler, who was to have directed, cast the picture. When Ford became involved, he used his own childhood memories as the basis for the characters. High production values here add a touch of extra class, turning the result into a Hollywood milestone despite its intrinsic inadequacies.

421
Genevieve

Two friendly rivals engage in a race on the way back from the Brighton veteran car rally.

This engaging movie was close to the style of an Ealing comedy, from a director and screenwriter who had both worked for the studio. It was one of those happy films in which, for no very good or expected reason, a number of modest elements merge smoothly to create an aura of high style and memorable moments. A charmingly witty script, carefully pointed direction, attractive actors and locations, an atmosphere of light-hearted British sex and a lively harmonica theme, turned it, after a slowish start, into one of Britain's biggest commercial hits and most fondly remembered comedies.

Horse Feathers
US   1932   69m   bw
Paramount (Herman J. Mankiewicz)

w Bert Kalmar, Harry Ruby, S. J. Perelman, Will B. Johnstone d Norman Z. McLeod ph Ray June m/ly Bert Kalmar, Harry Ruby
☆ *Groucho Marx* (Professor Wagstaff), *Chico Marx* (Chico), *Harpo Marx* (Harpo), *Zeppo Marx* (Zeppo), *Thelma Todd* (Connie Bailey), Robert Greig (Professor Hornsvogel)

'The current Marx comedy is the funniest talkie since the last Marx comedy, and the record it establishes is not likely to be disturbed until the next Marx comedy comes along. As for comparisons, I was too busy having a good time to make any.' – *Philip K. Scheuer*

● Groucho: 'You have the brain of a four-year-old child, and I'll bet he was glad to get rid of it.'

420
Horse Feathers

A college needs to win at football, and its corrupt new president knows just how to do it.

Possibly the Marxes' wildest yet most streamlined kaleidoscope of high jinks and irreverence, with at least one bright gag or line to the minute and lively musical interludes to boot. The story is just a hook on which to hang some memorable routines, including the opening introduction of Groucho as the new president of Huxley College, and his later attempt to guess the password so that Chico will let him into the speakeasy ('What'sa matter? You no understand English? You can't come in here unless you say swordfish. Now, I give you one more guess'). It is a classic of zany comedy.

Monty Python's Life of Brian
GB   1979   93m   Eastmancolor
Hand Made Films (John Goldstone)

w John Cleese, Graham Chapman, Eric Idle, Michael Palin, Terry Gilliam, Terry Jones d Terry Jones ph Peter Biziou m Geoffrey Burgon ad Roger Christian ed Julian Doyle
☆ Graham Chapman (Brian etc), John Cleese (Reg etc), Terry Gilliam, Eric Idle (Stan/Loretta etc.), Michael Palin (Pontius Pilate etc), Terry Jones (The Virgin Mandy etc), Kenneth Colley (Jesus the Christ), Gwen Taylor (Mrs. Big Nose etc.), Carol Cleveland (Mrs Gregory)

419
Monty Python's Life of Brian

A contemporary of Jesus is mistaken for him and crucified.

Monty Python's middle-eastern romp caused immense controversy on its first release. It has many funny moments, but much of the humour is laboured. Having set up the initial joke, which is a good one, the group seems hesitant about how to develop it; they draw back from causing real offence and keep most of their satire for such soft targets as revolutionaries who form committees and make reports rather than doing anything. The hilarious *Spartacus*-like finale, with a crucified choir singing 'Look on the Bright Side of Life' hints at what might have been: a brilliant comedy rather than just a good one.

Dumbo

♟ US 1941 64m Technicolor
Walt Disney
⬛ ≣ @ ⊚ ⊚ ∩

w Joe Grant, Dick Huemer *story* Helen Aberson, Harold
Pearl *d* Ben Sharpsteen *m* Frank Churchill, Oliver Wallace
☆ Featuring the voices of Sterling Holloway, Edward
Brophy, Verna Felton, Herman Bing, Cliff Edwards

'See the most genial, the most endearing, the most
completely precious cartoon feature film ever to
emerge from the magical brushes of Walt Disney's
wonder-working artists!' – *Bosley Crowther, New
York Times*

♟ music
♟ song, 'Baby Mine' (*m* Frank Churchill, *ly* Ned
Washington)

418
Dumbo

A baby circus-elephant finds that his big ears have a use after all.

Disney's animated movie is a childish delight. It is a simple, straightforward story with some excellent set pieces, notably Dumbo's nightmare after accidentally drinking champagne, with its superb sequence of pink elephants on parade, and Dumbo's slip that brings a tower of elephants crashing down to wreck the circus. There is little dialogue so that the visuals carry the story with its charming message of mother love and the value of self-confidence.

'You don't assign him to murder cases –
you just turn him loose!'

Dirty Harry
US 1971 103m Technicolor Panavision
Warner/Malpaso (Don Siegel)
⬛ ≣ @ ⊚ ⊚ ∩

w Harry Julian Fink, Rita M. Fink, Dean Riesner *d* Don
Siegel *ph* Bruce Surtees *m* Lalo Schifrin *ad* Dale
Hennesy *ed* Carl Pingitore
☆ *Clint Eastwood* (Harry Callahan), Harry Guardino (Lt
Bressler), Reni Santoni (Chico), John Vernon (The Mayor),
Andy Robinson (Killer), John Larch (Chief), John Mitchum
(De Georgio), Mae Mercer (Mrs Russell)
● Paul Newman was originally cast in the lead; after he
withdrew, the script was rewritten for Clint Eastwood.

417
Dirty Harry

A violently inclined San Francisco police inspector is the only cop who can bring to book a mad sniper. When the man is released through lack of evidence, the cop takes private revenge.

Paul Newman turned down the lead in this savage cop show that became a cult because of his political views. For Clint Eastwood, it was merely a more talkative extension of the laconic loner he had played in the Sergio Leone Westerns that had made him a star. Dirty Harry is an urban variation on Eastwood's established character. Siegel directed with great flair, emphasizing the fact that cop and killer are virtually indistinguishable from one another. The movie's success led to a spate of dirty cop movies, with Eastwood starring in four lesser sequels.

'Where were you in '62?'

American Graffiti
US   1973   110m   Techniscope
Universal/Lucasfilm/Coppola Company (Francis Ford Coppola, Gary Kurtz)
▭▭ ▬ ◔ ◠ ◠
wd George Lucas *ph* Ron Eveslage, Jan D'Alquen
m popular songs *ad* Dennis Clark *ed* Verna Fields, Marcia Lucas
☆ *Richard Dreyfuss* (Curt), Ronny Howard (Steve), Paul le Mat (John), Charlie Martin Smith (Terry), Cindy Williams (Laurie), Candy Clark (Debbie), Mackenzie Phillips (Carol)

'A very good movie, funny, tough, unsentimental ... full of marvellous performances.' – *Roger Greenspun, New York Times*

● The film cost $750,000, and grossed $55 million.
♟ picture; George Lucas (as writer); George Lucas (as director); Candy Clark

416
American Graffiti

In 1962 California, four young men about to leave for college gather for a night's girl-chasing and police-baiting.

This is a nostalgic comedy recalling many sights and sounds of the previous generation and carefully crystallizing a particular time and place. Made quickly on a low budget, shot at night for authenticity, with its soundtrack of rock songs and a cast of unknowns (most of whom soon became very much better known) and lots of vintage cars, it had both a nostalgia and a freshness that captivated audiences at the time, and since. Successful in itself, it led to many imitations.

A Taste of Honey
GB   1961   100m   bw
British Lion/Bryanston/Woodfall (Tony Richardson)
▭▭ ▬ ◎
w Shelagh Delaney, Tony Richardson *play* Shelagh Delaney *d* Tony Richardson *ph* Walter Lassally *m* John Addison *pd* Ralph Brinton *ad* Ralph Brinton *ed* Antony Gibbs
☆ *Rita Tushingham* (Jo), *Dora Bryan* (Helen), *Murray Melvin* (Geoffrey), Robert Stephens (Peter), Paul Danquah (Jimmy)

'Tart and lively around the edges and bitter at the core.' – *Peter John Dyer*

'Rich, full work, directed with an unerring sense of rightness.' – *New Yorker*

● A Region 2 DVD includes commentary by Dora Bryan, Rita Tushingham and Murray Melvin.
👑 best British picture; Dora Bryan; Rita Tushingham; screenplay

415
A Taste of Honey

Adventures of a pregnant Salford teenager, her sluttish mother, black lover and homosexual friend.

Part of the British new wave that enlivened the local industry in the 1960s, this was a film that brought to the screen the sort of working-class characters that had never been seen before. It is a fascinating off-beat comedy drama with memorable characters, sharply etched backgrounds, and succeeds in its determination to wring poetry out of squalor.

Shanghai Express
US   1932   84m   bw
Paramount
◫ ▤ ◎~

w *Jules Furthman* d *Josef von Sternberg* ph *Lee Garmes*
m W. Franke Harling ad Hans Dreier

☆ *Marlene Dietrich* (Shanghai Lily), Clive Brook (Capt.
Donald 'Doc' Harvey), Warner Oland (Henry Chang), Anna
May Wong (Hui Fei), Eugene Pallette (Sam Salt), Lawrence
Grant (Rev. Carmichael), Louise Closser Hale (Mrs.
Haggerty), Gustav von Seyffertitz (Eric Baum)

'Good programme picture bolstered by the Dietrich
name … Excellent camerawork overcomes really
hoke melodramatic story.' – *Variety*

'A limited number of characters, all meticulously
etched, highly atmospheric sets and innumerable
striking photographic compositions.' – *Curtis
Harrington, 1964*

● Remade in 1951 as *Peking Express*.
♟ Lee Garmes
♟ best picture; Josef von Sternberg

414
Shanghai Express

Old lovers meet on a dangerous train ride in China

Josef von Sternberg's superbly pictorial melodrama swoons over
Marlene Dietrich as a woman who meets her old lover, a British officer,
on a train which is waylaid by Chinese bandits. Dietrich is a figure of
mystery, photographed through veils and looking most alluring for a
woman who lives by her wits along the Chinese coast. The film set the
pattern for innumerable train movies to come, though none matched
its deft visual quality and few sketched in their characters so neatly.
Plot and dialogue were silent style, but refreshingly so.

L'Atalante
France 1934 89m bw
J. L. Nounez-Gaumont
📽 ▦ ⊚ ⊛
w Jean Guinée, Jean Vigo, Albert Riera *d* Jean Vigo
ph Boris Kaufman, Louis Berger *m* Maurice Jaubert
ed Louis Chavance
☆ Jean Dasté (Jean), Dita Parlo (Juliette), *Michel Simon*
(Pere Jules), Giles Margarites (Peddler)

'The singular talent – for once I think I may say genius – of the film lies in its translation into visual images of the mysterious and terrible and piteous undertones of even the simplest human life.'
– *Dilys Powell*

413

L'Atalante

A barge captain takes his new wife down river.

Jean Vigo's final masterpiece is a simple, slow-moving tale. The barge captain's wife becomes tired of her routine life and longs to enjoy the pleasures of Paris. He grows jealous when other men flirt with her; the couple quarrel, part and reconcile. Gaumont's executives thought it a piece of trash; they cut it and added new music before releasing it to an apathetic audience. It was re-released six years after Vigo's death in 1934 with the original music and some scenes restored. The film works on a poetic level, with Kaufman's camera capturing mysterious dreamlike images of river life, while Michel Simon's deckhand is one of the great screen performances.

Que la Bête Meure
France/Italy 1969 110m colour
La Boétie/Rizzoli (André Génovés)
📽 ▦ ⊚
US title: *This Man Must Die*
aka: *The Beast Must Die; Killer!*
w Paul Gégauff *novel The Beast Must Die* by Nicholas
Blake *d* Claude Chabrol *ph* Jean Rabier *m* Pierre Jansen,
Brahms *ad* Guy Littaye *ed* Jacques Gaillard
☆ Michel Duchaussoy (Charles Thenier), Caroline Cellier
(Helene Lanson), Jean Yanne (Paul Decourt), Anouk Ferjac
(Jeanne), Marc di Napoli (Philippe Decourt), Maurice Pialat
(Police Inspector), Jean-Louis Maury (Peasant/Charles'
Friend), Louise Chevalier (Mme. Levenes), Guy Marly
(Jacques Ferrand)

'The movie is so attenuated and unhurried that it dies on the screen.' – *Pauline Kael*

412

Que la Bête Meure

A father decides to find and murder the hit-and-run driver who killed his young son.

Claude Chabrol's psychological study is a revenge drama, but the director ignores the thriller aspects of the story to concentrate on relationships of love and hatred. It is a complex and absorbing drama: Charles (Michel Duchaussoy) infiltrates the family of the driver (Jean Yanne, in a memorable performance as an uncouth villain) and discovers that the man's son shares his hatred. The youth becomes a substitute for his dead child and an instrument of murder.

Hobson's Choice

GB 1953 107m bw
British Lion/London (Norman Spencer)

⬛ ▤ ◌ ⊘

w Norman Spencer, Wynard Browne *play* Harold
Brighouse *d* David Lean *ph* Jack Hildyard *m* Malcolm
Arnold *ad* Wilfrid Shingleton *ed* Peter Taylor

☆ *Charles Laughton* (Henry Horatio Hobson), *Brenda de
Banzie* (Maggie Hobson), *John Mills* (Willie Mossop),
Richard Wattis (Albert Prosser), Helen Haye (Mrs.
Hepworth), Daphne Anderson (Alice Hobson), Prunella
Scales (Vicky Hobson)

● Previously filmed in 1931 by Thomas Bentley for BIP
from a screenplay by Frank Launder, with James Harcourt,
Viola Lyel and Frank Pettingell.

🎦 British film

411
Hobson's Choice

*In the 1890s, a tyrannical Lancashire bootmaker is brought to heel by
his plain-speaking daughter and her simple-minded husband.*

David Lean was a surprising choice to direct this classic northern
English working-class comedy, since he was not noted for his sense of
humour. Charles Laughton, however, was ideally cast as the bullying
Victorian boot-shop proprietor whose eldest daughter Maggie, facing
spinsterhood, is anxious to marry and escape from home. The only
candidate is her father's timorous assistant, who becomes a success
with her help, while her father goes downhill without her. It is brilliantly
played, memorably set and photographed; one regrets only the slight
decline of the predictable third act.

'Makes *Ben-Hur* look like an epic!'

Monty Python and the Holy Grail

GB 1975 90m Technicolor
EMI/Python (Monty) Pictures/Michael White (Mark
Forstater)

⬛ ▤ ◌ ⊘ ◎ ◠

w Graham Chapman, John Cleese, Terry Gilliam, Eric Idle,
Michael Palin *d* Terry Gilliam, Terry Jones *ph* Terry
Bedford *m* Neil Innes *pd* Roy Smith *ed* John Hackney

☆ Graham Chapman (King Arthur etc), John Cleese
(Lancelot etc.), Terry Gilliam (Patsy etc.), Eric Idle (Sir Robin
etc.), Michael Palin (Galahad etc.)

'The team's visual buffooneries and verbal
rigmaroles are piled on top of each other with no
attention to judicious timing or structure, and a
form which began as a jaunty assault on the well-
made revue sketch and an ingenious misuse of
television's fragmented style of presentation,
threatens to become as unyielding and unfruitful as
the conventions it originally attacked.' – *Geoff
Brown*

410
Monty Python and the Holy Grail

King Arthur and his knights seek the Holy Grail.

This is the funniest of the features made by the Monty Python team. It
is a *Hellzapoppin*-like series of linked sketches on a medieval theme.
There is a siege with a vituperative French soldier ('Your mother was a
hamster and your father smelt of elderberries') who catapults a cow at
the knights, a minstrel singing the praise of his master ('Brave Sir
Robin bravely ran away …') and a great deal of general silliness and
private jokes. It is often uproariously funny and has a remarkable visual
sense of the Middle Ages.

409

Tootsie

Tootsie
US   1982   116m   colour
Columbia/Mirage/Punch (Sydney Pollack, Dick Richards)

⌗ ▤ ℚ～ ⓒ ⓒ ⌒

w Larry Gelbart, Murray Shisgal story Don McGuire
d Sydney Pollack ph Owen Roizman *m* Dave Grusin
pd Peter Larkin *ed* Frederic and William Steinkamp
☆ *Dustin Hoffman* (Michael Dorsey/Dorothy Michaels),
Jessica Lange (Julie), Teri Garr (Sandy), Dabney Coleman
(Ron), Charles Durning (Les), Sydney Pollack (George
Fields), George Gaynes (John Van Horn)

'It's a toot, a lark, a month in the country.'
– *Vincent Canby*

👤 Jessica Lange
🏆 best picture; Dustin Hoffman; Teri Garr; Sydney Pollack
as director; original screenplay; cinematography; editing;
song, 'It Might Be You' (*m* Dave Grusin, *ly* Alan Bergman,
Marilyn Bergman); sound
🏆 Dustin Hoffman

An out-of-work actor pretends to be a woman in order to get a job in a soap opera.

Dustin Hoffman gives his best comedy performance and, in its attention to detail, it is one of his finest moments. As with *Genevieve* and *Whisky Galore*, an unlikely comedy subject made an instant classic. It is all in the handling, in the way that putting on a dress turns Hoffman's actor into a feminist, who notices for the first time the way men can condescend to women.

'The 1931 nut crop is ready!'

Monkey Business

US   1931   81m   bw

Paramount (Herman J. Mankiewicz)

w S. J. Perelman, Will B. Johnstone, Arthur Sheekman
d Norman Z. McLeod *ph* Arthur L. Todd
☆ *Groucho Marx* (Groucho), *Chico Marx* (Chico), *Harpo Marx* (Harpo), *Zeppo Marx* (Zeppo), Thelma Todd (Lucille), Rockcliffe Fellowes (Joe Helton), Ruth Hall (Mary Helton), Harry Woods ('Alky' Briggs)

'Surefire for laughs despite working along familiar lines … picture has started off by doing sweeping business all over, and no reason why it shouldn't continue to tickle wherever it plays.' – *Variety*

408
Monkey Business

Four ship's stowaways crash a society party and catch a few crooks.

This is one of their most hectic films and Groucho ('I've worked myself up from nothing to a state of extreme poverty') hardly ever draws breath as he rattles out his repartee at manic speed. The shipboard part of this extravaganza is one of the best stretches of Marxian lunacy, but after the Maurice Chevalier impersonations it runs out of steam. But who is grumbling?

Être et Avoir

France   2002   colour

Metro Tartan/Maia/Arte France/Films d'Ici/Centre National de Documentation Pedagogique (Gilles Sandoz)

aka: *To Be and To Have*
d Nicolas Philibert *ph* Nicolas Philibert, Katell Djian, Laurent Didier, Hugues Gemignani *m* Philippe Hersant
ed Nicolas Philibert
☆ Georges Lopez, Alize, Axel, Guillaume

'It is, simply and stirringly, a kind of beau ideal of education, a vision of how the process can work at its best.' – *Joe Morgenstern, Wall Street Journal*

'Its patient accumulation of detail is breathtaking.' – *Anthony Quinn, Independent*

407
Être et Avoir

A year in the life of a one-room school in rural France.

Nicolas Philibert's film is nothing more dramatic than the changing of the seasons, seen through the windows. Children learn, quarrel and throw tantrums. Their teacher, quietly and patiently attempts to school them in behaviour at the same time as he tries to stimulate their minds. He takes a couple of older children to the bigger school they will be attending in the next year and tries to explain what is expected of them. Out of this small change of everyday life, Philibert extracts a treasure of humanity. The film is full of a quiet charm and unobtrusive observation that make it a gentle delight.

O Lucky Man!

'Smile while you're makin' it/Laugh while you're takin' it/Even though you're fakin' it/Nobody's gonna know …'

O Lucky Man!
GB   1973   174m   Eastmancolor
Warner/Memorial/Sam (Michael Medwin, Lindsay Anderson)

w David Sherwin *d* Lindsay Anderson *ph* Miroslav Ondricek *m* Alan Price *pd* Jocelyn Herbert *ad* Alan Withy *ed* David Gladwell

☆ *Malcolm McDowell* (Mick Travis), *Arthur Lowe* (Mr. Duff/Charlie Johnson/Dr. Munda), *Ralph Richardson* (Monty/Sir James Burgess), Rachel Roberts (Gloria Rowe/Mme. Paillard/Mrs. Richards), Helen Mirren (Patricia Burgess), Mona Washbourne (Sister Hallett/Usher/Neighbor), Dandy Nichols (Tea Lady/Neighbor)

'A sort of mod Pilgrim's Progress.' – *New Yorker*

🎭 Alan Price; Arthur Lowe

The odyssey of a trainee salesman who, after a while as an international financier, settles down to be a do-gooder.

Lindsay Anderson's episodic satire takes aim at many establishment targets through the odyssey of Mick Travis, a trainee salesman who becomes a subject for medical research, personal assistant to a millionaire who lands him in prison, and a do-gooder, until he reaches his apotheosis as a film star. The role is played with beguiling naivety by Malcolm McDowell who, like Travis, began as a coffee salesman. It is a modern revue-style version of *Candide*: very hit or miss in style and effect, but with good things along the way. Alan Price's musical comments on the action add a jaunty cynicism to the proceedings.

They Shoot Horses, Don't They?
US 1969 129m DeLuxe Panavision
Palomar/Chartoff-Winkler-Pollack

w James Poe, Robert E. Thompson *novel* Horace McCoy
d Sydney Pollack *ph* Philip Lathrop *m* John Green
md John Green, Albert Woodbury *pd* Harry Horner
ed Fredric Steinkamp
☆ *Gig Young* (Rocky), Jane Fonda (Gloria Beatty),
Susannah York (Alice), Michael Sarrazin (Robert Syverton),
Red Buttons (Sailor), Bonnie Bedelia (Ruby), Bruce Dern
(James)

'Although *They Shoot Horses, Don't They?* does
not, as a whole, reach the domain of art, many of
its aspects and an aura that lingers on establish it
as a true and eminent cinematic achievement.'
– *John Simon*

♟ Gig Young
♟ script; John Green, Albert Woodbury; Sydney Pollack;
Jane Fonda; Susannah York
Ⓣ Susannah York

405

They Shoot Horses, Don't They?

Tragedy during a six-day marathon dance contest in the early Thirties.

Sydney Pollack's unrelievedly harrowing melodrama is set in the early
Thirties at a marathon dance contest in which the last couple standing
will win a prize. As the contest continues, couples quarrel and collapse
while the master of ceremonies stages events to keep the audience
amused. At the end, the winning couple, finding they face further
humiliations, leave and one helps the other to kill herself. There is a
brilliant performance from Gig Young as the exploitative master of
ceremonies, and it is full of skilled technique and entertaining detail.

Henry V

GB 1989 137m Technicolor
Curzon/Renaissance Films (Bruce Sharman)

📽 📽 ▨ ☚ ◎ 🎧

w Kenneth Branagh *play* William Shakespeare *d* Kenneth Branagh *ph* Kenneth MacMillan *m* Patrick Doyle *pd* Tim Harvey *ed* Mike Bradsell

☆ Kenneth Branagh (Henry V), Derek Jacobi (Chorus), Simon Shepherd (Gloucester), James Larkin (Bedford), Brian Blessed (Exeter), James Simmons (York), Paul Gregory (Westmoreland), Charles Kay (Archbishop of Canterbury), Alec McCowen (Bishop of Ely), Edward Jewesbury, Ian Holm, Michael Williams, Geoffrey Hutchings, Robert Stephens, Judi Dench and also Paul Scofield, Harold Innocent, Emma Thompson, Geraldine McEwan

'The film's visual tedium, vulgarity and musical mediocrity would be more bearable if Branagh himself were a more persuasive lead actor.' – *MFB*

'The more I thought about it, the more convinced I became that here was a play to be reclaimed from jingoism and its World War Two associations.' – *Kenneth Branagh*

♟ best costume design (Phyllis Dalton)
♟ Kenneth Branagh (as best actor and best director)
♟ Kenneth Branagh (as director)

Hiroshima Mon Amour

France/Japan 1959 91m bw
Argos/Comei/Pathé/Daiei

📽 ▨ ◎

w Marguerite Duras *d* Alain Resnais *ph* Sacha Vierny, Takahashi Michio *m* Giovanni Fusco, Georges Delerue *ed* Jasmine Chasney, Henri Colpi, Anne Sarraute
☆ Emmanuele Riva (She), Eiji Okada (He)

'Suddenly a new film. Really new, first-hand: a work which tells a story of its own in a style of its own. One is almost afraid to touch it.' – *Dilys Powell*

♟ Marguerite Duras

404
Henry V

After his claim to the throne of France is refused, King Henry invades the country and wins a famous victory.

Kenneth Branagh's version of Shakespeare's *Henry V* was much darker than Laurence Olivier's celebrated patriotic film that was made during World War II. While Olivier celebrated righteous war with a stirring call to arms, as a king who, after his claim to the throne of France is refused, invades the country and wins a famous victory, Branagh shows the muddy and bloody brutality of war. He plays the king as a serious-minded politician, who needs a war to unite a kingdom and distract attention from other problems; he is determined to fight and to win. In his way, Branagh's Henry is a hero for modern times, as Olivier's was for the 1940s.

403
Hiroshima Mon Amour

A French actress working in Hiroshima falls for a Japanese architect and remembers her tragic love for a German soldier during the occupation.

On its first appearance, Alain Resnais' poetic remembrance of the destruction of Hiroshima was hailed as a work of art in an innovative new style. Its jumbled mixture of flashbacks and flashforwards can now be recognized as typical of this director. Marguerite Duras's script approaches the subject obliquely. 'All one can do is talk about the impossibility of talking about Hiroshima,' she said at the time. Resnais used two different cinematographers for the Japanese and French sequences; their integration into a complex and compelling whole, one that gives equal emphasis to the past and present, was made during a difficult editing process.

Le Souffle au Coeur

France/Italy/West Germany   1971   118m
colour
NEF/Marianne Films/Video Films/Seitz (Maurice Urbain)
🎞 📼 🔊
US title: *Murmur of the Heart*
aka: *Dearest Love*
wd Louis Malle *ph* Ricardo Aronovich *m* Gaston Frèche, Sidney Bechet, Henri Renaud, Charlie Parker *pd* Jean-Jacques Caziot, Philippe Turlure *ad* Jean-Jacques Caziot, Philippe Turlure *ed* Suzanne Baron
☆ Léa Massari (Clara Chevalier), Benoit Ferreux (Laurent Chevalier), Daniel Gelin (the Father), Michel Lonsdale (Father Henri), Ave Ninchi (Augusta), Gila von Weitershausen (Freda)
♟ Louis Malle (writer)

402
Le Souffle au Coeur

Recovering from an illness at a spa, a 15-year-old boy overcomes his sexual problems after sleeping, almost inadvertently, with his mother.

Louis Malle based the film on his own remembrances of his childhood. The accidental incest never happened in real life, but Malle did have a heart murmur and also what he called a 'strange and very passionate relationship with my mother'. It is a witty and observant study of middle class attitudes to love, sex and adolescent traumas, with the incest only forming a minor theme.

'James Bond 007 Back In Action!'
Goldfinger
🚹🚹   GB   1964   112m   Technicolor
UA/Eon (Harry Saltzman, Albert R. Broccoli)
🎞 📼 📼 🔊 ◉ ◉ 🎧
w Richard Maibaum, Paul Dehn *novel* Ian Fleming *d* Guy Hamilton *ph* Ted Moore *m* John Barry *pd* Ken Adam *ad* Peter Murton *ed* Peter Hunt *titles* Robert Brownjohn
☆ *Sean Connery* (James Bond), *Honor Blackman* (Pussy Galore), Gert Frobe (Goldfinger), Harold Sakata (Oddjob), Shirley Eaton (Jill Masterson), Bernard Lee ("M"), Lois Maxwell (Moneypenny), Desmond Llewellyn ("Q")

'A dazzling object lesson in the principle that nothing succeeds like excess.' – *Penelope Gilliatt*

'A diverting comic strip for grown-ups.' – *Judith Crist*

401
Goldfinger

James Bond prevents an international gold smuggler from robbing Fort Knox.

This was the third in the James Bond series and it is still the most accomplished, being lively and amusing. Sean Connery was the best of the many Bonds. The movie was made when 007 was still an unreconstructed male chauvinist, and before the series became formulaic, though all the ingredients that brought predictability to many of the later films had their origins here: beautiful, disposable women, hi-tech gadgets, and smart quips. Ken Adam's production design was a delight, as was Honor Blackman as Pussy Galore. Shirley Eaton had her five minutes of fame as the girl smothered to death in gold paint, Gert Frobe made a convincing villain, and Harold Sakata's Oddjob, with his lethal bowler hat, was a relishable assassin.

Red River

US 1948 133m bw
UA/Monterey (Howard Hawks)

▭ ▤ ⌕ ◉ ◉

w Borden Chase, Charles Schnee d Howard Hawks
ph Russell Harlan m Dimitri Tiomkin ad John Datu
Arensma ed Christian Nyby

☆ John Wayne (Tom Dunson), Montgomery Clift
(Matthew Garth), Joanne Dru (Tess Millay), Walter Brennan
(Groot Nadine), Coleen Gray (Fen), John Ireland (Cherry
Valance), Noah Beery Jnr (Buster McGee), Harry Carey Jnr
(Dan Latimer)

● It was remade as a TV film in 1988, directed by Richard
Michaels and starring James Arness, Bruce Boxleitner and
Gregory Harrison.

⚑ original story (Borden Chase); editing

400
Red River

How the Chisholm Trail was developed as a cattle drive.

Howard Hawks's large scale, brawling Western deals with an Oedipal conflict between a father, Thomas Dunson (John Wayne), and his adopted son, Matt (Montgomery Clift), on the first cattle drive from Texas to Kansas. Hawks thought it was the best Western he made, and certainly none of the others had such scope and ambition. There are some splendid action scenes, including a cattle stampede. Wayne's physicality and Clift's sensitivity provide an interesting contrast on the trail, while there is visual beauty in the images of the cowboys at work. The German director Rainer Werner Fassbinder, claimed that Hawks's films were about repressed homosexuality and there is an homoerotic undertone in Dunson's efforts to make a man of Matt, as there is when Matt and Cherry (John Ireland) compare guns.

Ride the High Country

US 1962 94m Metrocolor Cinemascope
MGM (Richard E. Lyons)

▭ ▤ ⌕

GB title: Guns in the Afternoon

w N. B. Stone Jnr d Sam Peckinpah ph Lucien Ballard
m George Bassman ad George W. Davis, Leroy Coleman
ed Frank Santillo

☆ Joel McCrea (Steve Judd), Randolph Scott (Gil
Westrum), Edgar Buchanan (Judge Tolliver), Mariette
Hartley (Elsa Knudsen), James Drury (Billy Hammond)

'A nice little conventional unconventional Western.'
– Stanley Kauffmann

399
Ride the High Country

Two retired lawmen help transport gold from a mining camp to the bank, but one has ideas of his own.

Elegiac Western in which two old-timers, both former lawmen, are paid to guard a gold shipment from a mining settlement in the Sierra Nevada, and then fall out over whether to deliver the gold or keep it for themselves. The arguments between the two encapsulate the history of the West and the problems of administering law with a gun. MGM executives hated the film and relegated it to second-place on a double-bill; it has outlasted all of them. Set in the early 1900s, as horses gave way to automobiles, it is a valediction not only to the frontier spirit (and, to a great extent, to Westerns as well), but also to the long career of Scott, whose last film it was. What a way to bow out.

The Killers
US 1964 95m Pathécolor
U-I (Don Siegel)
▇ ◉

w Gene L. Coon *story* Ernest Hemingway
d Don Siegel
ph Richard L. Rawlings *m* Johnny Williams *ad* Frank
Arrigo, George Chan *ed* Richard Belding
☆ John Cassavetes (Johnny North), *Lee Marvin* (Charlie),
Clu Gulager (Lee), Angie Dickinson (Sheila Farr), Ronald
Reagan (Browning), Claude Akins (Earl Sylvester)
● This was Ronald Reagan's last feature film and the first in
which he played a bad guy.
Ⓣ Lee Marvin

398
The Killers

A man waits to be killed.

Don Siegel's zesty, brutal remake of a 1946 movie, adapted from Ernest Hemingway's short story, was intended for television, but was released theatrically because of its violence. Siegel was determined not to copy the earlier film, nor did he use any of Hemingway's dialogue. His approach was to tell the story of a man waiting to be killed from the killers' point of view. It worked well, especially in the black comedy of the final moments when Sheila (Angie Dickinson) tries to explain to the dying Charlie (Lee Marvin), who holds a gun on her, why she double-crossed him. 'Lady, I just haven't got the time,' he says as he shoots her.

The Gospel According to St Matthew
Italy/France 1964 142m bw
Arco/Lux (Alfredo Bini)
▭ ▇ ◔ ◉ ◉

original title: *Il Vangelo Secondo Matteo*
wd Pier Paolo Pasolini *book* Gospel according to St
Matthew *ph* Tonino delli Colli *m* Bach, Mozart, Prokofiev,
Webern *md* Luis Enrique Bacalov *ad* Luigi Scaccianoce
ed Nino Baragli *cos* Danilo Donati
☆ Enrique Irazoqui (Jesus Christ), Susanna Pasolini
(Mary, as a woman), Mario Socrate (John the Baptist),
Margherita Caruso (Mary, as a girl), Marcello Morante
(Joseph), Settimo Di Porto (Peter), Otello Sestili (Judas)

'One of the most effective films on a religious
theme I have ever seen, perhaps because it was
made by a nonbeliever who did not preach, glorify,
underline, sentimentalize or romanticize his famous
story.' – *Roger Ebert, Chicago Sun-Times*

'Some find the slow rhythm fascinating, others
think it punishing.' – *Pauline Kael*

♟ Luis Enrique Bacalov; Luigi Scaccianoce; Danilo Donati

397
The Gospel According to St Matthew

The life of Christ seen almost as a ciné-vérité documentary.

Pasolini's film must be the only one to have been written by a saint, since all the dialogue comes from Matthew's gospel, which he follows with great literalness without compromising his own Marxist outlook. Filmed in the rocky landscape of southern Italy, with a cast drawn from friends and locals, and with Christ played by a Spanish student who looks as though he might have stepped out of an El Greco painting, the result is a calm, slow-paced film, a succession of carefully composed images that concentrate on the individuality of faces as much as Fellini might have done. Pasolini attempted to create 'a pure work of poetry, risking even the perils of aestheticism', and, to a large extent, succeeded.

The Big Parade

US   1925   115m approx (24 fps)   bw   silent
MGM

🎞 ▦ 🔍

w Laurence Stallings, Harry Behn *d* King Vidor *ph* John Arnold *m* William Axt, David Mendoza *ad* Cedric Gibbons, James Basevi *ed* Hugh Wynn
☆ John Gilbert (James Apperson), Renée Adorée (Melisande), Hobart Bosworth (Mr. Apperson), Karl Dane (Slim), George K. Arthur

'The human comedy emerges from a terrifying tragedy.' – *King Vidor*

'A cinegraphically visualized result of a cinegraphically imagined thing … something conceived in terms of a medium and expressed by that medium as only that medium could properly express it.' – *National Board of Review*

'The extraordinary impression of the rush of lorries, the queer terror of the woods … it was amazing how much fear could be felt in the mere continuous pace of movement.' – *Bryher, Close Up*

● The biggest grossing silent film of all.

396
The Big Parade

Encouraged by his fiancée, a young American joins up in 1917; he experiences the real nature of war and is wounded but recovers to find his true love.

King Vidor's desire to make a film that had lasting appeal resulted in this story of a young American who enlists in 1917, learns the realities of war, and is wounded but survives. He wanted a film about an average person who cannot control the situation in which he finds himself, someone who, in Vidor's words, 'goes along for the ride and tries to make the most of each situation as it happens.' The story was written by Laurence Stallings, a young playwright who had lost a leg in the war. One of the most effective scenes, the march of soldiers nearing the front-line, was filmed to the beat of a metronome to give it the measured step of a funeral procession. Enormously successful commercially, this 'anti-war' film survives best as a thrilling spectacle and a well-considered piece of film-making.

Last Orders

GB/Germany   2001   110m   DeLuxe
Metrodome/Winchester/MBP/Scala (Fred Schepisi, Elisabeth Robinson)

🎞 ▦ 🔍 ◉

wd Fred Schepisi *ph* Brian Tufano *m* Paul Grabowsky
pd Tim Harvey *ed* Kate Williams *cos* Jill Taylor
☆ Michael Caine (Jack), Bob Hoskins (Ray), Tom Courtenay (Vic), David Hemmings (Lenny), Ray Winstone (Vince), Helen Mirren (Amy), JJ Field (Young Jack), Anatol Yusef (Young Ray), Cameron Fitch (Young Vic), Nolan Hemmings (Young Lenny), Kelly Reilly (Young Amy), Laura Morelli (June)

'A moving study of the pleasures and obligations of friendship.' – *Philip French, Observer*

'A subtly powerful drama that finally tells us that not only is death not the end, sometimes it makes for new beginnings.' – *Kevin Courrier, Boxoffice*

'*Last Orders* is low-grade plot engineering but is endurable because we wait for some revelation that will justify the mechanics. But nothing of the kind comes our way.' – *Stanley Kauffmann*

395
Last Orders

Lifelong pals reflect on love and betrayal as they travel to the seaside to fulfil the last wish of an old friend.

A moving, working-class remembrance of things past, as three elderly Londoners look back on their lives and loves while preparing for a trip to the seaside to scatter the ashes of a mutual friend. A gently humorous, unsentimental account, tinged with melancholy, of the pleasures and pains of ordinary life; it gets excellent ensemble acting from its fine cast.

Howards End

GB 1992 140m Technicolor Super35
Widescreen
Merchant Ivory/Film Four (Ismail Merchant)
⊙⊙ 🎬 🔍 ⊙ ⊙ 🎧

w *Ruth Prawer Jhabvala* novel E. M. Forster d *James Ivory* ph Tony Pierce-Roberts m Richard Robbins pd Luciana Arrighi ad John Ralph ed Andrew Marcus
☆ Anthony Hopkins (Henry Wilcox), Vanessa Redgrave (Ruth Wilcox), Helena Bonham Carter (Helen Schlegel), *Emma Thompson* (Margaret Schlegel), James Wilby (Charles Wilcox), Sam West (Leonard Bast), Jemma Redgrave (Evie Wilcox), Nicola Duffett (Jacky Bast), Prunella Scales (Aunt Juley), Simon Callow (Music Lecturer)

'A most compelling drama, perhaps the best film made during the 30-year partnership of Ismail Merchant and James Ivory.' – *Variety*

'A handsome and intelligent piece of work: a faithful, well-paced, and carefully crafted dramatization of a very good story.' – *Terrence Rafferty, New Yorker*

👤 Emma Thompson; Ruth Prawer Jhabvala; Luciana Arrighi
👥 Best picture; James Ivory; Vanessa Redgrave; Tony Pierce-Roberts; Richard Robbins; Jenny Beavan, John Bright (costume design)
🏆 best picture; Emma Thompson

394
Howards End

The fortunes of two middle-class families overlap and interlock.

Of all Merchant-Ivory's adaptations of the novels of E. M. Forster, this is the best. In its story of the fortunes of two middle-class families overlapping and interlocking, the period nostalgia is undercut by an examination of the moral bankruptcy of the ruling class. The country landowner Henry Wilcox (Anthony Hopkins) is prepared to lie and cheat to keep his grip of the family inheritance, though he comes to regret it; his family's entrenched attitudes lead to the death of the poor young clerk Leonard Bast (Samuel West), who cannot afford the luxury of indolence he sees when he becomes involved with the impulsive, middle-class Helen (Helena Bonham Carter). It is a telling portrait of an age in transition to modern times.

The Eclipse

Italy/France 1962 125m bw
Interopa-Cineriz/Paris Film (Robert and Raymond Hakim)
⊙⊙ 🎬

original title: *L'Eclisse*
wd *Michelangelo Antonioni, Tonino Guerra, Elio Bartolini, Ottiero Ottieri* ph Gianni di Venanzo m Giovanni Fusco ad Piero Poletto ed Eraldo Da Roma
☆ *Monica Vitti* (Vittoria), Alain Delon (Piero), Francisco Rabal (Riccardo)

'The first time I saw the film I thought it magnificent but chill, played glitteringly … At a second visit the passion breaks through.' – *Dilys Powell*

393
The Eclipse

A young Roman woman breaks off one affair and begins another.

Antonioni's third film with Monica Vitti explores the same themes of ennui and anguish as his earlier two *L'Avventura* and *La Notte*. The narrative is a slight one of a young Roman woman breaking off one affair with an older man and beginning another with a young stockbroker. It is a portrait in depth, superbly done, apart from one largely irrelevant stock-market sequence that presumably makes a point about the deadening power of money. Vitti brings a vibrant quality to her playing of the woman, adding a luminous quality to the sterile, geometric settings she occupies.

The Life and Death of Colonel Blimp

GB   1943   163m   Technicolor
GFD/Archers (Michael Powell, Emeric Pressburger)

●● ▬ ◎~ ◎ ◎

US title: *Colonel Blimp*

wd Michael Powell, Emeric Pressburger *ph* Georges Perinal *m* Allan Gray *ad* Alfred Junge *ed* John Seabourne

☆ Roger Livesey (Clive Candy), Anton Walbrook (Theo Kretschmar-Schuldorff), Deborah Kerr (Edith Hunter/Barbara Wynne/Johnny Cannon), Roland Culver (Col. Betteridge), James McKechnie (Spud Wilson), Albert Lieven (Von Ritter), Arthur Wontner (Embassy Counsellor), A. E. Matthews (President of Tribunal), David Hutcheson (Hoppy), Ursula Jeans (Frau von Kalteneck), John Laurie (Murdoch), Harry Welchman (Maj. Davis)

'There is nothing brilliant about the picture, but it is perceptive, witty and sweet-tempered.' – *James Agee*

'No one else has so well captured English romanticism banked down beneath emotional reticence.' – *Time Out, 1985*

'It stands as very possibly the finest film ever made in Britain.' – *David Kehr, Chicago Reader*

392
The Life and Death of Colonel Blimp

A British soldier survives three wars and falls in love with three women.

Although based on David Low's cartoons that mocked a reactionary old soldier, Powell and Pressburger's Colonel Blimp was quite different in character: a sympathetic man involved in warm, consistently interesting if idiosyncratic love stories covering forty years against a background of three wars. His closest friend is a German officer, who is equally sympathetic and arrives in Britain as a refugee from the Nazis. The film was intended as propaganda, but upset Winston Churchill, who tried to have production halted and, after that failed, did his best to prevent it being seen outside Britain; the version that reached America was heavily cut. It is a curiously endearing film about the eccentricity of the British. Its conclusion may have been what upset Churchill; that there is no longer such a thing as a gentleman's war, where principles are more important than winning.

Short Cuts

US   1993   188m   colour   Panavision
Artificial Eye/Spelling/Fine Line/Avenue (Cary Brokaw)

●● ●● ▬ ◎~ ◎ ◠

w Robert Altman, Frank Barhydt *story* Raymond Carver *d* Robert Altman *ph* Walt Lloyd *m* Mark Isham *pd* Stephen Altman *ad* Jerry Fleming *ed* Geraldine Peroni

☆ Andie MacDowell (Ann Finnigan), Bruce Davison (Howard Finnigan), Jack Lemmon (Paul Finnegan), Zane Cassidy (Casey Finnigan), Julianne Moore (Marian Wyman), Matthew Modine (Dr. Ralph Wyman), Anne Archer (Claire Kane), Fred Ward (Stuart Kane), Jennifer Jason Leigh (Lois Kaiser), Chris Penn (Jerry Kaiser), Joseph C. Hopkins (Joe Kaiser), Josette Macario (Josette Kaiser), Robert Downey Jnr (Bill Bush), Madeleine Stowe (Sherri Shepard), Tim Robbins (Gene Shepard) and also Lily Tomlin, Tom Waits, Frances McDormand, Peter Gallagher, Annie Ross, Lori Singer, Lyle Lovett, Buck Henry

'A film with no dud line, flawed performance or slick piece of editing in all its 188 minutes … Only at a second viewing can one fully appreciate the magnificence of the film's grand design, which is the presentation of life as a mutually shared tragicomedy.' – *Philip French, Observer*

♟ Robert Altman (as director)

391
Short Cuts

In Los Angeles, the lives of nine dysfunctional, suburban couples interwine.

Robert Altman's ensemble film follows the intertwining lives of nine dysfunctional, suburban couples. It is an excellent, continually fascinating examination of people living on the edge, cut off from the truth of their emotions. The complexity of the cross-cutting between one scene and another is brilliantly achieved; what mars the film is its tendency to melodrama, particularly in its treatment of an alcoholic jazz singer and her equally disturbed cello-playing daughter.

'There never was a woman like Gilda!'

Gilda
US 1946 110m bw
Columbia (Virginia Van Upp)

📷 ▦ ⌨ ⊚ ⊚ 🎧

w Marion Parsonnet *story* E. A. Ellington *d* Charles
Vidor *ph* Rudolph Maté *m* Hugo Friedhofer *md* Morris
Stoloff, Marlin Skiles *ad* Van Nest Polglase, Stephen
Goosson *ed* Charles Nelson
☆ *Rita Hayworth* (Gilda), *Glenn Ford* (Johnny Farrell),
George Macready (Ballin Mundson), *Steve Geray* (Uncle
Pio), *Joseph Calleia* (Obregon), Joe Sawyer (Casey), Gerald
Mohr (Capt. Delgado), Ludwig Donath (German)

'From a quietly promising opening, the film settles
into an intractable obscurity of narrative through
which, as in a fog, three characters bite off at each
other words of hate.' – *Richard Winnington*

● Rita Hayworth's singing was dubbed by Anita Ellis.

390
Gilda

A gambler in a South American city resumes a love-hate relationship with an old flame … but she is now married to his dangerous new boss.

Rita Hayworth was never able to get away from her role as a *femme fatale* in this archetypal Hollywood *film noir*. 'Every man I knew had fallen in love with Gilda and wakened with me,' she once complained. The story of a gambler and his former lover – 'isn't it nice. No one has to apologize since we're both stinkers,' Gilda says to him – is complicated by the fact that, when they meet again, Gilda is married to his dangerous new boss. The production is wholly studio-bound and the better for it, with dialogue that would seem risible if it did not happen to be dealt with in this style and with these actors, who keep the mood brilliantly balanced between suspense and absurdity.

'Just another day of lying, cheating and stealing.'

The Grifters
US 1990 110m CFI color
Palace/Cineplex Odeon (Martin Scorsese, Robert
Harris)

📷 ▦ ⌨ ⊚ ⊚ 🎧

w Donald Westlake *novel* Jim Thompson *d* Stephen
Frears *ph* Oliver Stapleton *m* Elmer Bernstein *pd* Dennis
Gassner *ad* Leslie McDonald *ed* Mick Audsley
☆ *Anjelica Huston* (Lilly Dillon), *John Cusack* (Roy
Dillon), *Annette Bening* (Myra Langtry), Pat Hingle (Bobo
Justus), Henry Jones (The Desk Clerk), Michael Laskin
(Irv), Eddie Jones (Mints), J. T. Walsh (Cole Langtry),
Charles Napier (Hebbing)

'A brilliant, immensely seductive mix of
Kammerspiel, *film noir* and naturalistic slice-of-
life.' – *Tom Milne, MFB*

⚖ Anjelica Huston; Stephen Frears; Annette Bening;
Donald Westlake

389
The Grifters

A mother, who is robbing her gangster boss, is reunited with her son and his girlfriend, both confidence tricksters.

The plot of this bleakly invigorating vision of the underside of the American dream was taken from a novel by pulp writer Jim Thompson, and was spelled out by him as, '*Grifters* it seemed, suffered an irresistible urge to beat their colleagues.' So it is with three confidence tricksters: Lilly (Angelica Huston), the successful, selfish mother, who is robbing her gangster boss Roy (John Cusack), the son she had had at the age of fourteen, who is strictly a small-time operator; and his aging girlfriend Myra (Annette Bening). Only one of the three survives in a tightly-plotted adaptation that is directed with stylish confidence and no tricks.

Strike
USSR   1924   70m approx (24 fps)   bw
silent
Goskino/Proletkult
📽 🎞 ⓒ ⓟ
wd *Sergei M. Eisenstein* ph Edouard Tissé, Vassili
Khvatov *ad* Vasili Rakhals
☆ Grigori Alexandrov (Factory Foreman), Maxim Strauch
(Police Spy), Mikhail Gomarov (Worker)

388
Strike

In 1912, metal workers organize a peaceful strike after bullying and humiliation by the plant owners, but the bosses use thugs and Cossack troops to crush the strikers.

Eisenstein's brilliant propaganda piece of a 1912 strike of factory workers that is brutally put down by the authorities had superbly cinematic sequences. It was the first, and only, film in what was going to be a series called 'Towards the Dictatorship of the Proletariat'. The film mixes actuality with over-the-top performances from the actors, but the images themselves form a coherent and surprising whole.

Juliet of the Spirits
Italy/France   1965   145m   Technicolor
Federiz/Francoriz (Clemente Fracassi)
📽 🎞 ⓒ～ ⓟ 🎧
original title: *Giulietta degli Spiriti*
w Federico Fellini, Tullio Pinnelli, Brunello Rondi, Ennio
Flaiano *d* Federico Fellini *ph* Gianni di Venanzo *m* Nino
Rota *ad* Piero Gherardi *ed* Ruggero Mastroianni
☆ *Giulietta Masina* (Juliet), Mario Pisu (Giorgio), Sandra
Milo (Susy/Iris/Fanny), Valentina Cortese (Valentina), Sylva
Koscina (Sylva)

'A kaleidoscope of fantasy, a series of cerebral inventions, of which only a few are artistically justified … an extravagant illusion, a huge confidence trick, with little new to say and an often pedantic way of saying it.' – *David Wilson, MFB*

387
Juliet of the Spirits

Caught in an unhappy marriage with an ambivalent husband, a middle-aged woman invokes spirits who show her the possibilities of sensual pleasure.

Federico Fellini's fascinating patchwork of autobiographical flashbacks offers the distaff side of his *Eight and a Half*: a bored middle-aged woman finds she can conjure up spirits who lead her into a life of sensual gratification. He created the film for Giulietta Masina, his wife, because she wanted to return to acting. Its success depends upon its dreamlike imagery, the set designs of Piero Gherardi and the photography of Gianni di Venanzo rather than any deep exploration of feelings.

The Hospital
US 1971 101m DeLuxe Panavision
UA/Simcha (Howard Gottfried)
▀ ⊚

w *Paddy Chayefsky* d Arthur Hiller *ph* Victor Kemper
m Morris Surdin *ad* Gene Rudolf *ed* Eric Albertson
☆ George C. Scott (Dr. Herbert Bock), Diana Rigg (Barbara Drummond), Barnard Hughes (Drummond), Nancy Marchand (Mrs. Christie), Richard Dysart (D.r Welbeck), Stephen Elliott (Sundstrom), Donald Harron (Milton Mead), Roberts Blossom (Guernsey), Frances Sternhagen (Mrs. Cushing)

'A civilian mis-MASH.' – *Variety*

♟ Paddy Chayefsky
♟ George C. Scott

386
The Hospital

A city hospital suffers a series of strange events, and it is discovered that there is a killer at large.

Paddy Chayefsky's black comedy deals with sex and medical ethics in a city hospital beset by weird mishaps, where there is a killer is on the loose. In the same genre as *M*A*S*H*, it is very funny due to sharp writing and George C. Scott's angry, panic-striken chief of medicine. As he is beset by dying patients, demonstrators picketing the hospital and drop-out children he despises, he cries at one point, 'How am I expected to maintain my feeling of meaningfulness in the face of all this?' Chayefsky's answer is that he can do so, and will, but it won't mean much.

My Darling Clementine
US 1946 98m bw
TCF (Samuel G. Engel)
▀▀ ▀ ⊚ ⊚

w Samuel G. Engel, Winston Miller *book Wyatt Earp, Frontier Marshal* by Stuart N. Lake *d John Ford ph* Joe MacDonald *m* Cyril Mockridge *ad* James Basevi, Lyle Wheeler *ed* Dorothy Spencer
☆ *Henry Fonda* (Wyatt Earp), *Victor Mature* (Doc Holliday), *Walter Brennan* (Old Man Clanton), Linda Darnell (Chihuahua), Cathy Downs (Clementine), Tim Holt (Virgil Earp), Ward Bond (Morgan Earp), *Alan Mowbray* (Granville Thorndyke), John Ireland (Billy Clanton), Jane Darwell (Kate)

'Every scene, every shot is the product of a keen and sensitive eye.' – *Bosley Crowther*

'Considerable care has gone to its period reconstruction, but the view is a poetic one.' – *Lindsay Anderson*

385
My Darling Clementine

After suffering a personal loss, Wyatt Earp makes Tombstone safe for decent folk and confronts the Clanton gang at the OK corral.

John Ford's archetypal Western mood piece is full of nostalgia for times gone by and crackling with memorable scenes and characterizations. The subject was one that Hollywood has often returned to, and this time around Ford was remaking Fox's 1939 movie *Frontier Marshall*: Wyatt Earp cleans up Tombstone and wipes out the Clanton gang at the OK corral. Darryl Zanuck had a hand in the finished film, removing half-an-hour's footage from Ford's leisurely first cut and clarifying the narrative. Ford claimed that the final gunfight was authentic, filmed in the way that Earp himself had explained on one of his visits to Hollywood early in Ford's career, when he was working as an assistant prop boy.

Rocco and His Brothers

Italy/France   1960   180m   bw
Titanus/Les Films Marceau (Goffredo Lombardo)
🎞 ▦ ⊗ ⊘ 🎧

w Luchino Visconti, Suso Cecchi d'Amico, Vasco Pratolini
d Luchino Visconti *ph* Giuseppe Rotunno *m* Nino Rota
ad Mario Garbuglia *ed* Mario Serandrei
☆ Alain Delon (Rocco Parondi), Renato Salvatori (Simone
Parondi), Annie Girardot (Nadia), Katina Paxinou (Rosaria
Parondi), Roger Hanin (Morini), Paolo Stoppa (Boxing
Impresario), Suzy Delair (Luisa), Claudia Cardinale (Ginetta)

'Joins the band of films which, these last months,
have given one new hope for the cinema.' – *Dilys
Powell*

384
Rocco and His Brothers

*A peasant family moves into Milan, and each of its five brothers has
his problems.*

Visconti's epic and episodic drama, of a peasant family's move from
the south of Italy to Milan, was his own favourite among his films. It is
a complex work, following the activities of five brothers and their rivalries. Rocco (Alain Delon) is the brother who attempts to take responsibility for the family, contrasting with Simone (Renato Salvatore),
whose jealousy and involvement with a prostitute lead him to murder.
It is another brother who betrays Simone to the police and so splinters
the family group. The film works as both a multi-layered character
study and an account of a particular problematic moment in Italy's
social history of a mass migration from rural areas to the cities.

The Truman Show

US   1998   102m   DeLuxe
Paramount (Scott Rudin, Andrew Niccol, Edward S.
Feldman, Adam Schroeder)
🎞 ▦ ⊗ ⊘ 🎧

w Andrew Niccol *d* Peter Weir *ph* Peter Biziou
m Burkhard Dallwitz *pd* Dennis Gassner *ad* Richard L.
Johnson *ed* William Anderson
☆ Jim Carrey (Truman Burbank), Laura Linney (Meryl),
Noah Emmerich (Marlon), Natascha McElhone
(Lauren/Sylvia), Holland Taylor (Truman's Mother), Ed
Harris (Christof)

'An emerging genre of cheerfully subversive
movies finds its first near-masterpiece.' – *David
Thomson, Esquire*

Peter Weir; Andrew Niccol; Ed Harris
Peter Weir; Andrew Niccol; Dennis Gassner

383
The Truman Show

*Truman Burbank leads an enviable existence on the island of Seahaven
– then he discovers that there are cameras in every part of his lfe and
that all the people around him are actors.*

Andrew Niccol's clever script took reality television a step further: a
man who lives happily in an island community discovers that he is the
star of an all-day TV soap opera, and that his wife, friends and neighbours are all acting their parts. It was a clever (if implausible) conceit
that can be taken several ways: as a satire on our all-controlling media,
as a comment on television's pervasiveness and the way everyone
wants to appear on it, or as an instance of the situationists' desire to
disrupt the spectacle, to tear away the false tinsel of everyday life, and
reveal the real tinsel beneath. Whichever way, deftly directed by Peter
Weir, it was a pleasure to watch.

Shane

US 1953 118m Technicolor
Paramount (George Stevens)

w A. B. Guthrie Jnr *novel* Jack Schaefer *d George Stevens* ph Loyal Griggs *m* Victor Young *ad* Walter Tyler, Hal Pereira *ed* Tom McAdoo, William Hornbeck

☆ *Alan Ladd* (Shane), Jean Arthur (Marion Starrett), Van Heflin (Joe Starrett), *Jack Palance* (Wilson), Brandon de Wilde (Joey), Ben Johnson (Chris), Edgar Buchanan (Lewis), Emile Meyer (Ryker), Elisha Cook Jnr (Torrey), John Dierkes (Morgan)

'A kind of dramatic documentary of the pioneer days of the West.' – *MFB*

'Westerns are better when they're not too self-importantly self-conscious.' – *New Yorker, 1975*

'Stevens managed to infuse a new vitality, a new sense of realism into the time-worn story through the strength and freshness of his visuals.' – *Arthur Knight*

• The Regions 1 and 2 DVD releases include commentary by George Stevens Jnr and Ivan Moffat.
🎬 Loyal Griggs
🏆 best picture; A. B. Guthrie Jnr; George Stevens; Jack Palance; Brandon de Wilde

382
Shane

A family of homesteaders is helped in their struggle against a land-grabbing rancher by an enigmatic stranger.

George Stevens' archetypal family Western was much slower and statelier than most, as though to emphasize its own quality, which is evident anyway. It provided two memorable roles; for Alan Ladd as a mysterious stranger who helps a family of homesteaders, and for Jack Palance as a sneering, sadistic gunfighter for hire. Despite the mythic nature of the story, Stevens strove for authenticity in his depiction of the West, creating a dusty, nondescript town and filming in all weathers.

Earth

USSR 1930 63m approx (24 fps) bw
silent
VUFKU

original title: *Zemlya*
wd *Alexander Dovzhenko* ph *Danylo Demutsky* ad Basil Krichevski *ed* Alexander Dovzhenko

☆ Semyon Svashenko (Basil), Stephan Shkurat (Opanas), Mikola Nademsky (Grandfather Simon), Yelena Maximova (Basil's Fiancee)

'Stories in themselves do not interest me. I choose them in order to get the greatest expression of essential social forms.' – *Dovzhenko*

'A picture for filmgoers who are prepared to take their cinema as seriously as Tolstoy took the novel.' – *James Agate*

381
Earth

Trouble results in a Ukrainian village when a landowner refuses to hand over his land for a collective farm.

Alexander Dovzhenko almost ignores the melodramatic little plot of this film about unrest in a Ukrainian village when a landowner refuses to hand over his land for a collective farm. Lyrical sequences of rustic beauty, illustrating life, love and death in the countryside carry the message. It is a pantheistic one, of the cycle of life and its renewal by sacrifice, which the film celebrates in a succession of memorable images, from a dying man's pleasure in eating an apple to a funeral procession passing by an orchard.

Dog Day Afternoon

US   1975   130m   Technicolor
Warner/AEC (Martin Bregman, Martin Elfand)

⏚ ▤ ◉~ ◎ ◎

w Frank Pierson *book* Patrick Mann *d* Sidney Lumet
ph Victor J. Kemper *m* none *ad* Douglas Higgins
ed Dede Allen
☆ *Al Pacino* (Sonny Wortzik), John Cazale (Sal), *Charles Durning* (Det. Sgt. Moretti), Sully Boyar (Mulvaney), James Broderick (Sheldon), *Chris Sarandon* (Leon)

> 'There is plenty of Lumet's vital best here in a film that at least glancingly captures the increasingly garish pathology of our urban life.' – *Jack Kroll*

> 'A long and wearying case history of the beaten, sobbing, despairing and ultimately powerless anti-hero.' – *Karyn Kay, Jump Cut*

> 'Full of galvanic mirth rooted in human desperation.' – *Michael Billington, Illustrated London News*

> 'Brisk, humorous and alive with urban energies and angers fretting through the 92 degree heat.' – *Sight and Sound*

🏃 Frank Pierson
⚖ best picture; Sidney Lumet; Al Pacino; Chris Sarandon
🏆 Al Pacino

380
Dog Day Afternoon

Two incompetent robbers are cornered in a Brooklyn bank.

Two incompetent robbers, including one who wants the money to pay for his homosexual lover's sex-change operation, hold up a bank, but things go wrong and it becomes a media event in Sidney Lumet's *Dog Day Afternoon*. Based on a true story, this tragicomic thriller is a fascinating and acutely observed film for most of its length, but then bogs itself down in a surplus of talk. Al Pacino's nervy performance as a robber who begins to bond with his hostages, adds a memorable character study to this urban drama, where bad guys become stars through the television news coverage and achieve mythic status.

La Belle et la Bête

France   1946   96m   bw
Discina (André Paulvé)

⏚ ▤ ◉~ ◎ ◎ ♫

aka: *Beauty and the Beast*
wd Jean Cocteau *story* Madame LePrince de Beaumont
ph Henri Alekan *m* Georges Auric *ad* Christian Bérard
ed Claude Ibéria
☆ Jean Marais (Avenant/The Beast/The Prince), Josette Day (Beauty), Mila Parély (Adelaide), Marcel André (Merchant), Nane Germon (Felice), Michel Auclair (Ludovic)

> 'Perhaps the most sumptuously elegant of all filmed fairy tales.' – *New Yorker, 1980*

> 'Absolute magic: diamond cold and lunar bright.' – *CBS*

> 'A sensuously fascinating film, a fanciful poem in movement given full articulation on the screen.' – *Bosley Crowther, New York Times*

379
La Belle et la Bête

The Beast kidnaps Beauty's father but is redeemed through her love and becomes a handsome prince.

Jean Cocteau's stunning-looking adaptation of the fairy tale, set in the 17th century, has Beauty giving herself to the Beast who has kidnapped her father; through love the monster turns into a handsome prince. As he wrote, he was appealing to what remained of the child in his audience; he required faith in the belief that Beauty could tame the Beast. Cocteau transforms the monster's castle into a magical place, where hands stretch through walls to hold candles and doors open and close on their own. Within this surreal setting, the fairy tale unfolds sensuously and realistically to provide an unusual, poetic experience.

The Fallen Idol

GB 1948 94m bw
British Lion/London Films (Carol Reed)
≣ ◎~
US title: *The Lost Illusion*
w Graham Greene *story* *The Basement Room* by Graham
Greene *d* Carol Reed *ph* Georges Périnal *m* William
Alwyn *ad* Vincent Korda *ed* Oswald Haffenrichter
☆ *Ralph Richardson* (Baines), Michèle Morgan (Julie),
Bobby Henrey (Felipe), Sonia Dresdel (Mrs. Baines), Jack
Hawkins (Detective Ames)

'A short story has become a film which is compact
without loss of variety in pace and shape.' – *Dilys
Powell*

'It's too deliberate and hushed to be much fun …
you wait an extra beat between the low-key lines of
dialogue.' – *Pauline Kael, 70s*

Graham Greene; Carol Reed
British film

378
The Fallen Idol

An ambassador's small son nearly incriminates his friend the butler in the accidental death of his shrewish wife.

A near-perfect piece of small-scale cinema, built up from clever nuances of acting and cinematic technique. Carol Reed coaxed an excellent performance from Bobby Henrey as an ambassador's small son who nearly incriminates his friend the butler in the accidental death of his shrewish wife, and Ralph Richardson was at his best as the weak, boastful and kindly butler. Graham Greene worked closely with Reed on the script and produced a tightly constructed thriller of a child's misunderstandings of the adult world and his loss of innocence.

Padre Padrone

Italy 1977 113m Eastmancolor
Radiotelevisione Italia (Tonino Paoletti)
▣ ◎
aka: *Father and Master*
wd Paolo Taviani, Vittorio Taviani *book* Gavino Ledda
ph Mario Masini *md* Egisto Macchi *pd* Gianni Sbarra
ad Gianni Sbarra *ed* Robert Perpignani
☆ Omero Antonutti (Gavino's Father), Saverio Marconi
(Gavino), Marcella Michelangeli (Gavino's Mother), Fabrizio
Forte (Gavino as a Child)

'Its sense of loneliness is frighteningly profound,
while its simple, straightforward style depends on a
shrewd choice of telling, sometimes surreal detail.'
– *David Kehr, Chicago Reader*

● It won the Palme d'Or at cannes Film Festival in 1977.

377
Padre Padrone

The author tells how, after 14 years a shepherd, he leaves his tyranical father, joins the army, attends university and becomes one of Italy's most famous poets.

The Taviani brothers' vivid film was based on the autobiography of Gavino Ledda, who was taken out of school by his harsh father to look after the family's flock of sheep. Unable to read or write and speaking only a Sardinian dialect, the boy's salvation comes when he joins the army and gets an education. He remains on uneasy terms with his father, but studies for a degree and returns home to write his life story. A low-budget film, it is shot in an update of the neo-realist style, using folk song as a background to the fierce conflict between father and son.

The Elephant Man

US 1980 124m bw Panavision
EMI/Brooksfilms (Stuart Cornfeld)

w Christopher de Vore, Eric Bergren, David Lynch, from various memoirs *d* David Lynch *ph* Freddie Francis *m* John Morris *pd* Stuart Craig *ad* Robert Cartwright *ed* Anne V. Coates

☆ *Anthony Hopkins* (Dr. Frederick Treves), *John Hurt* (John Merrick), John Gielgud (Carr Gomm), Anne Bancroft (Mrs. Kendal), Freddie Jones (Bytes), Wendy Hiller (Mothershead), Michael Elphick (Night Porter), Hannah Gordon (Mrs. Treves)

'If there's a wrong note in this unique movie – in performance, production design, cinematography or anywhere else – I must have missed it.' – *Paul Taylor, Time Out*

'In an age of horror movies this is a film which takes the material of horror and translates it into loving kindness.' – *Dilys Powell, Punch*

⍏ best film; screenplay; David Lynch; editing (Anne V. Coates); art direction (Stuart Craig, Bob Cartwright, Hugh Scaife); John Morris; costume design (Patricia Norris); John Hurt

♔ best film; production design; John Hurt

376
The Elephant Man

In 1884 London, a penniless man deformed by a rare illness is rescued by a doctor from a fairground freak show and becomes a member of fashionable society.

David Lynch's film dealt with a curious, true story from Victorian England that had first been dramatized on stage in Bernard Pomerance's 1977 play *The Elephant Man*: in 1884 London, a penniless man deformed by a rare illness is rescued by a doctor from a fairground freak show, and becomes a member of fashionable society. It fails to move quite as it should, perhaps because the central figure, with his grotesque deformity is treated as a horrific come-on, like the hunchback of Notre Dame. Lynch, however, sets the scene superbly, and allows room for splendid performances, notably from John Hurt as the sweet-spirited Merrick, and Anthony Hopkins as his rescuer.

Farewell My Concubine

Hong Kong/China   1993   156m   colour
Artificial Eye/Thomson/China Film/Beijing Film (Hsu Feng)

⬚ ▤ ⬚ ⬚ ⬚ ⬚

w Lilian Lee, Lu Wei *novel* Lilian Lee *d* Chen Kaige
ph Gu Changwei *m* Zhaao Jiping *ad* Chen Huaikai
ed Pei Xiaonan

☆ *Leslie Cheung* (Cheng Dieyi), *Zhang Fengyi* (Duan Xiaolou), Gong Li (Juxian), Lu Qi (Guan Jifa), Ying Da (Na Kun), Ge You (Master Yuan), Lin Chun (Xiao Si (teenager)), Lei Han (Xiao Si (adult)), Tong Di (Xiao Si (adult))

'Chinese cinema ceases to be an acquired taste and becomes a required one … Its vast running time contains some episodes of pleasure, pain, adventure, vice or instructive insight for every taste or brow – high and low.' – *Alexander Walker, London Evening Standard*

'Chen's attempt to reach a wider audience with a bigger, less ambiguous film is still a formidable success. It's a kind of opera in itself, conducted by a director whose visual power is matched by an emotional force that few others in world cinema can match.' – *Derek Malcolm*

● The film was joint winner of the Palme d'Or at the Cannes Film Festival in 1993.
⚲ best foreign-language film; Gu Changwei

375
Farewell My Concubine

The lifelong relationship of two boys trained at the Peking Opera, whose popularity shields them initially from the monumental changes affecting China, are forced to confront reality when Mao's Cultural Revolution takes hold.

Chen Kaige's beautiful, epic film followed the careers of two boys who train together at the Peking Opera. They form a lifelong relationship, both on-stage – one playing masculine roles, the other in feminine parts – and off, through the political upheavals from the 1930s onwards until their final performance in the Sixties. Kaige recorded the social changes of Chinese life, including the Japanese occupation of the country, the Communist takeover and the Cultural Revolution, with an unblinking eye and from the viewpoint of the endlessly persecuted. It is a glorious achievement.

Eight Men Out

US   1988   119m   colour
Rank/Orion (Sarah Pillsbury, Midge Sandford)

⬚ ▤ ⬚ ⬚ ⬚ ⬚

w John Sayles *book* Eliot Asinof *d* John Sayles
ph Robert Richardson *m* Mason Daring *pd* Nora Chavooshian *ed* John Tintori

☆ John Cusack (Buck Weaver), Clifton James (Charles Comiskey), Michael Lerner (Arnold Rothstein), Christopher Lloyd (Bill Burns), John Mahoney (Kid Gleason), Charlie Sheen (Hap Felsch), David Strathairn (Eddie Cicotte), D. B. Sweeney ('Shoeless' Joe Jackson)

374
Eight Men Out

In 1919 members of the great Chicago White Sox baseball team take bribes to lose the World Series.

John Sayles' film would make a good companion piece to *Field of Dreams* that appeared a year later. While that film conjures up the ghost of 'Shoeless' Joe Jackson, Sayles puts Jackson and other members of the great Chicago White Sox baseball team at the centre of his drama, as they take bribes to lose the World Series. An absorbing drama, excellently filmed, with good ensemble acting, Sayles provides background to the scandal, from the mean-spirited owner of the club, and the big-spending gamblers who circled the players like sharks, to the players themselves, who became the scapegoats, sacrificed in the interests of commerce.

Repentance

Repentance
USSR 1984 155m colour
Cannon/Sovexportfilm/Gruziafilm
■ ◎~ ◎
original title: *Pokjaniye, Monanieba*
w Nana Djanelidze, Tengiz Abuladze, Rezo Kveselava
d Tengiz Abuladze *ph* Mikhail Agranovich *m* Nana
Djanelidze *pd* Georgy Mikeladze *ed* Guliko Omadze
☆ *Avtandil Makharadze* (Varlam Aravidze/Abel Aravidze),
Ia Ninidze (Guliko, Varlam's Daughter-in-law), Merab
Ninidze (Tornike, Varlam's Grandson), Zeinab Botsvadze
(Katevan Barateli, Sandro's Daughter), Ketevan Abuladze
(Nino Baratelli, Sandro's Wife), Edisher Giorgobiani (Sandro
Baratelli, Painter), Kakhi Kavsadze (Mikhail Korisheli), Nino
Zakariadze (Elena Korisheli)

'Its significance as a social and historical document
far outstrips its value as art.' – *Washington Post*

● The film did not receive a release until 1987. It was the
third part of a trilogy that began with *The Plea* (1968) and
The Wishing Tree (1976).

373

Repentance

*The body of a town's mayor – a man held in high esteem – is regularly
exhumed by a woman who is required to explain her actions in court.*

A woman explains to a court why she keeps exhuming the body of the
town's long-serving and much respected mayor in Tengiz Abuladze's
bleak and blackly humorous account of a society's complicity in a rule
of terror. She exposes a lifetime of power abused and opposition
silenced, evidence that makes others begin to consider their own past
behaviour. Abuladze uses dreams and other non-realistic techniques to
create a biting allegory of the corruption of a society by Stalinism.

Sons and Lovers

'The first experiences of a young man in
the mysteries of woman!'

Sons and Lovers
GB 1960 103m bw Cinemascope
TCF/Company of Artists/Jerry Wald
◌
w Gavin Lambert, T. E. B. Clarke *novel* D. H. Lawrence
d Jack Cardiff *ph* Freddie Francis *m* Mario Nascimbene
ad Tom Morahan
☆ *Dean Stockwell* (Paul Morel), *Trevor Howard* (Walter
Morel), *Wendy Hiller* (Mrs. Morel), Mary Ure (Clara Dawes),
Heather Sears (Miriam Lievers), William Lucas (William),
Donald Pleasence (Pappleworth), Ernest Thesiger (Henry
Hadlock)

'An album of decent Edwardian snapshots.' – *Peter
John Dyer*

'A rare, remarkable and courageous film.' – *Daily
Herald*

♟ Freddie Francis
♟ best picture; script; Jack Cardiff; Trevor Howard; Mary
Ure; art direction

372

Sons and Lovers

A Nottingham miner's son learns about life and love.

Jack Cardiff captured much of the atmosphere of D. H. Lawrence's
novel of a Nottingham miner's son learning about life and love by filming on location in Nottinghamshire. The drama of Paul Morel (Dean
Stockwell), a sensitive boy torn between his blunt father and his poses-
sive mother gained from the performances of Trevor Howard and
Wendy Hiller. It was one of the most faithful and successful translations
of Lawrence to the screen.

'A quiet little town not far from here.'

Dogville
Denmark/Sweden/France/GB/Germany/Finland/Italy/
Netherlands 2003 178m colour
Icon/Zentropa/Isabella/Something Else/Memfis/
Trollhattan/Pain Unlimited/Sigma/Zoma/Slot Machine/
Liberator2
🎞 ▦ ◎ ◎
d Lars von Trier *ph* Anthony Dod Mantle *pd* Peter Grant
ed Molly Malene Stensgaard
☆ Nicole Kidman (Grace), Harriet Anderson (Gloria),
Lauren Bacall (Ma Ginger), Jean-Marc Barr (The Man With
the Big Hat), Paul Bettany (Tom Edison), Blair Brown (Mrs
Henson), James Caan (The Big Man), Patricia Clarkson
(Vera), Jeremy Davies (Bill Henson), Ben Gazzara (Jack
McKay), Philip Baker Hall (Tom Edison Snr), Udo Kier (The
Man in the Coat), Chloe Sevigny (Liz Henson), Stellan
Skarsgard (Chuck), John Hurt (Narrator)

'Pedantic, obtuse, and unwatchable.' – *David
Denby, New Yorker*

'While you watch the movie, it can seem
ridiculously long-winded. But once it's over, its
characters' miserable faces remain etched in your
memory, and its cynical message lingers.'
– *Stephen Holden, New York Times*

'This galvanizing cinematic work is also gorgeous,
experimental, alive with a Scandinavian strain of
chutzpah, and artistically elegant.' – *Lisa
Schwarzbaum*

The General
Ireland/GB 1998 123m bw Panavision
Warner/Merlin Films/J&M (John Boorman)
🎞 ▦ ◎
wd John Boorman *ph* Seamus Deasy *m* Richie Buckley
pd Derek Wallace *ed* Ron Davis
☆ *Brendan Gleeson* (Martin Cahill), Adrian Dunbar (Noel
Curley), Sean McGinley (Gary), Maria Doyle Kennedy
(Frances), Angeline Ball (Tina), Jon Voight (Inspector Ned
Kenny)

'Both challenges and entertains the audience at a
variety of levels, as well as reviving the vitality and
freshness of the helmer's earliest, mid-'Sixties
pics.' – *Derek Elley, Variety*

● John Boorman won the prize for best director at the 1998
Cannes Film Festival.

371
Dogville

In the 1930s, a fugitive from gangsters is first sheltered by the inhabitants of a small town and later abused, as the risk of protecting her increases.

Among the most controversial films of recent times and one that requires patience, which is eventually rewarded, Lars von Trier's film is reminiscent in some respect of two plays, Friedrich Durrenmatt's *The Visit* and Thornton Wilder's *Our Town*. As in *The Visit*, a woman exacts a terrible revenge on a town for her mistreatment. Here, fleeing from gangsters, Grace (Nicole Kidman) is first sheltered by the inhabitants of a small town and later abused, as the risk of protecting her increases. *Our Town* created a community on an almost bare stage. Von Trier's film is acted as if in a rehearsal, on a soundstage where streets or buildings are indicated by lines of white paint, a method that emphasizes the gap between public and private behaviour. His provocative drama has a disturbing power.

370
The General

In Dublin of the early 1990s, Martin Cahill, a charming and brutal gangster, pulls off a succession of daring robberies until he betrays himself and is killed by an IRA gunman.

John Boorman made a knowing, witty throwback to the street-smart, socially aware gangster films of the Thirties in his drama of Martin Cahill, a charming and brutal Dublin gangster of the early 1990s, who pulls off a succession of daring robberies until he betrays himself and is killed by an IRA gunman. Although 'torn from today's headlines', the film follows a classic tragic trajectory of a man taking on the world until he is undone by his own overweening pride.

Le Feu Follet

France 1963 107m bw
Lux/Nouvelles éditions (Jean Pieuchot)
◧◧ ▇
US title: *The Fire Within*
aka: *Will-O'-The-Wisp; A Time to Live and a Time to Die*
wd Louis Malle *novel* Pierre Drieu La Rochelle
ph Ghislain Cloquet *m* Erik Satie *ad* Bernard Evein
ed Suzanne Baron, Monique Nana
☆ *Maurice Ronet* (Alain Leroy), Léna Skerla (Lydia), Jeanne Moreau (Jeanne), Yvonne Clech (Mademoiselle Farnoux), Hubert Deschamps (d'Avereau), Alexandra Stewart (Solange)

'An epitaph for all the beautiful young men, the semi-intellectual "gilded mediocrities" who skim through their days to their doom unchanged save for a surface tarnish. A latter-day parable of a Dorian Gray, superbly acted and beautifully filmed.'
– Judith Crist

369
Le Feu Follet

After time in a private clinic, a recovering alcoholic walks Paris looking for old friends but appalled by the compromises they have made, kills himself.

A recovering alcoholic, urged to be positive, visits his old friends and, horrified by the compromises they have made, kills himself. Louis Malle's uncompromising film is also a compassionate and fascinating film. Shot in an understated way, Malle began the project after a friend killed himself, and then turned to adapting a novel, which was based on the suicide of a surrealist poet, Jacques Rigaut. Maurice Ronet as the suicidal Alain gives a sensitive performance of a man who decides that he does not want to grow up and take life seriously.

Arsenic and Old Lace

US 1944 118m bw
Warner (Frank Capra)
◧◧ ▇ ◷ ◷ ◷
w Julius J. and Philip G. Epstein, with help from Howard Lindsay, Russel Crouse *play* Joseph Kesselring *d* Frank Capra *ph* Sol Polito *m* Max Steiner
☆ *Cary Grant* (Mortimer Brewster), *Josephine Hull* (Abby Brewster), *Jean Adair* (Martha Brewster), Priscilla Lane (Elaine Harper), Raymond Massey (Jonathan Brewster), *John Alexander* (Teddy Brewster), Peter Lorre (Dr. Einstein), James Gleason (Lt. Rooney), Jack Carson (Officer O'Hara), Edward Everett Horton (Mr. Witherspoon), Grant Mitchell (Reverend Harper)
● Made in 1942 but not released immediately.

368
Arsenic and Old Lace

Two gentle, elderly ladies are assisted in their murderous activities by their mad brother. Then their homicidal nephew arrives …

Joseph Kesselring's only success as a playwright was this black farce about two dear, well-meaning old ladies who invite lonely old men to their Brooklyn home, poison them with elderberry wine, and have their mad brother, who believes the corpses are yellow fever victims, bury them in the cellar. A homicidal nephew then turns up with bodies of his own. It is said Kesselring intended it as a serious thriller; it was turned into a comedy during rehearsal. Frank Capra added his own flair for perpetual hubbub, creating a frenzy of hilarious activity. He coaxed some perfect if overstated performances from his star cast. The film's flippant attitude to death was better received in wartime than would have been the case earlier or later.

Limelight

↟↟ US 1952 144m bw
Charles Chaplin
◐◐ ▤ ⊚ ⊚

wd Charles Chaplin *ph* Karl Struss *m* Charles Chaplin,
Raymond Rasch, Larry Russell *ad* Eugene Lourié *ed* Joe
Inge *photographic consultant* Rollie Totheroh
☆ *Charles Chaplin* (Calvero), *Claire Bloom* (Terry, a Ballet
Dancer), *Buster Keaton* (Piano Accompanist), Sydney
Chaplin (Neville, a Composer), Nigel Bruce (Postant, an
Impresario), Norman Lloyd (Stage Manager)

'From the first reel it is clear that he now wants to
talk, that he loves to talk … where a development
in the story-line might easily be conveyed by a
small visual effect, he prefers to make a speech
about it … it is a disturbing rejection of the nature
of the medium itself.' – *Walter Kerr*

'Surely the richest hunk of self-gratification since
Huck and Tom attended their own funeral.' – *New
Yorker, 1982*

'His exhortations about life, courage, consciousness
and "truth" are set in a self-pitying, self-glorifying
story.' – *Pauline Kael, 70s*

👤 Charles Chaplin, Raymond Rasch, Larry Russell
🏆 Claire Bloom (newcomer)

367
Limelight

*A washed up music hall comedian is helped by a young ballerina to
achieve a last moment of glory.*

A sentimental drama in a highly theatrical London East End setting of a
broken-down music hall comedian, who is stimulated by a young ballerina to a final hour of triumph. In other hands it would be very hokey,
but Chaplin's best qualities, as well as his worst, are in evidence, and in
a way the film sums up his own career. Chaplin based the comedian on
aspects of himself and his life. The film's fault is that Chaplin is no
longer a silent, or even a quiet, clown: he talks incessantly. When he
stops, in some early dream sequences and in his final performance in
the company of Buster Keaton, the magic is still there.

A Brighter Summer Day

Taiwan 1991 237m colour
ICA/Yang and His Gang (Yu Welyan)
original title: *Guling Jie Shaonian Sha Ren Shijan*
w Edward Yang, Yan Hongya, Yang Shunqing, Lai Mingtang
d Edward Yang *ph* Zhang Hulgong, Li Longyu *pd* Yu
Welyan, Edward Yang *ed* Chen Bowen
☆ Lisa Yang (Ming), Zhang Zhen, Zhang Guozhu (Father),
Elaine Jin (Mother), Wang Juan (Older Sister), Zhang Han
(Older Brother)

'One of the major feats of non-American cinema of
its time … Gathers an extraordinary momentum,
showing that you really can delineate the lives of
ordinary people in an extraordinary way without
either flashiness or pretension.' – *Derek Malcolm,
Guardian*

● The film also exists in a version that is 50m shorter. The
longer version is the director's preferred cut.

366
A Brighter Summer Day

*In the early 1960s, a 14-year-old boy falls in love with the girlfriend of
a young gang leader.*

Edward Yang's long but engrossing film has the qualities of a novel as
it details Taiwan's society in the early 1960s, a troubled time dominated
by the fear of Communist China. He depicts a country in search of identity and swamped by other cultures (the film's title comes from a song
by Elvis Presley). It was inspired by an actual event, the murder of a
14-year-old girl by a high school student. Yang focuses on a 14-year-
old boy, the son of a civil servant and refugee from mainland China,
who falls in love with the girlfriend of a young gang leader and, in a
moment of jealousy and frustration, kills her. The events, often taking
place in the dark, which is illuminated by sudden flashes of light, are
observed by Yang's camera from a little distance so that no close-ups
distract from the film's bustling life.

Family Life

GB 1971 108m Technicolor
EMI/Kestrel (Tony Garnett)

w David Mercer *play In Two Minds* by David Mercer
d Ken Loach *ph* Charles Stewart *m* Marc Wilkinson
ad William McCrow *ed* Roy Watts
☆ Sandy Ratcliff (Janice), Bill Dean (Baildon), Grace Cave
(Mrs. Baildon), Malcolm Tierney (Tim)

365
Family Life

Psychological problems cause a 19-year-old girl to enter a mental health institution, where harsh treatment only exacerbates her situation

A 19-year-old girl is driven into a mental collapse by emotional and family problems in Ken Loach's extraordinarily vivid and harrowing drama, in which the screenwriter David Mercer makes use of the theories of psychiatrist R. D. Laing on the relationship between schizophrenia and family life, that madness might be a strategy to make it possible to live in an unlivable situation. Put together with unknown actors and probing television techniques, it was both a slice of suburban life and an indictment of it.

Kagemusha

Japan 1980 179m Eastmancolor
TCF/Toho (Akira Kurosawa)

aka: *The Double*
aka: *Shadow Warrior*

w Akira Kurosawa, Masato Ide *d* Akira Kurosawa
ph Kazuo Miyagawa, Asakazu Nakai *m* Shinichiro Ikebe
ad Yoshiro Muraki
☆ Tatsuya Nakadai (Shingen Takeda/Thief), Tsutomu Yamazaki (Nobukado Takeda), Kenichi Hagiwara (Katsuyori Takeda), Kota Yui (Takemaru Takeda), Hideo Murata (Nobuharu Baba), Takayuki Shiho (Masatoyo Natio), Shuhei Sugimori (Masanobu Kosaka), Noboru Shimizu (Masatane Hara)

'Probably the director's most physically elaborate, most awesome film, full of magnificent views of lines of mounted soldiers slowly crossing grand landscapes.' – *Vincent Canby, New York Times*

☃ best foreign language film; art direction
Ⓣ direction; costume design

364
Kagemusha

When a warlord is mortally wounded, he decides that after his death his place will be taken by a double, thereby ensuring the continuity of the dynasty.

A fascinating Japanese epic centring on stately ritual and court intrigue: on the death of a clan chief his place is taken by the lookalike thief hired to overlook battlefields while the chief is really busy elsewhere. Tatsuya Nakadai gave distinctive performances as the chief and his double. Kurosawa demonstrated his mastery of large-scale action with some spectacular battles, especially the final conflict, where riflemen annihilate an enemy army. It is one of the director's most impressive works.

'Pits the dead against the living in a struggle for survival!'

The Night of The Living Dead
US   1968   98m   bw
Image Ten
🎞 ▤ ⓔ ⓖ ⓘ
w John A. Russo *d* George A. Romero *ph* George A. Romero *ed* George Romero
☆ Judith O'Dea (Barbara), Duane Jones (Ben), Karl Hardman (Harry Cooper), Keith Wayne (Tom), Russell Streiner (Johnny)

'The best film ever made in Pittsburgh.' – *Anon.*

'Casts serious aspersions on the integrity of its makers … the film industry as a whole and exhibs who book the pic, as well as raising doubts about the future of the regional cinema movement and the moral health of filmgoers who cheerfully opt for unrelieved sadism.' – *Variety*

● The Region 1 millennium edition DVD release includes commentary by Romero and the entire cast and the shooting script.

363
The Night of The Living Dead

Flesh-eating zombies, activated by radiation from a space rocket, ravage the countryside.

With this low-budget masterpiece, George A. Romero made one the most influential, and most imitated, of modern horror movies. His flesh-eating zombies, activated by radiation from a space rocket and ravaging the countryside were a new kind of horror. There was no real explanation of what had brought the ghouls from their graves; they were just there. There was an unusual relentlessness about the movie that had never been seen before: the zombies just keep coming and coming. It was gruesome and comic and terrifying and there was no happy ending. Neither Romero nor others who have remade or copied the film since have been able to achieve its powerful effect.

Distant Thunder

India 1973 100m colour
Balaka (Sarbani Bhattacharya)
🇺🇸
original title: *Asani Sanket*
wd Satyajit Ray *novel* Bibhutibhusan Banerjee
ph Soumendu Ray *m* Satyajit Ray *ad* Asok Bose
ed Dulal Dutta
☆ Soumitra Chatterjee (Gangacharan Chakravarti), Babita (Ananga), Ramesh Mukherjee (Biswas), Chitra Banerjee (Moti), Gobinda Chakravarti (Dinabandhu), Sandhya Roy (Chutki)

'I don't know when I've been so moved by a picture that I knew was riddled with flaws. It must be that Ray's vision comes out of so much hurt and guilt and love that the feeling pours over all the cracks in *Distant Thunder* and fills them up.' – *Pauline Kael, New Yorker*

● It won the Golden Bear award for Best Film at the Berlin Film Festival in 1973.

362
Distant Thunder

In 1943, a Brahmin teacher-priest and his wife experience in their small village the beginnings of a famine in Bengal.

A potent account of the breakdown of traditional values under the pressure of terrible events, as, in 1943, a Brahmin teacher-priest and his pretty young wife experience in their small village the beginnings of a famine in Bengal. Satyajit Ray explored the disaster that starved to death thousands at a personal level, focusing on the effect it had on individuals, whose ignorance or greed made it impossible for them to deal with the situation. He filmed the hunger in rich colours amid a glorious landscape, a contrast that was deliberately shocking.

Snow White and the Seven Dwarfs

🚶 US 1937 82m Technicolor
Walt Disney
📷 🇺🇸 🔎 ⊚ ⊚ 🎧
w Ted Sears, Otto Englander, Earl Hurd, Dorothy Ann Blank, Richard Creedon, Dick Richard, Merrill de Maris, Webb Smith, from the fairy tale by the brothers Grimm *m* Frank Churchill, Leigh Harline, Paul Smith *ad* Hugh Hennesy, Hazel Sewell, Gustaf Tenggren, Kendall O'Connor, Tom Codrick, Ken Anderson, Terrell Stapp, Charles Philippi, McLaren Stewart, Harold Miles *supervising d* David Hand *songs* Larry Morey, Frank Churchill
☆ Featuring the voices of Adriana Caselotti, Harry Stockwell, Lucille La Verne, Billy Gilbert

'Sustained fantasy, the animated cartoon grown up.' – *Otis Ferguson*

● Adriana Caselotti (1916–97) was the voice of Snow White, chosen after 150 teenagers, including Deanna Durbin, had auditioned for the role. Snow White's appearance was based on dancer Marjorie Belcher, who was later better known as Marge Champion.
🎵 'Bluddle-Uddle-Um-Dum'; 'Heigh Ho'; 'I'm Wishing'; 'One Song'; 'Some Day My Prince Will Come'; 'Whistle While You Work'; 'With a Smile and a Song'
👤 Special Award to Walt Disney for 'a significant screen innovation'. He was given one Oscar and seven miniature statuettes.
♫ Frank Churchill, Leigh Harline, Paul Smith

361
Snow White and the Seven Dwarfs

Thought by many to be doomed to failure, Disney's first feature cartoon created a world populated by a huge range of characters which was nevertheless firmly rooted in the fairy-tale tradition.

Disney's first feature cartoon was a mammoth enterprise, which no one in the business thought would work. The romantic leads were wishy-washy but the splendid songs and the marvellous comic and villainous characters turned the film into a worldwide box-office bombshell, which is almost as fresh today as when it was made. It had a darkness about it, in the person of the Wicked Queen, that was true to the fairy-tale tradition and tended to be lost in some later Disney films. It was a cinematic milestone and remains an extraordinary work.

Robocop
US   1987   103m   DuArt
Rank/Orion (Arne Schmidt)

w Edward Neumeier, Michael Miner *d* Paul Verhoeven
ph Jost Vacano *m* Basil Poledouris *pd* William Sandell
ad Gayle Simon *ed* Frank J. Urioste
☆ Peter Weller (Alex J. Murphy/Robocop), Nancy Allen
(Anne Lewis), Ronny Cox (Richard "Dick" Jones), Kurtwood
Smith (Clarence J. Boddicker), Dan O'Herlihy (The Old
Man), Miguel Ferrer (Robert Morton)

'The greatest science-fiction film since Metropolis.'
– *Ken Russell*

'A comic book film that's definitely not for kids.'
– *Daily Variety*

'Very violent and very funny.' – *Time Out*

'Essentially, it's just a hipper, more bam-bam
version of the law-and-order hits of the Seventies
… The picture keeps telling you that its
brutishness is a terrific turn-on, and maybe it is if
you're hooked on Wagnerian sci-fi comic books.'
– *Pauline Kael, New Yorker*

● A Region 2 special edition DVD includes the original
theatrical version and the director's cut, and commentary by
Paul Verhoeven and Ed Neumeier.
♟ editing (Frank J. Urioste)

360
Robocop

*Detroit in the future: a badly injured cop is reconstructed by science,
and defeats the forces of evil.*

Paul Verhoeven's gleefully dark vision of the future shows corporate
power controlling cities and citizens' lives, with only a badly injured
cop, reconstructed by science as a robot, on the side of justice.
Verhoeven directs with flair, mixing romance, thriller, some philosophizing, comedy and satire. It takes its audience to unexpected places
and, even while over-indulging in violence, raises serious questions
about the future of cities and the problems of policing them.

Being John Malkovich

US/GB   1999   112m   colour
Universal/Gramercy/Propaganda/Single Cell (Michael Stipe, Sandy Stern, Steve Golin, Vincent Landay)
📽 ▤ ⊚ ⊚ ⌂

w *Charlie Kaufman* d *Spike Jonze* ph Lance Acord
m Carter Burwell pd K. K. Barrett ad Peter Andrus
ed Eric Zumbrunnen
☆ John Cusack (Craig Schwartz), Cameron Diaz (Lotte Schwartz), Catherine Keener (Maxine), Orson Bean (Dr. Lester), Mary Kay Place (Floris), John Malkovich (John Horatio Malkovich), Charlie Sheen (Charlie)

> 'Touches on questions of love, identity, sex, gender and penetration with a playful perverseness few other semi-mainstream productions would ever dare to dabble in. Devilishly inventive and so far out there it's almost off the scale.' – *David Rooney, Variety*

> 'Manages any number of resourceful riffs on the cult of success without losing its own sweetness.' – *Adam Mars-Jones, The Times*

• Sean Penn, Brad Pitt and Christopher Bing appear uncredited as themselves.
⚖ Catherine Keener; Spike Jonze; Charlie Kaufman
Ⓣ Charlie Kaufman

359
Being John Malkovich

Having discovered a portal that allows him to spend time inside the brain of John Malkovich, an unhappily married, unsuccessful puppeteer decides to exploit the situation.

A witty, highly original comedy that manages to be both surreal and ordinary. Having discovered a portal that allows him to spend time inside the brain of John Malkovich, an unhappily married, unsuccessful puppeteer decides to exploit the situation. Spike Jonze depicts a recognizable world and the everyday oddballs that inhabit it, though it does disappear up its own inventiveness towards the end.

The Life of Oharu

Japan   1952   110m   bw
Shin Toho
📽 ▤ ⊚

original title: *Saikaku Ichidai Onna*
w Yoshikata Yoda, Kenji Mizoguchi novel Saikaku Ihara
d *Kenji Mizoguchi* ph Yoshima Kono, Yoshimi Hirano
m Ichiro Saito ad Hiroshi Mizutani ed Toshio Goto
☆ *Kinuyo Tanaka* (Oharu), Hisako Yamane (Lady Matsudaira), Toshiro Mifune (Katsunosuke), Yuriko Hamada (Yoshioka)

358
The Life of Oharu

A samurai's daughter is reduced to prostitution through her relationship with a servant in seventeenth-century Japan.

In the 1680s, the daughter of a samurai recalls her descent to prostitution through her love for a servant in Kenji Mizoguchi's superbly photographed and acted tragedy of a woman trapped by a remorseless fate. Made under difficult circumstances, the film is centered on the performance of the director's favourite actress Kinuyo Tanaka as the long-suffering and frequently humiliated Oharu. Her harsh treatment by a variety of men, and her resignation to her lowly condition, is set against a beautifully detailed portrait of the period.

Tunes of Glory

GB 1960 107m Technicolor
UA/Knightsbridge (Albert Fennell)

w James Kennaway *novel* James Kennaway *d* Ronald
Neame *ph* Arthur Ibbetson *ed* Anne V. Coates

☆ Alec Guinness (Lt. Col. Jock Sinclair), John Mills (Lt.
Col. Basil Barrow), Susannah York (Morag Sinclair), Dennis
Price (Maj. Charlie Scott), Kay Walsh (Mary), *Duncan
Macrae* (Pipe Maj. MacLean), Gordon Jackson (Capt.
Jimmy Cairns), John Fraser (Cpl. Piper Fraser), Allan
Cuthbertson (Capt. Eric Simpson)

'The picture is persuasive. But I daresay one does it
wrong by looking too hard for social reflections.
Lucky enough to find a film which has life in it.' –
Dilys Powell

♟ James Kennaway

357
Tunes of Glory

*The new disciplinarian CO of a Highland regiment crosses swords with
his lax, hard drinking predecessor.*

A confrontation between two officers became a fascinating contest
between two actors in this well-made, wintry barracks melodrama, of a
new disciplinarian CO of a Highland regiment crossing swords with his
lax, hard drinking predecessor. Alec Guinness and John Mills played
against type, with Guinness as the outgoing, rough battle-hardened
soldier who has made it to the top from the ranks and Mills as the
uptight, educated officer who expects everything to be done by the
book, an attitude he takes to a tragic conclusion.

Master and Commander: The Far Side of the World

US 2003 139m DeLuxe Panavision
TCF/Miramax/Universal (Samuel Goldwyn Jnr, Peter
Weir, Duncan Henderson)

w Peter Weir, John Collee *novels* Patrick O'Brian *d* Peter
Weir *ph* Russell Boyd *m* Iva Davies, Christopher Gordon,
Richard Tognetti *pd* William Sandell *ad* Bruce Crone,
Mark Mansbridge *ed* Lee Smith *sp* Industrial Light and
Magic *cos* Wendy Stites

☆ Russell Crowe (Captain Jack Aubrey), *Paul Bettany* (Dr.
Stephen Maturin), Billy Boyd (Barrett Bonden), James
D'Arcy (1st Lt .Thomas Pullings), Lee Ingleby (Hollom),
George Innes (Joe Plaice), Mark Lewis Jones (Mr Hogg),
Chris Larkin (Captain Howard, Royal Marines), David
Threlfall (Killick), Max Pirkis (Lord Blakeney)

'Much of the film is not sufficiently interesting.'
– *Stanley Kauffmann, New Republic*

● The action in the novels was shifted back seven years, to
1805, so that the enemy Captain Aubrey fights could be
altered from the United States to France.
♟ Russel Boyd; sound editing (Richard King)
♟ picture; Peter Weir; Lee Smith; art direction (William
Sandell, Robert Gould); Wendy Stites; makeup (Edouard F.
Henriques, Yolanda Toussieng); sound (Paul Massey, Doug
Hemphill, Art Rochester); visual effects (Daniel Sudick,
Stefen Fangmeier, Nathan McGuinness, Robert Stromberg)
♟ Peter Weir; William Sandell; Wendy Stites; sound

356
Master and Commander: The Far Side of the World

*After his ship is almost destroyed in an attack, a British sea captain
chases a faster French warship across the oceans.*

A handsome movie of derring-do on the high seas, with an exciting
story, of a British captain chasing a faster French warship across the
oceans after his ship is almost destroyed in an attack. It also found
time for quieter, reflective moments: there was a convincing relationship between Russell Crowe, as a man of action, and Paul Bettany, as a
man of science, both united in their love of music. It was an epic drama
that convincingly brought to life the past, brilliantly recreating the horrors of sea battles, as cannonballs splintered ships and crushed limbs.

Jean de Florette
France   1986   121m   Eastmancolor
Technovision
Renn/Films A2/RAI2/DD
⊙⊙ ⊙⊙ ▬ ◎⌁ ◎ ◠
w Claude Berri, Gérard Brach *novel* Marcel Pagnol
d Claude Berri *ph* Bruno Nuytten *m* Jean-Claude Petit
pd Bernard Vezat *ed* Arlette Langmann, Herve de Luze,
Noelle Boisson
☆ Yves Montand (Cesar Soubeyran/"Le Papet"), Gérard
Depardieu (Jean de Florette/Cadoret), Daniel Auteuil
(Ugolin Soubeyran/"Galignette"), Elisabeth Depardieu
(Aimee Cadoret)
⊕ best picture; adapted screenplay; cinematography;
Daniel Auteuil

Manon des Sources
France   1986   114m   colour   Technovision
Renn Productions/A2/RAI 2/DD Productions (Roland
Thenot)
⊙⊙ ⊙⊙ ▬ ◎⌁ ◎ ◎ ◠
w Claude Berri, Gérard Brach *novel* Marcel Pagnol
d Claude Berri *ph* Bruno Nuytten *m* Jean-Claude Petit
pd Bernard Vizat *ed* Geneviève Louveau, Hervé de Luze
☆ *Yves Montand* (Cesar "Le Papet" Soubeyran), *Daniel
Auteuil* (Ugolin Soubeyran), *Emmanuelle Béart* (Manon
Cadoret), Hippolyte Girardot (Bernard Olivier), Margarita
Lozano (Baptistine), Gabriel Bacquier (Victor)

355
Jean de Florette

Elemental story of feuding over water supplies in rural France in the Twenties. Stunning performances and detailed depiction of Provençal farming life made it a wild success in France, repeated to a remarkable extent abroad.

Manon des Sources

A young girl avenges the wrong done to her father by a farmer and his nephew.

Claude Berri's two-part film, based on Marcel Pagnol's novel of Provençal farming life is an absorbing story of peasant cunning, greed, love and revenge. In the 1920s a farmer and his nephew, who covet the land and water adjoining their property, block a spring so that their new hunchbacked neighbour, who has moved from the city, has no easy supply of water for his farm. In *Manon des Sources*, the two prosper because they have succeeded in buying the land and unblocking the spring. When the dead man's daughter discovers the treachery, she avenges the wrong done to her and her father. Played out against wide landscapes, photographed in medium shot for the most part, this is a tragic story beautifully told and excellently acted.

Jean de Florette

Amores Perros
Mexico   2000   154m   colour
Optimum/Zeta Film/AltaVista (Alejandro Gonzalez Inarritu)

aka: *Love's a Bitch*

w Guillermo Arriaga Jordan *d* Alejandro Gonzalez Inarritu
ph Rodrigo Prieto *m* Gustavo Santaolatta *pd* Brigitte Broch *ed* Alejandro Gonzalez Inarritu, Luis Carballar, Fernando Perez Unda

☆ Emilio Echevarria (El Chivo), Gael Garcia Bernal (Octavio), Goya Toledo (Valeria), Alvaro Guerrero (Daniel), Vanessa Bauche (Susana), Jorge Salinas (Luis), Marco Pérez (Ramiro)

'Feels like the first classic of the new decade, with sequences that will probably make their way into history.' – *Elvis Mitchell, New York Times*

'The individual stories, which weave in and out of each other with true-life untidiness, are so gripping you'll go along with them until everything becomes clear.' – *Kim Newman, Empire*

foreign language film
foreign language film

354
Amores Perros

A fatal car crash in Mexico City links three people: an unemployed teenager, an injured model and an ex-terrorist turned hit man.

In Mexico city, a car crash alters the lives of a teenager in love with his brother's wife, a model, who is disfigured in the accident, and a bored hitman in this dazzling, brutal movie of love and death. Its three stories cleverly intertwine, all of them involving dogs, from a pampered pet to a Rottweiler, a vicious champion dogfighter. The film depicts a macho dog-eat-dog world, where brothers casually betray one another, violence stalks the streets, the powerful are corrupt and family life offers no refuge. The final moments provide a small hope, as a redeemed assassin forswears violence, but he is a small figure overwhelmed by a bleak landscape through which he stumbles to an uncertain future.

Richard III

GB 1955 161m Technicolor Vistavision
London Films (Laurence Olivier)

📽 ▤ 🎞 ⊚ ⓟ

w William Shakespeare (adapted by Laurence Olivier, Alan
Dent, with additions) d *Laurence Olivier* ph *Otto Heller*
m *William Walton* pd *Roger Furse* ad *Carmen Dillon*
ed Helga Cranston

☆ *Laurence Olivier* (King Richard III), Claire Bloom (Lady
Anne), *Ralph Richardson* (Buckingham), *Cedric Hardwicke*
(King Edward IV), Stanley Baker (Henry Tudor), Alec Clunes
(Hastings), John Gielgud (Clarence), Mary Kerridge (Queen
Elizabeth), Pamela Brown (Jane Shore), Michael Gough
(Dighton), Norman Wooland (Catesby), Helen Haye
(Duchess of York), Patrick Troughton (Tyrell), Clive Morton
(Rivers), Andrew Cruickshank (Brackenbury)

'Wherever the play was loose-jointed or ill-fitting,
Sir Laurence has been its tinker and its tailor, but
never once its butcher.' – *Paul Dehn, News
Chronicle*

● A Region 1 two-disc set includes commentary by Russell
Lees and John Wilders, and a BBC interview, *Great Acting:
Laurence Olivier.*
⚖ Laurence Olivier
🎬 film; British film; Laurence Olivier

353
Richard III

*Shakespeare's play about Richard Crookback, his seizure of the throne
and his defeat at Bosworth.*

Laurence Olivier preserved in this film his celebrated stage performance as Shakespeare's deformed Richard Crookback, who seizes the
English throne but dies fighting to keep it at the battle of Bosworth.
Olivier's sinister portrayal, with a black comic edge, was based in part
on Disney's Big Bad Wolf and the American theatrical producer Jed
Harris, whom Olivier once called the most loathsome man he had ever
met. It is a necessarily theatrical, but highly satisfying filming of a
splendidly melodramatic view of history, with interesting but not fussy
camera movement, delightful sets (followed by a disappointingly 'realistic' battle) and superb performances.

Ace in the Hole

US 1951 111m bw
Paramount (Billy Wilder)
aka: The Big Carnival
w *Billy Wilder, Lesser Samuels, Walter Newman* d *Billy
Wilder* ph Charles B. Lang Jnr m Hugo Friedhofer
☆ *Kirk Douglas* (Chuck Tatum), Jan Sterling (Lorraine),
Porter Hall (Boot), Bob Arthur (Herbie), Richard Benedict
(Leo), Ray Teal (Sheriff), Frank Cady (Federber)

'Few of the opportunities for irony, cruelty and
horror are missed.' – *Gavin Lambert*

'Style and purpose achieve for the most part a
fusion even more remarkable than in *Sunset
Boulevard*.' – *Penelope Houston*

'As stimulating as black coffee.' – *Richard Mallett,
Punch*

'Americans expected a cocktail and felt I was giving
them a shot of vinegar instead.' – *Billy Wilder*

'Some people have tried to claim some sort of
satirical brilliance for it, but it's really rather nasty,
in a sociologically pushy way.' – *New Yorker, 1980*

'A brilliant arrangement of cause and effect …
unique as a mirror of the morbid psychology of
crowds … revolting but incontrovertibly true.'
– *New York Times*

● Locations were at Gallup, New Mexico.
⚖ script

352
Ace in the Hole

*In order to prolong the sensation and boost newspaper sales, a self-
seeking journalist delays the rescue of a man trapped in a cave.*

One of Billy Wilder's masterworks, in which he was in a serious mood,
exposing the sensationalism of the tabloid press. In order to prolong
the drama and boost newspaper sales, a self-seeking journalist delays
the rescue of a man trapped in a cave. Wilder's target was not merely
the press, radio and television but also its readers, listeners and viewers who enjoyed nothing so much as a dramatic disaster. With hindsight, Wilder felt he should have listened to Kirk Douglas, who
complained that his role as the journalist he played (and played well)
was too unsympathetic. The film did badly at the box office in America,
but won prizes in Europe. Time has confirmed that it is an incisive,
compelling melodrama.

Zéro de Conduite
France 1933 45m approx bw
Gaumont/Franco Film/Aubert
⊙⊙ ▨
wd Jean Vigo *ph* Boris Kaufman *m* Maurice Jaubert
ad Henri Storck *ed* Jean Vigo
☆ Jean Dasté (Monitor Huguet), Louis Lefébvre (Caussat),
Gilbert Pruchon (Colin), le nain Delphin (Principal)

'One of the most poetic films ever made and one of
the most influential.' – *New Yorker, 1978*

351
Zéro de Conduite

*In an unpleasantly stilted boarding school where the headmaster is a
tyrant and the staff are malevolent eccentrics, the returning boys
consider revolution.*

A clear forerunner of *If* ... as boys return from the holiday to a nasty
little boarding school, where the headmaster is an unpleasant dwarf
and all the staff are hateful: and a revolution breaks out. One of the
most famous of surrealist films, it pales beside Buñuel and is chiefly
valuable for being funny. It was banned in France for three years as an
attack on the educational system.

Lolita
GB 1962 152m bw
MGM/Seven Arts/AA/Anya/Transworld (James B.
Harris)
⊙⊙ ▨ ⊛ ⊚ ⊘
w Vladimir Nabokov *novel* Vladimir Nabokov *d* Stanley
Kubrick *ph* Oswald Morris *m* Nelson Riddle *ad* Bill
Andrews *ed* Anthony Harvey
☆ *James Mason* (Humbert Humbert), *Shelley Winters*
(Charlotte Haze), Sue Lyon (Lolita Haze), *Peter Sellers*
(Clare Quilty)

'The director's heart is apparently elsewhere.
Consequently, we face the problem without the
passion, the badness without the beauty, the agony
without the ecstasy.' – *Andrew Sarris*

'A diluted *Blue Angel* with a teenage temptress
instead of a tart.' – *Stanley Kauffmann*

'So clumsily structured that you begin to wonder
what was shot and then cut out, whether the
beginning was intended to be the end; and it is
edited in so dilatory a fashion that after the first
hour, almost every scene seems to go on too long.'
– *Pauline Kael*

● Before Mason was cast, Noël Coward and Laurence
Olivier were sought for the role of Humbert Humbert.
♟ Vladimir Nabokov

350
Lolita

*A middle-aged lecturer falls for an adolescent and marries her mother
to be near her.*

Censorship meant that Kubrick could not deal with the main subject
matter of Nabokov's novel, which was a middle-aged man's obsessive
lust for a 12-year-old girl that leads him to marry her mother to be near
her. Nor was the theme of child-molestation helped by the casting of
Sue Lyon as the prepubescent Lolita; she was sixteen and looked it.
Beginning with a bang, as one rival for the love of Lolita murders the
other, the story was told in flashback, and became something else: an
engrossing and blackly comic confrontation between two men. James
Mason as Humbert Humbert, is outwardly charming while inwardly
raging, and Peter Sellers essays a series of dazzling impersonations
and improvisations as his rival, Quilty. Sellers brings a sinister quality
to his lethal teasing, a manic matador to Mason's bull.

Red Sorghum

China 1987 92m Eastmancolor
Palace/Xi'an Film Studio (Li Changqing)
📷 ▦
original title: *Hong Gaoliang*
w Chen Jianyu, Zhu Wei, Mo Yan *d* Zhang Yimou *ph* Gu
Changwei *m* Zhao Jiping *ad* Yang Gang *ed* Du Yuan
☆ Gong Li (Nine, the Grandmother), Jiang Wen (Yu, the
Grandfather), Teng Rujun (Luohan), Liu Ji (Their Son), Qian
Ming, Ji Chunhua (Sanpao, the Bandit Chief), Zhai Chunhua

'A rough, proletarian belch of a film, a gleeful
assertion of peasant vitality, founded on amoral
(but fully justified) acts of transgression.' – *Tony
Rayns, MFB*

349
Red Sorghum

A man recalls his grandparents' love affair and violent times.

A revelation of a film, an exuberant tragicomic folk tale, told with immense panache, as a man recalls his grandparents' love affair and violent times. It announced the arrival of splendid new Chinese talent in Zhang Yimou, who made a film of exceptional originality. It is a celebration of the vitality of peasant life, through its hero, a chair-carrier who impregnates the bride of a rich leper and may afterwards have murdered her husband. His independence is matched by that of his love Nine (Gong Li), who refuses to yield to her leprous husband, runs a successful distillery and is prepared to take on the invading Japanese army. The photography is as colourful as the story and has as majestic a sweep.

Sansho the Bailiff

Japan 1954 132m bw
Daiei (Masaichi Nagata)
📷 ▦ ✎
original title: *Sansho dayu*
w Fuji Yahiro, Yoshikata Yoda *novel* Ogai Mori *d* Kenji
Mizoguchi *ph* Kazuo Miyagawa *m* Fumio Hayasaka
ad Kasaku Ito *ed* Mitsuji Miyata
☆ Eitaro Shindo (Sansho), Kinuyo Tanaka (Tamaki),
Yoshiaki Hanayagi (Zushio), Kyoko Kagawa (Anju), Akitaka
Kono (Taro), Keiko Enami (Anju as a Girl), Masahiko Kato
(Young Zushio)
● The film was awarded a Silver Lion at the Venice Film
Festival in 1955.

348
Sansho the Bailiff

In medieval Japan, a provincial governor is exiled for his integrity and honesty, only for a similar tragic destiny to befall his wife and children seven years later.

Kenji Mizoguchi's tough tale of oppression and injustice is set in medieval Japan, where a provincial governor is exiled for trying to protect the peasants from exploitation; in following him seven years later, his wife is forced into prostitution and his son and daughter bought as slaves by the ruthless Sansho. Based on a 12th-century legend, this story of cruelty, sacrifice and redemption is told simply but with great skill, the beauty of its images alleviating some of the narrative's harshness but not its power.

The Samurai

France 1967 95m colour
Filmel/CICC/Fida (Raymond Borderie, Eugene
Lepicier)

⬛ ▬ ⌕

original title: *Le Samourai*
US title: *The Godson*

wd Jean-Pierre Melville *ph* Henri Decaë *m* François de
Roubaix *pd* Georges Casati *ad* François de Lamothe
ed Monique Bonnot, Yo Maurette

☆ Alain Delon (Jef Costello), François Périer (The
Inspector), Nathalie Delon (Jan Lagrange), Caty Rosier
(Valerie), Jacques Le Roy (The Gunman), Michel Boisrond
(Wiener), Robert Favart (Barman)

● A dubbed version released in Britain in 1971 ran for
86m.

347
The Samurai

A hired assassin who lives by a code of self-sufficiency betrays himself by falling in love with the woman who witnessed him commit a murder.

Jean-Pierre Melville's existential thriller is dominated by Alain Delon's melancholy portrait of a self-sufficient hired assassin who betrays himself by falling in love with the woman who witnessed his murder of a night-club owner. Shot in tones of greys and blues, it is a moodily atmospheric, engrossing, low-key film with minimal dialogue. Melville transforms the thriller into a mythic tale of death as a seductive woman, finding poetry in the familiar gestures of gangster movies.

Ikiru

Japan 1952 143m bw
Toho

⬛ ▬ ⌕ ◉ ◎

aka: *Living*
aka: *Doomed*

w Hideo Oguni, Shinobu Hashimoto, Akira Kurosawa
d Akira Kurosawa *ph* Asaishi Nakai *m* Fumio Hayasaka
ad So Matsuyama *ed* Akira Kurosawa

☆ *Takashi Shimura* (Kanji Watanabe), Nobuo Kaneko
(Mitsuo Watanabe), Kyoko Seki (Kazue Watanabe)

346
Ikiru

A clerk learns that he is dying and spends his last months creating a children's playground.

Akira Kurosawa's moving and beautifully made personal drama concerned a clerk who learns that he has six months to live. Up to that moment, he had been someone who had shirked work as much as possible. He decides to give his life some purpose by spending his last months creating a children's playground. He succeeds and dies, finding a moment of peace and redemption, though others try to take credit for his work. It is a film of quiet charm and a celebration of a good deed. The final image is touching in its simplicity: the clerk sitting on a swing in the playground and singing 'Life is Short' as snow begins to fall.

Apocalypse Now

US 1979 153m Technicolor Technovision
Omni Zoetrope (Francis Coppola)

w John Milius, Francis Coppola d Francis Coppola
ph *Vittorio Storaro* m Carmine Coppola, Francis Coppola
pd Dean Tavoularis ad Angelo Graham ed Richard Marks,
Walter Murch, Gerald B. Greenberg, Lisa Fruchtman
☆ Martin Sheen (Capt. Willard), Robert Duvall (Lt. Col.
Kilgore), Frederic Forrest (Chef), Marlon Brando (Col.
Kurtz), Sam Bottoms (Lance), Dennis Hopper
(Photojournalist)

'The characters are living through Vietnam as pulp
adventure fantasy, as movie, as stoned humour.'
– *New Yorker*

'Emotionally obtuse and intellectually empty.'
– *Time*

● Coppola said at the Cannes Film Festival: 'It's more of an
experience than a movie. At the beginning there's a story.
Along the river the story becomes less important and the
experience more important.'
● *Apocalypse Now Redux*, a version running at 202m,
was released in 2001.
● Harvey Keitel was replaced by Martin Sheen.
🎙 Vittorio Storaro; sound (Walter Murch, Mark Berger,
Richard Beggs, Nat Boxer)
🏆 picture; John Milius, Francis Coppola (script); Francis
Coppola (as director); Robert Duvall; art direction; editing
🎖 Francis Coppola; Robert Duvall

Do the Right Thing

US 1989 120m colour
UIP/Forty Acres And A Mule Filmworks/Spike Lee

w Spike Lee d *Spike Lee* ph Ernest Dickerson m Bill Lee
pd Wynn Thomas ed Barry Alexander Brown
☆ Danny Aiello (Sal), Ossie Davis (Da Mayor), Ruby Dee
(Mother Sister), Richard Edson (Vito), Giancarlo Esposito
(Buggin Out), Spike Lee (Mookie), Bill Nunn (Radio
Raheem), John Turturro (Pino), John Savage (Clifton), Rosie
Perez (Tina)

'A very unusual movie experience – two hours of
bombardment with New York-style stimuli.'
– *Terrence Rafferty, New Yorker*

● The Region 1 two-disc DVD set from Criterion includes
commentary by Spike Lee, Ernest Dickerson, Wynn Thomas
and Joie Lee.
🏆 best original screenplay; Danny Aiello

345
Apocalypse Now

A Vietnam captain is instructed to eliminate a renegade colonel who has created his own army and is fighting his own war.

Francis Ford Coppola felt as though he was going to die during the making of this film; Martin Sheen nearly did, a heart attack. Post-production took so long that it missed its original release date by two years. The tone of near-madness and paranoia which raged behind the camera seeped into the film itself. It vividly captures the insanity of the Vietnam war and transfers to it the feeling of unimaginable horror that marked Joseph Conrad's novel *Heart of Darkness*, which was its first inspiration. It uses hyperbole and overstatement to convey in great detail the true nature of the first drugs and rock 'n' roll war, a hallucinatory, terrifying, jungle nightmare accompanied by an insistent beat.

344
Do the Right Thing

A white pizza parlour owner in a black neighbourhood sparks off a riot.

Spike Lee's witty, street-wise and passionate film about racism is set in a mainly black neighbourhood in New York, where a Italian-American pizza parlour owner sparks off a riot. An episodic account, it reveals the frustrations of black and white individuals in a changing world, where entrenched attitudes conflict with raised expectations. It is not words but actions that start the trouble: a black power enthusiast refuses to switch off his ghetto-blaster in the pizza parlour, and loses his temper when the owner smashes it. The film ends with an image of further, and more complex, troubles in the future: the Korean owner of a just-opened shop watching the pizza parlour burn.

Death by Hanging

Japan 1968 117m bw VistaVision
Academy/Connoisseur/Sozosha (Masayuki Nakajima,
Takuji Yamaguchi, Nagisa Oshima)
original title: *Koshikei*
w Tsutomu Tamura, Mamoru Sasaki, Michinori Faukao,
Nagisa Oshima *d* Nagisa Oshima *ph* Yasuhiro Yoshioka
m Hikaru Hayashi *ad* Jusho Toda *ed* Sueko Shiraishi
☆ *Nagisa Oshima* (Narrator), Yun-Do Yun (The Convict),
Kei Sato (Prison Warden), Fumio Watanabe (Education
Officer), Toshiro Ishido (Priest), Masao Adachi (Chief of
Guards), Mutsuhiro Toura (Doctor)

'For three-quarters of its length, the film can be
read as a brilliantly, insolently witty Brechtian
parable; an alienation effect taking one away from
the appalling realities of death by hanging, the
better to make one understand the implications of
those realities.' – *Tom Milne*

343
Death by Hanging

*Although he survives being hanged for the rape and killing of two
Japanese girls, a Korean student loses his memory and refuses to
accept responsibility for his past actions.*

A Korean student survives being hanged for the rape and killing of two
Japanese girls. After losing his memory, however, he refuses to accept
responsiblity for his crimes in Nagisa Oshima's complex and challenging film. A blackly comic examination of oppression, guilt and justice, it
is filmed as a succession of re-enacted episodes, complete with chapter headings, in the life of the central character. Basing the film on a
true story, Oshima uses the re-enactment of the student's life to point
up the institutionalized racism endemic in Japan, finally accusing the
audience of its guilty involvement in capital punishment.

La Stanza del Figlio

Italy/France 2001 87m colour
Momentum/Sacher/Bac/Canal+/RAITelepiu (Angelo
Barbagallo, Nanni Moretti)
◙ ▤ ⊚ ⊚
aka: *The Son's Room*
w Linda Ferri, Nanni Moretti, Heidrun Schleef *d* Nanni
Moretti *ph* Giuseppe Lanci *m* Nicola Piovani
ad Giancarlo Basili *ed* Esmeralda Calabria
☆ Nanni Moretti (Giovanni), Laura Morante (Paola),
Jasmine Trinca (Irene), Giuseppe Sanfelice (Andrea), Silvio
Orlando (Oscar), Claudia Della Seta (Raffaella), Stefano
Accorsi (Tommaso), Sofia Vigliar (Arianna)

'A measured, decorous, at times pat film that
manages to be quietly moving because it touches
on something real.' – *Kenneth Turan, Los Angeles
Times*

'Superbly acted, refreshingly direct and blessed
with an ingenious, unexpected final act.' – *Peter
Bradshaw, Guardian*

● It won the Palme D'Or at the Cannes Film Festival in
2001

342
La Stanza del Figlio

*After the accidental death of thier son, an outwardly happy middle-
class family begin to disintegrate.*

An apparently happy middle-class family begins to fall apart when the
teenage son dies in an accident in Nanni Moretti's moving, often
humorous, low-key drama of love and loss. It achieves its ends without
ostentation, but with undeniable truth and power. There are truthful
performances from Moretti himself as the boy's father, a psychiatrist
who finds it necessary to abandon his patients, and from Laura
Morante as the mother.

The Usual Suspects
US 1995 105m Technicolor Panavision
Polygram/Spelling/Blue Parrot/Bad Hat Harry/Rosco
(Bryan Singer, Michael McDonnell)
🎞️ 🎞️ ▦ ◎ ◎ ◎
w Christopher McQuarrie *d* Bryan Singer *ph* Newton
Thomas Sigel *m* John Ottman *pd* Howard Cummings
ad David Lazan *ed* John Ottman
☆ Gabriel Byrne (Dean Keaton), Stephen Baldwin
(McManus), Chazz Palminteri (Kujan), Kevin Pollak
(Hockney), Pete Postlethwaite (Kobayashi), Kevin Spacey
(Roger "Verbal" Kint), Suzy Amis (Edie), Giancarlo Esposito
(Jack Baer), Dan Hedaya (Sgt. Rabin), Benicio del Toro
(Fenster), Paul Bartel (Smuggler)

'What is most rewarding about *The Usual Suspects*
is not method acting or directorial flair, but its
vivid, audacious, relentless intelligence.' – *Stephen
Amidon, Sunday Times*

'An ironic, bang-up thriller about the wages of
crime. A terrific cast of exciting actors socks over
this absorbing complicated yarn.' – *Todd McCarthy,
Variety*

● Regions 1 and 2 special edition DVD releases include
commentary by Bryan Singer and Christopher McQuarrie,
and offer full-screen and widescreen anamorphic formats.
♟ Kevin Spacey; Christopher McQuarrie
♟ Christopher McQuarrie

Y Tu Mamá También
Mexico 2001 105m colour
Icon/Anhelo (Jorge Vergara)
🎞️ ▦ ◎ ◎ 🎧
GB and US title: *And Your Mother Too*
w Alfonso and Carlos Cuarón *d* Alfonso Cuarón
ph Emmanuel Lubezki *ad* Miguel Alvarez *ed* Alfonso
Cuarón, Alex Rodriguez
☆ Maribel Verdu (Luisa Cortes), *Gael Garcia Bernal* (Julio
Zapata), *Diego Luna* (Tenoch Iturbide), Diana Bracho (Silvia
Allende de Iturbide), Emilio Echevarria (Miguel Iturbide),
Ana Lopez Mercado (Ana Morelos), Maria Aura (Cecilia
Huerta), Andres Almeida (Diego "Saba" Madero)

'Outrageous without being offensive, provocatively
and unapologetically sexual, alive to the
possibilities of life and cinema.' – *Kenneth Turan,
Los Angeles Times*

'The movie is fast, funny, unafraid of sexuality and
finally devastating.' – *Elvis Mitchell, New York
Times*

♟ Carlos Cuarón; Alfonso Cuarón

341
The Usual Suspects

Five crooks meet in a police line-up and decide to work together on a couple of robberies.

An excellent, gripping thriller that plays tricks with its audience, leading it down one blind alley after another, as five crooks, who meet in a police line-up and decide to work together on a couple of robberies, come to believe that they are being manipulated by a mysterious master criminal. The film deals in deliberate confusion and double-cross. Its refusal to come clean until its final revelation may infuriate some, but it is part of its appeal, aided by some nicely edgy performances from the actors.

340
Y Tu Mamá También

Two Mexican youths learn about life and love from an older woman .

Alfonso Cuarón provided a joyous and sexy odyssey through Mexico as two Mexican youths learn about life and love from an older woman while on a road trip to find the perfect beach. Cuarón glanced lightly at the country's political corruption and social divisions, and also used an omniscient narrator to add a little gravity to the high-spirited proceedings. The film marked the arrival of two new stars in Gael Garcia Bernal and Diego Luna.

The Burmese Harp
Japan   1956   116m   bw
Nikkatsu (Masayuki Takagi)
▄▄ ◐~
original title: *Biruma no tategoto*
w Natto Wada *novel* Michio Takeyama *d* Kon Ichikawa
ph Minoru Yokoyama *m* Akira Ifukube *ad* Takashi
Matsuyama *ed* Masanori Tsujii
☆ Shoji Yasui (Private Yasushiko Mizushima), Rentaro
Mikuni (Captain Inouye), Tatsuya Mihashi (Commander),
Tanie Kitabayashi (Old woman)

'The film has a good narrative style, but has over-
simplified storytelling and intermittently taking
action. It is too downbeat.' – *Variety*

⚖ best foreign language film

339
The Burmese Harp

A shell-shocked Japanese soldier stays in the Burmese jungle to bury the unknown dead.

Kon Ichikawa's deeply impressive and horrifying film is concerned with the aftermath of war, taking place just after the Japanese surrender. One Japanese soldier, who becomes separated from his company, stays behind in the Burmese jungle to bury the war dead. He disguises himself as a Buddhist priest and gradually assumes that role in reality. It has an epic, folk-tale quality about it, particularly towards the end when Mizushima (Shoji Yasui) and his friends in a prisoner of war camp use parrots to communicate with each other. Ichikawa, who began by making lightweight comedies, achieves greatness here by superbly controlled direction. It was the best of many anti-war films that came out of Japan in the late Forties and Fifties. Ichikawa remade the story in 1985, in a version almost as good.

Lady for a Day
👫 US   1933   95m   bw
Columbia (Frank Capra)
👓 ▄▄ ◐~ ◉
w Robert Riskin *story* Madame La Gimp *by* Damon
Runyon *d* Frank Capra *ph* Joseph Walker *ad* Stephen
Goosson *ed* Gene Havlick
☆ May Robson (Apple Annie), Warren William (Dave the
Dude), Guy Kibbee (Judge Blake), Glenda Farrell (Missouri
Martin), Ned Sparks (Happy), Jean Parker (Louise), Walter
Connolly (Count Romero), Nat Pendleton (Shakespeare)

'Exceptionally adroit direction and scenario … sell
it with plenty of adjectives as it will please
everybody.' – *Variety*

⚖ best picture; Robert Riskin; Frank Capra; May Robson

338
Lady for a Day

Gangsters help an old apple seller to pose as a rich woman when her daughter visits.

Frank Capra's splendid sentimental comedy is full of cinematic resource. From a simple story of gangsters helping an old apple seller to pose as a rich woman when her daughter visits, Robert Riskin wrote a witty script of communal good will that cheered audiences in the Depression. It is a well-judged ensemble piece, without big star names; its character actors, given a chance to flower for once, give richly detailed performances. It remains the best translation of the world of Damon Runyon to the screen.

The Pianist
France/Poland/Germany/GB   2002   148m   colour
Pathé/RP/Heritage/Babelsberg/Runteam (Roman Polanski, Robert Benmussa, Alain Sarde)
🔳 ▬ ⊚ ⊚ ଋ
w Ronald Harwood *book* Wladyslaw Szpilman *d* Roman Polanski *ph* Pawel Edelman *m* Wojciech Kilar *pd* Allan Starski *ed* Hervé de Luze *cos* Anna B. Sheppard
☆ *Adrien Brody* (Wladyslaw Szpilman), Thomas Kretschmann (Captain Wilm Hosenfeld), Frank Finlay (The father), Maureen Lipman (The mother), Emilia Fox (Dorota), Ed Stoppard (Henryk), Julia Rayner (Regina), Jessica Kate Meyer (Halina), Ruth Platt (Janina)

'Surprisingly lacks a feeling of personal urgency and insight that would have made it a distinctive, even unique contribution to the considerable number of films that deal with the war in general and Holocaust in particular.' – *Todd McCarthy, Variety*

● It won the Palme D'Or at the Cannes Film Festival.
♟ picture; Ronald Harwood; Roman Polanski; Adrien Brody
🎞 Pawel Edelman; Anna B. Sheppard; Hervé de Luze
🏆 film; Roman Polanski

337
The Pianist

In Warsaw after the Nazi invasion, a Jewish pianist escapes from the ghetto and goes into hiding in a ruined part of the city.

Roman Polanski's moving, dispassionate account of survival based on a true story of a Jewish pianist who escaped from the Warsaw ghetto after the Nazi invasion and went into hiding in a ruined part of the city. It is told in the style of a 1950s war movie, with often searing imagery. Although it eventually becomes digressive and over-long, it has a haunting power, not the least in Adrien Brody's intense performance as the gaunt and troubled pianist.

☆ Terry Jones Writer, Actor, Director ☆

1. Annie Hall (Allen)
2. Apocalypse Now (Coppola)
3. Duck Soup (McCarey)
4. Fanny and Alexander (Bergman)
5. Groundhog Day (Ramis)
6. Guys and Dolls (Mankiewicz)
7. Jour de fête (Tati)
8. Napoléon (Gance)
9. Pathfinder (Salkow)
10. Steamboat Bill, Jr. (Riesner)

☆ Aki Kaurismaki Director ☆

1. L'Age d'Or (Buñuel)
2. L'Atalante (Vigo)
3. Au Hasard Balthazar (Bresson)
4. Broken Blossoms (Griffith)
5. Casque d'Or (Becker)
6. Greed (von Stroheim)
7. Mon Oncle (Tati)
8. Nanook of the North (Flaherty)
9. Rome, Open City (Rossellini)
10. Tokyo Story (Ozu)

☆ Alex Proyas Director ☆

1. Citizen Kane (Welles)
2. Dr. Strangelove (Kubrick)
3. The Exorcist (Friedkin)
4. The Godfather (Coppola)
5. It's a Wonderful Life (Capra)
6. Lawrence of Arabia (Lean)
7. North by Northwest (Hitchcock)
8. One Flew Over the Cuckoo's Nest (Forman)
9. The Third Man (Reed)
10. The Wizard of Oz (Fleming)

My Fair Lady

👫 US 1964 175m Technicolor Super Panavision 70

CBS/Warner (Jack L. Warner)

▭▭ ▭▭ ▬ ◈ ◎ ◎ ◉ ∩

w Alan Jay Lerner *play* Pygmalion by Bernard Shaw
d George Cukor *ph* Harry Stradling *m* Frederick Loewe
md André Previn *ch* Hermes Pan *ad* Gene Allen
ed William Ziegler *cos* Cecil Beaton

☆ *Rex Harrison* (Prof. Henry Higgins), Audrey Hepburn (Eliza Doolittle), Stanley Holloway (Alfred P. Doolittle), Wilfrid Hyde-White (Col. Hugh Pickering), Gladys Cooper (Mrs. Higgins), Jeremy Brett (Freddy Eynsford-Hill), Theodore Bikel (Zoltan Karpathy), Isobel Elsom (Mrs. Eynsford-Hill), Mona Washbourne (Mrs. Pearce), Walter Burke (Main Bystander)

● A Region 1 special edition two-disc DVD included commentary by Gene Allen, Marni Nixon, Robert A. Harris and James C. Katz.

♫ 'Why Can't the English'; 'Wouldn't It Be Luvverly'; 'I'm an Ordinary Man'; 'With a Little Bit of Luck'; 'Just You Wait'; 'The Rain in Spain'; 'I Could Have Danced All Night'; 'Ascot Gavotte'; 'On the Street Where You Live'; 'Get Me to the Church on Time'; 'I've Grown Accustomed to Her Face'

🏅 best picture; George Cukor; Harry Stradling; Rex Harrison; André Previn (scoring of music); costumes; sound

🏆 Alan Jay Lerner; Stanley Holloway; Gladys Cooper; editing

🏛 best picture

336
My Fair Lady

Musical version of Pygmalion, *about a flower girl trained by an arrogant elocutionist to pass as a lady.*

Rex Harrison's superb stage performance as Professor Higgins was fortunately preserved in George Cukor's elegant transference of the musical, based on Shaw's *Pygmalion*, about a young girl trained to pass as a lady. (Cary Grant was offered the role and turned it down, saying that he would not even go to see the film if Harrison was not given the role.) Harrison, knowing he could not sing, was taught an old music hall technique of delivering patter songs by talking on pitch and turned it into a virtuoso style, insisting, to the benefit of the film, on doing his songs live rather than miming to pre-recorded versions in the usual Hollywood way. Audrey Hepburn's singing was dubbed by Marni Nixon. In the restored 30th-anniversary laser disc edition, Hepburn can be heard singing two songs – 'Wouldn't It Be Luvverly' and 'Show Me' – on alternate tracks on the disc. Stanley Holloway was another excellent hold-over from the stage (Warner had wanted James Cagney) and Audrey Hepburn coped well as a Cockney. Harrison rightly considered that Cukor's direction was 'masterly'.

The Straight Story

France/US 1999 111m FotoKem 'Scope
Buena Vista/Les Films Alain Sarde/Canal+/Picture
Factory (Alain Sarde, Mary Sweeney, Neal Edelstein)

w John Roach, Mary Sweeney *d* David Lynch *ph* Freddie
Francis *m* Angelo Badalamenti *pd* Jack Fisk *ed* Mary
Sweeney
☆ *Richard Farnsworth* (Alvin Straight), Sissy Spacek
(Rose), Jane Galloway Heitz (Dorothy), Everett McGill (Tom
the Dealer), Jennifer Edwards-Hughes (Brenda), John Farley
(Thorvald), John Lordan (Priest), Harry Dean Stanton (Lyle)

'A lyrical poem to America's vast land and country
folks.' – *Emanuel Levy, Variety*

'This must be the strangest road movie ever made,
but it is also one of the most lovable.' – *Adam
Mars-Jones, The Times*

⚖ Richard Farnsworth

335
The Straight Story

*An elderly widower makes a 300-mile trip to see his ailing brother on
the only transport available to him: a lawn mower.*

Director David Lynch deserted the sinister and twisted places of his
usual imaginings to tell a a straightforward story about a man named
Straight (Richard Farnsworth), an elderly widower, who makes a 300-
mile trip to see his ailing brother on the only transport available to him,
a lawn mower. A gentle, folksy road movie that takes its time but establishes a mood of quiet enjoyment for simple pleasures, mixed with a
little regret for some past events; Farnsworth epitomizes a man who
knows his own worth and that of the others he meets on his journey.

A Touch of Zen

Taiwan 1969 180m colour
International Film (Hsia Wu Liang-fang)

original title: *Hsia Nu*
wd King Hu *story* P'u Sung-ling *ph* Hua Hui-ying *m* Wu
Ta-chiang *ed* King Hu
☆ Hsu Feng (Yang Hui-ching), Shih Chun (Ku Shen
Chai), Pai Ying (Shih), Tien Peng, Hsueh Han (Dr. Lu
Meng), Chiao Hung, Chang Ping-yu

'Kung fu gets its just recognition as a genre that
can be used in a serious, thoughtful film and have
its exciting, dynamic effects and drive
undiminished.' – *Variety*

● The film won the Grand Prize at the Cannes Film Festival
in 1975.

334
A Touch of Zen

*In 14th-century China, a poor artist becomes involved with the fugitive
daughter of a high-ranking official murdered by a powerful enemy.*

King Hu was the first, and remains the best, director to treat martial
arts movies with flair and seriousness. This is a compelling period
drama, set in 14th-century China, in which a poor, 30-year-old portrait
painter, who lives with his nagging mother in a derelict, haunted fort,
becomes involved with the fugitive daughter of a high-ranking official
murdered by a powerful enemy. It is a sprawling colourful epic with a
superb visual style.

'He's having the day of his life … over and over again.'

Groundhog Day
US   1993   101m   Technicolor   Panavision
Columbia TriStar/Columbia (Trevor Albert, Harold Ramis)

⊕⊕ ▬ ⊚~ ⊘ ⊚ ⌒

w Danny Rubin, Harold Ramis   *d* Harold Ramis   *ph* John Bailey   *m* George Fenton   *pd* David Nichols   *ad* Peter Lansdown Smith   *ed* Pembroke J. Herring

☆ *Bill Murray* (Phil), Andie MacDowell (Rita), Chris Elliott (Larry), Stephen Tobolowsky (Ned), Brian Doyle-Murray (Buster), Marita Geraghty (Nancy), Angela Paton (Mrs. Lancaster), Rick Ducommun (Gus)

'A major studio Hollywood comedy that both delights and surprises.' – *Sight and Sound*

'Something of a comedy classic, and a film which, for sheer entertainment value, you'd be hard pushed to beat.' – *Empire*

🏆 best original screenplay

333
Groundhog Day

Sent to cover an annual small-town Groundhog ceremony, a self-centred weatherman is forced to relive his day over and over again until he gets it right.

A cynical weatherman, sent to cover an annual small-town Groundhog ceremony, finds himself reliving his day over and over again until he becomes a better person, in Harold Ramis' sparkling comedy. Bill Murray's role as the knowing TV forecaster took full advantage of his world-weary air and brilliant comic timing. It was a version for modern times of *It's A Wonderful Life*: tougher, smarter, more knowing and successfully avoiding corn to provide an unexpectedly witty and warming comedy.

Hail the Conquering Hero
US   1944   101m   bw
Paramount (Preston Sturges)

▬

wd Preston Sturges   *ph* John Seitz   *m* Werner Heymann   *ad* Hans Dreier   *ed* Stuart Gilmore

☆ *Eddie Bracken* (Woodrow Lafayette Pershing Truesmith), *William Demarest* (Sergeant), Ella Raines (Libby), *Franklin Pangborn* (Committee Chairman), Elizabeth Patterson (Libby's Aunt), *Raymond Walburn* (Mayor Noble), *Alan Bridge* (Political Boss), Georgia Caine (Mrs. Truesmith), Freddie Steele (Bugsy), Jimmy Conlin (Judge Dennis), Torben Meyer (Mr. Schultz)

'First rate entertainment, a pattern of film making, not to be missed.' – *Richard Mallett, Punch*

'The energy, the verbal density, the rush of Americana and the congestion seen periodically in *The Miracle of Morgan's Creek* stagger the senses in this newest film.' – *James Ursini*

'It tells a story so touching, so chock-full of human frailties and so rich in homely detail that it achieves a reality transcending the limitations of its familiar slapstick.' – *James Agee*

'He uses verbal as well as visual slapstick, and his comic timing is so quirkily effective that the dialogue keeps popping off like a string of firecrackers.' – *New Yorker, 1977*

♟ Preston Sturges (as writer)

332
Hail the Conquering Hero

An army reject is accidentally thought a hero when he returns to his small-town home.

Preston Sturges' comedy made fun of patriotism and all the small town virtues in this comic romp of an army reject who is accidentally thought a hero when he returns to home. Skilfully orchestrated, it featured his repertory of comic actors at full pitch. Sturges satirizes local corruption and the politician's empty rhetoric, while suggesting that the townsfolk deserve no better. It is slightly marred by an overdose of sentiment at the end, which seems out-of-key, though some critics, such as Manny Farber, claim that it is 'tongue-in-cheek'. But Farber thought 'American mores well-nigh impervious to any kind of satire', which suggests a refusal to take seriously Sturges' comic invention.

The Go-Between

GB   1970   116m   Technicolor
EMI/World Film Services (John Heyman, Norman Priggen)

🔲 🇺🇸

w Harold Pinter *novel* L. P. Hartley *d* Joseph Losey
ph Geoffrey Fisher *m* Michel Legrand *ad* Carmen Dillon
ed Reginald Beck
☆ Alan Bates (Ted Burgess), Julie Christie (Marian Maudsley), Michael Redgrave (The Older Leo), Dominic Guard (Leo Colston), Michael Gough (Mr. Maudsley), Margaret Leighton (Mrs. Maudsley), Edward Fox (Hugh Trimingham)

'It's an almost palpable recreation of a past environment, and that environment is the film's real achievement, not the drama enacted within it.'
– Stanley Kauffmann

● The film won the Palme D'Or at the 1971 Cannes Film Festival beating Visconti's *Death in Venice*, much to Visconti's disgust.
♫ Margaret Leighton
Ⓣ Harold Pinter; Edward Fox; Margaret Leighton; Dominic Guard

331
The Go-Between

Staying at a stately home around the turn of the last century, 12-year-old Leo carries love letters from a farmer to his friend's sister.

'The past is another country. They do things differently there,' wrote the novelist L. P. Hartley, whose words open this film. It is the past that haunts Leo (Michael Redgrave), an old man whose ability to love ended around the turn of the last century, when he was 12 years old. Then, staying at a stately home, young Leo carries love letters from a farmer to his friend's sister, whose affair ends in tragedy. Filming Harold Pinter's screenplay of Hartley's novel, Joseph Losey lays bare the social structure of Edwardian society, the power of love to cross class boundaries, and a young boy's misplaced emotion. It is a lush work of painful nostalgia.

The Spirit of the Beehive

Spain   1973   98m   Eastmancolor
Elias Querejeta

🔲 🇪🇸 📷 ⊘

original title: *El Espíritu de la Colmene*
w Francisco J. Querejeta *d* Victor Erice *ph* Luis Cuadrado
m Luis de Pablo
☆ Fernando Fernan Gomez, Teresa Gimpera, Ana Torrent, Isabel Telleria

330
The Spirit of the Beehive

In 1940 in a remote village, two children see a travelling film show of Frankenstein, *and their imaginations run riot; or do they?*

Spanish director Victor Erice made this beautiful and sensitive story of childish imagination during Franco's regime. It is reminiscent in some ways of another film about childhood, *Jeux Interdits*, which also managed to blend seemingly unrelated elements into a satisfying whole, for this is also a meditation on the disastrous consequences of Franco's victory in Spain's Civil War. Erice set the film in a remote village in 1940. A wide-eyed seven-year-old village girl sees a travelling film show of *Frankenstein* and believes she can summon the monster. Then, in a barn nearby, she finds a wounded Republican soldier and believes he is the creature. Behind the events, and the withdrawal of the girl's parents – her father spends his time with his bees, her mother in writing letters to an exiled friend – lies the effects of the Civil War on imaginative life.

Black Robe

Canada/Australia 1991 100m Eastmancolor
Samuel Goldwyn/Alliance/Samson/Telefilm Canada
(Robert Lantos, Stephane Reichel, Sue Milliken)

⊞ ▤ ◎ ◎ ◎

w Brian Moore novel Brian Moore d Bruce Beresford
ph Peter James m Georges Delerue pd Herbert Pinter
ad Gavin Mitchell ed Tim Wellburn
☆ Lothaire Bluteau (Father Laforgue), Aden Young
(Daniel), Sandrine Holt (Annuka), August Schellenberg
(Chomina), Tantoo Cardinal (Chomina's Wife), Frank Wilson
(Father Jerome)

'A magnificently staged combination of top talents
delivering a gripping and tragic story.' – Variety

'An adventure story in the truest sense: the
filmmakers lead us into unknown territory and keep
pushing us farther and farther on, until, by the end,
we find ourselves deep in the wilderness of the
seventeenth-century consciousness.' – Terrence
Rafferty, New Yorker

329
Black Robe

In the 17th century, a Jesuit priest travels through Quebec to convert the Indians.

Bruce Beresford's tough-minded, compassionate, excellently acted account of inadvertent tragedy deals with an idealistic Catholic priest in Quebec who journeys to a mission post that has been set up to convert the Indians. Brian Moore researched the Jesuits' field reports of the time to create his drama of a young priest who is captured and tortured by the Iroquois and who begins to realize that his activities are damaging the people he has come to save. (A note at the end of the film points out that the Hurons who converted to Christianity were later slaughtered by the Iroquois.) The epic journey along a river wilderness is beautifully captured, and Beresford is even-handed in his depiction of the clash of two uncomprehending cultures.

Lancelot du Lac

France/Italy 1974 85m Eastmancolor
Mara/Laser/ORTF/Gerico Sound (Jean Yanne, Jean-
Pierre Rassam)

⊞ ▤ ◎

aka: Le Graal
aka: The Grail
wd Robert Bresson ph Pasqualino de Santis m Philippe
Sarde ad Pierre Charbonnier ed Germaine Lamy
☆ Luc Simon (Lancelot), Laura Duke Condominas (Queen
Guinevere), Humbert Balsan (Gawain), Vladimir Antolek-
Oresek (King Arthur), Patrick Bernard (Modrick), Arthur de
Montalembert (Lionel)

'Like so much of Bresson's work this is not so
much a movie more a religious experience, but you
don't have to be religious to enjoy it.' – Tom
Hutchinson, Film Review

328
Lancelot du Lac

The few remaining Knights of the Round Table return demoralized, having abandoned the Grail quest and Lancelot resumes his love affair with Guinevere, wife of King Arthur.

Robert Bresson's version of the Arthurian myths had the high ideals of chivalry withering as Lancelot, with the few remaining Knights of the Round Table, returns disillusioned from the failed quest to find the Holy Grail and resumed his love affair with Guinevere, wife of King Arthur. It was an austerely impressive drama of the loss of faith, conjuring up a medieval world with great economy of means.

Claire's Knee

Claire's Knee
France   1970   106m   Eastmancolor
Gala/Les Films du Losange (Pierre Cottrell)
🔲 ▬ ◕~ ◎ ◉
original title: *Genou de Claire*
wd Eric Rohmer *ph* Nestor Almendros *ed* Cécile Decugis
☆ Jean-Claude Brialy (Jerome), Aurora Cornu (Aurora),
Béatrice Romand (Laura), Laurence de Monaghan (Claire),
Michèle Montel (Mme. Walter), Gérard Falconetti (Gilles),
Fabrice Luchini (Vincent)

'Rohmer's quiet, complacent movie-novel game is
pleasing.' – *Pauline Kael, New Yorker*

327
Claire's Knee

*A 35-year-old diplomat who is about to be married, confides to a
female friend that he is attracted to a 16-year-old girl and her 17-year-
old half-sister.*

A witty and perceptive conversation piece, this is probably the best of
Eric Rohmer's explorations of the ambiguities of love and desire, in
which a 35-year-old diplomat, who is about to be married, succumbs
to temptation while at the same time resisting it. He confides to a
female friend, who is a writer, that he is attracted to a 16-year-old girl
and to Claire, her 17-year-old half-sister. Both girls show only a cur-
sory interest in him, though he does achieve his desire to caress
Claire's knee. Rohmer's characters here are all absorbed in their own
lives in a way that illumines the lives of others.

'See them all in a film about fantasy. And
reality. Vice. And versa.'

Performance
GB   1970   105m   Technicolor
Warner/Goodtimes (Donald Cammell)
🔲 ▬ ◕~ ◖
w Donald Cammell *d* Nicolas Roeg, Donald Cammell
ph Nicolas Roeg *m* Jack Nitzsche *md* Randy Newman
ad John Clark *ed* Antony Gibbs, Brian Smedley-Aston
☆ James Fox (Chas Devlin), Mick Jagger (Turner), Anita
Pallenberg (Pherber), Michèle Breton (Lucy), Stanley
Meadows (Rosebloom), Allan Cuthbertson (The Lawyer)

'A humourless, messy mixture of crime and
decadence and drug-induced hallucination.' – *New
Yorker, 1980*

'You don't have to be a drug addict, pederast, sado-
masochist or nitwit to enjoy it, but being one or
more of these things would help.' – *John Simon*

326
Performance

A vicious gangster moves in with an ex-pop star.

It was appropriate that this rock and gangster movie should have two
directors in Nicolas Roeg and Donald Cammell, since one of its themes
is doubles: Chas Devlin (James Fox), a tough gangland enforcer, needs
somewhere to hide after killing a friend of his boss, and moves into a
basement flat belonging to Turner (Mick Jagger), a reclusive and decadent rock star. Before long, they merge identities, becoming reflections
of each other. A dense, Pinteresque melodrama, it is lurid and noisy
and seems to be on the cusp of two eras, both reflecting the recent past
and projecting into the future with its mix of decadence and violence.
Warner's executives hated the film and put it on a shelf for two years
before releasing it.

Triumph of the Will
Germany   1936   120m   bw
Leni Riefenstahl/Nazi Party
🎞 ▤ ◎ ◎
d Leni Riefenstahl ph Sepp Allgeier and 36 assistants
m Herbert Windt ed Leni Riefenstahl

'Its length and lack of variety scream incompetence … Interminable, self-indulgent, repetitive – in a word, turgid.' – *Brian Winston, Sight and Sound, 2002*

● A Region 1 special edition DVD includes commentary by Dr Anthony Santoro, and a Riefenstahl short *Day of Freedom*.

325
Triumph of the Will

The official record of the Nazi party congress held at Nuremberg in 1934.

Leni Riefenstahl's official record of the Nazi party congress held at Nuremberg in 1934 is a devastatingly brilliant piece of film-making – right from the opening sequence of Hitler descending from the skies, his plane shadowed against the clouds. The rally scenes are a terrifying example of the camera's power of propaganda. After World War II it was banned for many years because of general fears that it might inspire a new Nazi party.

Playtime

ϯϯ France 1968 152m Eastmancolor
70mm
Specta Films (René Silvera)
▦ ▤ ⊚
w Jacques Tati, Jacques Lagrange *d* Jacques Tati *ph* Jean
Badal, Andreas Winding *m* Francis Lemarque *pd* Eugène
Roman
☆ *Jacques Tati*, Barbara Dennek, Jacqueline Lecomte,
Henri Piccoli

'Tati still seems the wrong distance from his
audience: not so far that we cannot see his gifts,
not close enough so that they really touch.'
– *Stanley Kauffmann*

'How sad that the result of all this, though it
includes a great deal of intermittent pleasure,
comes at times so dangerously close to boredom.'
– *Brenda Davies, MFB*

'A series of brilliant doodles by an artist who has
earned the right to indulge himself on such a
scale.' – *Alexander Walker*

324
Playtime

Hulot and a group of American tourists are bewildered by life in an airport, a business block and a restaurant.

Jacques Tati's film is almost an abstract work, for it has no actors, no story, no hero or heroine, and no dialogue to speak of. It is a human comedy, an observation of the oddities of everyday life, as his camera follows, in an easily distracted way, a group of American tourists through a day spent at an airport, a home show and a restaurant. There are moments of clowning, such as M. Hulot's startled expression as he discovers the room he has entered is actually a lift. But mostly the screen is just crammed with activity of one kind or another. It was Tati's folly, in which he invested his own money. The film took nearly four years to complete and its commercial failure meant he lost everything, including his home and the rights to his films. It remains, though, as a gleaming monument to a comic genius.

Funny Games

Germany 1997 108m colour
Metro Tartan/Wega (Veit Heiduschka)
▦ ▤ ⊚ ⊚
wd Michael Haneke *ph* Jurgen Jurges *pd* Christoph
Kanter *ed* Andreas Prochaska
☆ Susanne Lothar (Anna Schober), Ulrich Muhe (Georg
Schober), Frank Giering (Peter), Arno Frisch (Paul), Stefan
Clapczynski (Georgie Schober)

'Why would anyone stay when the film so explicitly
challenges them to leave?' – *Mark Kermode, Sight
and Sound*

323
Funny Games

Holidaying in their lakeside cottage, an affluent family at first welcome, but are then terrorized by, two strangers.

The plot of Michael Haneke may sound like a typical modern thriller: a wealthy family in their holiday home are terrorized by two strangers. But Haneke's intentions are far removed from the usual. It is intended as a polemic against film-makers and audiences who enjoy gratuitous violence. The violence here is presented in a way to make it seem painful rather than thrilling. Haneke has explained, 'The problem is not: how do I show violence, but how do I show the viewer his own position in relation to violence and its portrayal?' Audiences, he thinks, see so many images of violence that they have ceased to react to them in any meaningful way. It is a powerful and provocative film that challenges and disturbs.

Christ Stopped at Eboli
Italy/France   1979   155m   Technospes
Cinematografica/RAI/Action Film/Gaumont/Vides
(Franco Cristaldi, Nicola Carraro)

w Francesco Rosi, Tonino Guerra, Raffaele La Capria
book Carlo Levi *d* Francesco Rosi *ph* Pasqualino de
Santis *m* Piero Piccioni *ad* Andrea Crisanti *ed* Ruggero
Mastroianni
☆ Gian Maria Volonte (Carlo Levi), Alain Cuny (Baron
Rotundo), Paolo Bonacelli (Don Luigi Magalone), Lea
Massari (Luisa Levi), Irene Papas (Giulia), François Simon
(Don Traiella)

🏆 best foreign language film

322
Christ Stopped at Eboli

In 1935, an Italian doctor is exiled because of his political views.

Carlo Levi's autobiographical account of Fascist Italy and rural deprivation was faithfully and attractively adapted by Francesco Rosi, one of the country's best and most politically committed directors. It is set in 1935, when an Italian doctor is exiled because of his political views to a remote, southern part of the country. There, he finds a new purpose in using his medical knowledge to help the locals. The film, like the book, mixed personal statement and political opinions with descriptions of rural life in an area out of step with city life and politics, where superstition and tradition remained strong.

The Conversation
US   1974   113m   Technicolor
Paramount/Francis Ford Coppola

wd Francis Ford Coppola *ph* Bill Butler *m* David Shire
pd Dean Tavoularis *ed* Walter Murch, Rcihard Chew
☆ *Gene Hackman* (Harry Caul), John Cazale (Stan), Allen
Garfield (Bernie Moran), Frederic Forrest (Mark), Cindy
Williams (Ann)

'A private, hallucinatory study in technical expertise
and lonely guilt.' – *Sight and Sound*

'A terrifying depiction of a ransacked spirit.' – *New
Yorker, 1977*

'Alert, truthful, unarty and absolutely essential
viewing.' – *Michael Billington, Illustrated London
News*

● Regions 1 and 2 DVDs include commentary by Francis
Ford Coppola, and by Walter Murch.
♟ best picture; Francis Ford Coppola (as writer)

321
The Conversation

A surveillance expert becomes involved with one of his cases; he is faced with the true nature of personal responsibilities and the emerging consequence.

A bugging device expert lives only for his work, but finally develops a conscience in Francis Ford Coppola's absorbing, Kafkaesque suspense story with a brilliant central performance from Gene Hackman. This personal, timely (in view of Watergate) exercise in paranoia is deliberately baffling in its detail. Hackman's surveillance expert is himself a blank, a technician who resists personal interrogation but ends up being bugged by forces outside his control. It is a closely observed, melancholy account of the intrusive power of guilt.

Last Year at Marienbad

France/Italy 1961 94m bw Dyaliscope
Terra/Tamara/Cormoran/Precitel/Como/Argos/Cinetel/
Silver/Cineriz (Raymond Froment)

original title: *L'Année Dernière à Marienbad*
w Alain Robbe-Grillet *d* Alain Resnais *ph* Sacha Vierny
m Francis Seyrig *ad* Jacques Saulnier *ed* Jasmine
Chasney, Henri Colpi
☆ Delphine Seyrig (A/Woman), Giorgio Albertazzi
(X/Stranger), Sacha Pitoeff (M/Escort/Husband)

'Elaborate, ponderous and meaningless.'
– *Newsweek*

'Clearly the film's creators know exactly what they
want to do and have done it with complete
success. Whether one responds to the result is
entirely a matter of temperament.' – *John Russell
Taylor, MFB*

☖ Alain Robbe-Grillet

320
Last Year at Marienbad

*A man meets a woman in a sumptuous resort hotel – did they have an
affair the previous year in Marienbad?*

In a vast old-fashioned hotel, a man meets a woman who may or may
not have had an affair with him the previous year in Marienbad – or
was it Frederiksbad? Alain Resnais' enigmatic film presents a puzzle
with no solution. It is a dreamy work in which reality and fantasy blur
and the past and present are co-existent. Sacha Vierny's photography
captures the scenes in superb black and white photography, especially
in the extraordinary image of the formal gardens at Frederiksbad,
where the people cast long shadows but the surrounding shrubs and
statues do not. The formality extends to the film's lovers, who play
their game of attraction with a chill elegance.

The Conformist

Italy/France/West Germany 1969 108m
Technicolor
Mars/Marianne/Maran (Giovanni Bertolucci)

original title: *Il Conformista*
wd Bernardo Bertolucci *novel* Alberto Moravia
ph Vittorio Storaro *m* Georges Delerue *ad* Ferdinando
Scarfiotti *ed* Franco Arcalli
☆ *Jean-Louis Trintignant* (Marcello Clerici), Stefania
Sandrelli (Giulia), Gastone Moschin (Manganiello), Enzo
Taroscio (Professor Quadri), Dominique Sanda (Anna
Quadri), Pierre Clementi (Lino Semirama, the Chauffeur)

'It's a triumph of feeling and of style – lyrical,
flowing, velvety style, so operatic that you come
away with sequences in your head like arias.'
– *New Yorker*

☖ Bernardo Bertolucci (as writer)

319
The Conformist

*In 1938, an inhibited young man tries to conform to the prevailing
mood of Fascism but gets out of his depth when he turns informer.*

Bernardo Bertolucci's brilliantly realized recreation of an age explores
the nature of Fascism through an inhibited young man who tries to
conform to the prevailing mood of 1938. After a traumatic childhood
incident, he rejects everything that does not conform to what his society regards as normal life, marries a woman he does not love, and
becomes a killer for the party. While in Paris as an assassin, he begins
to have doubts, but only with the fall of Fascism does he realize that he
has been living a lie. Elegantly photographed by Vittorio Storaro,
Bertolucci's film was an engaging and teasing, psychological drama.

And Then There Were None

US 1945 97m bw
Popular Pictures/Harry M. Popkin (René Clair)

GB title: *Ten Little Niggers*

w *Dudley Nichols* novel Agatha Christie (aka: Ten Little Niggers) d *René Clair* ph *Lucien Andriot* m *Mario Castelnuovo-Tedesco* ad Ernst Fegte ed Harvey Manger
☆ *Walter Huston* (Dr. Armstrong), *Barry Fitzgerald* (Judge Quincannon), *Louis Hayward* (Philip Lombard), June Duprez (Vera Claythorne), *Roland Young* (Blore), *Richard Haydn* (Rogers), C. Aubrey Smith (General Mandrake), Judith Anderson (Emily Brent), Queenie Leonard (Mrs. Rogers), Mischa Auer (Prince Starloff)

'Rich in the elements which have made mystery melodramas popular, yet not in the precise form of any previously made.' – *Hollywood Reporter*

'The efforts at sprightly, stylish comedy don't gain much momentum.' – *Pauline Kael, New Yorker, 70s*

318
And Then There Were None

Ten people are invited to a house party on a lonely island, only to be murdered one by one.

René Clair and screenwriter Dudley Nichols improved upon Agatha Christie's classic mystery of ten people who are invited to a house party on a lonely island and murdered one by one. Adapted not so much from Christie's novel as from her play, which had a happier ending, and directed with the utmost care, their version offered playful black comedy that made a game of the succession of murders, stylish puzzlement, and some splendid acting cameos, notably from Walter Huston, Barry Fitzgerald, Louis Hayward and Richard Hadyn.

Animal Crackers

US 1930 98m bw
Paramount

w *Morrie Ryskind* musical play Morrie Ryskind, George S. Kaufman d Victor Heerman ph George Folsey m/ly Bert Kalmar, Harry Ruby ad Ernst Fegte
☆ Groucho (Captain Jeffrey Spaulding), *Chico* (Signor Emanuel Ravelli), *Harpo* (The Professor), *Zeppo* (Horatio Jamison), *Margaret Dumont* (Mrs. Rittenhouse), Lillian Roth (Arabella Rittenhouse), Louis Sorin (Roscoe W. Chandler), Robert Greig (Hives, the Butler), Hal Thompson (John Parker)

'A hit on the screen before it opened, and in the money plenty.' – *Variety*

317
Animal Crackers

Thieves covet a valuable oil painting unveiled at a swank party.

An excuse for the Marx Brothers to create comic mayhem, and a lively one in patches, though sedate and stagebound in treatment. The story hardly matters: at a party at the Rittenhouse Manor, the hostess plans to unveil a valuable painting, which goes missing, and introduce a celebrated explorer, Captain Spaulding to the guests, most of whom turn out to be as fraudulent as the Captain. The brothers are all in top form, and many of the dialogue exchanges are classics. Confusion reigns, polite society is confounded, Groucho makes fun of pretentious plays in a couple of monologues and a good time is had by all.

Animal Crackers

Black Narcissus

GB   1947   100m   Technicolor
GFD/The Archers (Michael Powell, Emeric Pressburger)

⊞ ▤ ◉~ ◉ ◉

wd Michael Powell, Emeric Pressburger *novel* Rumer Godden *ph* Jack Cardiff *m* Brian Easdale *pd* Alfred Junge *ed* Reginald Mills *cos* Hein Heckroth

☆ Deborah Kerr (Sister Clodagh), David Farrar (Mr. Dean), Sabu (Young General), Jean Simmons (Kanchi), Kathleen Byron (Sister Ruth), Flora Robson (Sister Philippa), Esmond Knight (Old General), Jenny Laird (Sister Honey), May Hallatt (Angu Ayah), Judith Furse (Sister Briony), Nancy Roberts (Mother Dorothea), Eddie Whaley Jnr (Joseph Anthony), Shaun Noble (Con)

'An artistic accomplishment of no small proportions.' – *New York Times*

👤 Jack Cardiff

316
Black Narcissus

In the Himalayas, Anglo-Catholic nuns are seduced by the atmosphere of their convent school cum hospital, which was once a harem.

One of the cinema's most beautiful films, despite its unlikely theme: Anglo-Catholic nuns in the Himalayas have trouble with climate, morale, and one of their number who goes mad with sexual frustration. Despite its mountainous setting, Powell shot it in Pinewood studios and in a sub-tropical garden in southern England. Powell, who regarded it as the most erotic film he made, achieved something new for him: the sequence that ends with Sister Ruth falling to her death was shot in time to Brian Easdale's music so that, as he wrote, 'music, emotion and acting made a complete whole, of which music was the master.' Despite some narrative uncertainty, the film remains a visual and emotional stunner.

Who Framed Roger Rabbit

↟↟ US 1988 103m Rank
Colour/Metrocolor/DeLuxe
Warner/Touchstone/Amblin (Robert Watts, Frank
Marshall)

⬭ ▤ ◕ ⊘ ⊙ ⊘ ⌒

w Jeffrey Price, Peter S. Seaman *book Who Censored
Roger Rabbit?* by Gary K. Wold *d* Robert Zemeckis
ph Dean Cundey *m* Alan Silvestri *pd* Elliot Scott
ed Arthur Schmidt *animation Richard Williams*
☆ Bob Hoskins (Eddie Valiant), Christopher Lloyd (Judge
Doom), Joanna Cassidy (Dolores), Stubby Kaye (Marvin
Acme) and also the voices of Charles Fleischer, Kathleen
Turner, Amy Irving, Lou Hirsch, Mel Blanc

'A deplorable development in the possibilities of
animation – and a melancholy waste of the gifts of
one of our most gifted actors.' – *Dilys Powell*

● A Region 1 two-disc set includes commentary by Robert
Zemeckis, Frank Marshall, Jeffrey Price, Peter Seaman,
Steve Starkey and Ken Ralston, and three shorts, *Tummy
Trouble, Rollercoaster Rabbit* and *Trail Mix-Up.* The Region
2 DVD release includes the three shorts.
♟ Arthur Schmidt; visual effects
♟ Dean Cundey; art direction

315
Who Framed Roger Rabbit

*Cartoon characters and live actors become involved in Dashiel
Hammett-style whodunnit.*

The seamless integration of animation and live-action, as cartoon characters became involved in a Dashiel Hammett-style whodunnit, was the main enchantment of Robert Zemeckis' clever comedy, with animation by Richard Williams. Never before had live actors looked at home in the two-dimensional world of animation, or cartoon characters seemed at ease in a real world of three dimensions. Both actors and character here occupy a new universe, an exaggerated version of their usual habitats. In some respects the cartoon characters almost outshine the live actors. Roger Rabbit's wife Jessica exudes sex appeal like few actresses can, and it is not often audiences can see Donald and Daffy Duck working together. It is a whole, new, enjoyable experience.

Day of Wrath

Denmark 1943 105m bw
Palladium

⬭ ▤ ⊘

original title: *Vredens Dag*
w Carl Dreyer, Poul Knudsen, Mogens Skot-Hansen
play Anne Pedersdotter by Hans Wiers Jenssen *d* Carl
Dreyer *ph* Carl Andersson *m* Poul Schierbeck *ad* Erik
Ases, Lis Fribert *ed* Edith Schlussel, Anne Marie Petersen
☆ Thorkild Roose (Absalon Pedersson), Lisbeth Movin
(Anne Pedersdotter, His Wife), Sigrid Neiiendam (Meret, His
Mother), Preben Lerdoff Rye (Martin, Son by His First
Marriage), Anna Svierkier (Herlofs Marte)

'An exceptional piece of cinema … the film will, I
think, be remembered for its realistic treatment of
the incredible; for its vicious tension; for the
unrivalled horror of its picture of human
callousness.' – *Dilys Powell*

314
Day of Wrath

*In 1623, two women, including the pastor's widow, are burnt as
witches in a Danish village.*

Carl Dreyer's harrowing, spellbinding melodrama with a message is set in the 17th century: an old woman is burned as a witch and curses the pastor who judged her. He dies and his mother accuses her daughter-in-law, in love with another man, of using witchcraft to kill him. It moves in a series of Rembrandtesque compositions from one horrifying sequence to another. Depressing but marvellous, it was filmed during the Nazi occupation of Denmark, and its theme of individuals trapped in a repressive society was an apposite one. Dreyer's meditation on the power that institutions have to create and encourage intolerance has lost none of its fearful power in the sixty or so years since it was made.

O Brother, Where Art Thou?

US   2000   106m   DeLuxe
Universal/Touchstone/StudioCanal/Working Title
(Ethan Coen)
🎬 ▦ ◎ ◉ 🎧
w *Ethan and Joel Coen* poem The Odyssey *by Homer*
d *Joel Coen* ph Roger Deakins m T Bone Burnett
pd Dennis Gassner ed Roderick Jaynes, Tricia Cooke
cos Mary Zophres
☆ *George Clooney* (Everett Ulysses McGill), John Turturro
(Pete), Tim Blake Nelson (Delmar), Charles Durning (Pappy
O'Daniel), John Goodman (Big Dan Teague), Michael
Badalucco (George Nelson), Holly Hunter (Penny), Stephen
Root (Radio Station Man), Chris Thomas King (Tommy
Johnson), Wayne Duvall (Homer Stokes), Daniel Von
Bargen (Sheriff Cooley)

'The pace of the action, the brilliance of the
dialogue, the spinning of a narrative out of scraps
of Faulkner and *Moby Dick*, all consolidate the
reputation that the brothers have earned.' – *Adam
Mars-Jones, The Times*

'It's such a charming, happy and beautiful film that
the only possible response is one of admiration
and gratitude.' – *Edward Porter, Sunday Times*

● The title is taken from the serious movie that the hero of
Preston Sturges' *Sullivan's Travels* intended to make.
● George Clooney's singing is dubbed by Dan Tyminski.
♟ script (Ethan Coen, Joel Coen)

Casque d'Or

France   1952   96m   bw
Speva/Paris (Robert Hakim)
◎
aka: *Golden Marie*
w Jacques Becker, Jacques Companeez d *Jacques Becker*
ph Robert Le Fèbvre m *Georges Van Parys* ed Marguerite
Renoir
☆ *Simone Signoret* (Marie), *Serge Reggiani* (Manda),
Claude Dauphin (Felix Leca), Raymond Bussières
(Raymond), Gaston Modot (Danard)

'Takes its place alongside *Le Jour Se Lève* among
the masterpieces of the French cinema.' – *Karel
Reisz*

'A screen alive with sensuousness and luminous
figures.' – *Dilys Powell*

🎭 Simone Signoret

313

O Brother, Where Art Thou?

*The adventures of three escaped jailbirds who go in search of treasure
in 1930s America.*

In a comedy that its makers claim to be based on Homer's *Odyssey*,
three convicts escape from a chain gang in Mississippi in the 1930s
and go in search of buried treasure. It is rooted in myth, but not of
ancient Greece. Instead, it journeys through modern American legends
and dreams with a lightly satirical touch and enormous charm that is
matched by the performances. It also comes closer than most modern
movies to re-inventing the musical as a potent form of entertainment.
The music underscores the story's Americana, from Charles Durning's
performance as a thinly disguised Jimmie Davis, the singing governor
of Louisiana, to songs in the folk tradition. They range from spirituals,
work songs and blues to bluegrass and other styles of country music.
A Ku Klux Klan gathering is choreographed in the style of a Busby
Berkeley spectacular, with just a hint of a Nuremberg rally.

312

Casque d'Or

*1898. In the Paris slums, an apache finds passionate love but is exe-
cuted for murder.*

An impeccable piece of film-making, of a tragic romance which seemed
bathed in a golden glow on its first release. Jacques Becker's masterpiece was based on a turn-of-the-century sensational story involving
Parisian apaches, then a new slang expression for the gangsters inhab-
iting the city's slums. Simone Signoret has her finest role as a courtesan; she enjoys a brief time with the man she loves, an honest man
who falls among thieves, before he is betrayed to the police by a jealous
gang leader. Becker's detailed recreation of the past is matched by his
observation of individuals; eschewing pyrotechnics, he re-creates a
believable past and its unbridled passions.

Central Station
Brazil/France   1998   110m   colour   'Scope
MACT/Videofilms/Riofilme/Canal+ (Arthur Cohn,
Martine de Clermont-Tonnerre)
☒ ☰ ⊛ ⊘

original title: *Central Do Brasil*
w João Emanuel Carneiro, Marcos Bernstein *idea* Walter
Salles *d* *Walter Salles* *ph* Walter Carvalho *m* Antonio
Pinto, Jaques Morelembaum *pd* Cassio Amarante, Carla
Caffe *ed* Isabelle Rathery, Felipe Lacerda
☆ *Fernanda Montenegro* (Dora), Marilia Pera (Irene),
Vinicius de Oliveira (Josue), Soia Lira (Ana), Othon Bastos
(Bastos), Otavio Augusto (Pedrao), Stela Freitas (Yolanda),
Matheus Nachtergaele (Isaias), Caio Junqueria (Moises)

'A melancholy Brazilian road movie shot through
with gently stressed cultural commentary.' – *Todd
McCarthy, Variety*

'Shrewd, tough and big-hearted.' – *David Denby,
New Yorker*

● A Region 1 DVD has commentary by Walter Salles,
Fernanda Montenegro, and Arthur Cohn.
⚖ foreign-language film; Fernanda Montenegro
🏆 foreign-language film

311
Central Station

*An elderly woman travels with a young boy on a journey across Brazil
in search of his father.*

A cynical, elderly, former schoolteacher accompanies a young boy
across Brazil in search of his father in Walter Salles', charming but
tough, study in loss and redemption. Dora (Fernanda Montenegro)
scrapes a living writing letters for the illiterate, and destroys most of
them as not worth posting. Josue (Vinicius de Oliveira) is a young boy
who turns to her for help when his mother is killed. She first sells him
to an adoption agency before discovering that he will be killed for his
organs, and then reluctantly agrees to help him. It is a wise, witty and
compassionate film that does not lose touch with the harsher realities
of life. Salles and his cinematographer Walter Carvalho brilliantly capture the teeming urban and isolated rural visions of Brazil, providing
fascinating glimpses into the ugliness and beauty of the country.

'When they speak of heroes – of villains -
of men who look for action, who choose
between honor and revenge – they tell
the story of Breaker Morant.'

'Breaker' Morant
Australia   1980   107m   Eastmancolor
Panavision
South Australian Film Corporation (Matthew Carroll)
☒ ☰ ⊛~ ⊘

w Jonathan Hardy, Bruce Beresford, David Stevens
play Kenneth Ross *d* Bruce Beresford *ph* Donald
McAlpine *md* Phil Cuneen *ed* William Anderson
☆ Edward Woodward (Lt. Harry Morant), Jack Thompson
(Maj. J.F. Thomas), John Waters (Capt. Alfred Taylor),
Charles Tingwell (Lt. Col. Denny), Terence Donovan (Capt.
Simon Hunt), Vincent Ball (Lt. Ian (Johnny) Hamilton)

'It is impossible to suppress a feeling that the spirit
of Stanley Kramer is abroad on the veldt.' – *Tim
Pulleine, MFB*

⚖ screenplay

310
'Breaker' Morant

*Three Australian officers, part of a British army guerilla unit, become
scapegoats and are courtmartialled for murder during the Boer War.*

During the Boer War, three Australian officers were court-martialled for
shooting prisoners, an event that Bruce Beresford re-creates in this
careful, moving military drama. Under his direction, it becomes an
anti-imperialist film, though it retains a wider resonance in depicting
the dehumanization of enemy captives during war. The trio, though
acting on orders, become political scapegoats to demonstrate the
integrity of the British army. The film switches between the trial and the
events that led up to it, becoming a complex study of divided loyalties.

Queen Christina
US   1933   101m   bw
MGM (Walter Wanger)

w Salka Viertel, H. M. Harwood, S. N. Behrman d Rouben
Mamoulian ph William Daniels m Herbert Stothart
ad Alexander Toluboff ed Blanche Sewell cos Adrian
☆ Greta Garbo (Queen Christina), John Gilbert (Don
Antonio De la Prada), Ian Keith (Magnus), Lewis Stone
(Chancellor Oxenstierna), C. Aubrey Smith (Aage), Reginald
Owen (Prince Charles), Elizabeth Young (Ebba Sparre)

'The shortcomings, such as they are, are so far
overshadowed by the potency of the premier
satellite, the sterling support, the Mamoulian
montage and the Behrman crisp dialogue that
they're relatively unimportant; for Christina is cinch
b.o.' – Variety

'Garbo, as enchanting as ever, is still enveloped by
her unfathomable mystery.' – Photoplay

'An unending series of exceptional scenes.'
– Modern Screen

• The leading male role was announced in turn for Leslie
Howard, Franchot Tone, Nils Asther, Bruce Cabot and
Laurence Olivier: Garbo turned them all down.

309
Queen Christina

*When faced with a political marriage, the queen of 17th-century
Sweden escapes the restrictions of her life by disuising herself as a
man and wandering her country, where she falls in love with the new
Spanish Ambassador.*

The star vehicle *par excellence*, superb to look at and one of Greta
Garbo's most fondly remembered films. Historically it is nonsense, but
the story is put across with great style: the queen of 17th-century
Sweden, distressed at the thought of a political marriage, goes wandering through her country in men's clothes and falls in love with the new
Spanish ambassador. Rouben Mamoulian created highly romantic
moments for her, as when, in love, she almost dances round her bedroom ('In my memory, I shall live a great deal in this room,' she murmurs) caressing the furniture and other objects. Mamoulian ends with
a close-up of her face, held for a long time. He wanted her to be a
beautiful mask for the audiences' imagination to animate.

Things to Come

GB   1936   113m   bw
London Films (Alexander Korda)

w H. G. Wells book *The Shape of Things to Come* by H. G. Wells *d* William Cameron Menzies *ph* Georges Périnal *m* Arthur Bliss *pd* William Cameron Menzies *ad* Vincent Korda *ed* Charles Crichton, Francis Lyon *sp* Harry Zech, Ned Mann

☆ Raymond Massey (John Cabal/Oswald Cabal), Edward Chapman (Pippa Passworthy/Raymond Passworthy), Ralph Richardson (The Boss), Margaretta Scott (Roxana/Rowena), Cedric Hardwicke (Theotocopulos), Sophie Stewart (Mrs. Cabal), Derrick de Marney (Richard Gordon), John Clements (The Airman)

'Successful in every department except emotionally. For heart interest Mr Wells hands you an electric switch … It's too bad present-day film distribution isn't on a Wells 2040 basis, when the negative cost could be retrieved by button pushing. It's going to be harder than that. It's going to be almost impossible.' – *Variety*

'A leviathan among films … a stupendous spectacle, an overwhelming, Dorean, Jules Vernesque, elaborated Metropolis, staggering to eye, mind and spirit, the like of which has never been seen and never will be seen again.' – *Sunday Times*

308
Things to Come

H.G. Wells' vision of the future includes a world war in 1940 and the exploration of outer space.

Alexander Korda approached H.G. Wells to prophesy what the future held. Wells's vision was of a war in 1940, followed by plague, rebellion, a new glass-based society, and the first rocketship to the moon. William Cameron Menzies brought it to life in a series of fascinating, chilling and dynamically well-staged vignettes. Bits of the script and acting may be wobbly, but the sets and music are magnificent, the first part of the prophecy chillingly accurate, and the whole mammoth undertaking almost unique in film history. The film ends with Wells vision of man's eternal quest: 'First this little planet and its winds and ways, and then all the laws of mind and matter that restrain him. Then the planets about him, and at last, out across the immensity to the stars …'

Metropolis

Germany   1926   120m approx (24 fps)   bw
silent
UFA (Erich Pommer)

w Thea von Harbou *d* Fritz Lang *ph* Karl Freund, Günther Rittau *ad* Otto Hunte, Erich Kettelhut, Karl Volbrecht *sp* Eugene Schüfftan

☆ Brigitte Helm (Maria/The Robot), Alfred Abel (Joh Frederson), Gustav Fröhlich (Freder Frederson), Rudolf Klein-Rogge (Rotwang), Fritz Rasp (The Man of Black)

'It goes too far and always gets away with it.' – *New Yorker, 1978*

'A wonderful, stupefying folly.' – *New Yorker, 1982*

● In 1984 Giorgio Moroder put out his own new version, with tinted sequences and a re-edited running time of 83 minutes. It was received with a mixture of distaste, respect and caution. The latest version on video is 139m long.

307
Metropolis

In the year 2026, enslaved workers toil underground for the benefit of the wealthy living in the upper city.

Fritz Lang's futuristic fantasy was set in the year 2026, when the workers in a modernistic city live underground and unrest is quelled by the persuasion of a saintly girl, Maria; but a mad inventor creates an evil Maria to incite them to revolt. Always somewhat overlong, and certainly heavy-going in places, this not only has many brilliant sequences that created genuine excitement and terror, but it inspired a great many Hollywood clichés to come, notably the Frankenstein theme. Its portrait of a de-humanised society, reduced to the level of slavery by mechanization and made insignificant by architectural grandiosity, still resonates. Lang, together with Thea von Harbou, his wife at the time, created a vision of the future that has not dimmed with time.

'Revealing the amazing things a woman will do for love!'

Morocco
US   1930   97m   bw
Paramount (Louis D. Lighton)

w Jules Furthman *novel Amy Jolly* by Benno Vigny
d Josef von Sternberg *m* Karl Hajos
ad Hans Dreier *ed* S.K. Winston
☆ *Marlene Dietrich* (Amy Jolly), Gary Cooper (Tom Brown), Adolphe Menjou (Mons. Le Bessiere), Ullrich Haupt (Adjutant Caesar), Juliette Compton (Anna Dolores), Francis McDonald (Cpl. Tatoche)

'Lightweight story with good direction … needs plenty of exploitation to do over average.' – *Variety*

'A definite step forward in the art of motion pictures.' – *National Board of Review*

'A cinematic pattern, brilliant, profuse, subtle, and at almost every turn inventive.' – *Wilton A. Barrett*

'Enchantingly silly, full of soulful grand passions, drifting cigarette smoke, and perhaps a few too many pictorial shots of the Foreign Legion marching this way and that.' – *New Yorker, 1979*

♟ Josef von Sternberg; Lee Garmes; Marlene Dietrich; Hans Dreier

306
Morocco

A promiscuous woman finds true love in North Africa with a Foreign Legionnaire.

Marlene Dietrich's first American film revealed her quintessence as a cabaret singer who arrives in Morocco and continues her wicked career by enslaving all the men in sight; but true love reaches her at last. Gary Cooper, as a soldier in the Foreign Legion, made an admirable foil for her, though he disliked the fact that von Sternberg ignored him to lavish total attention on Dietrich. It ended with a famous image of Dietrich removing her shoes and walking into the desert so she can follow the man she loves. Although wildly dated in subject matter, the film remains a perversely enjoyable entertainment.

Foreign Correspondent
US   1940   120m   bw
Walter Wanger

w Charles Bennett, Joan Harrison, James Hilton, Robert Benchley *novel Personal History* by Vincent Sheean
d Alfred Hitchcock *ph* Rudolph Maté *m* Alfred Newman
pd William Cameron Menzies *ad* Alexander Golitzen
ed Dorothy Spencer, Otho Lovering *sp* Lee Zavitz
☆ *Joel McCrea* (Johnny Jones/Huntley Haverstock), Laraine Day (Carol Fisher), *Herbert Marshall* (Stephen Fisher), *Albert Basserman* (Van Meer), Edmund Gwenn (Rowley), *George Sanders* (Scott Ffolliott), *Eduardo Ciannelli* (Krug), Robert Benchley (Stebbins), *Harry Davenport* (Mr. Powers), Martin Kosleck (Tramp)

'A masterpiece of propaganda, a first class production which no doubt will make a certain impression upon the broad masses of the people in enemy countries.' – *Joseph Goebbels*

'This juxtaposition of outright melodramatics with deadly serious propaganda is eminently satisfactory … Hitchcock uses camera tricks, cinematic rhythm and crescendo to make his points.' – *Howard Barnes, New York Herald Tribune*

'Easily one of the year's finest pictures.' – *Time*

♟ best picture; script; Rudolph Maté; Albert Basserman; Alexander Golitzen

305
Foreign Correspondent

As war threatens Europe in 1938, an American journalist arrives to report on the situation but is caught up in a spy ring.

An American journalist is sent to Europe in 1938 and becomes involved with spies in Alfred Hitchcock's thoroughly typical and enjoyable adventure. The rambling, episodic script builds up into brilliantly managed suspense sequences: an assassination, a windmill that is the spies' headquarters, an attempted murder in Westminster Cathedral, and a plane crash at sea. The final speech, which is made by the journalist as bombs fall on London, ended 'Hello, America! Hang on to your lights! They're the only lights left in the world!' It was quickly written by Ben Hecht and added at the last moment as an attempt to encourage America into the war.

Once Upon a Time in the West

Italy/US 1969 165m Techniscope
Paramount/Rafran/San Marco (Fulvio Morsella)

w Sergio Leone, Sergio Donati *d* Sergio Leone *ph* Tonino Delli Colli *m* Ennio Morricone *pd* Carlo Simi *ad* Carlo Simi *ed* Nino Baragli

☆ Henry Fonda (Frank), Claudia Cardinale (Jill McBain), Jason Robards (Cheyenne), Charles Bronson (The Man "Harmonica"), Gabriele Ferzetti (Morton), Keenan Wynn (Sheriff), Paolo Stoppa (Sam), Lionel Stander (Barman), Jack Elam (Knuckles), Woody Strode (Stony)

'The paradoxical, but honest 'fun' aspect of Leone's previous preoccupation with elaborately-stylized violence is here unconvincingly asking for consideration in a new 'moral' light.' – *Variety*

• This film has the longest credits of all: they sprawl through the first twelve minutes.

A Face in the Crowd

US 1957 126m bw
(Warner) Newton (Elia Kazan)

w Budd Schulberg story *Your Arkansas Traveller* by Budd Schulberg *d* Elia Kazan *ph* Harry Stradling, Gayne Rescher *m* Tom Glazer

☆ *Andy Griffith* (Lonesome Rhodes), *Lee Remick* (Betty Lou Fleckum), *Walter Matthau* (Mel Miller), *Patricia Neal* (Marcia Jeffries), Anthony Franciosa (Joey Kiely), Percy Waram (Colonel Hollister), Marshall Neilan (Sen. Fuller)

'Savagery, bitterness, cutting humour.' – *Penelope Houston*

'If Kazan and Schulberg had been content to make their case by implication, it might have been a completely sophisticated piece of movie-making. Instead, everything is elaborately spelled out, and the film degenerates into preposterous liberal propaganda.' – *Andrew Sarris*

'Some exciting scenes in the first half, but the later developments are frenetic, and by the end the film is a loud and discordant mess.' – *Pauline Kael, 70s*

304
Once Upon a Time in the West

A beautiful woman is threatened by a gunman who has been hired by the railroad to kill her.

Sergio Leone's epic Western played against preconceptions by starring Henry Fonda as a bad man. Made on a bigger budget than usual because of his collaboration with an American studio, it is even more baroque in style than his previous spaghetti Westerns. The story is a simple one: a lonely woman in the old West is in danger from a band of gunmen. The underlying theme is the death of the West with the coming of the railroad. It is this that will end the lives of the gunmen and the businessman who would replace them. Beautifully made and very violent, Leone's film seemed intended to signal not only the end of a way of life but also the death of the Western itself. It was his farewell to the genre.

303
A Face in the Crowd

A nonentity becomes an overnight sensation on television and develops delusions of lasting power.

Andy Griffith was exceptional in this brilliantly cinematic melodrama as a small-town hick who becomes a megalomaniac when television turns him into a cracker-barrel philosopher; he is finally destroyed by the woman who discovered and loved him. Elia Kazan, in his memoir, commented that Budd Schulberg's script was ahead of its time in anticipating Ronald Reagan. But its luridly entertaining satire of modern show business seems more an illustration of the power of media exposure to elevate nonentities, and of the dangers of the cult of celebrity in which television is complicit.

L'Argent

Switzerland/France 1983 84m colour
EOS/Marion's Films/FR3 (Jean-Marc Henchoz)

📽 ▦

wd Robert Bresson *story The False Note* by Leo Tolstoy
ph Emmanuel Machuel, Pasqualino de Santis *m* Bach
ad Pierre Guffroy *ed* Jean Francois Naudon
☆ Christian Patey (Yvon Targe), Sylvie Van Den Elsen (Old
Woman), Michel Briguet (The Woman's Father), Caroline
Lang (Elise Targe)

302
L'Argent

A man's life is ruined after he unwittingly passes a forged note.

Bresson's bleak study of conscience, fate and atonement concentrates on a tragic chain of events that is started when a forged note is passed in a photographer's shop. It is handed to a delivery man, who is arrested when he innocently tries to use it to pay for a drink. He loses his job, his wife and his child and is sentenced to prison. Bresson's pared-down style and intense focus is as vital as ever – it was his last film at the age of 84 – and manages to achieve a rare spiritual quality. He condemns a materialist viewpoint that condones an ambivalent attitude towards money, while stressing its symbolic qualities as a means through which society expresses so many of its values. The banknote that passes from hand to hand and corrupts those who touch it is a fake, but its effect is the same as if it were real.

'Some Memories Are Best Forgotten.'

Memento

US 2000 116m FotoKem
Pathé/Newmarket/Summit/Team Todd (Suzanne Todd,
Jennifer Todd)

📽 ▦ ⊚ ⊚

wd Christopher Nolan *story* Jonathan Nolan *ph* Wally
Pfister *m* David Julyan *pd* Patti Podesta *ed* Dody Dorn
cos Cindy Evans
☆ Guy Pearce (Leonard), Carrie-Anne Moss (Natalie), Joe
Pantoliano (Teddy), Mark Boone Jnr (Burt), Stephen
Tobolowsky (Sammy), Harriet Sansom Harris (Mrs. Jankis),
Callum Keith Rennie (Dodd)

'A remarkable psychological puzzle film.' – *Sight
and Sound*

'Exciting, intriguing and exhausting.' – *Empire*

Å Christopher Nolan (Screenplay); Dody Dorn

301
Memento

In Los Angeles, an insurance investigator who has lost his short-term memory searches for the man who raped and murdered his wife.

An exceedingly clever, complex drama about identity and its meaning, told through the experiences of a Los Angeles insurance investigator who has lost his short-term memory, but still tries to find the man who raped and murdered his wife. Christopher Nolan has constructed the drama so that the audience, too, experiences events without at first understanding their implications, and has to search for a meaning in the actions, in the same way as its hero looks for a purpose in life.

A Clockwork Orange
GB   1971   136m   colour
Warner/Polaris (Bernard Williams)

wd Stanley Kubrick *novel* Anthony Burgess *ph* John Alcott *m* Walter Carlos *pd* John Barry *ad* Russell Hagg, Peter Shields *ed* Bill Butler

☆ Malcolm McDowell (Alex), Michael Bates (Chief Guard), Adrienne Corri (Mrs. Alexander), Patrick Magee (Mr. Alexander), Warren Clarke (Dim)

'Very early there are hints of triteness and insecurity, and before half an hour is over it begins to slip into tedium … Inexplicably the script leaves out Burgess' reference to the title.' – *Stanley Kauffmann*

'It might be the work of a strict and exacting German professor who set out to make a porno violent sci-fi comedy.' – *New Yorker, 1980*

'Kubrick handles his medium with a confidence almost insolent. For the rest – the flashes of farce, the variations on distance and distortion and dream-imagery – he has given us the most audacious of horror-films. And the most inhuman.' – *Dilys Powell*

↧ best picture; Stanley Kubrick (as writer and director)

300
A Clockwork Orange

In the future, a young thug is brainwashed to hate violence in a government experiment that goes wrong.

Stanley Kubrick's fantastic meditation on a violent future has seemed more prescient with every passing year. Based on Anthony Burgess' novel that was as much an experiment in language as social comment, he posits a future, desolate Britain, in which a young gangster guilty of rape and murder obtains a release from prison after being experimentally brainwashed to abhor sex and violence; he discovers that society has become even more violent and, reverting to his old self, finds his proper place in the world with the aid of a smooth government minister. In extraordinary images of clown-like delinquents, Kubrick orchestrates to electronic music mindless street violence, which leads to mindful state violence and political manipulation. It is like a socially conscious Punch and Judy puppet show.

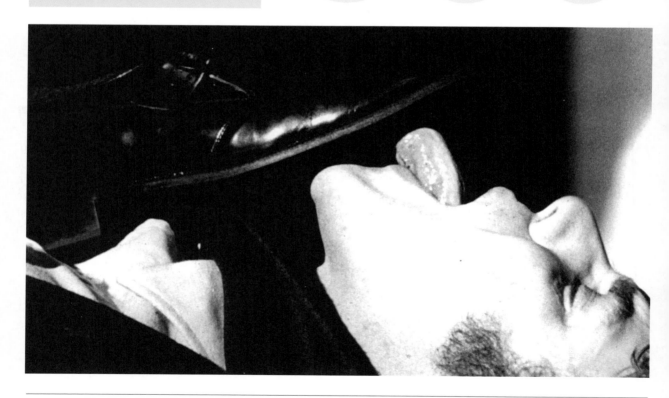

Angels with Dirty Faces

Angels with Dirty Faces
US   1938   97m   bw
Warner (Sam Bischoff)

w John Wexley, Warren Duff *story* Rowland Brown
d Michael Curtiz *ph* Sol Polito *m* Max Steiner *ad* Robert Haas *ed* Owen Marks
☆ *James Cagney* (Rocky Sullivan), *Pat O'Brien* (Jerry Connelly), *Humphrey Bogart* (James Frazier), *The Dead End Kids*, *Ann Sheridan* (Laury Ferguson), George Bancroft (Mac Keefer), Edward Pawley (Guard Edwards)

'Should do fair business, but the picture itself is no bonfire.' – *Variety*

'A rousing, bloody, brutal melodrama.' – *New York Mirror*

⚔ Rowland Brown; Michael Curtiz; James Cagney

A Brooklyn gangster is admired by slum boys, but for their sake pretends to be a coward when he goes to the electric chair.

In this shrewd, slick entertainment, Cagney had one of his best roles. As an actor, he wasn't fond of the Dead End Kids because of their scene-stealing tendencies, once slapping one for ad-libbing during a take. It is a seminal movie for all kinds of reasons. It combined gangster action with fashionable social conscience; it confirmed the Dead End Kids as stars; it provided archetypal roles for its three leading players and catapulted the female lead into stardom. It also showed the Warner style of film-making, all cheap sets and shadows, at its most effective.

Billy Liar

Billy Liar
GB   1963   98m   bw   CinemaScope
Vic Films (Joe Janni)

w Keith Waterhouse, Willis Hall *play* Keith Waterhouse, Willis Hall *novel* Keith Waterhouse inspired by Thurber's *Walter Mitty* d John Schlesinger *ph* Denys Coop *m* Richard Rodney Bennett *ad* Ray Simon *ed* Roger Cherrill
☆ *Tom Courtenay* (Billy Fisher), *Julie Christie* (Liz), Wilfred Pickles (Geoffrey Fisher), Mona Washbourne (Alice Fisher), *Ethel Griffies* (Florence), Finlay Currie (Duxbury), Rodney Bewes (Arthur Crabtree), Leonard Rossiter (Shadrack)

'John Schlesinger's direction, I am delighted to say, is rich in wit.' – *Dilys Powell*

● It was later turned into a TV series and a successful stage musical, making Billy a universal figure of the period.
● A Region 1 DVD release includes commentary by John Schlesinger, Tom Courtenay and Julie Christie.

In a drab North Country town, an undertaker's clerk lives in a world of fantasy.

Flawed only by its unsuitable CinemaScope ratio, this is a brilliant urban comedy of its time, seminal in acting, theme, direction and permissiveness. Tom Courtenay, who had taken over from Albert Finney in a stage version of Keith Waterhouse's novel, brought a diffident, dreamy quality to the role of the undertaker's clerk who lives in a world of fantasy where he is the machine-gun toting ruler of Ambrosia. 'I didn't need to imagine Billy's fantasy world. It was in every molecule of my body and I have been practising it since childhood,' Courtenay later wrote. As the old gives way to the new, with terraced housing coming down and high-rise flats going up, he remains stuck in his innate conservatism; freedom, personified by the carefree, spirited Julie Christie, is just another fantasy.

'His goal was freedom ... his strategy was peace ... his weapon was his humanity!'

Gandhi
GB 1982 188m Technicolor Panavision
Columbia/Goldcrest/Indo-British/International Film Investors/National Film Development Corporation of India (*Richard Attenborough*)
⬚ ▬ ◎ ⊙ ⊙

w John Briley *d* Richard Attenborough *ph* Billy Williams, Ronnie Taylor *m* George Fenton *pd* Stuart Craig *ad* Robert Laing, Norman Dorme, Ram Yedekar *ed* John Bloom
☆ *Ben Kingsley* (Mahatma Gandhi), Candice Bergen (Margaret Bourke-White), Edward Fox (Gen. Dyer), John Mills (The Viceroy), John Gielgud (Lord Irwin), Trevor Howard (Judge Broomfield), Martin Sheen (Walker), Ian Charleson (Charlie Andrews), Athol Fugard (Gen. Smuts), Saeed Jaffrey (Sardar Patel)
● Opening dedication: 'No man's life can be encompassed in one telling ... what can be done is to be faithful in spirit to the record and try to find one's way to the heart of the man.'
👤 best picture; Ben Kingsley; Richard Attenborough as director; John Briley; cinematography; costume design (John Mollo, Bhanu Athalya); art direction (Stuart Craig, Bob Laing); editing (John Bloom)
♫ music
🏆 best film; best direction; best actor; best supporting actress (Rohini Hattangady); outstanding newcomer (Ben Kingsley)

297
Gandhi

The life of the young Indian advocate who became a revolutionary, a saint and a martyr.

Richard Attenborough's film of the life of Gandhi was remarkable for two reasons. First, that it was made at all in an age which regards inspirational epics as very old hat, though it did take Attenborough twenty years to find anyone to finance it; and secondly, that it brought into life so splendid a leading performance from Ben Kingsley. It is a measure of the achievement of both that the most haunting images are not of the epic scenes, nor the moments of wide-screen natural beauty, but of a lean, brown, grizzled face in close-up – close enough so that, from the ascetic mask, the eyes blaze with a mischievous intelligence and wit.

Face to Face
Sweden 1976 136m Eastmancolor
Ingmar Bergman/De Laurentiis/Sveriges Radio (Ingmar Bergman, Lars-Owe Carlberg)
▬

wd Ingmar Bergman *ph* Sven Nykvist *m* Mozart *ad* Anne Terselius-Hagegòrd, Anna Asp, Maggie Strindberg *ed* Siv Lundgren
☆ *Liv Ullmann* (Dr. Jenny Isaksson), Erland Josephson (Dr. Tomas Jacobi), Gunnar Björnstrand (Grandpa), Aino Taube-Henrikson (Grandma)

'After one has detailed its shortcomings, a wonderful fact remains: it's a work possible only to a first-class artist who has invested his life with other artists.' – *Stanley Kauffmann*

♫ Ingmar Bergman (as director); Liv Ullmann

296
Face to Face

A psychiatrist staying with her grandparents finds herself in need of guidance.

Bergman's drama began as a four-part television series. He put in the script elements and memories from his own early life, as if he were trying to come to terms with his childhood and past. It gave an extra depth to the story of a seemingly happily married, professionally successful woman who suffers a sudden and unexpected breakdown. Liv Ullmann invests her with a intense reality, conveying her doubts, fears and contradictory feelings with total conviction. Her dream sequences, which the director regarded as 'extensions of reality', spell out the traumas that haunt her and lead her to attempt suicide. Bergman's drama throws light not only on his own upbringing but on the difficulties of loving relationships between parent and child and the old and the young.

Les Amants
France 1958 88m bw Dyaliscope
Nouvelles Editions (Louis Malle)
📽 ▥
aka: *The Lovers*
w Louis Malle, Louise de Vilmorin *novel Point de Lendemain* by Dominique Vivant *d* Louis Malle *ph* Henri Decaë *m* Brahms *ad* Jacques Saulnier, Bernard Evein *ed* Léonide Azar
☆ Jeanne Moreau (Jeanne Tournier), Alain Cuny (Henri Tournier), Jean-Marc Bory (Bernard Dubois-Lambert), Judith Magre (Maggy Thiebaut-Leroy)

295
Les Amants

A wife conceals from her husband a secret life that includes a romance with a younger man.

'If only for her, it deserved to be made,' said Louis Malle of Jeanne Moreau's performance in his film of a passionate romance that was treated as scandalous on its first release. It was banned in several American states and condemned as obscene in Ohio, though the Supreme Court later overturned the decision. Moreau is beautifully convincing as a rich provincial wife who has a secret life in Paris, but finds real satisfaction in an affair with a young man. For much of its running time, the film observes with an ironic eye French upper-middle-class ways before dissolving into a wildly romantic interlude of the wife's affair and ending in the uncertainty of an untried relationship with a new lover. The unknown and whatever it may hold, the audience is led to realize, is preferable to the stultifying familiarity of the rituals of bourgois life.

10
France/Iran 2002 93m colour
ICA/MK2/Abbas Kiarostami
◉
wd Abbas Kiarostami *ph* Abbas Kiarostami *m* Howard Blake *ed* Abbas Kiarostami
☆ Mania Akbari (Driver), Amin Maher (Amin), Roya Arabshahi, Katayoun Taleidzadeh, Mandana Sharbaf, Amene Moradi

'By the end you feel that the lives of the characters, and the complicated society they inhabit, have been illuminated.' – *A. O. Scott, New York Times*

'There's no doubt that this movie is, as the network executives say, a tough watch. But it repays the investment of attention a thousandfold.' – *Peter Bradshaw, Guardian*

'No ordinary moviegoer, whether Iranian or American, can be expected to relate to his films. They exist for film festivals, film critics and film classes.' – *Roger Ebert*

294
10

In Tehran, a woman driver and her passengers discuss their lives.

Abbas Kiarostami's minimalist film reduced filmmaking to its basics, putting two fixed cameras in the car with no director present, recording ten conversations between a woman driver and the people to whom she gives lifts over a period of two days. Kiarostami auditioned people for the film and discussed their characters and what they might say before he sent them on their way. The resulting film was edited from 23 hours of digital camera tapes. And it worked, providing intriguing glimpses into everyday lives, and the role of women in Islamic society: a young boy argues arrogantly with the driver, who is his mother; one woman tells how her boyfriend left her, weeps and then removes her scarf to reveal that she has cut off her hair; we hear, but do not see, a prostitute and an elderly religious woman. It has the revelatory fascination of eavesdropping on the conversation of others.

'She was his woman! And he was her man! That's all they had to fight with – against the world, the flesh, and the devil!'

The Southerner
US 1945 91m bw
(UA)
📇 ⊘

wd Jean Renoir *novel* Hold Autumn in Your Hand by George Sessions Perry *ph* Lucien Andriot *m* Werner Janssen *ad* Eugene Lourie *ed* Gregg Tallas
☆ Zachary Scott (Sam Tucker), Betty Field (Nona Tucker), *Beulah Bondi* (Granny Tucker), J. Carrol Naish (Henry Devers), Percy Kilbride (Harmie Jenkins), Blanche Yurka (Ma Tucker), Norman Lloyd (Finlay Hewitt)

'I cannot imagine anybody failing to be spellbound by this first successful essay in Franco-American screen collaboration.' – *Richard Winnington*

'You can smell the earth as the plough turns it up; you can sense the winter and the rain and the sunshine.' – *C. A. Lejeune*

● Some sources state that the script was by William Faulkner.
♟ Jean Renoir (as director); Werner Janssen

293
The Southerner

Problems of penniless farmers in the deep South.

Jean Renoir's film concerned the struggle of one famer in the deep South to grow his own cotton. He confessed that what attracted him to the story was that there was no story, merely a series of impressions. He planned a film in which man, animals, and the natural world would come together in harmony. Joel McCrea was to have starred, but did not like the script and withdrew, which almost lost the film its financing. An impressive, highly pictorial outdoor drama, it is more poetic than *The Grapes of Wrath*, but lacks the acting strength. It has, though, an undeniable feeling for the reality of a sharecropper's backbreaking struggle. Sam Tucker contends with a jealous neighbour and the deprivations of poverty as well as such natural forces as rain and floods. French-born cinematographer Lucien Andriot, who had begun his career in 1911, captures the harsh beauty of an unyielding landscape.

'The damnedest thing you ever saw!'

Nashville
US 1975 161m Metrocolor Panavision
Paramount/ABC (Robert Altman)
📇 ⊘ ⊘ 🎧

w Joan Tewkesbury *d* Robert Altman *ph* Paul Lohmann *md* Richard Baskin *ed* Sidney Levin, Dennis M. Hill
☆ Geraldine Chaplin (Opal), David Arkin (Norman Chauffeur), Barbara Baxley (Lady Pearl), Ned Beatty (Delbert Reese), Karen Black (Connie White), Keith Carradine (Tom Frank), Henry Gibson (Haven Hamilton), Keenan Wynn (Mr. Green), Lily Tomlin (Linnea Reese), Ronee Blakley (Barbara Jean)

'A gigantic parody … crammed with samples taken from every level of Nashville society, revealed in affectionate detail bordering on caricature in a manner that would surely delight Norman Rockwell.' – *Philip Strick*

'Wildly over-praised Altman, with all the defects we once looked on as marks of healthy ambitiousness: terrible construction, messy editing, leering jokes at its own characters, unending pomposity.' – *Time Out, 1980*

● The Region 1 DVD release includes commentary by Altman.
👤 song 'I'm Easy' (*m/ly* Keith Carradine)
♟ best picture; Robert Altman; Lily Tomlin; Ronee Blakley

292
Nashville

A political campaign in Nashville organizes a mammoth pop concert to gain support.

Robert Altman's kaleidoscopic, fragmented, multi-storied musical melodrama is a mammoth movie with many exciting moments. The country music capital of America forms a background to the interwoven stories of singers, musicians, would-be singers and misfits who congregate at a rally and concert for a presidential candidate. Loudspeaker vans circle the city blaring out political slogans as singers have breakdowns, seize a moment of fame, or are seduced, and a stripper fails to perform satisfactorily. It ends with an attempted assassination and the feeling that American society, its hopes and dreams have been explored with a knowing and satirical eye.

The Big Red One

US 1980 111m colour
UA/Lorimar (Gene Corman)

📽 🎬 🔊 ⊘

wd Samuel Fuller *ph* Adam Greenberg *m* Dana Kaproff
ad Peter Jamison *ed* David Bretherton, Morton Tubor
☆ Lee Marvin (Sergeant), Mark Hamill (Griff), Robert
Carradine (Zab), Bobby DiCicco (Vinci), Kelly Ward
(Johnson), Stéphane Audran (Walloon), Serge Marquand
(Ransonnet)

'A picture of palpable raw power which manages
both intense intimacy and great scope at the same
time.' – *Variety*

'Like all Fuller movies, about an inch from cliché all
the way.' – *Guardian*

291
The Big Red One

Five foot-soldiers survive action in several theatres of war between 1940 and 1945.

Samuel Fuller spent years trying to make this, his most personal film, based on his experiences as a private in the US Army's 1st Infantry Division during the Second World War. (In the late Sixties, he once acted out the entire film in my sitting room, moving armchairs and sofas to represent tanks, caves and foxholes.) The original release was a heartfelt account of young soldiers led by a tough, compassionate sergeant (Lee Marvin in an excellent, untypical performance) through four years of war, from North Africa to the death camps of Central Europe, but it lacked Fuller's usual visceral qualities. It was not the film Fuller intended; Warners had butchered his original cut. A restored version, running at 158 minutes, was released in 2004, revealing it to be one of Hollywood's best war movies, concentrating on the isolation of battle and the craziness of combat.

The Crowd

US 1928 98m bw silent
MGM (King Vidor)

🎬 🔊

w King Vidor, John V. A. Weaver, Harry Behn *d* King Vidor
ph Henry Sharp *ad* Cedric Gibbons, Arnold Gillespie
ed Hugh Wynn
☆ James Murray (John), Eleanor Boardman (Mary), Bert
Roach (Bert), Estelle Clark (Jane)

'No picture is perfect, but this comes as near to
reproducing reality as anything you have ever
witnessed.' – *Photoplay*

⚖ King Vidor; Unique and Artistic Picture

290
The Crowd

Episodes in the life of a city clerk.

King Vidor's deliberately humdrum story began as a discussion with Irving Thalberg when he remarked, 'the average fellow walks through life and sees quite a lot of drama taking place around him. Objectively, life is like a battle, isn't it?' Vidor was trying to show that drama can exist in the lowliest surroundings. Though some of the director's innovations have become clichés, the film retains much of its original power, from its opening scene with the camera panning from a crowd at the entrance of an office building up to a high window through which many clerks can be seen sitting at desks, then moving through the window and focusing on one particular clerk. It ends in the same manner, with the clerk, laughing with his family, as one of a crowd in a theatre audience.

'A picture for anyone who has ever dreamed of a second chance'

Alice Doesn't Live Here Any More
US   1974   112m   Technicolor
Warner (David Susskind, Audrey Maas)

w Robert Getchell *d* Martin Scorsese *ph* Kent L. Wakeford *m* various *md* Richard La Salle *pd* Toby Carr Rafelson *ed* Marcia Lucas
☆ *Ellen Burstyn* (Alice Hyatt), *Alfred Lutter* (Tommy Hyatt), Kris Kristofferson (David), Billy Green Bush (Donald Hyatt), *Diane Ladd* (Flo), Lelia Goldoni (Neighbour Bea), Jodie Foster (Audrey)

'What Scorsese has done is to rescue an American cliché from the bland, flat but much more portentous naturalism of such as *Harry and Tonto* and restore it to an emotional and intellectual complexity through his particular brand of baroque realism.' – *Richard Combs*

'Full of funny malice and breakneck vitality.' – *New Yorker*

'A tough weepie, redeemed by its picturesque locations and its eye for social detail.' – *Michael Billington, Illustrated London News*

● The film inspired the TV sitcom *Alice* (1976–85).
👤 Ellen Burstyn
👥 Robert Getchell; Diane Ladd
🏆 picture; Robert Getchell; Ellen Burstyn; Diane Ladd

The Man Who Shot Liberty Valance
US   1962   122m   bw
Paramount/John Ford (Willis Goldbeck)

w James Warner Bellah, Willis Goldbeck *d* John Ford *ph* William H. Clothier *m* Cyril Mockridge *ad* Eddie Imazu, Hal Pereira *ed* Otho Lovering
☆ James Stewart (Ransom Stoddard), John Wayne (Tom Doniphon), Vera Miles (Hallie Stoddard), Lee Marvin (Liberty Valance), Edmond O'Brien (Dutton Peabody), Andy Devine (Link Appleyard), Jeanette Nolan (Nora Ericson), John Qualen (Peter Ericson), Ken Murray (Doc Willoughby), Woody Strode (Pompey), Lee Van Cleef (Reese), Strother Martin (Floyd), John Carradine (Maj. Cassius Starbuckle)

'Like Queen Victoria, John Wayne has become lovable because he stayed in the saddle into a new era.' – *Judith Crist*

'A heavy-spirited piece of nostalgia.' – *Pauline Kael, 1975*

'A film whose fascination lies less in what it is itself than in what it reveals about the art of its maker.' – *William S. Pechter*

289
Alice Doesn't Live Here Any More

A widow sets off with her young son for Monterey and a singing career.

Martin Scorsese's film seems almost an aberration in his career, taking him away from his familiar New York and its street life into an old-fashioned odyssey of a woman attempting to fulfill her childhood dreams. Alice, suddenly widowed at 35, sells her home in New Mexico and sets off with her 12-year-old son for California and her home-town of Monterey to become a singer. She is a woman taking charge of her own life, even if she does it in a way others might find irresponsible. She moves through an impermanent if unchanging landscape, of motels and drive-in restaurants, working as a waitress and, though not making it over the rainbow, finding the possibility of contentment. Realistically squalid and foul-mouthed, it is an endearing look at a slice of America, with excellent performances. If it was an aberration, it remains a welcome one.

288
The Man Who Shot Liberty Valance

A tenderfoot becomes a hero for shooting a bad man, but the shot was really fired by his friend and protector.

John Ford's elegiac Western was conceived in a spirit of nostalgia. It marked the passing of the old West and the arrival of more civilized values that were replacing the pioneer spirit. The change was epitomized by the image of a stage-coach without wheels, while travellers arrived by train. James Stewart was the new man, who brought with him the spirit of learning and democracy. John Wayne was the old West; he rarely enters a domestic setting, remaining outside the door. It was also a celebration of myth over reality. Stewart insisted on a gun belt being put on the body of his friend, despite the fact that Wayne had not carried a handgun for many years. As the newspaper editor put it, 'when the legend becomes fact, print the legend.'

Amadeus
US   1984   160m   Technicolor   Panavision
Saul Zaentz

⧈ ⧈ ▤ ⓠ ⓖ ⓢ ⌒

w Peter Shaffer *play* Peter Shaffer *d* Miloš Forman *ph* Miroslav Ondricek *md* Neville Marriner *pd* Patrizia Van Brandenstein *ad* Josef Svoboda, Karel Cerny, Francesco Chianese *ed* Nena Danevic, Michael Chandler
☆ F. Murray Abraham (Antonio Salieri), Tom Hulce (Wolfgang Amadeus Mozart), Elizabeth Berridge (Constanze Mozart), Simon Callow (Emanuel Schikaneder), Roy Dotrice (Leopold Mozart), Christine Ebersole (Katerina Cavalieri)

'A major achievement, especially in films where genius is usually represented and dramatized as some kind of ill-humored, social eccentricity.' – *Vincent Canby*

'A visual and aural treat … an enjoyable, well-made movie of a seriousness currently lacking in our cinema.' – *Philip French, Observer*

● A director's cut, released in 2002, added 20m to the running time.
♟ picture; direction; F. Murray Abraham; adapted screenplay; make-up
♟ Tom Hulce; photography; editing; art direction
🎭 Miroslav Ondricek

287
Amadeus

Dying in 1823, the jealous composer Salieri claims to have murdered Mozart.

Peter Shaffer softened the hard edge of his play in adapting it for the cinema, but took full advantage of the scope that film provided in his drama of the musical and social competition between Mozart and the jealous Salieri. What was performed with economy on the stage became an exciting baroque film with spectacular images that was like an opera in high-pitched dialogue. Forman found that Mozart's music alone could make a dramatic point. He cut one scene in which Salieri sexually humiliated Constanze, Mozart's wife, after he studied Mozart's scores and realized his own inferiority. In the film, it was enough for Mozart's music to be heard: it, wrote Forman in his memoir, 'suddenly flattened the fine, titillating scene of high drama into a petty, anticlimactic redundancy'.

Jeux Interdits

France 1952 84m bw
Robert Dorfmann (Paul Joly)
🎧
aka: *Forbidden Games*
aka: *The Secret Game*

w Jean Aurenche, Pierre Bost *novel* François Boyer
d René Clément *ph* Robert Julliard *m* Narciso Yepes
ad Paul Bertrand *ed* Roger Dwyre
☆ *Brigitte Fossey* (Paulette), *Georges Poujouly* (Michel
Dolle), Amédée (Francis Gouard), Laurence Badie (Berthe
Dolle), Jacques Marin (Georges Dolle), Suzanne Courtal
(Mme Dolle), Lucien Hubert (Dolle, the Father)

'A truly imposing achievement of blending several
seemingly unrelated elements into a totally
meaningful whole.' – *John Simon, 1967*

👤 foreign film
⚖ François Boyer (original story)
Ⓥ picture

286
Jeux Interdits

*During World War II, an orphaned five-year-old girl from Paris seeks
refuge from the Nazis with a peasant family.*

René Clément deliberately chose unknown actors for this poignant
anti-war film, set in 1940, about childhood loss and adult betrayal: after
a little Parisian girl sees her fleeing parents killed by Nazi aircraft, she
takes refuge with a peasant family, whose young son helps her to bury
a dead puppy. They make a game of building a cemetery for dead animals, which leads to a village feud and the girl being sent to an orphanage. Clément, who used with great sensibility the delicate vulnerability
of Brigitte Fossey as the girl, wonderfully creates a child's view of the
world, whose games provide a momentary consolation in face of what
the director called the greatest of all forbidden games – war. In the final
moments, as the inconsolable little girl waits at the railway station for
the train to the orphanage, the camera sweeps up and away to show
her lost in a crowd of refugees.

The Killing Fields

GB 1984 141m colour
Goldcrest/Enigma (*David Puttnam*)
📷 ▬ 🎞 ⊙ ⊚ 🎧
w Bruce Robinson, from the article 'The Death and Life of
Dith Pran' by Sidney Schanberg *d* Roland Joffé *ph* Chris
Menges *m* Mike Oldfield *pd* Roy Walker *ad* Steve
Spence, Roger Murray Leach *ed* Jim Clark
☆ *Sam Waterston* (Sidney Schanberg), *Haing S. Ngor*
(Dith Pran), John Malkovich (Al Rockoff), Julian Sands (Jon
Swain), Craig T. Nelson (Military Attache)
👤 Haing S. Ngor (supporting actor); photography; editing
⚖ best picture; Sam Waterston; adapted screenplay; Roland
Joffe
Ⓥ best picture; adapted screenplay; Haing S. Ngor
(supporting actor)

285
The Killing Fields

*An American journalist is engulfed in the horror of Cambodia, and his
native adviser disappears and is thought to be dead.*

Ronald Joffé's brilliantly filmed true adventure tells a story of war and
heroism without resorting to the clichés of action movies: when Sidney
Schanberg, an American journalist, flees the country as the Khmer
Rouge take over, Dith Pran, his native adviser, stays behind and disappears. Schanberg fails to discover what happened to Pran until, four
years later, Pran turns up in a refugee camp, having survived by working as a peasant. Joffé does not flinch, though his audience may, at the
horror of modern war and the brutal regime of the Khmer Rouge. Amid
the slaughter and the destruction of a country, the story of a friendship
provides a momentary comfort.

La Beauté du Diable

Italy/France   1949   96m   bw

AYJM

w René Clair, Armand Salacrou *d* René Clair *ph* Michel Kelber *m* Roman Vlad *ad* Léon Barsacq *ed* James Cuenet

☆ *Michel Simon* (Prof. Faust/Mephisto), *Gérard Philipe* (Young Faust), Raymond Cordy (Servant), Nicole Besnard (Marguerite), Gaston Modot (Gypsy), Paolo Stoppa (Official)

284
La Beauté du Diable

The Faust story with the protagonists agreeing to change places.

In this richly enjoyable fantasy an ageing alchemist, regretting that he has still not explored science enough, is made young again by Mephistopheles, who takes on the appearance of the elderly Faust. But the young Faust decides that women are more interesting than learning. Gérard Philipe and Michel Simon are both at their considerable best in Clair's display of dazzling plot twists and cinematic virtuosity.

The Army in the Shadows

France/Italy   1969   143m   colour

Films Corona/Fono Roma (Jacques Dorfman)

original title: *L'Armée Des Ombres*

wd Jean-Pierre Melville *novel* Joseph Kessel *ph* Pierre l'Homme *m* Eric de Marsan *ad* Théobald Meurisse *ed* Françoise Bonnot

☆ Lino Ventura (Philippe Gerbier), Simone Signoret (Mathilde), Jean-Pierre Cassel (Jean Francois), Paul Meurisse (Luc Jardie), Claude Mann (Le Masque), Paul Crauchet (Felix), Christian Barbier (Le Bison)

283
The Army in the Shadows

A group of Resistance fighters in Lyon try to discover the traitors in their midst.

Jean-Pierre Melville brought his skills as a director of thrillers to this wartime story. A moving, harrowing and, in its depiction of a bungled execution, horrific account of the French Resistance at work, it is notable for the excellence of the direction and acting. Pierre l'Homme's photography maintains a subdued palette in keeping with the sombre narrative. Based on Joseph Kessel's documentary novel, Melville's drama concerns the early days of the French Resistance and the efforts of a group to rescue a member who is arrested by the Gestapo and to deal with those who are betraying them to the Nazis. Melville takes a low-key approach, showing the day-to-day activities of the group without false heroics, which makes the action, and the eventual fate of the resistance fighters, all the more affecting.

'Suspense and shock beyond anything you have ever seen or imagined!'

The Birds
US   1963   119m   Technicolor
Universal/Alfred Hitchcock
▭ ▣   ◎   ◉   ◉
w Evan Hunter story Daphne du Maurier d Alfred Hitchcock ph Robert Burks m Bernard Herrmann pd Robert Boyle ed George Tomasini sp Lawrence A. Hampton, Ub Iwerks sound consultant Bernard Herrmann cos Edith Head
☆ Rod Taylor (Mitch Brenner), Tippi Hedren (Melanie Daniels), Jessica Tandy (Lydia Brenner), Suzanne Pleshette (Annie Hayworth), Ethel Griffies (Mrs Bundy), Charles McGraw (Sebastian Sholes), Ruth McDevitt (Mrs MacGruder), Doodles Weaver (Fisherman)

''The dialogue is stupid, the characters insufficiently developed to rank as clichés, the story incohesive.' – Stanley Kauffmann

'We must sit through half an hour of pachydermous flirtation between Rod and Tippi before the seagull attacks, and another fifteen minutes of tedium … before the birds attack again. If one adds later interrelations between mother, girlfriend and a particularly repulsive child actress, about two-thirds of the film is devoted to extraneous matters. Poe would have been appalled.' – Dwight MacDonald

282
The Birds

In a Californian coastal area, flocks of birds unaccountably make deadly attacks on human beings.

Hitchcock's thriller is a curiously absorbing work. It begins as light comedy and ends as apocalyptic allegory. For once, Hitchock did without music, though Herrmann was responsible for scoring electronically the birds' songs and shrieks. Robert Boyle's production design was inspired by Edvard Munch's bleak painting *The Scream*. The resulting piece of Hitchcockery has no visible point except to tease the audience and provide plenty of opportunity for shock, offbeat humour and special effects (which despite the drumbeating are not quite as good as might be expected). The actors are pawns in the master's hand.

'Ever get the feeling you're being watched?'

Todo Sobre Mi Madre
Spain/France   1999   101m   colour
Panavision
Pathé/El Deseo/France2/Via Digital (Agustin Almodovar)
▭ ▣   ◎   ◎   ◠
aka: *All About My Mother*
wd Pedro Almodóvar ph Affonso Beato m Alberto Iglesias ad Antxon Gomez ed Jose Salcedo
☆ Cecilia Roth (Manuela), Eloy Azorin (Esteban), *Marisa Paredes* (Huma Rojo), Penelope Cruz (Sister Rosa), Candela Pena (Nina), *Antonia San Juan* (La Agrado), Rosa Maria Sarda (Rosa's Mother), Toni Canto (Lola, La Pionera)

'Weaves a silky web of emotional truths wrapped up in a shimmering cascade of glossy photography, glamorous close-ups and glorious acting from the cream of Spanish cinema.' – Alan Jones, Film Review

🚶 foreign film
🏆 Pedro Almodóvar (as director); foreign film

281
Todo Sobre Mi Madre

After the death of her teenage son, an actress and single mother goes in search of the boy's father, a transsexual prostitute.

Drawing on the themes of *All About Eve* and *A Streetcar Named Desire*, Pedro Almodóvar details an enthralling melodrama of love and death. It is a film about the difference between real and imagined emotions, of the kindness of strangers and the waywardness of life. Almodovar uses the collision of extremes to add an irrepressible excitement to his story. Both fathers in the drama are forgetful, one unable to recognize his daughter, the other having no memory of his son. Characters who display sexual confusion are contrasted with those who have confidence in their gender, a dead son is replaced by a live baby, the artifice of theatrical emotion is contrasted with the reality of actual feelings, though both often approach states of extreme drama.

'The Egos. The Battles. The Words. The Music. The Women. The Scandal. Gilbert & Sullivan & So Much More'

Topsy-Turvy
GB 1999 160m colour
Pathé/Thin Man/Greenlight Fund/Newmarket (Simon Channing-Williams)
🎦 📺 ⦿ ⦿ 🎧
wd *Mike Leigh* ph *Dick Pope* m Carl Davis, based on the works of Arthur Sullivan *md* Gary Yershon *pd Eve Stewart ed* Robin Sales *cos* Lindy Hemming
☆ *Jim Broadbent* (W.S. Gilbert), Allan Corduner (Sir Arthur Sullivan), Lesley Manville (Lucy Gilbert), Eleanor David (Fanny Ronalds), Ron Cook (Richard D'Oyly Carte), Timothy Spall (Richard Temple), Martin Savage (Grossmith), Lely (Kevin McKidd), Shirley Henderson (Leonora Braham), Jessie Bond (Dorothy Atkinson), Wendy Nottingham (Helen Lenoir)

''An overlong, overdressed and over-indulgent re-creation of an over-familiar story.' – *Alexander Walker, London Evening Standard*

● A Region 2 DVD release includes commentary by Mike Leigh.
👤 Lindy Hemming; make-up (Christine Blundell, Trefor Proud)
👤 Mike Leigh (as writer); Eve Stewart
📺 make-up/hair (Christine Blundell)

Topsy-Turvy

Gilbert and Sullivan clash over the creation of a new operetta.

Mike Leigh's detailed account of the trials and tribulations behind Gilbert and Sullivan's creation of *The Mikado* is an engrossing, witty and colourful drama. It concentrates on a clash between three giant egos, of writer, composer and producer, but takes time to explore the characters of those involved. It also provides an entertaining glimpse of backstage life and rivalries within a social and political context. The pair face a professional crisis, though their private lives are also in turmoil. Their last production was a failure and they need to find new inspiration: Gilbert's solution comes by way of a Japanese exhibition that allows him to add a newly fashionable exoticism to his libretto. Leigh explores not only creativity but also British responses to, and appropriations of, other cultures in an exuberantly acted, multi-layered extravaganza.

In the Mood for Love

Hong Kong   2000   97m   colour
Metro Tartan/Block 2/Paradis/Jet Tone (Wong Kar-wai)

original title: *Huayang Nianhua*
wd *Wong Kar-wai* *ph* Christopher Doyle, Mark Li Ping-bing   *m* Michael Galasso, Umebayashi Shigeru
pd *William Chang* *ad* Man Lim-chung, Alfred Yau   *ed* William Chang
☆ *Tony Leung Chiu-wai* (Chow Mo-wan), *Maggie Cheung* (Su Li-zhen), Lai Chin (Mr Ho), Rebecca Pan (Mrs Suen), Siu Ping-lam (Ah-ping)

'Dazzles with a heady atmosphere of romantic melancholy and ravishing visuals straight out of a Sixties Vogue spread but neglects to construct the kind of dramatic complexity to provide any lasting emotional resonance.' – *David Rooney, Variety*

● Tony Leung won the Best Actor award at the Cannes Film Festival in 2000 for his performance.

279
In the Mood for Love

In Hong Kong in the early 1960s, a newspaper editor and a secretary form a tentative relationship after they discover that their respective partners are having an affair.

Wong Kar-wai's sad drama, set in Hong Kong in the early 1960s, is almost a Chinese version of *Brief Encounter*. A delicate, subdued study in unrequited love, in which the reluctant couple almost merge into the background of a life that is long gone; it has about it an affecting air of broken-hearted nostalgia.

Angi Vera

Hungary   1978   93m   Eastmancolor
Mafilm/Objektiv

English title: *The Education of Vera*
wd *Pál Gábor* *story* Endre Vészi   *ph* Lajos Koltai
m György Selmeczi   *ad* Andras Gyorky   *ed* Éva Karmentö
☆ *Veronika Papp* (Vera Angi), Erzsi Pásztor (Anna Trajan), Eva Szabó (Maria Muskat), Tamás Dunai (Istvan Andre), László Horváth (Josef Neubauer)

278
Angi Vera

In the late Forties, an idealistic 18-year-old girl becomes a dedicated Communist Party worker and learns that betrayal is part of the system.

A courageous film when it was made, Pál Gábor's drama remains a deft and moving examination of the totalitarian mind-set, expressed in human terms. Gábor, who died relatively young from heart problems, was a humanist, more interested in people than dogma, and reveals here the wintry drabness of a totalitarian state, where fear of exposure is constant; but he also allows characters to blossom in individual ways.

'Eve Sure Knows Her Apples!'
The Lady Eve
US   1941   97m   bw
Paramount (Paul Jones)
▬ ◔ ◉

wd Preston Sturges *play* Monckton Hoffe *ph* Victor Milner *m* Leo Shuken, Charles Bradshaw *ad* Hans Dreier, Ernst Fegte *ed* Stuart Gilmore

☆ *Barbara Stanwyck* (Jean Harrington), *Henry Fonda* (Charles Pike), *Charles Coburn* ("Colonel" Harry Harrington), *Eugène Pallette* (Mr. Pike), William Demarest (Muggsy-Ambrose Murgatroyd), Eric Blore (Sir Alfred McGlennan Keith), Melville Cooper (Gerald), Martha O'Driscoll (Martha), Janet Beecher (Mrs. Pike), Robert Greig (Burrows), Luis Alberni (Pike's Chef), Jimmy Conlin (Steward)

'This time Preston Sturges has wrapped you up another package that is neither very big nor very flashy, but the best fun in months.' – *Otis Ferguson*

'The brightest sort of nonsense, on which Preston Sturges' signature is written large. The result has a sustained comic flavour and an individual treatment that are rarely found in Hollywood's antic concoctions.' – *New York Herald Tribune*

'A more charming or distinguished gem of nonsense has not occurred since *It Happened One Night*.' – *New York Times*

Ω Monckton Hoffe (original story)

Turkish Delight
Netherlands   1973   106m   colour
Columbia-Warner/Rob Houwer (Mia van't Hof)
▥ ▬ ◉ ◉

original title: *Turks Fruit*
w Gerard Soeteman *novel* Jan Wolkers *d* Paul Verhoeven *ph* Jan de Bont *m* Rogier van Otterloo *ad* Ralf van der Elst *ed* Jan Bosdriess

☆ Monique van de Ven (Olga Stapels), Rutger Hauer (Eric Vonk), Tonny Huurdeman (Olga's mother), Wim van den Brink (Olga's father), Dolf de Vries (Paul)

'Repulsive and meaningless' – *Clyde Jeavons, MFB*

'Underscored by a romanticism which slowly accumulates as time goes by. The difficulties of combining scatology and tenderness are neatly handled.' – *Derek Elley, Films and Filming*

● It was the winner of the Best Dutch Film of the Century at the 1999 Nederlands Film Festival.
Ω foreign film

277
The Lady Eve

A lady cardsharper and her father are outsmarted on a transatlantic liner by a millionaire simpleton; she plans an elaborate revenge.

The title of the film gives away the fact that Sturges's hectic romantic farce was a variation on the story of the Garden of Eden, about paradise lost and found. It was the first feature to show its director's penchant for mixing up sexual innuendo, funny men and pratfalls. After being outsmarted, the lady cardsharper impersonating an English Lady seduces the millionaire into marriage. Sturges said of Stanwyck that she 'had an instinct so sure that she needed almost no direction'; she returned the compliment by giving a perfect performance in the title role as a tough but vulnerable woman. It is scintillating entertainment.

276
Turkish Delight

A promiscuous young sculptor marries unhappily but falls in love with his wife again during her terminal illness.

Paul Verhoeven's scabrous satire on Dutch middle-class attitudes was combined with shock tactics and as much sex as the director could get past the censor and was a box-office success in Holland. Rutger Hauer is charismatic as the establishment-baiting artist, allowing genuine emotion to show through his teasing of convention. From the opening moments of a double murder, which turns out to be a violent fantasy of Hauer's sculptor, followed by his masturbation over his former wife's photograph and his love-making to a casual pickup amid the squalor of his studio, Verhoeven displays his hero's exuberant desire to offend middle-class sensibilities. But the film also encompasses feelings of tenderness, and never more so than in its final moments.

Les Diaboliques

France 1954 114m bw
Filmsonor (Henri-Georges Clouzot)
😎 🔊 ◎ ⊙ ⊙
aka: *Diabolique*
GB title: *The Fiends*

w Henri-Georges Clouzot, G. Geronimi *novel The Woman Who Was* by Pierre Boileau and Thomas Narcejac *d Henri-Georges Clouzot ph* Armand Thirard *m* Georges Van Parys *ad* Leon Barsacq *ed* Madeleine Gug
☆ Simone Signoret (Nicole Horner), Vera Clouzot (Christina Delasalle), Charles Vanel (Inspector Fichet), Paul Meurisse (Michel Delasalle)

'Scary, but so calculatedly sensational that it's rather revolting.' – *New Yorker, 1978*

'It depends very much on the intimate details of the seedy fourth-rate school, with its inadequate education and uneatable food, its general smell of unwashed children, hatred and petty perversions.' – *Basil Wright, 1972*

● Remade in 1976 as a TV movie, *Reflections of Murder.*

275
Les Diaboliques

A sadistic headmaster's wife and mistress conspire to murder him; but his body disappears and evidence of his presence haunts them.

Henri-Georges Clouzot's highly influential, suspenseful and scary thriller has become a minor classic. Slow to start and shabby-looking, as befits its grubby setting of a boarding school for boys, it gathers momentum with the murder and turns the screw with fine professionalism. The much-copied twist was typical of its authors and will still fool an audience seeing it for the first time. Its other qualities, of bleak humour and a disquieting view of human nature, skilfully presented survive subsequent viewings.

The Dresser

GB 1983 118m colour
Columbia/Goldcrest/World Film Services (Peter Yates)
🔊 ◎
w Ronald Harwood *play* Ronald Harwood *d* Peter Yates *ph* Kelvin Pike *m* James Horner *pd* Stephen Grimes *ad* Colin Grimes *ed* Ray Lovejoy
☆ *Albert Finney* (Sir), *Tom Courtenay* (Norman), Edward Fox (Oxenby), Zena Walker (Her Ladyship), Eileen Atkins (Madge), Michael Gough (Frank Carrington), Betty Marsden (Violet Manning), Lockwood West (Geoffrey Thornton)

'The best sort of drama, fascinating us on the surface with colour and humour and esoteric detail, and then revealing the truth underneath.' – *Roger Ebert*

'It is not an American picture; it is not like *42nd Street*. It is British and therefore tells a tale not of effortless overnight success but of day by day humiliation and defeat … It is utterly joyless. I can only claim that it tells its grim tale with sparks of humor and in merciless detail.' – *Quentin Crisp*

🏆 best picture; Tom Courtenay; Albert Finney; Peter Yates as director; Ronald Harwood (adaptation)

274
The Dresser

An exhausted Shakespearean actor-manager has a wild last day on tour, comforted and restrained by his homosexual dresser.

The interplay of Albert Finney, as an exhausted Shakespearean actor-manager, and Tom Courtenay, as his homosexual dresser, at the end of a tour was the greatest delight of this intensely theatrical film. Sir, as the dresser calls him, bears some resemblance to Sir Donald Wolfit, a great but unfashionable actor who was closer in temperament to Victorian actor-managers than his contemporaries. (Ronald Harwood, who wrote the screenplay and the original play on which it was based, was Wolfit's dresser for a time and his biographer.) Finney has a wonderful orotund and imperious manner, enough for one shout to halt a train as it leaves a station without him. Courtenay flutters around him beautifully, like a moth to a large flame. It is a pleasure for anyone interested in theatre, or in the intimacies of an affecting relationship.

The Big Sleep

US   1946   114m   bw
Warner (Howard Hawks)
🔲 ▬ ▧ ⌾ ⌾

w William Faulkner, Leigh Brackett, Jules Furthman
novel Raymond Chandler d Howard Hawks ph Sid
Hickox m Max Steiner ad Carl Jules Weyl ed Christian
Nyby

☆ Humphrey Bogart (Philip Marlowe), Lauren Bacall
(Vivian Sternwood Rutledge), John Ridgely (Eddie Mars),
Martha Vickers (Carmen Sternwood), Dorothy Malone
(Proprietress), Regis Toomey (Bernie Ohls), Charles
Waldron (General Sternwood), Charles D. Brown (Norris),
Elisha Cook Jnr (Harry Jones), Louis Jean Heydt (Joe
Brody), Bob Steele (Canino), Peggy Knudsen (Mona Mars),
Sonia Darrin (Agnes)

'A sullen atmosphere of sex saturates the film,
which is so fast and complicated you can hardly
catch it.' – Richard Winnington

'A violent, smoky cocktail shaken together from
most of the printable misdemeanours and some
that aren't.' – James Agee

'Harder, faster, tougher, funnier and more laconic
than any thriller since.' – NFT, 1974

'Wit, excitement and glamour in generous doses.'
– Francis Wyndham

● Remade Britain in 1977.

273

The Big Sleep

*Private eye Philip Marlowe is hired to protect General Sternwood's
wild young daughter from her own indiscretions, and finds several
murders later that he has fallen in love with her elder sister.*

An inextricably complicated, moody thriller from a novel whose author
claimed that even he did not know 'who done it'. Humphrey Bogart is
at his peak as laconic private eye Philip Marlow and the film is arguably
the best adaptation of a Raymond Chandler novel. The scenes between
Bogart and Bacall, made at the time before they married, have a palpable sexual charge. The film is vastly enjoyable for its slangy script, star
performances and outbursts of violence, suspense and sheer fun.

Sanger Fran Andra Vaningen

Sweden/France/Denmark/Norway/Germany   2000
99m   colour
ICA/Roy Andersson/Sveriges TV/Danmarks Radio/
Norsk Rikskringkasting/Arte France/SPDP/Essential/
Easy/ZDF/La Sept (Lisa Alwert)
🔲 ⌾
aka: Songs From the Second Floor
wd Roy Andersson ph Istvan Borbas, Jesper Klevenas
m Benny Andersson ed Roy Andersson cos Leontine
Arvidsson

☆ Lars Nordh (Kalle), Stefan Larsson (Stefan), Torbjörn
Fahlström (Pelle Wigert), Sten Andersson (Lasse), Lucio
Vucino (Magician), Hanna Eriksson (Mia), Peter Roth
(Tomas), Tommy Johansson (Uffe), Sture Olsson (Sven)

'Rapidly wears out its welcome after the first few
reels to finish up as a perplexing objet d'art.'
– Derek Elley, Variety

'Here is a film to try the patience of the nonbeliever, but astonish everyone else. Some might
find it a curate's egg of strangeness. But it's one of
the Fabergé variety.' – Peter Bradshaw, Guardian

'Audacious, offensive, original.' – Roger Ebert

272

Sanger Fran Andra Vaningen

A European city slips into barbarism during a financial crisis.

Swedish director Roy Andersson's film is an extraordinary work, set in
an unidentified European city, where financial experts fiddle with
unlikely solutions to an economic crisis while individuals suffer.

It looks unflinchingly but with a deadpan wit at the collapse of a
society built on wealth, and the desperate acts that result when the
money runs out: a woman walks the plank to her death while businessmen watch; a sacked worker clutches at the ankles of his boss, who
strides off dragging the man with him; a shopkeeper burns down his
furniture store, telling the insurance assessors that the piles of ash
were once valuable antiques. Andersson's surrealist satire proceeds by
discontinuous scenes that were shot in long takes with an immobile
camera that turn the action into a bizarre dream, a collaboration
between Karl and Groucho Marx.

My Childhood

GB 1972 48m bw
Connoisseur/BFI (Geoffrey Evans)

👓

wd Bill Douglas *ph* Mick Campbell *ed* Brand Thumim
☆ Stephen Archibald (Jamie), Hughie Restorick (Tommy),
Jean Taylor Smith (Grandmother), Karl Fieseler (Helmuth),
Paul Kermack (Jamie's Father), Helena Gloag (Father's
Mother)

'The story unfolds with pathos, tension and
considerable humour.' – *MFB*

My Ain Folk

GB 1973 55m bw
Connoisseur/BFI (Nick Nascht)

👓

wd Bill Douglas *ph* Gale Tattersall *ed* Peter West
☆ Stephen Archibald (Jamie), Hughie Restorick (Tommy),
Jean Taylor Smith (Grandmother), Bernard McKenna
(Tommy's Father), Mr Munro (Jamie's Grandad), Paul
Kermack (Jamie's Father), Helena Gloag (Father's Mother),
Jessie Combe (Father's Wife)

'A very considerable work of art, more profound,
more terrible and ultimately more inspiring than
My Childhood, all of whose virtues it shares.' –
Elizabeth Sussex, MFB

My Way Home

GB 1979 72m bw
BFI (Judy Cottam, Richard Craven)

👓

wd Bill Douglas *ph* Ray Orton *ad* Oliver Bouchier, Elsie
Restorick *ed* Mick Audsley
☆ Stephen Archibald (Jamie), Paul Kermack (Jamie's
father), Jessie Combe (Father's wife), William Carrol (Their
son, Archie), Morag McNee (Father's girl friend), Lennox
Milne (Grandmother), Gerald James (Mr. Bridge)

271
The Bill Douglas Trilogy

My Childhood

An eight-year-old boy lives with his half-brother and ailing grand-mother in dire poverty in a Scottish mining village.

My Ain Folk

Following the death of his maternal grandmother, a boy is reluctantly taken in by his father's mother until he goes away to an orphanage.

My Way Home

Leaving a children's home to become a miner and then a tramp, a young man's miserable life changes for the better when he is called up for National Service and goes to Egypt.

Bill Douglas's autobiographical trilogy began with *My Childhood* in which an eight-year-old boy lives with his ailing grandmother in dire poverty in a Scottish mining village. In *My Ain Folk*, the boy is reluctantly taken in by his father's mother following the death of his maternal grandmother, until he goes away to an orphanage. Finally in *My Way Home*, he leaves the children's home to become a miner and then a tramp; his miserable life changes for the better when he is called up for National Service and goes to Egypt. The bleakness and poverty of the lives depicted is told with an intense sympathy and a scrupulous honesty, which are mirrored by the directorial style – austere, spare, non-committal – to create a Calvinist masterpiece illumined by a little hope.

Little Caesar

US 1931 77m bw
Warner

▣ ▤ @~ ◎

w Francis Faragoh, Robert N. Lee *novel* W. R. Burnett
d Mervyn Le Roy *ph* Tony Gaudio *m* Erno Rapee
ad Anton Grot *ed* Ray Curtiss
☆ *Edward G. Robinson* (Cesare Enrico Bandello/'Little Caesar'), Douglas Fairbanks Jnr (Joe Massara), Glenda Farrell (Olga Strassoff), William Collier Jnr (Tony Passa), Ralph Ince (Diamond Pete Montana), George E. Stone (Otero), Thomas Jackson (Lt. Tom Flaherty), Stanley Fields (Sam Vettori), Sidney Blackmer (The Big Boy)

'It has irony and grim humour and a real sense of excitement and its significance does not get in the way of the melodrama.' – *Richard Dana Skinner*

'One of the best gangster talkers yet turned out … a swell picture.' – *Variety*

● Edward G. Robinson in reality was afraid of guns and had to have eyelids taped to prevent him from blinking every time he pulled the trigger.
♟ Francis Faragoh, Robert N. Lee

270
Little Caesar

The rise and fall of a vicious gangster.

Mervyn LeRoy's film had a central character clearly modelled on Al Capone and played with snarling gusto by Edward G. Robinson, who was forever identified with his role. LeRoy wanted the then unknown Clark Gable for the tough Joe Massara, but studio executives refused to sign him because they thought that his ears were too big. The film, though technically dated, moves fast enough to still maintain interest. It also has historical value as the vanguard of a spate of noisy gangster films in the 1930s.

The Loneliness of the Long Distance Runner

GB 1962 104m bw
British Lion/Bryanston/Woodfall (Tony Richardson)

▣ ▤ @~ ◎

w *Alan Sillitoe story* Alan Sillitoe *d* Tony Richardson
ph Walter Lassally *m* John Addison *ad* Ted Marshall
ed Anthony Gibbs
☆ *Tom Courtenay* (Colin Smith), Michael Redgrave (The Governor), James Bolam (Mike), Avis Bunnage (Mrs. Smith), Alec McCowen (Brown), Joe Robinson (Roach), Julia Foster (Gladys)
🎭 Tom Courtenay

269
The Loneliness of the Long Distance Runner

The only thing a Borstal boy does well is run, and as he trains he thinks back to his depressing life.

This is another of the British new wave's individual films of working-class life of the early 1960s. It is an unusual take on class war as the rebellious delinquent takes part in a climactic race against a team of public schoolboys. In his film debut, Tom Courtenay, scrawny with an expression like a clenched fist, contrasts wonderfully with the complacency of Michael Redgrave's governor. The film had the ideal cinematographer, creating images both lyrical and bleak, in Walter Lassally, who had worked on documentaries with such other new talents as Karel Reisz and Lindsay Anderson and had photographed *A Taste of Honey* for Tony Richardson.

'Much much more than a musical!'

Oliver!

GB 1968 146m Technicolor
Panavision 70
Columbia/Warwick/Romulus (John Woolf)

w Vernon Harris *play* Lionel Bart *novel Charles Dickens*
d Carol Reed ph Oswald Morris *m* Lionel Bart *md* John
Green *ch Onna White pd* John Box *ad* Terence Marsh
ed Ralph Kemplen

☆ *Ron Moody* (Fagin), Oliver Reed (Bill Sikes), Harry
Secombe (Mr. Bumble), Mark Lester (Oliver Twist), Shani
Wallis (Nancy), *Jack Wild* (The Artful Dodger), Hugh Griffith
(The Magistrate), Joseph O'Conor (Mr. Brownlow), Leonard
Rossiter (Mr. Sowerberry), Hylda Baker (Mrs. Sowerberry),
Peggy Mount (Widow Corney), Megs Jenkins (Mrs. Bedwin)

'Only time will tell if it is a great film but it is
certainly a great experience.' – *Joseph
Morgenstern*

♫ 'Food Glorious Food'; 'Where Is Love'; 'Boy for Sale';
'Consider Yourself'; 'You've Got to Pick a Pocket'; 'It's a Fine
Life'; 'I'd Do Anything'; 'Be Back Soon'; 'Who Will Buy'; 'As
Long As He Needs Me'; 'Reviewing the Situation'; 'Oom-
Pah-Pah'; 'Oliver'

🏆 best picture; Carol Reed; John Green; Onna White;
sound

🏆 Vernon Harris; Oswald Morris; Ron Moody; Jack Wild;
costumes (Phyllis Dalton); editing

268
Oliver!

A musical version of Oliver Twist.

Carol Reed's direction of this sing-a-long *Oliver Twist*, from Lionel
Bart's stage musical, does credit both to the show and the original
novel, though eclipsed in style by David Lean's straight version. Reed
had tried to buy the rights when the musical first opened in London,
but had been unable to afford them. He had wanted Shirley Bassey to
play Nancy; he was told that the murder of a black woman would not
play well in America. Otherwise, he got his own way with the casting,
including the incomparable Moody as Fagin. Reed's ability to inspire
child actors, and the excellent playing of the adult roles, resulted in a
richly satisfying film.

Early Summer

Japan 1951 125m bw
Shochiku

original title: *Bakushu*
w Kogo Noda, Yasujiro Ozu *d Yasujiro Ozu ph* Yuharu
Atsuta *m* Senji Ito *ad* Toshio Hamada *ed* Yoshiyasu
Hamamura

☆ *Setsuko Hara* (Noriko), *Chishu Ryu* (Koichi), Chikage
Awajima (Aya Tamura), Kuniko Miyake (Fumiko), Ichiro
Sugai (Shukichi), Chieko Higashiyama (Shige), Haruko
Sugimura (Tami Yabe)

267
Early Summer

*A family breaks up when the daughter rejects the man chosen as her
husband and marries someone else.*

Ozu's complex, compassionate, beautifully observed study of family
tensions involves three generations living together. The family members agree it is time the daughter, Noriko, married and they pick a suitable husband for her with the help of her boss. But she rejects him and,
on impulse, marries a childhood friend, the widowed son of a neighbour, who is about to leave to work in a distant province. Having lost
her income, the family breaks up and her parents have to move away.
The loss of tradition and the acceptance of what life brings lie behind
the action; much is left unspoken and unseen in this ensemble piece,
forcing its audience to ponder on the enigmatic dynamics of family life.

A One and a Two...

Taiwan/Japan 2000 173m Eastmancolor
ICA/1+2 Seisaku Iinkai/Pony Canyon/Omega/
Hakuhodo/Atom (Shinya Kawai, Naoko Tsukeda)
🎬 📷 📀
original title: *Yi Yi*
wd Edward Yang *ph* Yang Wei-han *m* Peng Kai-li
pd Peng Kai-li *ed* Chen Bo-wen
☆ Wu Nien-jen (NJ Jian), Elaine Jin (Min-Min), Issey
Ogata (Mr Ota), Kelly Lee (Ting-Ting), Jonathan Chang
(Yang-Yang), Chen Hsi-sheng (A-Di), Ko Su-yun (Sherry),
Michael Tao (Da-Da), Hsiao Shu-shen (Xiao Yan), Adrian
Lin (Lili)

> 'No narrative outline can hope to convey anything
> of the novelistic density of character and incident in
> Edward Yang's wonderful film.' – *Tony Rayns,
> Sight and Sound*

> 'A movie of formidable intelligence and
> observation, marbled with moments of magical
> abstraction.' – *Derek Elley, Variety*

● It won the Palme D'Or as best film at the Cannes Film
Festival in 2000.
— Region 1 and Region 2 DVD releases include
commentary with Edward Yang.

266
A One and a Two ...

A man with family and business problems contemplates what might have been when he meets a former girlfriend.

Edward Yang's sprawling saga coolly dissects three generations of a family that is going through a crisis. It begins at a wedding at which the bride is pregnant and the groom drunk, and concentrates on the problems of a middle-aged man whose computer firm is failing. While his mother-in-law lapses into a coma, his wife goes to a spiritual retreat, his daughter begins troubled relationships with boys and his son is in difficulties at school, he meets an old flame and wonders whether his life might have been different had he married, instead of abandoning, her. In a key moment, his eight-year-old son photographs the backs of people's head, to show them what they can not see. During the course of the narrative, the family begins to realize the value of those aspects of life that they have ignored. As the camera circles at a little distance from its characters, the film provides many pleasures, as well as insights into the human condition.

'I don't care what you do to me, Mike – just do it fast!'

'Blood red kisses! White hot thrills! Mickey Spillane's latest H-bomb!'

Kiss Me Deadly

US 1955 105m bw
UA/Parklane (Robert Aldrich)
🎬 📼 📷 📀
w A. I. Bezzerides *novel* Mickey Spillane *d* Robert Aldrich
ph Ernest Laszlo *m* Frank de Vol *ad* William Glasgow
ed Michael Luciano
☆ Ralph Meeker (Mike Hammer), Albert Dekker (Dr.
Soberin), Cloris Leachman (Christina Bailey/Berga Torn),
Paul Stewart (Carl Evello), Juano Hernandez (Eddie Yeager),
Wesley Addy (Pat Chambers), Maxene Cooper (Velda),
Gaby Rodgers (Gabrielle/Lily Carver)

> 'This meeting of "art" and pulp literature is, to say
> the least, curious.' – *MFB*

265
Kiss Me Deadly

By helping a girl who is nevertheless murdered, Mike Hammer prevents crooks from stealing a case of radioactive material.

An exuberant and harsh thriller set in an unlovely world and shot with brutal close-ups and unusual camera angles that create a disquieting effect. Based on Mickey Spillane's ugly thriller, it featured Ralph Meeker as a two-fisted private eye. Robert Aldrich never lets up the tension in what may be the ultimate *film noir*, stripped of any literary pretension and solely peopled by characters who are driven by dubious desires. Gaby Rodgers, in the last of her only two films, suggests a femme fatale who is not so much seductive as sick. The film is as unremittingly tough as its thuggish hero. Aldrich uses stark lighting and deep focus so that action seems to be happening in a theatrical space in which Spillane's characters act out their fears and fantasies. The ending, in which a woman's curiosity gets the better of her, so that she opens a deadly briefcase as if it were Pandora's box, remains justly famous.

'The shadow of this woman darkened their love.'

Rebecca
US   1940   130m   bw
David O. Selznick
📽 ▤ ▨ ◐ ◉ 🎧

w Robert E. Sherwood, Joan Harrison *novel* Daphne du Maurier *d* Alfred Hitchcock *ph* George Barnes *m* Franz Waxman *ad* Lyle Wheeler *ed* Hal C. Kern
☆ *Laurence Olivier* (Maxim de Winter), *Joan Fontaine* (Mrs. de Winter), *George Sanders* (Jack Favell), *Judith Anderson* (Mrs. Danvers), *Nigel Bruce* (Maj. Giles Lacy), *Gladys Cooper* (Beatrice Lacy), *Florence Bates* (Mrs. Van Hopper), *Reginald Denny* (Frank Crawley), *C. Aubrey Smith* (Col. Julyan), Melville Cooper (Coroner), Leo G. Carroll (Dr. Baker), Leonard Carey (Ben)

'Riveting and painful – a tale of fear and guilt, class and power.' – *Time Out, 1988*

● Original casting thoughts, all rejected, were Ronald Colman, William Powell and Leslie Howard for Maxim; Anne Baxter, Margaret Sullavan, Loretta Young, Vivien Leigh and Olivia de Havilland (for the second Mrs de Winter).
● A Region 1 two-disc DVD release includes commentary by film scholar Leonard J. Leff.
● Hitchcocl makes a cameo appearence near a phone box.
🏆 best picture; George Barnes
👤 script; Alfred Hitchcock; Franz Waxman; Laurence Olivier; Joan Fontaine; Judith Anderson; Lyle Wheeler; Hal C. Kern

264
Rebecca

The naive young second wife of a Cornish landowner is haunted by the image of his glamorous first wife Rebecca.

Daphne du Maurier's novel, became the supreme Hollywood entertainment package. Set in Monte Carlo and Cornwall, with generous helpings of romance, comedy, suspense, melodrama and mystery, Hitchcock added his own embellishments to the story: Manderley resembles a haunted house or where Norman Bates might live and strange shadows lie on the curtains in Rebecaa's bedroom. With strongly-drawn characters, and directed by the English wizard from a novel which sold millions of copies, it really could not miss, and it did not. In his first American film, Hitchcock was able to gather a cast of excellent actors, most of them British, although the Americans acquitted themselves well. Joan Fontaine, in the title role, gives her best performance as the naive newly-wed and her confrontations with Judith Anderson's Mrs Danvers are among the best moments in this Gothic romance.

The Ladykillers
🚹 GB 1955 97m Technicolor
Ealing (Michael Balcon)
📽 ▤ ◐ ◉ 🎧

w William Rose *d* Alexander Mackendrick *ph* Otto Heller *m* Tristram Cary *ad* Jim Morahan *ed* Jack Harris
☆ Alec Guinness (Professor Marcus), *Katie Johnson* (Mrs. Wilberforce), Peter Sellers (Harry), Cecil Parker (The Mayor), Herbert Lom (Louis), Danny Green (One-Round), Jack Warner (Police Superintendent), Frankie Howerd (Barrow Boy), Kenneth Connor (The Cab Driver)

'To be frivolous about frivolous matters, that's merely boring. To be frivolous about something that's in some way deadly serious, that's true comedy.' – *Alexander Mackendrick*

'The acting is triumphant … Artistically, I suspect, *The Ladykillers* needs a shade more of the macabre; it would be a better film if it were blacker. But I am beginning to find that I can see a joke better in twilight than midnight.' – *Dilys Powell*

● The role of Professor Marcus, played by Alec Guinness, was originally intended for Alistair Sim. It has been claimed, though Guinness has denied it, that his toothy appearance was based on the critic Kenneth Tynan who worked for Ealing as a script editor.
👤 William Rose
🏆 Katie Johnson; William Rose

263
The Ladykillers

An old lady takes in a sinister lodger who, with his four friends commits a robbery. When she finds out, they plot to kill her, but are hoist with their own petards.

A witty black comedy, shot in muted colours, which approaches the grotesque without damaging its acerbic humour or sense of fantasy. The old lady's decaying house at the end of a dull street was intended as a symbol of postwar Britain, with its ethos of muddling through. It is one of the few films where death is both shocking and funny. Ken Russell, looking back on British cinema, thought that it may have been the film that killed off the cosy tradition of Ealing comedies. 'If so,' he wrote, 'it was a glorious black way to go.' The performances are a joy, from the ensemble playing of the criminal gang to Katie Johnson, who had spent her long acting life in bit parts, as the indomitable old lady, whose innocence triumphs over wickedness. Alec Guinness' toothy academic mastermind is one of his finest comic portraits, at once sinister and benign.

The Wages of Fear

France/Italy 1953 140m bw
Filmsonor/CICC/Vera

original title: *Le Salaire de la Peur*
wd Henri-Georges Clouzot *novel* Georges Arnaud
ph Armand Thirard *m* Georges Auric *pd* Rene Renoux
ed Henri Rust, Madeleine Gug, Etienne Muse
☆ Yves Montand (Mario), Folco Lulli (Luigi), Peter Van
Eyck (Bimba), *Charles Vanel* (Jo), Vera Clouzot (Linda),
William Tubbs (Bill O'Brien)

'As skilful as, in its preoccupation with violence and
its unrelieved pessimism, it is unlikeable.'
– *Penelope Houston, Sight and Sound*

'It has some claim to be the greatest suspense
thriller of all time; it is the suspense not of mystery
but of Damocles' sword.' – *Basil Wright, 1972*

picture

262
The Wages of Fear

The manager of a Central American oilfield offers big money to drivers who will take nitroglycerine into the jungle to put out an oil-well fire.

Henri-Georges Clouzot's film is a masterpiece of suspense, and showed that France could make a big commercial thriller as well as anybody. After an extended introduction to the less than admirable characters, this fascinating film resolves itself into a shocker with one craftily managed bad moment after another. 'Art for me is provocation,' Clouzot once said, defending the cruelty often found in his films, though here the target is also exploitative corporations. The film was damagingly and extensively cut for its original American release. It was also disastrously remade by William Friedkin as *Sorcerer* in 1977.

'It begins with the scream of a train whistle – and ends with screaming excitement!'

Strangers on a Train
US   1951   101m   bw
Warner (Alfred Hitchcock)
📷 ▦ 🔍 ⊙ ◎ 🎧

w Raymond Chandler, Czenzi Ormonde *novel* Patricia Highsmith *d* Alfred Hitchcock *ph* Robert Burks *m* Dimitri Tiomkin *md* Ray Heindorf *ad* Ted Haworth *ed* William Ziegler
☆ Farley Granger (Guy Haines), *Robert Walker* (Bruno Antony), Ruth Roman (Anne Morton), Leo G. Carroll (Sen. Morton), Patricia Hitchcock (Barbara Morton), *Marion Lorne* (Mrs. Antony), Howard St John (Capt. Turley), Jonathan Hale (Mr. Antony), Laura Elliot (Miriam)

'You may not take it seriously, but you certainly don't have time to think about anything else.' – *Richard Mallett, Punch*

'The construction seems a little lame, but Hitch takes delight in the set pieces.' – *Time Out, 1985*

● Remade 1970 as *Once You Kiss A Stranger*.
● Hitchcock makes a cameo appearance boarding a train carrying a double bass.
♫ Robert Burks

261
Strangers on a Train

A tennis star is pestered on a train by a psychotic who wants to swap murders, and proceeds to carry out his part of the bargain.

This quirky melodrama has the director at his best, sequence by sequence, but the story is basically unsatisfactory. In his conversations with François Truffaut, Hitchcock pointed out that the flaws were the weakness of the final script – he found working with Raymond Chandler unsatisfactory – and the ineffectiveness of the two main actors. It is still superior suspense entertainment, however. Its theme of shared guilt between two contrasting personalities is a potent one; it is as if Dr Jekyll were to meet Mr Hyde and be compelled to associate with him. Hitchcock links the two men when they are far apart by cutting from one to the other, each copying or finishing the other's gesture or words. The film is about the mystery of the doppelganger, the dread other that haunts even the innocent.

WR – Mysteries of the Organism
Yugoslavia   1971   86m   colour
Neoplanta
📷 ▦

original title: *WR Misterije Organizma*
wd Dusan Makavejev *ph* Pega Popovic, Aleksandar Petkovic *ad* Dragoljub Ivkov *ed* Ivanka Vukasovic
☆ *Milena Dravic* (Milena), Ivica Vidovic (Vladimir Ilyich), Jagoda Kaloper (Jagoda), Tuli Kupferberg (US Soldier), Zoran Radmilovic (Radmilovic), Jackie Curtis (Herself), Miodrag Andric (Soldier)

'The point of view is so unstable that it seems to be more sophomoric than anything else.' – *Pauline Kael, New Yorker*

● The version released on video in Britain is the TV version 'improved by the author for Channel 4', which mainly meant that the scenes showing an erect penis – the first time an erection had been passed by the British Board of Film Censors for exhibition on the screen of a public cinema – were obscured by digital effects.

260
WR – Mysteries of the Organism

A free-wheeling exploration of the life and teachings of Wilhelm Reich.

The Serbian director Dusan Makavejev gained an international reputation with this witty, iconoclastic examination of sex and politics that juxtaposes the love affairs of a Russian skater with an examination of the life of psychoanalyst Wilhelm Reich, who suffered imprisonment and the burning of his books in America. He uses documentary techniques, newsreel footage and fiction to illuminate sexual attitudes in the USA and Yugoslavia in the late Sixties and early Seventies. To an extent it both exalts and demystifies sex; it also made sex funny and the notion that repression was bad, not only for the individual but for society as a whole. Makavejev examines what he regards as the pornography of power, the means by which those in authority control what others may see or do. He achieves his effects by masterly montage, cutting between documentary and fictional film to create a invigorating polemic.

'A big city cop who knows too much. His only witness – a small boy who's seen too much!'

Witness
US   1985   112m   Technicolor
Paramount/Edward S. Feldman

▭ ▆ ◷ ◉ ◉ ∩
w Earl W. Wallace, William Kelley *d* Peter Weir *ph* John Seale *m* Maurice Jarre *pd* Stan Jolley *ed* Thom Noble
☆ *Harrison Ford* (John Book), Kelly McGillis (Rachel), Josef Sommer (Schaeffer), Lukas Haas (Samuel), Jan Rubes (Eli Lapp), Alexander Godunov (Daniel Hochleitner)

'It's pretty to look at and it contains a number of good performances, but there is something exhausting about its neat balancing of opposing manners and values.' – *Vincent Canby*

🏆 editing; original screenplay
🏆 best picture; direction; Harrison Ford; photography; music; art direction
🏆 music

259
Witness

A young Amish boy witnesses a murder, and a big-city detective hides out in the community to protect him.

Peter Weir's gripping thriller was as much about the meeting of cultures as about cops and robbers. Harrison Ford's twentieth-century cop discovered the Amish sect whose life has remained unchanged since the eighteenth century. It was one of those lucky movies that works out well on all counts and shows that there are still craftsmen lurking in Hollywood. It is not only a thriller but also a love story and a modern-day version of the Western. The attraction that grows between Harrison Ford's beleaguered detective and Kelly McGillis' Amish widow is both delicately done and utterly believable, as both come to realize that there is no future for them together. Weir's film illumines the effects on a wider society of moral choices made by individuals.

'Imagine if you had three wishes, three hopes, three dreams and they all could come true.'

Aladdin
👥 US   1992   90m   Technicolor
Buena Vista/Walt Disney (John Musker, Ron Clements)

▭ ▆ ◷ ◉ ∩
w John Musker, Ron Clements, Ted Elliott, Terry Rossio *d* John Musker, Ron Clements *m* Alan Menken *m/ly* Alan Menken, Howard Ashman, Tim Rice *pd* R. S. Vander Wende *ed* H. Lee Peterson
☆ voices of: Scott Weinger (Aladdin), Brad Kane (Aladdin's singing), Robin Williams (Genie), Linda Larkin (Jasmine), Lea Salonga (Jasmine's singing), Jonathan Freeman (Jafar), Frank Welker (Abu/Narrator), Gilbert Gottfried (Iago), Douglas Seale (Sultan)

'Floridly beautiful, shamelessly derivative and infused with an irreverent, sophisticated comic flair.' – *Variety*

'A rollicking, bodaciously choreographed fantasy right out of Busby Berkeley.' – *Washington Post*

● It was followed by two sequels released direct to video: *Return of Jafar*, edited from an animated TV series, and *Aladdin and the King of Thieves*.
🏆 Alan Menken (score); song: 'Whole New World' (*m* Alan Menken, *ly* Tim Rice)
🏆 song: 'Friends like Me' (*m* Alan Menken, *ly* Howard Ashman); sound; sound effects editing

258
Aladdin

An urchin with a magic lamp falls in love with a runaway princess.

Disney's take on the familiar story was another brilliant return to classic form, with some innovative computer-generated animation. What made it especially memorable were the witty songs of Alan Menken and Howard Ashman, and its quick-change genie to match the free-flowing exuberance of Robin Williams' characterization. If Aladdin and his princess Jasmine are the usual bland teenage characters of Disney's movies, they are surrounded by a plethora of animated delights, including a flying carpet with attitude.

Heimat

West Germany   1984   924m   bw/colour
Edgar Reitz/WDR/SFB

aka: *Homeland*
w Edgar Reitz, Peter Steinbach   *d* Edgar Reitz   *ph* Gernot Roll   *m* Nikos Mamangakis   *ad* Franz Bauer   *ed* Heidi Handorf
☆ Marita Breuer (Maria), Michael Lesch (Paul Simon), Dieter Schaad (Paul), Karin Kienzler (Pauline), Eva Maria Bayerswaltes (Pauline), Rüdiger Weigang (Eduard), Karin Rasenach (Lucie)

257
Heimat

An epically conceived story of life in a German village between 1919 and 1982.

Edgar Reitz's production was essentially a very superior soap opera with pretensions of grandeur. It followed in eleven episodes the family of a blacksmith, and the fluctuating fortunes of his children, particularly the mayor's daughter, who married into the family, was abandoned by her husband and had several affairs before dying at the age of 82 in the last episode. Beautifully photographed, it had moments of magic amid much that was unexplained. Despite the symbolism and the irony (a village idiot is ever present), its audiences found that it had much to say, though no one could explain its lapses from colour to black-and-white and back again.

Le Boucher

France/Italy   1969   94m   Eastmancolor
La Boétie/Euro International (André Génoves)

aka: *The Butcher*
wd Claude Chabrol   *ph* Jean Rabier   *m* Pierre Jansen   *ed* Jacques Gaillard
☆ Stéphane Audran (Helene), Jean Yanne (Popaul), Antonio Passalia (Angelo), Mario Beccaria (Leon Hamel)

'A thriller, but a superlative example of the genre.'
– *Times*

256
Le Boucher

Murders in a small French town are traced to the inoffensive-seeming young butcher who is courting the local schoolmistress.

In Chabrol's curious, mainly charming film, the portrait of everyday village life at a time of crisis is full of sharp observation, and there is an intriguing contrast between Stéphane Audran's intelligent but introverted schoolteacher and Jean Yanne's earthy butcher. While Chabrol can not quite make up his mind whether he is filming an eccentric character study or a Hitchcock thriller, the film works on both levels. It is a study of damaged people and the damage they do to others. Audran's schoolteacher is emotionally distant, unable to commit herself to a relationship because of a past, unhappy love affair, Yanne's butcher is an overgrown child, haunted by the horrors he witnessed during his time as a soldier, and in love with her. Each fails the other in a thriller that offers no redemption.

Hannah and Her Sisters
US   1986   106m   Technicolor
Orion/Charles R. Joffe, Jack Rollins (Robert Greenhut)
📼 ▦ ◎~ ⓒ ⓞ
wd Woody Allen *ph* Carlo di Palma *m* popular and classical extracts *pd* Stuart Wurtzel *ed* Susan E. Morse
☆ Woody Allen (Mickey Sachs), Mia Farrow (Hannah), Dianne Wiest (Holly), Michael Caine (Elliot), Carrie Fisher (April), Barbara Hershey (Lee), Maureen O'Sullivan (Norma), Lloyd Nolan (Evan), Max von Sydow (Frederick), Daniel Stern, Sam Waterston (David), Tony Roberts (Mickey's ex-partner), Julie Kavner (Gail)

'A loosely knit canvas of Manhattan interiors and exteriors.' – *Sight and Sound*

'One of Woody Allen's great films.' – *Variety*

🏆 best original screenplay; Dianne Wiest; Michael Caine
🏆 best picture; Woody Allen (as director); Susan E. Morse; art direction
Ⓣ best original screenplay; direction

255
Hannah and Her Sisters

Relationships intermingle for a New York family over a two-year period between Thanksgiving dinners.

Even though it has nowhere in particular to go, and certain scenes are over the top, this is a brilliantly assembled and thoroughly enjoyable mélange of fine acting and New Yorkish one-liners, with particularly sharp editing and a nostalgic music score. It dealt in depth with more people than other of Allen's films. According to some, Allen modelled his characters on Mia Farrow's family, so that Maureen O'Sullivan was playing a role based on herself (it was one of her best performances). Allen later disliked the film's happy ending, but it worked and it is one that his characters have earned. Allen's examination of the lives of three sisters is acute. At the centre is the umarried Lee (Barbara Hershey), with whom her sister Hannah's husband Elliot (Michael Caine) is in love. A bewildered witness to it all is Hannah's former husband Mickey (Woody Allen), who observes the family's upheavals with a neurotic fascination and a disbelief in their pleasures.

'He'll Steal Your Heart!'
The Thief
Russia/France   1997   97m   colour
NTV Profit/Le Pont/Roissy (Igor Tolstunov)
📼 ▦ ⓞ
original title: *Vor*
wd Pavel Chukhrai *ph* Vladimir Klimov *m* Vladimir Dashkevich *pd* Victor Petrov *ed* Marina Dobrianskaja, Natalia Kucerenko
☆ Vladimir Mashkov (Tolyan), Ekaterina Rednikova (Katya), Misha Philipchuk (Sanya), Dima Chigarev (Sanya, 12 years-old), Amalia Mordvinova (Doctor's Wife), Lidia Savchenko (Baby Sanya)
🏆 foreign language film

254
The Thief

At the end of World War II, a fatherless boy gradually discovers that the soldier he and his mother love is a deserter, a cheat and a thief.

Pavel Chukhrai's film can be seen as a political fable about Stalin's own betrayals. Tolyan (Vladimir Mashkov) is a charmer who robs the poor, joining them in communal boarding houses, inviting them all out for a good time, and then returning to the empty house to rob them of their few possessions before he moves on. It is a compassionate, acutely observed study in love, betrayal and childhood disillusionment that also manages to find humour in painful situations. It is a tragedy of wasted emotion. Tolyan is loved by Katya, a widow with a young son, who becomes his accomplice in his thefts. She is unable to forget him and follows him even after he is arrested by the police. It results in her destruction and the likely ruin of her son. It is both a moving personal drama and an examination of a time of totalitarian mendacity.

'They'll take this town by storm …
fighting, laughing, loving, breaking every
law of the seven seas!'

Mutiny on the Bounty
US   1935   135m   bw
MGM (Irving Thalberg, Albert Lewin)

w Talbot Jennings, Jules Furthman, Carey Wilson
book Charles Nordhoff, James Hall *d* Frank Lloyd
ph Arthur Edeson *m* Herbert Stothart *ad* Cedric Gibbons,
Arnold Gillespie *ed* Margaret Booth
☆ *Charles Laughton* (Capt. William Bligh), *Clark Gable*
(1st Mate Fletcher Christian), Franchot Tone (Roger Byam),
Movita (Tehani), Dudley Digges (Bacchus), Henry
Stephenson (Sir Joseph Banks), Donald Crisp (Burkitt),
Eddie Quillan (Ellison), Francis Lister (Capt. Nelson),
Spring Byington (Mrs. Byam), Ian Wolfe (Maggs)

'Nothing to stand in the way of a box office
dynamite rating.' – *Variety*

'Incidents are made vivid in terms of the medium –
the swish and pistol crack of the lash, the sweating
lean bodies, the terrible labour, and the ominous
judgment from the quarterdeck.' – *Otis Ferguson*

● Remade in 1962 and in 1984 (as *The Bounty*)
🏆 best picture
🏆 script; Frank Lloyd; Herbert Stothart; Charles Laughton;
Clark Gable; Franchot Tone (whose role was originally to
have been played by Robert Montgomery); Margaret Booth

253
Mutiny on the Bounty

*An 18th-century British naval vessel sets off for South America, but
during a mutiny the captain is cast adrift and the mutineers settle in the
Pitcairn Islands.*

Charles Laughton's performance as a bullying, sadistic, repressive
Captain Bligh remains one of the best known of all screen performances;
it was to be endlessly parodied by two generations of comedians.
Laughton's acting is not diminished by these comic memories; he is monstrously believable and completely compelling (if he had played Captain
Ahab, he would have wiped the floor with Moby Dick). There was tension
between him and Clark Gable during filming which gave Gable's performance more of an edge than usual. The movie is a still-entertaining adventure film that seemed at the time like the pinnacle of Hollywood's
achievement.

Contempt
France/Italy   1963   103m   Technicolor
Franscope
Rome-Paris/Concordia/CCC (Carlo Ponti, Joseph E.
Levine)

original title: *Le Mépris*
wd Jean-Luc Godard *novel A Ghost at Noon* by Alberto
Moravia *ph* Raoul Coutard *m* Georges Delerue *ed* Agnès
Guillemot, Lila Lakshmanan
☆ Brigitte Bardot (Camille Javal), Michel Piccoli (Paul
Javal), Jack Palance (Jeremiah "Jerry" Prokosch), Fritz Lang
(Himself), Giorgia Moll (Francesca Vanini), Jean-Luc
Godard (Lang's Assistant Director)

'Portentous without having anything to say,
improvisatory without imagination, full of esoteric
references without relevance and in-group
allusions without interest. Its puppets behave with
meaningless meanness if not with sheer
meaninglessness.' – *John Simon*

● The disdain for producers shown in the film was
mirrored by real events: Godard had his name removed from
the Italian version owing to cuts imposed by the producers
and other changes, which included redubbing to remove the
different languages spoken by the participants, and a new
musical score by Piero Piccioni.

252
Contempt

*In Rome, a screenwriter has troubles with his wife as he tries to set up
a film of* The Odyssey *with a philistine American producer.*

Jean-Luc Godard's film is a clever and engrossing account of a marital
crisis and of film-making. In both of the enterprises, none of the princi-
pals are able to communicate with the others. Contempt is what
Camille (Brigitte Bardot) feels for her husband Paul (Michel Piccoli)
when it becomes clear that he is prepared to tolerate the possibility of
her affair with the American producer if it means he is hired to write the
script. Unease, too, came from Godard, who was pressed during filming by producers Carlo Ponti and Joseph E. Levine to show Bardot
naked. Part variation on Odysseus's Homeric homecoming and part a
contemplation of the compromises involved in filming, it is never less
than intriguing.

'Together For The First Time!'

It Happened One Night
US 1934 105m bw
Columbia (Frank Capra)

w *Robert Riskin* story *Night Bus* by Samuel Hopkins
Adams *d Frank Capra ph* Joseph Walker *md* Louis
Silvers *ad* Stephen Goosson *ed* Gene Havlick
☆ *Clark Gable* (Peter Warne), *Claudette Colbert* (Ellie
Andrews), Walter Connolly (Alexander Andrews), Roscoe
Karns (Oscar Shapeley), Alan Hale (Danker), Ward Bond
(Bus Driver), Jameson Thomas (King Westley), Arthur Hoyt
(Zeke)

'Something to revive your faith in a medium which
could belong among the great arts.' – *Robert
Forsythe*

'One of the most entertaining films that has ever
been offered to the public.' – *Observer*

● Remade 1956 (badly) as *You Can't Run Away From It.*
● Robert Montgomery was the first choice for the Gable
role, but he refused it because he had been on a bus in
Fugitive Lovers. The Colbert role was first offered to Myrna
Loy, Margaret Sullavan and Constance Bennett. Colbert was
lured by a $40,000 fee.
● Steven Spielberg paid $607,500 at a 1996 auction for
Clark Gable's Oscar, which he then presented to the
Academy of Motion Picture Arts and Sciences.
👤 best picture; Robert Riskin; Frank Capra; Clark Gable;
Claudette Colbert

251
It Happened One Night

*A runaway heiress falls in love with the reporter who is chasing her
across America.*

This is a highly influential romantic comedy, with Claudette Colbert and
Clark Gable at their best. It was the first film of its kind to use buses
and motels as background and still come up sparkling. It is a comedy
built on differences in class and expectations that found a ready audience in Depression America and has been kept alive by its witty take on
gender differences and the way both suspect the other of double-
dealing. The stars had the gift of empathy with their audience. 'If the
audience doesn't like your people, they won't laugh at them and they
won't cry with them,' as director Frank Capra rightly said. Its success
began the genre of screwball comedies that enlivened the Thirties and
Forties.

The Blood of a Poet

France 1931 58m bw
Vicomte de Noailles

original title: *Le Sang d'un Poète*
wd Jean Cocteau *ph* Georges Périnal *m* Georges Auric
ad Jean Gabriel d'Aubonne *ed* Jean Cocteau
☆ Lee Miller (Statue), Enrique Rivero (Poet), Pauline
Carton, Feral Benga, Jean Desbordes (Louis XV Friend),
Barbette, Odette Talazac

'It must be placed among the classic masterpieces
of the seventh art.' – *Revue du Cinéma*

Orphée

France 1949 112m bw
André Paulvé 1/Films du Palais Royal

wd Jean Cocteau *play* Jean Cocteau *ph* Nicolas Hayer
m Georges Auric *ad* Jean d'Eaubonne *ed* Jacqueline
Sadoul
☆ Jean Marais (Orpheus), François Périer (Heurtebise),
Maria Casarès (The Princess), Marie Déa (Eurydice),
Edouard Dermithe (Cegeste), Juliette Greco (Aglaonice)

'It is a drama of the visible and the invisible … I
interwove many myths. Death condemns herself in
order to help the man she is duty bound to
destroy. The man is saved but Death dies: it is the
myth of immortality.' – *Jean Cocteau*

• The film was dedicated to its designer Christian Bérard
(1902–49).

Le Testament d'Orphée

France 1959 83m bw
Editions Cinégraphiques (Jean Thullier)

aka: *The Testament of Orpheus*
wd Jean Cocteau *ph* Roland Pointoizeau *m* Georges
Auric and others *ad* Pierre Guffroy *ed* Marie-Josephe
Yoyotte
☆ Jean Cocteau (Himself, the Poet), Edouard Dermithe
(Cegeste), Maria Casarès (The Princess), François Périer
(Heurtebise), Henri Crémieux (The Professor), Yul Brynner
(The Court Usher), Jean-Pierre Léaud (The Schoolboy),
Daniel Gélin (The Intern), Jean Marais (Oedipus), Pablo
Picasso (Himself), Charles Aznavour (Himself)

The Blood of a Poet

Aspects of a poet's vision, taking place while a chimney is falling down.

Orphée

Death, represented by a princess, falls in love with Orpheus, a poet, and helps him when he goes into hell in pursuit of his dead love.

Le Testament d'Orphée

The poet, as an 18th-century man, dies, enters spacetime, is revived, and seeks his identity.

Cocteau identified with Orpheus, the mythic Greek poet who could charm everything with his music, in a play written when he was an opium addict, and *Orphée* resembles an opium dream: Death, represented by a princess, falls in love with Orpheus, a poet, and helps him when he goes into hell in pursuit of his dead love. It is the closest the cinema has come to poetry, with its memorable scenes and cinematic tricks, such as the entry to the hereafter through a mirror. *The Blood of the Poet*, crammed with striking images, is a blueprint for the later film, while the *Testament of Orpheus* is his defence of his artistic credo. None respond to literal examination. As Cocteau put it, 'if a housewife were given a literary work of art to rearrange, the end result would be a dictionary.'

Being There
US 1979 130m Metrocolor
Lorimar/North Star/CIP (Andrew Braunsberg)
▤ ▨ ▨ ▨

w Jerzy Kosinski *novel* Jerzy Kosinski *d* Hal Ashby
ph Caleb Deschanel *m* John Mandel *pd* Michael Haller
ad James Schoppe *ed* Don Zimmerman
☆ Peter Sellers (Chance), Shirley MacLaine (Eve Rand), *Melvyn Douglas* (Benjamin Rand), Jack Warden (President Bobby), Richard Dysart (Dr. Robert Allenby), Richard Basehart (Vladmir Skrapinov)

'It pulls off its long shot and is a confoundingly provocative movie.' – *Roger Ebert*

👤 Melvyn Douglas
☆ Peter Sellers
🏆 screenplay

249
Being There

An illiterate gardener is taken for a homespun philosopher and becomes a national celebrity.

Peter Sellers rarely had a role as good as Chance, the illiterate gardener who is taken for a homespun philosopher and becomes a national celebrity. There is a blankness about the character, as if waiting for others to force an identity upon him, that matched Seller's own personality, to which here he adds a touch of the comic unworldliness of Stan Laurel. Chance is someone whose knowledge of the world is taken entirely from television; out for the first time in a street he tries to use his TV's remote control to switch channels and so get rid of unpleasant people. Aided by Seller's imperturbable acting, Ashby and Kosinski make this one idea enough for a wonderfully satirical movie.

Death in Venice
Italy 1971 128m Technicolor Panavision
Warner/Alfa (Mario Gallo)
▣ ▤ ▨ ▨ 🎧

original title: *Morte a Venezia*
w Luchino Visconti, Nicola Badalucco *novel* Thomas Mann *d* Luchino Visconti *ph* Pasquale de Santis
m Gustav Mahler *md* Franco Mannino *ad* Ferdinando Scarfiotti *ed* Ruggero Mastroianni
☆ Dirk Bogarde (Gustav Von Aschenbach), Bjorn Andresen (Tadzio), Silvana Mangano (Tadzio's Mother), Marisa Berenson (Frau Von Aschenbach), Mark Burns (Alfred)

'Maybe a story as elusive as *Death in Venice* simply can't be filmed. Visconti has made a brave attempt, always sensitive to the original; but it's finally not quite the same thing.' – *David Wilson, MFB*

'Camp and miscalculated from start to finish ... a prime contender for the title Most Overrated Film of All Time.' – *Time Out, 1985*

👗 costumes (Piero Tosi)
🏆 Pasquale de Santis; Ferdinando Scarfiotti

248
Death in Venice

On holiday in Venice, a middle-aged composer becomes infatuated with a beautiful young boy.

Burt Lancaster, John Gielgud and Alec Guinness were among those who turned down the role of Mann's pathetic genius von Aschenbach before Visconti acquired the rights and persuaded Dirk Bogarde to play the part. The story was one of a comfortable middle-aged existence being wrecked by a self-destructive urge: how, in a lush Venetian hotel one summer in the early years of the century, a middle-aged German composer became infatuated with the charms of an angelic young boy and stayed in the city too long to escape the approaching plague. Bogarde's appearance was based on Gustav Mahler, whose behaviour had helped inspire the novella. Bogarde's part was a gruelling one, almost silent and requiring everything to be expressed by the eyes. Mahler's music adds a depth to this extended fable enriched by moments of great beauty and directorial style.

The Wizard of Oz

US 1939 102m Technicolor
MGM (Mervyn Le Roy)

w Noel Langley, Florence Ryerson, Edgar Allan Woolf *book* L. Frank Baum *d* Victor Fleming *ph* Harold Rosson *md* Herbert Stothart *ad* Cedric Gibbons, William A. Horning *ed* Blanche Sewell *songs* E. Y. Harburg, Harold Arlen

☆ *Judy Garland* (Dorothy), *Frank Morgan* (Prof. Marvel/The Wizard/Guard/Coachman), *Ray Bolger* (Hunk/The Scarecrow), *Jack Haley* (Hickory/The Tin Woodsman), *Bert Lahr* (Zeke/The Cowardly Lion), *Margaret Hamilton* (Miss Gulch/The Wicked Witch), Billie Burke (Glinda), Charley Grapewin (Uncle Henry), Clara Blandick (Auntie Em)

'There's an audience for it wherever there's a projection machine and a screen.' – *Variety*

'I don't see why children shouldn't like it, but for adults there isn't very much except Bert Lahr.' – *Richard Mallett, Punch*

'As for the light touch of fantasy, it weighs like a pound of fruitcake soaking wet.' – *Otis Ferguson*

● Ray Bolger was originally cast as the tin man but swapped roles with Buddy Ebsen who was to have been the scarecrow. Ebsen then got sick from the aluminium dust and was replaced by Jack Haley. Edna May Oliver was originally cast as the wicked witch. For Dorothy MGM wanted Shirley Temple

247
The Wizard of Oz

After a series of fantastic adventures, a young girl decides that there is no place like home.

MGM's classic fantasy was made notable by the performances of Judy Garland and the trio of Cowardly Lion (Bert Lahr), Scarecrow (Ray Bolger) and Tin Woodsman (Jack Haley). Its excellent score also helped. as did its story, in which unhappy Dorothy escapes from her home, has adventures in a fantasy land, but finally decides that happiness was in her own back yard all the time. The fairy tale is given vigorous straightforward treatment and adventurous art direction. The switch to Technicolor fantasy, after a sepia opening sequence, is a masterly touch ('I have a feeling we're not in Kansas any more,' says Dorothy as she steps out into Oz). Depite all the other pleasures, it is Garland's performance and her singing that has given the film its lasting appeal. As composer Harold Arlen put it, 'she sang not just to your ears, but to your tear ducts.'

Ugetsu Monogatari

Japan 1953 94m bw
Daiei (Masaichi Nagata)

w Matsutaro Kawaguchi, from 17th-century collection by Akinara Ueda, Tales of a Pale and Mysterious Moon after the Rain *d* Kenji Mizoguchi *ph* Kazuo Miyagawa *m* Fumio Hayasaka *ad* Kisaku Ito *ed* Mitsuji Miyata

☆ Masayuki Mori (Genjuro), Machiko Kyo (Lady Wukasa), Sakae Ozawa (Tobei), Mitsuko Mito (Ohama)

'Heavy going in spots, but with marvellous passages that are worth a bit of patience.' – *New Yorker*

246
Ugetsu Monogatari

During a civil war in the 16th century, two peasants seek their fortunes and bring disaster on their families.

Kenji Mizoguchi's film carries the subtitle 'Tales of the Pale Moon After a Rain', which suggests its delicate mix of the lyrical and the supernatural. Two peasants, a potter and his brother-in-law, a farmer, leave their village in search of fortune during troubled times. One seeks riches, the other to become a samurai; in the process both destroy their families. After a beautiful, wealthy woman admires his work, the potter falls in love with her and goes to live in her house, only discovering later that she is a ghost. The farmer becomes a warrior, but when he celebrates at a geisha house, he finds his wife has been forced to work there. These two cautionary tales both emphasize the weakness of men and the self-sacrifice of women and the redeeming power of their love. They are told in a wonderful visual style, notable for its fluidity, as the camera swoops around the action.

Boudu Sauvé des Eaux

France 1932 87m bw
Michel Simon/Jean Gehret
📧 🎬 ⊚

aka: *Boudu Saved from Drowning*

wd Jean Renoir *play* René Fauchois *ph* Marcel Lucien *m* from Raphael and Johann Strauss *ad* Jean Castanier, Hugues Laurent *ed* Marguerite Renoir

☆ *Michel Simon* (Boudu), *Charles Granval* (Monsieur Lestingois), Marcelle Hainia (Madame Lestingois), Séverine Lerczinska (Anne-Marie), Jean Dasté (Student), Jacques Becker (Poet on a Bench)

'A beautifully rhythmed film that makes one nostalgic for the period when it was made.' – *New Yorker, 1977*

● Remade 1985, more or less, as *Down and Out in Beverly Hills*.

245
Boudu Sauvé des Eaux

A scruffy tramp is not grateful for being rescued from suicide, and plagues the family who invite him to stay.

A minor classic of black comedy, interesting equally for its characterizations, its acting, and its film technique. Renoir delighted in the anarchic comedy of a scruffy tramp who was, he thought, the perfect hippy forty years before his time. Not even marriage can tame him, as he jumps out of the wedding party's boat to swim ashore, pinch clothes from a scarecrow and return to a disreputable life. This rejection of bourgeois concerns has a life-enhancing quality, while Michel Simon's grizzled performance as the tramp is in a class of its own.

Blue Velvet

US 1986 120m colour J-D-C Scope
De Laurentiis (Richard Roth)
📧 📧 🎬 ⊚~ ⊚ ◉ 🎧

wd David Lynch *ph* Frederick Elmes *m* Angelo Badalamenti *pd* Patricia Norris *ed* Duwayne Dunham

☆ Kyle MacLachlan (Jeffrey Beaumont), Isabella Rossellini (Dorothy Vallens), Dennis Hopper (Frank Booth), Laura Dern (Sandy Williams), Hope Lange (Mrs. Williams), Dean Stockwell (Ben)

'Horrifying in ways that genre horror movies never are … Lynch's nightmare has a sort of irregular, homemade quality, as if it had been cooked up with familiar but not entirely wholesome ingredients – a fresh apple pie with a couple of worms poking through the crust.' – *Terrence Rafferty, Nation*

⚐ David Lynch

244
Blue Velvet

Murder, mutilation and sexual perversion in Middle America.

In David Lynch's subversive film, a naïve man finds on some wasteland a severed ear – what Lynch once called 'a ticket to another world' – and is soon involved with a wan singer, a brutal psychopath and a detective's daughter. Lynch involves his audience in the voyeurism of his protagonist, who spends more time than most spying from cupboards. Frederick Elmes' photography emphasizes the contrast between the unnaturally bright colours of the outside world and the dark interiors, where shadows loom and obscure in this bizarrely stylish exercise. It is a small-town nightmare, a devastating examination of what horrors may lie behind neat white picket fences. It is also a warning to the curious. Kyle MacLachlan's ingenuous student inquisitiveness leads to his involvement in the activities of a sadistic sexual degenerate and a masochistic singer, Dorothy. Her name reveals the movie's gleeful deconstruction of *The Wizard of Oz*. Lynch shows there is no place like home, which is also no place to be.

Trainspotting

GB   1996   94m   colour
Polygram/Channel 4/Figment/Noel Gay (*Andrew Macdonald*)

▭▭ ▭▭ ▤ @▱ ▱ ∩

w John Hodge *novel* Irvine Welsh *d* Danny Boyle
ph Brian Tufano *pd* Kave Quinn *ad* Tracey Gallacher
ed Masahiro Hirakubo

☆ *Ewan McGregor* (Mark Renton), Ewen Bremner (Spud), Jonny Lee Miller (Sick Boy), Kevin McKidd (Tommy), *Robert Carlyle* (Begbie), Kelly Macdonald (Diane), Peter Mullan (Swanney), Irvine Welsh (Mikey)

'Spends far too much time with its nose pressed up against the glass of American cinema, desperate for a piece of the action, but merely fogging up the screen with longing. Until British cinema kicks this habit, it will continue to churn out films such as this, which bear the same relation to real film-making that drugs do to real pleasure. It's utterly empty: a cold turkey, despite the fancy trimmings' – *Tom Shone, Sunday Times*

'An extraordinary achievement and a breakthrough British film.' – *Derek Malcolm, Guardian*

• The film cost $3m and grossed more than $64 million worldwide.

👤 John Hodge
🎬 John Hodge

243
Trainspotting

A group of young Scots indulge in drugs and petty crime.

This adaptation of Irvine Welsh's novel was a dark and ironic take on young junkies at their antisocial worst, as four Scottish friends enjoy the highs, and suffer the lows, of heroin addiction, while indulging in petty theft, sex, booze and violence whenever they are capable of it. Directed by Danny Boyle with terrific energy and style, it was a witty subversion of the usual documentary approach to such subjects, and excellently acted by its ensemble cast. Boyle's stylized approach, which sometimes uses distorted visuals to suggest the effects of drug-taking, paid off brilliantly, allowing him to create a horribly effective scene from Ewan McGregor's dive into Edinburgh's filthiest toilet. It makes the group's rejection of conventional life seem almost heroic, because they are doomed to fail for all the usual reasons, despite their mantra, 'who needs reasons when you've got heroin?'

Brighton Rock

GB   1947   92m   bw
Associated British/Charter Films (Roy Boulting)

▭▭ ▤ @

US title: Young Scarface

w Graham Greene, Terence Rattigan *novel* Graham Greene *d* John Boulting *ph* Harry Waxman *m* Hans May *ad* John Howell *ed* Peter Scott

☆ Richard Attenborough (Pinkie Brown), Hermione Baddeley (Ida Arnold), *Harcourt Williams* (Prewitt), William Hartnell (Dallow), Alan Wheatley (Fred Hale), Carol Marsh (Rose Brown), Nigel Stock (Cubitt)

'The film is slower, much less compelling, and, if you get me, less cinematic than the book, as a child's guide to which I hereby offer it.' – *Richard Winnington*

'It proceeds with the efficiency, the precision and the anxiety to please of a circular saw.' – *Dilys Powell*

'False, cheap, nasty sensationalism … in my view, no woman will want to see it. No parents will want their children to see it.' – *Reg Whitley, Daily Mirror*

242
Brighton Rock

A young hoodlum decides to get rid of the waitress he married in order to prevent her giving evidence against him.

Graham Greene's 'entertainment' was given a properly seedy setting for his story of a teenage leader of a racetrack gang, who uses a waitress as alibi to cover a murder, marries her and later decides to be rid of her. It was very flashily done, with a trick ending which allowed the heroine to keep her illusions for a while. The Boulting Brothers filmed it on location in Brighton and, from the tense opening, captured an atmosphere of sleaze and easy money. Richard Attenborough was impressive as a nasty young thug with religious convictions, and Hermione Baddeley, as an end-of-the-pier entertainer, had all the bustle and vulgarity of the British seaside at its raucous best. Harry Waxman's photography makes Brighton almost another character, bringing to life its race course, concert parties, and shabby cafes of the time.

The Exterminating Angel
Mexico 1962 95m bw
Uninci Films 59 (Gustavo Alatriste)

original title: *El Angel Exterminador*
wd Luis Buñuel (story assistance from Luis Alcoriza)
ph Gabriel Figueroa *ad* Jesus Bracho *ed* Carlos Savage Jr.
☆ Silvia Pinal (Letitia–'The Valkyrie'), Enrique Rambal (Esmundo Nobile), Jacqueline Andere (Senora Alicia Roc), Jose Baviera (Leandro)

'An unsound and unsightly mixture of spurious allegory and genuine craziness.' – *John Simon*

241
The Exterminating Angel

Guests at a social event find that they are unable to leave the drawing room.

This is a fascinating surrealist fantasia on the theme of upper-class social rituals that was elaborated with even more panache in *The Discreet Charm of the Bourgeoisie*. Nevertheless, it is one of its director's key films, in which dinner guests find themselves unable to leave the room, stay there for days, and go totally to the bad before the strange spell is broken; when they go to church to give thanks, they find themselves unable to leave. Events are repeated during the film: people are introduced to one another several times. Luis Buñuel offers no explanation for his guest's paralysis of will, though it's possible to see it as the enervating result of conformist living, or the way people do repeat their actions day after day. It is best enjoyed for its bizarre qualities and black humour.

Morgan – A Suitable Case for Treatment
GB 1966 97m bw
British Lion/Quintra (Leon Clore)

US title: *Morgan!*
w David Mercer *play* David Mercer *d* Karel Reisz
ph Larry Pizer, Gerry Turpin *m* Johnny Dankworth
ad Philip Harrison *ed* Victor Proctor, Tom Priestley
☆ Vanessa Redgrave (Leonie Delt), *David Warner* (Morgan Delt), Robert Stephens (Charles Napier), Irene Handl (Mrs. Delt), Newton Blick (Mr. Henderson), Nan Munro (Mrs. Henderson)

'Poor Morgan: victim of a satire that doesn't bite, lost in a technical confusion of means and ends, and emerging like an identikit photograph, all bits and pieces and no recognizable face.' – *Penelope Houston*

'The first underground movie made above ground.' – *John Simon*

'I think Morgan is so appealing to college students because it shares their self-view: they accept this mess of cute infantilism and obsessions and aberrations without expecting the writer and director to resolve it and without themselves feeling a necessity to sort it out.' – *Pauline Kael*

Vanessa Redgrave
David Mercer

240
Morgan – A Suitable Case for Treatment

A young woman determines to leave her talented but half-mad artist husband, who has a fixation on gorillas and behaves in a generally uncivilized manner.

Morgan (David Warner), a gorilla-obsessed working-class artist attempts to prevent his middle-class wife from remarrying in Karel Reisz' frequently very funny movie, from an anarchic screenplay by David Mercer, one of Britain's leading playwrights of the Sixties, who often dealt with society's misfits. Morgan, whose mother regards him as a traitor to his class, booby-traps his wife's home to convince her that he still needs her, causes chaos at his ex-wife's wedding dressed as a gorilla, and ends up in an asylum. Reisz made of it an archetypal Sixties marital fantasy, an extension of *Look Back in Anger* in the mode of swinging London.

Southern Comfort
US   1981   106m   DeLuxe
EMI/Phoenix/Cinema Group Venture (David Giler)
◨ ▤ ◎ ⊘ ⊘
w Michael Kane, Walter Hill, David Giler *d* Walter Hill
ph Andrew Laszlo *m* Ry Cooder *pd* John Vallone
ed Freeman Davies
☆ Keith Carradine (Spencer), Powers Boothe (Hardin), Fred Ward (Reece), Franklyn Seales (Simms), T. K. Carter (Cribbs), Lewis Smith (Stuckey)

'As an action director Walter Hill has a dazzling competence. *Southern Comfort* comes across with such immediacy that it had a near-hypnotic hold on me and I felt startled – brought up short – when it ended.' – *Pauline Kael, New Yorker*

239
Southern Comfort

National Guardsmen on a routine exercise into swampland find themselves involved in a life-and-death struggle with the Cajun inhabitants.

Walter Hill's tough thriller puts some National Guardsmen in the Louisiana swamplands where they encounter hostile locals, the Cajuns, whom they have antagonized. Conflict soon develops. Andrew Laszlo's atmospheric photography brings out the sinister beauty of the swamps and Hill keeps the tension high. It is a brilliant, compelling, tightly-constructed thriller that manages also to be an allegory of American involvement in Vietnam.

Fantasia
↟↟ US   1940   135m   Technicolor
Walt Disney
◨ ▤ ◎ ⊘ ⊘ ◠
md Edward H. Plumb *supervisor* Ben Sharpsteen
☆ Leopold Stokowski, the Philadelphia Orchestra, Deems Taylor

'Dull as it is towards the end, ridiculous as it is in the bend of the knee before Art, it is one of the strange and beautiful things that have happened in the world.' – *Otis Ferguson*

'It is ambitious, and finely so, and one feels that its vulgarities are at least unintentional.' – *James Agate*

'Disney sometimes at his worst, often at his very best; and the best is on a level which no other cinematographic designer has reached. It takes over two hours, but somehow or other I'm afraid you will have to find the time.' – *Dilys Powell*

● Multiplane cameras, showing degrees of depth in animation, were used for the first time. The film was re-released in a print restored to its original freshness in 1990.
🏆 Special Award to Walt Disney, Leopold Stokowski

238
Fantasia

A concert of classical music is given cartoon interpretations.

Walt Disney's *Fantasia* was intended to give respectability to animation by marrying it to classical music. Disney later admitted that, while he did not regret making it, he would not do it over again. But it did offer some of his best animators the opportunity to demonstrate their skills with a greater freedom than a fairy tale would have provided. It is brilliantly inventive for the most part, especially in the dance of the Chinese mushrooms in 'The Nutcracker Suite', the low comedy of 'The Dance of the Hours' and Mickey Mouse as 'The Sorcerer's Apprentice'. The least part ('The Pastoral Symphony') can be forgiven.

Intolerance

US 1916 115m approx (24 fps) bw silent
D. W. Griffith

⊶ ▤ ◷ ◉ ◉

wd D. W. Griffith *ph* Billy Bitzer, Karl Brown *ad* Walter L. Hall *ed* Rose Smith, James Smith
☆ Mae Marsh (The Dear One), Lillian Gish (Woman Who Rocks the Cradle/Eternal Mother), Constance Talmadge (Marguerite de Valois/The Mountain Girl), Robert Harron (The Boy), Elmo Lincoln (The Mighty Man of Valour), Eugene Pallette (Prosper Latour)

'A mad, brilliant, silly extravaganza. Perhaps the greatest movie ever made. In it one can see the source of most of the major traditions of the screen: the methods of Eisenstein and von Stroheim, the Germans and the Scandinavians, and, when it's bad, de Mille.' – *New Yorker, 1980*

237
Intolerance

Four stories illustrate varieties of man's inhumanity to man over a period of two thousand years.

D. W. Griffith's grandiose epic, which at the time was by far the most expensive film ever made, deals with four stories – including Belshazzar's feast and the massacre of St Bartholomew – of intolerance through the ages, which are intercut and linked by the image of a mother and her baby, 'out of the cradle, endlessly rocking'. It was a massive enterprise of which audiences at the time and after were quite intolerant. Hard to take in parts, it is often ambitious and spectacular. Griffith conceived it on a vast scale: the siege of Babylon, with its massive walls and many thousands of extras, is still awe-inspiring. The film rises to a fine climax as all the stories come to a head, including a modern one with a race between a car and train. It has been called 'the only film fugue' and is an astonishing achievement for its time.

La Belle Noiseuse

France 1991 240m colour
Artificial Eye/Pierre Grise

⊶ ▤ ◉ ◉

w Pascal Bonitzer, Christine Laurent, Jacques Rivette *story* Le Chef d'Oeuvre Inconnu (The Unknown Masterpiece) by Honoré de Balzac *d* Jacques Rivette *ph* William Lubtchansky *m* Stravinsky *ad* Emmanuel de Chauvigny *ed* Nicole Lubtchansky
☆ Michel Piccoli (Edouard Frenhofer), Jane Birkin (Liz), *Emmanuelle Béart* (Marianne), Marianne Denicourt (Julienne), David Bursztein (Nicolas), Gilles Arbona (Porbus)

'Perhaps the most meticulous and seductive depiction in movies of the hard work of making art.' – *Richard Corliss, Time*

● Artist Bernard Dufour, whose hand is the only part of him to be seen, did the painting.
● *La Belle Noiseuse: Divertimento*, a two-hour version of the film using different takes, was produced for French TV and also given a cinema and video release.

236
La Belle Noiseuse

The beautiful young mistress of a friend inspires a famous artist to finish a painting, for which his wife modelled, that he put aside ten years before.

This gripping and penetrating movie on the themes of obsession, art and love, offers little in the way of conventional narrative. The tensions and interplay, artistic and erotic, slowly build during the film's four-hour length. William Lubtchansky's camera, in a series of beautiful images, gets as close as possible to the artist and his model. An audience has the privilege of not just observing a painter at work, but also a film-maker, so watching two masterpieces in the process of creation.

Bringing Up Baby
US 1938 102m bw
RKO (Howard Hawks)
⊡ ▤ ◔ ⊚ ◉

w Dudley Nichols, Hagar Wilde *d* Howard Hawks
ph Russell Metty *m* Roy Webb *ad* Perry Ferguson, Van Nest Polglase *ed* George Hively
☆ *Katharine Hepburn* (Susan Vance), *Cary Grant* (David Huxley), *May Robson* (Aunt Elizabeth), *Charles Ruggles* (Maj. Horace Applegate), *Walter Catlett* (Constable Slocum), *Fritz Feld* (Dr. Fritz Lehman), Jonathan Hale, Barry Fitzgerald (Mr. Gogarty)

'Harum-scarum farce comedy … definite box-office.' – *Variety*

'I am happy to report that it is funny from the word go, that it has no other meaning to recommend it … and that I wouldn't swap it for practically any three things of the current season.' – *Otis Ferguson*

'It may be the American movies' closest equivalent to Restoration comedy.' – *Pauline Kael*

'Crazy comedies continue to become crazier, and there will soon be few actors and actresses left who have no straw in their hair.' – *Basil Wright*

● The dog George was played by Asta from *The Thin Man* movies.
● Howard Hawks re-used portions of the script in *Man's Favourite Sport*.

All About Eve
US 1950 138m bw
TCF (Darryl F. Zanuck)
⊡ ▤ ◔ ⊚ ◉

wd Joseph L. Mankiewicz *ph* Milton Krasner *m* Alfred Newman *ad* Lyle Wheeler, George Davis *ed* Barbara McLean
☆ *Bette Davis* (Margo Channing), *George Sanders* (Addison de Witt), Anne Baxter (Eve), Celeste Holm (Karen Richards), Thelma Ritter (Birdie), Gary Merrill (Bill Sampson), Hugh Marlowe (Lloyd Richards), Gregory Ratoff (Max Fabian), Marilyn Monroe (Miss Caswell), Barbara Bates (Phoebe), Walter Hampden (Speaker at dinner)

'The wittiest, the most devastating, the most adult and literate motion picture ever made that had anything to do with the New York Stage.' – *Leo Mishkin*

● The idea for the film came from a short story, 'The Wisdom of Eve', by Mary Orr.
● A Region 1 special edition DVD includes commentary by Celeste Holm, Christopher Mankiewicz and Kenneth Geist, and interviews with Bette Davis and Ann Baxter.
👤 picture; Joseph L. Mankiewicz (as writer); Joseph L. Mankiewicz (as director); George Sanders
👤 Milton Krasner; Alfred Newman; Bette Davis; Anne Baxter; Celeste Holm; Thelma Ritter; art direction; editing
📺 picture

235
Bringing Up Baby

A zany girl causes a zoology professor to lose a dinosaur bone and a pet leopard in the same evening.

This is an outstanding screwball comedy, which barely pauses for romance and ends up with the whole splendid cast in jail. Cary Grant and Katharine Hepburn play brilliantly together, he as a serious scientist who needs loosening up, she as a impulsive woman who needs straightening out. Howard Hawks keeps the pace fast, the slapstick fresh and piles one outrageous situation on another in a breathlessly successful dash for laughs. Apart from the witty dialogue, there are splendid moments of physical comedy, as when, in a restaurant, Grant inadvertently steps on Hepburn's dress and tears off the back, so that he is forced to walk close behind her in a lockstep so that they exit with dignity intact. It is a comedy of love with no obvious romance; the couple never exchange kisses, but involve each other in mishaps and misunderstandings.

234
All About Eve

An ageing Broadway star suffers from the hidden menace of a self-effacing but secretly ruthless and ambitious young actress.

A basically unconvincing story with thin characters is transformed by a screenplay scintillating with savage wit and a couple of waspish performances into a movie experience to treasure. The story about the rivalry between an ambitious young actress and a temperamental star has been seen by some as based on Joseph Mankiewicz's relationship with his witty, elder brother Herman, who wrote *Citizen Kane*. With its epigrammatic exchanges ('Do they have audition for television?' 'That's all television is, my dear. Nothing but audition'), it is a joy to listen to, as well as watch. Bette Davis was at her bitchy best and there was genuine chemistry between her and Gary Merrill; they began an affair during filming and married later.

Shoah
France 1985 566m colour
Aleph/Historia
⬛ ▆ ◎
d Claude Lanzmann
● Part 1 is 274m, Part 2 292m.

233
Shoah

Massive documentary history of the Holocaust, using survivors' testimony and some re-enactment but no historical footage.

The title is a Hebrew word for annihilation, which is what is movingly described. The film cuts from the faces of those Claude Lanzmann interviewed, remembering their experiences to the places where they suffered; there grass now grows where the camps stood, and bodies lie buried beneath in mass graves. He has testimony not only from the Jews who survived, but the Germans who organized their transport to the death camps. It is an invaluable, life-affirming witness to that terrible time.

'The dawn of a new art!'
The Birth of a Nation
US 1915 185m approx (16 fps) bw silent
Epoch (D. W. Griffith, Harry E. Aitken)
⬛ ▆ ◎ ◎ ◎ ◠
w D. W. Griffith, Frank E. Woods *novel The Klansman* by Thomas Dixon Jnr *d* D. W. Griffith *ph* G. W. Bitzer
☆ Henry B. Walthall (Col. Ben Cameron), Mae Marsh (Flora Cameron), Miriam Cooper (Margaret Cameron), Lillian Gish (Elsie), Robert Harron (Tod), Wallace Reid (Jeff), Donald Crisp (Gen U.S. Grant), Joseph Henaberry (Abraham Lincoln), Raoul Walsh (John Wilkes Booth), Eugene Pallette (Union Soldier), Walter Long (Gus)

'A film version of some of the melodramatic and inflammatory material contained in *The Clansman* ... a great deal might be said concerning the sorry service rendered by its plucking at old wounds. But of the film as a film, it may be reported simply that it is an impressive new illustration of the scope of the motion picture camera.' – *New York Times*

'Griffith was, in his prime, a nineteenth-century humanist working in a twentieth-century medium. And, speaking for myself, I should welcome today some infusion of that unashamed humane sentiment into the smart machine-made films I see every week.' – *Dilys Powell, 1945*

● The soundtrack album features a recording of the score written by Joseph Carl Breil to accompany the film in 1915.

232
The Birth of a Nation

Northern and Southern families are caught up in the Civil War.

The cinema's first and still most famous epic, many sequences of which retain their mastery, despite its black villains and Ku Klux Klan heroes. Even at the time of its making, its extreme racism troubled many. (Assistant cameraman Karl Brown called the story 'the usual diatribe of a fire-eating Southerner'). The acting is melodramatic, influenced by Griffith's own experience in the theatre. The props department kept small bottles of hydrogen peroxide available so that Walter Long, in minstrel-style blackface as the lustful Gus, could foam at the mouth to suggest sexual passion. Nevertheless, it retains an irresistible sweep and power, and Griffiths's innovative use of the vocabulary of film, from close-ups and tracking shots to his editing, cross-cutting between events, is remarkable.

Gigi

US 1958 119m Metrocolor Cinemascope
MGM (Arthur Freed)

▭ ▬ ⌕ ⌾ ⊚ ⌂

w Alan Jay Lerner *d* Vincente Minnelli *ph* Joseph Ruttenberg *m/ly* Frederick Loewe, Alan Jay Lerner *md* André Previn *ad* Preston Ames, William A. Horning *ed* Adrienne Fazan *pd/cos* Cecil Beaton

☆ *Leslie Caron* (Gigi), *Louis Jourdan* (Gaston Lachaille), *Maurice Chevalier* (Honore Lachaille), *Hermione Gingold* (Mme Alvarez), Isabel Jeans (Aunt Alicia), Jacques Bergerac (Sandomir), Eva Gabor (Liane D'Exelmans), John Abbott (Manuel)

'It has the sureness expected when a group of the most sophisticated talents are able to work together on material entirely suited to them.' – *Penelope Houston*

● Leslie Caron's vocals were dubbed by Betty Wand.
♫ 'Thank Heaven for Little Girls'; 'It's a Bore'; 'The Parisians'; 'Gossip'; 'She is Not Thinking of Me'; 'The Night They Invented Champagne'; 'I Remember It Well'; 'Gigi'; 'I'm Glad I'm Not Young Anymore'; 'Say a Prayer for Me Tonight'
♟ best picture; Alan Jay Lerner; Vincente Minnelli; Joseph Ruttenberg; André Previn; Cecil Beaton; editing; Preston Ames and William A. Horning (art directors); title song; Maurice Chevalier (special award)

231
Gigi

In 1890s Paris, a young girl is trained by her aunt to be a cocotte.

Colette's story, was cleaned up in this delightfully set, costumed and performed musical. Alan Jay Lerner attributed the later decline of screen musicals to the absence of great entertainers who could set the film's musical style. This had one of the last, Maurice Chevalier. The songs were a development of that half-spoken approach developed in *My Fair Lady* so that the transition from dialogue to song and back seemed natural. Minnelli did not include any elaborate dance-filled production numbers that would have broken the elegantly casual mood. The result was an innovative musical, one of the last great showpieces from Arthur Freed's production unit.

Smiles of a Summer Night

Sweden 1955 105m bw
Svensk Filmindustri

▭ ▬ ⌕ ⌾ ⊚

original title: *Sommarnattens Leende*
wd Ingmar Bergman *ph* Gunnar Fischer *m* Erik Nordgren *ad* P.A. Lundgren *ed* Oscar Rosander

☆ *Gunnar Bjornstrand* (Fredrik Egerman), Eva Dahlbeck (Desirée Armfeldt), Ulla Jacobsson (Anne Egerman), Harriet Andersson (Petra), Margit Carlqvist (Charlotte Malcolm), Naima Wifstrand (Madame Armfeldt), Jarl Kulle (Count Carl-Magnus Malcolm)

230
Smiles of a Summer Night

A lawyer and his young wife join a house party at the invitation of his former mistress.

Ingmar Bergman's comedy of high period manners was a joy to look at thanks to Gunnar Fischer's cinematography. It was an elegant dissection of the varieties of love from an admirably detached viewpoint, as a country lawyer meets again a touring actress who was once his mistress, and accepts an invitation for him and his young wife to stay at her mother's country home for a weekend. By the time the weekend is over, most participants have changed partners. Bergman's inspiration, other than his playing with form, was his realization that it was possible for two people to love another without being able to live together. The series of sexual entanglements for guests and servants exposes class differences – the lower classes are far more uninhibited than their masters – as well as revealing the dangers of repressing feelings and the melancholia of getting what you desire.

An Autumn Afternoon
Japan   1962   113m   Agfa-Shochikucolor
Shochiku

original title: *Samma no Aji*
w Kogo Noda, Yasujiro Ozu *d* Yasujiro Ozu *ph* Yuharu
Atsuta *m* Kojun Saito *ad* Tatsuo Hamada *ed* Yoshiyasu
Hamamura
☆ Shima Iwashita (Michiko Hirayama), Chishu Ryu
(Shuhei Hirayama), Keiji Sada (Koichi), Mariko Okada
(Akiko), Shinichiro Mikami (Kazuo), Teruo Yoshida (Yutaka
Miura), Noriko Maki (Fusako Taguchi), Nobuo Nakamura
(Shuzo Kawai), Eijiro Tono (Sakuma, The 'Gourd')

229
An Autumn Afternoon

A widower encourages his daughter to marry and leave home.

Ozu's last film, in which form matters as much as content, is an elegiac account of the disintegration of family life and the prospect of lonely old age. A widower, horrified by the thought of his daughter becoming an old maid by looking after him, is encouraged by his friends to find her a husband. He succeeds, but then has to face life without her. Chishu Ryu, who appeared in nearly all of Ozu's films, plays the father in the perfect unobtrusive manner that the director's works required. Ozu's unhurried, meticulous direction allows room for the characters to emerge with total reality, as if partaking in everyday life rather than in a domestic drama. As with other of Ozu's films, it ends on a quiet note, of acceptance of whatever life brings, even if all that is on offer is loneliness.

The Bank Dick
US   1940   73m   bw
Universal

GB title: *The Bank Detective*
w Mahatma Kane Jeeves (W. C. Fields) *d* Edward F. Cline
ph Milton Krasner *md* Charles Previn *ad* Jack Otterson
ed Arthur Hilton
☆ *W. C. Fields* (Egbert Sousè), Franklin Pangborn (J.
Pinkerton Snoopington), Una Merkel (Myrtle Souse),
Shemp Howard (Joe Guelpe), Jack Norton (A. Pismo Clam),
Grady Sutton (Og Oggilby), Cora Witherspoon (Agatha
Souse)

'One of the great classics of American comedy.' –
Robert Lewis Taylor

'When the man is funny he is terrific … but the story is makeshift, the other characters are stock types, the only pace discernible is the distance between drinks or the rhythm of the fleeting seconds it takes Fields to size up trouble coming and duck the hell out.' – *Otis Ferguson*

'Individualistic display of broad comedy … adequate program supporter.' – *Variety*

● Fields's writing nom-de-plume was allegedly borrowed from noble characters in old English plays he squirmed through as a youth. They kept saying: 'M'hat, m'cane, Jeeves.'

228
The Bank Dick

In Lompoc, California, a ne'er-do-well accidentally stops a hold-up, is made a bank detective, acquires deeds to a worthless mine and interferes in the production of a film.

W.C. Fields is at his comic best as Egbert Sousè, an idle put-upon husband and father. There are delicious moments and very little padding in a movie that is almost an anthology of his best work of the past, echoing previous films and improving upon them. Fields seems to have believed that his movies had all the standard Hollywood ingredients; it took Paramount's executives to point out that they were about 'cheating and robbery and terrible people'. They should have added that such subject matter, once it had been filtered through Fields's inventive mind, was what made them so funny, and never more so than here.

Le Jour Se Lève

France 1939 95m bw
Sigma
📽 ▦ ⊚ ⊚ 🎧
aka: *Daybreak*
w Jacques Viot, Jacques Prévert d Marcel Carné ph Curt
Courant, Philippe Agostini, André Bac m Maurice Jaubert
ad Alexander Trauner ed Rene Le Henaff
☆ Jean Gabin (Francois), Jules Berry (M. Valentin), Arletty
(Clara), Jacqueline Laurent (Francoise)

'The man walks about his room, moves a few
things, lies on his bed, looks out of the window,
chain-smokes … and one is genuinely interested in
him all the time (remembering afterwards that
there exist directors who contrive to be boring even
when they use fifteen characters in a motor car
chase crackling with revolver shots).' – *Richard
Mallett, Punch*

227
Le Jour Se Lève

*A murderer is besieged by police in his attic room, remembers his past
through the night, and shoots himself.*

A model of French poetic realism, and a much-praised film which was
almost destroyed when it was bought for a mediocre American remake
(*The Long Night*). Marcel Carné's interest was in an ordinary man at
the mercy of an implacable and evil fate, which would have resonated
with a French audience just before the outbreak of war. It was the story
of a lonely man, who discovers that the woman he loves is involved
with an unpleasant music-hall performer. In a confrontation between
the two, he is provoked into shooting his rival, and as the police
besiege him in his attic room, remembers his past through the night,
and shoots himself. It was banned in France as 'demoralizing', though
its worth was quickly recognized elsewhere.

The Face

Sweden 1958 100m bw
Svensk Filmindustri (Allan Ekelund)
▦ ⊚
original title: *Ansiktet*
US title: *The Magician*
wd Ingmar Bergman ph Gunnar Fischer m Erik Nordgren
ad P. A. Lundgren ed Oscar Rosander
☆ Max von Sydow (Vogler), Ingrid Thulin (Manda Aman),
Gunnar Björnstrand (Vergerus), Naima Wifstrand
(Grandmother), Uke Fridell (Tubal), Lars Ekborg (Simson),
Bengt Ekerot (Spegel)

226
The Face

A mesmerist takes his revenge on those who expose him as a fraud.

Ingmar Bergman's virtually indecipherable parable involved a mesmerist and his troupe who, in 19th-century Sweden, are halted at a
country post to be examined by three officials. After he is partly
exposed as a fraud, he takes a frightening revenge. The film may be
about the survival of Christianity (and may not). It can equally be taken
as a celebration of the delusive power of artistic imagination, as personified by Max von Sydow's sinister charlatan; or it may express
Bergman's feeling that his audience misunderstands his intentions,
reading their own meanings into his work. It is a wholly personal
Bergman fancy that has to be enjoyed chiefly for its surface *frissons*,
for its acting and its look, which are sufficient compensation.

Fury
US 1936 94m bw
MGM (Joseph L. Mankiewicz)

w Bartlett Cormack, Fritz Lang *story* Norman Krasna
d Fritz Lang *ph* Joseph Ruttenberg *m* Franz Waxman
ad Cedric Gibbons, William A. Horning, Edwin B. Willis
ed Frank Sullivan
☆ Spencer Tracy (Joe Wheeler), Sylvia Sidney (Katherine Grant), Bruce Cabot (Bubbles Dawson), Walter Abel (District Attorney), Edward Ellis (Sheriff), Walter Brennan (Buggs Meyers), Frank Albertson (Charlie)

'The surface of American life has been rubbed away: *Fury* gets down to the bones of the thing and shows them for what they are.' – *C. A. Lejeune*

'Since the screen began to talk, no other serious film except *The Front Page* has so clearly shown that here is a new art and what this new art can do.' – *John Marks*

'Everyday events and people suddenly took on tremendous and horrifying proportion; even the most insignificant details had a pointed meaning.' – *Lewis Jacobs*

'Astonishing, the only film I know to which I have wanted to attach the epithet of *great*.' – *Graham Greene*

♟ Norman Krasna

'Even the moon is frightened of me – frightened to death!'

The Invisible Man
US 1933 71m bw
Universal (Carl Laemmle Jnr)

w R. C. Sherriff, Philip Wylie *novel* H. G. Wells *d* James Whale *ph* Arthur Edeson *ad* Charles D. Hall *ed* Ted J. Kent *sp* John P. Fulton
☆ Claude Rains (Jack Griffin/The Invisible One), Gloria Stuart (Flora Cranley), William Harrigan (Doctor Kemp), Henry Travers (Dr. Cranley), E. E. Clive (Jaffers), Una O'Connor (Mrs. Jenny Hall), Forrester Harvey (Mr. Herbert Hall), Dudley Digges (Chief of Detectives), Holmes Herbert (Chief of Police)

'Well made and full of intentional and unintentional laughs. Should do well.' – *Variety*

● Sequels, successively less interesting, were (all qv) *The Invisible Man Returns* (1940), *Invisible Woman* (1941), *Invisible Agent* (1942), *The Invisible Man's Revenge* (1944), *Abbott and Costello Meet the Invisible Man* (1951) and *Memoirs of an Invisible Man* (1992). A TV series with an anonymous hero was made by ATV in 1955; a Universal one with David McCallum followed in 1975, and was restructured as *The Gemini Man* in 1976.
Boris Karloff had been first choice for the role, but he turned it down.

225
Fury

The survivor of a lynch mob attempts to revenge himself on his persecutors.

Fritz Lang's first American film was also the best he made after leaving Germany. Norman Krasna's story was based on a true incident in San Jose, in which two suspects on a murder charge were taken out of jail and lynched by a mob which was never brought to justice. In Lang's version, a traveller in a small town is mistaken for a murderer and apparently lynched; he escapes in a fire but determines to have his persecutors hanged for his murder. It was a powerful, satisfying drama with Spencer Tracy at his best as an ordinary man driven to a raging madness by his near escape from death; it is possible that some of the intensity of his performance may have been a result of his extreme dislike of the autocratic director. (His loathing was nothing compared to that of the film's electricians who had to be dissuaded from dropping a heavy light on Lang's head.)

224
The Invisible Man

A scientist discovers a means of making himself invisible, but in the process becomes a megalomaniac.

A superb blend of eccentric character comedy, melodrama and trick photography in a Hollywood English setting that is remarkably faithful to the spirit of H. G. Wells's story about a scientist who discovers a means of making himself invisible, and in the process becomes a megalomaniac. There is a sense of genuine horror, when he first demonstrates his invisibility and announces his plans: 'We'll start with a few murders,' he says. 'Great men. Small men. Just to show we're not choosy.' It made a star of Claude Rains in his first film, even though he is seen for only a couple of seconds.

The Navigator

👥 US 1924 63m approx (24 fps) bw silent

Metro-Goldwyn/Buster Keaton (Joseph M. Schenck)

📼 ▤ ◉~ ⊚

w Jean Havez, Clyde Bruckman, J. A. Mitchell *d* Buster Keaton, Donald Crisp *ph* Elgin Lessley, Byron Houck
☆ *Buster Keaton* (Rollo Treadway), Kathryn McGuire (Betsy O'Brien), Frederick Vroom ('Cappy' John O'Brien)

'Studded with hilarious moments and a hundred and one adroit gags.' – *Photoplay*

223

The Navigator

A millionaire and his girl are the only people on a transatlantic liner marooned in mid-ocean.

Buster Keaton chartered a derelict ocean liner to make this comedy. It was to make him internationally famous and its succession of hilarious sight gags shows him in top form. At first, neither he nor the girl know there is anyone else aboard; then each discovers signs of life and goes in search, just missing finding the other in a wonderfully timed perambulation of the ship. Other sequences show Keaton trying to tow the liner from a rowing boat, which promptly sinks, and his valiant battle with a folding chair that folds in all the wrong places. It is among his greatest films.

'6 Reels of Joy.'

The Kid

👥 US 1921 52m approx (24 fps) bw silent

First National/Charles Chaplin

📼 ▤ ◉~ ⊚ ⊚

wd Charles Chaplin *ph* Rollie Totheroh
☆ *Charles Chaplin* (A Tramp), *Jackie Coogan* (The Child), Edna Purviance (The Woman)

'Has all the hallmarks of having been carefully thought out and painstakingly directed, photographed and assembled.' – *Variety*

222

The Kid

A tramp brings up an abandoned baby, and later loses him to his mother; but there is a happy ending.

Chaplin's sentimental comedy, set in the slums, is much less painful than the synopsis would suggest. The comedy is very sparingly laid on, but the production is comparatively smooth, Jackie Coogan as the child is sensational, and the film contains much of the quintessential Chaplin. He never had a better on-screen partner than Coogan and their scenes together are unforgettable. The scene where the kid is taken away in a wagon by an orphanage and rescued by Chaplin brilliantly combines pathos and comedy.

Blow-Up

GB 1966 110m Eastmancolor
MGM/Carlo Ponti
🎬 ⬛ ◎~ ◎ ◎ ◎ ∩

wd Michelangelo Antonioni *ph* Carlo di Palma *m* Herbert Hancock *ad* Assheton Gorton *ed* Frank Clarke
☆ David Hemmings (Thomas), Sarah Miles (Patricia), Vanessa Redgrave (Jane)

'A beautiful and startling film, startling because if the credits didn't say it was coauthored and directed by Michelangelo Antonioni you'd never believe it on the basis of the movie itself, and beautiful because in his first made-in-England English-language film the Italian director proves himself a master of the use of color, both literally and figuratively.' – *Judith Crist*

👤 Michelangelo Antonioni (as writer and director)

221
Blow-Up

A London fashion photographer thinks he sees a murder, but the evidence disappears.

Antonioni's film of a fashionable photographer roaming through swinging London hints at a thriller. A fashionable think-in on the difference (if any) between fantasy and reality, it is also a camera's eye view of a city at a particular time in its life, of frantic lives leading nowhere, of conspicuous consumption and hidden desires. Antonioni's startling use of colour and his almost documentary detailing of urban activity transform his minor mystery into a vivid historic document. Antonioni investigates a superficial world, one of brightly coloured surfaces where what matters is style. Its impulsive hero is a man who sees everything through the eye of his camera, but understands nothing, since he is incapable of regarding anything in depth.

'Weird sex. Obsession. Comic books.'

Crumb
US   1994   120m   colour
Artificial Eye/Superior (Lynn O'Donnell, Terry Zwigoff)
📷 ≣ ℚ~ ⊚ ⊚   🎧

d Terry Zwigoff *ph* Maryse Alberti *ed* Victor Livingston
☆ Robert Crumb (Himself), Charles Crumb (Himself, Robert's Older Brother), Maxon Crumb (Himself, Robert's Younger Brother), Aline Kominsky (Herself, Robert's Wife), Dana Crumb (Herself, Robert's First Wife), Beatrice Crumb (Herself, Robert's Mother)

'By turns gripping and appalling, *Crumb* is one of the most complete pictures of an artist ever made.' – *Clark Collis, Empire*

220
Crumb

A documentary account of the life of underground cartoonist Robert Crumb.

A fascinating, intimate and revealing documentary of an artist called 'the Breughel of the 20th century' by one interviewee, critic Robert Hughes. Robert Crumb, celebrated underground cartoonist and creator of such characters as Fritz the Cat and Mr Natural, discusses his life and work and plays ragtime and jazz from his vast collection of 78 rpm records, as he prepares to leave California to settle in France. He is seen in context with his somewhat dysfunctional brothers who, also talented, have failed to come to terms with society in the way that he has. (Charles, his older brother, committed suicide a year after being filmed.) Terry Zwigoff takes his audience into a strange place, where obsessives live at an odd angle to the conventional world. Crumb's strategies for survival often seem adolescent here. He combines a raw-nerved sensitivity with an compulsive honesty so that his art becomes a refuge from, and a comment on, the wider world.

Ivan's Childhood
USSR   1962   95m   bw
Mosfilm (G. Kuznetsov)
📷 ≣ ℚ~ ⊚

original title: *Ivanovo Detstvo*
w Vladimir Bogomolov, Mikhail Papava *novel* Vladimir Bogomolov *d* Andrei Tarkovsky *ph* Vadim Yusov *m* Vyacheslav Ovchinnikov *ad* Evgeni Cherniaev *ed* G. Natanson
☆ Kolya Burlyaev (Ivan), Irma Takovskaya (Ivan's Mother), Valentin Zubkov (Capt. Kholin), E. Zharikov (Lt. Galtsev), S. Krylov (Cpl. Katasonych), Nikolai Grinko (Col. Gryaznov), L. Malyavina (Masha), Andrey Mikhalkov Konchalovsky

'The film is not disfigured by the unnaturally cheery or the conventionally hysterical. With one blow it annuls a whole cinémathèque of the war films of all lands.' – *Ivor Montagu, Sight and Sound*

● It won the Golden Lion for best film at the Venice Film Festival in 1962.
● Tarkovsky replaced director Eduard Abalov, who was fired from the film, and began again with a new crew and cast, and a smaller budget.

219
Ivan's Childhood

A vengeful 12-year-old escapes from a concentration camp and becomes an army scout after his family is killed by the Nazis.

A lyrical opening, of a young boy laughing at the pleasure of a sunny, butterfly-filled spring day is abruptly shattered as he wakes to the horror of his actual situation: Ivan has been robbed of his childhood. The sole survivor of his family, and of a death camp, he is a grimy, half-starved,vengeful scout for the Russian army, stranded in a bleak war-scarred landscape near the German front line. Tarkovsky took over the film after its first director was sacked and his footage scrapped. Left with little money to spend, he brilliantly uses the limited means at his disposal – a ruined church, a burnt-out home, a sluggish marsh and river – to show the terrible nature of war, as seen through the eyes of a child.

'It's the love story of an unsung hero!'

Marty
US 1955 91m bw
UA/Hecht-Hill-Lancaster (Harold Hecht)
■ ⊛ ⊙ ◎
w *Paddy Chayefsky play* Paddy Chayefsky *d Delbert Mann ph* Joseph LaShelle *m* Roy Webb *ad* Edward S. Howarth, Walter Simonds *ed* Alan Crosland Jr.
☆ *Ernest Borgnine* (Marty), *Betsy Blair* (Clara), *Esther Minciotti* (Mrs. Pilletti), *Joe Mantell* (Angie), Karen Steele (Virginia), Jerry Paris (Thomas)

'Something rare in the American cinema today: a subtle, ironic and compassionate study of ordinary human relationships.' – *Gavin Lambert*

'A warm and winning film, full of the sort of candid comment on plain, drab people that seldom reaches the screen.' – *Bosley Crowther, New York Times*

● The original 1953 television version was also directed by Delbert Mann and starred Rod Steiger.
👤 picture; Paddy Chayefsky; Delbert Mann; Ernest Borgnine
👤 Joseph LaShelle; Betsy Blair; Joe Mantell; art direction
🏆 Ernest Borgnine; Betsy Blair

218
Marty

A butcher who fears he will never get a girl meets a girl who fears she will never get a man.

The first of the filmed teleplays which in the mid-fifties seemed like a breath of spring to Hollywood (they were cheap) and also brought in a new wave of talent of actors, directors and writers. Paddy Chayefsky was the best of them. His script concerned a 34-year-old Bronx butcher, who fears he will never get a woman because he is unattractive, but at a Saturday night dance he meets a girl with similar fears. Rod Steiger had starred in the TV version, but Ernest Borgnine replaced him in the film because Steiger refused to sign a long term contract with Burt Lancaster's production company. It remains one of the best of its kind. Its new naturalistic dialogue fell happily on the ear; but it has been so frequently imitated since that its revolutionary appearance is hard to imagine. It encouraged a new realism and still works as a tentative love story between the kind of everyday people that Hollywood had forgotten.

'A man went looking for America and couldn't find it anywhere!'

Easy Rider
US 1969 94m Technicolor
Columbia/Pando/Raybert (Peter Fonda)
▥ ■ ⊛ ⊙ ◎ ♫
w Peter Fonda, Dennis Hopper, Terry Southern *d* Dennis Hopper *ph* Laszlo Kovacs *m* various recordings *ad* Jerry Kay *ed* Donn Cambern
☆ Peter Fonda (Captain America/Wyatt), Dennis Hopper (Billy), *Jack Nicholson* (George Hanson), Antonio Mendoza (Jesus), Phil Spector (Connection), Robert Walker (Jack)

'*Cinéma-vérité* in allegory terms.' – *Peter Fonda*

'Ninety-four minutes of what it is like to swing, to watch, to be fond, to hold opinions and to get killed in America at this moment.' – *Penelope Gilliatt*

● Both the Regions 1 and 2 DVD releases include a commentary by Dennis Hopper.
👤 script; Jack Nicholson

217
Easy Rider

Two drop-outs ride across America on motorcycles.

Much imitated, though never equalled in its casual effectiveness, this was a seminal movie that opened the doors of Hollywood to many young movie-makers and made Jack Nicholson a star. A hipper version of Roger Corman's B features, in which both Peter Fonda and Jack Nicholson had appeared, it was an existential road movie that hit the mood of the moment with the rebellion of its anti-heroes against the established order. They revelled in America's wide-open spaces even if they under-estimated the dangers that lurked there. The introduction of Jack Nicholson's unhappy lawyer adds substance to what was, until that point, a road movie about two drug-dealing drop-outs in search of the easy life, who discover the pleasure of open roads and natural beauty and the hostility of closed minds. It becomes a critique of the American dream and the choices open to those who seek it.

Easy Rider

'The Man With The Barbed Wire Soul!'

Hud
US 1963 112m bw Panavision
Paramount/Salem/Dover (Martin Ritt, Irving Ravetch)

w Irving Ravetch, Harriet Frank *novel* Horseman Pass By
by Larry McMurtry *d* Martin Ritt *ph* James Wong Howe
m Elmer Bernstein *ad* Hal Pereira, Tambi Larsen *ed* Frank
Bracht

☆ *Paul Newman* (Hud Bannon), *Patricia Neal* (Alma
Brown), *Melvyn Douglas* (Homer Bannon), Brandon de
Wilde (Lon Bannon)

'So uncompromising in its portrait of an amoral
man and his impact upon three people that I am
tempted to reach for that dangerous adjective
"unique".' – *Judith Crist*

James Wong Howe; Patricia Neal; Melvyn Douglas
script; Martin Ritt; Paul Newman; Hal Pereira, Tambi
Larsen

Patricia Neal

216

Hud

*Life is hard on a Texas ranch, and the veteran owner is not helped by
his sexually arrogant ne'er-do-well son, who is a bad influence on the
household.*

Superbly set in an arid landscape, this incisive character drama was
extremely well directed and acted. As Hud, a hard-working Texas
rancher's sexually arrogant ne'er-do-well son, Paul Newman has a
seductive charm. He is in revolt against his father and the moral code
of the old West that he represents. Hud has no sentiment about the
ranch and what it represents – it is just something else to be exploited.
It is the hero-worshipping Brandon de Wilde, as Hud's younger
nephew, who is the moral arbiter of the movie and will assess the worth
of Hud's philosophy: 'This world is so full of crap, a man's gonna get
into it sooner or later whether he's careful or not.'

Whisky Galore

GB   1948   82m   bw

Ealing (Monja Danischewsky)

US title: *Tight Little Island*

w Compton Mackenzie, Angus MacPhail *novel* Compton Mackenzie *d* Alexander Mackendrick *ph* Gerald Gibbs *m* Ernest Irving *ad* Jim Morahan *ed* Joseph Sterling

☆ Basil Radford (Capt. Paul Waggett), Joan Greenwood (Peggy Macroon), Jean Cadell (Mrs. Campbell), Gordon Jackson (George Campbell), James Robertson Justice (Dr. MacLaren), Wylie Watson (Joseph Macroon), John Gregson (Sammy MacConrum), Morland Graham (The Biffer), Duncan Macrae (Angus MacCormac), Catherine Lacey (Mrs. Waggett), Bruce Seton (Sgt. Odd), Henry Mollinson (Mr. Farquharson), Compton Mackenzie (Capt. Buncher), A. E. Matthews (Col. Linsey-Woolsey)

'Brilliantly witty and fantastic, but wholly plausible.' – *Sunday Chronicle*

● Fourteen whisky bottles, said to be the last surviving from the wreck of the SS *Politician*, the real-life shipwreck that inspired the film, were sold in 1993 at a Glasgow auction for £12,012, with a bottle of Haig Dimple fetching £1,210.

215
Whisky Galore

Thirsty Hebridean islanders hide from the excise man a cargo of whisky washed up from a shipwreck.

This marvellously detailed, fast-moving, well-played and attractively photographed comedy firmly established the richest Ealing vein of ordinary men against the forces of bureaucracy. It was based on Compton Mackenzie's novel of a ship full of whisky being wrecked during World War II on a small Hebridean island which had run dry of the drink, to the consternation of the locals. They grab the bottles for themselves, and then have to keep it away from the local customs and excise man. Ealing's head Michael Balcon didn't like the script, saying 'All I can see is a lot of Scotsmen sitting by the fire and saying "Och aye."' Alexander Mackendrick used locals as well as actors when filming on location in the Hebrides and the result has a mellow authenticity and geniality that remains a pleasure to experience.

'The world as they knew it was slipping away from them. Time was running out for the human race. And there was nothing to hold on to – except each other!'

Invasion of the Body Snatchers

US   1955   80m   bw   Superscope

Allied Artists/Walter Wanger

w Daniel Mainwaring *novel* Jack Finney *d* Don Siegel *ph* Ellsworth Fredericks *m* Carmen Dragon *ad* Ted Haworth *ed* Robert S. Eisen

☆ *Kevin McCarthy* (Miles Bennel), *Dana Wynter* (Becky Driscoll), Larry Gates (Dr. Dan Kauffmann), *King Donovan* (Jack), Carolyn Jones (Theodora), Virginia Christine (Wilma Lentz), Sam Peckinpah (Charlie Buckholtz)

● The Region 1 DVD release includes an interview with Kevin McCarthy.

214
Invasion of the Body Snatchers

A small American town is imperceptibly taken over by an alien force.

Don Siegel's film, from Jack Finney's story, is a parable of conformity: a small American town is imperceptibly taken over by an alien force that replaces people with their exact likenesses except that they possess no soul, emotion or culture. Siegel wrote in his autobiography that many of his associates were already like that, incapable of love or passion. He was unhappy that studio executives edited out all the humour from his final cut. But it remains persuasive, thoroughly satisfying, low-budget science fiction, put across with subtlety and intelligence in every department. It was remade to lesser effect by Philip Kaufman in 1978 and by Abel Ferrara in 1994.

Come and See

USSR   1985   142m   colour
Byelarusfilm, Mosfilm

original title: *Idi i Smotri*

w Elem Klimov, Ales Adamovich *book The Story of Khatyn and Others* by Ales Adamovich *d* Elem Klimov *ph* Alexi Rodionov *m* Oleg Yanchenko *ad* Viktor Petrov *ed* Valeriya Belova

☆ Aleksei Kravchenko (Florya Gaishun), Olga Mironova (Glasha), Lyubomiras Lautsiavitchus (Kosach), Vladas Bagdonas, Victor Lorentz

'Taps into that hallucinatory nether world of blood and mud and escalating madness.' – *Rita Kempley, Washington Post*

213
Come and See

In Bylorussia during World War II, a young boy joins the resistance against the invading Nazis and witnesses the atrocities of war.

There is no more pitiless film about war than Klimov's masterpiece. The terrible atrocity of World War II is seen in two close-ups here. One is at the beginning, as a 12-year-old boy, happy and laughing, goes to join the resistance to the Nazi invasion of Bylorussia. The second is towards the end, when, traumatized by what he has seen, his face is a mask of horror, wide-eyed and scarcely human. The early scenes show the partisans playing at war. It is only when the boy goes home to his mother and finds a deserted house that the terror begins – as he runs away, the audience see what he does not: a heap of slaughtered bodies lying by a barn. By the end the boy has lost his humanity, and is more interested in binding the split stock of his rifle than in helping a wounded girl.

'The planet where nightmares come true …'

Solaris

USSR   1972   165m   Sovcolor   'Scope
Mosfilm

w Andrei Tarkovsky, Friedrich Gorenstein *novel* Stanislaw Lem *d* Andrei Tarkovsky *ph* Vadim Yusov *m* Eduard Artemyev *ad* Mikhail Romadin

☆ Natalya Bondarchuk (Harey), Donatas Banionis (Kris), Yuri Yarvet (Snaut), Anatoli Sonlonitsin (Sartorius)

212
Solaris

A psychologist is sent to investigate the many deaths in a space station orbiting a remote planet.

Andrei Tarkovsky's imaginative science fiction meditation on guilt and remembrance concerns a psychologist who discovers that a planet's ocean can materialize ghosts aboard the space station, who are clones of people known to the members of the crew. He is confronted by a manifestation of a woman he once loved, who killed herself after he left her. A haunting, metaphysical movie, it raises philosophical and ethical questions that end with a strange and startling image. It is of a scientist seeing a recreation of his family life on Earth; he is standing outside, looking through the window of his home, where it is raining indoors. Like others before him, Tarkovsky uses science fiction with its alien environments to explore what it means to be human.

The Best Years of Our Lives
US   1946   182m   bw
Samuel Goldwyn
🔲 ▭ ◑ ◐

w Robert Sherwood *novel* Glory for Me by Mackinlay Kantor *d* William Wyler *ph* Gregg Toland *m* Hugo Friedhofer *ad* George Jenkins, Perry Ferguson *ed* Daniel Mandell

☆ Fredric March (Al Stephenson), Myrna Loy (Milly Stephenson), Teresa Wright (Peggy Stephenson), Dana Andrews (Fred Derry), Virginia Mayo (Marie Derry), Cathy O'Donnell (Wilma Cameron), *Hoagy Carmichael* (Butch Engle), *Harold Russell* (Homer Parrish), Gladys George (Hortense Derry), Roman Bohnen (Pat Derry), Ray Collins (Mr. Milton)

'One of the best pictures of our lives!' – *Variety*

'Easily the best film from Hollywood on the warrior's return.' – *Sunday Graphic*

● In 1977 came a TV remake *Returning Home* but it did not lead to the expected series.
● Harold Russell was a handless veteran, with no training as an actor, whose only film this was until *Inside Moves* in 1980.

👤 picture; Robert Sherwood; William Wyler; Hugo Friedhofer; Fredric March; Harold Russell; Daniel Mandell

🎬 picture

La Grande Illusion
France   1937   117m   bw
Réalisations d'Art Cinématographique (Frank Rollmer, Albert Pinkovitch)
🔲 ▭ ◑ ◐

w Jean Renoir, Charles Spaak *d* Jean Renoir *ph* Christian Matras *m* Joseph Kosma *m/ly* Vincent Telly, Albert Valsien *md* Emile Vuillermoz *ad* Eugène Lourie *ed* Marguerite Renoir, Marthe Huguet

☆ *Pierre Fresnay* (Capt de Boeldieu), *Erich von Stroheim* (Von Raffenstein), *Jean Gabin* (Marechal), Julien Carette (Cartier), Marcel Dalio (Rosenthal), Gaston Modot (Surveyor), Jean Dasté (Teacher), Dita Parlo (Peasant woman)

'The story is true. It was told to me by my friends in the war ... notably by Pinsard who flew fighter planes. I was in the reconnaissance squadron. He saved my life many times when the German fighters became too persistent. He himself was shot down seven times. His escapes are the basis for the story.' – *Jean Renoir*

'Artistically masterful.' – *Variety*

'One of the true masterpieces of the screen.' – *Pauline Kael, 70s*

♟ best picture

211
The Best Years of Our Lives

Three men come home from war to a small middle-American community, and find it variously difficult to pick up where they left off.

Goldwyn had commissioned from Mackinlay Kantor a story about the resettlement of ex-servicemen in a small American town; but he had lost interest when Kantor wrote it in blank verse. Wyler liked it, though, and Sherwood turned it into a compelling screenplay about the alienation many servicemen felt on coming back to civilian life. To achieve some authenticity, Wyler cast the non-professional Harold Russell, a veteran who had lost both hands in a training accident. The situations and even some of the characters now seem a little obvious, but this was a superb example of high-quality film-making in the Forties, with smiles and tears cunningly spaced, and a film which said what was needed on a vital subject.

210
La Grande Illusion

During World War I, three captured French pilots have an uneasy relationship with their German commandant.

Goebbels called this First World War prison camp drama 'public cinematograph enemy number one' and came near to destroying the original negative. Renoir saw it as a confrontation between different types of men. It also concerns the way class can transcend nationality: the aristocratic French pilot de Boeldieu has more in common with his German captor than he has with his compatriots, one from the working class, the other a Jewish banker. The film is concerned with escape, literal and metaphorical, and with that illusory belief in the brotherhood of man that could not withstand the impact of a war meant to end all wars. Impeccably directed and acted, it enshrines what may be Von Stroheim's finest performance.

The Hunchback of Notre Dame

★★ US 1939 117m bw
RKO (Pandro S. Berman)

⊟ ▤ ⊕~ ⊙

w Sonya Levien, Bruno Frank *d* William Dieterle
ph Joseph H. August *m* Alfred Newman *ad* Van Nest
Polglase *ed* Robert Wise, William Hamilton

☆ *Charles Laughton* (The Hunchback), *Cedric Hardwicke*
(Frollo), *Maureen O'Hara* (Esmeralda), *Edmond O'Brien*
(Gringoire), *Thomas Mitchell* (Clopin), *Harry Davenport*
(Louis XI), Walter Hampden (Claude), Alan Marshal
(Phoebus), George Zucco (Procurator), Katherine Alexander
(Mme. De Lys), Fritz Leiber (A Nobleman), Rod la Rocque
(Phillipo)

'A super thriller-chiller. Will roll up healthy grosses
at the ticket windows.' – *Variety*

'Has seldom been bettered as an evocation of
medieval life.' – *John Baxter, 1968*

'It exceeds in sheer magnificence any similar film
in history. Sets are vast and rich in detail, crowds
are immense, and camera uses of both are
versatile, varied and veracious.' – *Motion Picture
Herald*

● Other versions: *Esmeralda* (1906, French); *Notre Dame
de Paris* (1911, French); *The Darling of Paris* (1917, US,
with Theda Bara); in 1923 (US) with Lon Chaney; in 1956
(France/Italy) with Anthony Quinn..

♬ Alfred Newman

When Harry Met Sally

US 1989 95m DuArt
Palace/Castle Rock/Nelson Entertainment (Rob
Reiner, Andrew Scheinman)

⊟ ▤ ⊕~ ⊙ ∿ ∩

w Nora Ephron *d* Rob Reiner *ph* Barry Sonnenfeld
m Harry Connick Jnr and others *pd* Jane Musky
ed Robert Leighton

☆ Billy Crystal (Harry Burns), Meg Ryan (Sally Albright),
Carrie Fisher (Marie), Bruno Kirby (Jess), Steven Ford
(Joe), Lisa Jane Persky (Alice), Michelle Nicastro (Amanda)

'A love story with a form as old as the movies and
dialogue as new as this month's issue of Vanity
Fair.' – *Roger Ebert, Chicago Sun-Times*

'Ravishing, romantic lark brimming over with style,
intelligence and flashing wit.' – *Rolling Stone*

♬ Nora Ephron
✍ Nora Ephron

209

The Hunchback of Notre Dame

*The deformed Notre Dame bellringer rescues a Gypsy girl from the evil
intentions of her guardian*

A superb version of Victor Hugo's novel that is one of the best examples of Hollywood expertise at work: art direction, set construction, costumes, camera, lighting and above all direction brilliantly support an irresistible story and bravura acting. Laughton took his role with great seriousness; on the first day of shooting, with Laughton in his makeup and heavy hump and a thousand extras in position, he told the director that he could not go on. 'I thought I was ready, but it just did not come,' he said. 'But it will come and it will be good.' And it was, in a performance filled with pain and demanding empathy. His biographer Simon Callow called it in 1987 'a cornerstone of this century's dramatic achievement; it is a yardstick for all acting.'

208

When Harry Met Sally

*Over a period of 12 years, a couple meet occasionally to debate
whether there can be friendship without sex between a man and a
woman.*

A bitter-sweet, often funny romantic comedy that approached the subject of love from an unusual angle. This off-key comedy about love was as good of its kind as we're likely to get these days. There's a melancholy tinge as the two see their friends in successful relationships, while theirs with other people always go wrong. It has become famous for its scene in a crowded restaurant where Meg Ryan demonstrates to Billy Crystal's Harry what a fake orgasm sounds like; there is at least a suggestion that it is something he has heard before.

Ran

Japan 1985 161m colour
Herald-Ace/Nippon-Herald/Greenwich (Masato Hara,
Serge Silberman)

▣▣ ▣▣ ▤ ◉~ ◉ ◉ ∩

w Akira Kurosawa, Hideo Oguni, Masato Ide *d* Akira
Kurosawa *ph* Takao Saito *m* Toru Takemitsu *ad* Yoshiro
Muraki *ed* Akira Kurosawa

☆ Tatsuya Nakadai (Lord Hidetora Ichimonji), Satoshi
Terao (Tarotakatora Ichimonji), Jinpachi Nezu (Jiromasatora
Ichimonji), Daisuke Ryu (Saburonaotora Ichimonji), Peter
(Kyoami)

'Prepare to be astonished … a towering
achievement in any language.' – *People*

🛇 costumes (Emi Wada)
🛇 direction, photography, art direction
🏆 best foreign film

207
Ran

A Japanese version of King Lear, *with three sons instead of three daughters.*

Akira Kurosawa took until the age of 75 to film his long-cherished project. The narrative follows a similar pattern to Shakespeare's *King Lear.* Lord Hidetora bequeaths his power to two of his sons after the third tells him he is making a mistake. They both betray him, slaughtering his followers and sending him mad. Kurosawa's version ends in tragedy and chaos, with most of the participants dead and Hidetora's clan destroyed. As ever, he orchestrates the battles with great skill, working on an epic scale with more than a thousand extras, and using colour to marvellous effect. He also scores with the more intimate scenes between Hidetora and his transvestite court entertainer Kyoami.

Bambi

👫 US 1942 72m Technicolor
Walt Disney

▣▣ ▤ ◉~ ◉ ∩

w Larry Morey, Perce Pearce *story* Felix Salten *d* David
D. Hand *m* Frank Churchill, Edward Plumb

☆ voices of: Bobby Stewart (Bambi), Peter Behn
(Thumper), Paula Winslowe (Bambi's Mother), Stan
Alexander (Flower), Cammie King (Faline)

'The ultimate stag movie.' – *anon*

'The film, charming and touching as it can be,
belongs more to the Disney of whimsy and
sentiment than it does to the creative artist; and
those who remember the Schubert in *Fantasia* will
know what I mean when I say that a good deal of
this tale of a forest deer is in Disney's Ave Maria
manner.' – *Dilys Powell*

'Sheer enchantment.' – *C. A. Lejeune*

🛇 Frank Churchill, Edward Plumb; song 'Love Is a Song'
(*m* Frank Churchill, *ly* Larry Morey); sound recording (Sam
Slyfield)

206
Bambi

The story of a forest deer, from the book by Felix Salten.

One of Disney's most memorable, sentimental and brilliant achievements, this animated feature follows a forest deer from birth to maturity. The theme, of the circle of life, was one the studio returned to in The Lion King. Although death intrudes, when Bambi's mother is shot by hunters, it's an otherwise paradisiacal forest, in which all animals live in harmony and man and his dogs are the only predators. The misty landscapes draw on sources as varied as Maxfield Parrish and Chinese art; instead of the songs of later Disney features, there's a symphonic score, and when a song is used, it's marvellously matched with imagery as in the April showers sequence. It has a great comic character in Thumper the rabbit, a splendid stag fight done in an impressionistic manner and a forest fire sequence that is genuinely thrilling.

Trouble in Paradise
US   1932   86m   bw
Paramount (Ernst Lubitsch)
◉

w Samson Raphaelson, Grover Jones *play* The Honest Finder by Laszlo Aladar *d* Ernst Lubitsch *ph* Victor Milner *m* W. Franke Harling *ad* Hans Dreier
☆ *Herbert Marshall* (Gaston Monescu/La Valle), *Miriam Hopkins* (Lily Vautier), *Kay Francis* (Mariette Colet), *Edward Everett Horton* (Francois Filiba), *Charles Ruggles* (The Major), C. Aubrey Smith (Adolph Giron), Robert Greig (Jacques the Butler), Leonid Kinskey (Radical)

> 'Swell title, poor picture. Better for the class houses than the subsequents.' – *Variety*

> 'One of the gossamer creations of Lubitsch's narrative art … it would be impossible in this brief notice to describe the innumerable touches of wit and of narrative skill with which it is unfolded.' – *Alexander Bakshy*

> 'A shimmering, engaging piece of work … in virtually every scene a lively imagination shines forth.' – *New York Times*

> 'An almost continuous musical background pointed up and commented on the action. The settings were the last word in modernistic design.' – *Theodor Huff, 1948*

● A Region 1 DVD release includes commentary by Lubitsch biographer Scott Eyman

205
Trouble in Paradise

Jewel thieves insinuate themselves into the household of a rich Parisienne, and one falls in love with her.

Ernst Lubitsch's witty movie was intended as a satire on detective stories and was based on a famous Hungarian thief. It is a pacy story of cross and double cross among society jewel thieves: Herbert Marshall plays the jewel thief who falls in love with a rich Parisienne, while planning with his partner-in-crime, Miriam Hopkins, to rob her. However, when Marshall exposes a company director as a thief and nothing is done because of the scandal involved, he leaves the lady he has fallen for and returns to his old partner in crime. For connoisseurs, it can not be faulted with its sparkling dialogue, innuendo, great performances and masterly cinematic narrative. It is one of the jewels of American sophisticated cinema.

> 'Uncle Leo's bedtime story for you older tots! The things they do among the playful rich – oh, boy!'

The Philadelphia Story
US   1940   112m   bw
MGM (Joseph L. Mankiewicz)
▥ ▤ ◕ ⌁

w Donald Ogden Stewart *play* Philip Barry *d* George Cukor *ph* Joseph Ruttenberg *m* Franz Waxman *ad* Cedric Gibbons *ed* Frank Sullivan
☆ *Katharine Hepburn* (Tracy Lord), *Cary Grant* (C.K. Dexter Haven), *James Stewart* (Macauley Connor), *Ruth Hussey* (Elizabeth Imbrie), *Roland Young* (Uncle Willie), *John Halliday* (Seth Lord), *Mary Nash* (Margaret Lord), *Virginia Weidler* (Dinah Lord), *John Howard* (George Kittredge), *Henry Daniell* (Sidney Kidd)

> 'There are just not enough superlatives sufficiently to appreciate this show.' – *Hollywood Reporter*

> 'An exceptionally bright job of screenplay writing … though films like this do little to advance the art of motion pictures, they may help to convince some of the more discerning among cultural slugabeds that when movies want to turn their hand to anything, they can turn it.' – *Otis Ferguson*

● Cary Grant donated his salary to war relief.
● Remade in 1956 as *High Society* (musical version)
♟ Donald Ogden Stewart; James Stewart
♔ best picture; George Cukor; Katharine Hepburn; Ruth Hussey

204
The Philadelphia Story

A stuffy heiress, about to be married for the second time, turns human and returns gratefully to number one.

Hollywood's most wise and sparkling comedy is a delight from start to finish. Philip Barry wrote the play for Katharine Hepburn and she bought the film rights so that she would be able to play it again on screen, at a time when Hollywood regarded her as box-office poison. Donald Ogden Stewart's script was an improvement on the original play, and George Cukor's direction was so discreet that you could hardly sense it. All the performances were just perfect. MGM recorded a stage performance to see where the laughs came. After Cukor had made the film he checked one against the other and found that the laughs were in a different place in the film, because of added visual jokes.

'They're Dancing Cheek-To-Cheek
Again!'

Top Hat
👫 US 1935 100m bw
RKO (Pandro S. Berman)
⬚ ▤ ◔ ◉

w Dwight Taylor, Allan Scott *d* Mark Sandrich *ph* David
Abel, Vernon Walker *m/ly* Irving Berlin *ch* Hermes Pan
ad Van Nest Polglase, Carroll Clark *ed* William Hamilton
☆ *Fred Astaire* (Jerry Travers), *Ginger Rogers* (Dale
Tremont), *Edward Everett Horton* (Horace Hardwick), *Helen
Broderick* (Madge Hardwick), *Eric Blore* (Bates), *Erik
Rhodes* (Alberto Beddini)

'The theatres will hold their own world series with
this one. It can't miss.' – *Variety*

'In 25 years *Top Hat* has lost nothing of its gaiety
and charm.' – *Dilys Powell, 1960*

♫ 'No Strings'; 'Isn't This a Lovely Day'; Top Hat, White Tie
and Tails'; 'Cheek to Cheek'; 'The Piccolino'
⚬ best picture; song 'Cheek to Cheek'; Hermes Pan; art
direction

203
Top Hat

The path of true love is roughened by mistaken identities.

A marvellous Astaire-Rogers musical which has Fred and Ginger at
their peak. It has a more or less realistic London supplanted by a totally
artificial Venice, and show-stopping numbers in a style which is no
more, separated by amusing plot complications lightly handled by a
team of deft *farceurs*. The slow double-takes of Edward Everett
Horton's befuddled impresario, Eric Blore's supercilious butler, and,
above all, Helen Broderick's worldly-wise wife add considerably to the
amusement. What matters, though, are the dances, the way Astaire and
Rogers do not merely step out superbly together, but express the most
delicate of emotions while doing so. Their collaboration reached its
apotheosis with the deliciously romantic 'Cheek to Cheek', with Rogers
fluttering in peacock feathers. Irving Berlin's score was one of his best,
with the songs tailored to Astaire's particular style. It was an elegant
one – the title song, 'Top Hat, White Tie and Tails' sums it up perfectly.

Sons of the Desert
👫 US 1934 68m bw
Hal Roach
⬚ ▤ ◔ ◉ ◉
GB title: *Fraternally Yours*
w Frank Craven, Byron Morgan *d* William A. Seiter
ph Kenneth Peach *m/ly* Marvin Hatley *ed* Bert Jordan
☆ *Stan Laurel* (Himself), *Oliver Hardy* (Himself), *Charley
Chase* (Himself), Mae Busch (Mrs. Lottie Chase Hardy),
Dorothy Christie (Mrs. Betty Laurel), Lucien Littlefield (Dr.
Horace Meddick)

'Funny all the way through.' – *New York Times*

202
Sons of the Desert

*Stan and Ollie want to go to a Chicago convention, but kid their wives
that they are going on a cruise for health reasons.*

An archetypal Laurel and Hardy comedy that is unsurpassed for gags,
pacing and sympathetic characterization, as Stan and Ollie, hen-pecked
as always, devise frantic schemes to get to a Chicago convention, and
then wish they had not. Its story of marital discord was reflected in real
life, with both men contemplating divorce. The mood of the film,
though, is light-hearted and happy. There is less slapstick than usual;
the emphasis is on character and situation. Stan Laurel is as other-
worldly as ever, contentedly munching on decorative wax fruit as Ollie
fails to persuade his wife to let him attend the convention. It is the dialogue, and interplay of the duo's gestures, that carry the comedy, particularly in the two miscreants' explanation to their knowing wives of
their entirely fictitious escape from a shipwreck.

Pygmalion

GB 1938 96m bw
Gabriel Pascal
▆ ◎~ ◎

w Anatole de Grunwald, W. P. Lipscomb, Cecil Lewis, Ian Dalrymple *play* Bernard Shaw *d* Anthony Asquith, Leslie Howard *ph* Harry Stradling *m* Arthur Honegger *ad* Laurence Irving *ed* David Lean
☆ *Leslie Howard* (Henry Higgins), *Wendy Hiller* (Eliza Doolittle), *Wilfrid Lawson* (Alfred Doolittle), *Scott Sunderland* (Colonel Pickering), *Marie Lohr* (Mrs Higgins), *David Tree* (Freddy Eynsford-Hill), *Esmé Percy* (Count Aristid Karpathy), *Everley Gregg* (Mrs Eynsford-Hill), *Jean Cadell* (Mrs Pearce)

'Ought to have big potentialities in the US, with some cutting … An introductory title briefly gives the source of the play, which was Shakespeare's *Pygmalion*.' – *Variety*

'Every possible care has been taken in the presentation of what may well prove to have a significant effect on future British film production, for it is live, human entertainment, flawlessly presented and making an obvious appeal to all kinds of audiences.' – *The Cinema*

● Remade in 1964 as *My Fair Lady* (Musical version)
♟ Bernard Shaw; Ian Dalrymple, Cecil Lewis, W. P. Lipscomb
♙ best picture; Leslie Howard; Wendy Hiller

201
Pygmalion

A professor of phonetics takes a bet that he can turn a Cockney flower seller in six months into a lady who can pass as a duchess.

A perfectly splendid Shavian comedy of bad manners, extremely well filmed and containing memorable lines and performances. As Eliza Doolittle, the victim of the professor's experiment, Wendy Hiller has never been bettered. Shaw was not happy with Leslie Howard's performance, thinking him too weak; he would have preferred Charles Laughton in the role. But he admitted, 'the public will like him and probably want him to marry Eliza, which is just what I don't want.' It was one of the most heartening and adult British films of the Thirties.

M

Germany 1931 118m bw
Nero Film (Seymour Nebenzal)
▆▆ ▆▆ ▆ ◎~ ◎ ◎

w Thea von Harbou, Paul Falkenberg, Adolf Jansen, Karl Vash *d* Fritz Lang *ph* Fritz Arno Wagner *m* Adolf Jansen *ad* Karl Vollbrecht, Emil Hasler *ed* Paul Falkenberg
☆ *Peter Lorre* (Franz Becker), Otto Wernicke (Inspector Karl Lohmann), Gustav Gründgens (Schraenker)

'Visual excitement, pace, brilliance of surface and feeling for detail.' – *New Yorker, 1977*

● Of Lang's later work, *Fury* comes closest to the feeling and style of *M*.

200
M

A psychopathic murderer of children evades the police but is caught by the city's criminals who find his activities giving them a bad name.

Fritz Lang's first sound film is an unmistakable classic. It is part social melodrama and part satire, but entirely unforgettable, with most of its sequences brilliantly staged. With his soft, lisping voice, melancholy manner and oddly disturbing looks, Peter Lorre, who had already played a sex maniac on the stage, was ideal casting, as the murderer, based on the real-life serial killer Peter Kürten. He gives one of the greatest of screen performances. Lorre's performance as a man who is powerless to control his urges is unforgettable. He is mostly a supremely unhealthy, heavy breathing presence, not much given to speaking, until his final, dramatic outburst at his trial by fellow criminals, 'I haven't any control over this evil thing that's inside me. The fire! The voices! The torment!… Who know's what it's like to be me?'

Rembrandt
GB   1936   85m   bw
London Films (Alexander Korda)
📽 🎬 ⊙

w Lajos Biro, June Head, Carl Zuckmayer *d* Alexander
Korda *ph* Georges Perinal, Richard Angst *m* Geoffrey Toye
ed William Hornbeck, Francis D. Lyon
☆ *Charles Laughton* (Rembrandt van Rijn), Elsa
Lanchester (Hendrickje Stoffels), Gertrude Lawrence (Geertje
Dirx), Edward Chapman (Fabrizius), Walter Hudd (Banning
Cocq), Roger Livesey (Beggar Saul), Herbert Lomas (Miller
Harmen van Rijn), Allan Jeayes (Dr. Tulp), Sam Livesey
(Auctioneer), Raymond Huntley (Ludvig), John Clements
(Gavaert Flink)

'Never exciting, and only partly believable … a
feature film without a story plot.' – *Variety*

'Amazingly full of that light which the great master
of painting subdued to his supreme purpose.' –
James Agate

'The film is ruined by lack of story and continuity: it
has no drive. Like *The Private Life of Henry the
Eighth* it is a series of unrelated tableaux.' –
Graham Greene

199
Rembrandt

Episodes in the life of the 17th-century painter.

This was another of Charles Laughton's versions of famous men for
producer Alexander Korda. Gone was the exuberance of his Henry VIII;
instead he presented an austerely comic, gently tragic character piece.
Laughton is convincing as a painter and his wife Elsa Lanchester
played opposite him with great poignancy. The film did not draw audiences, though Korda offered free admission to anyone owning a
Rembrandt; but it survives on the quality of its acting and its superb
staging and photography.

The Thief of Baghdad

ⁿⁿ GB 1940 109m Technicolor
London Films (Alexander Korda)
■ ⊛~ ⌒

w Miles Malleson, Lajos Biro *d* Michael Powell, Ludwig Berger, Tim Whelan *ph* Georges Périnal, Osmond Borradaile *m* Miklos Rozsa *ad* Vincent Korda *ed* Charles Crichton, William Hornbeck *sp* Lawrence Butler

☆ *Conrad Veidt* (Jaffar), *Sabu* (Abu), John Justin (Ahmad), June Duprez (Princess), Morton Selten (King), Miles Malleson (Sultan), *Rex Ingram* (Djinni), Mary Morris (Halima)

'The true stuff of fairy tale.' – *Basil Wright*

'Both spectacular and highly inventive.' – *NFT, 1969*

'Magical, highly entertaining, and now revalued by Hollywood moguls Lucas and Coppola.' – *Time Out, 1980*

● Previously filmed in 1924 with Douglas Fairbanks Snr. Remade in 1960 (Italy/France) with Steve Reeves.
👤 Georges Périnal; Vincent Korda
🏆 Miklos Rozsa

198
The Thief of Baghdad

A boy thief helps a deposed king thwart an evil usurper.

This is a marvellous blend of magic, action and music, the only film to catch on celluloid the overpowering atmosphere of the Arabian Nights. Alexander Korda, its producer, wanted to make the film to exploit the talents of his two biggest stars, Sabu and Conrad Veidt, both of whom went on to give performances to match any in their careers. It ended up with two directors because Ludwig Berger was good with actors, but not spectacle, which Michael Powell handled brilliantly. In the event Korda and Berger quarreled and most of his footage never made it into the final cut.

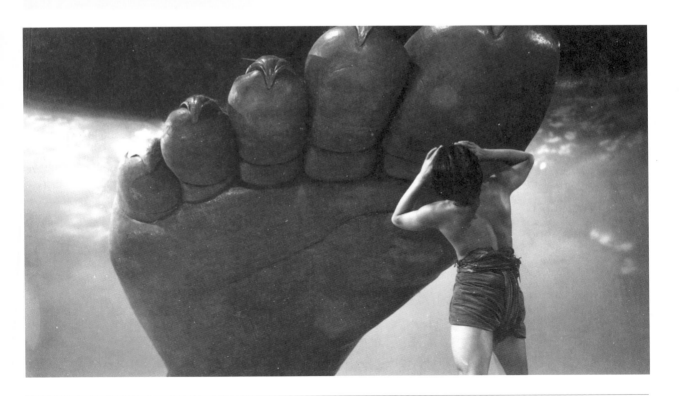

Love Me Tonight
US   1932   104m   bw
Paramount (Rouben Mamoulian)
🇺🇸 ◉

w Samuel Hoffenstein, Waldemar Young, George Marion
Jnr play Tailor in the Château by Leopold Marchand and
Paul Armont d Rouben Mamoulian ph Victor Milner
ad Hans Dreier ed William Shea songs Rodgers and Hart
☆ Maurice Chevalier (Maurice Courtelin), Jeanette
MacDonald (Princess Jeanette), Charles Butterworth (Count
de Savignac), Charles Ruggles (Vicomte Gilbert de Vareze),
Myrna Loy (Countess Vantine), C. Aubrey Smith (The
Duke), Elizabeth Patterson (Aunt), Ethel Griffies (Aunt),
Blanche Frederici (Aunt), Robert Greig (Major-Domo
Flamond)

'A musical frolic, whimsical in its aim and delicately
carried out in its pattern.' – Variety

'Gay, charming, witty, it is everything that the
Lubitsch musicals should have been but never
were.' – John Baxter, 1968

''A rich amalgam of filmic invention, witty
decoration and wonderful songs.' – NFT, 1974

● The Region 1 DVD release includes audio commentary
by Miles Kreuger, Chevalier singing 'Louise' and Jeanette
MacDonald singing 'Love Me Tonight'.
♫ 'Song of Paree'; 'Isn't It Romantic'; 'Lover'; 'Mimi'; 'A
Woman Needs Something Like That'; 'Love Me Tonight';
'The Son-of-a-Gun Is Nothing But a Tailor'; 'Poor Apache'

197
Love Me Tonight

A Parisian tailor accidentally moves into the aristocracy.

This is possibly the most fluently cinematic comedy musical ever made, a wonderful edifice built on a slight plot. Sounds and words, lyrics and music are deftly blended into a compulsively and consistently laughable mosaic of sophisticated nonsense; one better than the best of Lubitsch and Clair. Rouben Mamoulian's direction weaves songs and action together brilliantly and ends with a splendid romantic joke as Jeanette MacDonald gallops on horseback so that she can stand in the middle of a railway track to stop the train carrying Maurice Chevalier away from her.

The Player
US   1992   124m   DeLuxe
Guild/Avenue (David Brown, Michael Tolkin, Nick
Wechsler)
📼 🇺🇸 ◎ ◉ ◉ ∩

w Michael Tolkin novel Michael Tolkin d Robert Altman
ph Jean Lepine m Thomas Newman pd Stephen Altman
ad Jerry Fleming ed Geraldine Peroni, Maysie Hoy
☆ Tim Robbins (Griffin Mill), Greta Scacchi (June
Gudmundsdottir), Fred Ward (Walter Stuckel), Whoopi
Goldberg (Detective Avery), Peter Gallagher (Larry Levy),
Brion James (Joel Levison), Cynthia Stevenson (Bonnie
Sherow), Vincent D'Onofrio (David Kahane), Dean Stockwell
(Andy Civella), Richard E. Grant (Tom Oakley), Sydney
Pollack (Dick Mellen)

'The movie has the exhilarating nonchalance of the
director's seventies classics, and its tone is volatile,
elusive: with breathtaking assurance, it veers from
psychological-thriller suspense to goofball comedy
to icy satire.' – Terrence Rafferty, New Yorker

● The film featured more than 60 stars playing themselves,
including Harry Belafonte, James Coburn, Peter Falk, Teri
Garr, Angelica Huston, Jack Lemmon, Nick Nolte, Burt
Reynolds, Julia Roberts, Susan Sarandon, Rod Steiger and
Bruce Willis.
● The Region 1 and 2 DVD releases include commentary
by Robert Altman and Michael Tolkin.
🏆 Robert Altman; Michael Tolkin; Geraldine Peroni
🏅 Robert Altman; Michael Tolkin

196
The Player

A Hollywood studio executive gets away with murder.

Robert Altman's satirical look at Hollywood filmmaking is a great pleasure, from its opening virtuoso sequence, a nine-minute crane shot that circles a studio building and peers at its inhabitants as if they were creatures in a zoo, to its final parody of an action movie. In between, the movie is witty, surprising and intelligent. It observes the power games and the doubts and insecurities of people with inflated egos and larger expense accounts. It is a deft and dazzling satire on the film industry and, by extension, on America itself.

Pinocchio

US   1940   77m   Technicolor
Walt Disney

d Hamilton Luske, Ben Sharpsteen *m/ly Leigh Harline, Ned Washington, Paul J. Smith* ad Al Zinnen, Ken Anderson, Thor Putnam, Charles Philippi, McLaren Stewart, Kendall O'Connor, Hugh Hennesy, John Hubley, Terrell Stapp, Dick Kelsey *supervisors* Ben Sharpsteen, Hamilton Luske
☆ voices of: Dickie Jones (Pinocchio), Christian Rub (Geppetto), *Cliff Edwards* (Jiminy Cricket), Evelyn Venable (The Blue Fairy), Walter Catlett (J. Worthington Foulfellow), Frankie Darro (Lampwick)

'A film of amazing detail and brilliant conception.'
– *Leonard Maltin*

'A work that gives you almost every possible kind of pleasure to be got from a motion picture.'
– *Richard Mallett, Punch*

♫ 'When You Wish Upon A Star'; 'Give a Little Whistle'; 'Hi-Diddle-Dee-Dee (An Actor's Life for Me)'; 'I've Got No Strings'
Leigh Harline, Ned Washington, Paul J. Smith (*m*); song 'When You Wish Upon a Star' (*m* Leigh Harline, *ly* Ned Washington)

195
Pinocchio

The blue fairy breathes life into a puppet, which has to prove itself before it can turn into a real boy.

Disney's version of this charming tale is a fascinating, superbly organized and streamlined cartoon feature without a single second of boredom. There is wit in the foxy Foulfellow and his sidekick Gideon persuading Pinocchio to become an actor, horror in Pleasure Island, where bad boys are turned into donkeys, some of Disney's most brilliant animation in the sequence with Monstro the Whale, and plenty of emotion in the reunion of the puppet with Geppetto and his transformation into a real boy. Sheer delight.

Kwaidan

Japan 1964 164m Eastmancolor
Tohoscope
Ninjin Club/Bungei
⬚ ▤ ◉ ◎

w Yoko Mizuki d Masaki Kobayashi ph Yoshio Miyajima
m Toru Takemitsu ad Shigemasa Toda ed Hisashi Sagara
☆ Rentaro Mikuni (Samurai), Ganjiro Nakamura (Head
Priest), Katsuo Nakamura (Hoichi), Keiko Kishi (Yuki/Snow
Woman), Tatsuya Nakadai (Minokichi), Kanemon Nakamura
(Kannai)
⚱ best foreign film

194
Kwaidan

Four elegant ghost stories by Lafcadio Hearn.

This literally haunting film is among the most beautiful ever made.
Masaki Kobayashi creates a succession of exotic, perfectly composed
images and strange narratives. The supernatural tales are ones of loss,
usually of love, though in one instance, of a blind storyteller's ears.
Kobayashi spent a year filming the stories, using antiques from the
period of the stories to give them an aesthetic authenticity. Toru
Takemitsu's percussive and eerie score brilliantly evoke an other-
worldly atmosphere to set off a work of great, decorative artifice.

'The scenes! The story! The stars! But
above all – the suspense!'

The Night of the Hunter

US 1955 93m bw
UA/Paul Gregory
⬚ ▤ ◉ ◎ ◉ ◎

w James Agee novel Davis Grubb d Charles Laughton
ph Stanley Cortez m Walter Schumann ad Hilyard Brown
ed Robert Golden
☆ Robert Mitchum (Preacher Harry Powell), Shelley
Winters (Willa Harper), Lillian Gish (Rachel), Don Beddoe
(Walt Spoon), Evelyn Varden (Icey Spoon), Peter Graves
(Ben Harper), James Gleason (Birdie)

'One of the most frightening movies ever made.'
– Pauline Kael, 1968

'A genuinely sinister work, full of shocks and over-
emphatic sound effects, camera angles and
shadowy lighting.' – NFT, 1973

'One of the most daring, eloquent and personal
films to have come from America in a long time.'
– Derek Prouse

193
The Night of the Hunter

*A psychopathic preacher goes on the trail of hidden money, the secret
of which is held by two children.*

Charles Laughton's only film as a director was this strange, manic fantasy; an allegory of good and evil. Laughton saw it as a child's nightmare and evil finally comes to grief against the forces of sweetness and
light (the children, an old lady, water, animals). Although the narrative
does not flow smoothly, there are splendidly imaginative moments,
and no other film has ever quite achieved its texture. Many of its
images are unforgettable, from Shelley Winters drowned in her car, her
hair floating like weeds in the water, to the children escaping down the
misty river. Robert Mitchum gives what he regarded as his best performance as the seductively menacing preacher with 'love' and 'hate'
tattooed on his knuckles. The sadness for Laughton was that it took
many years for the film's unusual quality to be appreciated.

'A recollection of evil...'

Picnic at Hanging Rock

Australia 1975 115m Eastmancolor
Picnic Productions/Australia Film Corporation (Hal and Jim McElroy)

🎞 ▦ ⊘ ◉

w Cliff Green *novel* Joan Lindsay *d* Peter Weir
ph Russell Boyd *m* Bruce Smeaton *ad* David Copping
ed Max Lemon

☆ Rachel Roberts (Mrs. Appleyard), Dominic Guard (Michael Fitzhubert), Helen Morse (Dianne De Poiters), Jacki Weaver (Minnie), Vivean Gray (Miss Greta McGraw), Kirsty Child (Dora Lumley)

'Atmospherically vivid, beautifully shot, and palpably haunting.' – *Michael Billington, Illustrated London News*

'If this film had a rational and tidy conclusion, it would be a good deal less interesting. But as a tantalizing puzzle, a tease, a suggestion of forbidden answer just out of earshot, it works hypnotically and very nicely indeed.' – *Roger Ebert*

🏆 Russell Boyd

192
Picnic at Hanging Rock

In 1900, schoolgirls set out for a picnic; some disappear and are never found.

Peter Weir's intriguing mystery is a film that ventures successfully into metaphysical realms and bravely offers no answer to its central puzzle, which remains as an unsettling question that continues to haunt the mind. The opening scenes concentrate on the incongruity, and the wrongness, of a college, run like an English public school, in the Australian bush. The girls' innocence is stressed, as is their curiosity about sex, a matter that both fascinates and frightens them. The day is one given over to love, St Valentine's Day. And in the heat of the day, three girls climb the high, thrusting volcanic rock that provides some shade for their picnic. They are unexpectedly joined by their prim teacher and all vanish. Whether you want to regard the drama as a parable of sexual awakening or of colonial repression, it successfully retains its own enigma.

The Piano

Australia 1993 120m Eastmancolor
Entertainment/CIBY 2000/Jan Chapman

🎞 ▦ ⊘~ ◉ ◉ 🎧

wd Jane Campion *ph* Stuart Dryburgh *m* Michael Nyman
pd Andrew McAlpine *ed* Veronika Jenet

☆ Holly Hunter (Ada McGrath), Harvey Keitel (George Baines), Sam Neill (Stewart), Anna Paquin (Fiona McGrath), Kerry Walker (Aunt Morag), Genevieve Lemon (Nessie), Tungla Baker (Hira), Ian Mune (Reverend)

'A riveting excursion into 19th-century sexuality, a movie that takes the conventions of the Gothic romance and refracts them through a dark contemporary lens.' – *David Ansen, Newsweek*

'Not since the early days of cinema, when audiences trampled over each other towards the exit to avoid the train emerging from the screen, could I imagine the medium of film to be so powerful.' – *Lizzie Francke, Sight and Sound*

'An emotionally devastating tour de force, both heart-rending and heart-warming.' – *Film Review*

● The film shared the Palme d'Or as best film, and Holly Hunter won the award as best actress, at the Cannes Film Festival in 1993.
🏃 Holly Hunter; Anna Paquin; Jane Campion (as writer)
🏆 best picture; Jane Campion (as director); Stuart Dryburgh; Veronika Jenet; costume design (Janet Patterson)
🏆 Holly Hunter; Andrew McAlpine

191
The Piano

A mute Scottish widow travels with her young daughter for an arranged marriage to a landowner in New Zealand, where she is forced to leave her most-treasured possession, her piano, on a beach.

The strange opening of Jane Campion's film is followed by equally striking images of life in a simple, isolated community. It is a complex drama of lust and love, and of a woman emerging from an emotional silence in a repressive community into a self-determined and fulfilled life. The powerful and moving melodrama is beautifully photographed and impeccably acted, with an astonishing performance from Anna Paquin as the wilful daughter.

Throne of Blood

Japan   1957   105m   bw
Toho (Akira Kurosawa, Sojiro Motoki)

📽 ▦ @~ ⊚ ◉

original title: *Kumonosu-Jo*

w Hideo Oguni, Shinobu Hashimoto, Ryuzo Kikushima, Akira Kurosawa *play* William Shakespeare *d* Akira Kurosawa *ph* Asaichi Nakai *m* Masaru Sato *ad* Yoshiro Muraki, Kohei Ezaki *ed* Akira Kurosawa

☆ Toshiro Mifune (Taketoki Washizu), Isuzu Yamada (Asaji, Lady Washizu), Takashi Shimura (Noriyasu Odagura), Minoru Chiaki (Yoshiaki Miki), Akira Kubo (Yoshiteru), Takamaru Sasaki (Kunimaru), Chieko Naniwa (Witch)

'Its final impression is of a man who storms into a room with an impassioned speech to deliver and then discovers that he has forgotten what he came to say.' – *Kenneth Cavander, MFB*

'You should be strangely stimulated and have some fun at this film.' – *Bosley Crowther*

● A Region 1 DVD release includes audio commentary by Japanese film expert Michael Jeck and two alternative subtitle translations.

190
Throne of Blood

A samurai, spurred on by his wife and an old witch, murders his lord at Cobweb Castle.

Akira Kurosawa's version of Shakespeare's *Macbeth* retains the same plot as the original, but has been transposed to medieval Japan with the Samurai Washizu (Toshiro Mifune) in the Macbeth part. The equivalent of Lady Macbeth is Lady Washizu, a woman who is even more ferocious and determined. Kurosawa tells the tragedy in a series of stunning images, atmospheric and fog-laden, culminating in a savage and horrifying final sequence.

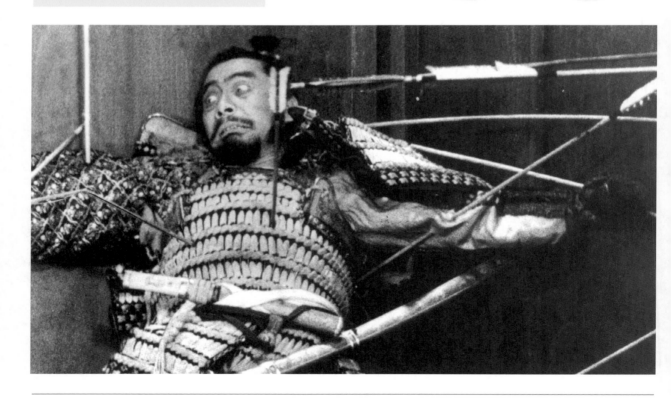

The Diary of a Country Priest

France 1950 120m bw
Union Générale Cinématographique (Léon Carré)

original title: *Journal d'un Curé de Campagne*
wd Robert Bresson *novel* Georges Bernanos *ph* L. Burel
m Jean-Jacques Grunenwald *ad* Pierre Charbonnier
ed Paulette Robert
☆ *Claude Laydu* (Priest of Ambricourt), Jean Riveyre
(Count), Armand Guibert (Priest of Torcy), Nicole Ladmiral
(Chantal)

189
The Diary of a Country Priest

A lonely young priest fails to make much impression in his first parish; and, falling ill, he dies alone.

Robert Bresson's striking, bleak, slow and austere film has little dialogue, and what there is comes straight from Bernanos' novel, but considerable visual beauty in the telling, using close-ups to display the priest's interior suffering, his spiritual anguish, as he attempts to convince his grudging parishioners of the need for faith and grace. Bresson's preferred cut ran for 160m, but he trimmed it by 40m at the urging of its producers; it was cut further, to 95m, when released in America, which made it harder to appreciate.

'Spies! Playing the game of love – and sudden death!'

The Lady Vanishes

GB 1938 97m bw
Gaumont British/Gainsborough (Edward Black)

w Sidney Gilliat, Frank Launder *novel* *The Wheel Spins* by
Ethel Lina White *d* Alfred Hitchcock *ph* Jack Cox
md Louis Levy *ed* R.E. Dearing, Alfred Roome
☆ *Margaret Lockwood* (Iris Henderson), *Michael Redgrave* (Gilbert Redman), *Dame May Whitty* (Miss Froy),
Paul Lukas (Dr. Hartz), *Basil Radford* (Charters), *Naunton Wayne* (Caldicott), *Catherine Lacey* (The Nun), *Cecil Parker* (Eric Todhunter), *Linden Travers* (Margaret Todhunter),
Googie Withers (Blanche), *Mary Clare* (Baroness), Philip
Leaver (Signor Doppo)

'Directed with such skill and velocity that it has
come to represent the very quintessence of screen
suspense.' – *Pauline Kael, 70s*

● Hitchcock was actually second choice as director. The
production was ready to roll as *Lost Lady*, directed by Roy
William Neill, with Charters and Caldicott already in place,
when Neill became unavailable and Hitch stepped in.
● Hitchcock makes a cameo appearance at a railway station
in London.
● Remade badly in 1974
● A Region 1 DVD release from Criterion includes audio
commentary by film historian Bruce Eder.

188
The Lady Vanishes

En route back to England by train from Switzerland, an old lady disappears and two young people investigate.

Hitchcock and his screenwriters brilliantly refurbished the disappearing lady trick in an exuberant comedy thriller. They even get away with a horrid model shot at the beginning. Michael Redgrave and Margaret Lockwood add high-spirited wit to the mystery. Along the way, it takes a dig at the policy of appeasement, as an English gentleman waves a white handkerchief to parlay with the enemy and is promptly shot. It is superb, suspenseful, brilliantly funny, meticulously detailed entertainment.

Passport to Pimlico

↟↟ GB 1949 84m bw
Ealing (E. V. H. Emmett)

w T. E. B. Clarke *d* Henry Cornelius *ph* Lionel Banes *m* Georges Auric *ad* Roy Oxley *ed* Michael Truman
☆ Stanley Holloway (Arthur Pemberton), *Margaret Rutherford* (Prof. Hatton-Jones), Basil Radford (Gregg), Naunton Wayne (Straker), Hermione Baddeley (Eddie Randall), John Slater (Frank Huggins), Paul Dupuis (Duke of Burgundy), Jane Hylton (Molly), Raymond Huntley (Mr. Wix), Betty Warren (Connie Pemberton), Barbara Murray (Shirley Pemberton), Sydney Tafler (Fred Cowan)

'One of the most felicitous and funny films since the age of the René Clair comedies.' – C. A. Lejeune

● The film was based on a genuine news item. The Canadian government presented to the Netherlands the room in which Princess Juliana was to bear a child.
● The Region 2 DVD release is available only as part of four-disc set, *Ealing Comedy Classics 2*.
🏅 T. E. B. Clarke

187
Passport to Pimlico

Part of a London district is discovered to belong to Burgundy, and the inhabitants find themselves free of rationing restrictions.

This was a delightful postwar escapist fantasy which benefited from T. E. B. Clarke's witty and inventive screenplay and fine performances from a notable gallery of character players. A cleverly detailed little comedy, it inaugurated the best period of Ealing in its preoccupation with suburban man and his foibles. It was not exactly satire, but it was great fun, and kindly with it. The film has a postwar nostalgia for less restricted and brighter times – the sun shines constantly on that corner of the English district that is briefly foreign without seeming different – as they explain, 'it's just because we are English that we're sticking up for our right to be Burgundian.' The wartime spirit of camaraderie is evoked and a good time is had by all.

Oh Mr Porter

↟↟ GB 1937 84m bw
GFD/Gainsborough (Edward Black)

w Marriott Edgar, Val Guest, J. O. C. Orton *story* Frank Launder *d* Marcel Varnel *ph* Arthur Crabtree *md* Louis Levy
☆ *Will Hay* (William Porter), *Moore Marriott* (Jeremiah Harbottle), *Graham Moffatt* (Albert Brown), Dave O'Toole (Postman), Dennis Wyndham (Grogan)

'That rare phenomenon: a film comedy without a dud scene.' – *Peter Barnes, 1964*

'Behind it lie the gusty uplands of the British music-hall tradition, whose rich soil the British film industry is at last beginning to exploit.' – *Basil Wright*

● The Region 2 DVD release is part of a two-disc set with *Convict 99*.

186
Oh Mr Porter

The stationmaster of an Irish halt catches gun-runners posing as ghosts.

This is Will Hay's finest comedy, in which he is partnered by his familiar and excellent stooges, the wily, senile Moore Marriott and the plump and lazy Graham Moffatt. Hay was always at his best playing a seedy incompetent, who covers up his many mistakes with a self-confident pomposity. Here, given a job out of harm's way as the stationmaster of an Irish halt, he catches gun-runners posing as ghosts more by luck than skill. The plot is borrowed from *The Ghost Train*, but each line and gag brings its own inventiveness. There is a splendid runaway train finale, with Hay and his crew fending off terrorists as the engine speeds through the countryside, crashing through level-crossing gates and narrowly avoiding collisions with oncoming expresses. It is a delight of character comedy and cinematic narrative.

The Tin Drum

West Germany/France 1979 142m
Eastmancolor
UA/Franz Seitz/Bioskop/GGB 14 KG/Hallelujah/
Artemis/Argos/Jadran/Film Polski

original title: *Die Blechtrommel*
w Jean-Claude Carrière, Franz Seitz, Volker Schlöndorff
novel Günter Grass *d* Volker Schlöndorff *ph* Igor Luther
m Maurice Jarre *pd* Nicos Perakis *ad* Nicos Perakis
ed Suzanne Baron
☆ David Bennent (Oskar Matzerath), Mario Adorf (Alfred
Matzerath), Angela Winkler (Agnes Matzerath), Daniel
Olbrychski (Jan Bronski), Katharina Thalbach (Maria),
Andrea Ferreol (Lina Greff)

'A big, sweeping film that does its best to serve the
torrential imagination of one of the most original,
most gifted German writers of our day.' – *Vincent
Canby, New York Times*

🏅 best foreign film

185
The Tin Drum

*Not caring for the world he is growing up in, a small boy determines to
remain a child.*

A brilliantly made version of a labyrinthine satire on German national-
ism and the rise of the Nazis, as seen from the viewpoint of a child. The
emphasis is sometimes on sex and scatological detail, for it is intended
to be disturbing viewing, and succeeds in its aim of depicting a frightening world where reason is overthrown. David Bennent, an eleven
year-old who was no bigger than a five-year-old child, gives a frightening, wide-eyed intensity to the role of Oskar, who refuses to accept any
responsibility for the society into which he is born by remaining a
small boy. Günter Grass' view that Nazism resulted in the infantilism of
an era is brilliantly conveyed in Volker Schlöndorff's film, which
restricts its view of the world to one that is witnessed from a child's
limited perspective.

October

USSR 1927 95m approx bw silent
Sovkino

w Sergei M. Eisenstein, Grigory Alexandrov *d* Sergei M.
Eisenstein *ph* Edouard Tissé, V. Popov
☆ Vasili Nikandrov (Lenin), N. Popov (Kerensky), Boris
Livanov (Minister Tereschenko)

'The film lacks excitement and may leave you cold.'
– *Pauline Kael*

'Some of the action scenes are genuinely stirring –
when he wasn't editorializing, the man really could
cut film.' – *David Kehr, Chicago Reader*

184
October

In 1917, the Kerensky regime is overthrown by the Bolsheviks.

Sergei Eisenstein made a propaganda masterpiece of the beginning of
the Russian revolution. Its images have all too often been mistaken and
used for genuine newsreel, so dynamic and realistic do they seem. The
storming of the Winter Palace is filmed as a stirring spectacle and there
are other memorable images, such as the opening of a bridge with dead
bodies sliding off it into the water below, including that of a horse that
dangles high in the air before plunging down. Cinematically, it is an
undoubted masterpiece.

A Night at the Opera

US   1935   96m   bw
MGM (Irving Thalberg)

w George S. Kaufman, Morrie Ryskind *d* Sam Wood
ph Merritt Gerstad *md* Herbert Stothart *ad* Cedric
Gibbons, Ben Carre *ed* William LeVanway
☆ *Groucho Marx* (Otis B. Driftwood), *Chico Marx*
(Fiorello), *Harpo Marx* (Tomasso), *Margaret Dumont* (Mrs
Claypool), Kitty Carlisle (Rosa Castaldi), Allan Jones
(Riccardo Baroni), Walter Woolf King (Rodolfo Lassparri),
Sig Rumann (Herman Gottlieb)

'Corking comedy with the brothers at par and biz
chances excellent … songs in a Marx picture are
generally at a disadvantage because they're more
or less interruptions, the customers awaiting the
next laugh.' – *Variety*

● Zeppo Marx absented himself from here on.

183
A Night at the Opera

Three zanies first wreck, then help an opera company.

The Marx Brothers' switch to MGM's glossier production machine gave them a bigger budget to play with as well as musical interludes by other than themselves for a change of pace. It also brought more outside control and discipline to their working methods. This first venture was certainly among the best of the Marxian extravaganzas. It includes Groucho and Chico's contract routine ('There ain't no Sanity Clause!') and the stateroom crush, where dozens of people pile into the same small space, which are enough on their own to bring joy. The brothers tried out their material on the road before audiences so that they could discover which scenes worked best, so the result was more polished than usual and with a softening of the Marx's anarchic attitudes to the world but no lessening of their comic spirit

'Television will never be the same!'

'Prepare yourself for a perfectly
outrageous motion picture!'

Network
US   1976   121m   Metrocolor   Panavision
MGM/UA (Howard Gottfried, Fred Caruso)

w Paddy Chayefsky *d* Sidney Lumet *ph* Owen Roizman
m Elliot Lawrence *ed* Alan Heim
☆ *Peter Finch* (Howard Beale), *William Holden* (Max
Schumacher), Faye Dunaway (Diana Christensen), Robert
Duvall (Frank Hackett), Wesley Addy (Nelson Chaney), Ned
Beatty (Arthur Jensen), Beatrice Straight (Louise
Schumacher), John Carpenter (George Bosch)

'The cast of this messianic farce take turns yelling
at us soulless masses.' – *New Yorker*

'Too much of this film has the hectoring stridency
of tabloid headlines.' – *Michael Billington,
Illustrated London News*

● The theme was taken up a year later in the shortlived TV
series *W.E.B.*
● Peter Finch died shortly after the film was released and
was first actor to be awarded a posthumous Academy Award.
👤 Paddy Chayefsky; Peter Finch; Faye Dunaway; Beatrice
Straight
🏆 best picture; Sidney Lumet; Owen Roizman; William
Holden; Ned Beatty
Ⓣ Peter Finch

182
Network

A network news commentator begins to say what he thinks about the world and becomes a new messiah to the people and an embarrassment to his sponsors.

Paddy Chayefsky's deliberately melodramatic satire on media corruption is hectic to the point of hysteria. His script recieved appropriate treatment from director Sidney Lumet and his cast, with both Peter Finch and William Holden at their finest. It is passionate and compulsively watchable in its attack on demagoguery and in its depiction of the dangerous madness exploited by the mass media. What once seemed overheated satire has come, with time, to resemble accurate reporting. Its very existence in a commercial system is as remarkable as its box-office success.

'They make the fighting sinful west blaze into action before your eyes!'

Destry Rides Again
US   1939   94m   bw
Universal (Joe Pasternak)
◨ ▤ ⚲ ~

w Felix Jackson, Gertrude Purcell, Henry Myers
novel Max Brand   *d* George Marshall   *ph* Hal Mohr
m Frank Skinner   *m/ly* Frederick Hollander, Frank Loesser
md Charles Previn   *ad* Jack Otterson   *ed* Milton Carruth
cos Vera West

☆ *James Stewart* (Tom Destry), *Marlene Dietrich* (Frenchy), *Brian Donlevy* (Kent), *Charles Winninger* ('Wash' Dimsdale), *Samuel S. Hinds* (Judge Slade), *Mischa Auer* (Boris Callahan), Irene Hervey (Janice Tyndall), Jack Carson (Jack Tyndall), *Una Merkel* (Lily Belle Callahan), Allen Jenkins (Bugs Watson), Warren Hymer (Gyp Watson), *Billy Gilbert* (Loupqerou)

'Makes the b.o. grade in a big way … just plain, good entertainment.' – *Variety*

'I think it was Lord Beaverbrook who said that Marlene Dietrich standing on a bar in black net stockings, belting out *See What the Boys in the Back Room Will Have*, was a greater work of art than the Venus de Milo.' – *Richard Roud*

● An early sound version in 1932 starred Tom Mix; *Frenchie* (1950) was a slight variation. See also *Destry*.

181
Destry Rides Again

A mild-mannered sheriff finally gets mad at local corruption and straps on his guns.

A film that brought sex to the Western, this represents Hollywood expertise at its very best. Its story manages to encompass suspense, comedy, romance, tenderness, vivid characterization, horseplay, songs and standard Western excitements, without moving for more than a moment from a studio main street set. Dietrich plays against her usual image as a tough and raucous singer at the Last Chance Saloon, engaging in a furious fist-fight with Una Merkel. (The censor cut one of her lines after the first showing, when she murmurs, 'There's gold in them thar hills', as she stuffs dollar bills down her cleavage.) It starts with a sign reading 'Welcome to Bottleneck' and an outburst of gunfire; it ends with tragedy followed by a running joke.

'It's no laughing matter.'

King of Comedy
US   1983   109m   Technicolor
TCF/Embassy International (Arnon Milchan)
◨ ▤ ⚲ ◎ ◎

w Paul D. Zimmerman   *d* Martin Scorsese   *ph* Fred Shuler
m various   *md* Robbie Robertson   *pd* Boris Leven
ad Lawrence Miller, Edward Pisoni   *ed* Thelma Schoonmaker

☆ *Robert DeNiro* (Rupert Pupkin), *Jerry Lewis* (Jerry Langford), Diahnne Abbott (Rita), Sandra Bernhard (Masha)

'This is a very frightening film, and in retrospect nothing about it seems funny at all.' – *Variety*

'Unquestionably one of the films of the year.' – *Guardian*

'A most eerie and memorable picture.' – *Spectator*

🏆 best original screenplay

180
King of Comedy

Obsessed with becoming a chat-show host, an aspiring comedian kidnaps his idol and ransoms him for a spot in the show.

Martin Scorsese's meditation on celebrity culture had Robert DeNiro as an aspiring comedian who kidnaps a chat show host, played by Jerry Lewis. An amusing, underplayed farce with a tragic lining, it provided a very convincing picture of today's media and the potential nastiness of fan worship. There was a disquieting ambivalence about it; as screenwriter Paul Zimmerman said, 'People knew the movie was funny as they were watching it, but they didn't feel safe enough to laugh.'

Les Misérables

US 1935 109m bw
Twentieth Century (Darryl F. Zanuck)

w W. P. Lipscomb *novel* Victor Hugo *d* Richard Boleslawski *ph* Gregg Toland *m* Alfred Newman *ed* Barbara McLean

☆ *Fredric March* (Jean Valjean), *Charles Laughton* (Javert), Cedric Hardwicke (Bishop Bienvenu), Rochelle Hudson (Big Cosette), Frances Drake (Eponine), John Beal (Marius), Jessie Ralph (Mme. Magloire), Florence Eldridge (Fantine)

'Brilliant filmization, sure fire for heavy money.' – *Variety*

'Unbelievably thrilling in all the departments of its manufacture … a memorable experience in the cinema.' – *New York Times*

'A superlative effort, a thrilling, powerful, poignant picture.' – *New York Evening Post*

'Deserving of rank among the cinema's finest achievements.' – *New York World Telegram*

● Other versions of the story: 1909, 1913 (French); 1917 (William Farnum); 1923 (French: Gabriel Gabrio); 1929 as *The Bishop's Candlesticks* (Walter Huston); 1934 (French: Harry Baur); 1946 (Italian: Gino Cervi); 1952 (US); 1956 (French: Jean Gabin); 1978 (British: Richard Jordan)

♟ best picture; Gregg Toland; editing

179
Les Misérables

A convict who makes good is hounded by a ruthless policeman with a fanatical sense of duty.

A solid, telling, intelligent version of Victor Hugo's much-filmed classic novel of the unjustly convicted Jean Valjean, who, sentenced to years in the galleys, emerges to build up his life again but is hounded by a cruel and relentless police officer. As the fanatical, pursuing Javert, Charles Laughton suggested repressed anger and guilt in a powerful performance that contrasted with Fredric March's strong Valjean. In acting and adaptation, it is hard to see how this film could be bettered. Its Polish-born director Richard Boleslawski, who trained in Moscow, responds to the drama of two conscience-stricken opponents (though Javert's better nature only pricks him late in the movie, just before his tragic death) with an almost religious intensity, aided by Gregg Toland's exceptional cinematography.

Le Million

France 1931 89m bw
Tobis (Frank Clifford)

wd René Clair *musical comedy* Georges Berr, M. Guillemaud *ph* Georges Périnal *m* Georges Van Parys, Armand Bernard, Philippe Parès *ad* Lazare Meerson

☆ Annabella (Beatrice), René Lefèvre (Michel), *Paul Olivier* ('Father Tulipe' Crochard), Louis Allibert (Prosper), Vanda Gréville (Vanda), Raymond Cordy (Taxi Driver)

'A good musical farce that ought to do well everywhere … it has speed, laughs, splendid photography and a good cast.' – *Variety*

'René Clair at his exquisite best; no one else has ever been able to make a comedy move with such delicate inevitability.' – *New Yorker, 1978*

'I wanted an atmosphere of foolishness … we put gauze between the actors and the sets, which created an illusion of unreality.' – *René Clair*

● The style of this film was developed and expanded in Hollywood by Lubitsch in *One Hour with You* and by Mamoulian in *Love Me Tonight*.

178
Le Million

An artist and an ingratiating crook search Paris for a lost lottery ticket.

René Clair's comic masterpiece combines slapstick and satire in a zany tale about a search for a lost lottery ticket. A wonderful chase film, with its delicate touch, perfect sense of comedy timing and infectious use of recitative and song, it is superb screen entertainment using most of the medium's resources. Clair and his artistic director, Lazare Meerson, emphasized the unreality of their *jeu d'esprit* in some sequences by hanging gauze between the actors and the sets. In like manner, Clair replaces dialogue with many varieties of song, from popular melodies to operetta. It remains one of the most lighthearted, delightful and inventive of films, with an operatic finale that becomes a rugby game as the cast dash, tackle and scrummage in search of the jacket containing the missing ticket.

'The screen's master of suspense moves his camera into the icy blackness of the unexplained!'

'Don't give away the ending – it's the only one we have!'

Psycho
US   1960   109m   bw
Shamley/Alfred Hitchcock
▣ ▤ ◎ ◉ ◉ ◠

w Joseph Stefano *novel* Robert Bloch *d* Alfred Hitchcock (and Saul Bass) *ph* John L. Russell *m* Bernard Herrmann *ad* Joseph Hurley, Robert Clatworthy *ed* George Tomasini
☆ *Anthony Perkins* (Norman Bates), Vera Miles (Lila Crane), John Gavin (Sam Loomis), Janet Leigh (Marion Crane), John McIntire (Sheriff Chambers), Martin Balsam (Milton Arbogast), Simon Oakland (Dr. Richmond)
● Hitchcock makes a cameo appaearance standing outside an estate agency
● This is the beginning of Hitchcock's trailer, in which he audaciously wandered round the sets and practically gave away the entire plot: 'Here we have a quiet little motel, tucked away off the main highway, and as you see perfectly harmless looking, whereas it has now become known as the scene of a crime … This motel also has an adjunct, an old house which is, if I may say so, a little more sinister looking. And in this house the most dire, horrible events took place.'
● Janet Leigh's book *Psycho: Behind the Scenes of the Classic Thriller* (1995) chronicles the making of the film.
♟ Alfred Hitchcock; John L. Russell; Janet Leigh; art direction

177
Psycho

At a lonely motel, vicious murders take place and are attributed to the manic mother of the young owner.

A curious shocker devised by Hitchcock as a tease and received by most critics as an unpleasant horror piece in which the main scene, the shower stabbing, was allegedly directed not by Hitchcock but by Saul Bass. After enormous commercial success, over the years it has achieved classic status over the years; despite effective moments of fright, it has a childish plot and script, and its interest is that of a tremendously successful confidence trick, made for very little money by a TV crew. When asked by the press what he used for the blood in the bath, Mr Hitchcock said: 'Chocolate sauce.'

'To tell you the truth, I ain't a real cowboy. But I'm one helluva stud!'

Midnight Cowboy
US   1969   113m   DeLuxe
UA/Jerome Hellman
▣ ▤ ◎ ◠ ◉ ◠

w Waldo Salt *novel* James Leo Herlihy *d* John Schlesinger *ph* Adam Holender *md* John Barry *pd* John Robert Lloyd *ed* Hugh A. Robertson
☆ *Jon Voight* (Joe Buck), *Dustin Hoffman* (Enrico 'Ratso' Rizzo), Brenda Vaccaro (Shirley), Sylvia Miles (Cass), John McGiver (Mr. O'Daniel)

'If only Schlesinger's directorial self-discipline had matched his luminous sense of scene and his extraordinary skill in handling actors, this would have been a far more considerable film.' – *Arthur Schlesinger Jnr (no relation)*

'A great deal besides cleverness, a great deal of good feeling and perception and purposeful dexterity.' – *Stanley Kauffmann*

♟ best picture; Waldo Salt; John Schlesinger
♟ Dustin Hoffman; Jon Voight; Sylvia Miles
♟ best picture; Waldo Salt; John Schlesinger; Dustin Hoffman; Jon Voight

176
Midnight Cowboy

A would-be Texan stud spends a hard winter helping a tubercular con man.

John Schlesinger's outsider's view of New York life reflects that of his main character, Joe Buck (Jon Voight), a naive, slightly dim-witted Texan who comes to the city to offer his services as a stud for rich women; he is at once isolated from, and fascinated by, the teeming life around him. Joe spends his time helping Ratso (Dustin Hoffman), a tubercular con man, whose hope it is to go to Florida. Schlesinger conveys the seedy-aggressive reality of New York street life not only through what he shows but the often brutal style of editing, with montage and flashbacks marked by jump cuts. The heart of the film is the relationship between two contrasting men: Joe Buck, who is big, blond and naive, and Rizzo, a small, limping, vulnerable man who has found no refuge in the lowest depths of society. The relationship between these two vulnerable dreamers is sensitively explored against the background of an unfeeling city.

Mephisto

Hungary 1981 144m Eastmancolor
Mafilm/Manfred Durniok

◨ ⬛ ◉

w Peter Dobai, István Szabó *novel* Klaus Mann *d* István Szabó *ph* Lajos Koltai *m* Zdenko Tamassy *ad* Jozsef Romvari *ed* Zsuzsa Csakany

☆ *Klaus Maria Brandauer* (Hendrik Hofgen), Ildikó Bánsági (Nicoletta Von Niebuhr), Krystyna Janda (Barbara Bruckner)

'Shows extraordinary period flair for the Germany of the 1920s and 1930s, balanced acting by a multinational cast, and exemplary direction.'
– *Variety*

● A Region 1 DVD release includes conversations with István Szabó and Klaus Maria Brandeur.

👤 best foreign film

175
Mephisto

An idealistic left-wing actor sells out to the Nazis.

István Szabó's film is a chilling and fiercely compelling melodrama of moral corruption, as an actor, who is committed to the idea of a workers' theatre, becomes a puppet of the Nazis in 1920s Germany. Klaus Maria Brandauer, as a man who willingly sells his soul gives a bravura performance in the role, showing the vanity, ruthlessness and self-deception that enables him to justify his behaviour as necessary for survival. Ironically, it is his performance in *Faust* that first attracts the attention of the Nazi hierarchy, and in similar fashion he sells his soul. Like Faust, too, it is an action he comes to regret but cannot alter. Szabó demonstrates how easy it is to slip from integrity to complicity with evil.

A Man for All Seasons

GB 1966 120m Technicolor
Columbia/Highland (Fred Zinnemann)

◨ ⬛ ◉

w Robert Bolt *play* Robert Bolt *d* Fred Zinnemann *ph* Ted Moore *m* Georges Delerue *pd* John Box *ad* Terence Marsh *ed* Ralph Kemplen

☆ *Paul Scofield* (Sir Thomas More), *Wendy Hiller* (Alice More), Susannah York (Margaret More), *Robert Shaw* (King Henry VIII), Orson Welles (Cardinal Wolsey), Leo McKern (Thomas Cromwell), Nigel Davenport (Duke of Norfolk), John Hurt (Richard Rich), Corin Redgrave (William Roper), Cyril Luckham (Archbishop Cranmer), Jack Gwillim (Chief Justice)

'Mr Zinnemann has crystallized the essence of this drama in such pictorial terms as to render even its abstractions vibrant.' – *New York Times*

'A beautiful and satisfying film, the ultimate demonstration, perhaps, of how a fine stage play can be transcended and, with integrity and inspiration, turned into a great motion picture.'
– *Judith Crist*

● Reports indicate that Charlton Heston badly wanted the role of Sir Thomas More.

👤 best picture; Robert Bolt; Fred Zinnemann; Ted Moore; Paul Scofield

👤 Wendy Hiller; Robert Shaw

🏆 best picture; best British film; Ted Moore; John Box; Paul Scofield

174
A Man for All Seasons

Sir Thomas More opposes Henry VIII's divorce, and events lead inexorably to his execution.

An irreproachable film version of a play that has had its narrative tricks removed but stands up remarkably well. The film marks an encouraging example of a sober, literate and thoughtful work gaining wide public acceptance. Acting, direction, sets, locations and costumes all have precisely the right touch. It is surprising now to recall that studio executives thought they were taking an immense risk in financing a film that starred Paul Scofield, an actor they regarded as unknown.

A Matter of Life and Death

GB 1946 104m Technicolor
GFD/Archers (Michael Powell, Emeric Pressburger)
▬ ◉ ◎
US title: *Stairway to Heaven*

wd Michael Powell, Emeric Pressburger *ph* Jack Cardiff
m Allan Gray *pd* Hein Heckroth *ad* Arthur Lawson
ed Reginald Mills
☆ David Niven (Squadron Leader Peter D. Carter), *Roger
Livesey* (Dr. Reeves), *Kim Hunter* (June), *Marius Goring*
(Conductor 71), *Raymond Massey* (Abraham Farlan),
Abraham Sofaer (The Judge)

'A dazzling mesh of visionary satire, postwar
politics and the mystical side of English
romanticism.' – *Tony Rayns, Time Out, 1979*

'Beautifully written, beautifully acted, beautifully
executed … you would think such formidable
merits would add up to quite a film – and darned if
they don't.' – *Time Out*

'This film, whether or not you find its philosophy
half-baked, is downright good cinema, doing things
that couldn't be done in any other medium.'
– *Tribune*

'It compelled attention and created emotion.'
– *Basil Wright, 1972*

● A Region 2 DVD release includes commentary with Jack
Cardiff.

173
A Matter of Life and Death

An injured pilot hovers between this world and the next.

This is an outrageous fantasy of a brain-damaged pilot who is torn
between this world and the next after bailing out of his plane. On one
level, he is receiving treatment, falling in love and complaining of
headaches; on another, he is appealing against the decision of a higher
bureaucracy that he should join the rest of his crew in heaven. The film
seemed more in keeping after the huge death toll of a world war.
Powell and Pressburger had learned the Hollywood lesson of eating its
cake and still having it, since the supernatural elements are capable of
explanation as the result of the pilot's injuries. A mammoth technical
job in the heavenly sequences, it deserves high praise for its sheer
arrogance, wit, style and film flair.

The Manchurian Candidate

US 1962 126m bw
UA/MC (Howard W. Koch)
▥ ▬ ◔ ◉ ◎ ◌

w George Axelrod *novel* Richard Condon *d* John
Frankenheimer *ph* Lionel Lindon *m* David Amram
pd Richard Sylbert *ad* Richard Sylbert, Philip Jefferies
ed Ferris Webster
☆ Frank Sinatra (Bennett Marco), Laurence Harvey
(Raymond Shaw), Janet Leigh (Rosie), James Gregory (Sen.
John Iselin), Angela Lansbury (Raymond's Mother), Henry
Silva (Chunjim), John McGiver (Sen. Thomas Jordon)

'The unAmerican film of the year.' – *Penelope
Houston*

'An intelligent, funny, superbly written, beautifully
played, and brilliantly directed study of the all-
embracing fantasy in everyday social, emotional
and political existence.' – *Philip Strick, 1973*

'Although it's a thriller, it may be the most
sophisticated political satire ever to come out of
Hollywood.' – *Pauline Kael, 70s*

● Angela Lansbury as 'Raymond's Mother' was in reality
only three years older than her screen son, Lawrence
Harvey.
● Remade in 2004.
● The Regions 1 and 2 DVD releases include an audio
commentary by the director, and interviews with Frank
Sinatra and George Axelrod.
♟ Angela Lansbury

172
The Manchurian Candidate

*A Korean war 'hero' comes back a brainwashed zombie triggered to kill
a liberal politician, his control being his own monstrously ambitious
mother.*

John Frankenheimer's paranoid thriller, based on Richard Condon's
novel, had a melodramatic and implausible plot that in the political
atmosphere of the time rang true. Frankenheimer's direction stressed
the reality of the situation, with performances and dialogue that never
strayed from actuality; the political rhetoric resembled that which could
be heard on television any day of the week. George Axelrod's script
added wit to the suspense. It was both exciting and thought-provoking.

171
12 Angry Men

12 Angry Men
US 1957 95m bw
(UA) Orion-Nova (Henry Fonda, Reginald Rose)
⊞ ▤ 🝙 ⊚ ⊚

w Reginald Rose *play* Reginald Rose *d* Sidney Lumet
ph Boris Kaufman *m* Kenyon Hopkins *ad* Robert Markell
ed Carl Lerner

☆ Henry Fonda (Juror No. 8), Lee J. Cobb (Juror No. 3),
E. G. Marshall (Juror No. 4), Jack Warden (Juror No. 7), Ed
Begley (Juror No. 10), Martin Balsam (Juror No. 1), John
Fiedler (Juror No. 2), Jack Klugman (Juror No. 5), George
Voskovec (Juror No. 11), Robert Webber (Juror No. 12),
Edward Binns (Juror No. 6), Joseph Sweeney (Juror No. 9)

'Holds the attention unquestioning. It is one of the
most exciting films for months.' – *Dilys Powell*

'Generates more suspense than most thrillers.'
– *New Yorker*

🏆 picture; Reginald Rose; Sidney Lumet
🏆 Henry Fonda

*A murder case jury about to vote guilty is convinced otherwise by one
doubting member.*

Though unconvincing in detail, this is a brilliantly tight character melodrama adopted from Reginald Rose's television play by Rose himself and director Sidney Lumet, with Henry Fonda epitomizing liberal conscience at the film's centre. It is never less than absorbing to experience. Acting and direction are superlatively right, and the film was important in helping to establish television talents in Hollywood.

170
Alien

'In space, no one can hear you scream!'
Alien
GB 1979 117m Eastmancolor Panavision
TCF/Brandywine (Walter Hill, Gordon Carroll, David
Giler)
⊞ ▤ ▤ 🝙 ⊚ ⊚ ◠

w Dan O'Bannon *d* Ridley Scott *ph* Derek Vanlint
m Jerry Goldsmith *pd* Michael Seymour *ed* Terry
Rawlings, Peter Weatherley *sp* visual fx: H. R. Giger, Carlo
Rambaldi, Brian Johnson, Nick Allder, Denys Ayling *chief
designer* H. R. Giger

☆ Tom Skerritt (Dallas), Sigourney Weaver (Ripley), John
Hurt (Kane), Veronica Cartwright (Lambert), Harry Dean
Stanton (Brett), Ian Holm (Ash), Yaphet Kotto (Parker)

'It was not, as its co-author admitted, a think piece.
The message he intended was simple: Don't close
your eyes or it will get ya.' – *Les Keyser,
Hollywood in the Seventies*

● It was followed by three sequels, *Aliens*, *Alien3* and
Alien Resurrection.
● A Region 1 and 2 DVD release includes commentary by
Ridley Scott, cast and technical crew, two versions of the
film with an extended one running 137m, as well as deleted
scenes and storyboards etc.
🏆 visual effects (H. R. Giger, Carlo Rambaldi and others)
🏆 art direction
🏆 production design (Michael Seymour)

*Astronauts returning to Earth visit an apparently dead planet and are
infected by a violent being which has unexpected behaviour patterns
and eliminates them one by one.*

Ridley Scott took the standard ingredients of a horror movie set in an old dark house, shifted them to a new gleaming spaceship and created a deliberately scarifying and highly commercial shocker. The plot is close to Agatha Christie's *Ten Little Indians*, except we know the guilty party (or, indeed to a 1958 B movie *It! The Terror from Beyond Space*). There's not much room for characterization, but the performances are excellent within the limitations of the genre, and it set Sigourney Weaver, playing a strong-minded astronaut, on a trajectory of three sequels. On its own terms, it is a classic of suspense – and art direction.

Alien

Paths of Glory
US 1957 86m bw
UA/Bryna (James B. Harris)

w Stanley Kubrick, Calder Willingham, Jim Thompson *novel* Humphrey Cobb *d* Stanley Kubrick *ph* Georg Krause *m* Gerald Fried *ad* Ludwig Reiber *ed* Eva Kroll
☆ Kirk Douglas (Col. Dax), *Adolphe Menjou* (Gen. Broulard), *George Macready* (Gen. Mireau), Wayne Morris (Lt. Roget), Richard Anderson (Maj. Saint-Auban), Ralph Meeker (Cpl. Paris), Timothy Carey (Pvt. Ferol)

'A bitter and biting tale, told with stunning point and nerve-racking intensity.' – *Judith Crist*

'Beautifully performed, staged, photographed, cut and scored.' – *Colin Young*

● Because of its anti-militarist stance the film was banned in parts of Europe and in US military movie theatres for some years.

169
Paths of Glory

In 1916 in the French trenches, three soldiers are court-martialled for cowardice.

This is an incisive melodrama chiefly depicting the corruption and incompetence of the high command and is a harsh attack on the futility of war in general. The trench scenes are the most vivid ever made, and the rest is shot in genuine castles, with resultant difficulties of lighting and recording; the overall result is an overpowering piece of cinema. Kubrick's theme is of class warfare as much as actual battles against the enemy, with the ordinary soldiers suffering to act as a cover-up for the mistakes of the officers. The infantrymen are 'lions led by donkeys', to use A. J. P. Taylor's description of British soldiers of the time. The paths of glory of the title refer to the generals' self-advancement, not to battlefield bravery. Kubrick contrasts the command's field HQ, an impressive, over-decorated chateau, with the horrific conditions of the men in the trenches.

Persona
Sweden 1966 81m bw
Svensk Filmindustri (Lars-Owe Carlberg)
📼 ▦ ◎ ◉

wd Ingmar Bergman *ph* Sven Nykvist *m* Lars Johan
Werle *ad* Bibi Lindström *ed* Ulla Ryghe
☆ *Liv Ullmann* (Actress Elisabeth Vogler), *Bibi Andersson*
(Nurse Alma), Margaretha Krook (Dr. Lakaren), Gunnar
Björnstrand (Mr. Vogler)

'Reactions have ranged from incomprehension to
irritation with what is dismissed as a characteristic
piece of self-indulgence on Bergman's part –
Bergman talking to himself again.' – *David Wilson,
MFB*

'A puzzling, obsessive film that Bergman seems not
so much to have worked out as to have torn from
himself.' – *New Yorker, 1977*

168
Persona

*A nurse begins to identify with her mentally ill patient, and herself has
a nervous breakdown.*

Ingmar Bergman wrote of his script for this intense clinical study that it
was not like a normal script but 'more like the melody line of a piece of
music'. It is a mysterious film and basically is a duet for two actresses.
Its stars, Bibi Andersson and Liv Ullmann, who resemble one another,
seem to be playing mirror images of themselves. Bergman presents the
drama in a very complex cinematic manner which tends to obscure the
main theme while providing endless fascination for cinéastes.

Touch of Evil
US 1958 95m bw
U-I (Albert Zugsmith)
▦ ◕ ◎ ◉ ∩

wd Orson Welles *novel* Badge of Evil by Whit Masterson
ph Russell Metty *m* Henry Mancini *ad* Alexander
Golitzen, Robert Clatworthy *ed* Virgil Vogel, Aaron Stell
☆ Charlton Heston (Ramon Miguel 'Mike' Vargas), Orson
Welles (Hank Quinlan), Janet Leigh (Susan Vargas),
Marlene Dietrich (Tanya), Akim Tamiroff ('Uncle Joe'
Grandi), Joseph Calleia (Pete Menzies), Ray Collins (District
Attorney Adair), Dennis Weaver (Motel Clerk)

'Pure Orson Welles and impure balderdash, which
may be the same thing.' – *Gerald Weales, Reporter*

167
Touch of Evil

*A Mexican narcotics investigator honeymooning in a border town
clashes with the local police chief over a murder.*

This is an overpoweringly atmospheric melodrama. It is crammed with
Wellesian touches, such as the opening virtuoso scene done in one
long take, but it is sometimes cold and unsympathetic, with rather
restrained performances (especially his) and a plot which takes some
following. It was hardly the most auspicious return to Hollywood for a
wanderer, but it has become a deserved cult classic.

Touch of Evil

Pelle the Conqueror

Denmark/Sweden 1987 150m colour
Curzon/Danish Film Institute/Swedish Film Institute/
Svensk Filmindustri/Per Holst

🎬 🎞 📽 🎦 🎧

original title: *Pelle Erobreren*

wd Bille August *novel* Martin Andersen Nexö *ph* Jörgen
Persson *m* Stefan Nilsson *pd* Anna Asp *ed* Janus
Billeskov Jansen

☆ *Max von Sydow* (Pappa Lasse), *Pelle Hvenegaard*
(Pelle), Erik Paaske (Farm Foreman), Kristina Tornqvist
(Little Anna), Morten Jørgensen (Farming trainee), Alex
Strøbye (Kongstrup), Astrid Villaume (Mrs. Kongstrup),
Björn Granath (Farmhand Erik)

'A vividly recreated, minutely detailed panorama of
a particular time (the turn of the century), place
(rural Denmark), and circumstance (life on a great
farm) in the course of four seasons.' – *Vincent
Canby*

● It won the Palme D'Or at the 1988 Cannes Film Festival.
● It was released on video in two versions, one subtitled,
one dubbed by American actors.

🏆 best foreign film
🏆 Max von Sydow

166
Pelle the Conqueror

*In the early 1900s, the young son of a Swedish immigrant worker
enduring hardship on a Danish farm learns to be self-sufficient.*

Bille August's coming-of-age story is set at a harsh time. The world, as
seen through the observant eyes of young Pelle, is hard: an old man
loses his mind after being hit over the head, a wife castrates her husband after he seduces her niece, his father takes to the bottle. Against
this, is set the natural rhythm of farm work through the season and the
pleasures of the countryside. The film matches an epic scope with
domestic detail in a finely acted, beautifully photographed movie.

461

Marius

France 1931 125m bw
Marcel Pagnol/Paramount

w *Marcel Pagnol* play Marcel Pagnol *d* Alexander Korda
ph Ted Pahle *m* Francis Grammon *ed* Roger Mercanton
☆ *Raimu* (Cesar Olivier), *Pierre Fresnay* (Marius),
Charpin (Honore Panisse), Orane Demazis (Fanny)
• Two sequels with the same players and from the same
pen made this a famous trilogy: *Fanny* (qv) and *César* (qv).
• *Port of Seven Seas* (MGM 1938) was a hammy and
stagey Hollywood compression of the trilogy. See also
Fanny (1960), a dull version of the stage musical, with the
songs removed.

Fanny

France 1932 128m bw
Les Films Marcel Pagnol/Braunberger-Richebé

w *Marcel Pagnol* play Marcel Pagnol *d* Marc Allégret
ph Nicolas Toporkoff, André Dantan, Roger Hubert,
Georges Benoit, Coutelain *m* Vincent Scotto *ed* Raymond
Lamy
☆ *Raimu* (Cesar Olivier), Orane Demazis (Fanny), Pierre
Fresnay (Marius), *Fernand Charpin* (Honore Panisse), Alida
Rouffe (Honorine Cabanis), Robert Vattier (M. Brun),
Auguste Mouriès (Aunt Claudine Foulon), Milly Mathis
(Aunt Claudine Foulon), Maupi (Chauffeur), Edouard
Delmont (Dr. Felicien Venelle)
• This was the first film Pagnol made as his own producer.
After its success he was able to build his own studio. An
Italian version, directed by Mario Almirante, was made in
1933 and a German version starring Emil Jannings in 1934.
It followed on from *Marius* and was followed by a sequel,
César (qqv).

César

France 1936 117m bw
La Société des Films Marcel Pagnol

wd Marcel Pagnol *ph* Willy *m* Vincent Scotto
ad Galibert *ed* Suzanne de Troeye, Jeanette Ginestet
☆ *Raimu* (Cesar Olivier), Orane Demazis (Fanny), Pierre
Fresnay (Marius), Fernand Charpin (Honore Panisse), André
Fouché (Cesariot), Alida Rouffe (Honorine Cabinis), Robert
Vattier (M. Brun), Auguste Mouriès, Milly Mathis (Aunt
Claudine Foulon), Maupi (Chauffeur), Edouard Delmont (Dr.
Felicien Venelle), Paul Dulac (Felix Escartefigue)
• This was the third film in Pagnol's Marseilles trilogy,
following *Marius* and *Fanny* (qqv)

Marius

The son of a Marseilles waterfront café owner gives up his sweetheart to go to sea.

Fanny

After her lover returns to sea, Fanny discovers that she is pregnant and agrees to marry a wealthy widower.

César

A son sets out to find his real father, who returns home after 20 years of unhappy exile.

Although Marcel Pagnol directed only the final film of the trilogy, he exercised artistic control over all three, as they follow the fortunes of the restless Marcel and Fanny, the woman he loves. Marcel goes to sea not knowing that Fanny is pregnant by him. She marries a wealthy older man to provide security for her and her son; after much tribulation, the lovers are re-united. Pagnol's actors were comfortable in their roles, since they had played in the stage version of *Marius* for some 800 performances. The films have wit, wonderful observation and humanity and superb ensemble playing. They communicate the pleasures of everyday moments – as the dying Panisse enumerates, from enjoying a drink under the plane trees to shaving at a open window overlooking the sea. There is an authenticity about them that, despite their occasional staginess, prefigures the later Italian neo-realist masterpieces.

The Lavender Hill Mob

↟↟ GB 1951 78m bw
Ealing (Michael Truman)

⬛ ▬ ◎～ ◎ ◎

w T. E. B. Clarke *d* Charles Crichton *ph* Douglas Slocombe *m* Georges Auric *ad* William Kellner *ed* Seth Holt

☆ *Alec Guinness* (Henry Holland), *Stanley Holloway* (Pendlebury), Sidney James (Lackery), Alfie Bass (Shorty), Marjorie Fielding (Mrs. Chalk), Edie Martin (Miss Evesham), John Gregson (Farrow), Gibb McLaughlin (Godwin), Sydney Tafler (Clayton), Audrey Hepburn (Chiquita)

'Amusing situations and dialogue are well paced and sustained throughout: the climax is delightful.'
– *MFB*

'An outrageous comedy, of course, but the observations of detail and character are so true, the sense of a familiar place so sharp, that few will resent the gusto with which the outrage is perpetrated.' – *C. A. Lejeune*

● Region 2 DVD release is available only as part of a four film set, *Ealing Comedy Classics*.

♟ T. E. B. Clarke
♟ Alec Guinness
♖ British film

164
The Lavender Hill Mob

A timid bank clerk conceives and executes a bullion robbery.

A superbly characterized and inventively detailed comedy, one of the best ever made at Ealing or in Britain. It is a cozy criminal film, pure escapism with an intent only to amuse. It involves two genial masterminds, Alec Guinness as a timid, bank clerk, and Stanley Holloway as the small businessman he enlists to turn gold into souvenirs of the Eiffel Tower. Guinness used hand-washing gestures, a difficulty in pronouncing his 'r's, and padding to make him look plump in order to give the clerk some individuality. The film's most daring moment was to parody the police car chase from Ealing's crime drama *The Blue Lamp*, which had also been scripted by T. E. B. Clarke.

'In 1959 a lot of people were killing time. Kit and Holly were killing people.'

Badlands
US   1973   94m   CFI color
Warner/Pressman/Williams/Badlands (Terrence Malick)

🔲 🔲 ▦ ⊙ ⊙
wd Terrence Malick *ph* Brian Probyn, Tak Fujimoto, Stevan Larner *m* George Tipton, James Taylor *ad* Jack Fisk *ed* Robert Estrin
☆ Martin Sheen (Kit), Sissy Spacek (Holly), Warren Oates (Father), Ramon Bieri (Cato), Alan Vint (Deputy), Gary Littlejohn (Sheriff)

'One of the finest literate examples of narrated cinema since the early days of Welles and Polonsky.' – *Jonathan Rosenbaum*

'So preconceived that there's nothing left to respond to.' – *New Yorker*

163
Badlands

A teenage girl and a young garbage collector wander across America leaving a trail of murder behind them.

Terrence Malick's first feature was a violent folk tale for moderns. It quickly became a cult and has proved to be a seminal film in its depiction of aimless anger as a means of attempting to connect with the world. A voice-over narration by Sissy Spacek gives it a naive tone, as of children playing at violence. Martin Sheen is effective as the damaged killer who can not quite understand how he got himself into such a mess. The feature was based on Charles Starkweather and Caril Ann Fugate, who killed eleven people in a chase across country in 1958. Starkweather was executed in 1959, and Caril Fugate sentenced to life imprisonment.

An American in Paris
US   1951   113m   Technicolor
MGM (*Arthur Freed*)

🔲 ▦ ⊙ ⊙ ⊙ 🎧
w Alan Jay Lerner *d* Vincente Minnelli *ph* Al Gilks, John Alton *m/ly* George Gershwin, Ira Gershwin *md* Saul Chaplin, Johnny Green *ch* Gene Kelly *ad* Cedric Gibbons, Preston Ames *ed* Adrienne Fazan *cos* Walter Plunkett, Irene Sharaff
☆ Gene Kelly (Jerry Mulligan), Oscar Levant (Adam Cook), Nina Foch (Milo Roberts), Leslie Caron (Lise Bouvier), Georges Guetary (Henri Baurel)

'Spangled with pleasant little patches of amusement and George Gershwin tunes.' – *Bosley Crowther, New York Times*

● Chevalier was originally paged for the Georges Guetary role, but turned it down because he lost the girl.
● The production cost $2,723,903, of which $542,000 went on the final ballet
♫ 'I Got Rhythm'; 'Embraceable You'; 'By Strauss'; 'Swonderful'; 'Tra La La'; 'Our Love Is Here to Stay'; 'Stairway to Paradise'; 'Concerto in F' (instrumental); 'An American in Paris' (ballet)
👤 picture; Alan Jay Lerner; Al Gilks, John Alton; musical arrangement (Saul Chaplin, Johnny Green); art direction; costumes (Walter Plunkett, Irene Sharaff)
👤 Vincente Minnelli; Adrienne Fazan

162
An American in Paris

A carefree young artist scorns a rich woman's patronage and wins the love of a gamine.

Altogether delightful musical holiday, one of the highspots of the Hollywood genre, with infectious enthusiasm and an unexpected sense of the Paris that was. All the music was by George Gershwin, including his 'Concerto in F' played by the concert pianist and wit Oscar Levant, in which, as a joke at his vanity, he also appears as the conductor, instrumentalists and audience. At the end comes the moment it is best remembered for, an eighteen-minute ballet danced by Gene Kelly with Leslie Caron and based on the work of Impressionist painters.

The Last Picture Show

US 1971 118m bw
Columbia/LPS/BBS (Stephen J. Friedman)
🔲 ▭ ◎~ ◦ ◎ 🎧

w Larry McMurtry, Peter Bogdanovich *d* Peter
Bogdanovich *ph* Robert Surtees *m* original recordings
pd Polly Platt *ad* Walter Scott Herndon *ed* Donn
Cambern

☆ Timothy Bottoms (Sonny Crawford), Jeff Bridges
(Duane Jackson), Cybill Shepherd (Jacy Farrow), *Ben
Johnson* (Sam the Lion), *Cloris Leachman* (Ruth Popper),
Ellen Burstyn (Lois Farrow)

'The most important work by a young American
director since *Citizen Kane*.' – Paul D. Zimmerman

'So many things in it are so good that I wish I liked
it more.' – *Stanley Kauffmann*

'Colour always had a tendency to prettify, and I
didn't want that. I didn't want it to be a nostalgic
piece.' – *Peter Bogdanovich*

● *Texasville* (qv), a sequel featuring many of the same
actors, was filmed by Bogdanovich in 1990.
● Regions 1 and 2 DVD releases include a documentary on
the film and eight minutes of additional footage.
🎗 Ben Johnson; Cloris Leachman
♟ best picture; script; Peter Bogdanovich (as director);
Robert Surtees; Jeff Bridges; Ellen Burstyn
🏆 script; Ben Johnson; Cloris Leachman

161
The Last Picture Show

*Teenage affairs in a small Texas town in 1951, ending with the hero's
embarkation for Korea and the closing of the tatty cinema.*

The 1950s were a time of social shifts, notably in entertainment, when
it looked as though cinema might wither away and television take over.
It is that moment, with the closing of the dilapidated cinema in a small
Texas town, that Peter Bogdanovich concentrated on, with penetrating
nostalgia. In 1951, high-school students Sonny (Timothy Bottoms) and
Duane (Jeff Bridges), who are approaching graduation, have nothing
but sex on their minds, though by the end one has gone off to war and
the other is running a pool hall. It is a bitter-sweet account of growing-
up, of shattered dreams and lost illusions, symbolized by the cinema,
the death of its avuncular owner and its closure.

Stagecoach

US 1939 99m bw
(UA)
🔲 ▭ ◎~ ◎

w Dudley Nichols *story* Stage to Lordsburg by Ernest
Haycox *d* John Ford *ph* Bert Glennon *m* Richard
Hageman, W. Frank Harling, John Leopold, Leo Shuken,
Louis Gruenberg *md* Boris Morros *ad* Alexander Toluboff
ed Otho Lovering, Dorothy Spencer

☆ *Claire Trevor* (Dallas), *John Wayne* (The Ringo Kid),
Thomas Mitchell (Dr. Josiah Boone), *George Bancroft*
(Sheriff Curly Wilcox), Andy Devine (Buck Rickabaugh),
Berton Churchill (Henry Gatewood), Louise Platt (Lucy
Mallory), *John Carradine* (Hatfield), *Donald Meek* (Mr.
Samuel Peacock), Tim Holt (Lt. Blanchard), Chris-Pin
Martin (Chris)

'It displays potentialities that can easily drive it
through as one of the surprise big grossers of the
year.' – *Variety*

'The basic western, a template for everything that
followed.' – *John Baxter, 1968*

'A motion picture that sings a song of camera.'
– *Frank S. Nugent, New York Times*

● Remade in 1966.
● The original story was clearly inspired by Guy de
Maupassant's *Boule De Suif*.
🎗 music; Thomas Mitchell
♟ best picture; John Ford; Bert Glennon; art direction;
editing

160
Stagecoach

*Various Western characters board a stagecoach in danger from an
Indian war party.*

This combines many themes of Westerns both before and after it:
Cowboys versus Indians, the cavalry riding to the rescue in the last
reel, a gun duel in an empty street. In dealing with redemption and
revenge, it conforms to another favourite genre, of putting a disparate
group in a single location. This is *The Petrified Forest* in hectic motion,
or *Grand Hotel* on wheels. Ford, shooting for the first of many times in
Monument Valley, emphasizes class distinctions. At the beginning, a
tart with the heart of gold and a drunken doctor are run out of town by
grimly devout women. In stops on the way, the respectable gather
together isolating the others. Only in the stagecoach are social differences blurred, because death makes no such distinctions. Firm characterization, restrained writing, an exciting climax and a star performance
from John Wayne combine to make it a classic.

The Last Metro

France 1980 131m Fujicolour
Les Films du Carrosse/Andrea/SEDIF/TF1/SFP (Jean-José Richer)

original title: *Le Dernier Métro*
w François Truffaut, Suzanne Schiffman d François Truffaut ph Nestor Almendros m Georges Delerue
ad Jean-Pierre Kohut Svelko ed Martine Barraque
☆ *Catherine Deneuve* (Marion Steiner), *Gérard Depardieu* (Bernard Granger), Jean Poiret (Jean-Loup Cottins), Heinz Bennent (Lucas Steiner)

'A dazzlingly subversive work … a gently comic, romantic meditation on love, loyalty, heroism and history.' – *Vincent Canby, New York Times*

● A Region 2 DVD release includes audio commentary by historian Jean-Pierre Azema and an interview with Truffaut.
☖ best foreign film

159
The Last Metro

A Jew hides from the Nazis in the cellar of the Parisian theatre he manages.

François Truffaut had come full circle when he made this, his greatest success. Having begun as an aggressive critic of large-scale star vehicles, now, towards the end of his career, he was making precisely that kind of movie, here featuring Catherine Deneuve and Gérard Depardieu. You could ascribe the change to maturity or mellowing, but whatever the reason, this is a handsome, tightly enclosed, symbolic melodrama of a Jewish manager, who hides in the cellar of his theatre during the Nazi occupation of Paris, while his wife, its leading actress, takes over the running of the place. War is merely a backdrop to the characters' obsession with their craft, which provides a refuge from the madness that engulfs the outside world.

'A provocative new comedy about sex, friendship, and all other things that invade our lives.'

The Barbarian Invasions

Canada 2003 99m Technicolor 'Scope
UIP/Cinemaginaire/Pyramide (Denise Robert, Daniel Louis)

aka: *Les Invasions Barbare*
wd *Denys Arcand* ph Guy Dufaux m Pierre Aviat
pd François Seguin ed Isabelle Dedieu
☆ *Remy Girard* (Remy), Stephane Rousseau (Sebastien), *Marie-Josée Croze* (Nathalie), Marina Hands (Gaelle), Dorothee Berryman (Louise), Johanne Marie Tremblay (Sister Constance), Dominique Michel (Dominique), Louise Portal (Diane)

'The dialogue often has the violet luster of teenage playwriting. Shear away the film's pretensions, and it's a soap opera of assholes.' – *Michael Atkinson, Village Voice*

● The film features many of the same characters as Arcand's *The Decline of the American Empire*, which he directed in 1986.
● Marie-Josée Croze won the best actress award, and Denys Arcand the best screenwriter at the Cannes Film Festival in 2003.
♟ foreign language film
☖ Denys Arcand (as screenwriter)

158
The Barbarian Invasions

In Montreal, a dying, womanizing left-wing academic is gradually reconciled with his son, a wealthy city trader.

Denys Arcand revisits, at the point of death, Remy, the womanizing, left-wing academic who was a central character of his *The Decline of the American Empire*. As Remy's estranged son, a wealthy city trader, uses his money in dubious ways to ensure that his father ends his life at peace, you could take this witty and moving account of death and rebirth as a hymn to the power of capitalism, though it is richer and deeper than that. Set against the terrorist attack on America's World Trade Center, it is also a study in the behaviour of powerful nations (what historian Cesare Blado defined as 'peoples possessed by civilized barbarism'), and in the pleasures to be derived from opposing the established order, whatever that might be.

'You are cordially invited to George and Martha's for an evening of fun and games!'

Who's Afraid of Virginia Woolf?
US   1966   129m   bw
Warner (Ernest Lehman)
🔘 ▬ ◗ ◉ ◖
w Ernest Lehman *play* Edward Albee *d* Mike Nichols
ph Haskell Wexler *m* Alex North *pd* Richard Sylbert
ed Sam O'Steen
☆ *Richard Burton* (George), *Elizabeth Taylor* (Martha),
George Segal (Nick), *Sandy Dennis* (Honey)

'A magnificent triumph of determined audacity.'
– Bosley Crowther

'One of the most scathingly honest American films
ever made.' – Stanley Kauffmann

● A Region 1 DVD release includes commentary by Haskell
Wexler.
🕯 Haskell Wexler; Elizabeth Taylor; Sandy Dennis
⚓ best picture; Ernest Lehman; Mike Nichols; Alex North;
Richard Burton; George Segal
🎟 best picture; Richard Burton; Elizabeth Taylor

157
Who's Afraid of Virginia Woolf?

A college professor and his wife have an all-night shouting match and embarrass their guests.

A milestone in cinematic permissiveness, Edward Albee's play of a viciously combative marriage gained even more notoriety when filmed for the casting in the leading roles the most famous married couple in the world, who were also noted for titanic rows. As an entertainment, it is sensational for those in the mood. Burton and Taylor pull out all the stops in this scarifying portrait of a marriage and of the damage people can do to each other. The film provides its audience with a domestic version of the Cold War that was the concern of international politics at the time. It is a fearsome game of intimidation and bluff, with Haskell Wexler's cinematography providing scrupulous observation of two combatants' every slight grimace or tic that might be a sign of a momentary defeat in their continual skirmishes.

'Out of the hushed strangeness of these lives, and out of the shadows that hid their shame, filmdom has fashioned a drama most unusual, most touching and most wonderful!'

'The town they talk of in whispers!'

Kings Row
US   1942   127m   bw
Warner (Hal B. Wallis)
▬ ◗ ◖
w Casey Robinson *novel* Henry Bellamann *d* Sam Wood
ph James Wong Howe *m* Erich Wolfgang Korngold
pd William Cameron Menzies *ad* Carl Jules Weyl
ed Ralph Dawson
☆ *Ann Sheridan* (Randy Monoghan), *Robert Cummings*
(Parris Mitchell), Ronald Reagan (Drake McHugh), *Claude
Rains* (Dr. Alexander Tower), Betty Field (Cassandra Tower),
Charles Coburn (Dr. Henry Gordon), Nancy Coleman
(Louise Gordon), *Maria Ouspenskaya* (Mme. Von Eln),
Harry Davenport (Col. Skeffington), Judith Anderson (Mrs.
Harriet Gordon), Karen Verne (Elise Sandor)

'Half masterpiece and half junk.' – *James Agate*

● The film was made in 1941, but its release was delayed
for a year because the studio thought it too downbeat. It was
not a great box-office success.
⚓ best picture; Sam Wood; James Wong Howe

156
Kings Row

In a small American town during the early years of the century, three children grow up into a world of cruelty and madness.

A superb Hollywood melodrama; a revealing soap opera in the mould of *Peyton Place*, except that it is set in the early 1900s. The film toned down the best-seller on which it was based, only hinting at incest, but keeping mutilation, murder and suicide. Ronald Reagan had the best role of his career as a playboy who has his legs needlessly amputated by a sadistic surgeon and laughs off his disability. Despite the moral squalor of its story, it still managed a happy ending. Sam Wood's direction, James Wong Howe's photography and William Cameron Menzies' sets gave it great visual strength, and there is haunting music and a wholly absorbing if incredible plot.

The Man in the White Suit
GB   1951   81m   bw
Ealing (Sidney Cole)
▱ ▤ ◕ ◉
w Roger MacDougall, John Dighton, Alexander
Mackendrick *d* Alexander Mackendrick *ph* Douglas
Slocombe *m* Benjamin Frankel *ad* Jim Morahan
ed Bernard Gribble
☆ *Alec Guinness* (Sidney Stratton), *Joan Greenwood*
(Daphne Birnley), *Cecil Parker* (Alan Birnley), Vida Hope
(Bertha), *Ernest Thesiger* (Sir John Kierlaw), Michael Gough
(Michael Corland), Howard Marion Crawford (Cranford),
Miles Malleson (Tailor), *George Benson* (The Lodger), *Edie
Martin* (Mrs. Watson)

'The combination of an ingenious idea, a bright,
funny and imaginative script, skilful playing and
perceptive brisk direction has resulted once more
in a really satisfying Ealing comedy.' – *Richard
Mallett, Punch*

● The Region 2 DVD release is available only as part of a
four-disc set, *Ealing Comedy Collection*.
𐐋 script

The Man in the White Suit

*A scientist produces a fabric that never gets dirty and never wears out.
Unions and management are equally aghast.*

Alexander Mackendrick made a brilliant, wide-ranging satirical comedy
about a scientist who produces an indestructible fabric which antago-
nizes Unions and management. Every character was intended as a caricature, including Alec Guinness' scientist, who never considers the
consequences of his invention. It is played as farce and put together
with meticulous cinematic counterpoint, so that every moment counts
and all concerned give of their very best, including Benjamin Frankel,
who composed witty music to underscore the satire.

'Everything Is Suspect … Everyone Is For Sale … And Nothing Is What It Seems.'

LA Confidential

US 1997 136m Technicolor Panavision
Warner/Regency (Arnon Milchan, Curtis Hanson, Michael Nathanson)

📷 ▬ ❀ ⊚ ⌐

w *Brian Helgeland, Curtis Hanson* novel James Ellroy
d *Curtis Hanson* ph *Dante Spinotti* m Jerry Goldsmith
pd Jeannine Oppewall ad Bill Arnold ed Peter Honess
☆ *Kevin Spacey* (Jack Vincennes), *Russell Crowe* (Bud White), *Guy Pearce* (Ed Exley), James Cromwell (Dudley Smith), David Strathairn (Pierce Patchett), *Kim Basinger* (Lynn Bracken), Danny DeVito (Sid Hudgens), Graham Beckel (Dick Stensland)

'It's not quite the full-strength java Ellroy writes, but it's about as hard as a 1990s studio picture can be.' – *Kim Newman, Empire*

'An irresistible treat with enough narrative twists and memorable characters for a half-dozen films.' – *Variety*

● It grossed around $38m in the US and another $30m elsewhere.

♟ Kim Basinger; Curtis Hanson, Brian Helgeland
♟ best picture; Curtis Hanson (as director); Dante Spinotti; Jerry Goldsmith; Jeannine Oppewall; Peter Honess; sound
🎗 Peter Honess

154
LA Confidential

In Los Angeles in the early Fifties, an incorruptible cop learns that you cannot always play by the rules.

Curtis Hanson made a period thriller with a modern theme. His exemplary, excellently acted film took in not only the insidiousness of corruption, but also the dangers of celebrity in a city dedicated to fame in one way or another. At the centre were three cops: the honest Ed Exley (Guy Pearce), the rule-breaking Bud White (Russell Crowe), and the corrupt Jack Vincennes (Kevin Spacey). Pearce is the one who receives an education in the ways of the world, and Vincennes is the self-deceiver who believes in his own invulnerability. The film is full of surprises; only the coda disappoints.

The 39 Steps

GB 1935 81m bw
Gaumont British (Ivor Montagu)

📷 ▬ ❀ ⊚

w *Charles Bennett, Ian Hay, Alma Reville* novel John Buchan d *Alfred Hitchcock* ph Bernard Knowles m Hubert Bath, Jack Beaver md Louis Levy ad Otto Wendorff, Albert Jullion ed Derek Twist
☆ *Robert Donat* (Richard Hannay), *Madeleine Carroll* (Pamela), Godfrey Tearle (Prof. Jordan), Lucie Mannheim (Miss Smith/Annabella), Peggy Ashcroft (Margaret), John Laurie (John), *Wylie Watson* (Mr. Memory), *Helen Haye* (Mrs. Jordan), Frank Cellier (Sheriff Watson)

'A narrative of the unexpected – a humorous, exciting, dramatic, entertaining, pictorial, vivid and novel tale told with a fine sense of character and a keen grasp of the cinematic idea.' – *Sydney W. Carroll*

'Such is the zest of the Hitchcock plot that the original point of the title was totally forgotten, and half a line had to be added at the end by way of explanation.' – *George Perry, 1965*

● Hitchcock makes a cameo appearance passing on a street.
● Remade in 1959 and 1978
● A Region 1 DVD release includes commentary by Hitchcock scholar Marian Keane, the broadcast of the 1937 Lux Radio Theater adaptation and a documentary, *The Art of Film: Vintage Hitchcock*. A Region 2 special edition DVD release includes a documentary on Hitchcock.

153
The 39 Steps

A murder suspect flees from London to Scotland to track down the real killers.

A marvellous comedy thriller with most of the gimmicks found not only in Hitchcock's later work but in anyone else's who has tried the same vein. It has little to do with the original novel, though the outline remains similar: a spy is murdered; the man who has befriended her is suspected, but eludes the police until a chase across Scotland produces the real villains. Hitchcock extracted both comedy and eroticism from the scenes in which the fugitive Robert Donat is handcuffed to the reluctant Madeleine Carroll, who then has to remove her wet stockings. The film barely sets foot outside the studio, but it makes every second count, and is unparalleled in its use of timing, atmosphere and comedy relief.

The Knack
GB   1965   84m   bw
UA/Woodfall (Oscar Lewenstein)
▬ ◉ ⌒
w Charles Wood *play* Ann Jellicoe *d* Richard Lester
ph David Watkin *m* John Barry *ad* Assheton Gorton
ed Anthony Gibbs
☆ *Michael Crawford* (Colin), *Ray Brooks* (Tolen), *Rita Tushingham* (Nancy Jones), Donal Donnelly (Tom)

'The whole film has the anarchic quality modish today and at all times appealing to a new generation understandably bent on overturning the ideas which have hardened in the minds of their elders.' – *Dilys Powell*

'The running jokes and gags never come off.' – *Pauline Kael*

● The film won the Palme D'Or at the 1965 Cannes Film Festival.

152
The Knack

A sex-starved young teacher lets one room of his house to a successful womanizer, another to an innocent girl from the North.

Richard Lester's frantic comedy is a a kaleidoscope of images of swinging London in which anything goes. There is even a chorus of elders to make disapproving comments on the action. Michael Crawford displays a gift for physical comedy, and Charles Wood's script is full of witty lines. An excuse for an anarchic series of visual gags, it is brilliantly done in the style of *A Hard Day's Night*.

The Lost Weekend
US   1945   101m   bw
Paramount (*Charles Brackett*)
▬ ◔ ◉ ⌒
w Charles Brackett, Billy Wilder *novel* Charles Jackson
d Billy Wilder *ph* John F. Seitz *m* Miklos Rozsa *ad* Hans Dreier, Earl Hedrick *ed* Doane Harrison
☆ *Ray Milland* (Don Birnam), Jane Wyman (Helen St. James), Philip Terry (Nick Birnam), *Howard da Silva* (Nat the Bartender), *Frank Faylen* (Bim)

'A reminder of what celluloid is capable of achieving when used by a good director.' – *Spectator*

'Most to be admired are its impressions of bare dreadful truth: the real crowds in the real streets as the hero-victim lugs his typewriter to the pawnshop, the trains screaming overhead, the awful night as he makes his escape from the alcoholics' ward.' – *Dilys Powell*

'A distinguished film, rich in cinematic ingenuity.' – *The Times*

👤 best picture; script; Billy Wilder (as director); Ray Milland
♟ John F. Seitz; Miklos Rozsa; editing

151
The Lost Weekend

An alcoholic writer goes on a drunken binge.

Startlingly original on its release, this is a stark little drama of two days in the life of a young dipsomaniac writer. No film had treated alcoholism seriously before; a drunk was a joke or even a hero, as in William Powell's enjoyable, ever-tipsy private eye *Thin Man* films, which were successful comedies of the 1930s. Don (Ray Milland) is not funny but a falling-down drunk who will do anything to get a drink and tries to kill himself after experiencing terrifying hallucinations. It keeps its power, especially in the scenes on New York streets and in a dipso ward. It could scarcely have been more effectively filmed. (Ray Milland claimed that he was sent a letter by an alcoholic who wrote that he was so moved by Milland's masterly portrayal of a drunk, he had decided to give up movies.)

Mean Streets

US 1973 110m Technicolor
Taplin-Perry-Scorsese (Jonathan T. Taplin)
🔳 ▦ ◉ ⊙ ⊙

w Martin Scorsese, Mardik Martin *d* Martin Scorsese
ph Kent Wakeford *ed* Sid Levin
☆ *Harvey Keitel* (Charlie), *Robert DeNiro* (Johnny Boy),
David Proval (Tony), Amy Robinson (Teresa), Richard
Romanus (Teresa)

'Lacks a sense of story and structure ... unless a
film-maker respects the needs of his audience, he
can't complain if that audience fails to show up.'
– *Variety*

'A thicker-textured plot than we have ever had in an
American movie, and a deeper sense of evil.'
– *New Yorker*

'Extraordinarily rich and distinguished on many
levels.' – *Joseph Gelmis*

150
Mean Streets

Four young Italian-Americans use Tony's Bar as a base for drinking, brawling and hustling.

Martin Scorsese's film which tells the story of a group of friends who pursue a lifestyle of boozing, fighting and crime, had its origins in his own experiences as a young man growing up in Little Italy. It was the first film in which Scorsese announced himself as a major talent and discovered the subject matter that has served him so well. He reveals a good eye for realistic detail within a relentlessly sordid melodrama of the street life of small-time gangsters. It also teamed him with Robert DeNiro, who has been a major presence in his best movies.

'The monster demands a mate!'
The Bride of Frankenstein

US 1935 90m bw
Universal (Carl Laemmle Jnr)
🔳 ▦ ◉ ⊙ ⊙ ◠

w John L. Balderston, William Hurlbut *d* James Whale
ph John Mescall *m* Franz Waxman *ad* Charles D. Hall
ed Ted Kent
☆ *Boris Karloff* (The Monster), Colin Clive (Henry
Frankenstein), *Ernest Thesiger* (Dr Septimus Pretorius),
Valerie Hobson (Elizabeth Frankenstein), *E. E. Clive*
(Burgomaster), Dwight Frye, O. P. Heggie (Hermit), Una
O'Connor (Minnie), *Elsa Lanchester* (Mary Shelley and the
monster's mate), Gavin Gordon (Byron), Douglas Walton
● The regular release version runs 75m, having dropped
part of the Mary Shelley prologue and a sequence in which
the monster becomes unsympathetic by murdering the
burgomaster.
● The title was originally to have been *The Return of
Frankenstein*.
● The Region 1 DVD is available as part of a five-disc set
Frankenstein: The Legacy Collection that includes
commentary on the film by historian Scott MacQueen and a
documentary on its making. The Region 2 DVD is available
as a two-disc set with *Frankenstein*; it also includes the
documentary and commentary by MacQueen.
🔊 sound recording (Gilbert Kurland)

149
The Bride of Frankenstein

Baron Frankenstein is blackmailed by Dr Praetorious into reviving his monster and building a mate for it.

Frankenstein was startlingly good in a primitive way; this sequel is the screen's sophisticated masterpiece of black comedy, with all the talents working deftly to one end. Every scene has its own delights, as Baron Frankenstein is forced to reanimate the monster he had created in the first film and to make its female counterpart. It is all woven together into a superb if wilful cinematic narrative which, of its gentle mocking kind, has never been surpassed. An early script, from John L. Balderston, had a female monster with the 'head and shoulders of a hydrocephalic circus giantess who has committed suicide in a fit of sexual despondency'. Fortunately, Whale had Elsa Lanchester in the role, looking like Nefertiti on a bad hair day.

The Enigma of Kaspar Hauser

West Germany 1974 110m colour
Contemporary/Zud Deutscher Rudfunk/Werner
Herzog

original title: *Jeder für sich und Gott gegen alle*
aka: *The Mystery of Kaspar Hauser; Every Man for Himself and God against All*
wd Werner Herzog *ph* Jörg Schmidt-Reitwein
m Pachelbel, Albinoni and others *ad* Henning V. Gierke
ed Beate Mainke-Jellinghaus
☆ *Bruno S.* (Kaspar Hauser), Walter Ladengast (Daumer), Brigitte Mira (Kathe), Willy Semmelrogge (Circus Director), Gloria Dör (Madame Hiltel), Volker Prechtel (Hiltel), Hans Musaus (Unknown Man)

'A double fable, intermingling the stultifying effects of bourgeois society and the cruelty of a demonic universe.' – *Pauline Kael*

'Herzog's direction is not free of the hallmarks of contemporary German film-making, an estheticism, a slow pace, an arrogance toward dramatic concept that almost supply an imaginary soundtrack accompanying the picture saying: "You can see that this film was made by an intellectual, can't you?"' – *Stanley Kauffmann*

● The film was awarded the Special Jury Prize at the Cannes Film Festival in 1975.
● The Region 1 DVD includes commentary by Werner Herzog and Norman Hill.

148
The Enigma of Kaspar Hauser

In the 1820s, a 16-year-old boy who has spent his life isolated from others is found abandoned in the town square of Nuremberg.

Werner Herzog's compelling film was based on a true story from the 1820s. One day the residents of Nuremberg discover a destitute teenage boy in their town. Apparently he has grown up with little or no human contact. A disturbing and affecting account of an untouched mind confronting humanity at its best and worst, it exposed the limitations of society's response. Bruno S., a man who spent many years in various mental institutions, after suffering an abusive childhood, gives a fiercely convincing performance in the title role.

Way Out West

US 1937 66m bw
Hal Roach (Stan Laurel)

w Jack Jevne, Charles Rogers, James Parrott, Felix Adler *d* James Horne *ph* Art Lloyd, Walter Lundin *m* Marvin Hatley *ad* Arthur I. Royce *ed* Bert Jordan
☆ *Stan Laurel* (Himself), *Oliver Hardy* (Himself), *James Finlayson* (Mickey Finn), *Sharon Lynne* (Lola Marcel), Rosina Lawrence (Mary Roberts)

'Thin returns indicated … for added feature on duallers.' – *Variety*

'Not only one of their most perfect films, it ranks with the best screen comedy anywhere.' – *David Robinson, 1962*

'The film is leisurely in the best sense; you adjust to a different rhythm and come out feeling relaxed as if you'd had a vacation.' – *New Yorker, 1980*

♫ Marvin Hatley

147
Way Out West

Laurel and Hardy come to Brushwood Gulch to deliver the deed to a gold mine.

In these six reels of perfect cinematic joy, the famous comic duo get involved in some hilarious antics in a small town in the American West. Laurel and Hardy are at their very best in some brilliantly-timed routines. The film begins and ends with the same joke: as they and their mule cross a shallow river, Hardy suddenly steps into a pothole and is submerged. There are some magic moments: a charming soft shoe shuffle, the rendition of 'The Trail of the Lonesome Pine' and a scene where Laurel is tickled to make him give up an heirloom. It is enough to make anyone laugh.

'They got a murder on their hands ... they don't know what to do with it.'

In the Heat of the Night
US   1967   109m   DeLuxe
UA/Mirisch (Walter Mirisch)
▭ ▬ ▣ ⌾ ⊚ ⌒
w Stirling Silliphant *d* Norman Jewison *ph* Haskell Wexler *m* Quincy Jones *ad* Paul Groesse *ed* Hal Ashby
☆ *Sidney Poitier* (Virgil Tibbs), *Rod Steiger* (Bill Gillespie), Warren Oates (Sam Wood), Quentin Dean (Delores Purdy), William Schallert (Webb Schubert)

'A very nice film and a very good film and yes, I think it's good to see a black man and a white man working together ... but it's not going to take the tension out of New York City; it's not going to stop the riots in Chicago.' – *Rod Steiger*

'A film that has the look and sound of actuality and the pounding pulse of truth.' – *Bosley Crowther, New York Times*

● Poitier subsequently starred in a couple of very inferior sequels, *They Call Me Mister Tibbs* and *The Organization* (both qv).
♟ best picture; Stirling Silliphant; Rod Steiger; Hal Ashby; sound
♟ Norman Jewison; sound effects (James A. Richard)
🏆 Rod Steiger

146
In the Heat of the Night

In a small Southern town, the bigoted and bombastic sheriff on a murder hunt grudgingly accepts the help of a black detective.

In this tense and exciting thriller set in the American South, Rod Steiger and Sidney Poitier give pitch-perfect performances as the racially prejudiced small-town sheriff and the brilliant young city detective. The film explores racism through the explosive clash of two contrasting personalities, who begin to have a grudging respect for one another. The acting, and Stirling Silliphant's sharp script, gives the two characters humanity. Under Norman Jewison's firm direction and Haskell Wexler's cinematography, capturing the shabbiness of the town and the beauty of the surrounding countryside, the film is as enjoyable as it is disturbing.

'To break the driver, the cop was willing to break the law.'

The Driver
US   1978   91m   DeLuxe
TCF/EMI/Lawrence Gordon
▭ ▬ ⌾
wd Walter Hill *ph* Philip Lathrop *m* Michael Small *pd* Harry Horner *ad* David M. Haber *ed* Tina Hirsch, Robert K. Lambert
☆ Ryan O'Neal (The Driver), Bruce Dern (The Detective), Isabelle Adjani (The Player), Ronee Blakley (The Connection)

'Comic book cops and robbers existentialism.' – *Pauline Kael*

'Because of the quiet and mysterious mood of this picture, it has a pretentious quality to it.' – *Variety*

145
The Driver

A detective determines to catch an old enemy from the criminal underworld.

Walter Hill's existentialist thriller is a deft and clever work that has been stripped of all redundancies and reduced to its core: two obsessional men on different sides of the law locked in deadly conflict – a detective is prepared to use whatever means he can to apprehend his old adversary, a getaway driver who is the best in the business. It is a movie in which character is defined by action, notably the scene in an underground garage in which the driver nonchalantly demolishes a Mercedes to demonstrate his skills. A simple, pared down story of bleak lives, it is brilliantly told.

Don't Look Now
GB   1973   110m   Technicolor
BL/Casey/Eldorado (Peter Katz)
▭ ▬ ✆ ◎ ◉ ⌒
w Allan Scott, Chris Bryant *story* Daphne du Maurier
d Nicolas Roeg *ph* Anthony Richmond *m* Pino Donaggio
ad Giovanni Soccol *ed* Graeme Clifford
☆ Donald Sutherland (John Baxter), Julie Christie (Laura
Baxter), Hilary Mason (Heather), Clelia Matania (Wendy),
Massimo Serrato (Bishop)

'The fanciest, most carefully assembled enigma yet
seen on the screen.' – *New Yorker*

'A powerful and dazzling visual texture.' – *Penelope
Houston*

Ⓣ Anthony Richmond

144
Don't Look Now

*After the death of their small daughter, John and Lewis Baxter go to
Venice and there meet two old sisters who claim mediumistic connection with the dead girl. The husband scorns the idea, but repeatedly
sees a little red-coated figure in shadowy passages by the canals. Then
he confronts it …*

Daphne du Maurier's macabre short story became, under the direction
of Nicolas Roeg, a piece of high cinematic art, full of vague suggestions and unexplored avenues. It deals with the effect of loss on the
relationship of a husband and wife. John Baxter is sceptical about the
old sisters' claim that they are supernaturally in touch with his
deceased daughter, but despite his doubts, he keeps seeing what
appears to be a child in a red coat here and there around the city.
Fascinatingly set in wintry Venice, and filmed with brilliant surface
detail, this movie has to be seen to be appreciated.

'Strange desires! Loves and hates and
secret yearnings … hidden in the
shadows of a man's mind!'
Doctor Jekyll and Mr Hyde
US   1931   98m   bw
Paramount (Rouben Mamoulian)
▬ ✆ ◎ ◉
w Samuel Hoffenstein, Percy Heath *novel* Robert Louis
Stevenson *d* Rouben Mamoulian *ph* Karl Struss *ad* Hans
Dreier *ed* William Shea
☆ *Fredric March* (Dr. Henry Jekyll/Mr. Hyde), Miriam
Hopkins (Ivy Pearson), Rose Hobart (Muriel Carew), Holmes
Herbert (Dr. Lanyon), Halliwell Hobbes (Brig-Gen. Carew),
Edgar Norton (Poole)

'Promises abundant shocks and returns now that
the fan public is horror conscious. Probably loses
something on popular appeal by highbrow
treatment.' – *Variety*

'As a work of cinematic imagination this film is
difficult to fault.' – *John Baxter, 1968*

● The screenplay with 1,400 frame blow-ups was
published in 1976 in the Film Classics Library (editor
Richard J. Anobile).
● The film was subsequently edited down to 80m, and this
is the only version remaining.
👤 Fredric March
👥 Samuel Hoffenstein, Percy Heath; Karl Struss

143
Doctor Jekyll and Mr Hyde

*A Victorian research chemist finds a formula which separates the good
and evil in his soul; when the latter predominates, he becomes a rampaging monster.*

There have been many films inspired by Robert Louis Stevenson's
famous psychological horror story about a nineteenth-century scientist
who perfects a chemical means of dividing good and evil in the human
psyche. However, when Jekyll tests the formula on himself, the evil in
his soul proves to be more powerful than the good, with the result that
he is transformed into a bestial psychopath. This is the most exciting
and cinematic version by far. The make-up is slightly over the top, but
the gas-lit London settings, the pace, the performances and the clever
camera and sound tricks make it a film to enjoy over and over again.
Subjective camera is used at the beginning, and for the first transformation the actor wore various layers of make up which were sensitive
to different colour filters and thus produced instant change.

Napoleon
France 1927 378m approx (24 fps) bw
(some colour) silent
WESTI/Société Générale de Films

wd Abel Gance *ph* various *m* Arthur Honegger
ad Schnitt, Schildnecht, Alexandre Benois, Jacouty,
Meinhardt, Eugene Lourie *ed* Abel Gance
☆ Albert Dieudonné (Napoleon Bonaparte), Antonin
Artaud (Marat), Pierre Batcheff (General Lazare Hoche)
● The 1934 version ran 140m and included three-
dimensional sound.

142
Napoleon

The early life of Napoleon.

Abel Gance's biographical epic on the young Napoleon is brilliant in most particulars, but owes its greatest interest to its narrative sweep, its flair for composition and its use of triptych screens which, at the end, combine to show one giant picture, the clear precursor of Cinerama. He revised the film in 1934 and added stereophonic sound. One must see it on a large screen to appreciate its visionary magnificence and brilliant camerawork that has hardly ever been bettered.

Open City

Open City
Italy 1945 101m bw
Minerva
◧ ▤ ◉
original title: *Roma, Città Aperta*
w Sergio Amidei, Federico Fellini *d* Roberto Rossellini
ph Ubaldo Arata *m* Renzo Rossellini
☆ Aldo Fabrizi (Don Pietro Pellegrini), Anna Magnani
(Pina), Marcello Pagliero (Giorgio Manfredi), Maria Michi
(Marina)
⚘ script

141
Open City

Italian workers defy the Nazis in Rome towards the end of World War II.

Roberto Rossellini's neo-realist film about underground workers in Rome resisting the Nazis during the final phase of the war has the quality of a vivid newsreel. It was made under great difficulties with little money; for a time Rossellini could not afford to have his footage developed. He shot it on the streets and in actual interiors because there were no studio facilities available. It helped to give this nerve-stretching melodrama a feeling of actuality, with all the background detail as real as care could make it.

All that Money Can Buy

All that Money Can Buy
US 1941 106m bw
RKO/William Dieterle (Charles L. Glett)
◧ ▤ ◉ ◉
aka: *The Devil and Daniel Webster*
aka: *Daniel and the Devil; Here Is a Man*
w Dan Totheroh story *The Devil and Daniel Webster* by
Stephen Vincent Benet *d* William Dieterle *ph* Joseph
August *m* Bernard Herrmann *ad* Van Nest Polglase
ed Robert Wise *sp* Vernon L. Walker
☆ *Walter Huston* (Mr Scratch), James Craig (Jabez
Stone), Anne Shirley (Mary Stone), Simone Simon (Belle),
Edward Arnold (Daniel Webster), Jane Darwell (Ma Stone),
Gene Lockhart (Squire Slossum), John Qualen (Miser
Stevens), H. B. Warner (Justice Hawthorne)

'Some of those in the movie industry who saw it
restively called it a dog; but some of them cried it
was another catapult hurling the cinema up to its
glorious destiny.' – *Cecilia Ager*

♟ Bernard Herrmann
⚘ Walter Huston

140
All that Money Can Buy

A hard-pressed farmer gives in to the Devil's tempting, but is saved from the pit by a famous lawyer's pleading at his 'trial'.

Stephen Vincent Benét's short story of a struggling farmer who succumbs to temptation by the Devil, but is rescued from damnation by the skill of a clever lawyer, was given superlative treatment in this brilliant Germanic *Faust* set in 19th-century New Hampshire. Walter Huston gives his best ever performance as the diabolical Mr Scratch, dangerously charming at one moment and menacing the next. Using historical figures, alienation effects, comedy asides and the whole cinematic box of tricks which Hollywood had just learned again through *Citizen Kane*, it is a magic act in more ways than one.

Kind Hearts and Coronets

Kind Hearts and Coronets
GB 1949 106m bw
Ealing (Michael Relph)
👓 ▦ ⊚∼ ⊚ ⊚

w Robert Hamer, John Dighton *novel* Israel Rank by Roy Horniman *d* Robert Hamer *ph* Douglas Slocombe *md* Ernest Irving *ad* William Kellner *ed* Peter Tanner ☆ *Dennis Price* (Louis Mazzini), *Alec Guinness* (Lord D'Ascoyne/Henry D'Ascoyne/Canon D'Ascoyne/General D'Ascoyne/Admiral D'Ascoyne/Ascoyne D'Ascoyne/Lady Agatha D'Ascoyne/Duke of Chalfont), *Valerie Hobson* (Edith), *Joan Greenwood* (Sibella), Miles Malleson (Hangman), Arthur Lowe (Reporter), Audrey Fildes (Mrs Mazzini), John Penrose (Lionel), Hugh Griffith (Lord High Steward), Clive Morton (Prison Governor)

'A brilliant misfire for the reason that its plentiful wit is literary and practically never pictorial.'
– *Richard Winnington*

'The film in general lacks a visual style equal to its script … All the same, *Kind Hearts and Coronets* is a very funny film and it gets away with a great deal. With so much, in fact, that its makers deserve salutation as pioneers in the little-explored territory of adult British cinema.' – *Lindsay Anderson*

'A film which can be seen and seen again with undiminished pleasure.' – *Basil Wright, 1972*

An impecunious heir eliminates eight D'Ascoynes who stand between him and the family fortune.

A witty, genteel black comedy that is enlivened by Alec Guinness's virtuoso turn playing the eight members of an aristocratic family who are murdered by an impoverished relative who is determined to inherit the family's wealth. Well set in the stately Edwardian era, it deserves its high reputation for wit and style. Robert Hamer's comedy, for all its elegance, has a bitter edge. The determined murderer, Louis Mazzini (the silkily witty Dennis Price), finds that the woman he desires chooses to marry for money, not love, and he learns early on that the high society he wishes to join is built on hypocrisy and snobbery.

'Like Nothing In This World You've Ever Thrilled To Before.'

Dead of Night
GB   1945   104m   bw
Ealing (Sidney Cole, John Croydon)
▣ ▤ ◉~ ⊚ ⊙

w John Baines, Angus MacPhail, based on stories by themselves, H. G. Wells, E. F. Benson *d* Alberto Cavalcanti, Charles Crichton, Robert Hamer, Basil Dearden *ph* Douglas Slocombe, Stan Pavey *m* Georges Auric *ad* Michael Relph *ed* Charles Hasse
☆ *Mervyn Johns* (Walter Craig), *Roland Culver* (Eliot Foley), Mary Merrall (Mrs. Foley), Judy Kelly (Joyce Grainger), Anthony Baird (Hugh Grainger), *Sally Ann Howes* (Sally O'Hara), *Frederick Valk* (Dr. Van Straaten), *Googie Withers* (Joan Courtland), Ralph Michael (Peter Courtland), Esmé Percy (Dealer), Basil Radford (George Parratt), Naunton Wayne (Larry Potter), Miles Malleson (Hearse Driver), *Michael Redgrave* (Maxwell Frere), Hartley Power (Sylvester Kee) and also Elizabeth Welch

'One of the most successful blends of laughter, terror and outrage that I can remember.' – *James Agee*

● Region 1 DVD is only available in a two-disc set with *The Queen of Spades* and has no extras. The Region 2 DVD is available only as part of a four-film box set, *Ealing Classics*; it has no extras.

138
Dead of Night

In recurring dreams, a man is told stories of the supernatural.

A chillingly successful and influential compendium of stories of the macabre. The film was especially effective in Basil Dearden's low-key handling of the linking sequence with its circular ending: an architect is caught up in an endless series of recurring dreams, during which he is told other people's supernatural experiences and finally murders the psychiatrist who is trying to help him. Of the various stories, Robert Hamer's *The Haunted Mirror* is a gripping account of a destructive passion. Charles Crichton provides some comic relief with that reliable double act of Basil Radford and Naunton Wayne as golfing friends who play a game to decide who marries the girl they both love, with the loser committing suicide, and Alberto Cavalcanti's *The Ventriloquist's Dummy* has a notably effective performance from Redgrave as an ventriloquist who has an obsessional relationship with his dummy.

A Hard Day's Night
👫   GB   1964   85m   bw
UA/Proscenium (Walter Shenson)
▣ ▤ ◉~ ⊚ ⊙ 🎧

w Alun Owen *d* Richard Lester *ph* Gilbert Taylor *m/ly* The Beatles *md* George Martin *ad* Ray Simm *ed* John Jympson
☆ *The Beatles*, Wilfrid Brambell (Grandfather), Norman Rossington (Norm), *Victor Spinetti* (TV Director)

'A fine conglomeration of madcap clowning … with such a dazzling use of camera that it tickles the intellect and electrifies the nerves.' – *Bosley Crowther*

'All technology was enlisted in the service of the gag, and a kind of nuclear gagmanship exploded.' – *John Simon*

'The *Citizen Kane* of Jukebox movies' – *Andrew Sarris*

● It has also been released on CD-ROM for Apple Macintosh computers, together with the script and an essay on the movie.
♟ Alun Owen; George Martin

137
A Hard Day's Night

Harassed by their manager and Paul's grandpa, the Beatles embark from Liverpool by train for a London TV show.

A comic fantasia with music that was an artistic and enormous commercial success. Richard Lester used every cinematic gag in the book, as the Beatles, nagged by their manager and Paul McCartney's grandfather, catch a train from Liverpool to London to appear in a TV pop show. It led directly to all the kaleidoscopic swinging-London spy-thrillers and comedies of the later Sixties, and so has a lot to answer for; but at the time it was a sweet breath of fresh air, and the Beatles even seemed willing and likeable.

The Marriage of Maria Braun
West Germany   1978   119m   Fujicolour
Albatros/Trio/WDR/FdA (Michael Fengler)
📽 ▨ ⊘
original title: *Die Ehe der Maria Braun*
w Peter Märthesheimer, Pea Fröhlich *d* Rainer Werner
Fassbinder *ph* Michael Ballhaus *m* Peer Raben
ad Norbert Scherer, Claud Kottmann, Georg Borgel, Helga
Ballhaus *ed* Juliane Lorenz, Franz Walsch
☆ Hanna Schygulla (Maria Braun), Klaus Löwitsch
(Hermann Braun), Ivan Desny (Oswald), Gottfried John
(Willi)

Lola
West Germany   1982   113m   colour
Rialto-Trio (Horst Wendlandt)
⊚ ⌔
w Peter Marthesheimer, Pea Froelich, Rainer Werner
Fassbinder *d* Rainer Werner Fassbinder *ph* Xaver
Schwarzenberger *m* Peer Raben *ad* Rolf Zehetbauer
ed Juliane Lorenz, Rainer Werner Fassbinder
☆ Barbara Sukowa (Lola), Mario Adorf (Schuckert), Armin
Mueller-Stahl (Von Bohm), Matthias Fuchs (Esslin)

Veronika Voss
West Germany   1982   104m   bw
Maura/Tango/Rialto/Trio/Maran (Thomas Schühly)
📽 ▨ ⊘
w Peter Märthesheimer, Pea Fröhlich, Rainer Werner
Fassbinder *d* Rainer Werner Fassbinder *ph* Xaver
Schwarzenberger *m* Peer Raben *ed* Juliane Lorenz
☆ Rosel Zech (Veronika Voss), Hilmar Thate (Robert
Krohn), Annemarie Düringer (Dr. Katz), Doris Schade
(Josefa), Cornelia Froboess (Henriette)

'A dazzling parable of all cinema, of the penalties of
living out one another's fantasies.' – *Sight and
Sound*

● It was inspired by the life of the drug-addicted Sybille
Schmitz, a star of the Nazi era.

The Marriage of Maria Braun

*The vicissitudes of a post-war bride who is eventually blown up in a
gas explosion.*

Lola

A cabaret singer leads a double life.

Veronika Voss

*In the Fifties, a distraught star of the previous decade flees from her
own image, but finds that her psychiatrist is her own worst enemy.*

Fassbinder's impressive trilogy, a collaboration with screenwriters
Peter Marthesheimer and Pea Frohlich, deals with three women at a
particular moment in history: Germany's economic miracle 1950s. The
women seek love but fail to find it, and are destroyed by a male-domi-
nated system, demonstrating Fassbinder's belief that 'man can oppress
a woman simply by letting her know she's a woman'. For all her vitality,
Maria Braun, who emerges from the chaos of the Third Reich, discovers the fatal cost of survival, while waiting for better times to arrive.
Based on Sybille Schmitz, a forgotten actress who was a star in the
Nazi era and later died from her morphine addiction, Veronika Voss is
exploited by an unscrupulous doctor, who is protected by civil authorities. In Lola, a variation on the Josef Sternberg/Marlene Dietrich *The
Blue Angel* an idealistic civil servant comes to realise, through his love
for a woman who turns out to be a prostitute, that civic corruption is
necessary for economic growth. Fassbinder uses different approaches
in each film: the rich palette used in *Maria Braun* suggests the
Hollywood melodramas of the German-born Douglas Sirk; in *Lola*, the
garish colours of the brothel bleed into everyday life; in *Veronika Voss*,
the luminous black and white photography makes its protagonist seem
as pale as a ghost.

La Strada

Italy 1954 94m bw
Ponti/de Laurentiis

aka: The Road

w Federico Fellini, Ennio Flaiano, Tullio Pinelli *d* Federico Fellini *ph* Otello Martelli *m* Nino Rota *ad* Mario Ravasco, E. Cervelli *ed* Leo Catozzo, Lina Caterini

☆ Giulietta Masina (Gelsomina), Anthony Quinn (Zampano), Richard Basehart (Matto 'The Fool')

🏆 best foreign film
♟ script

135

La Strada

A half-witted peasant girl is sold to an itinerant strongman and ill-used by him.

Federico Fellini's curious attempt at a kind of poetic neo-realism was saved by its style and performances from Antony Quinn as an itinerant strong-man, Giulietta Masina as the simple-minded country girl he buys as his assistant and then abuses, and Richard Basehart as a gentle circus clown who befriends her. Masina's delicate, clown-like performance, hovering between laughter and tears, brings true and moving emotion to the film's themes of loneliness and of a woman's suffering redeeming a brutal man.

The Dead

GB 1987 83m Foto-Kem
Vestron/Zenith/Liffey Films (Wieland Schulz-Keil, Chris Sievernich)

w Tony Huston *book* Dubliners by James Joyce *d* John Huston *ph* Fred Murphy *m* Alex North *pd* Stephen Grimes, Dennis Washington *ed* Roberto Silvi *cos* Dorothy Jeakins

☆ Anjelica Huston (Gretta Conroy), Donal McCann (Gabriel Conroy), Rachel Dowling (Lily), Cathleen Delany (Aunt Julia Morkan), Dan O'Herlihy (Mr. Browne), Helena Carroll (Aunt Kate Morkan), Donal Donnelly (Freddy Malins)

'A delicate coda in a minor key to an illustrious 46-year career.' – *Daily Variety*

'A small masterpiece, perfectly achieved.' – *Time Out*

♟ best adapted screenplay; Dorothy Jeakins

134

The Dead

Two Irish spinster sisters throw a winter dinner for their relatives and friends.

John Huston's last film is a warm and somehow invigorating reminiscence of things past, in which two women give a dinner party on a snowy night in Ireland in 1904. It is based on James Joyce's story of a middle-aged man wondering at his wife's remembrance about the frail dead boy who loved her dearly when she was young. Huston tells his tale with the buttonholing insistence of some ancient mariner about to set out on his final voyage. He is blessed with a cast sensitive to the drama, who provide some inspired ensemble playing.

Lacombe, Lucien

France 1974 141m Eastmancolor
Rank/NEF/UPF/Vides/Hallelujah Films (Louis Malle)
●●
w Louis Malle, Patrick Modiano *d* Louis Malle *ph* Tonino
Delli Colli *m* Django Reinhardt *ad* Ghislain Uhry
ed Suzanne Baron
☆ Pierre Blaise (Lucien), Aurore Clement (France), Holger
Lowenadler (Albert Horn), Thérèse Gieshe (Bella Horn)

'Malle's film is a long, close look at the banality of
evil; it is – not incidentally – one of the least banal
movies ever made.' – *Pauline Kael, New Yorker*

'Easily Mr Malle's most ambitious, most
provocative film.' – *Vincent Canby, New York Times*

♟ best foreign film
🏆 best film

133

Lacombe, Lucien

A boy is rejected by the French resistance and joins the Gestapo instead.

Louis Malle's tragic fable of collaboration caused controversy in France and led him to leave the country. It was a provocative film about a young peasant who works for the Gestapo, having been spurned by the French resistance. Malle researched the subject extensively before writing his fictional treatment. For his central role he used a non-professional, Pierre Blaise, a local youth who had never been to a cinema or read a book in his life but understood Lucien's background (he subsequently made three more films before dying in a car accident at the age of 23). Malle's film deals sympathetically with the vulnerability and pride of youth, and with the banality of evil.

'They beat him. They deprived him. They
ridiculed him. They broke his heart. But
they couldn't break his spirit.'

Kes

👪 GB 1969 109m Technicolor
UA/Woodfall (Tony Garnett)
●● ⊚
w Barry Hines, Ken Loach, Tony Garnett *novel* A Kestrel
for a Knave by Barry Hines *d* Ken Loach *ph* Chris Menges
m John Cameron *ad* William McCrow *ed* Roy Watts
☆ David Bradley (Billy Casper), Lynne Perrie (Mrs.
Casper), Colin Welland (Mr. Farthing), Freddie Fletcher
(Jud), Brian Glover (Mr. Sugden)

'There emerges a most discouraging picture of life
in the industrial north … infinitely sad in its total
implications, it is also immensely funny in much of
its detail.' – *Brenda Davies*

'Particularly to be admired is the way in which the
dialogue has been kept flowing, as if it were always
spontaneous, something proceeding from the
moment.' – *Dilys Powell*

🏆 Colin Welland; David Bradley

132

Kes

In a northern industrial town, a boy learns about life from the fate of his pet bird.

Ken Loach's deceptively simple drama, about a boy living in the North of England who gains wisdom by observing the life of his pet kestrel, is one of the key British films of its period. In a neo-realist tradition, it uses some non-professional actors and deals with working-class life in an honest and uncondescending way. It is a passionate work about the waste of human potential, of individuals trapped by circumstances in an uncaring system. It was perhaps symptomatic of the failures of Britain's film industry that its distributors put the film on a shelf for a year before releasing it to critical acclaim.

Jour de Fête
France 1948 87m bw
Francinex (Fred Orain)

w Jacques Tati, Henri Marquet *d* *Jacques Tati* *ph* Jacques Mercanton *m* Jean Yatove *ad* Rene Moullaert *ed* Marcel Morreau

☆ *Jacques Tati* (Francois), Guy Decomble (Roger), Paul Fankeur (Marcel), Santa Relli (Roger's Wife)

'You could watch it with a bout of toothache and it would make you laugh.' – *Daily Express*

'It is not progressive; it won't be a landmark in the history of the cinema; but it gives me more pleasure than any film for the last five years.' – *Dilys Powell*

● A reissue version had colour items hand-painted in each frame, and proved quite effective.
● A restored version in colour, made by Tati on experimental Thomsoncolour film but never printed at the time due to technical problems, was released in 1994 as part of France's celebration of the centenary of cinema. It has also been released on video-cassette.

131
Jour de Fête

A village postman sees a film about the efficiency of the American postal service and decides to smarten himself up.

Jacques Tati's first feature is an undiluted joy, an episodic account of a French rural postman who, having heard about the US Post Office's impressive organization, resolves to improve his own professional performance. The film, which made use of jokes from an earlier short, is a mix of hilarious slapstick and local colour, as a fair makes its annual visit to the village. Tati's comic vision was a nostalgic one, though he used sound in new ways. There is a constant background noise of the countryside, from dogs, cows, roosters and geese, and dialogue is incidental. The comedy is brilliantly physical.

Three Colours: Blue

France 1993 98m Eastmancolor
Artificial Eye/MK2/CED/France 3/CAB/TOR/Canal
(Marin Karmitz)
🎞 ▤ ⊚～ ⊘ ⊙ ⌒
original title: *Trois Couleurs: Bleu*
w Krzysztof Pisiewicz, Krzysztof Kieslowski d Krzysztof
Kieslowski ph Slawomir Idziak m Zbigniew Preisner
ad Claude Lenoir ed Jacques Witta
☆ Juliette Binoche (Julie), Benoît Régent (Olivier),
Florence Pernel (Sandrine), Charlotte Véry (Lucille), Hélène
Vincent (Journalist), Philippe Volter (Estate Agent), Claude
Duneton (Doctor), Hugues Quester (Patrice), Emmanuelle
Riva (The Mother)

'What lifts it out of the doldrums is Kieslowski's
fascinating use of reflections, focusing techniques
and camera angles to give the somewhat
pedestrian material a profound and otherworldly
East European feel.' – *Kim Newman, Empire*

● The music for the film was written first and the action
was filmed to match its rhythms.

Three Colours: White

France/Poland 1993 92m Eastmancolor
Artificial Eye/MK2/France 3/Cab/TOR/Canal (Marin
Karmitz)
🎞 ▤ ⊚～ ⊘ ⊙ ⌒
original title: *Trois Couleurs: Blanc*
w Krzysztof Piesiewicz, Krzysztof Kieslowski d Krzysztof
Kieslowski ph Edward Klosiński m Zbigniew Preisner
ad Halina Dobrowolska, Claude Lenoir ed Urszula Lesiak
☆ Zbigniew Zamachowski (Karol Karol), Julie Delpy
(Dominique), Janusz Gajos (Mikolaj), Jerzy Stuhr (Jurek),
Juliette Binoche (Julie), Florence Pernel (Sandrine)

'A fairly straightforward black comedy that skirts
pretentiousness and goes easy on the symbolism
while retaining Kieslowski's eerie gift for spinning
mystical narrative gold from the simplest of
ingredients.' – *Lisa Nesselson, Variety*

● This second part of a trilogy, based on the colours of the
French flag, deals with equality.

Three Colours: Red

France/Switzerland/Poland 1994 99m
Eastmancolor
Artificial Eye/MK2/France 3/CAB/Tor (Marin Karmitz)
🎞 ▤ ⊚～ ⊘ ⊙ ⌒
original title: *Trois Couleurs: Rouge*
w Krzysztof Piesiewicz, Krzysztof Kieslowski d Krzysztof
Kieslowski ph Piotr Sobocinski m Zbigniew Preisner
pd Claude Lenoir ed Jacques Witta
☆ Irene Jacob (Valentine), Jean-Louis Trintignant (Judge
Joseph Kern), Jean-Pierre Lorit (Auguste), Frédérique Feder
(Karin), Juliette Binoche (Julie), Julie Delpy (Dominique)

'If it's true – as the helmer has announced – that
this opus will be his last foray into film directing,
Kieslowski retires at a formal and philosophical
peak.' – *Variety*

● It is the last part of a trilogy based on the French
tricolour and deals with fraternity.
♟ Krzysztof Kieslowski (director); Krzysztof Piesiewicz
(screenplay); Piotr Sobocinski

Three Colours: Blue

A secretive woman, the wife of a composer, whose husband and child are killed in a car crash, destroys his final work, sells all their possessions and sets out to remake her life.

Three Colours: White

A Polish hairdresser suffers a series of humiliations in Paris – he becomes impotent, his French wife divorces him and he is reduced to penury – and returns to Warsaw with the aim of becoming rich and winning back his wife.

Three Colours: Red

A model confides her fears about her life to a lonely and inquisitive retired judge, who secretly arranges a meeting between her and a young lawyer.

Krzysztof Kieslowski's trilogy, based on the colours of the French tricolour, is concerned with the theme of liberty. In the first part (*Blue*), the wife of a composer, after both he and their child die in an accident, takes drastic steps to create a new life for herself. The second part (*White*) is an elegant and acid comedy of a Chaplinesque little man at large in an entrepreneurial Poland – 'home at last,' says our hero, regaining consciousness on a Warsaw rubbish dump after a nightmare trip from France. In the third (*Red*), a retired judge lends a sympathetic ear to a fearful young woman in a delicate and intricate study of coincidence and destiny that brings an impressive trilogy to a stylish and intriguing end.

Bicycle Thieves

Italy 1948 90m bw
PDS-ENIC (Umberto Scarparelli)

original title: *Ladri di Biciclette*
US title: *Bicycle Thief*
w Cesare Zavattini *d* Vittorio de Sica *ph* Carlo Montuori
m Alessandro Cicognini *ad* Antonio Traverso *ed* Eraldo
Da Roma
☆ *Lamberto Maggiorani* (Antonio Ricci), *Enzo Staiola*
(Bruno Ricci)

'A film of rare humanity and sensibility.' – *Gavin
Lambert*

'A memorable work of art with the true flavour of
reality. To see it is an experience worth having.'
– *Richard Mallett, Punch*

'My idea is to de-romanticize the cinema.' –
Vittorio de Sica

👤 foreign film
Cesare Zavattini
🏆 picture

129
Bicycle Thieves

*An Italian workman, long unemployed, is robbed of the bicycle he
needs for his new job, and he and his small son search Rome for it.*

Vittorio de Sica's film is the epitome of Italian neo-realism: a man has
just got the first job he has had in a long while, but his bicycle has
been stolen. Since he needs it to do his new job, he and his young son
scour Rome in search of it. Strangely, when de Sica was having trouble
raising the finance to make the film, David Selznick offered to back it
provided that Cary Grant played the leading role. The part went to a
non-professional, a factory worker who had brought his son to an
audition to play the boy in the film. Carlo Montuori's camera superbly
captures the seedier parts of Rome, the soup kitchen and flea market.
The slight human drama is developed so that it has all the force of
King Lear, and both the acting and the backgrounds are vividly compelling.

'Everybody laughs but Buster!'

The General

👥 US 1926 80m approx (24 fps) bw
silent
UA/Buster Keaton (Joseph M. Schenck)
📽 🎞 🔊 ⊙ ⊚

w Al Boasberg, Charles Smith *d* Buster Keaton, Clyde Bruckman *ph* J. Devereux Jennings, Bert Haines *ad* Fred Gabourie *ed* Harry Barnes, J. Sherman Kell

☆ Buster Keaton (Johnnie Gray), Marion Mack (Annabelle Lee), Glen Cavander (Captain Anderson)

'It has all the sweet earnestness in the world. It is about trains, frontier America, flower-faced girls.' – *New Yorker, 1977*

'The production itself is singularly well mounted, but the fun is not exactly plentiful … here he is more the acrobat than the clown, and his vehicle might be described as a mixture of cast iron and jelly.' – *Mordaunt Hall, New York Times*

● The story is based on an actual incident of the Civil War, treated more seriously in *The Great Locomotive Chase* (qv).
● The screenplay with 1,400 freeze frames was issued in 1976 in the Film Classics Library (editor, Richard Anobile).
● The Region 1 DVD is available as part of a two-film set with *Steamboat Bill Jr.* The Region 2 release includes two shorts, *Cops* and *The Balloonatic.*

128

The General

A confederate train driver gets his train and his girl back when they are stolen by Union soldiers.

Buster Keaton's film about a train driver in the Confederate army who, after his train and his girlfriend are captured by Union troops, succeeds in regaining both, is a slow-starting, then hilarious action comedy, often voted one of the best ever made. It was an expensive production, with its spectacular train crash becoming the most costly single shot in silent films. At the time of its original release, it was a critical and popular failure. It took thirty years before it was recognized as a classic of comedy. Its sequence of sight gags, each topping the one before, remains an incredible joy to behold.

Ossessione

Italy 1942 135m bw
ICI
📽 🇺🇸 ⊚ ◎

w Antonio Pietrangeli, Giuseppe de Santis, Gianni Puccini, Luchino Visconti, Mario Alicata *d Luchino Visconti* ph Aldo Tonti, Domenico Scala *m* Giuseppe Rosati *ad* Gino Rosati *ed* James M. Cain

☆ Massimo Girotti (Gino), Clara Calamai (Giovanna), Elio Marcuzzo (Lo Spagnuolo)

● Other versions: *Le Dernier Tournant* (France 1939); *The Postman Always Rings Twice* (US 1945); *The Postman Always Rings Twice* (US 1981).

127
Ossessione

A wanderer falls for the wife of an innkeeper and together they murder her husband, but fate takes a hand.

Luchino Visconti's unofficial remake of *The Postman Always Rings Twice* is a powerful melodrama credited with starting the neo-realist movement in Italy, although it was barely released outside that country. It is a raw account of sex and murder, as a drifter falls in love with the wife of an innkeeper and joins her in killing him. Visconti starred Massimo Girotti, an actor he desired (though his love was not reciprocated) and Clara Calamai as the couple, who give off an intense erotic heat. It was not as glossy as the Hollywood versions of the story and was in stark contrast to the glamorous movies being turned out under Italy's Fascist government.

Day for Night

France/Italy 1973 116m Eastmancolor
Films du Carrosse/PECF/PIC (Marcel Bébert)
📽 🇺🇸 ◎

original title: *La Nuit Américaine*

w François Truffaut, Jean-Louis Richard, Suzanne Schiffman *d François Truffaut* ph Pierre-William Glenn *m* Georges Delerue *ad* Damien Lanfranchi *ed* Yann Dedet, Martine Barraque

☆ Jacqueline Bisset (Julie Baker), Valentina Cortese (Severine), Jean-Pierre Aumont (Alexandre), Jean-Pierre Léaud (Alphonse), Dani (Lilianna), Alexandra Stewart (Stacey), Jean Champion (Bertrand), François Truffaut (Ferrand), David Markham (Dr. Nelson)

'Made with such dazzling craftsmanship and confidence that you can never quite believe Truffaut's point that directing a movie is a danger-fraught experience.' – *Michael Billington, Illustrated London News*

● Graham Greene, as Henry Graham, played an insurance representative.
● A Region 1 DVD release includes three documentaries, two interviews with Truffaut and an interview with Valentina Cortese.

🏆 best foreign film
🏆 script; François Truffaut (as director); Valentina Cortese
🏆 best picture; François Truffaut; Valentina Cortese

126
Day for Night

Frictions and personality clashes beset the making of a film in Nice.

The movie-obsessed François Truffaut depicted the human tensions that can plague the production of a romantic film in this richly detailed, insider's eye-view of film-making. Setting the action in a film studio in Nice, Truffaut plays a director much like himself directing a cast that includes Jean-Pierre Léaud, his most regular collaborator, in a performance that also seems to draw on personal experience. One of Truffaut's contemporaries, Jean-Luc Godard, thought he had sold out with this film, perhaps because the film-within-the-film is obviously a piece of commercial trash. It is, though, an immensely enjoyable, fun film with melodramatic asides.

Festen

Festen
Denmark   1998   105m   colour
October/Nimbus/DR TV/SVT Drama (Brigitte Hald)
🔜 🎌 ⓖ ⓞ
aka: *The Celebration*
w Thomas Vinterberg, Mogens Rukov   *d* Thomas
Vinterberg   *ph* Anthony Dod Mantle   *ed* Valdis Oskarsdottir
☆ Ulrich Thomsen (Christian), Henning Moritzen (Helge),
Thomas Bo Larsen (Michael), Paprika Steen (Helene), Birthe
Neumann (Elsa), Trine Dyrholm (Pia), Helle Dolleris (Mette),
Therese Glahn (Michelle), Klaus Bondam (Master of
Ceremonies), Bjarne Henriksen (Kim), Gbatokai Dakinah
(Gbatokai)

'As smart, sharp and stinging as a slap around the
face.' – *Tom Shone, Sunday Times*

• The film was made under the dictates of Dogma 95, of
which Vinterberg was a signatory; its conditions laid down
for film-making include location shooting, direct sound, and
hand-held camerawork.

125
Festen

A son reveals terrible secrets about his father at a family gathering.

Thomas Vinterberg's film is enough on its own to more than justify the activities of the Dogme group, who insisted on going back to basics in their film-making, shooting on location, using only available light, using music only if it occurred within the scene being shot, and similar 'vows of chastity'. It was set in a large house, at a formal dinner to celebrate a patriarch's 60th birthday. There, his eldest son makes a speech claiming that his father sexually abused him as a child, and drove his twin sister to kill herself. Brilliantly done, it was an unsettling, nervy drama, in which the edgy acting and twitchy camera-work combined to give a raw, emotional power to the narrative.

The Colour of Pomegranates

The Colour of Pomegranates
USSR   1969   73m   colour
Armenfilm
🔜 🎌 ⓞ
original title: *Tsvet Granata*
wd Sergei Paradjanov   *ph* Suren Shakhbazian   *m* Tieran
Mansurian   *ad* Stepan Andranikan
☆ Sofiko Chiaureli (Young Poet/Poet's Love/Nun with
White Lace Angel W), M. Alekian (Poet as a Child), V.
Glastian (Poet in the Cloister), G. Gegechkori (Poet as an
Old Man), O. Minasian (The Prince)

124
The Colour of Pomegranates

Biopic of the 18th-century Armenian poet Sayat Nova, as he rises from a child working as a wool dyer to courtier and monk, told in the manner of his poems.

The Georgian director Sergei Paradjanov was imprisoned in the 1970s by the Soviet authorities and forbidden to make films on his release, though he was able to direct two further films in the mid-1980s before his sudden death from a heart attack. This extraordinary and lyrical film was made before he fell completely out of favour. It was based on the llife of the poet Sayat Nova, who, living in Armenia in the eighteenth century, rose from humble beginnings as a wool dyer and finally became a courtier and a monk. The film's story is told in the style of Nova's poems – its richly coloured, emblematic images are like a succession of animated icons.

The Colour of Pomegranates

'Positively The Most Hilarious Picture
You've Ever Seen!!!'

A Day at the Races
US   1937   109m   bw/blue-tinted ballet
sequence
MGM (Lawrence Weingarten)

w *Robert Pirosh, George Seaton, George Oppenheimer*
d *Sam Wood* ph *Joseph Ruttenberg* m Franz Waxman
ch Dave Gould ad *Cedric Gibbons* ed *Frank E. Hull*
☆ Groucho (Dr. Hugo Z. Hackenbush), *Chico* (Tony),
Harpo (Stuffy), *Margaret Dumont* (Mrs. Upjohn), Maureen
O'Sullivan (Judy), Allan Jones (Gil), *Douglass Dumbrille*
(Morgan), *Esther Muir* ('Flo'), Sig Rumann (Dr. Steinberg)

'The money is fairly splashed about; the capitalists
have recognized the Marx Brothers; ballet
sequences, sentimental songs, amber fountains,
young lovers. Easily the best film to be seen in
London, but all the same I feel a nostalgia for the
old cheap rickety sets.' – *Graham Greene*

♫ 'All God's Chillun Got Rhythm'; 'On Blue-Venetian
Waters'; 'A Message From the Man in the Moon'; 'Tomorrow
Is Another Day'
♟ Dave Gould

123

A Day at the Races

The Marx Brothers help a girl who owns a sanatorium and a racehorse.

Though this film lacks the Marx Brothers' zaniest inspirations, *A Day at the Races* is a top-quality production and contains several of their funniest routines, as well as a racecourse climax that is spectacularly well integrated. The musical and romantic asides are a matter of taste but are delightfully typical of their time. Sam Wood's directorial approach, which often resulted in as many as twenty takes of a scene, sometimes inhibited the brothers' comedy, but they still lived up to Dadaist Hans Richter's description of them as showing 'one way in which fools may speak the truth.'

'One of the greatest stories of love and adventure ever told is brought to the screen as Dickens himself would wish it!'

David Copperfield
🏃 US 1934 132m bw
MGM (David O. Selznick)
📹 ▤ 🔍

w Hugh Walpole, Howard Estabrook *novel* Charles Dickens *d* George Cukor *ph* Oliver T. Marsh *m* Herbert Stothart *ad* Cedric Gibbons *ed* Robert J. Kern *montage* Slavko Vorkapich

☆ *Freddie Bartholomew* (young David), *Frank Lawton* (David as a man), *W. C. Fields* (Micawber), *Roland Young* (Uriah Heep), *Edna May Oliver* (Aunt Betsy), *Lennox Pawle* (Mr Dick), *Basil Rathbone* (Mr Murdstone), Violet Kemble Cooper (Miss Murdstone), Maureen O'Sullivan (Dora), Madge Evans (Agnes), Elizabeth Allan (Mrs Copperfield), *Jessie Ralph* (Peggotty), Lionel Barrymore (Dan Peggotty), Hugh Williams (Steerforth), Lewis Stone (Mr Wickfield) and also *Herbert Mundin* (Barkis), Elsa Lanchester (Clickett), Jean Cadell (Mrs Micawber), Una O'Connor (Mrs Gummidge), John Buckler (Ham), Hugh Walpole (the Vicar), Arthur Treacher (donkey man)

● Charles Laughton was originally cast as Micawber, but resigned from the role after two days of shooting. It was said at the time that 'he looked as though he were about to molest the child'.

⚖ best picture; editing

Au Revoir Les Enfants
France 1988 107m Eastmancolor
Nouvelles éditions de Films/MK2/Stella Films (Louis Malle)
📹 ▤ 🔍 ⊙ 🎧

wd Louis Malle *ph* Renato Berta *ad* Willy Holt *ed* Emmanuelle Castro

☆ Gaspard Manesse (Julien Quentin), Raphaël Fejtö (Jean Bonnet), Francine Racette (Mme Quentin), Stanlislas Carre de Malberg (François Quentin), Philippe Morier-Genoud (Father Jean), François Berleand (Father Michel), François Negret (Joseph)

'Malle has said of *Au Revoir*, "I reinvented the past in the pursuit of a haunting and timeless truth." Maybe that's why I felt as if I were watching a faded French classic, something I dimly recalled.' – *Pauline Kael, New Yorker*

⚖ best foreign film; Louis Malle (as writer)
🏆 Louis Malle (as director)

122
David Copperfield

An orphan grows up to become a successful writer.

Dickens' semi-autobiographical novel of an orphan who, disliked by his cruel stepfather and helped by his eccentric aunt, grows up to become an author and eventually to marry his childhood sweetheart, is conveyed better than the screen has normally managed in this small miracle of compression. George Cukor achieved the difficult feat of making the characters, as he put it, 'slightly grotesque, at time caricature, yet completely human'. It is a particularly pleasing example of Hollywood's handling of literature and of the deployment of a great studio's resources (Cukor thought the white cliffs in California, near Malibu, were whiter and cliffier than the ones at Dover). It also overflows with memorable character cameos and scenes of dramatic power.

121
Au Revoir Les Enfants

During the German occupation of France, a boy at a Catholic school inadvertently betrays his Jewish schoolfriend to the Nazis.

Louis Malle indulges in no false heroics or grand gestures in his intensely personal, semi-autobiographical movie about a French schoolboy who unintentionally betrays his Jewish friend to the Nazis during World War II. Malle's approach is cooly understated, concentrating on creating the everyday life of both the school and the upper-middle-class society of the time; into both, the realities of war slowly intrude. It is only at the close of the film, which won the Golden Lion award for best film at the Venice Film Festival, that Malle reveals the story is true, and that the Jewish boy, along with two others, died at Auschwitz and the school's head, a priest, at Mauthausen. The title comes from the priest's final words as he left the school.

Cinema Paradiso

Italy/France   1989   122m   colour
Palace/Films Ariana/RAI TRE/Forum/Franco Cristaldi
⚎ ⚎ ▤ ⊗ ⊙ ⊙ ⌒
original title: *Nuovo Cinema Paradiso*
wd Giuseppe Tornatore *ph* Blasco Giurato *m* Ennio Morricone, Andrea Morricone *pd* Andrea Crisanti *ed* Mario Morra
☆ Antonelli Attli (Young Maria), Enzo Cannavale (Spaccafico), Isa Danieli (Anna), Leo Gullotta (Bill Sticker), Marco Leonardi (Toto as a Teenager), Pupella Maggio (Older Maria), Agnese Nano (Elena), Leopoldo Trieste (Fr. Adelfio), Salvatore Cascio (Toto as a Child), Jacques Perrin (Toto as an Adult), *Philippe Noiret* (Alfredo)
● A director's cut lasting 175m was released in 1994.
● Region 1 and 2 DVD releases include two versions of the film, the theatrical version and the longer director's cut.
🏃 best foreign film
🏆 best foreign film; original screenplay; Philippe Noiret; Salvatore Cascio; Ennio and Andrea Morricone

120
Cinema Paradiso

A film director remembers his early life and his boyhood friendship with the projectionist at his local cinema.

In Giuseppe Tornatore's semi-autobiographical celebration of the communal joys of film in the time before television, a movie director recalls his childhood friendship with a cinema projectionist in the 1950s. Philippe Noiret, one of the greatest of screen actors, is magnificent as the grizzled projectionist, passing on his knowledge of film and life to the boy. Nostalgic in its celebration of the cinema, it is beautifully detailed in its enjoyment of the rituals of small-town life with, underneath it all, a toughness in its depiction of a child's growth to maturity.

'What Is The One Memory You Would Take With You?'

After Life

Japan   1998   118m   colour
ICA/TV Man Union/Engine (Shiho Sato, Masayuki Akieda)
⚎ ▤ ⊙
aka: *Wonderful Life*
original title: *Wandafuru Raifu*
wd Hirokazu Kore-Eda *ph* Yamazaki Hiroshi *m* Yasuhiro Kasamatsu *ad* Toshihiro Isomi, Hideo Gunji *ed* Hirokazu Kore-Eda
☆ Arata (Takashi Mochizuki), Erika Oda (Shiori Satonaka), Susumu Terajima (Satoru Kawashima), Tsuyoshi Naito (Ichiro Watanabe), Kyoko Kagawa (Kyoko Watanabe), Kei Tani (Ken-nosuke Nakamura), Takashi Naito (Takuro Sugie), Sadao Abe (Ichiro Watanabe, as student)

'A profound meditation on life's meaning and value and the relationship of movies, memories and dreams.' – *Stephen Holden, New York Times*

119
After Life

After they die, people are processed by bureaucrats who allow them to take one memory of their life, in the form of a film re-creation, into eternity.

Hirokazu Kore-Eda's moving drama is based on a clever notion of life after death in which the deceased are dealt with by other-worldly administrators who permit them to take with them into eternity a single memory of their earthly lives, encapsulated in film format. A simple, straightforward drama, mixing actual memories with imagined ones, it manages to touch deep feeling. It is both witty and moving in its depiction of the newly dead and the stranded officials who attempt to deal both with their lives and those fleeting moments that gave them meaning.

The Chant of Jimmie Blacksmith

Australia 1978 122m Eastmancolor
Panavision
Film House (Fred Schepisi)

wd Fred Schepisi *novel* Thomas Keneally *ph* Ian Baker
m Bruce Smeaton *pd* Wendy Dickson *ed* Brian Cavanagh
☆ Tommy Lewis (Jimmie Blacksmith), Ray Barrett
(Constable Farrell), Jack Thompson (Rev. Neville), Freddy
Reynolds (Mort), Angela Punch McGregor (Gilda), Steve
Dodds (Tabidgi), Peter Carroll (McCready)

'One of the greatest pieces of political film making I
know, because it doesn't impose rhetorical nobility
on its characters or twist their lives into social
statement.' – *Stephen Schiff*

'This is a large scale film – a visually, impassioned
epic.' – *Pauline Kael*

'A big film intended for a big audience. On its own
terms, it is a powerful indictment of the insidious,
pervasive canker of white racism.' – *David Wilson,
Sight and Sound*

118
The Chant of Jimmie Blacksmith

Provoked by his white employers, an aborigine becomes a killer.

Fred Schepisi's powerful film deals with the tragedy of an outcast at
home in no society, who is torn between the world he has lost and the
one he cannot gain. Jimmy Blacksmith (based on a real life outlaw and
killer Jimmy Governor) is a half-caste who works for white farmers but,
provoked by them, goes berserk and slaughters their families. Filmed
against the vast Australian landscape, Schepisi investigates notions of
identity and racism within a colonial society. The violence is shocking,
as it is meant to be. It is one of the great achievements of Australian
cinema. Thomas Keneally, on whose novel the film was based, praised
Schepisi for his courage in challenging Australian attitudes and for producing 'a grand flawed film, a fine film'.

Oliver Twist

GB 1948 116m bw
GFD/Cineguild (Ronald Neame)

w David Lean, Stanley Haynes *novel* Charles Dickens
d David Lean *ph* Guy Green *m* Arnold Bax *md* Muir
Mathieson *pd* John Bryan *ed* Jack Harris *cos* Margaret
Furse
☆ *Alec Guinness* (Fagin), *Robert Newton* (Bill Sikes),
Francis L. Sullivan (Mr Bumble), *John Howard Davies*
(Oliver Twist), *Kay Walsh* (Nancy), *Anthony Newley* (The
Artful Dodger), *Henry Stephenson* (Mr Brownlow), *Mary
Clare* (Mrs Corney), *Gibb McLaughlin* (Mr Sowerberry),
Diana Dors (Charlotte)

'A thoroughly expert piece of movie entertainment.'
– *Richard Winnington*

'A brilliant, fascinating movie, no less a classic than
the Dickens novel which it brings to life.' – *Time*

117
Oliver Twist

*A foundling falls among thieves but is rescued by a benevolent old
gentleman.*

David Lean's simplified, brilliantly cinematic version of a voluminous
Victorian novel is beautiful to look at and memorably played. Dickens'
classic story of the young boy who becomes involved with thieves but
is saved from a life of petty crime by a kind elderly man, is given the
perfect maximum impact in every scene. Lean filmed the murder of
Nancy by Sikes without showing anything but, as the sound of cries
and bangs begins, Sikes' bull terrier scrabbles at a door to get out of
the room. Alec Guinness' Fagin, though it became as controversial as
Shakespeare's Shylock, is a memorable portrait, full of sly humour, and
Robert Newton, as the villainous Sikes, and Francis L. Sullivan as the
pompous beadle could not be bettered.

Oliver Twist

On the Town

US 1949 98m Technicolor
MGM (Arthur Freed)

w Betty Comden, Adolph Green *ballet* Fancy Free by
Leonard Bernstein *d* Gene Kelly, Stanley Donen
ph Harold Rosson *m* Saul Chaplin, Roger Edens, Leonard
Bernstein *md* Lennie Hayton, Roger Edens *ch* Gene Kelly,
Stanley Donen *ad* Cedric Gibbons, Jack Martin Smith
ed Ralph E. Winters *cos* Helen Rose

☆ *Gene Kelly* (Gabey), *Frank Sinatra* (Chip), *Jules
Munshin* (Ozzie), *Vera-Ellen* (Ivy Smith), *Betty Garrett*
(Brunhilde Esterhazy), *Ann Miller* (Claire Huddesen), Tom
Dugan (Officer Tracy), Florence Bates (Mme. Dilyovska),
Alice Pearce (Lucy Shmeeler)

'The speed, the vitality, the flashing colour and
design, the tricks of timing by which motion is
fitted to music, the wit and invention and
superlative technical accomplishment make it a
really exhilarating experience.' – *Richard Mallett,
Punch*

♪ 'New York, New York'; 'Prehistoric Man'; 'I Can Cook
Too'; 'Main Street'; 'You're Awful'; 'On the Town'; 'Count on
Me'; 'Pearl of the Persian Sea'

♟ Lennie Hayton, Roger Edens

116
On the Town

Three sailors enjoy 24 hours' leave in New York.

Although it was based on a Broadway show, many changes were made
for this brash location musical, which is among the best things ever to
come out of Hollywood. While its narrative of three sailors enjoying a
day's shared leave in New York was kept, their characters were rewritten to suit the personalities of Gene Kelly, Frank Sinatra and Jules
Mushin. Arthur Freed, the producer, did not like Leonard Bernstein's
score and left out as much of it as he could. It marked a change in
musicals, since elaborate production numbers were dropped in favour
of a more intimate approach. The serious ballet towards the end is an
acquired taste, but the film otherwise contains a great deal to be
thankful for.

City Lights

US   1931   87m   bw   silent (with music and effects)
UA/Charles Chaplin

wd Charles Chaplin *ph* Rollie Totheroh *m* Charles Chaplin *md* Alfred Newman

☆ Charles Chaplin (A Tramp), Virginia Cherrill (A Blind Girl), Florence Lee (Her Grandmother), Harry Myers (An Eccentric Millionaire)

'Chaplin has another good picture, but it gives indications of being short-winded, and may tire fast after a bombastic initial seven days … he has sacrificed speed to pathos, and plenty of it.' – *Variety*

'Even while laughing, one is aware of a faint and uneasy feeling that Chaplin has been pondering with more than a bit of solemnity on conventional story values, and it has led him further than ever into the realms of what is often called pathetic.' – *National Board of Review*

115
City Lights

A tramp befriends a millionaire and falls in love with a blind girl.

There are several delightful sequences in Chaplin's best manner in this sentimental comedy about a vagrant who befriends a wealthy man and falls in love with a blind girl. Chaplin found the film difficult, as he did Virginia Cherrill, but both survived the experience (although Cherrill was suspended for a time and would only return for more money). Chaplin's comic moments, which include the opening discovery of the tramp sleeping in the lap of a statue as it is unveiled, a boxing match and a life-and-death struggle with a suicidal millionaire, are well polished routines. But nothing he did before, or after, compared to the closing scene here; a brilliant moment of recognition and loss that is enough, as James Agee put it, 'to shrivel the heart to see'.

'In a strange and horrifying playground the innocents act out their game of life and death …'

Walkabout

Australia   1970   100m   DeLuxe
Max L. Raab/Si Litvinoff

w Edward Bond *novel* James Vance Marshall *d* Nicolas Roeg *ph* Nicolas Roeg *m* John Barry *pd* Brian Eatwell *ad* Terry Gough *ed* Antony Gibbs, Alan Pattillo

☆ Jenny Agutter (Girl), Lucien John (Boy), David Gulpilil (Aborigine), John Meillon (Father)

'The film is rich enough, especially at a second look, to make you forget the flaws. You are left with the impression of a fresh, powerful and humane imagination.' – *Dilys Powell*

● A Region 1 DVD release has commentary by Nicolas Roeg and Jenny Agutter.

114
Walkabout

A man kills himself in the desert and his children trek among the Aborigines to safety.

Nicolas Roeg achieves a great deal with this pared-down drama in the vast, open spaces of the Australian outback. There, two children, whose father, after failing to kill them, commits suicide, walk to safety with the help of an Aboriginal youth. He is undergoing his right of passage, sent into the wilderness by the elders of his tribe to survive for six months on his own. A director's and photographer's experimental success, from Edward Bond's spare script, the film also ends in tragedy. The contrast between city and native life, between artificial restrain and natural response is sometimes forced, but the power of its images makes it a film not easily forgotten.

Walkabout

A Kind of Loving

GB   1962   112m   bw
Anglo-Amalgamated/Waterhall/Vic Films (Joe Janni)

w *Keith Waterhouse, Willis Hall* novel *Stan Barstow*
d *John Schlesinger* ph *Denys Coop* m *Ron Grainer*
ad Ray Simm ed Roger Cherrill

☆ *Alan Bates* (Vic Brown), *June Ritchie* (Ingrid Rothwell),
Thora Hird (Mrs. Rothwell), *Bert Palmer* (Mr. Brown), *Gwen Nelson* (Mrs. Brown)

'You will be shocked by this highly moral film only if you are shocked by life.' – *Evening News*

113
A Kind of Loving

A young North Country draughtsman is forced into marriage, has to live with his dragon-like mother-in-law, and finally sorts out a relationship with his unhappy wife.

A blunt melodrama with strong kinship to *Saturday Night and Sunday Morning*: a young man in the North of England, having been coerced into marriage, has a difficult relationship with his wife's dominating mother, but eventually he and his wife achieve a measure of happiness together. There were effectively low-key performances from Alan Bates and June Ritchie as the two lovers trying to come to an accommodation with each other and with life. In his first feature film, John Schlesinger, who had come from making television documentaries, stressed the realism of the setting in his striking direction, photographed amid urban grime and suburban conformity.

'... maybe it's better for both of us to leave each other alone.'

The Hustler
US 1961 135m bw Cinemascope
TCF/Robert Rossen

w Robert Rossen, Sidney Carroll *novel* Walter Tevis *d* Robert Rossen *ph* Eugene Schufftan *m* Kenyon Hopkins *ad* Albert Brenner, Harry Horner *ed* Dede Allen
☆ Paul Newman ('Fast' Eddir Felson), *Jackie Gleason* (Minnesota Fats), *George C. Scott* (Bert Gordon), *Piper Laurie* (Sarah Packard), *Myron McCormick* (Charlie Bums), Murray Hamilton (Findlay), Michael Constantine (Big John)

'There is an overall impression of intense violence, and the air of spiritual decadence has rarely been conveyed so vividly.' – *David Robinson*

'The supreme classic of that great American genre, the low-life movie.' – *Observer*

● A Region 1 and Region 2 DVD release includes commentary by Paul Newman and critic Richard Schikel.
♟ Eugene Schufftan
♗ best picture; script; Robert Rossen (as director); Paul Newman; Jackie Gleason; George C. Scott; Piper Laurie
♟ best picture; Paul Newman

112
The Hustler

A pool-room con man comes to grief when he falls in love.

Robert Rossen's downbeat melodrama traces the education of a pool-room hustler who discovers that winning is not everything. It is a Faustian story of a con-man who loses his soul by being tempted to join forces with a big-time gambler so that he can beat the best pool player in the business. The matches between Paul Newman's Fast Eddie and Jackie Gleason's Minnesota Fats are brilliantly handled, capturing the seedy atmosphere that is the hustler's world, and the sweat and tension of a contest that determined money and status. Newman conveys charm and desperation in his role; as the crippled Sarah (Piper Laurie), the woman he picks up and destroys, tells him, 'You're too hungry.' With superb supporting performances from George C. Scott as the brutal, manipulative manager and Gleason as the self-possessed champion player, this is a gripping, stylish film of disillusionment.

'Not that it matters, but most of it is true!'

Butch Cassidy and the Sundance Kid
US 1969 110m DeLuxe Panavision
TCF/Campanile (John Foreman)

w William Goldman *d* George Roy Hill *ph* Conrad Hall *m* Burt Bacharach *ad* Jack Martin Smith, Philip Jefferies *ed* John C. Howard
☆ Paul Newman (Butch Cassidy), *Robert Redford* (The Sundance Kid), Katharine Ross (Etta Place), Strother Martin (Paercy Garris), Henry Jones (Bike Salesman), Jeff Corey (Sheriff Bledsoe), Cloris Leachman (Agnes), Ted Cassidy (Harvey Logan), Kenneth Mars (Marshal)

'A mere exercise in smart-alecky device-mongering, chock-full of out of place and out of period one-upmanship, a battle of wits at a freshman smoker.' – *John Simon*

● Region 1 and 2 DVD releases include commentary by director George Roy Hill, Hal David, Robert Crawford and cinematographer Conrad Hall.
♟ William Goldman; Conrad Hall; Burt Bacharach; song 'Raindrops Keep Fallin' on My Head' (*m* Burt Bacharach, *ly* Hal David)
♗ best picture; George Roy Hill; sound (William Edmondson, David Dockendorf)
♟ best picture; George Roy Hill; Conrad Hall; Burt Bacharach; William Goldman; Robert Redford; Katharine Ross; sound track

111
Butch Cassidy and the Sundance Kid

A hundred years ago, two Western train robbers keep one step ahead of the law until finally tracked down in Bolivia.

A humorous, cheerful, poetic, cinematic account of two semi-legendary Western outlaws and train robbers, who manage to escape the grasp of the long arm of the law until finally being cornered by the Bolivian army. Winningly acted by Paul Newman and Robert Redford and stylishly directed by George Roy Hill, it was one of the great commercial successes of the 1960s, not least because of Newman and Katharine Ross' lighthearted bicycle-ride to the song 'Raindrops Keep Fallin' on My Head'. Death is kept at a distance even at the end, when the wounded Butch and Sundance emerge from their hideout to be mown down by the guns of the Bolivian army: the film freezes, leaving them in flight, though the sound of firing continues until the image fades to sepia.

The Gold Rush

↟↟ US 1925 72m bw
Charles Chaplin
▣▣ ▤ ◈~ ◉ ◉

wd Charles Chaplin *ph* Rollie Totheroh *m* Charles Chaplin *md* Max Terr (1942 version) *ad* Charles D. Hall *ed* Harold McGhean (1942 version)

☆ *Charles Chaplin* (The Lone Prospector), Georgia Hale (Georgia), Mack Swain (Big Jim), Tom Murray (Black Larson)

♟ Max Terr

110
The Gold Rush

A lone prospector in the Yukon becomes rich after various adventures.

Chaplin's comedy about an impoverished gold prospector who becomes eventually rich, is essentially a succession of slowly but carefully built visual gags. It is his finest example of comedy drawn from utter privation; as such it appealed vastly to the poor of the world. As a clown, Chaplin himself is near his best, though as usual there is rather too much straining for pathos. There are priceless comic moments: the hungry Mack Swain imagining that Chaplin is a giant chicken, the little tramp genteelly eating his boot, his delicate tap dance with two bread rolls skewered on forks, and the suspenseful scene in which his cabin is precariously balanced on the edge of a precipice.

'It spans a whole new world of entertainment!'

The Bridge on the River Kwai

GB 1957 161m Technicolor Cinemascope
Columbia/Sam Spiegel
▣▣ ▣▣ ▤ ◈~ ◉ ◉ ◌

w Carl Foreman, Michael Wilson *novel* Pierre Boulle *d* David Lean *ph* Jack Hildyard *m* Malcolm Arnold *ed* Peter Taylor

☆ *Alec Guinness* (Colonel Nicholson), William Holden (Shears), Jack Hawkins (Major Warden), Sessue Hayakawa (Colonel Saito), James Donald (Major Clipton), Geoffrey Horne (Lieut. Joyce), Andre Morell (Col. Green), Percy Herbert (Grogan)

'Brilliant is the word, and no other, to describe the quality of skills that have gone into the making of this picture.' – *Bosley Crowther, New York Times*

● Cary Grant was originally sought for the William Holden role.
● Michael Wilson should also have been credited for the script but he was blacklisted at the time.
● A Region 1 and 2 limited edition two-disc set includes a documentary on the making of the film, and an appreciation and discussion by filmmaker John Milius.

♟ picture; adaptation (now credited to Carl Foreman, Michael Wilson and Pierre Boulle); David Lean; Jack Hildyard; Malcolm Arnold; Alec Guinness; editing
♟ Sessue Hayakawa
♟ film; British film; Alec Guinness; Pierre Boulle

109
The Bridge on the River Kwai

British POWs in Burma are forced by the Japs to build a bridge; meanwhile British agents seek to destroy it.

David Lean's first epic, and the first he made in CinemaScope, was an ironic adventure with many fine moments, set in the blistering heat of the Burmese jungle. It was distinguished by Alec Guinness's portrait of Colonel Nicholson, the English commanding officer whose men, prisoners of war, are used by the Japanese to build an essential bridge; he is heroic in his initial stand against his captors, but finally cannot bear to see his bridge blown up. There were other excellent performances, from Sessue Hayakawa as the Japanese commandant and William Holden as an American who helps British agents to destroy the bridge. Behind the drama of the confrontation between Colonel Nicholson and his friends and enemies lies a darker story of the ease with which opposition can give way to collaboration with the enemy. The physical detail of the production was beyond criticism.

The Blue Angel

The Blue Angel
Germany   1930   98m   bw
UFA (Erich Pommer)

w Robert Liebmann, Carl Zuckmayer, Karl Vollmoeller
novel *Professor Unrath* by Heinrich Mann d Josef von
Sternberg ph Günther Rittau, Hans Schneeberger
m Frederick Hollander (inc 'Falling in Love Again', 'They
Call Me Wicked Lola') ad Otto Hunte, Emil Hasler ed S.K.
Winston
☆ *Emil Jannings* (Prof. Immanuel Rath), *Marlene Dietrich*
(Lola Frohlich), Kurt Gerron (Kiepert), Hans Albers
(Mazeppa), Rosa Valetti (Guste)

'It will undoubtedly do splendidly in the whole of
Europe and should also appeal strongly in the
States … only fault is a certain ponderousness of
tempo which tends to tire.' – *Variety*

'At the time I thought the film was awful and vulgar
and I was shocked by the whole thing. Remember,
I was a well brought up German girl.' – *Marlene
Dietrich*

• The two-disc Region 1 and 2 DVD includes the 104m
German and the 94m English versions of the film,
commentary by Werner Sudendorf of the Berlin Film
Museum and interview footage of Marlene Dietrich.

108
The Blue Angel

A strait-laced academic falls in love with a cabaret performer.

Von Sternberg's masterwork of late Twenties German grotesquerie
concerns a fuddy-duddy professor who is infatuated with a tawdry
night-club singer. She marries him but is soon bored and contemptu-
ous; humiliated, he leaves her and dies in his old classroom. After a
slowish beginning, the film becomes an emotional powerhouse, set in
a dark nightmare world which could be created only in the studio. Shot
also in English, it was highly popular and influential in Britain and
America. It instantly catapulted Dietrich to international stardom,
emphasizing her sexual mystery and ambiguity.

It's a Wonderful Life

It's a Wonderful Life
US   1946   129m   bw
RKO/Liberty Films (Frank Capra)

w Frances Goodrich, Albert Hackett, Frank Capra d Frank
Capra ph Joseph Walker, Joseph Biroc m Dimitri Tiomkin
ad Jack Okey ed William Hornbeck
☆ *James Stewart* (George Bailey), *Henry Travers*
(Clarence), Donna Reed (Mary Hatch), Lionel Barrymore
(Mr. Potter), Thomas Mitchell (Uncle Billy), Beulah Bondi
(Mrs. Bailey), Frank Faylen (Ernie), Ward Bond (Bert), Gloria
Grahame (Violet Bick), H. B. Warner (Mr. Gower), Frank
Albertson (Sam Wainwright), Samuel S. Hinds (Pa Bailey),
Mary Treen (Cousin Tilly)

''The most brilliantly made motion picture of the
1940s, so assured, so dazzling in its use of screen
narrative.' – *Charles Higham*

'In its own icky, bittersweet way, it's terribly
effective.' – *New Yorker, 1977*

'At its best all this seems to me insipid, and at its
worst an embarrassment to both flesh and spirit.'
– *Richard Winnington, News Chronicle*

⚖ best picture; Frank Capra; James Stewart; editing

107
It's a Wonderful Life

*A man is prevented from committing suicide by an elderly angel who
takes him back through his life to show him what good he has done.*

With constant repetition on television, Capra's superbly assembled
small-town comedy in a fantasy framework has become a perennial
favourite. It is perfect Christmas entertainment with its story of a man
who is persuaded not to kill himself after an angel shows him all the
good he has done in his life. It was Capra's first movie after his wartime
service and the last that showed him working at a high creative level. It
is cosier than his earlier films, extolling family and home as the place
where virtue resides. Stewart's performance as an embittered would-be
suicide gives it an honesty that it might otherwise lack and provides its
conclusion with a heart-warming geniality.

E.T. The Extra-Terrestrial

US   1982   115m   DeLuxe
Universal (Steven Spielberg, Kathleen Kennedy)

w Melissa Mathison *d* Steven Spielberg *ph* Allen Daviau
m John Williams *pd* James D. Bissell *ed* Carol Littleton
sp Creator of E.T.: Carlo Rambaldi
☆ Dee Wallace (Mary), Henry Thomas (Elliott), Peter
Coyote (Keys), Robert MacNaughton (Michael), Drew
Barrymore (Gertie), K. C. Martel (Greg), Sean Frye (Steve),
Tom Howell (Tyler)

'*E.T.* is the closest film to my own sensibilities, my
own fantasies, my own heart.' – *Steven Spielberg*

● The movie was reissued in 2002 with its special effects
enhanced, and walkie-talkies substituted for the FBI agents'
guns. One line of dialogue was also changed in the
Halloween scene. Spielberg explained, 'There's no reason
why the word terrorist belongs in a film like *ET*, and we were
being glib in the early Eighties with Mary saying, "You will
not go out dressed as a terrorist." Now she says, "You will
not go out dressed as a hippy."'
● A Region 1 two-disc DVD release includes the 1982 and
the 2002 versions, and has an introduction by Spielberg.
♟ John Williams; visual effects (Carlo Rambaldi, Dennis
Murren, Kenneth F. Smith); sound (Buzz Knudson, Robert
Glass, Don Digirolamo, Gene Cantamessa); sound effects
editing (Charles L. Campbell, Ben Burtt)
♟ picture; Steven Spielberg; Melissa Matheson; Allen
Daviau; Carol Littleton
♟ John Williams

106
E.T. The Extra-Terrestrial

*When an alien spacecraft is disturbed in a Los Angeles suburb, one of
its crew members is left behind and befriended by a small boy.*

Steven Spielberg's belief in a benign future full of happy people living
in suburban comfort, what you could call a spiritual suburbanity,
extended to outer space in this stupefyingly successful box-office fairy
tale. People, or more specifically government agents in search of scientific knowledge, were the frightening species here, as an alien being,
accidently left behind in Los Angeles, becomes the friend of a small
boy. The film was about love and friendship, designed to appeal to the
child in everyone, and it worked wonderfully. Spielberg was taken to
the world's heart because he dared to make a film without sex, violence
or bad language.

'A guy without a conscience! A dame without a heart!'

'He's as fast on the draw as he is in the drawing room!'

The Maltese Falcon
US   1941   101m   bw
Warner (Henry Blanke)
⬛ ▤ ▤ ⬕ ⓖ ⓟ

wd John Huston *novel* Raymond Chandler *ph* Arthur Edeson *m* Adolph Deutsch *ad* Robert Haas *ed* Thomas Richards
☆ *Humphrey Bogart* (Sam Spade), *Mary Astor* (Brigid O'Shaughnessy), *Sydney Greenstreet* (Kasper Gutman the Fat Man), *Elisha Cook Jnr* (Wilmer Cook), *Barton MacLane* (Det. Lt. Dundy), Lee Patrick (Effie Perine), *Peter Lorre* (Joel Cairo), Gladys George (Iva Archer), *Ward Bond* (Det. Tom Polhaus), *Jerome Cowan* (Miles Archer)

'The trick which Mr Huston has pulled is a combination of American ruggedness with the suavity of the English crime school – a blend of mind and muscle – plus a slight touch of pathos.' – *Bosley Crowther, New York Times*

'Admirable photography of the sort in which black and white gives full value to every detail, every flicker of panic.' – *Francis Wyndham*

⚖ best picture; John Huston (as writer); Sydney Greenstreet

105
The Maltese Falcon

A private eye is hired to find a black sculpture of a bird.

John Huston's version of Raymond Chandler's novel is near-perfection: a brilliant cast, interesting characters, smart dialogue and every nuance subtly stressed. Bogart as Sam Spade, a private detective who has been hired to track down a sculpture of a falcon, possessed the right world-weary integrity. As John Huston recalled, 'Something happened when he was playing the right part. Those lights and shadows composed themselves into another, nobler personality'. Mary Astor was seductively untrustworthy, and Sydney Greenstreet and Peter Lorre were everything villains should be; charmingly unsavoury. Of its kind, it has never been bettered.

Unforgiven
US   1992   131m   Technicolor   Panavision
Warner (Clint Eastwood)
⬛ ▤ ⬕ ⓖ ⓟ ⌒

w David Webb Peoples *d* Clint Eastwood *ph* Jack N. Green *m* Lennie Niehaus *pd* Henry Bumstead *ad* Adrian Gorton, Rick Roberts *ed* Joel Cox
☆ *Clint Eastwood* (William Munny), *Gene Hackman* (Sheriff 'Little Bil' Daggett), *Morgan Freeman* (Ned Logan), *Richard Harris* (English Bob), Jaimz Woolvett (The Schofield Kid), Saul Rubinek (W.W. Beauchamp), Frances Fisher (Strawberry Alice), Anna Thomson (Delilah Fitzgerald), David Mucci (Quick Mike), Rob Campbell (Davey Bunting), Anthony James (Skinny Dubois)

'Eastwood climbs back into the saddle to make a classic western.' – *Ian Johnstone, Sunday Times*

'A tense, hard-edged, superbly dramatic yarn that is also an exceedingly intelligent meditation on the West, its myths and its heroes.' – *Variety*

● A Regions 1 and 2 two-disc special edition DVD set includes a commentary by Richard Schickel, documentaries on Eastwood and the making of the film and *Duel at Sundown*, an episode of the TV series *Maverick*.
👤 best picture; Clint Eastwood (as director); Gene Hackman; Joel Cox
⚖ Clint Eastwood (as actor); Henry Bumstead; Jack N. Green; David Webb Peoples; best sound
🏆 Gene Hackman

104
Unforgiven

A former hired killer sets out with two other men to collect a thousand-dollar reward for killing the cowboys who slashed the face of a prostitute.

Clint Eastwood's harsh and impressive Western revived the genre to spectacular effect. He starred as a former gunman turned unsuccessful farmer, who was a weary, defeated version of the impassive characters he played in Sergio Leone's spaghetti Westerns. Together with a young would-be gunfighter and an old friend, he sets out to collect a hefty reward for killing the men who wounded a prostitute. The drama of revenge and needless slaughter shows the reality of a brutal way of life, which is opposed to the myths of glamorous killers peddled by pulp writers. Here people die badly after failing to live well.

Z

France/Algeria 1968 125m Eastmancolor
Reggane/ONCIC/Jacques Pérrin
▣ ▤ ◎～ ◉ ◠

w Costa-Gavras, Jorge Semprun *novel* Vassili Vassilikos
d Costa-Gavras *ph* Raoul Coutard *m* Mikis Theodorakis
pd Jacques D'Ovidio *ad* Jacques d'Ovidio *ed* Françoise
Bonnoi
☆ Jean-Louis Trintignant (The Examining Magistrate),
Jacques Pérrin (Photojournalist), Yves Montand (The
Deputy), François Périer (Public Prosecutor), Irene Papas
(Helene), Charles Denner (Manuel)

'One of the fastest, most exciting melodramas ever
made.' – *Pauline Kael*

🏆 best foreign film
   best picture; director; script
   Mikis Theodorakis

*In Greece, a magistrate proves that the death of a politician was
murder.*

Costa-Gavras' exciting police suspense drama dealt with the murder of
a Greek leading opposition MP at a rally. The police were anxious to
establish the event as an accident, but the examining magistrate
proved otherwise. The film recalled events during the rule of the Greek
colonels and was therefore highly relevant for a while, both as entertainment and as a political *roman à clef*. Its more general point, about
the corruption of moral values and the way governments attempt to
cover up their misdeeds, has lost none of its pertinence. Costa-Gavras
made the investigation as gripping a political thriller as it was in real
life, as a honest man tried to discover the truth, at whatever cost.

'… look closer'

American Beauty

US 1999 122m Technicolor Panavision
DreamWorks (Bruce Cohen, Dan Jinks)
▣ ▤ ◎ ◉ ◠

w Alan Ball *d* Sam Mendes *ph* Conrad L. Hall
m Thomas Newman *pd* Naomi Shohan *ed* Tariq Anwar,
Christopher Greenbury
☆ *Kevin Spacey* (Lester Burnham), *Annette Bening*
(Carolyn Burnham), Thora Birch (Jane Burnham), Wes
Bentley (Ricky Fitts), Mena Suvari (Angela Hayes), Peter
Gallagher (Buddy Kane), Allison Janney (Barbara Fitts),
Scott Bakula (Jim Olmeyer), Sam Robards (Jim Berkley),
Chris Cooper (Colonel Fitts)

'A film of incredible flair and formal, compositional
brilliance.' – *Peter Bradshaw, Guardian*

'The picture is a con. Can't educated liberals see
that it sucks up to them at every plot turn?'
– *Pauline Kael*

● The film cost $15m to make and took $277m at the box
office world wide.
● The Region 1 and 2 DVD releases include commentary
by Sam Mendes and Alan Ball.
🏆 picture; Kevin Spacey; Sam Mendes; Alan Ball; Conrad
L. Hall
   Annette Bening; Thomas Newman; Tariq Anwar,
Christopher Greenbury
   picture; Annette Bening; Kevin Spacey; Conrad L. Hall;
Tariq Anwar, Christopher Greenbury; Thomas Newman

American Beauty

A suburban American recalls the events that led to his murder.

Sam Mendes made, from Alan Ball's perceptive script, a terrific, biting
comedy of a man dealing, in an adolescent way, with a midlife crisis
and the arid existence he and those around him, including his ambitious but unsuccessful wife, are living. It is told by a dead suburban
husband and father as he reviews his life and the events that led to his
murder. The crisis comes when he quits his boring job but cannot find
an interesting alternative. While he merely lusts after one of his daughter's school friends, his wife begins an affair with a rival and successful
real-estate agent. The film manages not only to expose the inanities of a
conformist society, but also to suggest an alternative, in the small
pleasures that existence affords. There is not a false note in either the
acting or the direction.

American Beauty

☆ **John Dahl**
Director☆

1. Chinatown (Polanski)
2. A Clockwork Orange (Kubrick)
3. Crimes and Misdemeanors (Allen)
4. Double Indemnity (Wilder)
5. The Godfather (Coppola)
6. Once Upon a Time in the West (Leone)
7. Schindler's List (Spielberg)
8. Sunset Blvd. (Wilder)
9. The Treasure of the Sierra Madre (Huston)
10. Unforgiven (Eastwood)

☆ **Joel Schumacher**
Director ☆

1. Battleship Potemkin (Eisenstein)
2. Lawrence of Arabia (Lean)
3. The Cook, The Thief, His Wife & Her Lover (Greenaway)
4. Bicycle Thieves (De Sica)
5. Breaking the Waves (von Trier)
6. A Clockwork Orange (Kubrick)
7. The Conversation (Coppola)
8. Sunset Boulevard. (Wilder)
9. Stalker (Tarkovsky)
10. The Conformist (Bertolucci)

☆ **Wesley Strick**
Writer☆

1. Bonnie and Clyde (Penn)
2. Chinatown (Polanski)
3. 8 1/2 (Fellini)
4. Goldfinger (Hamilton)
5. The Night of the Hunter (Laughton)
6. North by Northwest (Hitchcock)
7. Rosemary's Baby (Polanski)
8. Tirez sur le Pianiste (Truffaut)
9. Touch of Evil (Welles)
10. Vertigo (Hitchcock)

The Adventurer
US   1917   21m approx (24 fps)   bw   silent
Mutual
⊚   ⊚
wd Charles Chaplin ph William C. Foster, Rollie Totheroh
☆ Charles Chaplin, Edna Purviance, Eric Campbell,
Henry Bergman

The Cure
👫 US   1917   20m approx   bw   silent
Mutual/Charles Chaplin
▤ ⊚ ⊚
wd Charles Chaplin ph William C. Foster, Rollie Totheroh
☆ Charles Chaplin, Edna Purviance, Eric Campbell,
Henry Bergman

Easy Street
👫 US   1917   22m approx   bw   silent
Mutual/Charles Chaplin
▤ ⊚ ⊚
wd Charles Chaplin ph William C. Foster, Rollie Totheroh
☆ Charles Chaplin, Edna Purviance, Albert Austin, Eric
Campbell
● The film is available as part a Region 1 seven-disc set,
Charlie Chaplin Short Comedy Classics, and as a Region
2 compilation DVD, *Charlie Chaplin - The Mutual Films
Vol. 1*.

101
Chaplin Shorts

The Adventurer

An escaped convict rescues two wealthy women from drowning and is invited to their home.

The Cure

A dipsomaniac sent to a spa gets his booze mixed up with the spa water.

Easy Street

In a slum street, a tramp is reformed by a dewy-eyed missionary, becomes a policeman, and tames the local bully.

W. C. Fields once referred to Chaplin as 'a goddamned ballet dancer', and he was right. Chaplin did conceive of his short films as dance, working them out in improvisations of a hilarious choreography. They are ballets of a sort, pantomime taken to wonderous, fleet-footed heights that have never been reached again. *The Adventurer* is joyfully knockabout with his physical gags at their most streamlined as he plays an escaped convict who rescues two wealthy women from drowning and is invited to their home. *The Cure*, in which a dipsomaniac sent to a spa gets his booze mixed up with the spa water, is one of the funniest, with no pathos intervening (nor come to that much plot); it is simply a succession of balletic slapstick scenes of the highest order. *Easy Street*, set in a deprived neighbourhood is quintessential Chaplin, combining sentimentality and social comment with hilarious slapstick.

The Graduate
US   1967   105m   Technicolor   Panavision
UA/Embassy (Lawrence Turman)

w Calder Willingham, Buck Henry *novel* Charles Webb
d *Mike Nichols* ph *Robert Surtees* m Dave Grusin
m/ly *Paul Simon (sung by Simon and Art Garfunkel)*
pd Richard Sylbert *ed* Sam O'Steen
☆ *Dustin Hoffman* (Ben Braddock), *Anne Bancroft* (Mrs Robinson), Katharine Ross (Elaine Robinson), Murray Hamilton (Mr Robinson), William Daniels (Mr Maguire), Elizabeth Wilson (Mrs Braddock), Richard Dreyfuss (Student)

'Seeing *The Graduate* is a bit like having one's most brilliant friend to dinner, watching him become more witty and animated with every moment, and then becoming aware that what one may really be witnessing is the onset of a nervous breakdown.'
– *Renata Adler*

● Robert Redford was considered for the role of Benjamin Braddock; Doris Day turned down the role of Mrs Robinson.
♟ Mike Nichols
♟ best picture; script; Robert Surtees; Dustin Hoffman; Anne Bancroft; Katharine Ross
🎬 best picture; Mike Nichols; Calder Willingham, Buck Henry; Dustin Hoffman

100
The Graduate

A wealthy young graduate searches for a different future for himself.

Richly reflecting the anything-goes mood of the late Sixties, this lushly-filmed comedy opened a few new doors, looked ravishing, was well acted and had a popular music score. Dustin Hoffman was an inspired, if quirky, casting as a rich Californian ex-student, a person he described as 'a walking surfboard'. He brought to the role a confusion and sense of panic that was exactly what was needed for someone who is led into an affair with the wife of his father's friend, then falls in love with her daughter. His indecision is contrasted with the older generation's certainties, which are ones he does not share; it is a friend of his father who offers him that generation's vision of the future: 'Plastics.' A comedy of its time, it has also stood the test of time.

Bad Day at Black Rock

US 1955 81m Eastmancolor
Cinemascope
MGM (Dore Schary)

🎞 📼 ⊛ 🔊

w Millard Kaufman *story* Bad Time at Hondo by Howard
Briskin *d* John Sturges *ph* William C. Mellor *m* André
Previn *ad* Malcolm Brown, Cedric Gibbons *ed* Newell P.
Kimlin

☆ *Spencer Tracy* (John J. MacReedy), *Robert Ryan* (Reno
Smith), Dean Jagger (Tim Horn), Walter Brennan (Doc
Velie), Ernest Borgnine (Coley Trimble), Lee Marvin (Hector
David), Anne Francis (Liz Wirth), John Ericson (Pete Wirth),
Russell Collins (Mr Hastings)

'A very superior example of motion picture
craftsmanship.' – *Pauline Kael*

'The movie takes place within twenty-four hours. It
has a dramatic unity, an economy of word and
action, that is admirable in an age of flabby
Hollywood epics that maunder on forever.'
– *William K. Zinsser, New York Herald Tribune*

'The skill of some sequences, the mood and
symbiosis between man and nature makes this film
sometimes superior to *High Noon*.' – *G. N. Fenin*

♟ Millard Kaufman; John Sturges; Spencer Tracy

99
Bad Day at Black Rock

*A stranger arrives in a desert town to make inquiries about a Japanese
farmer and finds the townsfolk strangely unhelpful.*

A Western underneath its post-World War II setting, this can also be
read, like *High Noon*, as an attack on McCarthyism and the Un-
American Activities Committee. A one-armed stranger gets off the train
in a shabby, sun-scorched desert town on a simple errand, and meets
with hostility from the locals, who have something to hide and are, as
one admits, 'consumed with apathy'. Slowly he discovers the guilty
secret and, prevented from leaving, confronts them in a superb showdown. There is not a moment wasted in this tightly-written thriller
about an individual at odds with an entire community, as Sturges
screws up the tension almost unbearably before releasing it in sudden
moments of violence.

This Is Spinal Tap

US 1984 82m CFI color
Mainline/Embassy (Karen Murphy)

🎞 📼 ⊛ ⊚ ⊚ 🎧

w Christopher Guest, Michael McKean, Harry Shearer, Rob
Reiner *d* Rob Reiner *ph* Peter Smokler *m* Christopher
Guest, Michael McKean, Harry Shearer, Rob Reiner
pd Dryan Jones *ed* Robert Leighton

☆ Christopher Guest (Nigel Tufnel), Michael McKean
(David St. Hubbins), Harry Shearer (Derek Smalls), Rob
Reiner (Marty DiBergi), R. J. Parnell (Mick Shrimpton),
David Kaff (Viv Savage), Tony Hendra (Ian Faith), Bruno
Kirby (Tommy Pischedda)

'It stays so wickedly close to the subject that it is
very nearly indistinguishable from the real thing.'
– *Janet Maslin, New York Times*

● The Regions 1 and 2 special edition DVD releases
include an hour of extra footage, audio commentary by the
band (in character) and an interview with the director. It was
also available on an interactive CD-ROM, which included
extra audio commentary on the film and out-takes.
● *This Is Spinal Tap: The Official Companion*, edited by
Karl French, was published by Bloomsbury in 2000.

98
This Is Spinal Tap

*The ultimate send-up of rock stars on tour and the documentary
makers who take them seriously.*

A witty, wickedly accurate satire that skewers the pretensions of rock
musicians and their hangers-on, as it follows the adventures of a
British heavy metal rock group on tour in America. Done in a documentary style, with interviews with the band and its manager, who respond
to questions with incomprehensible answers. Distracted by their self-
importance, they are gloriously unaware of their own ineptitude. They
do not mind when they discover that their Boston gig has been can-
celled, because it is not a big college town. The movie hits its target
with total precision and provides some terrific visual jokes, such as the
moment when the band do a number involving a mock-up of
Stonehenge.

Henry V

GB 1944 137m Technicolor
Rank/Two Cities (Laurence Olivier)

w Laurence Olivier, Alan Dent *play* William Shakespeare
d Laurence Olivier *ph* Robert Krasker *m* William Walton
ad Paul Sheriff, Carmen Dillon *ed* Reginald Beck
☆ Laurence Olivier (Henry V), *Robert Newton* (Pistol),
Leslie Banks (Chorus), *Esmond Knight* (Fluellen), Renée
Asherson (Katherine), George Robey (Falstaff), *Leo Genn*
(Constable of France), Ernest Thesiger (Duke of Beri), Ivy St
Helier (Alice), Ralph Truman (Mountjoy), Harcourt Williams,
Max Adrian, Valentine Dyall (Duke of Burgundy), Felix
Aylmer (Archbishop of Canterbury), John Laurie and also
Roy Emerton, Michael Shepley, George Cole

'His production – it was his first time out as a
director – is a triumph of colour, music, spectacle,
and soaring heroic poetry, and, as actor, he brings
lungs, exultation, and a bashful wit to the role.'
– *Pauline Kael, 70s*

● The Region 1 DVD release includes a commentary by by
film historian Bruce Eder.
▮ Special Award to Laurence Olivier
♟ best picture; William Walton; Laurence Olivier (as actor);
art direction

97
Henry V

Shakespeare's historical play is seen in performance at the Globe Theatre in 1603; as it develops, the scenery becomes more realistic.

Laurence Olivier's immensely stirring, patriotic version of Shakespeare's play opens as a performance at the Globe Theatre in 1603; as it develops, it becomes more realistic. It is an almost wholly successful production of Shakespeare on film, sturdy both in its stylization and its command of more conventional cinematic resources for the battle of Agincourt. It worked both as a call to arms of a beleaguered country ('We few, we happy few, we band of brothers/For he today that sheds his blood with me/Shall be my brother') and as a reminder of what was at stake, and the traditions that were worth fighting for. The combination of Olivier's oration and William Walton's music was irresistible.

Duck Soup

↟↟ US 1933 68m bw
Paramount
■ ◎~ ◎ ◎

w Bert Kalmar, Harry Ruby, Arthur Sheekman, Nat Perrin
d Leo McCarey ph Henry Sharp m/ly Bert Kalmar, Harry
Ruby ad Hans Dreier, Wiard Ihnen ed LeRoy Stone
☆ Groucho Marx (Rufus T. Firefly), Chico Marx
(Chicolini), Harpo Marx (Pinky), Zeppo Marx (Bob Roland),
Margaret Dumont (Mrs Teasdale), Louis Calhern
(Ambassador Trentino), Edgar Kennedy (Lemonade man),
Raquel Torres (Vera Marcal)

'Practically everybody wants a good laugh right
now, and this should make practically everybody
laugh.' – Variety

'So much preliminary dialogue is necessary that it
seems years before Groucho comes on at all; and
waiting for Groucho is agony.' – E. V. Lucas, Punch

'The most perfect of all Marxist masterpieces.' –
Time Out, 1984

● The Region 2 DVD release is part of a four-disc set, The
Marx Brothers Collection.
♫ Hail. Hail Freedonia; His Excellency is Due; Just Wait
'til I Get Through With It; Freedonia's Going to War.

96
Duck Soup

A country's newly-elected president starts a war for the hell of it.

The satirical aspects of this film about presidential politics and war are fascinating but appear to have been unintentional: an incompetent becomes President of Fredonia and wages war on its scheming neighbour just for the hell of it. It is also the most satisfying and undiluted Marx Brothers' romp, albeit the one without instrumental interludes. For the first, and only, time, the brothers were under the attempted control of an excellent comedy director, Leo McCarey, although he is on record as not enjoying the film. It does include such classic moments as the lemonade stall sequence, with Harpo paddling in the seller's jar, the mirror bit, with Groucho's unexpected movements being aped by Harpo in disguise, and an endless array of one-liners and comedy choruses.

Manhattan

US 1979 96m bw Panavision
UA/Jack Rollins/Charles H. Joffe
◙◙ ◙◙ ■ ◎~ ◎ ◎ ◠

w Woody Allen, Marshall Brickman d Woody Allen
ph Gordon Willis md Tom Pierson ed Susan E. Morse
☆ Woody Allen (Isaac Davis), Diane Keaton (Mary Wilke),
Meryl Streep (Jill), Mariel Hemingway (Tracy), Michael
Murphy (Yale)

'Given that the identity of his films has increasingly
been determined by his compulsion to talk about
the things he finds important, but also by his fear
of having them come out as anything but a joke, it
is not surprising that he has scarcely been able to
decide on a form for his "art": from the anything-
for-a-laugh skittering of his early films, to the
broad parodies and pastiches of his middle period,
to the recent confessional/psychoanalytical mode.'
– Richard Combs, MFB

'A masterpiece that has become a film for the ages
by not seeking to be a film of the moment.'
– Andrew Sarris

⚥ script; Mariel Hemingway
🏆 best picture

95
Manhattan

Episodes in the sex life of a TV comedy writer with an obsession about New York.

This is as close to a summation of Woody Allen's views and *oeuvre* as we are likely to get. It is both a celebration of New York and George Gershwin's popular songs and a smart, half despairing comment on the lives we lead. His love of the city was never more lyrically exposed, his character's anxieties never put to better comic use. Allen's neurotic comedy writer here makes things difficult for himself by fancying other women over the one he is with, but it does not make the loss of his girl-friend (Diane Keaton) to the sisterhood any less painful. It may be his most personal film; it is certainly one of his wittiest and the most romantic.

His Girl Friday

His Girl Friday
US   1940   92m   bw
Columbia (Howard Hawks)
▣ ▤ ◉ ◎

w Charles Lederer *play* The Front Page *by* Charles MacArthur, Ben Hecht *d* Howard Hawks *ph* Joseph Walker *m* Sydney Cutner *md* Morris Stoloff *ad* Lionel Banks *ed* Gene Havlik

☆ *Rosalind Russell* (Hildy Johnson), *Cary Grant* (Walter Burns), *Ralph Bellamy* (Bruce Baldwin), Gene Lockhart (Sheriff Hartwell), Porter Hall (Murphy), *Ernest Truex* (Bensinger), Cliff Edwards (Endicott), *Clarence Kolb* (Mayor), *Roscoe Karns* (McCue), *Frank Jenks* (Wilson), Abner Biberman (Louis), Frank Orth (Duffy), John Qualen (Earl Williams), Helen Mack (Molly Malloy), *Billy Gilbert* (Joe Pettibone) and also Alma Kruger (Mrs Baldwin)

'The kind of terrific verbal slam-bang that has vanished from current film-making.' – *New Yorker, 1975*

'The main trouble is that when they made *The Front Page* the first time, it stayed made.' – *Otis Ferguson*

● The Rosalind Russell role had first been turned down by Jean Arthur, Ginger Rogers, Claudette Colbert and Irene Dunne.
● A Region 1 and Region 2 DVD release includes a commentary by critic Todd McCarthy.

94
His Girl Friday

An editor tries to stop his former wife, who is the paper's star reporter, from marrying again.

Howard Hawks gave a sex-change to *The Front Page*, the classic story of Chicago newspapermen covering a hanging. The story's star reporter not only became a woman, but was also the former wife of the newspaper's managing editor. It provided an extra frisson to the couple's relationship, adding sourly-sweet romantic misunderstandings to the screwball comedy, while preserving the cynical wit of the original play. It gets expert comedy acting from Cary Grant and Rosalind Russell as the bickering couple, who can only express their love through insults. It is possibly the fastest comedy ever filmed, and one of the funniest, a frantic and hilarious black farce with all participants at their best.

High Noon

'When the hands point up … the excitement starts!'

High Noon
US   1952   85m   bw
Stanley Kramer
▣ ▤ ◕ ◎ ◉

w Carl Foreman *story* The Tin Star *by* John W. Cunningham *d* Fred Zinnemann *ph* Floyd Crosby *m* Dimitri Tiomkin *ad* Ben Hayne *ed* Elmo Williams, Harry Gerstad *singer* Tex Ritter

☆ *Gary Cooper* (Will Kane), Grace Kelly (Amy Kane), Thomas Mitchell (Jonas Henderson), Lloyd Bridges (Harvey Pell), Katy Jurado (Helen Ramirez), Otto Kruger (Percy Mettrick), Lon Chaney (Martin Howe), Henry Morgan (William Fuller)

'A Western to challenge *Stagecoach* for the all-time championship.' – *Bosley Crowther*

'The most un-American thing I've ever seen in my whole life.' – *John Wayne*

● The leading role was turned down by John Wayne, Charlton Heston, Marlon Brando and Gregory Peck.
● The Region 1 DVD release includes commentary by Maria Cooper-Janis, Jonathan Foreman, Tim Zinneman, John Ritter and David Crosby and two documentaries.
🎖 Dimitri Tiomkin; Gary Cooper; title song (*m* Dimitri Tiomkin, *ly* Ned Washington); editing
♟ best picture; Carl Foreman; Fred Zinnemann

93
High Noon

A principalled marshal is left exposed by an ungrateful town in his own hour of need.

The playwright Simon Gray has advanced the theory that Gary Cooper's stiff-legged walk and anguished expression was due not to acting, but to the effect of piles, from which he was suffering at the time. Whatever, he is effective as a marshal who gets no help when he determines to defend his town against revengeful badmen. It is possible to see this Western as a comment on the McCarthy era, when little was done to combat the political witchhunts that damaged many lives. John Wayne was not alone in regarding it as un-American. It has become to be a classic simply because it was very well done, with every scene and performance clearly worked out. Cinematically it was pared to the bone, and photographed like a newsreel in a flat light; Dimitri Tiomkin's hypnotic, repetitive theme tune also helped.

'Only the rainbow can duplicate its brilliance!'

The Adventures of Robin Hood

👫 US 1938 102m Technicolor
Warner (Hal B. Wallis)

📷 🇺🇸 ▭ 🎬 ⊙ ⊙ 🎧

w Seton I. Miller, Norman Reilly Raine *d* William Keighley, Michael Curtiz *ph* Tony Gaudio, Sol Polito, W. Howard Greene *m* Erich Wolfgang Korngold *ad* Carl Jules Weyl *ed* Ralph Dawson

☆ *Errol Flynn* (Sir Robin of Locksley), *Basil Rathbone* (Sir Guy of Gisbourne), *Claude Rains* (Prince John), Olivia de Havilland (Maid Marian), *Alan Hale* (Little John), Patric Knowles (Will Scarlet), *Eugene Pallette* (Friar Tuck), *Ian Hunter* (King Richard), *Melville Cooper* (Sheriff of Nottingham), Una O'Connor (Bess), Herbert Mundin (Much the Miller's Son), Montagu Love (Bishop of Black Canons), Howard Hill (Captain of Archers)

● At the time of its release this was Warner's most expensive film, costing more than $2m. Chico, California, stood in for Sherwood Forest; the archery contest was shot at Busch Gardens, Pasadena. Curtiz took over direction when it was felt that the action lacked impact.

● James Cagney nearly played the title role, but was dropped following a dispute over money.

● A two-disc Region 1 and 2 DVD release includes documentaries, a cartoon *Katnip Kollege*, and commentary by film historian Rudy Behlmer.

🏆 Erich Wolfgang Korngold; Carl Jules Weyl; Ralph Dawson
♟ best picture

92
The Adventures of Robin Hood

The outlaw Robin Hood saves the English throne for the absent King Richard.

Errol Flynn was still enthusiastic about films when he made this exciting adventure story. As a result, he did all his own stunts. He revealed in his autobiography, 'As I lost interest in the vehicles I was cast in, I let the stunt men take over. Especially if there was swordplay.' Here, he wields his sword with great panache, especially in his duel with the splendidly villainous Basil Rathbone. The dialogue has a wit to it – 'You speak treason,' says Marian. 'Fluently', replies Robin. Rousingly operatic in treatment, with dashing action highlights, fine comedy balance, much of it supplied by Eugene Pallette as Friar Tuck, and incisive acting all round, it is historically notable for its use of early three-colour Technicolor; also for convincingly recreating Britain in California.

'Your eyes – your ears – your senses will be overwhelmed!'

Days of Heaven
US   1978   95m   Metrocolor
Paramount/OP (Bert and Harold Schneider)
⬚ ▦ ⊘ ⊚ ⊙
wd Terrence Malick *ph* Nestor Almendros *m* Ennio Morricone *ad* Jack Fisk *ed* Billy Weber
☆ Richard Gere (Bill), Brooke Adams (Abby), Sam Shepard (The Farmer), Linda Manz (Linda), Robert Wilke (Farm Foreman), Jackie Shultis (Linda's Friend), Stuart Margolin (Mill Foreman)

'It's serious, yes, very solemn, but not depressing.' – *Roger Ebert*

'Superbly directed and acted; see it for a second time and its hold is still more relentless.' – *Dilys Powell, Punch*

'One of the great cinematic achievements of the 1970s.' – *Variety*

'Terrence Malick's innocently convoluted parable of love lost and found, and reconciliation achieved and then fatally broken, is superbly counterpointed, thanks to Nestor Almendros' photography, by the burgeoning expansiveness of Texas during the First War.' – *Sight and Sound*

♟ Nestor Almendros
♟ Ennio Morricone
🛡 Ennio Morricone

91
Days of Heaven

Itinerant workers looking for employment leave Chicago for the rural midwest.

Terrence Malick's reputation as a great director rests on no more than the four feature films he has managed to make in the past thirty-two years. This may be his best, the story of three young immigrants, who leave Chicago for the wheatfields in the early days of the last century. Visually a superb slice of period life, it has an emotional force that emerges slowly from the conjunction of the vast landscape and its reticent intruders, who have fled from the dark of the city to find no peace in the country, but only back-breaking, hand-shredding work.

'As boys they said they would die for each other. As men, they did.'

Once Upon a Time in America
US   1984   228m   Technicolor
Warner/Embassy/Ladd/PSO (Arnon Milchan)
⬚ ⬚ ▦ ⊘ ⊚ ⊙ 🎧
w Leonardo Benvenuti, Piero de Bernardi, Enrico Medioli, Franco Arcalli, Franco Ferrini, Sergio Leone *novel The Hoods* by David Aaronson ('Harry Grey') *d* Sergio Leone *ph* Tonino Delli Colli *m* Ennio Morricone *ad* Carlo Simi, James Singelis *ed* Nino Baragli
☆ Robert De Niro (Noodles), James Woods (Max), Elizabeth McGovern (Deborah), Treat Williams (Jimmy O'Donnell), Tuesday Weld (Carol), Burt Young (Joe), Danny Aiello (Police Chief Aiello), William Forsythe (Cockeye)

'It is, finally, a heart-breaking story of mutual need. By matching that need with his own need to come to terms with his own cultural memories, Leone has made his most oneiric and extraordinary film.' – *Tony Rayns, MFB*

🛡 Ennio Morricone

90
Once Upon a Time in America

The lives of four immigrant gangsters seen over forty years become an energetic commentary on the development of modern America.

A vast, sprawling, violent crime-saga that is both the epitome and summation of gangster movies; a powerful, almost operatic drama of waste and despair. Leone follows the lives of four gangsters between 1922 and 1968 in a dense and elaborately structured movie on an epic scale. It opens at a halfway point in the story, and then moves into the future and the past, though whether it is an actual past and future or merely the opium dreams of Noodles (Robert De Niro), remembering his childhood and imagining what is to come, is never quite resolved. Ambiguity is part of Leone's method. Warners cut the film to a running time of two hours and rearranged the story in chronological order on its first US release, but it has been restored almost to its original length on video and DVD releases.

'A divinely decadent experience!'

Cabaret
US   1972   123m   Technicolor
ABC Pictures/Allied Artists (Cy Feuer)

📷 ▦ 🎞 ⊚ ◉ 🎧

w Jay Presson Allen *novel Goodbye to Berlin* by
Christopher Isherwood *d* Bob Fosse *ph* Geoffrey
Unsworth *m/ly* John Kander, Fred Ebb *md* Ralph Burns
ch Bob Fosse *pd* Rolf Zehetbauer *ad* Rolf Zehetbauer,
Jurgen Kiebach *ed* David Bretherton
☆ *Liza Minnelli* (Sally Bowles), *Joel Grey* (Master of
Ceremonies), *Michael York* (Brian Roberts), Helmut Griem
(Maximilian von Heune), Fritz Wepper (Fritz Wendel),
Marisa Berenson (Natalia Landauer), Elisabeth Neumann-
Viertel

'A stylish, sophisticated entertainment for grown-
up people.' – *John Russell Taylor*

'Film journals will feast for years on shots from this
picture; as it rolled along, I saw page after
illustrated page from a not-too-distant book called
The Cinema of Bob Fosse.' – *Stanley Kauffmann*

👤 Bob Fosse (as director); Geoffrey Unsworth; Ralph
Burns; Liza Minnelli; Joel Grey
🏆 best picture; Jay Presson Allen
🏆 best film; Rolf Zehetbauer; Geoffrey Unsworth; Bob
Fosse; Liza Minnelli; Joel Grey

89
Cabaret

In pre-war Berlin, the atmosphere is an uneasy mixture of sex and anti-Semitism. In the Kit Kat Klub, the performers and their friends live and work under the growing Nazi threat.

The decadence of Berlin in the early Thirties, when it was a hot-bed of vice and anti-Semitism, is brilliantly evoked in this musical version of Christopher Isherwood's stories about Sally Bowles, a singer in the Kit Kat Klub, who shares her English lover with a homosexual German baron, while her Jewish friend Natalia has troubles of her own. Liza Minnelli has never had a part to compare to her performance here, and Fosse's choreography has a sharp, angular quality. It regrettably follows the plot line of the play *I Am a Camera* rather than the Broadway musical on which it is allegedly based, but the very smart direction creates a near-masterpiece of its own, and most of the songs are intact.

'Small Town … Big Crime … Dead Cold.'

Fargo
US   1996   98m   DuArt
Polygram/Working Title (Ethan Coen)
▣ ▤ ≡ @. ⊚ ⊚ ∩

w Joel and Ethan Coen *d* Joel Coen *ph* Roger Deakins
m Carter Burwell *pd* Rick Heinrichs *ad* Thomas P.
Wilkins *ed* Roderick Jaynes (Joel and Ethan Coen)
☆ *Frances McDormand* (Marge Gunderson), *William H.
Macy* (Jerry Lundegaard), Steve Buscemi (Carl Showalter),
Peter Stormare (Gaear Grimsrud), Harve Presnell (Wade
Gustafson), Kristin Rudrüd (Jean Lundegaard), Tony
Denman (Scotty Lundegaard)

'Written and directed with the verve, painstaking
nuance and outrageously black humour that have
become the mainstay of a Coen movie.' – *Ian
Nathan, Empire*

'I came away feeling what a great film it was as it
had managed to make the basically bland triumph
of decency over evil a most rivetting affair.'
– *Marianne Gray, Film Review*

● A subtitle claims that the film is based on a true story,
but it is more likely an invention of its authors.
● Region 1 and 2 DVD releases include commentary by
Roger A. Deakins and an interview with the Coen brothers.
⚱ Frances McDormand; Ethan and Joel Coen (screenplay)
⚱ best picture; William H. Macy; Joel Coen (as director);
Roger Deakins; Roderick Jaynes
🏆 Joel Coen (as director)

88
Fargo

*In wintry Minnesota an insolvent car salesman plans the kidnap of his
wife, hoping to prise a ranson from her affluent father.*

Originality in thrillers is always welcome though not often encountered.
Here the setting is unfamiliar – a small Minnesotan town deep in winter
snow, where a car salesman with money troubles hires two criminals
to kidnap his wife so that her wealthy father will pay a ransom. This
deft and witty movie also pits a pregnant, rural police chief against two
city slickers. Frances McDormand, as the slow-moving but quick thinking cop, and William H. Macy as the panicked salesman both give
ripely individual performances. The violence, when it comes, is properly shocking, but it is the humanity that sticks in the mind.

'What did happen on the Cahulawassee
River?'

Deliverance
US   1972   109m   Technicolor   Panavision
Warner/Elmer Enterprises (John Boorman)
▣ ▣ ≡ @. ⊚ ⊚ ∩

w James Dickey *novel* James Dickey *d* John Boorman
ph Vilmos Zsigmond *m* Eric Weissberg *ad* Fred Harpman
ed Tom Priestley
☆ Burt Reynolds (Lewis), Jon Voight (Ed), Ned Beatty
(Bobby), Ronny Cox (Drew), James Dickey (Sheriff Bullard),
Billy McKinney (Mountain Man)

'There is fundamentally no view of the material, just
a lot of painful grasping and groping.' – *Stanley
Kauffmann*

'A simple, brutally physical movie.' – *Michael
Atkinson, Movieline*

⚱ best picture; John Boorman

87
Deliverance

*Four businessmen spend a holiday weekend shooting the rapids of a
dangerous river, but find that the real danger to their lives comes from
themselves and other humans.*

This journey into the heart of American darkness by four city friends,
who had intended a holiday weekend canoeing down a dangerous river,
is well set up by director John Boorman. The first disquieting moment
of their vulnerability comes when one of the high-spirited group
indulges in a guitar and banjo duel with a simple hillbilly boy; at first he
condescends to the boy, who then rips into some virtuoso playing that
defeats him. It is a sign of terrors to come in a vigorous drama of survival that is an almost apocalyptic vision of man's inhumanity, disguised as a thrilling adult adventure.

Brief Encounter

GB   1945   86m   bw
Eagle-Lion/Cineguild (Anthony Havelock-Allan, Ronald Neame)

▨ ▤ ◎~ ◎ ◎

w Noël Coward, David Lean, Ronald Neame, Anthony Havelock-Allan *play* Still Life *by* Noël Coward *d* David Lean *ph* Robert Krasker *m* Rachmaninov *md* Muir Mathieson *ad* L. P. Williams *ed* Jack Harris
☆ *Celia Johnson* (Laura Jesson), *Trevor Howard* (Alec Harvey), Stanley Holloway (Albert Godby), Joyce Carey (Myrtle Bagot), Cyril Raymond (Fred Jesson)

'Both a pleasure to watch as a well-controlled piece of work, and deeply touching.' – *James Agee*

'Polished as is this film, its strength does not lie in movie technique, of which there is plenty, so much as in the tight realism of its detail.' – *Richard Winnington*

'A celebrated, craftsmanlike tearjerker, and incredibly neat. There's not a breath of air in it.' – *Pauline Kael, 70s*

● A TV film version was made in 1975 by ITC, starring Richard Burton and Sophia Loren and directed by Alan Bridges. It was an unqualified disaster.
● A Region 1 DVD release includes commentary by historian Bruce Eder.
♟ Anthony Havelock-Allan, Ronald Neame, David Lean (script); David Lean (director); Celia Johnson

86
Brief Encounter

A suburban housewife on her weekly shopping visits develops a love affair with a local doctor; but he gets a job abroad and they agree not to see each other again.

The theme of *Brief Encounter* now seems ordinary: two middle-aged strangers meet and tremble on the edge of an adulterous romance, but at the time it was the first British film to deal with such concerns and was in danger of being censored. It works well because of the tremulous Celia Johnson as the suburban housewife and Trevor Howard as the doctor (though Howard himself couldn't understand why the couple didn't consummate the affair when they had the opportunity). It's an outstanding example of good middle-class cinema turned by sheer professional craft into a masterpiece; even those bored by the theme must be riveted by the treatment, especially the use of a dismal railway station and its trains.

Yojimbo

Japan   1961   110m   bw
Toho

▨ ▤ ◎~ ◎ ◎

w Ryuzo Kikushima, Akira Kurosawa *d* Akira Kurosawa *ph* Kazuo Miyagawa *m* Masuru Sato *ad* Yoshiro Muraki
☆ *Toshiro Mifune* (Sanjuro Kuwabatake), Eijiro Tono (Gonji the Sake Seller), Kamatari Fujiwara (Tazaemon), Takashi Shimura (Tokuemon), Seizaburo Kawazu (Seibei), Isuzu Yamada (Orin), Hiroshi Tachikawa (Yoichiro)

'One of the rare Japanese movies that is both great and funny to American audiences.' – *New Yorker*

● A Region 2 DVD release includes commentary from film historian Philip Kemp.

85
Yojimbo

A masterless samurai offers his services in a town divided by two rival gangs with the intention of tricking them into annihilating each other.

A wandering samurai tricks two rival gangs of cut-throats into destroying one other in Kurosawa's masterful, beautifully composed and witty movie. It has a great opening scene that sets the tone: Toshiro Mifune's unemployed swordsman walks into a small town and is passed by a dog carrying a human hand. The game of double- and triple-cross that goes on throughout the film is a delight. It was the inspiration for the 'spaghetti Western' cycle when it was remade by Sergio Leone as *A Fistful Of Dollars* with Clint Eastwood in the Mifune role.

The Band Wagon

US 1953 112m Technicolor
MGM (Arthur Freed)

📽️ ▦ 🔍 ⊕ 🎧

w Adolph Green, Betty Comden *d* Vincente Minnelli
ph Harry Jackson *m* Adolph Deutsch *m/ly* Howard Dietz,
Arthur Schwartz *ch* Michael Kidd *ad* Cedric Gibbons,
Preston Ames *ed* Albert Akst *cos* Mary Ann Nyberg
☆ Fred Astaire (Tony Hunter), Jack Buchanan (Jeffrey
Cordova), Oscar Levant (Lester Marton), Cyd Charisse
(Gaby Gerard), Nanette Fabray (Lily Marton)

'The best musical of the month, the year, the
decade, or for all I know of all time.' – Archer
Winsten

● The Jack Buchanan character, Jeffrey Cordova, was first
offered to Clifton Webb. It was loosely based on José Ferrer,
who in the early Fifties produced four Broadway shows all
running at the same time, and acted in a fifth.
♫ 'A Shine on Your Shoes', 'By Myself', 'That's
Entertainment', 'Dancing in the Dark', 'Triplets', 'New Sun in
the Sky', 'I Guess I'll Have to Change My Plan', 'Louisiana
Hayride', 'I Love Louisa', 'Girl Hunt' ballet.
♟ Adolph Green, Betty Comden; Adolph Deutsch; Mary
Ann Nyberg

84
The Band Wagon

*A Broadway musical is put on by a highly strung producer and a
washed-up Hollywood dancer who has decided to try his luck on the
stage.*

Arthur Freed's production unit at MGM was responsible for many of the
best Hollywood musicals. This, which was recognized as a classic on
its first release, is simple but sophisticated, with the bare minimum of
plot: a has-been Hollywood dancer joins forces with a temperamental
stage producer to put on a Broadway musical. It was clothed in witty
dialogue, clever design and costumes, good songs and splendid
dances, including a ballet based on Mickey Spillane's tough thrillers.
And, of course, a terrific cast and meticulous direction.

North by Northwest

North by Northwest
US   1959   136m   Technicolor   Vistavision
MGM (Alfred Hitchcock)

▭ ▀ ✑ ⊙ ⊙ ⌒

w Ernest Lehman *d* Alfred Hitchcock *ph* Robert Burks
m Bernard Herrmann *ad* William A. Horning, Robert
Boyle, Merrill Pye *ed* George Tomasini

☆ Cary Grant (Roger O. Thornhill), Eva Marie Saint (Eve
Kendall), James Mason (Phillip Vandamm), Leo G. Carroll
(Professor), Martin Landau (Leonard), Jessie Royce Landis
(Clara Thornhill), Adam Williams (Valerian)

'It is only when you adopt the basic premise that
Cary Grant could not possibly come to harm that
the tongue in Hitchcock's cheek becomes plainly
visible.' – *Hollis Alpert, Saturday Review*

'*North by Northwest* is never brutal. Mr Grant calls
it a comedy; I would agree that it is consistently
entertaining, its excitement pointed by but never
interrupted by the jokes.' – *Dilys Powell*

'You get a lot of entertainment for your money. You
get a couple of clever, sophisticated screen actors
and an elegant actress with a fine-drawn, exciting
face. You get one scene that will be talked about as
long as people talk about films at all.' – *C. A.
Lejeune*

● The Region 1 and 2 DVD releases include commentary
by Ernest Lehman.
⚖ Ernest Lehman; art direction; editing

83
North by Northwest

*An advertising executive is pursued across America by enemy agents
who have mistaken him for a spy.*

A delightful chase comedy-thriller with a touch of sex, a kind of compendium of its director's best work, with memories of *The 39 Steps*, *Saboteur* and *Foreign Correspondent* among others. It has some of the most fondly remembered moments from Hitchcock's movies, notably Cary Grant's fleeing from the crop-spraying plane and the fight to the death on Mount Rushmore. Grant brings a bewildered charm to his role of an advertising man who is mistaken for a spy, and then becomes a target for enemy agents because he knows too much. It is a role-playing thriller where nothing is what it seems; deceit has rarely been so entertaining.

Fanny and Alexander
Sweden/France/West Germany   1982   188m
Eastmancolor
AB Cinematograph/Swedish Film Institute/Swedish
TV One/Gaumont/Persona Film/Tobis (Jörn Donner)

▭ ▀ ✑ ⊙ ⊙

wd Ingmar Bergman *ph* Sven Nykvist *m* Daniel Bell
pd Anna Asp *ad* Anna Asp, Susanne Lingheim *ed* Sylvia
Ingemarsson

☆ Gunn Walgren (Helena Ekdahl), Ewa Fröling (Emilie
Ekdahl), Jarl Kulle (Gustav-Adolph Ekdahl), Erland
Josephson (Isak Jacobi), Allan Edwall (Oscar Ekdahl), Börje
Ahlstedt (Prof. Carl Ekdahl), Mona Malm (Alma Ekdahl),
Gunnar Björnstrand (Filip Landahl), Jan Malmsjö (Bishop
Edvard Vergerus)

'It's as if Bergman's neuroses had been tormenting
him for so long that he cut them off and went
sprinting back to Victorian health and domesticity.'
– *New Yorker*

♟ cinematography; best foreign-language film; art
direction; costume
⚖ direction; screenplay
🏆 cinematography

82
Fanny and Alexander

*An affluent Uppsala family comes together to celebrate Christmas
1910.*

Bergman described this as like a huge tapestry 'filled with masses of colour and people, houses and forest, mysterious haunts of caves and grottoes, secrets and night skies.' As a description of his saga of a well-to-do Uppsala family experiencing happiness and misery in 1910, it will do as well as any other. It is a kind of Bergman compendium, and impossible to describe exactly for those who have not seen it. It took six months to shoot, with a large cast that included more than sixty speaking parts and many extras. It harks back to memories of Bergman's own childhood, especially a scene where a young boy gets up early on Christmas morning to try out his new magic lantern. Though he has made some TV movies since, it was Bergman's farewell to feature film directing, which demonstrated his magic for the last time.

All Quiet on the Western Front
US   1930   130m approx   bw
Universal (Carl Laemmle Jnr)
🎞 🇺🇸 💬 ⊚ ⊚

w Lewis Milestone, Maxwell Anderson, Del Andrews,
George Abbott *novel* Erich Maria Remarque *d Lewis
Milestone ph Arthur Edeson m* David Broekman
ad Charles D. Hall, William R. Schmidt *ed* Milton Carruth,
Edgar Adams
☆ Lew Ayres (Paul Baumer), Louis Wolheim (Katczinsky),
Slim Summerville (Tjaden), John Wray (Himmelstoss),
Raymond Griffith (Gerard Duval), Russell Gleason (Muller),
Ben Alexander (Kemmerick), Beryl Mercer (Mrs. Baumer)

> 'A magnificent cinematic equivalent of the book …
> to Mr Milestone goes the credit of effecting the
> similitude in united and dynamic picture terms. The
> sound and image mediums blend as one, as a form
> of artistic expression that only the motion screen
> can give.' – *National Board of Review*

> 'A trenchant and imaginative audible picture …
> most of the time the audience was held to silence
> by its realistic scenes.' – *New York Times*

● ZaSu Pitts originally played the role of Mrs. Baumer in
the film. When preview audiences, used to seeing her in
comedies, were confused by her performance, her scenes
were reshot with Beryl Mercer in the part.
🏆 best picture; Lewis Milestone (as director)
🏅 Lewis Milestone, Maxwell Anderson, Del Andrews,
George Abbott; Arthur Edeson

'The most magnificent picture ever!'
Gone with the Wind
US   1939   220m   Technicolor
MGM/Selznick International (David O. Selznick)
🎞 🇺🇸 💬 ⊚ ⊚ 🎧

w Sidney Howard (and others) *novel* Margaret Mitchell
d Victor Fleming (and George Cukor, Sam Wood)
ph Ernest Haller, Ray Rennahan *m* Max Steiner
pd William Cameron Menzies *ad* Lyle Wheeler *ed* Hal C.
Kern, James E. Newcom *sp* Jack Cosgrove, Fred Albin,
Arthur Johns
☆ *Clark Gable* (Rhett Butler), *Vivien Leigh* (Scarlet
O'Hara), Olivia de Havilland (Melanie Hamilton), Leslie
Howard (Ashley Wilkes), Thomas Mitchell (Gerald O'Hara),
Barbara O'Neil (Ellen O'Hara), *Hattie McDaniel* (Mammy),
Butterfly McQueen, Victor Jory, Evelyn Keyes, Ann
Rutherford, Laura Hope Crews, Harry Davenport, Jane
Darwell, Ona Munson and also Ward Bond

> 'Perhaps the key plantation movie.' – *Time Out,
> 1980*

● The best account of the film's making is in Gavin
Lambert's 1975 book, *GWTW*.
● In the early seventies a stage musical version toured the
world, with music by Harold Rome.
🏆 best picture; Sidney Howard; Victor Fleming; best
cinematography; Lyle Wheeler; Vivien Leigh; Hattie
McDaniel; best film editing; William Cameron Menzies
(special award)
🏅 Max Steiner; Clark Gable; Olivia de Havilland; special
effects

81
All Quiet on the Western Front

*Fired with patriotism, a young German boys volunteer in 1914 but
quickly become disillusioned when faced with the horror and futility of
the trenches.*

Lewis Milestone's anti-war film concerns a group of German teenagers
who volunteer for action on the Western Front in 1914, but they
become disillusioned, and none of them survives. A landmark of
American cinema, it was Universal's biggest and most serious undertaking until the Sixties. This highly emotive war film with its occasional
outbursts of bravura direction, reminiscent of Eisenstein and Fritz
Lang, fixed in millions of minds the popular image of what it was like in
the trenches, even more so than James Whale's *Journey's End*, which
had shown the Allied viewpoint. Despite dated moments, it retains its
overall power and remains a great pacifist work.

80
Gone with the Wind

*Although the Civil War lays waste to the American states, a self-centred
Southern girl survives, only to lose the man she cares for.*

David O. Selznick's sweeping period romance is the only film in history
that could be profitably revived for forty years: 'still pure gold', said the
Daily Mirror in 1975, and the sentiment has been repeated with its
release on DVD. Many books have been written about the filming of
this story of an egotistic Southern girl who survives the Civil War but
finally loses the only man she loves; and about its troubled production:
scripts were written and rewritten, directors and cinematographers
came and went, and Gable did not want to play Rhett Butler because
the girl does not fall for him at first sight. Its essential appeal is that of
a romantic story with strong characters and an impeccable production.

Gone with the Wind

'Out-leaping the maddest imaginings!
Out-thrilling the wildest thrills!'

King Kong

👫 US   1933   100m   bw
RKO (Merian C. Cooper)

▢   ▤   ⊙   ⊚   ⌒

w James Creelman, Ruth Rose *story* Edgar Wallace
d Merian C. Cooper, Ernest Schoedsack *ph* Edward
Linden, Vernon Walker, L. O. Taylor *m* Max Steiner
ad Carroll Clark, Al Herman, Van Nest Polglase *ed* Ted
Cheesman *sound effects* Murray Spivak *chief
technician* Willis J. O'Brien

☆ *Robert Armstrong* (Carl Denham), *Fay Wray* (Ann
Darrow), Bruce Cabot (John Driscoll), Frank Reicher (Capt.
Englehorn), Sam Hardy (Charles Weston), Noble Johnson
(Native Chief), Steve Clemento (Witch King)

'If properly handled, should gather good grosses in
a walk … and may open up a new medium for
scaring babies via the screen.' – *Variety*

'Just amusing nonsense punctuated by such
reflections as why, if the natives wanted to keep the
monster on the other side of the wall, they should
have built a door big enough to let him through.'
– *James Agate*

79
King Kong

*A film producer on safari brings back a giant ape which terrorizes New
York.*

By today's standards, the stop-motion special effects of this classic
horror movie are clumsy: Kong's size changes from one moment to
another and his movements are jerky. Yet, thanks to O'Brien's animation, he seems real. The sense of adventure that fills the picture derived
from its producers. Cooper and Schoedsack were both men of action
who enjoyed taking risks and learned their trade making documentary
films in the wilder places of the world. Against all the odds, this fable of
beauty and the beast retains a mythic power. Its themes of love and
betrayal have the raw power of fantasy and a childlike quality of make-
believe that still enchants. For all its quaintness, it contains some of the
most memorable images in film history. No more enthralling adventure
has been filmed.

517

Cabiria
Italy/France   1957   110m   bw
Dino de Laurentiis/Les Films Marceau
▣ ▦ ⊙ ⊙ ⌂
original title: *Le Notti di Cabiria*
aka: *Nights of Cabiria*
w Federico Fellini, Ennio Flaiano, Tullio Pinelli *d* Federico
Fellini *ph* Aldo Tonti *m* Nino Rota *ad* Piero Gherardi
ed Leo Catozzo
☆ Giulietta Masina (Cabiria), François Périer (Oscar
D'Onofrio), Amedeo Nazzari (Alberto Lazzari), Franca Marzi
(Wanda), Dorian Gray (Jessy)

'Any nobility in the original conception slowly
suffocates in an atmosphere of subjective
indulgence bordering dangerously on self-pity.'
– *Peter John Dyer*

'Stylistically the whole film with its dejected setting
and its riotously fluent movement is brilliant. And
the acting is superb.' – *Dilys Powell*

🎖 best foreign language film

78
Cabiria

*A prostitute ekes out an existence in Rome, constantly betrayed by
those around her but still able to dream of romance.*

Fellini's bitter Cinderella story, of a Roman prostitute dreaming of
romance and respectability, gave Giulietta Masina one of her greatest
roles. Her hapless escapades at the hands of her clients include being
dumped in a lake, hidden in a bathroom, hypnotized and humiliated,
and robbed by the man she happily marries. Fellini was influenced by
Chaplin's *City Lights* in making the film, and Masina's performance
reflects aspects of Chaplin's little tramp, even in her dancing. At each
disaster, she reveals not only a pathetic dignity but also an irrepressible
spirit and just a touch of optimism.

'The most devastating detective story of
the century!'
All the President's Men
US   1976   138m   Technicolor   Panavision
Warner/Wildwood (Robert Redford, Walter Coblenz)
▣ ▦ ⊙ ⊙ ⊙
w William Goldman *book* Carl Bernstein, Bob Woodward
d Alan J. Pakula *ph* Gordon Willis *m* David Shire
pd George Jenkins *ed* Robert L. Wolfe
☆ *Robert Redford* (Bob Woodward), *Dustin Hoffman* (Carl
Bernstein), Jason Robards Jnr (Ben Bradlee), Martin Balsam
(Howard Simons), Hal Holbrook (Deep Throat), Jack
Warden (Harry Rosenfeld), Jane Alexander (Bookkeeper),
Meredith Baxter (Debbie Sloan)

'It works as a detective thriller (even though
everyone knows the ending), as a credible (if
occasionally romanticized) primer on the prosaic
fundamentals of big league investigative
journalism, and best of all, as a chilling tone poem
that conveys the texture of the terror in our nation's
capital during that long night when an aspiring
fascist regime held our democracy under siege.'
– *Frank Rich, New York Post*

🎖 William Goldman; Jason Robards Jnr; art direction;
sound (Arthur Piantadosi, Les Fresholtz, Dick Alexander,
Jim Webb)
🎖 best picture; Alan J. Pakula; Jane Alexander; Robert L.
Wolfe

77
All the President's Men

*A reconstruction of the discovery of the White House link with the
Watergate affair by two young reporters from the* Washington Post.

Alan J. Pakula's absorbing drama reconstructs the investigative journalism of two young reporters from the *Washington Post* that revealed
a link between the White House of President Nixon and the break-in at
the Democrat headquarters at the Watergate building in Washington. It
is a terrific political thriller, all the more riveting for being based on a
real scandal, that brings out the best in its two contrasting stars,
Redford and Hoffman, and also gets a scintillating performance from
Jason Robards Jnr as their gruff editor. Pakula treats it as if it were a
documentary with a restrained intelligence that makes it authentic history and diverting entertainment.

Viskningar och Rop

Sweden 1972 91m Eastmancolor
Cinematograph (Ingmar Bergman)

🔲 ▤ ⓐ ⓦ

aka: *Cries and Whispers*

wd Ingmar Bergman *ph* Sven Nykvist *m* Chopin, Bach
ad Marik Voss *ed* Siv Lundgren

☆ *Harriet Andersson* (Agnes), *Kari Sylwan* (Anna), *Ingrid Thulin* (Karin), *Liv Ullmann* (Maria/Her Mother)

> 'Harrowing, spare and perceptive, but lacking the humour that helps to put life and death into perspective.' – *Michael Billington, Illustrated London News*

👤 Sven Nykvist
♟ best picture; Ingmar Bergman (as writer); Ingmar Bergman (as director)

76
Viskningar och Rop

As a young woman dies slowly and painfully from cancer, she is tended by her sisters and her maid – the only person able to express compassion.

A quiet, chilling, classical chapter of doom which is variously reminiscent of Chekhov, Tolstoy and Dostoievsky but is also essential Bergman. Tough but important viewing, it lingers afterwards in the mind like a picture vividly painted in shades of red. It is an intimate story: a young woman dying of cancer in her family home is tended by her two sisters. It grew out of a vision Bergman had, of a large red room, with three women in white whispering together, and the finished work has some of the qualities of a dream from which it would be pleasant to wake. The two sisters are selfish and tormented and the mood is often despairing, though the film ends wonderfully on an image of reconciliation.

'M*A*S*H Gives A D*A*M*N.'

M*A*S*H

US 1970 116m DeLuxe Panavision
TCF/Aspen (Ingo Preminger, Leon Ericksen)

🔲 🔲 ▤ ⓐ⌁ ⓐ ⓦ 🎧

w Ring Lardner Jnr *novel* Richard Hooker *d* Robert Altman *ph* Harold E. Stine *m* Johnny Mandel *md* Herbert Spencer *ad* Arthur Lonergan, Jack Martin Smith *ed* Danford B. Greene

☆ Donald Sutherland (Hawkeye Pierce), Elliott Gould (Trapper John McIntyre), Tom Skerritt (Duke Forrest), Sally Kellerman (Major Hot Lips Houlihan), Robert Duvall (Major Frank Burns), Jo Ann Pflug (Lt Hot Dish), René Auberjonois (Dago Red), Gary Burghoff (Radar O'Reilly), Roger Bowen (Col. Henry Blake)

> 'Bloody funny. A hyper-acute wiretap on mankind's death wish.' – *Joseph Morgenstern*

> 'The laughter is blood-soaked and the comedy cloaks a bitter and terrible truth.' – *Judith Crist*

> 'A foul-mouthed, raucous, anti-establishment comedy, combining gallows humour, sexual slapstick and outrageous satire.' – *Les Keyser, Hollywood in the Seventies*

● Regions 1 and 2 two disc DVD release includes audio commentary by Robert Altman.
👤 Ring Lardner Jnr
♟ best picture; Robert Altman; Sally Kellerman; Danford B. Greene

---

75
M*A*S*H

Surgeons at a mobile hospital in Korea spend what spare time they have chasing women and bucking authority.

Robert Altman once told me, 'M*A*S*H was not released. It escaped.' Appropriate for a movie about the idiocy of war, and irreverence in the face of death, that studio executives wanted to shelve. Its two stars, also unhappy, tried to have Altman sacked, and its screenwriter was furious because no one stuck to his script. It was only in post-production that the episodic narrative gained shape by the addition of its shots of camp loudspeaker announcements. Out of this chaos came a savagely funny film on the shambles of war. Its randy, life-enhancing surgeons, forever bucking authority, operate in a world where reason no longer holds. There are no battles, but the waste and horror is present in all its brutality, and caring humanity, in the blood-drenched hospital scenes. Korea and Vietnam may be past history, but M*A*S*H retains its resonance.

A Short Film About Killing

Poland 1988 84m colour
Gala/Film Unit 'Tor'/Zespoly Filmowe (Ryszard Chutkowski)

original title: *Krótki Film O Zabijaniu*
w Krzysztof Piesiewicz, Krzysztof Kieslowski *d* Krzysztof Kieslowski *ph* Slawomir Idziak *m* Zbigniew Preisner *ad* Halina Dobrowolska *ed* Ewa Small
☆ Miroslaw Baka (Jacek Lazar), Krzysztof Globisz (Piotr Balicki), Jan Tesarz (Waldemar Rekowski), Zbigniew Zapasiewicz (Bar Examiner)

'A powerful rebuke to a world that pretends to deter violence through ritualized capital punishment, but dramatizes, sensationalizes and perpetuates it instead.' – *Edward Guthmann, San Francisco Chronicle*

74
A Short Film About Killing

A brutal and pointless murder is committed by an indifferent youth; his case is unsuccessfully defended by an idealistic lawyer.

Krzysztof Kieslowski was not merely the leading Polish film director from the 1980s until his death in 1996; he was also one of the greatest directors of his time. He once said that he did not have any feelings about society as a whole, but what he did care for was the individual human being. That passion is evident in this powerful and unremittingly bleak drama. Originally part of a series of television films on the ten commandments, it concerns a disenchanted youth who commits a bungled and motiveless murder and is defended by an idealistic lawyer opposed to capital punishment. The film is unforgettable in its condemnation of killing, whether criminal or judicial.

Aguirre, Wrath of God

West Germany 1972 95m colour
Hessicher Rundfunk/Werner Herzog

original title: *Aguirre, der Zorn Gottes*
wd Werner Herzog *ph* Thomas Mauch *m* Popol Vuh *ed* Beate Mainka-Jellinghaus
☆ *Klaus Kinski* (Don Lope de Aguirre), Ruy Guerra (Don Pedro de Ursua), Helena Rojo (Inez), Cecilia Rivera (Flores), Del Negro (Brother Gaspar de Carvajal), Peter Berling (Don Fernando de Guzman), Alejandro Repulles (Gonzalez Pizarro)

'It ingeniously combines Herzog's gift for deep irony, his strong social awareness, and his worthy ambition to fashion a whole new visual perspective on the world around us via mystical, evocative, yet oddly direct imagery. It is a brilliant cinematic achievement.' – *David Skerritt, Christian Science Monitor*

● The Region 1 DVD release includes a commentary by Werner Herzog. A Region 1 and 2 box set of five Herzog/Kinski films includes commentary by Herzog and Norman Hill and Herzog's documentary *My Best Friend* on his relationship with Kinski.

73
Aguirre, Wrath of God

In 1560, one of Pizaro's conquistadors, accompanied by soldiers, a monk and two women, embarks upon a doomed attempt to find the legendary city of El Dorado.

Klaus Kinski was the perfect actor to play Lope de Aguirre, a conquistador in Peru, who ignores Pizarro's orders, takes over a band of soldiers, and plans to rule the coutry; as he brings his party of forty down river by raft, he succumbs to megalomania. Kinski conveys his insane desire with a power few other actors could match. In the final moments of the film the camera circles around his mad, lone figure on the raft, over which hundreds of monkeys swarm. In this absorbing drama, vividly assembled and impossible to forget, Herzog wittily points up the contrast between the harsh reality of the jungle and the band of sophisticated Europeans, out of their depth and consumed by all-conquering, self-destructive vanity.

Rear Window
US 1954 112m Technicolor
Paramount/Alfred Hitchcock

w John Michael Hayes *novel* Cornell Woolrich *d* Alfred Hitchcock *ph* Robert Burks *m* Franz Waxman *ad* Jospeh MacMillan Johnson, Hal Pereira *ed* Geroge Tomasini
☆ James Stewart (L.B. "Jeff" Jeffries), Grace Kelly (Lisa Carol Fremont), Raymond Burr (Lars Thorwald), Judith Evelyn (Miss Lonely Hearts), Wendell Corey (Det. Thomas J. Doyle), Thelma Ritter (Stella)
☖ John Michael Hayes; Alfred Hitchcock; Robert Burks

72
Rear Window

Confined to his room by a broken leg, a news photographer believes he witnesses a murder committed in a nearby apartment.

Hitchock sets himself a problem with this thriller. Its restricted setting – an apartment room in which a news photographer, confined by a broken leg, sees a murder committed in a room on the other side of the court – means that all depends upon the script and the acting. Hitchcock teasingly uses the photographer's voyeurism to remind his audience that cinema also makes them voyeurs, implicit in an activity that, as a nurse points out to James Stewart's crippled hero, used to be punished by having one's eyes burned out. Like Stewart, the audience wants something exciting to happen in one of the other apartments; when it does, it is caught up in the suspense. With John Michael Hayes's tautly-written script, Stewart at his irascible best and Kelly as the perfect Hitchcock heroine, it succeeds as an artificial but gripping suspenser of an unusual kind.

'Tea At Four. Dinner At Eight. Murder By Midnight.'
Gosford Park
US/GB 2001 137m Technicolor
Panavision
Entertainment/Capitol/Film Council/Sandcastle 5/Chicagofilms/Medusa (Robert Altman, Bob Balaban, David Levy)

w Julian Fellowes *idea* Robert Altman, Bob Balaban *d* Robert Altman *ph* Andrew Dunn *m* Patrick Doyle *pd* Stephen Altman *ed* Tim Squyres *cos* Jenny Beavan
☆ Eileen Atkins (Mrs. Croft), Michael Gambon (Sir William McCordle), Jeremy Northam (Ivor Novello), Clive Owen (Robert Parks), Bob Balaban (Morris Weissman), Maggie Smith (Constance, Countess of Trentham), Ryan Phillippe (Henry Denton), Alan Bates (Jennings), Helen Mirren (Mrs. Wilson), Kelly Macdonald (Mary Maceachran), Richard E. Grant (George), Tom Hollander (Lt Commander Anthony Meredith), Kristin Scott Thomas (Lady Sylvia McCordle), Emily Watson (Elsie), James Wilby (The Hon. Freddie Nesbitt) and also Derek Jacobi (Probert), Geraldine Somerville (Louisa, Lady Stockbridge), Sophie Thompson (Dorothy), Camilla Rutherford (Isobel McCordle), Claudie Blakley (Mabel Nesbitt), Stephen Fry (Inspector Thompson), Ron Webster (Constable Dexter)
♟ Julian Fellowes
☖ best picture; Robert Altman; Helen Mirren; Maggie Smith; Stephen Altman; Jenny Beavan
♙ best British film; Jenny Beavan

71
Gosford Park

In the early 1930s, a large party of guests and their servants assemble for a country house weekend; when their host is murdered all come under suspicion.

Robert Altman's satire of British upper-class life in the early 1930s uses the form of an old-fashioned mystery story, set in a country house over a weekend. Aristocratic guests and their servants come under suspicion when their host is killed twice. It is, as with Altman's best films, an ensemble piece, using a dazzling cast of British actors. A witty, acute, splendidly acted dissection of a way of life at the point of its disintegration, it captures not only the antagonism between the working- and upper-classes, but also their complicity in the continuation of a decadent social system.

Star Wars

♁♁ US 1977 121m Technicolor
Panavision
TCF/Lucasfilm (Gary Kurtz)
▭▭ ▭▭ ▤ ◍ ◉ ◎ ◉ ◎ ⌂
aka: *Star Wars IV: A New Hope*
wd George Lucas *ph* Gilbert Taylor *m* John Williams
pd John Barry *ed* Paul Hirsch, Marcia Lucas, Richard
Chew *sp* Rick Baker, John Dykstra
☆ Mark Hamill (Luke Skywalker), Harrison Ford (Han
Solo), Carrie Fisher (Princess Leia Organa), Peter Cushing
(Grand Moff Tarkin), Alec Guinness (Obi-Wan Kenobi),
Anthony Daniels (C-3PO), Kenny Baker (R2-D2), Dave
Prowse (Darth Vader), Phil Brown (Owen Lars)
● The voice of Darth Vader was supplied by the uncredited
James Earl Jones.
● The film was re-released in 1997, with its sound
remixed and digital technology used to improve battle
sequences and the size of the city of Mos Eisley. Some
unused footage from the original was added, together with
computer animation, to show a meeting between Han Solo
and Jabba the Hutt. It took more than $46m in the first week
of its re-release, and became the first film to gross more
than $400m at the US box office.
♟ John Williams; John Barry; editing; costumes (John
Mollo); visual effects (John Stears, John Dykstra and
others); sound
♟ best picture; script; direction; Alec Guinness
Ⓣ John Williams

The Empire Strikes Back

♁♁ US 1980 124m Eastmancolor
Panavision
TCF/Lucasfilm (Gary Kurtz)
▭▭ ▭▭ ▤ ◍ ◉ ◎ ⌂
w Leigh Brackett, Lawrence Kasdan *story* George Lucas
d Irvin Kershner *ph* Peter Suschitzky *m* John Williams
pd Norman Reynolds *ed* Paul Hirsch
☆ Mark Hamill, Harrison Ford, Carrie Fisher, Billy Dee
Williams (Lando Calrissian), Anthony Daniels (C-3PO),
Peter Mayhew (Chewbacca), Kenny Baker (R2-D2), Frank
Oz (Yoda), Alec Guinness (Obi-Wan Kenobi)
♟ John Williams; art direction
Ⓣ music

Return of the Jedi

♁♁ US 1983 132m DeLuxe
Panavision
TCF/Lucasfilm (Howard Kazanjian)
▭▭ ▭▭ ▤ ◍ ◉ ◎ ⌂
aka: *Star Wars: Episode VI - Return of the Jedi*
w Lawrence Kasdan, George Lucas *d* Richard Marquand
ph Alan Hume *m* John Williams *pd* Norman Reynolds
ed Sean Barton, Duwayne Dunham, Marcia Lucas, Arthur
Repola
☆ Mark Hamill, Harrison Ford, Carrie Fisher, Billy Dee
Williams, Anthony Daniels, Peter Mayhew, Kenny Baker
♟ John Williams; art direction

Star Wars Trilogy

Star Wars

A rebel princess in a distant galaxy escapes, and with the help of her robots and a young farmer overcomes the threatening forces of evil.

The Empire Strikes Back

The Rebel Alliance takes refuge from Darth Vader on a frozen planet.

Return of the Jedi

'Episode 6' of the Star Wars *serial: our heroes combat Darth Vader and Jabba the Hutt.*

George Lucas's original Star Wars trilogy has been diminished by its three prequels, which have often seemed little more than well-illustrated toy catalogues. A long time ago (and it may have been in a galaxy far, far away) the first films did provide cinematic excitement and simple pleasures. In the first, Lucas deftly borrowed his plot and viewpoint from Kurosawa's *The Hidden Fortress*, with its war experienced by two squabbling robots. The adventure continued with death-defying escapes, sword play, gun battles, dogfights in space and a little light romance, all the ingredients of old-fashioned science fiction serials lovingly brought up to date. Well cast, with Alec Guinness adding a little gravitas, it was delightful escapist fare. Its influence on Hollywood may not have been for the good, leading to a succession of mediocre juvenile blockbusters, but the trilogy itself remains a pleasure, and not a guilty one.

'Slightly encumbered by some mythic and neo-Sophoclean overtones, but its inventiveness, humour and special effects are scarcely less inspired than those of its phenomenally successful predecessor.' – *New Yorker*

'I admire the exquisite skill and talent which have been poured into these films, while finding the concepts behind these gigantic video games in the sky mindlessly tedious.' – *Margaret Hinxman, Daily Mail*

'An impersonal and rather junky piece of moviemaking.' – *Pauline Kael, New Yorker*

'Only the effects are special.' – *Sight and Sound*

Chinatown
US 1974 131m Technicolor Panavision
Paramount/Long Road (Robert Evans)

w Robert Towne d Roman Polanski ph John A. Alonso
m Jerry Goldsmith pd Richard Sylbert ad Stewart
Campbell ed Sam O'Steen
☆ Jack Nicholson (J.J. Gittes), Faye Dunaway (Evelyn
Mulwray), John Huston (Noah Cross), Perry Lopez
(Escobar), John Hillerman (Yelburton), Roman Polanski
(Man with Knife), Darrell Zwerling (Hollis Mulwray), Diane
Ladd (Ida Sessions)

'You are swept along as helpless as any of the
corpses so unaccountably drowned in empty lake-
beds.' – *Dilys Powell*

'The success of *Chinatown* – with its beautifully
structured script and draggy, overdeliberate
direction – represents something dialectically new:
nostalgia (for the thirties) openly turned to rot, and
the *celebration* of rot.' – *Pauline Kael*

👤 Robert Towne
🏆 best picture; Roman Polanski; John A. Alonso; Jerry
Goldsmith; Jack Nicholson; Faye Dunaway
🏆 Roman Polanski; Robert Towne; Jack Nicholson

69
Chinatown

In 1930s Los Angeles, a cop-turned-private eye who searches only for the truth discovers only cynicism, corruption and scandal.

Polanski puts his audience in the position of his hapless Los Angeles private eye who, in 1937, takes on a simple case and burrows into it until it leads to murder and a public scandal. Both are led up blind alleys together, and begin to understand the mystery at the same time. Robert Towne's script uses the conventions of detective stories to explore civic and personal corruption in the style of Raymond Chandler, but adds a more modern perspective. It is eminently watchable, with effective individual scenes and performances, and photography which is lovingly composed though tending to suggest period by use of an orange filter. This teasing, complex film is among the best of Hollywood's thrillers.

Two Tars

US   1928   20m   bw   silent
Hal Roach

w Leo McCarey, H. M. Walker *d* James Parrott
ph George Stevens *ed* Richard Currier
☆ Stan Laurel, Oliver Hardy, Edgar Kennedy, Charley Rogers, Thelma Hill, Ruby Blaine, Charlie Hall

Big Business

US   1929   20m   bw   silent
Hal Roach

w Leo McCarey, H. M. Walker *d* James W. Horne
ed Richard Currier
☆ Stan Laurel, Oliver Hardy, James Finlayson
● The Region 2 DVD release is on a disc with *Way Out West*.

You're Darn Tootin'

US   1929   20m   bw   silent
Hal Roach

w H. M. Walker *d* Edgar Kennedy *ph* Floyd Jackman
ed Richard Currier
☆ Stan Laurel, Oliver Hardy, Agnes Steele, Otto Lederer

Hog Wild

US   1930   20m   bw
Hal Roach

w H. M. Walker, Leo McCarey *d* James Parrott
ph George Stevens *ed* Richard Currier
☆ Stan Laurel, Oliver Hardy, Fay Holderness, Dorothy Granger

Laughing Gravy

US   1931   20m   bw
Hal Roach

w H. M. Walker *d* James W. Horne *ph* Art Lloyd
ed Richard Currier
☆ Stan Laurel, Oliver Hardy, Charlie Hall, Harry Bernard

Helpmates

US   1932   20m   bw
Hal Roach

w H. M. Walker *d* James Parrott *ph* Art Lloyd
ed Richard Currier
☆ Stan Laurel, Oliver Hardy, Blanche Payson, Robert Callahan

The Music Box

US   1932   30m   bw
Hal Roach

w H. M. Walker *d* James Parrott
☆ best short

68
Laurel and Hardy Shorts

Two Tars

Two sailors in an old banger cause a traffic jam and a consequent escalation of violence.

Big Business

Stan and Ollie fail to sell a Christmas tree to a belligerent householder.

You're Darn Tootin'

Two musicians get into trouble at work, in their digs and in the street.

Hog Wild

Stan helps Ollie to put a radio aerial on the roof of his house.

Laughing Gravy

Stan and Ollie retrieve their dog when the landlord throws it out into the snow.

Helpmates

Stan helps Ollie clean up after a wild party while the wife was away.

The Music Box

Two delivery men take a piano to a house at the top of a flight of steps.

Towed in a Hole

🏃 US 1932 20m bw
Hal Roach
w Stan Laurel *d* George Marshall *ph* Art Lloyd
ed Richard Currier
☆ Stan Laurel, Oliver Hardy, Billy Gilbert

Dirty Work

🏃 US 1933 20m bw
Hal Roach
w H. M. Walker *d* Lloyd French *ph* Kenneth Peach
ed Bert Jordan
☆ Laurel and Hardy, Lucien Littlefield, Sam Adams

Blockheads

🏃 US 1938 60m bw
Hal Roach/Stan Laurel
📷 ▦ ◉ ✿
w James Parrott, Harry Langdon, Felix Adler, Charles Rogers, Arnold Belgard *d* John G. Blystone *ph* Art Lloyd
m Marvin Hatley
☆ *Stan Laurel, Oliver Hardy*, Billy Gilbert, Patricia Ellis, Minna Gombell, James Finlayson

'Hodge-podge of old-fashioned slapstick and hoke.' – *Variety*

👤 Marvin Hatley

Towed in a Hole

Two would-be fishermen wreck the boat they have just bought.

Dirty Work

Chimney sweeps cause havoc in the house of an eccentric scientist.

Blockheads

Twenty years after World War I, Stan is still guarding a trench because nobody told him to stop. Ollie takes him home to meet the wife, with disastrous consequences.

From their early *You're Darn Tootin',* with its surreal pants-ripping contest, to *Blockheads*, their last first-class comedy that includes encounters with a tip-up truck and an automatic garage, Laurel and Hardy provided nearly a decade of superb slapstick that never fails to bring laughter. Their short films follow a similar pattern, whether they are putting a radio aerial on the roof of a house in *Hog Wild,* or being chimney sweeps in *Dirty Work*, or failing to sell a Christmas tree to a belligerent householder in *Big Business*, or wrecking the boat they have just bought in *Towed in a Hole*. There will be a contest with inanimate objects, which they will lose, followed by tit-for-tat destruction of their surroundings and each other. Yet each film is full of new comic invention and perfectly timed gags. The violence they inflict upon each other is never malicious. Even at their most destructive, there is a gleeful innocence about them. If one of their shorts had to be singled out, it would be *The Music Box,* the most consistently hilarious display of brilliantly sustained slapstick on film.

Monsieur Hulot's Holiday

France 1953 91m bw
Cady/Discina (Fred Orain)

original title: *Les Vacances de Monsieur Hulot*
w *Jacques Tati*, Henri Marquet d Jacques Tati ph Jacques
Mercanton, Jean Mouselle m Alain Romans ad Henri
Schmitt, R. Brian Court ed Charles Bretoneiche, Suzanne
Baron, Jacques Grassi
☆ *Jacques Tati* (M. Hulot), Nathalie Pascaud (Martine),
Michèle Rolla (The Aunt), Valentine Camax (Englishwoman)

'The casual, amateurish air of his films clearly adds
to their appeal: it also appears to explain their
defects.' – *Penelope Houston, MFB*

'It had me laughing out loud with more enjoyment
than any other comedy film this year.' – *Daily
Express*

'Its humour is gentle, innocent and charming and
the semi-silent idiom is superbly managed. The
movie is perfectly composed with a light touch that
is the work of a certain kind of gravity and
sophistication.' – *Peter Bradshaw, Guardian*

⚖ script

67
Monsieur Hulot's Holiday

*Arriving at the seaside, an eccentric bachelor causes chaos but
remains blithely unaware of the uproar as catastrophe follows
catastrophe.*

Jacques Tati's inimitable, accident-prone, ever-curious M. Hulot made
his debut in a film to set the whole world laughing. On a simple outline,
of a bachelor arriving at a seaside resort and unwittingly causing havoc
for himself and everyone else, Tati strung a succession of amiable
jokes, mostly magnificently timed, that pointed up the absurdities of
everyday life. There is hardly any dialogue, though it is far from silent.
One of its triumphs is the brilliantly comic use of sound, from deflating
tyres and snatches of conversation to creaking doors and mistuned
radios. There is charm and a guileful innocence about Tati's great creation, seen here at his unadulteratedly comic best.

'Stirring – in the seeing! Precious – in the
remembering'

Mr Smith Goes to Washington

US 1939 130m bw
Columbia (Frank Capra)

w *Sidney Buchman* story Lewis R. Foster d *Frank Capra*
ph Joseph Walker m Dimitri Tiomkin ad Lionel Banks
ed Al Clark, Gene Havlick montage Slavko Vorkapich
☆ *James Stewart* (Jefferson Smith), *Claude Rains* (Sen.
Joseph Paine), *Jean Arthur* (Saunders), *Thomas Mitchell*
(Diz Moore), *Edward Arnold* (Jim Taylor), Guy Kibbee (Gov.
Hubert Hopper), Eugene Pallette (Chick McGann), Beulah
Bondi (Ma Smith), *Harry Carey* (President of the Senate), H.
B. Warner (Sen. Fuller), Astrid Allwyn (Susan Paine), Ruth
Donnelly (Mrs. Emma Hopper), Charles Lane (Nosey),
Porter Hall (Sen. Monroe)

'It says all the things about America that have been
crying out to be said and – and says them
beautifully.' – *Los Angeles Times*

'The great American picture.' – *Billboard*

'A totally compelling piece of movie-making,
upholding the virtues of traditional American
ideals.' – *NFT, 1973*

♟ Lewis R. Foster
⚖ best picture; Sidney Buchman; Frank Capra; Dimitri
Tiomkin; James Stewart; Claude Rains; Harry Carey; Lionel
Banks

66
Mr Smith Goes to Washington

*An innocent local hero is made a senator and the career politicians who
had thought him a useful dupe find he cannot be manipulated.*

Washington's youngest senator exposes corruption in high places,
almost at the cost of his own career in Capra's archetypal high-flying
vehicle, with the little man coming out on top as he seldom does in life.
It is hard to believe that Joseph Breen, who acted as censor to
Hollywood, warned the studio not to touch such 'loaded dynamite',
since it endorses the system it criticizes. Supreme gloss hides the corn,
helter-skelter direction keeps one watching, and all concerned give
memorable performances. A cinema classic.

The Four Hundred Blows
France 1959 94m bw Dyaliscope
Films du Carrosse/SEDIF (Georges Charlot)
📽 ▦ ⦿~ ⊘ ⊘
original title: *Les Quatre Cents Coups*
wd François Truffaut *ph* Henri Decaë *m* Jean Constantin
ad Bernard Evein *ed* Marie-Josèph Yoyotte
☆ *Jean-Pierre Léaud*, Claire Maurier, Albert Rémy

'The narrative is boldly fluent. Sympathetic, amused, reminded, occasionally puzzled, you are carried along with it. I don't think you will get away before the end.' – *Dilys Powell*

● The film is said to be based on Truffaut's own childhood.
♟ script

Stolen Kisses
France 1968 91m Eastmancolor
Films du Carrosse/Artistes Associés (Marcel Berbert)
▦ ⊘
original title: *Baisers Volés*
w François Truffaut, Claude de Givray, Bernard Revon
d François Truffaut *ph* Denys Clerval *m* Antoine Duhamel
☆ Jean-Pierre Léaud (Antoine Doinel), Delphine Seyrig (Fabienne Tabard), Michel Lonsdale (Georges Tabard), Claude Jade (Christine Darbon)
♟ best foreign film

Bed and Board
France/Italy 1970 97m Eastmancolor
Columbia/Les Films du Carrosse/Valoria/Fida Cinematografica (Marcel Berbert)
📽 ▦ ⊘
original title: *Domicile Conjugal*
w François Truffaut, Claude de Givray, Bernard Revon
d François Truffaut *ph* Nestor Almendros *m* Antoine Duhamel *ad* Jean Mandaroux *ed* Agnès Guillemot
☆ Jean-Pierre Léaud, Claude Jade, Hiroko Berghauer, Daniel Ceccaldi, Claire Duhamel, Barbara Laage

Love on the Run
France 1979 95m Eastmancolor
Les Films du Carrosse (François Truffaut)
📽 ▦ ⊘
w François Truffaut, Marie-France Pisier, Jean Aurel, Suzanne Schiffman *d* François Truffaut *ph* Nestor Almendros *m* Georges Delerue *pd* Jean-Pierre Kohut Svelko *ed* Martine Barraqué
☆ Jean-Pierre Léaud, Marie-France Pisier, Claude Jade, Rosy Varte

65
Antoine Doinel Tetralogy

The Four Hundred Blows

A 12-year-old boy, unhappy at home, finds himself in a detention centre but finally escapes and keeps running.

Stolen Kisses

An ineffective young man can find neither work nor love.

Bed and Board

Antoine Doinel, becomes a husband, father, writer and adulterer.

Love on the Run

Antoine Doinel, separated from his family, is still having girl trouble.

Truffaut's fascinating four features, together with his lighthearted 30m short, *Antoine and Collete*, are almost unique in cinema for featuring the same character, played by the same actor, Jean-Pierre Léaud, at the ages of 13, 19, 24, 28 and 33. (Czech director Dusan Klein is achieving something similar in his ongoing series *Poets*.) Moving from an unhappy childhood to a hapless, sort of maturity, Doinel's is a story of failed relationships, though the final film, *Love on the Run*, ends with the possibility of happiness, after flashbacks covering his many mistakes. The high spot remains the earliest movie, *The Four Hundred Blows*, a sensitive portrait of anguished adolescence that drew on Truffaut's own experiences as a disturbed young delinquent. Truffaut stopped at Doinel's early thirties because he realised that Antoine might grow older but was failing to grow up, a view of masculinity that may be more pertinent these days than then.

A Nous la Liberté

France 1931 95m bw
Tobis
■ ⦿ ◎
US title: *Freedom for Us*
wd René Clair *ph* Georges Périnal *m* Georges Auric
pd Lazare Meerson *ad* Lazare Meerson *ed* René Clair,
Rene Le Henaff
☆ Raymond Cordy (Louis), Henri Marchand (Emile), Rolla
France (Jeanne), Paul Olivier (Paul Imaque), Jacques Shelly
(Paul), Andre Michaud (Foreman)

'Different from the usual run ... easily
understandable even to those who do not know
French.' – *Variety*

'He demonstrates that sound pictures can be as
fluid as silents were, and the picture is rightly
considered a classic.' – *Pauline Kael, 1970s*

'I was close to the extreme left ... I wanted to
attack the Machine, which led men into starvation
instead of adding to their happiness.' – *René Clair*

• Region 1 and 2 DVD releases include a video interview
with Madame Bronja Clair and a short film *Entr'acte*.
⦾ Lazare Meerson

64

A Nous la Liberté

A man succeeds in business after escaping from jail but when his old accomplice appears the two take to the road.

In terms of sheer film flair, this is a revelation, an operetta-style satirical comedy with leftish attitudes and several famous sequences later borrowed by Chaplin for *Modern Times*. It lampoons the mechanization of humanity through its tale of a factory owner who is blackmailed about his past, and with the help of an old prison friend, finally takes to the road. The film was sparked by Clair noticing, in an industrial quarter of Paris, wild flowers growing against the background of smoking factory chimneys. The climax of the film wittily encapsulates Clair's attitudes: at the opening of a new factory, money from a stolen suitcase is blown into the yard; the top hatted officials forget their dignity and begin to dash for the cash.

Ashes and Diamonds

Poland 1958 104m bw
Film Polski
⟺ ■ ◎
original title: *Popiol y Diament*
wd Andrzej Wajda *novel* Jerzy Andrzejewski *ph* Jerzy
Wojcik *m* Aroclaw Radio Quintet *ad* Roman Mann
ed Halina Nawrocka
☆ Zbigniew Cybulski (Maciek), Ewa Krzyzanowska
(Krystyna), Adam Pawlikowski (Andrzej), Waclaw
Zastrzezynski (Szczuka), Bogumil Kobiela (Drewnowski)

'Wajda has created some vivid iideas through
imagery–ideas that carry cynicism, melancholia,
wistfulness, and shock,' – *Bosley Crowther, New
York Times*

63

Ashes and Diamonds

As the war ends in 1945, the Polish Resistance order a partisan to murder a leading Communist.

A Polish partisan is confused by the apparent need to continue killing after the war is over in Wajda's chilling account of the intellectual contradictions to which war leads. In a small Polish town reduced to rubble, a gunman is told to find and kill a fellow Pole, who is a leading Communist. Another partisan fears that he, too, will be killed, as resistance fighters are being shot for holding the wrong opinions. The assassin would rather be making love than war, though he still obeys orders. Wajda's harrowing account, a moving and sensitive film in its own right, is given intensity by Zbigniew Cybulski (once known as the Polish James Dean for he, too, died young) as the compassionate, despairing killer.

'The List Is Life. The Man Was Real. The Story Is True.'
Schindler's List
US   1993   195m   bw/colour
Universal/Amblin (Steven Spielberg, Gerald R. Molen, Branko Lustig)
🔊 🔊 ▦ 🔍 ⊚ ⊚ ⊙ ⌒

w Steven Zaillian *novel* Thomas Keneally *d* Steven Spielberg *ph* Janusz Kaminski *m* John Williams *pd* Allan Starski *ad* Ewa Tarnowska, Maciej Walczak, Ryszard Melliwa, Grzegorz Piatkowski *ed* Michael Kahn
☆ *Liam Neeson* (Oskar Schindler), *Ben Kingsley* (Itzhak Stern), *Ralph Fiennes* (Amon Goeth), Caroline Goodall (Emilie Schindler), Jonathan Sagalle (Poldek Pfefferberg), Embeth Davidtz (Helen Hirsch), Malgosha Gebel (Victoria Klonowska), Shmulik Levy (Wilek Chilowicz), Mark Ivanir (Marcel Goldberg)

'Evinces an artistic rigor and unsentimental intelligence unlike anything the world's most successful filmmaker has demonstrated before.' – *Variety*

'Indiana Jones in the Cracow Ghetto.' – *Will Tremper, Die Welt*

👤 best picture; Steven Spielberg; Steven Zaillian; Janusz Kaminski; Michael Kahn; John Williams; Allan Starski
♟ Liam Neeson; Ralph Fiennes; costume design (Anna Biedrzycka-Sheppard); make-up
📺 best film; adapted screenplay; Steven Spielberg; Ralph Fiennes; Janusz Kaminski; John Williams

62
Schindler's List

During World War II, an Austrian businessman employs Jewish slave labour so that he can save more than a thousand from the Nazi death camps

Steven Spielberg's coming of age as an adult-film maker was marked by this film, which was based on a true story: during the Second World War, an Austrian businessman persuaded the Nazis to let him use Jewish slave labour in his factory; and then, with the money he earned, bribed a brutal SS commandant to save 1,100 Jews from the concentration camps. It is a brilliantly realized, fiercely controlled and restrained treatment, using monochrome photography for the most part to achieve a documentary feel. Harsh and compassionate, it avoids sentimentality until the end and is a notable achievement.

The Leopard
US/Italy   1963   205m   Technirama
TCF/Titanus/SNPC/GPC (Goffredo Lombardo)
⊚ ⌒
original title: *Il Gattopardo*
wd Luchino Visconti *novel* Giuseppe de Lampedusa *ph* Giuseppe Rotunno *m* Nino Rota *ad* Mario Garbuglia *ed* Mario Serandrei
☆ Burt Lancaster (Prince Don Fabrizio Salina), Claudia Cardinale (Angelica Sedara/Bertiana), Alain Delon (Tancredi), Paolo Stoppa (Don Calogero Sedara), Serge Reggiani (Don Ciccio Tumeo), Leslie French (Cavalier Chevally)

'That rare thing - a great film based on a great book.' – *Philip French, Observer*

'One of the most moving meditations on individual mortality in the history of the cinema.' – *David Kehr*

● A restored version of the film running for 205m was released in 2003.
● The three disc Region 1 DVD release from Criterion includes the film in its original 187m Italian version, in its 161m English language version, a documentary on the background and a commentary by critic Peter Cowie.

61
The Leopard

An Italian aristocrat faces the changes affecting his position as the country is unified by Garibaldi.

Giuseppe di Lampedusa's novel of the family life of an Italian nobleman at the time of Garibaldi was an ideal subject for the aristocratic Visconti, who created from it his most sumptuous film. The elaborate, complex family saga was painted like an old master, with great care and attention to detail. Visconti had wanted Brando to star; he got Burt Lancaster, which despite his excellent performance, proved a disastrous choice. As a result Twentieth Century Fox picked up the international release but couldn't make head or tail of it commercially; they even ruined its high quality by releasing a dubbed, shortened version in CinemaScope and DeLuxe colour of poor standard. It was Lancaster who supervised the dubbing, which was crudely done and in unsuitable accents. It is only recently that Visconti's version has been restored to its original dramatic force.

Great Expectations

👥 GB 1946 118m bw
Rank/Cineguild (Anthony Havelock-Allan)
📼 ▬ ◎~ ◎ ◎

w Ronald Neame, David Lean, Kay Walsh, Cecil McGivern,
Anthony Havelock-Allan *d David Lean ph Guy Green*
m Walter Goehr *ad* John Bryan *ed* Jack Harris
☆ John Mills (Pip), Bernard Miles (Joe Gargery), *Finlay
Currie* (Abel Magwitch), *Martita Hunt* (Miss Havisham),
Valerie Hobson (Estella), *Jean Simmons* (Young Estella),
Alec Guinness (Herbert Pocket), Francis L. Sullivan
(Jaggers), Anthony Wager (Young Pip), Ivor Barnard
(Wemmick), Freda Jackson (Mrs. Joe Gargery), Hay Petrie
(Uncle Pumblechook), O. B. Clarence (Aged Parent), George
Hayes (Compeyson), Torin Thatcher (Betley Drummle) and
also Eileen Erskine (Biddy)

'The first big British film to have been made, a film
that sweeps our cloistered virtues out into the
open.' – *Richard Winnington*

'The best Dickens adaptation, and arguably David
Lean's finest film.' – *NFT, 1969*

● It was remade as a less than memorable TV movie in
1974, directed by Joseph Hardy and starring Michael York,
Sarah Miles and James Mason.
● Robert Krasker was the original cinematographer, but
was replaced after Lean found his photography flat and
uninteresting.
👤 Guy Green; John Bryan
♟ best picture; script; David Lean (as director)

60
Great Expectations

*A boy meets an escaped convict on the Romney Marshes, with strange
consequences for both of them.*

David Lean realized the possibilities of filming Dickens's novel after
seeing Alec Guinness's stage adaptation of the story of a young boy
whose life is changed by meeting an escaped convict on the Romney
Marshes. He returned the favour by giving Guinness a role in his film.
On John Bryan's stylized sets, using forced perspective, Lean successfully encouraged slightly larger-than-life performances from his cast.
Despite the inevitable simplifications, it is a superbly pictorial rendering
of the much-loved novel, with all the famous characters in safe hands
and masterly judgement in every department.

'The thousands who have read the book
will know why WE WILL NOT SELL ANY
CHILDREN TICKETS to see this picture!'

The Grapes of Wrath
US 1940 128m bw
TCF (Darryl Zanuck, Nunnally Johnson)
📼 ▬ ◎~

w Nunnally Johnson *novel* John Steinbeck *d John Ford
ph* Gregg Toland *m* Alfred Newman *ad* Richard Day, Mark
Lee Kirk *ed* Robert Simpson
☆ *Henry Fonda* (Tom Joad), *Jane Darwell* (Ma Joad),
John Carradine (Casy), Charley Grapewin (Grandpa), Dorris
Bowdon (Rosasharn), Russell Simpson (Pa Joad), Zeffie
Tilbury (Grandma), O. Z. Whitehead (Al), John Qualen
(Muley), Eddie Quillan (Connie), Grant Mitchell

'A genuinely great motion picture which makes one
proud to have even a small share in the affairs of
the cinema.' – *Howard Barnes*

'The most mature motion picture that has ever
been made, in feeling, in purpose, and in the use of
the medium.' – *Otis Ferguson*

'A sincere and searing indictment of man's cruel
indifference to his fellows.' – *Basil Wright*

👤 John Ford; Jane Darwell
♟ best picture; Nunnally Johnson; Henry Fonda; Robert
Simpson

59
The Grapes of Wrath

*After the dust-bowl disaster of the Thirties, Oklahoma farmers trek to
California in the hope of a better life.*

'We keep a-comin'. We're the people that live. Can't nobody wipe us
out. Can't nobody lick us. We'll go on forever,' says Ma Joad in her
populist outburst at the end of John Ford's superb film, which could
scarcely be improved upon. The sentiment might be at odds with
Steinbeck's novel of Oklahoma farmers trekking to California in the
hope of a better life after the dust-bowl disaster of the Thirties, but it
fits the film. As does Jane Darlow's doughty performance in the role
and, especially, Henry Fonda's as the angry Tom Joad. Acting, photography, and direction combine to make this an unforgettable experience,
a poem of a film.

Saturday Night and Sunday Morning

GB 1960 89m bw
Bryanston/Woodfall (Harry Salzman, Tony Richardson)

📷 🇺🇸 ◎

w Alan Sillitoe novel Alan Sillitoe d Karel Reisz
ph Freddie Francis m Johnny Dankworth ad Ted Marshall
ed Seth Holt

☆ Albert Finney (Arthur Seaton), Shirley Anne Field
(Doreen Gretton), Rachel Roberts (Brenda), Bryan Pringle
(Jack), Norman Rossington (Bert), Hylda Baker (Aunt Ada)

'Here is a chance for our own new wave.'
– Evening Standard

'This study of working-class energies and
frustrations has been overdirected.' – Pauline Kael

● Warwickshire never showed the film because the
producers refused to delete two love scenes. David Kingsley
of British Lion said: 'We are not prepared to agree that a film
of outstanding importance and merit should be re-edited by
the Mrs Grundies of the Warwickshire County Council. It is
fortunate for the world that Warwickshire's greatest and often
bawdy son, William Shakespeare, was not subject in his day
to the restrictions of prim and petty officialdom.'
● A Region 2 DVD release includes commentary from film
historian Robert Murphy, Alan Sillitoe and Freddie Francis.
🏆 best British film; Albert Finney; Rachel Roberts

58
Saturday Night and Sunday Morning

A defiant and dissatisfied factory worker alienates his friends by his rebellious behaviour but eventually has to conform.

Albert Finney burst onto British screens as a Nottingham factory worker, dissatisfied with his lot, who gets into trouble through an affair with a married woman but finally settles for convention. His disdainful attitude is summed up in his telling his father, slumped in front of the TV, about an accident at work: 'This fellow got his hand caught in a press. Of course, he's only got one eye. He lost the sight of the other looking at telly day in and day out.' Startling when it emerged, it is a raw melodrama with sharp detail and strong comedy asides. Matching the mood of the times, and displaying a new attitude to sex, it transformed British cinema.

West Side Story

🚶 US 1961 155m Technicolor
Panavision 70
(UA) Mirisch/Seven Arts (Robert Wise)

📷 🟦 ◎ ◎ ◎ 🎧

w Ernest Lehman play Arthur Laurents, after William
Shakespeare d Robert Wise, Jerome Robbins ph Daniel L.
Fapp m/ly Leonard Bernstein, Stephen Sondheim
ch Jerome Robbins pd Boris Leven ed Thomas Stanford
cos Irene Sharaff

☆ Natalie Wood (sung by Marni Nixon) (Maria), Richard
Beymer (sung by Jimmy Bryant) (Tony), Russ Tamblyn
(Riff), Rita Moreno (sung by Betty Wand) (Anita), George
Chakiris (Bernardo), Simon Oakland (Lt Schrank), Bill
Bramley (Officer Krupke), Tucker Smith (Ice), Tony
Mordente, Tony Winters, Eliot Feld

'The irony of this hyped-up, slam-bang production
is that those involved apparently don't really believe
that beauty and romance can be expressed in
modern rhythms.' – Pauline Kael

'Nothing short of a film masterpiece.' – Bosley
Crowther, New York Times

● Jerome Robbins also received an honorary Oscar for 'his
brilliant achievements in the art of choreography on film.'
🏆 best picture; Robert Wise, Jerome Robbins; Daniel L.
Fapp; Rita Moreno; George Chakiris; Thomas Stanford;
Irene Sharaff; musical direction (Saul Chaplin, Johnny
Green, Sid Ramin, Irwin Kostal); art direction; sound
👤 Ernest Lehman

57
West Side Story

Romeo and Juliet's star-crossed lovers play out their dramas through rival gangs of the New York docklands.

Leonard Bernstein's Romeo and Juliet story in a New York dockland setting presented difficulties in keeping the original choreography from the stage production when transferring it to the screen. The decision to use determinedly realistic settings does not help Robbins's stylized dances, but their pace and energy make up this deficiency. The production values are fine and the song numbers electrifying, so that it forms a lasting memorial to an important musical that took to the streets and celebrated rebellious youth.

On the Waterfront
US   1954   108m   bw
Columbia/Sam Spiegel
▭ ▤ ⌖ ◉ ◎

w Budd Schulberg *novel* Budd Schulberg *d* Elia Kazan
ph Boris Kaufman *m* Leonard Bernstein *ad* Richard Day
ed Gene Milford

☆ *Marlon Brando* (Terry Malloy), Eva Marie Saint (Edie
Doyle), *Lee J. Cobb* (Johnny Friendly), Rod Steiger (Charley
Malloy), Karl Malden (Father Barry), Pat Henning ("Kayo"
Dugan), Leif Erickson (Glover), James Westerfield (Big
Mac), John Hamilton ("Pop" Doyle)

'An uncommonly powerful, exciting and
imaginative use of the screen by gifted
professionals.' – *New York Times*

'A medley of items from the Warner gangland
pictures of the thirties, brought up to date.'
– *Steven Sondheim, Films in Review*

• The Regions 1 and 2 DVD releases include commentary
by film critic Richard Schickel and Elia Kazan biographer
Jeff Young.
🏆 best picture; Budd Schulberg; Elia Kazan; Boris
Kaufman; Richard Day; Marlon Brando; Eva Marie Saint;
editing
🏆 Leonard Bernstein; Lee J. Cobb; Rod Steiger; Karl
Malden
🏆 Marlon Brando

56
On the Waterfront

After the death of his brother, a young stevedore breaks the hold of a waterfront gang boss.

Elia Kazan's film can be seen in personal terms as his defence of his naming names of his left wing associates to the Un-American Activities Committee in 1952. There is an obvious analogy between Kazan's action and that of Marlon Brando's Terry Malloy, a young stevedore who breaks the hold of a waterfront gang boss by testifying against him. Taken as an intense, brooding dockyard thriller, it is a compelling, emotionally satisfying work, noted for its great performances from Brando, Steiger, Eva Marie Saint and Lee J. Cobb. Brando and Steiger's dialogue in the back of a taxi has become a deserved classic of American film, and a masterclass in method acting, as Brando berates Steiger, his gangland brother, for forcing him to lose a boxing match: 'See! You don't understand! I could've been a contender. I could've had class and been somebody. Real class, instead of a bum.'

'The whole world loves him!'

Tom Jones
GB   1963   129m   Eastmancolor
UA/Woodfall (Tony Richardson)
▭ ▤ ⌖ ◉ ◎

w John Osborne *novel* Henry Fielding *d* Tony
Richardson *ph* Walter Lassally, Manny Wynn *m* John
Addison *pd* Ralph Brinton *ad* Ted Marshall *ed* Antony
Gibbs

☆ *Albert Finney* (Tom Jones), Susannah York (Sophie
Western), Hugh Griffith (Squire Western), Edith Evans (Miss
Western), Joan Greenwood (Lady Bellaston), Diane Cilento
(Molly Seagrim), George Devine (Squire Allworthy), Joyce
Redman (Mrs. Waters/Jenny Jones), David Warner (Blifil),
Wilfrid Lawson (Black George), Freda Jackson (Mr.
Seagrim), Rachel Kempson (Bridget Allworthy)

'Uncertainty, nervousness, muddled method …
desperation is writ large over it.' – *Stanley
Kauffmann*

'I just felt I was being used. I wasn't involved … I
was bored most of the time.' – *Albert Finney*

• The narrator was Michael MacLiammoir.
🏆 best picture; John Osborne; Tony Richardson; John
Addison
🏆 Albert Finney; Hugh Griffith; Edith Evans; Diane Cilento;
Joyce Redman; production design
🏆 best film; best British film; John Osborne

55
Tom Jones

In 18th-century England an abandoned illegitimate boy is raised by the squire and has many amorous adventures before marrying.

Henry Fielding's 18th-century classic novel, of a foundling who is brought up by the squire and marries a lady after many adventures, was given a riotously updated treatment by Tony Richardson, aided by John Osborne's iconoclastic script and Albert Finney's exuberant hero. It became a fantasia on Old England, at some distance from the original, with Richardson trying every possible jokey approach against a meticulously realistic physical background. Despite trade fears, the *Hellzapoppin* style made it an astonishing box-office success (the sex helped). Richardson later reflected that it had not been a happy or cohesive production; fortunately, that does not show on the screen.

Annie Hall
US 1977 93m DeLuxe
UA/Jack Rollins-Charles H. Joffe (Fred T. Gallo)
◧ ▤ ◷ ◎ ◉
Sub-title: *A Nervous Romance*
w Woody Allen, Marshall Brickman *d* Woody Allen
ph Gordon Willis *m* various *ad* Mel Bourne *ed* Wendy
Greene Bricmont, Ralph Rosenblum
☆ *Woody Allen* (Alvy Singer), *Diane Keaton* (Annie Hall),
Tony Roberts (Rob), Carol Kane (Allison), Paul Simon (Tony
Lacey), Shelley Duvall (Pam), Colleen Dewhurst (Mom
Hall), Christopher Walken (Duane Hall)

'The film's priceless vignettes about the difficulties
in chitchatting with strangers, the awkward
moments in family visits, and the frequent
breakdowns in communication and failures in
intimacy, its reminiscences about the palpable
horrors of growing up in Brooklyn, and its comic
encounters with lobsters in the kitchen or spiders
in the bathroom, all seem like snapshots from Allen
and Keaton's own romance.' – *Les Keyser,
Hollywood in the Seventies*

● The narrative supposedly mirrors the real-life affair of the
stars, who separated before the film came out. (Diane
Keaton's family name is Hall.)
▲ best picture; script; direction; Diane Keaton
♟ Woody Allen (as actor)
Ⓣ best film; script; Woody Allen (as director); Diane
Keaton

54
Annie Hall

*A Jewish comedian reflects on his childhood and failed marriages as
he relates his latest doomed relationship.*

The success of this comedy turned its creator from a minority performer to a superstar. Its story, of a Jewish comedian who has an affair
with a midwestern girl set against the neuroses of New York and Los
Angeles, was a semi-serious collage of jokes and bits of technique,
some of the former very funny and some of the latter very successful.
As Alvy Singer, who is very much Woody Allen's alter ego, shuffles
through his life and failures at love, the film's non-linear structure
forces juxtapositions that add to its emotional resonance; it is a funny
film, but is not without moments of pain.

The Red Shoes
GB 1948 136m Technicolor
GFD/The Archers (Michael Powell, Emeric
Pressburger)
◧ ▤ ◷ ◎ ◉ ◠
wd Michael Powell, Emeric Pressburger *ph* Jack Cardiff
m Brian Easdale *pd* Hein Heckroth *ad* Arthur Lawson,
Hein Heckroth *ed* Reginald Mills
☆ *Anton Walbrook* (Boris Lermontov), *Moira Shearer*
(Victoria Page), Marius Goring (Julian Craster), Robert
Helpmann (Ivan Boleslawsky), Albert Basserman (Sergei
Ratov), Frederick Ashton, Leonide Massine (Grischa
Ljubov), Ludmilla Tcherina (Irina Boronskaja), Esmond
Knight (Livy)

'In texture, like nothing the British cinema has ever
seen.' – *Time Out, 1981*

▲ Brian Easdale; Hein Heckroth
♟ best picture; original story (Michael Powell, Emeric
Pressburger); editing

53
The Red Shoes

*Tragic consequences ensue when a young ballerina becomes a star
and is forced to choose between love and her career.*

Never was a better film made from such a penny-plain story of a girl
student who becomes a great ballet star but commits suicide when
torn between love and her career. The splendour of the production is in
the intimate view it gives of life backstage in the ballet world with its
larger-than-life characters. The ballet excerpts are very fine, and the
colour discreet; the whole film is charged with excitement. It is a study
in high romanticism, a story of art as something to die for. The executives of J. Arthur Rank, its British distributor, hated the film so much
that they hardly released it; it was the Americans who first recognized
its qualities. It remains a sport among British films, an intensely cinematic work that owed nothing to the naturalistic tradition of local
cinema but was a compelling work of dark fantasy, of art for death's
sake.

'Nine men who came too late and stayed too long!'

'The land had changed. They hadn't. The earth had changed. They couldn't!'

The Wild Bunch
US   1969   145m   Technicolor   Panavision
Warner Seven Arts/Phil Feldman
▣ ▣ ▤ ◎ ⊚ ◉ ⌒
w Walon Green, Sam Peckinpah *d* Sam Peckinpah
ph Lucien Ballard *m* Jerry Fielding *ad* Edward Carrere
ed Lou Lombardo
☆ William Holden (Pike Bishop), Ernest Borgnine (Dutch Engstrom), Robert Ryan (Deke Thornton), Edmond O'Brien (Sykes), Warren Oates (Lyle Gorch), Jaime Sanchez (Angel), Ben Johnson (Tector Gorch), Strother Martin (Coffer), L. Q. Jones (T.C.), Albert Dekker (Pat Harrigan)

'A western that enlarged the form aesthetically, thematically, demonically.' – *Stanley Kauffmann, 1972*

''The bloody deaths are voluptuous, frightening, beautiful. Pouring new wine into the bottle of the western, Peckinpah explodes the bottle; his story is too simple for this imagist epic.' – *Pauline Kael, New Yorker*

'One of the most moving elegies for a vanished age ever created within the genre.' – *Time Out, 1984*

♟ script; Jerry Fielding

52
The Wild Bunch

In 1914, Texas bandits are ambushed by an old enemy and die bloodily in defence of one of their number against a ruthless Mexican revolutionary.

Peckinpah called his blood-soaked epic "a simple story about bad men in changing times", but it is also about changing men in bad times. From the opening, with smiling children stirring scorpions into an ant's nest, he plunges into a world of casual, haphazard violence. There is a gradual re-awakening among its world-weary, saddle-sore killers, of a sense of honour or, at least, loyalty. For all its many slow-motion deaths, it is a movie driven by character rather than action, and it is this that gives it both interest and abiding excitement, aided by a grizzled cast that included some of the best character actors in American cinema.

If ...
GB   1968   111m   Eastmancolor
Paramount/Memorial (Lindsay Anderson, Michael Medwin)
◧ ▦ ◕~

w David Sherwin d Lindsay Anderson ph Miroslav Ondricek m Marc Wilkinson pd Jocelyn Herbert ad Brian Eatwell ed David Gladwell
☆ Malcolm McDowell (Mick Travers), David Wood (Johnny), Richard Warwick (Wallace), Robert Swann (Rowntree), Christine Noonan (The Girl), Peter Jeffrey (Headmaster), Arthur Lowe (Mr. Kemp, Housemaster), Anthony Nicholls (Gen. Denson)

'The school ... is the perfect metaphor for the established system all but a few of us continue to accept.' – David Wilson

'It's something like the Writing on the Wall.' – Lindsay Anderson

'Combines a cold and queasy view of youth with a romantic view of violence.' – New Yorker

● It won the Palme D'Or at the 1969 Cannes Film Festival.

51
If ...

Discontent at a boys' public school breaks out into rebellion.

Lindsay Anderson catches perfectly a mood of rebellion and dissatisfaction with the status quo in his fable of discontent that escalates to a full-scale revolt at a boys' public school, which is a microcosm of a class-ridden larger society. His allegorical treatment of school life puts the emphasis on a direct narrative enhanced by clever cutting and a variety of pace. The change from colour to monochrome and vice versa began because it was too expensive to shoot some sequences in colour; Anderson then decided that colour was enhanced when it was used intermittently. The film deals with revolution as style, epitomized by Malcolm McDowell's swaggering performance as the leading anarchist.

Fitzcarraldo
West Germany   1982   158m   colour
Werner Herzog/ProjectFilmproduktion/Zweite Deutsches Fernsehen/Wildlife Films, Peru (Werner Herzog, Lucki Stipetic)
◧ ◨ ▦ ◷ ◔

wd Werner Herzog ph Thomas Mauch m Popol Vuh ad Henning von Gierke ed Beata Mainka-Jellinghaus
☆ Klaus Kinski (Brian Sweeney Fitzgerald/Fitzcarraldo), Claudia Cardinale (Molly), José Lewgoy (Don Aquilino), Paul Hittscher (Capt. Orinoco Paul), Miguel Angel Fuentes (Cholo the Mechanic), Huerequeque Enrique Bohorquez (Cook)

'A fine, quirky, fascinating movie. It's a stunning spectacle, an adventure-comedy not quite like any other, and the most benign movie ever made about nineteenth century capitalism running amok.' – Vincent Canby, New York Times

● 'Fitzcarraldo' is the nearest the natives can get to 'Fitzgerald'.
● The Region 1 and Region 2 DVD releases include commentary by Werner Herzog and Lucki Stipetic.

50
Fitzcarraldo

An Irish adventurer is determined to establish an opera house in the middle of the Amazonian jungle – but first he has to haul a steamboat over a mountain.

In Peru at the turn of the century, an eccentric Irishman succeeds against all odds in establishing an opera house in the jungle in Werner Herzog's strange and brilliant film. Its centrepoint is the hero's successful attempt to drag his massive boat from one river to another by way of a mountain, a feat matched with great difficulty by the filmmakers themselves. There is a palpable sense of strain and tension present, much of it stemming from the passionate performance of the extraordinary Klaus Kinski, whose love-hate relationship with his director intensified the air of benign madness that hangs over the finished film.

Wings of Desire

Wings of Desire
France/West Germany 1987 127m
bw/colour
Road Movies/Argos films
🎞 📼 📀~ 💿 📀 🎧
original title: *Der Himmel über Berlin*
w Wim Wenders, Peter Handke *d* Wim Wenders *ph* Henri
Alekan *m* Jürgen Knieper *ad* Heidi Ludi *ed* Peter
Przygodda
☆ Bruno Ganz (Damiel), Solveig Dommartin (Marion),
Otto Sander (Cassiel), Curt Bois (Homer), Peter Falk
(Himself)

'A friend of mine says that he loved every second
of this movie and he couldn't wait to leave. To put it
simply, *Wings of Desire* has a visual fascination but
no animating force – that's part of why it's being
acclaimed as art.' – *Pauline Kael, New Yorker*

'A soaring vision that appeals to the senses and the
spirit.' – *Desson Thomson, Washington Post*

● The Region 1 and 2 DVD releases include commentary
by the director.

49
Wings of Desire

*One of Berlin's guardian angels decides to become human after falling
in love with a trapeze artist.*

In this benign fantasy, Wim Wenders imagined angels hovering over
Berlin and offering comfort to its unhappy inhabitants. One of a pair of
these guardian spirits decides he wants to be human after falling in
love with a circus performer. Wenders' marvellously photographed
encounter with humanity and recent German history is full of a quiet
joy. The angels discover the history of the city, the many nationalities
that live there, and their hopes and fears, before their own closer
involvement with earthly life. They are instructed in the ways of
humankind by a former angel, played by Peter Falk, since Wenders
needed for the role an actor who was recognizable the world over. Falk
was also not thrown by the fact there was no script so that he had to
improvise most of his lines. The film achieves a rare and generous
spirituality.

'They're young … they're in love … and
they kill people!'

Bonnie and Clyde
US 1967 111m Technicolor
Warner/Seven Arts/Tatira/Hiller (*Warren Beatty*)
🎞 📼 📀~ 💿 📀
w David Newman, Robert Benton *d* Arthur Penn
ph Burnett Guffey *m* Charles Strouse, using 'Foggy
Mountain Breakdown' by Flatt and Scruggs *ad* Dean
Tavoularis *ed* Dede Allen *cos* Theodora Van Runkle
☆ *Warren Beatty* (Clyde Barrow), *Faye Dunaway* (Bonnie
Parker), Gene Hackman (Buck Barrow), Estelle Parsons
(Blanche), *Michael J. Pollard* (C.W. Moss), Dub Taylor (Ivan
Moss), Denver Pyle (Frank Hamer), Gene Wilder (Eugene
Grizzard)

'It is a long time since we have seen an American
film so perfectly judged.' – *MFB*

'A film from which we shall date reputations and
innovations in the American cinema.' – *Alexander
Walker*

'It works as comedy, as tragedy, as entertainment,
as a meditation on the place of guns and violence
in American society.' – *Roger Ebert*

👤 Burnett Guffey; Estelle Parsons
🏆 best picture; David Newman, Robert Benton; Arthur
Penn; Warren Beatty; Faye Dunaway; Gene Hackman;
Michael J. Pollard; Theodora Van Runkle
🎭 Faye Dunaway; Michael J. Pollard

48
Bonnie and Clyde

*In the early Thirties, a thief and his girlfriend became America's most
ruthless bank robbers.*

At the time of its original release, many critics were horrified by this
very influential movie, with Bosley Crowther of the *New York Times*
calling it 'strangely antique, sentimental claptrap'. Its technically brilliant evocation of a glamorous couple of outlaws in 1930s sleepy mid-
America brought much of the energy and style of the French New Wave
to American cinema. It used every kind of cinematic trick, including
fake snapshots, farcical interludes, dreamy soft-focus and a jazzy score
to provide an ironic picture of a car thief and the daughter of his
intended victim, who team up to become America's most feared and
ruthless bank robbers and popular folk-heroes. Warren Beatty and Faye
Dunaway add a touch of glamour that lifts the outlaws out of the
ordinary. The film even made extreme violence quite fashionable (and
very bloody it is).

A Bout de Souffle

France 1960 90m bw
SNC (Georges de Beauregard)
🔲 ▬ 🔳 ◎ ◎ ◑
aka: *Breathless*

w Jean-Luc Godard *story* François Truffaut *d* Jean-Luc Godard *ph* Raoul Coutard *m* Martial Solal *ad* Claude Chabrol *ed* Cécile Decugis

☆ *Jean-Paul Belmondo* (Michel Poiccard/Laszlo Kovacs), Jean Seberg (Patricia Franchini), Daniel Boulanger (Police Inspector), Jean-Pierre Melville (Parvulesco), Jean-Luc Godard (Informer), Liliane Robin (Minouche)

'A film all dressed up for rebellion but with no real tangible territory on which to stand and fight.' – *Peter John Dyer*

'A chunk of raw drama, graphically and artfully torn with appropriately ragged edges out of the tough underbelly of modern metropolitan life.' – *Bosley Crowther, New York Times*

● See also *Breathless* (1983), American remake.
● The Region 1 DVD release has a commentary by David Sterritt. The Region 2 release includes Godard's short *Charlotte et Son Jules.*

47
A Bout de Souffle

A cop-killer and his American girlfriend go on the run in Paris.

Godard's gangster movie of a young car-thief who kills a policeman and goes on the run with his American girlfriend was one of the first and most influential works of the French New Wave. In doing something new, Godard returned to techniques that had been long disused. He shot the film silently, adding the sound in post-production; he made it on the streets of Paris using available light and sometimes pushed his cameraman along the road in a wheelchair. He wanted to suggest that the techniques of making a movie had only just been discovered. The improvised nature of the actual filming was matched by the haphazard script, in which scenes were quickly scribbled by Godard at the start of each day, and the impulsive performances of Jean-Paul Belmondo and Jean Seberg. Though the result is reminiscent of both *Quai des Brumes* and innumerable American gangster thrillers (the film is dedicated to Monogram), his approach gave it a casual charm that has not faded.

Jules et Jim

France 1962 105m bw Franscope
Films du Carrosse/SEDIF (Marcel Berbert)
🔲 ▬ 🔳 ◎ ◎ ◑

w François Truffaut, Jean Gruault *novel* Henri-Pierre Roché *d* François Truffaut *ph* Raoul Coutard *m* Georges Delerue *ed* Claudine Bouche

☆ Oskar Werner (Jules), *Jeanne Moreau* (Catherine), Henri Serre (Jim), Vanna Urbino (Gilberte), Boris Bassiak (Albert), Anny Nelsen (Lucie)

'The sense is of a director intoxicated with the pleasure of making films.' – *Penelope Houston, MFB*

'An arch and arty study of the perversities of women and the patience of men.' – *Bosley Crowther, New York Times*

● The Region 2 DVD release includes audio commentary by Jeanne Moreau.

46
Jules et Jim

A young woman maintains loving relationships with two men.

In Paris before World War I, a girl alternates between a French and a German student, and after the war they meet again to form a constantly shifting triangle in François Truffaut's quintessentially French period romance. Truffaut once called Jeanne Moreau 'the greatest sweetheart in French cinema', and she proves it with an enchanting star performance. The film is charming and melancholy, technically interesting, emotionally uplifting, and acted and directed with verve and feeling. It opens with a brisk montage that creates a period style and a fast-paced narrative suggesting the exuberance of youth before settling into a deft and leisurely examination of romance and the varieties of love.

Jules et Jim

Weekend
France/Italy   1968   103m   Eastmancolor
Comacico/Copernic/Lira/Ascot

◖◗ ▆

wd Jean-Luc Godard *ph* Raoul Coutard *m* Antoine
Duhamel, Mozart *ed* Agnes Guillemot

☆ Mireille Darc (Corinne), Jean Yanne (Roland), Jean-
Pierre Kalfon (Leader of FLSO), Valerie Lagrange (His Moll),
Jean-Pierre Léaud (Saint-Just/Man in Phone Booth), Yves
Beneyton (Member of FLSO), Paul Gegauff (Pianist)

'Though deeply flawed, this film has more depth
than any of Godard's earlier work. It's his vision of
Hell and it ranks with the greatest.' – *Pauline Kael,
New Yorker*

'The film must be seen, for its power, ambition,
humor and scenes of really astonishing beauty.'
– *Renata Adler, New York Times*

45
Weekend

*A Parisian couple is trapped in an endless traffic jam along a French
country road.*

Jean-Luc Godard's brilliant black satire is at the expense of consumerism and conventional values. He sets it in the ultimate gridlocked
traffic jam, in which a bourgeois Parisian couple gets stuck while trying
to escape the city for a country weekend. The scene is set with a
superbly executed ten-minute tracking shot along the unmoving cars
stuck on a French country road that ends in the horror of a multiple
pile-up that has left bloody bodies lying on the road. As cars crash,
tempers fray and savagery takes over, culminating in cannibalism.
Interspersed with lectures on revolutionary matters that do not much
matter, it is otherwise a bleak and apocalyptic vision of the false values
of present day society, filmed with venomous and deadly invention. It
was, wrote Godard, 'a film found on a scrap heap.'

One Flew over the Cuckoo's Nest
US   1975   134m   DeLuxe
UA/Fantasy Films (Saul Zaentz, Michael Douglas)
▭▭ ▭▭ ▬ ◷ ⊚ ⊚ ⌒
w Lawrence Hauben, Bo Goldman *novel* Ken Kesey *play*
d Milos Forman *ph* Haskell Wexler, Bill Butler, William
Fraker *m* Jack Nitzsche *pd* Paul Sylbert *ad* Edwin
O'Donovan *ed* Richard Chew, Sheldon Kahn, Lynzee
Klingman
☆ *Jack Nicholson* (Randle Patrick McMurphy), *Louise
Fletcher* (Nurse Mildred Ratched), William Redfield
(Harding), Will Sampson (Chief Bromden), Brad Dourif
(Billy Bibbit), Christopher Lloyd (Taber), Scatman Crothers
(Turkle), Danny DeVito (Martini)
● Kirk Douglas bought the rights to the book and starred in
a Broadway adaptation of it, but he was unable to obtain
backing for a film version. When Michael Douglas obtained
finance from outside the movie industry, his father was too
old to play the lead role. James Caan turned down the role.
Louise Fletcher's role was turned down by Anne Bancroft,
Angela Lansbury and Ellen Burstyn.
● Regions1 and 2 two-disc Special Edition DVD releases
include commentary by Milos Forman, Michael Douglas
and Saul Zaentz.
🏆 best picture; script; Milos Forman; Jack Nicholson;
Louise Fletcher
⚖ Haskell Wexler; Jack Nitzsche; Brad Dourif; editing
🏆 best picture; Milos Forman; Jack Nicholson; Louise
Fletcher; Brad Dourif; editing

44

One Flew over the Cuckoo's Nest

A harrowing but darkly comic film about a cheerful immoralist subverting the regime of a state mental hospital.

The crux of Milos Forman's anti-authoritarian film is a power battle between a harshly repressive nurse and McMurphy, a hell-raising convict who fakes madness in the belief he will have an easier time in a mental hospital. It ends in a defeat that is also a victory. McMurphy's rebellion finally leads to his destruction, but his example sets others free. This wildly and unexpectedly commercial film, of a project which had lain dormant for 14 years, is amusing and horrifying. Its success depends upon its two beautifully matched leading performances. The film has a bigger purpose; it suggests that the mental ward is a microcosm of society in general. Whether or not it convinces on that level, it is certainly impossible to ignore.

'You can't kiss away a murder!'

Double Indemnity
US   1944   107m   bw
Paramount (Joseph Sistrom)
▣ ▤ ◉ ◎
w Billy Wilder, Raymond Chandler *novel* James M. Cain
d Billy Wilder *ph* John Seitz *m* Miklos Rozsa *ad* Hans
Dreier, Hal Pereira *ed* Doane Harrison
☆ *Fred MacMurray* (Walter Neff), *Barbara Stanwyck*
(Phyllis Dietrichson), *Edward G. Robinson* (Barton Keyes),
Tom Powers (Mr Dietrichson), Porter Hall (Mr. Jackson),
Jean Heather (Lola Dietrichson), Byron Barr (Nino Zachette),
Richard Gaines (Mr Norton)

'The sort of film which revives a critic from the
depressive effects of bright epics about the big
soul of America or the suffering soul of Europe and
gives him a new lease of faith.' – *Richard
Winnington*

'The most pared-down and purposeful film ever
made by Billy Wilder.' – *John Coleman, 1966*

'Profoundly, intensely entertaining.' – *Richard
Mallett, Punch*

'One of the highest summits of *film noir* … without
a single trace of pity or love.' – *Charles Higham,
1971*

♟ best picture; script, direction; John Seitz; Miklos Rozsa;
Barbara Stanwyck; sound recording (Loren L. Ryder)

43
Double Indemnity

A wife seduces an insurance agent into murdering her husband.

Raymond Chandler, writing his first Hollywood script in collaboration
with Billy Wilder, thought the agonizing experience had shortened his
life; but it gave immortality to the resulting movie, in which an insurance agent connives with the glamorous wife of a client to kill her husband and collect. Based on a novel by another detective story writer,
James M. Cain (whose books Chandler disliked), it is the archetypal
film noir of the Forties. The hero who is also the villain was almost a
new concept, and he tells his story in flashback, dictating it in his office
as he bleeds to death from a gunshot wound. Brilliantly made and inci-
sively written, it perfectly captures the decayed Los Angeles atmosphere of a Chandler novel but using a simpler story and more
substantial characters.

The Battleship Potemkin
USSR   1925   75m approx (16 fps)   bw
silent; sound version 65m
Goskino
▣ ▤ ◉ ◎ ◎
original title: *Bronenosets Potemkin*
wd Sergei Eisenstein *ph* Edouard Tissé, V. Popov
ad Vasili Rakhals *ed* Sergei Eisenstein
☆ A. Antonov (Vakulinchuk), Grigori Alexandrov (Senior
Officer Gilyarovsky), Vladimir Barsky (Commander Golikov),
Aleksandr Levshin (Petty Officer), Ivan Bobrov (Humiliated
Soldier), Mikhail Gomorov (Sailor Matyushenko)

'One of the fundamental landmarks of cinema.'
– *Roger Ebert*

'Great as it undoubtedly is, it's not really a likable
film; it's amazing, though – it keeps its freshness
and excitement, even if you resist its cartoon
message.' – *Pauline Kael*

42
The Battleship Potemkin

*In 1905, sailors mutiny in Odessa at the start of the revolution in
Russia.*

As part of the Soviet Union's 20th anniversary celebrations of the
mutiny at Odessa, an episode in the 1905 revolution, Eisenstein made
his partly fictitious account of the sailors' revolt. It is a textbook cinema
classic, and masterpiece of creative editing, especially in the famous
Odessa Steps sequence (copied by, among others, Brian de Palma in
his film *The Untouchables*) in which innocent civilians are mown down
by Tsarist troops; the bloody happenings of a minute are lengthened to
five by frenzied cross-cutting. The film contains 1,300 separate shots,
and was judged the best film ever made in 1948 and 1958 by a panel of
international judges.

'To have seen it is to wear a badge of courage!'

'A monster science created but could not destroy!'

Frankenstein
US   1931   71m   bw
Universal (Carl Laemmle Jnr)

w Garrett Fort, Francis Edwards Faragoh, John L. Balderston *play* Peggy Webling *novel* Mary Wollstonecraft Shelley *d* James Whale *ph* Arthur Edeson *m* David Broekman *ad* Charles D. Hall *ed* Clarence Kolster, Maurice Pivar

☆ *Boris Karloff* (The Monster), *Colin Clive* (Henry Frankenstein), *Mae Clarke* (Elizabeth), John Boles (Victor Moritz), *Edward Van Sloan* (Dr Waldman), *Frederick Kerr* (Baron Frankenstein), *Dwight Frye* (Fritz, the Dwarf)

'Still the most famous of all horror films, and deservedly so.' – *John Baxter, 1968*

'The horror is cold, chilling the marrow but never arousing malaise.' – *Carlos Clarens*

41
Frankenstein

A scientist creates a living creature from corpses, but it becomes a monster.

Whole books have been written about this film and its sequels, in which a research scientist creates from corpses a living monster, which then runs amok. Apart from being a fascinating if primitive cinematic work in its own right, it set its director and star on interesting paths and established a Hollywood attitude towards horror. It was a European approach. The director and most of the actors were British, and the style was largely borrowed from German silents such as *The Golem*. Colin Clive as Frankenstein provided the model for all future mad scientists and Boris Karloff brought a peculiar poignancy to his portrayal of the monster. A seminal film indeed, which at each repeated viewing belies its age.

'There's no speed limit and no brake When Sullivan travels with Veronica Lake!'

Sullivan's Travels
US   1941   90m   bw
Paramount (Paul Jones)

wd Preston Sturges *ph* John Seitz *m* Leo Shuken *ad* Hans Dreier, Earl Hedrick *ed* Stuart Gilmore

☆ *Joel McCrea* (John L. Sullivan), *Veronica Lake* (The Girl), *Robert Warwick* (Mr Lebrand), William Demarest (Mr. Jones), Franklin Pangborn (Mr Casalais), Porter Hall (Mr Hadrian), Byron Foulger (Mr Valdelle), Eric Blore (Sullivan's Valet), Robert Greig (Sullivan's Butler), Torben Meyer (The Doctor), *Jimmy Conlin* (Trusty), Margaret Hayes (Secretary)

'A brilliant fantasy in two keys – slapstick farce and the tragedy of human misery.' – *James Agee*

'The most witty and knowing spoof of Hollywood movie-making of all time.' – *Film Society Review*

'A deftly sardonic apologia for Hollywood make-believe.' – *New York Times*

'Reflecting to perfection the mood of wartime Hollywood, it danced on the grave of Thirties social cinema.' – *Eileen Bowser, 1969*

● A Region 1 DVD release includes a documentary on Preston Sturges and commentary by Kenneth Bowser, Noah Baumbach, Christopher Guest and Michael McKean.

40
Sullivan's Travels

A Hollywood director tires of comedy and goes out to find real life.

This marvellously sustained tragi-comedy ranges from pratfalls to a chain gang and never loses its grip or balance. It is also a defence of Hollywood's escapist entertainment. Sturges's story of a Hollywood director who grows tired of making trivial movies and goes out into the world to experience the realities of life, was in part a defence of his own attitudes and artistic beliefs. His hero longs to make films of social realism with a little sex. He decides to find out how the poor live by disguising himself as a hobo and discovers, after being thrown in jail, that comedy brightens the dreariness of many people's lives. In this instance, he was right.

'Love is a mighty power.'

Breaking the Waves
Denmark/Sweden/France/Netherlands   1996
159m   colour   Super 35
Guild/Zentropa/Trust/Liberator/Argus/Northern Lights
(Vibeke Windelöv, Peter Aalbaek Jensen)
🎞 ▦ ⊚ ⊚ ⌒

w Lars von Trier, Peter Asmussen d Lars von Trier
ph Robby Müller m Joachim Holbek ad Karl Juliusson
ed Anders Refn
☆ Emily Watson (Bess), Stellan Skarsgård (Jan), Katrin
Cartlidge (Dodo), Jean-Marc Barr (Terry), Udo Kier (Man on
the Trawler), Adrian Rawlins (Dr Richardson), Jonathan
Hackett (The Minister), Sandra Voe (Bess's Mother)

'An astonishing film, so well thought-out and
passionately executed that it's only afterwards, if
then, that audiences will wonder exactly what they
have been persuaded to think and feel.' – Adam
Mars-Jones, Independent

'Acted with a conviction you rarely find, it's one of
those movies that affects you in such a profound
way. Believe me, this one's a life-altering
experience.' – Alan Jones, Film Review

● The film won the Grand Jury Prize at the Cannes Film
Festival in 1996.
● The Region 2 DVD release includes commentary by Lars
von Trier and Anders Refn.
♟ Emily Watson

39
Breaking the Waves

A young woman prostitutes herself to save her husband's life.

Lars von Trier's film of a young woman in a remote part of Scotland,
who humiliates herself in the hope of saving the life of her husband,
paralyzed in an accident on an oil rig, is a remarkable and striking
work, though in some ways a dislikeable one. It has a raw, emotional
power rarely encountered on film, owing to Emily Watson's soulful and
guileless central performance and the restlessly casual, close-up
camera work. But its theme, an apparent celebration of self-sacrifice
through sexual degradation, is often unlovely and hard to take. The
ending suggests that von Trier may have been watching *Ordet*, a film
by his fellow countryman Carl Dreyer, that also deals with the effects of
an irrational faith.

'Real life screened more daringly than it's
ever been before!'

The Magnificent Ambersons
US   1942   88m   bw
RKO/Mercury (Orson Welles)
🎞 ▦ ⊚ ⌒

wd Orson Welles novel Booth Tarkington ph Stanley
Cortez m Bernard Herrmann ad Mark-Lee Kirk ed Robert
Wise, Mark Robson
☆ Joseph Cotten (Eugene Morgan), Dolores Costello
(Isabel Amberson Minafer), Agnes Moorehead (Fanny
Amberson), Tim Holt (George Amberson Minafer), Anne
Baxter (Lucy Morgan), Ray Collins (Jack Amberson),
Richard Bennett (Major Amberson), Erskine Sanford
(Benson), Donald Dillaway (Wilbur Minafer)

'Rich in ideas that many will want to copy,
combined in the service of a story that few will care
to imitate.' – C. A. Lejeune

'Nearly every scene is played with a casual
perfection which could only come from endless
painstaking planning and rehearsals, and from a
wonderful sense of timing.' – Basil Wright, 1972

● Previously filmed in 1925 as *Pampered Youth*.
● The credits are all at the end and all spoken, ending with:
'I wrote and directed the picture. My name is Orson Welles.'
♟ best picture; Stanley Cortez; Agnes Moorehead; art
direction–interior decoration (Albert D'Agostino, A. Roland
Fields, Darrell Silvera)

38
The Magnificent Ambersons

A proud family falls on hard times.

Orson Welles' film of the decline of a proud family, which loses its
wealth and its control of the neighbourhood, might well have been his
masterpiece. But he had not reckoned with the studio butchering the
editing, weakening the latter half of the film, while Welles was out of the
country. It remains a fascinating period drama of a family riven with
rivalries and dominated by the snobbish, callow son who prevents his
widowed mother finding happiness with the man she loves. Told in brilliant cinematic snippets, the whole is a treat for connoisseurs and a
delight in its fast-moving control of cinematic narrative.

Tristana

Spain/Italy/France 1970 105m Eastmancolor
Academy/Connoisseur/Epoca/Talia/Selenia/Les Films
Corona (Juan Estelrich)

▣ ▤

w Luis Buñuel, Julio Alejandro *novel* Benito Pérez Galdós
d Luis Buñuel *ph* José F. Aguayo *ad* Enrique Alarcón
ed Pedro Del Rey
☆ Catherine Deneuve (Tristana), Fernando Rey (Don
Lope), Franco Nero (Horacio), Lola Gaos (Saturna), Antonio
Casas (Don Cosme), Jesús Fernández (Saturno)

'It is Buñuel at his most majestic.' – *Tom Milne,
MFB*

'A marvellously complex, funny and vigorously
moral movie that also is, to me, his most perfectly
cast film.' – *Vincent Canby, New York Times*

♟ best foreign film

37
Tristana

A womanizing aristrocrat comes to regret seducing his young ward.

Buñuel created a complex black comedy of obsessive behaviour, in which an impoverished, womanizing aristocrat seduces his young ward and pays the price for his action. He set the story in provincial Spain of the 1920s to emphasize the repressive environment in which both live. Don Lope (Fernando Rey) is a suffocating presence in the life of Tristana (Catherine Deneuve), and she finds herself able to escape him only briefly, with a younger man who lacks courage. She returns as she loses a leg to cancer, an event that gives her the strength to dominate Don Lope by marrying him. Buñuel's style and humour enliven this, by his standards, straightforward narrative that also provides him with the opportunity to mock religion and other forms of consolation.

'Three Decades of Life in the Mafia.'
GoodFellas

US 1990 146m Technicolor
Warner (Irwin Winkler)

▣ ▤ ⊛ ◉ ◎ ⌂

w Martin Scorsese, Nicholas Pileggi *novel Wiseguy* by
Nicholas Pileggi *d* Martin Scorsese *ph* Michael Ballhaus
pd Kristi Zea *ad* Maher Ahmad *ed* Thelma Schoonmaker
☆ Robert De Niro (James Conway), *Ray Liotta* (Henry
Hill), *Joe Pesci* (Tommy DeVito), Lorraine Bracco (Karen
Hill), Paul Sorvino (Paul Cicero), Frank Sivero (Frankie
Carbone), Tony Darrow (Sonny Bunz), Mike Starr (Frenchy),
Frank Vincent (Billy Batts), Chuck Low (Morris Kessler)

'Simultaneously fascinating and repellent.'
– *Variety*

'In its own narrow, near-claustrophobic
perspective, however, driven along by a classic
soundtrack and with no shortage of master
directorial brush strokes, it is hard to imagine a
bigger picture than this.' – *Empire*

♟ Joe Pesci
♟ film; Martin Scorsese; script (Martin Scorsese, Nicholas
Pileggi); Lorraine Bracco; Thelma Schoonmaker
♟ film; Martin Scorsese; script (Martin Scorsese,
Nicholas Pileggi)

36
GoodFellas

A gangster recalls his life before he turned police informer.

Scorsese's Mafia movie deals in an original way with an original subject, a gangster who turns informer and gives up to the police his friend and mentor. It concentrates on the ordinary, everyday life of its criminal fraternity; it shows workaday finagling, not big time robbery. A brilliant, unsparing delineation of the sub-culture of crime and the corruption of the spirit it entails, it also showcases some virtuoso direction. The scenes of emotional give-and-take during the gang's table talk are superbly done, as is the way the camera weaves down corridors and into dim-lit rooms in pursuit of its unlovely, amoral characters.

Casablanca

US 1942 102m bw
Warner (Hal B. Wallis)
▢▢ ▤ 🔊 @ ⊙ ℧ ⌂

w *Julius J. Epstein, Philip G. Epstein, Howard Koch* play *Everybody Comes to Rick's* by Murray Burnett, Joan Alison d *Michael Curtiz* ph *Arthur Edeson* m *Max Steiner* ed *Owen Marks*
☆ *Humphrey Bogart* (Rick Blaine), *Ingrid Bergman* (Ilse Lund), Paul Henreid (Victor Laszlo), *Claude Rains* (Captain Louis Renault), Sydney Greenstreet (Ferrari), Peter Lorre (Ugarte), S. Z. Sakall (Carl), *Conrad Veidt* (Major Strasser), *Dooley Wilson* (Sam), *Marcel Dalio* (Croupier), Joy Page, John Qualen, Ludwig Stossel, Leonid Kinskey, Helmut Dantine and also Ilka Gruning

'It's far from a great film, but it has an appealingly schlocky romanticism, and you're never really pressed to take its melodramatic twists and turns seriously.' – *Pauline Kael, 70s*

● Originally named for the leads were Ronald Reagan, Ann Sheridan and Dennis Morgan
♪ 'As Time Goes By', 'Knock on Wood'
🏆 best picture; Julius J. and Philip G. Epstein, Howard Koch; Michael Curtiz
🎭 Arthur Edeson; Max Steiner; Humphrey Bogart; Claude Rains; Owen Marks

35
Casablanca

Cynical café owner Rick Blaine abandons his neutrality to help an old love escape the Nazis with her idealistic husband.

This romantic movie is cinema *par excellence*: a studio-bound Hollywood melodrama, which, after various chances, just fell together impeccably into one of the outstanding entertainment experiences of cinema history. From the basis of an unproduced play, the screenwriters fashioned a story that gave Bogart one of his great roles as Rick, whose café in Casablanca is a centre for war refugees awaiting visas for America. It enabled him to be at first a world-weary cynic ('I stick my neck out for nobody. I'm the only cause I'm interested in.') and then transcend his bitterness to help an old love escape the Nazis with her underground-leader husband. What more could you ask for than love, intrigue, excitement, suspense and humour cunningly deployed by master technicians and a perfect cast?

Belle de Jour

France/Italy 1967 100m Eastmancolor
Paris Film/Five Film (Robert and Raymond Hakim)
▢▢ ▤ @~ ⊙ ⊙

w *Luis Buñuel, Jean-Claude Carrière* novel Joseph Kessel d *Luis Buñuel* ph *Sacha Vierny* m none ad Robert Clavel ed Louisette Hautecoeur, Walter Spohr
☆ *Catherine Deneuve* (Séverine Serizy), Jean Sorel (Pierre Serizy), Michel Piccoli (Henri Husson), Genevieve Page (Madame Anais), Pierre Clémenti (Marcel)

'Oppressively powerful. Like being buried alive in Sarah Bernhardt's dressing room.' – *Wilfred Sheed*

'The rhythm of the writing, the color changes, acting tempos, camera angles, the whole editing – all this is perfect. There is not one extraneous shot, nor one that is missing. Disparate elements are embraced in a self-possessed, lucidly enchanting flow.' – *John Simon*

● It won the Golden Lion for best film at the Venice Film Festival in 1967.
● The Region 1 DVD release includes an interview with Catherine Deneuve and commentary by Buñuel scholar Julie Jones.

34
Belle de Jour

A surgeon's wife with masochistic tendencies finds sexual fulfilment working in a brothel.

Buñuel's fascinating film about a respectable woman who finds herself drawn to afternoon work in a brothel was ideally cast. Catherine Deneuve, as Séverine, had the perfect self-contained quality to suggest a woman who needed the admiration of others on her own terms. The film's erotic tension stems from this masochistic fantasy life, free from the restraints of her bourgeois marriage. Buñuel, impeccably weaving a mixture of fact and fantasy into a rich fabric, also wanted an imaginative response from his audience. Often asked about its best known scene and what it was that the Asian client had in his little box that horrified the other prostitutes and intrigued Séverine, he would answer, 'Whatever you want there to be.'

Alexander Nevsky

Alexander Nevsky
USSR   1938   112m   bw
Mosfilm

w Pyotr Pavlenko, Sergei Eisenstein *d* Sergei Eisenstein *ph* Edouard Tissé *m* Sergei Prokofiev *ad* I. Shpinel, N. Soloviov, K. Yeliseyev
☆ *Nikolai Cherkassov* (Prince Alexander Yaroslavich Nevsky), Nikolai Okhlopkov (Vassily Buslai), Andrei Abrikosov (Gavrilo Olexich), Dmitri Orlov (Ignat, Master Armourer), Vasili Novikov (Pavsha, Governor of Pskov)

'The picture will meet with good results wherever its political sentiments find established adherents. Otherwise it's almost nil for general appeal.'
– *Variety*

'Superb sequences of cinematic opera that pass from pastoral to lamentation and end in a triumphal cantata.' – *Georges Sadoul*

33
Alexander Nevsky

In 1242, Prince Alexander Nevsky defeats the invading Teutonic Knights in a battle on the ice of Lake Peipus.

Eisenstein's first sound film is a splendid historical and patriotic pageant about Prince Alexander Nevsky, who, in 1242, defeated the invading Teutonic Knights in a battle on the ice of Lake Peipus. It shows the director at his most inventively pictorial and climaxes in a superb battle sequence, using music instead of natural sound, that has since inspired many other movie combats, from *Henry V* to *The Lord of the Rings*. The movie's almost musical construction is enhanced by Sergei Prokofiev's dramatic score, with the vivid action edited to the music.

'The Revolt That Stirred The World!'
The Battle of Algiers
Algeria/Italy   1965   135m   bw
Casbah/Igor (Antonio Musi, Yacef Saadi)

original title: *La Battaglia di Algeri*
w Franco Solinas *d* Gillo Pontecorvo *ph* Marcello Gatti *m* Ennio Morricone, Gillo Pontecorvo *pd* Sergio Canevari *ed* Mario Morra, Mario Serandrei
☆ Brahim Haggiag (Ali La Pointe), Jean Martin (Colonel), Yacef Saadi (Kader), Tommaso Neri (Captain), Samia Kerbash (One of the Girls), Ugo Paletti (Captain)

'An astonishing piece of work in directorial technique processing to achieve not merely a newsreel tempo but a grainy realism unmatched by the average news film and all too rarely approached by even the better ventures into cinéma vérité. What is equally noteworthy is Pontecorvo's objectivity in showing both the exhilaration and the heart-break of a fight for liberation, with neither the oppressed nor the oppressor able to survive at ease with his conscience.' – *Judith Crist*

● The Region 2 DVD release includes an interview with Gillo Pontecorvo.
⚿ best foreign film; Franco Solinas; Gillo Pontecorvo (as director)

32
The Battle of Algiers

In 1954 Algiers, an ex-convict joins the terrorists in rebellion against the French government.

Before the invasion of Iraq in 2003, American military personnel saw a screening at the Pentagon of Pontecorvo's brilliant reconstruction of a bitter period of French colonial history. It was a tribute to its accuracy and lasting relevance. In documentary style, Pontecorvo detailed the Algerian uprising for independence of the 1950s, and the harsh struggle that developed between the French forces, using conventional military tactics, including torture, and the unorthodox nationalist guerrillas, who blew up restaurants and shot policemen on sight. The film is remarkably even-handed in its treatment of the atrocities committed by both sides. Yet the most chilling moment is a remark by the French commander who points out that his only duty is to win, and adds, 'I would now like to ask you a question: should France remain in Algeria? If you answer yes, then you must accept the consequences.'

2001: A Space Odyssey

GB 1968 141m Metrocolor Panavision
MGM/Stanley Kubrick (Victor Lyndon)

w Stanley Kubrick, Arthur C. Clarke *story The Sentinel* by Arthur C. Clarke *d* Stanley Kubrick *ph* Geoffrey Unsworth, John Alcott *m* Richard Strauss, Johann Strauss and other classics *pd* Tony Masters, Harry Lange, Ernie Archer *ad* John Hoesli *ed* Ray Lovejoy

☆ Gary Lockwood (Frank Poole), Keir Dullea (David Bowman), William Sylvester (Dr Heywood Floyd), Leonard Rossiter (Smyslov), Robert Beatty (Halvorsen), Daniel Richter (Moon-watcher), Douglas Rain (voice of HAL), Margaret Tyzack (Elena)

> 'Somewhere between hypnotic and immensely boring.' – *Renata Adler*

> 'Morally pretentious, intellectually obscure and inordinately long … intensely exciting visually, with that peculiar artistic power which comes from obsession … a film out of control, an infuriating combination of exactitude on small points and incoherence on large ones.' – *Arthur Schlesinger Jnr*

● Alex North's rejected score for the film has also been released on compact disc.

🎖 special visual effects (Stanley Kubrick)
🏆 script; Stanley Kubrick; art direction
🏆 cinematography; production design

31
2001: A Space Odyssey

A mind-blowing cinematic experience, Kubrick's voyage encompassed past, present and future – and about four million years.

Kubrick's psychedelic masterpiece offered a trip without the benefit of LSD to its first audiences, who enjoyed its spaced-out images, culminating in the final, obscurely symbolic sequence that ends with a enigmatic star child. Its overarching theme – from ape to modern space scientist, mankind has striven to reach the unattainable – is easier to understand than the detail of Kubrick's meditation on the future. If all art constantly aspires to the condition of music, then Kubrick got closer than most in this symphonic work of interrelated images, which has more in common with silent cinema, documentaries such as Vertov's *Man with the Movie Camera* or the lyrical features of Murnau, than with present day features.

'The Legend Comes to Life'

The Lord of the Rings: The Fellowship Of the Ring

US/New Zealand   2001   178m   DeLuxe
Super 35

Entertainment/New Line/Wingnut (Barrie M. Osborne, Peter Jackson, Fran Walsh, Tim Sanders)

📽 ▦ ⌖ ◎ ⌒

w Fran Walsh, Philippa Boyens, Peter Jackson *d* Peter Jackson *ph* Andrew Lesnie *m* Howard Shore *pd* Grant Major *ed* John Gilbert *sp* Taylor/WETA Workshop *cos* Ngila Dickson, Richard Taylor

☆ Elijah Wood (Frodo Baggins), Ian McKellen (Gandalf), Liv Tyler (Arwen), Viggo Mortensen (Aragorn), Sean Astin (Sam), Cate Blanchett (Galadriel), John Rhys-Davies (Gimli), Billy Boyd (Pippin), Dominic Monaghan (Merry), Orlando Bloom (Legolas), Christopher Lee (Saruman), Hugo Weaving (Elrond), Sean Bean (Boromir), Ian Holm (Bilbo Baggins), Andy Serkis (Gollum)

● The film was re-released in 2003 in a version that ran for 208m.

👤 Andrew Lesnie; Howard Shore; Peter Owen, Richard Taylor; visual effects (Jim Rygiel, Randall William Cook, Richard Taylor, Mark Stetson)

♟ picture; Peter Jackson; Ian McKellen; Grant Major; Ngila Dickson, Richard Taylor; John Gilbert; sound (Christopher Boyes, Michael Semanick, Gethin Creagh, Hammond Peek); song 'May It Be' (m/l Enya, Nicky Ryan, Roma Ryan)

Ⓣ film; Peter Jackson; visual effects; make up/hair

'A New Power Is Rising.'

The Lord of the Rings: The Two Towers

US/New Zealand/Germany   2002   179m
DeLuxe   'Scope

Entertainment/New Line/Wingnut (Barrie M. Osborne, Fran Walsh, Peter Jackson)

📽 ▦ ⌖ ◎ ⌒

w Fran Walsh, Philippa Boyens, Peter Jackson *novel* J.R.R. Tolkien *d* Peter Jackson *ph* Andrew Lesnie *m* Howard Shore *pd* Grant Major *ed* Michael Horton, Jabez Olssen *sp* Richard Taylor *cos* Ngila Dickson, Richard Taylor

☆ Elijah Wood (Frodo), Ian McKellen (Gandalf), Liv Tyler (Arwen), Viggo Mortensen (Aragorn), Sean Astin (Sam), Cate Blanchett (Galadriel), John Rhys-Davies (Gimli), Bernard Hill (Theoden), Christopher Lee (Saruman), Billy Boyd (Pippin), Dominic Monaghan (Merry), Orlando Bloom (Legolas), Hugo Weaving (Elrond), Miranda Otto (Eowyn), Brad Dourif (Wormtongue) and also Andy Serkis (Gollum)

● The film was re-released in 2003 in a version that ran for 214m.

👤 visual effects (Jim Rygiel, Joe Letteri, Randall William Cook, Alex Funke); sound editing (Ethan Van der Ryn, Mike Hopkins)

♟ picture; Michael Horton; Grant Major (with Dan Hennah, Alan Lee); sound (Christopher Boyes, Michael Semanick, Michael Hedges, Hammond Peek)

Ⓣ Ngila Dickson, Richard Taylor; visual effects (Jim Rygiel, Joe Letteri, Randall William Cook, Alex Funke)

The Lord of the Rings: The Fellowship of the Ring

A hobbit inherits a magic ring that could enslave all the races of Middle Earth unless it is destroyed.

The Lord of the Rings: The Two Towers

The Fellowship of the Ring is split into three groups, each facing different dangers, as the evil Saruman launches his armies in a bid to control Middle Earth.

'A grand, even visionary entertainment.' – *Sight & Sound*

'Looks to please the book's legions of fans with its imaginatively scrupulous rendering of the tome's characters and worlds on the screen, as well as the uninitiated with its uninterrupted flow of incident and spectacle.' – *Todd McCarthy, Variety*

The Lord of the Rings: The Return of the King

As the hobbits struggle to reach Mount Doom to dispose of the cursed ring, others prepare for the final battle to free Middle Earth from evil.

'Such a crowning achievement, such a visionary use of all the tools of special effects, such a pure spectacle, that it can be enjoyed even by those who have not seen the first two films.' – *Roger Ebert, Chicago Sun-Times*

'Represents that film-making rarity – a third part of a trilogy that is decisively the best of the lot.' – *Todd McCarthy, Variety*

The Lord of the Rings: The Return of the King

New Zealand/Germany/US   2003   201m
DeLuxe   Super 35
Entertainment/New Line/Wingnut/Lord Dritte (Barrie
M. Osborne, Peter Jackson, Fran Walsh)
🎞 🎬 ⊚ ⊚ ⌒
w *Fran Walsh, Philippa Boyens, Peter Jackson*
novel J.R.R. Tolkien d *Peter Jackson* ph *Andrew Lesnie*
pd *Grant Major* ed *Jamie Selkirk* sp *Jim Rygiel; Weta*
cos *Ngila Dickson, Richard Taylor*
☆ Elijah Wood (Frodo), Ian McKellen (Gandalf), Liv Tyler
(Arwen), Viggo Mortensen (Aragorn), Sean Astin (Sam),
Cate Blanchett (Galadriel), John Rhys-Davies (Gimli),
Bernard Hill (Theoden), Billy Boyd (Pippin), Dominic
Monaghan (Merry), Orlando Bloom (Legolas), Hugo
Weaving (Elrond), Miranda Otto (Eowyn), Andy Serkis
(Gollum), Ian Holm (Bilbo)
👤 picture; Peter Jackson (as director); script; art direction;
Jamie Selkirk; Howard Shore; visual effects (Jim Rygiel, Joe
Letteri, Randall William Cook, Alex Funke); costume
design; sound (Christopher Boyes, Michael Semanick,
Michael Hedges, Hammond Peek); makeup (Richard Taylor,
Peter King); song 'Into the West' (m/l Frances Walsh,
Howard Shore, Annie Lennox)
🎗 film; script; Andrew Lesnie; visual effects

Tolkien's trilogy of a small band of friends – the Fellowship of the Ring – facing an overwhelming enemy often reads like a cross between Norse myths and *Scouting for Boys*. His heroic hobbits emulate Baden Powell's paen to the average Briton as 'our stolid, pipe-sucking manhood, reliable in the tightest of places'. Peter Jackson, in his magnificent, bravura epic, powerfully conveys the conviction that this fantasy truly deals in matters of life and death. Enhanced by the detailed design, beautifully creating different cultures, and by powerful performances, it carries the action through its occasional *longueurs*. By the third film, the struggle has become internalized: each surviving member of the fellowship has to struggle to find within himself the strength to continue in what seems to be a lost cause. Jackson orchestrates the set pieces with dazzling skill; the final battle ranks with the most thrilling and brilliant sequences on film.

Sunrise

US 1927 97m (24 fps) bw silent
Fox

⬚ ▬ ⊙ ⊚ ⌾

w Carl Mayer *novel* A Trip to Tilsit by Hermann
Sudermann *d* F. W. Murnau *ph* Karl Struss, Charles
Rosher *m* (sound version) Hugo Riesenfeld *ad* Rochas
Gliese *ed* Harold D. Schuster

☆ Janet Gaynor (The Wife), George O'Brien (The Man),
Margaret Livingston (The Woman From the City), Bodil
Rosing (The Maid), J. Farrell MacDonald (The
Photographer)

'Not since the earliest, simplest moving pictures,
when locomotives, fire engines and crowds in
streets were transposed to the screen artlessly and
endearingly, when the entranced eye was rushed
through tunnels and over precipices on runaway
trains, has there been such joy in motion as under
Murnau's direction.' – *Louise Bogan, The New
Republic*

'The story is told in a flowing, lyrical German
manner that is extraordinarily sensual, yet perhaps
too self-conscious, too fable-like, for American
audiences.' – *Pauline Kael, 70s*

👤 Karl Struss, Charles Rosher; Janet Gaynor; Unique and
Artistic Picture
♟ Rochas Gliese

29
Sunrise

*A villager in love with a city woman is torn between her and his wife,
whom he resolves to murder.*

Murnau's romantic drama was subtitled 'A Song for Two Humans' and
carried an opening title, 'You might hear it anywhere, and at any time.'
It was his most lyrical work, dealing with one of the oldest of stories, of
a man driven by his love for two women. A farmer becomes infatuated
with a holiday-making city woman and agrees to kill his wife and go to
the city with her; but instead of carrying out the crime, he repents and
the couple are reconciled. The film was among the first-ever Oscar winners, for 'artistic quality of production'. Its high romantic style, the
contrast of simplicity and sophistication in country and urban life and,
above all, its visual quality, its use of light and shade, combined to give
it a lasting vitality.

To Be or Not to Be

US 1942 99m bw
Alexander Korda/Ernst Lubitsch

⬚ ▬ ⊙

w Edwin Justus Mayer *story* Ernst Lubitsch, Melchior
Lengyel *d* Ernst Lubitsch *ph* Rudolph Maté *m* Werner
Heymann *ad* Vincent Korda *ed* Dorothy Spencer

☆ *Jack Benny* (Joseph Tura), *Carole Lombard* (Maria
Tura), Robert Stack (Lt. Stanislav Sobinski), *Stanley Ridges*
(Prof. Alexander Siletsky), *Felix Bressart* (Greenberg),
Lionel Atwill (Rawitch), *Sig Rumann* (Col. Erhardt), *Tom
Dugan* (Bronski), Charles Halton (Dobosh)

'The comedy is hilarious, even when it is
hysterically thrilling.' – *Commonweal*

'As effective an example of comic propaganda as
The Great Dictator and far better directed.' –
Charles Higham, 1972

'The actual business at hand … is nothing less
than providing a good time at the expense of Nazi
myth … Lubitsch distinguishes the film's zanier
moments with his customary mastery of sly
humour and innuendo, and when the story calls for
outright melodrama he is more than equal to the
occasion.' – *Newsweek*

● A Region 2 DVD release includes a documentary on
Lubitsch.
♟ Werner Heymann

28
To Be or Not to Be

*As the Nazis invade Poland, a troupe of actors in Warsaw is recruited
to help kill a traitor.*

This marvellous free-wheeling entertainment starts as drama and
descends through romantic comedy and suspense into black farce.
Jack Benny never had a better role than this, as vain Polish actor Josef
Tura, one of a company stuck in Warsaw who get involved in an underground plot and an impersonation of invading Nazis, including Hitler.
Lubitsch chose Benny for the role because he regarded him not as a
comedian but an actor who always played the part of a comedian. The
film was accused of bad taste at the time. The line in which a Nazi says
about Tura's acting 'What he did to Shakespeare we are now doing to
Poland', shocked audiences. Miklos Rozsa disliked the film so much
that he refused to compose the score (though he did write the music
for one scene). Now it is seen as an outstanding example of satirical
comedy, one that exposes the banality of evil.

Wild Strawberries

Sweden 1957 93m bw
Svensk Filmindustri (Allan Ekelund)
🔲 ▤ ◉~ ◉ ◉
original title: *Smultronstället*
wd Ingmar Bergman *ph* Gunnar Fischer *m* Erik Nordgren *md* E. Eckert-Lundin *ad* Gittan Gustafsson *ed* Oscar Rosendar
☆ *Victor Sjöström* (Prof. Isak Borg), *Ingrid Thulin* (Marianne Borg), Gunnar Bjornstrand (Evald Borg), Bibi Andersson (Sara), Naima Wifstrand (Isak's Mother), Jullan Kindahl (Agda)

'The work of a man obsessed by cruelty, especially spiritual cruelty, trying to find some resolution.' – Kenneth Cavander, MFB

'Wonderfully composed movie in which Bergman is able to vary the tone from melancholy to gaiety in the most deeply satisfying way.' – Peter Bradshaw, Guardian

● It won the Golden Bear award at the Berlin Film Festival in 1958.
● The Region 1 DVD release has commentary by film scholar Peter Cowie.
♟ script

27
Wild Strawberries

An elderly professor has a nightmare which causes him to think back over his long life.

The aged and ailing Victor Sjostrom, a seminal figure in Swedish cinema as actor and director, gives a remarkable performance as an elderly professor who thinks back over his long life in Ingmar Bergman's beautifully paced drama. The professor's memories, not all pleasant, are sparked by a nightmare, and he travels into his past on the road to self-revelation. This psychic journey is deepened by the people he meets on an actual trip, who include a girl reminiscent of his first love and an unhappily married couple. At the end, he is reconciled with his past. Bergman noted in his diary of these final close-ups of Sjostrom, 'Never before or since have I experienced a face so noble and liberated.'

Rashomon

Japan 1951 83m bw
Daiei (Jingo Minoura)
🔲 ▤ ◉~ ◉ ◉ 🎧
aka: *In the Woods*
wd Akira Kurosawa *stories* In a Grove; Rashomon by Ryunosuke Akutagawa *ph* Kazuo Miyagawa *m* Fumio Hayasaka *ad* So Matsuyama
☆ Toshiro Mifune (The bandit), Machiko Kyo (Masago, the samurai's wife), Masayuki Mori (The samurai), Takashi Shimura (The woodcutter), Minoru Chiaki (The priest)

'A masterpiece, and a revelation.' – Gavin Lambert, MFB

'An artistic achievement of such distinct and exotic character that it is difficult to estimate it alongside conventional story films' – Bosley Crowther, New York Times

● The Region 1 DVD release includes commentary by Japanese film historian Donald Richie.
🏆 best foreign film
♟ art direction

26
Rashomon

Four witnesses to a murder remember it differently.

Kurosawa's indescribably vivid drama introduced to cinema the novel concept of the unreliability of witnesses: in medieval Japan, four people have different versions of an incident in which a bandit attacked a nobleman in the forest. Genuinely strange (one of the versions is told by a ghost), *Rashomon* reintroduced Japanese films to the West after a gap of twenty years, creating a furore at the Venice Film Festival. Even though it is now familiar, and was even remade (badly) in Hollywood as *The Outrage* and became a Broadway play, it has lost none of its original force in its dazzling depiction of the subjectivity of truth. Despite the glimmer of hope at the end of the film, it offers a bleak and despairing view of humanity.

'Hang on for the comedy that goes to infinity and beyond!'

Toy Story
†† US 1995 80m Technicolor
Buena Vista/Walt Disney/Pixar (Ralph Guggenheim, Bonnie Arnold)
◧ ▤ ◲. ◎ ◎ ◠

w Joss Whedon, Andrew Stanton, Joel Cohen, Alec Sokolow *story* Joe Ranft, John Lasseter, Pete Docter, *d* John Lasseter *m* Randy Newman *ad* Ralph Eggleston *ed* Robert Gordon, Lee Unkrich
☆ voices of: Tom Hanks (Woody), Tim Allen (Buzz Lightyear), Don Rickles (Mr Potato Head), Jim Varney (Slinky Dog), Wallace Shawn (Rex), John Ratzenberger (Hamm)

'A visionary roller-coaster ride of a movie.' – *Roger Ebert, Chicago Sun-Times*

'Magically witty and humane entertainment, a hellzapoppin fairy tale.' – *Owen Gleiberman, Entertainment Weekly*

'A winning animated feature that has something for everyone on the age spectrum.' – *David Ansen, Newsweek*

♟ John Lasseter (special achievement)
♟ Randy Newman; song 'You've Got a Friend' (*m/ly* Randy Newman); screenplay

25
Toy Story

A toy cowboy, the long-time favourite of a small boy, is jealous of a new arrival, an astronaut figure who refuses to believe that he is a toy, and replaces him in the boy's affections.

A dazzling comedy that was the first computer-animated feature and remains the best so far. It is one of the few family films that can actually be enjoyed by all the family. Its story, of toys who come to life when people are not around, touches on sibling rivalry, jealousies and insecurities. It is crammed with good jokes, both verbal and visual ('Hey, look, I'm Picasso,' says Mr Potato Head, rearranging his features so that one eye is above the other), does not ignore the darker side of childhood, and has a happy ending. Its hyper-realistic style and glossy textures, its wit and invention, as well as its innovation, mark it out as something special.

Viridiana
Spain/Mexico 1961 91m bw
Uninci/Films 59/Gustavo Alatriste (Munoz Suay)
◧ ▤

w Luis Buñuel, Julio Alajandro *d* Luis Buñuel *ph* José F. Agayo *m* Gustavo Pittaluga *pd* Francisco Canet *ad* Francisco Canet *ed* Pedro del Rey
☆ Silvia Pinal (Viridiana), Francisco Rabal (Jorge), Fernando Rey (Don Jaime), Jose Calvo (The Beggar), Margarita Lozano (Ramona), José Manuel Martin (The Beggar), Victoria Zinny (Lucia)

'One of the cinema's few major philosophical works.' – *Robert Vas*

'An extraordinary film, a superb film.' – *Dilys Powell*

● It won the Palme d'Or at the 1961 Cannes Film Festival.

24
Viridiana

A religious young woman invites beggars to live in her uncle's house.

Luis Buñuel's often hilarious and surrealist melodrama concerns a novice who, about to take her vows, is corrupted by her wicked uncle and installs a load of beggars in his house. Buñuel explained his inspiration as combining the story of a little-known saint he remembered from his school days and an old erotic fantasy about making love to the queen of Spain when she was drugged. Amid the perverse happenings, he strove for authenticity by including in the cast an actual beggar, who ignored all instructions, and dressing them in clothes bought from the poor of Madrid. It is a film packed with shades of meaning, most of them sacrilegious and fascinating to contemplate.

The Passion of Joan of Arc

France   1928   110m   bw   silent
Société Générale des Films

original title: *La Passion de Jeanne d'Arc*
w Carl Dreyer, Joseph Delteil *d* Carl Dreyer *ph* Rudolph
Maté *ad* Hermann Warm, Jean Hugo *ed* Carl Dreyer
☆ *Renée Falconetti* (Joan of Arc), Eugène Silvain (Bishop
Cauchon), Maurice Schutz (Nicholas Loyseleur), Michel
Simon (Jean Lemaitre), Antonin Artaud (Jean Massieu),
Louis Ravet (Jean Beaupere), André Berley (Jean d'Estivet),
Jean d'Yd (Guillaume Erard)

'One of the greatest of all movies … Falconetti's
Joan may be the finest performance ever recorded
on film.' – *Pauline Kael*

'Isn't worth a dollar to any commercial regular
picture theatre in the US.' – *Variety*

● Lillian Gish was first considered for the role of Joan.
Falconetti never made another film. After its first showing
the film was cut by the French authorities and was banned
by the British until 1930.
● A Region 1 DVD release includes commentary by Dreyer
scholar Casper Tybjerg.

23
The Passion of Joan of Arc

Joan of Arc is found guilty of heresy by a French court and burned at the stake.

In her only film role, Falconetti gives one of the greatest of screen performances as Joan who, on her last day on Earth, is subjected to five increasingly threatening interrogations before being burned at the stake. Dreyer opens with a shot of the actual transcript of the trial and uses this contemporary account as a basis for his film, though compressing the three months it lasted into a single day. In this austerely moving drama, the actors were not allowed make-up so that their features were exposed to intense scrutiny in the almost continuous close-ups Dreyer prefers, thus drawing in the audience to become involved in the increasingly emotional action. Without deviating from the transcript of the trial, Dreyer is able to suggest character through these close-ups. The appearance of the inquisitors – narrow-faced fanatics or fleshy cynics – contrasts with the openness and innocence of Joan.

Andrei Rublev

USSR   1966   181m   bw/colour
Cinemascope
Mosfilm

w Andrei Mikhalkov-Konchalovsky, Andrei Tarkovsky
d Andrei Tarkovsky *ph* Vadim Yusov *m* Vyacheslav
Tcherniaiev *ad* Evgeny Chernyaev *ed* Ludmila Feyganova
☆ *Anatoly Solonitsin* (Andrei Rublev), *Ivan Lapikov*
(Kirill), Nikolai Grinko (Daniel Chorny), Nikolai Sergeyev
(Theophanes the Greek)

'The one indisputable Russian masterpiece of the
last decade.' – *Nigel Andrews, MFB, 1973*

'With the exception of the great Eisenstein, I can't
think of any film which has conveyed a feeling of
the remote past with such utter conviction … a
durable and unmistakable masterpiece.' – *Michael
Billington, Illustrated London News*

● The film was later released in a 'director's cut' running for
205m.
● The Region 1 DVD iincludes the director's cut, interviews
with Tarkovsky and audio essays by Professor Petric over
selected scenes. The Region 2 release has interviews with
Yuri Nazarov and Tasrkovsky's sister.

22
Andrei Rublev

Imaginary episodes from the life of a medieval icon painter.

Tarkovsky's imaginative re-creation of the life of a 15th-century monk and icon painter is also a superb evocation of medieval Russia that dramatizes the eternal problem of the artist, whether to take part in the life around him or merely comment on it. In this film about faith, Tarkovsky contrasts the serene achievement of Rublev's work with the violence and turmoil of the times. Told in separate episodes, it includes such magnificent set pieces as the sack of the city and Cathedral of Vladimir and the massacre of inhabitants, and the casting of a great bell that releases Rublev from a vow of silence and sends him back to his painting. A note Tarkovsky wrote in his diary in 1971 throws an oblique light on the film, for it is the basis of Rublev's spiritual dilemma: 'Talent is a misfortune, for on the one hand it entitles a person to neither merit nor respect, and on the other it lays on him tremendous responsibilities.'

The Discreet Charm of the Bourgeoisie

France/Spain/Italy   1972   105m   Eastmancolor
Greenwich (Serge Silberman)
🔲 🎞 📷 🔊

original title: *Le Charme Discret de la Bourgeoisie*
w Luis Buñuel, Jean-Claude Carrière *d* Luis Buñuel
ph Edmond Richard *ad* Pierre Guffroy *ed* Hélène
Plemiannikov
☆ *Fernando Rey* (Don Raphael, Ambassador of Miranda),
Delphine Seyrig (Simone Thevenot), *Stéphane Audran* (Alice
Senechal), Bulle Ogier (Florence), Jean-Pierre Cassel (Henri
Senechal), Paul Frankeur (François Thevenot), Julien
Bertheau (Bishop Dufour)

'A perfect synthesis of surreal wit and blistering
social assault.' – *Jan Dawson, MFB*

'Extraordinarily funny and brilliantly acted.'
– *Vincent Canby, New York Times*

🎖 best foreign film
🏆 Luis Buñuel, Jean-Claude Carrière (script)
🏆 Stéphane Audran; script

Les Enfants du Paradis

France   1945   195m   bw
Pathé (Fred Orain, Raymond Borderic)
🔲 🔲 🎞 📷 🔊 🔊

US title: *Children of Paradise*
w Jacques Prévert *d* Marcel Carné *ph* Roger Hubert
m Maurice Thiriet, Joseph Kosma, G. Mouque
ad Alexandre Trauner, Léon Barsacq, Raymond Gabutti
ed Henri Rust, Madeleine Bonin *cos* Mayo
☆ *Arletty, Jean-Louis Barrault, Pierre Brasseur, Marcel
Herrand, Maria Casarès*, Louis Salou, Pierre Renoir, Gaston
Modot, Jane Marken

'A magnificent scenario … Prévert is as adept with
wit as with poignancy … I don't believe a finer
group of actors was ever assembled on film'
– *John Simon*

'Few achievements in the world of cinema can
equal it.' – *Roger Ebert, Chicago Sun-Times*

● A Region 1 two-disc set includes commentaries by film
scholars Brian Stonehill and Charles Affron.
🏆 Jacques Prévert

21
The Discreet Charm of the Bourgeoisie

The efforts of a group of friends to dine together are continually frustrated.

Buñuel's light-hearted, wickedly satirical comedy of the self-interested rich begins with four guests arriving at a dinner party, only to discover that their hostess is not expecting them. (In a nice touch, one guest snatches back the flowers she has brought when the maid attempts to take them away.) From that moment, there is no let-up in the comic invention as the group try, and fail, to have a meal together. They are frustrated by a funeral, lust and military manoeuvres as their adherence to social ritual is mercilessly mocked. The director's touch is delightfully deft: he can suggest the horror of torture simply by showing cockroaches tumbling on to piano keys. It is a film without a straightforward narrative, proceeding by way of interrupted dinner parties, ghost stories and dreams, told by a master storyteller who never disappoints.

20
Les Enfants du Paradis

In Paris' street of theatres, a mime falls in love with a beautiful actress.

A magnificent evocation of a place and a period, this thoroughly enjoyable epic melodrama is flawed only by its lack of human warmth. It remains nevertheless one of the cinema's most memorable films. Set in the 'theatre street' of Paris in the 1840s, its elaborate and highly theatrical story is centred around Baptiste, a mime, who falls in love with the elusive Garance, but her problems with other men prevent them from being more than acting partners. Made in wartime Paris, disrupted by air raids and electricity cuts and including Jewish actors and technicians who had been forbidden to work, it shows no sign of these difficulties. Graced with superb performances from Arletty, as Garance, a woman pursued by many men, and Jean-Louis Barrault as the moonstruck mime, it remains a glorious celebration of romantic love in all its guises.

Pather Panchali
India   1955   115m   bw
Government of West Bengal (Satyajit Ray)
📽 ▬ ◉ ◎
wd Satyajit Ray *novels* Bhibuti Bashan Bannerjee
ph Subrata Mitra *m* Ravi Shankar *ad* Banshi
Chandragupta *ed* Dulal Dutta
☆ Kanu Banerjee (Harihar), Karuna Banerjee (Sarbajaya),
Uma Das Gupta (Durga), Subir Bannerjee (Apu), Chunibala
(Indir Thakrun)

'It has been left to the Indian cinema to give us a
picture of a childhood which preserves under the
shadow of experience not only its innocence but
its gaiety.' – *Dilys Powell*

'Not to have seen the cinema of Ray means
existing in the world without seeing the sun or the
moon.' – *Akira Kurosawa*

'Any picture as loose in structure or as listless in
tempo as this one is would barely pass as a
"rough cut" with the editors in Hollywood.' –
Bosley Crowther, New York Times

Aparajito
India   1956   113m   bw
Epic Films Private Ltd (Satyajit Ray)
📽 ▬ ◉ ◎
aka: The Unvanquished
wd Satyajit Ray *novel* Aparajita by Bibhutibhusan
Bandapadhaya *ph* Subrata Mitra *m* Ravi Shankar
ad Bansi Chandragupta *ed* Dulal Dutta
☆ Pinaki Sen Gupta (Apu as a boy), Karuna Banerjee
(Mother), Kanu Banerjee (Father), Smaran Ghosal (Apu as
an adolescent), Ramani Sen Gupta (Bhahataran)
● It won the Golden Lion at the 1957 Venice Film Festival.

The World of Apu
India   1959   106m   bw
Satyajit Ray Productions
📽 ▬ ◉
original title: Apur Sansar
wd Satyajit Ray *novel* Aparajita by Bibhutibhusan
Banerjee *ph* Subrata Mitra *m* Ravi Shankar *ad* Bansi
Chandragupta *ed* Dulal Dutta
☆ Soumitra Chatterjee (Apu), Sarmila Tagore (Aparna),
Alok Chakravarti (Kajal), Swapan Mukherjee (Pulu),
Dhiresh Majumdar (Sasinarayan), Sefalika Devi
(Sasinarayan's Wife), Dhires Ghosh (Landlord)

'Rich and contemplative, and a great, convincing
affirmation.' – *Pauline Kael, New Yorker*

19
The Apu Trilogy

Pather Panchali

In a small Bengal village, the son of a would-be writer grows up in poverty and tragedy before setting off with what remains of the family to seek a living in Benares.

Aparajito

After his father's death, a poor country boy is helped by his mother to study for university.

The World of Apu

An impoverished writer, working as a clerk, who agrees to an arranged marriage, is devastated by the death of his wife in childbirth and rejects his son.

Ray's sensitive trilogy, based on two classic Bengali novels, follows the life of a poor village boy, from his birth to his progress to the city, school, university and an unexpected marriage during three decades to the 1940s, mirroring India's shift from a rural to an urban society. The poverty shown in *Pather Panchali* matched that of its director, who several times had to suspend filming as he ran short of cash. (He never earned any money from the film.) Slow-paced, episodic, often reflective and tragic, the films also allow room for peripheral characters to flourish. Its underlying theme, centred on the pleasures and tribulations of family relationships, is of individuals struggling to retain their integrity. Though it is forty years or more since its first release, the trilogy continues to communicate a life-affirming humanity.

'Hunted by men ... Sought by women!'

The Third Man
GB   1949   100m   bw
British Lion/London Films/David O. Selznick/
Alexander Korda (Carol Reed)
■■ ▬ ⊛ ⦿ ⦿

w Graham Greene *d* Carol Reed *ph* Robert Krasker
m Anton Karas *ed* Oswald Hafenrichter
☆ Joseph Cotten (Holly Martins), *Trevor Howard* (Maj.
Calloway), *Alida Valli* (Anna Schmidt), *Orson Welles* (Harry
Lime), *Bernard Lee* (Sgt. Paine), *Wilfrid Hyde-White*
(Crabbin), Ernst Deutsch (Baron Kurtz), Siegfried Breuer
(Popescu), Erich Ponto (Dr. Winkel), Paul Hoerbiger (Porter)

'Sensitive and humane and dedicated, [Reed]
would seem to be enclosed from life with no
specially strong feelings about the stories that
come his way other than that they should be
something he can perfect and polish with a
craftsman's love.' – *Richard Winnington*

'Reaffirms Carol Reed as our foremost film-maker
and one of the best three or four in the world'
– *Fred Majdalany*

'Crammed with cinematic plums which could do
the early Hitchcock proud.' – *Time*

👤 Robert Krasker
👤 Carol Reed; editing
🏆 British film

'It happened in Hollywood ... a love story
... a drama real and ruthless, tender and
terrifying!'

Sunset Boulevard
US   1950   110m   bw
Paramount (Charles Brackett)
■■ ▬ ⊛ ⦿ ⦿

w Charles Brackett, Billy Wilder, D. M. Marshman Jnr
d Billy Wilder *ph* John F. Seitz *m* Franz Waxman
ad Hans Dreier, John Meehan *ed* Arthur Schmidt, Doane
Harrison
☆ Gloria Swanson (Norma Desmond), *William Holden*
(Joe Gillis), *Erich von Stroheim* (Max von Mayerling), *Fred
Clark* (Sheldrake), *Nancy Olson* (Betty Schaefer), Jack Webb
(Artie Green), Lloyd Gough (Morino), *Cecil B. de Mille*
(Himself), H. B. Warner (Himself), Anna Q. Nilsson
(Herself), Buster Keaton (Himself), Hedda Hopper (Herself)

'Miss Swanson's performance takes her at one
bound into the class of Boris Karloff and Tod
Slaughter.' – *Richard Mallett, Punch*

● Montgomery Clift was to have played the role taken by
William Holden, but decided against it at the last moment,
because his real-life affair with an older woman, Libby
Holman, was too close to the situation in the film.
👤 script; Franz Waxman; art direction
👤 best picture; Billy Wilder (as director); John F. Seitz;
Gloria Swanson; William Holden; Erich von Stroheim;
Nancy Olson; editing

18
The Third Man

*An American pulp fiction writer goes to Vienna to meet an old friend
and finds that he has disappeared in sinister circumstances.*

Carol Reed's totally memorable and irresistible romantic thriller concerns an unintelligent but tenacious writer of Westerns, who arrives in
post-war Vienna to join his old friend Harry Lime, but discovers that
Harry has a sinister reputation and seems to have met with an accident.
The drama is full of cynical characters but is not without humour;
Hitchcock with feeling, if you like. Graham Greene explored the sewers
beneath the city before making clever use of them in his story, which
bore some resemblance to the plot of Robert Montgomery's now forgotten thriller *Ride the Pink Horse*. Cinematographer Robert Krasker
shot the action at odd angles to emphasize feelings of unease and
uncertainty. The film is stylish from the first to the last, with inimitable
backgrounds, of zither music and war-torn buildings, pointing up a
then-topical story of black market corruption.

17
Sunset Boulevard

*A young scriptwriter recalls his fatal involvement with a reclusive star
of the silent screen.*

The film that ended Billy Wilder's long partnership with screenwriter
Charles Brackett was concerned with a subject both knew intimately:
Hollywood. Told by a corpse, a luckless, young Hollywood scriptwriter,
who goes to live with a wealthy older woman, a slightly dotty and
extremely possessive relic of the silent screen, it is an incisive melodrama of a disturbing world. The malicious observation throughout is a
treat – when MGM's head Louis B. Mayer saw it, he screamed that
Wilder should be tarred and feathered and run out of town. Wilder originally wanted Mae West for the role of the silent star, but she fortunately turned it down. Gloria Swanson is perfect as the diva, though
Wilder films her cruelly (it was the way he directed her scenes that led
to blows with Brackett) and Holden, who had to be forced into making
the movie, gives a star-making performance as her equally reluctant
lover.

'This is the story of J.J. – but not the way he wants it told!'

Sweet Smell of Success
US   1957   96m   bw
UA/Norma/Curtleigh (James Hill)
🎞 ▦ ◎, ⊚ ⊚ 🎧
w Clifford Odets, Ernest Lehman *d* Alexander Mackendrick *ph* James Wong Howe *m* Elmer Bernstein *ad* Edward Carrere *ed* Alan Crosland Jnr
☆ Burt Lancaster (J.J. Hunsecker), *Tony Curtis* (Sidney Falco), Martin Milner (Steve Dallas), Sam Levene (Frank D'Angelo), Susan Harrison (Susan Hunsecker), Barbara Nichols (Rita), *Emile Meyer* (Harry Kello)

'A sweet slice of perversity, a study of dollar and power worship.' – *Pauline Kael*

'The last of the great films noir, and among the sharpest, most uncompromisingly dark Manhattan street movies.' – *Peter Bogdanovich*

16
Sweet Smell of Success

An ambitious press agent helps a powerful New York columnist break up his sister's romance.

This dark melodrama of a corrupt, megalomaniac gossip columnist was based on the style of Walter Winchell, the man who can be said to have invented celebrity journalism. Along with *The Front Page*, it remains the definitive picture of the sleazy side of newspapers. Burt Lancaster and Tony Curtis, as preening columnist and hustling, ambitious publicist, give their best-ever performances. Alexander Mackendrick used aspects of the actors' own personalities to flesh out their characters, recognizing that Curtis was extremely vain but lacked ego, whereas Lancaster was all ego. The film moves fast, and the predatory, low-angled camera is rarely still, capturing the bitter-sweet tang of the street life of New York and its febrile creatures of the night. The plot matters less than the photographic detail and the skilful manipulation of decadent characters, larger than life-size.

The Seventh Seal
Sweden   1957   95m   bw
Svensk Filmindustri (Allan Ekelund)
🎞 ▦ ◎, ⊚ ⊚
original title: *Det Sjunde Inseglet*
wd Ingmar Bergman *ph* Gunnar Fischer *m* Erik Nordgren *pd* P. A. Lundgren *ed* Lennart Wallen *cos* Manne Lindholm
☆ *Max von Sydow* (Antonius Block), *Bengt Ekerot* (Death), Gunnar Bjornstrand (Jons), Nils Poppe (Jof), Bibi Andersson (Mia), Gunnel Lindblom (Girl)

'The most extraordinary mixture of beauty and lust and cruelty, Odin-worship and Christian faith, darkness and light.' – *Alan Dent, Illustrated London News*

'You know where they dance along the horizon? We'd packed up for the evening and were about to go home. Suddenly I saw a cloud, and Fischer swung his camera up. Some actors had gone, so grips had to stand in. The whole scene was improvised in ten minutes flat.' – *Ingmar Bergman*

• A Region 1 DVD release has commentary by film historian Peter Cowie.

15
The Seventh Seal

Death comes for a knight, who challenges him to a game of chess while he tries to show illustrations of goodness in mankind: but Death takes them all away in the end.

Few films have been parodied as much as Bergman's account of a disillusioned knight returning home from the Crusades, who meets the cloaked figure of Death, with whom he plays a game of chess for his own life as he travels through a country scourged by plague and witch-hunts. It survives triumphantly because of its high seriousness, its probing of the significance of existence. The images, including some of the most astonishing ever put on the screen, conjure an intensity of emotion, ending in an amazing unforgettable moment: the film's characters silhouetted on a hillside against an ominous sky as they join the dance of death. Apart from the superstitious, medieval horrors, a dark world irrationally sustained by religion, it is a lyrically beautiful work, a celebration of the joys of living.

'He had to find her … he had to find her…'

The Searchers
US   1956   119m   Technicolor   Vistavision
Warner/C. V. Whitney (Merian C. Cooper)

w Frank S. Nugent *novel* Alan le May *d* John Ford
ph Winton C. Hoch *m* Max Steiner *ad* Frank Hotaling, James Basevi *ed* Jack Murray
☆ John Wayne (Ethan Edwards), Jeffrey Hunter (Martin Pawley), Natalie Wood (Debbie Edwards), Vera Miles (Laurie Jorgensen), Ward Bond (Capt. Rev. Samuel Clayton), John Qualen (Lars Jorgensen), Henry Brandon (Chief Scar), Antonio Moreno (Emilio Figueroa)

'You can read a lot into it, but it isn't very enjoyable.' – *Pauline Kael, 70s*

'A ripsnorting Western, as brashly entertaining as they come.' – *Bosley Crowther, New York Times*

14
The Searchers

A former Confederate soldier searches for his niece who has been abducted by an Indian war party.

This disturbing Western of obsession and racism has become Ford's most influential film. John Wayne gives his most ambiguous performance as a Confederate war veteran who tracks down the Indians who have slaughtered his brother and sister-in-law and carried off their daughter. He is no longer a simple gung-ho hero, but a tormented, vengeful loner, out of step with his society. Ford's great themes of loss and reconciliation are echoed in many films that followed (not the least being Scorsese's *Taxi Driver*, in which another loner attempts to redeem a young girl for reasons that he does not fully understand). The film's last shot has become an iconic one: after seven years, Wayne returns the girl to her home; as they welcome her, he crosses his arms, turns and walks out the open door, which closes behind him, excluding him from the family gathering.

Taxi Driver
US   1976   114m   Metrocolor
Columbia/Italo-Judeo (Michael and Julia Philips)

w Paul Schrader *d* Martin Scorsese *ph* Michael Chapman *m* Bernard Herrmann *ad* Charles Rosen *ed* Tom Rolf, Melvin Shapiro, Marcia Lucas
☆ Robert De Niro (Travis Bickle), Jodie Foster (Iris Steensman), Cybill Shepherd (Betsy), Peter Boyle (Wizard), Leonard Harris (Charles Palantine), Harvey Keitel (Sport)

'I don't question the truth of this material. I question Scorsese's ability to lift it out of the movie gutters into which less truthful directors have trampled it.' – *Stanley Kauffmann*

'A vivid, galvanizing portrait of a character so particular that you may be astonished that he makes consistent dramatic sense.' – *Vincent Canby, New York Times*

● Schrader says the story was modelled after the diaries of would-be assassin Arthur Bremer.
♫ best picture; Bernard Herrmann; Robert De Niro; Jodie Foster
🎭 Bernard Herrmann; Jodie Foster

13
Taxi Driver

A New York taxi driver is driven mad by the pimps, prostitutes and drug dealers he sees on the city streets.

Scorsese's unlovely but brilliantly made film haunts the mind and paints a most vivid picture of a hell on earth. De Niro's Travis Bickle is a lonely Vietnam veteran who becomes a New York taxi driver and allows the violence and squalor around him to explode in his mind. He becomes involved with two women, one that he desires who rejects him, and a 14-year-old prostitute, who he could have but does not want. He comes to regard himself as the lone arbiter of morality in a corrupt world and, seeking to redeem it through violence, is reduced by it to a momentary celebrity. Scorsese concentrated on the disintegrating character of Bickle, filming the drama from his point of view. He shot it quickly, from an intense script by Paul Schrader, in much of the manner of a horror movie. It is not surprising that Bernard Herrmann's score should recall his music for *Psycho*, another film about a disturbed loner.

Singin' in the Rain
US   1952   102m   Technicolor
MGM (Arthur Freed)

w Adolph Green, Betty Comden *d* Gene Kelly, Stanley
Donen *ph* Harold Rosson *m* Nacio Herb Brown
md Lennie Hayton *ch* Gene Kelly, Stanley Donen
ad Cedric Gibbons, Randall Duell *ed* Adrienne Fazan
ly Arthur Freed
☆ *Gene Kelly* (Don Lockwood), *Donald O'Connor* (Cosmo
Brown), *Debbie Reynolds* (Kathy Seldon), *Millard Mitchell*
(R.F. Simpson), *Jean Hagen* (Lina Lamont), Rita Moreno
(Zelda Zanders), Cyd Charisse (Dancer), *Douglas Fowley*
(Roscoe Dexter)

> 'Perhaps the most enjoyable of all movie musicals.'
> – *New Yorker, 1975*

● Debbie Reynolds singing 'Would You' was dubbed by
Betty Royce.
● A Regions 1 and 2 two-disc special edition DVD
included commentary by Debbie Reynolds, Donald
O'Connor, Cyd Charisse, Kathleen Freeman, Stanley Donen,
Betty Comden, Adolph Green, Baz Luhrmann and Rudy
Behlmer.
♫ 'Make 'Em Laugh'; 'Moses'; 'Fit as a Fiddle'; 'Singin' in
the Rain'; 'All I Do Is Dream of You'; 'I've Got a Feelin' You're
Foolin'; 'Should I'; 'You Were Meant For Me'; 'Good
Morning'; 'Would You'; 'You Are My Lucky Star'
⚖ Lennie Hayton; Jean Hagen

12

Singin' in the Rain

*When talkies are invented, the reputation of one female star shrivels
while another grows.*

The best movie musical made so far, a marvel from Arthur Freed's
wonderful production unit at MGM, bursting with exuberant wit. It has
everything: a great script about the end of silent films and the beginning of talkies, terrific songs, slick choreography, excellent direction
and stars who spark each other to flashes of brilliance. An affectionate
satire of Hollywood, it parodies earlier styles but also shows how song
and dance sequences could and should be filmed. It has pace and style
and brightens the dullest day.

**Dr Strangelove; or, How I Learned to
Stop Worrying and Love the Bomb**
GB   1963   93m   bw
Columbia/Stanley Kubrick (Victor Lyndon)

w Stanley Kubrick, Terry Southern, Peter George
novel Red Alert by Peter George *d* Stanley Kubrick
ph Gilbert Taylor *m* Laurie Johnson *ad* Ken Adam
ed Anthony Harvey
☆ *Peter Sellers* (Lionel Mandrake/Merkin Muffley/Dr.
Strangelove), *George C. Scott* (Gen. 'Buck' Turgidson), Peter
Bull (Ambassador de Sadesky), Sterling Hayden (Gen. Jack
D. Ripper), Keenan Wynn (Col. 'Bat' Guano), Slim Pickens
(Maj. T.J. 'King' Kong), James Earl Jones (Lt. Lothar Zogg),
Tracy Reed (Miss Scott)

> 'Scarcely a picture of relentless originality; seldom
> have we seen so much made over so little.' – *Joan
> Didion*

● *Fail Safe* (qv), which took the same theme more
seriously, was released almost simultaneously.
● The Regions 1 and 2 DVD release includes a
documentary and a split-screen interview with Peter Sellers
and George C. Scott.
⚖ best picture; script; Stanley Kubrick (as director); Peter
Sellers
🏆 best picture; best British film; Ken Adam

11

Dr Strangelove; or, How I Learned to
Stop Worrying and Love the Bomb

*A comic nightmare in which stupidity and madness in high places
causes an atomic bomb to be dropped on Russia.*

Historically an important film in its timing, its nightmares being those of
the early Sixties, Stanley Kubrick's black comedy involves a mad USAF
general launching a nuclear attack on Russia. When recall attempts fail
and retaliation is inevitable, all concerned sit back to await the destruction of the world. The film resolves itself into a series of sketches with
imperishable moments. Sellers gives three excellently observed performances as the US president, a stereotyped RAF captain, and a mad
German-American scientist. Revelations by former United States
defense secretary, Robert S. McNamara, in the recent documentary *The
Fog of War* about General Curtis Le May, whose advice to President
Kennedy over Cuba was 'fry it', make the film seem less like satire than
reportage. Either way, it is to be treasured and enjoyed.

Eight and a Half

Italy 1963 138m bw
Cineriz (Angelo Rizzoli)

original title: *Otto e Mezzo*
w Federico Fellini, Ennio Flaiano, Tullio Pinelli, Brunello Rondi d *Federico Fellini* ph Gianni di Venanzo m Nino Rota ad Piero Gherardi ed Leo Catozzo
 ☆ *Marcello Mastroianni* (Guido Anselmi), Claudia Cardinale (Claudia), Anouk Aimée (Luisa Anselmi), Sandra Milo (Carla), Rossella Falk (Rossella), Barbara Steele (Gloria Morin), Madeleine Lebeau (French Actress)

'The whole may add up to a magnificent folly, but it is too singular, too candid, too vividly and insistently alive to be judged as being in any way diminishing.' – *Peter John Dyer, MFB*

'Fellini's intellectualizing is not even like dogs dancing; it is not done well, nor does it surprise us that it is done at all. It merely palls on us, and finally appals us.' – *John Simon*

● A Region 1 two-disc set includes a commentary by Gideon Bachmann and professor of film Antonio Monda, two documentaries and interviews with Sandra Milo, Lina Wertmuller and Vittorio Storaro.
 🎖 best foreign film; Piero Gherardi (cos)
 🏆 Federico Fellini (as director); script; Piero Gherardi (art direction)

10
Eight and a Half

Confused by his inability to think of a subject for his new film, a director resorts to fantasy.

A successful film director on the verge of a nervous breakdown has conflicting fantasies about his life, in this Fellini self-portrait. Marcello Mastroianni, as the director's alter ego, is plagued by producers, his wife and his mistress. He recalls his childhood and has sexual reveries involving whores. When he meets his ideal woman in actress Claudia Cardinale, she fails him and he dreams of killing himself, an act that releases him from his doubts so that he can make the film we watch. It is a coruscating, melancholy, self-reflecting spectacle of a man beginning to be at his wit's end. Mastroianni, who used many of Fellini's characteristic gestures and tone of voice in his portrayal, saw his role as 'a symbol of a generation that had nothing more to give'. Fellini's own directorial exuberance and visual style here, though, are evidence that he had not exhausted his talent.

'The movie too HOT for words!'

Some Like It Hot

👫 US 1959 122m bw
UA/Mirisch (Billy Wilder)

w Billy Wilder, I. A. L. Diamond d *Billy Wilder* ph Charles Lang Jnr m Adolph Deutsch ad Ted Howarth ed Arthur P. Schmidt cos Orry-Kelly
 ☆ *Jack Lemmon* (Jerry/Daphne), Tony Curtis (Joe/Josephine), *Marilyn Monroe* (Sugar Kane), *Joe E. Brown* (Osgood E. Fielding III), George Raft (Spats Columbo), Pat O'Brien (Mulligan), Nehemiah Persoff (Little Bonaparte), George E. Stone (Toothpick Charlie), Joan Shawlee (Sweet Sue)

'A comedy set in the Prohibition era, with transvestism, impotence, role confusion, and borderline inversion – and all hilariously innocent, though always on the brink of really disastrous double-entendre.' – *Pauline Kael*

'Most of the time Billy Wilder's new piece – a farce blacker than is common on the American screen – whistles along at a smart, murderous pace.' – *Dilys Powell*

🎖 Orry-Kelly
 🏆 script; Billy Wilder (as director); Charles Lang Jnr; Jack Lemmon; art direction
 🏆 Jack Lemmon

9
Some Like It Hot

Two musicians who witness a gangland killing disguise themselves as members of an all-girl band.

A milestone of film comedy that keeps its central situation alive with constant and fresh invention. Its wit, combined with a sense of danger, has rarely been duplicated and never equalled. Wilder took the element of disguise from an early German musical, but that was a much more conventional work. There are not many comedies that could begin, as this does, with its two unemployed musicians witnessing the St Valentine's Day Massacre before fleeing to Miami disguised as women. But even sudden death cannot quench its droll virtuosity. It is also perfectly cast. Marilyn Monroe was worth all the trouble she caused Wilder during its making, and Curtis and Lemmon are a brilliantly contrasting pair, the one smooth, confident and ladylike, the other panic-stricken and broad. 'Nobody's perfect', is the last line, hilarious in its context, but on this occasion, cast, script and director all were.

Vertigo

US   1958   128m   Technicolor   Vistavision
Paramount (Alfred Hitchcock)

w Alec Coppel, Samuel Taylor *novel D'entre les Morts* by
Pierre Boileau, Thomas Narcejac *d* Alfred Hitchcock
ph Robert Burks *m* Bernard Herrmann *ad* Hal Pereira,
Henry Bumstead *ed* George Tomasini *cos* Edith Head
☆ James Stewart (John Ferguson), Kim Novak (Madeleine
Elster/Judy Barton), Barbara Bel Geddes (Midge), Tom
Helmore (Gavin Elster), Henry Jones (Coroner)

> 'One of the two or three best films Hitchcock ever
> made' – *Roger Ebert, Chicago Sun-Times*

> 'There's nothing else like *Vertigo* in the Hitchcock
> canon – nothing so urgent, so feverish and also,
> paradoxically, so contrived.' – *Janet Maslin, New
> York Times*

> 'Through all of this runs Alfred Hitchcock's
> directorial hand, cutting, angling and gimmicking
> with mastery. Unfortunately, even that mastery is
> not enough to overcome one major fault - that the
> film's first half is too slow and too long.' – *Variety*

• Regions 1 and 2 collectors edition DVD releases include
commentary by Herbert Coleman, Robert A. Harris, James
C. Katz and Steven Smith.

♟ art direction; sound (George Dutton)

8
Vertigo

*An acrophobic detective becomes the victim of a murder conspiracy
when he meets the double of a woman who killed herself.*

Hitchcock used a combination of a forward zoom and a reverse tracking shot to create a feeling of vertigo in this double identity thriller. It
was as unsettling as the phobia it dealt with and kept its audience dizzy
and off balance throughout the puzzling events and was perfectly complemented by Bernard Herrmann's unsettling score. Often filmed in
sickly colours, as if reflecting the mental condition of its characters, it
concerns a detective with a fear of heights, who is drawn into a complex plot in which the woman he loves apparently falls to her death.
Then he meets her double, and tries to make her into the person he
lost. James Stewart, playing a character far removed from his more
usual good guy roles, brought out the detective's fear, depression and
near madness with impeccable control. Hitchcock's study of an obsessive and haunted love is the darkest of his films, and the best.

Raging Bull

US   1980   119m   bw/colour
UA/Chartoff-Winkler

w Paul Schrader, Mardik Martin *d* Martin Scorsese
ph Michael Chapman *m* from library sources *pd* Gene
Rudolf *ad* Kirk Axtell, Sheldon Haber, Alan Manser
ed Thelma Schoonmaker
☆ Robert De Niro (Jake La Motta), Cathy Moriarty (Vickie
La Motta), Joe Pesci (Joey), Frank Vincent (Salvy), Nicholas
Colasanto (Tommy Como)

> 'Scorsese makes pictures about the kind of people
> you wouldn't want to know.' – *Variety*

> 'A bravura display of cinematic skill.' – *Daily Mail*

♟ editing (Thelma Schoonmaker); Robert De Niro
♟ best film; best direction; Cathy Moriarty; Joe Pesci;
Michael Chapman; sound (Donald O. Mitchell, Bill
Bicholson, David J. Kimball, Les Lazarowitz)
🅣 editing; Joe Pesci

7
Raging Bull

*Boxer Jake La Motta recalls his days as middle-weight champion of the
world.*

Martin Scorsese's best film so far is a tough, powerfully made ringside
melodrama about the rise to fame of an unlikable middle-weight boxer.
Based on the autobiography of Jake La Motta, it was uncompromising
in its depiction of the savagery of the ring. A poll of American critics
voted it the best movie of the 1980s and it has a visceral dynamic that
made it the finest movie about boxing, one that does not pull its
punches. De Niro's dazzling performance in the title role encompasses
both La Motta as a savage fighter and his later incarnation as an overweight would-be comedian. Scorsese brought to the film what he called
a 'kamikaze' approach, in which he put everything he knew and felt in
the expectation that after it he would have to find another way of life.
Fortunately, he did not crash and burn, but survived to provide a compelling portrait of a man who could only express himself with his fists.

Citizen Kane

US 1941 119m bw
RKO (Orson Welles)
📷 ▦ ⊛ ⊚ ⊚ ⌒

w Herman J. Mankiewicz, Orson Welles *d* Orson Welles *ph* Gregg Toland *m* Bernard Herrmann *ad* Van Nest Polglase *ed* Robert Wise *sp* Vernon L. Walker

☆ *Orson Welles* (Kane), *Joseph Cotten* (Jedediah Leland), *Dorothy Comingore* (Susan Alexander), *Everett Sloane* (Bernstein), *Ray Collins* (Boss Jim Geddes), *Paul Stewart* (Raymond), *Ruth Warrick* (Emily Norton), *Erskine Sanford* (Herbert Carter), *Agnes Moorehead* (Kane's mother), *Harry Shannon* (Kane's father), *George Coulouris* (Walter Parks Thatcher), *William Alland* (Thompson), *Fortunio Bonanova* (music teacher)

'On seeing it for the first time, one got a conviction that if the cinema could do that, it could do anything.' – *Penelope Houston*

● The Region 1 DVD two-disc special edition includes commentary by Peter Bogdanovich and by Roger Ebert, a two-hour documentary *The Battle Over Citizen Kane* and the radio broadcast *The War of the Worlds*. A three-disc gold edition adds the HBO feature *RKO 281* about the making of the film.

🏃 Herman J. Mankiewicz, Orson Welles (script)
⚖ best picture; Orson Welles (as director); Gregg Toland; Bernard Herrmann; Orson Welles (as actor); art direction; Robert Wise

6
Citizen Kane

The life and death of a newspaper tycoon is recalled by those who knew him best.

A newspaper tycoon dies, and a magazine reporter interviews his friends in an effort to discover the meaning of his murmured last word, 'Rosebud'. From this simple story, came a brilliant piece of Hollywood cinema. Although the movie's technical innovations – deep focus, overlapping dialogue, fractured narrative, fake newsreels – might now seem run-of-the-mill, Orson Welles, aided by ex-journalist Herman Mankiewicz's script, identified and exposed a type of megalomaniacal media mogul who is with us still today. What is often overlooked in the frequent solemn discussions of the movie's many merits, is how funny the film is, particularly in the scenes of Kane's mistress attempting to become an opera singer. But it is the whole that is so satisfying in its devastating portrait of the corruption of an individual and his times. Almost every shot and every line is utterly absorbing both as entertainment and as craft.

The Seven Samurai

Japan 1954 155m bw
Toho (Shojiro Motoki)
📷 ▦ ⊛ ⊚ ⊚ ⌒

original title: *Shichi-nin no Samurai*
w Akira Kurosawa, Shinobu Hashimoto, Hideo Oguni *d* Akira Kurosawa *ph* Asaichi Nakai *m* Fumio Hayasaka *ad* Takashi Matsuyama *ed* Akira Kurosawa

☆ *Toshiro Mifune* (Kikuchiyo), *Takashi Shimura* (Kambei), *Kuninori Kodo* (Gisaku), *Yoshio Inaba* (Gorobei), *Seji Miyaguchi* (Kyuzo), *Minoru Chiaki* (Heihachi)

'It is as sheer narrative, rich in imagery, incisiveness and sharp observation, that it makes its strongest impact … It provides a fascinating display of talent, and places its director in the forefront of creative film-makers of his generation.' – *Gavin Lambert, Sight and Sound*

'This, on the surface, is a work of relentless, unmitigated action, as epic as any film ever made, and, again on the surface, sheer entertainment. Yet it is also an unquestionable triumph of art.' – *John Simon*

● A Region 1 DVD release has commentary by Japanese film expert Michael Jeck. A Region 2 DVD release has commentary on key scenes by film historian Philip Kemp.
⚖ art direction

5
The Seven Samurai

A wandering samurai recruits a band of warriors to defend a village from bandits.

Kurosawa's magnificent movie, the greatest of all samurai films, is a superbly strange medieval adventure. His genius was to bring together two groups who needed one another: fearful villagers requiring protection from bandits, and ronin, footloose samurai who, in the general disintegration of feudal society, no longer owed allegiance to a clan lord and were mercenaries in need of employment. The film later served as the basis for the Western *The Magnificent Seven* and the science-fiction film *Battle Beyond the Stars*, but they pale in comparison to this vivid and violent drama. The actors give the seven warriors a vital individuality; they are men who understand that they have no place in settled society, and the battle scenes are thrilling. The film exists in several versions, being cut from its 208m to 155m for its release in the West. The most complete version now available runs for 190m, which is not a second too long.

The Godfather
US 1972 175m Technicolor
Paramount/Alfran (Albert S. Ruddy)
🎞 ▤ ⚲ ⊚ ⊚ ⌒
w Francis Ford Coppola, Mario Puzo *novel* Mario Puzo
d Francis Ford Coppola *ph* Gordon Willis *m* Nino Rota
pd Dean Tavoularis *ad* Warren Clymer *ed* Paul Zinner,
Marc Laub, William Reynolds, Murray Solomon *cos* Anna
Hill Johnstone
☆ Marlon Brando (Don Vito Corleone), *Al Pacino*
(Michael Corleone), Robert Duvall (Tom Hagen), James
Caan (Sonny Corleone), Richard Castellano (Clemenza),
Diane Keaton (Kay Adams), Talia Shire (Connie Rizzi),
Richard Conte (Barzini), John Marley (Jack Woltz)
🏆 best picture; script; Marlon Brando
⚖ Francis Ford Coppola (as director); Al Pacino; Robert
Duvall; James Caan; Anna Hill Johnstone; sound (Charles
Grenzbach, Richard Portman, Christopher Newman)
Ⓣ Nino Rota

The Godfather Part II
US 1974 200m Technicolor
Paramount/the Coppola Company (Francis Ford
Coppola)
🎞 ▤ ⚲ ⊚ ⊚ ⌒
w Francis Ford Coppola, Mario Puzo *d* Francis Ford
Coppola *ph* Gordon Willis *m* Nino Rota, Carmine Coppola
pd Dean Tavoularis *ad* Angelo Graham *ed* Peter Zinner,
Richard Marks, Barry Malkin *cos* Theodora Van Runkle
☆ Al Pacino (Michael Corleone), *Robert De Niro* (Vito
Corleone), Diane Keaton (Kay Adams), Robert Duvall (Tom
Hagen), John Cazale (Fredo), Lee Strasberg (Hyman Roth),
Michael V. Gazzo (Frank Pentangeli), Talia Shire (Connie
Rizzi), Troy Donahue (Merle Johnson)
● The two films were eventually combined and extended
for television into a ten-hour serial, *The Godfather Saga*.
🏆 best picture; script; Francis Ford Coppola (as director);
Nino Rota, Carmine Coppola; Robert De Niro; art direction
⚖ Al Pacino; Lee Strasberg; Michael V. Gazzo; Talia Shire;
Theodora Van Runkle
Ⓣ Al Pacino

'Real Power Can't Be Given. It Must Be Taken.'

The Godfather Part III
US 1990 161m Technicolor
Paramount/Zoetrope (Francis Ford Coppola)
🎞 ▤ ⚲ ⊚ ⊚ ⌒
w Mario Puzo, Francis Ford Coppola *d* Francis Ford
Coppola *ph* Gordon Willis *m* Carmine Coppola, Nino
Rota *pd* Dean Tavoularis *ad* Alex Tavoularis *ed* Barry
Malkin, Lisa Fruchtman, Walter Murch
☆ Al Pacino (Michael Corleone), Diane Keaton (Kay
Adams), Talia Shire (Connie Rizzi), Andy Garcia (Vincent
Mancini), Eli Wallach (Don Altobello), Joe Mantegna (Joey
Zasa), George Hamilton (B.J. Harrison), Bridget Fonda
(Grace Hamilton), Sofia Coppola (Mary Corleone), Raf
Vallone (Cardinal Lamberto), Franc D'Ambrosio (Tony
Corleone), Donal Donnelly (Archbishop Gilday), Richard
Bright (Al Neri), Helmut Berger (Frederick Keinszig), Don
Novello (Dominic Abbandando)
⚖ best picture; Francis Ford Coppola; Andy Garcia; best
song 'Promise Me You'll Remember' (*m* Carmine Coppola, l
John Bettis); best art direction; best cinematography, best
film editing

4
The Godfather Trilogy

The Godfather

*When, after ruling for two generations, the Mafia's New York head dies
of old age, his son takes over reluctantly but later learns how to kill.*

The Godfather Part II

*The story moves on, with Michael Corleone consolidating his position,
while the film also looks back to the early career of his father, Vito.*

The Godfather Part III

*Michael Corleone attempts to become a legitimate businessman while
grooming his brother's violent and illegitimate son as his successor.*

It is the first two parts of Francis Ford Coppola's intriguing trilogy that
make it an undoubted classic. He used America's finest screen actors,
including Brando, and his heirs apparent, De Niro and Pacino, in what
are still are among their best performances. The brilliantly made first
episode has the Mafia's ageing New York head passing on the succession to his reluctant son. In the second, the son reflects on the problems of himself and his father before him in a complex movie,
explaining the present in terms of the past and providing a comprehen-
sive view of American society. The third completes the story, with the
family's move into legitimate business, but Coppola's control slackens.
Nevertheless, as a whole, the three have all the fascination of a snake
pit: a warm-hearted family saga except that the members are thieves
and murderers.

Lawrence of Arabia

GB 1962 221m Technicolor Super
Panavision 70
Columbia/Horizon (Sam Spiegel)

🎬 🎬 🎞 🎥 📀 🔊 🎧

w Robert Bolt, Michael Wilson *book The Seven Pillars of
Wisdom* by T.E. Lawrence *d David Lean ph Frederick A.
Young m Maurice Jarre pd John Box ad John Stoll
ed* Anne V. Coates

☆ *Peter O'Toole* (T.E. Lawrence), *Omar Sharif* (Sherif Ali
Ibn El Kharish), *Arthur Kennedy* (Jackson Bentley), Jack
Hawkins (Gen. Allenby), Donald Wolfit (Gen. Murray),
Claude Rains (Mr Dryden), Anthony Quayle (Col. Harry
Brighton), *Alec Guinness* (Prince Feisal), Anthony Quinn
(Auda Abu Tayi), José Ferrer (Turkish Bey), Michel Ray
(Ferraj), Zia Mohyeddin (Tafas)

> 'Lean has managed to market epics as serious
> entertainment rather than as the spectacles they
> are.' – *Time Out, 1980*

● Marlon Brando was originally announced as the star, but
backed out. Albert Finney turned down the role before
O'Toole was offered it.
● Michael Wilson was uncredited at the time for his work
on the script because he had been blacklisted.
🏆 best picture; David Lean; Frederick A. Young; Maurice
Jarre
🏆 Robert Bolt; Peter O'Toole; Omar Sharif
🏆 best picture; best British picture; Robert Bolt; Peter
O'Toole

3

Lawrence of Arabia

*An adventurer's life with the Arabs, told in flashbacks after his acciden-
tal death in the Thirties.*

The real hero here is director David Lean, in overcoming immense difficulties to create an overwhelming epic experience. Historically accurate
it is not: the diminutive Lawrence was at least a foot shorter than Peter
O'Toole. (It could have been worse, since the role was first offered to
Marlon Brando.) O'Toole, a great actor at his charismatic best, achieves
both Lawrence's bravado and his disenchantment. Yet it is not his performance that captures the attention, nor Robert Bolt's intelligent
script, so much as Lean's own meticulous flamboyance, orchestrating,
for example, the dramatic entrance of Sharif, first seen as a wavering
dot in an immensity of sky and sand, and the bravura of the magnificent battles. The post-production of the film had to be completed
quickly, since producer Sam Spiegel had arranged a royal premiere.
Lean and his editor had no time for second thoughts in cutting the film;
fortunately, they got it right first time.

La Règle du Jeu
France   1939   113m   bw
La Nouvelle Edition Française (Claude Renoir)
🔳 ▬ ◎~ ◎ ◎
aka: *The Rules of the Game*
w Jean Renoir, Carl Koch d Jean Renoir ph Jean Bachelet, Alain Renoir *m* Joseph Kosma, Roger Desormières *ad* Eugène Lourié, Max Douy *ed* Marguerite Renoir, Marthe Huguet
☆ *Marcel Dalio* (Robert de la Chesnaye), Nora Gregor (Christine de la Chesnaye), Jean Renoir (Octave), Mila Parély (Genévieve de Marrast), Julien Carette (Marceau), Gaston Modot (Schumacher), Roland Toutain (Andree Jurieu)

'It is a question of panache, of preserving a casual indifference to the workings of fate.' – *The Times*

'How brilliantly Renoir focuses the confusion! The rather fusty luxury of the chateau, the constant mindless slaughter of wild animals, the minuets of adultery and seduction, the gavottes of mutual hatred or mistrust...' – *Basil Wright, 1972*

● The film was originally banned as indicting the corruption of France, and during the war the negative was destroyed during an air raid; but eventually a full version was pieced together from various materials.

2
La Règle du Jeu

A count organizes a weekend shooting party which results in complex love intrigues among servants as well as masters.

It took more than 20 years for Renoir's film to be recognized as his masterpiece; on its release, audiences hated it, some even ripping up cinema seats in protest, because they could not bear to see their own irrelevance and corruption reflected on the screen. (As Renoir said, 'People who commit suicide do not care to do it in front of witnesses.') It was originally banned as demoralizing, but remains triumphantly, morally bracing and richly comic. The subject matter of a thousand boulevard comedies – a shooting party at a country mansion, where everyone is preoccupied with love-affairs – becomes a devastating portrait of the society of his time; snobbish, racist and mendacious, whose obsessive frivolity leads to death and destruction. The chilling central section, where the guests mechanically slaughter rabbits and pheasants, prefigured the coming war. At the film's end, its characters are reduced to shadows on a wall, fading to oblivion.

☆ **Gillian Armstrong**
Director ☆

1. Citizen Kane (Welles)
2. Raging Bull (Scorsese)
3. La Strada (Fellini)
4. The Godfather Part II (Coppola)
5. Rashomon (Kurosawa)
6. Chinatown (Polanski)
7. Bicycle Thieves (De Sica)
8. 8 1/2 (Fellini)
9. Singin' in the Rain (Kelly, Donen)
10. Vertigo (Hitchcock)

☆ **Catherine Breillat**
Director ☆

1. Ai No Corrida (Oshima)
2. Sawdust and Tinsel (Bergman)
3. Baby Doll (Kazan)
4. Lost Highway (Lynch)
5. Vertigo (Hitchcock)
6. Salò (Pasolini)
7. L'avventura (Antonioni)
8. Ordet (Dreyer)
9. Lancelot du Lac (Bresson)
10. Ten (Kiarostami)

☆ **Howard Maxford**,
Film Editor ☆

1. North by Northwest (Hitchcock)
2. Marathon Man (Schlesinger)
3. Victor/Victoria (Hughes)
4. Chitty Chitty Bang Bang (Edwards)
5. Carry On Screaming (Thomas)
6. Singin' in the Rain (Kelly, Donen)
7. On Her Majesty's Secret Service (Hunt)
8. The Spy Who Loved Me (Gilbert)
9. Moonraker (Gilbert)
10. Lawrence of Arabia (Lean)

Tokyo Story
Japan   1953   135m   bw
Shochiku (Takeshi Yamamoto)
▣ ▤ ⊘
original title: *Tokyo Monogatari*
w Kogo Noda, Yasujiro Ozu *d* Yasujiro Ozu *ph* Yuharu Atsuta *m* Kojun Saito *ad* Tatsuo Hamada *ed* Yoshiyasu Hamamura
☆ *Chishu Ryu* (Shukishi Hirayama), *Chieko Higashiyama* (Tomi Hirayama), Setsuko Hara (Noriko), Haruko Sugimura (Shige Kaneko), Nobuo Nakamura (Kurazo Kaneko), So Yamamura (Koichi), Kuniko Miyake (Fumiko), Eijiro Tono (Sanpei Numata)

'Masterpiece: tender, profoundly mysterious and desperately sad.' – *Peter Bradshaw, Guardian*

'The supreme masterpiece of one of the cinema's greatest masters. As a study of family life and generational relationships, the film can be mentioned in the same breath as *King Lear*.' – *Philip French, Observer*

● A Region 1 two-disc DVD release includes two documentaries and a commentary by Ozu scholar David Desser

1

Tokyo Story

An elderly couple, who travel to Tokyo to visit their married son and daughter, discover that their children have little time for them.

Ozu was the most classical and contemplative of directors. He serves a rebuke to those who think that, because a film is moving pictures, the camera should be in motion all the time, tracking and panning and zooming. In this understated, beautifully composed classic of domestic disillusionment, the editing is unobtrusive and the camera's gaze is steady; it moves only three times during the film and is kept at a low angle, looking up at the characters. Director Masahiro Shinoda, who worked as an assistant to Ozu, described it as the point of view of a small deity observing human action. In his formal concentration on everyday family life, Ozu discovers universal truths about the human condition. Here, an elderly couple face the painful fact that they are a burden to their children and grandchildren. But the most devastating comment comes at the end of the film, from their daughter; 'Isn't life disappointing.' It may be, but at least Ozu never disappoints.

Index